GARIBALDI

By the same author

NICHOLAS RIDLEY
THOMAS CRANMER
JOHN KNOX
LORD PALMERSTON

Jasper Ridley

GARIBALDI

The Viking Press
New York

Published in 1976 by The Viking Press, Inc.
625 Madison Avenue, New York, N.Y. 10022

Library of Congress Cataloging in Publication Data
Ridley, Jasper Godwin.
Garibaldi.
Bibliography: p.
Includes index.
1. Garibaldi, Giuseppe, 1807-1882.
DG552.8.G2R52   1976   945'.08'0924   [B]   75-41366
ISBN 0-670-33548-7

Printed in U.S.A.

*The illustration on the title page is from
a portrait of Garibaldi by Giuseppe Fraschere.*

To my son
BENJAMIN

CONTENTS

CONTENTS

ILLUSTRATIONS

MAPS

FOREWORD

IT is ninety-two years since Garibaldi died, but he is almost as popular today as he was during his lifetime. In Italy his reputation has withstood even the iconoclastic instinct of the younger generation to disparage a national hero whom they have been taught from childhood to regard as an Establishment figure, not as the revolutionary whom his contemporaries knew. The Catholic Church has forgotten or forgiven his invectives against the Papacy and the priesthood. Fascists, Communists and Liberals have all claimed him as one of their own. On the centenary of his triumph of 1860, the United States honoured the man to whom Abraham Lincoln offered a high command and the rank of Major-General in the US army, and the Soviet Union acclaimed the supporter of the Paris Commune and Marx's First International. Garibaldi is the only man who, at the height of the Cold War, appeared on a postage stamp in both the USA and the USSR.

He has not been forgotten in those two countries – Britain and Uruguay – where he was almost as greatly admired, during his lifetime, as he was in his native Italy. No foreigner has ever aroused such enthusiasm in Britain as Garibaldi did during his Sicilian campaign in 1860 and his visit to London four years later; and he is still remembered, not only because of the Garibaldi biscuit and the inns named after him. In Uruguay, where the statue of José Garibaldi, Commander-in-Chief of the Naval Forces of the Republic from 1842 to 1848, stands in the old harbour of Montevideo, I discovered during my first encounter with the immigration and customs officials at Montevideo Airport the love which is felt for the 'hero of both worlds' and the kindness which is extended to his biographer. It is natural that the invader of Entre-Ríos should be less popular in Argentina; but here, too, I met with nothing but kindness, even from the Irish-Argentine compatriots of Admiral Brown. The controversy which was aroused seventy years ago by the erection of his statue in the Plaza Italia in Buenos Aires has not entirely passed away; but the mention of his name in Argentina first and foremost brings back happy memories of a childhood song: 'Is it true that Garibaldi is dead? Poom!'

Since the first biography of Garibaldi, by his friend Cuneo, was published in Turin in 1850, a vast number of other books have appeared; but strangely enough in view of Garibaldi's popularity in Britain, no comprehensive life has ever been published in English. The two-volume biography by his secretary Guerzoni, which was published in Italy in 1882 within a few months of Garibaldi's death, was not translated into English, perhaps because Garibaldi's friend from Gosport, Jessie White Mario, who might well have translated it, wrote a shorter life in English which was published as a Supplement to the English translation of Garibaldi's memoirs.

In the twentieth century, though many shorter biographies have been published in Britain – not all of them of the quality of Christopher Hibbert's *Garibaldi and his Enemies* in 1965 – no comprehensive work has appeared. This is certainly because of the existence of Trevelyan's three great volumes, which have been repeatedly reprinted since they were first published nearly seventy years ago, and have achieved nearly as high a reputation in Italy as in Britain. Most English people have learned what they know of Garibaldi from Trevelyan. Although it is generally thought that Trevelyan wrote a biography of Garibaldi, in fact he expressly refused to do so, stating that he was a historian, not a biographer; and his *Garibaldi's Defence of the Roman Republic, Garibaldi and the Thousand,* and *Garibaldi and the Making of Italy* deal only with the four years 1848–9 and 1859–60, the rest of Garibaldi's life being covered in two prefaces and one epilogue. Mr Mack Smith, who has succeeded Trevelyan as the greatest English Garibaldi expert of his day, has written about the year 1860 in even greater depth than Trevelyan; but, apart from a very short biography, he has treated Garibaldi's activities during the next decade only incidentally to his study of Italian politics in the 1860s, and has written almost nothing on the earlier period. With regard to 1848–9 and 1859–60, it is not easy to compete with the brilliance of Trevelyan or the erudition of Mack Smith, but even in the chapters dealing with these familiar years I have discovered new material which was not used by my illustrious predecessors.

Garibaldi's twelve eventful years in South America have been almost entirely ignored by English biographers, and it is not generally known in Britain that he went there. In Italy there is sufficient interest in his South American career to make it profitable to organise cheap excursion trips from Italy to Uruguay for visitors to the Garibaldi house, and for the Museo del Risórgimento to maintain a permanent representative in Montevideo to undertake researches into the subject of 'Garibaldi in America'. But these researches have tended to concentrate on only a few aspects of Garibaldi's South American career, and have shown a reluctance to use the contemporary hostile sources of the Rosista propagandists, which, however untrustworthy, are obviously important and, in their own way, revealing for the biographer of Garibaldi.

'The twelve years which Garibaldi spent in South America,' wrote Trevelyan in 1911, 'is a period of his career which has never yet been subjected to close historical investigation. Whether, if it were investigated on the spot, many new facts would be now forthcoming, I am unable even to guess.' My own investigations on the spot showed that more new facts were forthcoming than I had dared to hope for.

As Trevelyan pointed out, Garibaldi's memoirs have hitherto been the chief source of information about his years in South America. There are four versions of the memoirs – the English edition published in New York by Dwight in 1859; the French edition of Alexandre Dumas the elder; the German edition of Garibaldi's mistress Esperanza von Schwartz (Elpis Melena); and the Italian edition which Garibaldi edited himself in 1872, and which was translated into English by Werner and published in London in 1889. Werner's translation is in many ways unsatisfactory; not only does he give a distorted impression of Garibaldi's style when he translates, for example, 'una giovine' (a girl) as 'a fair damsel', but he is guilty of several actual mistranslations and errors.

Thanks to the assistance of Mr E. F. F. de Testa, I was able to trace and gain access to a copy of the very rare Dwight edition, as well as the other three versions; and though I did not attempt a detailed concordance of Dwight, Dumas, Melena and the *Edizione Definitiva*, I have in every case of conflict followed the version which internal and other evidence indicated was the most reliable. I have adopted this principle with regard to the controversial Dumas edition, which is radically different from the other versions. The Dwight edition, which Garibaldi wrote in Tangier in 1850–1 and which ends with his departure from Montevideo in April 1848, and the 1872 edition, which carries the story up to 1871, are almost identical for the period up to 1848; and Melena's German edition is not very different. But Dumas's incorporates whole episodes which are not found in the other editions; the chief of these are Garibaldi's encounter with the Saint-Simonian Socialists, his escape from Genoa to Marseilles in 1834, his merciful treatment of Millan, who had tortured him at Gualeguay, and his friendly meeting with his old enemy, Admiral Brown, in Montevideo. There has been a great difference of opinion among scholars about the authenticity of these passages. Some authorities have suggested that Dumas invented them, and Trevelyan stated that the Dumas version is almost valueless; but others have warmly defended it, and Luzio has gone so far as to say that it is the most authentic version of the memoirs.

One matter seems to have been overlooked. In the account of the Battle of Costa Brava in 1842, Dumas's version (which is written, in the first person, ostensibly by Garibaldi himself) places the battle off the island of Martín García. Although Garibaldi's memory sometimes failed him on matters of detail, it would have been impossible for him to confuse a minor engagement at the mouth of the Paraná with a very bloody battle fought seven weeks later four hundred miles up-river, and there can be no doubt that Garibaldi did not write this chapter. It must be a forgery by Dumas. This throws grave doubt on the validity of the Dumas version, as does the fact that when Garibaldi edited the final edition of 1872, he incorporated none of the material which Dumas had added to Garibaldi's original manuscript of 1850.

This does not mean that all the Dumas memoirs are valueless. Dumas had met Garibaldi before he published his edition of the memoirs, and he may well have included in them an account of episodes which Garibaldi had told him personally. In many cases there is confirmation of Dumas's supplementary material from other sources. The story of Garibaldi's voyage from Marseilles to Constantinople with the Saint-Simonians is confirmed by other contemporary writers, and Admiral Brown's visit to Montevideo was reported at the time in the Montevidean newspapers. On the other hand, Dumas's story of Garibaldi's generous treatment of Millan seems to me to be obviously based on a confusion in Dumas's mind between Gualeguay and Gualeguaychú, and I have rejected it, though this will distress some of Garibaldi's admirers. There is no confirmation of Dumas's account of Garibaldi's adventures on the journey from Nice to Marseilles in 1834, but as there is no reason for doubting it, I felt justified in including this entertaining story.

My work on this book has been hampered by strikes in Britain, Italy, Argentina and Uruguay; and once, during a riot, I was driven out of a library by tear-gas, after demonstrators had used the library as a first-aid post. But I have been treated with great kindness by everyone whom I have met, including police and strikers, while carrying on my research in eight countries, and I am most grateful to all those who have helped me in connexion with the book.

Her Majesty the Queen graciously permitted me to read, quote and use information contained in Queen Victoria's Journal and correspondence and other documents in the Royal Archives at Windsor Castle.

Garibaldi's great-granddaughter Mrs Anita Hibbert (Ricciotti's granddaughter) helped me with her encouragement and gave me private information about Garibaldi and his family, and I am grateful to her and to her stepmother, Signora Erica Garibaldi.

Senhor Wolfgang Ludwig Rau, of Florianópolis in Brazil, was good enough to allow me to read and transcribe unpublished documents which he had managed to acquire in connexion with his biography of Anita Garibaldi, which was published in Brazil in June of 1975. He also helped me to evaluate the importance of local traditions at Laguna about Anita Garibaldi's first marriage and early life, as well as giving me hospitality and other help at Florianópolis and Laguna.

Captain Alex McAdam of Bedlay Castle in Scotland allowed me to read and transcribe the unpublished manuscripts of his grandfather, John McAdam, who for many years was regarded as Garibaldi's unofficial representative in Britain, and was his closest British friend.

Señora Laura Pirretti de Novikov of Buenos Aires allowed me to transcribe and quote from an unpublished letter of Garibaldi in her possession.

My work has been greatly facilitated by Dr Anthony Campanella of Geneva, who was good enough to give me a copy of his two-volume bibliography of all published writings on Garibaldi up to 1970, with its 16,141 entries, at a time when his book was unobtainable in England. I am also grateful to Dr Campanella for his willingness to answer my requests for information at all times, and for the hospitality which he and Signora Campanella showed to me in Geneva.

Señor Jorge Luis Borges not only showed me great kindness at the Biblioteca Nacional in Buenos Aires, where he allowed me to take up much of his valuable time, but gave me private information about the experiences of his grandfather, who fought under Garibaldi at the siege of Montevideo.

I am grateful to the Honourable John Lodge, the United States Ambassador in Buenos Aires, for his help and hospitality at the embassy; to Mrs Francesca Lodge for her encouragement and for putting me in touch with a valuable source of information; and to His Excellency Giuseppe de Rezo Thesauro, the Italian Ambassador in Buenos Aires, for doing so much to facilitate my researches in Italy.

I am grateful to Professor Enrique de Gandía of the Argentine National Academy of History for his encouragement and for his willingness to consult other distinguished Argentine historians about documents and information for which I was searching.

Professor Alberto M. Ghisalberti gave me every assistance at the Museo del Risorgimento in Rome.

This book could not have been written in its present form without the help of the late Sir Eugen Millington-Drake, Mr Willie Anderson of Buenos Aires, and Mr Robert Martin of the British Embassy in Montevideo, who were responsible for my contacts in South America and made the arrangements for my visit there. I am grateful to Mr Anderson, to Mr and Mrs Martin, and to all my other friends in Argentina and Uruguay for their hospitality.

Mr Noel Blakiston helped and encouraged me at every stage, and he and Mr Malcolm Deas were good enough to read my manuscript and help me with their advice.

I was helped with advice on translation from Italian by Mrs Nuccia Foulkes; from Spanish, by Señorita Lucía Santa Cruz; from Danish, by Mrs Ulla Lindsay; and from Dutch by Mr Martin de Block.

My thanks are due to Comandante Napoleone Coltelletti (the grandson of Luigi Coltelletti), Señorita Sara Lussich, Señorita Gisele Shaw and Mr E. F. F. de Testa for private information about Garibaldi; to Mrs Georgina Battiscombe, Dr Richard Blaas (the Archiv-Direktor of the Osterreichisches Staatsarchiv in Vienna), Mrs Penelope Chilton, Padre Claudino of Laguna, Father Francis Edwards, sj, Mrs Rose Gardom, Don Isidoro Giuliani of Mandriols, Mr Alex Glasgow, Señora Luisa Mercedes Levinson, Miss Moira McAdam, Mr Donald Murray of the Lodge St Clair in Glasgow, Signor Armando Pirotto of the Museo del Risorgimento in Montevideo, Signor Antonio Putzu of Caprera, Mrs Diana Raymond, Mr Maurice Rickards, Mr Harold Rosenthal, the Hon. Giles St Aubyn, Mr John Saville of the University of Hull, Mr Richard Seligman of Melbourne, Australia, Dr Michael Smith, Señor Spencer-Tailleboys, Señor R. J. Suarez, Mr Nicholas Walter, Señora Manon Weaver (a great-niece of Colonel John Peard), and Mr Andrew Graham-Yooll of the *Buenos Aires Herald*, for supplying me with information or drawing my attention to material and sources; to Señor Patricio Gannon for assistance with photographs and in other ways, and for hospitality at his *estancia* near Gualeguaychú; to Mr Charles Cooper and the staff of R.C.F. Tools Ltd., to Ozalid Ltd. of East Grinstead, and to Mr Herbert Tout for help in developing Peruvian microfilm; to Mr Michael Sandler for information about French military equipment and practice in the nineteenth century; to Senhor and Senhora Luiz Antonio Pompeia and Mr and Mrs Christopher Small for hospitality in São Paulo and Glasgow; to my cousin Geoffrey Waller for all his help in Buenos Aires; to Mrs John Coates for useful advice as to how to reach the battlefield of San Antonio in her native Salto; to Signor M. A. Alpino of the Museo del Risorgimento in Rome; Señorita Beatriz Bosch, the staff of the British Council in London, Paris, Rome and Lima, Mr Kenneth Coates, Señor Dellapena and the staff of *Histonium* in Buenos Aires, Mr Peter MacDonald and the staff of the British Council in Montevideo, Señorita Matilde

Machao Garciarena and Señorita María de las Mercedes Chaparro of the Instituto Magnasco in Gualeguaychú, Signor Erich Linder of the Agenzia Letteraria Internazionale in Milan, Señor Mario Alarcon Muñiz of *El Debate* in Gualeguay, Mr John Press, Señor Celso Rodríguez, Señor Lawrence Smith, Señor Manuel Veiravé of the Museo Gualeguay, and Mr C. H. Whistler and the staff of the British Council in Buenos Aires.

To Senhora Edmée Bastian and the staff of the Instituto Histórico e Geográfico Brasileiro of Rio de Janeiro; Capitán de Navio Laurio H. Destefani and the staff of the Departmento de Estudios Historicos Navales at the Secretaria de Marina in Buenos Aires; Señor Armando Dilernia and the staff of the Biblioteca Nacional in Buenos Aires; Señor A. M. Garcia Viera and the staff of the Archivo General de la Nación in Montevideo; Signorina Paola Gessa and the staff of the Biblioteca di Storia Moderna e Contemporanea in Rome; Mr Robert Mackworth-Young, Miss Jane Langton and the staff of the Royal Archives at Windsor Castle; Señor R. J. Suarez and the staff of the Escuela Mecanica de la Marina in Buenos Aires; Señor Roberto Couture de Troismonts, Señorita Mabel Vignart and the staff of the library of the Universidad Nacional in La Plata; to the Librarian and staff of the Archivo General de la Nación, the Biblioteca del Congreso and the Museo Mitre in Buenos Aires; the Bibliothèque Publique et Universitaire in Geneva; the University Library in Leicester; the British Museum, the British Museum Newspaper Library in Colindale, the Institute of Latin American Studies, the London Library, the Public Record Office and the Westminster City Library in London; the Museo del Risorgimento in Milan; the Biblioteca Nacional and the Museo Histórico Nacional in Montevideo; the Central Library in Newcastle-upon-Tyne; the Biblioteca Nacional in Rio de Janeiro; and the Biblioteca Municipal in São Paulo.

The frontispiece is reproduced by kind permission of Comandante Napoleone Coltelletti; the photograph of the portrait of Anita Garibaldi by kind permission of Mrs. Anita Hibbert, and the other illustrations by arrangement with the Mansell Collection and the Radio Times Hulton Picture Library.

My mother and Mr Peter Grant for their advice on the typescript; Vera, for her help with the proofs, advice on translation from German, and in many other ways; and the Hon. John Jolliffe and the staff of Constable, and my agent Mr Graham Watson and the staff of Curtis Brown, for their help and encouragement at all times.

GARIBALDI

CHAPTER 1

THE MERCHANT SEAMAN

G IUSEPPE Maria Garibaldi was born at Nice at six o'clock in the
morning on 4 July 1807, which was the seventy-third birthday
of his grandfather, Angelo Garibaldi.[1]

The town of Nice had for two thousand years played an important
part in the history of Provence. From 1388 until fifteen years before
the birth of Giuseppe Garibaldi it had been in the territory of the
independent sovereign state of Savoy, which stretched from the Lake
of Geneva in the north to the territory of the Republic of Genoa in the
south. Nice was its chief seaport, and from here a busy trade was
carried on with the other ports of the Mediterranean. The Duke of
Savoy was an important power in European politics, and was usually
the ally of the Holy Roman Emperor, and the Habsburgs in Austria
and Spain, against the King of France. In 1718 he was granted the
island of Sardinia as a reward for his assistance to the Allies in the
War of the Spanish Succession, and took the title of King of Sardinia.
Henceforth the Duchy of Savoy was officially known as the Kingdom
of Sardinia, though it was often referred to, informally, as Piedmont,
where its capital, Turin, was situated.

In 1792 the armies of the French Revolution invaded Savoy and
captured Nice. After Napoleon's victories in Italy the old frontiers
were redrawn; and while most of the Kingdom of Sardinia was formed
into the Cisalpine Republic, which afterwards became the Kingdom
of Italy with Napoleon as king, the province of Savoy in the north,
and the town of Nice, were incorporated into the territory of the
French Republic. In 1804 the French Republic became the French
Empire when Napoleon took the title of Emperor; so Garibaldi was
born a subject of the Emperor Napoleon, and when he was christened
in the church of St Martin in Nice on 19 July 1807, when he was
fifteen days old, the official records gave his Christian names in their
French form, Joseph Marie.[2] Napoleon was at the height of his power.
On the day when Garibaldi was born he was at Tilsit on the Russian
frontier, finishing his series of interviews with Tsar Alexander 1 which
led, two days later, to the treaty of alliance by which Russia agreed

to adopt a policy of pro-French and anti-British neutrality. Across the Atlantic the seven million citizens of the United States were celebrating the thirty-first anniversary of their Declaration of Independence.

Although some writers have stated that Garibaldi was the son of a poor fisherman – a story which appeals both to Radicals and to romantics – his father, Domenico Garibaldi, was in fact a sailor and a small trader who was wealthy enough to own one small ship – the *Santa Reparata*, of 29 tons. Giuseppe Garibaldi's grandfather, Angelo Garibaldi, had also been a shipowner; he came from Chiavari in the Republic of Genoa, where Domenico was born in 1766. Domenico Garibaldi had not received any formal education, having gone to sea in his father's ship at an early age; in 1871 Giuseppe Garibaldi wrote that Domenico was much less well educated than the average sea-captain and shipowner of the late nineteenth century. But Domenico, like his brother, could read and write, which his brother's wife could not do; she was unable to sign her name on the baptismal register when she was godmother at Giuseppe Garibaldi's christening.

The name Garibaldi suggests that the family may originally have come from Germany; and though Giuseppe Garibaldi's secretary and biographer, Guerzoni, was at pains to deny this, and stated that the Garibaldis were descended from Garibaldo, Duke of Turin, in the seventh century, Guerzoni's story is as far-fetched as the theory of the German Radical, Karl Blind, that the family was descended from the Dukes of Bavaria. Garibaldi's English friend and biographer, Jessie White, who married the Italian revolutionary Alberto Mario, believed that she detected traces of his Teutonic origin in his red-blonde hair, his slow, heavy tread when he walked, his calm and slow method of talking, without any gesticulation, and in his preference for country life to city life.[3]

Domenico Garibaldi, like his son Giuseppe himself, was not a good business man. When he was a young man he had bought a ship of his own, but he had incurred such heavy losses that he had been compelled to go back to working as a sailor on his father's ship. In due course, he had taken over the *Santa Reparata* from Angelo Garibaldi, and managed to run it sufficiently successfully to remain solvent; but he did not improve the family business, and always blamed himself for not having done sufficiently well to be able to leave a decent fortune to his sons.[4]

Soon after Domenico Garibaldi was born, his father moved to Nice, where Domenico in 1794 married Rosa Raimondi, a girl from the fishing village of Loano in the Gulf of Genoa, whose family had also moved from Genoese territory to Nice. Their first child, a girl named

Maria Elisabetta, was born in 1797 and died at the age of two. Their second child was a boy, born in July 1804, who was called Angelo after his grandfather. The third child and second son was Giuseppe, who was just three years younger than Angelo. When Giuseppe was nearly three, another son, Michele, was born in June 1810; and when he was five and a half, a fourth son, Felice, was born in January 1813. Garibaldi was nearly ten when the first sister that he knew, Teresa, was born in May 1817.[5]

All the sons were successful, in their different ways, in later life, though they tended to die young. All four began by going to sea, and then followed different courses. Angelo emigrated to the United States, became a wealthy business man in New York, and ended as Sardinian Consul in Philadelphia, where he died in 1853, when he was forty-nine. Michele, who was more single-minded than any of his brothers in his devotion to the sea, became one of the most experienced and respected sea-captains in the Mediterranean. He died in 1866, aged fifty-six. Felice was less ambitious than the other members of the family. He was very handsome, charming and kind, and was so successful with women that he did not trouble to seek for success in any other field. He took a desk job with a shipping firm in Naples, and died at the age of forty-two in 1855. Giuseppe, who became a revolutionary and a soldier in Europe and South America, lived a far more hazardous life than any of his brothers, but was the only one of them to reach old age. When he died in his bed aged nearly seventy-five, he was already being called 'the hero of both worlds' – the Old and the New.

Like many other Italian families of the period, the Garibaldis and their relatives all lived together in one house at Nice. Domenico and Rosa with their children, and the grandfather Angelo Garibaldi, lived in the house of Rosa's uncle, Gustavini, with Gustavini's wife and children. It was in this house that Giuseppe Garibaldi, and all Domenico's children except Teresa, were born. The house was on the front of the harbour at Nice, near the head of Porto Olimpio. In 1897 the whole street was demolished when the harbour was enlarged and the spot where Garibaldi was born is today covered by the water on the north side of the harbour.[6]*

In 1814 Napoleon was overthrown, the Bourbons were restored to the throne of France, and the victorious Allied statesmen at the

---

*There appears to be no truth in the statement in Dumas's edition of the memoirs that Garibaldi was born in the same house as Napoleon's general, Massena, who was almost certainly born in another part of the town; and as the statement does not appear in either the Dwight or the 1872 editions of the memoirs, it is probably one of the additions which Dumas inserted in the memoirs.[7]

Congress of Vienna set about restoring the old frontiers and the old régimes in Europe. Nice was once again part of the Kingdom of Sardinia. The Garibaldis became subjects of King Victor Emanuel 1, and the seven-year-old Joseph Garibaldi became officially Giuseppe Garibaldi. He had always been Peppino to his family and friends. In March 1815 Napoleon returned from Elba – it was the first political event which Peppino, then aged seven, remembered;[8] but he did not have time to reconquer Nice during the Hundred Days, and after the battle of Waterloo the plans of the Congress of Vienna were finally put into force. But the statesmen at Vienna did not like republics, and although the Kingdom of Sardinia was restored, the republics of Venice and Genoa were not. The town of Venice and the province of Venetia were given to Austria, along with Lombardy, which was restored to her. The territory of the former Republic of Genoa was given to the King of Sardinia. Sardinia now had the flourishing port of Genoa as well as Nice.

South of the Kingdom of Sardinia and the Austrian provinces of Lombardy and Venetia were the independent duchies of Modena, Parma and Lucca, and Tuscany, ruled by its Grand-Duke at Florence. To the south-east of the duchies were the Papal States under the sovereignty of the Pope in Rome. These extended from the Romagna and Bologna in the north to the Patrimony of St Peter in the south, and to the frontier with the Kingdom of Naples in the Abruzzi and in the Gulf of Terracina. The Kingdom of Naples, which was officially known as the Kingdom of the Two Sicilies, was the largest territorial unit in the Italian peninsula, covering the whole of southern Italy and the island of Sicily. The capital was the city of Naples, which had a population of 400,000 and was the largest city in Italy.

In this same year, 1815, a change occurred in the life of the Garibaldi family. One of Gustavini's sons married, and it proved too much even for the capacity of Gustavini's house to absorb new members of the family. The Garibaldis were asked to leave, and moved from the north to the east side of the harbour, into a large, rambling tenement house with innumerable passages and small rooms, known as Aburarum House, at No. 3, Quai Lunel. Domenico and Rosa Garibaldi lived here for the rest of their lives. It was here that their youngest child, Teresa, was born, and that Peppino and his brothers spent their childhood. Before Peppino died, a plaque had been erected in his honour on the front of the house.[9]

Peppino grew up on the waterfront, and from the very first he wanted to be a sailor. But there were two sides to his character. When he grew up, he became a successful man of action; but he was also a Utopian visionary. He took rapid decisions, and achieved spectacular results while the theoreticians and the politicians were talking; but sometimes, when he was at a gay and noisy dinner party or social gathering, he would stare dreamily into space, utterly oblivious to what was going on around him. This unusual combination of a starry-eyed idealist and a successful general was there from birth. When Garibaldi was a child, he would often walk across the street from his house to the ships in the harbour, where he would talk to the sailors, and learn to trim the sails and tie knots, and coax the fishermen to take him with them to the tunny-fish festival at Villefranche, to the sardine hauls at Limpia, or when they went oyster-dredging. But on other days he would lie under the olive trees reading a book, or wander off by himself into the hills above Nice, and walk for hours alone in the woods, dreaming day-dreams, and acquiring a love for nature and for animals. As a boy, he already had a great compassion for all kinds of suffering, and could not bear to see a person or an animal in pain.

His compassion was emotional, not logical. All his life he was a man of war, volunteering for one military campaign after another, and often fighting a particularly bloody kind of war, ordering soldiers, many of them young boys, into action in the face of murderous rifle fire; but he was deeply affected when he came face to face with the sufferings of a dying soldier. He presided at one of the first international pacifist congresses that was ever held, and told Gladstone that he could not watch a military parade without thinking of the horrors of war; but he wrote in his memoirs that, although 'lovers of peace, right and justice, we are nevertheless forced to agree with the axiom of an American general: "War is the true life of man"'. He was a strong opponent of capital punishment; but his soldiers knew, as one of them put it, that he was capable of ordering them to be shot without putting down his cigar.* As a boy, he enjoyed going on hunting expeditions to shoot game in the woods; but once, when he was aged seven, on one of his solitary walks he found a grasshopper, and picked it up and brought it home, clutching it tenderly, only to find that he had broken one of its legs by holding it too tightly. He retired to his room, and wept for several hours.[10]

He was a quick-witted child. When he was eight he went on a shooting expedition with his cousin in the Var district, which was now just across the frontier in France, and came on a woman washing clothes in a wide ditch. Suddenly the woman lost her balance, pitched forward, and fell head first into the water; but Peppino, realizing that

*The vivid and well-known phrase that Garibaldi ordered men to be shot 'without taking his cigar out of his mouth' is unfortunately an incorrect translation of Hoff-stetter's original German.

she was in danger of being drowned, immediately rushed to her assistance. Though he was encumbered by the game-bag on his shoulder, he managed to help pull her out of the ditch. All his life Garibaldi was proud of the fact that he had saved a woman from drowning at the age of eight. When he was twelve he went to the aid of some boys whose boat had capsized, and pulled them out of the water; and when he grew up and became a strong swimmer he saved a man or a child from being drowned on three other occasions.[11]

When Garibaldi was twelve a terrible disaster occurred in his family. On 17 January 1820 his sister Teresa, who was two years and eight months, was sleeping in her bed with her nurse when the bed caught fire, and both Teresa and the nurse were burned to death. As the nurse had locked the bedroom door on the inside, no one could do anything to help them. The tragedy seems to have affected Peppino very deeply. He does not mention it in any of the editions of his memoirs; he was always inclined to be reticent about his private griefs. His secretary Guerzoni had heard about it, but did not know any of the details or the child's name. But when the English explorer, Theodore Bent, visited Garibaldi at his home on the island of Caprera a few years before Garibaldi's death, Garibaldi objected because Bent had locked his bedroom door during the night, and asked: 'What do you fear in the house of Garibaldi that makes you lock your door?' As Bent seemed surprised, Garibaldi told him about the circumstances in which his sister had died some sixty years before, and explained that because of this he did not like a bedroom door to be kept locked. Bent misunderstood what Garibaldi had said, and thought that it was Garibaldi's daughter Rosita, who died when she was a small child in Montevideo in 1845, who had been burned to death.[12]

This fatal accident to their daughter may have increased the great love, and the tender care amounting to over-protectiveness, which Domenico and Rosa Garibaldi showed to their surviving children, especially Peppino. In his memoirs, Garibaldi wrote that his father and mother were over-protective, though he stated that his mother 'might have been a model to all mothers, and I can say no more'. Rosa Garibaldi was very religious, as might have been expected from an emotional Italian woman of humble origin and the wife of a sailor; she was a devoted and orthodox member of the Roman Catholic Church, and made Peppino, like all her other children, attend church regularly when he was a boy. Peppino rejected her religious doctrines when he grew up; but he attributed his love of humanity, and his patriotic love for Italy, to the fact that his mother had implanted in him her compassion for those who were suffering. He even spoke with respect of her religious views.

Though I am certainly not superstitious [he wrote in his memoirs] yet not infrequently at the most difficult moments of my stormy life – as when I escaped unharmed from the waves of the ocean, or from the leaden hail of the battlefield – I seemed to see my loving mother bending and kneeling before the Infinite, a suppliant for the life of the child of her womb. And, though I had no great belief in the efficacy of her prayers, I was moved by them, and felt happier, or less unhappy.[13]

Garibaldi's parents gave him love, security and a happy childhood, which fortified him to meet with courage and equanimity the hatreds, dangers and suffering which he encountered in adult life. The over-protectiveness had no harmful results, and incited him to deeds of daring.

This led to a conflict with his parents at quite an early age. Both his father and mother, noticing Peppino's intelligence, and the gentle, dreamy side of his character, thought that these qualities would be wasted if he became a sailor, like the other members of his family. They wanted him to become a priest, a lawyer or a doctor. As they could not afford to send him to a *gymnasium*, where he would have received higher education, they arranged for him to receive a good education from three private teachers, two of whom were priests, and one a layman, Monsieur Arena, who, after serving in Napoleon's army, had opened a private school which had been closed down by the authorities, probably because Arena was considered to be politically unreliable. Arena taught Peppino proper Italian, which he had not learned as a small child, his first language having been the mixture of Italian and Provençal French which was spoken in Nice at that time; but it was not until he was already a young man that he made a serious effort to study Italian, when his brother Angelo wrote to him from the United States and suggested that he should study the Italian language and Roman and Italian history. Arena also taught him writing and mathematics.

In later life, Garibaldi was violently prejudiced against priests, and in his memoirs he contrasts the good education which he received from Arena with the education provided by the priests, who trained him to be nothing except either a priest or a lawyer, and not fit for 'any useful employment'; but he speaks favourably of one of the priests, who taught him English. He described him as 'an unprejudiced priest, very well read in Byron's beautiful language'. In his memoirs, he regrets that he did not learn to speak English better, and says that if he had known, as a child, that he would have such friendly relations with English people in the future, he would have made greater efforts to learn the language. Garibaldi realized that his English was far from perfect, as did many English people who met him during his visit to

7

England in 1864. But he spoke four languages perfectly. Apart from French and Italian, he learned to speak fluent Spanish and Portuguese in South America; and Bent says that he spoke excellent German.[14]

His slowness in learning Italian from Arena was due to the fact that he did not wish to become an intellectual, but was determined to go to sea, like his grandfather and father and his three brothers. He was annoyed that he was taught academic subjects instead of things that would be useful to him at sea. He decided to teach himself what he needed to know in order to obtain a ship's master's certificate, and bought books on mathematics, astronomy, geography and commercial law. He also complained that his tutors did not teach him gymnastics, fencing or riding, and that he had to learn these skills in other ways. 'I learned gymnastics by climbing the ship's rigging and sliding along the ropes; fencing, by protecting my head and trying my best to hit other people's heads; and riding from the best horsemen in the world, the *gauchos*.' But he learned to swim as a very small child, and became a very strong swimmer.[15]

Although Domenico Garibaldi could not afford to send Peppino to a *gymnasium*, he was determined to provide him with a better education than he could obtain in Nice, and sent him to some kind of school in Genoa. Garibaldi states this in the first edition of his memoirs, and also mentioned it to Gladstone at a dinner party in London in 1864, when he told him that he refused to go with his school-fellows to watch the military parades in Genoa, because of his horror of war. He soon grew very bored with sitting at a desk in school, and as his father would not send him to sea, but insisted that he should continue at his school in Genoa, he decided one day, when he was at Nice in the school holidays, to run away to sea and sail to the Levant with three or four boys of his own age. They decided to seize a ship and sail her as far as Genoa, and then see what further adventures they would have there. The first part of the plan was surprisingly successful. The boys collected some food and provisions for the voyage, and also some fishing tackle, and then seized one of the ships in the harbour at Nice, and sailed off eastwards for Genoa. When they were off Monaco, a coastguard clipper came up behind them, boarded them, and brought their ship and the boys back to Nice. An *abbé* had discovered the boys' design, and told Domenico Garibaldi, who had sent the coastguards to bring them back. In later life, Peppino realized that it was very fortunate for him that he had been caught, and was even grateful to the *abbé* who had warned his father. 'An *abbé* had revealed our flight,' he wrote in the 1872 edition of his memoirs. 'What a coincidence! an *abbé*, an embryo priest, had perhaps helped to save me from ruin, and I am ungrateful enough to pursue those poor priests! All the same, a priest is an impostor, and I am devoted to the sacred worship of truth.'[16]

In the end, his parents gave way. Giuseppe Garibaldi became a sailor like his brothers. In his memoirs, he complains that this did not occur until he was 'about fifteen', and goes on to say that he thinks that boys who want to be sailors should be allowed to go to sea at the age of eight; but Garibaldi was always bad at remembering dates, and, if the maritime records of Nice are correct, his name was inscribed on the register of seamen on 12 November 1821, when he was fourteen, though he did not sail on his first voyage until more than two years later. But the happy day came at last. On 29 January 1824 his mother tearfully packed his bags, and he sailed in the *Costanza* to Odessa. Most of the maritime trade of Nice was with the other Italian Mediterranean ports; but trade was also carried on with the Levant and North Africa. The *Costanza* was commanded by Acting-Captain Pesante, who, though he had not yet been awarded his master's certificate, impressed Garibaldi as being the best captain he ever knew. Garibaldi was very happy. He was at sea, and he loved to hear the crew, who, like Captain Pesante, were nearly all men from San Remo, singing their Ligurian love-songs. He says that he was too young to understand the sexual emotions to which the words of the songs referred; but the music moved him deeply. Many years later he remembered every detail of his first ship – the shape of the masts, the large deck, and the carved figure-head at the prow.[17]

He returned from Odessa in July, and four months afterwards went on his second voyage. On 11 November 1824 he was granted his sailor's matriculation documents by the authorities at Nice, and on the same day he sailed in his father's ship, the *Santa Reparata*, with his father in command. His mother had persuaded his father to take Peppino; if the boy had to go to sea, she preferred it to be in his father's ship than in any other captain's. His first voyage with his father was a short journey westwards along the French coast to St Tropez, Toulon, Bandol and Martigues; but on 26 March 1825 he sailed from Nice in the *Santa Reparata*, under his father, bound for Rome. After calling at Leghorn and other ports they reached Fiumicino on 12 April, and went on by land to Rome, where they stayed for more than a month, as Domenico Garibaldi had some legal business to transact there, finally leaving on 19 May and reaching Nice on 1 June.

It was the first time in his life that Peppino had been to Rome, and it so happened that he did not go there again until he went to fight for its revolutionary government in 1848. At the time of this first visit, he did not yet hold any strong opinions about Italian unity and liberation; but Rome already meant a great deal to him, as it did to so many other Italians. Apart from its position, in the eyes of devout Catholics, as the seat of the Papacy, it was a symbol of the days, fifteen hundred years before, when it had been the capital of an empire which had united all Italy, as well as ruling many subject peoples. When Garibaldi first saw Rome – or so, at least, he wrote in later years – he had a vague vision of the Rome of the future, the capital of a united Italy and free from Papal rule. But in 1825, despite such vague yearnings, he had no serious hopes that Italian unity would ever be achieved, and no idea of doing anything active to bring it about. 'We had grown to be like the Jews,' he wrote in later years, 'we looked for no prize or goal in life except gold.' This was, he thought, inevitable in view of the fact that they had grown up without a country, and that their only teachers had been priests.[18] Like other nineteenth-century Radicals – including some of Jewish origin – Garibaldi sometimes expressed opinions of this kind about Jews. They were dictated, not by racial prejudice, but by disapproval of the outlook of the middle-class Jewish merchant and capitalist.

For the next nine years, Garibaldi continued his life as a sailor in the Mediterranean, sometimes in his father's ship and sometimes in those of other owners and under other masters.[19] He was a keen and skilful sailor, and soon rose to the rank of first mate. He was liked and respected both by the officers and by the men. 'You could tell when the deck had been swabbed or the cables coiled by Peppino,' said one of his shipmates, 'he would help us all with our work; never got us into any trouble with the skipper, but neither aided nor abetted indiscipline.'[20]

Most of Garibaldi's voyages were short journeys along the French Mediterranean coast, or across the Gulf of Genoa to the Ligurian ports; but he made several journeys to Turkey and the Black Sea, usually in the ships of the Gioan company of Nice, carrying wine, sugar and olive-oil to the east, and corn and flour to the west. All his voyages were made in sailing ships, for although steamships were already operating in the English Channel, and occasionally in the North Atlantic, they did not appear in the Mediterranean for another ten years. The ships were about 200 tons, and had a crew of about ten or twelve. Only once did Garibaldi sail out through the Straits of Gibraltar into the Atlantic. This was in 1827, when he went on a voyage to the Canary Islands, sailing from Nice on 5 January and docking at Genoa on the return journey on 15 May.[21]

He was less fortunate on a voyage to the Levant in the autumn in the *Cortese* under Captain Semeria. They sailed from Nice on 12 September, bound for the Black Sea. It was late in the year to sail to the Black Sea, because many Black Sea ports were ice-bound during at least part of the winter; but they hoped to be able to reach them before the ice set in.[22] While they were off Cape Matapan they were stopped by Greek pirates.[23] Piracy had greatly increased in the eastern Mediterranean during the Greek War of Independence against Turkey. Many of the pirates were Greek patriots who were acting as privateers under letters of marque from the Greek revolutionary authorities, but who did not always distinguish between Turkish and neutral vessels, or between their patriotic duty and their desire to steal.

Captain Semeria ordered his crew not to resist the pirates, and to Garibaldi's disgust they surrendered without a struggle. The pirates took their weapons and ammunition, and then proceeded to loot the ship with great thoroughness, taking everything which was of the slightest value. They even took Garibaldi's shoes. After the pirates had sailed away, the *Cortese* made for the nearest port to try to find new supplies. They landed at St Nicholas on the island of Cythera, which, along with the rest of the Ionian Islands, had been ceded to Britain at the Congress of Vienna. Garibaldi was sent ashore to get help, and on his way to the British captain's office he met an English private, who noticed that Garibaldi was barefoot, and gave him a pair of his own shoes. Forty-two years later, Garibaldi remembered this act of friendship, and told the readers of *Cassell's Magazine* that it was the first of many acts of kindness which had been done to him by English-men. But they were able to obtain only a minimum of essential supplies at St Nicholas.

Garibaldi and his shipmates sailed away, but as soon as they came out of the harbour they met another gang of pirates, who had been hiding behind Dragonera Island, waiting for them to leave St Nicholas. The *Cortese* could not make any resistance, because the first pirates had taken all their arms, and they had not obtained any weapons on Cythera. As the ship had been looted so thoroughly by the first pirates, there was nothing of value for the second gang to take; but they allowed the crew of the *Cortese* to go on their way on condition that they sailed out to sea and did not return to St Nicholas to report the presence of the pirates at Dragonera Island to the British authorities.

Next day they were attacked for a third time by pirates. These pirates were led by a captain named Tombasi, who commanded a well-armed man-of-war with a crew of 150, and claimed to be an officer of the revolutionary Greek navy. In later years, Garibaldi might have been expected to have had sympathy for privateers who were fighting in a revolutionary war for national freedom; but although he already sympathized with the Greek national struggle, he did not like Tombasi, either at the time or when he described the incident in *Cassell's Magazine* in 1870. Tombasi and his men were much more unpleasant than the pirates off Dragonera Island. When they found that there was nothing of value in the *Cortese*, some of them suggested slitting the throats of Garibaldi and all the rest of the captured crew. But some of the other pirates objected violently to this, and after a long argument among the pirates Tombasi allowed the crew of the *Cortese* to go, after taking the clothes that they were wearing, as well as the ship's equipment and navigation instruments. They made new clothes for themselves as best they could out of some matting which they found in the ship's hold; but they had no food on board and were in grave difficulties when they were lucky enough to meet an English ship, whose commander, Captain Taylor, gave them food, and helped them to get to Melos. In Melos they were re-equipped by some English and American warships, and were able to sail on 1 November to Constantinople.[24]

It was now too late in the year to go to the Black Sea, so they decided to winter in the Aegean, and go to the Black Sea in the spring. On 13 March 1828 they docked at Smyrna, where they stayed for nearly two months. While they were there, one of the crew fell overboard, and would have drowned if Garibaldi had not dived in and saved him.[25]

On 6 May they left Smyrna for Constantinople, and sailed on into the Black Sea, and through the Straits of Kertch into the Sea of Azov, where they docked at Taganrog, which was now accessible after having been ice-bound for five months. They then sailed for home, and reached Constantinople on the return journey on 24 August.[26] During their stay in Constantinople, Garibaldi fell ill. His illness was so prolonged that the ship had to sail without him. When he had recovered from his illness, he found that he could not go home, because war had broken out between Turkey and Russia, and this seriously disrupted communications by sea between Italy and Constantinople. He was stranded in Constantinople with very little money. But he accepted the situation very cheerfully, without worrying in the least, being convinced, as he always was when in difficulties, that everything would turn out all right. He joined the Italian Working Men's Club in Pera, the district across the Golden Horn which is now called Beyoglu. He met an Italian family who helped him. He was particularly grateful to the lady of the house, Signora Luigia Sauvaigo, who came from Nice. He writes that Signora Sauvaigo, who was so devoted to her excellent husband and her charming family, was 'one of those women who have so often made me say: Woman is the most perfect of creatures, whatever men may claim.'

Other members of the Italian community in Constantinople came to his help. One of them, Dr Diego, found him a job, recommending him to a widow named Signora Timoni as a tutor to her three boys. He taught the boys Italian, French and mathematics. The academic education, which he had so reluctantly received at his parents' insistence, now came in useful. He decided to improve it by learning as well as teaching. He began learning Greek while he was staying in Signora Timoni's house, though he afterwards forgot it, along with the Latin which he had learned as a boy. His chief reason for learning Greek was his admiration for the Greek struggle for independence against Turkey. He said that if the Italians could produce guerrilla leaders like Constantine Eparca, Karioskaki and Kolokotrones, Italy would be free. He was fascinated by the songs of the Greek revolutionaries, both by the words and the music.

Garibaldi wrote in his memoirs that throughout his life he was always lucky enough, whenever he was in danger or difficulties, to find people who were willing to help him.[27] His charm and personality must have had something to do with this. Those people who helped him, like Signora Sauvaigo in Constantinople, were usually women; but most people of either sex who met him formed a very favourable impression of him, unless they were either personal rivals or political enemies. No photograph or portrait of Garibaldi exists earlier than 1842, when he was aged thirty-four;* but his physical features were duly recorded on four occasions in the registers of the merchant and royal navies in Nice and Genoa when he was between the ages of fourteen and twenty-six. 'Height: $39\frac{3}{4}$ oncie (5 ft $6\frac{1}{2}$ in). Hair: chestnut, or fair. Eyebrows: fair. Eyes: light brown. Forehead: high. Nose: regular. Mouth: average. Chin: round. Beard: fair. Face: oval. Complexion: good. Special marks: none.'[28] The most striking thing about him was his simple dignity of manner, his relaxed frankness, his obvious sincerity, and his quiet courtesy, which could give way to outbursts of violent anger if he were subjected to injury or insult.

*The earliest known portrait of Garibaldi, painted by Bettinotti in 1842, must have been painted in Montevideo before Garibaldi left on the Paraná expedition in June, and was therefore painted a few months before his thirty-fifth birthday. Three other portraits of Garibaldi in South America, all published for the first time in 1848, were probably painted in 1847. These are the portrait by Salucci, published in the *Correo del Ultramar* in Paris; the anonymous portrait published in the *Mondo Illustrato* of Turin; and the portrait of the Italian Legion at Montevideo, including Garibaldi, by Rugéndas; see J. M. Fernandez Saldana's article on the portraits of Garibaldi in *La Prensa* (Buenos Aires), 16 November 1941. The many pictures of Garibaldi as a young man engaged in some adventurous exploit were of course all painted from imagination many years afterwards. According to Comandante Coltelletti, the portrait of Garibaldi painted by Giuseppe Fraschere in the house of the Comandante's grandfather, Luigi Coltelletti, in Genoa on 2 June 1855 (for which Coltelletti paid Fraschere 65 lire) was the only occasion on which Garibaldi ever sat for his portrait. (See frontispiece.) During the latter half of his life he was often photographed.

It is not quite clear for how long Garibaldi remained in Constantinople, but there is every indication that he stayed there for two and a half years.[29] There must have been some reason, which he does not mention in his memoirs, which kept him in Constantinople, because the war between Russia and Turkey ended in September 1829. Eventually he sailed for home in the brig *Nostra Signora delle Grazie*, under Captain Casabona, and reached Nice in the spring of 1831.

Some years before, Garibaldi had fallen seriously in love for the first time. The girl was Francesca Roux, of Nice. Before Garibaldi left for the Levant in September 1827, he and Francesca agreed to marry when he returned. When he reached Nice after an absence of nearly four years, he called first on his parents, and then hurried round to Francesca's house. Finding her garden gate locked, he vaulted the wall of the garden, and found Francesca nursing a baby. He then noticed that she had a wedding ring on her finger. She had married someone else a year before, and had just given birth to her first child. Garibaldi immediately understood what had happened. He kissed Francesca, told her not to try to explain anything, wished her every happiness, and left. Many years afterwards, Garibaldi told this story to his little girl, Clelia, his daughter by his mistress, Francesca Armosino. After living for many years with Francesca Armosino, he married her on 26 January 1880, when Clelia was nearly thirteen; and on his wedding day he told Clelia about Francesca Roux, saying that both his first and his last love had been called Francesca.[30]

Garibaldi usually managed to adopt a philosophical attitude about his unhappy love affairs. On one occasion, when he was aged about fifty, he was discussing with Jessie White Mario the case of a young relative of his who had committed suicide because the girl he loved had rejected him. 'How very foolish,' he said, 'for a man to kill himself for one woman when the world is full of women. When a woman takes my fancy, I say: "Do you love me? I love you. You don't love me? More fool you!"' Jessie White Mario was sure that he never asked any woman twice.[31] But he was not always able to be indifferent, and act rationally, when he was in love.

CHAPTER 2

THE SAINT-SIMONIANS

THOUGH Garibaldi, on his home-coming, had met with a disappointment in love, he had a success in his career. Soon after his return to Nice, he was granted his master's certificate, second grade, and given his first command. He was appointed master of the ship in which he had returned from Constantinople, and commanded the *Nostra Signora delle Grazie* on a voyage to Port Mahon in Minorca and to Gibraltar. After this he made several other voyages along the Ligurian coast, sometimes as captain and sometimes as first mate.[1]

On 24 February 1832 he sailed from Nice as mate of the *Clorinda*, 223 tons, bound for Taganrog, under Captain Clary, who was only a few years older than Garibaldi. In the Aegean they were attacked by two Greek pirate ships off the island of Amorgos. But Captain Clary was more courageous than Captain Semeria of the *Cortese* five years before, or perhaps was merely better armed. He gave orders to fire at the pirates with his two eight-pounder cannon, which, as usual in merchant ships in the Aegean, were always kept loaded. A brief skirmish followed, in which the crew of the *Clorinda* shot at the pirates with their cannon and muskets, and in which Garibaldi was slightly wounded in the right hand; and the pirates beat a hasty retreat. Many years later, Garibaldi jotted down, in pencil, on a sheet of paper a list of all the battles in which he had been engaged during his life in Europe and South America; and the first battle on the list is this fight with Greek pirates in the Aegean. The lessons of his experiences with the pirates under Captain Semeria and Captain Clary were not lost on Garibaldi. 'I relate this last anecdote,' he wrote in *Cassell's Magazine* in 1870, 'in support of my own opinion, that it is always better to fight when one is attacked than to yield without a struggle.'[2]

They reached Constantinople early in May, and Taganrog by the middle of June.[3] While they were in port at Taganrog, Garibaldi became involved in some trouble with the Russian police. He did not mention the incident in his memoirs, but the story was told long afterwards by Captain Antonio Figari of the Italian merchant navy, who was a friend of Garibaldi. Figari was then aged fifteen, and a cabin boy in another ship that was docked at Taganrog.

The Tsar of Russia, Nicholas I, was a stern autocrat and strict disciplinarian, and he imposed his ideal of military discipline on every aspect of civilian life throughout his empire. The authorities at Taganrog had promulgated police regulations which prohibited any kind of noise or disorderly behaviour in the streets; and the gay Italian sailors came into conflict with the law. One evening, Garibaldi and some of his comrades, returning to their ships after a jolly spree in the town, started singing their Italian sailors' songs, with Garibaldi singing louder than anyone. Garibaldi loved singing, and had a good tenor voice; he believed that if his voice had been trained, he could have become an opera singer. The singing was interrupted by the arrival of the Russian police, who arrested Garibaldi on a charge of riotous behaviour. Captain Clary approached Antonio Rossi, an important Italian merchant who had lived for many years in Taganrog and was a friend of the Governor of the town. Rossi saw the Governor, and also the Governor's wife, and persuaded them to intervene with the police in Garibaldi's favour; and the police released Garibaldi, on condition that he remained on board ship until he left Taganrog.

But Garibaldi resented the attitude of the police, and was in defiant mood. A few evenings later, he and one of his friends, who was the mate on another of the Gioan company's ships in Taganrog, went on shore together, intending to visit a place of entertainment. But the place had been closed by the police, and when Garibaldi and his friend arrived there, they found the police waiting and warning people not to enter. The police recognized Garibaldi, and arrested him, and charged him with disobeying the order to stay on board his ship. The Chief of Police was very angry, and spoke of sending Garibaldi to Siberia as a lesson to all foreign seamen; but Rossi went again to the Governor, and again the Governor's wife used her influence on Garibaldi's behalf. Garibaldi was released a second time, with a severe caution, and stayed on board the *Clorinda* until she sailed for home, reaching Constantinople at the beginning of July and Villefranche on 1 September. We must have some reservations about accepting Captain Figari's story. It was first published nearly eighty years afterwards, when Figari, though still alive, was aged ninety-four. Figari says that the incident occurred in 1831, when it is very unlikely that Garibaldi was in Taganrog; he wrongly states that the name of Garibaldi's ship was the *Generale Massena;* he says that immediately on returning to Nice, Garibaldi entered the Royal Sardinian Navy, which he did not do until more than a year later, after he had made two more voyages as a merchant seaman; and he says that Garibaldi was aged twenty at the time of the incident in Taganrog, whereas in fact he was nearly twenty-five in June 1832. But there is probably at least some truth in Figari's story.[4]

The *Clorinda* had hardly reached home when she turned round, and went back to the Black Sea, with Garibaldi again as mate. The crew included his younger brother, Michele, who was aged twenty-two, and Edoardo Mutru, a sailor from Nice of Garibaldi's age with whom he became very friendly. On 10 September they sailed for the Aegean, and on 5 November left Salonika for Odessa, returning to Constantinople in January 1833, and reaching Marseilles in March.[5] Garibaldi then sailed again almost immediately for the Black Sea in the *Clorinda*; but from his point of view, this voyage was to be different from all the others.

While Garibaldi had been pursuing his career as a merchant seaman, the *Risorgimento* had begun in Italy. For a long time there had been a feeling among certain intellectuals that there was some kind of link between the people of the different states of Italy, where everyone spoke some Italian dialect, though the whole area had not been united under one ruler since the downfall of the Roman Empire in the fifth century. Metternich said that Italy was only a geographical expression; but it was an expression which was in general use, and had some meaning for the inhabitants, like the word 'Scandinavia' today. As early as 1764 Count Gian Rinaldo Carli had written about the stranger who entered a café in Milan, and was asked whether he was a Milanese or a foreigner. 'I am neither a Milanese nor a foreigner,' he replied, and explained to his puzzled questioner that he was an Italian, and that an Italian was not a foreigner anywhere in Italy.[6]

But the *Risorgimento* only developed as a serious force after 1789. Like all the revolutionary movements of the nineteenth century, it arose out of the French Revolution, and the march of Napoleon's armies. The French Revolution was welcomed more enthusiastically in Italy than anywhere else abroad. In Naples, Napoleon established his general, Murat, as king. In the north, he himself became king of the Kingdom of Italy. It was the first time since the tenth century that a state had been named 'Italy'. Napoleon abolished the archaic laws of the old régime, introduced religious toleration and divorce, built roads, abolished torture, the discriminatory laws against the Jews, and the antiquated system of measurements. His government became unpopular, even with the Radicals, because he suppressed republican and Jacobin movements, taxed and exploited the Italians for France's benefit, and ignored the national feelings of the people; but the Italian Radicals never turned against Napoleon, like the Spanish and German Radicals did, and the contingents from the Kingdom of Italy proved to be the most reliable of the foreign units in his army.

Napoleon was more unpopular in Piedmont than anywhere else in Italy. Unlike the other Italian rulers, the King of Sardinia was welcomed enthusiastically when he returned in 1814, particularly in those territories, such as Nice, which had been directly annexed by France. Jessie White Mario stated that though she sometimes heard Mazzini and the other Italian revolutionaries speak favourably of Napoleon and pay tribute to his role in furthering the liberation of Italy from the old absolutist governments, she could not remember ever hearing Garibaldi say a good word for Napoleon. She thought that his childhood prejudices against the foreign oppressor of the Italian people of Nice was too strong for him to be able to judge Napoleon objectively. But in fact Garibaldi, in the first edition of his memoirs, condemned both Napoleon and the Allied powers with equal objectivity and truth. He stated that Napoleon had betrayed the cause of liberty which he had proclaimed on entering Italy, while the Allies, including Protestant Prussia and England, had reimposed the Papacy as well as the monarchy and the aristocracy. Yet 'the Italians were vilified as a degenerate race, and falsely accused of having brought their misfortunes upon themselves, by their ignorance, fanaticism and pusillanimity'.[7]

When Napoleon fell, the Congress of Vienna re-established the old régimes in every part of Italy. Some of these régimes were much more oppressive than others. The King of Naples and the Duke of Modena established a ferocious tyranny; the King of Sardinia and the rulers of Parma and Tuscany were relatively mild.

In the Papal States, the government was almost entirely in the hands of clerics, only the lowest grades in the civil service being held by laymen. Here, like in other Italian states, religious toleration, which had existed in the time of Napoleon, was abolished, and only the Roman Catholic religion was permitted. Books and newspapers were censored, and the expression of revolutionary, heretical and immoral opinions was punished. The laws against the Jews were not only reintroduced, but in some cases made more severe, the Jews being forced to live in ghettos, forbidden to own property, and compelled to attend a Catholic church service once a week. Torture was once again allowed in judicial processes. Vaccination was made illegal. The street lighting in Rome was suppressed. Popular education, which had to some extent been encouraged by Napoleon, was restricted by the Papal government, which carried its opposition to progress so far as to prevent the building of railways in the Papal States, believing, with reason, that this would disturb the tranquillity of the isolated valleys where the peasants, though very poor, were on the whole contented and were strongly attached to Catholic religious observances and their parish priest. This attitude of the Papal government about railways annoyed the neighbouring governments, as it prevented the construction of railway lines which could have linked the other Italian states; and the Pope eventually gave way, under pressure from Austria, and allowed the lines to be built.

The rulers of Europe, having beaten Napoleon and 70,000 French soldiers at Waterloo, and sent 'General Buonaparte' to St Helena, thought that they had defeated the Revolution and re-established order in Europe; and to ensure the stability of the old régimes, the Tsar of Russia, the Emperor of Austria and the King of Prussia formed the Holy Alliance, by which they agreed that it was their sacred duty to intervene by force to restore any European sovereign who was overthrown by a revolution of his subjects. But within a few years they were challenged by a small group of unarmed Italian Radicals, who eventually succeeded where Napoleon and his armies had failed. Less than five years after Waterloo, Radical students were demonstrating in the universities and high schools against their kings and dukes. They broke up their classes and lectures, and demonstrated in the streets. As a sign of protest they grew beards and moustaches, wore their hair longer than the usual fashion, and smoked cigars. The authorities expelled the most unruly students, and reacted strongly to the beards and moustaches. At the least excuse, the police would seize a student, march him off to the barber's, and have him forcibly shaved.[8]

But there was a more organized and sinister form of opposition than the student demonstrations. Unable to fight the monarchs of Europe in the open on the battlefield, the revolutionaries fought them clandestinely, and formed secret societies. The political secret society – the revolutionary underground cell – first arose in Italy after Waterloo. Secret societies with no political connexions, like the Mafia in Sicily and the Camorra in Naples, had existed in Italy for some time. The revolutionary Radicals now formed a secret society with political objectives – the Carbonari. Some of the members were idealistic students; others were tough criminals. It had branches in Spain and France as well as in Italy, and its leader was Filippo Buonarroti, an Italian aristocrat who had become a naturalized Frenchman, a friend of Robespierre, and the founder of modern revolutionary Socialism. Its objective was to overthrow the despotic kings and establish an egalitarian republic; its method was political assassination.

The Carbonari were the pioneers of the modern revolutionary underground organization. They were followed in due course by Mazzini's Young Italy; by Bakunin, the Nihilists and Lenin's Bolshevik Party in Russia; by the illegal Communist parties; by the resistance organizations in occupied Europe during the Second World War; by the IRA in Ireland; and by the Tupamaros in South America. At about the same time as the Carbonari, a counter-revolutionary secret society called the Sanfedisti was formed. Its aim was to murder Radicals and members of the Carbonari.

One of the young idealists who joined the Carbonari was Giuseppe Mazzini. He was born on 28 June 1805, and so was almost exactly two years older than his great disciple, Giuseppe Garibaldi. Like Garibaldi he was a subject of the King of Sardinia, his father being a doctor in Genoa. After studying law at the university, he joined the Carbonari; but he soon left them, and founded his own organization, which he called Young Italy. He would probably in any case have left the Carbonari, because he showed throughout his life that he could not work in any group which he did not dominate, and was psychologically incapable of collaborating with anyone who was intellectually his equal; but he disapproved of the practice of the Carbonari of killing traitors and informers, though, like the Carbonari, he justified the assassination of kings and tyrants. Mazzini was far superior as a theoretician and writer to anyone in the Carbonari, and in his journals and pamphlets he put forward the philosophical justification of tyrannicide. It was chiefly because of this that during his life he was hated and feared, not only by governments but also by all men of moderate opinions, in every country of Europe.

At many periods of history, noble-minded men and women have been prepared to become cold-blooded murderers out of selfless devotion to a cause. During the religious wars of the sixteenth and seventeenth centuries, both John Knox on the Protestant side, and the Jesuit de Mariana on the Catholic, found many texts in the Old Testament to justify the murder of the leaders of the other side. During the French Revolution, Charlotte Corday became a heroine in the eyes of the French Royalists and of Tory society in London when she murdered the Jacobin leader, Marat, in his bath. Mazzini similarly justified the assassination of despots, at least if it was done in order to precipitate a revolution. 'Sacred in the hand of Judith was the sword that took the life of Holofernes; sacred was the dagger which Harmodius encircled with roses; sacred the dagger of Brutus; sacred the stiletto of the Sicilian who began the Vespers; sacred the arrow of Tell!'[9]

Garibaldi – at least in his younger days – supported Mazzini's doctrine of assassination. He praised Brutus and the men of the Vespers. In South America, his political colleagues, the Unitarians of Uruguay, who were Radicals like Mazzini, called for the assassination of Rosas, the dictator of Argentina; and in 1848 Garibaldi, like Mazzini, applauded the murder of Count Rossi, the Pope's Conservative minister, which sparked off the revolution in Rome.

Mazzini was the greatest political thinker that the international Radical movement produced during the nineteenth century, and he expressed more clearly than anyone else their doctrines of revolutionary nationalism. He believed passionately in his country, Italy; but he was an internationalist as well as a nationalist. His aim was a federation of the world. He thought that Italian patriots, fighting to free their country, should make common cause with patriots of foreign countries who were working for the liberation of their own peoples, as there was no conflict between them; for wars were not caused by patriots, but by cosmopolitan kings who used their subjects for their own ends. He not only supported the nationalist struggles of the Poles and Hungarians against Austria, but joined with the Radicals of other countries who had followed his example in founding Young Italy. In April 1834 the leaders of Young Germany and Young Poland met Mazzini in Geneva and formed Young Europe, with a programme drafted by Mazzini. Soon afterwards, Young France, Young Switzerland and Young Austria joined Young Europe. The revolutionary nationalists of Ireland were absent. Mazzini sympathized with the Irish struggle against British oppression, but the strong Catholic feeling among the Irish revolutionaries usually made them take the anti-revolutionary side in Europe. Garibaldi, in particular, was hated in after years by the Irish nationalists.

Mazzini, like Garibaldi and all the Italian Radicals, was bitterly opposed to the Catholic Church and to all organized religion, though he was not an atheist. He was deeply religious, and believed passionately in his deistic God. This was one of the main causes of his disagreement with the Socialists, whom he condemned, in any case, as a diversionary body who weakened the Liberal nationalist struggle against absolutism and Conservatism. But though Young Italy was supported by many Catholics, including several priests, it came into conflict with the Catholic Church hierarchy.

The contest had its roots in the French Revolution. The revolutionary leaders, Hébert and Camille Desmoulins, had claimed to be followers of the 'sans-culotte Jesus'; but the Papacy had thrown its influence against the revolution, which had originally been supported by most of the parish priests in France. Pope Pius VI had excommunicated the Catholic priests who supported the revolution, and had encouraged the émigré French bishops who called for a counter-revolutionary crusade of Catholic Austria and Protestant Prussia against France; and the French Revolution had led to the burning of churches in France and the worship of the Goddess of Reason. After 1815 the Radicals saw the Pope and the Church hierarchy working together with the Austrian Catholic Metternich, the ultra-Protestant

Tory government of Britain, and the Greek Orthodox Tsar of Russia, to suppress Liberalism and revolution everywhere. The issue was joined between Catholicism and Liberalism, and their conflict dominated the history of Europe in the nineteenth century.

Garibaldi accepted many of Mazzini's doctrines. After 1848 he often disagreed with Mazzini, not only on questions of strategy and tactics, but on such fundamental matters as their attitude to the Sardinian monarchy and to Socialism. But in the essential principles of Radicalism, his Italian patriotism, his internationalism, and his attitude to religion and the Catholic hierarchy, Garibaldi all his life was a Mazzinian.

In 1821 some officers in the Sardinian army, who were members of the Carbonari, organized a military insurrection in Piedmont at the same time as revolution broke out in Naples. Metternich sent the Austrian army to suppress both revolts. The King of Naples and the King of Sardinia were restored to power. The heir to the throne of Sardinia, Prince Charles Albert, who held Liberal opinions and had been sympathetic to the rebels, submitted to the King, and was denounced as a traitor by the revolutionaries. The leaders of the revolution were sentenced to be hanged after having their right hands cut off, and though the sentences were commuted, and no executions took place, they were removed to Austrian prisons and kept for years chained up in the dungeons of the Spielberg fortress in Moravia. The Italian *Risorgimento* had its first martyrs.

The revolution in Paris in July 1830 triggered off a series of revolts and revolutionary demonstrations all over Europe. Once again, as in 1792, the European Radicals looked to France for assistance, though the new French King, Louis Philippe, whom the revolutionaries had placed on the throne instead of his more reactionary cousin, Charles x, soon showed that he was far from being a revolutionary supporter. In February 1831 revolts organized by the Carbonari broke out in Modena, in Bologna, and in the Romagna in the Papal States. Again, as in 1821, Metternich sent the Austrian army to suppress the revolution. In Bologna and the Romagna, where the revolutionaries demanded a constitution and elected assemblies in place of government by a Cardinal-Governor appointed by the Pope, the Swiss Guards of the Pope moved in after Austrian soldiers had crushed the revolt, and undoubtedly committed some atrocities, even if these were exaggerated in the revolutionary propaganda; and Cardinal Bernetti instituted a severe repression of all political and religious dissent.

The repression in 1831 was more severe than in 1821. This time a number of death sentences were carried out. One of those executed was Ciro Menotti, a young revolutionary tradesman of Modena, who was optimistic enough to think that the notoriously reactionary Duke of Modena might agree to become the leader of the Italian *Risorgimento*. The Duke encouraged him for a while, and then arrested him and handed him over to the Austrians, who hanged him. Nine years later, Garibaldi called his eldest son Menotti in honour of Ciro Menotti. More arrests and executions followed in the two years after 1831. The most serious incident was in Piedmont, where the Carbonari organized a revolutionary plot in the Sardinian army against the new king, Charles Albert, who was especially hated by the revolutionaries because of his betrayal of the revolution of 1821. The plot was discovered, and at the personal insistence of Charles Albert, fourteen of the conspirators were shot. As a result, the Carbonari organization was practically wiped out, and the field was left clear for Young Italy.

Garibaldi was slower to join the revolutionary movement than were many young Italians of his generation. He was only thirteen at the time of the revolutionary outbreaks of 1821, and was not affected by them as was the fifteen-year-old Mazzini; but even the disturbances ten years later found him a passive spectator. He never joined the Carbonari. As a sailor, he was not in touch with the revolutionary youth as he would have been in the universities or in the cities of Turin and Genoa. But isolated though he was on the merchant ships in the Mediterranean and the Black Sea, the execution of Menotti affected him deeply. Whenever he went ashore at any Italian port, he tried to find revolutionary books and pamphlets in which he could read more about the martyrs and the cause for which they had died. The new series of executions in Piedmont two years later decided Garibaldi. Jessie White Mario states that it was the executions of 1833 which drove him into the revolutionary movement.[10]

Garibaldi now came into contact with another creed which had arisen at the beginning of the nineteenth century. In the spring of 1833 he met the Saint-Simonian Socialists. Socialism, like revolutionary Radicalism, had grown out of the French Revolution of 1789. Two forms of Socialism emerged – the revolutionary Socialism of Babeuf and Buonarroti, and the peaceful Socialism of Robert Owen in Britain and of Saint-Simon in France. The Count de Saint-Simon, an elderly aristocrat who had barely escaped with his life during Robespierre's rule, wrote a number of books in which he put forward a plan for equal distribution of wealth and the ownership of goods in common, and proposed, surprisingly enough, that this system should be introduced and supervised by a government consisting of big business men under the presidency of King Louis XVIII. After Saint-Simon's death, his movement continued, and became more bizarre. Under their new leader, Enfantin, the Saint-Simonians founded a new religion, and set out to shock the great majority of their contemporaries by violating the established social and moral conventions. Like a number of other isolated groups and individuals of the period, the Saint-Simonians advocated the equality of the sexes and the liberation of women from the chains of marriage, and they aroused more opposition by this than by any of their other doctrines.

The revolution of 1830 was a stimulus to the Saint-Simonians, as it was to all other unorthodox groups. They formed a hippy commune in Paris, wore loose-hanging robes and other extraordinary garments quite unlike the clothes worn by ordinary people at the time, practised as well as preached the doctrine of free love, and worshipped Enfantin as a kind of God. They proclaimed that a spiritual regeneration of the world was necessary, in which Enfantin would be the Father of Humanity, and searched and advertised for a suitable girl to cohabit with Enfantin and be the Mother of Humanity. Their exhibitionist behaviour in Paris caused a public scandal, and the leaders were charged with offences against public decency. At their trial in Paris, which was widely reported in the press, Enfantin was sentenced to a year's imprisonment and banishment from France; the other defendants were to be banished forthwith. Thirteen of them were taken to Marseilles, and on 22 March 1833 were put in a ship bound for Constantinople. The ship was the *Clorinda*, and the mate was Garibaldi.

The voyage to Constantinople took twenty-three days, and during this time Garibaldi became very friendly with Emile Barrault, who was one of Enfantin's chief assistants and the leader of the party of Saint-Simonians in the *Clorinda*. Barrault was aged thirty-four. Like all the Saint-Simonian leaders, he was intellectually brilliant. He had been a professor of rhetoric, and had written a play which had been performed at the Comédie Française. Barrault found Garibaldi a sympathetic listener to his propaganda.

Garibaldi was first attracted to the Saint-Simonians because he sympathized with them as a persecuted minority. The French press had for some months been conducting a vicious campaign against the Saint-Simonians, and when they arrived at Marseilles on their way to exile, the local newspapers attacked and ridiculed them. Large crowds came out to stare and jeer at the cranks in strange clothes who were marched through the streets to the port, singing their 'Song of the Woman' – the ideal woman who was to be the bride of Enfantin – and put on board the *Clorinda*. Garibaldi reacted in their favour. 'I had heard very little about the Saint-Simonian sect,' he wrote in his memoirs, 'I only knew that these men were the persecuted apostles of a new religion.'

On the voyage to Constantinople, Barrault taught Garibaldi the Saint-Simonian doctrines.

[He] proved to me that the man who defends his country, or who attacks other people's country, is in the first example a virtuous soldier, and in the second example an unjust one; but the man who, becoming a cosmopolitan, adopts this second land as his country, and goes and offers his sword and his blood to all peoples who are struggling against tyranny, he is more than a soldier; he is a hero.[11]

These words, which Garibaldi's Fascist admirers during the Mussolini era had difficulty in explaining away, are only to be found in the Dumas version of the memoirs; but they are consistent with his action in fighting for liberty and the Radical cause in Brazil, Uruguay and France, as well as in Italy.

Barrault gave Garibaldi his copy of Saint-Simon's book, *Le Nouveau Christianisme*. Garibaldi kept the book all his life, and it is still in his bedroom at Caprera, with Barrault's autograph on the first page. But Barrault did not convert Garibaldi to Saint-Simonian Socialism. Garibaldi enthusiastically accepted the Saint-Simonians' internationalist principles, but not their Socialist economic theories. He reacted in exactly the same way forty years later, when he came into contact with Marx and the First International.

Garibaldi's reaction to the Saint-Simonians was typical of him, and shows the difference between him and Mazzini. Mazzini, with his keen intellect and philosophical approach, detected all the weaknesses in the Saint-Simonian doctrine, and subjected it to a devastating analysis in his pamphlet *Thoughts upon Democracy in Europe*.[12] Garibaldi was merely impressed by the sincerity and idealism of Barrault, and moved to compassion and indignation at the persecution of the Saint-Simonians. This was Garibaldi's strength and weakness as compared with Mazzini. Garibaldi made friends, overlooked disagreements, and achieved results, while Mazzini was finding subtle points of theoretical difference with potential allies, and entering into bitter polemics with them which split the movement and achieved nothing; but Garibaldi's naïve approach and trusting disposition sometimes caused him to be used as a tool by unscrupulous persons and to fight for objects for which he did not really intend to fight.

Garibaldi remembered the Saint-Simonians, and they remembered him. One of them, the composer Félicien David, witnessed an example of Garibaldi's skill and courage. He was talking to Garibaldi one warm evening on the deck, when they saw a turtle in the water. After commenting on how unusual it was to find a turtle so far from the shore, Garibaldi described to David the two safe ways of capturing a turtle, and then said that there was a third way which was unsafe, because it was better to get your thigh or arm caught between two Sheffield razors than in the jaws of a turtle. He then told David that he would give him a practical illustration of this third way of capturing a turtle, and leaped into the sea, fully clothed. Soon afterwards he reappeared on the bridge of the ship, very wet and bleeding a little, but holding the turtle, and said to David: 'You can have turtle-soup.' Barrault saw the other side of Garibaldi's character. On Easter Sunday, Captain Clary invited all the passengers and crew to dinner, and to celebrate Easter they ate a paschal lamb. Garibaldi did not join them at dinner. When Barrault asked if he were not hungry, Garibaldi said that it had been his job to feed the lamb before it was slaughtered, and that he had grown fond of the animal, and could not bear to eat it.[13]

On 15 April they reached Constantinople, where Barrault and his companions landed, determined to search for the bride of Enfantin. The Turkish authorities objected as much as those in France to the practices of the Saint-Simonians, which angered the Mohammedans even more than the French Catholics, and within a week the Turkish government had told the French Ambassador that they would be deported immediately.[14] They went to Egypt, where Mehemet Ali allowed them to stay, and took these very gifted men into his service. Some years later, the Saint-Simonians returned to France, convinced that the wicked world was not ripe for spiritual rebirth, and that they had better do as well as possible for themselves in competitive capitalist society. Enfantin became a very successful business man, and as a director of the Paris–Lyons Railway Company played a leading part in the development of the PLM line. Several of the other Saint-Simonians became prominent industrialists. Barrault became a Liberal MP in the French Parliament, and later wrote several books on railways, as well as a biography of Christ. David wrote several successful operettas.

CHAPTER 3

GENOA, 4 FEBRUARY 1834

FROM Constantinople, the *Clorinda* sailed on into the Black Sea, and after docking at Odessa went on to Taganrog. Here, for the second time on this eventful voyage, Garibaldi met a man who influenced his life. One evening, while they were at Taganrog, Garibaldi entered an Italian seamen's club in the port area, and found that a meeting was in progress in one of the rooms. A young sailor was making a speech about the liberation of Italy and the doctrines of Mazzini and Young Italy; and Garibaldi sat down near the back of the room, and listened. The speaker was Giovanni Battista Cuneo, a young sailor aged twenty-four – two years younger than Garibaldi – who came from Oneglia on the Ligurian coast. He had joined Young Italy, and had been instructed by Mazzini to carry on propaganda in the merchant navy. Cuneo's speech was followed by general discussion. Garibaldi took no part in the discussion; but after the meeting he went up to Cuneo, and told him how greatly he had been impressed by his speech. Cuneo was very pleased with this new convert, and during the rest of Garibaldi's stay in Taganrog the two young men often met, and talked about the *Risorgimento* and Young Italy. 'I am sure that Columbus did not feel so much satisfaction at the discovery of America,' wrote Garibaldi in his memoirs, 'as I felt on meeting someone who was working for the redemption of our country.'[1] Cuneo gave Garibaldi the names and addresses of his political contacts in Marseilles, where Mazzini was in exile and had established the headquarters of Young Italy.

Garibaldi returned from Taganrog to Nice in the summer of 1833, and went to Marseilles. Here he met a member of Young Italy named Covi, whose address he had been given by Cuneo; and he states in his memoirs that Covi introduced him to Mazzini.[2] Mazzini had been living in Marseilles in the house of the French Radical politician, Demosthènes Ollivier, in secrecy, because since the political reaction in France which followed the labour unrest of 1832, the government of Louis Philippe had become almost as hostile to revolutionaries as the governments of the Holy Alliance.

Garibaldi refers to his meeting with Mazzini in Marseilles in two editions of his memoirs. Mazzini also wrote that he first met Garibaldi at this time; and Jessie White Mario, who knew both men very well, says that they met in Ollivier's house in Marseilles in the autumn of 1833. 'Would Italy today,' she wrote, 'be . . . a nation peerless among her peers, had Joseph Mazzini and Joseph Garibaldi never met that autumn in Marseilles?' The story of this first meeting of Mazzini and Garibaldi became part of the mythology of the *Risorgimento*, and pictures by Matania and other *Risorgimento* painters of the two great patriots, at their first encounter, looking at each other in instant mutual admiration, were already hanging in hundreds of Italian homes soon after Garibaldi and Mazzini died. But it is very unlikely that the meeting took place, and Garibaldi and Mazzini probably met for the first time in 1848. Garibaldi's ship did not return from Taganrog until 17 August 1833, when it docked at Villefranche. Mazzini, after spending the early summer in Marseilles, left for Geneva at the end of June, and had arrived in Geneva by 28 June. He did not return to Marseilles for many years. As Garibaldi and Mazzini were both using false names during their stay in Marseilles in 1833, it would not be surprising if they both came to believe, when they eventually met fifteen years later, that the other was one of the revolutionaries whom they had met on one occasion, under another name, in 1833.[3]

Someone – either Mazzini or somebody else – initiated Garibaldi into Young Italy in Marseilles in the autumn of 1833, and administered the oath of loyalty to him. All the members of Young Italy were known by false names in the organization, and Garibaldi took the name of Giuseppe Borel.[4] He was a most useful acquisition for Young Italy, for he already had a sense of realism and a practical ability which were rare among Radical revolutionaries. Jessie White Mario wrote that Garibaldi 'knew far more of the world and its ways at six and twenty than did Mazzini at the age of twenty-nine', because whereas Mazzini had lived a secluded life at home with a doting mother, Garibaldi's experiences as a seaman had taught him when to take risks and when to be cautious, and had made him familiar with fraudulent traders, with shipowners who oppressed their crews and cheated the insurance companies, and with seamen who stole from their employers. 'With regard to the courage and constancy of the masses he probably had his doubts.' Mazzini and the refugees at Marseilles 'believed that every Italian felt as they felt; even in those days we suspect Garibaldi of putting all this enthusiasm into quarantine'.[5]

Garibaldi had joined the organization at the right time, for Young Italy had an important task for him to perform. Mazzini had made plans for a revolution to take place in the Kingdom of Sardinia. Seven hundred revolutionaries, most of whom were Poles who had been living as refugees in Switzerland since the defeat of the Polish revolution in 1831, were to invade Sardinian territory by crossing the Lake of Geneva from the Swiss side and attacking Savoy. At the same time, the members of Young Italy were to launch an insurrection in Genoa. Garibaldi and other sailors who supported Young Italy were to join the Sardinian Royal Navy and organize a mutiny in support of the revolution. As soon as the revolution broke out in Genoa, they were to seize their ships and join the revolutionaries.

But serious difficulties had already arisen. Mazzini had chosen General Ramorino to lead the invasion from Switzerland. Ramorino was an Italian revolutionary who had served with distinction at Wagram and in Russia in 1812 in the Italian contingent of Napoleon's army, and had held a high command in the Polish forces during the revolution of 1831. But he was at loggerheads with Mazzini almost from the start, and had taken so long in raising the necessary money for the invasion in Paris that some of Mazzini's friends began to say that he had embezzled the funds for himself. Some of the revolutionaries urged Mazzini to remove Ramorino from the command; but Mazzini refused, as he did not know anyone else who had Ramorino's military experience and prestige. Eventually it was decided to fix the date of the invasion on the Lake of Geneva for 31 January 1834. The revolt in Genoa was timed for 11 February, by which time it was hoped that the invaders from the north, having been joined by large numbers of the people and of the royal garrisons, would be approaching Genoa.

The subjects of the King of Sardinia were liable for compulsory military service in the land forces or in the Royal Navy. But any sailor in the merchant navy could have his call-up deferred, provided that he served a total of five years in the Royal Navy before he reached the age of forty. Garibaldi now notified the Sardinian authorities that he wished to do his service in the Royal Navy at this time. On 16 December 1833 he received orders to report to Genoa, where he was to join the warship *Eurydice*. On the 26th he began his service there, putting on the close-fitting dress-coat uniform, with sword-belt hanging from the shoulder, and high top hat. His friend Edoardo Mutru, who had sailed with him on the *Clorinda*, joined the Royal Navy on the same day. Mutru was not a member of Young Italy, but was a strong sympathizer.

Sailors joining the Royal Navy were required to have a *nom-de-guerre*, a pseudonym which they used in the service. They could choose their own pseudonym, but it had to begin with the same letter of the alphabet as their real name. Garibaldi chose the name of Cleombroto, the King of Sparta in the fourth century BC, which he was allowed to adopt, although it began with a C, not a G, presumably because it sounded close enough. The choice of the name is interesting in the circumstances, as King Cleombroto was killed at the Battle of Leuctra fighting for despotic Sparta against the revolutionary, freedom-loving armies of Thebes. The naval authorities at Genoa duly noted that Garibaldi Giuseppe Maria, captain second grade in the merchant navy, seaman third grade in the Royal Navy, was to be known as Cleombroto. They did not know that he was also Borel of Young Italy, and that he had joined the Royal Navy, as Jessie White Mario put it, 'in the service of the Revolution'.[6]

Garibaldi was ideally suited for the task which he had been allotted by Young Italy. His skill as a sailor, his knowledge of the character and habits of seamen, and his friendly personality made him an excellent person to conduct revolutionary propaganda in the navy; and he was very successful, winning over many of the sailors in the *Eurydice* to the cause of the revolution. One day in January 1834 he was given shore-leave, and contacted Vittore Mascarelli, a twenty-four-year-old captain of the merchant navy who was a native of Nice and a member of Young Italy. Garibaldi and Mascarelli went into a café in the town. An NCO of the artillery, whom Garibaldi and Mascarelli did not know, but whose name was Medici, came and sat down at their table. They started talking, and Garibaldi and Mascarelli told Medici about the need for a revolution, and urged him to join Young Italy and organize a mutiny in the artillery. Medici was a very sympathetic listener, and appeared to be won over by their arguments. Unfortunately he was an agent of the secret police. He sent a full report to the police on what Garibaldi and Mascarelli had said, alleging that they had offered him money if he organized a mutiny in the artillery. The story about the money sounds very unlikely, and was probably invented in order to discredit the idealism of the revolutionaries.[7]

After many delays and postponements, the day came at last for the start of the invasion of Savoy. On the night of 31 January some of the Poles, who formed the advance guard, seized two boats and crossed the Lake of Geneva; but they lost their way, and were intercepted by a force of Swiss policemen, who marched them off to the local police station and locked them up. On the next night, 1 February, Mazzini and Ramorino with 223 men – the rest of the 700 did not materialise – set off to join the first contingent at the agreed meeting-place. Their comrades did not come. Mazzini, who was temperamentally unsuited to be a revolutionary leader, was so nervous and excited that he forgot to take his overcoat, though it was a cold winter's night, and he soon developed a temperature, which rose higher when he indulged in heated arguments about tactics with Ramorino. When it became clear that the others would not be coming, Ramorino suggested that they should call off the whole project. Mazzini became so indignant that he finally collapsed and lost consciousness, and Ramorino and the others marched back into Switzerland. When Mazzini came to, and found that he was still in Switzerland, and had not even succeeded in crossing the frontier, he returned to Geneva in despair, convinced that all was lost.[8]

The news of the attempted invasion spread quickly over Europe. It caused great excitement in Genoa, where the Young Italy organization was thrown into confusion, and the public believed that a revolution was about to begin. Suddenly, on 3 February, Garibaldi was transferred from the *Eurydice* to the *Conte des Geneys*, which was the Admiral's flagship and the largest ship in the Sardinian fleet. This was a heavy blow to Garibaldi. As in other navies, discipline tended to be stricter in larger than in smaller warships, and Garibaldi's facilities for revolutionary propaganda, right under the Admiral's nose, would be less than in the *Eurydice*. A few hours before the revolution in Genoa was expected to start, he was being moved from his friends and sympathizers in the *Eurydice*, where his propaganda had been so successful, to the *Conte des Geneys*, where, in the short time at his disposal, he would have no chance of persuading his new shipmates to mutiny. He therefore decided to desert from the navy. As he had no chance of organizing a mutiny in the *Conte des Geneys*, he could at least join the civilian revolutionaries in Genoa, and add one more to the number of fighters on the barricades.

He slept only one night in the *Conte des Geneys*. Next morning, on 4 February, he and his friend Mutru pretended to be ill, and reported sick. The duty petty officer had not been told that Garibaldi was suspected of being a revolutionary agitator, and, having no reason for suspicion, gave him and Mutru a pass to go ashore to see the doctor. They made off into the town, and went to the Piazza Sarzano, having heard a rumour that the revolution would begin with an attack on the military barracks there. But they saw no sign of any revolution – no barricades, not even a street demonstration. They spent the day wandering around Genoa; but though the town was swarming with troops and police, everything was quiet. Mutru then suggested that, as there was obviously not going to be a revolution, they had better return to their ship, and face the consequences of having been absent without leave for a few hours rather than become deserters. But Garibaldi thought that they had gone too far to turn back, and was sure that he would not have been transferred from the *Eurydice* to the *Conte des Geneys* unless the authorities had suspected him of being a revolutionary. In the evening, they looked in at a dance-hall – always a good hiding-place for revolutionaries on the run from the police – and found it crowded; and they wryly decided that the people of Genoa were more interested in dancing than in revolution. They stayed in the dance-hall until midnight, and then made their way to the house of a woman, who was no doubt a supporter of Young Italy, where they spent the night.

Garibaldi appears to have suffered from a certain nervousness during these days in Genoa. Like other persons who have faced a similar situation, he seems to have felt more anxiety when hiding from the police in a house in a town, where he might be caught like a rat in a trap, than he did on a battlefield, or when facing the perils of the sea, or when he was being hunted by the authorities in the open country-side. He could not get off to sleep that night in Genoa until 5 am, and he woke only an hour later with a sense of imminent danger. He woke Mutru, and suggested that they should leave the house at once. But Mutru did not share Garibaldi's apprehensions, and insisted on going to sleep again. Garibaldi then went off by himself. Again he walked round the town, but there was still no sign of the revolution. He was thinking about returning to find Mutru at the house where they had spent the night, when he met a friend who told him that, a few minutes after Garibaldi had left the house, the police had arrived and had arrested Mutru. This convinced Garibaldi that his premonition of danger had been justified; but in fact the story was untrue. Mutru, after a good sleep, had returned to the *Conte des Geneys;* but as soon as he reached the ship, he was arrested and charged with being a party to an attempted insurrection.

Garibaldi had now definitely decided to desert from the navy, and thought that he had better acquire some civilian clothes. As a start, he went into a hatter's shop, and bought a large black hat, like the kind worn by university professors; without his top hat and sword, his coat looked less conspicuously like naval uniform. He then sought out another friend in Genoa, a woman named Teresina who owned a fruit shop in Carlo Felice Street. He asked Teresina to hide him from the police, and she agreed to do so, and hid him in an inner room in the shop.

He had made up his mind to return to Nice, and as he knew that both the port and the highway would be watched by the police, he could not go either by sea or along the coast road. He would have to go by an inland route, walking along the byways and footpaths. Teresina gave him a suit of her husband's clothes, which he put on;

they were working men's clothes, and more suitable for walking in the fields than his university professor's hat. The hat could still serve a useful purpose, for Teresina filled it with bread and cheese. He left the shop, and set out on his journey; but when he reached the Piazza di Banchi, he heard everyone talking about the arrests which were taking place, and somebody said that the police were looking for a man called Garibaldi. He decided to take refuge with a woman whom he knew named Caterina, and stayed in her house till nightfall. At about 8 pm he slipped out of the house, and made his way to the edge of the city by the small alleys and back-gardens of the houses. He had to climb many walls and hedges, but after about an hour he had completed this – the most dangerous – part of his journey, and left Genoa by the Porta della Lanterna.

This, as far as we can judge, is what happened to Garibaldi in Genoa on 4 and 5 February 1834. In 1850, when he wrote the first edition of his memoirs which were published nine years later, he described his experiences on this occasion; and in 1851, when he travelled in a ship from New York to Panama, he talked about them to another traveller, Edoardo Reta, who wrote it down in his diary. In 1866, after he had become a national hero, he received letters from several women in Genoa, who identified themselves as the women who had helped him on 4 and 5 February 1834; and he wrote short, but charming, letters of thanks to all of them. In these various accounts he mentions several facts which he omits in the other versions; but there is nothing contradictory in the various accounts, unless it is a contradiction because a man cannot remember, nearly twenty years later, if he did something on 4 or 5 February, and confuses the sequence in which he visited a number of women helpers and the streets in which they lived.[9]*

After leaving Genoa, he walked across country, through the Sestri Mountains to Nice. He walked at night, finding his direction by the

*The well-known story of how, when the troops surrounded the Piazza Sarzano, he ran into a fruit shop, where the woman who owned the shop, though she did not know him, decided on the spur of the moment to hide him, is inconsistent with the story which Garibaldi told Reta; but a careful reading of the Dumas and Melena versions of Garibaldi's memoirs, which are the sources of this story, shows that Garibaldi never actually says that the shop was situated in the Piazza Sarzano, that his entry into the shop followed immediately after the surrounding of the square by the soldiers, or that the woman who owned the shop was a stranger to him. She was, in fact, his friend Teresina. Nor is there any evidence for the story told by several modern biographers that Garibaldi spent 4 and 5 February 1834 making love to three women in Genoa, beyond the fact that one of these women, according to Reta, addressed him as 'tu', not 'voi', which was natural among members of a revolutionary organization, and that Garibaldi commented: 'Women are angels in such circumstances.' But these words are Reta's comment, not Garibaldi's.

stars; during the day, he slept under bushes and in other concealed places. After ten days he had covered the two hundred miles, and reached Nice. Meanwhile his brother Felice, who lived in Genoa, where he worked for a business firm, had been arrested. On 10 February the Marquis Paolucci, the Military Governor of Genoa, ordered the arrest of 'Francesco' Garibaldi, brother of Giuseppe Garibaldi, 'one of the heads of the insurrectionary movement'. Felice, though he sympathized with the *Risorgimento*, had never been actively interested in anything except girls; and after a few days he was released, and allowed to go to Corsica.[10]

Domenico and Rosa Garibaldi were very distressed at what had happened; all their ambitions for their intelligent son Peppino, who they had hoped would become a priest, a doctor or a lawyer, had been dashed. The mother, who became more devoutly religious and Catholic with each disaster that confronted her, had been pained to hear Peppino speak favourably of the Saint-Simonians when he had returned from his voyage in the *Clorinda* six months before. Now she was convinced that it was all the fault of the Saint-Simonians that Peppino had got into trouble, and told all her friends and neighbours in Nice: 'The Saint-Simonians ruined my son.'[11]

Garibaldi realized that it would not be safe for him to stay for long at home, or anywhere else in Nice. He decided to go to Marseilles where he knew many members of Young Italy who were living there in exile, and who, although occasionally troubled by the French police, were much safer than in the Kingdom of Sardinia. He said goodbye to his family and friends, and set off for the French frontier, again avoiding the coast road, and going inland through the hills. He did not return home for more than fourteen years. He never saw his father again.

His cousin Angelo Gustavini, and another friend, went with him as far as the frontier on the River Var, some five miles from Nice. The river was higher than usual because of the recent heavy rains, but Garibaldi swam across, and as he stood on French soil, and waved goodbye to his friends on the other side of the river, he felt that he had at last reached safety. Like many other Radicals of his generation, he thought of France as the country of the Revolution. He did not appreciate, as Mazzini did, the reactionary character of Louis Philippe and his new government.

He walked up to the first frontier post that he came to in France, and told the immigration officials who he was, and how he had escaped from Genoa, and asked for political asylum. The officials told him that as he had entered France illegally, they would have to detain him until they received instructions from higher authority as to what to do with him. The officials took him to the town of Draguignan, forty miles from the frontier. He had no idea what would happen to him, but he realized that he might be taken back to the frontier and handed over to the Sardinian authorities. He decided to try to escape if he got the chance.

At the police station at Draguignan, he was held in a room on the first floor of the building, which was not more than ten feet above the street level. There was one policeman in the room with him; as it was a warm day in early spring, the window was open. Garibaldi walked casually over to the window, as if he were looking at the view, and then suddenly jumped down into the street. The policeman, who had less at stake than Garibaldi, preferred to run down the stairs, and by the time he reached the street, Garibaldi was disappearing round the corner. He ran out of the town into the fields and got away.

He walked in the direction of Marseilles, through the hills of the Var district, and on the evening of the following day he arrived at a small village. He went into the village inn and ordered food and drink. The innkeeper was very friendly, and invited Garibaldi to sit down to a meal at the table with him and his wife; and Garibaldi told the innkeeper the whole story of his escape from Genoa and Draguignan. He probably believed that even if the French police had not been too friendly, the people of France were ardent supporters of the revolution; but the innkeeper said, a little gruffly, that if Garibaldi had escaped from the French police, it was his duty to capture Garibaldi and hand him over to the police. Garibaldi was not sure, from the innkeeper's tone of voice, if he meant this seriously; but he treated the matter as if the innkeeper were joking, and as the innkeeper was physically a weaker man than he, he felt confident of his ability to overpower the innkeeper in any tussle if he tried to apprehend him. So Garibaldi continued happily eating his supper.

After a little while a number of villagers came into the inn. Garibaldi talked to them and drank with them, and they were all very friendly; but as the inn filled up, it occurred to Garibaldi that if the innkeeper really wished to hand him over to the police, he would now be able to do so, because if there were a struggle between Garibaldi and the innkeeper, all the other guests in the inn, being acquaintances of the innkeeper, would obviously come to the innkeeper's assistance, and Garibaldi would not be able to beat them all. Then the company began to sing. They sang the Provençal songs that Garibaldi had known since his childhood, and he joined in, with his fine tenor voice. Afterwards he sang the song *Le Dieu des bonnes gens*, the words of which were written by the French Radical poet, Béranger, though it was a drinking song with hardly any political significance. His song was received with great applause, and the guests demanded an *encore*. After this, he had no more anxiety that he would be handed over to the police. They sat up drinking, singing and playing cards all night. When dawn came, he said goodbye to the innkeeper, and walked out with the other guests.[12]

He reached Marseilles without any more adventures, and found his friends of Young Italy. He was, of course, an illegal immigrant, but so were many other foreigners in Marseilles, and he was safe enough in the district around the harbour which was later known as the *vieux port*. He could rely on the help of the Italian political refugees and their French Radical and Socialist friends. They found an English sailor named Joseph Pane, who was willing to sell his identity papers to Garibaldi, and Garibaldi passed himself off as Joseph Pane. This was a little risky, because Garibaldi could hardly speak a word of English, but it was a risk which had to be taken.

One day in June 1834, after Garibaldi had been in Marseilles for about three months, he happened to see a local newspaper, *Le Peuple Souverain*. 'It was the first time,' he wrote in his memoirs, 'that I had the honour of seeing my name printed in a newspaper.'[13] It contained a report of Garibaldi's court martial by the naval authorities in Genoa on 3 June. Nine defendants, the eldest of whom was thirty-six, had been tried together, six being present in court and three in their absence. One of the six defendants present was Mutru. The three tried in their absence were Garibaldi, Mascarelli and a civilian inhabitant of Genoa named Caorsi. Garibaldi, Mascarelli and Caorsi were accused of plotting in the months of January and February last an insurrection in the forces against His Majesty the King, Garibaldi and Mascarelli having tried to corrupt with money an NCO of the artillery – this was Medici, whom Garibaldi and Mascarelli had met in the café in Genoa – and Caorsi having tried to obtain ammunition and weapons for the revolutionaries. The sentence of the court, dated 16 June, found Garibaldi and the two other absent defendants guilty, and sentenced them to 'ignominious death and exposed them to the public vendetta as enemies of the Fatherland and of the State, and liable to all the pains and penalties imposed by the King's laws against bandits of the first degree'. The six defendants present in court, however, had all been acquitted; so the court had been more lenient than might have been expected, and Mutru was safe.[14]

Garibaldi had to get employment of some kind, and he returned to his old occupation of a merchant seaman. He signed on for a voyage to the Levant in the French ship *L'Union* under the name of Joseph Pane. He could not sail officially as master or mate, because Joseph Pane had no master's certificate, and could only be an ordinary seaman. On 22 April 1834 the merchant navy authorities at Nice had duly entered in their records that Garibaldi had gone absent without leave from the Royal Navy on 4 February; and more than a year later, on 11 August 1835, they struck his name off the register of seamen on grounds that only bureaucrats could have thought of – that he had left the area of their jurisdiction and gone into the jurisdiction of the authorities at Genoa. But Garibaldi states in his memoirs that he sailed as mate in the *Union*, so he obviously took the master, Captain Cazan of Antibes, into his confidence, and carried out the mate's duties, although he is not entered as mate in the ship's logbook.[15]

While the *Union* was still in port at Marseilles, Garibaldi saved a fourteen-year-old French schoolboy, Joseph Rambaud, from drowning. The boy, feeling a little bored during the summer holidays, had been amusing himself by jumping from one ship to another, and had slipped and fallen into the water between the ship and the shore, and had become trapped under the *Union*. Garibaldi, who had just changed into his best clothes before going ashore for a Sunday evening's leave, dived into the sea. At first he could not find the boy; but at the third attempt, by what he describes as 'great good luck', he got hold of him and brought him to the shore. There were many people on the waterfront on the summer Sunday evening, and a large crowd had gathered to watch the rescue drama. They gave Garibaldi a great cheer when he succeeded in saving the boy, and Garibaldi was warmly thanked by the boy's mother. He told Madame Rambaud and Joseph that his name was Joseph Pane. When he published his memoirs, he wondered whether Joseph Rambaud was still alive, and whether he would now discover, for the first time, that Joseph Pane who had saved his life was the famous General Garibaldi.[16]

On 25 July 1834 he sailed in the *Union* from Marseilles to Constantinople and Odessa, and after spending the winter in the East, returned to Marseilles on 2 March. His next voyage was to Tunis. The Bey of Tunis had ordered a corvette to be built for him at Marseilles. When the ship, which was named the *Hélène*, was finished, she had to be delivered to the Bey, and Garibaldi was one of the crew who was chosen to sail her to Tunis. This is the only germ of truth in the tales which were told by Garibaldi's biographers in later years about Garibaldi's adventures in Tunis. When Garibaldi came to England in 1864, one of the popular biographies of him, which were sold in the streets of London, told the story of how Garibaldi had offered his services to the Bey, who had refused to employ him because he could not appreciate Garibaldi's virtues. The book contained a picture, called 'Garibaldi offers his services to the Bey of Tunis', showing the fat, coarse Bey sitting in a drunken stupor on a settee, unable to appreciate the qualities of the clean-limbed young Garibaldi who stands before him. A better version was told by the German writer, Ludwig von Alvensleben, who in 1859 published the most fantastic of all the romantic biographies of Garibaldi. Alvensleben wrote that Garibaldi entered the Bey's navy, and that the Bey's favourite Sultana, Leila, fell in love with him. The Bey discovered their secret assignations; but Leila, by a clever ruse of which Garibaldi knew nothing, surrendered herself to the vengeance of the Bey in order to enable Garibaldi to escape. There is unfortunately not a word of truth in this story. Garibaldi never met either the Bey or the Sultana. He merely sailed from Marseilles to Tunis in the *Hélène* on 17 May 1835, and after handing the ship over to the naval officials at Tunis, returned to Marseilles in a Tunisian warship of the Turkish navy.[17]

Cholera was raging in Marseilles. The disease, which had begun in South Russia in 1831, and had been carried into Poland by the Russian troops who marched in to suppress the insurrection, became the great scourge of Europe in the 1830s. The wealthy classes reacted by leaving the towns, whenever possible, for their country estates, often at a speed which amounted to a panic flight. The nursing of the sick was left to a few devoted nuns, and to people of the lowest classes who would do anything for a little money.

The cholera arrived in Marseilles in December 1834, and increased during the next six months, reaching its peak in July 1835. The usual panic developed, and great religious processions were held in the streets, interceding for the end of the cholera. The municipal authorities appealed for volunteers to join the city Ambulance Corps to carry the cholera patients to the hospitals, and to perform the unskilled work in the wards. When Garibaldi returned from Tunis, he volunteered for the Ambulance Corps, together with a man from Trieste with whom he had become friendly when they travelled in the Tunisian warship from Tunis to Marseilles. For a fortnight they lived at the hospital, spending the nights in the wards watching by the bedsides of the cholera victims. There were no recognized precautions which Garibaldi could take against catching the disease; but he took a herbal medicine which was approved of only by quacks, and was convinced that this would provide an absolute protection against the cholera.[18]

His action in joining the Ambulance Corps was typical of Garibaldi – of his self-sacrifice, his desire to help his fellow-men, and his readiness to face danger, not only in the exciting form in which it comes at sea or on the battlefield, but also in the sordid cholera hospitals. It was this side of his character which made some people say that if Garibaldi had lived in a different age, he would have been a Catholic saint. In his case, such acts of self-sacrifice, which for others were so often caused by religious convictions, were prompted by his belief in nineteenth-century humanism, and had been set in motion by his meeting with the Saint-Simonian Socialists.

In the summer of 1835 Garibaldi decided to go to South America. Neither Garibaldi himself, in his letters or memoirs, nor any of his intimate friends who wrote his biography, have stated the reasons why he went there, though Guerzoni speculated on them, and they are obvious enough. Thousands of Italians emigrated to America in the 1820s and 1830s, some of them driven by poverty at home and a desire for adventure, and some as political refugees. The incentives for the political refugees to go increased after the collapse of Mazzini's Savoy expedition in February 1834, when every government in Europe tightened the police surveillance of the refugees and clamped down more strictly than ever on any kind of political activity by the revolutionaries in exile. Life was becoming more difficult for those of them, like Garibaldi, who were living illegally in Marseilles with false papers. But in view of the indifference to danger which Garibaldi always showed, Guerzoni is probably right in thinking that he went to South America, not in order to escape from the risks which he ran in France, but because he wished to travel further afield than the Aegean and the Black Sea.[19]

There seemed to be little opportunity of engaging in political work in Italy. The executions and arrests had weakened Young Italy, and the Savoy fiasco had discouraged them. After three years of continuous revolts and attempted assassinations of rulers, revolutionary activity stopped after February 1834, and did not revive for some years. More and more Italian exiles were going to America. Many went to the United States; some, like Garibaldi's friend Cuneo, whom he had met at Taganrog, went to Montevideo in the newly-established Oriental Republic of Uruguay. But most went to Rio de Janeiro, where there was a large Italian settlement.

At the end of August or the beginning of September 1835, Garibaldi sailed from Marseilles for Rio de Janeiro in the *Nautonnier*, a French ship owned by a firm in Nantes, and commanded by Captain Beauregard. He signed on as Giuseppe Pane. In his memoirs, he states that he served as mate on the voyage; but he did not receive a mate's pay. A captain's salary was 200 francs a month, a mate's 130 francs, the cook's 73 francs, the ship's carpenter's 65 francs, and the ordinary seaman's 45 francs. The ship's records show that Garibaldi was paid 85 francs a month, which was not an official rate of pay for any grade, but was more than was paid to anyone else in the *Nautonnier* except the master. So it is clear that Captain Beauregard took advantage both of Garibaldi's skill and experience, and of the awkward predicament in which he had placed himself through his revolutionary activities, and used his services as mate at a reduced salary. Beauregard had the excuse that it would not have been easy to explain to the shipowners and to the authorities why he had paid more than 85 francs a month to the ordinary seaman, Giuseppe Pane.[20]

In the *Nautonnier*, a fifteen-year-old ship of 204 tons, they set off on the 5,000-mile voyage to Rio de Janeiro. In 1820 a ship had sailed from Lisbon to Rio in fifty-one days, but this record run was not often equalled, and the journey from Europe usually took between seventy and eighty days. The usual route was by the Canaries and Cape Verde Islands; but only the bigger ships had compasses and instruments, and in most cases the captains navigated by the stars. The *Nautonnier* may have been blown off course and gone as far north as the Azores, because a ship bound for Rio, which from its description closely resembled the *Nautonnier*, called at the Azores in the autumn of 1835. The date of the *Nautonnier*'s arrival in Rio is not known; but it was probably in November, at the beginning of the South American summer, that Garibaldi saw the famous view of Sugar Loaf Mountain and the white eighteenth-century houses on the waterfront, which so impressed European travellers of the period, as he sailed into the Bay of Guanabara, and was rowed ashore by negro slaves at Rio de Janeiro.[21]

CHAPTER 4

RIO DE JANEIRO

WHEN Garibaldi was born, nearly the whole of South and
Central America was part of the Spanish and Portuguese
colonial empires. The Spanish colonies stretched in an unbroken line
along the Pacific coast through ninety-eight degrees of latitude from
Cape Horn to Oregon; and an enormous expanse of territory in the
north-east of South America – the colony of Brazil – belonged to
Portugal. In 1810 the local aristocracy in Buenos Aires revolted against
the government of the King of Spain, and by 1821 the Spanish Empire
on the American continent had disappeared. Thirty years after the
revolution of 1810, the territory which had been ruled from Madrid
had become sixteen independent republics, several of which were at
war with each other, and most of which were engaged in civil wars.

In the Portuguese colony, events took a different course, owing to
the fact that during the Napoleonic wars the King of Portugal transferred his court from Lisbon to Rio de Janeiro, and remained there
after the war was over. When a Liberal revolution broke out in Brazil
in 1822, Dom Pedro, the King's son and heir, joined the revolutionaries
and proclaimed the independence of Brazil with himself as Emperor.
But Pedro's Radical politics angered the Conservatives; and in 1831
he abdicated in favour of his five-year-old son, Pedro II, and returned
to Portugal to lead the Liberal forces to victory in the civil war against
his brother, King Miguel, and to place his daughter Maria on the
Portuguese throne.

In Brazil the empire was governed during Pedro II's infancy by a
Regent, Antonio de Feijó, who was a constitutional Conservative
politician. He pleased the wealthy classes by his strong Conservative
policies, but aroused jealousy and resentment by his arrogant treatment of his political colleagues and of Parliament. The empire, which
covered an area almost as large as Europe including Russia, had a
population of 4,000,000, of whom more than half were negro slaves.
Many foreigners, chiefly Italians and Chinese, had come to Brazil by
the time that Garibaldi arrived in 1835.

The capital, Rio de Janeiro, was the largest city in South America;

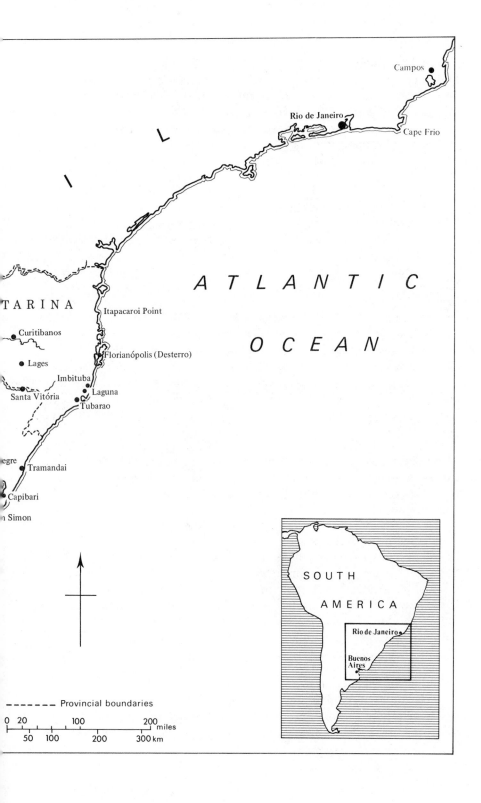

Campos

Rio de Janeiro

Cape Frio

ATLANTIC

OCEAN

I L

I

TARINA

Itapacaroi Point

Curitibanos

Lages

Imbituba

Florianópolis (Desterro)

Santa Vitória

Laguna

Tubarao

egre

Tramandai

Capibari

n Simon

SOUTH

AMERICA

Rio de Janeiro

Buenos
Aires

- - - - - - - Provincial boundaries

0 20   100   200 miles
                                  miles
   50   100   200   300 km

it had a population of 170,000 in 1835. Its two and three storey buildings were in white granite, which gave it a completely different appearance from any other city in the world. Its system of street lighting was in advance of most cities of Europe, for though gas light had not yet come, torches burned at night in the streets at very frequent intervals. The many fountains in the squares provided an adequate water supply, with which the town was kept remarkably clean by the standards of 1835. Rio was full of people, especially of negro slaves going about their masters' business with no great urgency. Only the large expanse of sand known as Copacabana, on the southern edge of Rio, was deserted. In 1835 there were only a few ruined buildings there, though old men could remember a time when it had been quite populated.[1]

Garibaldi, as he states in his memoirs, was lucky enough to find in Rio de Janeiro the most essential requirement for a stranger arriving in a foreign country – a good friend. One day, soon after his arrival, he was walking in the Lago do Passo, the Palace Square, near the harbour, where the crowds assembled and strolled in the evenings and on Sundays. He caught the eye of a young man of about his own age, and immediately had a feeling of happiness and recognition, so that he thought that it must be a friend whom he had met somewhere before. He spoke to him, and discovered that he was an Italian journalist called Luigi Rossetti. Garibaldi and Rossetti had in fact never met before, but they took an immediate liking to each other, and became close friends. Rossetti wrote to Mazzini on 26 January 1836 to tell him how pleased he was to have met Garibaldi. Two days earlier, another member of Young Italy had written to Mazzini that Borel, as he called Garibaldi, had joined the Rio branch of Young Italy and had taken the oath.[2]

Garibaldi did not wait long before engaging in political activity. Soon after he arrived in Rio, he wrote an article for a very obscure Brazilian newspaper in which he attacked King Charles Albert of Sardinia. No copy of this journal appears to be in existence. Presumably Garibaldi's article, if not anonymous, was published under his Young Italy name of Borel; but the Sardinian Minister in Brazil, Count Palma di Borgofranco, somehow discovered that Garibaldi was the author. On 1 February Borgofranco wrote to the government in Turin: 'A certain Garibaldi, a subject of His Majesty, together with the said Cuneo, a Genoan, has marked his arrival in this capital by an article published in the newspaper *Paquet du Rio* against His Majesty.' Like most Sardinian diplomats, Borgofranco wrote his reports to his government in French, and the *Paquet du Rio* is obviously a French translation of the name of the newspaper, because Borgofranco wrote that the article was written in Portuguese. Garibaldi's article must have been translated into Portuguese by someone else, as Garibaldi did not yet know enough Portuguese to be able to write in the language; and the publication was probably arranged by Cuneo, who was in Montevideo, but was in constant communication with the members of Young Italy in Rio de Janeiro.

Count Borgofranco also reported that a very large red, white and green tricolour, which Mazzini and Young Italy had adopted as the flag of Republican Italy, was flying over the house in Rio where the 'Italian Liberals', as he called them, had their headquarters. He had complained to the Brazilian Foreign Minister, Baron de Aiser; but the Baron had said that though he regretted that the flag was flying, there was nothing that he could do about it, though he added that he might perhaps be able to do something later.[3]

Garibaldi was not satisfied with writing articles against Charles Albert in Brazilian newspapers. On 27 January 1836 he wrote to Mazzini, addressing him as Strozzi – one of his names in Young Italy – and signing himself Borel. He suggested that he should get hold of a ship and attack and rob all Sardinian and Austrian ships that he might meet outside Brazilian territorial waters, and offered to do this if Mazzini would send him letters of marque signed by the leaders of Young Europe.[4] Mazzini was always prone to rush into rash revolutionary adventures, but he was sensible enough to reject this proposal, and he apparently did not reply to Garibaldi's letter.

Garibaldi's suggestion that he might attack Sardinian and Austrian ships off the Brazilian coast was a feasible one, because about thirty-five Sardinian and fourteen Austrian ships called at Rio de Janeiro every year; but if he had put his plan into operation, he would have been regarded as a pirate under international law, and hunted down by all the navies of the world. The system of privateering, which was permitted under international law until the Great Powers agreed to ban it at the Congress of Paris in 1856, permitted a private subject of a state to attack and pillage the ships of nationals of a state at war with his own country, provided that he was issued with letters of marque by his government; but the governments of the world would not have recognized the Executive Committee of Young Europe as having any lawful authority to issue letters of marque. To Garibaldi, what he was proposing to do was very different from piracy. He was not proposing to rob indiscriminately from all merchantmen, but only those flying the Sardinian or Austrian flag; and he intended to apply the proceeds of his robberies for the good of the cause. But it is unlikely that the governments would have shown him any consideration on this account, and he would probably not have survived for long if he had carried out his project.

Instead of becoming a privateer for Young Europe, Garibaldi was reduced to trying to earn a living in Rio de Janeiro. Some of the Italians in Brazil had opened restaurants, which had previously been almost unknown there. Apart from the Italians who had come to Rio, a smaller number had settled in Cabo Frio, a coastal town ten miles north of Cabo Frio itself, which was the promontory where the coastline turns northwards, eighty miles east of Rio. Cabo Frio was one of the earliest European settlements in Brazil, and had changed very little since the early seventeenth century. Rossetti proposed to Garibaldi that they should open a business of selling and carrying supplies, chiefly macaroni, to the Italian restaurant-proprietors in Rio and Cabo Frio. Rossetti was to run the office in Rio and manage the business side of the venture, while Garibaldi sailed between Rio and Cabo Frio with the macaroni. They hoped that they would be able to sell some of their macaroni to the native Brazilians, but here they were disappointed. The Brazilians, who did not like foreigners, were very suspicious of foreign innovations. An American from the United States had recently tried to make money by selling lumps of ice which could be put in cold drinks on the hot summer days; but the Brazilians had refused to take the ice, and the American soon went bankrupt.

The journey from Rio de Janeiro across the Bay of Guanabara to Cabo Frio took between twelve and eighteen hours, according to the wind, for no steamships had yet appeared in South America, and all sea voyages were made under sail. Cabo Frio was a perilous place for sailors, because the strong currents often carried a ship on to the rocks at the cape, especially in the dark. Foreign merchants had for long been asking the Brazilian government to erect a lighthouse on Cabo Frio; but it was not until 1839 that Brazil at last allowed the British Navy to build the lighthouse, at the expense of the British taxpayer.[5]

The risks of the Cabo Frio route were not enough to satisfy Garibaldi's desire for adventure, and he soon grew tired of being a commercial traveller in macaroni. The only satisfaction which he derived from the occupation was that he was at sea, and could name his ship the *Mazzini*, and fly the Italian Republican tricolour. This greatly annoyed the Sardinian Minister. On 26 March 1836 Count Borgofranco wrote to his government complaining that there were three ships – the *Mazzini*, the *Giovine Italia* (Young Italy) and the *Giovine Europa* (Young Europe) – which were always sailing in and out of the harbour at Rio de Janeiro flying the Italian tricolour. The captains of these three ships behaved in as provocative a manner as possible, deliberately sailing near any Sardinian ships in the harbour, and shouting revolutionary slogans and insults to the Sardinian sailors as they passed. Borgofranco discussed the situation with the Austrian Minister in Rio, and they agreed that it would be a mistake to send a note of protest to the Brazilian government, because the government would not only refuse their demands, but would publish the exchange of diplomatic notes in the Brazilian newspapers, and would make them look ridiculous. Borgofranco had a better idea. He wrote to the Sardinian Foreign Minister:

> If ever the *Giovine Europa* and the *Mazzini* should sail out to sea with the flag that they have hoisted on their boats, I will take advantage of the good will of two captains of our merchant navy, discreetly armed, who have offered to follow them and finish them off. It is a little liberty that one is entitled to take in America in order to deliver our shipping from the anxieties which these new kind of pirates are causing.

But Count Borgofranco, like Garibaldi, did not put his plans of violence into operation.[6]

Garibaldi's chief comfort in Rio was the friendship of his brother Italians, many of whom were members of Young Italy, and included some whom he had known in Europe. His old colleague Edoardo Mutru, whom he had last seen in Genoa on 5 February 1834, came to Rio after he had been acquitted by the military court and had completed his term of service in the Sardinian Royal Navy. Garibaldi also became friendly with Luigi Dalecazi, an engineer from Verona. Dalecazi had emigrated to Switzerland as a young man, but had thrown up his prospects as an engineer in Switzerland to take part in Mazzini's revolutionary projects in February 1834, and, after escaping from Genoa with the help of the French Consul, had come to Rio. Garibaldi spent many hours at Dalecazi's house in Rio at No. 7, Via Fresca, where he met two little girls, Dalecazi's daughter Emilia and Annita de Lima Barreto, who was Signora Dalecazi's niece. When she grew up, Annita married a United States naval officer, Thomas Walker of Boston, and they settled in Calcutta. In 1900 Mrs Walker met the Brazilian novelist Virgilio Varzea, and told him about Garibaldi. She remembered the sturdy, blond young sailor because he was so different from the other Italians who came to Dalecazi's house. He would sometimes sit in the middle of a group who were engaged in animated conversation, and stare dreamily into space; but on other occasions he would play boisterous games with the two little girls, who would climb on his knee, and clamber all over him, and pull his hair and beard.[7]

Garibaldi formed another link in Rio de Janeiro which lasted all his life. He joined a Freemasons' lodge. Freemasonry played a very different role in South America, and in the European Radical movement of the nineteenth century, than in England, where masonic lodges had developed in the early years of the Hanoverian dynasty as organizations of business men, formed for mutual aid, with a secret ritual for which there were both historical and psychological reasons, and a loose religious doctrine to which Anglicans, Nonconformists and Jews could all subscribe. The most rigid members of the Church of England found it possible to reconcile their tributes, in their masonic lodges, to the Great Architect of the Universe, with their acceptance of the Thirty-nine Articles of the Church, even at a time when these Articles were very rigidly interpreted. Freemasonry in Britain was always respectable, and the masons took care to elect royal Princes of the House of Hanover as their Grand Masters.

Before the middle of the eighteenth century, masonic lodges were being formed in Italy and France. They were usually started by English noblemen who resided there; but they inevitably assumed a very different significance in autocratic Catholic countries. Both the Papacy and the autocratic sovereigns were very suspicious of a secret organization in which freethinkers, Protestants and Jews met and worshipped in an unorthodox way, and the fact that it had been started by Englishmen increased their suspicions. As the rationalists and humanists, the followers of Voltaire and Rousseau, were able to accept the non-denominational religion of the Freemasons, they, too, joined the organization, and Freemasonry became revolutionary. In the Napoleonic Empire it was favoured by the government, and the masons elected Napoleon's brothers to be their Grand Masters as regularly as the British masons chose the sons of George III. But this Bonaparte connexion made Freemasonry more dangerous than ever in the eyes of the rulers of Europe after 1815. The Pope anathematized the Freemasons, and Catholic spokesmen, either in good or bad faith, confused them with the Carbonari. This caused more revolutionaries and Radicals to join the Freemasons. The Freemasons were not in fact, as their opponents claimed, a revolutionary and seditious organization; but they were what would now be called a 'front organization', where the revolutionaries of the Carbonari and Young Italy joined in a non-political organization with men who were sympathetic to their aims, but not active revolutionaries.

By 1835 there were Freemasons' lodges all over Italy, France and Spain; and though the lodges in the United States were non-revolutionary, like the British lodges, those in Rio de Janeiro, Montevideo and Buenos Aires followed the European pattern. Many of the leaders of the Italian *Risorgimento*, including Mazzini and Cuneo, were Freemasons; and when Garibaldi was in Rio in 1836 he joined the local lodge. The Rio lodge was part of the Brazilian masonic organization, the *Asilo de la Vertud* (the Shelter of Virtue), and was not connected with the *Grand Orient*, which controlled the masonic lodges in France and Italy and elsewhere in South America. The *Asilo de la Vertud* was regarded by the *Grand Orient* as an unorthodox, deviationist group; but its doctrine and nature were fundamentally the same as those of all the continental European, and South American, lodges.[8]

When Garibaldi had been in Brazil for a year, and faced his second summer there, he was very dissatisfied that he was doing nothing except trading and trying to make money. The only way in which he was able to satisfy his desire to help his fellow-men was by once again engaging in his life-saving activities. One day he was on the waterfront in Rio de Janeiro when a negro slave fell into the sea. Garibaldi went to the rescue and saved him from drowning. Such solicitude for the life of a slave was rare in Brazil in 1836. The slaves seemed happy enough as they walked about the streets, laughing and singing, in their bright-coloured clothes; but they were not allowed to wear shoes, or to travel in the public buses, drawn by mules, which began about this time, and when they died, instead of receiving the elaborate funerals accorded to free Brazilians, their bodies were unceremonially thrown into a pit. The Irish abolitionist, the Reverend Robert Walsh, was shocked at the cruel treatment to which the slaves were subjected, and wrote, perhaps with some exaggeration, that he had never walked along a street in Rio without hearing the cries of pain and the sound of whips emanating from one of the houses. But Garibaldi did not hesitate to leap into the water when he saw a slave drowning, in the sight of interested and indifferent onlookers, because, as Cuneo wrote, 'a negro was for Garibaldi a brother no less than a white'.[9]

In view of Garibaldi's feelings about making money, it is not surprising that he had no ability to do this, and that the macaroni enterprise did not prosper. All his life he was much better at guerrilla warfare than at commercial transactions, and he and Rossetti came to the conclusion that neither of them had a good head for business. They were cheated by people whom they had trusted, and made mistakes because of their ignorance of local conditions. Their affairs improved after December 1836, when they secured a contract with a company that held a monopoly of flour and millet-seed to carry their produce to the ports of Macaé and Campos, about fifty and a hundred miles north of Cabo Frio; and by February 1837 they were making money. But Garibaldi was still dissatisfied. He wished to engage in some revolutionary activity on behalf of Italian freedom; and in many letters to Cuneo in Montevideo – some of them written in code, and others in veiled language – he returned to his old scheme of privateering on behalf of Young Europe. But for this he needed a bigger, and a better armed, ship than the vessel in which he was trading between Rio de Janeiro and Campos; and to buy such a ship he needed money.[10]

On 17 October he wrote to Cuneo from Cabo Frio:

Brother, this is only to tell you of our arrival here on the 15th, and that the daughter of our caulker is beautiful, but so beautiful, of a beauty which your romantic imagination has often painted, and that I am head over heels in love with her. I assure you that if I were not so out of practice, I should rub up our tools again, grown rusty by disuse; but, alas! we shall go on doing nothing, as usual. *Dinè! dinè!* [money, in Genoese dialect] is what we want; and with that, in Italy, we should also find beauties.

Jessie White Mario – herself a beautiful woman – was at pains to point out that Garibaldi was speaking metaphorically, and referring not to a woman, but to a ship that he wanted to buy. She writes that ' "the daughter of the caulker", had she been a woman in flesh and blood, might have been easily won without *dinè* by the handsome young sailor'.[11]

The only suggestion which Cuneo could make in reply to Garibaldi's complaints was that Garibaldi should leave Rio de Janeiro and come to Montevideo; but by the time that Cuneo's suggestion reached him, a new development had completely changed the outlook for Garibaldi. In March or April 1837 he wrote to Cuneo that he could not come to Montevideo, 'because it is impossible for me to do so; nor can I, without risk, explain the reason by letter. All that I can tell you is that I am setting out upon a new path, guided always by our principles, with that goal in view which you first put before me.'[12] Garibaldi had made contact with the rebels in Rio Grande do Sul.

Revolution and civil war had broken out in Brazil. All the political pundits had been expecting this; they had forecast that the empire could not possibly survive, and believed that Brazil would inevitably split up into four independent republics.[13] The problem of communications seemed to make unity impossible, once the traditional link with the Portuguese crown had gone. Apart from a few rough cart-tracks, there were no roads at all, and the only way to make long inland journeys was on horseback through the mountains and tropical forests. There was communication by sea between the ports on the Atlantic seaboard; but because of the changeability and unpredictability of the winds, and the strong currents, this took so long, with sailing ships, that news of revolts and other incidents in the far north of Brazil often reached Rio de Janeiro first in the European newspapers,[14] though these were usually about three months out of date. So no one was surprised when two of the eighteen provinces of the empire revolted in 1835 – Pará in the north, and Rio Grande do Sul in the south.

Rio Grande do Sul is geographically different from the rest of Brazil. Apart from uplands in the west, the whole province is flat, being part of the great plain which stretches through the whole of

Uruguay and beyond the River Plate into Argentina. The frontier with Uruguay was a wholly artificial one, a line on a map drawn in 1777 by Spanish and Portuguese statesmen as a compromise settlement of an international dispute; in many places it ran across individual properties and was crossed as readily by men as by cattle. Many people in Rio Grande do Sul began to think that their province, like its southern neighbour, could survive as an independent republic, free from distant Rio de Janeiro.

On 20 September 1835, while Garibaldi was on his way from Marseilles to Rio de Janeiro, General Bento Gonçalves da Silva Pilho in Porto Alegre began the struggle for the independence of Rio Grande do Sul. Bento Gonçalves was descended from an old aristocratic Portuguese family, and was one of the largest landowners in the province. He had had a distinguished career in the Brazilian army under both the King of Portugal and the Emperor. The people of all classes in Rio Grande do Sul looked on him as their leader, and followed him both from their love of independence and their respect for Gonçalves. One of Gonçalves's most active supporters was an Italian refugee, Count Tito Livio Zambeccari, the son of the famous aviator who had been the first man ever to fly in a balloon in England. Tito Livio Zambeccari was a member of Young Italy, and he associated the independence movement in Rio Grande do Sul with the Italian *Risorgimento*.

The Brazilian government in Rio de Janeiro was not an autocratic or brutal one. It was a mildly Conservative government of a constitutional monarchy. But in the 1830s the difference between a monarchy and a republic was a burning political issue. People had not yet got used to the idea of a Conservative republic. Conservatives were royalists, Republicans were revolutionaries. So Zambeccari and the members of Young Italy supported the struggle of Rio Grande do Sul to overthrow the rule of the Emperor of Brazil and set up an independent republic. Zambeccari became the chief propagandist for the Riograndenses, whose political slogans were in line with the tradition of Rousseau, of the French revolutionaries of 1789, and Mazzini. Their only difference was on the religious question, because Gonçalves and his followers were devoutly Catholic, and had none of the anti-Papal and anti-clerical attitude of Young Italy. In all their proclamations, they declared that Roman Catholicism must be the state religion, and although they permitted freedom of worship for all religious denominations, only Catholics could hold office in their republic. Zambeccari kept quiet on the religious issue.

It was not easy for the government in Rio de Janeiro, a thousand miles away, to deal effectively with the revolt in Rio Grande do Sul.

But they contacted General Bento Manoel Ribeiro, another leading army officer and large landowner in the province, and authorized him to wage war against Gonçalves. They also sent a naval squadron to Rio Grande do Sul under the command of Captain John Pascoe Grenfell, the English boy from Battersea who became Commander-in-Chief of the Brazilian navy. On 4 October 1836 Manoel defeated Gonçalves with the help of Grenfell's fleet, and Gonçalves and Zambeccari and three other Riograndense leaders – Onofre Pires, Afonso Côrte Real and Pedro Boticário – were captured and sent to Rio de Janeiro. Gonçalves and Boticário were imprisoned in Fort Laje on an island at the entrance to the harbour at Rio; Zambeccari, Pires and Côrte Real were put in Fort Santa Cruz on the waterfront on the mainland on the northern outskirts of the city. In Rio Grande do Sul, Manoel entered Porto Alegre in triumph; but the Republican forces withdrew to the hills, under the command of General Lima, their Deputy Commander-in-Chief under Gonçalves.[15]

Rossetti and Garibaldi, and all the members of Young Italy in Rio de Janeiro, sympathized with the Riograndense cause; and Garibaldi was filled with a desire to help in some way. This led him to revise his previous idea of turning corsair in the cause of the revolution. He now wished to act, not under the Italian tricolour, but under the red, yellow and green flag of Rio Grande do Sul, with letters of marque from Gonçalves's government. Meanwhile Rossetti had heard that Zambeccari, whom he had known in Italy, was imprisoned in the Santa Cruz fortress and wished to visit him, to bring him some comforts in his captivity. He was granted permission to do so, and told Zambeccari that Garibaldi was eager to turn privateer for Rio Grande do Sul. Zambeccari was very interested in the idea, which he thought might link up with more ambitious plans which he and Gonçalves were hatching. They were able to keep in secret contact, from their prisons, with their supporters in the south, and were hoping to win over General Manoel himself to the cause of the revolution. Their plan was that the five leaders in the forts at Rio should escape from prison, and that at the same time Manoel in Rio Grande do Sul should declare for them. They welcomed the idea of a third *coup* – that Garibaldi should set out as a privateer to rob Brazilian shipping.

According to the Brazilian novelist, Virgilio Varzea, Rossetti obtained permission to visit Zambeccari again in February 1837, and this time he took Garibaldi with him. Garibaldi, in the Dumas edition of his memoirs, and Cuneo and Guerzoni, state that Zambeccari introduced him in Fort Santa Cruz to Gonçalves, who gave him letters of marque; but in the 1872 edition of the memoirs, which he edited himself, Garibaldi says that he met Gonçalves for the first time in Rio Grande do Sul in 1838, and as Gonçalves was in Fort Laje, not in Fort Santa Cruz, it is clear that Garibaldi visited only Zambeccari, Onofre Pires and Côrte Real. Zambeccari obtained letters of marque for Garibaldi, but they were signed, not by Gonçalves, but by General Lima in Rio Grande do Sul. It is not surprising, in the circumstances, that it took some time before Garibaldi received the letters of marque, and though they were dated 14 November 1836, they only reached him on 4 May 1837.[16]

While Garibaldi was waiting for the letters of marque, he had to prepare the ship. His ship, the *Mazzini*, of 20 tons, small though she was, would serve as a vessel for a privateer, provided that she was properly armed and equipped. A secret collection of funds was made among the Italians in Rio, and £8,000 was raised. According to Colonel Mancini, Garibaldi's Deputy-Commander of the Italian Legion in Montevideo, who deserted to the enemy in 1844, Garibaldi induced one poor man to contribute to the fund by promising that he would regard it as a loan, and then afterwards refused to repay the money; but no reliance can be placed on the scurrilous allegations that Mancini made in order to justify his desertion.

Garibaldi enlisted a crew of eight, of whom six were Italians and two Maltese. One of the Italians was his old colleague Mutru; another was Luigi Carniglia, the boatswain; and a third was named Maurizio Garibaldi, though he was no relation of Garibaldi. Rossetti, though he was not a sailor, was to go with them as a passenger. The work of arming the ship was carried out in the harbour at Rio, alongside the Fish Market, but in such a way that none of the port officials knew what was going on under their noses. On 7 May, three days after Garibaldi received the letters of marque, the *Mazzini* sailed out of the harbour of Rio de Janeiro, having obtained clearance from the port authorities. The statements that Garibaldi made to obtain the clearance were false in nearly every particular. He stated that he was sailing to Campos with a cargo of meat and one passenger, whom he correctly named as Rossetti. He gave the names of only five members of his crew, and stated that his own name was Cipriano Alves.[17]

The rest of the plans laid in the Santa Cruz prison were nearly as successful. Three days after Garibaldi sailed, on the night of 10 May, Onofre Pires and Côrte Real escaped from Santa Cruz by leaping into the water from their prison cell and swimming to a boat manned by their supporters, who had intended to rescue Gonçalves from Fort Laje, but, after failing in this attempt, had gone to Fort Santa Cruz to save the others. Zambeccari, who could not swim, had been unable to escape with his two colleagues. Soon afterwards Gonçalves was removed from Fort Laje to Bahia in the north. On 10 September he was

53

permitted by the Governor of his new prison to go swimming in the river near the prison. He swam out to one of the small boats which were in the river at the time, and was taken away before the guards at the prison could intervene; in due course, he reached safety in Rio Grande do Sul. The Brazilian government later discovered that the Governor of his prison at Bahia was a Freemason. Meanwhile on 8 April 1837 General Manoel in Rio Grande do Sul surrendered to the Republican General Netto, and three days later joined with Netto in besieging Porto Alegre. The Imperial government now held no territory in Rio Grande do Sul except the two ports of Porto Alegre and Rio Grande, which were controlled by Grenfell's fleet. The only thing that went wrong with Zambeccari's plans was that he himself, and Boticário, were unable to escape. Zambeccari was released from prison in 1839 on condition that he returned to Italy.[18] There he took part in the revolutionary movement, and in 1860 served under Garibaldi in Naples.

As soon as Garibaldi had left the harbour at Rio de Janeiro, he sailed, not towards Campos, but south towards Rio Grande do Sul. He had not gone more than twenty miles before he met a ship flying the Brazilian flag off the Ilha Grande. She was the *Luisa* (60 tons), and was sailing to Europe carrying a few passengers, a small cargo of furniture, and a large supply of coffee. Among her crew were a number of negro slaves, who were often employed in the Brazilian merchant navy. Garibaldi stopped the *Luisa*, and fired a few shots across her bows. Although the *Luisa* was larger than the *Mazzini*, she was not armed, and surrendered without a struggle. When Garibaldi boarded her, one of the passengers took him aside and offered him his jewels if he would spare his life; but Garibaldi told him that he had no intention of robbing the passengers, and assured him that he need not fear either for his life or his jewels.[19]

Garibaldi did not have enough men to navigate both the *Luisa* and the *Mazzini*, and, as the *Luisa* was the better ship, he transferred all his armaments and equipment to the *Luisa*, and scuttled his own ship. In the Dumas edition of his memoirs, he states that he renamed the *Luisa* the *Farroupilha*, and all his biographers have repeated this; but they were confusing it with the name of the ship which he navigated a year later, and in fact he renamed the *Luisa* the *Mazzini*. He sailed south for about a week, and on 17 May came in to shore near Itapacaroi Point, north of Itajaí, where he told the captured crew and passengers that they could take the ship's boat and row themselves to shore, taking their personal belongings and valuables with them; but he offered the negro slaves the opportunity to gain their freedom by staying with him and joining his crew, and five of them accepted his offer.[20] Garibaldi's prisoners could consider themselves lucky; most privateers in his position would have killed them, rather than lose his only ship's boat for their convenience and give them the chance of reporting his whereabouts to the Brazilian authorities much earlier than would otherwise have been done.

When the Brazilian government heard about the capture of the *Luisa*, they labelled it as an act of piracy; and by his action Garibaldi acquired a reputation of being a pirate. He retained this reputation for the whole of his stay in South America, and still retains it today among many sections of opinion in Argentina. But Garibaldi was never a pirate; all his seizures of vessels during his years in South America were lawful acts of privateering under letters of marque from an established government, and though occasionally he exceeded his legal rights by inadvertently capturing a neutral ship, an apology and reparation were promptly made.[21] Most of these captures – all those made after 1841 – were carried out under letters of marque from the government of Montevideo, which was recognized as the legal government of Uruguay by nearly every other state in the world. When he captured the *Luisa* in 1837 he was acting under the authority of the government of Rio Grande do Sul, which, though it was not recognized by any foreign government, was in *de facto* control of nearly the whole of the province – an area of 91,000 square miles, a little larger than England, Scotland and Wales.

Garibaldi now had to take a decision, and, for reasons for which he cannot be blamed, he made an error of judgement which had very unfortunate consequences for him. It was necessary to overhaul and revictual the ship. He could not put into any of the ports in Rio Grande do Sul, in the great lagoon of Lagoa dos Patos, because Grenfell's fleet controlled Porto Alegre, Rio Grande and the lagoon; but he could have landed somewhere on one of the Atlantic beaches in Rio Grande do Sul, and tried to find the necessary food and other requirements there. This plan had the drawback that he could not be sure whether the Republicans or the Imperial forces controlled any particular part of the coast at the moment; and it was obviously preferable, if possible, to put into a port. His friends in Rio de Janeiro had told him that the government of Uruguay was neutral in the Brazilian civil war, and would be prepared to receive in its ports the ships of both belligerents. So Garibaldi sailed south past the coast of Rio Grande do Sul, and on 28 May entered the old port of Maldonado, which is now the fashionable seaside resort of Punta del Este, at the entrance to the estuary of the River Plate, some three miles from the town of Maldonado.[22] He thereby entered for the first time the political world of the River Plate – the world that was dominated by Juan Manuel de Rosas.

CHAPTER 5

THE ORDEAL AT GUALEGUAY

THE revolution of 1810, which resulted in the collapse of the Spanish Empire in South America, was led by the intellectual élite of Buenos Aires. After they had won their independence, and the frontiers of the new states had been settled, a disagreement arose as to the form of the constitution of the Republic of Argentina. The Liberal leader, Rivadavia, wanted the republic to be governed from Buenos Aires; but many local leaders favoured a federal system in which the provincial governments would have a great deal of regional autonomy. The politicians formed into two factions – the Unitarians and the Federalists – and a bitter party conflict ensued.

Outside the capital city of Buenos Aires, with its 80,000 inhabitants, and a number of very small provincial towns, there was the pampas, where there lived nearly a million gauchos and at least 12,000,000 cattle. The gauchos lived by catching the cattle, on horseback with a lasso, and slaughtering them, and eating their meat and sending their hides to Buenos Aires for export. Apart from a handful of village crafts-men and tavernkeepers, no man on the pampas did anything except catch and slaughter cattle, and drink and gamble at the village wine-shop. There was virtually no cultivation of land, and all the household labours were performed by women.

In Buenos Aires, the dispute between the Federalists and the Unitarians led to violence, and culminated in a mutiny of the Unitarian army officers, and a battle in which the Unitarian leader, Lavalle, captured the Federalist leader, Dorrego, and had him shot without trial – an act which was used by the Federalists to justify every atrocity which they committed during the next twenty-four years. In their war with the Unitarians, the Federalists called in the help of the gauchos. The leader of the gauchos was Juan Manuel de Rosas, who was born in Buenos Aires, but had lived all his life on the pampas. Though Rosas was in many ways more of a Buenos Aires politician than a gaucho, he posed as the head of the gauchos, and could honestly claim to be as good a horseman as any of them. In 1829 he took power in Buenos Aires, and exercised an iron rule over all the city intellectuals, both Unitarians and Federalists. The Liberal writer, Sarmiento, saw Rosas's triumph as the victory of the gaucho over the middle class, of the countryside over the town, of barbarism over civilization.[1]

As leader of the Federalist party, Rosas took care to observe the proper forms of Federal government. Officially he was only Governor of the province of Buenos Aires; but his followers in the other provinces invited him to be the protector of the interests of the whole Argentine Confederation, and in practice he was the dictator of Argentina. His private army of thugs – called the Mashorca by their opponents – terrorized the Buenos Aires middle classes, and murdered many of Rosas's critics in the streets and in their houses at night. The badge of the Rosistas was a round red cap – darker in colour and different in shape from the red cap of liberty of the Radicals in Europe – and on Sunday mornings the Mashorca patrolled the streets after mass, threatening any woman who was not wearing a strand of red ribbon in her hair.[2] But Rosas was at some pains to make a good impression on foreign governments and merchants. He himself rarely emerged from his palace at Palermo on the banks of the River Plate, which was then some three or four miles outside Buenos Aires; but his daughter Manuelita became the leader of fashionable society and the patroness of every charitable institution, and made a very favourable impression on foreign diplomats.

Rosas attached a great deal of importance to propaganda, which he placed under the direction of an Italian journalist, Pedro de Angelis. Apart from his daily newspaper, the *Gaceta Mercantil*, he had a quarterly journal, the *Archivo Americano,* which was published in Spanish, English and French, and was designed to influence public opinion in Britain, France and the United States; while the English-language daily newspaper of the British merchants in Buenos Aires, the *British Packet*, which was edited by an English immigrant, Thomas Love, was nothing but a Rosas propaganda sheet, though it claimed to speak on behalf of the British community. Rosas himself gave frequent directives on policy, and even on matters of detail, to Pedro de Angelis and the journalists.[3] He also succeeded in building up a powerful lobby in Britain, the leader of which was Alfred Mallalieu, jp, of Highgate. But the layer of civilization, put on for the benefit of foreign sympathizers, was thin. Rosas depended for his power in Argentina on the gauchos who hated the culture of cities. Many of his subordinate commanders were men like Fecundo Quiroga, who habitually flogged his prisoners with his own hand, and on one occasion, if the accusation of his enemies is correct, bit off the ear of one of them.[4]*

*Quiroga, however, has many admirers in present-day Argentina who claim that the allegations made against him by the Liberal propagandists were lies.

57

The Buenos Aires Unitarians fled for their lives to Uruguay, where they became a powerful political influence in Montevideo. About this time, the native Uruguayans formed two political parties, the Blancos and the Colorados, which are still today the two largest parties in Uruguay. The Argentine Unitarians linked up with the Liberal Colorados, while the Conservative Blancos were friendly to Rosas and the Federalists in Argentina. The leader of the Colorados was General Fructuoso Rivera; the leader of the Blancos was General Manuel Oribe. In 1837 Oribe was President of Uruguay, and the Blancos were in power.

The people of northern Uruguay were in close contact with the inhabitants of Rio Grande do Sul, and the Uruguayan politicians took an interest in the struggle of the Riograndenses against Brazil. The Colorados and the Unitarians were sympathetic to the Riograndenses. The attitude of the Blanco and Federalist governments of Uruguay and Argentina was more complex. Uruguay and Argentina had recently been allies in a war against Brazil, and diplomatic relations with the empire were often strained. Ideologically, Rosas and Oribe were against the Riograndenses; on nationalist grounds they were happy to see the Riograndenses prolong their war against the Imperial government. Garibaldi's friends in Rio de Janeiro had therefore good grounds for their belief that Oribe's government would adopt an attitude of neutrality towards any Riograndense privateer who entered a Uruguayan port.

When Garibaldi put into port at Maldonado, he found the local Uruguayan officials very friendly. He revictualled the ship, while Rossetti went off by land to Montevideo, some eighty miles to the west, to make arrangements for selling the cargo of coffee which he had captured, and to get in touch with Cuneo and the other members of Young Italy in Montevideo. Garibaldi sold some of the coffee of the *Luisa* to a merchant in Maldonado. He stayed in Maldonado for a fortnight. There was a French whaling ship in port, and Garibaldi and his men spent several evenings drinking and feasting with the French crew. But as soon as the Brazilian Minister in Montevideo discovered that the captors of the *Luisa* were in Maldonado, he asked Oribe's government to arrest the ship and crew, and hand over both the *Luisa* and the pirates to Brazil. Oribe agreed to this request, and sent orders to this effect to the officials at Maldonado; and at the same time, the Brazilian Minister in Montevideo ordered a Brazilian warship, the *Imperial Pedro*, to sail for Maldonado to intercept the *Luisa* if Garibaldi and his men should try to sail away and escape.

The news of Oribe's decision leaked out prematurely, and reached the authorities in Maldonado before the official order arrived. The

Governor of Maldonado had become friendly with Garibaldi, and told him that he had better sail away quickly before the order to arrest him arrived. Garibaldi lost no time in preparing to sail, but he had not yet been paid by the merchant in Maldonado to whom he had sold the coffee. He went to the merchant's house; but the merchant, who had heard that Garibaldi was about to be arrested, refused to pay him, and warned Garibaldi by signs to keep away, intimating that there were police in the house who had come to arrest him. Garibaldi rightly guessed that the merchant was bluffing, and, as he was in no position to sue the man in the law courts, and was in a desperate situation, he adopted desperate remedies. He drew a pistol, levelled it at the merchant's head, and went round the house with him from room to room, until the merchant had produced the money. He then went quickly back to his ship, and sailed out of Maldonado.

He got away before the Brazilian warship arrived, to the annoyance of the Rio de Janeiro newspaper, the *Jornal do Commercio*, which reported on 30 June that 'the pirate who has made people talk so much about him recently' – they did not know Garibaldi's name – had got away, because contrary winds had prevented the *Imperial Pedro* from arriving at Maldonado in time. In Rio de Janeiro, the authorities took their revenge on Garibaldi's friends, and prohibited both the *Giovine Italia* and the *Giovine Europa* from using the port.

But the winds which had frustrated the Brazilian warship made things very difficult for Garibaldi. He had to put to sea in the face of a strong north-easterly gale, which prevented him from sailing to Rio Grande do Sul, or out into the Atlantic, as well as making navigation very dangerous even in the River Plate. He therefore sailed up the River Plate in the direction of Montevideo, keeping as near as he dared to the Uruguayan shore. Meanwhile the captain of the *Imperial Pedro*, finding that Garibaldi had left Maldonado, set out to search for him in the River Plate; but it was mid-winter in South America, and the weather was foggy, as it often is in the River Plate at that time of year. The *Imperial Pedro* searched in vain for the *Mazzini*.[5]

Garibaldi had not had time to take in many stores before his hurried departure from Maldonado, and he was therefore short of food – except, of course, for the coffee. He could not put into any Uruguayan port; but, seeing a deserted house on a desolate part of the coast, about four miles inland, he decided to land on the beach and go to the house in search of food. Landing was difficult, as the only boat on the *Luisa* had been taken by the original crew when Garibaldi put them ashore off Itapacaroi; but he and his namesake Maurizio Garibaldi succeeded in getting ashore by using one of the tables in the ship as a raft, and Garibaldi, leaving Maurizio to repair the table, walked inland to the house. Here he found the wife of the owner, a beautiful and cultured woman from Montevideo who had married a gaucho after her family had lost their money; and she wrote poetry. Garibaldi could speak very little Spanish, but he and the woman were able to understand each other, and though they never met again, she impressed him sufficiently for him to write about her at some length in his memoirs thirty-four years later. They discussed Dante and Italian poetry, and she read him some of her own poems, which he greatly admired; and she gave him a book of Quintana's poems. When her husband returned, he turned out to be uneducated and uncouth as compared with his charming wife; but he was friendly enough, and gave Garibaldi a bullock's carcass to take back to his ship. He and Maurizio managed with difficulty to get back to the *Mazzini* on the table with the bullock.[6]

The *Mazzini* continued to sail westwards up the River Plate, and passed Montevideo. In the estuary they met another ship, the *Bilandra,* and persuaded the crew to sell them their boat; being unable to put into port, they had to make their purchases from other ships in midstream. But the *Mazzini* had been sighted from the shore, and the Uruguayan authorities had no difficulty in identifying her as the captured Brazilian ship, the *Luisa*. The Commander of the Port of Montevideo sent Lieutenant Errazquim, in the gunboat *Maria* with a crew of twenty-four men, to arrest the pirates. He sailed out of Montevideo at 8 pm on 14 June, and twelve hours later, at 8 am on the 15th, he encountered the *Mazzini*. As Garibaldi refused to obey his order to heave to, he opened fire, and a fierce fight took place. Garibaldi says in his memoirs that all his Italians fought bravely, except one, whom he does not identify beyond saying that he was a Venetian, and that two of the Maltese also fought well, but that the five negroes whom he had freed behaved in a most cowardly fashion, and fled into the hold when the battle began.

Garibaldi and his men repulsed a boarding party from the *Maria* with musket fire and their cutlasses, and the Uruguayans then settled down to an exchange of musket fire between the decks of the two ships. Garibaldi's helmsman, Fiorentino, was shot dead as Garibaldi stood beside him on the bridge. Garibaldi then seized the helm himself, but a moment later a bullet struck him below the ear and lodged in his neck, and he fell senseless on the deck. If the bullet had been an inch higher, it would have killed him; and as it was, it inflicted the most serious wound that he ever received in battle. His boatswain, Luigi Carniglia, Maurizio Garibaldi and two other Italians carried on the fight for nearly an hour, until the *Maria* abandoned the attack when the *Mazzini* disengaged and slipped away to the south out into the middle of the estuary. Lieutenant Errazquim had three men wounded, two slightly and one severely, and he decided to return to Montevideo. At 1.30 pm he met another Uruguayan gunboat, the *Lobo*, which was also looking for Garibaldi; and shortly afterwards he met the Brazilian warship, the *Imperial Pedro*. He told both these ships the direction in which the pirates had gone, and the *Lobo* and the *Imperial Pedro* set off in pursuit.[7]

On board the *Mazzini*, Garibaldi recovered consciousness, but was in great pain, and quite unable to carry out his duties. The crew brought the map to him as he lay in his bunk, and asked him for orders. They were in a very dangerous predicament, and there was only one possible course for them to adopt: to sail for an Argentine port, hoping that they would receive better treatment there than in Uruguay. Garibaldi looked at the map, and gave orders to sail for Santa Fé on the River Paraná, because, as he says in his memoirs, it was the first place he saw on the map. The boatswain, Carniglia, though he had no previous experience as a helmsman, took charge of the navigation. Garibaldi pays him the warmest tribute in his memoirs, both for his courage in the sea-fight, when he held the enemy at bay with his blunderbuss, and for his navigation afterwards. With his captain wounded, in waters where neither he nor any other member of the crew, except Maurizio Garibaldi, had ever sailed, with hardly any provisions on board except coffee, and with two warships in pursuit, he brought the ship to safety.

Garibaldi himself was in a sorry plight. There was no doctor in the ship who could extract the bullet from his neck, and he was in constant pain. Carniglia, who as well as steering the ship acted as Garibaldi's special nurse, fed him on coffee, though the bullet in his neck affected his larynx and made it very difficult for him to swallow. Garibaldi became very depressed when the body of Fiorentino was thrown into the sea, although he knew that this was the accepted form of burial for a sailor, because he had been moved by a poem of Ugo Foscolo about the significance of being remembered on a gravestone; and he made Carniglia promise that if he died of his wound, his body would not be thrown into the sea.[8]

On 18 June they reached the island of Martín García, near the place where the Rivers Paraná and Uruguay meet in the River Plate. As they were passing the island they met another ship, and bought some food and wine from them, and then, taking the left-hand fork in the river, sailed up the Paraná towards Santa Fé. The sailors who had sold them the supplies landed at Colonia in Uruguay, and gave the first definite news for three days of the whereabouts of the hunted pirates. The *Imperial Pedro* and the *Lobo* had seen no sign of them, and Rosas's newspapers in Buenos Aires, which had reported the sea-fight quite impartially, were speculating as to where the 'Riograndense pirate' had gone. On 20 June the Governor of Colonia wrote to Oribe's Prime Minister in Montevideo that the captured *Luisa*, with thirteen pirates on board and their captain severely wounded, was sailing for Santa Fé; but the Paraná was in Argentine territorial waters, and no Uruguayan or Brazilian warship would venture to fight a battle there without permission from Rosas.[9]

Some days later, the *Mazzini* reached the point where the little River Gualeguay flows into the Paraná. There they met a ship from Buenos Aires, and asked the captain for supplies. The captain was friendly, but had no supplies to give them, and suggested that they should sail up the Gualeguay to the town of Gualeguay, where supplies would be available. As they had to put into some Argentine port, Gualeguay was as good as any, and here their painful journey ended. They reached Gualeguay on or before 27 June, twelve days after the sea-fight.[10]

Gualeguay is in Entre-Rios, the province which is surrounded on three sides by the Rivers Paraná and Uruguay, and in 1837 – and for a hundred and thirty years afterwards – could only be approached by water except from the province of Corrientes in the north. The capital of Entre-Rios has often been changed, but in 1837 it was Paraná – then called Bajada – as it is in 1974. The flat and slightly undulating grasslands of Entre-Rios, well interspersed with trees and copses, contained more cattle than human beings. There were seven towns in the province, the largest of which, Paraná, had 5,000 inhabitants. The rest of the population lived in scattered *estancias,* and the central part of Entre-Rios was almost uninhabited. There were some Spanish, French and Italian immigrants who engaged in trade in some of the small towns, and English, Scottish and Irish settlers had acquired land in Entre-Rios, chiefly in the east, along the banks of the Uruguay. There were wanted criminals, and army deserters, who roamed about the countryside. But most of the population had been born in Entre-Rios, and had never left it. The Governor of Entre-Rios was Colonel Pascual Echague, who was an old friend, as well as a loyal officer, of Rosas. Under him, the town of Gualeguay, and its 2,000 inhabitants, were governed by Major Leonardo Millan, a rough gaucho who was very typical of the officers in Rosas's armies.[11]

When Garibaldi arrived at Gualeguay, Echague was on a visit to the town, so he was able to deal at once, himself, with the problems raised by the arrival of the Brazilian ship and the Riograndense privateers. As important questions of foreign policy were involved, he had to refer the matter to Rosas; and on 6 July he sent a copy of a petition to Rosas signed by Garibaldi, asking to be granted asylum.

The petition, 'from the commander of the Riograndense privateer *Mazzini*', was obviously drafted for Garibaldi by one of Echague's secretaries. Apart from the fact that Garibaldi was hardly in a fit state of health to draft a delicately worded petition, it was written in Spanish, and it began, in the correct style, 'Long live the Federation', and was dated '27 June 1837, Year 28 of Liberty, 23 of the Entre-Rios Federation, 26 [*sic*] of Independence and 8th of the Argentine Confederation' – that is to say, the eighth year after Rosas's coming to power in Buenos Aires. But the petition most fairly expressed Garibaldi's opinions, and after stating that he was acting in support of the liberty and independence of the province of Rio Grande from the tyranny of the empire, it recapitulated truthfully all the events which had occurred since he left Rio de Janeiro.[12]

The most urgent thing for Garibaldi was to obtain medical treatment for his neck-wound, and Echague hastened to provide this. He sent his own doctor, young Ramon del Arco, who later became an eminent surgeon in Buenos Aires, to treat Garibaldi, and provided lodgings for him in the house of a Spanish merchant from Catalonia, Jacinto Abreu. Dr del Arco extracted the bullet from Garibaldi's neck. The operation, which in 1837 had to be carried out without an anaesthetic, was performed in Abreu's house; it lasted half an hour, and caused Garibaldi extreme pain. Afterwards he was nursed by Señora Abreu, and also by Carniglia, who continued the care which he had shown for Garibaldi on board ship. Within a few months Garibaldi had completely recovered. After he was cured, he was allowed to remain in Abreu's house, and was placed on parole, being allowed to go freely wherever he would, and to ride up to eighteen miles from Gualeguay, on condition that he gave his word of honour not to try to escape. He accepted the condition. His ship and cargo were held by the authorities; but in compensation Garibaldi was paid one peso per day – one United States dollar at the current rate of exchange – which was substantially more than the majority of the people of Gualeguay received each day.[13]

Garibaldi could certainly not complain of the treatment which he received at Gualeguay, and when he wrote his memoirs he expressed his gratitude to Echague. He wrote that although Echague was his political enemy, who had supported the wrong cause by fighting for Rosas, he must publicly thank him for his kindness. It never occurred to Garibaldi that the hated Rosas, as well as Echague, was responsible for his good treatment, and all his life he assumed, as his biographers have done, that it was only because of the slowness of communication between Gualeguay and Buenos Aires, and Rosas's dilatoriness in dealing with correspondence, that Echague was able to continue for six months treating Garibaldi well. In fact it was Rosas himself who was ultimately responsible for the kind treatment that Garibaldi received. After receiving Echague's report of 6 July on the arrival of the captured *Luisa*, and Garibaldi's petition, Rosas wrote to Echague on 5 August:

> My dear friend, With regard to the Imperial ship *Luisa*, of which you wrote to me on 6 July last, taken by a Riograndense privateer . . . without interfering with the detention of the crew which you have ordered, I would like you to show them every consideration which is compatible with their safe detention.

Echague replied on 21 August that he had already complied with Rosas's wish; he had allowed the captain of the privateer to go riding and had seen to it that he lacked nothing. The instructions of Rosas and Echague were duly carried out by the local commander at Gualeguay, Millan, though he was not particularly friendly to Garibaldi, who hardly ever saw him.[14]

Rosas had meanwhile reached a decision about the *Luisa*. He would hand back the ship to the Brazilians, but allow all the crew, except Garibaldi, to go free. Garibaldi himself would not be handed over to the Brazilians, but would be detained for the time being, on parole, at Gualeguay. All the crew thereupon sailed to Montevideo in one of the ships which were always going between there and Paraná, except for Carniglia, who remained at Gualeguay until Garibaldi had completely recovered from his wound; then he, too, went to Montevideo. From there, Carniglia and the Italians made their way to Rio Grande do Sul, where they joined the Republican forces; the Maltese and the negroes disappeared somewhere, and the negroes presumably retained the freedom from slavery which was their recompense for the dangers and hardships which they had endured in Garibaldi's company. When Rosas told the Brazilian Minister in Buenos Aires of his decision, the Minister arranged for the former master of the *Luisa*, Captain Manoel de Conseição, to go with four men to Gualeguay to fetch the ship. On 20 October Conseição arrived at Buenos Aires in the *Luisa* with 157 bags of coffee and some furniture on board.[15] A good deal of the coffee had disappeared from the ship at Gualeguay before she was handed over to Captain Conseição, and for some time afterwards the people of Gualeguay remembered that coffee had been cheap in 1837 because there was a larger quantity than usual in the shops.[16] The *Luisa*'s anchor, and Garibaldi's telescope, had also for some reason been removed from the ship, and are today in the local history museum in Gualeguay.

Garibaldi remained for six months in Gualeguay, in Abreu's house. He became very friendly with a number of families in Gualeguay, and was on general terms of friendship with most of the local inhabitants, thanks as usual to his frank and charming personality. He learned two skills in Gualeguay which were to be of the greatest value to him afterwards; he learned to speak Spanish, and to ride a horse. As a sailor, and a member of a lower-middle class, urban, seafaring family, Garibaldi had never learned to ride, and had made most of his inland journeys on foot; but on the great flat grasslands of Entre-Rios he acquired the art of horsemanship, which was still, in the nineteenth century, an essential requirement for anyone holding high military command on land.

He wrote a poem while he was in Gualeguay about the oppression of Italy by the hated Austrians; he composed it when riding in the copses, while he halted to let his horse graze. He spent his time walking, riding and reading in the beautiful surroundings and under the cloudless skies of spring and early summer in Entre-Rios. He occasionally saw a French newspaper, which must always have been at least four months out of date, and was happy to read about attempted revolutions in Calabria, the Abruzzi and Sicily, and of the refusal of the British government to expel Mazzini from England or the Young Italy refugees from Malta. He would have been happy in Gualeguay if he had been a man of quieter temperament; but he resented the forced inactivity, and wished to be in Rio Grande do Sul, fighting for the Riograndenses on land and sea. He was in regular communication with his Italian friends in Montevideo, the letters travelling freely by the sea-route. After his crew arrived in Montevideo, and Rossetti and Cuneo knew where he was, they were eager to help him escape from Gualeguay; but his parole prevented this. 'About escaping,' he wrote to Cuneo, 'suffice it to say that I am here on my word of honour.'[17]

The events which followed seem to have been caused by a tragic misunderstanding. At about midsummer – it must have been at the end of December 1837 or the beginning of January 1838 – Garibaldi broke his parole and tried to escape.[18] Among officers of European armies – and none more than in the British army – a breach of parole was regarded as an utterly dishonourable and unpardonable action; and it says much for the extraordinary popularity which Garibaldi enjoyed in later years among the British aristocracy that his breach of parole at Gualeguay was completely overlooked and forgiven, although the story had been widely publicized in his memoirs and in other books. It is surprising that Garibaldi, who always had a great sense of honour, and shortly before had written to Cuneo explaining that he could not escape because he had given his word, should soon afterwards have violated parole.

Cuneo, in his biography of Garibaldi, wrote that Garibaldi had

heard, the evening before his escape, that he was to be taken next day
to Paraná, and that he felt that these changed circumstances released
him from his parole. But Garibaldi's own explanation, in his memoirs,
is more convincing. He says that all his friends in Gualeguay had been
urging him to escape, telling him that he was a fool to feel bound by
his parole, and that they had explained to him that the authorities
would not have placed him on parole unless they had wanted him to
escape. Their granting him parole, he was told, was in fact an invitation
to him to go, so that the government would be spared the expense of
keeping him a prisoner in Gualeguay and from the necessity of making
a decision about what to do with regard to the Brazilian demand for
his extradition.[19] The code of honour of every man, however upright,
will be influenced by the general opinion of his neighbours. Men will
do things in one country which they would not do in another; and they
change their standard of morality quite rapidly if they find that what
they had regarded as an honourable act is seen by their neighbours
as being only the conduct of a fool.

All Garibaldi's friends urged him to escape while he had the chance.
Eventually the warning that it was now or never, as he was to be moved
to Paraná next day and extradited, turned the scale. Afterwards
Garibaldi thought that some of the people who had told him to go
were *agents provocateurs;* but this seems unlikely, as no one would have
had a motive for doing such a thing. It is much more likely that the
tempters were his friends who honestly believed that they were acting
in his interests, though they were certainly mistaken, for the events
that followed show that the authorities had not in fact decided to extra-
dite him, and had probably not even decided to take him to Paraná.

The escape was hurriedly planned by Garibaldi and his friends.
In his memoirs, Garibaldi denies that Abreu was involved, and
mentions only that he received help from an old man who lived about
five miles outside the town. Local tradition identifies the old man as
Bernardo Gallo, and firmly implicates Abreu in the plot, as well as
another friend of Garibaldi, Gregorio Correa. According to this
tradition, it was Abreu who provided Garibaldi with a horse and a
pistol. Garibaldi and his friends discussed the details at a meeting at
Gallo's house. It was decided that he should ride west towards the
Paraná, to the *estancia* of an English settler where he would be sheltered
until he could be smuggled on to a boat going to Montevideo. Correa
is said to have offered to go with him as a guide, and Garibaldi to
have refused to agree, out of consideration for Correa's safety; but he
certainly set off with a professional guide – one of those *baqueanos* who,
by experience and intuition, knew every inch of the trackless pampas,
and could therefore always obtain high payments for their services.

Garibaldi and the guide set off at dusk – about 8.30 pm at that time of year – and rode all night, through heavy wind and rain, almost at a gallop, towards the Paraná. They had about eighty miles* to cover before they reached the Englishman's *estancia*, and Garibaldi believed that, when morning came, they were within sight of it. The guide then told Garibaldi to wait in a wood while he went on to the Englishman's house to make sure that Garibaldi could safely go there. Garibaldi, who was feeling tired after his long night ride – he was still an inexperienced horseman – dismounted, tied his horse to an acacia tree, and lay down to sleep. He awoke three hours later, but the guide had not yet returned. Garibaldi walked to the edge of the wood to see if there was any sign of him. Suddenly he heard a noise behind him, and found a squad of soldiers on horseback with drawn swords charging towards him. The leader called on him to surrender. Resistance was impossible, and Garibaldi could not try to escape, as the soldiers were between him and the place where he had left his horse. So he handed over his pistol, and gave himself up. Garibaldi never accused the guide of having betrayed him to the soldiers; but the circumstances of his capture – the disappearance of the guide and the sudden arrival of the soldiers – are very suspicious, and local tradition has no doubt about it. It says that the guide was named Juan Pérez, that he had led Garibaldi during the night, not towards the Paraná and the Englishman's *estancia*, but round in circles to the vicinity of an army camp, and had then gone to the camp and told the soldiers where Garibaldi was waiting.

The soldiers put Garibaldi on his horse, tied his arms behind his back and his feet under the horse, and took him back to Gualeguay. As they rode along the banks of the River Gualeguay in the heat of the summer day, the mosquitoes were active, and they plagued Garibaldi mercilessly, as he could not brush them away because his hands were tied behind his back. When they reached Gualeguay, they went to the house of the commandant, Millan. When Millan saw Garibaldi, he struck him across the face with a whip, which was the almost automatic reaction of Rosas's gaucho officers when they first encountered a prisoner. He asked Garibaldi the names of the people who had provided him with his horse and pistol. Garibaldi refused to tell him,

*Garibaldi (*Memoirs, Scritti*, II.49), states that the distance was 54 '*miglia*', which Dwight (p. 34) and Werner (I.45) translated as 54 'miles', Melena (I.46) as 54 '*Miglien*', and Dumas (I.105) as 54 '*milles*'. Garibaldi was almost certainly referring to the Piedmontese mile of 2,466 metres, which would correspond with the actual distance from Gualeguay to the River Paraná. All the references in Garibaldi's memoirs to '*miglia*' are interpreted here as being to the Piedmontese mile, and the necessary alteration has been made so as to give the distance in each case in English miles.

so he struck repeatedly at Garibaldi's face, which was already swollen with the mosquito bites. As Garibaldi still said nothing, Millan ordered him to be tortured. He was taken to an adjacent building, and tied by his two wrists, which were still bound together, to a long beam in the roof, so that he was hanging with his whole weight on his arms, with his feet about four or five feet from the ground. He was told that he would remain in this position until he revealed the names of his accomplices.

After a while Millan came in, and asked Garibaldi if he would now give the information. As Millan stood immediately beneath him, Garibaldi had the satisfaction of being able to spit in his face, where-upon Millan coolly said that in view of his attitude Garibaldi would remain hanging there, and left the room. Garibaldi hung on the beam for two hours. His wrists were cut by the rope, and the pain was intense. He felt a violent thirst, and asked for water. His guards took pity on him, and gave him water, but he found that it seemed to burn his stomach and caused the worst suffering of all. After two hours he lost consciousness. When he came to, he was lying in a prison cell, chained to another prisoner, who had been convicted of a murder.

Garibaldi's treatment had aroused great sympathy in Gualeguay, where so many of the inhabitants had come to know him and like him. This angered Millan and his officials so much that they let loose a reign of terror in the town, which the Rosista gaucho commanders were always very ready to do at the slightest excuse. Suspicion had naturally fallen on Abreu, and though Garibaldi said nothing to incriminate either him or anyone else, he was arrested, along with a few other suspects. But despite the general panic among the local population, a woman of Gualeguay, Señora Rosa Sanabria de Alemán, risked the wrath of the officials by visiting Garibaldi in prison, and bringing him all the comforts which were permitted.[20]*

After a few days, Garibaldi was transferred to the provincial jail

---

*The house where Garibaldi was tortured was probably destroyed in 1848 (see Villanueva, p. 81), and replaced by another building, which was widely believed to be the original building where Garibaldi had suffered, and was preserved as such until 1970, when it was demolished to make way for a block of flats which was under construction in January 1972. According to the article by The Old Creole in 1937 (Villanueva, pp. 133-4), Millan's secretary Salustiano Moreiro ordered Garibaldi to be hung up for a second time, for one hour more, and this time by one wrist only; but Garibaldi says nothing about this in his memoirs, and on such a point local tradition can hardly be relied on. The well-known story, that the guards refused Garibaldi the water for which he called, and that it was given to him by Señora Alemán, who was standing among a crowd of jeering spectators at the entrance to the building, is not only improbable, but conflicts with Garibaldi's story in all the editions of his memoirs. It appears to be the invention of Garibaldi's more imaginative biographers, and is not even upheld by the more reliable local tradition.

in Paraná. He was put in charge of an escort under a negro officer, and taken to Paraná with his hands bound behind his back and his feet tied under his horse. On the way, they stopped to buy some refreshments at the *estancia* of an Englishman. The Englishman was impressed by the dignity of the prisoner in the party, and asked the guards to unbind him and allow him to share in the refreshments. The guards said that they had orders to keep his hands and legs bound; but the Englishman suggested that they could safely leave him unbound until they approached Paraná, and offered to supply them with the refreshments free of charge if they did this; and the guards agreed to the bargain.[21]

In the prison in Paraná, Garibaldi recovered from the immediate effects of the torture; but he never got rid of the long-term effects. In after-years he sometimes felt spasms of pain in his arms in certain types of weather, which may well have been due to the torture, though the rheumatism and arthritis in his legs, from which he also suffered in later years, must have been due to other causes. He felt great indignation at the way in which he had been treated. He described it in a letter to Cuneo in February 1838 from his prison in Paraná, and wrote:

> I ought not to end without recording the name of that monstrous abortion of nature under the auspices of Hell, and to tell you at least his name, so that it can be held up to the execration of the whole Universe. Yes, Leonardo Millan had your brother hung up for two hours by the hands![22]

After he had been in prison in Paraná for two months, he was suddenly told that he was to be released, and was free to go wherever he wished. He felt deeply grateful to Echague for this, which he considered was the greatest of all the benefits he had received from the Governor of Entre-Rios, as he had feared that he might be kept in prison for many years. He lost no time in leaving Paraná, and took ship for Montevideo.[23]

CHAPTER 6

RIO GRANDE DO SUL

GARIBALDI sailed from Paraná to Montevideo; but his troubles were not over. When he contacted his friends in Montevideo, they warned him that the Uruguayan government had not forgotten his fight with the gunboat *Maria*. In the eyes of the authorities he was a criminal who had opened fire on Uruguayan naval officials while resisting arrest, and had severely wounded one of them. He therefore remained concealed in the house of Angelo Pesante, who had been the master of the ship in which Garibaldi had made his first journey as a sailor from Nice to Odessa in 1824. Here he was visited by Cuneo and by Rossetti. Rossetti, after leaving Garibaldi's ship at Maldonado in the previous May, had made his way from Montevideo to Rio Grande do Sul, but after contacting the Riograndense revolutionaries had returned to Montevideo to make arrangements for publishing a newspaper for the Riograndenses.

Garibaldi stayed in Pesante's house for a month, and then set off with Rossetti for Rio Grande do Sul. The distance from Montevideo to the frontier was about 300 miles. It was the first time that he had ever made a long journey on horseback, but he very much enjoyed it, as he had already begun to feel a great love for the Uruguayan plains, for the horses of the pampas – 'the true Sultan of the desert', as he called them – and for the other animals that roamed there. He was shocked at the cruelty with which the South Americans treated their animals, and felt that the long series of terrible civil wars that they endured was their punishment for this.

After entering Rio Grande do Sul, Garibaldi and Rossetti went to the little village of Piratini in the highlands to the west of Pelotas on the Patos lagoon, about seventy miles from the Uruguayan frontier. The revolutionary government had made Piratini its temporary capital. There, in a cottage that was named, for the moment, the Ministry of Finance, they were warmly welcomed by the Minister, Almeida, who told them that President Bento Gonçalves had left Piratini to take command of the Republican army that was engaging the Imperial government forces along the San Gonçalves river.

Garibaldi asked to be allowed to join the President's army, and after spending a few days at Piratini he set off for Gonçalves's headquarters. Rossetti remained in Piratini editing the newspaper *O Povo* (*The People*), which became the official organ of the Republican government of Rio Grande do Sul. A few months later, the seat of the government, and the editorial office of *O Povo*, were moved from Piratini to Caçapava, a hundred miles to the north-west.[1]

The fighting in Brazil, Uruguay and Argentina, in which Garibaldi was to be involved almost continually during the next ten years, had its peculiar features, because of the vast size of the territory and the sparsity of population. To people in Europe, South American warfare seemed both romantic and ridiculous. Garibaldi himself contributed to the romantic idea. When he published his memoirs, after he had returned to Europe and had become famous as an Italian patriot, both he himself and his editors, translators and publishers hoped that the book would be a best-seller, which it was. The account of his life in South America was therefore made to sound romantic. The popular biographies of Garibaldi were a good deal more romantic than the memoirs, and much further from the truth. These biographies, embellished with romantic illustrations, showed an invincible hero performing deeds of prodigious valour, a beautiful heroine riding wildly through tropical forests, and a world of melodramatic unreality which has made it difficult for Garibaldi's later biographers to treat his years in South America seriously.

On the other hand, the small numbers of forces involved, and the simple weapons used, made South American warfare seem ridiculous to European observers. 'In Rio Grande,' wrote the British writer, Alfred Mallalieu, 'battles last a whole day, and the triumph must be dearly purchased indeed which costs half a dozen killed and twice as many wounded.' A French traveller, Chavagnes, who was present at the Battle of Caëthe in Brazil during the revolt in the province of São Paulo in 1843, reported mockingly that after a battle which lasted five days, no one had been killed, and only two men had been wounded, both of them by the bursting of their own guns.[2] In fact, the battles in the Brazilian civil wars were often very fierce, and, on their own small scale, bloody. The number of casualties was certainly small. This is obvious from the great distress which Garibaldi showed, in his letters and in his memoirs, whenever he had to report that one of his men had been killed. He viewed losses with the personal concern of a platoon commander, not with the necessary detachment of an army general.

The casualties were small because the armies were small, and this was because the population was small. The total armed forces of the Brazilian government in 1844, with which they controlled an area of three and a quarter million square miles and a population of 4,170,000, were 24,000 officers and men, of whom 17,000 were regulars and the rest reserves. At no time did the Imperial government feel able to send more than 10,000 men against the rebels of Rio Grande do Sul. The Riograndenses claimed – and it may have been an exaggerated claim – to have a total armed force of 9,372 men in October 1839, of whom 4,296 were front-line troops and 5,076 reserves of the National Guard. Of the front-line troops, 1,827 were cavalry and 2,247 infantry; and though there were – at least on paper – 222 men in the artillery corps, these did not often manage to go into action in the conditions of warfare which prevailed in Rio Grande do Sul. The 5,076 reserves of the National Guard were all cavalry, and were in fact the local gauchos who could be called up, with their horses, to serve in an emergency in their districts. There were never more than about 6,000 Riograndenses under arms at any one time, which was by no means an insignificant number out of a total population of 160,000.[3]

With these small armies operating in a vast territory, the chief problem was to find the enemy, and often the hostile forces did not meet for many months at a time. When they did, fierce battles took place, in which no quarter was given. The chief weapon of the cavalry was the lance, about 18 feet long, which apart from the blade at the spear-point, also had a steel spike at the rear end with which a horseman, without dismounting, could finish off a wounded enemy who was lying on the ground. The cavalry also carried sabres and pistols. The infantry fought with carbine and bayonet. As the conditions of warfare in the remote plains of the pampas made it almost impossible to guard prisoners, the captors had the alternative of killing the prisoners or letting them go free. Most commanders adopted the course which military prudence and common sense suggested, and killed the prisoners. Garibaldi, who found this very distasteful, often let his prisoners go, and on at least one occasion angered his comrades-in-arms by doing so.

The prospects for the wounded were almost as grim as for the prisoners of war. There were few doctors attached to the army, and no facilities for nursing or performing operations on the battlefields of the pampas. The slightly wounded men were given first-aid treatment by their comrades, and carried, or helped, to a base camp where they received more elaborate treatment. Seriously wounded men were past helping, and, rather than leave them to die on the battlefield in the heat of the sun, or to be found, when still alive, by an enemy force, one of their comrades would often comply with the wounded man's request and shoot him after a tender farewell.*

*Garibaldi's statement that the seriously wounded soldiers were sometimes shot by their own comrades appears only in the Dumas edition of Garibaldi's memoirs (*Memoirs*, Dumas, I.126). It is cut out of Melena's German edition, and the whole

When Garibaldi arrived in Rio Grande do Sul, the Imperial government was making a serious attempt to reconquer the province. An army of several thousand men had been sent to Porto Alegre, which the Imperialists still held, and from there marched out to find and destroy the Riograndense forces. Near Pelotas they met a superior force under Bento Gonçalves, and retreated northwards towards Porto Alegre. Garibaldi, coming from Piratini, caught up with Gonçalves as he was pursuing the retreating enemy. He was received as warmly as he had been at Piratini. Gonçalves invited him to a simple meal – the President shared his soldiers' rations when on campaign – and treated him with the kindness and honour which he deserved in view of the services which he had rendered and the sufferings which he had undergone for the Riograndense cause.

Garibaldi immediately took a liking to Gonçalves, and formed a high opinion of him. Gonçalves, who was aged fifty – not nearly sixty, as Garibaldi states in his memoirs – was tall and slim, and still active enough, as he had recently shown, to be able to escape from prison by swimming; and he remained one of the best horsemen in Rio Grande do Sul. But in Garibaldi's opinion he lacked the necessary determination as a military commander, and seems to have been like one of those generals whom Napoleon criticized for not being lucky.

> He was unlucky in battle [wrote Garibaldi] a fact which has always made me think that chance plays a great part in the events of war. One quality, indeed, which the gallant general of the Republic lacked was perseverance in battle. I consider this to be a grave defect. Before starting a fight you ought to think matters over carefully; but, having once begun, you should never give up hope of victory until you have tried your utmost efforts and brought your last reserves into action.[4]

Garibaldi went with Gonçalves as he pursued the enemy. The Imperialists succeeded in avoiding them, and could not be brought to battle; but 170 miles to the north, the Riograndenses won a great victory over an Imperialist force on the Rio Pardo. The Imperialists lost over a thousand men. This put an end, for the time being, to their hopes of reconquering Rio Grande do Sul, and left Gonçalves in control of the province. While the indignant members of Parliament in Rio de Janeiro denounced the Brazilian government for its military incompetence and its failure to suppress the rebellion, the remaining Imperialist forces in Rio Grande do Sul were reduced to holding the ports of Porto Alegre, Rio Grande and San José do Norte, and to carrying on small-scale guerrilla warfare. This they did quite effect-

section in which it comes is omitted in the Dwight and 1872 editions; but in a footnote to his novel *Clelia* (p. 458n.), Garibaldi states that this happened at the battle of San Antonio in Uruguay in 1846 (see *infra*, p. 198).

ually under the command of a brave and skilful leader, Lieutenant-Colonel Francisco de Abreu, afterwards Baron de Jacuhy, who was known as 'Moringue'* – the marten – on account of his ferocity and cunning, and was particularly hated by the Republicans because he was himself a native of Rio Grande do Sul. This made Garibaldi eager to cross swords with him, particularly when he heard that Moringue's small band of mercenaries and adventurers included many Austrians.[5]

But Garibaldi was planning to fight on sea, not on land. He wished to pursue his project of the previous year and raid Brazilian shipping, which he could now do much more easily, as he could operate from a base in the friendly territory of Rio Grande do Sul. On sea, unlike on land, the Riograndenses had no forces which could compete with the Brazilian government's. The Brazilian Imperial Navy, with 67 ships of the line, carrying a total of 2,830 men and 350 guns,[6] was the largest in South America, and could hold its own with any navy in the world except those of the great European powers or the United States. The Riograndenses had no real navy at all; they had only two ships and two daring and enthusiastic foreigners – Garibaldi and John Grigg. Grigg was a citizen of the United States, a young man from a very wealthy family, who had come to fight for Rio Grande do Sul out of a desire for adventure and Republican sympathy. When Garibaldi met Grigg, he admired his abilities and character.[7]

Gonçalves and his government found two ships for Grigg and Garibaldi. Grigg's ship was named the *Republicano*, and was 25 metric tons. Garibaldi was given a slightly bigger ship, which was named the *Farroupilha* – from the word 'riff-raff', which had been applied to the Riograndense privateers by the Imperialists, and proudly accepted by them. The name was later changed to the *Rio Pardo* in honour of the Republican victory. Garibaldi was placed in command over Grigg, with the rank and title of Lieutenant-Captain Garibaldi, Commander of the Naval Forces of the Republic.[8]

The crews of his two ships – that is to say, the total man-power of the Riograndense navy – consisted of about sixty men. Seven of them were Italians – Garibaldi's old comrades, Mutru, Carniglia and the others who had been with him on the *Mazzini* at Maldonado and Gualeguay. Some of the others were negro slaves, who had been granted their freedom on condition that they joined the navy. The rest were what Garibaldi called 'that class of seafaring adventurers known on the Atlantic and Pacific coasts of America as *frères de la côte*' – men of all nations who had been pirates, smugglers, or, more often, crews of

---

*Garibaldi states that 'Moringue' means 'marten', and that Colonel Abreu was so called on account of his ferocity and cunning; but in fact the word means an ear-shaped jar. Abreu had inherited the nickname from his father, who was given it because he had large ears.

74

ships engaged in the illegal slave trade, but were now happy enough
to serve with the former slaves in Garibaldi's ships. Garibaldi found
the freed negroes more reliable, on the whole, than the *frères de la côte*.
Apart from the negroes, there were very few native-born South
Americans in the crews.[9]

Apart from the insignificant size of the Riograndense navy, it was
restricted in its sphere of operations. The Republican capital, Caçapava, and the area to the south-west of Porto Alegre where their main
forces were stationed is on the western side of the Lagoa dos Patos.
Garibaldi's two ships were in this lagoon, which is 200 miles long from
north to south, and 30 or 40 miles from east to west. The only entrance
to the lagoon is at the south-east end, through the straits between Rio
Grande and San José do Norte, which are less than a mile wide. As
both Rio Grande and San José do Norte were held by the Imperialists,
and their navy was in the straits, it was impossible for the Republican
ships in the lagoon to reach the open sea. They could, however, hamper
the shipping which passed between Rio Grande and Porto Alegre on
the northern shore of the lagoon. The unchallenged control of the
lagoon by the Imperialist navy was an important factor in the war,
because it meant that they could without difficulty maintain and supply
their garrison in Porto Alegre by sea, and hold this bridgehead for
future operations by land against the Riograndense armies to the west
of the lagoon. Garibaldi and Grigg decided to disturb the supply line
to Porto Alegre.

From their base near Camaqua, about half-way down the lagoon
on the western shore, Garibaldi and Grigg made raids on Brazilian
merchantmen sailing in the lagoon between Rio Grande and Porto
Alegre. At first the Imperialist navy laughed at the activities of the two
small ships. But Garibaldi and Grigg succeeded in intercepting and
plundering an increasing number of Brazilian merchant ships during
the winter of 1838. They brought their prizes to a landing-place near
Camaqua, which they regularly used, as there was no proper port on
that part of the lagoon. Here, on the beach, the captures were legalized
in proper form; a lawyer appointed by Gonçalves's government sat as
judge in a prize court, and after hearing Garibaldi's evidence and
examining his credentials, ruled that the captured ships and goods
were lawful prize under international law, and could therefore be
retained by the Republic of Rio Grande do Sul. Garibaldi and his
men were permitted to retain part of the booty for themselves, under
the usual provisions of the law of prize. This they greatly appreciated,
as their pay from the Republican Ministry of War and Marine was
usually in arrears.

On 4 September 1838 Garibaldi and Grigg met a large Brazilian merchant ship, the *Mineira*. Garibaldi reported to his government that he had captured the ship with one cannonade and two musket shots; but the crew scuttled the ship before making off in their boats towards the desolate sands and marshland on the eastern side of the lagoon. The Riograndenses could not save the ship, but were able to retrieve the whole of the cargo and bring it in to Camaqua. This success angered and alarmed the Brazilian naval authorities, who issued orders that in future no merchant ships were to sail in the lagoon without a naval escort. This was a tribute to the success of the Riograndense sailors whom the Brazilians had been ridiculing; but it seriously hampered the operations of Garibaldi and Grigg, who were not strong enough to attack a convoy of Brazilian warships.[10]

The supremacy of the Imperialists at sea, and of the Riograndenses on land, caused comparative military and naval inactivity during the summer of 1838-9, and the Riograndense authorities were able to turn their attention to more peaceful activities. They organized an effective administration, collected the taxes, and made preparations for drafting a constitution for the new Republic and organizing a general election for a Parliament. In the tradition of the French revolutionaries of 1793, they adopted a new calendar, in which the years were reckoned from 20 September 1835, the date on which the Republic had been proclaimed; but the days of the week and the months were not altered, and all the festivals of the Church were kept, as the government was at pains to emphasize its devotion to the Catholic faith.[11] Slavery, which played an important part in economic and social life on the *estancias* and in the private houses of the wealthy landowners, was retained; but slaves who volunteered for the armed forces were freed from slavery.

The chief propaganda instrument of the Riograndense cause was *O Povo*, a rather badly printed newspaper which Rossetti edited and published every Saturday at Caçapava. The first number, on 1 September 1838, contained, as the opening words of the first article on the front page, a long quotation from Mazzini's manifesto of Young Italy, which was reprinted in a box on the front page in every subsequent issue. Though the news in *O Povo* was, in the main, accurate, Rossetti considered that his job was to help the war effort and bolster up morale. Reports of successes were exaggerated a little, and news of setbacks was sometimes suppressed for as long as possible, or not reported at all.

There was also time, that summer, for a social life among the leading members of the government and Riograndense society. Gonçalves's two sisters, Doña Antonia and Doña Anna, were the chief hostesses. These two middle-aged ladies had both spent a few seasons at the court in Lisbon in the days of the old régime. They both owned large houses and *estancias* on the western shore of the Patos lagoon, Doña Antonia near Camaqua and Doña Anna further south at Arroyo Grande, on the smaller inner lagoon, the Lagoa Mirim, which runs out of the Lagoa dos Patos on the south-west. Here they entertained their brother's civil and military officers in appropriate style. Garibaldi was an honoured guest at these parties. He was charmed by Doña Anna, who still retained a youthful grace and elegance, and had the most delightful manners. She had living with her, at Arroyo Grande, the family of Don Paulo Ferreira, a Riograndense landowner whose house and *estancia* near Pelotas had been sacked by the Imperial forces. Ferreira had three beautiful young daughters, who assisted Doña Anna to entertain the officers on her *estancia*. Though Garibaldi states in his memoirs that each of the three girls was more beautiful than the others, he had no doubt where his own preference lay. He fell in love with Doña Manuela, the youngest daughter. She was engaged to Gonçalves's son, and Garibaldi says that this prevented him from making love to her, as he could not steal the girl of a friend and brother-officer whom he admired as much as young Gonçalves.

Despite his humble birth and his Radical political opinions, Garibaldi felt completely at home in these elegant aristocratic surroundings. In his letters of thanks to Doña Anna, which were written in a most courtly style, he told her how much he and his men appreciated her hospitality whenever they returned to Arroyo Grande after their operations in the lagoon. In his memoirs he described the joy with which they saw the tall palm trees at the mouth of the stream leading to Doña Anna's *estancia* whenever a contrary wind or some naval duty brought them to the *estancia;* and whenever they were required to transport Doña Anna and the young ladies of her household to Doña Antonia's house at Camaqua, 'there was a hurrying to and fro, and busying oneself in attentions to the beautiful travellers, an eager rivalry in showing devotion, respect and veneration to the dear creatures'.[12]

On Doña Antonia's *estancia* at Camaqua there was a large storehouse near the shore of the lagoon, about twelve miles from Doña Antonia's house. It was used by Doña Antonia's labourers for storing the *maté* tea which they produced on the *estancia*. Doña Antonia placed the storehouse at Garibaldi's disposal for building ships, and he and his sixty men used the place, which was full of timber and scrap metal, as their chief base when on active service. On 17 April 1839 Garibaldi and about a dozen of his men were sitting having their breakfast and drinking *maté* in front of the storehouse, on a misty early morning in the South American autumn. The rest of his men were scattered around the area, doing their work. They had not seen an enemy on land for nearly a year, and their security had become very lax. None of them were carrying their weapons, which they had left inside the storehouse. Without warning Moringue, with a force of 150 cavalry and infantry, emerged from the mist and began firing at them. Perhaps one of Moringue's men started firing too early, because Garibaldi and his men just had time to race for the shelter of the storehouse, which Garibaldi reached at the moment when one of the enemy horsemen lunged at him with a lance and pierced his *poncho* – the South American cloak which he always wore. As soon as he reached the storehouse, Garibaldi snatched up one of the carbines which were stored there and fired at the enemy, bringing down two or three of them. Most of his handful of men succeeded in reaching the storehouse; but two or three, who were unable to reach it, ran off in the opposite direction. One of these was Mutru, who managed to escape; another of them was captured by Moringue's men, and killed at once, although he was unarmed.

Garibaldi and his few companions held the storehouse for several hours against the greatly superior numbers of the enemy. In his memoirs, he named the chapter 'Fourteen against One Hundred and Fifty'; but in the report which he wrote at the time to the regional Political Chief, he put the odds against him even higher, stating that he had only eleven men, including himself. But his original letter has not survived, and we know it only in the form in which it was published by Rossetti in *O Povo* on 22 May 1839. Rossetti, who was quite shameless as a propagandist, may have understated the number of Garibaldi's men in order to magnify their achievement; but perhaps the fourteen included Mutru and the other men who ran off, so that only eleven of them reached the storehouse and took part in the fight.

Moringue's men included eighty of his Austrians, who, according to Garibaldi's very hostile testimony, were the best soldiers in the Imperial forces. The Austrians lay down on the ground, as they had been trained to do, and fired at Garibaldi's men inside the storehouse. Garibaldi, writing after a lifetime of experience as a commander who so often owed his success to his aggressive, unorthodox and daring tactics, stated in his memoirs that the enemy made a great mistake in following the rules of the book on this occasion, because if they had immediately rushed the storehouse they would have overwhelmed and exterminated the defenders. As it was, he and his men had time to take up their positions, and put up a stout defence. Though outnumbered by more than ten to one, they had the advantage of the better cover; and they sang the new Riograndense national anthem as loudly as possible so as to make it sound as if there were more men in the storehouse than in fact there were. Their morale was as high as it always

GARIBALDI'S BIRTH-PLACE AT NICE

GENERAL ROSAS

ANITA GARIBALDI

was with Garibaldi's men, so that Garibaldi's chief problem was to prevent them from leaving the cover of the storehouse and charging out on the enemy. After a while, Moringue sent some men to climb on the roof of the storehouse and set it on fire; but the defenders stabbed at them through the smokeholes with their lances and bayonets, and dislodged them from the roof before they had succeeded in igniting the timbers. Then by a lucky chance one of Garibaldi's musketeers – a freed negro named Procopio – fired a shot which hit Moringue himself as he was directing operations, and broke his arm; and Moringue then ordered the retreat. He was perhaps influenced by the knowledge that, though he temporarily outnumbered his adversary, he was deep in enemy territory, and might himself be overwhelmed if Riograndense reinforcements arrived. He left six dead behind and carried off a number of wounded with him. Garibaldi had one man killed, and six slightly wounded.

Garibaldi wrote his report on the engagement to the regional Political Chief that same night. After describing his victory over the 'slaves and assassins' who had attacked him, he asked the Political Chief to inform the government of the heroism shown by 'our eleven brave men . . . which shows how men will fight to the death in defence of the infant Riograndense Republic against an enemy, although the numbers were so unequal, and which proves once more that one free man is worth twelve enslaved ones'. This reference to 'slaves' and 'assassins' may seem inappropriate in the case of volunteer mercenaries who had merely been fighting in war for the government they served; but Garibaldi – or perhaps Rossetti in O Povo – was thinking along the lines of Rouget de Lisle in the Marseillaise – 'Que veut cette horde d'esclaves?' – and expressing the feelings of nineteenth-century Radicals that, though men who fought for the cause of a free republic were heroes, those who fought for kings and despots were contemptible slaves who were murdering patriots at the behest of their tyrannical masters. Garibaldi was very happy, after the battle, when he discovered that the lovely Manuela had expressed great concern for his safety when she heard about the danger which he had faced.[13]

The Republican government had formed an ambitious plan for taking the offensive and carrying the war into enemy territory. To the north of Rio Grande do Sul was the state of Santa Catarina, one of the smallest provinces in the Brazilian Empire, with an area about the size of Scotland, and a population in 1839 of 66,000, of which only 12,000 were slaves.[14] This population of horsemen and fishermen had hitherto remained loyal to the Emperor; but in the small coastal towns of Laguna and Desterro (the modern Florianópolis) there were Radical intellectuals who sympathized with the Republican movement in Rio Grande do Sul. They made secret contacts with Bento Gonçalves and planned an invasion of Santa Catarina by the Riograndenses to coincide with a Republican rising in Laguna and Desterro, which would lead to the establishment of a free Republic of Santa Catarina allied to the Republic of Rio Grande do Sul.

The key move in the operation was to be an attack on Laguna, and though the main attack was to be by the Riograndense land forces, Garibaldi's ships could play a useful part in making a simultaneous attack from the sea, provided that no larger number of Brazilian warships happened to be in the area at the time. The difficulty was that Garibaldi's two ships were in the Lagoa dos Patos, and that, as the mouth of the lagoon was completely controlled by the Imperial navy at Rio Grande and San José do Norte, it was impossible for the Riograndense ships to get out of the lagoon. So Garibaldi formed another plan. On the east side of the lagoon there is a strip of land separating the lagoon from the Atlantic. In 1839, as in 1974, this land was virtually uninhabited; it consisted of sandy wastes, and rough grasslands interspersed with canals and marshes. Garibaldi now proposed that his two ships, which had been renamed the *Rio Pardo* and the *Seival*, after the Republican victories at these places, should be dragged overland from the lagoon and refloated in the Atlantic. At its narrowest point the peninsula is less than ten miles across, but here, and at most places, the land was so soft and marshy that the operation would have been impossible. Garibaldi therefore selected a longer route to the north of the Lagoa dos Patos, between the Bay of Capibari and Tramandai, which is the only part of the district where it has been possible, in more recent times, to build a railway. The distance at this point is about fifty miles.

Garibaldi sailed north-east across the lagoon to the Bay of Capibari, and consulted a local resident named Abreu, who was said to be a clever engineer. Abreu designed two vehicles which could be lowered into the water, placed under the ships, and levered up on land with the ships on them. The vehicles were then fastened together by a shaft, and two hundred oxen, assisted by Garibaldi's men, dragged the vehicles, with the ships on them, for three days across the fifty miles. The operation was successfully carried out, and on 14 July the ships were lowered into the Atlantic on the other side.[15]

This exploit has become one of the famous incidents in Brazilian history. The well-known picture by Lucílio Albuquerque of the ships being drawn overland, with the oxen heaving, the men pushing, and Garibaldi riding alongside on his horse waving his hat in the air, and exhorting the men, with great gestures, to even greater efforts, is as inaccurate as most other nineteenth-century pictures, in all countries, of romantic episodes from the nation's wars. The vehicles on which the ships were placed, which can be seen today in Porto Alegre, had four wheels under each of the two vehicles, each wheel being ten feet in diameter, and all four being placed under the front part of each vehicle. Because of the design of the vehicles, the oxen could draw the ships without undue effort. No doubt Garibaldi was right when he modestly wrote in his memoirs that the incident shows how small his ships were; but it was nevertheless a great achievement. It is a credit not so much to the physical efforts of the men as to the boldness of Garibaldi's conception and the engineering skill of Abreu, the local handyman of a village in a very remote part of Rio Grande do Sul.

This success was followed by a bitter and undeserved disaster. Garibaldi and Grigg, with their ships in the Atlantic, immediately sailed north towards Santa Catarina to be in readiness for the attack on Laguna. Garibaldi, in the *Rio Pardo*, had thirty men on board, some of them landsmen who were going to take part in the operations at Laguna, but had never been to sea, and lay in the holds feeling very sick. The ship was well laden with food supplies and equipment. But next day, 15 July – the day after they had completed their overland journey and reached the Atlantic – they encountered a *pampero*, the violent hurricane which arises so suddenly off the coast of South America. Garibaldi found that he was unable to get the ship to land, and as he realized that she could not keep afloat much longer, he gave the order to abandon ship, and seizing a plank, jumped into the sea and tried to swim to shore. He was making progress, with difficulty, against the waves, when he saw that Carniglia was still clinging to the ship, being fastened to the deck by his heavy coat, which he was unable to undo and discard. Garibaldi swam to him, and, drawing out a knife which he was carrying, tried to slit Carniglia's coat and cut it away; but the knife broke, and at that moment a wave carried Garibaldi deep under, and when he came up again Carniglia had disappeared. Then Garibaldi saw that Mutru was in great trouble. He shouted instructions to Mutru, as to how best to hold his plank, and swam over to him; but just before he reached him, Mutru was carried under by a wave, and did not emerge again.

Garibaldi managed to reach the shore. He found that out of the thirty men on the *Rio Pardo*, sixteen had been drowned and fourteen had survived. All his closest friends and best seamen were among the dead. Carniglia, who had served so well on the voyage to Gualeguay and had nursed him there when he was wounded, had been drowned; so had Mutru, his old school friend who had shared his experiences during the abortive revolution in Genoa, and the negro Procopio, who had fought so well a few weeks earlier in the defence of the storehouse and had hit Moringue. Garibaldi was the only one of the seven Italians to survive. On the other hand, several of the seasick landsmen, who had never been to sea before and could not swim, had survived, having got hold of a plank and been carried safely to the shore. As they sat on the shore, soaked through on the cold winter's day, they saw that a cask of brandy from their ship had been washed ashore. Garibaldi told his men to console and hearten themselves by drinking the brandy; but their hands were so cold that they could not open the cask, and Garibaldi had to make them run for an hour in order to warm themselves and dry their clothes. Eventually they found their way to a cottage some four miles inland, which was inhabited by a poor family, who treated them with great kindness.

John Grigg, in the *Seival*, had been more fortunate or more skilful than Garibaldi. He had succeeded in bringing his ship safely to land a little way up the coast, without losing a single man or any of his cargo.[16]

The forces of nature had struck a heavy blow at the tiny Riograndense navy. Rossetti, who went with the Republican forces to Laguna as a war correspondent, did not report the disaster in *O Povo*, but instead, after mentioning Garibaldi's great exploit in dragging the ship overland between 11 and 14 July, stated that Garibaldi and his men in the *Farroupilha*** and the *Seival* had safely arrived at Laguna.[17] But the shipwreck did not seriously impede the plans for the attack on Laguna. The operation was planned by General Netto and carried out by Colonel David Canabarro, an enormously fat man who could move his armies with more rapidity than his own great bulk. Garibaldi had been given a captured vessel, the *Itaparica*, and he and Grigg in the *Seival* sailed into the harbour at Laguna on 22 July 1839, exactly a week after the shipwreck, while Canabarro stormed the town from the land side. The Imperial forces in Laguna under Colonel Villas Boes put up a sharp resistance, but it had ceased before the end of the day. The Imperialists lost 15 killed, and the Riograndenses took 77 prisoners,

---

*There is some confusion as to the names of Garibaldi's ships. In his memoirs, he states that he named the captured *Luisa* in 1837 the *Farroupilha* (see *supra*, p. 54), and that the ship in which he sailed on the Lagoa dos Patos in 1838 and 1839 was the *Rio Pardo*; and this is confirmed by his letter of 5 September 1838 (see *supra*, pp. 75–6), which was dated as being written from the *Rio Pardo*. Doria (in Doria-Bandi, p. 25) cites a letter from Castilhos to Monteiro (both of them majors in the Riograndense army) written in July 1839, describing the shipwreck and naming Garibaldi's ship as the *Farroupilha*; and she is also called the *Farroupilha* in Lt-Col Meroes's bulletin (published in *O Povo*, 10 August 1839). But the official Santa Catarina Register of Wrecks (entry for 15 July 1839) names the ship the *Rio Pardo*. This manuscript contains an entry of all wrecks off the coast of Santa Catarina since 1516. The latest entry is for the year 1944.

including 5 officers. They captured – or claimed to have captured – 4 warships and 14 merchant ships, 463 carbines, 16 crates of wheat, and 36,620 rounds of ammunition.

In view of the Imperialists' control of the entry to the Lagoa dos Patos, news of the events in Santa Catarina could only be taken overland to the Riograndense authorities in the south, and it travelled slowly. It took a fortnight for the report of the victory to reach Netto's headquarters at Villa Setembrini, and a month before it was known at Caçapava. Netto's order of the day of 3 August, announcing the victory at Laguna on 22 July, which was published in *O Povo* at Caçapava on 20 August, named five officers of Canabarro's 'liberating division', as well as Canabarro himself, to whom the Fatherland owed a debt of gratitude, among them Lieutenant-Captain José Garibaldi, commander of the naval squadron.[18]

Thus Garibaldi, for the first time, entered the town of Laguna, whose chief claim to fame today, both in Brazil and abroad, is its association with him and with the woman whom he met there. When, twenty years later, the story of Garibaldi and Anita was published and avidly read throughout Europe and the United States, the readers conjured up a picture of Laguna as a romantically remote place, far beyond the pale of civilization in a dark and wild continent. In fact, the small town of some 4,000 inhabitants, situated in a remarkably beautiful inlet of the sea, surrounded on four sides by mountains, and where, on most days of the year, both the sea and sky are of an almost identical dark blue colour, was a fashionable seaside resort for wealthy merchants, whose elegant furniture and elaborate clockpieces rivalled the best examples of their kind in London and Paris. The wealthy merchants of Laguna were divided in their political sympathies. Most of them felt that they had no reason to be dissatisfied with their condition under the government of the Emperor of Brazil; but there were others who were eager to be the leading figures in an independent republic of Santa Catarina.

The Riograndenses did their best to encourage this feeling. Four days after the capture of Laguna, Canabarro issued a proclamation on 26 July, which he signed on a massive oak table at a ceremony in the Town Hall at which Garibaldi and his other top-ranking officers were present. 'Long live the Catarinense nation,' it proclaimed, 'long live the Republican system!' By 5 September in Year I of Catarinense Independence they had succeeded in forming a provisional government of Santa Catarina, headed by a priest and composed chiefly of local Laguna politicians, though Rossetti, who had accompanied the Riograndense army, became Secretary of State. The provisional government proceeded to appoint 22 July as the national day, renamed the town of St Antonio of the Angels of Laguna as the 'July city of Laguna', and appointed Colonel Canabarro of the Riograndense forces to be General Commander-in-Chief of the army of Santa Catarina. Many inhabitants of the province felt that all this smelled more of conquest by Rio Grande do Sul than liberation from Brazil. The Riograndenses and their supporters occupied a number of other towns in the province further north along the coast; but the attempt of the Radicals to seize power in Desterro was suppressed by the firm and rapid action of the local Governor. The Riograndense forces began to meet opposition and passive resistance in the areas under their control.[19]

The capture of Laguna turned out to be the high water mark of the Riograndense struggle. It aroused anger and fear in Rio de Janeiro, and made the Imperial government set about in real earnest the reconquest of Santa Catarina and Rio Grande do Sul. Garibaldi wrote in his memoirs that it was a favourite saying of Canabarro's 'that a hydra should rise from the lagoon of Laguna to devour the Empire', and Garibaldi thought that this might have proved true; but 'our haughty attitude towards the good Catarinenses – our friends at first, and afterwards our bitter enemies' – had 'led to our losing the fruits of a most brilliant campaign, which might have brought about the fall of an empire and the triumph of the Republic over the whole American continent'.[20]

CHAPTER 7

ANITA

As long as the Riograndenses held Laguna, Garibaldi was able to wage war against Brazilian shipping much more effectively than he had done before. With Laguna as a base, he could raid along the Atlantic coast as far north as Desterro, or even São Paulo, and intercept the Brazilian trade with Europe as well as their coastal commerce. Between the end of July and the end of October 1839 he made several successful expeditions. It was when he was returning to Laguna from one of these expeditions that he first saw Anita.

Anita Garibaldi has become a legendary figure. Her life and death made her a national heroine in both Brazil and Italy, and a heroine of romance in many other countries of the world. Books about her were widely read, and she was the subject of several well-known pictures. These pictures showed Anita's first meeting with Garibaldi, which for some reason was set beside a garden well, with Garibaldi gazing at her with bold admiration, and she at him with a mixture of fascination and resistance; Anita galloping bareback through the Brazilian forest, with her long hair streaming – an incident which was at least based on fact; Anita and Garibaldi escaping in a rowing boat along a shaded river from the fierce soldiers who threaten them from the bank – one which had no basis in fact whatever; and the death of Anita in the house in the Italian marshes, with the sobbing Garibaldi kneeling at her bedside and desperately clasping her hand. All this made her seem as romantic and remote a figure as a character in a Nordic saga or an ancient Greek myth; but her grand-daughter survived until 1971, and there are many persons living in Laguna today who have spoken to people who knew Anita.

Anita was born Anna Maria de Jesus. Guerzoni, who wrote many untrue things about Anita, calls her a Creole. Admiral Winnington-Ingram, who was in Montevideo when he was a young officer in 1845, said the same thing in his memoirs; but though Winnington-Ingram saw Garibaldi and Anita in Montevideo, he did not write his memoirs until 1889, and was perhaps merely repeating what was already an accepted story. Other writers stated that she was the daughter of a high-ranking English officer. In fact, she seems to have come from pure Portuguese stock. Her father, Bento Ribeiro da Silva de Jesus, was a poor Brazilian peasant from the province of São Paulo. In 1815, like many other poor peasants, he moved south in the hopes of avoiding the destitution which faced him in São Paulo, and crossed the state border into Santa Catarina, where he settled in a village near Tubarão which was then named Morrinhos, but today is called Annita Garibaldi. There has been some dispute as to where Anita was born, because there were three villages called Morrinhos in the district; but Garibaldi, in a short biographical note about Anita which he wrote in 1850, said that it was Morrinhos near Tubarão.[1]

Bento da Silva de Jesus and his wife Maria Antonia had several children, apart from Anita, though two people who claimed to know the family well have made conflicting statements about the number and names of these children, and neither statement agrees with the official records. Anita was probably born in 1821, but there is no surviving record of her birth, though the registers of the baptisms of her brother Manoel in 1822 and of her sister Sicilia in 1824 have survived.* The house in which she was born in Morrinhos, like most of the other houses in the village, was built on wooden piles which had been placed in the water of the slow-flowing stream among the banana trees of the village.

Bento da Silva died while Anita was still a child, and soon afterwards her mother moved with her family from Morrinhos to the town of Laguna. Apart from the rich merchants and their negro slaves, there was a poor white community in Laguna. One of them was a young man called Manoel Duarte di Aguiar. According to one story, Duarte was a fisherman; but the weight of local tradition says that he was a shoe-maker,[2] though no doubt, like nearly all the inhabitants of Laguna, he fished in his spare time and ate fish as his main food. As well as being fishermen, the people of Laguna, like all the population of Santa Catarina, were excellent horsemen. Foreign visitors were particularly surprised that the women were also excellent riders, that they rode everywhere unattended, and were quite unabashed if strangers spoke to them.[3] Anna Maria de Jesus – Aninha Bentos, or Annita Bentos, as she was usually called – learned, like the other girls, to be a good horse-woman at an early age. She probably did not learn to read or write

*Anacleto Bittencourt states that Anita had two brothers, Francesco and Antonio, and three sisters, Bernarda, Antonia and Felicità (Varzea, pp. 242–3n). Maria Fortunata (in Boiteux, p. 52) says that she had two brothers, Salvator and Barnardo; but perhaps Maria Fortunata did not mean to suggest that Anita had no other brothers or sisters. Her brother Manoel was baptized at Lages on 27 December 1822, and her sister Sicilia on 19 September 1824. The children may of course have been known by different names from those with which they were baptized.

until a few months before her death in Italy, when she started to learn, and managed at least to sign her name. After she met Garibaldi she learned, in due course, to speak Spanish and Italian, but she seems to have had difficulty in remembering to pronounce her name, Garibaldi, in the Italian and Spanish way, and not to call it 'Ga-ree-bough-zhee', as all the Brazilians did.*

Despite all the contradictory stories about her, nearly everyone who knew her agreed that she was not beautiful in the usually accepted sense of the word. An inhabitant of Laguna, Anacleto Bittencourt, who knew her when he was a young man, described her as being 'tall, a little stout, with long and protruding breasts, an oval face covered with freckles, large black and slanting eyes, and thick flowing black hair'.[4] Bittencourt's description has been considered to be inaccurate and spiteful, but part of it at least is confirmed by the two etchings of the drawings for which Anita appears to have sat. 'From early life she was distinguished by a vivacious disposition', wrote Garibaldi.[5] As she emerged from childhood, she was already an extremely determined and powerful personality, and this made her mother eager to marry her off as soon as possible, though she was only about fourteen. Manoel Duarte was an obvious choice, though he was more than ten years older than Anita; but Anita was not eager.

Anita's most intimate friend was a young girl of her own age, Maria Fortunata. Though Anita died in 1849, Maria was still living on 30 March 1900 at Conceição near São Paulo, when she described an incident in which Anita had been involved in about 1835. A young man who admired Anita, and had been pursuing her unsuccessfully, waylaid her in a wood near Laguna when she was walking home. He dismounted from his horse, and when Anita arrived he tried to rape her. Anita snatched his whip, gave him a sound flogging, jumped on his horse, and rode off to lodge a complaint at the police station in Laguna.[6] After the rumpus caused by this event, her mother increased her pressure to persuade Anita to marry Duarte, and eventually Anita reluctantly agreed, though she told Maria Fortunata about her misgivings and anxieties. The marriage took place in the parish church of Santo Antonio dos Anjos in Laguna, which like many South American churches was built of white marble, and dated from the end of the

*The three surviving letters of Anita (all written from Nice in 1848) are written in different hands, and signed by the same illiterate hand, thus suggesting that Anita asked someone else to write the letters for her, but was able, with difficulty, to sign her name. Garibaldi wrote at least one letter to Anita as early as 1845; but it is suggested that it might have been read to her by someone else. In one of Anita's three letters, she signed her name 'Anita Garibau', probably because she was confused as to the way in which the name 'Garibaldi' was written and pronounced in Italian.

seventeenth century. An enormous gilded and ornate Baroque altar-piece had been installed in 1803, and was much boasted of by the inhabitants of Laguna. On 30 August 1835 Aninha Bentos walked up the aisle along the brown, yellow and red carpet with the twenty-five-year-old shoemaker, Manoel Duarte, and they were pronounced man and wife.[7] If Anita was born in 1821, she was only fourteen, and this is quite likely; at any rate, she cannot have been more than sixteen. The wedding party took place in a cottage just across the road from the church, which had been built some years before by the negro slaves of a local builder.

Anita had been married for just four years when she first met Garibaldi. Although it has been stated that she had a daughter by Duarte,[8] this is certainly not true, for there were no children of the marriage. Duarte continued in his trade as a shoemaker, but he also enrolled in the local detachment of the National Guard. When the Riograndense forces invaded Santa Catarina in 1839, he was called up for active service by the Brazilian government, and sent to join the Imperial army which was resisting the invasion. It is not known whether he took part in the battle for Laguna, or whether he had been stationed elsewhere.

Garibaldi described his first meeting with Anita in the most famous passage of his memoirs. The romantic style of his language, which is even more romantic in the English translation than in the Italian original, has led some modern readers to doubt the reality of the incident; but there was really nothing remarkable or unusual about it. Garibaldi was walking on the quarter-deck of the *Itaparica*, thinking sadly of the loss of his Italian friends in the shipwreck of the *Rio Pardo*. He decided that he would 'look out for a woman' to comfort him in his loneliness. He happened to look through his telescope at the cottages on the Barra, the hill behind Laguna, and saw a girl. He decided immediately to go and look for her, and climbed to the houses on the Barra; but he could not find her, and had given up hope of seeing her again when he met a local inhabitant whom he had known ever since his first arrival in Laguna. This man invited Garibaldi into his house for a cup of coffee, and there Garibaldi saw the girl for whom he was searching.

We both remained enraptured and silent, [he wrote in his memoirs] gazing on each other like two people who had met before, and seeking in each other's faces something which makes it easier to recall the forgotten past.

At last I greeted her, and said to her: 'You must be mine.' I could only speak a little Portuguese, and uttered the bold words in Italian. But my insolence was magnetic. I had formed a tie, pronounced a decree, which

only death could annul. I had come upon a forbidden treasure, but yet a
treasure of great price!!!

If there was guilt, it was mine alone. And there was guilt. Two hearts
were joined in an infinite love; but an innocent existence was shattered.
She is dead! I am unhappy! and he is avenged, yes, avenged! On the day
when, vainly hoping to bring her back to life, I clasped the hand of a
corpse, with bitter tears of despair, then I knew the great wrong that I
had done. I sinned greatly and I sinned alone![9]

This account is inaccurate in at least one point. It is not true that in
1839 Garibaldi could speak only a little Portuguese. During the previous twelve months he had been writing military reports and charming
letters to Gonçalves's sister, in fluent Portuguese;[10] and even if we
assume that these letters were translated or perfected for him by a
friend, there is very little doubt that after eighteen months in Rio de
Janeiro and another eighteen months in Rio Grande do Sul and Santa
Catarina, Garibaldi would have been able to say 'You must be mine'
in Portuguese.

Garibaldi's first meeting with Anita is described in all the editions
of his memoirs, and although these accounts are very similar, there are
subtle differences between them which are not accidental. The world
first heard about the encounter when the first edition of the memoirs
was published, in English, by Garibaldi's American friend, Dwight, in
New York in 1859. In this version, Garibaldi's first meeting with Anita
is almost respectable; for Garibaldi states that after seeing Anita through
his telescope, he hesitated to approach her because 'I knew of no one to
whom I could apply for an introduction'. Dumas's account, in his French
edition of the memoirs, was less respectable than Dwight's, but more
romantic; having seen Anita from his ship, he went at once to the house.

My heart was beating, but despite its agitated state it had formed a resolution which did not weaken.

A man asked me in; I would have gone in, even if he had forbidden it;
I had seen this man once before; I saw the girl, and said to her: 'Virgin,
you will be mine.'

I had formed, by these few words, a link which only death could break;
I had found a forbidden treasure, but a treasure of how great a price! If
a wrong was committed, the wrong was mine alone. It was my wrong if
two hearts, by joining together, tore the soul of an innocent person. But
she is dead, and he is avenged.

When Dumas published the memoirs, he added a footnote to this
passage:

This chapter is deliberately wrapped in a veil of obscurity, because, after
I had read it, I said to Garibaldi: 'Read this, dear friend, it does not seem

clear to me.' He read it, and then, after a moment's pause, said with a sigh: 'It must stay as it is.' Two days later, he sent me a notebook headed 'Anita Garibaldi'.[11]

Dumas never published this notebook, and it cannot now be traced; but it was probably another copy of the document about Anita which Garibaldi gave to Dwight, and which Dwight published, as an appendix to the memoirs, under the title 'Biographical Sketch of Anna Garibaldi, written in Italian by her husband, Gen. Giuseppe Garibaldi'. If so, it throws no fresh light on the meaning of the words which perplexed Dumas.

Many readers of this passage in the Dumas edition of the memoirs thought that it meant that Garibaldi had eloped with another man's wife. Their suspicions were increased when the Baroness Esperanza von Schwartz, under the name of Elpis Melena, published the German edition of the memoirs in 1861. Here the account of Garibaldi's first meeting with Anita was very nearly the same as that which Garibaldi afterwards published in the 1872 Italian edition,* but it also contained words which appeared in no other edition: 'I was guilty because the love that then joined our hearts together broke the heart of a poor innocent, who had greater rights than I had.'[12] Rumours that Anita was a married woman when she met Garibaldi were circulating during Garibaldi's lifetime. Some people even interpreted Garibaldi's statement that he alone was guilty as meaning that he had abducted Anita by force against her will – a preposterous idea, which is not borne out either by the memoirs or by any other evidence.

Garibaldi never made any attempt to deny that he had eloped with a married woman. On the contrary, the passage in the 1872 edition did nothing to counteract the interpretation that had been put on the passage in the earlier editions, but rather the reverse. But when his secretary Guerzoni published his biography in 1882, a few months after Garibaldi's death, he expressly denied that Anita had been a married woman, and put forward a new explanation of Garibaldi's words. 'The man whom Garibaldi met on the doorstep was her father, and those who say that it was her husband are wrong. Anita had been betrothed by her father's wish to a man whom she did not love; but she was not married, as people believed.' And Guerzoni added: ' "If guilt there was," exclaimed Garibaldi, "it was entirely mine. If the spirit of an innocent man was injured, the responsibility should be mine alone, and I accept responsibility. She is dead, and her father is vindicated." '[13] Guerzoni stated that this was a quotation from the Baroness von Schwartz's German edition of Garibaldi's memoirs,

*See pp. 88–9, supra.

volume I, pages 84–5, which was a deliberate deception, because Garibaldi made no reference at all to Anita's father in this passage or anywhere else.

Jessie White Mario wrote even greater nonsense, both in her Italian book *Garibaldi e i suoi tempi* in 1884 and in her English biography of Garibaldi which was published in 1889 as a Supplement to the English translation of the 1872 edition of the memoirs. After describing Garibaldi's first meeting with Anita, she proceeded:

> That he would have married her then and there if he could have obtained the consent of her family is certain; but her father, a proud, severe man, accustomed to implicit obedience, had betrothed his daughter to a very wealthy and very old man. Could Anita have hoped, either by open opposition or by persuasion, to regain her freedom, naturally she would have preferred that her lover should have wedded her and taken her from her home to his heart in proper orthodox fashion; but she knew that she would have been compelled to marry the old man whom she had never loved and now abhorred, so she fled with her true love on board the schooner *Itaparica*.[14]

Jessie White Mario must have been as conscious as Guerzoni that she was lying in order to save Garibaldi's reputation. There is no reason to believe that Bentos da Silva was a 'proud, severe man accustomed to implicit obedience', and in any case he had died before Anita married Duarte. As for the statement that she was forced to marry an old man, it is true that Duarte was nearly twice Anita's age when she married him; but so was Garibaldi. When Garibaldi first met Anita, she was eighteen, or at the most twenty, and he was thirty-two, a little older than Duarte. But Jessie White Mario's nonsense was exceeded by the incomparable Alvensleben, who as usual reached the heights of absurdity in his life of Garibaldi in 1859, where he stated that the man to whom Anita was engaged to be married against her will was General Rosas in Buenos Aires.[15]

Twenty years after Garibaldi's death, the Brazilian novelist and poet Virgilio Varzea wrote his book *Garibaldi in America*. The book was apparently never published in the original Portuguese text, but an Italian translation by Clemente Pitti was published in Rio de Janeiro in 1902. Varzea was not a historian, and though his book has achieved the reputation of being one of the leading authorities on Garibaldi's life in South America, this is probably because very few people have read it, as only four copies of the book can be traced today.[16] Varzea usually gives no authority for his statements, and in some cases introduces conversations which are obviously imaginary. He does, however, make an interesting contribution to the solution of the mystery of

Anita Garibaldi. He states that his friend, the Brazilian poet Araujo Figueiredo, had met a few years previously Anacleto Bittencourt, an old man aged over ninety, who had known Anita at the time when she met Garibaldi; and Figueiredo took down in writing a statement which Bittencourt made to him, which is published in Varzea's book.

Bittencourt stated that Garibaldi first met Anita when he was visiting houses in Laguna and billeting his troops on the householders. When he knocked at Duarte's door, Anita opened it and told him that Duarte, who had been serving in the Imperial army, was lying in bed in the house, severely wounded. Garibaldi offered to take Duarte to the Riograndenses' military hospital, and Anita accepted on condition that she could accompany him. Garibaldi took Duarte and Anita to the hospital, where Anita nursed her husband, and also took her turn in nursing the other wounded soldiers of both the armies. A few days later, Duarte died of his wounds; but Anita stayed in the hospital nursing the other wounded patients. In the course of the next few weeks she and Garibaldi fell in love, and when Garibaldi left Laguna, Anita went with him on his ship.[17]

Bittencourt's statement, as published by Varzea in Pitti's translation, is accurate with regard to a number of details which can be confirmed by written records and other documents; but his account of Garibaldi's first meeting with Anita is obviously wrong, and no one in Laguna, then or now, believes his story about Duarte dying in hospital. They do not believe that Bittencourt told Figueiredo this, and think that it was invented by Varzea and Pitti in order to shield the reputations of Garibaldi and Anita. But Bittencourt's statement was resented most by the people who believed the tales of Guerzoni and Jessie White Mario and refused to accept that Anita had ever been married before she met Garibaldi. Foremost among these was Ricciotti Garibaldi, the son of Garibaldi and Anita, who stoutly maintained that his mother had never been married to anyone except his father. The attitude of the Garibaldi family was sufficient to convince Trevelyan and other historians. The Brazilians at first rejected the story of the marriage even more vehemently than the Italians; but it is conclusively proved by the official record in the Laguna church register of Duarte's marriage to Anita on 30 August 1835, which was discovered by the Brazilian historian J. A. Boiteux in 1932, and since then has been seen by several historians, including the present author; and the fact of the marriage has become generally accepted everywhere, though it is still rejected by many members of the Garibaldi family, chiefly because of Ricciotti Garibaldi's attitude.[18]

Although the marriage records conclusively prove Anita's marriage to Duarte, this passionate belief of Ricciotti's that Anita had been only engaged, and not married, to Duarte, was so strong that it must raise a slight doubt; and there are other reasons to believe that this was not simply a case of Garibaldi eloping with another man's wife. Ever since it became accepted that Anita was married to Duarte, it has generally been assumed that they were living together when Garibaldi first met Anita, and that it was Duarte who invited Garibaldi into his house for a cup of coffee. But this is almost certainly wrong, and Guerzoni's statement that the man who offered Garibaldi the coffee was not Anita's husband is the only truth in his whole story. After Anita married Duarte, she lived with him in his house in Rua de Praia in Laguna, which is now No. 42 Rua Fernando Machado. In 1839 the house was on the waterfront, the present market square and waterfront having been built on land reclaimed from the sea at a later date.[19] The houses up on the Barra, where Garibaldi first met Anita, are a long way from Duarte's house. The man who offered Garibaldi the coffee was probably one of Anita's brothers, or perhaps one of Duarte's brothers, unless – which there is no reason to believe – he was her lover. Duarte was serving in the Imperial army, and was not at home; and unless he was one of the seventy-seven prisoners of war who were captured by the Riograndenses at Laguna, he must have retreated from Laguna with the Imperial forces. This, however, raises the question as to why Anita had stayed in Laguna. It was the usual practice for the wives and families of the soldiers to follow their husbands on campaign as camp-followers. Their presence in the Imperial army during the fighting in Santa Catarina is commented upon in several contemporary documents.[20] These facts confirm the local tradition in Laguna that Duarte had deserted Anita before Garibaldi met her.

This theory would not have been good enough to please Ricciotti Garibaldi; but it can at least be plausibly argued, even if it cannot be proved, that Garibaldi eloped with a woman who had already been abandoned by her husband. It is argued that in that case Garibaldi would not have felt the sense of guilt which he expressed in the memoirs; but if the ferocious young Amazon, who, shortly before her marriage to Duarte, had horse-whipped a man who tried to rape her, and who was not in love with Duarte, had refused to permit Duarte to exercise his marital rights, and Duarte had left her for this reason, Garibaldi might well have felt that he had built his happiness on the unhappiness of another; and if Anita never allowed Duarte to consummate the marriage, it would explain why Garibaldi told Ricciotti that Anita had only been engaged, and not married, to Duarte. There is no proof whatever of this theory, which is only put forward speculatively; for unless new documents are discovered, no one will know the whole truth about Garibaldi and Anita.

CHAPTER 8

FROM LAGUNA TO MONTEVIDEO

A T the end of October 1839, Canabarro ordered Garibaldi to make a new raid on Brazilian shipping further north along the coast. The Brazilian government had sent a number of ships to blockade the harbour of Laguna in order to stop Garibaldi's expeditions; but he and Canabarro were sure that he would be able to slip out at night. He had three ships under his command – the *Rio Pardo*, a new ship which he named after the wrecked one, and commanded himself; the *Seival*, Grigg's ship, which was now placed under an Italian commander; and the *Caçapava*, of which Grigg took charge. Anita insisted on sailing with Garibaldi in the *Rio Pardo*.[1] She was breaking completely with her life at Laguna, and intended from now on to follow Garibaldi everywhere. Before leaving Laguna, she gave her sewing scissors to her friend Anna Garcia, who, after Anita had become famous throughout the world, passed them on to her brother-in-law, whose family presented them to the local museum.[2]

Garibaldi's three ships slipped out of the harbour under cover of darkness, and sailed as far north as the province of São Paulo. They succeeded in capturing a number of valuable prizes including a merchant vessel with a large cargo of rice. On their journey home with their prizes, they met a large Brazilian warship off the island of Santa Catarina. This warship carried seven guns against the solitary cannon in the *Rio Pardo*; and as Grigg, in the *Caçapava*, had become separated during the previous night from the other two ships, Garibaldi faced the Imperial warship without his help.

Garibaldi reacted to the situation in the way in which he was usually to react in his military campaigns in future operations; seeing that he could not avoid the superior forces, he attacked, firing the first shot in what developed into a fierce conflict. In the end, Garibaldi and the *Seival* got away, but he lost two of the three merchant ships which he had captured as prizes. He made for the coast, and landed at Imbituba, some twenty miles north of Laguna, where he set up a cannon on the shore, and erected some hasty bulwarks around the harbour in preparation for an attack from the Brazilian ships which were pursuing him.

The attack came at dawn next day. The *Rio Pardo* and the little *Seival* defended themselves for five hours, with the assistance of the covering fire from their cannon on the shore, against three better-armed Brazilian warships. They suffered many casualties, and some of Garibaldi's crew lost their nerve, and fled below deck. Before the battle began, Garibaldi had tried to persuade Anita to go on shore while the fight lasted; but she refused. When the fight was at its hottest, she picked up a musket and fired at the enemy. Soon afterwards, she and two of the sailors were knocked down by the blast of a cannon ball which exploded near them; but though the two men were killed, Anita was unhurt. Garibaldi then urged Anita to go below. She replied that she would do so, but only to make the cowards who were hiding there return to their duty. She soon came back on deck with two or three sailors whom she had shamed into returning to the battle area by her taunts and insults, and she fought on alongside Garibaldi and the men. Eventually, to Garibaldi's surprise, the enemy broke off the engagement, and sailed away. He later discovered that it was because their commander had been killed. Garibaldi returned safely to Laguna with his two ships, and Grigg, in the *Caçapava*, also found his way home.[3]

The Brazilian government, stung by the loss of Laguna and the criticism in Rio de Janeiro, now made a determined effort to regain the province of Santa Catarina. They sent a new army under General Andrea, who had recently suppressed a revolt of Indians and mulattos in the province of Pará with great brutality. Andrea could rely, not only on superior regular forces to those of the Republicans, but also on the sympathy and assistance of the majority of the Catarinenses. All over the province there were risings of supporters of the Imperial government. One of them took place in the small fishing port of Imarui, less than ten miles north of Laguna at the head of the little lagoon. The rising was premature. Canabarro sent Garibaldi and a squad of his sailors to suppress the revolt; and as the Riograndenses and their Catarinense supporters regarded the people of Imarui as rebels against the Republican government of Santa Catarina, Garibaldi was ordered to punish them for their rebellion by sacking the town.

The people of Imarui had erected defences in the harbour, expecting the Riograndenses to attack them from the sea. Garibaldi therefore landed with his men a little way down the coast, and attacked Imarui from the land side. The defenders were taken completely by surprise, and Garibaldi captured the little town without difficulty. He then ordered his men to sack the place. They carried out their orders very happily, but Garibaldi was disgusted with the operation. 'I was obliged to obey orders,' he wrote in his memoirs, 'but, even under a Republican government, it is very repugnant to have to obey blindly . . . I hope that neither I, nor anyone else who retains any feelings of humanity, will ever have to sack another town.'[4]

His men began by looting the wine-shops and getting drunk. Garibaldi himself had given up drinking wine since he had been in South America, and drank nothing but water; and he and a few senior officers were the only men who remained sober. The men wrecked the town. Garibaldi decided to concentrate on saving the lives and persons of the inhabitants, and made no attempt to save the property. As his men got more and more drunk and out of hand, he began to feel not only disgust, but also anxiety as to what would happen if the enemy troops, who were on the heights near the town, were to appear and suddenly attack them. He gave the word out, untruthfully, that the enemy were coming; but his men paid no attention. He was sure that if a force of fifty Imperialists had attacked him at that moment, they could have wiped out his men. He eventually succeeded in making his men return to their ships, but only by using his sabre on them.

On the return journey to Laguna an incident occurred which brought home to Garibaldi the kind of men whom he had under his command. A German sergeant who had fought well at Imarui had been killed in the fighting. Garibaldi wished to bury him on the spot, but his men asked him to take the body back to Laguna so that the sergeant could have proper burial there. That evening, in the ship, Garibaldi heard a great noise, and found the men drinking and gambling across the sergeant's corpse, which they used as a table on which they placed candles that they had stuck into bottles.[5]

The Imperialists were advancing rapidly on Laguna from the north. On 15 November a fleet of twenty-two Brazilian warships, mostly small craft, but carrying substantial numbers of well-armed soldiers, sailed towards Laguna with reinforcements for the Imperial land forces; and Canabarro prepared to evacuate the town, and retreat inland. He ordered Garibaldi to prepare for the retreat by transferring all the stores and equipment in his ships to the shore. About midday, Garibaldi climbed to the top of the Barra to view and assess the situation, and saw, from the movements of the Imperial ships and land forces, that they were planning to attack the Barra. He sent word to Canabarro about the enemy movements, and advised him to station his infantry in a position where they could have inflicted heavy losses on the enemy; but for some reason this was not done, and Garibaldi thought that a great opportunity had been lost.

Before Garibaldi could return to the ships, the Brazilian fleet had entered the harbour. His sailors who had come on shore with the supplies, seeing the enemy's superiority, refused to return to their ships; and those who were on board, thinking that the struggle was hopeless, hesitated to open fire. But Anita, who was on board the *Rio Pardo*, fired the cannon at the enemy, and once the first shot had been fired, the sailors opened up with cannon and small arms. Garibaldi did not lose many of his crew, because so few of them were in the ships; but the losses among his officers were very heavy, Garibaldi himself being the only officer who was unhurt. He saw Grigg cut to pieces by grapeshot, which killed him instantly; and the dead and wounded were lying on the deck of his own ship. Anita was firing the cannon of the ship, and Garibaldi sent her on shore to find Canabarro and ask him for orders – partly in order to get her to a place of safety, and partly because he thought that if he sent any of his men, the man would run away once he had arrived on land, and make no attempt to report to the General.

Towards evening, Canabarro sent him word that they were evacuating the town. He ordered Garibaldi to land as much as possible of his stores and equipment, and then set fire to all his ships and to join the retreating land forces. Anita took charge of the landing of the supplies, going repeatedly backwards and forwards with the men in the rowing boats under heavy fire, while Garibaldi directed the action against the enemy to cover the evacuation operation. He and Anita and the other survivors then joined the Riograndense army, and marched out of Laguna with them.[6]

During the next three months the Riograndenses retreated slowly 450 miles to the south-west in a great semicircle, fighting rearguard actions, chiefly of a guerrilla character, with the superior numbers of the pursuing Imperial forces, and hampered all the way by pro-Imperialist guerrillas among the people of Santa Catarina. In less than a month they had reached and abandoned Lages, the chief town of Santa Catarina, and were on the borders of Santa Catarina and Rio Grande do Sul. The force of events had turned Garibaldi from a sailor into a soldier, and rendered his post of Commander of the Republican Navy an empty title; but he said that as long as he had a carbine and a sabre lying across his horse's saddle, he was happy and could render useful service. Anita was at his side throughout the whole campaign. 'She looked upon battles as a pleasure,' wrote Garibaldi, 'and the hardships of camp life as a pastime.'[7]

On 14 December 1839 the Republicans won a victory at the ford of Santa Vitória on the River Pelotas, some forty miles south of Lages. According to the Brazilian government's announcement, their defeat occurred because the local Imperialist commander, in defiance of orders, had tried to cross the river with 200 men to attack 600 'rebels' on the other side. Gonçalves's order of the day claimed that the Imperialists had lost 50 men killed, and that the Republicans, who had lost 25 'patriots', captured 15 prisoners, including 'the traitor Lieutenant Basilio', who was a deserter from the Republican forces. The prisoners were granted their lives on condition that they enlisted in the Republican cavalry. The scale of military operations in South American warfare is shown by the fact that this small engagement was hailed as a great victory by the Republicans, and was prominently reported in the press in Rio de Janeiro and Montevideo. Anita did not take part in the battle, but she watched it on horseback, remaining in the saddle all day, and dismounting only to render first-aid to the wounded. This was all that could be done for them, as there were no ambulances or medical corps on the battlefield. When the fight was over, in the evening – so Garibaldi believed – he and Anita conceived their first child.[8]

The Republicans were able to follow up their victory by taking the offensive, and in January, with the help of reinforcements from Rio Grande do Sul under General Manoel, they recaptured Lages. The Rio de Janeiro newspaper, *Despertador*, admitted that, as a result of the Battle of Santa Vitória, 'the municipality of Lages is once more occupied by the Anarchists'.[9] Garibaldi and Anita were in action several times during the counter-attack which recaptured Lages. They were marching through a wood on the summit of the Serra do Espinasso when they were ambushed by a larger force of Imperialists, but drove them off after a prolonged exchange of musket fire. After the battle, the local inhabitants raised wooden crosses over the graves of the dead soldiers, some of which are still there today; but for many years afterwards they would not enter the wood at night, because they believed that the wood was haunted by the ghosts of the soldiers.[10]

The fight on the Capão da Mortandade, by the Forquilhas stream, near Curitibanos, was the occasion which gave rise to one of the most famous stories about Anita which twenty years later found its way into the popular literature of Europe. The Imperialists beat off an attack by Garibaldi's troops, in the course of which Anita's horse was shot beneath her, and she was taken prisoner. When she was brought before the commanding officer of the Imperial forces, he taunted her about the defeat of the Republicans, to which Anita replied by violently denouncing him and the Brazilian government. Her captors then told her that Garibaldi was dead, and presumably believed this to be true, because they allowed her to inspect the corpses on the battlefield; but when Anita found that Garibaldi was not among the dead, she was inspired to new exertions. She managed to escape that night, when her captors were drunk, and ran off into the forest. She travelled for four days and nights, living on berries and on some food which she obtained from some cottagers, one of whom gave her a horse; and she eventually reached Lages, which was then in the hands of the Riograndenses. She stayed in Lages only long enough to drink one cup of coffee, and then rode off to join the anxious Garibaldi, who was with his men at Vacaria, some seventy miles away across the border in Rio Grande do Sul.[11]

The Republicans held Lages and the surrounding district for about a month. During this time, Garibaldi was one of the Commissioners appointed to organize the collection of taxes in the area, being responsible for the Maçao district. This taxation may have made the Republicans unpopular, because Garibaldi observed that though they had been welcomed as liberators by the inhabitants when they retook Lages, the people were equally glad to see them go, and cheered the Imperial troops who recaptured the town for the second time in a new offensive which drove the Republicans over the state boundary into Rio Grande do Sul, leaving the whole of Santa Catarina in the hands of the Brazilian armies. Even after the Riograndenses had entered Rio Grande do Sul, they had trouble with pro-Imperialist guerrillas in the hilly districts of the north; but they rejoined Gonçalves's forces at the President's military headquarters at Villa Setembrina near Porto Alegre.[12]

Soon afterwards, Garibaldi took part in the biggest battle in which he had hitherto fought. An Imperial force under General Calderon advanced westwards from Porto Alegre, and Gonçalves met them in a pitched battle at Pinheirinho, six miles from Taquari. Garibaldi states, in his memoirs, that the Republicans had 6,000 men, 5,000 of them cavalry, against the Imperialists' 4,000 infantry and 3,000 cavalry, and adds that the Imperialists had also a few pieces of artillery. The Brazilian newspapers, at the time, reported that the Imperialists had 1,014 men against 2,000 Republicans;[13] but this referred only to one section of the battlefield, and was an attempt to minimize the effect of the battle. The Imperialists suffered from the disadvantage that General Calderon was killed in a skirmish a few days before the battle.

The right wing of the Republican army was commanded by General Netto, the left wing by Canabarro, and the whole army by Gonçalves himself. Now that they were campaigning in more regular conditions, Anita was not allowed to take part in the battle; but she protested strongly against Gonçalves's suggestion that she leave the battlefield, and was allowed to stay. Garibaldi was stationed on a hill in the centre with the infantry, nearly all of whom were negroes and mulattos. In the 1872 edition of his memoirs he described how, as he waited for the battle to begin, he looked down from the hill at the plain below; and he expressed the contradictory attitude to war, with its blend of pacifism and militarism, which he adopted in 1872, if not in 1840.

> Our hearts felt the throb of battle and the confidence of victory. I have never seen a more beautiful day, or a more magnificent sight . . . Very soon the blood, the broken limbs, and the corpses of so many splendid young fellows will disfigure the beautiful and virgin fields. And yet we were panting with eagerness for the signal for battle. . . . What a strange attitude for a disciple of Beccaria, who hated war. But what can you expect? On my road through life I have met Austrians, priests and despotism.[14]

On 3 May 1840 the Battle of Taquari was fought, and resulted in a victory for the Riograndenses. The decisive role in the battle was played by a body of lancers in Canabarro's division composed entirely of freed negro slaves. Garibaldi criticized Gonçalves for not pursuing the defeated enemy with sufficient energy, thus letting the fruits of the victory escape him; but Garibaldi, though he always favoured a policy of attack, was not a blind and unreasoning advocate of it. When others criticized Gonçalves for having selected a defensive position at Pinheirinho, and waiting for the enemy to attack instead of attacking himself, Garibaldi disagreed. He was sure that Gonçalves's policy had been right, and had been responsible for the victory.[15]

The Riograndenses celebrated the glorious day of Taquari, and thought that they had won the war. Rossetti, who had made only one passing reference in O Povo to the fall of Laguna and the retreat from Santa Catarina, now proclaimed in the paper that God and men had judged and condemned the Brazilian Empire at Taquari.[16] The Imperialists were again reduced to holding the ports in the Lagoa dos Patos and to waging the guerrilla warfare of Moringue and his band. During the winter of 1840 the Riograndenses sent an expedition to capture the port of San José do Norte on the northern side of the entrance to the Lagoa dos Patos. Some new canoes and small craft were built and given to Garibaldi, so that he could take part in the operation, because San José do Norte could be approached by land only from the north along the barren strip of land which separated the Lagoa dos Patos from the Atlantic. Gonçalves himself commanded the Riograndense forces, with Garibaldi acting as one of his three subordinate commanders. The plan was to capture the port immediately by a surprise attack; but the attempt failed, and the Riograndenses were forced to lay siege to the place. They won some successes in a few skirmishes, but were eventually obliged to abandon the siege and withdraw.[17]

During the operations at San José do Norte, Garibaldi's men once again showed the savagery of which they were capable. By South American standards, the war in Rio Grande do Sul was not exceptionally cruel – much less so than the campaigns in Uruguay and Argentina in which Garibaldi was later to take part; but the Imperialists had committed some atrocities against Republican prisoners of war, civilians and women, to which Rossetti had given publicity in *O Povo*.[18] At San José do Norte, one dark and rainy night, Garibaldi's men made a surprise attack on one of the forts held by the defenders. While the frightened civilians, alarmed at the noise of the shooting, flocked to the church in the main square of the town, and prayed for divine protection, Garibaldi's soldiers surrounded an enemy unit and took about twenty prisoners. The prisoners were made to stand in line, and one by one were taken away and had their throats cut. After the first four had been killed, their captors came for the fifth in the line, who was a young boy who had just joined the army; but at that moment Garibaldi arrived and stopped the executions, telling his soldiers that the boy might yet be able to render good service to the community. Ninety years later, the boy's son met Garibaldi's grand-daughter Italia, and told her that his father, for the rest of his life, had always been eager to do a good service to any Italian whom he met, out of gratitude to Garibaldi.[19]

After the withdrawal from San José do Norte, Garibaldi was sent to San Simon, about a hundred miles north of San José do Norte on the peninsula, with orders to supervise the building of canoes which could be used as warships during the next campaign. Most of the country around San Simon is desolate sandy waste; but Garibaldi found a pleasant *estancia* which had belonged to a wealthy landowner who supported the Imperial government and had therefore fled from the district, and he commandeered the property as a suitable place for building the canoes. Anita was in the eighth month of her pregnancy, and she moved into the house of a friendly family in the village of Mustarda, near San Simon. The house is no longer standing, but there is a tree in the garden which must have been there in 1840, under which Garibaldi and Anita are supposed to have walked. Garibaldi bought a small herd of cattle, and in his spare time from building the canoes became an *estancia* owner. Their only complaint at Mustarda was the cold, because the winter was exceptionally severe for Rio Grande do Sul, with temperatures sometimes falling to freezing point, and with a great deal of rain.

On 16 September 1840 Anita gave birth to a son, whom they called Menotti in honour of Ciro Menotti, the Italian patriot who had been executed by the Duke of Modena in 1831. He was born with a scar on his head, which Garibaldi believed had been caused by the fact that when Anita was carrying him – it was in the first month of her pregnancy – she had fallen from her horse when she was taken prisoner near Curitibanos. Medical evidence decisively rejects this possibility; but if Menotti suffered no effects from this prenatal experience, he had a series of extraordinary adventures almost from birth, and it is remarkable that he survived. Menotti was only twelve days old when Moringue attacked the village of Mustarda. Garibaldi was away at the time, having gone to Villa Setembrina in connexion with his naval duties; and Anita fled from the house, on horseback, in the bitter weather, with Menotti on her saddle, to escape from the raiders, and hid in the woods with some of Garibaldi's men until Moringue had gone.[20]

Menotti soon had to face even greater dangers, because a few weeks later the Imperialists launched another drive against Rio Grande do Sul. In July 1840 a revolution had taken place in Rio de Janeiro against the unpopular Conservative Regent, Araújo Lima. He was denounced in Parliament by the Opposition leader, Andrade Machado, and capitulated when enormous street demonstrations demanded his resignation. The fourteen-and-a-half-year old Emperor was proclaimed to be of age, the Regency was abolished, and Andrade became head of a constitutional Liberal government. The new government tried to solve the problem of Rio Grande do Sul by negotiation, offering the Riograndenses an amnesty and a measure of home rule if they gave up their claim to independence. Gonçalves refused the offer. The Brazilian government then prepared, on the one hand, to carry on the war with more efficiency and determination than under the old régime, and at the same time to pursue a more conciliatory political policy. They sent a new army to Porto Alegre under General Caixas, the best general who had so far appeared on either side in the war. He periodically renewed his offer of amnesty as he marched against Gonçalves's main force to the west of Porto Alegre. Although Garibaldi says that the offers of amnesty 'were scornfully rejected by the nobler part of the army', he admits that the Republicans would have been wiser to accept them in view of their military position, and that many of their followers wished to do so.[21]

Caixas drove the Riograndense forces into the highlands of the west. The Republican ministers, the newly-elected Parliament of Rio Grande do Sul, the government archives, the staff and printing-presses of *O Povo*, and all the Republican sympathizers who were not prepared to accept the Imperial amnesty, with their wives and children, all followed the army in its retreat. Garibaldi, Anita and Menotti went with the army, taking their small herd of cattle with them. Garibaldi and his sailors were attached to Canabarro's division, with which they had served in Santa Catarina. This division led the retreat, while Gonçalves's formed the rearguard, which was continually harassed by Moringue's guerrillas. At Villa Setembrina Moringue made a sudden raid on them, and the editorial staff of O Povo, who had been trained to fight if necessary, became involved in the fighting. In this action, Rossetti was killed. In the course of fifteen months, Garibaldi had lost four of his best friends – Mutru and Carniglia in the shipwreck, Grigg at Laguna, and now Rossetti.

The retreating army suffered great hardships on the march. The cold weather continued longer than usual, and in the high sierras of western Rio Grande do Sul the temperature at night fell well below freezing. The rains were exceptionally heavy, and drenched them thoroughly, as well as impeding their progress by raising the waters of the flooded rivers and mountain streams. At times they were short of food, especially the infantry. The cavalry chased the cattle which they met, and caught them with their lassos, but, as usual in South American armies, they ate most of the carcasses themselves, instead of sharing them with the infantry. When they were passing through the forest of Las Antas, there were no cattle, and everyone went hungry, being forced to live on the smaller forest animals and on berries. Caixas sent a division of Imperial troops, which was commanded by a French man, General Labattue, to cut off the retreating Riograndenses; but Labattue's men got the worst of the encounter, and themselves retreated to the west before the retreating Riograndenses. This made matters worse for the Republicans, because it meant that Labattue's men had consumed most of the meagre supplies before the Riograndenses arrived.

The women and children suffered especially, and many of the children died. Other children were abandoned when they could not keep up with the army, though in many cases their mothers stayed behind with them, so that the mothers as well as the children were lost. Babies like Menotti, who was a month old, had a slightly better chance than the older children, because they could be carried more easily; but Anita lost her usual cool composure in the face of danger because of her anxiety about Menotti, and she and Garibaldi considered that it was almost a miracle that he survived. Garibaldi got hold of two mules on which he placed Anita and Menotti; but on one occasion, when they were passing down a gorge in the forest of Las Antas, Garibaldi had to carry Menotti in a large handkerchief which he had tied round his neck to form a big sling in which the baby could be put, and he tried to keep Menotti warm by breathing on to his face. Anita, too, sometimes carried Menotti in a handkerchief tied round her neck.

His men helped him all they could, for Menotti was a great favourite with the soldiers, who often wrapped their coats around him to protect him from the cold. The only consolation for the Republican army was that the wild Indian tribes in the forests, who knew nothing of the issues involved in the war of Rio Grande do Sul against Brazil, chose to be friendly to Canabarro's men and to attack Labattue's troops. On the edge of the forest, the Republicans met a Riograndense woman who had been kidnapped and held prisoner by the Indians for many years. She attached herself to the Republican army, and so escaped from her captors.

After a march which Garibaldi stated, in his memoirs of 1872, was the most terrible that he ever experienced, they emerged from the forests into the plateau of Cima da Serra. Here they suddenly encountered warm spring weather, and an abundance of cattle, and they were in much better spirits by the time that they reached Cruz Alta. But things were going badly for the Republicans. Gonçalves was stoutly refusing all the Brazilian proposals for negotiations, but more and more of his supporters were accepting Caixas's offers of an amnesty, and abandoning the struggle. After a short pause at Cruz Alta, the Republicans marched south to San Gabriel, where at last the retreat ended. They had come 400 miles from Porto Alegre. Garibaldi set to work to build huts as temporary accommodation for the army. In San Gabriel he met for the first time an Italian immigrant, Francesco Anzani, who later became a close colleague and friend.[22]

After he had stayed for a few months in San Gabriel, Garibaldi asked Gonçalves to be released from the service of Rio Grande do Sul. His biographers have given a misleading impression about this, suggesting that the resistance of the Riograndenses finally ended at San Gabriel, and that Gonçalves disbanded his forces and told Garibaldi to go. In fact, the Republican resistance continued for nearly four years, though an increasing number of Riograndenses were submitting to Caixas's lenient rule. The fighting flared up again in 1843, and it was not until February 1845 that the Riograndense resistance finally collapsed. Garibaldi, in his memoirs, does not claim that he left because the fighting was over. He states that after living a life of hardship for several years, he wished for a rest; but his chief reason was that he wanted to hear news of his parents and of Italy, with whom he had completely lost touch since he had been in Rio Grande do Sul. He therefore decided to go to Montevideo, where he would be in contact with Nice, even though letters took three months each way. Perhaps even Anita, with a six-month-old baby, thought that it would be better to live, for a while at least, in a house in a town instead of following an army on campaign.

Garibaldi therefore asked Gonçalves's permission to go to Montevideo, at least for a time.[23] He had not definitely decided to leave Rio Grande do Sul for ever, and thought that after a few months' rest in Montevideo, he might well return to the Riograndense service. In Uruguay, Oribe had been replaced as President by the Liberal Unitarian leader, General Fructuoso Rivera, who was very sympathetic to the cause of Rio Grande do Sul; so Garibaldi knew that he would no longer be in any danger in Montevideo. Gonçalves gave Garibaldi permission to go, and also to collect a herd of cattle to pay for the cost of his journey. Garibaldi spent three weeks rounding up the cattle, and assembled a herd of nine hundred. He engaged some drivers for the cattle, and at the end of April 1841 set off with Anita and Menotti and the cattle for Montevideo.

But Garibaldi experienced the usual ill-luck which he always had when he was engaged in commercial, as opposed to military, activities, and lost all the cattle before he reached Montevideo. Nearly half of his herd were drowned when they were crossing the Rio Negro in Uruguay, and the remaining five hundred cattle were so exhausted by the journey and the crossing of the rivers, and owing to shortage of fodder there was so much difficulty in feeding them, that on the advice of his drivers – whom he afterwards suspected of defrauding him – he slaughtered all the remaining cattle, skinned them, and, abandoning the carcasses, kept nothing except the hides. The result was that after taking fifty days to cover the 400 miles from San Gabriel, and suffering considerably from the winter cold on the journey, they reached Montevideo with 300 hides instead of 900 cattle; and as the hides sold for very little, they were almost penniless.[24]

After reporting his arrival to the police, who noted that 'José Garibalde' with his wife and one son had arrived in Montevideo from San Gabriel on 17 June,[25] Garibaldi contacted his Italian friends in the city. He stayed for a short time in the house of Napoleone Castellini, and then moved into a house in what was then called Porton Street; but in May 1843, when Garibaldi was still living there, the streets in Montevideo were renamed, and Porton Street became the street of 25 de Mayo,[26] in honour of the rising in Buenos Aires against Spanish authority on 25 May 1810, which was celebrated in Uruguay as well as in Argentina as the day of South American Independence – which is the name that the street still bears today. Montevideo had spread beyond the old city walls which the Spaniards had erected in the early eighteenth century, and now stretched as far as the cemetery and to what is today Ejido Street, but included only a very small part of the modern city. In 1841, Montevideo was surrounded on three sides by water – on the south by the open sea, on the west and north by the bay and the harbour. Across the bay to the west was the fortified hill of the Cerro. The population was just over 40,000.[27]

The house in which Garibaldi lived for nearly seven years, which is a museum today, is virtually a one-storey house, built of white stone, with a flat roof, on the edge of which there are two very small rooms which can barely be called a second storey. On entering by the front door the visitor comes into a covered courtyard surrounded by ivy, on the right of which are four moderate-sized interconnecting rooms, while there is also one room on the left-hand side. Garibaldi and his family lived in one of these rooms – which one is not known – and other families occupied the other rooms. At the far end, on the right, is a small kitchen, built in dark red brick, which Anita shared with the other women in the house. All the occupants were presumably entitled to sit and walk on the roof.

Garibaldi had hoped that he would be able to live for a time in Montevideo on the proceeds of the sale of his cattle; but as he had lost them all on the way, he had to find another way of earning a living. After taking a job for a short time as a ship's broker, he fell back on the course which he had adopted when he had found himself penniless in Constantinople; he became a teacher, teaching mathematics to some pupils in the house of an Italian friend of Cuneo's named Semidei. He held this post for about six months. But war had broken out between Uruguay and Argentina, and in January 1842 Garibaldi gave up his teaching job and became an officer in the Uruguayan navy.[28]

Nine months after they arrived in Montevideo, when Menotti was eighteen months old, Garibaldi and Anita were married. The ceremony took place on 26 March 1842 in the church of San Francisco de Asis, a large, sunlit Baroque church just around the corner, not more than a hundred yards from Garibaldi's house. Their marriage certificate recorded that Don Zenón Aspiazu, the curate of the rector of the church, had married 'Don José Garibaldi, native of Italy, legitimate son of Don Domingo Garibaldi and of Doña Rosa Raimunda, with Doña Ana Maria de Jesus, native of Laguna in Brazil, legitimate daughter of Don Benito Riveiro de Silva and of Doña Maria Antonia de Jesus', after they had received a dispensation from the further proclamations of the banns, and not receiving the nuptial benediction because it was Lent. Garibaldi's headmaster at the school where he had taught, Don Pablo Semidei, and a Doña Feliciana García Villagran, were the witnesses.[29] No mention was made of either Duarte or Menotti.

In later years, Guerzoni and Garibaldi's other biographers thought it necessary to explain why Garibaldi, who was known to be a free-thinker and an opponent of Roman Catholicism, had been married in a Roman Catholic church; it was because at that time civil marriage had not been established in Uruguay, and the only place where it was possible to marry was in a Catholic church.[30] In fact, it was not so very surprising that Garibaldi married in a Catholic church. Whatever his opinions on religion may have been, he was nominally a Catholic, having been baptized into the Catholic Church; otherwise he would not have been able to hold the post of Commander of the Naval Forces of the Republic under the constitution of Rio Grande do Sul.

After the publication of Garibaldi's memoirs, with the passage about Garibaldi's guilt with regard to Anita, it was widely believed in Europe that Garibaldi and Anita had never been through a marriage ceremony. Another rumour was that when Garibaldi and Anita went to Nice in 1848, Garibaldi's pious Catholic mother was shocked to find that they were not married, and insisted on them going to church and getting married before she would allow them to live together in her house. There does not appear to be any truth in this story, though it was believed by Mrs Chambers, an Englishwoman who was a close friend of Garibaldi.[31] Garibaldi did nothing to counter these rumours; but two years before his death some of his friends, who were more eager to deny the rumours than Garibaldi was himself, obtained from Montevideo a certified copy of the marriage register, which was sent to Italy and widely publicized. It has been published in several books about Garibaldi, and the original can be seen in the manuscript book of marriages in the church of San Francisco de Asis. The wide publicity given to the certificate distracted attention from the real grounds on which it might be argued that Garibaldi and Anita were never married – because Duarte was still alive, and the marriage was therefore bigamous.

This remains an unsolved mystery, because no one has been able to discover when Duarte died. Duarte completely disappears from view after Garibaldi and Anita left Laguna in November 1839, and nothing more is known about him except contradictory rumours. There is Bittencourt's story – or Varzea's and Pitti's – that he died in the military hospital in 1839. A few people in Laguna believe that he was killed by the Riograndense troops just before they evacuated Laguna, either on the express orders of Garibaldi, or by chance in a military operation or a brawl; but this is not widely accepted. The matter would be settled if Duarte's death certificate could be found. Few documents have been searched for more assiduously; but no trace of it has been found. Hopes of finding it were revived when a new batch of nineteenth-century documents were discovered at Tubarão in 1971; but they had been so badly gnawed by woodworm that they were indecipherable. It is unlikely that Duarte's death certificate will ever be found. In nineteenth-century Brazil there were too many Freemasons who would have been prepared to destroy any document which proved that Duarte had died after 26 March 1842, and too many Catholic priests who would have been equally ready to destroy any which proved that he had died before this date.

No one knows why Garibaldi and Anita, after living together for twenty months in Santa Catarina and Rio Grande do Sul, and for nine months in Montevideo, decided to get married in March 1842. Jessie White Mario's story, that they married at the first opportunity, is absurd. Even if they could not have found a priest to marry them in the chaos of the last days at Laguna and the campaign in Santa Catarina, they could easily have found one after they had arrived in Rio Grande do Sul, during the lull in the war in the winter of 1840, or at San Gabriel next summer; and they had lived in Montevideo since June 1841, within a hundred yards of the church of San Francisco de Asis. Less charitable writers have suggested that when Garibaldi took a position as a schoolmaster, his employer made difficulties about Anita, and that he therefore decided to marry her bigamously. This theory might be plausible if it were true, as Pereda and Garibaldi's biographers believed, that Garibaldi arrived in Montevideo at the beginning of 1842; but in fact he arrived on 17 June 1841, and in January 1842, two months before the marriage, he had ceased to be a teacher and had joined the Uruguayan navy,[32] though there is no reason whatever to assume, as one author has done, that he used his position as a high-ranking naval officer to terrorize the priest into performing a bigamous ceremony.[33]

The most likely reason why Garibaldi and Anita married in March 1842 was because they had just heard news of Duarte's death. This would have been perfectly possible, because ships sailed often between Laguna and Montevideo – they afterwards played an important part during the siege of Montevideo – and sailors could have brought news from Laguna of Duarte's death to his widow in Montevideo.[34] Against this, it is said that in that case Anita would have stated on the marriage certificate that she was a widow, not single; but she might have preferred to say nothing about her first marriage, even though she believed that Duarte was dead.

CHAPTER 9

COSTA BRAVA

THE war in Rio Grande do Sul, though it had aroused strong passions in the province, was a purely Brazilian affair, which was hardly noticed in the outside world. The war in which Garibaldi fought in Uruguay had important international repercussions, and the course of the war was influenced to a considerable extent by the foreign policy of the great powers. Jessie White Mario and Garibaldi's other biographers have given a rather misleading impression about the nature of the war and Garibaldi's attitude to it. They say that there was a struggle for power in Uruguay between Rivera and Oribe, and that Garibaldi took no interest in it until Oribe asked Rosas for help, after which Garibaldi felt bound to fight for the freedom and independence of Uruguay against Rosas and the Argentine invaders. Garibaldi himself suggests in the later editions of his memoirs that this was what happened, but the story is a product of Unitarian propaganda and of Garibaldi's later disillusionment with Rivera. The war in Uruguay was in fact a civil war between Rosas's dictatorship and the forces of Liberalism, which was the reason why Garibaldi took part in it.[1]

The struggle in Uruguay was also to some extent a struggle between France and Argentina, and at one time between France and Great Britain. In 1838 the French government quarrelled with Rosas because Rosas's government had not repaid the loans which it had borrowed from French capitalists, and the French sent their navy to blockade Buenos Aires until the money was repaid. Rosas refused to submit, and the French blockade increased his popularity in Argentina. He held out for two and a half years, during which the blockade continued, before complying with the French demands. France asked Oribe's government in Uruguay to allow their ships to use the Uruguayan ports and other facilities while they were blockading Buenos Aires; but Oribe, who was on very friendly terms with Rosas, refused. The French action against Rosas, and disagreement with Oribe encouraged the Uruguayan Colorados and the Argentine Unitarian refugees who had come to Montevideo; and they deposed Oribe, and installed

Rivera as President in his place. Oribe fled to Argentina. In 1839 Rivera, egged on by the Argentine Unitarian refugees and secretly encouraged by France, declared war on Argentina, and granted France the use of the Uruguayan ports.

The British Foreign Secretary, Lord Palmerston, was concerned at these developments. The French blockade of the River Plate interfered with British trade, and Palmerston was suspicious that the French were seeking to establish a zone of influence in Uruguay.[2] He recognized the blockade, and did not actively interfere in the River Plate; but he gave moral support to Rosas against France and the Unitarians of Uruguay.

In 1840 Rivera sent an army under the Argentine Unitarian General Lavalle to invade Argentina; and soon afterwards General Ferré, the Governor of the Argentine province of Corrientes, joined the Unitarians. Lavalle, who had been particularly hated by the Rosistas ever since he had ordered the Federal leader, Dorrego, to be shot in 1828, was defeated by an army of Rosistas commanded by Oribe and was himself captured and shot; but Ferré held out in Corrientes, and invaded Entre-Rios.

The war was also fought at sea, where the Uruguayan navy was commanded by a former United States citizen, John H. Coe, and the Argentine navy by Admiral Brown. William Brown was born in Foxford in County Mayo in Ireland in 1777, had emigrated with his parents to the United States at the age of nine, had joined the United States merchant navy, and was captured on the high seas by the British and pressed into the British navy during the Napoleonic Wars, where he served with such distinction that he became an officer. He was taken prisoner by the French, escaped twice, and eventually found his way to England by way of St Petersburg. In 1809 he left the British navy and went to Argentina, where he became Commander-in-Chief of the revolutionary fleet during the war against Spain, and won a reputation second only to General San Martín as a hero of national independence. After gaining further glory in several wars in South America, Brown was appointed in 1841, at the age of sixty-four, to command the Argentine fleet against the Uruguayan navy under Coe, who had served under him in earlier campaigns. The two met in a sea-battle off Montevideo in November 1841, when Brown was victorious, and virtually destroyed the whole of Coe's fleet.[3]

Rivera's government and Coe promptly set about building a new navy, and one of the officers whom they chose for it was Garibaldi. As the Uruguayan government was sympathetic to the Republicans of Rio Grande do Sul – Rivera was a personal friend of Bento Gonçalves – Garibaldi's record of service in the Riograndense navy was a good

GIUSEPPE MAZZINI

recommendation for obtaining a commission in the Uruguayan navy, and in January 1842 he was appointed a colonel in the navy. At this period, in both the Uruguayan and Argentine navies, the officers officially held military, not naval, rank; thus Brown, though then and afterwards always referred to as Admiral Brown, was officially Brigadier-General Brown, and Coe was a colonel. The rank of colonel was the third highest in the Uruguayan armed forces, the only higher ranks being the rank of Brigadier-General and that which was officially known as Colonel-Major, and unofficially as General.*

Within a few months Garibaldi had been entrusted with a very important duty. The Uruguayan government wished to send their navy to link up with the Unitarians in Corrientes. The south-eastern point of the province of Corrientes is 450 miles north of Montevideo, where it touches the frontiers of both Uruguay and Rio Grande do Sul on the River Uruguay. The city of Corrientes, the capital of the province, is 200 miles further to the north-west, a few miles from the River Paraná, which is the western boundary of Corrientes. The best method of communication between Montevideo and Corrientes was to sail up the River Uruguay and then cross the province of Corrientes by land, thus avoiding a march of 450 miles across the plains of Uruguay. This river journey involved the risk, in the early stages after leaving Montevideo, of meeting the Argentine fleet in the River Plate, and of passing under the guns of the Argentine island fortress of Martín García near the point where the rivers Uruguay and Paraná run into the River Plate; but in the later stages of the journey the Unitarians could sail through friendly territory, as the left bank of the River Uruguay was held by the Unitarians of Uruguay, and higher up-river by the friendly Republicans of Rio Grande do Sul, and the right bank, north of Concordia, by Ferré's followers in Corrientes.

But the government of Montevideo had thought out a more daring plan. They proposed to send their fleet, not up the River Uruguay, but up the River Paraná to the city of Corrientes. This was a much more dangerous operation, because it involved, after encountering the Argentine fleet in the Plate and the fortress of Martín García,

*The officer ranks in the Uruguayan and Argentine army and navy at this time, with their equivalent in the British army, were as follows:

Brigadier-General (addressed as General) – Lieutenant-General
Coronel-Major (addressed as General) – Major-General
Coronel – Colonel
Teniente-Coronel (addressed as Coronel) – Lieutenant-Colonel
Sergiente-Major (or Comandante) – Major
Capitán – Captain
Teniente – Lieutenant
Sub-Teniente – 2nd Lieutenant

sailing for 600 miles up the Paraná through Argentine territory. For the first 250 miles of this stretch, both banks of the river were held by Rosas's forces; for the last 350 miles, the left bank was occupied by Ferré's Unitarians and the right bank by the Unitarians of Santa Fé. But the Paraná route was not selected merely because it avoided the overland march across the province to the town of Corrientes. Twenty miles north of the town of Corrientes, the River Paraguay flows into the Paraná on the frontier between Argentina and the independent neutral republic of Paraguay. Paraguay's only outlet to the sea is along the rivers Paraguay, Paraná and Plate, and all its international trade went this way. It had always been essential for Argentina to keep open this trade route with Paraguay; but the Uruguayan navy, joined with the smaller Correntino vessels and operating from bases in Corrientes, could do great damage to Argentine shipping in the Paraná, and cripple her trade with Paraguay.

After the Paraná expedition had ended in disaster, Garibaldi wrote about it with great bitterness in his memoirs. 'The real motive for the expedition was not to bring help to the inhabitants of Corrientes and to revictual them,' he wrote in 1850, 'the real motive was to get rid of me.' This is a far-fetched theory. By 1847 there were many politicians in Montevideo who would have been pleased to get rid of Garibaldi, but in 1842 he was not yet sufficiently prominent to have made any powerful enemies. He himself realized this, for he adds in the memoirs: 'How did it happen that, being still so unimportant, I had already made such powerful enemies? This is a mystery that I have never been able to solve.'

Apart from the fact that, as a serving soldier, he bitterly resented the bungling of a campaign by the politicians at home, the Prime Minister and Foreign Minister in Montevideo who planned the Paraná expedition was Vidal, who later became very unpopular with the Radical political group in Montevideo with which Garibaldi was associated. In his memoirs, he calls Vidal 'a man of painful and despicable memory'. The portrait of this handsome gentleman, with his clean-shaven face, his well-cut coat and his elegant cravat, suggests that he would have felt more at home in the company of Wellington and Metternich than with the bearded revolutionaries of Montevideo; and he had the misfortune to be Prime Minister in the opening stages of a war when everything was going wrong, and to be replaced in the darkest hour by the men who eventually led the nation to victory. Garibaldi denounces Vidal for having fled to Europe in the middle of the war with a large part of the Treasury funds, and for riding around the European capitals in an expensive coach; but although this is largely true, it would have been fairer to point out that after Vidal had fallen from power, the new government of Montevideo did everything possible to persuade him to leave the country.[4]

The Paraná expedition might have been a great success had it not been for a lamentable failure of Uruguayan intelligence and a piece of bad luck. The River Paraná, though very wide, is shallow, and in summer it is not navigable higher than the town of Paraná, except for very small craft. In winter, ships can go a little further upstream. If the Uruguayan government could have sent a flotilla of small ships, which had succeeded in evading the Argentine fleet in the River Plate and reaching Corrientes, they would have been safely out of reach of Admiral Brown's larger warships, and could have operated there very successfully for a time. But the government in Montevideo did not know that the water level in the Paraná in the winter of 1842 was lower than it had been in any winter for fifty years. Vidal decided to send Garibaldi to the Paraná with three ships, the largest of which, the *Constitución*, drew 18 feet of water, and in the winter of 1842 could not sail further north than Costa Brava on the boundary of Entre-Rios and Corrientes, more than 300 miles south of their destination, the town of Corrientes. As the larger Argentine vessels could also reach Costa Brava, this meant that when Garibaldi arrived there, he would be unable to do anything except wait, like a rat caught in a trap, till Brown's ships arrived to destroy him.

Though the Uruguayan intelligence was deplorable, their security was good. Garibaldi and the naval authorities knew that many of the inhabitants of Montevideo were secret supporters of Oribe, and were sending information to him and to Rosas; but they were very successful in deceiving the spies. The three warships were not anchored together in the harbour at Montevideo, but were interspersed among the many Uruguayan and foreign merchant ships which were preparing to sail to Europe and elsewhere; and Garibaldi took steps to ensure that even if the spies found out that an expedition was being prepared, they should not know its destination. He engaged pilots who had spent their whole careers in piloting ships on the River Uruguay; and when the Argentine spies at last discovered about the expedition, they believed that it was going to sail up the Uruguay. It was only on 22 June, the day before Garibaldi sailed, that the authorities in Buenos Aires heard anything about the expedition; and they were then informed that the government of Montevideo were preparing to send an expedition of three ships, under the command of Garibaldi, to take supplies to the Unitarians in Corrientes by way of the River Uruguay.[5]

At 3 pm on 23 June 1842 Garibaldi sailed from Montevideo with his flagship, the *Constitución*, carrying eighteen guns, the *Pereyra* with two guns, and the unarmed *Prócida*, which was used as a hospital and transport ship. The *Prócida* had been renamed the *Libertad*, but, as usual when ships were given a new name which the politicians in the government thought more suitable, the sailors who served in her continued to call her by her old name. The three ships carried a total of 510 men.[6] Some of them had fought with Garibaldi in Rio Grande do Sul; others had distinguished themselves in the Uruguayan wars against Spain and Brazil. But the majority of the crew were men of the most disreputable kind, who had been discharged from the army and sent to the navy as a punishment for crimes. Most of them had been convicted of murder.[7] The ships carried supplies and munitions for Corrientes, the most important part of the cargo being a large stock of gunpowder. Only a handful of people in Montevideo knew that they would be sailing up the Paraná, and Garibaldi was the only man on board who knew.

On 23 June the Montevidean politician, Alsina, wrote to Ferré at Corrientes that the expedition had sailed that day. 'Garibaldi has been in the squadron since January,' he wrote, 'he is an Italian, a former chief of the forces of the Farrapos; it is said that he is a swashbuckler with the nerve of a Fourier' – a reference to Charles Fourier, the revolutionary from San Domingo, who had been one of the wildest of the extremists during the French Revolution of 1792. 'Some think that he is going to the Uruguay, but who knows why; others think that he is planning a surprise, or a sudden blow, but who knows where.'[8]

It was only after Garibaldi had sailed that Ferré was officially informed by Vidal of the instructions which had been given to Garibaldi. He was to sail up the River Paraná to the town of Paraná, capturing as many Argentine merchant ships as possible; and if he had succeeded in evading Rosas's warships, he was to proceed upriver to the ports of Corrientes, and hand over his prizes to the Correntino authorities. He was to give all possible assistance to any land forces from Rivera's army that he might encounter, and to the Unitarians of Corrientes and Santa Fé. On reaching Corrientes, he was to place himself under Ferré's orders for future operations. He was also to carry supplies and munitions to the Unitarians in Corrientes.[9]

Admiral Brown had been patrolling the River Plate since 24 April; but owing to the delay in receiving the reports from the spies in Montevideo, he had no idea that an enemy expedition was being planned, and had returned to port in Buenos Aires. As soon as he heard the news on 22 June, he prepared to sail with a fleet of seven ships in order to stop the Uruguayan squadron from sailing up the Uruguay. He had at first assumed that Coe would be in command, and was looking forward to another round against his old enemy; and he had been disappointed when he was informed that his opponent was Garibaldi, a subordinate commander of whom he had never heard.[10]

The Montevidean squadron, after anchoring off Colonia on 23 June, reached Martín García at 10.15 am on the 26th. At this point, where the water of the River Plate, on most days of the year, is dark red in colour from the red sandstone soil of South America, navigation is difficult because of sandbanks and shoals. Garibaldi sailed through the channel to the north of Martín García between the island and the Uruguayan coast, within range of the Argentine artillery on the rock. According to a story which was published in the Montevidean newspaper, *El Nacional*, he had disguised his ships so as to make them look like the ships of the Argentine navy; but though this story has been accepted by some eminent historians, it seems quite clear that it is not true.[11] He sent his two smaller ships through the channel at full sail as near as possible to the Uruguayan shore, while he covered them in the *Constitución*, which engaged in an exchange of gunfire with the fortress which lasted for two hours. Garibaldi's losses were light, but one of them was a heavy blow, both militarily and personally, for his friend Pocaroba, an Italian officer on the *Constitución*, was killed, his head being blown off by a cannon ball.

Soon after he had passed Martín García, the *Constitución* ran on to a sandbank. Garibaldi and his men made repeated efforts to get the ship afloat, but she was stuck in three feet of sand, and the tide was going out, and after twenty-four hours they had still not succeeded in freeing her. Garibaldi then decided to lighten the ship by transferring the eighteen guns in the *Constitución* to the *Prócida*. This was a very hazardous step to take with an enemy fleet in the vicinity, because it meant that the guns of the *Constitución* were out of action for a time during which only the two guns of the *Pereyra* were operational. But Garibaldi felt that he had to take the risk. He was only five miles from Martín García, but out of range of the guns of the fortress, which like all naval guns of the period could not hit objects at more than about 600 yards; and he could only hope that Brown's fleet would not appear until the *Constitución* had been refloated and her guns were back in position.

But the guns were still in the *Prócida*, and the *Constitutión* was still aground, when Brown's seven ships with their 73 guns appeared on the horizon. They had sailed from Buenos Aires on 26 June, a few hours after Garibaldi had passed Martín García. They were greeted with loud cheers from the garrison of Martín García; but before they were within shooting range, Brown's flagship, the *General Belgrano*, ran on to a sandbank. This temporarily disorganized the Argentine fleet, and while the *Belgrano* was being freed from the sandbank, Garibaldi's men succeeded in refloating the *Constitución* and getting her guns back in place; and they sailed up the River Plate with Brown's ships in pursuit. Suddenly a thick fog came down, and Brown lost sight of the Uruguayan squadron. Garibaldi commented, in his memoirs, that on this, as on other occasions in his life, he was lucky. Part of his luck, though he never knew this, was that the enemy did not appreciate the difficulty which he was in; because on 27 June Captain Crespo, the commandant of Martín García, wrote to Brown describing the gun-battle which had taken place on the previous day, and adding that the three ships of the 'savage Unitarian traitors' had passed through the channel and were out of Brown's reach.[12]

Under cover of the fog, Garibaldi's ships sailed up the Paraná on 29 June. Brown was sure that they had gone up the Uruguay. He is supposed to have said, afterwards, that only a Garibaldi would have dared to sail up the Paraná; but apart from the fact that his spies had told him that Garibaldi was bound for the Uruguay, he could not have expected that a ship the size of the *Constitución* would try to sail up the Paraná to Ferré's territory that winter. Brown therefore sailed up the Uruguay in pursuit of Garibaldi while Garibaldi sailed up the Paraná. Garibaldi's first need was to find a pilot who knew the Paraná. Having deliberately taken on pilots who knew the Uruguay in order to deceive Rosas's spies in Montevideo, he was relying on picking up a local pilot on his journey up the Paraná; but he found that the local men, whether from Argentine patriotism, Rosista zeal, or fear of the consequences, refused to serve as his pilots. He therefore used more forceful arguments to persuade them to serve, and wrote in his memoirs: 'My sabre soon removed all obstacles, and we had a pilot.'

From time to time on his journey along the Paraná, Garibaldi landed and seized cattle, or entered a village and demanded food and information. 'We were compelled to bully them,' he wrote, 'our difficult position left us no choice.' At San Nicolás, the first Argentine village which they reached on the right bank of the Paraná, they seized a number of local residents as prisoners, in order to compel them to act as pilots and give them information about enemy dispositions. One of the least obstinate of the pilots was an Austrian, who was prepared to be quite co-operative. When the inhabitants of the villages refused to give them supplies and information, Garibaldi threatened to sack the village; and as his threats were unavailing, he frequently carried them out. When he reached the important trading town of Rosario, he found that the business men and citizens were more concerned about the risk of damage to property, or perhaps more sympathetic to the Unitarian cause, than the tougher gauchos and Rosistas of the villages. In Rosario, alone of all the places at which he called, he found that the population was prepared to collaborate, and he left them un-harmed.[13]

On 19 July Garibaldi reached the town of Paraná, where he had spent two months in prison four years before. Here he found his route barred by a small Argentine squadron under Major Seguí, who nine years later, as Urquiza's secretary, played a leading part in the military revolt which led to the overthrow of Rosas. Garibaldi was expecting to meet this opposition, because as early as 2 July he had elicited the information from his reluctant prisoners that Seguí's flotilla at Paraná was the only Argentine naval force in the river.[14] Seguí was supported by a few land batteries at Paraná, but though he had more ships than Garibaldi, they were inferior in man-power and fire-power. His six ships – the *Vigilante*, the *Argentina*, the *Libertad*, the *Federal*, the *Santa-fecino* and the *Camila* – had a total strength of 275 men against the 500 on Garibaldi's ships; and although he had 22 guns against Garibaldi's 20, they were of smaller calibre.

For two hours, from 10.30 am to 12.30 pm, Garibaldi exchanged fire with Seguí, and got much the best of the encounter. Seguí, either through a genuine mistake or from a desire to excuse his defeat, wrote to Oribe that Garibaldi had 20 guns in the *Constitución*, 10 in the *Pereyra*, and 5 in the *Prócida*, and claimed that, although much inferior to the enemy in power and weapons, 'the great people of the Paraná hurled themselves in contempt and revenge against the miserable slaves of the usurper of the Oriental State, the mulatto Rivera'. The local Rosista newspaper, the *Federal Entreriano*, referred to the 'natural cowardice' of Garibaldi's men, and claimed that the action had shown the difference between 'Argentine soldiers and the mercenary adventurers suborned by the gold of the filthy savage mulatto Rivera'.[15]

At 6 am on 27 July Garibaldi arrived at El Cerrito, an islet on the left bank of the Paraná some twenty miles north of the town of Paraná. After avoiding the fire of a shore battery by passing so close to it that they were out of range and the battery fired over their heads, the Montevidean ships seized a number of small merchant craft at Cerrito and took a few prisoners. According to the Rosistas, Garibaldi's men seized and spoiled a neutral Paraguayan ship at Cerrito; and they also seized the *Joven Esteban* (Young Stephen), a private yacht belonging to Esteban Rams, a merchant of the town of Paraná, who at the time was sailing in the yacht with his family. The Buenos Aires newspaper, the *Gaceta Mercantil*, accused Garibaldi of an act of inhumanity in turning Rams adrift in a boat with several women and children, including one very old woman, without any food or other necessaries. But although Garibaldi's Paraná campaign, and his campaign on the River Uruguay three years later, aroused a hatred in Argentina which to some extent still exists today, no one ever accused him of killing civilians or prisoners, though the Rosistas themselves often killed prisoners. Garibaldi's rough crew – the criminals who had been sent to the fleet as punishment for murder and other crimes – robbed and looted; but though Garibaldi allowed them to sack in enemy territory, he managed to stop them from killing the inhabitants, and even from raping the women. The bitterly hostile Rosista newspapers never accused them of this.

Garibaldi sailed on to La Paz – then called Caballú Cuatiá – and a few miles further north, on 6 August, he met four Correntino ships – three armed launches and a transport ship. They were commanded by Ferré's secretary, Lieutenant Alberto Villegas, and Ferré had sent them to meet the Montevidean squadron. The link-up was hailed by the Unitarians as a great success, but almost immediately afterwards Garibaldi discovered the fact that was to foil the whole expedition. On the Costa Brava, thirty miles to the north of La Paz, he found the water was too shallow for the *Constitución*. The river was only 21 feet deep, which was not enough for the *Constitución*, which drew 18 feet of water. She could not go on. Garibaldi had guessed that by now Brown would be coming up the Paraná after him, and that he could not escape him. He therefore decided to wait for Brown at Costa Brava and fight him when he arrived. He was still more than 250 miles from the town of Corrientes – it had taken Villegas seventeen days to come from there to Costa Brava – but he sent on as many as possible of the supplies which he had brought for the Correntinos in the smaller craft which he had captured on his journey and in the Correntino transport ship which Villegas had brought from Corrientes.[16]

He then carefully selected the best position for the battle with Brown. He found it at the point where the little river San Juan flows into the Paraná, three miles north of Costa Brava, on the exact spot where the boundary lies between the provinces of Entre-Rios and Corrientes. He assembled his ships together on the left bank of the Paraná, up against the eastern shore, so that he could not be surrounded by Brown's superior number of ships. In front, facing the enemy, was the *Constitución*, with her 18 guns. He placed next to her, at right angles and facing the left bank of the river, the *Pereyra* with her 2 guns and the captured yacht, the *Joven Esteban*, which he had turned into a fighting ship by transferring to her some of the small calibre guns from the ships of the Correntino squadron. Behind, he placed his hospital ship, the *Prócida*, which had sailed with him from Montevideo, the three Correntino ships under Villegas, and two of the prizes which he had not yet sent on to Corrientes. The Correntino guns were of too short range to be of any use in the first stages of the battle, but he hoped to use them, and their crews of brave and keen young sailors, if it came to fighting at close quarters and boarding the enemy ships.[17]

Brown was only eight days behind Garibaldi. He had sailed up the Uruguay as far as Gualeguaychú and a little further north before coming to the conclusion that as no one had seen any sign of the Montevidean squadron they could not have come this way, and must have gone up the Paraná. But Brown knew the Paraná better than Garibaldi, and would not sail up the Paraná in the *Belgrano*, though she drew only 14 to 16 feet of water against the 18 feet of Garibaldi's *Constitución*. He sent the *Belgrano* back to Buenos Aires, and sailed up the Paraná with five ships – the *Echague*, the *Americano*, the *Republicano*, the *Chacabuco* and the *9 de Julio*, which he chose as his flagship, though she was the smallest of the five ships.[18]

As soon as Brown entered the Paraná, he found plenty of traces of Garibaldi, for all along the river, at Baradero, San Nicolás, San Lorenzo, El Chapetón, Hernandarias, and even at Rosario, he heard bitter complaints about the havoc which the 'pirates' had caused. He and his men were therefore in fighting mood as they sailed up river, knowing that eventually they were certain to catch up with Garibaldi. At the town of Paraná he met Seguí with his battered flotilla, and two of Seguí's ships which had fought Garibaldi a week before – the *Argentina* and the *Libertad* – joined Brown's expedition. He was also joined by three smaller ships of the auxiliary naval division of Paraná, and sailed up to Costa Brava with ten ships carrying a total of 693 men and 57 guns. His two largest ships, the *Echague* and the *Americano*, both of which carried 14 guns, were smaller vessels than Garibaldi's *Constitución;* but his total fire-power was nearly three times Garibaldi's, and he had a small superiority in numbers of fighting men. He had also another and more decisive advantage which Garibaldi had not yet appreciated; the guns of his five leading ships had a longer range than any of Garibaldi's.[19]

On 14 August Brown arrived at Costa Brava. In his report to Rosas, Brown gave the date of the battle, which was fought on the two days following his arrival, as 15 and 16 August. Garibaldi, in his despatch to Ferré, stated that the fight was on the 16th and 17th. For many years it was a point of honour for Argentine historians to accept Brown's dates, and for the Uruguayans to accept Garibaldi's, and the dispute was carried on with surprising vehemence, though nothing whatever depends on it. Brown's dates are almost certainly correct.*[20]

*Brown's dates are more likely to be correct because he wrote his report to Rosas on the day after the battle ended, whereas Garibaldi wrote three (or four) days later, from Esquina on 20 August. Garibaldi's dates of 16th and 17th are given by Ferré

When Brown arrived at Costa Brava, the wind was against him, so he decided to make no attempt to attack that day, but waited out of range of Garibaldi's guns. Garibaldi did not wish to leave his good defensive position in order to sail after him; but he sent a landing party under Major Pedro Rodriguez to march down the left bank of the Paraná and attack Brown's ships as they lay at anchor near the shore. Brown had realized that Garibaldi might do this, and had posted Major Montana with a hundred men – not 500, as Garibaldi thought – to guard his ships against any attack from the land. After a sharp exchange of musket fire with Montana's men, Rodriguez was obliged to retire. There was no more action that day, and the night was quiet, except for an occasional musket shot fired by one side or the other.

Next day, 15 August, the wind having changed, Brown sailed upstream at noon, and attacked. As he approached, he observed Garibaldi's guns through his telescope, and realized that their range was shorter than his own. He therefore withdrew a little way until he had reached a position where he was out of range of Garibaldi's guns, but Garibaldi was within range of his. The Montevidean press afterwards condemned him for this, and commented that the cowardly Rosista cut-throats had not dared to fight Garibaldi on equal terms; but Garibaldi himself could appreciate and praise these sound tactics of his enemy.

> The old English admiral was well aware of the range of our artillery, and its marked inferiority compared with his own; and therefore, sacrificing the brilliant spectacle of a storm of grapeshot and a hand-to-hand encounter, he consulted the safety of his men by taking advantage of the longer range of his guns, and remained at a distance, which did not suit us at all.[21]

Garibaldi, like many of his biographers, did not realize that Brown was an Irishman, not an Englishman.

in his letter to the Military Commandant of Goya on 3 September 1842 (Pereda, II.76), and by Rivera and Bustamante in their letter to Ferré, 3 September 1842 (Ferré, p. 933), in reply to Ferré's letter giving them news of the battle; but they, like Ferré, were obviously relying on the date given to Ferré by Garibaldi. The strongest confirmation of Brown's dates of 15th and 16th is Ferré's letter to the Military Commandant of Esquina of 22 August (in Pereda, II.70), which states that the Commandant wrote to Ferré on 18 August, telling him that Garibaldi had arrived in Esquina. As Garibaldi says that it took him three days to march from Costa Brava to Esquina after the battle, he could not have arrived in Esquina by the 18th if the battle had only ended on the afternoon of the 17th, but might have done so if in fact it ended twenty-four hours earlier, and Garibaldi counted the 16th (the day on which he began his march) as the first of the three days.

Naval historians have criticized Garibaldi for allowing Brown to carry out this manoeuvre, and for adopting too defensive a tactic, which is an unusual criticism to be levelled at Garibaldi. They say that he should have sailed into the attack on 14 August with the wind behind him, and grappled with the enemy at close quarters. Brown himself would not have agreed, because in his letters he attributed most of his difficulties to the strong defensive position which Garibaldi had chosen.

The battle continued all the afternoon and evening of 15 August. By the evening the *Constitución* had been badly battered, and Garibaldi had suffered considerable losses, including his Italian friend, Lieutenant Borzone, who had been killed. His other two ships of the line, the *Pereyra* and the *Joven Esteban*, had escaped almost undamaged. He transferred his wounded to the hospital ship, the *Prócida*, and placed some of them in one of the captured prizes, and sent them up river to Corrientes. His stocks of ammunition were beginning to get low. It occurred to him that he could still go on firing, after his ammunition had run out, by using pieces of chain, and all other kinds of metal that he could find, as ammunition, and he ordered his men to cut up the chains so that they could be used for this purpose.

In the evening Lieutenant Villegas came on board the *Constitución* to see Garibaldi. Garibaldi invited Villegas into his cabin and poured out two glasses of wine; he still occasionally drank wine, though he usually drank water. While they were talking, a shell hit the *Constitución*, splintering the flag-mast, bringing down the flag and upsetting the two glasses of wine in Garibaldi's cabin. Garibaldi went out to inspect the damage, and then returned, as cool as ever, and refilled the wine-glasses. Villegas had come to suggest to Garibaldi that they should abandon the *Constitución* and retreat upstream with their remaining ships under cover of night. Garibaldi refused. Villegas then asked permission to move his ships of the Correntino squadron to a slightly different position; but this was a trick, because after Villegas got back to his ship, he sailed away with the three Correntino ships, and returned to Corrientes.

Garibaldi was indignant. He pursued Villegas for a little way in one of the small prize ships which he had in the rear, but was unable to catch him; and in his memoirs he vigorously denounced Villegas as a deserter, and commented: 'Desertion in the hour of danger is the most heinous of all crimes.' A Correntino historian has stoutly defended Villegas, arguing that if Garibaldi had been under the orders of a wise general like Canabarro, as he had been at the Battle of Laguna, he would have burned the *Constitución* and retreated on the night of 15 August, after the first day's fighting, and thus saved the other ships;

and he claims that Villegas saved the Correntino ships from the total destruction which Garibaldi's folly brought on the Montevidean squadron. As against this argument, Garibaldi's action in fighting to a finish at Costa Brava had a great moral effect, both in Montevideo and among the enemy. Garibaldi felt that he had no choice in the matter. 'Even with the certainty of defeat,' he wrote in his memoirs, 'we had to fight, at least for the honour of our arms. And fight we did.'[22]

The night of 15 August was not as quiet as the night before, for Brown's bombardment was kept up intermittently throughout the night. At 2 am Garibaldi sent Captain Arana Urioste, the Spanish commander of the *Pereyra*, with fifty men to attack Brown's ships from the land and try to set them on fire. Arana's party was observed as they approached the enemy, and was met with heavy musket fire. Arana was hit in the head and killed, and his men retreated. Garibaldi then sent Manuel Rodriguez, who had served with him in Rio Grande do Sul and was one of the survivors of the shipwreck of July 1839, with a small body of men, to set fire to Brown's ships by towing some of their prizes, loaded with combustible material, alongside the enemy squadron and setting fire to them there. The first part of the operation was successfully carried out, and the prizes burned well; but Brown's men succeeded in keeping the fire under control, and it did not do much damage to their ships.

At 4 am Garibaldi made a third attempt to destroy Brown's ships. He could not try to set them on fire again, because he had no more inflammable material; but he put some of the stock of gunpowder, which he was taking to Corrientes, into one of the prizes, and sent some of his men to take it alongside the *9 de Julio* and blow her up. Brown saw what they were doing, and realized the necessity of extinguishing the fuse before it reached the gunpowder. He himself climbed into the boat which contained the gunpowder and the burning fuse, accompanied by three of his men, one of whom was a boy named Bartolomé Cordero, who was still one week short of his twelfth birthday. He had been in the navy since the age of ten, and had already fought in two major battles before Costa Brava. He now succeeded, under Brown's directions, in putting out the fuse before it reached the gunpowder. Brown is supposed to have said, as he watched Bartolomé at work, that the boy would one day become a famous admiral; but, like other historical prophecies, this one was not remembered until after it had been fulfilled.

As dawn approached, Garibaldi realized that the situation was very serious. The *Constitución* was shot full of holes, which his men had only managed to caulk with great difficulty. Many of his crew had been killed, and many more wounded; and as his hospital ship, the *Prócida*, was full to capacity with the wounded, others had to lie around in the *Constitución*, where their cries of pain were continuously heard. Several of his men had deserted to the enemy during the night, and gave them useful and encouraging information about the state of the Montevidean ships and crews. At daybreak Garibaldi sounded the reveille and, assembling his men on deck, climbed on a pump and spoke to them what he calls 'a few words of comfort and encouragement'. The men responded splendidly, and ran to their posts with a new determination. This encouraged Garibaldi in his resolve to fight on.

The battle continued with greater intensity after daybreak on 16 August. Brown sent a force to attack the *Constitución* from the land. He gave the command of this force to Lieutenant Mariano Cordero, a young officer aged twenty-three, who was the elder brother of Bartolomé Cordero, and who also, in due course, became an admiral. Mariano Cordero's attack was repulsed by musket fire from the *Constitución*. Cordero attacked again, and though he was again driven back, he renewed the attack several times. He eventually abandoned it, and withdrew, after he had lost a third of his men.

Garibaldi's ammunition had now run out, but he loaded his guns with the pieces of chain which his men had prepared the night before, and he went on firing the chain, and any scrap metal which he could find, at the enemy. At last, in the afternoon of 16 August, after fighting for more than forty-eight hours, he decided to blow up his own ships, and retreat overland. He had lost more than 300 men killed and seriously wounded, two-thirds of his total force. The *Constitución* had taken very heavy punishment, and the *Pereyra*, which was almost undamaged after the first day's fighting, had been badly battered on the second day. The pleasure yacht which he had commandeered from the family of Paraná, the *Joven Esteban*, was still virtually unharmed; but she was now to go with the others. He distributed all his stocks of gunpowder in the three ships and in the remaining prizes, and transferred his wounded men to the shore. Then he blew up the ships, and marched away overland on the left bank of the Paraná.

The *Constitución* went up with a tremendous explosion which staggered the enemy. Garibaldi, who watched it from the land, wrote afterwards that it was a most extraordinary sight; there was hardly a ripple on the surface of the waters of the Paraná, but the débris was thrown far and wide on to both the banks of the river, even on to the right bank, on the Santa Fé side, a mile away. The *Joven Esteban* merely caught fire. Brown thought that she might be saved, and sent parties of his men to try to put out the flames. He told Bartolomé Cordero that as he had put out the burning fuse in the boat the night before, he could now try again in the *Joven Esteben*. When his elder brother Mariano saw that Bartolomé was going to the burning ship, he asked Brown's permission to go too. There had always been a friendly rivalry between the brothers, both at home and in the navy, and Mariano set out to catch up with Bartolomé; but Bartolomé's boat was lighter and faster, and he reached the *Joven Esteban* first. Mariano beat his younger brother in the final competition of their lives, becoming a Vice-Admiral, whereas Bartolomé only reached the rank of Rear-Admiral. But neither of them managed to put out the fire in the *Joven Esteban*, which burned as effectively as Garibaldi wished.[23]

The Argentine sailors found traces of human corpses in the *Constitución* and the *Pereyra*, and deduced that Garibaldi had blown up his ship with his wounded men still on board. The *Gaceta Mercantil* of Buenos Aires reported on 20 September that the cruel pirate had set fire to his ships and burned his own wounded men alive; and some of the later Argentine historians have repeated this story, expressing a mixture of horror at Garibaldi's cruelty and of reluctant admiration for his ruthless devotion to duty. Garibaldi himself, in his memoirs, admits that some of his men were in the ships when he blew them up. He says that some of the more disreputable members of his crew, when ordered to pour alcohol on inflammable material in the ships in order to make them burn better, drank the alcohol instead, and became so drunk that they collapsed in a stupor, and, unknown to Garibaldi and their comrades, were lying in the holds of the ships when they were blown up.[24]

Garibaldi transferred all his wounded from the three fighting ships before they were blown up. Those who were well enough to be moved were taken to the left bank, so that their comrades could carry them on their overland march; the more seriously wounded were taken to the *Prócida*, which was not blown up. If Villegas had not deserted, Garibaldi would have used his ships to transport the wounded to Corrientes; as it was, he was forced to leave them to fall alive into the enemy's hands. They were fortunate that their captors were commanded by Brown and not by Rosas's other generals. Brown treated them with every consideration, and sent his personal physician, his fellow-Irishman Dr Hugh Thomas Sheridan, to care for them.[25]

The Rosista newspaper, the *Federal Entreriano*, went one better than the *Gaceta Mercantil*, though the *Gaceta* hastened to follow suit by reprinting the article from the *Federal Entreriano* on 3 October under the heading 'Characteristic act of barbarous inhumanity'. They accused Garibaldi of burning, not only his own wounded, but also the prisoners whom he had captured at San Nicolás and El Cerrito and at other places along the Paraná.

The pirate Garibaldi [they wrote] having been sent to the waters of the Paraná by the savage mulatto Rivera, held as prisoners on board the corvette *Constitución* ten men who would have dearly loved to escape from the power of that wicked man. These unhappy creatures and the wounded men in the brig *Pereyra* were left on board when the two ships were set on fire by our enemies. Their shrieks of despair could be clearly heard at that moment, and these unfortunate wounded men were seen trying to crawl to the ship's side. But their martyrdom did not last long; the atrocity of the pirate was accomplished . . . the ships blew up, and the Paraná became a horrible spectacle.[26]

These allegations have been repeated in more recent times, not only by pro-Rosas writers in Argentina, but also by the Correntino historian Roibón in his attempt to justify Villegas and the desertion of the Correntino squadron. Ignoring the fact that the wounded might have been carried safely to Corrientes if Villegas's ships had remained at Costa Brava, he accused Garibaldi of blowing up both his own wounded and the prisoners, and lists this as one of the horrors which would have been avoided if Garibaldi had followed Villegas's advice and retreated on the night of 15 August.[27] Garibaldi makes no mention, in his memoirs, about what happened to the pilots whom he pressed into his service, or to the other prisoners; but he probably sent them to Corrientes before the battle began, or placed them with the seriously wounded men on the *Prócida*. Everything that we know about Garibaldi's conduct on other occasions suggests that, if he could not send them to Corrientes, it is much more likely that he would have set them free at the last moment and allowed them to make their way, if they could, to Brown's squadron, rather than that he would have blown them up or burned them.

The Argentines made no serious attempt to pursue Garibaldi. Garibaldi writes in his memoirs that Brown put 500 men ashore, which would have been the greater part of his total force, with orders to hunt down Garibaldi and his men, but that they were so shaken by the explosion when the *Constitución* blew up that they abandoned the pursuit. According to a well-established tradition in Argentina, Rosas had given Brown orders to capture Garibaldi alive and to bring him and his other prisoners to Buenos Aires where they were to be publicly hanged; but when, after the battle, one of Brown's officers urged the admiral to allow him to pursue Garibaldi overland, Brown replied: 'No, let them go; Garibaldi is a brave fellow' ('*Garibaldi es un valiente*'). Some historians have pointed out that this is an unlikely story. Brown certainly conceived a great admiration for Garibaldi's valour as a result of Costa Brava, and in later years he visited his old adversary in Montevideo and shook hands in a most friendly fashion;

but this does not mean that he would have disobeyed orders from Rosas – if indeed he received them – to capture Garibaldi, and would deliberately have allowed him to escape. Brown was an honourable warrior, and was not guilty of the cruelty which was shown by most of Rosas's commanders; but he disappointed his admirers in Montevideo, who respected him for his part in the fight for South American independence from Spain, by remaining loyal to Rosas, and refusing to become 'the General Monck, or Bernadotte', of Argentina. Next year, at Montevideo, Brown obeyed Rosas's orders, though most reluctantly, and handed over some of his prisoners of war to Rosas for execution.[28]

Nor did Brown feel any sympathy for Garibaldi in August 1842. He had been primed with stories, on his journey up the Paraná, of the looting and destruction in which Garibaldi's men had indulged. On the day after the battle, he wrote in his report to Rosas: 'The behaviour of these men, Most Excellent Señor, has been very like pirates, because they sacked and destroyed every house and creature that fell into their power, without reckoning on the fact that there is a Supreme Power who rewards and punishes our actions.' Two days later, on 19 August, he wrote to Oribe: 'The behaviour of the enemy has been more disgraceful than could be imagined, all the laws of humanity and of peoples have been violated by these men; but already they have been punished, the waters have submerged them for their misconduct, like scoundrels and men from whom our Heavenly Father has withdrawn his protection.' Brown wrote much the same in a private letter to his wife.

> They fought like tigers, being confident of success because of their strong position; but they had to finish the farce with a pair of fuses and gunpowder. . . . The behaviour of these men has been much more like pirates than like fighting men belonging to a civilized people; they sacked and destroyed every little creature or valuable thing which had the misfortune to fall into their power; it is difficult to imagine how much damage they have done. After what they have done, it is not surprising that they were defeated, because there is a Supreme Power which always, sooner or later, rewards or punishes our actions.[29]

If Brown had sent a party of men to pursue Garibaldi in his retreat from Costa Brava, he would probably have either killed or captured him; but Brown's attitude, throughout the whole of the Rosas wars, was that of the professional naval officer. He did not deliberately allow Garibaldi to escape, but he did not, like so many of the Rosistas, feel a strong desire for revenge on the savage Unitarians; and so, having destroyed the enemy fleet twice in nine months, he did not wish to go to any great trouble to capture a small body of scattered fugitives.

The news of the victory reached Buenos Aires on 27 August. The artillery of the city fired a twenty-one-gun salute, and next day the streets were decorated, and guns fired salutes repeatedly throughout the day. Costa Brava had been a great triumph for the Rosista cause, and according to Brown's report to Rosas he had suffered very few casualties. Rosas's English-language newspaper, the *British Packet,* gave Brown's losses as 8 killed and 12 wounded; but this was obviously inaccurate, because Mariano Cordero's private diary states that he lost one-third of the force with which he attacked Garibaldi from the land, so the Argentines must have lost a total of at least 50 killed, or 7 per cent of their total man-power.[30]

On 3 September the *British Packet,* which was always a little more restrained in its propaganda than the vernacular Rosista press, reported the victory, and paid tribute to the bravery of Garibaldi's men, though it condemned them for their piratical behaviour. When Garibaldi had sailed to Gualeguay in the *Luisa* five years before, the Buenos Aires press had never discovered his name, and had referred to him as 'the Riograndense privateer'; but during the Paraná campaign they discovered that he was named 'Garribaldi', and that he was an Italian by birth, though the *British Packet* must have thought that he was much older than thirty-five, because they stated that they understood that he had commanded a corvette in Murat's navy when Murat was King of Naples during the Napoleonic Wars. The *British Packet* added that 'his late expedition to the Paraná shows that he is intrepid'.[31]

In Montevideo, where the press had been reporting Garibaldi's victorious advance up the Paraná, the news of Costa Brava was first published in the English-language paper, *The Britannia,* on 3 September. They reported that Garibaldi had fought with his two warships against eight of Brown's, and that, after sinking two of Brown's ships, he had burned his own ships and marched away overland. Two days later, *El Nacional* in Montevideo stated that Garibaldi had fought with 300 men against Brown's 1,600, this figure of 1,600 being in fact the total personnel of the Argentine navy. 'Our Garibaldi succumbed, but with glory,' they wrote on 9 September. They forecast that 'Garibaldi seems to be destined to accomplish great things'.[32]

On 9 September, a glorious spring day, Brown arrived in Buenos Aires in the *9 de Julio* to a tumultuous welcome. He landed near the place in the Plaza Colon where his statue now stands, and was greeted by cheering crowds and the music of the military band of the Victoria Theatre. Manuelita de Rosas had come to meet him, and he drove in an open carriage with Manuelita and his wife through the streets decorated with flags, with the guns firing continuously in salute, to Rosas's palace at Palermo, where he was received by Rosas. In the evening the city was illuminated, and the people roasted beef on open fires in the streets. On the Alameda, which today is the Avenida del Libertador, they burned two effigies, which were presumably those of Rivera and Garibaldi, though very few people in Buenos Aires can have had any idea of what Garibaldi looked like. There is a well-known story, which seems improbable, that Brown was shocked that an effigy of Garibaldi was burned, and commented: 'What an outrage! to burn a brave fellow!'

While the people were eating the *asado* and burning the effigies in the streets, Buenos Aires society was attending a great ball in Rosas's palace at Palermo. One of those present was the future Admiral Farragut, who commanded the naval forces of the North during the American Civil War. In 1842 he was a Commander and in charge of a United States warship which was visiting Buenos Aires. He was not impressed with the beauty of Manuelita as she opened the ball; and he was taken aback at the decorations in the ballroom, which was covered, not only with the slogan 'Death to the savage Unitarians!' but also with realistic pictures of patriotic Rosistas kneeling on their Unitarian prisoners and cutting their throats.[33]

Meanwhile Garibaldi, having landed on the left bank of the Paraná at Costa Brava, set out to march towards the north into the province of Corrientes. Of the 510 men who had sailed with him from Montevideo, only 160 remained, and these included the wounded. They were 250 miles south of the town of Corrientes, and 600 miles north-west of Montevideo. They had not one horse between them; they had to carry their wounded; and they had so little food that Garibaldi had to ration them to one biscuit a day. Their immediate destination was Esquina, the first village in the province of Corrientes; but their march was impeded by a large number of streams and small rivers which they had to cross, and as they marched across the pampas, with its coarse grass and occasional small copses, they could barely manage, in a day's march, to reach the horizon which they had seen in the morning. It took them more than two days to cover the thirty miles to Esquina, which they reached on the evening of 18 August. They found the people of Esquina very friendly.

From Esquina, Garibaldi wrote his report on the Battle of Costa Brava to Ferré. He ended his letter with a terse comment on the action of Villegas: 'With the greatest disgust, the undersigned announces that Commandant Villegas deserted us with the force under his command on the first night of the combat.'[34]

After spending about a week at Esquina, Garibaldi and his men marched on to the little town of Goya, about a hundred miles to the north. This time they travelled in greater comfort, because Ferré had sent a ship to carry the wounded to Corrientes, and they had obtained a supply of food and a few horses before setting out. Garibaldi wrote to Ferré, asking for instructions, and told him that he would wait in the neighbourhood of Goya until he heard from him.[35]

Soon afterwards, Garibaldi moved to the little town of Santa Lucía de los Antos, five miles from Goya, and he stayed there for about two months. According to local tradition, he had a love affair in Santa Lucía with a girl named Lucía Esteche, the daughter of a local land-owner. He is said to have met her when he first arrived at Santa Lucía and called at her father's *estancia* to ask for a drink of water for himself and his men, and fell in love at first sight. While he was in Santa Lucía, he carved his name on the church door. After he had left the district, Lucía Esteche gave birth to his daughter, who in later years was proud to call herself Margarita Garibaldi. Garibaldi never returned to Santa Lucía; he never saw Lucía Esteche again, and never met his daughter. But he corresponded with both Lucía and Margarita, and a few years before his death, when he was living in retirement on the island of Caprera off the coast of Sardinia, he wrote to Margarita in Santa Lucía and invited her to visit him. Margarita, who was now a married woman, felt unable to accept, as she could not leave her husband and children.[36]

Ferré told Garibaldi to build up a new flotilla of small Correntino craft on the River Paraná at Goya; but though Garibaldi waited for two months at Goya and Santa Lucía, the boats from which he was to create the flotilla did not arrive, and he wrote in his memoirs that he did nothing during this period except waste a great deal of time. He pressed Ferré for action, but he heard nothing more till he received new instructions at the end of October. He was to march across the province of Corrientes to the River Uruguay, and join Rivera's army at San Francisco near Paysandú in Uruguay, where he was to take charge of the Unitarian flotilla on the River Uruguay. He marched 200 miles to the River Uruguay at Higo, and sailed down-river to San Francisco.[37] He arrived just too late to take part in one of the decisive battles of the war.

CHAPTER 10

THE SIEGE OF MONTEVIDEO:
THE REGIS INCIDENT

O N 6 December 1842 the Unitarian army under Rivera met a
Federalist army under Oribe, composed partly of his Uruguayan
supporters, but largely of Argentine soldiers whom Rosas had sent
to his aid. Rivera's army was decisively defeated at Arroyo Grande,
losing 1,500 men killed and 1,000 taken prisoner,[1] and the rest of his
force fled in panic. The prisoners were dealt with by the *degollador* – the
cut-throat. Rosas and Oribe had made this an official position in their
armies, one cut-throat, with the rank of NCO, being attached to each
battalion. His duty was to kill the prisoners after the battle. The cut-
throat passed down the long line of kneeling prisoners, holding his knife
in his right hand, and putting his left arm tenderly round each prisoner
in turn, would slit his throat, whispering soothingly as he did so:
'A woman suffers more in childbirth.'[2]*

When Garibaldi arrived at Visillac, near San Francisco, to report
for duty to Rivera, he found the town almost deserted. He was told
that all the troops had crossed the river to fight a great battle against
Oribe in Entre-Rios, and he set off with his men to join them. But he
did not find the battlefield, or get nearer than twenty-five miles to it.[3]

Rivera's army fell back in disorder. They crossed the River Uruguay
into the territory of the Oriental state, and then, without making any
attempt at a stand, made for Montevideo. Many civilians, and women
and children, accompanied the army, because the troops of Rosas
and Oribe killed some Unitarian civilians in the territory which they
occupied, and their enemies thought that there would be wholesale
massacres of Unitarians. General Urquiza, the commander of Rosas's
army in Entre-Rios, made it clear to the Unitarians what they were
to expect. Nine years later, Urquiza turned against Rosas, and won
the war for the Unitarians. He thereby ensured that a statue of himself,
as a liberator of his country, should be erected in nearly every town
in Argentina; and he increased his reputation by establishing the
tradition that he was the father of 102 bastards. But in 1842 he was one

*The author is indebted for this information to the eminent Argentine writer, Jorge
Luis Borges, whose grandfather fought in the Unitarian army.

of Rosas's most ferocious generals. 'Parricides and robbers are not prisoners of war,' he told his soldiers, 'nor objects of clemency. You have sworn to exterminate them; fulfil your vow and avenge your country. It is the will of Heaven and the express order of your General, compatriot and friend, Justo J. de Urquiza.'[4]

While Oribe advanced on Montevideo, Urquiza marched against the Unitarians in Corrientes, and quickly crushed them. Ferré fled to Paraguay, but was refused asylum there, and took refuge with the rebels of Rio Grande do Sul; and the province of Corrientes passed once again under the control of Rosas.

Garibaldi was ordered to take charge of the Unitarian squadron on the River Uruguay and to try to interfere with the operations of the Argentine and Oribe navies there. But before he had encountered any of the enemy vessels, he received new instructions—to burn all his ships, and make his way back to Montevideo overland. He carried out his orders, and commented in his memoirs that though this was the third time that he had had to burn his own ships, at least on the other two occasions – he was referring to Laguna and Costa Brava – he had been allowed to fight a battle first. He reached Montevideo before the end of the year.[5]

Oribe advanced more slowly than the Unitarians expected; but he marched across Uruguay without meeting any resistance, taking Salto, Paysandú and Colonia, and by the beginning of February was forty-five miles from Montevideo. On 2 February Admiral Brown arrived off Montevideo with a squadron of five ships of the line – a sixth ship arrived later – to assist Oribe's land forces in capturing the town. Garibaldi went into action against the Argentine navy on the very first day. As Brown's ships sailed down to Montevideo, one of his supply ships, the *Oscar*, with three guns, was wrecked on the rocks off Point Yaguas at the entrance to Montevideo harbour. After the crew of the *Oscar* had abandoned the ship, Garibaldi approached the wreck with five of his smaller ships, and boarded the *Oscar*, removing all the stores, guns and ammunition which he found there. Brown sent the *Palmar* and five smaller vessels to attack Garibaldi, who engaged them in a brisk gun-battle; but as the Argentine ships were considerably superior in fire-power to Garibaldi's vessels, Garibaldi retreated with the stores which he had taken from the *Oscar*.[6]

As the people of Montevideo watched Brown's ships blockading the harbour, they were encouraged to read in the newspapers that Rivera's army was barring Oribe's road to the capital; but in fact Rivera offered no resistance, and allowed Oribe to bypass him, and at 4 pm on 16 February Oribe arrived outside Montevideo. He encamped on the hill of the Cerrito, which today is in the middle of Montevideo, but was then just outside the city. Oribe greeted Brown's fleet with a salvo of guns, to which Brown's artillery responded with an answering salute. Oribe optimistically at once renamed the Cerrito the 'Cerrito de la Vitoria', and thought that Montevideo, like all the other towns that he had taken, would surrender without a struggle. Since crossing the frontier of Uruguay on 27 December, he had advanced 300 miles in fifty-one days, and was now four miles from Montevideo. He tried in vain for the next nine years to advance those last four miles.[7]

The Montevideans had begun building defences, but these were not nearly ready by 16 February, when Oribe reached the Cerrito. Nor had they completed the organization of the army, and they had no navy to oppose Brown's fleet. They had a total of 6,137 men defending Montevideo, of whom 5,397 were infantry and 140 cavalry, against Oribe's army of 3,500 infantry and 9,000 cavalry; and though they had 600 artillerymen against Oribe's 500, they had only 23 guns against Oribe's 30.[8] But the morale of the defenders was magnificent, though both the Chief of Police and a prominent general, Nuñez, deserted to Oribe. The government and the press roused the resistance of the citizens by stirring proclamations, appealing to them to fight to the death against Rosas. Vidal, who had only just survived a vote of censure in Parliament after the Paraná expedition, resigned and went to Europe; and Vazquez became the new Prime Minister. The organization of the defence of Montevideo was given to General Paz.

General Cesar Diaz, who was one of the foremost commanders in the defence, afterwards wrote that if Oribe had attacked as soon as he arrived at the Cerrito, Montevideo must have fallen. Garibaldi says the same thing in his memoirs. But Oribe expected the city to surrender without a fight if he waited for a few days, and he wished to avoid the destruction involved in taking it by assault. He made no serious attack on the defenders, and engaged only in minor reconnaissances. By the end of March the fortifications had been put into a strong state, the guns of the artillery had been increased from 23 to 170, and the defenders were confident that Montevideo would never fall.[9]

In his memoirs, Garibaldi wrote that the true patriotic Uruguayan did not see the war as a personal fight for power between Rivera and Oribe, but as a war of the Oriental nation against Rosas's Argentines and their henchmen, the Uruguayan traitors who supported Oribe.[10] The Rosistas, on the other hand, claimed that Oribe was the lawful President of the Oriental Republic of the Uruguay, from which he had been illegally ousted by the rebel Rivera, and denied that the Unitarians were in any sense fighting a national war for Uruguay. They emphasized, in their propaganda, that the city and the government of Montevideo were controlled by aliens and not by native Uruguayans. Large numbers of Oribe's supporters had left Montevideo as the siege began, though many others had remained as his secret agents inside the city; and as a result of this, the percentage of foreigners among the population increased. At the beginning of the siege, the population of Montevideo was 42,000, of whom two-thirds were native Uruguayans and one-third immigrants, 21,854 immigrants having arrived during the previous four years. 10,200 – nearly a quarter of the whole population – were French. There were 6,376 Italians and 3,200 Spaniards. By October 1843 the population of the city had fallen to 31,189, of whom only 11,431 were native-born; a year later, it had fallen to 20,000.[11]

Rosas and Oribe also made great play in their propaganda about a sinister syndicate of foreign speculators who were controlling the government of Montevideo. The leading figure of this syndicate was Samuel Lafone, an English immigrant. The syndicate was the main financial prop of the Montevidean government. During the siege, the government sold to the syndicate the right to collect the customs revenues for the next few years, in return for an immediate loan, an arrangement which temporarily saved the government of Montevideo from bankruptcy, but was a very profitable transaction for Lafone and his colleagues. Lafone and the British merchants in Montevideo published an English-language newspaper, *The Britannia*, which waged a war of words with Love's *British Packet* of Buenos Aires.

The large number of foreigners in Montevideo made it essential for the Unitarians to enlist them in the army. The volunteers were not offered any pay, but they were to be provided with free rations and necessaries for themselves and their families, and an Act of Parliament was passed granting each volunteer 60 square miles of land in the Republic and 25,000 head of cattle, as a gift from the state, after the war.[12] As soon as Oribe threatened Montevideo, many foreigners volunteered. The French, with their military and Radical traditions and memories of Napoleonic glories, were particularly eager to enlist. But on 1 April Oribe issued a proclamation, in which he said that any foreigner who actively helped or encouraged the Unitarians to resist would cease to be entitled to the privileges granted to neutrals, and would be treated as an enemy.[13] Oribe argued that there was nothing unreasonable in announcing that soldiers in the enemy army would not be treated as neutrals; but the Montevidean government and press, making the maximum propaganda out of Oribe's proclamation, reminded the people of how Oribe had treated his prisoners at Arroyo Grande, and interpreted his proclamation as a threat to murder all the foreigners who fought for Montevideo, or who even helped the government by lending it money. The Unitarians told the foreigners that they ought now to enlist not only to protect the cause of Liberalism and freedom, but to save themselves and their compatriots from massacre.

The Italians were less eager than the French to enlist in the Montevidean army; but Garibaldi thought that, bearing in mind the lack of military tradition among the Italians as compared with the French, it was remarkable that they got so many volunteers. While 2,000 French enlisted at once, and the newspapers praised the French for their zeal, a small item in the press announced that a recruiting office for Italian volunteers would be opened at 8 am on Thursday 13 April, and that Garibaldi would be there to enlist the volunteers. By 24 April he had enrolled 215 men; but by 13 May 2,904 Frenchmen, out of a total French population of 5,300, had enlisted, as against 400 who had joined the Italian Legion by 19 May out of 4,200 Italians in Montevideo.[14] This difference between the French and Italian record led to difficulties between the two Legions, for the French despised the Italians as a nation of men who could not fight, but could only stab with a dagger in the dark, or from behind.

The government, the press, and the leaders of the French and Italian Legions did all they could to counter this ill-feeling, and to show the solidarity which existed between the French and the Italians. Garibaldi prevented his men from sending a challenge to a duel to the Frenchmen who said that Italians could only stab in the dark.[15] Not a hint of the disagreements appeared in the press, and the French-language newspaper, *Le Patriote Français*, which was published in Montevideo for the French volunteers and civilians, took every opportunity to praise the Italians and Garibaldi personally. On 5 January 1844 Garibaldi and some of his officers were guests of the French Legion at a dinner. The *Patriote Français* declared that the evening showed that the French and Italians could collaborate as closely at the dinner table as they did on the battlefield, and gave the lie to those 'who dared to spread the rumour that the Italians and the French had ceased to understand each other; as if this were possible'.[16] But at lower levels the feelings were not always so friendly, and the letters and diaries of the inhabitants of Montevideo refer to the friction, though it was greatly exaggerated in the Buenos Aires press and in Oribe's newspaper, the *Defensor de la Independencia Americana*.

The French Legion eclipsed the Italian in the efficiency of its propaganda. The Italians tried to launch a newspaper in Italian for their Legion, with Cuneo as editor; but it never rivalled the *Patriote Français*. Before the siege began, Cuneo had published *L'Italiano*, which was supposed to be a weekly and appeared irregularly on Saturdays, twenty-three issues being published between May 1841 and September 1842, when it packed up. During the siege, Cuneo's efforts were even less successful. Whereas the *Patriote Français* appeared regularly every day except on Mondays throughout nearly the whole of the siege, Cuneo managed to produce only four numbers of the *Legionario Italiano* between October 1844 and March 1846, when he finally abandoned his attempts to publish a paper.[17]

But from the point of view of his ultimate objective, the liberation of Italy, Cuneo did more good by sending exaggerated accounts of the achievements of Garibaldi and the Italian Legion to Mazzini in London. Mazzini published the reports which he received from Cuneo in his paper *L'Apostolato Popolare*, which was read, not only by the refugees in London, but illegally in Italy; and though Mazzini's part in publicizing Garibaldi's achievements in South America was afterwards greatly exaggerated by Jessie White Mario and the Mazzinians, he made the name of Garibaldi known in Italy, particularly after Garibaldi's victory at San Antonio in 1846.[18]

The French Legion was the most important factor in the defence of Montevideo, because the 3,000 Legionaries amounted to nearly half the total personnel of the Army of the Capital. Their commander, Thiebaut, was a French Basque from the Pyrenees, who had fought in the French Revolution of 1830 and in the Spanish civil war on the Isabelino, Liberal, side. Most of the Legionaries were Republicans and Radicals, and Adolphe Delacour, the editor of the *Patriote Français*,[19] put over Republican, Radical, and occasionally even Socialist propagand . This made the French Legion suspect in the eyes of Louis Philippe and his ministers, which was embarrassing for the government of Montevideo, as they relied on the diplomatic support of France against Argentina. The French government demanded that the French Legion be disbanded, as it violated the French neutrality laws, and eventually sent an ultimatum in April 1844 threatening war unless the Legion was disbanded within forty-eight hours. The government of Montevideo got out of this very difficult predicament by dissolving the Legion, granting Uruguayan citizenship to all the Legionaries, and re-forming them in a corps which was officially known as the Second Battalion of the National Guard, but which everyone in Montevideo continued to call the French Legion. Fortunately for the government of Montevideo, the French government were prepared to accept this situation.[20]

There was a Basque Legion, under Colonel Brie, which with 700 men was a little larger than the Italian Legion, composed of Spanish Basques who had emigrated to Montevideo. There were not enough volunteers from among the 600 British residents in Montevideo to make it possible to form a separate British Legion; but a handful of British subjects joined the Montevidean forces. These included Joseph

Mundell, a Scotsman who had lived all his life in South America, and who was greatly respected by Garibaldi, and a London docker named Sam, who was bitterly hated by the Rosistas, and was often denounced in the *British Packet* for the terrible crimes which he had committed.*[21] There was also a corps of former negro slaves. The number of slaves in Uruguay was much smaller than in Brazil, and as all slaves born in Uruguay since 1814 had already been freed, there were only 6,000 slaves remaining in 1842. In December 1842, at the most critical moment of the war, the government of Montevideo abolished slavery, thereby winning the support of the negro population and the goodwill of the powerful abolitionist movement in Britain. Oribe was also liberating any slave who joined his army. In Buenos Aires, Rosas was liberating any slave who denounced his master for treason against the state.[22]

In the critical weeks of March 1843, the government of Montevideo entrusted Garibaldi with two important duties. He was appointed Commander-in-Chief of the Uruguayan navy, under the Minister of War and Marine, and given the task of building up a new navy which could operate against the Argentine ships with which Admiral Brown was blockading Montevideo; and he was also given the task of creating the Italian Legion in the land forces. As he could not personally organize and lead the Italian Legion while he was commanding the fleet, the government appointed a Commission of three, consisting of Garibaldi and two other prominent Italians, Frugoni and Castellini, to be the ultimate authority, under the Minister of War and Marine, for the Legion. The Commission appointed Mancini to be the Commander of the Legion. Mancini, like Garibaldi, held the rank of full Colonel; under Mancini, the Deputy-Commanders were Lieutenant-Colonel Anzani and Major Danuzio.[23]

Garibaldi had met Anzani at San Gabriel in Rio Grande do Sul just before he left for Montevideo in 1841, and had met him again briefly in Salto on his journey from Goya to Paysandú after the battle of Costa Brava. Anzani was an old revolutionary who had escaped from Italy after being involved in the revolt of 1821, and had fought for the Greeks in their War of Independence against Turkey, for the French Socialists on the barricades in Paris on 5 June 1832, for Dom Pedro and the Liberals at the siege of Oporto in the Portuguese civil war, and for the Riograndenses against Brazil. He then went to

*A less useful volunteer for the Montevidean cause was George Henry Strabolgi Neville Plantagenet Harrison, an English enthusiast who completely deceived the Montevidean authorities and journalists about his ancestry and his military prowess, and made it possible for the Argentine press to enjoy a good laugh at the expense of the gullible Unitarians.

Uruguay, and traded as a merchant at Salto, and had just moved to Buenos Aires, of all places, when the siege of Montevideo began.

Garibaldi had formed a very favourable impression of Anzani in their meetings at San Gabriel and Salto, and was convinced that he was the man who could organize and discipline the Italian Legion. He wrote to Anzani in Buenos Aires, inviting him to come to Montevideo for this purpose; and Anzani accepted the invitation. Anzani was a devoted and hardened revolutionary of the classical type. General Rodríguez, who played a prominent part in the defence of Montevideo, wrote in his memoirs that he had never seen Anzani laugh or smile; but though Anzani was a strict disciplinarian, he never used foul language, and always spoke softly in his North Italian accent. Rodríguez states that Anzani's personality was such that Garibaldi always addressed his subordinate commander as 'Signor Anzani', though he called most of the other Legionaries by their names or Christian names. Jessie White Mario goes so far as to say that, though Garibaldi was the 'military leader' of the Italian Legion, Anzani was its 'moral head and chief'.[24]

Garibaldi's other two Deputies, Mancini and Danuzio, were less desirable characters. Garibaldi was honest enough to admit, in his memoirs, that it was on his recommendation that Mancini was appointed as Commander of the Legion;[25] but this appointment, like Danuzio's, turned out to be very unfortunate, as both Mancini and Danuzio deserted to Oribe the next year. This was perhaps an example of Garibaldi's over-trusting nature, which, in the opinion of many friendly critics, often made him the dupe of unscrupulous men; but no one else in Montevideo seems to have had any suspicions of the loyalty of Mancini and Danuzio until it was too late. Throughout 1843 Mancini was issuing the most inspiring orders of the day, and the most eloquent proclamations, to the Italian volunteers and residents.

Garibaldi himself turned his attention to naval operations. It was essential for the Montevidean government to break Brown's blockade, because they depended on supplies from other parts of Uruguay, and from abroad, for food and arms, though surprising progress was made, during the siege, in setting up factories to manufacture arms inside Montevideo.[26] It was also important to break the blockade because of the moral effect on the governments of Britain and France, which always acted on the recognized rule of international law that a blockade was only legal if it could be effectively enforced. Oribe claimed to be in occupation of the whole of Uruguay except for Montevideo, but the people in the villages along the coast were very willing to smuggle beef and other commodities into Montevideo harbour; and ships from ports in Brazil, particularly from Laguna and Desterro, also brought in supplies. These blockade-runners slipped in, in small vessels, mostly at night.

When Garibaldi took over the command of the Montevidean fleet, after the disaster of Costa Brava, there was only one warship, the *25 de Mayo*, and four or five small craft, which were ready for service; but he built up a flotilla of small ships, and by February 1844 had a squadron of 17 warships under his command, with a total personnel of 316.[27] With this flotilla he gave as much protection as possible to the blockade-runners, though his ships were too small to venture on an open battle with the Argentine navy; and they attacked any merchant vessels that were carrying supplies to Oribe's forces at the Buceo, a fortress on the point some four miles to the east of Montevideo. Across the bay, to the west of Montevideo, the fortress of the Cerro was held by the Unitarians, though it was surrounded on the land side by Oribe's troops. Communication between Montevideo and the Cerro could only be maintained by sea; but Garibaldi succeeded in keeping these communications open at all times. He also succeeded in holding the tiny islet in the bay which was officially named Liberty Island, but which was usually referred to by its old name of Rats Island.

The crews of Garibaldi's ships were composed of men of the same type as those whom he had led in Rio Grande do Sul and on the Paraná expedition. The Montevidean land forces consisted of Uruguayan and Argentine Unitarians, who were inspired by the military traditions of South America, and of the French and Italian Legionaries with their revolutionary and Napoleonic ideals; but the navy was the receptacle for the worst elements of the armed forces who had been sent there as a punishment, for naval deserters from warships of other nations, and for common criminals.[28]

Ever since the first occasion on which Garibaldi commanded a squadron of Montevidean ships, on the Paraná expedition of 1842, the Rosas and Oribe press had labelled him and his crew as pirates. They would almost certainly have done this in any case, because as they refused to recognize that the government of Montevideo was a lawful authority, it followed that the sailors who fought for the rebels were pirates. But the conduct of Garibaldi's crew gave some justification for the designation. Garibaldi himself admitted, in his memoirs, that they were an unruly and pillaging gang, and though he claimed that he could keep them in order, he was not always able to do so.

In Garibaldi's ships, there was none of the spit-and-polish discipline which was found in other navies, and regular officers criticized Garibaldi for his laxity. Some of them thought that Garibaldi's democratic beliefs and his ideas of equality prevented him from enforcing a strict discipline and authority over his men; and Garibaldi's dislike of capital punishment, and his natural humanity, made it impossible for him to hang and flog his sailors like other naval commanders of the period. This also applied in the Italian Legion on land.

> He hated all unnecessary pedantry; [wrote Jessie White Mario] from first to last considered that barrack-life dulled the intellect, narrowed the sympathies, and fettered the souls of men. He deemed that if you could train a man to face and fight the enemy, never to fire in the air nor from a distance too great to hit him, nor turn his back on the field, nor yield to a panic, it was as much as you could expect from him; other peccadilloes might be condoned.

But in the case of the Italian Legion, matters were remedied by Anzani, who had none of Garibaldi's reluctance to punish indiscipline. General Rodríguez, who, as a regular army officer had much stricter ideas of discipline than Garibaldi, described Anzani's methods of enforcing discipline as 'cruelty'.[29]

The spirit of comradeship and slack discipline in Garibaldi's naval forces did not interfere with their fighting efficiency, for Garibaldi was always capable of maintaining the enthusiasm of his men under fire, despite the fact that on many occasions, like Costa Brava, he made demands on their courage and endurance which many regular military commanders would have hesitated to make; but there seems no doubt that he was not as successful as the martinets of the regular navies in preventing them from looting. Garibaldi seems eventually to have learned his lesson about this, because all the war correspondents and other commentators on his Italian campaigns in later years tell a very different story from those who had observed his activities in South America. They all speak of the very rigorous discipline which he imposed in Italy, where he went so far to the other extreme that he sometimes had men shot for stealing an apple from the civilian population.

Garibaldi's predecessor as commander of the Montevidean navy, the old North American sailor, Coe, was worried about the lack of discipline in Garibaldi's ships, and feared that when Garibaldi succeeded him as the naval Commander-in-Chief, this indiscipline would spread throughout the fleet. When he handed over his command to Garibaldi, he invited Garibaldi and Salvador Rombys, a retired Sardinian naval officer, to come on board his ship. Rombys accompanied Coe and Garibaldi as they walked round Coe's flagship, and after they had completed this tour of inspection, Coe asked Rombys what he thought of the ship. Rombys replied that he was greatly impressed by the smartness and discipline of the ship, which was much better than the discipline in Garibaldi's ships. Garibaldi made no comment, but after he and Rombys had left Coe, Garibaldi asked Rombys if he really meant what he had said about the lack of discipline in Garibaldi's ships, and Rombys said that he did. Rombys's son revealed in later years that Coe had rehearsed his conversation with Rombys in advance, because he thought that this would be the most tactful way of bringing the matter to Garibaldi's attention, as Garibaldi would be more ready to accept criticism of his lack of discipline from a neutral observer than from his retiring predecessor. The government obviously shared Coe's anxieties about the lack of discipline in Garibaldi's ships, because when they appointed Garibaldi to command the Paraná expedition they included an express instruction about discipline in their commission to Garibaldi: 'The government recommends the most rigorous discipline as the basis of self-preservation by a prudent severity which is its chief element.'[30]

The Montevidean leaders knew that the result of their war against Rosas and Oribe would be decided by Britain and France, and attached great importance to their diplomacy and propaganda in London and Paris. The war was interfering with British trade with Buenos Aires, Montevideo, and with Paraguay up the River Plate and the River Paraná; and after Sir Robert Peel's Conservative government replaced Lord Melbourne and the Whigs in 1841, Lord Aberdeen, Peel's Foreign Secretary, pursued a more friendly policy towards France, and consequently towards the Unitarians of Montevideo, than his predecessor, Lord Palmerston, had done. But by March 1843 the British and French governments had come to the conclusion that, as only Montevideo was still held by the Unitarians, the quickest way to end the hostilities, and to restore normal trading conditions in the River Plate, would be for Rosas and Oribe to win the war as soon as possible. But they did not recognize Oribe's government as the government of Uruguay.

The Unitarians tried to counteract the mood in London by mounting an intensive propaganda campaign, which at the time was almost unprecedented. They found three effective propagandists – Rivera Indarte and Agostin Wright, of the newspaper *El Nacional*, and Florencio Varela, the editor of another leading Montevidean journal, the *Comercio del Plata*. All three were Argentine Unitarians. Indarte, the youngest and least eminent of the three, was the most effective as a propagandist, though he was less respectable and truthful than Varela, who had become the leading intellectual of Montevideo. In his books *Ephemerides* and *Tables of Blood*, Indarte gave the names of 23,404 victims who had been murdered by Rosas, and though these figures may have been exaggerated, they were much nearer the truth than Indarte's scandalous stories about Manuelita de Rosas, whom he accused not only of being a prostitute, but also of committing incest with Rosas. Indarte sent a copy of *Tables of Blood* to every important newspaper, and to many MPs and prominent persons, in Britain, France and the United States.[31]

Rosas, too, was aware of the importance of influencing the policy of the great powers, and in both Britain and France there were newspapers and politicians who were instruments of propaganda for one side or the other. In Britain, Evers, the MP for Dalkeith, was a spokesman for Montevideo, while Mallalieu organized a strong counter-lobby in support of Rosas. A less open, but far more influential, supporter of Rosas in Britain was Palmerston, who in Opposition was attacking Aberdeen's policy of collaboration with France, and wrote powerful anonymous articles in the *Morning Chronicle* attacking the Unitarians of Montevideo and their French supporters. Palmerston, as always, was concerned only with British interests, and he did not think that British interests in the River Plate would be furthered by having a Liberal rather than a Rosista President in Uruguay. On 4 February 1846 the *Morning Chronicle*, in an anonymous article which bears every mark of Palmerston's style, wrote: 'For our own parts, whether Don Oribe or Don anybody else be President of Monte Video appears to us . . . a matter of such perfect insignificance, that we only wonder any British statesman can trouble himself about it.'[32] In the United States, where the British and French interest in the River Plate was viewed with great suspicion as threatening the Monroe Doctrine, the press, especially the *New York Weekly Herald*, tended to be favourable to Rosas and Oribe.

The position was complicated by the fact that both Britain and France maintained a naval squadron off Montevideo, and at the beginning of the siege, in February 1843, had landed a small body of marines to protect their traders during the hostilities. The commander of the British squadron, Commodore Purvis, became an enthusiastic supporter of the Unitarian cause, though this conflicted with the policy of Peel, Aberdeen, and the British Minister in Buenos Aires, Sir John Mandeville. Purvis was typical of many Englishmen of his time. He believed in upholding the honour of the British flag by adopting a truculent attitude towards foreigners, and in helping the cause of constitutional freedom by supporting Liberals all over the world. He also hated and despised Irishmen, including Admiral Brown. As it took three months for a letter to go from Montevideo to London, and another three months for a reply to arrive in Montevideo, Purvis knew that it would take at least six months before any action of his was disowned by his government.

Lafone and the English residents in Montevideo persuaded Purvis that the Unitarians represented the cause of constitutional freedom, and Purvis allowed his prejudices full rein. On 17 February 1843 – the day after Oribe arrived at the Cerrito, when the Montevidean government and press issued their stirring call for resistance – Purvis sent a letter to Brown. It was not addressed correctly to 'Brigadier-General Brown', but to 'Mr Brown, a British subject, commanding the naval forces of the Argentine Republic off Montevideo'. In the letter, Purvis informed Brown that the Queen of Great Britain desired all British subjects to remain neutral, and called on him to cease serving in the Argentine navy; and he enclosed a copy of the British Foreign Enlistment Act.[33]

On the night of 6 April, Brown sent a naval force to attack Rats Island, where Garibaldi had installed a garrison of sixty men. Garibaldi happened to be returning to Montevideo at the time from a visit of inspection to Rats Island, and had a lucky escape. A strong gale was blowing, and the sea was very rough in the bay. In the darkness, Garibaldi's boat passed very close to a large ship which Garibaldi recognized as Brown's flagship, the *Belgrano*. A sentry on the *Belgrano* heard them, and cried out 'Who goes there?' Garibaldi whispered an order to his men to row as quietly as possible, and passed on without replying to the challenge, expecting a hail of bullets from the *Belgrano*; but none came. Garibaldi afterwards realized that this was because the *Belgrano* was on her way to attack Rats Island, and Brown did not wish the garrison on the island to be warned of his approach by the noise that would be made if his crew fired at a passing boat.

Shortly before dawn on 7 April, Brown opened fire on the garrison of Rats Island. The garrison put up a stout resistance, but the Argentines landed, and removed a quantity of supplies, including some gunpowder. Garibaldi recaptured the island with a small flotilla that same night.[34] Next morning, on the 8th, Brown sent a larger force to attack Garibaldi and his men on Rats Island; but then Purvis intervened. He told Brown that the gunpowder that his men had seized on Rats Island was the property of a British subject, and must be returned immediately; and he also suggested that Brown should agree to make a truce with the Montevidean forces. Brown agreed, under protest, to hand over the gunpowder to Purvis, but rejected the proposal for a truce. Purvis then sent a note to 'Mr Brown, an English subject commanding the Buenos Aires vessels of war', and gave him notice 'that I will not tolerate the Argentine Squadron committing any act of hostility on the Town of Montevideo, whereby may be endangered the life or property of a British subject', and that if any natural-born British subject was responsible for such an attack, he 'will be by me deemed guilty of piracy and treated accordingly'.[35]

Brown, in a reply correctly addressed to 'Commodore' Purvis, acknowledged receipt of his note, and said that he had referred it to his government in Buenos Aires. He then resumed his attack on Rats Island; but Purvis promptly sent one of his ships, the *Daphne*, into the line of fire between Brown and Garibaldi, so that Brown could not continue the attack without firing on the British flag. Brown was not prepared to commit an act of war against Britain without the authority of his government, and therefore agreed to Purvis's suggestion for a truce. Garibaldi accepted the truce, but Brown afterwards alleged that he had made use of it to fortify Rats Island. Brown also complained that Garibaldi had attacked one of his unarmed boats which was carrying medical supplies to his ships.[36]

On 13 April Purvis sent another note to Brown. This time he addressed it, illogically, to 'Commodore Brown', and said that he would not permit Brown to continue the blockade unless Oribe withdrew his proclamation of 1 April against British subjects and other neutrals who helped Montevideo. Faced with this threat, and with repeated protests from the British and French Consuls, Oribe withdrew his proclamation; but Brown announced that in view of Purvis's attitude, he could not enforce the blockade of Montevideo, and at the beginning of May he withdrew his blockading fleet and anchored them some twenty miles away. The Buenos Aires press denounced Purvis, and in due course the pro-Rosas lobby in Britain took up the matter. Mandeville asked the British government to repudiate Purvis's actions, and to order him to recognize the blockade of Montevideo; but meanwhile Purvis remained in command of the British squadron at Montevideo.[37]

This was the first of several occasions on which Garibaldi received material help in his campaigns from the British navy. It was the beginning of a long collaboration between British naval officers and this long-haired Italian revolutionary, with his curious garments and his semi-Socialist theories. Whereas in South America, Italy, France and Austria, aristocrats and militarists thought of Garibaldi as a particularly obnoxious type of revolutionary trouble-maker, the English aristocracy and officer class, who had a low opinion of revolutionaries, Radicals and Socialists in general, had a great admiration for Garibaldi. In later years, this was partly because Garibaldi was against the Pope, which appealed to the Protestants in the British Establishment; but this did not apply in the South American period, and there was always something more than religious prejudice involved in the Garibaldi fervour which took hold of the British ruling classes. They admired his bravery, his absolute lack of guile and political cunning, his simple manners and sincerity, and his honest sailor's character.

Garibaldi spent most of his time with the fleet, but he also often fought on land, where his presence was needed to inspire the Italian Legion. On 2 June 1843 the Italians were in action for the first time when the Army of the Capital launched a moderately large-scale sortie. The first battalion of the Italian Legion, under Danuzio, captured the enemy outpost which they had been ordered to capture; but the other two battalions of the Legion refused to advance, and then ran away, giving as their excuse that they had no ammunition. They were jeered at as cowards by the French Legionaries, and the matter became the talk of Montevideo.

The authorities did their best to keep the matter quiet. The *Nacional*, in its report of the fighting, stated merely that the first battalion of the Italian Legion had carried out the attack in perfect order; and the *Patriote Français* published a message which they said had been sent to the French Legion by the Italian Legion, though it was not signed by Garibaldi or by any other Italian leader. The message emphasized the friendship which existed between the French and Italian Legions; but to illustrate this friendship it chose examples from the era of Napoleon and his infant son thirty years before. The Italians told 'our dear brothers of the French Legion' that 'France and Italy are the only two nations between whom no ill-feeling exists. Italy gave France an Emperor, and France gave Italy the most precious gift which she had received from Providence, the King of Rome, that young Caesar sitting on the throne of the Roman Emperors.' These sentiments were as alien to Garibaldi and the members of Young Italy as they were to the ordinary French Legionary who mocked the fighting ability of the Italians.[38]

Garibaldi, who had not been present during the battle of 2 June, was overcome with shame at the cowardice which his men had shown. Next day, the Minister of War and Marine, Pacheco y Obes, who afterwards became a close friend of Garibaldi, ordered that an inquiry should be held into the conduct of the second and third divisions of the Italian Legion; but on 4 June Garibaldi persuaded him to suspend the inquiry for the time being. Garibaldi felt that the only satisfactory solution was for the Legion to retrieve the disgrace of 2 June by distinguishing themselves in another battle as soon as possible.

On 8 June a force of 190 Italian Legionaries was sent across the bay to the Cerro, where the garrison was skirmishing with Oribe's troops; and Garibaldi left the fleet to accompany them. They manned the front line at the Cerro on 9 June and all that night. On 10 June Pacheco y Obes came to the Cerro to witness the skirmishing. The defending force was roughly equal in numbers to Oribe's forces in the area, but as Oribe's men were better trained, and the Montevidean commanders were not over-confident of the fighting ability of their men, they did not order any attack on the enemy. Garibaldi saw the chance for which he had been waiting. He went up to Pacheco and asked his permission to lead the Italian Legionaries against a detachment of enemy soldiers who had established themselves in a house in the village near the Cerro; and Pacheco consented. Garibaldi then made a short speech to his men, exhorting them to vindicate the honour of Italy; and he found, as he was to find so often in South America and Italy during the next twenty-five years, that he could inspire Italians to deeds of courage which they could not perform when he was absent. They stormed the enemy's position at the point of the bayonet, and after killing several of the enemy and putting them to flight, returned to the Cerro with 43 prisoners. Their only losses had been two sergeants seriously wounded and one other man slightly wounded.[39]

Next day they returned to Montevideo, having won the congratulations of Pacheco, commendation in the army orders of the day, and praise in the press for their courage. On 2 July the Italian and French Legions paraded side by side in the Plaza de la Constitución in Montevideo, and after taking the oath of loyalty to the Oriental Republic, which ironically was taken for the Italian Legion by Colonel Mancini, they were awarded their colours. The Italians chose as the flag of the Legion a black flag with a picture of Vesuvius in eruption in the centre of it.[40]

Garibaldi writes in his memoirs with justifiable pride of this engagement at the Cerro on 10 June when the Legion wiped out the disgrace of the previous week; but he makes no mention whatever of another incident which occurred in the same area a few days later, and which had unfortunate consequences both for him and for the government of Montevideo. Garibaldi led a guerrilla raid by the Italian Legionaries on the Oribe troops who were stationed in the village near the Cerro. A number of inhabitants of the village had continued to live in their houses despite the spasmodic fighting which was going on around them, and from time to time they were injured in some way through the activity of the soldiers. As several of the residents of the village were foreigners, this gave both sides the opportunity of accusing the other of committing atrocities against foreign civilians. In the course of this raid near the Cerro in the middle of June 1843, Garibaldi's men entered a number of civilian houses, including one which belonged to a

Brazilian subject, and committed some damage and depredations there.[41]

Apart from Britain, France and the United States, the foreign power which could exert most influence in the war in the River Plate was Brazil, and both in Buenos Aires and in Montevideo the government was working to win over Brazil from her policy of neutrality and to induce her to join in on their side. The Brazilian government was suspicious of Rosas's Argentina, which was their strongest rival in South America; but they were not friendly to Rivera, who had close contacts with the Republicans in Rio Grande do Sul. There was thus a conflict of opinion in Rio de Janeiro as to what policy they should pursue with regard to the River Plate.

In March 1843 the Argentine Minister in Rio de Janeiro negotiated a treaty of alliance with the Brazilian government, under which Argentina and Brazil were to co-operate in crushing the rebellions in Rio Grande do Sul and Uruguay, and in effect agreed that Uruguay should be subject to a joint Argentine-Brazilian sphere of influence. Rosas refused to ratify the treaty out of consideration for Oribe, who was a personal friend as well as a reliable ally, and stated that he would not make any treaty affecting Uruguay to which Oribe, as President of Uruguay, was not a party.[42] This strengthened the hand of the Liberal, pro-Unitarian politicians in Rio de Janeiro, and negotiations for an alliance began between Brazil and the government of Montevideo.

The Brazilian Minister in Montevideo, Regis, was opposed to the new policy of his government, and did not favour an alliance with the Unitarians of Uruguay. In June 1843, when the secret negotiations for the treaty between Brazil and Montevideo were getting well under way, he sent a harshly-worded note of protest to the Montevidean Prime Minister, Vazquez, complaining about the damage and depredations committed by Garibaldi and his men in the house of the Brazilian subject in the village near the Cerro. The Montevidean press claimed that the damage was unavoidable, as Garibaldi had found it necessary, in the course of his operations against the enemy, to enter and occupy the house of the Brazilian; but they admitted that, in the heat of battle, some irregularities might have been committed.

Regis not only protested, and demanded compensation for the Brazilian, but also mentioned the fact that the commander responsible for the outrage, Garibaldi, was a notorious pirate who had formerly committed acts of piracy in the service of the rebels of Rio Grande do Sul. Vazquez sent a copy of Regis's note to Garibaldi, so as to give Garibaldi an opportunity of investigating the matter. Garibaldi took great exception to the note. He called at the Brazilian legation, and demanded to see Regis; and on gaining admission to Regis's presence, he challenged him to a duel. Regis, who had formerly been a naval officer in the Imperial Brazilian navy, refused to fight Garibaldi, saying that as an officer and a gentleman and a diplomatic representative of his Emperor he could not meet a notorious pirate who owed his freedom to the fact that he had been graciously pardoned for his offences by the Emperor of Brazil. Regis was presumably referring to the periodical amnesties which Caixas had offered to the Republicans of Rio Grande do Sul, though Garibaldi had never taken advantage of them. Garibaldi replied by calling Regis a coward, and left the legation.

Regis protested to the Montevidean government that Garibaldi had violated his diplomatic immunity by challenging him to a duel on account of something which he had written in a diplomatic note. He demanded that Garibaldi should be dismissed from his posts in the armed forces, and banished from Uruguay, and that he should be kept under arrest until he left the country; and he threatened to leave Montevideo if his demands were refused. He was delighted to have an opportunity to exacerbate relations between Brazil and Montevideo, and to thwart the negotiations for the treaty. The government of Montevideo were very eager not to offend Brazil at this moment, and immediately sent Regis a handsome apology and arrested Garibaldi. But Garibaldi was released a few hours later and placed under open arrest pending further investigations into the incident. This meant that in the meantime he was free, and able to carry on his naval and military duties; but it was probably in order not to offend Regis that Garibaldi did not attend the parade on 2 July when the Italian Legion was awarded its colours.

When Regis heard that Garibaldi had been released, he announced that he was leaving Montevideo, and went on board a Brazilian warship which was at anchor in the harbour. Vazquez made one more attempt to pacify Regis. He sent him a note on board the ship, apologizing again for Garibaldi's action, and telling him that Garibaldi had explained that in challenging Regis to a duel, he had intended to challenge him only in his personal capacity, and not as the representative of Brazil, but that Garibaldi now realized that it was impossible to make this distinction, and admitted that his action had been wrong. Regis rejected this note, and sailed next morning for Rio de Janeiro.

The pro-Argentine faction in Brazil made the most of the incident, and so did the Rosas newspapers in Buenos Aires. The *Gaceta Mercantil* and the *British Packet* reported that when Regis refused to accept Garibaldi's challenge to a duel, and called him a pirate, Garibaldi drew a sword which he had concealed in a sword-stick, and would have killed Regis if the staff at the legation had not rushed in and ejected Garibaldi after a desperate struggle. In the succeeding months they produced a simplified version of the incident; the pirate Garibaldi had forced his way into the Brazilian legation, and had tried to murder the Minister.[43]

On 22 June Garibaldi wrote to the government from 'the war schooner *Emansipacion* [*sic*]', in Montevideo harbour, and gave his explanation of what had occurred. He denied that he had used any violence in the Brazilian legation, but admitted that he had called Regis a coward when he had refused to give him redress.

> Please accept, most excellent Señor, this protest [he wrote] and this declaration that Colonel Garibaldi knows the respect which he owes to the Imperial Government and its Ministers; that if, when he asked Señor Regis for satisfaction, he was in any way lacking in respect, he thinks that he was asking for what a man of honour is entitled to; and finally, that the unfortunate incidents which have occurred were caused by the insult of Señor Regis in calling him a pirate.

He ended by declaring that he submitted himself to justice and was loyal to the constitution, as befitted a Colonel of the Republic.[44]

On 5 July the *Gaceta Mercantil* published a long article on the subject, in which they claimed that it was not the Rosistas, but the Unitarians of Montevideo, who were the cut-throats.

> The representative of the government of His Imperial Majesty, and his subjects, have been barbarously insulted by the pirate Garibaldi, although this villain owes his life to the generous amnesty which was granted to him by His Majesty the Emperor of Brazil. As is well-known and notorious, this bandit, who has been proscribed in Italy on account of his crimes, sacked the shops and houses at the Cerro, committing barbarous atrocities on the bloody days of 12, 13 and 14 June – deeds of prowess worthy of a well-known pirate and murderer.

The Brazilian Minister had 'barely escaped being murdered by a foreign pirate, a savage Unitarian thirsting for gold and blood'. Yet the mulatto Rivera had not punished Garibaldi, who was the Admiral of the savage Unitarians in Montevideo; and 'a British Commodore is friendly with this pirate, and instead of condemning his crimes, he tolerates and authorizes them!'[45]

But the government of Brazil were determined not to allow this regrettable incident to deflect them from their policy of negotiating an alliance with Montevideo. On 17 July the Montevidean Minister in Rio de Janeiro wrote to reassure his anxious government that the Brazilian Foreign Minister had told him that the Regis-Garibaldi incident was only a storm in a teacup which could easily be settled. The Brazilian government sent Casançao de Sinimbú to replace Regis in Montevideo. Sinimbú was a rising Liberal politician who, after spending some months in Whig society in London and three years studying in the Liberal atmosphere of Jena University in Prussia, had returned to Brazil to become a well-known Liberal journalist and MP. He was given this diplomatic appointment in Montevideo at the age of thirty-two with the object of negotiating an anti-Rosas alliance.[46]

With goodwill on both sides, all that was necessary was to find a formula to settle the Garibaldi incident. On arriving in Montevideo, Sinimbú announced that he could not hold any talks with the government until Brazil had received satisfaction for the affront to Regis; but he explained to the Montevidean government that he was only adopting this high attitude in order to appease public opinion in Brazil, and to take the wind out of the sails of the pro-Argentine faction in Rio de Janeiro. The Montevidean government persuaded Garibaldi to visit Sinimbú at the Brazilian legation and apologize. Garibaldi told Sinimbú what the Montevidean government had already told Regis, that he had intended to challenge Regis in his personal capacity and not as the representative of Brazil, and that he now realized he had acted wrongly. Sinimbú accepted his explanation and apology, and he and Garibaldi shook hands. The Montevidean press adopted the line that Garibaldi had done wrong, but had acted under great provocation, that Regis had deliberately aggravated the incident by his arrogant notes and conduct, and that the matter was now closed, leaving Uruguayan-Brazilian relations in a very friendly state.[47]

Sinimbú and Vazquez then got down to business, and negotiated a secret treaty of alliance against Rosas. The Brazilian and Uruguayan navies were to mount a joint attack on the Uruguayan port of Colonia, which Oribe had occupied, and after Colonia had been captured it was to be leased to Brazil as a naval base for operations against Argentina. But the pro-Argentine faction in Rio de Janeiro succeeded in preventing the ratification of Sinimbú's treaty; and after it had been violently attacked in Parliament in Rio, in a debate in which Garibaldi's misconduct was frequently referred to, the Brazilian government announced that it would continue to pursue a policy of strict neutrality in the hostilities in the River Plate. Sinimbú resigned his position as Minister in Montevideo, and retired for a time from political life.[48] In due course he returned to it, and became Foreign Minister, and later Prime Minister, of Brazil. He finally retired as Viscount Sinimbú, being the last man to be created a Viscount before the downfall of the Empire in 1889.

When Varzea was writing his book *Garibaldi in America* at the beginning of the twentieth century, he got in touch with Sinimbú. Sinimbú did not feel capable of granting Varzea an interview, but he wrote him a letter in which he said that he still remembered very clearly his meeting with Garibaldi in Montevideo nearly sixty years before. Garibaldi, he wrote, was 'an attractive man, talkative, and with a lively and intelligent glance; but I would be untruthful were I to say that I suspected, at that time, that I was in the presence of the most glorious and disinterested of the creators of Italian unity.'[49] Sinimbú died in 1906, aged ninety-six.

CHAPTER 11

THE SIEGE OF MONTEVIDEO:
TREASON IN THE LEGION

THE collapse of the projected alliance with Brazil was one of several diplomatic set-backs which the Montevidean government encountered in the summer of 1843–4. In October 1843 Purvis received orders from the British government to recognize the blockade of Montevideo, and Brazil also recognized it. Purvis disregarded his orders as far as possible, and by his protests and threats succeeded in inducing Admiral Brown to exempt all British ships from the operation of the blockade; but he could not permanently thwart the policy of the British government.

On 8 March 1844 Peel stated in the House of Commons that Britain would not intervene in the River Plate. He said that the war 'was not properly a conflict between Monte Video and Buenos Ayres', but between the Federalists and the Unitarians, 'and therefore the war might be considered as rather between different parties in Buenos Ayres than between Buenos Ayres and Monte Video'.[1] This was almost the exact truth, but it was the Rosista, not the Unitarian, way of describing the war. In June, Purvis received orders recalling him immediately to London, and though his actions were not officially condemned by the British government, everyone knew that they had been repudiated.

With Britain and Brazil remaining strictly neutral, and France becoming less friendly, the Unitarians of Montevideo faced Rosas and Oribe with no prospect of receiving any outside help. The Unitarians held nothing except the city of Montevideo and the port of Maldonado, though Rivera, with the remnants of his army of Arroyo Grande, was lurking in Oribe's rear, and trying to wage at least a guerrilla war against him. Rivera had resigned the presidency of the republic when he took over the leadership of the army in the field in favour of the able but self-effacing President Joachim Suarez. But a powerful new leader now appeared in Montevideo. In January 1843 Colonel Melchor Pacheco y Obes, who had shown great energy in organizing the defence of Mercedes at the beginning of the war, was appointed Minister of War and Marine. Pacheco became a close friend of Garibaldi. Another important member of the government was Andres Lamas, who was in charge of the police, and showed great determination in suppressing Oribe's agents and sympathizers. Lamas, too, was friendly with Garibaldi.

According to Pacheco's friend Lorenzo Batlle – the first member of this distinguished family to play a leading part in Uruguayan politics – Pacheco, ever since his childhood, had been a passionate student of the history of the great French Revolution of 1793,[2] and his proclamations give the impression that he felt himself to be the Robespierre of Uruguay. He stimulated the spirit of 'the Fatherland in danger', and proclaimed the duty of every citizen to fight to the death for the country and the cause, and to show no weakness or mercy to traitors and cowards. Pacheco y Obes was a Radical, and this brought him into conflict with Rivera. A serious split developed between these two leaders, in which personal ambition played a part. Rivera had the support of the more moderate Liberals, of the officers of the regular Uruguayan army – that is to say, of those who had not joined Oribe – and of the majority of the Unitarians among the native Uruguayans and the Argentine refugees. Pacheco relied on the support of the Radicals, of Thiebaut and the French Legion, and of Garibaldi and the Italians.

Unlike his prototype, Robespierre, Pacheco did not institute a reign of terror in Montevideo; but he was responsible for a policy of reprisals which increased the savagery of the war, though it fell far short of what the Rosistas and Oribe's Blancos were doing. On 12 February 1843 the government of Montevideo issued a decree which provided that all captured Argentine officers and men would be granted the rights of prisoners of war, but that any Uruguayan fighting for Oribe, if taken prisoner, would be executed, by shooting in the back, as a traitor who had helped the foreign enemy. The British and French Consuls in Montevideo protested against this decree. But on 1 June Colonel Silva, at the head of a detachment from Rivera's army, slipped through Oribe's lines and arrived at the Cerro, bringing with him 37 prisoners – two officers and 35 men – whom he had captured on his march. Pacheco crossed the harbour to the Cerro to greet Silva, and saw the prisoners. He identified the two officers and two of the other prisoners as native Uruguayans, and ordered them to be shot from the back; and to Silva's disgust, the order was immediately carried out, before Pacheco returned to Montevideo with the other 33 prisoners. Meanwhile Oribe's men and the Argentine land forces continued in their usual fashion to cut the throats of many of their prisoners, though Admiral Brown treated all those whom he captured at sea as prisoners of war.[3]

In August 1843 Brown's men captured four Unitarian sailors,

including one young boy, who were trying to run the blockade. Brown held them as prisoners for two months on board one of his ships, granting them all the rights of prisoners of war; but when Oribe heard about them, he decided to execute them, and insisted that Brown hand them over to him. Brown obeyed orders, and the men were executed. Their corpses were mutilated and castrated, and during the night of 6 October were hung up on posts in the no-man's-land between the armies on the eastern outskirts of Montevideo, where they were seen at dawn on the 7th by the Montevidean soldiers. The men of the Italian Legion succeeded in retrieving the corpses, which were buried after a state funeral in the cathedral at five o'clock the same afternoon, before a large crowd which clamoured for vengeance. The Rosas and Oribe newspapers claimed that the mutilations of the corpses had been carried out by the Unitarians themselves, in order to use the incident for propaganda purposes.

On the same day, Pacheco issued a new decree. In retaliation for the murder of prisoners of war by the enemy, all Argentine officers who were captured would henceforth be executed, though Argentines of other ranks would be treated as prisoners of war unless they had been personally guilty of war crimes. All prisoners of Uruguayan nationality who had been serving with the enemy, whatever their rank, would be shot from the back under the earlier decree. A few weeks later, an Argentine officer, Captain García, was captured and shot under the order of 7 October. But the execution, and the orders of 12 February and 7 October, disturbed many Unitarians at the time, as well as bringing protests from the British and French Consuls; and when an Argentine naval officer, Lieutenant Cueli, was taken prisoner on 31 October, Pacheco announced that he would not be shot under the decree of 7 October, but would be released because of the considerate way in which Admiral Brown treated his prisoners.[4]

Pacheco was denounced throughout the rest of his life by the Rosistas and Blancos for his decrees of 12 February and 7 October. He defended himself by claiming that both reprisals and the execution of traitors were justified by the law of all civilized nations, and pointed out that the four men whom he had shot at the Cerro on 1 June were the only Uruguayan enemy soldiers to whom the decree of 12 February was applied, though over five hundred of them were taken prisoner in the course of the war; that Captain García was the only Argentine officer shot under the reprisal decree; and that there were only three other death sentences for political offences carried out in Montevideo during the siege, although the executions carried out by Rosas and Oribe during this time ran into thousands.[5]

Garibaldi greatly admired Pacheco, and all his life regarded him as a friend, as well as a political leader. But though he admired Pacheco's revolutionary zeal and energy, it is unlikely that he approved of the decrees of 12 February and 7 October. Garibaldi's merciful nature made him oppose capital punishment, though he sometimes shot mutinous soldiers on the battlefield. When a serious case of cowardice in the face of the enemy occurred in June 1844, and the offender, a native-born Uruguayan lieutenant, was sentenced to death by court-martial, Garibaldi interceded for his life with President Suarez, after the sentence had been confirmed by the Commander-in-Chief, and persuaded Suarez to commute the sentence to one year's service in the ranks on Rats Island.[6]

The only mitigation in the ferocity of the war was at sea, where the accepted laws of war were nearly always observed. This was thanks to the personalities of the two naval commanders, Brown and Garibaldi. The Montevidean newspapers, repaying the compliment of the Rosas and Oribe press, which consistently referred to 'the pirate Garibaldi', dubbed Brown a pirate, and occasionally attacked him fiercely, arguing that he had forfeited all the respect which he had won in the Wars of Independence by his conduct as Rosas's Admiral. They particularly attacked him for handing over to Oribe the prisoners who were executed and mutilated in October 1843, and denounced him again when, two months later, he opened fire on a fleet of unarmed fishermen who were blockade-running. But on other occasions they acknowledged that Brown treated his prisoners well. The Unitarians did not know until after the war that Brown had prevented a concentrated bombardment of Montevideo, though shells were continually falling in the city, and someone was killed by them nearly every day. When Rosas ordered Brown to bombard the city from the sea, Brown persuaded him to withdraw the order on the grounds that it might damage the property of British and French subjects, which would have serious international repercussions. In April 1845 Brown sent a ship to save the lives of some Montevidean fishermen whose boat had been wrecked when they were trying to run the blockade. Garibaldi issued a statement thanking Brown for his humanitarian conduct, and the government of Montevideo ordered all the Montevidean newspapers to publish Garibaldi's statement.[7]

While Brown prevented the bombardment of Montevideo, Oribe, on his part, never tried to capture it by assault. At first he was convinced that, if he waited for a few weeks, the city would surrender without a struggle; but when it was clear that this would not happen, he still did not order a general attack, but confined himself to fighting minor skirmishes. The Unitarian General Iriarte was convinced that Oribe would try to take Montevideo by storm, and that, if the attack

154

were successful, he and his wife and children, along with all the Unitarians in the city, would be slaughtered; but the attack never came. Oribe did not think that he had enough troops to capture Montevideo by assault. He had 14,000 men against 8,000 for the defence; but 9,000 of his men were cavalry, who would be of little use in street fighting, and he was weaker in artillery than the defenders.[8] Historians have speculated as to why Rosas did not send him reinforcements, and have suggested that Rosas preferred to see Uruguay involved in a long civil war, rather than to have it secure under the dictatorship of an ally who might afterwards turn into an enemy. Others believe that Oribe, despite his hatred of the Unitarians, shrank from ordering an attack which would have resulted in a wholesale massacre of the Montevidean middle classes by his Uruguayan and Argentine gaucho soldiers. He hoped to starve Montevideo into submission by his blockade by land and sea.

As it was useless to prevent supplies from entering by land as long as ships could enter the harbour of Montevideo, the result of the war turned on the success of the blockade. But the blockade was largely ineffective. In order not to antagonize Britain and France, it was only half-heartedly enforced during the first two years of the siege; and it was also frustrated to a considerable extent by the successful blockade-running of the fishermen along the coast and of adventurous traders from Laguna and other ports in Brazil. Garibaldi's ships gave all the protection which they could to the blockade-runners, and frequently engaged in sharp skirmishes with Brown's larger ships. Garibaldi also seized several Argentine and neutral ships which were carrying supplies to Oribe's territory. One of them belonged to a poor immigrant from Croatia, Josef Lussich. Garibaldi promised that he would try to obtain compensation for Lussich, but the compensation was never paid. This set-back did not prevent Lussich from building up the business which is today the greatest shipowning company in South America.*

The siege of Montevideo continued for nine years. In 1850, the eighth year of the siege, Alexandre Dumas the elder published an account of it, in Paris, in a book which he called *Montevideo, or a new Troy*, comparing the siege to the ten-year siege of Troy of which Homer had written. He dedicated the book 'To the heroic defenders of Montevideo'; it was widely read, and was the apogee of the pro-Montevidean propaganda in France. Dumas was not the first man to compare the siege of Montevideo to the siege of Troy. The comparison had occurred five years before to an officer in Oribe's army, who, unlike Dumas, remembered that Troy had been captured in the end, and wrote on

*I am grateful to Señorita Sara Lussich for this information.

Christmas Eve 1844 that they would take the city, even 'if this siege of Montevideo lasts as long as that of Troy'.[9]

Dumas's book gave a vivid picture of life in Montevideo during the siege, though it is to some extent an inaccurate picture. He had not been in Montevideo himself, and relied on the book which Agostín Wright had published in Montevideo in 1845. He was undoubtedly influenced very largely by Pacheco y Obes, who by 1850 had been sent as the Montevidean Minister to Paris, and had become a friend of Dumas. Pacheco is the hero of Dumas's book, though Pacheco's friend Garibaldi, who is wrongly said to have been discovered and promoted by Pacheco, also receives a great deal of praise.

Dumas praised the heroism of the population of Montevideo, as they lived, day after day, within a few miles of the enemy, with every part of the city within earshot of the gunfire in the front line. He wrote about children who, when not in school, carried ammunition to the soldiers in the front line, and described how the women waited every day for a messenger to bring a letter from their husbands and sons at the front, knowing that it was just as likely that they would receive, not a letter, but the body of the loved one himself, dead or dying, on a stretcher. Dumas's book was a brilliant propaganda tract for Montevideo, the 'last bulwark of civilization' and of European culture in South America. His account is quite correct in one respect; many children joined the army. One of them was Borges, the grandfather of the great Argentine writer, Jorge Luis Borges. He was serving in the artillery before his fourteenth birthday.[10]

Dumas had not yet met Garibaldi when he wrote *Montevideo, ou une nouvelle Troie*: but though he is wrong in several of his statements about Garibaldi, there is no reason to doubt the account which he gives of Garibaldi's poverty. He states that in 1843 a well-known Montevidean business man, Francisco Agell, mentioned to Pacheco that Garibaldi was so poor that he could not afford to light a candle in his house at night. Pacheco then sent his ADC, Colonel Tajes, to Garibaldi with a hundred patacones; but Garibaldi accepted only half of this money, and told Tajes to take the other fifty patacones to a poor widow whom he named. On another occasion Garibaldi insisted that a thousand patacones, which was his share of prize money, should be given to the poor. Dumas undoubtedly heard about these incidents from Pacheco, who tells the same story in his own book.[11]

A very similar story is told by Colonel Danel. He was sent by Pacheco with a message to Garibaldi on what he describes as a very cold night in June 1844, though, being in Montevideo, it is unlikely that the temperature was much below freezing. He was shocked to see the poverty in which Garibaldi lived, with only one candle in the room.

He reported it to Pacheco, who told the Chief of Police, Lamas, and Pacheco and Lamas decided to send Garibaldi 100 pesos which they raised from their own pockets; but when Danel gave Garibaldi the money, Garibaldi was only willing to accept 12 pesos, and told Danel to keep the rest of the 100 pesos to relieve the needs of his own family.[12]

There are several other accounts of Garibaldi's extreme poverty in Montevideo, the story of the absence of candles being told in a slightly different form by five writers.[13] Obviously not all these stories are true in every detail; but there can be no doubt that Garibaldi was very poor, and on at least one occasion was very short of candles. The Unitarians and their supporters were eager to stress Garibaldi's poverty, and his refusal to derive any financial advantage from his high position in the navy, because of the constant allegations that Garibaldi and the foreign adventurers had come to South America to make their fortune, and were doing so at the expense of the unfortunate natives of Uruguay. These allegations were believed, not only by the Rosistas and Blancos, but by many of the Unitarians in Montevideo. Similar allegations were made against Thiebaut. It is difficult to know whether these allegations were as false in Thiebaut's case as they were in Garibaldi's, because Thiebaut has not had a succession of contemporary and posthumous biographers who were determined to vindicate his reputation. The anti-French feelings of Garibaldi's admirers made them unwilling to say anything good about Thiebaut and the French Legion; and Dumas was too much of a Pachecist to undertake the task after Pacheco had quarrelled with Thiebaut.

Garibaldi was not only determined to sacrifice his own personal interests, and those of his wife and family, but also insisted that his Legionaries should follow his example of self-sacrifice. When the French and Italian Legions were first formed in 1843, the government of Montevideo decided that instead of paying wages to the Legionaries they would recompense them by granting them lands in Uruguay after the war. In May 1843 a government decree, which was approved by the National Assembly, gave to each soldier in the French and Italian Legions sixty square miles of land in three of the most fertile regions of the republic, all of which were at the time in territory occupied by Oribe, as well as 25,000 head of cattle for each man. The measure aroused some muted criticism in Montevideo. On 17 July 1843 the *Nacional* published on its front page a long letter from a reader, which was reprinted on the following days in other Montevidean newspapers. The writer, who signed himself 'A friend of the Legionaries', pretended that he approved of the grant, but used statistics and arithmetic to show that the extent of the nation's gratitude to the brave Legionaries was so great that it had given them nearly all the land in Uruguay.[14]

In January 1845 Rivera sent an envoy from his headquarters in Northern Uruguay to Montevideo. Among other letters he carried one for Garibaldi, offering to give each soldier of the Italian Legion some land in Northern Uruguay. The Italian Legionaries were Pacheco's strongest supporters in his struggle for power with Rivera, and Rivera may have been hoping, by this gift, to win over the Italian Legionaries to his side. Garibaldi refused the offer with thanks in a letter to Rivera of 23 March. He told him that everyone in the Italian Legion believed 'that it is the duty of every free man to fight for freedom wherever it is attacked by tyranny, without distinction between land and peoples, because freedom is the patrimony of all humanity'. They therefore refused to accept any reward for performing their duty in fighting for the freedom of Montevideo.[15]

Garibaldi expressed his sincerest beliefs in this letter, but his action was open to misrepresentation. This was doubtless the reason why the letter was not published in any of the Montevidean newspapers. As the land had already been given to the Italians by law in May 1843, Garibaldi and his officers were hardly in a position to refuse to accept it on the Legion's behalf; and the French Legionaries would not have been too pleased if this example of self-sacrifice by the Italian Legionaries had become widely known. Garibaldi always tended to suffer the fate of a noble-minded idealist in a world of self-seeking cynics, and found that his most praiseworthy actions were resented and sneered at as self-advertising humbug by people who wished to have an excuse for not emulating him.

On 17 November 1843 Garibaldi and his men took part in the battle at Tres Cruces, outside Montevideo, which was afterwards described by Bartolomé Mitre in his famous article 'A Trojan Episode'. Mitre was an Argentine Unitarian who had come to Montevideo as a refugee, and at the age of twenty-two was serving as a major in the Army of the Capital. He later became one of the commanders of the army which overthrew Rosas at the Battle of Monte Caseros in 1852, and the greatest Liberal President of Argentina in the nineteenth century. Mitre met Garibaldi for the first time in 1841, soon after Garibaldi arrived in Montevideo from Rio Grande do Sul, at a party which was being held for the Italians in Montevideo. Garibaldi joined in the singing of patriotic Italian songs, singing the Hymn of Young Italy in his soft and vibrant tenor voice; but he drank nothing but plain water at the party, and ate bread which he dipped in garlic in the Genoese fashion. Mitre saw Garibaldi a second time during the siege of Montevideo, when Garibaldi was in action in one of his ships against Brown's squadron; and on 17 November 1843 he met him for the third and last time at the headquarters of the Italian Legion in the front line at

Montevideo. It is strange that the two men never met again, because in 1843 they were only just beginning a political and personal association which was carried on by correspondence, and which continued in spirit until the day in 1904 when Mitre unveiled a statue to Garibaldi in the Plaza Italia in Buenos Aires, not more than half a mile from the site of Rosas's palace at Palermo.*

Mitre has given a description of Garibaldi's appearance on this last occasion, on 17 November 1843, when Garibaldi was aged thirty-six. He was short and stocky, with the rounded shoulders and rolling walk of a sailor, and with his long red hair and beard looked like the traditional pictures of Christ. Like so many other observers, Mitre thought that his eyes were blue, though in fact they were brown.[16] He states that Garibaldi had not yet adopted the red shirt as a uniform for himself and his men, but wore a uniform consisting of a blue frock-coat without any insignia of rank, with a high military collar and a double row of gold buttons which were always buttoned up from top to bottom. He wore a tall cylindrical white beaver hat, which he would wave in the air at critical moments during a battle.

Anzani had decided that it was necessary to impose some summary field punishments on certain soldiers of the Italian Legion who had committed offences against military discipline. He knew that Garibaldi was too kind-hearted to punish them suitably, so he sent him out of the room, saying to him: 'Go away! this is no job for you.' This gave Mitre the opportunity to talk to Garibaldi, and he jotted down his recollections at the time in his army notebook. Garibaldi expounded his political doctrines, telling Mitre that the evils which were afflicting South America could only be remedied by new revolutions and new wars. Mitre thought that Garibaldi was a passionate Republican with 'a head and heart in disequilibrium', a 'true hero in flesh and blood, with a sublime ideal, who had exaggerated and misdirected ideas about liberty, but who contained the elements necessary to achieve great things'. If Mitre really noted this down at the time, and his conclusions were not re-written for publication in 1888, they are an extraordinarily shrewd analysis of Garibaldi's character for a young man of twenty-two to have made.

Suddenly, at about twelve noon, the trumpet for action sounded, because fighting had broken out in a sector of the front line near the place called Tres Cruces, which was about half-way between the centre of Montevideo and Oribe's headquarters at the Cerrito. The leader of the Montevideans on that sector of the line was Colonel Neira, a Spaniard by birth, who had emigrated to Argentina as a child and had

*After the overthrow of Rosas in 1852, the palace was pulled down, stone by stone, by the victorious Unitarians.

fought against the British at Buenos Aires in 1806 and 1807. He later became a naturalized citizen of Uruguay, and now, at the age of sixty, was playing an active part in the defence of Montevideo. He was a very popular figure with the Montevidean troops, as he sat on his black horse, with his abundant white hair and beard, and his red cloak. On this occasion, he led a detachment against a fortified position in the enemy lines, and his men carried it by storm and wiped out the unit that had been holding it; but Neira himself was killed in the fight. His men started to carry back his body to their lines, but were attacked by another band of enemy soldiers, who tried to snatch Neira's corpse from them. Neira's soldiers, thinking that if the Rosistas and Blancos captured the corpse they would mutilate it, like they had so recently mutilated the bodies of the prisoners on 7 October, fought fiercely to retain the corpse.

When Garibaldi was told of what was happening, he went at once to the rescue, accompanied by a small number of his men. They were getting the best of it when enemy reinforcements arrived; but Garibaldi ordered his men to fix bayonets, and, waving his sabre in his right hand and his white hat in his left, urged them to fight to the death to prevent the body of the gallant Neira from falling into enemy hands. Colonel Cesar Diaz, who was soon to become a general and one of the key figures in the defence of Montevideo, arrived with reinforcements for Garibaldi; but more reinforcements arrived from the Cerrito for Oribe's men, and both sides sent more and more reinforcements until about 1,500 men were engaged on each side. After fighting had continued, with muskets and bayonets, for more than an hour, Oribe's men retreated, leaving Neira's corpse in the hands of his comrades. Before the Montevideans had succeeded in reaching their lines with the corpse, another enemy force appeared; but they were driven off by the guns of the Montevidean artillery.

This fight over Neira's corpse, with more and more warriors joining in on both sides as neither would abandon their prey, reminded Mitre of the story in the *Iliad* of the fighting over the body of Patroclus, and inspired him to call his account of the battle 'A Trojan Episode'.[17] It was the biggest action between the armies on the Montevidean front during 1843.

Next year Garibaldi was involved in two other major engagements on land. He led the Italian Legion on 28 March 1844, when General Paz launched an attack from the Cerro on the village of Miguelete, which was the centre of Oribe's civil administration. The Legion fought a fierce action against the enemy troops at the ford of La Boyada, when the Legionaries were trying to cross the little River Miguelete. As usual in this war in which propaganda played such an important part, both sides claimed the victory. The Unitarians failed to capture Miguelete, and the Rosistas claimed that they had repulsed the attack; but General Nuñez, who had deserted from Montevideo at the beginning of the siege, and had become one of Oribe's senior commanders, was killed in the fighting.[18]

A month later, Garibaldi and his Legion were again in action in the fighting on 24 April, when Paz launched a combined attack from the Cerro and from Montevideo in an attempt to encircle a large part of Oribe's army. The Italians played a leading part in the fighting near the Cerro, while Thiebaut and the French Legion attacked at Tres Cruces from the city. Garibaldi took an enemy strong-point in a meat-salting factory in the village of Machado, and held it against the enemy counter-attacks; but the Unitarians did not achieve their main object, and again both sides claimed the victory.[19]

Garibaldi was dividing his time between fighting on land and on sea, and whenever there was no important land action to be fought he was with the navy, helping the blockade-runners, and trying to enforce a counter-blockade of the Buceo. He had a number of naval successes in August 1844, when he captured ten Argentine merchant ships in the River Plate, and brought them back to Montevideo with their cargoes of flour, timber and straw. On the night of 20 August he captured two Argentine ships, the *Josefina* and the *Juanita*, off Punta Carretas, near Montevideo. He found a sailor on the *Josefina* who was a deserter from a Unitarian regiment which had been stationed at Soriano, and he handed him over to the authorities at Montevideo. The man was sentenced to death by court martial, but Garibaldi interceded for him, and he was pardoned by President Suarez and returned to his regiment. One of the ships which Garibaldi captured was a Spanish vessel, the *Rosario*, which was found, on investigation, not to have contravened the regulations of the government of Montevideo prohibiting trade with Oribe's territory. The *Rosario* was therefore returned to her owners.

On the night of 25 August, a small detachment of the French Legion made a daring and successful raid on the enemy port of the Buceo, returning to the harbour of Montevideo at 3 am on the 26th with the Argentine merchant ship the *Maria Ana* and a considerable amount of equipment and provisions which they had seized in the Buceo. On another occasion, Garibaldi made a raid on the Buceo, and seized a merchant ship, *La Paloma*, which was owned by a Frenchman living at Paysandú who had been trading with Oribe's territory. Garibaldi turned the *Paloma* into his flagship, and renamed her the *28 de Marzo* after the battle at the ford of La Boyada on 28 March 1844.[20]

Most of these attacks on enemy shipping took place at night; but one of them, on 18 September 1844, was by day, when Garibaldi, with a flotilla of his small ships, fought a running battle with two Argentine warships, the *Chacapuco* and the *Palmar*, which he pursued for four hours in full view of the cheering spectators on the sea-front at Montevideo. By his audacity in these sea-fights, 'the valiant Colonel Garibaldi' won as much praise in Montevideo as 'the pirate Garibaldi' won abuse in Buenos Aires. But the greatest damage to both the hostile navies was caused, not by each other, but by the hurricane, the *pampero*, which in May 1844 blew for twenty-four hours with such force that it completely stopped all naval operations by both sides and destroyed a large quantity of friendly, enemy and neutral shipping. At the height of the storm, Garibaldi took charge of the rescue operations, and his men brought many people to safety, including the crew of a ship from Rio Grande do Sul which was in danger at the entrance to the harbour at Montevideo.[21]

Garibaldi's successes against Argentine shipping made the Rosistas very angry, and articles denouncing him appeared more frequently than before in their newspapers. The *Gaceta Mercantil* and the *British Packet* wrote that 'horrible crimes drove him from Italy, and from the gaols of Brazil he brought his horrible "arts" to the Rio de la Plata'. But a correspondent of the *British Packet*, who had watched his warships in action in the winter of 1843, wrote a less bitter description of him in a doggerel verse which the paper published:

> Costa Brava's brave son was seen in advance,
> His left bore a cutlass, his right grasped a lance.
> To view his red whiskers, Oh! horrid to tell!
> He seemed like a Demon emerging from Hell.[22]

The conditions during the siege, and the Radical sympathies of so many of the active elements among the defenders of the city, led the government to take many steps in advance of their time. After the *Patriote Français* had declared that it was intolerable that profiteers should be exploiting the people at a time when the soldiers were dying for their country and the cause of freedom, decrees were promulgated to control the price and uphold the quality of bread and other foodstuffs. A system of free state education was introduced for all children of serving soldiers. The cultural life of Montevideo flourished during the siege, with actors and opera singers performing at the Teatro de Comercio in the Calle 1 de Mayo, very close to Garibaldi's house, sometimes at special performances for the French or Italian Legionaries at which the proceeds went to the hospitals and to buying comforts for the troops. The medical services for the soldiers were much better than the services which prevailed in European armies before the days of

Florence Nightingale. In the hospital of the French Legion, the death rate was only about 15 per cent, as compared with the 40 per cent death rate in the hospitals at Scutari ten years later at the beginning of the Crimean War.[23]

The French hospital had been paid for by the contributions of the French residents in Montevideo for the use of the French Legionaries; but the wounded and sick Italian Legionaries, who did not have a hospital of their own, were cared for in the French hospital. In April 1844 Garibaldi wrote a letter of thanks to Thiebaut, which was published in the *Patriote Français,* in which he praised the nurses in the hospital, 'those sublime ladies who, trampling on the usual repugnance of their sex, have resigned themselves to the most painful duties, and have poured the balm of their consoling exhortations into the hearts of the children of an unhappy land [Italy] as well as into those of the sons of a country more favoured by Heaven [France]'. He promised the French that 'on the day of danger, the Italians will see in you their brothers, and cursed be he amongst us who will abandon you to the danger'.[24] Despite the bitter disillusionment of 1849, Garibaldi fulfilled this promise in 1870.

The organization of the hospital depended to a considerable extent on the voluntary efforts of nurses and other women helpers. This side of the arrangements was directed by the Philanthropical Society of Oriental Ladies, under the chairmanship of Rivera's wife, Doña Bernardina de Rivera. Her committee, which met regularly at Rivera's house in the Calle Zabala, issued appeals for aid which were signed by the wives of prominent personages in Montevideo, and published long lists of women whom the committee thanked for helping in the hospital or for sending money and comforts to the troops. One notable absentee from the committee, and from these lists, was Anita Garibaldi. As the wife of the Commander of the Naval Forces of the Republic, one would have expected Anita to have been a member of Doña Bernardina's committee, and in any case to have helped in some way, like so many of the women of Montevideo. She was occupied in keeping house, and in looking after her children, for she could not afford a servant, and now had three children under five – Menotti, Rosita and Teresita; but even if she could never find a baby-sitter, or make time to walk a hundred yards to Rivera's house to attend a meeting of Doña Bernardina's committee, she could have lent her name, and added her signature, to the activities and statements of the committee.

But Anita may have been cold-shouldered by the native-born, upper-class ladies who sat on the committee. Many of the regular army officers disliked the foreign Legionaries, and their wives may well have disliked the foreign peasant girl from Morrinhos. According to some of

Garibaldi's friends who knew Anita in Montevideo, she suffered from a feeling of inferiority and resentment towards the polished society ladies, and was very jealous because so many of these ladies were interested in Garibaldi. She made no attempt to hide her anger whenever she saw Garibaldi talking to any of these women.[25] This may have upset her so much that she did not respond to any of the appeals of Doña Bernardina's committee; or perhaps she found such activity too tame after her experiences in Brazil.

Despite her occasional outbursts of jealousy, Anita was a close companion and a great help to Garibaldi, who paid tribute to this side of her activities in Montevideo in the short biographical note about her which he wrote for Dwight when he was in New York in 1850.

> Anna, although superior to the trials and dangers of war, was amiable in domestic life. She assisted and consoled me in adverse fortune, in the trying circumstances which we endured in the capital of the Republic of Uruguay. During all the time I remained in the service of it, she left the city but seldom, taking no part in military operations, and devoting herself to the care of the family.

Apart from riding out on her horse in the evenings to meet Garibaldi when he returned to Montevideo with the Legion from the lines outside the town, Anita played no part in Garibaldi's campaigns.[26] It is interesting to note that, whether this is a coincidence or otherwise, Anita never actually fought in any battle except those which took place on the soil or in the harbours of her native province of Santa Catarina. In Rio Grande do Sul, and afterwards in Italy, she accompanied Garibaldi on his campaigns, but did not fight herself. In Montevideo she stayed at home and looked after the children.

The enthusiasm and self-sacrifice of the population of Montevideo, of which Dumas wrote so brilliantly, was one side of the story; but there was another side which he did not mention. Some of the citizens of Montevideo were secret supporters of Oribe, and though many of the Blancos left the city at the beginning of the siege, and others were expelled from time to time, a certain number still remained, and caused anxiety to the government. Pacheco and Lamas warned the people to be on their guard against enemy agents; but considering the severities of Rosas and Oribe, and the French revolutionary traditions of 1793, which meant so much to Pacheco and to the French Legionaries, it is remarkable that the government of Montevideo refrained from the widespread use of revolutionary tribunals and the firing squad to deal with the enemy in their midst. There was only one execution for treason in Montevideo in the whole course of the war, and this occurred at the height of the popular indignation after the mutilated corpses of the prisoners had been found between the lines on 7 October 1843. Pacheco was chiefly responsible for this execution, though the Rosista and Blanco press tried to throw the blame on Garibaldi.

In May 1843 Lamas had received reports which made him suspicious of the loyalty of Luis Baena, a wealthy native-born Uruguayan business man who had intimate commercial and social contacts with the foreign business community in Montevideo. Lamas recommended that Baena be expelled from Montevideo; but the foreign business men made representations on his behalf, and the government allowed him to stay. At the beginning of October Baena was overheard to say, in a conversation with a friend, that as soon as Oribe's army had entered Montevideo, the financial difficulties of the country would be solved. His words were reported to Pacheco, who summoned him to an interview but allowed him to go free, after warning him, in what the *Nacional* called a 'fatherly' way, that his offence deserved to be punished by death. A few days later – only three days after the discovery of the mutilated corpses on 7 October – Baena wrote to a friend in Oribe territory 'that the Cerrito was a monument of death and extermination for all those who plot against the legal government', and that 'the cursed foreigners were expiating their crimes'.

Baena tried to smuggle these letters out of Montevideo by sea; but his courier was stopped by one of Garibaldi's ships, and the letter was brought to Garibaldi. Garibaldi reported the matter to Pacheco, who ordered that Baena should be arrested. Pacheco offered to pardon Baena if he confessed his crime; but as Baena protested his innocence, Pacheco sent him for trial before a military court which convicted him of treason and sentenced him to death. Baena's friends then made every effort to obtain a reprieve, and the foreign business community offered the government a large sum of money if the death sentence were commuted. The government, which as usual was in serious financial difficulties, would have found the money useful; but the foreign merchants' offer decided Pacheco that the death sentence must be carried out, and he persuaded the government to reject the offer, and to declare that in the Oriental Republic of the Uruguay the rich were as much subject to the law as the poor. Baena was shot at 7 am on 17 October 1843.[27]

The Rosista and Blanco press was very indignant at the execution of Baena, and alleged that the letters which he was accused of writing had in fact been forged. They emphasized the part which Garibaldi had played in the affair in order to make out that respectable Uruguayans were being put to death by the foreigners in Montevideo. The *British Packet* wrote that Baena 'was denounced by the Italian proscript, Garribaldi', and that 'the denaturalized mercenaries peremptorily demanded the head of the accused'. The *British Packet* was outraged that the firing squad which executed Baena was composed of foreigners and former negro slaves.[28]

Next year the Oribe agents had their greatest success, when they persuaded the Commander and Deputy-Commander of the Italian Legion, Colonel Mancini and Major Danuzio, to desert to Oribe. Though Mancini and Danuzio made out that they had done this because of their admiration for Oribe and their disgust at the state of things in Montevideo, the Montevideans were convinced that they had been bribed with offers of money. A study of Oribe's private correspondence shows that this was indeed so, and that Oribe took a keen personal interest in the plot; eight days before Mancini and Danuzio deserted, one of Oribe's secret agents in Montevideo wrote to Oribe that he had received the 2,000 pesos for Mancini and Danuzio.[29]

On 28 June 1844 Mancini and Danuzio ordered the Italian Legion to occupy an enemy advance-post which they said had been abandoned by the enemy. The Legionaries stealthily approached the Blanco defences without being fired on; but when they reached the enemy lines, Mancini harangued his men, told them that he and Danuzio were going over to the enemy, and urged all the Legionaries to come with him. Only a few of the 600 Legionaries in the party followed Mancini; the rest refused, and some of them opened fire on the deserters, and made their escape back to their own lines under the fire of Oribe's soldiers, who, by prior arrangement with Mancini, were waiting to receive the deserters.

According to Garibaldi's order of the day to the Italian Legion, and the Montevidean newspapers, only 9 other Legionaries followed Mancini and Danuzio. The *British Packet* claimed that 35 had come over – 11 officers and 24 other ranks – though it admitted that 'the rest of the corps were, through some mismanagement, prevented from following the example of their comrades'. Lieutenant Odinici, the Legion's medical officer, noted in his diary that 11 officers, whom he named, took 14 other ranks with them; and six months later, the *Patriote Français* stated that 33 former members of the Italian Legion were fighting for Oribe. But if Garibaldi understated the number of the deserters, he could justly boast that all but a handful had remained loyal under very difficult circumstances. Next day, the treacherous Legionaries presented themselves in the front line of Oribe's army and appealed to their former comrades to join them; but the loyal Legionaries replied by opening fire on them.

Danuzio issued a statement, which the Blanco army printed on leaflets and scattered in the Montevidean lines, appealing to all the soldiers of the Italian Legion to desert to Oribe, who, he said, was certain to win the war, and whom he praised in such lavish terms that it must have been obvious to everybody that the statements had been drafted by Oribe's propaganda experts. At Pacheco's direction, the Montevidean newspapers published the text of the leaflet in order to show that the press of Montevideo was free, and that they had no need to suppress the lying propaganda of the enemy, since no one in Montevideo would believe it. They also published Garibaldi's order of the day to the Italian Legion, in which Garibaldi said that the traitors' desertion had only strengthened the Italian Legion, because it was better to have open enemies than hidden enemies in their midst.[30]

Thiebaut, who was perhaps worried that the desertions might cause friction between his men and the Italians, immediately made a gesture of support for Garibaldi. On the morning of 29 June he called a meeting of his officers, and proposed that they should pass a resolution of sympathy for Garibaldi, and that one of them should take a copy of the resolution to Garibaldi's house. One of the officers then suggested that they should all go, and all the officers of the French Legion arrived at Garibaldi's house, where Thiebaut presented him with the resolution and expressed their sympathy and respect for him and for the brave Italian Legion. Garibaldi was very moved, and thanked them in a short speech in which he praised the French Legion. The incident was well publicized in the *Patriote Français*.[31]

A fortnight later, Oribe's *Defensor de la Independencia Americana*, and the *Gaceta Mercantil* in Buenos Aires, published another statement by Danuzio and one by Mancini which, unlike the first statement which Danuzio issued after his desertion, was not published in the Montevidean press. They declared that in view of the attacks which Garibaldi had made on them, they must state, in reply, that Garibaldi was a worthless character, and that one of the reasons why they had joined Oribe was that they were ashamed to serve under a man like Garibaldi. Both Mancini and Danuzio wrote about Garibaldi in the most violent terms. Mancini stated that when Garibaldi first arrived in Rio de Janeiro, he set up in business as a butcher, but lost so much money that he decided to turn corsair; he borrowed the money which he needed to equip his ship from an old man with a large family, whom he promised to repay, but afterwards refused to do so, even when the old man wrote to beg him to repay the money as he and his family were in dire poverty. Mancini made an even more serious accusation against Garibaldi. When Garibaldi was serving with the so-called Republicans in Rio Grande do Sul, he had 'committed a crime which no man could commit unless he was as immoral and corrupted a pirate as Garibaldi; he had persecuted an honourable man, forcibly abducting his wife, whom he afterwards married in Montevideo'.

Danuzio, in his statement, accused Garibaldi of obtaining 6,000 pesos for his expedition to Corrientes by false promises that he would repay the money. He stated that Garibaldi received a large sum of money every month which he kept for himself while the soldiers of the Italian Legion had no clothes and went barefoot. On one occasion, a soldier of the Legion lost 4½ oz of gold in gambling with another soldier, and refused to pay the debt. The winner complained to his officer, who asked Garibaldi to investigate the matter; and Garibaldi ordered the loser to pay 2 oz to the winner, and kept the other 2½ oz for himself. Danuzio also asserted that Garibaldi kept a ship permanently ready in the harbour of Montevideo in which he and his family could escape to Marseilles.[32]

The Montevidean cause suffered more from internal dissension among its leaders than from the desertion of the commanders of the Italian Legion. The quarrel between the followers of Rivera and those of Pacheco y Obes was becoming increasingly serious. Two years earlier, Rivera had been the hero of all the Unitarians; but his complete inactivity since his defeat at Arroyo Grande had weakened his position. Ever since the beginning of the siege, the Montevidean newspapers had been encouraging the citizens by telling them that Rivera's army was coming to the rescue, that he was harrying Oribe's flank, and that one day soon the people of Montevideo would see his advance-guard; but he never came, and the people began to lose confidence in him when he made no attempt to relieve Montevideo. Meanwhile Pacheco had been appointed Commander-in-Chief of the Army of the Capital as well as Minister of War and Marine. The Prime Minister, Vazquez, and several members of the government resented Pacheco's influence; and in September 1844 they received a letter from Rivera urging them to get rid of him.[33] Their opportunity came in November, when Garibaldi once again caused an international incident with Brazil.

Brazil, like Britain, France and the United States, had sent war-ships to Montevideo to protect her nationals during the fighting in the River Plate. The squadron was commanded by its English Admiral, Grenfell, who had become Commander-in-Chief of the Brazilian navy. Some of Grenfell's men landed at Montevideo on shore leave, and three of them did not return to their ships. Grenfell discovered that they had enlisted in Garibaldi's navy. Garibaldi had several deserters from other navies among his men, because the discipline in his ships was less rigorous, and the prospects of enrichment greater, than in the more regular navies of other states; but Grenfell alleged that a sailor named Ravena had not deserted, but had been kidnapped, when he was drinking in an inn in Montevideo, by one of Garibaldi's officers,

Lieutenant Botero. Botero claimed that Ravena had deserted from the Brazilian navy a month before, and had voluntarily enlisted in the Montevidean navy, but had then also deserted from the Montevidean navy, and had been arrested in the inn as a deserter.

Grenfell sent an officer to Garibaldi, who was in his flagship the *28 de Marzo* in the harbour of Montevideo, and peremptorily demanded the return of the three Brazilian sailors. Garibaldi refused to hand them over. Grenfell then sent him an ultimatum that unless the men were handed over within an hour, he would open fire on Garibaldi's ships. Garibaldi ordered his men to action stations, trained his guns on the Brazilian squadron, and told Grenfell that he rejected the ultimatum and was ready for battle. This dissuaded Grenfell from carrying out his threat; but he informed the Brazilian Minister in Montevideo, who ordered Grenfell to take no action while he raised the matter with Vazquez.

Garibaldi had not consulted his government before calling Grenfell's bluff; but his action was endorsed by the Minister of War and Marine, Pacheco, who came on board Garibaldi's flagship and enthusiastically supported him. Pacheco sent a defiant note from the *28 de Marzo* to Grenfell, refusing to hand over the Brazilian seaman, accusing Grenfell of insulting the Uruguayan flag, and threatening to answer force with force. But the Montevidean government was in a difficult position. They did not wish to be involved in hostilities with Brazil, and knew that their position was weak in international law. Even if Grenfell's allegation about the pressganging of Ravena was untrue, and all the men concerned were deserters who had joined the Montevidean navy of their own free will, the Uruguayan government had signed a treaty with Brazil providing for the mutual surrender of all deserters from their navies. Vazquez therefore told the Brazilian Minister that though Grenfell had been wrong in threatening Garibaldi instead of raising the question through diplomatic channels, the government would comply with the Brazilian demand and hand over the sailors.

When Pacheco, who was still in Garibaldi's ship, heard that the government had given way, he wrote an angry note to Vazquez and President Suarez, accusing them of having betrayed the country by their cowardly surrender to Brazil, and resigning in protest from the government. His resignation was accepted, and General Bauzá was appointed Minister of War and Marine in his place.

The resignation of Pacheco split the Army of the Capital to a dangerous extent. The supporters of Rivera, and the more Conservative of the native Uruguayan officers, were pleased; but the French and Italian Legionaries, and the more Radical elements in the native units, were indignant. Next day, on 9 November, seven high-ranking officers – General Bauzá, Garibaldi, Cesar Diaz, Colonel Flores, Colonel Estivao and two other colonels – called on Vazquez and asked him to reinstate Pacheco. But Thiebaut was a notable absentee from the deputation; and on the same day he issued an order of the day to the French Legion, in which he stated that though the Legionaries deplored Pacheco's resignation, they would accept it in the public interest. This was an important success for the government, and they achieved another next day, when they won over Flores, who on 10 November issued an order of the day emphasizing the need for unity in the army and loyalty to the government.

The Italian Legion was under suspicion, because of the known friendship of Garibaldi for Pacheco. A special performance had been planned for the Italian Legion at the Teatro de Comercio on Sunday 10 November, when Donizetti's *Lucia di Lammermoor* and his *Elisir d'amore*, and Rossini's *Barber of Seville*, were to be performed; and, as if this were not enough for one evening's entertainment, Señora Teresa Lanaro was to sing the Italian Hymn between the operas. But a few hours before the show was due to begin, the theatre management announced that it had been banned by order of higher authority. In the nineteenth century, revolutions sometimes started with theatrical or operatic performances.

On the morning of 12 November, three leaders of the National Guard, Muñoz, Batlle and Solsona, called on President Suarez and demanded that Pacheco be reinstated. The government thereupon ordered Flores to arrest Muñoz and Pacheco. Pacheco was placed on board the French warship, *L'Africaine*, and taken to Rio de Janeiro, being ostensibly sent there on a diplomatic mission, though he protested against the appointment and asked to be allowed to serve in the army as a common soldier. The government issued a number of emergency decrees reminding the people of the laws against treason and threatening to enforce them against anyone who resisted the government; but there was no more resistance, and no further arrests, and on the following Sunday, 17 November, the government allowed the performance for the Italian Legion to take place at the Teatro de Comercio.[34]

The events of November 1844 brought the split among the defenders of Montevideo into the open, and exacerbated it. As well as a split between Rivera and Pacheco, there was now a split between the French and Italian Legions. The *Patriote Français* of 14 November stressed its respect for Pacheco; but the Italians felt that the French had betrayed him. On 10 November Odinici noted in his diary that nearly all the heads of battalions opposed the removal of Pacheco from the Ministry of War and the command of the troops, except

Thiebaut, who had been 'won over by the shameful Colorado party who wish to make the Oriental State the patrimony of Rivera'.[35]

The Rosistas and Blancos made the most of the division among their enemies, and tried to throw mud at them all indiscriminately. The *British Packet*, after first reporting that Garibaldi had gone into exile with Pacheco, later sneered at him for abandoning Pacheco after having been responsible for the clash with the Brazilian navy which led to Pacheco's resignation. 'Garribaldi, it seems,' they wrote on 23 November, 'after having got his hot-headed patron into a scrape, very chivalrously abandoned him to his fate, when he saw Flores determined on supporting Vazquez.' But Oribe's *Defensor* was prepared to give Garibaldi and the Italians the credit for maintaining honour among thieves, while they accused Thiebaut of having been won over to support the government by a gift of 6,000 patacones. 'There was more decency, if indeed such a thing exists among the savage Unitarians of Montevideo, in the conduct of those men who call themselves Italian Legionaries'; and though eventually, as they were outnumbered ten to one by the forces under the orders of Thiebaut and Flores, Vazquez forced them to submit without it costing him what he had had to pay to Thiebaut, 'the Italians nevertheless did not dirty themselves this time by performing the task of Judas Iscariot'. Thiebaut strongly denied the charge, and the *Patriote Français* published the *Defensor*'s article in full, along with Thiebaut's denial.[36]

Rivera's best chance of consolidating his position in Montevideo, and of reuniting the Unitarians under his leadership, would have been to win a major victory against Rosas and Oribe. In March 1845 he fought his first pitched battle since his defeat at Arroyo Grande, at India Muerta in Northern Uruguay; but again he was decisively defeated, losing many killed, and many prisoners, who, like at Arroyo Grande, were despatched by the Rosista cut-throats after the battle. As the siege of Montevideo entered its third year, the defenders faced the enemy without any foreign ally, with their leaders engaged in a bitter struggle for power, with a large section of their army discontented but still undefeated, and with no thought of surrender.

CHAPTER 12

THE EXPEDITION TO SALTO

THE triumph of Vazquez and the pro-Rivera forces had been chiefly due to the decisive action which Flores had taken as soon as he was appointed Commander-in-Chief of the Army of the Capital. But within a month Vazquez and Flores had a violent personal quarrel, as a result of which Vazquez dismissed Flores from his post and appointed General Martinez as Commander-in-Chief in his place, with Colonel Cesar Diaz as his Chief of Staff. Cesar Diaz was a Radical and a supporter of Pacheco; and though Pacheco himself remained in exile in Rio de Janeiro, his supporters held important positions in the government and the army command. Vazquez had appointed General Bauzá as Minister of War and Marine; but Cesar Diaz had no respect for Bauzá, and, relying on the Prime Minister's support, disregarded the orders which he received from Bauzá. Diaz liked Garibaldi and hated Thiebaut, and just as he promoted and favoured Pacheco's supporters in the native army in preference to Rivera's, so he supported the Italian Legion against the French. He singled out the Italians for praise in his orders of the day, and made no mention of the French.

By March 1845 Thiebaut and the French Legionaries had become so angry with Cesar Diaz that they mutinied. Thiebaut said that he had been insulted because Diaz had ignored him in his orders of the day, and he refused to lead his men into the front line. The government could not charge 40 per cent of its army with mutiny, and could therefore only try to cajole the French into returning to duty. For six days the French refused to man the defences of the city, but were eventually persuaded to do so. The quarrel between Thiebaut and Diaz flared up again in July 1845, and Thiebaut challenged Diaz to a duel. He asked Garibaldi to carry his challenge to Diaz. Garibaldi succeeded in patching up the quarrel between Thiebaut and Diaz, and they did not fight a duel.[1] Despite the increasing ill-feeling between the French and the Italians, Garibaldi and Thiebaut remained on fairly good terms; and the French Legionaries' paper, the *Patriote Français*, whose editor, Delacour, was very radical, continued to give Garibaldi very favourable coverage.

The intervention of the foreign Legions in the power struggle in Montevideo increased the resentment against the foreigners, and Rosas's propaganda against them began to have its effect. Week after week, the Argentine and Oribe newspapers played on this theme: the unfortunate native population of Montevideo was living under the military rule of foreign mercenaries who terrorized them into submission. While the Rosistas and Blancos directed their propaganda indiscriminately against all the foreign volunteers, Rivera's supporters in Montevideo, and the more Conservative sections among the Unitarians, tended to overlook the misdeeds of the French, and to concentrate their hatred on Garibaldi and the Italians.

An interesting example of the attitude of a Conservative regular officer of the Uruguayan army can be found in the diary of General Tomas de Iriarte. Iriarte had had a long and distinguished career in the struggle for independence against Spain and the war against Brazil, and had been entrusted with the task of organizing the building of the fortifications of Montevideo when Oribe marched on the city. Although he had performed this vital duty with great speed and determination, he had nevertheless been retired from active service soon afterwards, and henceforth devoted his abundant energies to keeping a voluminous diary, in which he sometimes wrote as many as 15,000 words under one day's entry. The diary was not intended for publication, and was kept secret by his family for more than a hundred years till Señor Luis Iriarte Udaonda rendered a great service to historical studies by allowing it to be published. General Iriarte unburdened himself in his diary, and expressed hostile and uncharitable opinions about most of his brother-officers; but though he was obviously a sour and cantankerous man, he was very intelligent. He rarely gave praise, but he gave it when he felt it was due, and was shrewd enough to spot that young Major Mitre had exceptional ability and a brilliant future.

Iriarte did not at first show any hostility to Garibaldi. He made a favourable comment about him when he heard the news of Costa Brava, and in a number of entries during 1843 and 1844 he praised him for the courage and skill which he had shown in some naval action. But after the events of November 1844 Iriarte became increasingly hostile to Garibaldi, whom he regarded as the main support of Pacheco, whom Iriarte detested. He felt no gratitude to Garibaldi and the foreign volunteers who were risking their lives in the defence of Montevideo, but only resentment at their interference in the affairs of his country, and disgust because, as he frankly admitted, the freedom and safety of Montevideo depended on them, and not on his compatriots. As a regular soldier, he was shocked at the lack of discipline in the fleet and in the Italian Legion, and at Garibaldi's practice of accepting in the navy and the Legion not only criminals wanted by the police, and deserters from foreign warships, but also deserters from other units of the Montevidean army who preferred the rough camaraderie of Garibaldi's forces to the spit-and-polish discipline of the regular Uruguayan army.

> The armed foreigners [he wrote in his diary on 17 April 1845] continually abuse the impunity and toleration which is granted to them, and the Italians especially have acquired such a domination that the police leave them alone, in order to avoid worse troubles, and submit passively to their bloody brawls and to their daily and gratuitous insults. These men are coarse, cruel, and have acquired immoral habits through leading a life of adventure, and they respect no authority except that of their leader, Colonel Garibaldi.

Iriarte was roused to fury when he heard a rumour, in April 1845, that Garibaldi was being appointed to succeed Martinez as Commander-in-Chief of the Army of the Capital. He resented this, not only because Garibaldi was a foreigner, 'a low-born adventurer whose background and place of origin are unknown', but also because he objected to a naval man being put in charge of the army. He distrusted Garibaldi as a strong partisan of Pacheco. He thought that Pacheco had promised Garibaldi that after they had won the war he would provide Garibaldi with a warship in which he could take his Legion to Italy and make a revolution there. 'Garibaldi, who belongs to a secret society, Young Italy, which has a branch in Montevideo, and is volcanic and headstrong and drunk with enthusiasm, became a passionate supporter of Pacheco.'[2]

Iriarte's reference to Garibaldi's membership in 'a secret society, Young Italy', was nearer the truth than the comments of some of the other Uruguayans, both Blancos and Unitarians, about foreign secret societies. Many Uruguayans feared that these secret societies were exercising a sinister control over Montevideo. Some saw the hidden hand of Freemasonry behind Samuel Lafone and the foreigners. The Rosistas did not launch a determined campaign against the Freemasons, like that which developed in Argentina at the end of the nineteenth century, when Right-wing nationalists accused Mitre, Sarmiento and the Argentine Liberals of associating with Garibaldi in a great masonic conspiracy to subvert the freedom and contaminate the morals of the Argentine people; but on 28 November 1845 the *Gaceta Mercantil*, in an article about Garibaldi's past career which was surprisingly accurate, accused him of being 'one of the leaders of the masonic lodge'.[3]

Garibaldi had in fact joined the Montevidean lodge, which was known as *Les Amis de la Patrie* and had been formed by French immigrants in 1827 under the auspices of the French Freemasons of the *Grand Orient*. Garibaldi did not join until he had been living for more than three years in Montevideo, because of difficulties caused by his previous membership in the dissident Brazilian masonic organization, the *Asilo de la Virtud*, which he had joined in Rio de Janeiro; but on 18 August 1844 he was admitted as an apprentice mason by the *Amis de la Patrie*, after he had sworn an oath that he no longer had any connexion with the *Asilo de la Virtud*. Of the 33 members present at this meeting of the lodge, 24 were Frenchmen, most of them merchants. There were two Italians, and the others were Swiss, Belgian or Hungarian.[4]

In January 1845 Rosas decided to intensify the half-hearted blockade of Montevideo. Admiral Brown announced that henceforth ships of all nations would be stopped and searched when entering Montevideo, and that only postal packets in foreign warships would be allowed to proceed. This proved to be a blessing in disguise for Montevideo, because it tipped the scales for Peel and Aberdeen. The *rapprochement* between Britain and France led both powers to decide on a joint intervention in the River Plate, where the continuation of hostilities was interfering with their trade.

In April and May 1845 Mr William Gore Ouseley and Baron Deffaudis arrived in the River Plate with instructions to present Rosas and the Unitarians of Montevideo with a joint Anglo-French plan for ending the war, and to use the British and French military and naval contingents at Montevideo to impose the terms by force if Rosas rejected them. The proposals were that the Argentine troops should evacuate Uruguayan territory, that Brown's fleet should raise the blockade of Montevideo, and that Rosas should recognize the independence of Uruguay. Both Oribe and the government of Montevideo were to resign, and an impartial caretaker government was to supervise free elections, on a franchise limited to the middle classes, to the National Assembly, which should then decide whether Oribe or Rivera, or someone else, should become President of Uruguay.

Ouseley and Deffaudis went to Buenos Aires, where they met Rosas and his Foreign Minister, Arana. Rosas very willingly agreed to recognize the independence of Uruguay, which he had never officially disputed, but rejected the other proposals. The United States Minister in Buenos Aires, Brent, who was alarmed at the prospect of British and French intervention in South America, offered to mediate between Argentina and Britain and France. Ouseley and Deffaudis agreed to meet Brent and Arana, but after a few meetings they broke off the talks and left Buenos Aires for Montevideo. Brent issued a public statement placing the entire responsibility for the breakdown in the negotiations on Britain and France; but the United States government, as Aberdeen and Guizot had foreseen, took no further action, though the press in the United States denounced the European powers for violating the Monroe Doctrine.[5]

The British and French naval commanders, Admiral Inglefield and Admiral Lainé, had already acted against the Argentines. On 21 July they sent a note to Oribe demanding that he cease all military action against Montevideo while the Anglo-French peace proposals were being considered, and warning him that if he did not agree, they would take action against him. When Oribe indignantly rejected the ultimatum, Inglefield and Lainé surrounded and boarded Brown's ships. They told Brown to abandon the blockade, and required all British-born officers and men in his force, including the Admiral himself, to sign a declaration promising not to continue serving in the Argentine navy. Brown was quite prepared to sign, because he was aged sixty-eight and was already thinking of retiring, and when he returned to Buenos Aires he relinquished his command and resigned from active service. The British and French seized three of the Argentine ships, the *General San Martín*, the *General Echagüe* and the *Maipú*, and handed them over to Garibaldi. They allowed the other Argentine ships, and all the Argentine crews, to return to Buenos Aires.[6]

The Anglo-French intervention was warmly welcomed in Montevideo. Vazquez hastened to accept the British and French peace proposals, though perhaps only because he knew that Rosas had rejected them. Ouseley and Deffaudis now proceeded to work closely with the government of Montevideo. Brazil decided to join the strongest side, and after picking a quarrel with Argentina, withdrew their Minister from Buenos Aires on 17 August, and placed their warships in the River Plate at the disposal of the British and French admirals. According to Ouseley, the government of Montevideo placed Garibaldi and their navy, with Garibaldi's full approval, under the command of the British and French admirals; but there does not seem to have been any formal agreement to this effect with the Montevidean government. Garibaldi did not view his position in this light; and he both acted at the time, and wrote afterwards in his memoirs, as if he had an equal position and an independent command as regards Inglefield and Lainé.[7]

The strength of the British, French and Unitarian land forces in Uruguay was a little inferior to the total which Rosas and Oribe had at their disposal, for the British, French and Unitarian land forces amounted to about 15,000 men against Rosas and Oribe's 9,000 men in Uruguay, and the 3,000 which Rosas had in Entre-Rios and his reserve army of 12,000 in the province of Buenos Aires. But Britain and France had complete naval superiority. France had ten warships with a total of 2,230 men and 282 guns, and Britain also had ten warships with 1,310 men and 138 guns. The Brazilians had eight warships with 1,150 men and 146 guns.[8] The Brazilians did not, in fact, take any active part in operations; but Inglefield, Lainé and Garibaldi made their plans to attack Rosas and Oribe during the summer of 1845–6. An expedition consisting of five British and five French warships and the captured Argentine ship, the *San Martín*, sailed up the River Paraná as a gesture to show Rosas that they could enter his territorial waters at will. At Obligado, a little south of Gualeguay, the Argentine naval and land forces refused to let them pass, and a battle was fought in which the British and French were victorious, but the Argentines fought with a heroism which is still commemorated every year in Argentina on 20 November. After this, the Anglo-French squadron remained in the Paraná, thus putting a stop to Argentine trade with Paraguay.

A larger expedition was to sail up the River Uruguay, capture the ports held by Oribe on the left bank in Oriental territory, and to raid the towns in Entre-Rios on the right bank. This force was to consist of five British warships under Admiral Inglefield, five French warships under Admiral Lainé, and seventeen Montevidean ships under Garibaldi. In addition to the crews, Garibaldi's ships carried land forces. These amounted to about 750 men, of whom just over one-third were members of the Italian Legion, and the rest were native Uruguayan units. About half the Italian Legion went with Garibaldi, while the other half remained in Montevideo.[9]

Garibaldi was eager that Colonel Rodríguez, who later became a General, should accompany him on the expedition to the River Uruguay; but Rodríguez was serving with the Army of the Capital, and though he was eager to go, he was unable to get the transfer arranged in time. He came to Garibaldi's house late one afternoon to tell him so. Garibaldi was not in the least put out. He suggested to Rodríguez that they go for a walk together, and they set off, just as it was getting dark, and walked round from Garibaldi's house in the Calle 25 de Mayo to the Calle Buenos Aires, not far away, where President Suarez lived. Garibaldi asked to see Suarez, and he and Rodríguez spoke to the President, Garibaldi asking him to sign the necessary papers then and there to allow Rodríguez to be transferred to the Uruguay expedition. Suarez said that it would have to go through the Ministry of War and Marine. Garibaldi argued with Suarez, remaining quite calm and unruffled, though Rodríguez was surprised at the casual way in which he addressed the President of the Republic. 'You are getting very old, Don Joaquin,' he said to Suarez in a kindly voice. But Suarez insisted that it was a matter for Bauzá at the Ministry of War and Marine; so Garibaldi set off with Rodríguez, and walked back to the Calle Colon, where Bauzá lived. They found Bauzá, and after he had demurred a little, he signed the necessary order. Garibaldi went home contented, and Rodríguez was with his expedition when it sailed.[10]

By this time, the Italian Legionaries were dressed in the red shirts which afterwards became so famous as the uniform of Garibaldi's men in Italy. The so-called red 'shirt' was in fact a loose-hanging robe which reached to the knees and was worn outside the trousers; it had no buttons and had merely holes for the head and arms. It was fastened with a belt round the waist. Although the red shirt attracted a great deal of attention in Europe when Garibaldi and his men appeared in it, no one seems to have attached much importance to it in Uruguay. Apart from Mitre, who merely says that when he saw Garibaldi he was not yet wearing it, none of Garibaldi's contemporaries in South America make any mention of it, except for the British Admiral, Winnington-Ingram, who served in Montevideo as a young naval officer from 1845 to 1847.

Strangely enough, Winnington-Ingram is the only writer who has given any explanation of the origin of the red shirt, for neither Garibaldi himself nor Cuneo nor Jessie White Mario explains why Garibaldi adopted this strange uniform for his Legion. Winnington-Ingram states that when the Italian Legion was first formed, which was in May 1843, the Montevidean authorities wished to dress the Legionaries as cheaply as possible. They found a stock of the red overalls which were manufactured in Montevideo for export to Buenos Aires, where they were worn by the slaughterers who killed the cattle in the slaughter-houses at Ensenada. The garments were red, so that it mattered less if they were stained with the blood of the cattle. Because of the war and the blockade, it was no longer possible to export the garments, and they were therefore lying unused in the factory in Montevideo. The government therefore bought them as a uniform for the Italian Legion. Jessie White Mario states that the Legionaries wore them for the first time on 2 July 1843, at the victory parade after the fight at the Cerro, though Mitre says that Garibaldi was not wearing the red shirt at the battle over Neira's corpse in November 1843.[11]

The colour of the uniform is almost more remarkable than its strange shape, because of the political significance of red as a colour. Red had been vaguely associated with revolution ever since 1789, when the French revolutionaries had adopted the red cap of liberty; but it was not until 1848 that red became accepted everywhere in Europe as the emblem of the Socialists and the extreme Left wing, after the French Socialists had demanded that the red flag should replace the tricolour of the Liberal Republicans as the French national flag. In 1848 the designation 'Red Republican' for the extreme Left wing came into general use. When Garibaldi's men became famous and feared as one of the most formidable revolutionary bodies in Europe, some Continental Conservatives, either sincerely or mischievously, confused the red shirt of the Garibaldini with the red flag of the Socialists, though it never occurred to Garibaldi's admirers among the British aristocracy that there was the slightest connexion between them.

In South America, red also had a political significance, but a completely different one. In Argentina, Rosas had adopted red as his colour, because of its association with blood and the cattle-killing activity of his gaucho supporters, though it had an additional point through its connexion with Rosas's name. In Uruguay, on the other hand, the Liberal Colorados had been associated with red, as against the white of Oribe's Blancos. But when the Argentine soldiers, in their red Rosista caps, appeared at the gates of Montevideo, red went quite out of fashion with the Colorados, and the women of Montevideo were not eager to wear the colour which the women of Buenos Aires were compelled to wear in their hair by the threats of Rosas's murder gangs. The decision of the government of Montevideo to dress the Italian Legionaries in red was a triumph of parsimony over political prejudice.

On 30 August 1845 Inglefield and Lainé took up their positions off Colonia, and waited for Garibaldi, who arrived with his squadron during the night. Colonia, both then and now, was a charming town surrounded on two sides by the sea, with white, eighteenth-century houses built in the Spanish colonial style, which was well suited to the beautiful climate of the district. In peace time, it was the port from which ships sailed by the shortest sea-route from the Oriental Republic to Buenos Aires. Colonia had been held by Oribe's men ever since they captured it on the way to Montevideo in January 1843. Garibaldi summoned Colonel Montero, the commander of the garrison, to surrender; but Montero, who was perhaps influenced by the fact that, as a native-born Uruguayan, he was liable to be shot from the back as a traitor if he fell into enemy hands, refused to surrender. Garibaldi and the Anglo-French squadron then bombarded the town from the sea. The bombardment began at 7 am on 31 August, and continued for three hours, during which time 1,507 shells were fired at Colonia. The French ship, the *Ducouadic*, under Captain Page, fired on Garibaldi's men by mistake, and wounded several of them; but no one was killed. In all, Garibaldi had only five men wounded, one of whom was Rodríguez.

While the firing was going on, the garrison and most of the civilian population evacuated the town and retreated inland. Before leaving, some of the inhabitants set fire to their houses. Others carried their furniture and belongings into the street, and burned them, or abandoned them there. The Blancos claimed that the whole population had destroyed their property and fled, rather than fall into the hands of the savage Unitarians; the Unitarians said that the people had been forced by Oribe's soldiers to burn the property and then to accompany the retreating garrison. Garibaldi pursued the enemy into the fields outside the town. 'But when we were engaged in the open plain,' he wrote in his memoirs, 'and had obtained some advantage, in spite of the superior strength of the enemy, the Allies – for what reason I do not know – retired within the walls, and obliged us to do the same, being unable to continue the fight unsupported.' It is not very surprising that the British and French broke off the action at Colonia. Apart from the fact that most military commanders tended to be more cautious than Garibaldi, Britain and France were not fighting an all-out war against Rosas and Oribe, but were undertaking a limited intervention with naval forces and a very small number of land troops.

After the Allies had occupied Colonia, a good deal of looting took place. In the Dumas edition of the memoirs, Garibaldi states that he gave the strictest orders against looting and that 'needless to say, the Legionaries scrupulously obeyed my orders'. This must be an addition and a falsification by Dumas, because in all the other editions of the memoirs Garibaldi admits that some looting took place.

> Between the confusion of the fire and that of the ruins, it was difficult to keep up such discipline as to prevent all plundering; and the French and English soldiers, in spite of strict orders from the Admirals, did not fail to make use at their pleasure of the things left in the houses and in the streets. Our men, on their return, partly followed their example, in spite of all that the officers could do to restrain them. The repression of disorder was not easy, because Colonia was a place well supplied with every kind of provisions, especially with alcoholic liquors, which inflamed the unlawful inclinations of the plunderers. However, the most important of all the things which our men took were food and some mattresses, which they carried into the church where they were quartered, to sleep on; and these were, of course, left behind when we went away a few days later. But without the example of our allies, which our soldiers naturally followed, such excesses would have been avoided.[12]

The Argentine and Blanco press told a different story. They raised a storm of protest about the havoc caused by Garibaldi's men, who had engaged in wholesale looting at Colonia, and had then set fire to the town; and Garibaldi was strongly denounced in Parliament in Buenos Aires. Garibaldi's opponents in Montevideo were very ready to believe this enemy propaganda. Iriarte first heard about the events at Colonia from a deserter from the Blanco garrison who made his way to Montevideo. The deserter told him almost exactly the same story which Garibaldi later wrote in his memoirs, describing how they had found the inhabitants' furniture burning or abandoned in the streets in front of their houses; but though Iriarte at first believed this story, he was soon writing about the 'atrocities' committed by the 'cruel', 'wicked' Italians, and pitying the population of the places which they passed.[13]

The theme was taken up, after the usual three months' time-lag, by the pro-Rosas press in Europe. For tactical reasons, it was obviously wiser, in Britain and France, to omit all references to looting by the British and French contingents, and concentrate entirely on the excesses of Garibaldi's Italians. While the *Gaceta Mercantil*, writing for the Buenos Aires public, denounced the sack of Colonia 'by the Anglo-French pirates and Garibaldi's savage Unitarians', Rosas's English-language newspapers, and his friends in Britain and France, presented a picture of the British and French admirals looking on complacently while Garibaldi's pirates committed their atrocities under the protection of the British and French navies. An indignant MP raised the matter in the French Chamber of Deputies, where there was a full-scale debate in January 1846. In Hamburg, where trade with the River Plate was affected, the newspaper *Bursenhalle* condemned the Anglo-French action.

In Portugal, the *Restauracion* of Lisbon made its readers' flesh creep with its description of Garibaldi's conduct at Colonia:

> The beautiful church of Colonia, so clean with its recently whitewashed walls, as simple in its style as a village chapel, did not escape the outrages. The victorious Condottieri established themselves there; they slept upon the marble floor of the choir, hanging up their caps and cartridge-boxes on the blessed chandeliers; the vaults re-echoed the sound of muskets and swords which rolled on the floor in the midst of this* sacrilegious and profane shouts; the altar served as a table of orgies.

After describing the strange appearance of the soldiers, with their long and straight moustaches, their Sicilian capotes, their caps with flowing plumes, and their pistols and daggers hanging from their belts, the *Restauracion*'s reporter declared that 'these men, eating, drinking and playing the fruits of their plunder at dice, brought to mind an epoch fortunately forgotten in Europe'. Oribe's *Defensor* added the detail that the Unitarians had amused themselves, in the church at Colonia, by cutting the throat of the statue of the Virgin of the Carmen, alleging that she was a Rosista supporter.[14]

*Sic. This passage from the *Restauracion* of 18 September 1846 is given here in the English translation published in Rosas's *Archivo Americano* on 20 March 1847.

The *British Packet* sneered at the 'triple alliance' of Great Britain, France and 'Young Italy', and wrote that the trophies of Colonia 'are not destined to grace alone the *Hotel des Invalides* and St Paul's, as a new associate has been admitted in the person of the Genoese outlaw, Garibaldi'. They tried to explain away the fall of Colonia by the bare-faced lie that it had been an undefended town without a garrison, and compared the horrors at Colonia with the sack of San Sebastian during the Peninsular War. In their propaganda to Brazil, which had not yet played an active part in the campaign against Argentina, the Rosas press denounced the Brazilian government for making an alliance with the pirate Garibaldi, who only two years before had tried to assassinate their Minister in Montevideo. They also accused Garibaldi of being a Socialist.[15]

The Allies sailed away, leaving a small force of native Uruguayan soldiers under Colonel Lorenzo Batlle to hold Colonia. The Blancos thereupon returned to Colonia, and besieged it for several months; but Batlle held out successfully, and won most of his skirmishes with the besiegers. The intervention of Britain and France had changed the balance of forces, and the consequences were immediate. The desertions from the Montevidean army almost stopped, but an increasing number of Oribe's soldiers deserted to the Unitarians, both at Montevideo and at Colonia.[16]

Inglefield, Lainé and Garibaldi then turned their attention to Martín García. Colonel Crispo, the Argentine commander of the island fortress, did not wait for their arrival, but evacuated it on the morning of 5 September, retiring to San Nicolás in the River Paraná, and leaving only one officer and 19 wounded soldiers on Martín García. Later on the same day, some of Garibaldi's ships and one French warship arrived and took possession of Martín García; and next day Inglefield and Lainé arrived with five more warships. The Argentine officer and the 19 wounded soldiers were put on board the British warship, the *Dolphin*, and taken to Buenos Aires. On 7 September Garibaldi himself arrived, and set foot on the rock from which he had been shelled on his expedition to the Paraná three years before. At the same time, the Argentines evacuated the Island of Flores, off the Buceo to the east of Montevideo.[17]

Garibaldi left a garrison of 14 men to hold Martín García, and set off up the River Uruguay. On 8 September he reached the island of Viscaino, where he found five small Argentine vessels. He sent the *Juanita* back to Montevideo laden with 1,550 hides, abandoned the *Emilia* and the *San Vicente*, and sailed on up the Uruguay, taking the *Manuelita* and the *Juan Isabel* with him as extra transport ships. On the same day he reached Yaguari, where he met a sergeant and two men from the force of Juan de la Cruz Ledesma, who, ever since Rivera's defeat at India Muerta in March, had been conducting guerrilla activities behind Oribe's lines; and some days later, they found Juan de la Cruz himself hiding up a tree. At Yaguari, Garibaldi heard stories, which were all too true, of the ill-treatment to which the Rosistas and Blancos were subjecting the French and British settlers and their families, who until now had been living peacefully in Entre-Rios and in the areas of Uruguay which Oribe held. They were being arrested and interned as enemy aliens, and in many cases treated with great brutality. 'The enemy,' wrote Garibaldi to Bauzá, 'have committed atrocities which horrify against the patriotic foreigners.' By 'patriotic foreigners', Garibaldi meant the foreign residents who sympathized with the Unitarian cause. But some of them, at least, had been rescued by the 'sons of heroism', as he called the soldiers under his command.[18]

At Yaguari, Garibaldi heard that a force of 20 enemy infantry, escorted by 18 cavalrymen, were in the neighbourhood, marching inland with a number of foreign civilians who were being taken to an internment camp. He pursued them, attacked them, and after killing 24 of the guards, took the remaining 14 guards, 8 of whom had been wounded, as prisoners, and freed the internees. A few days later, he was informed that another small party of foreigners from Mercedes had been brought under guard to the River Uruguay, and were now in a launch on the river, being carried off to internment in Entre-Rios. He sent five of his Italians to seize the launch. They boarded her, threw the captain into the river, along with all the guards who resisted, took the other guards prisoner, and released the internees.[19]

In his operations along the River Uruguay, Garibaldi drew a distinction between the left and the right banks of the river. The territory on the left bank, in the Oriental Republic of the Uruguay, he treated as friendly territory to be freed from the armies of Rosas and Oribe; and in many of the villages there he was acclaimed as a liberator.[20] Entre-Rios, on the right bank, was Argentine territory, where the inhabitants were to be regarded as enemies. He did not always, perhaps, make this distinction in practice, because his men had to live off the land, and took the cattle that they needed as meat wherever they found them on either bank; but in Entre-Rios they caused widespread damage, which aroused an even greater outcry in the Argentine press than that which had followed Garibaldi's depredations during the Paraná expedition of 1842.

Garibaldi's activities in Entre-Rios in 1845 are still remembered in Argentina, where his name is hated today by large sections of the population. Again, as in 1842, there was not a single case in which a specific allegation of murder or rape was made against his men; but they did extensive damage to property. They seized the cattle which they needed for food, and took them to their ships; and they entered the homes on the *estancias*, broke the doors and windows, and stole any valuables that they could find. These stories of looting may have been exaggerated; but though Garibaldi denies that his men stole, he admits that there were excesses, and in view of the circumstances and the character of many of his men, it can safely be assumed that some looting occurred. The thing that rankled most with the *estancia*-owners of Entre-Rios was the breaking of the fences. Only a small part of the thousands of cattle on the *estancias* could be accommodated in Garibaldi's ships and used for food; but Garibaldi's men broke down the fences around the stockades, either because it was the easiest way of driving the cattle to the ships, or out of a deliberate desire to do as much damage as possible to the enemy. The result was that the rest of the cattle got out, and strayed all over the pampas, so that the *estancia*-owners lost many more cattle than those which Garibaldi took.*

On 17 September Garibaldi arrived at Soriano, on the left bank of the River Uruguay. He sent a party of ten men ashore to reconnoitre; but finding the enemy were there in some strength, he sailed on. He makes no mention, in his memoirs, of his arrival and departure from Soriano, which was claimed as a victory by the Blancos; but his report about it to Bauzá was published in the Montevidean press.[21] On the evening of 19 September he reached Fray Bentos, at the mouth of the little stream that runs down from the town of Gualeguaychú, in Entre-Rios, some five miles from the River Uruguay. Here he was met by a local Unitarian supporter, Bernardino Gomez, and set off, with 250 of his men, to march overland, through the night, to Gualeguaychú, with Gomez acting as his guide.

They reached Gualeguaychú at midnight, and attacked the sleeping town. The enemy were taken completely by surprise, only nine of the garrison being awake, and these were quickly overcome in a short fight in which three of them were wounded, one seriously. The rest of the garrison surrendered without resistance. Their commander, Villagra, was captured when asleep in bed, and brought to Garibaldi in his nightshirt. Garibaldi set up his headquarters in the main square, in an attractive house, built in the usual Spanish colonial style, belonging to a wealthy inhabitant, Don Juan Gonzalez de Cossio. Every man in the town, including the foreigners, was arrested before daybreak, and brought to this house, where Garibaldi spoke to them, and assessed them for an appropriate contribution in bread, maize and linen. They

*This information was supplied by Señorita Gisele Shaw, whose great-grandfather's *estancia* was occupied by Garibaldi and his men.

were then all released, except for Villagra, the Mayor, the Borough Treasurer, and the local Chief of Police, who were kept in custody in Cossio's house.

Garibaldi remained for thirty-six hours in Gualeguaychú. For the inhabitants, they were thirty-six hours of terror, about which their descendants still speak today. Garibaldi's men looted the town, causing great destruction. Local tradition tells many stories of the excesses which they committed, remembering especially how they stole the silver pipes through which the wealthier citizens drank their *maté* tea. It also tells of how Señor and Señora Lapalma, the richest family in Gualeguaychú, placed their house at Garibaldi's disposal for use as a hospital for his wounded, and how they were rewarded by having all their valuables stolen by Garibaldi's men; while a wounded Italian Legionary was lying on their best table, his comrades looted all around him. But it seems unlikely that Garibaldi would have needed to use the house as a hospital, as there are no reports of his having suffered any casualties in the brief struggle with the nine Argentine soldiers when he captured the town; and though it is perhaps unfair to judge Señora Lapalma by her portrait at Gualeguaychú, it is difficult, after seeing it, to believe that she was an angel of mercy to the sick, as she looks an exceptionally disagreeable woman in the picture.

After his men had looted all day on 20 September, and on the next morning, Garibaldi left Gualeguaychú at 3 pm on the 21st. Before he left, he released Villagra and the other three prisoners whom he still held. The prisoners undoubtedly expected that they would have their throats cut, which is what they themselves would have done to their own prisoners. But the foreign merchants in Gualeguaychú signed an appeal to Garibaldi, asking him to show mercy and release the prisoners; and Garibaldi agreed. In his report to Bauzá, the Minister of War and Marine in Montevideo, he explained that he was doing this 'because of the humanitarian instructions of the supreme government of the Republic'. One of his soldiers put it more simply in a letter to a friend: 'The colonel treated all the prisoners very well.'[22]

Some of Garibaldi's supporters were not pleased at his humane decision. The murder of prisoners by the Blancos had caused a strong desire for revenge among the Unitarians, and a War Crimes Commission had been set up in Montevideo to investigate charges against men guilty of atrocities, so that they could be punished if captured. Villagra had gained a reputation of being a particularly savage Rosista, and had been involved in an incident in 1842 which had enraged the Unitarians. During the fighting in Corrientes and Entre-Rios in that year, the Rosistas captured a negro officer in the Unitarian army whom they alleged had been involved in an attempt to assassinate Echague five years before. Villagra announced that he would be executed for this crime. The Unitarians seized Villagra's brother-in-law as a hostage, threatened to kill him if the negro officer were put to death, and offered an exchange. Villagra, rejecting his wife's appeal on her brother's behalf, refused to agree to an exchange, and vowed vengeance against all Unitarians if his brother-in-law were killed. He was warmly congratulated on his attitude by Urquiza. 'If they sacrifice your innocent brother,' wrote Urquiza, 'I promise you that even the most insignificant of them shall be put to the sword.' But Villagra's brother-in-law was not executed; he was released by the Unitarians, who afterwards claimed that Villagra had secretly agreed to the exchange, but had then tricked them, and had killed the negro officer as soon as his brother-in-law was safe.[23]

The release of Villagra, when Garibaldi had him in his power, angered many of the Unitarians. Iriarte, in Montevideo, considered the matter coolly, and condemned Garibaldi's action as unwise, because it placed the Unitarians at a disadvantage; if Rosas's men knew that, if they were taken prisoner, they would always be immediately released, whereas all Unitarians captured by the Rosistas had their throats cut, there would be a great incentive for those who were concerned with their own safety to fight for Rosas and not for the Unitarians; while those Rosistas who, having been taken prisoner, were then released, would fight with renewed determination for Rosas in order to atone for having allowed themselves to be captured.

Three days later, Iriarte heard another explanation of Garibaldi's magnanimity at Gualeguaychú which he was very ready to accept. This was that Garibaldi had accepted a bribe of 400 oz of gold as a condition of releasing Villagra and the other prisoners.

> We cannot guarantee the truth of this story [wrote Iriarte in his diary] but we will say this: when we first heard of how Villagra and the garrison of Gualeguaychú had been set free, which has disgusted all of us, we attacked the idea that pecuniary interest had played any part in that unjustifiable decision of the Italian Garibaldi; but we must indicate our suspicions, because of our complete lack of confidence in him. . . . It is certain that Garibaldi is an unknown adventurer who, like many others, has come to this country to exploit it for his own profit; and that the government ought not to be so liberal in placing such absolute trust in men of this type, still less should it elevate them to positions of authority.[24]

It was perhaps because Garibaldi was aware that accusations of this kind were being made, not only by the enemy but even by people who were supposed to be his brothers-in-arms, that he condemned himself and his family to live in conditions of such poverty that he could not even afford to have an adequate supply of candles.

Just as Iriarte attributed the worst motives to Garibaldi's act of kindness, Urquiza believed the worst of Villagra for having been the beneficiary of it. He assumed that Garibaldi would not have released Villagra except as a reward for some act of treachery, and he could not, in any case, forgive Villagra for having allowed himself to be taken prisoner in his nightshirt. He never spoke to Villagra again until 1851, when Urquiza had joined the Unitarians and was leading them to victory in the final campaign against Rosas. Urquiza met Villagra in the street when he was passing through Gualeguaychú. 'You do not deserve my friendship since you lost to Garibaldi,' said Urquiza. 'Not deserve your friendship!' replied Villagra. 'I, who was fighting for my country when your Excellency was at your mother's breast.' Urquiza promptly embraced Villagra, and the two men were reconciled.[25]

In the Dumas edition of the memoirs, Garibaldi states that on one occasion, which must have been during the River Uruguay expedition of 1845, he took the whole garrison of Gualeguay prisoner, among them Major Millan, who had tortured him at Gualeguay eight years before. He states that he resisted the temptation to take revenge, and refused to see Millan, for fear lest the sight of Millan should evoke such bitter memories that it would overcome his better instincts and lead him to commit an act of vengeance. When the Scottish writer and Socialist, Robert Cunninghame-Graham, visited Argentina for the first time in 1870, he spent some months in Gualeguaychú. At this time, eighteen years after the downfall of Rosas, Sarmiento was President of a Liberal Argentina, and the triumphant Unitarians at Gualeguaychú regarded Garibaldi as a great hero, and followed his exploits in Europe with admiration. Many years later, Cunninghame-Graham wrote about Garibaldi, whom he greatly admired, and described how Garibaldi had captured Millan at Gualeguaychú, and, instead of taking revenge on him, had brought him a cup of coffee with his own hands. This story is not only too good to be true, but is in flat contradiction to Garibaldi's statement, in the Dumas edition of the memoirs, that he refused to see Millan when he held him prisoner; and Dumas's story itself is improbable. It does not appear that Millan was ever stationed at Gualeguaychú, though a sergeant named Millan was serving under Montero at Colonia in September 1845. In view of the fact that the story does not appear in any edition of the memoirs except Dumas's, it is probably one of Dumas's additions, based on a confusion between Gualeguaychú and Gualeguay, though Gualeguaychú is fifty miles from Gualeguay, and was the nearest point to Gualeguay that Garibaldi reached during the campaign of 1845–6.[26]

Garibaldi got no credit either from his friends or his enemies for his unparalleled generosity in releasing his captives instead of killing them.

Only his British and French Allies approved of his action and followed his example in their treatment of their prisoners and captured civilians; and Ouseley, in his reports to Aberdeen, strongly commended Garibaldi for his humanity. But the recipients of his kindness showed him no gratitude. Three hundred years before Garibaldi, a more cynical Italian, Machiavelli, had written that although a man may forgive you for killing his father, he will never forgive you for taking his property. This proved to be sadly true in Garibaldi's case. The people of Gualeguaychú, including the men whom he had released, immediately sent indignant reports to Buenos Aires of the terrible excesses committed by Garibaldi's troops, and the Rosista press renewed the outbursts with which they had greeted the actions of the Italians at Colonia. They denounced the 'base robberies committed by the bandit Garibaldi, the auxiliary and instrument of the Anglo-French', and added that 'it is impossible that the Ministers Ouseley and Deffaudis should ever be able to justify, even before England and France, the opprobrium with which they have tarnished the flags of those two European states, allying them to that of a pirate who has got out of the prisons of Genoa and Brazil'.[27]

The Argentine government appointed a commission of inquiry into the horrors of Gualeguaychú. It published a report containing the statements of thirty-seven foreign residents of Gualeguaychú, who all gave evidence of their personal experiences of the looting and destruction of property by Garibaldi's men. There is no mention of murder, rape or any kind of personal violence to prisoners or civilians; nor is there the slightest sign of gratitude for Garibaldi's action in releasing the prisoners. His generosity was not reciprocated. A few weeks later, a group of French and English residents near Paysandú, who had refused to fight in Oribe's army when they were called up for military service, were taken to an internment camp, and thirty-three of them were murdered on the way by their guards. Soon afterwards Rosas announced that if the Argentine forces captured any British, French or Montevidean soldiers or sailors conducting operations against Argentina, their commanders would immediately be punished as pirates.[28]

On 30 September Garibaldi reached Paysandú; but his attack on the town was repulsed by heavy fire from the land battery 'President Oribe'. He lost four men killed, as well as having six wounded and losing a number of horses who were hit on board ship by the gunfire. Garibaldi made only a passing reference to this set-back in his memoirs, nor was it mentioned in any of his reports to his government which were published in the Montevidean newspapers; but it is described at length in Garibaldi's letter to the Commissioners of the Italian Legion in Montevideo, as well as in letters from Anzani and from Colonel

Aleman, a Uruguayan officer who was serving under Garibaldi. All these letters were captured by the enemy, and sent to General Antonio Diaz, who was Oribe's Minister of War, but had taken personal command of the Blanco forces in Northern Uruguay. The defeat was greatly exaggerated by the Rosista press, which claimed that "the infamous Garibaldi' had been compelled to abandon his whole expedition to the River Uruguay.[29]

After leaving Paysandú, Garibaldi proceeded upriver with 19 ships. His largest ship, the *Cagancha*, had a crew of 74 and 14 guns; his flagship, the *28 de Marzo*, had a crew of 36, with 2 guns; and the captured Argentine ship, the *Maipú*, a crew of 27 and 5 guns. The rest of his ships varied in size from the *Resistencia* with 26 men and 2 guns to the whaleboat *Manuelita* with a crew of two, which had no armament and was used as a transport ship, giving a total Montevidean naval force of 16 fighting ships and 3 transport ships, with a total strength of 323 men and 39 guns. He had 226 men of the Italian Legion and 101 cavalry, which, excluding the officers and men whom he had left to garrison Martín García, gave him a total force of 651. He also had with him a British gunboat under Lieutenant Dench and a French one under Captain Morier.[30]

Garibaldi was now approaching his destination, the town of Salto. Thirty years before, Salto was an uninhabited area, but in 1817 a trading settlement of Uruguayan and European merchants had been established there, and it now had a population of 10,000. It was the key point in the operations in the north. It faced Concordia, in Entre-Rios across the river, and was the centre of communications between the remnants of Rivera's army in Northern Uruguay and the Unitarian armies in Corrientes, which Paz had been sent to command. After the battle of India Muerta in the previous March, Rivera and his men had retreated into Rio Grande do Sul; but the Riograndense resistance against the Imperial government of Brazil had finally collapsed in January, and Rivera and his army were interned by the Brazilian government. Rivera was taken to Rio de Janeiro, but most of his men slipped back into Northern Uruguay. Rivera, who knew that Brazil was on the point of entering the war on the side of Montevideo, did not resign his command, but prepared to re-enter Uruguay and take over the leadership of the army there as soon as Brazil declared war; but meanwhile Vazquez, in Montevideo, had been drifting towards the pro-Pacheco faction. In August 1845 the government of Montevideo ordered Rivera not to re-enter Oriental territory without permission; and a few months later, Pacheco returned to Montevideo from Rio de Janeiro, while Rivera remained in exile there. The command of Rivera's army in Northern Uruguay was given to General Medina. With

Garibaldi's squadron controlling the River Uruguay and the crossing from Salto to Concordia, the Unitarians could maintain the communications between Medina and Paz, and prevent the Rosistas in Entre-Rios from keeping contact with Urquiza's army, which was on the borders of Rio Grande do Sul, keeping watch over Medina.

Salto was held for Oribe by Colonel Manuel Lavalleja and a force of 700 men. On 6 October Garibaldi wrote to Lavalleja in an effort to persuade him to surrender Salto without fighting. His letter was drafted with considerable political cunning. In an attempt to gain some advantage from the split between Rivera and Pacheco, he pointed out to Lavalleja that Rivera, the hated enemy of the Blancos, was no longer in authority on the Unitarian side: 'Today the Oriental state has got rid of the man who was its harmful influence; today you will not meet among us Colorados any colour except the colours of the People.' He wrote that he did not suggest that Lavalleja should desert to the Unitarians, 'because I know the dignity of your character too well to think that you are capable of any baseness'; he merely proposed that he and Lavalleja should meet on the French warship *L'Eclair* to discuss what they could do to help the people of Uruguay. He ended the letter by assuring Lavalleja that the English and French forces had come to the River Plate only in order to protect their own nationals, and had no wish to violate the independence of the Oriental Republic.[31]

Despite all the blandishments in the letter, Lavalleja did not reply, but sent the letter to Oribe's government, who published it in the press. Garibaldi advanced to Hervidero, a village on the left bank of the River Uruguay, some twenty miles south of Salto. He landed and occupied the village, and leaving Anzani in charge of his forces there, pressed on up to Salto. While Garibaldi was sailing towards Salto, Lavalleja marched out of Salto and attacked the '*gringo* savage pirates'* at Hervidero. Anzani told his men to hold their fire until Lavalleja's troops were nearly on them, and then shot them down, and drove them back in disorder. The Blancos received such a mauling at Hervidero that they made no attempt to hold Salto, and both the garrison and the civilian population evacuated the town. Garibaldi, after linking up with the Scotsman, Mundell, who was commanding a Unitarian guerrilla band, entered Salto on the morning of 3 November. He found no one in the town except a few Brazilians and Sardinians. He proceeded to fortify it, in order to hold it as a base in Northern Uruguay, and to link up whenever possible with Medina and Paz.[32]

---

*'*Gringo*' is a derogatory word for 'foreigner' in South America. Although today it is applied chiefly to citizens of the United States, it was often used, in Garibaldi's time, to refer to Italian immigrants.

At 4 pm on 24 November Garibaldi marched out of Salto with 100 infantry of the Italian Legion and 200 cavalry to attack Lavalleja's forces, who had taken up their position on the River Itapebí, twenty miles north of Salto. Lavalleja, like Garibaldi, had 100 infantry, but had 250 horsemen against Garibaldi's 200. After marching all night, Garibaldi came on the enemy at dawn on 25 November. His cavalry were unable to cross the river through the ford, because the currents were difficult, and the horses became frightened; but he sent his infantry through the ford, after ordering them to put their cartridges round their necks, and the Legionaries reached the other side and routed the enemy with the bayonet, capturing many prisoners, one cannon, and 12,000 rounds of ammunition for muskets. Garibaldi lost only two men killed and five wounded.

After Lavelleja's men had fled, Garibaldi came up with the civilians from Salto who had been accompanying Lavalleja's army, with Lavalleja's wife and family, and thirty British and French internees. Garibaldi freed the internees, and sent Señora Lavalleja and her family, and the families of other officers and soldiers of Lavalleja's army, to the camp of the Blanco commander, General Garzón, because he wished to show himself 'as always, worthy of the principles of humanity which characterize the cause of the Oriental people'. The *Gaceta Mercantil*, who admitted for once that Lavalleja had been defeated by Garibaldi's 'numerical superiority', reported that 'the Anglo-French and Garibaldi robbed and committed every species of violence upon the families of the convoy in the most infamous and barbarous manner'; but the civilians told Garibaldi that they had been forced, against their will, to follow Lavalleja, and were happy to be liberated by him, and to return to Salto.[33]

The *Gaceta Mercantil* told horrifying stories of the sack of Salto by Garibaldi's men, and accused Garibaldi of setting a personal example in looting. 'With his band of marauders he ran from one habitation to another of the unfortunate families, opening their trunks, boxes, drawers and chests, whence he robbed with his own hands their money and jewels. He afterwards ordered a general pillage.' They reported that 'the pirates butchered in cold blood several respectable Oriental citizens', one of whom, Don Eustaquio Gonzalez, 'was cowardly and barbarously killed by that atrocious English ruffian Mundell'. They also accused the Anglo-French forces of converting a church in Salto into a barracks, and forcing a Spanish priest to work in chains on building the defences of Salto. Ouseley tried to persuade the British government to pay no attention to these stories. He wrote to his friend Lord Cowley, the Duke of Wellington's brother, who was the British Ambassador in Paris: 'Pray recollect that mendacious as is the Press in Europe it is truthful as compared with that of Rosas. He governs by a judicious use of lies and assassination.'[34]

Urquiza, after defeating Rivera at India Muerta, had remained in Northern Uruguay with his army; but he was now ordered by Rosas to crush the revolt in Corrientes. He marched west to Salto, but decided, before crossing to Concordia, to capture Salto and eliminate Garibaldi's forces holding the base.[35] He boasted that he would cross the river in Garibaldi's boats. On 3 December his advance-guard reached Salto. He was joined there by another Blanco army under Antonio Diaz. On 6 December Urquiza and Diaz, with a combined force of nearly 3,000 men, began the siege of Salto. Garibaldi and his 650 men had been joined by a force of 300 cavalry under Colonel Baez, who had come from Medina's army. If the Italians had any doubts as to what would happen to them if they were taken prisoner, it was removed with the arrival of Urquiza, who had publicly declared that he would murder every Unitarian whom he captured; but under Garibaldi's leadership, they were confident that they could hold Salto against these greatly superior forces. On 14 December Garibaldi wrote to Anita: 'We are holding the front against Urquiza and Antonio Diaz, and I think they will not trouble us much; our soldiers are the sons of victory in every part. At Tapiby [Itapebí] I treated Lavalleja's wife better than you were treated by the Curitibans.'[36] This was a reference to the occasion when Anita had been taken prisoner by the Brazilian forces near Curitibanos in Santa Catarina, and had escaped after her four days' ride through the forest.

Although most of Uruguay is completely flat, there are a number of small, steep hills in the country round Salto. One of them lies just outside the town on the east side. Garibaldi had realized that this would be an advantageous place for the besiegers to put their cannon; but as he had not enough men to hold it, and to extend his lines, he was forced to abandon it to Urquiza. As he had expected, Urquiza established a battery on the hill, from which he shelled the town; but Garibaldi, bringing in some of the guns from his ships, replied very effectively. Urquiza sent parties of men to probe the defences, but did not launch a general assault, and Garibaldi won most of the infantry skirmishes. Urquiza's only real success was to force his way into a stockade where the defenders had kept most of their captured cattle, and stampede the cattle into running off, so that Garibaldi lost most of his food supply; but Garibaldi, having control of the river, could replenish his stocks of food without difficulty, although Urquiza completely cut off the town from the land side. Urquiza was so unsuccessful that he was reduced to gloating over the deaths of 'two miserable *gringos*' in his report to Antonio Diaz.[37]

Garibaldi held Salto against Urquiza for eighteen days. After this, Urquiza decided that he could not afford to wait any longer, and on 23 December he crossed to Concordia and marched on against the Unitarians in Corrientes, taking all the horses in the district with him. 'He crossed the river above Salto,' wrote Garibaldi in his memoirs, 'but not in our vessels, as he had promised.' Urquiza left 700 men under Lamos and Vergara to continue the siege of Salto. As the besieging army was now weaker than Garibaldi's force, there was no danger of Salto falling, and there was no serious fighting, though Garibaldi sent out his cavalry to round up cattle in the neighbourhood and skirmish with the enemy. On 9 January, in a night sortie, he inflicted a sharp defeat on the besieging army.[38]

While Garibaldi was at Salto, he suffered a personal loss which affected him very deeply. His daughter Rosita died in Montevideo. Rosita was certainly a small child when she died, but there is a surprising contradiction of evidence about her age. According to a letter which Garibaldi wrote in later years to his secretary, Basso, she was aged between four and five when she died; but her death certificate in the church of San Francisco de Asis in Montevideo states that she died on 23 December 1845 aged one and a half years. The inscription on her gravestone in the cemetery at Montevideo, which also gives 23 December 1845 as the date of her death, gives her age as thirty months. Of the three contradictory records, Pereda preferred the tombstone, because he thought that Anita, who might well have sent a friend to register Rosita's death, would have been personally responsible for the wording on the tombstone. But Pereda overlooked the fact that, if Rosita was thirty months old when she died, Garibaldi could not have been her father, because this would place her birth in June 1843, and Garibaldi was absent from Montevideo, and from Anita, on the Paraná expedition between June and December 1842. It is difficult to believe that Garibaldi could say that a much-loved child had died at the age of four if she had really died at eighteen months; and so, despite the other evidence, it would seem that Garibaldi's version is the most likely and that Rosita was born at the end of 1841, soon after her parents arrived in Montevideo, when Menotti was a year old, and that Rosita was therefore just four when she died.

The cause of Rosita's death is not definitely known; but she probably died of scarlet fever, because a very serious epidemic of scarlet fever swept through Montevideo in 1845, causing heavy loss of life among a population whose resistance to disease had been weakened by food shortages and the other hardships of the siege. The conditions of life in Garibaldi's house in Calle 25 de Mayo, with all the family living in one room, made any child particularly prone to infection during the stifling summer heat.

Garibaldi first heard about Rosita's death in a letter from Pacheco y Obes. The manner in which Pacheco broke the news to him made the blow more painful, and caused him, for the only time in his life, to feel bitter resentment against the man who was a personal friend as well as a political leader. Pacheco wrote him a letter containing instructions about his military operations at Salto, and then added: 'Your daughter Rosita is dead; this you ought to know, at any rate.' This curt, brutal way of telling the bereaved father no doubt appealed to Pacheco, as it fitted in well with the image which he presented to himself and the world of the hard, incorruptible Robespierre of South America, who subordinated all personal feelings to his devotion to his country and the cause of freedom; but it went down badly with an emotional man like Garibaldi, who still resented it when he wrote about it to Basso in after years: 'That man was not a father, never had been, never could be; had he been a father, he would have been able to understand a father's love for a daughter.' He wrote that Pacheco, like Paz, deserved to be remembered in Montevideo as the brave defender of the New Troy; 'but I loved so dearly that little creature of mine, the loss of her would have grieved me by itself; and the way in which the news was communicated to me was so brutal, it hurt me so grievously, that I have never been able to forgive it.'

In Montevideo, Anita took the blow even harder than Garibaldi; and when Garibaldi heard about the extent of her grief, he was afraid that she might go mad. He therefore suggested that she should come to him at Salto, despite all the risks involved in the journey and in the battle-zone, so that he could help and comfort her.

When Anita arrived, Garibaldi heard from her the details of Rosita's last illness and death. In the account of it which he wrote for Basso, he showed that his hatred of priests and organized religion did not prevent him from believing in immortality, at least in moments of personal bereavement. 'Rosita was the most beautiful, the sweetest of little girls . . . Her intelligence was most precocious . . . She died without complaining, begging her mother not to grieve, telling her that they would meet again soon – meet to part no more.' He said to Anita: 'Yes, yes, we shall see our Rosita again; the soul is immortal, and this life of misery is only an episode of immortality – a divine spark, part of the infinite flame that animates the universe.'[39]

CHAPTER 13

SAN ANTONIO

O N 8 February 1846 Garibaldi fought his most famous battle in South America at San Antonio. Although he had less than 200 men involved in the action, it gained him a great reputation in Italy, and is the only incident during the whole of his residence in South America, apart from his meeting with Anita, which is widely remembered in Europe. A pictorial representation of it, which bears no relation whatever to the true facts, adorns the plinth of the Garibaldi statue in Buenos Aires. Garibaldi always considered it to have been one of his greatest victories, and all his biographers acclaim it as a great triumph. But at the time his enemies claimed that the victory had gone to them; and today in Argentina there are eminent historians who believe that it was a defeat for Garibaldi.

On 7 February, ten cavalrymen from General Medina's army arrived in Salto, and told Garibaldi that Medina, with part of Rivera's army of Northern Uruguay, was marching to the relief of Salto, and was thirty-five miles away to the north.[1] Next day Garibaldi marched out with some of his men to welcome Medina's advance-guard and escort them into Salto. He had 186 infantrymen of the Italian Legion with him and a body of 100 native Uruguayan cavalry under Colonel Baez.[2] They marched north along the banks of the River Uruguay till they reached a spot three miles from the centre of the town. The landscape at this point, on the east side of the River Uruguay, is flat, and the soil, like the greater part of Brazil and Uruguay, is red. A mile from the river there is a little hill, not more than 30 feet high, but with so steep an angle that the top of the head of a man walking up the hill on one side cannot be seen by people on the other side until he is less than ten steps from the summit. The area is open, but covered with small clumps of orange trees. At about noon on 8 February, Garibaldi and his men were crossing the plain, with the river on their left and the hill on their right. It was at the hottest part of the summer, and the day was an exceptionally warm one. Suddenly a force of about 1,000 men, both infantry and cavalry, came over the brow of the hill.

There are nine accounts of the battle of San Antonio by people who fought in it.[3] Four are by Garibaldi himself. He gave three different descriptions of the battle in the four editions of the memoirs, apart from the shorter account which he wrote two days after the battle to Muñoz, the Pachecist politician who had recently replaced Bauzá as Minister of War in Montevideo. Three other members of the Italian Legion wrote descriptions of San Antonio – the Legion's medical officer, Lieutenant Odinici, in his daily diary of the Italian Legion; an anonymous Legionary whose account was published by Cuneo in the *Legionario Italiano* about a month afterwards; and Sacchi, an officer of the Legion, who wrote an account of it in later years. Colonel Baez, the commander of the native Uruguayan cavalry in Garibaldi's force, wrote a report on the battle to Medina. On the other side, there is only the report of the Blanco commander, Colonel Servando Gomez, to Oribe.

Although the authors of these accounts draw different conclusions about the result of the battle, they all tell basically the same story. Garibaldi suddenly saw Gomez's Blanco forces emerge over the top of the hill, and realized at once that he was confronted with a very much larger force than his own. He estimated the enemy strength at 900 cavalry and 300 infantry, thus outnumbering his own force by more than four to one. Gomez, who stated that Garibaldi's force consisted of 250 infantry and 200 cavalry, did not give the numbers of his own men in his report to Oribe; but there is no doubt that, even if Garibaldi's estimate of the enemy numbers was exaggerated, they greatly outnumbered his own men. Baez suggested that they should retreat; but Garibaldi realized that they had no time to do this, and that if they attempted to retreat, it would merely mean that they would fight at a disadvantage and with weakened morale.

Fortunately there was some kind of derelict building on the flat ground, which must have been on or near the site of the cottage which stands there at the present day. Garibaldi and his infantry just had time to reach this ruin, which provided them with the cover of a wall on the east side facing the enemy, though it was open on the west side. Baez and the cavalry waited on their mounts for the enemy cavalry to charge. After one sharp encounter with their opponents, Baez's horsemen retreated towards Salto. Garibaldi wrote in his memoirs that the cavalry had fled in a most cowardly fashion, and had abandoned the Italian Legion to fight alone against both cavalry and infantry. He thought that if Baez's men were unable to fight Gomez's cavalry in the open space, they should have joined the infantrymen behind the wall. As it was, Garibaldi's remaining force was outnumbered, not four to one as they had been before Baez's retreat, but six to one. Garibaldi's feelings were shared by the other members of the Italian Legion. Sacchi complained bitterly that only seventeen of Baez's horsemen came and joined them in the ruined building.

Meanwhile the Italian Legion were facing the enemy infantry. Garibaldi wrote in his memoirs that if Gomez's cavalry had charged them, they would have ridden them down and wiped them out; but instead of sending in the cavalry, Gomez ordered his 300 infantrymen to advance, not in column, but in one long straight line, so that they presented an easy target to the defenders. The Blanco infantry advanced slowly, firing as they walked, and began shooting long before they were within range. Garibaldi, as usual, told his men to hold their fire, and when the enemy were within thirty yards the Legionaries opened up, and shot down many of them. The Blanco infantry fell back in some disorder. They attacked again, and repeatedly, throughout that hot afternoon, often coming close enough to engage in hand-to-hand fighting with the bayonet. As usual, the morale of Garibaldi's men was magnificent. They sang the national anthem of Uruguay, Garibaldi leading the singing in his fine tenor voice, just as he had made his men sing the Riograndense Republican song during the fighting at the storehouse at Camaqua seven years before. Once Gomez invited Garibaldi to surrender, sending in an envoy under a flag of truce; but Garibaldi refused to discuss surrender.

Later in the day, some of Gomez's cavalry returned from chasing Baez, and surrounded the Italian Legion. Some of the horsemen dismounted, and joined Gomez's infantry in renewed attacks on the Italians, while others charged, singly, on horseback; but there was no concentrated cavalry charge, such as Garibaldi expected; and the attackers always got the worst of the close fighting. A cavalryman rode up to the building with a torch in each hand, and tried to throw it on to the roof to set it on fire; but he was unsuccessful. According to the Dumas version of the memoirs – and the story is confirmed by Sacchi – the defenders could easily have shot the man, but were prevented by Garibaldi, who was filled with admiration for his courage.

Garibaldi's casualties began to mount up. The bugle-boy of the Italian Legion, a lad of fifteen, was with the Legion that day, and he continued to sound his bugle throughout the action. A Blanco cavalryman rode at him and stuck him through with his lance; but the dying boy threw himself on the cavalryman, and attacked him with his knife and his teeth. Another Legionary came up, and killed the cavalryman with his bayonet, though too late to save the boy. The corpses of the boy and the cavalryman were found locked together, the boy's body full of stab-wounds, and the cavalryman's bearing the marks of the boy's teeth. The worst hardship for Garibaldi's men was that they suffered greatly from thirst under the burning sun. This was a great ordeal, particularly for the wounded men.

After the battle had lasted for nine hours, at about half-past eight, when it was nearly dark, Garibaldi decided to try to retreat to Salto. They had about half a mile to go to the River Uruguay, where they would be under cover of the trees on the river bank once they had succeeded in crossing the open ground. They set off, carrying their wounded comrades, though one, who was too badly wounded to be moved, was shot at Garibaldi's orders to prevent him from falling alive into the enemy's hands.[4] As they moved slowly towards the river, they were shot at by Gomez's infantry and attacked by his cavalry; but whenever the Blancos came too close, the Italian Legion turned and drove them off by musket fire and bayonet. They reached the river bank, where at last they could relieve their thirst, taking it in turn to drink while their comrades stood guard over them. Then they marched back to Salto, still fighting off the attacks of the enemy, though these became much less frequent after they had reached the shelter of the trees by the river. It took them four and a half hours to cover the three miles from San Antonio to Salto, but by midnight they were safe within the defences of the town. They had lost 30 killed and 53 wounded. Every officer in the Legion, except Garibaldi himself, had been wounded. Eighteen of Baez's cavalrymen had been killed.

Anzani, who had been left in command of the Legionaries in Salto, was very pleased to see them. During the day, a force of Gomez's cavalry had come to Salto and summoned Anzani to surrender, telling him that Garibaldi and his whole force had been killed or captured at San Antonio, and that Anzani and the rest of the Legionaries had therefore no chance of holding out in Salto. But Anzani had replied that Italians do not surrender, and had successfully repulsed the enemy attacks which had followed. Medina's advance-guard reached Salto during the night, a few hours after Garibaldi. Gomez had already withdrawn his army towards Paysandú.

Garibaldi enlisted the help of two French medical officers from the French gunboat at Salto, and asked them to treat the wounded; but he stated that 'more welcome than anything else to our poor sufferers was the tender nursing of the gentle women of Salto'. Several of the severely wounded men died during the following days; and one sergeant, a man from Nice, had a leg amputated – an operation which still had to be performed without an anaesthetic. On the morning after the battle, Garibaldi marched out with his men to the battlefield, where they found some wounded soldiers of both sides still lying on the ground; and he provided medical treatment both for his own wounded and for the enemy's. The ground was covered with corpses. They were all carried back to Salto, and buried in a common grave, both friend and foe together, on the hill just outside the town where Urquiza had placed his battery during the siege. Garibaldi erected a mound and a cross over the grave.[5]

On 10 February Garibaldi wrote his report to the Minister of War and Marine in Montevideo of the 'very terrible combat' which had taken place on the 8th at San Antonio, between Gomez's 1,200 men and 200 men of the Italian Legion, 'to whom were joined 100 men of the Baez division'. He wrote that he and all his officers had 'never experienced a greater honour than to have been soldiers of the Italian Legion on the 8th on the field of San Antonio. The Legion has 30 dead and 53 wounded; the enemy has, without doubt, suffered many losses, particularly among his infantry, which was completely defeated.'

On the same day, he wrote a report on the battle to Castellini and Frugoni, his fellow-Commissioners for the Italian Legion, who had remained in Montevideo. He told them: 'I would not give up my title of Italian Legionary for a world of gold!'[6]

When the news of San Antonio reached Montevideo, the government and press hailed it as a great victory for Garibaldi and the Italian Legion. They published Garibaldi's communiqué of 10 February; but editorials in the press hastened to point out that the communiqué showed the modesty, as well as the valour, of Garibaldi, because in fact his success had been much greater than he made out. Cuneo, whose newspaper *Il Legionario Italiano* had been published in the closing months of 1844, but had collapsed after three issues, now brought out a fourth and last issue to commemorate San Antonio. He published what purported to be a letter from a French naval officer who was serving on the River Uruguay which stated that Garibaldi had lost 33 killed and 53 wounded out of a total of 200 men, and that the enemy, whose numbers were given as 1,500 men, had lost 500 killed, of whom 250 fell in the first attack on Garibaldi's position and 124 in the second, while four carts had been needed to carry away the wounded. Even if this French officer really existed, it is difficult to see how he could possibly have known the number of Gomez's soldiers who had fallen in the first, as opposed to the second and subsequent, assaults at San Antonio. On 27 February the *Patriote Français*, which, despite all the animosity between the French and Italian Legions, did not attempt to play down the extent of Garibaldi's achievement, published a statement by a Blanco soldier, Marcos Suarez, who had deserted to the garrison of Salto, that out of Gomez's 300 infantrymen who had fought at San Antonio, all except 40 had been killed or wounded.[7]

Meanwhile the Buenos Aires press had published Gomez's report to Oribe of 14 February on the action at San Antonio. He described how his brave infantry had advanced in the face of intensive enemy fire, and how, at the end of the day, the savage Unitarians had fled from their position and retreated to Salto. He gave a full list of the names and ranks of all his casualties, amounting to a total of 28 killed and 74 wounded. He claimed that Garibaldi had lost 135 killed, 'from which it is easy to calculate the number of wounded whom they carried off with them'. Gomez stated that he had captured 20 prisoners, 60 muskets, 30 carbines, 50 lances, 37 sabres and the scabbards of the sabres of several infantry officers, including the scabbard of the pirate Garibaldi.[8]

On 16 February Garibaldi was promoted to the rank of General. Nine days later, the Montevidean government issued the famous decree of 25 February 1846. 'Señor General Garibaldi and all those who were with him on that glorious day have deserved well of the Republic.' The words 'The feat of 8 February 1846 accomplished by the Italian Legion under the orders of Garibaldi' were to be inscribed in letters of gold on the flag of the Italian Legion. 'The names of those who fought on that day, after the departure of the cavalry', were to be inscribed on a plaque in Government House in Montevideo with a list of all those who had died. Their families were to receive a pension at double the usual rate. 'There shall be issued to those who took part in the combat after the cavalry departed a shield to be worn on the left arm, with this inscription in addition to a laurel of gold: "Invincible, they fought on 8 February 1846".' Until another army corps achieved an equally glorious feat of arms, the Italian Legion was to take the right-hand place of the infantry on parade. This decree was to be published in General Orders on every anniversary of San Antonio.[9]

The news of the victory of San Antonio and the decree of 25 February was sent by Cuneo to Mazzini in London. Mazzini wrote a letter to *The Times* about it, which to his indignation was not published. But no one could stop Mazzini from reporting it in the *Apostolato Popolare*. When the news was known in Italy, it had a great effect. A mention of Garibaldi's name at the Scientific Congress in Genoa was greeted with loud cheers, and a subscription was opened in Florence to purchase a sword of honour to be presented to him. In Montevideo, odes to Garibaldi and the Italian Legion, in Italian and in Spanish translation, were published in the press and recited at the Teatro de Comercio. Admiral Lainé added his praise in a letter to Garibaldi, in which he described San Antonio as 'a battle of which the soldiers of the

Grand Army which once controlled Europe might be proud'.[10]

There have not been many wars in history in which propaganda played so important a part as in the war in Uruguay. The most important thing for both belligerents was to persuade Britain and France that their side was winning, and that the quickest way for the great European powers to re-establish peaceful trading conditions in the River Plate was to help them to win as quickly as possible. It was therefore more important that people should believe in a victory than that the victory should actually have been won. When small armies, roaming over vast expanses of territory in Northern Uruguay, happened to meet each other and fought a battle or skirmish, there was ample scope for lying propaganda when no town changed hands to mark a victory or defeat, and there was nothing to indicate who had won and lost except the wildly conflicting claims about casualties issued by the commanders on both sides. So when news of San Antonio reached Montevideo, both sides claimed that they had won a great victory 300 miles away in Northern Uruguay.

Two days after the government of Montevideo had issued the decree of 25 February, Oribe's artillery on the Cerrito fired a twenty-one gun salute in honour of Gomez's victory at San Antonio. In Buenos Aires, the *British Packet* sneered that Garibaldi had been made a general 'to console him for the drubbing he received the other day' at San Antonio, and though they admitted that the Italians had always fought much more bravely than the French, it was only the walls of the building in which they sheltered that saved them from total destruction in the battle. These claims roused the Montevideans to fury. The *Patriote Français* wrote on 28 February: 'We do not deny the well-known bravery of Monsieur Gomez, but we question more than ever his military talents, and we consider the lying bulletin which led to the Orbist demonstrations yesterday to be a real blot on his reputation."[11]

They believed that Garibaldi had won a victory at San Antonio, and welcomed it, and praised Garibaldi for it; but at the same time, they reacted against the lavish praise which Garibaldi had received from the government of Montevideo, and thought that if so much honour had been shown to Garibaldi because of a fight in which such small numbers had been engaged, it was chiefly because Pacheco's supporters wished to pander to the Italian Legion, as against the French Legion and the native units, in order to win the support of the Italians in the struggle for power between Pacheco and Rivera. They also resented the silence and implied criticism about Baez. The *Patriote Français* of 26 February warmly praised Garibaldi, but did not expressly refer to the Italian Legion by name, and tried to give Baez an equal share of the glory.

> At the moment when Colonel Baez, after fantastic efforts and prodigies of valour, found himself forced to leave the battlefield, Garibaldi, left to his own resources and in a very exposed position, said to his comrades, to his soldiers: 'Friends, we must die, let us perish, eventually, with honour'. ...Glory to the brave men of San Antonio and to the men who commanded them! Baez and Garibaldi have given the cause of civilization and humanity yet another day of glory![12]

General Iriarte, despite all his prejudice against Garibaldi, paid full credit to his achievement at San Antonio as 'a brilliant feat of arms' by which Garibaldi and his 'valiant Legionaries' had won 'immortal fame'; but he was annoyed that the government were giving all the credit to Garibaldi and the Italians, and none to the native Uruguayan Baez. Iriarte was even more put out that Garibaldi had been made a general, which he linked with the promotion of a number of Pachecist lieutenant-colonels, including Anzani and Cesar Diaz, to the rank of full colonel. 'To give the rank of general to an obscure adventurer like Garibaldi, to a man who has given proof of valour, but has no military knowledge, who is, after all, a foreign upstart' showed the government's contempt for the higher ranks of the army, and would cause discontent, 'because there are many old colonels who have served with Rivera who are disgusted by the rise of the Italian Garibaldi to the rank of general; and in fact all these old leaders have realized that the government's object is to make new creatures of the new men who support them'. Iriarte thought that there were altogether too many generals in Uruguay; the United States, with a population of 20,000,000, had fewer generals than Uruguay, which had only 130,000 inhabitants.[13]

When Garibaldi heard about his promotion to general, he reacted with a typical gesture. He wrote to Muñoz, the Minister of War, refusing the rank of general.* This was undoubtedly a spontaneous action without any political motive, because Garibaldi could not have

---

*De-Maria (III.217–18) gives the date of Garibaldi's letter as 4 March 1846, and this is followed in *Scritti*; but this must be wrong, as Garibaldi refers in the letter to the government decree of 1 March, and it took at least ten days for news from Montevideo to reach Salto. The letter was undated in the French translation in the *Patriote Français* of 8 May 1846, which was the first occasion on which it was published. In Ximenes (I.9), where it is published in an Italian translation, it is dated 10 March 1846, which might be possible; but in Ximenes it is wrongly stated to have been written from Montevideo, not Salto.

known, at the time, of the resentment which his promotion had aroused in certain circles in Montevideo.

As Chief of the Italian Legion, whatever I have deserved as a reward, I give it to the mutilated men and to the families of the dead of the said Legion. Not only the rewards, but also the honours, would weigh on my soul, as they have been bought with Italian blood. . . . The Legion found me as a colonel in the army, and accepted me as such to be its head; and as such I shall leave the Legion when we have fulfilled our vows to the Oriental People.

He added that all the members of the Legion who had been promoted had refused their individual promotions, as they wished the honours to be awarded to the Legion as a unit.[14]

As soon as Cuneo, in Montevideo, heard that Garibaldi had refused to accept the rank of general, he wrote to him, urging him to change his mind and accept.[15] According to Jessie White Mario, Garibaldi wrote to Cuneo from Salto refusing to do so;* but he eventually accepted the promotion. He was henceforth officially known as Colonel-Major Garibaldi, and addressed as General Garibaldi, in Uruguay; and he called himself General Garibaldi for the rest of his life.

Garibaldi's letter refusing the rank of general was not published in the vernacular Montevidean newspapers; but the *Patriote Français*, after declaring on 5 May that Garibaldi had refused the rank of general, and expressing a wish that his letter should be known to the public, published a French translation of it on 8 May.[16] One cannot avoid a suspicion that the *Patriote Français* may have had an ulterior motive for publishing it. As the government of Montevideo were determined that Garibaldi should become a general, and managed to persuade him to agree, it is understandable why his letter refusing the promotion was not published in the Montevidean newspapers; but the resentment against Garibaldi's promotion could be expected to be particularly strong in the French Legion, because of the ill-feeling between the French and the Italians, and the fact that Thiebaut had not been made a general. The *Patriote Français* may have published Garibaldi's letter of refusal in order to appease the indignation of the French

---

*An undated extract from this letter, in English translation, was published by Jessie White Mario in her Supplement to Werner's translation of Garibaldi's memoirs (III.59). Like all Jessie Mario's quotations, it is very suspect. The passage 'I refused the title of Colonel Major, consequently I will not accept that of General', could hardly have been written by Garibaldi, who knew very well that these were two names for the same rank.

Legionaries, and to make it more difficult for Pacheco and the government to persuade Garibaldi to accept the rank. As late as September 1846 the *Patriote Français* was still referring to Garibaldi as 'Colonel Garibaldi', though they eventually called him 'General Garibaldi'; and another French-language newspaper, the *Courrier de la Plata*, called him 'Colonel Garibaldi' on one occasion in April 1848.[17]

Apart from the question of the number of casualties, there is very little doubt about what happened at San Antonio. By the elementary test of discovering who remained in possession of the battlefield, Oribe's men were victorious; but in every other sense it was a victory for Garibaldi. For nine hours he waged a defensive battle against an enemy who outnumbered him by about six to one, and after more than 40 per cent of his men had been killed or wounded, he succeeded in retreating to safety with the rest of his force, after crossing half a mile of open ground without cover of any kind, surrounded by superior numbers of the enemy who dared not launch a full-out attack. He and his Italians displayed extraordinary courage and endurance, though they owed their survival to the foolish tactics of the enemy, whose infantry advanced in line instead of in column, and who never used their cavalry effectively.

It is impossible to form a correct estimate of the number of casualties. There is no reason to doubt that the figure of 30 dead and 53 wounded, which Garibaldi gave for his own casualties, was substantially accurate. Any discrepancy between Garibaldi's figures and the slightly higher number of dead given in the *Nacional* and by Jessie White Mario can be explained by the fact that some of his wounded died of their wounds after he wrote his report of 10 February, though Sacchi, writing many years afterwards, states that 37 were killed on the battlefield, and that those who died of wounds in Salto brought the total deaths to 43. Nor is there any doubt as to the number of Baez's dead, as the various figures vary only between 18 and 20. But there is no reliable indication of the number of Gomez's casualties. The figure of 500 killed given in the Montevidean newspapers is obviously an exaggeration; but it is difficult to accept Gomez's own figures of 28 dead and 77 wounded. If Gomez in fact suffered more casualties, the names of some of his dead and wounded must have been deliberately omitted from the detailed casualty list in his report to Oribe which was published in the press. This is by no means impossible. The Uruguayan historian, Antonio Diaz, had no doubt that Gomez omitted the names of many of his dead and wounded from his report to Oribe. Diaz was sure that the attacking force must have suffered more casualties than the defenders, and suspected that Gomez's losses were very heavy.[18]

There is also the problem of Baez's role. Garibaldi and his Legionaries never forgave Baez for deserting them; but the Uruguayans insisted on giving him a share of the credit with Garibaldi. In his first report to the Minister of War, Garibaldi made no strictures on Baez's conduct; he did not denounce him as a deserter, as he had denounced Villegas for deserting him at Costa Brava in his first report of that battle. The first press reports, too, praised the valour of Baez, as well as the valour of Garibaldi in continuing the fight alone after the brave Baez had been forced to retreat. But the government decree of 25 February, which expressly awarded the honours for San Antonio to those who had fought on after Baez had left, was a pointed condemnation of Baez, and was much resented by the native Uruguayans as an example of the tendency of the Pachecists to favour the Italians. When Iriarte, who had at first assumed that this was the only explanation of why Baez had been ignored in the decree of 25 February, later discovered that it was because Baez was said to have run away, he refused to believe it, because he remembered that Baez had been a brave and cool officer in the war against Brazil.

There were suggestions that Baez had perhaps withdrawn his cavalry from the battlefield because he thought that the Blancos might be attacking Anzani in Salto, and had gone to their rescue; but whatever the truth of this, it seems clear that Baez, by his retreat, indirectly helped Garibaldi by drawing off Gomez's cavalry. The absence of the cavalry in the earlier stages of the battle may have been one of the reasons why the Italian Legion never had to face the cavalry charge which Garibaldi was expecting, though another was perhaps because Gomez, to judge from his report to Oribe, seems to have considered the ruined building to have been more of an obstruction to the horses than is suggested in the account of the fight in Garibaldi's memoirs. It must also be remembered that Baez lost 20 per cent of his men killed, which was almost exactly the same proportion that Garibaldi lost.[19]

The final verdict on San Antonio must rest with the Uruguayan historian, Antonio Diaz.

Señor Gomez suffered a reverse which caused him serious losses, thanks to his lack of skill, not only because of the resistance at San Antonio, but also because of the escape of Colonel Garibaldi, who was able to return to Salto. . . . The fight at San Antonio was a disgrace for the arms of General Oribe, and an indisputable glory for Garibaldi and for Colonel Baez, who was also a chief agent and an indefatigable leader of that defence. . . . The lack of skill of General Gomez, as compared with Garibaldi, was the cause of that glittering achievement, which may indeed be considered as one of the most glorious in the military career of that man in the Republics of the Plate.[20]

CHAPTER 14

COMMANDER-IN-CHIEF:
THE HOWDEN-WALEWSKI MISSION

THE two years which followed the Battle of San Antonio have been very largely neglected by Garibaldi's biographers, and more especially by Garibaldi himself. In the Dumas edition of the memoirs, he makes the extraordinary statement that San Antonio was the last thing of importance which happened to him in Uruguay. In the Dwight and 1872 editions of the memoirs, though he gives a very full description of the Battle of the Daimán three months after San Antonio, he stated that nothing of importance occurred between his return to Montevideo from Salto in September 1846 and his departure for Italy in April 1848. In fact, it was during this time that he waged his most successful naval campaign in South America, to which he makes only a passing reference in the memoirs. The reason for this silence is undoubtedly the disgust and disillusionment which he experienced during these years with the Unitarians of Montevideo, and particularly with Rivera and his adherents.

In February 1846 the supporters of Rivera, who were incensed at the banishment of Rivera and the domination of the government by the Pachecists, raised their voices in the National Assembly in Montevideo. They demanded that Rivera be permitted to return from Brazil, and made difficulties about renewing the government's emergency powers. Pacheco and the government replied by dissolving the National Assembly and suspending the constitution for the duration of the war. In place of the National Assembly they appointed an Assembly of Notables, who were nominated by the government, and proclaimed that the government assumed full responsibility for leading the nation to victory. The Conservatives considered that the government's action was illegal and unconstitutional.[1]

Suddenly, on 18 March, Rivera arrived in the harbour of Montevideo in a Spanish ship from Rio de Janeiro and asked permission to land. Demonstrations broke out in Montevideo in his support, the French Legionaries shouting 'Long live Rivera! Death to Pacheco!' as they returned to their homes at night. When the government refused to permit him to land, and ordered him to leave Montevideo immediately, a large part of the Army of the Capital, under the command of

Flores, rose in his support and overthrew the government. The French Legion, the negro regiments and part of the native Uruguayan units supported the military coup; but part of the army, under Colonel Estivao, who was Pacheco's brother-in-law, came out for the government and Pacheco. Street fighting broke out between the forces of Flores and Estivao, and several persons, including Estivao himself, were killed before Flores and the Riveristas were victorious. Pacheco went into exile. His position had been greatly weakened by the fact that his most reliable supporters, the Italian Legion, were hamstrung by the absence of Garibaldi and half the Legionaries in Salto; and those who were in Montevideo took no part in the fighting.

As soon as Rivera had gained control, he did all he could to win the goodwill of the Italian Legion. He issued a proclamation on 15 April, praising the valour of the Italians; and on 5 April the *Patriote Français*, which, like the French Legion, had supported Rivera's *coup d'état*, published an article in praise of Garibaldi, stating that in view of Garibaldi's absence in Salto, and the fact that the Italian Legion did not have a newspaper, it was taking on itself the task of defending Garibaldi's reputation against the lying allegations of the Rosista and Blanco press that Garibaldi and his Italians had misbehaved themselves at Colonia. But Rivera and the new government secretly contacted General Medina in Salto, and told him to take steps to prevent the Italian Legion there from declaring for Pacheco and holding the town on Pacheco's behalf.[2]

There had been no action of any kind on the Salto front after the Battle of San Antonio and Medina's arrival at Salto, because Gomez had withdrawn his troops towards Paysandú. There had therefore been plenty of opportunity for friction to develop between the garrison and the local population, and between Garibaldi and Medina. In his memoirs, Garibaldi claims that the relations between his soldiers and the civil population of Salto were excellent, and he is doubtless right when he states that the 'gentle *Saltegne*' – the women of Salto – were very friendly with his men; but Antonio Diaz may also be right when he states that there were complaints from many of the citizens of Salto about the misbehaviour of the troops, and the loose discipline which Garibaldi enforced. Garibaldi had never believed in the rigid discipline of regular army officers, and it is easy to believe that in the weeks after 8 February 1846 he was not inclined to use harsh methods against the heroes of San Antonio.

Garibaldi's attitude displeased General Medina, with his belief in military discipline, and his relations with Garibaldi became very bad. The meetings of the junta of army leaders at Salto turned into wrangles between Medina and Garibaldi; and when Medina received instructions from Montevideo to bridle Garibaldi and the Italians, he was very eager to do so. But this was easier said than done. Medina had brought 300 men with him from Rio Grande do Sul, and he had another 300 cavalry under Baez; but there were still nearly 600 survivors of the troops who had come from Montevideo with Garibaldi, and, though less than 200 of these were Italians, most of the others, though native-born Uruguayans, had become as devoted to Garibaldi as his own Legionaries. But Garibaldi was worried because the Italian Legion was weakened by being divided, with some in Montevideo and some in Salto. He wrote repeatedly to Cuneo and to the Commissioners of the Legion and urged them to bring all the Legionaries in Montevideo to Salto as soon as possible; but the government refused to allow them to go.[3]

At the beginning of May, Medina gave orders for the cavalry in Salto to leave the town and go on reconnaissance in Northern Uruguay. Garibaldi strongly objected to the order. He thought that it was dictated by a desire to weaken his position in Salto, both against Medina and against the Blancos. On 8 May he asked Medina to call a meeting of the junta of army leaders to discuss the order; but Medina refused. Garibaldi then wrote this letter to Medina:

> Most excellent Señor,
> In view of your Excellency's note, dated today, from which it is clear that your Excellency has no desire even to hold a meeting of the Junta of Leaders, which I had demanded in my previous note, I have decided to act myself, by virtue of the responsibility conferred on me by the supreme government in this area and of the forces stationed in it; and I must ask your Excellency not to take any contrary action, and inform you that I shall take all steps to prevent this.
> > God send your Excellency many years.
> > > J. Garibaldi[4]

In referring to the responsibility that the government had conferred on him in the Salto area, Garibaldi was taking advantage of the ambiguity which existed in his relationship with Medina. When Garibaldi first arrived in Salto, there were no other Montevidean troops in the area, and he exercised an independent command; but Medina had been appointed Commander-in-Chief of the forces in Northern Uruguay, and as Salto was in Northern Uruguay, he considered that Garibaldi was under his orders, and was now threatening to commit mutiny. Medina must have been delighted when Garibaldi marched out of Salto with his men a few days later to attack the enemy. The Blanco army had marched north and again approached Salto, having taken up its position some ten miles south-east of Salto on the River Daimán, which is one of the many little rivers, hardly wider than streams, which flow into the River Uruguay. From this position their commanders, Lamos and Vergara, sent out bands of cavalry to attack Garibaldi's cavalry when they went out from Salto to round up cattle. Garibaldi decided to drive away the Blanco army. With his cavalry, and with the infantry of the Italian Legion, who had been reduced to just over 100 fighting men, he marched at night, as he usually did, and came on the enemy encamped on the River Daimán on the morning of 20 May.

He caught them, completely unprepared, in a surprise attack, and scattered them, driving many of them into the Daimán. He then marched back to Salto; but, as he puts it in his memoirs, 'Fortune had not deserted us that day', and the enemy gave him the opportunity to win another and more decisive victory. It was one of those warm days, with a cloudless blue sky, which sometimes come in Uruguay as late in the autumn as May, and the visibility was excellent. As Garibaldi and his men marched across the slightly undulating pampas, they noticed that the enemy was hovering on their flank. They came to a point where they had to cross a field in which the grass was so high that it was taller than a man, and Garibaldi realized that if the enemy attacked him while he was crossing this field, he would be at a great disadvantage, and would probably be annihilated. He therefore decided to fight and beat the enemy first. He sent his cavalry against them, and the enemy counter-attacked, and soon a fierce battle was in progress, in which both Garibaldi's cavalry and the Italian Legion distinguished themselves. After withstanding the enemy attack for half an hour, Garibaldi's men advanced and drove them back in complete disorder.

In his memoirs, Garibaldi wrote with great pride about the Daimán. Though neither at the time, nor afterwards, was it regarded as a triumph comparable to San Antonio, Garibaldi gives it a little more space than San Antonio in the memoirs. From Garibaldi's account, it is clear that the Blancos fought with much greater courage at the Daimán than they had done at San Antonio. Garibaldi describes how one of Vergara's soldiers fought on, after being wounded, until he was fighting alone, on one knee, against six of Garibaldi's men. Garibaldi arrived in time to order his men to spare the life of their brave enemy.[5]

Garibaldi returned to Salto to deal with Medina. On 12 June he sent an order to Colonel Jauregui, the Chief of Police at Salto:

Señor Chief of Police,
   I send herewith the order to Señor Brigadier-General Don Anacleto Medina to transfer himself on board the French warship *Eclair*, and I hold you responsible for the prompt execution of this order.
God send you many years.
J. Garibaldi

Medina was escorted to the *Eclair*, and sent back to Montevideo. Garibaldi had thus quietly deposed his superior officer, and sent him out of the arena in which he had been appointed Commander-in-Chief.[6]

According to Antonio Diaz, the government of Montevideo disapproved of Garibaldi's conduct, but took no action, because Medina did not wish to return to Salto.[7] Apart from what Medina may have wished, the government was powerless to discipline Garibaldi. In his memoirs, Garibaldi wrote that he was so loved by the Uruguayan units at Salto, as well as by his own Italians, that he might easily have made himself dictator had he wished. His position was also strengthened by his friendship with Ouseley, Inglefield and Lainé, who had a high opinion of him, and in any case tended to prefer the Pachecists to the Riveristas. Whatever they might think of Pacheco's politics, they felt that the Pachecists were more determined and efficient than the Riveristas in carrying on the war against the Blancos.

Garibaldi was almost certainly right in thinking that Medina's hostility was chiefly caused, not because he disapproved of the disorderly conduct of the Italians, but because he wished to secure Salto for the Riveristas. Garibaldi thought that he had acted with great restraint. 'At Montevideo, after Rivera's ascendancy,' he wrote in his memoirs, 'the squares had been stained with blood. At Salto, they had some idea of playing the same farce; but it did not succeed. I contented myself, by way of reprisals, with assuming the command of the forces as before.'[8]

Rivera and the government decided to recall Garibaldi and the Italian Legion to Montevideo, thinking presumably that, despite all the disadvantages, it would be better to have them in the capital, where they would be outweighed by the French Legion and the other forces, rather than leaving them in control of Salto. A new commander arrived to take charge of a small garrison at Salto; and on 20 August 1846 Garibaldi and the survivors of the Italian Legion sailed from Salto to Montevideo. They arrived off the Cerro at about 10 pm on 4 September, and after staying the night on board, disembarked in Montevideo early next morning, though Garibaldi himself did not leave the ship till the afternoon. The authorities had made arrangements to give the Italian Legion a great welcome as they came ashore, with the Basque Legion, headed by its commander, Colonel Brie, lining up on the waterfront and playing them ashore with its band, and Thiebaut and the French being also present to welcome them; but by an unfortunate mistake – if it was a mistake – the Italians landed some hours before they were expected, and there was no one there to greet them. The *Patriote Français* hastened to explain the reason for the absence of the Basque and French Legions, and all the garrison turned out to honour Garibaldi and his men at a victory parade next day.[9]

The Italian Legionaries from Salto returned to their place in the ranks of the Army of the Capital, which was now commanded by General Correa under Colonel Costa, the Minister of War and Marine. Both Correa and Costa were sympathetic to Rivera. Meanwhile Garibaldi was given a naval command. The former Argentine warship, the *Maipú*, which the British had seized from Admiral Brown in August 1845, was fitted out for the expedition, and Garibaldi was ordered to raid Argentine shipping in the River Plate and as far up the Paraná as he thought it wise to venture.

It was probably while this expedition was being planned that Admiral Lainé paid his visit to Garibaldi's house one evening. The story is told by Jessie White Mario in a form which is certainly untrue, and by the Uruguayan Héctor Vollo in 1899 in a version which may well be true.* When Garibaldi's colleagues suggested to him that they should hold a meeting at his house, he usually proposed that they should meet at the Ministry of War or somewhere else instead, because of the primitive conditions which prevailed in his home. But once, on a summer evening – it was probably in October 1846 – he agreed that the meeting should be held at his house. The representatives from the Montevidean Ministry of War and Marine arrived, and began discussing the proposed naval operations with Garibaldi, while Anita played with the children at the other end of the room. After a while, as the children became too distracting, Anita took them up onto the roof. The conference continued until after dusk, when there was a knock at the front door, and Garibaldi opened it to admit a short, stout man whom he recognized, in the half-light, as Admiral Lainé. Lainé joined the conference. They pored over the maps at the table in Garibaldi's room, but had some difficulty in seeing them by the light of the only candle which Garibaldi possessed. Next day, the government sent Garibaldi a large stock of candles; but Garibaldi's colleagues agreed that in future these high-level conferences should be held at the Ministry of War and Marine.[10]

Garibaldi saw more of Ouseley than of Lainé or Inglefield, because the admirals were usually at sea, and whenever Garibaldi was in Montevideo it was more convenient for Ouseley to deal with him. This also had the advantage that whereas Inglefield spoke neither French, Spanish nor Italian, and found it difficult to talk to Garibaldi, Ouseley could speak fluent Spanish and French, and seems usually to have

* Vollo heard the story from Papini, who told him that Castagna, Piaggio and Lainé were present; but his statement that the meeting was held in the kitchen is improbable, because the shared kitchen is so small that there would hardly have been room for four people to sit in it. Jessie White Mario is quite wrong in describing Garibaldi's house as a 'poor hovel with no door'.

spoken to Garibaldi in French. In 1859, when Garibaldi became very prominent in European politics at the outbreak of the war in Italy, Ouseley, who was then stationed in Costa Rica, wrote a report about Garibaldi for the British government, which showed how differently Garibaldi was regarded by the British ruling class than by the military establishment in South America.

When the British and French intervened on the side of Montevideo in 1845, Iriarte's first reaction had been to hope that they would keep Garibaldi and his Italians in order, because he thought that British and French admirals, with their strict ideas about discipline, would be outraged at Garibaldi's lack of discipline.[11] But though Inglefield and Lainé were sceptical at first as to Garibaldi's ability to preserve order among his men, they soon changed their minds. At one of the meetings with Garibaldi which were held at Ouseley's house, Inglefield asked Ouseley to find out from Garibaldi how he proposed to keep his men in order. Garibaldi answered quietly that he never had any difficulty in maintaining discipline, and that as a last resort he would blow out the brains of a trouble-maker with his pistols, but that this occurred only rarely: '*Je lui brûle la cervelle, mais cela n'arrive que rarement.*' Ouseley thought that it happened more often than Garibaldi said. 'In fact,' wrote Ouseley in 1859, 'he had on more than one occasion been obliged to draw one of the pistols, always worn in his belt, and resort to the extreme remedy that he mentioned.'

One of Ouseley's main duties in Montevideo was to make sure that the subsidies which the British and French governments were paying to the Montevidean navy were properly accounted for. Ouseley found that Garibaldi, unlike all the Uruguayan government officials with whom he had to deal, was scrupulously honest. At first Ouseley, despite the good reports which he had heard of Garibaldi, tended to assume the worst, because he was firmly convinced that every government official in South America was dishonest. He therefore resorted to various tricks to test the accuracy of Garibaldi's accounts; but he found that Garibaldi was entirely honest, and thereafter paid no attention to the native Uruguayans who hated Garibaldi, and who were always trying to make Ouseley believe that Garibaldi was cheating him.

Garibaldi usually visited Ouseley in the evening, and always wore a poncho or cloak, which he never took off. Ouseley afterwards discovered that Garibaldi came after dark because, as he had no money to buy candles, he wished to write his reports and prepare his maps at home during the hours of daylight; and he wore the poncho to hide his threadbare clothes.[12]

Ouseley's wife, Maria, also became very friendly with Garibaldi.

She was a citizen of the United States by birth, the daughter of Cornelius Van Hess, who was at one time Governor of Vermont. Her tall, stately figure attracted attention everywhere she went, and to Anita's annoyance it attracted Garibaldi's attention. Mrs Ouseley, who was an excellent rider, often went to meet Garibaldi when he rode home in the evening from the front line at the head of his Legionaries. This may have been one of the reasons why Anita was also in the habit of riding out to meet Garibaldi on these occasions, and taking her place at his side, which, in her absence, was filled by Maria Ouseley. Garibaldi's friends in Montevideo thought that Anita had feelings of inferiority in the presence of the society ladies; but she knew that she could beat them all on horseback.[13]

Alfred de Brossard, who was a member of Deffaudis's staff in Montevideo in 1847, was less enthusiastic than Ouseley about Garibaldi, but in view of the fact that he was writing in France in 1850, just after Garibaldi had fought against the French in Rome, his tribute to Garibaldi is significant. 'His probity and disinterestedness is unblemished,' he wrote, 'and his austerity, though a little affected, reminds one of the ancient Romans.' As a sailor and soldier, his cool daring had won the confidence of his men. 'But his military ability ends here . . . He is very able at carrying out plans, but is incapable of rising to general conceptions of war. His intelligence is obviously shaped by political revelationism. Just to look at his face, noble and regular, but frozen by his usual absent-mindedness, his large blue eyes, piercing and dark, one can see that he is a persevering and determined man, but nothing more.' Brossard condemned Garibaldi for his failure to enforce discipline over his men, which he attributed to his false ideas of equality and his 'fraternal tolerance', and added: 'He knows how to get his men killed, but not how to flog them.'[14]

In October, Garibaldi sailed in the *Maipú* up the River Plate, and proceeded to attack Argentine shipping wherever he found it. For once he was not fighting against heavy odds. As the British and French had compelled Admiral Brown and his English-born officers to retire from the Argentine service, had confiscated three of the Argentine warships, and were blockading Buenos Aires, Garibaldi had little serious opposition to contend with, and he succeeded in seizing many prizes. After a number of successes off Colonia, he sailed up the lower reaches of the Paraná, and, entering the little ports along the river and on the south bank of the River Plate, he captured or destroyed the Argentine craft which he found there. The reports of Ximenes, the Captain of the Port of Buenos Aires, to Rosas, tell the tale of woe: the *Quecho*, the *Matildo*, the *Paula*, the *Victoria*, all met and seized by the pirate Garibaldi in the former Argentine ship, the *Maipú*. On 9 November the *Gaceta*

Mercantil reported that some days earlier, Garibaldi had sailed from Colonia to Montevideo with eighteen Argentine merchant ships as prize; and on 4 November he reached Montevideo with all of them. On the same day, the British warship, the steamer *Lizard*, also arrived in Montevideo with three Argentine ships which she had captured. A few of the ships which Garibaldi had taken were neutral foreign ships which he was not entitled to seize under international law, including one which belonged to a British merchant, Mr Lamb, who traded with Buenos Aires. These neutral ships were returned to their owners, with apologies, by the government of Montevideo.[15]

The success of Garibaldi in the *Maipú* aroused the greatest anger in Argentina. They were particularly angry because Garibaldi was conducting his operations in an Argentine ship. They denounced the action of Ouseley and Deffaudis in giving the Argentine ship *Maipú* to Garibaldi, and encouraging and assisting him to seize Argentine ships, as an outrage against America and an 'affront to humanity and to commerce'. This theme of the wickedness of the great European powers in sending Garibaldi to rob and burn along the internal rivers of Argentina was taken up by the press in other countries on the American continent. In Chile, the *Gaceta* of Valparaiso denounced this shameful Anglo-French intervention in 'the world of Columbus'; and in Washington, the *Daily Union* became very indignant about the action of Ouseley and Deffaudis in sending 'the Italian pirate Garibaldi' to attack Argentine shipping in an Argentine ship.[16]

Garibaldi's successful raids in the *Maipú* were the culmination of a successful year. But the new year was to see another sharp change of fortune. 1847 was a black year for the Montevidean cause. It opened badly on 9 January, when Servando Gomez captured Salto. Paysandú, which had been captured by Rivera some months earlier, fell to Gomez on 24 January, Soriano on the 26th, and Mercedes on the 27th. While Gomez was winning these victories in Uruguay, Urquiza crushed the Unitarians in Corrientes. By March, the Blancos had won back nearly all the territory that they had lost in 1845 and 1846, and the Unitarians held nothing except the towns of Montevideo and Colonia. But the Unitarian cause had suffered an even more serious set-back. In June 1846 Peel's government in Britain resigned, and Aberdeen was replaced as Foreign Secretary by Palmerston. Within a fortnight of taking office, Palmerston had quarrelled violently with France about the marriages of the Queen and Infanta of Spain, and Aberdeen's policy of an *entente cordiale* with France was in ruins.

Palmerston continued for a time to pursue Aberdeen's policy in the River Plate. The Unitarians of Montevideo, who had been alarmed at Peel's defeat over the Corn Laws in November 1845, relieved at Lord

John Russell's failure to form a government in December, and again alarmed at the change of government in June 1846, noticed no change in British policy for nearly a year. But Palmerston's suspicions of France, and his sympathy for Rosas, led him slowly to change the emphasis of British policy in the River Plate. He persuaded Guizot to make a new peace bid, and in May 1847 Lord Howden and Count Walewski arrived from Europe to replace Ouseley and Deffaudis, who sailed for home. The new Anglo-French peace proposals were almost the same as those which Guizot and Aberdeen had put forward in 1845: Rosas was to recognize the independence of Uruguay, to withdraw his troops from Uruguayan territory, and to cease all military operations against Uruguay; the foreign legions in Montevideo were to be dissolved; and a caretaker government was to be established in Uruguay to arrange for free elections to a new National Assembly, which would elect a new President of the Republic. But Howden, unlike Walewski, had instructions to withdraw all military support from Montevideo if Rosas accepted these proposals and Montevideo did not.[17]

Howden and Walewski began by suggesting that both sides agree to a truce while the peace proposals were being considered. This was accepted by Rosas, and rather reluctantly by the government of Montevideo, and on 22 May a truce came into force. It was to last for a month, and then to continue until denounced, with twenty-four hours' notice, by either side. Howden and Walewski then went to Buenos Aires, and put their peace proposals to Rosas. Despite the fact that the war had recently been going in his favour, Rosas was wise enough to accept. There was a strong difference of opinion in Montevideo as to whether to accept or not.

The population of Montevideo, after nine years of war and more than four years of siege, were eager for peace, and their hopes had been encouraged, and their will to fight weakened, by the truce. Many of the Riverista officers, like Flores, were in favour of the peace proposals. But the terms were unacceptable to the Argentine Unitarians in Montevideo, who had always seen the war as a crusade to liberate Argentina from Rosas as well as Uruguay from Oribe. The more radical and heroic of the Uruguayan Unitarians took the same attitude. This was not a policy with which Palmerston, or any British government, had the least sympathy. Even Aberdeen had decisively rejected it, and in one of his last letters before leaving office had criticized Ouseley for favouring it. 'Your great object,' he wrote to Ouseley on 2 July 1846, 'is the overthrow of Rosas; I should deeply regret this, and would not effect it if I could . . . We have no complaint whatever, in my opinion, to make against Rosas, except his reluctance to make peace with Mte Video.'[18]

Garibaldi, with his Liberal crusading zeal, his friendship with the Pachecists, and his inherent dislike of compromise and of anything which smacked, however remotely, of surrender, was in favour of continuing the war. In this, at least, he had the support of Thiebaut and the French Legion. There was probably some justification for the assertions of the Rosista propagandists that the foreign Legionaries in Montevideo had a personal interest in the continuation of the war, because even though the allegations about the looting and profiteering activities of the Legionaries were greatly exaggerated, many of the foreigners had no property or prospects, and had never had any successful career except as soldiers of Montevideo. There was also the possibility that the lands in Uruguay, which they had been promised after the war, might be confiscated by the new government which emerged under the peace proposals.

The struggle for power in Montevideo between the Pachecists and Riveristas was intensified during the truce. In order to stiffen the determination of the people to resist, the Pachecists formed a new political society, with Fernandez as provisional President, and Andrés Lamas, the Minister of the Interior, as Vice-President. The society held its inaugural meeting on 15 June, and invited about fifty prominent persons, including the military leaders, to attend. Garibaldi came with Anzani and Mundell, and Flores and some Riverista officers also attended. After the President had made the opening address, Flores rose and made a violent attack on Lamas, whom he accused of subverting the constitution and terrorizing the people of Montevideo. When Flores had finished speaking, he and his friends walked out, and the meeting became very disorderly; and soon afterwards Garibaldi, Anzani and Mundell walked out. Flores printed his denunciation of Lamas, and had it distributed in Montevideo. He also started a newspaper, the *Conciliador*, which agitated in favour of peace.[19]

In view of Flores's action, the war party considered it essential that the key positions in Montevideo should be held by men who were opposed to surrender. Garibaldi was therefore placed in command of the Army of the Capital. He was not officially given the title of Commander-in-Chief, perhaps because the Pachecists and the government realized that the appointment of a foreigner to this position might cause difficulties. Instead, a decree of 25 June 1847 reorganized the whole system of command in the Army of the Capital. The Commander-in-Chief, Correa, became Minister of War and Marine. The office of Commander-in-Chief was abolished. The Army of the Capital was divided into two parts; the first, containing the Italian Legion and the French Legion, was placed under the command of Thiebaut; the other part, containing all the other regiments, was placed under

Colonel Villagran. Both Thiebaut and Villagran were placed under the supreme command of Garibaldi, who was thus in charge of all the Army of the Capital, and Commander-in-Chief in all but name.[20] It was a well-earned reward for the bravest, most sincere and most successful of the Montevidean generals; but it was a very controversial step, and played into the hands of the Rosistas' propaganda, just at the time when resentment against the foreign Legionaries was growing in Montevideo because the Legionaries seemed to stand in the way of a negotiated peace.

The Pachecists probably did not foresee the extent of the opposition to Garibaldi's appointment; but Oribe's paper, the *Defensor*, in its editorial of 1 July, struck a note which met with a ready response in many quarters.

> The ultimate shame that could be inflicted upon those few Orientals who still reside in Montevideo was to force them to submit to a vile adventurer; and a decree of those infamous rulers who call themselves the government of the nation has condemned them to this infamy, by giving the post of Commander-in-Chief of the forces of this city to the Italian pirate José Garibaldi. We do not believe that it will be easy to find, in the history of civilized peoples, an example of such degradation; and one can only draw the conclusion that these sons of the country, who call themselves its leaders, have not only lost all ideas of honour and decency, but also the ability to blush, if they imagine that even the most abject slaves will agree to suffer this new humiliation and infamy.

The *Defensor* followed this up with an even longer, and even more vitriolic, article on 5 July, which filled the greater part of that issue of the paper, and ended by telling the Oriental people that they now faced the simple choice: did they wish to be ruled by General Oribe, 'the new Duke of Wellington', or by 'that *gringo* pirate'?[21]

At the height of the furore about Garibaldi's appointment, Howden and Walewski arrived in Montevideo. Howden had had a distinguished military and diplomatic career, having often been sent on special missions to trouble-spots in Greece, Belgium, Portugal and Spain. Walewski was the illegitimate son of Napoleon and the Polish Countess Maria Walewska; despite his Bonapartist family ties, he had entered the French diplomatic service under Louis Philippe. Howden had instructions from Palmerston to use all the means in his power to force the government of Montevideo to accept the Anglo-French proposals; Walewski's instructions from Guizot were merely to put forward the proposals, and to discover whether they were acceptable to Montevideo. Howden soon formed the opinion that the Unitarian leaders in Montevideo were a gang of power-seeking politicians, that there was nothing to choose between them and Rosas from a moral point of view, and that the Rosistas and Blancos were right in their allegations that Montevideo was completely under the control of the foreign Legionaries. He had a series of meetings with the leaders in Montevideo, and used all his experience, his charm and his firmness to induce them to accept his peace terms. He came to the conclusion that the chief obstacle to the acceptance of the terms was the presence of Garibaldi and his Italians.

On 6 July, Howden had an interview with Garibaldi. It is easy to imagine his feelings when he first saw the bearded, long-haired Radical in his extraordinary uniform who was frustrating the policy of the British government in the River Plate. He tried to persuade Garibaldi to dissolve the Italian Legion and to accept the peace terms; but Garibaldi refused, and told Howden that he and his Legion would continue the fight for freedom in Montevideo. After they had talked, Garibaldi departed, leaving Howden full of admiration for him. He was more than ever convinced that Montevideo was dominated by the armed foreigners, but was also sure that Garibaldi was the most admirable character that he had met on his mission to the River Plate. It is one of the most striking examples of the effect which Garibaldi always produced on the English aristocracy. At a time when not only the enemy, but also many of the Unitarians for whom Garibaldi was fighting, were conducting a vicious campaign of slander against him, Lord Howden, with that respect for eccentricity, courage and sincerity in an opponent which was more marked in the British ruling class than in their counterparts in other countries, was filled with admiration for the foreign revolutionary who was obstructing the object of his diplomatic mission.

Two years later, Howden spoke in a debate on the River Plate in the House of Lords. It was on 10 July 1849, seven days after the collapse of the Roman Republic, when Garibaldi, after his two months' defence of Rome, was retreating to the north on the march which ended in disaster and the death of Anita. Howden denounced the Unitarians of Montevideo and justified Rosas. He said that the war of Montevideo was not a fight for national independence, as the Unitarians made out, but a war which had begun as a party faction fight, and was only being prolonged because the foreign mercenaries who controlled Montevideo had a vested interest in the continuation of hostilities. He then added that he was glad to have the opportunity to pay a tribute to a man who 'stood a disinterested individual among those who only sought their own personal advantage . . . a person of great courage and military skill, who had a great claim upon their sympathies'. This man was

General Garibaldi. Howden's speech was welcomed in Buenos Aires; but the *British Packet* was perplexed by his references to Garibaldi, and believed, or pretended to believe, that when he praised Garibaldi he was speaking sarcastically.[22]

The day after Garibaldi's talk with Howden, he had an interview with Flores, who told him that unless he resigned as Commander-in-Chief, there would be a mutiny in the Montevidean army, as many of the native-born Uruguayan officers would refuse to serve under him. Garibaldi immediately offered to resign; he had never been interested in his own personal advancement, and did not hesitate to relinquish it for the public good. On 7 July 1847, twelve days after he had been appointed Commander-in-Chief, he wrote a very short letter to General Correa, the Minister of War and Marine:

Most excellent Señor,
I have the honour to express to your Excellency the great gratitude that I owe to the supreme government for the honourable post that they have conferred upon me, and I resign it.
God send your Excellency many years.
José Garibaldi

Correa accepted Garibaldi's resignation. He revoked the new chain of command which had been set up on 25 June, and returned to the previous arrangement, appointing old Colonel Villagran as Commander-in-Chief. Garibaldi's only comment, in his memoirs, on this whole episode was one sentence in the 1872 edition: 'During this time I was called to the honour of commanding the army of the Republic, and nothing of importance occurred during my command, which I handed over to the brave old veteran Villagran.'[23]

It was presumably an accident, and not arson by Garibaldi's enemies, when the tobacconist's shop next door to Garibaldi's house caught fire on the night of 16 July. The fire in the shop burned fiercely, and for a time it looked as if Garibaldi's house was in danger; but the fire brigade and the police made great exertions, and the fire was brought under control. Garibaldi himself played an active part in fighting the fire, and in urging the fire-fighters to act with even greater energy.[24]

During these days, Garibaldi received more signs of consideration from his opponents than from his allies. On 25 July Admiral Brown arrived in Montevideo. He was on his way to Ireland to visit his native town of Foxford, which he had not seen for sixty years. As the truce was still in force, Brown asked permission to land and stay for a few days in Montevideo. The permission was granted, and he was received with due honour at Government House. He lodged at a house in the Calle

Cerro, and though the authorities placed a guard in front of the house to protect him from any hostile demonstration, nothing of the kind took place. The *Comercio del Plata*, the new Montevidean newspaper which Varela had founded on his return home after completing his term as Uruguayan Minister in London, used the occasion to point out the generosity and humanitarianism of the Unitarians. Varela contrasted the honour which was being paid to Brown in Montevideo with the fate which would befall any Unitarian commander who set foot in Buenos Aires.

During his stay in Montevideo, Brown visited Garibaldi at his house. The two enemies talked in a most friendly fashion, expressed their admiration for each other, and discussed their campaigns, especially Costa Brava; and Brown told Anita of the high regard which he had for Garibaldi.[25]

On 15 July the government of Montevideo informed Howden and Walewski that they were rejecting the peace proposals, which Oribe had accepted on the same day. Next day Howden ordered Commodore Herbert, who had succeeded Inglefield in command of the British squadron, to embark all the British forces in Montevideo, raise the blockade of Buenos Aires, and return to England, 'as I consider . . . that the Orientals of Monte Video are not at this moment free agents, but entirely controlled by a foreign garrison'; and he told the Montevidean government that Britain was withdrawing all support from them. Howden left Montevideo on 26 July.

Anti-British demonstrations broke out in Montevideo. The slogan 'Death to the English' appeared on the gates of the barracks where the British marines were stationed, and snipers shot from out of the darkness at the British troops as they sat in the evenings in the garden of the barracks. But Garibaldi wrote a letter, on behalf of the Italian Legion, to Captain Martin, of the British ship *Eagle*, in which he thanked him for his collaboration and wished him success in the future, though he expressed his disappointment that the British government were abandoning their Montevidean allies. All the British troops had left within a few weeks. But France continued to support Montevideo. Walewski assured the Montevidean government that the French navy would be able to maintain the blockade of Buenos Aires without British help, and though he sailed for France on 3 August, he left behind him his successor, Devoize, who had instructions to support Montevideo more energetically than ever, now that this was, in Guizot's eyes, a way of striking at Palmerston.[26]

On 2 August the government of Montevideo gave Oribe the required twenty-four hours' notice that it was ending the truce which had been in force since 22 May. Within a few hours Oribe's artillery was bombarding the Montevidean outposts, an action which was denounced by the Unitarians as a violation of the truce terms, as the twenty-four hours' notice had not expired.[27] But for many of the inhabitants of Montevideo it was not the premature action of Oribe which aroused resentment, but the fact that their own government had decided to resume hostilities, and that they could again hear the familiar sound of the guns which had been silent for more than two months. There were demonstrations against the war in the streets of Montevideo.

On the night of 3 August a meeting of several high-ranking army officers and prominent civilian leaders was held at the house of Colonel Magariños. Flores, who was present, suggested that they organize a petition to the government demanding the opening of peace negotiations with Oribe. By next day the petition had been signed by 420 leading figures in Montevideo, including General Aguiar, one of the most distinguished of the older Uruguayan generals; Araucho, the President of the Court of Justice; and Isidore De-Maria, the editor of the *Constitucional*, as well as Flores and the organizers of the petition. Another petition by less eminent signatories was presented two days later. It declared that after the citizens of Montevideo had heroically resisted Oribe for fifty-three months, no one could doubt their zeal and loyalty, but that now a negotiated peace would be the best way of winning over the more moderate and Liberal elements among Oribe's supporters. On 5 August, a counter-petition, signed by thirty serving officers, including Villagran the Commander-in-Chief, Tajes and Batlle, declared their loyalty to the government, and their determination to continue the war. Garibaldi was not one of the officers who signed this declaration, but this can only have been because it was thought advisable that only native-born Uruguayans should sign.

On 7 August the government, having been stiffened by a new promise of French assistance from Devoize, rejected all demands for peace, and refused to meet any deputation from the petitioners. Four days later, at Devoize's instigation, the government resigned, and was replaced on 16 August by a new ministry composed of ardent Pachecists. On the same day, a mutiny broke out among the troops stationed at the Cerro. It was led by Captain Larraya, and involved the whole of the Second Battalion of the native-born army. It was not directly caused by a desire to end the war, because it was due to the fact that the battalion had not received any pay for the last four months; but it added to the general discontent, and the officers of the peace party, such as Flores, showed no great zeal in suppressing the mutiny. The government therefore entrusted the task to Garibaldi. According to

Jessie White Mario, who is mistaken about the date of the mutiny,* Garibaldi rode out alone on his horse to face the mutineers, and shamed them into surrendering, after all the other army commanders had been afraid to take any action. Garibaldi may have fearlessly faced the mutineers; but their capitulation was in fact arranged by the new French naval commander, Admiral Le Prédour, who negotiated a settlement under which the mutineers surrendered on the promise of their lives and liberty, Larraya agreeing to go into exile on a French warship.

A few days later, Garibaldi sent a memorandum to the government in which he complained of Flores's defeatism and unreliability, and denounced him for his readiness to negotiate with the enemy. As a result, Flores resigned his position in the army. He was presented with a passport and advised to leave the country, and left for Brazil.[28]

Throughout all these weeks Rivera himself had played no part in the events in Montevideo, because he was besieged by the Blancos in Maldonado. When he heard about Flores's resignation and exile, he wrote to President Suarez in some alarm. The government replied by sending Batlle to Maldonado with orders to remove Rivera. By a deft manoeuvre, he succeeded in arresting Rivera in the midst of his army, and quickly bundled him on board a French warship which took him once again to exile in Brazil.

In his memoirs, Garibaldi is most misleading about this incident, as he is about all the conflict between Rivera and Pacheco. He ignored the whole subject in the first editions of the memoirs, but in the 1872 edition he dealt with it briefly. He attributed all the disasters which befell the Montevidean cause to the 'revolution' of 1 April 1846, when the selfish, power-seeking Riveristas overthrew the patriotic and dis-interested Pachecists. He completely disregarded the fact that the revolution was a reply to the suppression of the constitution by Pacheco six weeks earlier; and his comment on the events at Maldonado in October 1847 is that Rivera, after being defeated repeatedly by the Argentines, retreated to Maldonado, where he embarked and left the country amid 'universal execration'.[29]

The Rosistas and Blancos hated Rivera so much that they could not conceal their joy at his downfall; but they interpreted it, and the events in Montevideo in July and August, as proof that the foreign

---

*She says (Werner, III.63) that the mutiny occurred on the day that Garibaldi was appointed Commander-in-Chief, which she places immediately after the return from Salto in September 1846. Her statement that no other general dared to try to suppress the mutiny because 'shortly before, Estibas [she means Estivao] had been killed in a mutiny', hardly suggests that Estivao had been killed in street-fighting when resisting the successful *coup d'état* of April 1846.

mercenaries had finally gained complete control over the Montevidean authorities. They painted a picture, which was not altogether a false one, of a war-weary population of native Uruguayans in Montevideo who were longing for peace, but were prevented from demanding it by the reign of terror exercised by the armed Europeans, backed by a handful of Argentine Unitarian refugees. They reported that when the armistice was ended, crowds of Montevideans had tried to cross the lines and fraternize with Oribe's forces, but had been driven back by the musket-fire and bayonets of the foreigners at the orders of Garibaldi.[30] Increasingly, they singled out two individuals for their attacks—Garibaldi and Varela. According to the Buenos Aires and Oribe newspapers, the Italian Garibaldi was the real ruler of Montevideo, and the Argentine traitor Varela – the leading representative of the middle-class Unitarian intelligentsia – was the chief propagandist and sedition-monger. They almost forgot to denounce Rivera, Pacheco, and Lafone and his international speculators, because they were so busy attacking Garibaldi and Varela.

But Rosas was secretly adopting a different attitude with regard to Garibaldi. When he heard that Garibaldi had been forced to resign as Commander-in-Chief in Montevideo, it occurred to him that as Garibaldi would be feeling aggrieved at the treatment which he had received, this might be a good moment to buy him over. He offered Garibaldi 30,000 dollars if he would desert the Montevideans and join the Argentine and Blanco forces, and wrote a personal letter to Oribe about it. 'You should try to win the *gringo* Garibaldi, who is the inspiration of the savage Unitarians besieged in Montevideo, without stinting the amount. You should give him all the money that he asks for, as the savages have not got any to give him, not even for candles.' But Oribe had already tried to buy Garibaldi without success, and he replied to Rosas: 'I have used all possible means to achieve this, but he cannot be won; he is a stubborn savage.'*

*The authenticity of these letters, with the surprising reference to the candles – it is strange that Rosas should have known about this in 1847 – would be established beyond all doubt if it were possible to find the original letters; but I have been unable to find them in either Buenos Aires or Montevideo, and am informed by Professor Irazusta, the editor of the five-volume edition of Rosas's correspondence, that he has never seen them. But the eminent Argentine historian, Carranza, cited these undated extracts from the letters, which he implies were written about July 1847, in a footnote to an article in the *Revista Nacional* of Buenos Aires in 1901 (XXXI.11n). He stated that he had found them among Rosas's private correspondence. Pereda (III.75), who cites them, gives Carranza as his reference. Carranza's reputation is high enough to justify us in accepting them on his word alone. The offer of a bribe to Garibaldi is confirmed by Ouseley, who referred, in his memorandum for Lord John Russell in 1859, to the offer of 30,000 dollars to Garibaldi (*Cornhill Mag.*, NS, XXX.394).

CHAPTER 15

THE RETURN TO ITALY

ALTHOUGH Garibaldi had refused to desert to Rosas, he was thinking of leaving Montevideo for Italy. He had never ceased to think about the liberation of Italy during all his years in South America, and had been deeply moved when he heard about the expedition of the Bandiera brothers in 1844, which revived the Italian fight for freedom after a ten-year interval. The two young Bandieras planned to land with a party of patriots at a lonely spot on the coast of Calabria and start a revolution against the King of Naples. Unfortunately Mazzini, who was a party to the plan, believed his English Liberal friends who told him that there was no postal censorship in Britain, and posted a letter to another Italian refugee in London, in which he revealed all the details of the plot. The British government had given orders that Mazzini's letters were to be secretly opened in the General Post Office at Mount Pleasant, and on learning the contents of Mazzini's letter they informed the Austrian and Neapolitan governments, who had already discovered about the plan. The Bandieras and their companions landed in Calabria, but they lost their way, the local peasants did not rise, and they were all captured. Nine of them, including young Nicola Ricciotti, were shot. As they faced the firing squad, they sang the chorus from Mercadante's *Donna Caritea*: 'He who dies for his country has lived long enough!'[1]

When Garibaldi's second son was born, he called him Ricciotti in honour of the martyr. Ricciotti Garibaldi was born on 24 February 1847, six months after Garibaldi and Anita had returned to Montevideo from Salto. They may have decided to have another child when they were in Salto in view of Rosita's death. Jessie White Mario says that Garibaldi was so poor that Lieutenant Odinici, the medical officer of the Italian Legion, had to organize a collection among Garibaldi's friends to pay for Ricciotti's christening. This may well be true, because either Garibaldi's poverty, or some other reason, had prevented him from having any of his other children christened. When Ricciotti was christened in the church of San Francisco de Asis on 28 March 1847, Teresita was christened at the same time, although she was already sixteen months old,* and there is no record of the christening of either Rosita in this church or of Menotti in Rio Grande do Sul.[2]

Garibaldi was certainly as poor as ever. One day about this time, he was on the point of going out to attend an interview with President Suarez when Teresita fell down the stairs and cut her forehead. Garibaldi decided to buy her a toy to console her, and went to their money box, where he found that they had only three pesos. He put the money in his pocket, and went off to meet Suarez, but the important public business which he discussed with the President made him forget completely about Teresita's toy. When he returned home, he found Anita in a state of great distress because someone had robbed their money box. Garibaldi was able to reassure her on this score, and handed back the three pesos to her.[3]†

Garibaldi's thoughts of returning to Italy seem, naturally enough, to have become stronger whenever he encountered some new example of Uruguayan ingratitude and bickering. In July 1846 he wrote from Salto to Cuneo in Montevideo, just after the successful outcome of his conflict with Medina. He told Cuneo that he was thinking of sending Anita and the children to Europe, and asked Cuneo to ask Ouseley and Lainé to help to get a passport for Anita. He sent Anita back to Montevideo in July 1846, a month before he himself left Salto; but he obviously abandoned, for the moment, his plan of sending her to Europe, perhaps because she was expecting the birth of Ricciotti. He revived the idea after the experiences of July and August 1847, and by this time was making definite plans for returning to Italy himself.[4]

At the very moment when Garibaldi was becoming increasingly disillusioned about affairs in Uruguay, the news from Italy was becoming more and more encouraging. In June 1846 Cardinal Mastai-Ferretti was elected Pope as Pius IX. The new Pope, who was the son of an Italian Count, and had spent a number of years on a diplomatic mission in Chile, had tried, as Archbishop of Spoleto and Bishop of Imola, to pursue as liberal a policy as possible under the reactionary rule of Pope Gregory XVI; and his election as Pope caused Metternich to have serious misgivings.

As soon as he became Pope, Pius IX introduced a series of bold, Liberal reforms. He immediately proclaimed an amnesty for all political prisoners in the Papal States. He greatly relaxed the censorship,

---

*According to the records in the church of San Francisco de Asis referring to Teresita's baptism, Teresita was born in November 1845; but there are reasons for believing that she was born in 1844 (see Pereda, III.23, 29).

†Though the story of Teresita's toy appears only in the Dumas edition of the memoirs, Dumas expressly states that he was told the story by Garibaldi himself.

abolished the discriminatory laws against the Jews, discontinued all persecution of heretics, introduced reforms which had long been demanded by the Liberals into the financial and administrative systems, and decreed that in future laymen, as well as priests, might serve in the higher branches of the government and judiciary. On the most important of all the Liberal demands, that he should introduce a constitution and elected assemblies in the Papal States, he proceeded more slowly, because here he was confronted with the determined opposition of the Church hierarchy, who were entrenched in the positions of political power; but in April 1847 he issued a decree establishing a legislative council for the city of Rome, some of whom were to be elected by the citizens and some appointed by the Pope. These measures were greeted with great popular enthusiasm, and provided a great spur to the revolutionary movement in Italy and to the *Risorgimento*. Demonstrations took place all over Italy, the people rallying to the slogan '*Viva Pio Nono e la liberta!*' Not surprisingly, the patriotic and revolutionary mobs sometimes committed acts of violence against reactionaries and the police, and Metternich made this the excuse for sending Austrian troops to restore order in the city of Ferrara, in the Papal territories, without Pius ix's consent, and despite his protests.

Mazzini in London watched developments in Italy with great hopes, and in September 1847 wrote a letter to Pius ix, encouraging him in his task of liberalising the Papal States, and offering him the support of Young Italy; and when the news of Pius ix's reforms and the Liberal movement in Italy reached Montevideo, Garibaldi and Anzani wrote to Monsignor Bedini, the Papal Nuncio in Montevideo, on 12 October 1847, congratulating Pius ix on his actions. After reminding the Nuncio that during the five-year siege of Montevideo their Italian Legion had succeeded in distinguishing itself, 'thanks to Providence and the ancient spirit which still enflames our Italian blood', they offered the services of the Legion to the Pope. 'If these hands, which are used to fighting, would be acceptable to His Holiness, it is unnecessary to say that we dedicate them most willingly to the service of him who has done so much for our country and the Church. We would indeed be very happy if we could co-operate in Pius ix's work of redemption . . . and we do not think that we would pay too high a price if it costs us our blood.' They ended by telling Bedini that they prayed that His Holiness 'may be granted many years for the happiness of Christianity and of Italy'. Bedini sent the letter on to Rome, and wrote to Garibaldi and Anzani 'that the devotion and generosity expressed in your letter towards our Supreme Pontiff is worthy of Italian hearts'.[5]

The letter of Garibaldi and Anzani makes strange reading today.

Within a few years Pius IX had become the most determined enemy of Italian Liberalism and the *Risorgimento*, and Bedini was endorsing the executions of Garibaldi's followers in the Papal States. But the letter of Garibaldi and Anzani was not only in line with Mazzini's policy towards the Pope in 1847, but also undoubtedly expressed the sincere enthusiasm which they had come to feel for Pius IX as a result of his reforming policy. Garibaldi had not yet developed that passionate hatred of the Catholic Church and of priests which followed from his experiences in 1849. He had rejected the Catholic dogma in which he had been brought up by his mother, and had adopted the deistic doctrines of Mazzini; but, like Mazzini himself and the other members of Young Italy, he was always ready to work together with the Catholic Church if it gave any indication that it had abandoned its reactionary attitude in temporal politics. His experiences in South America had probably not greatly affected his attitude towards the Catholic Church, because the Church had observed a strict neutrality in the war between Rosas and the Unitarians, and had remained silent, though both sides accused the other of being anti-Christian and against the Church.

In November 1847 Garibaldi again took part in naval operations in the River Plate in the *Maipú*, which was now renamed the *Fama*. He captured an Argentine merchant ship, the *Aquila*, which was sailing from Rio de Janeiro to Buenos Aires, off Punta del Espinillo, some fifteen miles west of Montevideo; and there was again trouble when he captured a Sardinian ship, which the government of Montevideo returned to its owners, with the usual apologies. But Garibaldi had definitely decided to return to Italy in the near future, and his desire to go was probably intensified after a very unpleasant incident later in November, when a nasty brawl broke out between soldiers of the Basque and Italian Legions, in which a Basque killed one of Garibaldi's Italians with a knife. The Rosista and Blanco newspapers made out that a serious rift had arisen between Garibaldi and Brie over the incident, with Garibaldi insisting that the government should inflict the severest punishment on the murderer, while Brie tried to shield him.[6]

At the beginning of December, the Sardinian ship *Carolina* arrived at Montevideo from Genoa with a supply of revolutionary newspapers, which were now, for the first time, being legally published in Piedmont. They were full of news of Liberal demonstrations and risings all over Italy. The Italians in Montevideo celebrated by holding a torchlight procession through the streets. It was led by Garibaldi and the officers of the Legion, with the Legionaries and the Italian civilians marching behind, while bands played and the marchers sang Italian patriotic and revolutionary songs.[7]

At the beginning of January 1848 Anita left Montevideo for Italy, with Menotti, Teresita and Ricciotti, and a number of other wives and children of Italian Legionaries. Garibaldi had decided to send her and the children to stay with his mother in Nice. Anita was distressed at being separated from Rosita's body in the cemetery in Montevideo; on the day before she left, she put flowers on the grave for the last time. Garibaldi was intending to follow Anita in the near future, though he was not sure whether he would go to Nice. He was under sentence of death in the kingdom of Sardinia for his actions in Genoa in February 1834, and as Charles Albert had given no indication of any change in his attitude to the revolutionaries of Young Italy, Garibaldi could not be sure that the fourteen-year-old sentence might not be carried out if he went to Nice. He was therefore considering going to the Papal States, or to Tuscany, and offering his services either to Pius IX or to the Grand-Duke of Tuscany, who had shown some signs of being willing to follow the Pope's Liberal lead. An alternative plan, if the Grand-Duke turned out to be hostile, was for Garibaldi to land at some place on the coast of Tuscany, with as many of his Legionaries as would accompany him, and to carry on guerrilla activities in Tuscany in the hopes of starting a revolution there. But his exact destination was to be arranged later, between Mazzini and Garibaldi's colleague, Giacomo Medici, who, after fighting for several years for the Liberals in Spain, had been sent to Montevideo by Mazzini in 1845 to contact the members of Young Italy there, and now returned to Europe with messages from Garibaldi to Mazzini.[8]

On 8 February 1848 Montevideo celebrated the second anniversary of the victory of San Antonio. Articles commemorating the victory, and praising Garibaldi and the Italian Legion, appeared in all the Montevidean newspapers, though the *Gaceta Mercantil* declared that it was notorious that on 8 February 1846, at San Antonio, the Orientals and Argentines had obtained a 'glorious triumph' over the foreign adventurers in a battle in which the forces on both sides had been equal, and which had ended in Garibaldi's 'defeat and flight'. The *Gaceta* particularly attacked Varela for pretending that San Antonio was a victory instead of a 'shameful defeat' for 'the foreigners who are the infamous and hateful instruments of European intervention against the most sacred principles and interests of America'. In honour of San Antonio, Garibaldi was appointed a member of the Assembly of Notables. Although the members of the Assembly were nominated, and not elected, Garibaldi was, most appropriately, nominated to be the member for Salto.

The appointment led to another outburst of criticism from the Rosistas, and the usual dissatisfaction in certain circles in Montevideo.

The *Defensor* denounced the appointment of Garibaldi, a man 'bathed in American blood'; but it was warmly defended in the *Conservador* of Montevideo, which declared that 'it is an act of justice, not a favour, which has been granted to the victor of San Antonio'.[9]

Neither the Montevideans who applauded, nor the Blancos who condemned, the appointment of Garibaldi as a member of the Assembly of Notables, seemed to be aware that the new member of the Assembly was intending to leave Uruguay for ever in two months' time. But the criticism which followed the appointment may have given Garibaldi an additional motive for leaving. On 20 February he wrote to Medici, telling him that he had decided to return to Italy with some of his Legionaries, and asking Medici to discuss with Mazzini which was the best place for them to land. He wrote that their object was to fight the Austrians in the open field, because the anger of all Italians should be ceaselessly directed against the Austrians.[10] Garibaldi was now using more nationalistic phrases in his letters than he did at most other periods of his life, though even at this time there were fewer chauvinistic expressions in his original text than in the very free English translations into which Jessie White Mario put them. In view of the way in which he had been treated in Uruguay, and the hostility which he had aroused, as an Italian, among the people for whom he was fighting in Montevideo, Garibaldi's internationalism was less to the fore at this moment.

On 15 February the Assembly of Notables met, and Garibaldi took his seat, swearing the oath of allegiance to the Oriental Republic. He was immediately appointed to his first and last Parliamentary duty. It had been reported to the Assembly that one honourable member had just fled from Montevideo to Oribe's territory, and a committee of five members, one of whom was Garibaldi, was appointed to consider whether he should be expelled from the Assembly. On inquiry into the case, it transpired that the MP had not intended to commit treason, but had murdered his wife after finding her with her lover, and had fled from Montevideo in order to avoid arrest. The court which tried the case found him guilty with extenuating circumstances, and sentenced him to be banished from the territory of the Republic; if he returned, he was to be imprisoned.[11]

Garibaldi was still in Montevideo on 20 March, when an event occurred which outraged all the Unitarians in the city. Two Spanish assassins, who had been hired by Oribe, slipped through the front line and murdered Varela by stabbing him in the back as he entered his house at No. 90 Calle de Misiones not more than a few hundred yards from Garibaldi's house. The murderers succeeded in escaping. The crime shocked the Unitarians, despite the fact that they themselves had publicly called for the assassination of Rosas – their spokesman, Rivera Indarte, having launched the slogan: 'It is a holy deed to kill Rosas.'[12] If Garibaldi had stayed on in Montevideo, he might have been the next victim; but his arrangements for departure were almost complete. The government of Montevideo not only gave him permission to go, but allowed him to take a ship with him. It was obviously necessary for him to have his own ship, because he could not travel in an ordinary passenger or cargo ship if he intended to land illegally in Tuscany and start a revolution; so the Montevidean authorities allowed him to buy a Montevidean ship. He raised the purchase-money by subscriptions from the Italians in Montevideo. The ship was named the *Bifronte*, and she flew the Sardinian flag.

Only a minority of the Italian Legion sailed with Garibaldi. The majority stayed in Montevideo. The prospects for those who embarked were very hazardous, because they were expecting to land in territory which was still controlled by their enemies, in the hopes of starting a revolution; but sixty-three of the Legionaries went with him.* They included Anzani and Sacchi, who was suffering so badly from the leg wound which he had received at Montevideo that Garibaldi had to carry him on board the ship. Most of the 63 had fought at San Antonio; but there were a few Uruguayans among them who came because of their affection for Garibaldi. One of these was a negro named Aguiar.[13]

Garibaldi had one more thing to do in Montevideo. After he had gone on board the ship, he sent one of his men, Lavagna, to the cemetery in Montevideo to dig up the coffin of Rosita, so that he could take it to Europe for Anita and himself. It was an illegal action, but Lavagna had no difficulty in squaring the cemetery authorities, and brought the coffin safely to Garibaldi.[14]

In his memoirs, Garibaldi wrote that when he left Montevideo, 'the people who had welcomed us with such enthusiasm, who had such quiet confidence in the courage of our soldiers, took every opportunity of showing their affection and gratitude'. Cuneo and Jessie White Mario quote a letter that was presented to Garibaldi and his men at their departure, signed by Colonel Tajes and many officers of the National Guard, expressing their gratitude for the Italians' services.[15] There can be no doubt that such feelings of gratitude were shown by many people in Montevideo, just as others felt a mixture of relief and

*The number who sailed with Garibaldi is given as 63 in the 1872 edition of the memoirs, as 56 in the Dumas edition, as 29 in Melena's edition, and as 73 by Garibaldi in his poem 'The Return of the Seventy-Three'. The ship sometimes flew the Uruguayan, and sometimes the Sardinian, flag. Garibaldi in his memoirs calls her the *Speranza*; but all the reports in the Montevidean and Buenos Aires press call her the *Bifronte*.

anxiety at the departure of these valuable but hated allies; but any manifestations of either gratitude or hostility were kept very private. Garibaldi's departure was very much played down by both the Unitarian and the Rosista press.

The silence of the Montevidean press may have been partly due to the fact that it was in a state of disarray in April 1848. The last number of Varela's *Comercio del Plata* had appeared on 21 March, the day after the assassination of its editor, and it did not resume publication until 2 June. The *Nacional* had carried on for nearly a year after the death of Rivera Indarte, but had closed down on 31 July 1846 at a time when all the Montevidean newspapers were reducing their size owing to a paper shortage. The *Constitucional* stopped publication on 31 August 1847 after Flores's exile and the trouble in Montevideo which followed the rejection of the Anglo-French peace proposals. But there were enough newspapers being published in Montevideo in April 1848 to make it clear that the silence about Garibaldi's departure was not due to a slip-up by one editor or reporter, but to the fact that the authorities in Montevideo did not wish to publicize the fact that they had lost the services of their most successful general on land and sea.

On 15 April, the day that Garibaldi sailed, the *Patriote Français* reported that a review of the Italian Legion, together with the Basque Legion, would be held on Sunday the 16th at 7 am, but said nothing about Garibaldi's departure. On the Sunday, a short notice appeared on the third page of the *Patriote Français*: 'The Sardinian brig *Bifronte* left for Italy on the night of 14th to 15th. She carries General Garibaldi, Colonel Anzani, and some officers and soldiers, very few in number.' A similar short report appeared on the same day in the French-language newspaper, the *Courrier de la Plata*, in an obscure place on an inside page. The *Conservador* did not report Garibaldi's departure on 15 April, and even omitted to mention the sailing of the *Bifronte* in its shipping column, where it usually published a list of all ships which arrived at and left Montevideo. On 18 April the Assembly of Notables met. If any tribute was paid to the distinguished member who had just left for Europe, either at this or at any subsequent meeting of the Assembly, it was not reported in the press.

On 19 April the *Conservador* gave the first real publicity to Garibaldi's departure by publishing a statement headed 'The Italian Legion to the people of Montevideo'. It declared that now, 'when the illustrious chief of the Italian Legion, the dauntless General Garibaldi, and other valiant comrades have reluctantly decided to leave this generous people, hearing the insistent call of their native land, we firmly and permanently renew, in the presence of heroic Montevideo and its brave defenders, our protestation that we will always remain filled with constancy and loyalty to the noble cause and its united defenders.' The declaration was said to be made on behalf of 'all the individuals of the Italo-Oriental Legion'. This was the first time that the phrase 'Italo-Oriental Legion' had been used.

The enemy press was also inclined to play down the news of Garibaldi's departure. Having repeatedly told their readers in recent months that Garibaldi was the dictator of Montevideo, it would not have been easy to explain why he had now quietly gone away, rendering superfluous the efforts of the Argentine and Blanco armies to liberate the native-born Uruguayans from his yoke. A fortnight before Garibaldi sailed, on 2 April, Oribe's *Defensor* gave the first news of his impending departure, reporting that 'the pirate Garibaldi is getting ready to leave soon' with all his Italians, and that the rations and equipment of the Italian Legion were being shared out between the French and Basque Legions. The *Defensor* always liked to publish letters and small news items from inside Montevideo, no doubt in order to frighten and impress the Montevideans as to the efficiency of their agents within the city; but none of Rosas's papers in Buenos Aires published this information about Garibaldi's departure, though they normally reprinted interesting news which had recently appeared in the *Defensor*. On 22 April the *Defensor* quoted the report that Garibaldi had sailed, which had appeared in the *Courrier de la Plata* on 16 April, and commented: 'It seems that this Condottiero has given up hope as to the outcome of a struggle in which he has played so bloody a part, and thinks that he has nothing to gain by pursuing his career as an adventurer.'

Rosas played the theme in an even quieter key than Oribe. The first mention of it in the Buenos Aires newspapers came on an inside page of the *British Packet* of 29 April: '*A good riddance*. Garibaldi, the chief of the Italian *condottieri* in Montevideo, his second in command, Ansani, and about sixty more, officers and men, sailed from Montevideo on 15th instant in the Sardinian brig *Bifronte* for Genoa.' On 2 May the *Gaceta Mercantil*, writing in a more restrained style than they had ever adopted about Garibaldi during the past five years, wrote that 'There seems no doubt that Garibaldi and his men embarked on the Saturday', and also reported briefly that one of Garibaldi's men had collected money for the journey by going around begging for alms at pistol point before he sailed. But far more space in the paper was devoted to an attack on Thiebaut and the French Legion.[16]

But the only press report which can have interested Garibaldi was the one that appeared in the *Conservador* on 13 April, two days before he sailed. It brought the first news to Montevideo of what was to be the first of the European revolutions of 1848 – the rising in Palermo on 12 January which overthrew for the time being the rule of the King of Naples in Sicily. Garibaldi did not know, when he sailed from Montevideo on 15 April, that revolutions had already occurred in Naples, Milan, Paris, Vienna and Berlin, because the first news of these events reached Montevideo on 30 April, when the newspapers arrived with the report of the fall of Louis Philippe and the proclamation of the Second Republic in France on 24 February.[17]

By this time, Garibaldi was way out in the Atlantic. Leaving Montevideo at dawn with a strong breeze behind them, though the weather was threatening, they made good progress, and by the evening of the first day they were passing Maldonado and Punta del Este. At dawn next morning they could only just see the coastline, and had their last sight of land for many weeks. Garibaldi felt a pang of sadness as he saw his last glimpse of the coast of South America; but once it had disappeared from view he thought only of the future, as they sailed north, bound for Gibraltar and then somewhere in Italy.[18]

CHAPTER 16

1848: THE LAKE MAGGIORE CAMPAIGN

THE voyage of the *Bifronte* – which Garibaldi renamed the *Speranza* – lasted sixty-eight days. Garibaldi and his men spent the time, when they were not performing their duties on board ship, doing physical exercises to keep themselves fit. Garibaldi also arranged for the less well-educated of his men to be taught to read and appreciate Italian literature. Every evening they assembled on deck and sang a revolutionary patriotic song which had been composed by one of the officers of the Legion, Cocelli, who led them in the singing; it was, wrote Garibaldi, their form of evening prayer.

The voyage was uneventful, except that on one occasion, when some brandy started burning, there was a false alarm that the ship was on fire. A fire on board ship was one of the greatest hazards of a sea-voyage in the days of wooden ships; but Garibaldi and Anzani succeeded in putting out the flames before anything except the brandy had caught fire. Garibaldi observed how even brave men may become frightened when faced with danger of a kind to which they are not accustomed, because some of his veterans, who had shown no sign of fear on the battlefield of San Antonio, were thrown into panic when confronted with the fire on the *Speranza*. Garibaldi was much more worried about the state of Anzani's health. Anzani had been severely wounded in the chest many years before when fighting in Spain, and was now suffering from a very serious attack of consumption, which became worse through the inadequate diet on the long sea voyage.

In the middle of June they passed through the Straits of Gibraltar, and put in to the Spanish port of Santa Pola, near Alicante, where Captain Gazzolo went on shore to buy more supplies. He returned in a state of great excitement, not only with supplies but with all the news of what had been happening in Italy and Europe in the first five months of 1848 – the revolts in Naples and Venice, the overthrow of Louis Philippe and Metternich in Paris and Vienna, and the rising in Milan, where the people rose on 18 March in the bloodiest of all the revolutions of 1848 and defeated the brutal Croat regiments of the Austrian army after five days' street fighting. That night there was great celebration in the *Speranza*.[1]

The King of Sardinia, Charles Albert, had decided to associate the royal house of Savoy with the cause of Italian Liberalism and unification. In April 1848 he declared war on Austria and marched into Lombardy in support of the revolutionary governments in Milan and Venice. Mazzini and Young Italy had never forgiven Charles Albert for his betrayal of the Carbonari revolutionaries of 1821 and for his stern suppression of the risings and plots after coming to the throne. They were disgusted at his cynical and belated adherence to the Italian cause, and did not trust him; but he could provide the *Risorgimento* with an army of 96,000 men, which was more effective than Mazzini's pamphlets or Garibaldi's sixty-three Legionaries from Montevideo. In every part of Italy, the revolutionaries accepted Charles Albert as their leader, and volunteers marched north to join his army. The revolutionary leaders in Milan and Venice, who at first had proclaimed that they were fighting to create independent republics of Lombardy and Venetia, both afterwards invited Charles Albert to incorporate the two provinces into the Kingdom of Sardinia.

The Commander-in-Chief of the Austrian army in Italy was Field-Marshal Count Radetzky. 'Father Radetzky', as his men called him, was eighty-two years old; but he was as energetic and determined as ever after sixty-two years in the army. Radetzky had only 70,000 men against Charles Albert's 96,000, and withdrew his army into the small area between the River Mincio and the River Adige, with his fortresses at Mantua and elsewhere, which was known as the Quadrilateral.

Everybody had turned against Austria except the Pope. Pius IX, who had started off the whole movement which had led to the upsurge in Italy and the revolutions of 1848, was the only Italian ruler who refused to join in the war against Austria. He had sincerely wished to introduce a more Liberal régime in the Papal States, but he had never been in favour of Italian unification, and had become alarmed at the extent of the movement which he had unleashed. When a brigade of volunteers from the Papal States enlisted in the Sardinian army, and announced that they were fighting for the Pope and the Church in a crusade against Austria, Pius issued a statement on 29 April dissociating himself from them. He said that as the unworthy representative on earth of the Prince of Peace he could not support a war against Austria, but that if his subjects in the Papal States wished to volunteer for the Sardinian army, he could not prevent them.[2]

The Pope's statement caused a violent change of feeling towards him among the Radicals and revolutionaries. They could not understand why, if the Pope was sincere, he had not supported the just cause in the war. Margaret Fuller, the American girl from Massachusetts who married the Count (afterwards the Marquis) of Ossoli, and was living in Rome, noticed the change. A few weeks earlier she had written about the 'child-like joy and trust' with which the people of Rome had greeted the Pope's reforms; now she reported that the people were calling the Pope 'traitor' and 'imbecile', and saying 'Death to the Cardinals and death to the Pope!'[3]

When Garibaldi, at Santa Pola, heard the news of these events, he changed his provisional plans to land in Tuscany, and instead set sail for Nice. In view of Charles Albert's attitude, he felt sure that there was no longer any danger of the death sentence imposed in 1834 being carried out; and, like most of the other Italian Radicals, he wished to fight against Austria under Charles Albert's leadership. He arrived at Nice at 1 pm on 21 June, and met with a great reception. Anita had had the same experience when she had landed at Genoa in April on her arrival from Montevideo. To her surprise, she had been met by cheering crowds, who cried 'Long live Garibaldi! Long live the family of our Garibaldi!' The Genoese newspapers had written at length about Anita and her two children. They did not notice the third child, Ricciotti, who was only thirteen months old, and was hidden in the folds of his mother's cloak.[4]

Garibaldi himself was equally surprised by the reception which he received at Nice. Crowds had assembled on the waterfront, and the harbour was full of small boats with people waving and cheering. They had all read about San Antonio in the Italian Radical newspapers. The first thing that Garibaldi saw as he entered the harbour was Anita in a boat, and they met again after their six months' separation. Ships arriving at Nice were subject to quarantine regulations, which were often in force at the Mediterranean ports in the middle of the nineteenth century as a precaution against the spread of cholera and other epidemics, and the passengers were not supposed to land for a fortnight or more; but Garibaldi and the other passengers on the *Speranza* paid no attention to this, as they felt that the crowds would not have permitted them to observe the regulations even if they had wished to do so.[5]

Garibaldi's father had died in 1843, but his mother was still alive, living in the same house in the Quai Lunel, Aburarum House, to which the family had moved when Garibaldi was eight, and which he had last seen fourteen years before. Anita and the children had been living there since their arrival from Montevideo. Garibaldi now moved in, along with Anzani, who was very ill with consumption, and was put to bed in the house. Despite their different views on religion and politics, Garibaldi and his mother had always been very fond of each other, and had a happy reunion; but she was not altogether happy about Garibaldi's relationship with Anita, and had qualms as to whether she should allow them to cohabit as man and wife in her house. Garibaldi and Anita must have told her enough to make her have doubts about the validity of the marriage ceremony in Montevideo, and she tried to persuade them to go through another ceremony in Nice; but though Mrs Chambers, an English woman who was a close friend of Garibaldi, wrote in later years that Rosa Garibaldi had insisted that they should be married again in Nice, it seems that they did not do so, as there is no record of any such marriage in the official records of Nice.[6]

Garibaldi would not stay more than a few days in Nice, because, as he put it, 'there was fighting on the Mincio'. He decided to enlist at once in Charles Albert's army. On 25 June he was the guest of honour at a banquet for 400 guests at the inn the Albergo di York in Nice. 'You know that I was never a supporter of the King,' he told them, 'but this was because in those days he did harm to Italy. But I am a realist, and with my men I will join the King of Sardinia, and if he will bring about the regeneration of our peninsula, I will shed my blood for him; and I am sure that all other Italians will think the same as I do.' He ended with the words: 'Long live Italy! Long live the King! Long live Nice!'[7]

He was joined by over a hundred volunteers in Nice, in addition to the sixty-three who had come from Montevideo, and set off with them by sea for Genoa in the *Speranza*, which was once again called the *Bifronte*. He told Anzani to stay in his mother's house at Nice, as he was much too ill to travel; but on the voyage to Genoa, the *Bifronte* was blown off course towards Corsica, and when she reached Genoa next day, Garibaldi, to his dismay, found Anzani there. Anzani had insisted on travelling to Genoa, and thanks to Garibaldi having been blown towards Corsica, he had arrived first; but he was so ill that he had been obliged to return to a sick-bed in Genoa. Garibaldi's Legion, including himself and Anzani, now numbered 169 men – 24 officers and 145 other ranks. He named them, as he had done in Montevideo, the Italian Legion.[8]

Garibaldi received an enthusiastic welcome from the Young Italy supporters and from large sections of the population in Genoa, and on 3 July he addressed a great rally at the revolutionary club, the Circolo Nazionale. He said that they would drive the Austrians out of Italy that year . . .

. . . if we forget about political systems, but not if we begin discussions about the forms of government and the future of political parties. The great, and only, question at the moment is the expulsion of the foreigner and the war of independence. . . . Men, arms, money, that is what we need, not idle arguments about political systems. I was a Republican; but when I discovered that Charles Albert had made himself the champion of Italy, I swore to obey him and faithfully to follow his banner. . . . Charles Albert is our leader, our symbol. . . . There is no salvation apart from him.[9]

Garibaldi's speech caused some disquiet among the members of Young Italy in Genoa. They supported the policy of a united front with the Sardinian monarchists against the Austrians, but thought that Garibaldi had been unnecessarily enthusiastic about Charles Albert. Mazzini had come from London to Milan after the revolution there, and was giving political guidance to Young Italy in his newspaper *L'Italia del Popolo*. He was also trying to influence the policy of the provisional revolutionary government of Lombardy. He realized that it was necessary 'to catch their hare before discussing the sauce in which it was to be cooked', and to defeat the Austrians before discussing the merits of a monarchy or a republic. But he argued that it was Charles Albert and the monarchists who were introducing political discussions about the forms of government when they called for the immediate union of Lombardy and Venetia with the Kingdom of Sardinia; and he tried unsuccessfully to persuade the revolutionaries in Milan and Venice to continue the war in the name of the Republic of Lombardy and the Venetian Republic. From his diametrically opposite point of view, Mazzini would have agreed with Queen Victoria, who did not share the pro-Italian sympathies of her Prime Minister and Foreign Secretary, Lord John Russell and Palmerston, and in May 1848 wrote to Palmerston: 'Why Charles Albert ought to get any additional territory the Queen cannot in the least see.'[10]

Medici, whom Garibaldi had first met in Montevideo three years before, and who had made the arrangements, on the Italian side, for Garibaldi's return from South America, was particularly worried about Garibaldi's enthusiasm for Charles Albert. He visited Anzani, who was sinking fast, and unburdened himself about his fears for Garibaldi's political development. Anzani tried to reassure Medici, and told him that though Garibaldi had often angered him, he was irreplaceable; and he strongly urged Medici not to quarrel with him.[11]

Garibaldi had decided to go at once to the front line, but before leaving Genoa he visited Anzani. Both Anzani and Garibaldi must have realized that this would probably be the last time that they would see each other. Anzani urged Garibaldi never to betray the people's cause. This hurt Garibaldi, who had not expected that his speeches in Nice and Genoa would make Anzani, of all people, suspect his loyalty to the Republican principles which they shared.

Two days later, Anzani died. It was a heavy blow for Garibaldi, who thought that Anzani was an irreplaceable loss. 'Had we been fortunate enough to have him at the head of our army,' he wrote in his memoirs in 1872, 'the peninsula would certainly have been cleared of all foreign rulers long ago.' He felt particularly bitter because Anzani's last words to him had been to urge him not to betray his principles; and this had the unfortunate result of making him even more resentful against the Mazzinians who had 'tormented poor dying Anzani to use his influence with me'.[12]

From Genoa, Garibaldi went to Charles Albert's army headquarters at Roverbella near Mantua, a few miles from the front line, and on 5 July he had an audience with the King. He wrote in his memoirs that it was a strange experience meeting the man who, fourteen years before, had confirmed the death sentence that had been passed on him for desertion and attempted high treason, and to whom he was now offering his loyal services; but Charles Albert was courteous and friendly. When Garibaldi tried to get the King and his staff to pass from words to deeds, things were less satisfactory. Garibaldi hoped that he and his Legionaries would be sent into action against the Austrians as soon as possible; but neither Charles Albert nor his officers were sympathetic to revolutionaries like Garibaldi, and having an army of 96,000 men under their command, they did not attach as much importance as Garibaldi did to the question of whether 168 volunteers from Montevideo and Nice should be sent into action this week or next. They did not respond at all favourably to the suggestion, which Garibaldi and his sympathizers were making, that Garibaldi should be entrusted with a high command in the army with the rank of general.[13]

They told Garibaldi to report to the War Office in Turin, who would arrange for him and his men to serve in some capacity; and Garibaldi reluctantly set out for the capital of the Kingdom of Sardinia, which was nearly 200 miles to the west of the battle area. On his way he went to Milan, where he stayed at the Albergo del Marina in the Piazza San Fedele. In Milan he met his friend, Dr Ripari, the surgeon, who asked if he were looking for Mazzini, because Mazzini was staying in the Albergo della bella Venezia, which was quite near the Albergo del Marina. Garibaldi replied that he was not looking for Mazzini, but for the provisional government of Lombardy, whom he hoped might appoint him to some position where he could fight the Austrians, if the Sardinian authorities would not do this. But though Garibaldi left Milan for Turin without seeing Mazzini, this did not prevent Mazzini from urging the Lombard authorities to give Garibaldi a high command in their forces.[14]

When Garibaldi reached Turin, he found that the War Office was

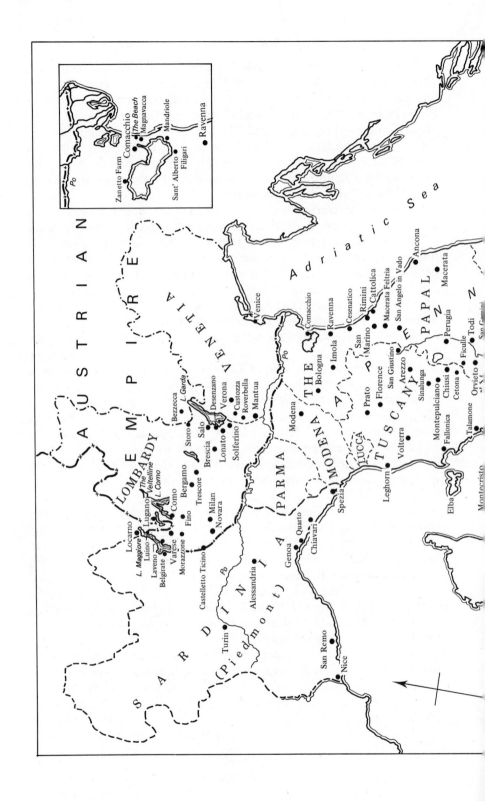

Inset map labels:

Po
Zanetto Farm
Comacchio
The Beach
Magnavacca
Mandriole
Ravenna
Sant' Alberto
Filigari

Main map labels:

A U S T R I A N   E M P I R E

LOMBARDY

VENETIA

Adriatic Sea

Locarno
Luino
L. Maggiore
Lugano
The Veltelline
L. Como
Como
Fino
Bergamo
Milan
Novara
Trescore
Lonato
Brescia
Salo
Storo
Bezzecca
L. Garda
Desenzano
Verona
Custozza
Roverbella
Mantua
Solferino
Venice

Laveno
Belgirate
Varese
Morazzone
Castelletto Ticino

SARDINIA

(Piedmont)

Turin
Alessandria
Genoa
Quarto
Chiavari
Spezia

PARMA

MODENA

Modena

Po
Po

THE

Bologna
Imola
San Marino
San Giustino
Cesenatico
Ravenna
Comacchio
Rimini
Cattolica
Macerata Feltria
San Angelo in Vado
Ancona
Macerata

PAPAL

Perugia
Todi
San Gemini

LUCCA

TUSCANY

Leghorn
Volterra
Prato
Florence
Arezzo
Sinalunga
Montepulciano
Fallonica
Chiusi
Cetona
Ficulle
Orvieto
Talamone

Elba

Montecristo

San Remo
Nice

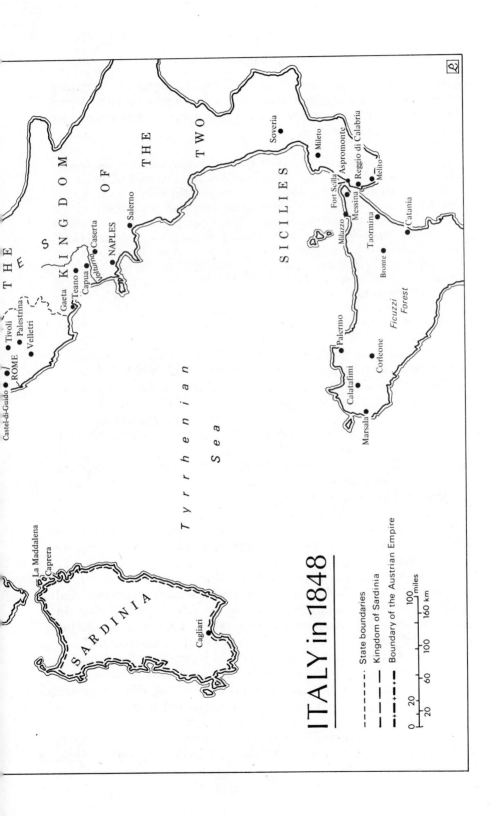

ITALY in 1848

------- State boundaries
------- Kingdom of Sardinia
-+-+-+- Boundary of the Austrian Empire

0 20   60   100   miles
0 20   60   100 160 km

Castel-di-Guido

ROME
Tivoli
Palestrina
Velletri

THE

KINGDOM

OF

THE

TWO

SICILIES

Gaeta
Teano
Capua Caserta
Volturno
NAPLES
Salerno

Tyrrhenian

Sea

La Maddalena
Caprera

SARDINIA

Cagliari

Palermo
Calatafimi
Marsala
Corleone

Ficuzzi
Forest

Bronte

Milazzo
Taormina
Messina
Catania

Fort Scilla
Aspromonte
Reggio di Calabria
Melito

Mileto

Soveria

as reluctant as the high command at the King's headquarters to employ the services of a dangerous Radical revolutionary. Charles Albert himself had written to Franzini at the War Office, a few hours after his interview with Garibaldi:

I hasten to warn you that I have today received in audience the famous General Garibaldi, who has come from America and arrived at Genoa, where he left sixty of his disciples, whom he offered to me along with himself. The antecedents of these gentlemen, and particularly of the self-styled general, and his famous republican proclamation, make it absolutely impossible for us to accept them in the army, and particularly to make Garibaldi a general. If there were a naval war he might be employed as a leader of privateers, but to employ him otherwise would be to dishonour the army. As I think he will be going to Turin, where he will not lack supporters, be ready for his attack. The best would be if they went off to any other place; and to encourage him and his brave fellows, they might perhaps be given a subsidy on condition that they go away.[15]

It is difficult to guess what Charles Albert meant by Garibaldi's 'famous republican proclamation', because since his return to Italy all Garibaldi's political declarations had been calls for unity under Charles Albert. Perhaps it was the antimonarchist article which Garibaldi had written twelve years before in the obscure Brazilian newspaper in Rio de Janeiro which still rankled with Charles Albert, and made it impossible, in the King's eyes, to employ his services against the enemy. In view of the King's letter, Franzini advised Garibaldi to go to Venice, where he could operate at sea in the Adriatic as a privateer.[16] This annoyed Garibaldi, but it was probably good advice, because Manin in Venice, who combined revolutionary Radical principles with a realistic support of a united national front under Charles Albert, was closer to Garibaldi in outlook than most of the other Italian leaders.

From Turin, Garibaldi returned to Milan, where he arrived on 14 July. He was greeted by a popular demonstration of support, and spoke to the crowd from the window of the Albergo del Marino. In Milan he was at last given something to do, though it was not the job that he had hoped for. Although the provisional government of Lombardy had decided to ask Charles Albert to incorporate Lombardy in Sardinia, there was still an independent administration in Milan, and they were more willing than the royal government officials to use Garibaldi's services. On 15 July he was appointed a general in the Lombard army; but to his disappointment he was given an office job concerned with organizing the formation of a new corps of volunteers, including his own Legionaries. He also met further obstruction from

General Salasco, Charles Albert's military representative in Milan. Salasco objected to the red shirt which Garibaldi and his followers were wearing, and argued that it would make them too conspicuous to the enemy; but though there may have been some truth in this, Salasco was in no hurry to provide them with any other uniform. To make matters worse, Garibaldi caught a fever in Milan, and for several days was confined to his bed.[17]

While he was in Milan, he met Mazzini. Although Garibaldi had considered himself to be a faithful disciple of Mazzini for fifteen years, relations between them were now a little strained. Garibaldi wrote in his memoirs that Mazzini suggested to him that Young Italy and the Radicals should make it clear that they would only join the army if Charles Albert agreed to fight for a free republic. Jessie White Mario, who was one of the few people to remain at all times on terms of close friendship with both Garibaldi and Mazzini, says that Garibaldi completely misrepresented Mazzini's attitude on this point, and claims, on the contrary, that it was due to Mazzini's efforts that Garibaldi was appointed a general by the provisional government in Milan.[18] But the disagreements between Garibaldi and Mazzini which now began continued, despite short periods of collaboration, until the end of their lives. Garibaldi and Mazzini respected each other's virtues; but Garibaldi always thought that Mazzini was an impractical Utopian theoretician who took the wrong decision in every crisis; and Mazzini thought that Garibaldi was too stupid to see that he was being led by the nose by the royal house of Savoy.

Within a week, Garibaldi was ordered by the provisional government of Lombardy to go to Bergamo, some forty miles north-east of Milan, where he was to train new recruits. This was a little better than being in an office in Milan, but he was still far from happy, as he was not fighting the enemy, but performing an organizational job for which, as he wrote in his memoirs, he was quite unfitted, because of his nature and his ignorance of military theory. While he was at Bergamo, Charles Albert attacked Radetzky at Custozza on 24 July. The Sardinian army, though it outnumbered the Austrians, suffered a heavy defeat, and fell back in disorder towards Milan. As Radetzky advanced, the provisional government of Lombardy prepared for a desperate defence of the city street by street.[19]

Ignoring Charles Albert and the Sardinian High Command, they quickly got together a force of 1,500 men and placed them under Garibaldi's command. This force was composed of personnel who were almost as undesirable as the 'frères de la côte' who served in the Uruguayan navy. They were mostly men who had deserted, or had been discharged as medically unfit, from the Sardinian and Lombard forces operating against the Austrians in the Alps; and though they were not actual criminals, like the crews in the Montevidean fleet, they proved to be less brave and reliable in action. The government of Lombardy ordered Garibaldi to lead these men and harry Radetzky's flank as he advanced on Milan. Garibaldi named his force the Anzani battalion.[20]

Garibaldi marched north to Monza, from where he intended to operate against Radetzky's flank; but here he heard disastrous news. The town council of Milan, fearing that the defence of the city would cause loss of civilian lives and great damage to property, had persuaded Charles Albert to evacuate Milan without fighting, despite the protests of the Radicals. When Garibaldi heard what had happened, he decided to disregard his orders, and to make for the mountains around Como in the north and carry on guerrilla warfare on his own against the Austrians. But he could not persuade all his men to follow him. When they heard that Milan was about to fall and the Sardinian army was in full retreat, many of them threw away their weapons and deserted. The others tried to stop them, and opened fire on them. Some of the deserters, who had retained their weapons, fired back, and as a regular battle developed between the loyal men and the deserters, Garibaldi thought that it was best to allow the deserters to go; and he marched off towards Como with those men who had remained faithful.[21]

On the way from Monza to Como they met Mazzini. He was marching along with a number of followers, with a musket slung over his shoulder, and carrying a banner bearing the words 'God and the People'. He was looking for Garibaldi, wishing to fight under his orders as a private soldier. Medici was with him and in command of the Mazzinian detachment. Mazzini and Medici placed themselves under Garibaldi's orders and marched with him to Como. On the way, Mazzini wrote articles for his paper, which he signed 'Giuseppe Mazzini, a soldier of Garibaldi's Legion'.

The weather was very bad, with heavy rain, and the marchers were often soaked to the skin. Mazzini was quite unfit for the rigours of such a campaign. He was never physically a strong man, and the sedentary life which he normally led meant that he was completely out of training. But he coped with the situation much better than he had done on the Savoy expedition of 1834, and forced himself by sheer will-power to keep up with the others. Medici wrote that the soldiers were filled with admiration for Mazzini. Garibaldi, in his memoirs, was much less enthusiastic about him.

> He joined us on the march, and continued with us as far as Como. From Como he crossed into Switzerland while I was making preparations to hold

the country in the Comaschi mountains. Many of his followers, or pretended followers, went with him and followed him on to foreign soil. This naturally encouraged others to desert.[22]

From Como, Garibaldi marched west by Varese to the River Ticino, and established himself in the village of Castelletto Ticino, ten miles south of Lake Maggiore. Here he heard that Charles Albert had asked Radetzky for an armistice, to which Radetzky had agreed on condition that Charles Albert withdrew his forces from Lombardy and Venetia and his fleet from the Adriatic. In view of the disastrous defeat which Charles Albert had suffered at Custozza, the terms were not unreasonable; but it was a blow to the Venetians, who lost the aid of the Sardinian navy, while Radetzky overran the whole of Venetia except for the city of Venice. Worst of all, on 6 August the City of the Five Days, as the revolutionaries called Milan, was reoccupied by Radetzky, which was a great moral defeat for the Italian national cause. At least thirty thousand refugees, fleeing from the Austrian vengeance and the atrocities of their Croat troops, fled from Lombardy into Piedmont with the retreating Sardinian army.

Garibaldi was contacted at Castelletto by an envoy from the Austrian unit in the district, who informed him that the armistice had been signed, and suggested that their men should meet and fraternize. Garibaldi agreed to observe the armistice, but refused to allow fraternization with the enemy, which was understandable, in view of the bad morale of his men and their readiness to desert. Desertions had by now reduced the numbers of his force to 1,700. He had a slight recurrence of the fever that had laid him up in Milan in July, and this and the news of the armistice made him very depressed. The parish clerk of Castelletto, who had the difficult task of dealing with Garibaldi's demands for food and other supplies, reported that Garibaldi's illness and depression made him rather difficult to deal with, though the parish clerk thought that he was at heart a decent fellow.[23]

Garibaldi's decision to observe the armistice was only temporary. On 13 August, at Castelletto, he issued his famous appeal to the Italian people. It began with Mazzini's slogan 'God and the People', and continued:

Chosen in Milan by the People and their representatives as leader of my men, with no aim except that of Italian independence, I am not able to conform to the humiliating convention which has been signed by the King of Sardinia with the hated foreigner dominating my country. If the King of Sardinia has a crown which he wishes to save by guilt and cowardice, my companions and I do not wish to save our lives by infamy, and to abandon, without sacrificing ourselves, our sacred soil to the mockery of those who oppress and ravage it.[24]

The Castelletto manifesto had an immediate effect in reviving the morale of the national forces after the defeat of Custozza, the fall of Milan and the armistice. Garibaldi managed to get the proclamation printed, and stuck copies on the walls of the towns where he passed; and copies were seen in other parts of Italy. It established Garibaldi as a national hero as far off as Florence and Rome, though Manin, in Venice, does not appear to have heard about it until afterwards. The Austrian and Sardinian generals obtained copies, and sent them to each other.[25]

As soon as the news reached the Austrian headquarters in Milan, General D'Aspre drew the attention of the Sardinian High Command to it, and complained that General Garibaldi's activities in the north were a violation of the armistice. This was the last occasion on which D'Aspre referred to Garibaldi as 'General Garibaldi'. General Salasco, who had never liked Garibaldi, hastened to assure the Austrians that Garibaldi was acting without authority from the Sardinian army. Writing in French, the language in which all the Sardinian government's official correspondence was conducted, he told General Hess that 'the King has been informed of the aggressions of Monsieur Garibaldi, who is in no way in the King's service', and that the King disapproved of Garibaldi's action, which stained the King's honour. The King was therefore sending troops to the Lake Maggiore area to arrest Garibaldi and his men, and to 'remove any possibility of their undertaking another adventure'. Meanwhile Radetzky sent D'Aspre, with a force of several thousand men, to find and destroy Garibaldi and his forces.[26]

Garibaldi decided to carry on the war by himself for as long as possible. He had no illusions that he would be able to do this effectively for very long; but he hoped that it would set an example to others, and lead to the development of a resistance movement throughout Italy. 'On this occasion, I revived the hope that I had nurtured for many years of inciting our fellow-citizens to that partisan warfare which, in the absence of an organized army, could lead to the general arming of the nation, if the nation really had an inner and resolute wish to redeem itself.'[27] This first campaign against the Austrians lasted only a fortnight; but though it did not lead to the development of a mass resistance movement on the scale that Garibaldi had hoped for, it made Garibaldi a popular hero, at least among the more militant and Radical elements, all over Italy.

Garibaldi showed himself to be a very skilful guerrilla leader.

Although he had considerable experience in South America of fighting skirmishes with a few hundred infantrymen on both sides, he had never waged guerrilla warfare with small groups of partisans against large bodies of regular troops, which would hardly have been possible on the open plains of Rio Grande do Sul and Uruguay. But the mountainous country of the Italian lakes was very suitable for partisan warfare, and Garibaldi hoped to adopt the well-known tactic of partisan groups, of carrying on his activities from bases in neutral territory, retreating into Switzerland when he was too hard pressed by the enemy, and emerging again to make raids across the border into Italy whenever possible. Less than a year before, the Swiss Radicals had won their short civil war against the Catholic cantons of the Sonderbund, and the Radical government in Berne sympathized with the Italian struggle against Austria. They might therefore be prepared to wink at border violations provided that these were not too flagrant.

Garibaldi and his depleted force at Castelletto were joined by Medici and some of Mazzini's friends who had crossed the frontier from Lugano to resume the struggle, though Mazzini himself remained at Lugano. But the number of deserters had increased when the news of the armistice was known, and even with Medici's troop Garibaldi had less than 1,300 men. With these he marched north to Lake Maggiore on the night of 13 August, and early next morning arrived at Arona, on the lake, where he served a requisition notice on the town clerk, demanding 1,286 rations of bread, 20 sacks of rice, 3 sacks of oats for his small number of horses, and 7,000 lire in cash.[28]

The Italian lakes were a famous holiday resort for wealthy Italian and foreign tourists, and in recent years steamships had begun to operate on the lakes for the use of the tourists. There were two steamships, the *Verbano* and the *San Carlo*, which navigated on Lake Maggiore. Garibaldi discovered that they were both due to arrive at Arona from the Swiss part of the lake during the course of the day, and he wrote out a short order to the Director of Shipping at Arona, requisitioning the ships for the use of his troops. When they arrived, he seized them, embarked his men, and sailed up the western side of the lake.[29]

The weather had now changed, and was the sunniest and warmest that can be found on Lake Maggiore in August. As they steamed past Intra and Cannobio and all the villages along the lake, the balconies of the houses at the lakeside were filled with beautiful women cheering and waving. Much heartened by the sight of these 'lovely faces so animated that it seemed as if they wished to fly to welcome the brave men who did not despair of snatching their hearths from the oppressor', Garibaldi crossed the lake to the little town of Luino, about half-way up the lake on the eastern side, and some seven miles from the frontier.

He had written to the town clerk of Luino two days before, ordering him to supply 1,300 rations of bread, wine and cheese within twenty-four hours. Garibaldi and his men spent the night in and around the Beccacia Inn at Luino, and next day, at last, went into action for the first time against the Austrian forces.[30]

The enemy consisted of a detachment of Croat infantry, who were particularly hated by the Italians for the cruelty which they had shown on various occasions, and particularly during the five days in Milan. The unit at Luino was commanded by Major Mollinary. Although some of Garibaldi's biographers have stated, from force of habit, that the Austrians greatly outnumbered Garibaldi's men at Luino, this is not so, because for once Garibaldi had a decisive superiority in man-power. Mollinary had come out with 700 men in the hope of finding traces of Garibaldi; but he had no idea that Garibaldi was present in the immediate neighbourhood in such strength, and he had divided his force into two parts, and sent half his men off scouting in another direction. On the morning of 15 August 1848 he found himself at Luino with 338 men. Garibaldi and his 1,300 men had just set off to march across country to Varese when the Croats came upon their rear, who were just leaving the inn. The inn became the centre of the fight, and as Garibaldi and his advance-guard could not get back in time to prevent the Croats from overpowering his rearguard and capturing the inn, it was necessary for Garibaldi to recapture the inn if he was to achieve the moral effect of a victory. He succeeded in doing this without too much difficulty, thanks to the valour of a Pavese unit among his force, and the Croats fled, leaving one officer and three men dead, and 33 prisoners, many of them wounded. Garibaldi regretted that he had not enough cavalry to pursue and annihilate the enemy; but he had won his first battle in Europe.

Mollinary either miscalculated the number of Garibaldi's men, or deliberately exaggerated them in order to excuse his defeat to Radetzky. He reported to headquarters that Garibaldi had had between 2,000 and 2,500 men, two cannon, two steamships, and 'a mass of smaller craft'. His chief consolation was that the inhabitants of Luino had made no attempt to help Garibaldi; they had hurried to the side of the lake and had stood there, watching the battle as if it were a show.

Garibaldi treated the prisoners well, and cared for the wounded on both sides. He entrusted them to the care of Signora Mantegazza, a lady who lived on the other side of the lake, but had crossed to Luino in her private boat, when she heard the firing in order to nurse the wounded. Garibaldi sent the seriously wounded prisoners to a hospital in Cannobio, and kept all his other prisoners in the two steamers, which he anchored at Luino. He left a detachment of sixty men at

Luino to guard the ships and the prisoners, and set off with the rest of his force for Varese, marching up and down the mountains between Lake Maggiore and Lake Como in weather which was nearly as hot as Salto in January.[31]

He now heard that a large Austrian force was marching against him. Realizing that he could not hope to win a pitched battle against them, he decided to split up into smaller groups, and to wage only guerrilla actions. He therefore told Medici to separate from him, and operate with his own independent group. Meanwhile Charles Albert had sent his brother, the Duke of Genoa, to the area to round up Garibaldi's men, as he had promised Radetzky that he would do. The Duke reached Arona on 16 August, two days after Garibaldi had left, and heard that Garibaldi had won a victory over the Austrians, and had shot all the prisoners whom he had captured. This was quite untrue. Nor was there any more truth in the story, which was published in the official journal of the Sardinian government, that Garibaldi had taken with him three inhabitants of Castelletto and Arona as hostages, and had had them shot at Luino 'against all the laws of humanity'. The journal also stated that the town council of Arona had appealed to Charles Albert to protect them against Garibaldi.[32]

Radetzky had realized that Garibaldi would try to operate from a haven in Switzerland, and was eager to cut him off and capture him before he could cross the frontier. He entrusted the operation to Acting Field-Marshal Baron von D'Aspre, with a brigade commanded by Major-General Baron von Simbschen, and another brigade under Lieutenant-General Prince von Schwarzenberg. While the two brigades closed in on Garibaldi, Radetzky warned the Swiss government and the cantonal authorities in the Ticino that if 'the revolutionary, Garibaldi' retreated into Switzerland and was not at once disarmed and interned, the Austrian troops would pursue him across the frontier.[33]

During this campaign, Garibaldi encountered some of the disappointments which confront partisan leaders. He had hoped that many of the local people would join his ranks, but hardly anyone did so, and many were too afraid of Austrian reprisals to give him any assistance. He discovered that peasants are not normally idealistic revolutionaries. They were not merely hostile, but in some cases gave information about Garibaldi's whereabouts to the Austrians for money. Garibaldi had two of them shot for spying. At Varese, where he fixed many copies of his Castelletto manifesto to the walls of the buildings, he addressed a large crowd from the balcony of the town hall; but according to an informer who reported on the meeting to D'Aspre, hardly anyone volunteered to join him. 'Except for an "*Enviva*" which was given him as a tribute,' wrote D'Aspre to Radetzky, 'the invitation to take up arms did not find much echo.'[34]

On the afternoon of 26 August, Garibaldi and his men entered the little town of Morazzone, where the streets were so narrow that Garibaldi had to order his men to stand sideways when he drew them up in file. They had had nothing to eat all day, and could not, at first, persuade the inhabitants to give them food; but just before 5 pm they obtained the food, and proceeded to eat their rations. They did not know that an Austrian force under Simbschen and Schwarzenberg was approaching the town. Garibaldi was sitting on a bench in the square, eating a chunk of bread and drinking a glass of wine, when the Austrians attacked. Simbschen had sent in a battalion of the Kinsky Regiment as an advance-guard, and thanks to the slackness of the sentries whom Garibaldi had posted, they had entered the town unobserved. Garibaldi's newer recruits began to panic; but Garibaldi drew his sabre, and with his officers rushed at the enemy, and after a mélée in the narrow and crowded streets the Austrians were driven out of the town, two of their officers being wounded. Simbschen then bombarded Morazzone with his artillery.

Both sides were completely mistaken as to the strength of their opponents. Jessie White Mario wrote that Garibaldi, with 500 men, fought all day against 10,000 Austrians with 18 guns and cavalry. Simbschen told D'Aspre that he had 700 men and only two cannon against Garibaldi's 1,500 men. In fact, both sides had about 700 men; but the Austrians, unlike the Garibaldini, had recently rested and eaten, they were more experienced soldiers, and they had their two cannon, with a range of 250 yards, which they repeatedly fired in rapid succession so as to make Garibaldi think that they had far more artillery than they really had.

Apart from bombarding Morazzone, the Austrians resorted to the method which they had adopted elsewhere against guerrillas, and, to the great indignation of the Italians, set fire to the houses on the outskirts of the town. By now, night had come, but the town was well illuminated by the burning houses. At 11 pm, after the battle had lasted for six hours, Garibaldi decided that he must retreat; but he needed a guide to show him the way. As he could not persuade any of the inhabitants of Morazzone to volunteer for this duty, he was obliged to force a priest in the town to act as their guide. The priest was made to walk between two of Garibaldi's men, but he nevertheless somehow managed to escape in the darkness soon after they left Morazzone. Garibaldi wrote in his memoirs in 1872 that the priest 'came with us after much resistance; this was natural; that class of vampires remain in Italy in order to act as go-betweens for the foreigner'.

They marched off through the night, as quietly as possible, and carrying their wounded. After a while, the advance-guard became separated from the rear, and although the column halted, the rear-guard, with the wounded, did not come up. Garibaldi went back nearly as far as Morazzone to look for them, but he could not find them, and eventually he had to order the advance-guard to go on. Some of the wounded were taken prisoner by the Austrians. According to Simbschen's report, the Austrians lost 3 killed and 16 wounded in the action, while Garibaldi lost 7 killed. Simbschen could not give the number of Garibaldi's wounded, because he thought that Garibaldi had carried them away.[35]

When dawn came, Garibaldi found that he had only 70 men with him, as all the rest had dispersed; and he decided to retreat into Switzerland. He set off along the footpaths in the mountains, but in such circumstances the seventy men could not keep together, and when Garibaldi reached the Swiss frontier he had only thirty men. He disbanded them, and told them to make their own way in Switzerland, and in due course to return to Italy and resume the struggle when this became possible. He himself went to Lugano. He was exhausted, and his fever had become worse. He took a room in a hotel in Lugano, and went to bed.[36]

On 29 August the Austrian High Command issued a communiqué about their victory over Garibaldi, which they forced the *Gazzetta di Milano* to publish in that part of the paper which was reserved for official government statements.

> The only man who, when faced with the victorious advance of our army to the frontiers of our territory, thought that he could rashly maintain the struggle with his band, and would not recognize the armistice which had been made with Piedmont, was the soldier of fortune, Garibaldi, who had given himself the title of Colonel, and commanded about 5,000 desperadoes, mostly foreigners of all nations, and treacherous deserters whom he had hastily assembled.

After describing the campaign at some length, in a version which was almost as inaccurate as the statement about the numbers, nationality and character of Garibaldi's men, they accused Garibaldi of having extorted 4,000 lire from the village of Gavirate, and of shooting a police sergeant at Gemona who had tried to stop him from stealing money there, though in fact this police sergeant was shot because he had acted as a spy for the Austrians. They claimed that Garibaldi had been driven across the Swiss frontier, and gave their own casualty figures as two officers wounded and forty to fifty other ranks killed and wounded throughout the whole campaign, which roughly tallied with the reports which they had received from their subordinate officers.[37]

Garibaldi still had one card to play; he held the two steamers and the 33 Croat prisoners whom he had taken at Luino. D'Aspre immediately realized the importance of this before Garibaldi told him. On 27 August, the day after the battle at Morazzone, he reported to Radetzky that he had captured a number of Garibaldi's men, and added: 'I would willingly have some of these prisoners shot. The only thing that prevents me is the thought that the 33 Croats who are prisoners in the ships would suffer the same fate.'[38]

When the garrison which Garibaldi had left at Luino heard that the Austrians were advancing, they sailed in the ships, with the prisoners, to Cannero on the other side of the lake. Garibaldi now ordered them to return the ships to Arona under a flag of truce, and to send sixteen of the prisoners to Luino, among them the Croats' medical officer, Winkelhofer. He had made Winkelhofer promise to propose to the Austrian commander that the Croats should be exchanged for Garibaldi's men who had been taken prisoner at Morazzone, placing Winkelhofer on parole to return to captivity at Cannero if the Austrians rejected the proposal. The Austrians agreed, and released the prisoners, though one of them, Demaestri, had to have his right arm amputated. The wounded Croat prisoners whom Garibaldi had sent to Cannobio had been found there by the Duke of Genoa's Sardinian troops when they occupied the town.[39]

A few days after Garibaldi arrived at Lugano, when he was feeling a little better, Medici arrived at the inn. Medici had crossed the frontier three days before Garibaldi, and had succeeded in finding him in Lugano. According to Garibaldi, he outlined to Medici his plans for organizing fresh incursions into Italy, but Medici said contemptuously: 'We can do much better.' Garibaldi then realized that Medici and Mazzini were determined to exclude him from all share in their plans. He therefore decided to return to Nice to recuperate from his illness before undertaking any military operation.[40]

Both Garibaldi and Mazzini wished to conduct guerrilla operations against the Austrians in Italy from bases in Switzerland; but they found it impossible to collaborate because of their personal differences. Their disagreements about the conduct of operations in August 1848 led to recriminations, with both the Garibaldians and the Mazzinians telling conflicting stories in later years. In the 1872 edition of the memoirs, Garibaldi made several criticisms of Mazzini and Medici. After criticizing Mazzini for going to Switzerland from Como at the beginning of August, which he said encouraged his men to desert, he gave full praise to Medici for returning from Lugano and joining him at Castelletto; but he said that many other Italians who had crossed into Switzerland were deterred from joining him in Italy by the fact that Mazzini, at Lugano, was making plans for more ambitious ventures in Italy, and that these men therefore held back in order to take part in these ventures, which in fact never materialized. Jessie White Mario, who came down firmly on Mazzini's side in these disputes, says that Mazzini's plans did materialize later in the year, in November, when Medici and the Mazzinians crossed the Italian frontier and conducted heroic operations against the Austrians in the mountain snows, during which three of the Mazzinians froze to death. She says that Mazzini had intended to ask Garibaldi to lead this expedition, but that Garibaldi had temporarily given up the fight and had returned to Nice.

It fell to Antonio Picozzo in 1882, after both Mazzini and Garibaldi were dead, to write an account of the 1848 guerrilla campaign which gave unstinted praise to both groups of partisans. Picozzo, after stating that Garibaldi at Morazzone held up 10,000 Austrians for a whole day with 500 men, told the equally untrue story of how Medici and 200 Mazzinians kept 5,000 Austrians at bay for four hours, though this was not as good as Dumas, who had claimed that Medici had achieved the feat with only 68 men.[41]

Garibaldi's generalship in the campaign of August 1848 was also criticized by Carlo Pisacane in his book *The War fought in Italy in the Years 1848–9*, which he published in Genoa in 1851. Pisacane was closer to Mazzini than to Garibaldi, though he was too much of a Socialist to be a true Mazzinian. He wrote that Garibaldi was not a good guerrilla leader, because he exhausted his men by long, pointless marches, made inadequate preparations for feeding them, and when he found a good defensive position waited there for the enemy to attack him, instead of attacking the enemy. He condemned Garibaldi for allowing himself to be bottled up in the Lake Maggiore district, instead of going the other side of Lake Como into the mountainous country of the Valteline, where he could have held out longer. At Morazzone, Garibaldi seems to have been out-generalled. He was compelled to make a retreat by night which ended in the complete dispersal of his force, by an enemy who was numerically no stronger than he was, because he had been put in a position where he had to fight a battle cooped up in a burning town and had been deceived into thinking that he was facing a greatly superior enemy force. But it is going much too far for Pisacane to describe Garibaldi's Legionaries as 'brave but badly led young men'.[42]

The defeat of the guerrillas ended the fighting in Italy for the time being. On 2 September Radetzky reported to the War Office in Vienna that he had driven Garibaldi over the frontier.

With this, Austrian territory has been completely freed from the enemy bands, and even this audacious and resourceful *condottiero* has renounced – at least for the time being – his plans to invade our territory. This renunciation is clearly shown by the voluntary restitution of the ships, which were so necessary for his raids and his requisitions.

Radetzky's victory spurred on the army and the counter-revolutionary forces in Austria to overthrow the Liberal government in Vienna, and to install the young Archduke Franz Josef as Emperor, with Prince Felix von Schwarzenberg as his Prime Minister; and 'Father Radetzky' was acclaimed by Johann Strauss, Grillparzer, Otto Prechtler and Alexander Kaufman as the hero who had slain 'the dragon Communism' and avenged the Five Days in Milan.[43]

CHAPTER 17

FROM LEGHORN TO ROME

GARIBALDI travelled from Lugano to Nice through Switzerland and France. In 1848 revolutionaries faced many difficulties, but they had two advantages over those of later times: it was much easier to obtain a false passport, and there were no difficulties about foreign currency for anyone who had a supply of gold coins in his pocket. The only difficulty which Garibaldi encountered on his journey was when he reached the Sardinian frontier on the River Var between Saint-Laurent and Nice. When he asked permission from the frontier officials to enter the country, they referred the matter to the Chief of Police for the Nice district, and received the solemn reply that Garibaldi would be permitted to enter the Kingdom of Sardinia if he had a permanent address in the Kingdom to which he could go, but that otherwise entry must be refused; and Garibaldi, having provided a permanent address, and waited for a few days at Saint-Laurent, was allowed to go to Nice, where he arrived on the evening of 10 September.[1]

On reaching Nice, he did not take up residence in his mother's house, but moved with Anita and the children to the cottage of an old sailor friend, Giuseppe Deidery, who lived just outside the town. There seems to have been some anxiety among his friends that Charles Albert might order him to be arrested for high treason because he had issued his manifesto at Castelletto against the armistice;[2] but Charles Albert, who was particularly eager at this time to retain and increase his support among the Radicals, was not contemplating any such step. Perhaps Garibaldi made this an excuse to move out of his mother's house in view of the difficulties which she was making about his relationship with Anita.

Garibaldi addressed a political rally in Nice, and then went to bed in Deidery's house, and had a complete rest.[3] It was one of the few occasions in his life when he was forced to take to a sick-bed, though from about this time onwards he was often troubled by painful attacks of rheumatism and arthritis in his legs. Some of his biographers have attributed the arthritis to a hereditary tendency in his family, but others have thought that it was caused by the torture to which he had been subjected at Gualeguay, and others again to the fact that he had been exposed to the wet in the tropical forests of Brazil. The torture theory would have been plausible if the arthritis had been confined to his arms, but could not have caused it in his legs; and as for the tropical forest theory, it overlooks the fact that except for the retreat to the west in Rio Grande do Sul in October 1840, which had not lasted for more than two or three weeks, Garibaldi had never camped out in forests during his twelve years in South America.

He stayed less than three weeks in Nice, and then, having fully recovered his health, he was off again. On 26 September he went to San Remo to address a patriotic rally. He travelled by sea in the ship of his old friend Captain Pesante, who had been the master of the ship *Costanza* in which he had made his first voyage as a merchant seaman in 1824. He was acclaimed by all classes in San Remo, being welcomed by a reception committee which included a Marquis, a Count and two middle-class lawyers, and cheered by the people, who greeted him with indiscriminate shouts of 'Long live Garibaldi! Long live Pius IX! Long live Charles Albert! Long live Italian independence!'[4]

From San Remo he went to Oneglia, where he made a speech, and then on to Genoa. A Parliament had been elected in the Kingdom of Sardinia; it was the first under the new constitution which Charles Albert had granted. Garibaldi was invited to stand as a candidate at Cicagna, a small town just outside Genoa, and he agreed. He issued a stirring patriotic address to the electors, and a number of other proclamations, in which he urged that the armistice with Austria should be ended and the war resumed as soon as possible. He was elected, although he had made it clear that he would not be able to take his seat in the National Assembly, as he was about to go off to fight for Italian independence.[5]

But he could not decide where to go. The most useful thing which he could have done would probably have been to go to Venice to organize a fleet for Manin, who was in great need of help at sea since Charles Albert had withdrawn the Sardinian navy; but while he was in Genoa he received a visit from the Sicilian revolutionary, Paolo Fabrizi, who invited him to come to the help of the Sicilians who were resisting an attempt by King Ferdinand to reconquer the island. Ferdinand, after carrying through a counter-revolution in Naples in May, had sent his troops against the Sicilians in September, and had earned the name of 'King Bomba' by his bombardment of the civilian population in Messina, which had continued for several hours after the city had surrendered. Garibaldi accepted Fabrizi's invitation. He assembled a party of 72 volunteers, including 38 of the Legionaries who had come with him from Montevideo, and prepared to go to the help of the Sicilians.[6]

Before he sailed, Anita arrived in Genoa, and demanded to accompany him on his campaign. She wished once more to ride and fight at his side, as she had done eight years before in Santa Catarina and Rio Grande do Sul. Perhaps she wished also to get away from her mother-in-law, or simply to be with Garibaldi; at any rate, she was less content to be a housewife and mother in Nice than she had been in Montevideo. Menotti, who was now eight, had been sent to a boarding school in Genoa, at Charles Albert's expense, when Anita had first arrived from South America;[7] and Teresita, who was three, and Ricciotti, who was eighteen months, were left in the care of the Deiderys in Nice.

On 24 October Garibaldi sailed from Genoa in a French steamer, the *Pharamond*, with Anita and the seventy-two volunteers, bound for Palermo. But next day the *Pharamond* put in to Leghorn for supplies, and Garibaldi found himself in the centre of a political storm. The Grand-Duchy of Tuscany had been one of the least reactionary of the Italian states before 1848, because though the Grand-Duke Leopold II was an autocratic sovereign and a nephew of the Emperor of Austria, he was more liberal than most of the other Italian rulers. When revolution broke out all around him in 1848, he granted a constitution, brought a government of moderate Liberals to power, and even reluctantly agreed to send detachments to take part in Sardinia's war against Austria. But he did not go far enough for the Radicals, and a powerful opposition movement developed, particularly in Florence and Leghorn. The leaders of the Radicals were Giuseppe Montanelli and Francesco Domenico Guerrazzi, the famous novelist, who, after Mazzini, was the most prominent figure in the Young Italy movement.

At the end of August, the dockers and artisans of Leghorn rose in revolt against the Grand-Duke and the government of Tuscany. The troops who were sent from Florence to suppress the revolt were driven out of the town; but Montanelli and Guerrazzi went to Leghorn and calmed the revolutionaries. The Grand-Duke felt obliged to appoint Montanelli as Prime Minister and Guerrazzi as Minister of the Interior. But some of the Radicals did not approve of this, and started a campaign against Montanelli's government under the leadership of a university professor, Carlo Pigli, who succeeded Guerrazzi as the chairman of the revolutionary Radical club, the Circolo del Popolo, and was thought to be a Communist by the French Minister in Florence.[8]

When the *Pharamond* arrived at Leghorn at 8 am on 25 October, the streets were decorated, flags were flying, and a great crowd had assembled on the waterfront to greet Garibaldi.[9] 'The Via Grande and the Piazza were decorated as if for a holiday,' wrote the *Corriere Livornese*, 'and an enormous crowd cheered the hero of Montevideo. . . . All the citizens of different classes are madly excited to see our Garibaldi and to know that he is here. He thinks he is about to leave for Sicily, but the people of Leghorn are begging him to stay in Tuscany.'

Garibaldi was immediately invited to stay in Tuscany by the local leaders in Leghorn, and to take command of the revolutionary Tuscan army. When Garibaldi explained that he was on his way to help the Sicilians, the Radicals in Leghorn suggested that he would be able to help the Sicilians best by taking command of the Tuscan army and leading it across the southern frontier, through the Papal States, into the Kingdom of Naples, thus attacking King Ferdinand in his rear. Garibaldi agreed to stay, if the government of Tuscany would appoint him to command their forces against Naples; and Menichetti and Isolani, the local leaders in Leghorn, sent a telegram to Montanelli in Florence asking him for an immediate reply, because the *Pharamond* was due to leave for Palermo the same evening.

But Montanelli and Guerrazzi were not at all enthusiastic. They feared that Garibaldi might become the centre of a more Radical revolutionary movement which might hamper their policy of conciliating the Grand-Duke by moderation and dissuading him from calling in the Austrian troops to restore him to absolute power. Montanelli and Guerrazzi gave a series of evasive replies to the series of telegrams which they received from Menichetti and Isolani. Time was getting short, with the *Pharamond* due to leave at 7 pm; so Isolani cabled to Montanelli that they must know the government's decision by that time. But they had heard nothing by 7 pm. Garibaldi then persuaded the *Pharamond* to delay her departure for a few hours, and at 7.15 pm sent a telegram to Montanelli: 'I ask will you take Garibaldi as commander of Tuscan forces to operate against Bourbons. Yes or No. Garibaldi.' At 8.06 pm Montanelli sent a reply, not to Garibaldi but to Isolani, stating that he agreed to Garibaldi's appointment, but could not confirm it officially without the authority of the Minister of War, which could not be obtained immediately. This was good enough for Garibaldi, who told the *Pharamond* to sail without him.

Garibaldi remained in Leghorn for a few days, waiting for confirmation of the government's decision. He was fêted by the Radical leaders, and when they took him to the opera on the evening of 29 October, the whole auditorium rose to their feet and cheered him. By this time, he was beginning to chafe at the delay, and to regret that he had not gone on to Palermo; but after toying with the idea of going to Lombardy to fight the Austrians there, he decided to go to Venice to help Manin. He had now been joined by nearly 300 volunteers in Leghorn, and had a total force of about 350. He arranged with the government of Tuscany to supply him with 300 overcoats, 300 pairs of boots, 250 muskets and bayonets, and 20 officers' sabres, and prepared to march across Tuscany and the Papal States to the Adriatic, and embark at Ravenna for Venice. On 3 November he travelled by train to Florence with Anita and his men. There were more demonstrations in his favour when he arrived in Florence. In a speech from the balcony of the house where he was staying, he saluted the Tuscan people, and told them that when he left South America his original intention had been to land in Tuscany.[10]

Pigli and the Opposition immediately got hold of Garibaldi. On the day before he arrived in Florence, he had been elected an honorary member of the Circolo del Popolo, and on 5 November the Club held a great rally. The speakers were Pigli, Carlo Bonaparte and Garibaldi. Carlo Bonaparte was the nephew of Napoleon I, and the son of Lucien Bonaparte, Prince of Canino. After achieving an international reputation as an ornithologist, he had become one of the most extreme of the Left-wing leaders in Italy. The rally was held, not in the usual meeting place of the Circolo del Popolo, but in the Leopold Theatre, the largest hall in Florence. The theatre was packed to full capacity.

Pigli made the opening speech at the meeting. He praised Garibaldi, who, he said, after being forced by circumstances to fight for freedom in a foreign country many thousands of miles from his native shores, had now come to fight for the freedom and independence of his own country. Carlo Bonaparte followed with a violent speech, denouncing Guerrazzi and the Tuscan government for their moderate policy. Garibaldi, the chief attraction, spoke last. He, too, criticized the government as 'the obstacle which prevents us from acting freely in accordance with our conscience', and said that it was 'necessary not merely to push the government, but to assault them if necessary in order to make them go forward'.[11]

The audience were enthusiastic about Garibaldi's speech, but Montanelli and Guerrazzi did not appreciate it. They did not supply Garibaldi with the coats, boots and weapons which they had promised him; and Montanelli told the French Minister in Florence that Garibaldi had not received any help or encouragement from the Tuscan government in connexion with his expedition to Venice. Garibaldi set off without them with his 350 Legionaries on an arduous march to Ravenna, which involved crossing the Apennines. He would not allow Anita to come, so she returned to Nice, and lived with Teresita and Ricciotti in Deidery's house.[12]

The winter had set in early, and as the Legionaries marched higher up the Apennines they found the snow was lying knee-deep. It was the first time for fourteen years that Garibaldi had encountered the rigours of a European winter, and he and his men, many of whom, like him, had become used to the climate of South America, felt the cold. They had no warm clothing suitable for this kind of weather, because when they left Genoa they had been expecting to go to Sicily, and they had not been given the warm overcoats which the Tuscan government had promised them. At Filigari, at the top of the pass, they reached the frontier of the Papal States, and found their way blocked by 400 Swiss soldiers in the Pope's service. The Papal authorities in Bologna had been notified by the Nuncio in Florence that the Legionaries were on their way, and had sent the Swiss troops to stop them from entering the Papal territory.

Garibaldi and his men had to wait at the frontier at the top of the pass in the snow. There was an inn there, and the innkeeper was very friendly. He allowed the 350 men to crowd into the inn and bivouac on the floor, and provided them with all the comforts that were available, for which Garibaldi and his officers paid out of their own pockets; but Garibaldi was very angry about the way in which he was being treated. He commented in his memoirs on the injustice of the world; men who had volunteered to join him, and were ready to give their lives to free their country, were being forced to suffer in the bitter cold, while the wealthy classes, the selfish business men, and the so-called patriots who cheered from the sidelines but would not go to fight themselves, were living in comfort and warmth in the cities. He also reflected bitterly on the fact that it was two men who had been hailed as the liberators of Italy, Pius IX and Guerrazzi, who were responsible for the sufferings of his Legionaries, because Pius would not let them go on, and Guerrazzi had refused to provide them with the warm clothing which would have protected them against the cold.

Though the commander of the Papal troops at Filigari refused to allow Garibaldi's men to cross the frontier, he permitted Garibaldi to go alone to Bologna to argue with General de Latour, the commander of the Papal forces in the area. The news that the Legionaries were held up at the top of the pass had immediately reached Bologna, and the action of the Papal government had been strongly condemned in the press. The Radicals organized a petition protesting against it, and prepared to give Garibaldi a great reception when he arrived in the city.

We demand the immediate and definite recall of the troops who have been sent against the General in a hostile attitude, and intend to honour the arrival of the hero of Montevideo in the manner that he deserves. . . . On this occasion, General de Latour should remember that he is a Bolognese, and that a single arbitrary action can ruin a reputation which it has taken years to achieve.

General de Latour acted on this advice. When Garibaldi arrived at Bologna on the evening of 9 November, Latour met him at the entrance to Bologna, and escorted him in state through the city, amid tumultuous cheering, to the Grande Albergo Reale, where accommodation had been booked for him. Latour was able to reassure Garibaldi. The day before, he had received a letter from Count Rossi, the Pope's Prime Minister, ordering him to allow Garibaldi's men to enter the Papal States and go to Ravenna in transit for Venice, but instructing him to do all he could to hurry them on their way and to get rid of them as soon as possible. Rossi's letter had been written two days before the Legionaries arrived at the frontier. The hold-up at Filigari, which had caused so much resentment among the Legionaries, was entirely due to a foolish decision of the subordinate authorities at Bologna, and not to Pius ix and his government.

In Bologna, Garibaldi discussed with General Zucchi, the Commander-in-Chief of the Papal army, the question of the length of their stay. Zucchi agreed that Garibaldi and his 350 men should go to Ravenna and stay there till another detachment of volunteers arrived from Mantua, after which they would all leave Ravenna at once for Venice.[13] But when Garibaldi and his Legionaries reached Ravenna, there were more difficulties. Ravenna was on the verge of revolution, and their arrival added to the political excitement. They were welcomed by the Radicals in the town, and became very friendly with the local population. Garibaldi liked the people of Ravenna, whom he found different from the inhabitants of the other cities through which he had passed. They were taciturn, cool and undemonstrative, but Garibaldi thought that this showed that they were men of deeds, not words. He was particularly pleased with one example of their taciturnity which he was told had occurred shortly before his arrival. A man had assassinated a police informer in the public square in daylight, in full view of hundreds of people, and none of them had been prepared to make any statement about the crime to the authorities.

The Papal authorities in Ravenna thought that the Legionaries were a very dangerous influence in an explosive situation, and wished to get rid of them at the earliest possible moment. But the Mantuan volunteers did not arrive in Ravenna; and as Garibaldi was determined to wait for them before sailing to Venice, as he had agreed with Zucchi, the authorities at Ravenna discovered to their dismay that the Garibaldinis' stay was likely to be prolonged. They decided to go back on the agreement that Zucchi had made. General de Latour told Garibaldi that the government insisted that the Legionaries should leave for Venice at once, without waiting for the Mantua contingent. When Garibaldi refused to go, Latour informed him that if necessary he would use force to disarm and arrest the Legionaries, as he had troops outside the town, with two small cannon, in sufficient strength to overcome resistance. Garibaldi said that if his men were attacked, they would fight, and he contacted his friends in the town. They called out the revolutionary National Guard, distributed arms, and prepared to fight at Garibaldi's side. At this moment, news arrived of the assassination of Rossi and the revolution in Rome.[14]

The Pope's refusal to join the war against Austria had led to a violent Radical revolutionary agitation in Rome against the Papal government. The movement had supporters among all classes of the population. Carlo Bonaparte of Canino and the Princess Belgiojoso, whom the Austrians called the 'Communist Semiramis',[15] were well-known revolutionaries; most of the leaders were middle-class lawyers and journalists; and the chief support came from the masses in the Trastevere, the poorest section of the city. A brilliant Radical journalist, Pietro Sterbini, wrote inflammatory articles in his paper; and a burly wine-merchant, Angelo Brunetti, who was known by his pet-name of Ciceruacchio, harangued the people, and became a second Danton. He made the name 'Trastevere' as ominous to the Conservatives in 1848 as the 'Faubourg Saint-Antoine' had been to the French aristocrats of 1792. There were many people of all classes in Rome who were opposed to the Radicals and to revolution; and outside the city, among the peasants throughout the Papal States, the revolutionaries had very little support.

In September 1848 the Pope appointed Count Rossi as his Prime Minister. Politically, Rossi was in almost complete sympathy with Pius IX. In the days of Gregory XVI, Rossi had been regarded with suspicion by the reactionary Papal government because he favoured certain reforms and had married a Protestant wife; but in 1848 he was in favour of keeping out of the war against Austria, and his political position, which had seemed Liberal as recently as a year before, now seemed Conservative to the Radicals of Rome. He also made many personal enemies by his haughty manner, and his habit of treating any criticism with silent contempt. He was attacked by Sterbini and Carlo Bonaparte and other Radicals, in speeches and in the press, in the violent and blood-curdling language which was the stock-in-trade of Radical journalists of the period.

On 15 November, nine days after he had authorized Garibaldi's Legionaries to enter the Papal States from Tuscany, Rossi went to address the opening of the new Parliament which the Pope had instituted. He was intending to make an uncompromising Right-wing speech insisting on the need to restore law and order in Rome. As he entered the Parliament building, he was attacked by hostile demonstrators, and someone stabbed him in the neck with a dagger. He died almost immediately. No one knows who the murderer was. At the time it was widely believed that he was a young man called Trentanove; but after he was executed for the murder by the counter-revolutionaries some years later, nearly everyone became convinced of his innocence. Both Ciceruacchio's son, Luigi Brunetti, and Carlo Bonaparte were accused of being the assassin, but this is unlikely.

The news of the assassination of Rossi was received with great enthusiasm by the Radicals. Trentanove, being rightly or wrongly thought to be the murderer, was carried through the streets on the shoulders of the mob. A procession marched around the city, with the dagger which had killed Rossi being held high in triumph; and the marchers took care to go to Rossi's house, where they called for his widow to show herself at the window, held up the dagger, and cried 'Long live the Italian Republic! Long live the dagger of Brutus!' and sang a new hymn which Sterbini had composed, beginning 'Blessed is the hand that killed Rossi'.[16] Next day the crowd stormed the Pope's palace and killed the Pope's confessor, who tried to keep them out, and was said to have fired on the people. They departed when Pius announced that he had appointed a new government under the Radical, Muzzarelli, in which Sterbini was one of the ministers.

Rossi's murder led to the revolution in Rome and was a political assassination fulfilling the requirements necessary to secure Mazzini's approval. It was not an act of vengeance against some obscure police infori er or some traitor who had betrayed the movement, but the elimination of a prominent political leader, of a 'tyrant' in circumstances which were delightfully reminiscent of the assassination of Julius Caesar by Brutus; and it had been the signal for a revolution, just as political assassinations were supposed to be in Mazzinian theory. The Mazzinians all over Italy applauded the deed, and a demonstration in Leghorn was addressed by Pigli, who said that Rossi had met the fate of enemies of the people.[17]

Garibaldi, like all the other members of Young Italy, approved of Rossi's assassination, and in his memoirs of 1872 he wrote about it in a passage which distressed his English supporters. After stating that 'as a disciple of Beccaria, I am opposed to the death penalty, and therefore I blame the dagger of Brutus', he continued:

The Harmodiuses, the Pelopidases and the Brutuses, the men who freed their country from tyrants, have not been painted by ancient history in colours so dirty as those in which the modern devourers of the peoples would like to exhibit any man who has touched the ribs of the Duke of Parma, Bourbon of Naples. . . . The ancient metropolis of the world, worthy on that day of her ancient glory, liberated herself from a satellite of tyranny, the most terrible one, and bathed the marble steps of the Capitol with his blood. A young Roman had recovered the steel of Marcus Brutus. . . . That dagger-stroke announced to the compromisers with the foreigner that the people knew them.[18]

Conservative supporters, and many moderate Liberals, were shocked by Rossi's murder, and so was everyone abroad except Radical revolutionaries. In England the assassination, like Garibaldi's words on the subject in later years, embarrassed the Liberal champions of Italian freedom, who would not realize that the Mazzinian patriots in Italy were as ready to use political assassination as a weapon as were the Irish Fenians, the Russian Nihilists, and the international Anarchists and their disciples in the twentieth century. Rossi's death convinced the Pope that this is what happens if a sovereign grants a constitution and political liberty to his people, and henceforth Pius became a determined opponent of Liberalism and the *Risorgimento* in all its forms.

On the night of 24 November Pius escaped from Rome with the connivance of several members of the foreign diplomatic corps, disguised as a servant in the livery of the Bavarian Minister. At six o'clock next morning he reached Gaeta in the Kingdom of Naples, where King Ferdinand and his court were in residence. Pius drove to the house of his Nuncio at Gaeta; but the Nuncio's servants refused to admit him, and did not believe that he was the Pope till the Nuncio appeared and went on his knees to him.[19] From Gaeta, where Ferdinand received him with great honour, Pius issued a proclamation denouncing the murder of Rossi and the events in Rome, and refused to receive the envoys who were sent by the ministers in Rome to urge him to return. The ministers then ordered that a general election should be held throughout the Papal States to elect the members of a Constituent Assembly who would decide the future form of government in the Papal States. Pius replied by denouncing the election as illegal, and threatening to excommunicate anyone who voted.

When Garibaldi heard about the events in Rome, he again changed his plans. Realizing that the new Roman government would soon be attacked by counter-revolutionary armies from foreign states, he decided, instead of going to Venice, to remain in the Papal States and fight in the Roman revolutionary army. He marched his men from Ravenna to Cesena, some twenty miles to the south, and leaving them there, went on by himself to Rome to see the ministers. It was only the second time in his life that he had been to Rome, having last been there twenty-four years before when, at the age of seventeen, he went with his father on his second voyage as a merchant seaman. In Rome he met Campello, one of the new Radical ministers, and Campello agreed that his Legionaries should be enrolled in the Roman army, and receive pay and equipment from the government; but Campello insisted that the numbers should be limited to 500, as the government could not afford to keep any more.

Meanwhile an incident occurred at Cesena which saddened Garibaldi. Two of his best officers, who had served with him in Montevideo, quarrelled, and one of them, Risso, struck the other, Ramorino, across the face with a whip. Ramorino thereupon challenged him to a duel. Garibaldi was very distressed that two veterans of Tres Cruces and La Boyada should now fight against each other instead of fighting the Austrians or the Neapolitans; but in the matter of duelling, and in a few other matters, Garibaldi adopted the attitude of an army officer, and not of a Radical revolutionary, of the period. 'I should certainly have expelled from the Legion the officer who would take a blow from anyone', he wrote in his memoirs. He therefore allowed the duel to take place, and Ramorino killed Risso. So Risso, who had miraculously survived a neck-wound which he had received in operations against the Rosistas at Montevideo, was killed by his own comrade after only one campaign in his native land.[20]

Garibaldi and his men spent Christmas and the New Year marching around the eastern parts of the Papal States trying to find a suitable place to take up their quarters, and eventually in the middle of January they reached Macerata. They had arrived there for the first time a few weeks earlier, but the inhabitants had refused to admit them, because they had heard stories – which Garibaldi says were lies spread by priests – that the Legionaries would misbehave themselves and cause damage in the town. On the return journey, Garibaldi insisted that he and his men should be admitted, and the people of Macerata were pleasantly surprised to find that the Legionaries behaved very well. Garibaldi states that the volunteers who had now joined him were mostly men of very respectable families and background, including many from aristocratic families. In fact, though he does not mention it, a number of them were from the criminal classes; but there is no doubt that the Legion now, and on all his future campaigns in Italy, contained a smaller proportion of disreputable characters than it had done in South America. Many of the volunteers were university students and schoolboys, some of them as young as twelve or fourteen years old. Not everyone approved of Garibaldi's practice of taking boys of this age from their parents, and allowing them to live, march, fight and die at the side of the criminal elements in the Legion; but Garibaldi's admirers claimed that Garibaldi was a father, as well as a commander, to the boys, and an excellent moral influence on them. The boys certainly adored him. The idea of boys of twelve going into battle was not a strange one to Garibaldi, because in South America they often fought at this age, both in the army and the navy.[21]

On 21 January 1849 the election to the Constituent Assembly took place throughout the Papal States. The franchise was the most democratic that had ever been adopted in any national election in any country, all male citizens over twenty-one being entitled to vote. The priests had spread the news around that anyone who voted would be excommunicated; but the government had launched a great campaign, calling on everyone to vote, and had used all kinds of propaganda, and in some cases pressure, to persuade them to do so. In Rome, voting was quite heavy, but there were many abstentions in the country districts. In two small towns, Castello and Corneto, no one voted at all; in Pius IX's home district of Sinigaglia, only 200 voted out of 27,552 electors; and even in Bologna less than half the electorate voted.[22]

Garibaldi was persuaded by the local Radical club, the Circolo Popolare, to stand as one of the sixteen candidates nominated by the club for the eastern region, which included Macerata. As a subject of the King of Sardinia, he was an alien in the Papal States; but the government had decreed that any Italian could be elected to the Constituent Assembly. The Pope's supporters, who were strong in Macerata, decided to boycott the elections in obedience to the Pope's command, and the Circolo Popolare were afraid that there would be many abstentions in Macerata. Garibaldi and his Legionaries had made their arrangements to leave Macerata and move to Rieti a few days before the election; but the Circolo Popolare persuaded them to stay in Macerata and vote there, so as to swell the total number of votes cast. Most of the Legionaries were not in fact entitled to vote, because, though the foreigners from other parts of Italy were allowed to stand as candidates, they had not been expressly allowed to vote; and the students and schoolboys under twenty-one in the Legion were not entitled to vote. But the Circolo Popolare brushed aside these objections; and at 11 am on Sunday, 21 January, the 528 Legionaries marched to the polling station, and all cast their votes for Garibaldi and the other fifteen candidates on the Circolo Popolare's list.

The result of the election was declared next day. A local Macerata Radical headed the poll with 3,928 votes; Garibaldi came thirteenth, with 2,069 votes; the lowest of the sixteen candidates elected obtained 1,873 votes. The Papal supporters denounced the election as illegal, because the Legionaries had voted. That night there was a demonstration in the square in Macerata, with cries of 'Long live Pius IX! Death to General Garibaldi and his Legionaries!' In the middle of the demonstration, the Legionaries arrived, and threatened to burn the houses of the demonstrators; but the local police succeeded in calming everyone, and restoring order.[23]

Next day Garibaldi issued a farewell message to the people of Macerata, in which he thanked them for the hospitality which they had shown to his men, and marched off with the Legion to Rieti, seventy miles to the south-west and about half-way to Rome. He himself travelled to Rieti with two or three companions by a different route from the rest of his men, because he wished to spy out the land along the Neapolitan frontier, which he expected would be the scene of fighting when the Neapolitan forces invaded the Papal States. He encountered cold weather and snow as he crossed the Apennines, and this brought on a painful attack of rheumatism. The Legionaries arrived at Rieti on 31 January. That evening they went to the theatre, and made a demonstration in the interval, shouting 'Long live the Republic! Death to the priests! Death to Pius ix!' According to the Papal propagandists and the Austrian press, they cut off the head of a statue of Pius ix in the main square at Rieti, insulted the priests, and in many cases cut off their hair.[24]

At Rieti, Garibaldi was joined by more volunteers, including Ugo Bassi, a priest from Bologna. Ugo Bassi was a passionate Christian and a passionate revolutionary, who combined a gentle kindness and a fiery eloquence. He was a spiritual descendant of Arnold of Brescia, and the spiritual ancestor of similar types in the twentieth century. Although he was now nearly fifty, he had lost none of his youthful enthusiasm. During the previous twenty-five years he had just managed to avoid getting into serious trouble with the Church, and had actually been received in audience by Gregory xvi and Pius ix, who had treated him as a harmless joke; but after his activities in 1848 and 1849 he was denounced by the hierarchy as a renegade priest. Garibaldi, like nearly everyone who met him, became very fond of him. Ugo Bassi persuaded Garibaldi to appoint him as chaplain to the Legion. Bassi wished to hold a service for the Legionaries in the cathedral at Rieti. Garibaldi agreed, but the parish priest would not permit it.[25]

The Legion remained at Rieti while Garibaldi went on to Rome to take his seat in the Constituent Assembly. When he arrived in Rome he received a great welcome from the Radicals, particularly from their younger supporters, and spoke at a political demonstration. The great question to be decided was the future government of the Papal States. Pisacane afterwards wrote that Garibaldi and his supporters had planned to march on the Capitol and proclaim Garibaldi as Dictator, and that Garibaldi was only dissuaded from doing so by some of the wiser Radicals; but Pisacane's story is very improbable.[26]

The Pope's attitude had increased the opposition and revolutionary spirit among the Radicals in Rome. Ciceruacchio had replied to the Pope's threat of excommunication by holding a procession, which the Pope's supporters denounced as blasphemous, in which men wearing cardinals' hats burlesqued religious ceremonies and ridiculed the rite of excommunication. On 2 February a mass rally in the Apollo Theatre had called for the establishment of a Roman Republic in the Papal States, and a young priest, the Abbé Arduini, had made a speech in which he declared that the temporal power of the Pope was 'a historical lie, a political imposture, and a religious immorality'.[27]

On 5 February the 150 elected deputies of the Constituent Assembly met in the Capitol in Rome, with the Prime Minister, Muzzarelli, presiding. Among them was the member for Macerata, who was still the member for Salto in the Parliament of the Oriental Republic of Uruguay and the member for Cicagna in the Parliament of the Kingdom of Sardinia. The first session was devoted to swearing-in the deputies, who began answering the roll-call of their names. When the name of Carlo Bonaparte, who was the member for Viterbo, was called, he replied to the roll-call by calling out 'Long live the Republic!', whereupon Garibaldi raised a point of order. He said that it was a waste of time to go on with the swearing-in ceremony, and that as they were the elected representatives of the nation, they should do what was expected of them, not only by the people of Rome, but by a million Italian brothers, and settle the destiny of the Italian nation. To delay for a minute would be a crime. 'Shall we waste time discussing formalities? I firmly believe that as the former system of government has come to an end, the most suitable form for Rome today would be the Republic.' There were cheers from many of the deputies, but shouts of protest from others; and Garibaldi continued: 'Are the descendants of the ancient Romans, the Romans of today, incapable of being Republicans? As someone in this hall has now uttered the trenchant word "republic", I repeat, Long live the Republic!' The dying Anzani need not have feared that Garibaldi was abandoning his Republican principles.

Carlo Bonaparte then proposed that they should proceed with the roll-call of deputies, but that as soon as this was finished they should proclaim the Republic, and not adjourn until they had done so; but Sterbini said that it was essential that Europe should see that the Romans today, like their ancient Senate, discussed things calmly and not under the influence of passion; and after Garibaldi had again intervened to say that the Roman people did not have to follow the example of their pupils, the English or the French, but could find enough examples from their own history, Sterbini asked the brave

General Garibaldi to curb his impatience, and the session was adjourned.

On 8 February, the Assembly proceeded to discuss the future form of government. Garibaldi's rheumatism was so bad that he could not walk, and had to be carried into the Assembly hall by Bueno, who had come with him from Montevideo. As they went in, Garibaldi told his friend Vecchi that it was the anniversary of San Antonio, and that he was now being carried by Bueno, just as they had carried the wounded back to Salto after the battle three years before. Seven thousand miles away in Montevideo, the decree of 25 February 1846 was being published in the order of the day, and the victory was being commemorated, while in Rome the Constituent Assembly proceeded to the proclamation of the Republic. After a discussion in which Garibaldi spoke and declared that the Roman cause was the same Italian cause as the cause of Sicily and Venice, the Assembly passed a resolution at one o'clock in the morning by 120 votes to 23 declaring that the Papal temporal power in the Roman state was at an end; that the Pope would be guaranteed all necessary facilities for exercising his spiritual functions; that the Roman state would be a pure democracy and should have 'the glorious name of the Roman Republic'; and that the citizens of the Roman Republic should have a common nationality with the people of the rest of Italy.[28]

A few days later, Garibaldi returned to his Legionaries at Rieti. Soon afterwards, Anita arrived there. She had heard that Garibaldi was stationed more or less permanently at Rieti, and came from Nice to be with him. They stayed in Rieti for two months, which was the longest time that they had been together since Anita left Montevideo just over a year before. At Rieti they decided to have their fifth child.[29]

Before he left Rome, Garibaldi had had an interview with the Minister of War, and persuaded him to allow him to increase the numbers in the Legion from 500 to 1,000. He appealed for new recruits at Rieti, and volunteers came in from all parts of Italy. The number of Legionaries rose to 1,264, and as the government in Rome had fixed 1,000 as the limit, Garibaldi had to maintain 1,264 men on the pay and rations allotted to 1,000. He was also short of muskets and ammunition; but he arranged with the blacksmiths at Rieti to make lances, so that all his men should have some weapon. He knew that they would soon be called on to defend the Roman Republic.[30]

CHAPTER 18

30 APRIL AND VELLETRI

THE Constituent Assembly turned, not to Sterbini, Ciceruacchio or Carlo Bonaparte and the leaders of the revolution of 16 November who had proclaimed the Republic, but to the man whom most of them regarded as their political and spiritual guide. They invited Mazzini to come to Rome and become the chief minister of the new republic. They entrusted the executive power to three Triumvirs – Mazzini, Armellini and Saffi; but the other two Triumvirs were completely dominated by Mazzini.

Mazzini lived as frugally in Rome as he had done as a refugee in Switzerland and London, dining in cheap restaurants, with his only luxury being the poor quality cigars which he constantly smoked. But his power was absolute, because though the Constituent Assembly remained in session it never went against his wishes. He issued decrees which transformed the Papal States into a modern democratic republic, and ended clerical control of the government; but he maintained the religious life of the country. He condemned all attempts to interfere with religious worship, and ordered that the traditional religious feast days should be observed, and that priests should be paid by the government, because they performed a service which was appreciated by the majority of the citizens of the Republic. But he could not prevent Ciceruacchio from holding his anti-religious processions, and occasional attacks on priests and monasteries by militant atheist groups and mobs.

Although the Papal and Conservative propagandists abroad became very indignant about the horrors of life in Rome and the persecutions of Catholics, they admitted that there was no political repression by Mazzini's government, which they blamed, not for being too severe, but for being too lenient. They condemned Mazzini for failing to suppress popular disorder, attacks on priests, blasphemous publications, and sexual licence; but there was no sign of the guillotine, the firing squad, the revolutionary tribunals, or a secret police. The only punishments which Mazzini inflicted on the Pope's supporters was to fine priests who, in obedience to the Pope's interdict, refused to hold religious services and perform their priestly duties. Mazzini claimed that this was an offence against the people, who were deprived of their desire for the solace of religion.

Garibaldi did not altogether agree with Mazzini's policy towards the clergy. He did not wish to persecute priests, and protected them from injury, if not always from insult, at the hands of his Legionaries. But he believed that except for a small minority of priests, like Ugo Bassi and Arduini, who had taken the side of the people against the Pope, the priests were agents of the counter-revolution and of the foreign armies which were threatening the Roman Republic; and he thought that they should be carefully watched and bridled. But he tried to avoid offending the religious susceptibilities of the people. When he was at Rieti, on Good Friday (6 April), he dismounted from his horse and took off his hat as a salute when a procession of monks passed by. Anita, who was sitting at his side on horseback, did not dismount or salute.[1]

Mazzini dealt firmly with the Radical extremists at Ancona, who, in the tradition of the Carbonari, had formed an association to assassinate their political opponents. They were led by a revolutionary priest. Many priests and Conservatives were put to death in Ancona. Mazzini sent Felice Orsini, who afterwards achieved notoriety when he tried to assassinate Napoleon III, to suppress the disorders in Ancona. Orsini declared that Republicanism did not mean assassination, and arrested thirty-five of the murderers, who were taken to Rieti and elsewhere to await trial.

This led to another disagreement between Mazzini and Garibaldi. On 9 April Garibaldi wrote to Mazzini and suggested that if the murderers were condemned to death, they should be pardoned and enrolled in his Legion. Garibaldi did not approve of the policy of assassinating priests and Conservatives; but, apart from the fact that he was opposed to capital punishment, he thought it a waste of much-needed man-power to execute these revolutionary supporters, who could redeem themselves by serving in the army; and he felt sure that he could keep them in order, as he had done with equally disreputable characters in his forces in South America. Mazzini refused to agree; but as capital punishment had been abolished in the Roman Republic, the men were sentenced to long terms of imprisonment.[2]

The Pope appealed to the Catholic governments to restore him to power, and to overthrow this 'so-called government of pure democracy'.[3] His host, the King of Naples, offered to send troops into the territory of the Roman Republic, and invited all the other Catholic states to join him. Charles Albert of Sardinia declined, and stated that he did not think that his Catholic faith required him to intervene in the temporal government of the Papal States. Portugal, where British influence was paramount, also refused, under pressure from Palmerston. The Right-wing military dictatorship in Spain sent a small force. Austria was eager to intervene. But the leading role was played by France. The unusual feature of the Italian scene in 1848 had been the absence of the usual French intervention. In the time of Napoleon, and in 1831, France had intervened in support of the Italian revolutionaries; but in 1848 her place as the champion of Italian freedom had been taken over by Sardinia. When the French Republican government offered to help Venice, Manin had refused, and had turned instead to Charles Albert. France now had the opportunity to intervene in Italy, but as a champion of counter-revolution. As soon as the Pope fled from Rome, before he had even issued his appeal for help, the head of the French government, General Cavaignac, had offered to send troops to restore him to power.

Cavaignac had always been a convinced Liberal and Republican; but he had been appointed Dictator in June 1848, when he suppressed a Socialist revolt in Paris with a ruthlessness which has made his name hated in the international Socialist movement for 125 years. In November 1848 he was nearing the end of his term of office, and elections for the President of the Republic were due to be held in a fortnight's time. Cavaignac was the candidate of the Liberal Republicans; his chief opponent was Louis Napoleon Bonaparte, the future Napoleon III. By his immediate offer to help the Pope against the revolutionaries in Rome, Cavaignac hoped to win Catholic support in the election. His policy was approved in the French National Assembly by 480 votes against 63. Louis Napoleon, playing for Socialist and Radical support, abstained. Cavaignac tried to use Louis Napoleon's abstention, and his relationship to Carlo Bonaparte, against him in the election; but Louis Napoleon was elected by a large majority.

Before Cavaignac's term of office ended, he had assembled an army of 9,000 men in Marseilles, ready to sail for Rome; but Louis Napoleon's victory halted these plans for the time being. Louis Napoleon had been a member of the Carbonari when he was a young man, and had strong sympathies with Italian nationalism; and for four months after he became President, he took no action against the Roman Republic while the expeditionary force waited in Marseilles. But he was faced with a powerful Catholic revival in France. After the revolution of 1848, large numbers of the French middle classes and peasants turned to the Catholic Church as the only bulwark against Socialism and atheism. The Bourbon and the Orleanist monarchies had gone, and the Liberal Republicans were detested by the Right and the Left; the Catholic Church seemed the only alternative to revolution. This

French Catholic revival was one of the most important external factors which influenced the Italian *Risorgimento* during the next twenty-two years, though fortunately for the Italian Radicals it was counterbalanced by Protestant and pro-Italian feeling in Britain.

The pressure of the French Catholics on Louis Napoleon became irresistible. They mounted a great campaign of propaganda against the Roman Republic. They emphasized that France was the eldest daughter of the Church – a title which she claimed because King Clovis in the fifth century had been the first monarch in Western Europe to convert to Christianity – and that it was her duty to overthrow the revolutionary atheists in Rome and restore the Pope to his rightful place. Louis Napoleon gave way and agreed to send the troops to Rome; but he tried to win the support of the Left-wing Republicans, and even of the Radicals, for his policy of intervention by claiming that if France intervened, it would prevent the Austrians from doing so. The French would restore the Pope as a constitutional ruler, and would save the Roman revolutionaries from the tortures and executions to which the Austrians would subject them if Austrian forces captured Rome and restored the Pope with absolute powers. This argument persuaded Radicals like Jules Favre to support the intervention, though Ledru-Rollin and Arago opposed it strongly, and after a heated debate, in which the government refused to admit that their troops were going to Rome to restore the Pope, the money for the expedition was voted in the National Assembly by 395 votes against 283.

On 22 April the 9,000 French troops in Marseilles sailed for Civita Vecchia. They were commanded by General Oudinot, Duke of Reggio, the son of Napoleon I's Marshal, who had himself served in Russia and in the campaign of 1814 as a young officer. He was a devout Catholic, and had no sympathy with the revolutionary Radicals; and he was a politician as well as a soldier, having been elected to the National Assembly. Oudinot arrived at Civita Vecchia on 24 April; and as he persuaded the local authorities there that he had come to protect Rome from the Austrians, he was allowed to disembark his troops without opposition. The King of Naples was ready to invade the Roman Republic from the south, and 9,000 Spanish troops and a small Spanish fleet had joined him.

Austria took no part in the campaign. At the end of March, Charles Albert, against the strong advice of Palmerston, had succumbed to the pressure of the nationalists and Radicals in Piedmont who demanded that he should intervene to help the Roman Republic, and had ended the armistice with Austria and resumed the war. Radetzky defeated him at Novara, and overwhelmed the Sardinian army in a four-day campaign. Charles Albert abdicated in favour of his son, Victor Emanuel II, who was forced to accept Radetzky's terms. After defeating the Sardinians, Radetzky was ready to march to the Pope's assistance; but Oudinot warned him, politely but firmly, to keep clear of Rome.

Oudinot sent a message to Mazzini, telling him that the French army would enter Rome, but that they came as friends, not enemies, and wished only to protect Rome from Austrian intervention and to restore peace between the Pope and his subjects. Mazzini replied that the Roman Republic wished to be friends with Republican France, but that if the French came as friends they should discuss with the Roman government the conditions under which their friendly forces should enter Rome.[4]

Mazzini, while still hoping to avoid a conflict with France, prepared to resist, and called on the people to defend the Republic. He appointed a Military Commission of Defence under the chairmanship of Pisacane. In every quarter of the city Committees of the Barricades were set up under the direction of Ciceruacchio. They called on the people to build barricades, while the volunteers spread sand across the streets to make them safer for the horses of the cavalry. The Committee of Ambulances was formed under the leadership of the Princess Belgiojoso, Henrietta Pisacane and other prominent revolutionary women; they organized medical assistance to the wounded and nursing in hospitals, and also propaganda and the encouragement of morale. Mazzini and the Triumvirs issued an appeal to the people:

> Brothers! to arms! Foreigners, enemies of the Roman people, are advancing. Republican Europe is watching you; their eyes are on you, these Poles, these Germans, and these Frenchmen, unfortunate apostles of Liberty, but not without glory in their misfortune; Lombards, Genoese, Sicilians and Venetians are watching you.[5]

But Oudinot thought that the Romans would not fight. The officers who had taken his letters to Mazzini had been approached by Papal supporters in Rome, who assured them that all the people were longing to be liberated by the French. This was also the opinion of the silly young French Chargé d'Affaires in Rome. He reported to Oudinot that all the preparations for resistance were bluff; and other foreign diplomats confirmed this, because, despite the events of 1848, it was an accepted myth that Italians do not fight.[6]

Mazzini appointed General Avezzana to be Minister of War and Commander-in-Chief of the army of the Roman Republic. Avezzana was an old revolutionary warrior of 1820 who, in the sneering words of a French Catholic writer, had 'spent twenty years of his life selling cigars in New York and a few days erecting barricades in Genoa';[7] but in fact he had also gained military experience in the Spanish revolutionary army of 1821, and in Mexico. The total forces under his command amounted to 19,000 men, of whom only 1,000 were in Rome. 4,000 were facing the Austrians in the Romagna in the north-east; 1,000 were keeping order in Ancona; Garibaldi and his 1,300 Legionaries were at Rieti; and the remaining 12,000 were spread along the Neapolitan frontier, because since the Pope had gone to Gaeta, the Romans were expecting the main attack to come from Naples.

Avezzana now hurriedly summoned many of these units to Rome, and Garibaldi, after being ignored for many weeks, suddenly became an object of interest to the government. Only eleven days before, one of his officers, Danerio, had complained to Mazzini that in five months the Republican government had not given a hundred muskets to Garibaldi; but on 23 April Avezzana appointed Garibaldi a General of Brigade, and next day ordered him to come to Rome at once with his Legion. Garibaldi had been expecting this, and a week before had sent Anita back to Nice. She had wanted to come to Rome with him, but he had insisted that she return to the children.[8]

On the march from Rieti, the Legionaries happened to arrive at an inn where Margaret Fuller from Massachusetts was staying. She had secretly married the Count, and future Marquis, of Ossoli, and was returning to Rome from a visit to her child at Rieti. Margaret was one of those women who loved Mazzini with that spiritual fervour which was all the greater because they believed that he could never love a woman like he loved Italy. 'Dearly I love Mazzini,' she wrote to Emerson, 'his soft, radiant look makes melancholy music in my soul; it consecrates my present life, that, like the Magdalen, I may, at the important hour, shed all the consecrated ointment on his head.' But she was less enthusiastic when the Garibaldini arrived in strength at the inn.

Her friend Mrs Story described what happened. The innkeeper rushed into the room in great alarm. 'We are quite lost! Here is the Legion Garibaldi! These men always pillage, and, if we do not give all up to them without pay, they will kill us.' Margaret looked out into the road, and saw the Legion marching on the inn; and she was worried that they might steal the horses of her carriage, and that she would then be unable to continue her journey to Rome.

On they came, and she determined to offer them a lunch at her own expense; having faith that gentleness and courtesy was the best protection from injury. Accordingly, as soon as they arrived, and rushed boisterously into the *osteria*, she rose, and said to the *padrone*, 'Give these good men wine and bread on my account; for, after their ride, they must need refreshment.' Immediately, the noise and confusion subsided; with respectful bows to her, they seated themselves and partook of the lunch, giving her an account of their journey. When she was ready to go, and her *vettura* was at the door, they waited upon her, took down the steps, and assisted her with much gentleness and respectfulness of manner, and she drove off, wondering how men with such natures could have the reputation they had. And, so far as we could gather, except in this instance, their conduct was of a most disorderly kind.[9]

At 6 pm on 27 April Garibaldi rode into Rome through the Porta Maggiore at the head of the Legionaries. They received a great ovation from the people, who cried out 'Garibaldi has come!' Garibaldi himself and those sixty Legionaries who had come with him from Montevideo, wore the red shirt, which attracted much attention; the other soldiers of the Legion wore various different uniforms, or none at all. Most of them wore, as headgear, not shakos like the French, but large hats with great plumes. The onlookers noticed particularly the negro, Aguiar, who had come from Montevideo and had become Garibaldi's batman, and rode at his side in his red shirt. The Legionaries took up their quarters in the convent of St Silvester, from which the nuns had been ejected. Garibaldi's horses were stabled in the palace of Prince Torlonia. More than fifty years later, an Italian living in Yorkshire remembered how, when he was a little boy working in the Palazzo Torlonia in 1849, Aguiar sometimes gave him rides on Garibaldi's horses.[10]

A young Dutch artist, J. P. Koelman, who was living in Rome, walked down to the convent to look at the Garibaldini of whom he had heard so much. He found an officer and some soldiers in the courtyard, and talked to them. Some cloth, which they had stolen, was lying on the ground, half covered with a pile of straw. While they were talking, Garibaldi arrived. The sentry, who was reclining in a half-sitting, half-lying position on his belly, did not bestir himself when he saw Garibaldi, though the officer and the other soldiers touched their caps in a slovenly way, to which Garibaldi vaguely responded. Garibaldi spoke briefly to the officer, and passed on, leaving Koelman with a vivid impression of his powerful personality. 'Thank God the General saw nothing', said the officer, kicking the straw over the stolen cloth so that it covered it more completely. Koelman asked the officer whether it was usual among the Garibaldini for the soldiers to pay so little attention to their superior officers. 'My dear fellow,' replied the officer, laughing, 'the General insists on discipline on the battlefield, not in the barracks.'[11]

Avezzana had now assembled about 7,000 men in Rome. Apart

from Garibaldi's 1,300 Legionaries, he had 1,400 Roman volunteers, who had already had military experience, having fought for Manin in Venice; 1,000 National Guards; 450 University students, who had volunteered a few days before, and had had no military training; 300 volunteers from the civil servants of the taxation department who had organized themselves under the leadership of the Radical extremist, Zambianchi; and 2,500 *carabinieri* of the old Papal Civil Guard. There had been considerable doubts as to whether the *carabinieri* would fight for the Republic; but the hopes of the Papalists, and the fears of the Republicans, proved to be groundless, as the *carabinieri* served loyally under the new régime.[12]

Next day another 600 volunteers arrived in Rome. They were a battalion from Lombardy under Major Manara, and were mostly men from aristocratic families who had fought under Charles Albert in 1848 and March 1849. They were not Republicans or Mazzinians, but were Italian nationalists. When they arrived at Civita Vecchia on 26 April, they found the French there, and were taken prisoner; but Oudinot released them after they had given their word of honour not to enter Rome before 4 May, as Oudinot was sure that within a week he would have occupied Rome without resistance. The Lombard volunteers entered Rome on 29 April, and placed themselves at Avezzana's disposal for the defence of the city. The French naturally accused the Lombards of breaking their word of honour; the Lombards claimed that there had been a series of misunderstandings. On their arrival in Rome, they were reviewed by Avezzana, who addressed them, and ended his speech with the words 'Long live the Republic!' The Lombards did not respond. Manara, with great presence of mind, immediately called out 'Long live Italy!', which his men echoed enthusiastically.[13]

On 28 April Oudinot set out for Rome from Civita Vecchia with his army. On the same day a Spanish gunboat captured a Republican fort on the coast, and next day the Neapolitan army crossed the frontier. Oudinot marched slowly on Rome. The Republicans had stuck up notices in French along the road, quoting the text of Article 5 of the French Republican Constitution with its pledge that France would never suppress the liberties of foreign peoples; but this did not impress Oudinot, who disliked the Republican Constitution, and thought that it was impertinent of foreigners to quote it at him. At one point on the route a small group of snipers fired at the French; but though the French returned their fire, they still did not expect to encounter serious resistance. The weather was unusually hot for so early in the summer. The French spent the night of the 29th at Castel-di-Guido, and next morning marched on towards Rome. It was even hotter than on the two previous days, and by 10.30 am the heat was intense. The French suffered much with their hot, heavy shakos on their heads.[14]

The western boundary of Rome in 1849 was the wall which had been built in the seventeenth century, running from St Peter's and the Vatican to the hill of Janiculum, and down to the city gate, the Porta San Pancrazio, immediately to the south of the Janiculum, and on towards the south. To the east of the Janiculum, inside the city, the ground fell sharply, past the old Aurelian Wall of the third century and the church of San Pietro in Montorio down to the working-class area of the Trastevere far below, behind which was the River Tiber and the city on the eastern bank. To the west of the Janiculum, outside the walls, there were the gardens of three residential villas; the entrance to the gardens, which began 250 yards outside the Porta San Pancrazio, was immediately adjacent to a little villa, the Vascello, just outside the gardens and next to the gate in the wall which surrounded the gardens. From this gate, the ground inside the gardens rose up a gentle slope for another 250 yards to the top of the ridge, which was nearly as high as the hill of the Janiculum 500 yards to the east. On this ridge there was a tall, four-storey building, the Villa Corsini, on the spot where today stands the memorial arch in honour of the heroes of 1849; because of its exposed position on the top of the ridge, the Villa Corsini was often called the *Casino dei Quattro Venti*, the House of the Four Winds. West of the Villa Corsini the gardens ran for nearly a mile, down a slope covered with trees and across a stream, to a large sixteenth-century villa, the Villa Pamfili, and beyond it to the western side of the gardens on the road to Civita Vecchia and the west coast. On the northern side of the gardens, near the Villa Valentini, there was a sharp drop over the wall to a sunken lane running, near the old aqueduct, up to the walls of Rome between the Janiculum and the Vatican.

Garibaldi had realized that it was essential to prevent the French from occupying the villa gardens. If the French could establish their cannon on the ridge at the Villa Corsini, they could bombard the Janiculum and the Porta San Pancrazio and cover the area between the gardens and the walls of Rome, making it very difficult and costly for the Romans to recapture the Villa Corsini and the ridge. Avezzana had therefore authorized Garibaldi to take possession of the gardens on 29 April. Garibaldi established his headquarters at the Villa Corsini, and on the morning of the 30th was waiting there for the French. He had 2,500 men, including the 450 University students. Avezzana had placed Colonel Galletti with 1,800 men, and Colonel Masi with 2,000, in reserve, behind Garibaldi.[15]

278

The French reached the western wall of the city at about noon, and advanced on the Cavalleggieri gate immediately to the south of the Vatican. Suddenly Garibaldi's artillery opened fire. A French officer, who knew Rome well, looked at his watch, and told Oudinot that it was the midday gun being fired in the city. There followed a second shot, and men fell dead around Oudinot. Only then did he believe that the Romans would fight.[16]

Garibaldi ordered his men to advance on the French, firing with their muskets and using their bayonets. The university students threw themselves on the enemy with enthusiasm. They had no military experience, but many of the French troops were new recruits who had never been in action before, and had the same lack of experience as the students without their revolutionary zeal. The French reeled under the assault, but they did not run, as a force of Oribe's Blancos would probably have done, and after hard hand-to-hand fighting for nearly an hour, they drove Garibaldi's men back along the sunken lane to the north of the villa gardens. Then Garibaldi, who was watching the battle from the height of the Villa Corsini, called on Galletti to send in his 1,800 men, while still holding Masi's 2,000 in reserve. Garibaldi rode forward, and, rising in the stirrups, drew his sabre, and ordered 2,000 of his men to charge with the bayonet; and the French broke, and retreated in disorder. The French gave their losses as 80 killed, 250 wounded and 250 taken prisoner; but they probably lost 500 men killed and wounded, and 365 of them were taken prisoner. Garibaldi lost 200 killed and wounded, and had one man taken prisoner – Ugo Bassi, who was captured while he was administering extreme unction to a dying soldier. Among the killed was Captain Montaldi, who had come from Montevideo, where he had fought with the Italian Legion in the first battle at the Cerro in June 1843 and in nearly all Garibaldi's battles in Uruguay.[17]

Garibaldi himself was struck in the thigh by a bullet as he sat on his horse. It was the first time that he had been wounded in battle since the serious neck-wound that he received in the fight with the gunboats off Montevideo in 1837, and from which he ultimately recovered at Gualeguay. He managed to hide the fact that he had been wounded from his men, although by the end of the battle his saddle was soaked with his blood. That evening he sent word to his doctor, Ripari, to come to his headquarters to tend the wound, but told him not to come until after dark, so that the troops should know nothing about it.[18]

The wound caused Garibaldi some pain and discomfort, but it was not serious, and he was fit for action next morning. He then urged Avezzana and the government to allow him to pursue the French, who had retreated to Castel-di-Guido. Garibaldi thought that if he attacked at once, before the French had recovered from their mauling of the day before, he would be able to annihilate them, or drive them back to their ships and away from Rome. But Mazzini forbade Garibaldi to pursue the enemy. Apart from the fact that he wished to hold the army in reserve for use against the Neapolitans, and did not wish it to be depleted by heavy losses in a new engagement against the French, there were more important political reasons for his decision. He still wished to avoid all-out war with France. He refused to believe that the country of the French Revolution and the Second Republic was an enemy in the sense that the Bourbon and Habsburg monarchies of Naples and Austria were enemies. He hoped that the Radical forces in France would be strong enough to prevent the resumption of hostilities against Rome if the Romans treated the battle of 30 April as a tragic mistake, and did not irrevocably antagonize French public opinion by inflicting a further humiliation on the French army. His agent in France issued a statement to the French press, announcing the Roman victory, but regretting the whole incident, and ending: 'May even the guilty be pardoned – they are sufficiently punished by remorse.' But Garibaldi, who always believed that attack was the best form of defence, thought that Mazzini was guilty of a serious error of judgement.[19]

There were great celebrations in Rome over the victory of 30 April, and the moral effect throughout Europe was considerable. Ten thousand soldiers of France, the leading military nation of Europe, who had believed that Italians were afraid to fight, had been defeated by an enemy who, though their total force available was about three-quarters of the French numbers, had in fact only sent some 4,000 of them into action against the 10,000 French. The Romans mocked that the French had been right when they had boasted that they would enter Rome, because they had entered it as prisoners. On the evening of the battle, the French prisoners were subjected to some ill-treatment by their captors; but Mazzini immediately ordered that they were to be treated with every consideration. The wounded were well cared for in the hospitals; the others were allowed to wander freely in Rome on parole, and protected from any insult; and they were subjected to a concentrated campaign of revolutionary propaganda, being told that as fellow-Republicans and brothers they should not fight against their Roman comrades. When Oudinot and the Catholics in France heard about this, they were angry and worried. The Catholic propagandists shamelessly misrepresented the acts of kindness shown by the Princess Belgiojoso and the women of her Ambulance Committees to the French prisoners as an attempt by beautiful but brazen Radical hussies to seduce the virtuous young Frenchmen, both in a sexual and a political sense, by inducing them to commit the sins of fornication and high treason.[20]

Mazzini arranged a demonstration of Franco-Roman solidarity, and invited the prisoners to take part. All the officers refused, but 250 other ranks agreed to march in a fraternization parade, at which the crowds shouted 'Long live the French people! Down with the government of priests! Long live the two sister Republics!' These 250 were then released, given 50,000 cigars as a gift of the Roman people, and escorted under a flag of truce to Oudinot's camp. Oudinot was not pleased at this development, but felt that the French could not be out-done by the Radicals of Rome in generosity, and released the garrison of Civita Vecchia whom he had been holding as prisoners, as well as Ugo Bassi. Mazzini hoped, as he told the Constituent Assembly, that the prisoners whom he had released would be apostles of revolution in Oudinot's camp; and he had some grounds for this hope. The French Catholics consoled themselves with stories of how their patriotic soldiers had repulsed the blandishments of Princess Belgiojoso's women, and had declared their devotion to their Fatherland and the Catholic Church; but *The Times* correspondent at Oudinot's headquarters, who had no sympathy for the Roman Republic, reported that the kind treatment which the prisoners had received in Rome had made a great sensation in the French camp, 'and more than one man inquires if it be just and right that a Republican government should compel another Republican government to accept the restoration of the spiritual head of the Roman Church'.[21]

In France the news of 30 April caused a hardening of the attitudes both of the Left and of the Right. In the National Assembly, Jules Favre, the Radical deputy who three weeks earlier had supported Oudinot's expedition because he believed the assurances of the government that the French troops were going to Rome to protect the Romans from the Austrians, strongly denounced the Prime Minister, Odilon Barrot, in the debate on the evening of 7 May, accusing him of deceiving the Assembly and the nation. The government, knowing that the Assembly would finish its term in a few days' time, and was likely to be replaced by a more Conservative Assembly after the forthcoming elections, hedged, and played for time. Barrot declared that Oudinot had exceeded his instructions by attacking Rome, and promised to send a Foreign Office official to Rome to try to negotiate a peaceful settlement with Mazzini. The official chosen for the mission was Ferdinand de Lesseps, who afterwards was responsible for the construction of the Suez Canal. By this declaration and this promise, Barrot escaped a direct vote of censure; but next day Louis Napoleon wrote a private letter to Oudinot, promising him that he would send him reinforcements and would ensure that the honour of France would be vindicated and the humiliation of 30 April avenged. Louis Napoleon put the whole blame for what had happened on Garibaldi. In a message to the National Assembly he declared that the Romans would have allowed the French troops to enter Rome peacefully on 30 April if Garibaldi and his Legion had not arrived a few days before and persuaded the people to fight.[22]

Meanwhile a Frenchman named Mangin, who had lived for many years in Rome, and like other French civilians was still living there free and unharmed, made a private attempt to arrange an armistice between the French and the Romans. Carrying a white handkerchief as a flag of truce, he tried to pass through the front line, but was fired on by the Roman sentries, and gave up the attempt. He tried a second time, but was stopped at the Roman outposts, and brought before an army captain, who worked himself up into a passion, abused him as a traitor, and threatened to have him shot. At this moment Garibaldi arrived on a tour of inspection of the front line, and on hearing Mangin's story ordered him to be released; but he refused to let him through the lines without authority from the government. Mangin then went to Mazzini, obtained his consent for his private peacemaking mission, and, armed with a pass signed by Mazzini, made his third attempt to get past the front-line sentries. This time he was successful, but when he reached Castel-di-Guido, Oudinot refused to receive him.[23]

Having temporarily knocked out Oudinot, the Roman Republic turned to deal with its other enemies. The Neapolitan army of 11,000 men, commanded by King Ferdinand himself, was at Velletri, less than twenty-five miles south of Rome. On 4 May Garibaldi left Rome with 2,300 men, with orders to stop the Neapolitan advance. His forces consisted of his own Legionaries, the university students, and Manara's Lombard volunteers and their cavalry.[24] It was inevitable that there should be some friction between the Republican Radicals and the young gentlemen from Lombardy, with their spotless uniforms and polished boots and perfect parade-ground discipline, who proudly wore the cross of Savoy on their sword-belts to show that they were not Republicans, and that their only object in coming to Rome was, as one of them, Emilio Dandolo, said, 'the ardent desire of defending an Italian city from a foreign invasion'.

Dandolo's feelings about Garibaldi were mixed, and very similar to those of General Iriarte and the other professional soldiers who had known Garibaldi in Uruguay. Dandolo admired his courage and energy in battle, but deplored his lack of discipline and his unorthodox and democratic methods. In his account of the campaigns in the Roman Republic in 1849, which he published the same year, Dandolo described how Garibaldi and his officers would ride on their horses with all their possessions heaped on their saddles, in the South American style. Apart from Garibaldi, who was looked after by Aguiar, none of the officers had a batman. When they arrived at their encampment, at the end of a day's march, the officers would often leap from their horses and attend themselves to their horses' needs; and sometimes Garibaldi himself would do this, if Aguiar was not available. 'The officers were chosen from among the most courageous,' wrote Dandolo, 'and raised at once from the lower to the highest ranks, that is, without any regard to precedence or regular order; today one might see an individual with a sword at his side, captain of his troops or company; tomorrow, for the sake of variety, he would shoulder his musket and enter the ranks, having again become a private soldier.' Dandolo thought that there were far too many officers in Garibaldi's Legion. 'The Quarter-Master was a Captain; the purveyor or private cook of the General was a Lieutenant; his orderly was also a Lieutenant. The staff was composed entirely of Colonels and Majors.' Other observers, apart from Dandolo, made adverse comments about the number of officers in Garibaldi's Legion, which was sometimes as high as one officer to every six men; but Dandolo admitted that most of these officers, and nearly the whole of Garibaldi's Legion, 'seemed to justify their high-sounding titles by the bravery of their conduct'.

Manara and the officers of the Lombard Brigade were afraid that the absence of distinctions between officers and men in Garibaldi's Legion would have a bad influence on the discipline of their own soldiers. By the time they reached Tivoli they were so worried that they sent a letter to Avezzana, asking to be transferred to another section of the army, and refusing to serve under Garibaldi or to march with Garibaldi's Legionaries. Avezzana promised to do all he could to meet their wishes, but asked them to continue serving under Garibaldi for a few more days; and they reluctantly agreed. Whatever they might think of each other in other respects, both the Garibaldini and Manara's men respected each other's courage. Dandolo, in his book, pays full tribute to the bravery of Garibaldi's Legionaries; and Garibaldi, in his memoirs, praised the valour and fighting ability of the Lombard Brigade. Relations between Garibaldi and Manara were probably never as bad as Dandolo made out. On at least one occasion during the campaign against the Neapolitans, Garibaldi invited Manara to dinner; and when he returned to Rome he appointed Manara as his Chief of Staff.[25]

At midnight on 7 May they reached Palestrina, about twenty-five miles south-east of Rome. It was pouring with rain. Garibaldi ordered that the Lombard Brigade should be quartered in the Augustinian monastery; he often put his men into monasteries and convents because they were large and suitable buildings to convert into barracks, and also, perhaps, because, as Dandolo put it, 'he made war on monks who were hostile to the Republic quite as much as on the Neapolitans'. The monks refused to let them in. The Lombard Brigade waited patiently for an hour in the rain, and then, at 1 am, called the pioneers, who blew in the doors, and the troops took possession of the monastery. Dandolo says that the monks, though very frightened, were pleasantly surprised to find that the troops behaved so well, and actually became quite friendly. Garibaldi quartered his other troops in the Capuchin monastery. According to Guerrazzi, who was not there, the troops found love-letters among the possessions of the monks in both monasteries; but Dandolo and Hoffstetter, who were there, say nothing about this.[26]

The King of Naples was at Albano with an army of 8,000 men. He had with him General Zucchi of the Papal army, who had negotiated with Garibaldi in Bologna about his embarkation at Ravenna for Venice; and he sent Zucchi with the bulk of the Neapolitan army to attack Garibaldi at Palestrina. Garibaldi spent 8 May reconnoitring, as he often did. Dandolo states that Garibaldi sometimes disguised himself as a peasant, and went out alone to reconnoitre; but more often he would sit for many hours on his horse, taking a careful look through his telescope at every detail of the terrain and at any enemy movements which could be observed. He ordered his men to occupy the hill, named the Monte di San Pietro, to the south of the village of Palestrina, and waited for the enemy attack.

It came at 2 pm on 9 May. The Neapolitans outnumbered Garibaldi's troops by nearly three to one; but the Neapolitans were very reluctant to fight, and Garibaldi could see, through his telescope, that their officers were having great difficulty in getting them into line and making them advance. Garibaldi used the tactics which he had used in South America, particularly at the Daimán, though at Palestrina there were larger numbers on both sides than in any of his battles in Uruguay. He made his men hold their fire until the enemy were near, and then drove them back with musket fire, while the few who came close enough were despatched with bayonets; and after repelling a number of successive attacks, he ordered his men to charge the decimated and demoralized enemy, and drove them back. Manara's cavalry pursued the retreating Neapolitans. Dandolo believed that they could have made the victory even more complete if they had been allowed to carry on with the pursuit; but Garibaldi noticed that his cavalry was straggling out in some disorder, and was afraid that they would be ambushed and destroyed by the enemy; and he therefore ordered them to be recalled and to break off the pursuit. He lost 12 men killed and 20 wounded. The enemy's losses were at least 100 killed and wounded, and 20 of them were taken prisoner.

The prisoners were brought before Garibaldi. They were frightened, and begged him to spare their lives. When Garibaldi had set their fears at rest, they told him that he was regarded with the greatest dread by the Neapolitans, and that King Ferdinand had sent Zucchi to Palestrina with the express object of taking him prisoner. Garibaldi and his troops then returned to the village of Palestrina. The Lombard Brigade again found the doors of the Augustine monastery locked. The monks had all gone away and had taken the keys with them. Manara's men had to break down the door again. This time, before they left, they sacked the monastery.[27]

On 15 May Lesseps arrived at Oudinot's headquarters, and told Oudinot that Louis Napoleon ordered him to make an armistice for fifteen days with the Romans while Lesseps negotiated with Mazzini. The Romans afterwards accused the French of making the armistice in order to deceive them while the French build-up went on; but in fact Louis Napoleon's object was not to make a build-up possible, but to appease the Left in France until after the elections for the new National Assembly. Oudinot strongly opposed the armistice, and thought that it was the Romans who were able to utilize it to build up their forces, because during the truce 7,000 volunteers came to Rome from other parts of Italy and from abroad. The newcomers included Polish volunteers, composed of those Polish refugees who were always ready to fight for revolutionary causes everywhere in Europe from Portugal to Hungary. The Prussian Radical, Haug, also came to Rome, and became one of Garibaldi's staff officers.[28]

As soon as the armistice was signed, Mazzini hastened to avail himself of the fortnight's breathing-space. Next day, 16 May, almost the whole of the forces in Rome were sent south against the Neapolitans. The troops who had been spread along the Neapolitan frontier, and stationed elsewhere outside the capital, were sent to the north-east to defend Ancona from the advancing Austrians, who captured Bologna on 16 May. Avezzana was sent to Ancona, and General Roselli was appointed Commander-in-Chief of the forces in Rome and on the Neapolitan front. The greatest merit of Roselli was that he was a Roman. The Pope's supporters in the republic, and the Catholic propagandists abroad, made great play with the fact that most of the Republican leaders were 'foreigners', among whom they included Italians from countries outside the Papal States. As Mazzini, Garibaldi and Avezzana were all Sardinian subjects by origin, it was useful to have a Roman as Commander-in-Chief in the south.

Garibaldi was annoyed at Roselli's appointment. He was happy to serve under Avezzana, whom he respected and praised as being chiefly responsible for the victory over Oudinot of 30 April. But he had no respect for Roselli, who had no experience of war; and he thought that if Avezzana was being removed from the command in the south, he himself ought to have been appointed in Avezzana's place. His relations with both Roselli and Mazzini became strained.[29]

Roselli marched with 10,000 men against the Neapolitans at Albano. But the Neapolitans were already retreating, as they had heard that Oudinot had signed an armistice with the Romans.[30] Roselli did not know this, but he discovered that the Neapolitans were marching south from Albano towards the frontier, and appeared to be retreating. He sent Garibaldi on ahead with 2,000 troops to keep contact with the enemy, but gave him no orders to engage them.

On the morning of 19 May Garibaldi came up with the Neapolitans two miles north of Velletri, and his cavalry began skirmishing with the Neapolitan rearguard. Garibaldi planted his artillery on a hill overlooking the town from where he could bombard the enemy; but the battle did not go entirely satisfactorily for Garibaldi. The Neapolitan cavalry charged Garibaldi's cavalry, and drove them back in disorder. Garibaldi, who was in the road a little in the rear, suddenly saw his cavalry galloping back in full flight, and on the spur of the moment acted in a manner which he afterwards realized was unwise. He faced the fleeing riders, sitting on his horse in the middle of the road, and ordered them to halt. But the onrush of the cavalry was too strong to halt, and Garibaldi and his horse were thrown to the ground, and the retreating cavalry rode over them. Aguiar, who had seen the danger in which Garibaldi stood, had also ridden out into the road to try to halt the cavalry, and he too had been thrown and ridden over. Many of the fleeing cavalrymen, when they rode over Garibaldi and Aguiar, were themselves brought down, and as horses and riders began to pile up in the road, the Neapolitan cavalry came down upon them, and began sabring them.

But a body of infantry of Garibaldi's own Legion, who were stationed in the orchards at the side of the road, opened fire on the Neapolitans, and launched a counter-attack. A unit of young boys – some of Garibaldi's twelve- and fourteen-year-olds – rushed forward to save Garibaldi, and somehow managed to drag him clear and carry him to the side of the road. The horses lying in the road completely blocked it, and thus prevented anyone from retreating or advancing any further; and under the fire of Garibaldi's infantry in the orchards, the Neapolitan cavalry fell back. Garibaldi was severely bruised, but otherwise unhurt, and Aguiar also escaped serious injury. After Garibaldi had realized, to his surprise, that he had no broken bones or ribs, he went to the house where the King of Naples had slept the night before, had a hot bath, and went to bed in Ferdinand's bed. He had practically recovered by the time that he awoke next morning.[31]

The Neapolitans, who had seen Garibaldi go down under the horses' hooves, believed that he had been killed, and the story of his death was cheerfully spread among the Pope's supporters and the Catholics in France. When Garibaldi reappeared in action a few days later, his enemies claimed that it was an impostor who resembled Garibaldi and had been substituted for him by the revolutionaries in order to maintain the morale of his men. They said that Anita had agreed to take this false Garibaldi as her husband in order to help the cause, as was to be expected from a devoted and immoral revolutionary woman. They said that the real Garibaldi had lost an ear in a battle or brawl in South America, and that the false Garibaldi wore his hair long in order to conceal the fact that he had two ears. The French Catholic writer, Mirecourt, was not prepared to vouch for the truth of this story; but he hoped that it was true, so that there would be two Garibaldis to share the guilt of their crimes and the punishment on the Day of Judgement.[32]

Garibaldi lost 100 men killed and wounded at Velletri. The Neapolitans lost more. At 4 pm Roselli arrived with the bulk of his army. He had not moved up earlier because he had waited at Zagarolo till his food supplies arrived from Rome, whereas Garibaldi had advanced without food supplies, seizing the cattle from an estate along the route which belonged to a cardinal, and rationing his men to make sure that the supplies were sufficient. Garibaldi despised Roselli for moving so slowly, and for leaving him to fight alone at Velletri. Roselli complained to Mazzini and Pisacane that Garibaldi had attacked the enemy without orders, and had risked the success of the operation and wasted the lives of his men by doing so.[33]

The Neapolitans retreated rapidly until they reached the frontier, and crossed it, completely evacuating the territory of the Roman Republic. Mazzini then ordered the army to return to Rome, where the armistice with France could be ended with twenty-four hours' notice by either side after 29 May. This led to another disagreement between Garibaldi and Mazzini. Garibaldi wished to pursue the Neapolitans across the frontier and invade Naples. He realized that this meant leaving Rome defenceless against Oudinot; but he believed that it would in any case be impossible to hold Rome for long. The walls and fortifications around Rome were eighteen miles in circumference; and the Roman Republic did not have enough men to hold so long a line even if they concentrated all their soldiers in the capital; and he was convinced that if Oudinot could not take Rome with 40,000 men, Louis Napoleon would send him 100,000 to do the job.

Garibaldi therefore advised Roselli and Mazzini to evacuate Rome. He suggested that the Triumvirs and the Assembly and government should withdraw to the mountainous districts of the republic in the Apennines with a small part of the army, where he thought that they would be able to hold out for a considerable time. Meanwhile he would lead the greater part of the army into the Kingdom of Naples. He knew that fighting the Neapolitans was a very different matter to fighting the French, and that Ferdinand's soldiers had no will to fight; and he believed that he would overrun Naples easily, that there would be a revolution there, and that the Neapolitan soldiers in Sicily would then be unable to continue their operations against the Sicilian revolutionaries, who would liberate their island. According to Jessie White Mario, he made the prophetic remark, at this time, that a victory under the walls of Capua would win the independence of the whole peninsula; but Garibaldi had no illusions that the triumph of 1860 could easily have been achieved in 1849. He wrote in his memoirs that the defeat of the Italian revolution in 1849 was probably inevitable in any case, but that if his strategy had been pursued, the Roman Republic would not have been defeated so soon, but would have outlasted the republics in Venice and Hungary, and would have had the honour of being the last to fall of the revolutionary régimes of 1848.[34]

Mazzini could not consider adopting Garibaldi's proposal. He did not see things primarily from the military point of view, but thought of the political and revolutionary significance of the defence of Rome. Apart from the diplomatic effect of the fall of Rome in international affairs, he was influenced by the revolutionary traditions which the men of 1848 had taken over from the French revolutionaries of 1789 and 1830, in which the revolution staked everything on the barricades in the capital city. Revolutionaries, as opposed to nationalist guerrillas like the Spanish partisans who fought Napoleon I, had never in recent times waged guerrilla warfare, though Mazzini, in one of his earliest writings, had suggested that they should do so. Increasingly after 1848 revolutionary military thinking became defensive; the object was not so much to win as to inspire future generations by their martyrdom on the barricades. Garibaldi was almost alone among nineteenth-century revolutionaries in favouring the offensive, and guerrilla war in the countryside, which became so widely accepted by revolutionaries in the twentieth century. It would have been politically impossible for Mazzini to agree to evacuate Rome in May 1849.

Garibaldi and the soldiers on the southern front reached Rome on 1 June. Garibaldi was suffering from arthritis, had a sudden attack of fever, and was feeling depressed. He went to bed in his lodgings in the Hôtel d'Angleterre in the Via di Rivoli. It was an unfortunate time for him to fall ill, because on 1 June Oudinot ended the armistice.

CHAPTER 19

THE VILLA CORSINI
AND THE FALL OF ROME

SINCE 15 May Lesseps had been negotiating with Mazzini. Lesseps was a conscientious Foreign Office official and a moderate Conservative. He thought that Mazzini was a dangerous revolutionary, though he liked him personally; but he was determined to carry out the instructions of the French government and reach a peaceful agreement if possible. 'If we were to enter Rome by brute force,' he told Oudinot, 'we should not only have to pass over the bodies of a few foreign adventurers, but we should have to leave dead on the ground the bourgeois, the shopkeepers, the young people of good family, all the classes, in fact, who defend order and society in Paris.'[1] When Lesseps told Mazzini that the French had come as friends to protect Rome from the Austrians, Mazzini replied that the Roman government would welcome them as allies and permit them to station their troops at Civita Vecchia or elsewhere in the territory of the republic, provided that they did not enter the city of Rome or try to interfere in the internal government of the republic. But Oudinot had been opposed to Lesseps's mission from the start. As a zealous Catholic, he was determined to restore the Pope to his temporal authority; and as a French soldier he believed that it was necessary to avenge the insult to French honour of 30 April, at least by a peaceful march into Rome, and preferably by fighting and winning a battle.

On 31 May, Lesseps and Mazzini signed a treaty under which French troops would be stationed at Castel-di-Guido, but would not enter Rome, and in which nothing was said about the Pope or the system of government in the Papal States, a formula having been found by which the French did not recognize the Roman Republic with which they were making the agreement. But when Lesseps returned to Castel-di-Guido, Oudinot told him that he was ending the armistice at once, and resuming hostilities. He showed the astonished Lesseps a letter which he had received from Louis Napoleon ordering him to do this, and recalling Lesseps to Paris. Lesseps returned to Paris at once to find that he had been dismissed in disgrace from the Foreign Office.

He was vilified in the press, and by the Foreign Minister in Parliament, as a weakling who had been prepared to betray French interests to Mazzini. Lesseps's mission was not, as the Romans thought, a trick from the beginning; but the Catholic Church and the army leaders in France had won over Louis Napoleon to a policy of a war to destroy the Roman Republic. A large part of the responsibility for this rests with Oudinot.[2]

On 1 June Oudinot wrote to Roselli to give him twenty-four hours' notice that he was ending the armistice, but adding that in order to give time for French civilians to leave Rome, he would not attack 'the place' until 4 June. On the evening of 2 June, just after the twenty-four hours expired, French troops occupied the villa gardens and the Villa Corsini, the House of the Four Winds, the vital point on the heights to the west of the Janiculum which Garibaldi had always realized was absolutely essential to the defence of Rome. On several occasions since 30 April, Garibaldi had pointed out to Roselli the vital necessity of fortifying the villas against a French attack; but nothing had been done, and Roselli, visiting the handful of men who were holding the villas on 2 June, told them that they need not be on the alert until midnight on 3 June, because Oudinot had written that he would not attack before the 4th. When the French troops moved in a few hours later, they easily overran the defenders in the Villa Pamfili and took it almost without resistance; and though the Romans hastily put up a desperate defence in the House of the Four Winds, this also fell to the French after some fierce fighting. But the Romans still held their outpost of the Vascello at the eastern entrance to the villa gardens.

The Romans accused Oudinot of capturing the villas by a deliberate fraud. But Oudinot, who still resented the fact that the Lombard Brigade had fought against him on 30 April in breach of their parole, replied that when he had written that he would not attack 'the place' until 4 June to allow time for the French civilians to leave, he meant the city itself, where the French were residing, and not the defence outposts in the villas, which he was free to attack as soon as his twenty-four hours' notice of the termination of the armistice had expired on 2 June.[3] Even Oudinot's admirers, who repudiate the charge of bad faith, agree that his wording of the letter was unfortunate; and everyone is agreed that, whatever may be said against Oudinot, it cannot excuse the gross negligence of Roselli in failing to fortify the villas and put the garrison there into a state of readiness.

A few hours before the French captured the villas, Garibaldi received a letter from Mazzini at the lodgings where he was lying ill. Mazzini, who had received Oudinot's letter ending the armistice, asked Garibaldi what measures he suggested should be taken for the defence of Rome when the fighting was resumed. Garibaldi immediately wrote a short reply:

Mazzini,
As you ask me what I wish, I will tell you: it is not possible for me to be of use to the Republic except in two ways; either as absolute dictator, or as a simple soldier.

Ever Yours,
G. Garibaldi

In suggesting that he should be made dictator, Garibaldi was using a word which did not have the pejorative meaning in 1849 which it has acquired today, since Mussolini adopted it in deliberate imitation of Garibaldi. The Republicans of the period had based their ideas of government on the system of the ancient Romans, who in times of great national emergency vested the powers of the Senate in a Dictator, who was to have absolute powers for six months and then surrender them again to the Senate. 'I demanded the dictatorship,' wrote Garibaldi in his memoirs, 'like on some occasions in my life I had demanded the helm of a boat that was being driven against the rocks by the tempest.' But Mazzini was not prepared to make Garibaldi either dictator or a private soldier, and he ordered him to return to duty as a general under Roselli. Garibaldi's letter increased the mistrust between him and Mazzini, and confirmed Mazzini's suspicions that Garibaldi was not a true Republican. Pisacane also condemned Garibaldi's attitude. Although Pisacane was a Duke by birth, his social and economic doctrines brought him nearer to Socialism and Anarchism than any other leader of the *Risorgimento*, and he is regarded by his admirers as one of the founders of Italian Socialism. He rejected Garibaldi's idea of a dictatorship as utterly opposed to the principles of Republicanism and democracy, and commented, very unfairly, that Rome did not need a Rosas or an Oribe.[4]

When Garibaldi heard of Mazzini's decision, he accepted the position; and when, a few hours later, he heard that Oudinot had captured the villas, he rose at once from his sick-bed and went to his headquarters in the Janiculum, just below the villas. He was sure that he could not hold Rome if the villas were lost, and decided that they must be recaptured at once, and at all costs. By 5 am on 3 June his troops were in position to begin the attack. Roselli had put him in charge of operations, and given him 6,000 of the total of 18,000 men in the army of the Republic in Rome. Oudinot had brought up more than half his total force from Castel-di-Guido, and had 16,000 men engaged.

The area between the Villa Corsini and the eastern entrance to the gardens at the Vascello was triangular in shape, with the garden walls running down the slope from the villa to the apex of the triangle at the garden gate next to the Vascello. The gate was only wide enough for about five men to pass abreast. To capture the villa by a frontal assault, Garibaldi's men had to run along the road for 250 yards from the walls of Rome at the Porta San Pancrazio to the garden gate, under the fire of the French soldiers in the villa, and then enter through the bottle-neck of the gate, on which all the fire-power of the French could be concentrated. Once inside the gate, there was another 250 yards to go up the garden path, with a box hedge six feet high on both sides of it, to the villa at the top of the ridge. Immediately in front of the villa there was a wall, covered with flower-pots, behind which the defenders could shelter and fire at the attackers. The Villa Corsini itself was four storeys high, with no windows facing towards Rome on the lower storeys, but with a wide outside staircase up which men and horses could climb to the entrance to the villa on the second floor. There were windows facing Rome on the upper two storeys, and from here, as well as from the wall with the flower-pots, the French could fire at the advancing Garibaldini. As an alternative to the frontal attack up the garden path, Garibaldi could have tried to climb the garden wall which ran along both sides of the triangle down to the garden gate at the Vascello; or he could have tried a wider flanking movement and entered the gardens from the sunken lane to the north, near the Villa Valentini. But both these operations would have entailed climbing walls and high banks under enemy fire.

The Villa Corsini was thus ideally placed for defence against the Roman attack. On the other hand, if the Romans succeeded in capturing the villa, they would not find it easy to hold against a French counter-attack, because the French, attacking from the west, could approach up the western slope through the gardens under cover of the trees all the way to the house. This put Garibaldi at a grave disadvantage. To capture and hold the villa against enemy forces more than two and a half times greater in numbers, with a positional advantage both in defence and in counter-attack, was an almost impossible task; but it was a task which had to be accomplished if Rome was to be saved.

The battle of 3 June 1849 lasted seventeen hours, from dawn till dusk on the hot summer Sunday. Garibaldi made one attack after the other, but his men were driven back with heavy losses. If they managed to reach the garden gate, they were mown down as they passed, five abreast, through the gate, or afterwards as they ran up the slope to the villa between the box hedges; and when checked, and forced to retreat, they were as much exposed to enemy fire in retreat as in advance.

Garibaldi directed the attack sitting on his white horse just outside the Porta San Pancrazio, being himself in the line of the enemy fire; but he was not wounded, though his *poncho* was pierced by enemy bullets. His army of young aristocrats, workers and students, all enthusiastic revolutionaries, commanded by officers who were nearly all under thirty years of age, charged, shouting '*Avanti!*' with a heroic disregard of the extreme danger; but they could not reach the Villa Corsini in the face of the French fire.

As each attack was repulsed, Garibaldi sent in more men, who were driven back in the same way, and then yet another attack, the brunt of the fighting falling on his own Legionaries and on Manara's Lombard Brigade. At last, at about three o'clock in the afternoon, after nearly ten hours of unsuccessful effort, the Lombard Brigade captured the Villa Corsini; but the French recaptured it within an hour with an attack through the orchards to the north of the villa. Garibaldi then renewed the attack from San Pancrazio, and the story of the morning was repeated. Towards evening, after many attacks had failed with heavy losses, the Lombards captured the Villa Corsini for the second time; but before nightfall the French had again recaptured it without much difficulty. At the end of the day the French were in possession of the villas, and Garibaldi knew that Rome was lost.

Garibaldi's losses were very heavy. Of the 1,000 men of his own Legion who took part in the attack, he had lost more than one-fifth killed and wounded, losing 23 officers and 200 men. One of them was Ramorino, who had killed Risso in the duel at Cesena, but was now able to give his own life in action against the enemy, and not against a comrade. Manara lost a third of his Lombards, having 200 killed and wounded out of 600. All Masina's small force of 40 Bolognese cavalry were wiped out. In all, Garibaldi probably lost about 1,000 killed and wounded out of his total force of 6,000. The French gave their casualties as 14 killed and 242 wounded, and 19 taken prisoner or unaccounted for; but the figures may well have been higher.

Garibaldi's losses, in proportion to the total number of his soldiers, were substantially less than the losses which he had suffered with his much smaller force at Costa Brava and San Antonio, where he had lost two-thirds and half respectively of his men killed and wounded.*

*Garibaldi's statement, 'I have seen some very terrible fights, I have seen our fights of Rio Grande, I have seen La Boyada, I have seen the Salto Sant-Antonio [*sic.*!], I have seen nothing comparable to the butchery of the Villa Corsini', appears only in the Dumas edition of the memoirs. The statement is factually inaccurate. The account of the battle of 3 June, in the Dumas edition, is written in a style completely unlike the cool, straightforward version in Garibaldi's own edition of 1872.

But the size of the losses, and the ultimate defeat, left feelings of bitterness among some of his soldiers, and his generalship on 3 June has been strongly criticized. Dandolo, who lost his brother and many of his friends in the Lombard Brigade on 3 June, and was wounded himself, condemned Garibaldi in the book which he wrote a few months later; and Pisacane made the same criticism in his book in 1851.

> Garibaldi [wrote Dandolo] in the engagement of 3 June, showed himself to be as incapable of being General of a division as he had proved himself to be an able and efficient leader in the skirmishes and marches against the Neapolitans . . . he was utterly incapable of directing the manoeuvres of men by which alone the scale can be turned in a field of battle.

Dandolo says that Garibaldi made an endless series of attacks with small bodies of men, whereas he would have done much better if he had thrown in all his troops in one great rush which would have overwhelmed the French. He sent in one company after another, holding the mass of his men in reserve, and often did not even send in a whole company at a time, but only units of twenty or thirty men. Yet when the commander of a unit of the Lombard Brigade, who had captured the Villa Valentini and was trying to hold it with twelve men against an enemy counter-attack, sent a man, towards evening, to ask Garibaldi for reinforcements, Garibaldi replied: 'I have not one more soldier; see if you can find any.' Dandolo comments: 'What, in the name of Heaven, had he done with all his soldiers? Scattered about, here, there, everywhere, they were engaged in heroic but partial combats, which, even when successful, could in no way decide the final success of the battle.'

Dandolo described the engagement in which he was wounded late in the evening, just after his brother had been killed by a French unit who pretended that they were revolutionaries who wished to surrender and then shot him dead at close range.

> At this moment of unspeakable suffering, Garibaldi came in our direction, and I heard him say: 'I shall require twenty resolute men and an officer for a difficult undertaking.' [Dandolo immediately volunteered.] 'Go,' said Garibaldi to me, 'with twenty of your bravest men, and take the Villa Corsini at the point of the bayonet.' Involuntarily I remained transfixed with astonishment – with twenty men, to hurry forward to attack a position which two of our companies, and the whole of Garibaldi's Legion, after unheard-of exertions, had failed in carrying. . . . I did not answer a word, but pointed to those who were to accompany me. 'Spare your ammunition, to the bayonet at once,' said Garibaldi.

Dandolo and his twenty companions set off from the Porta San Pancrazio to the garden gate and up the garden path. Eight of them fell before they reached the Villa Corsini. When they got there, Dandolo realized that there were several hundred Frenchmen holding the villa, and that he could not attack them with twelve men; so after a while he ordered the retreat. Seven more were killed on the way back, and Dandolo, who was wounded in the thigh during the retreat, reached the Roman lines with five companions. The other fifteen had fallen in this utterly pointless excursion.

No doubt Garibaldi made mistakes on 3 June. He had never before commanded so large a body of troops as 6,000 men, and he had risen from a sick-bed to take command of the operation. But it is difficult to believe that he was as foolish as Dandolo states. Dandolo had never liked Garibaldi and his military and political doctrines; he wrote with the natural resentment of a soldier against a general who had freely expended the lives of his comrades in an unsuccessful assault; and he was deeply affected by the loss of his brother. He wrote his book a few months later, when there was a good deal of recrimination among the defeated revolutionaries about who was to blame for everything. Garibaldi was certainly not a complete fool, and it is inconceivable that he would have ordered twenty men to take a position which he knew was held by several hundred, unless perhaps, knowing that near-miracles can sometimes happen in war, he thought that the French might be on the point of cracking, that Dandolo's twenty men might be the straw that would break the camel's back, and was willing to sacrifice the lives of twenty soldiers on the chance of thus gaining a strongpoint which had to be won if Rome was to be saved.

It is strange, in view of the heavy losses which Garibaldi suffered in the frontal attack on the Villa Corsini, that he did not at least try the alternative of a flank attack over the garden walls. He did detach a few units to attack the Villa Valentini on the north side of the gardens; but these attacks, like the frontal assault on the Villa Corsini, might have been undertaken by larger bodies of men. He could also perhaps have made better use of his artillery on the Janiculum, and subjected the French in the Villa Corsini to a concentrated bombardment before sending in his infantry, though the artillery was firing for most of the day, and had severely damaged the Villa Corsini by the end of the engagement. Perhaps Garibaldi's real mistake was that he believed that superior French forces, like Oribe's Blancos, could be defeated, without strategy, by heroism alone.

Whatever may be thought of Garibaldi's tactics, it is impossible to accept Dandolo's statement that if Garibaldi had sent in the whole of the 600 Lombards at the same time, in column, supported by half a company of riflemen, he could have taken the Villa Corsini 'after a short contest'. Garibaldi and his men could not have defeated an enemy nearly three times as strong, with more experience of fighting, and holding the superior position. In any case, Garibaldi's real failure on 3 June was not that he failed to capture the Villa Corsini, which he took several times, but that he failed to hold it.

The communiqué which Garibaldi issued after the battle of 3 June was a complete distortion of the truth.* It stated that 'a very fierce battle continued all day, always to the advantage of our men', that 'the enemy were beaten at all points', and that 'the night intervened, leaving the battlefield to us'. But though he claimed the victory in the communiqué, Garibaldi knew that he had lost the Villa Corsini and that it was now inevitable that Rome should fall. All that he could do was to hold out for as long as possible.[5]

He managed to do this for exactly a month. Oudinot settled down to plan the capture of Rome as a major military operation, because he and his men had learned to respect their enemy on 3 June. Even after 30 April the French had regarded the Roman soldiers as a revolutionary rabble who, though they had somehow managed to win a victory by a fluke, would nevertheless collapse at the first serious attack; but after 3 June they paid tribute, in their letters and comments, to the bravery of Garibaldi and his men. Oudinot did not invest Rome, because he thought that even with 30,000 men he did not have sufficient force to hold the line at all points along the eighteen-mile circumference of the city walls. He therefore massed his forces to the west, and sent out raiding parties of cavalry to harass peasants and other persons bringing supplies into Rome. He planted his artillery on the ridge at the Villa Corsini and, as Garibaldi had feared, bombarded the defences of the Janiculum and the city itself from these vantage points. Garibaldi answered with his artillery from the Pancrazio gate, but with less effect. He himself was under constant bombardment at his headquarters in the Villa Savorelli on the Janiculum, and impressed those who saw him by his coolness when the enemy artillery scored a near miss on the mess-room where he was dining, and when he stood on the parapet of the wall, lighting a cigar with the shells bursting all around him.[6]

The civilians in the city were also within range, and were bombarded nearly every night. Mazzini appointed a committee for the preserva-

---

*Trevelyan (I.172) states that Garibaldi issued this communiqué after he had captured the Villa Corsini and before the French recaptured it. This theory, which would acquit Garibaldi of untruthfulness, cannot be maintained, as the communiqué stated that the Romans were left in possession of the field when the fighting stopped at night. The communiqué, which is not dated, was published in the *Monitore Romano* on 8 June.

tion of ancient monuments, under Sterbini, to do all they could to protect the Roman antiquities from the French shells, and to make it known in Rome and abroad that the French gunners had damaged the façade of St Peter's. A number of foreign diplomats protested to Oudinot against the bombardment, thus giving Oudinot the pleasure of snubbing the British Consul, Freeborn, whom he considered to be a secret sympathizer with the revolutionaries of Rome. The civilian population carried on unconcernedly, strolling in the piazzas and drinking in the cafés during the bombardment. Arthur Hugh Clough, the English poet, enjoyed himself in Rome during the siege, his only complaint being that the museums were closed. He wrote cheerfully about the French to J. C. Shairp: 'They cannot get in; they banged away by moonlight most of last night.'[7]

The defence of Rome was having an important effect on the ordinary middle-class Englishman whose feelings always had a considerable influence in moulding the policy of the most powerful nation in the world. The middle-class Englishman did not like the French and did not like the Pope; but he strongly disapproved of Republicanism, and believed that Mazzini was a very dangerous revolutionary, even though a handful of intellectual cranks in England were silly enough to admire him. *The Times* was not happy about the French action, but their suspicion of France was not as strong as their fears of Red Republicanism. When Oudinot, instead of marching straight into Rome, was driven back on 30 April, *The Times* commented that 'no one, certainly, anticipated that this modern invasion would find an Horatius Cocles on the bridge', and sent a special correspondent to Oudinot's headquarters, though they had no reporter in Rome. The reports of their correspondent with Oudinot were written entirely from the French point of view. On 27 June he wrote that though he strongly disapproved of Oudinot's expedition, he nevertheless hoped that the French would capture Rome, because 'nothing will contribute so much to the general peace of the world as the capture of that band of Socialists who, under the name of liberty and by force of arms, have held possession so long of the Eternal City'.[8]

The Times reports were, however, sufficiently truthful to make the readers realize that Garibaldi had defeated superior numbers of Neapolitans and was holding out against the attacks of superior French forces; and whatever the middle-class Englishman might think about the Roman Republic, he developed a sneaking admiration for Garibaldi as a gallant underdog. The heroism of Garibaldi and his Legionaries on 30 April, at Velletri, on 3 June and during the last defence of Rome reaped valuable dividends, ten years later, for the cause of Italian freedom in Britain.

298

In France, the events in Rome had caused a final break between the Right and the Left. On 12 June Ledru-Rollin moved the impeachment of Louis Napoleon and the government for their betrayal of the French Constitution by their attempts to suppress the liberties of a foreign people; but once again he was decisively defeated in the Assembly. Next day he led what he called a peaceful demonstration in the streets of Paris, but which the government said was an attempted insurrection; it was dispersed by the army, who made many arrests. Ledru-Rollin fled to England. He had achieved nothing except to vindicate the honour and international solidarity of European Radicalism, and to boost for a short while the morale of the defenders of Rome. Mazzini, in a proclamation, declared that 'while Oudinot makes his last efforts, France rises in indignation, rejects from its breast and repudiates the soldiers who dishonour her. One more effort, and our Fatherland is saved for ever.'[9]

But Oudinot slowly edged forward towards the Janiculum and the Pancrazio gate, digging in and fortifying his advance posts and erecting, under heavy fire from Garibaldi's artillery, new batteries nearer the Roman positions. Garibaldi sent out small detachments to worry the French at their work, particularly at night, but the French got the best of these skirmishes. On the night of 17 June Garibaldi made a raid on the French positions, sending a battalion of Polish volunteers who fought in the white shirts which Polish troops had worn in the sixteenth century, and impressed both their allies and their enemies by their bravery. But they could not stop the French preparations.[10]

On 21 June Oudinot ordered a general assault on Garibaldi's position. There was fierce hand-to-hand fighting round the Pancrazio gate, with the Romans refusing to retreat or surrender, and dying at their posts when they were overrun. They drove back several attacks, but by next morning the French had captured three strongpoints to the south of the Porta San Pancrazio, though elsewhere along the western wall they were repulsed. Oudinot had gained less than he had hoped from the day's fighting, but he had won an important foothold in the Roman defences, and the position was serious for the Romans. Garibaldi withdrew a hundred yards to the east, behind the old Aurelian Wall, just a little below the top of the hill on the way down to the Trastevere. He still held the Janiculum and the Porta San Pancrazio and his outpost in the fort of the Vascello, at the entrance to the garden of the Villa Corsini, 250 yards beyond his front line. His headquarters in the Villa Savorelli, just below the summit of the Janiculum, had been badly damaged by bombardment during the last action, so he transferred his headquarters to the nearby Palazzo

Corsini, and two days later to the Villa Spada, fifty yards behind the Aurelian Wall.[11]

The loss of the bastions on 21 June put Rome in imminent danger of capture, and led to violent arguments among the revolutionaries as to what should be done to save the situation. For the first time, some of the Republican leaders openly criticized Mazzini's leadership; and on 22 June Sterbini, who had played such a prominent part in the early stages of the revolution in Rome, tried to organize a movement to have Garibaldi appointed as Dictator. After trying unsuccessfully to raise the matter in the National Assembly, he rode to Garibaldi's headquarters at the Palazzo Corsini and asked him to assume the dictatorship. Garibaldi rejected the suggestion. He told Sterbini that he had proposed, a few weeks earlier, that he should become Dictator, but that now it was too late for this, and that to raise the matter at this stage would do more harm than good.

Sterbini was not discouraged. He rode down to the Ponte Sisto, where he harangued the soldiers who were assembled there, and called for the dictatorship for Garibaldi; and he then went on to the Piazza Colonna, on the eastern bank of the Tiber, and addressed the crowds in the square. He denounced Roselli as an incompetent general, and said that only Garibaldi could save Rome. The crowds cheered enthusiastically at every mention of Garibaldi's name and the demand that he be given the dictatorship; but a young sculptor named Bezzi, who was dressed in the uniform of the University Division and was carrying a carbine, denounced Sterbini's proposal as treason to the Republican government. He seized the bridle of Sterbini's horse, threatened to shoot him as a traitor, and told him to go home and keep quiet. This effectively deflated Sterbini, who gave up his attempts to make Garibaldi Dictator.[12]

On the same day, Mazzini called a conference of his generals, and proposed to them that they should recapture the lost bastions to the south of the Porta San Pancrazio by a *levée en masse*. This idea had been part of the military thinking of revolutionary movements since the days of the French Revolution of 1792. It consisted of the whole people, that is to say, all men of military age, both civilians and soldiers, armed and unarmed, hurling themselves at the enemy and overcoming him by sheer weight of numbers, so that however many were killed, there would always be enough survivors to reach the enemy positions and win. It was considered by revolutionary theoreticians to be the ideal tactic for revolutionary masses to adopt, but it was never tried out in practice till it was used by the French defenders of Paris against the Germans in 1871, with disastrous results.

Mazzini proposed, on 22 June, that the people of Rome should storm the French positions at the Pancrazio gate and recapture them by a mass assault. Roselli agreed, and so did all the other generals except Garibaldi, who strongly opposed it. He said that it would fail with very heavy loss of life, and that the large masses of people would get in each other's way, and would prevent his troops from getting at the French. He was probably right, because in the confined area the crowds would have been unable to run forward, or even walk, and would have had to stand in an immovable mass, a target for the enemy artillery. Thanks to Garibaldi's opposition, Mazzini reluctantly abandoned the plan. He thought that Garibaldi had thwarted the last chance of saving Rome, and wrote a letter to Manara in which he bitterly reproached Garibaldi for his refusal to support the *levée en masse*. He told Manara: 'I regard Rome as having fallen.'[13]

Three days later, Garibaldi wrote to the Triumvirs and proposed an alternative plan. He suggested that Manara should be placed in command of the defence of the Janiculum, while he himself should secretly leave Rome at night with his own Legionaries and attack the French rear near Civita Vecchia, thus taking them by surprise and disorganizing their campaign against Rome. Mazzini and Roselli rejected the proposal, because they thought that it would be impossible for Garibaldi's men to leave Rome unobserved by the French. It was only after the siege was over that *The Times* correspondent with Oudinot revealed that the French had been expecting Garibaldi to do this, but had no idea how they could deal with it. They believed that if Garibaldi attacked their line of communication with Civita Vecchia, he would completely disrupt their plans, because in view of the length of the line and the geographical conditions, they would need to detach at least 10,000 troops to prevent Garibaldi's raids, and they could not spare these troops from the attack on the Janiculum. They could not understand why Garibaldi never came out. *The Times* correspondent thought that the only possible explanation must be that the Republican leaders feared that if Garibaldi's Legionaries left Rome, the people would rise in a counter-revolution in support of the Pope.

Garibaldi did not know about the French anxieties, but he was sure that Mazzini and Roselli had made a great strategic blunder, and he made his feelings plain. In this critical hour for the Roman Republic, the ill-feeling between Garibaldi and Mazzini had reached its highest point. Garibaldi said something to Mazzini which made Mazzini think, rightly or wrongly, that Garibaldi had refused to continue serving in the defence of the Janiculum, and on 26 June Mazzini appointed General Mezzacapo to succeed Garibaldi as commander of the defences there. But Manara made peace between Mazzini and

Garibaldi. He wrote to Mazzini and assured him that Garibaldi would do his duty and fight at the Janiculum. This was the last letter that Manara wrote before he was killed.[14]

Oudinot gave the Romans a week's respite after his success of 21 June before the next assault, but the bombardment continued day and night, except when the midday heat made it impossible to keep up the firing for fear lest the guns should seize up, and when the thunderstorms stopped operations for a few hours. The Romans strengthened their second line of defence on the Janiculum, and barricades were erected in the city streets by civilians working under the directions of Ciceruacchio's Committee of the Barricades. The Pope's supporters were shocked to see many women, wearing short skirts, helping the men build the barricades, and laughing and flirting with them as they did so, which convinced the Papalists that the revolutionaries were determined to subvert society and morality. Garibaldi, hiding his real opinion, joined with Avezzana and Roselli in signing an appeal to the people on 24 June. 'Behind the first bulwark the enemy will find a second wall, and behind that the barricades of the people ... God, who has inspired the people with constancy and faith, has decreed the triumph of right.' Morale was very high. 'The soldiers, I think, will fight to the last,' wrote Clough to F. T. Palgrave on 21 June, 'and though I suspect some base plotting is at work, yet the whole *basso popolo* will fight, and the middle classes mostly, and the "youth" almost universally will *at least* offer a passive resistance.'[15]

On 26 June Garibaldi was in his headquarters in the Villa Spada, which as usual was under bombardment, when, to his great surprise, Anita arrived. When the fighting in Rome began, she had written to him from Nice suggesting that she should join him; but he had written to her to dissuade her from coming. She had nevertheless come to Rome, travelling by ship to Leghorn, and from there by coach, entering Rome from the eastern side along the roads which were still open to civilian travellers. She had then persuaded someone to take her to Garibaldi's headquarters. A few minutes after she arrived, a shell hit the building, making a hole in the ceiling and bringing down the plaster in the room where she and Garibaldi were talking; but Anita was as cool under fire as she had been in the old days. Garibaldi managed to persuade her to keep out of the front line.[16]

Anita arrived at a time when the red shirt that she knew so well became more in evidence in Rome. Until now, only the handful of Legionaries who had come from Montevideo had worn the red shirt. The other members of the Legion had worn other uniforms, or none. But during the fighting in Rome, Garibaldi had decided that he wished all the troops of his Legion to wear the red shirt, though the Lombards and the *carabinieri* and the other troops under his command would naturally wish to retain their own uniforms. By the last week in June the new uniforms were ready, and all the surviving Legionaries under his command, who numbered about 1,000, put on the red shirt. Many of them only had the opportunity to wear it for a few days before they died.[17]

By 29 June, Oudinot was ready for the final attack. It was St Peter's Day, a traditional feast day in Rome. The Triumvirs ordered the clergy to hold the usual religious festivals, and the people kept the public holiday, dancing in the squares and cafés, and watching firework displays, which the government encouraged for the sake of morale. The festivities were ended by a thunderstorm at 10 pm. The storm also forced Oudinot to postpone his attack, which had been timed for midnight. At 2 am the rain stopped, and the attack began with an artillery barrage which eventually succeeded in breaching a gap in the fortifications of the Janiculum. At dawn Oudinot sent in the infantry. He had ordered them to give no quarter during the day's fighting, as it would be too inconvenient to deal with prisoners.[18]

The fighting of 30 June was the fiercest of the campaign. The French attacks were repeatedly repulsed, and always renewed. Garibaldi threw in all his reserves to try to hold the Aurelian Wall, which he knew was his last line of defence, because he had never believed that the barricades in the streets would hold up the French for long. The men fought with their bayonets, and their officers, including Garibaldi himself, joined them, fighting with their sabres. The French were greatly impressed by the courage of their enemies, and in several cases, despite Oudinot's order, offered quarter to some of the bravest of them. Among these were three officers of the Lombard Brigade, who made a last, suicidal charge, with cigars in their mouths and sabres in their hands. With them was a girl from their canteen, wielding a bayonet. The French offered them their lives, but all four, including the girl, refused, and went down fighting. The French showed no mercy to those French revolutionaries whom they found fighting for the Roman Republic. When one of them was taken prisoner, a French soldier strangled him, saying that the wretch did not deserve the honour of being killed with the bayonet. These revolutionary Frenchmen proudly declared that they were not fighting against France, but against reactionaries. There were men on both sides with strong ideological convictions. One of Oudinot's soldiers, who was killed on 30 June, asked his comrades to tell his mother that he died happy because he died fighting for religion.[19]

By 4 pm the French had captured the whole of the defences of the Janiculum and the Aurelian Wall, where nearly all Garibaldi's gunners were killed at their post; and the Roman outpost of the Vascello was finally captured during the following night. The losses on both sides on 30 June were heavy; and Garibaldi lost another personal friend when his negro batman, Aguiar, was killed. Oudinot and his artillery commander, General Vaillant, claimed that the defenders had greatly outnumbered their own men, and gave the Roman losses as 400 killed, and their own as 19 killed and 97 wounded; but these were certainly the usual propaganda figures which French generals were in the habit of issuing after battles, and were no nearer the truth than the communiqué which Garibaldi had issued on 3 June. The French Catholic writers even falsified the date of the action, in order to make out that it had been fought on the 29th, St Peter's Day. 'A marvellous coincidence,' wrote their propagandist, Balleydier, 'the eldest daughter of the Church crushes the revolutionary hydra on the very day of the feast of St Peter and the eve of the feast of St Paul.'[20]

In the Capitol, less than two miles from the French positions, the Constituent Assembly was in permanent session. On the evening of 30 June the deputies debated what to do. Garibaldi had gone there straight from the battle area, still wearing his red shirt in which he had fought on the Aurelian Wall that day. It was stiff with dried blood, though none of the blood was his own, as he had emerged unscathed from the battle of 30 June.

Three points of view were put forward in the Assembly. Many deputies asked the Triumvirs to capitulate to Oudinot. Mazzini suggested that they should withdraw to the Tiber, abandoning the western part of the city, and call on the people to defend the eastern part of Rome street by street, on every barricade. The Republic should go down fighting in a blood-bath which would be remembered for centuries and be an inspiration to their successors to continue the struggle for liberty – the course which was adopted twenty-two years later by the Paris Commune. Garibaldi said that if they adopted Mazzini's plan and withdrew across the Tiber, they could prolong resistance only for a few days at the most. He suggested instead that the government, the Assembly and the army should leave Rome and carry on the war in the countryside. The Assembly rejected Mazzini's plan. One great weakness in it was that the working-class district of the Trastevere, where there was so much revolutionary enthusiasm, was in that part of the city west of the Tiber which Mazzini proposed to abandon; and the Trasteverians, like the revolutionary workers of Paris in the nineteenth century, were ready to die on the barricades in defence of their own districts, but not elsewhere. A majority of the deputies were clearly in favour of surrender, and decided to ask Oudinot to grant them an armistice while they made up their minds what to do. Oudinot, realizing the way that the Assembly was moving, agreed to an armistice for twenty-four hours, but no longer.

On 2 July, a few hours before the armistice expired, the Assembly decided to end all resistance in Rome. Finding that Roselli was only too eager to resign as Commander-in-Chief, they appointed Garibaldi to succeed him, and gave him leave to withdraw from Rome with as many volunteers as were prepared to follow him; but the government and the Assembly would stay in Rome. Mazzini and the other two Triumvirs resigned, and Cernuschi, a zealous Republican who had played a great part in organizing the defence of Rome, formed a new government to perform the painful duty of surrendering to Oudinot.[21]

Many of the revolutionary leaders thought that the time had come to escape. There was nowhere in Italy for them to go, unless they could somehow manage to reach Venice, where Manin was still holding out; because the counter-revolution had triumphed in every Italian state except Sardinia, where the new King, Victor Emanuel, having been forced to make peace with Radetzky after the defeat of Novara, was anxious to do nothing to offend Austria, and in any case did not like Mazzinian Republicans. But the revolutionaries in Rome were helped by the diplomatic representatives of the only three countries whose governments regarded them with any degree of sympathy – Switzerland, Britain and the United States. The Swiss Radical government offered them asylum. The British Consul in Rome, Freeborn, who had so annoyed Oudinot by his sympathies with the Romans that Oudinot had deliberately requisitioned his villa outside the walls during the siege, gave British passports to many of the revolutionary leaders to enable them to escape and travel through hostile territory to Britain or Malta, though *The Times* complained that British passports, which were so much respected in Italy, were being degraded by being issued to foreign revolutionaries in the name of 'the old humbug, "humanity" '; and Palmerston ordered Freeborn to stop issuing them. By the time that Freeborn received Palmerston's directive, he had already saved the lives of many revolutionaries, though he assured Palmerston that he had given out fewer passports than the Swiss and United States Consuls.[22]

The Republican aims of the Roman revolutionaries aroused much more sympathy in the United States than in Britain, and a committee for the defence of Italian freedom was formed in New York. The committee was very critical of the conduct of the United States Minister in Rome, Cass, whom they accused of being hostile to Mazzini and the Republican government throughout the siege of Rome, and contrasted his actions with those of the United States Consul in Rome, Governor Brown, who had issued United States' passports to the escaping revolutionaries. It was unfortunate that when Theodore Dwight published the first edition of Garibaldi's memoirs in New York in 1859, he included, as an appendix, some writings of his own about the siege of Rome, in which he attacked Cass; because Cass had in fact tried to help Garibaldi to escape from Rome. Garibaldi did not mention this in Dwight's edition of the memoirs, which ended with his departure from Montevideo; but in the 1872 edition he paid full tribute to Cass.

On the afternoon of 2 July 1849, just after the National Assembly had decided to capitulate, Garibaldi received a message from the United States legation that Cass wished to see him at once. He walked to the legation, but on his way he met Cass himself in the street. Cass offered to put him on board a United States warship at Civita Vecchia, which would take him to safety in the United States or anywhere else where he wished to go. Garibaldi was very grateful to Cass, but he refused the offer.[23] He had decided to fight on in Italy. He planned to march out of Rome with as many volunteers as would follow him, to retreat into the country districts of the Papal States, and, if they could not hold out there, to try to get to Venice to join Manin.

At 5 pm, Garibaldi assembled the army in St Peter's Square. He addressed them, sitting on his horse, with Anita on horseback at his side. Several people who were present wrote down his words afterwards as far as they could remember them; and although all the reports naturally differ as to his exact words, they all agree as to the sense. 'This is what I have to offer to those who wish to follow me: hunger, cold, the heat of the sun; no wages, no barracks, no ammunition; but continual skirmishes, forced marches and bayonet-fights. Those of you who love your country and love glory, follow me!'[24]

Four thousand seven hundred men decided to follow him. 'The more prudent,' wrote Dandolo, 'could not conceive what Garibaldi could hope to accomplish with a handful of dispirited soldiers against four armies'; and Pisacane, with his usual dislike of Garibaldi, wrote that many soldiers refused to go when they heard that Garibaldi would be leading the expedition. Some of Garibaldi's best officers, like Nino Bixio, were too badly wounded to go; but Sacchi, Cocelli, and others who had come from Montevideo, were able to accompany him. Ciceruacchio and his sons went with him, as did Zambianchi, whom the Pope's supporters and even the Mazzinians denounced as a blood-thirsty ruffian because he had executed some priests in the Trastevere whom he suspected of being counter-revolutionaries. Garibaldi's doctor, Ripari, was eager to come, but Garibaldi made him stay in Rome to care for the wounded. Anita came. She rushed off from St Peter's Square to cut her hair short and change into men's clothes. Her action on that day, and in the next five weeks, made her a national heroine in a country in which she lived for only four months of her life.*

At 7 pm on 2 July, Garibaldi and his followers left Rome by the Porta San Giovanni on the Tivoli road. Twenty-one hours later, the French marched into Rome.[25]

*Anita lived for only four months in present-day Italy. This excludes the twelve months during which she lived at Nice.

CHAPTER 20

THE MARCH TO SAN MARINO

AT midday on 3 July the Constituent Assembly, which had been occupied since February in drafting the republican constitution, completed its work, and the constitution was proclaimed in the Capitol amid shouts of 'Long live the People's Republic!' It was the last Mazzinian gesture before the French entered Rome. The official journal of the Republic, the *Monitore Romano*, spent the last three days of its existence in proclaiming the overthrow of the Papal throne. 'Today, when on that throne, stigmatized by civilization, flows the blood of so many victims, who will dare to raise it again? . . . Can the Pope, like the tyrants, sit upon a seat of bayonets?'[1]

The Pope succeeded in sitting on a seat of bayonets for more than twenty-one years, though he did not dare to return to Rome until nine months after Oudinot entered it. The French were masters of Rome, cutting down the Republican tricolour flags from the balconies of the houses, prohibiting all assemblies and Republican newspapers, and cuffing youths and other civilians who insulted them in the streets or in the cafés. A number of prominent Republicans were arrested, including Garibaldi's surgeon, Dr Ripari, and some men were executed under martial law for attacks on the occupying forces; but there were no wholesale executions. Mazzini remained in Rome for a few days in order to show his supporters that he was prepared to be arrested; but he then decided to escape, with the aid of the British passport which Freeborn had given him, and made his way by sea to Marseilles, disguised as a ship's cook, and then through Switzerland to London.[2]

When Louis Napoleon had first decided to intervene, he had justified his action to the French Republicans by claiming that if the Pope were restored by the French, and not by the Austrians, he would return as a constitutional, not an absolute, sovereign. But after the experiences of 1848 and 1849, Pius IX had had enough of constitutions; and under the pressure of Catholic opinion in France, Louis Napoleon abandoned his attempts to persuade Pius to adhere to the constitutional reforms which he had granted in 1847. In the French National Assembly the former Liberal, Montalembert, demanded that the Holy Father should be restored to his throne without conditions. If France did otherwise, he declared, amid the applause of the Catholic MPs, she would 'exchange the role and the glory of Charlemagne for a pitiable imitation of Garibaldi'.[3] In the Papal States, and everywhere in Italy except the Kingdom of Sardinia, the old autocracy was restored as if the events of the past two years had never occurred.

From the French point of view, only one thing spoilt the victory of 3 July 1849: the fact that Garibaldi and his band had been allowed to escape. At 4 pm on 2 July General Vaillant noticed that the red shirts of the Garibaldini, who were holding the front line on the Aurelian Wall during the twenty-four-hour armistice, had been replaced by the blue uniforms of the other Roman units; but he did not know that Garibaldi was preparing to leave Rome on the far side of the city in a few hours' time, and it was not until the French entered Rome next day that they discovered that he had gone. They then suspected that the Romans had asked for the twenty-four-hour armistice in order to allow him time to escape. *The Times* correspondent with Oudinot was disappointed that the French had not moved fast enough to surround Rome and cut off Garibaldi's retreat, before 'this roving son of liberty and rapine' could escape.[4]

But Oudinot had little doubt that he would be able to dispose of Garibaldi quite easily. The 4,700 Garibaldini faced four armies totalling 86,000 men. Oudinot had 40,000 men in Rome and Civita Vecchia. Twenty thousand Neapolitans were in arms on the frontiers of the Papal States. The Spanish expeditionary force near Rome numbered 9,000. In the north of the Papal States, and in Tuscany, there were 2,000 men in the Tuscan forces of the restored Grand-Duke and 15,000 Austrians under the command of D'Aspre and Gorzkowski, apart from Radetzky's armies in Lombardy and Venetia. Oudinot thought that 20,000 men would be enough to deal with less than 5,000 Garibaldini. He sent General Morris with 7,000 French troops to pursue them. He had not permitted the Spanish expeditionary force to play any part in capturing Rome; but he now allowed 7,000 of the Spaniards to join in the pursuit of Garibaldi. On the Neapolitan frontier 7,000 Neapolitan soldiers were detailed to find and destroy the Garibaldini. *The Times* correspondent wrote confidently that 'the worst enemies of the country will probably be annihilated', and as Garibaldi 'is now nothing better than a brigand, making war on his own account, it is probable that if caught much ceremony will not be used in respect of him'; but Arthur Hugh Clough's sympathies were with Garibaldi and Anita. 'There is a Mrs Garibaldi,' he wrote to Palgrave on 6 July, 'she went out with him to the Abruzzi. I hope the French won't cut them to pieces, but *vice versa*.'[5]

Clough was not the only person who thought on 6 July that Garibaldi was heading for the Abruzzi province of the Kingdom of Naples. This was what Garibaldi wished his enemies to believe. His real plan was to avoid all the hostile armies and go north-east from Rome into the mountainous areas of the Papal States. If he could not rally the people there, he would cross into Tuscany and try to win the support of the Tuscans; and if he failed here too, he would try to reach Venice, where Manin's men, alone of all the revolutionary forces of 1848, were still holding out, though desperately pressed by the Austrians by land and sea. It was not easy for a force of nearly 5,000 men, who could only move as fast as the slowest foot-soldier, to march from Rome to Venice without being tracked down by the pursuing French, Neapolitans and Spaniards; but Garibaldi hoped to deceive the enemy as to his whereabouts. When he marched out of the Porta San Giovanni on the south-east side of Rome on the evening of 2 July, he headed for Tivoli, eighteen miles almost due east of Rome. The Garibaldini marched all night in absolute silence. Garibaldi told his officers to pass their orders down the line in whispers, and forbade his men to smoke.[6]

They reached Tivoli early next morning, and rested. The population of Tivoli were very friendly to the Garibaldini, because, though they were not good Republicans, they were very angry with the French. There had been an important gunpowder factory at Tivoli, which had supplied Rome with gunpowder during the siege. Four days before, a French unit had arrived at Tivoli, and though the population welcomed them warmly, and asked them to take over the factory, the French had insisted on blowing it up, thus depriving the local inhabitants of their livelihood.[7]

On the evening of 3 July – just as the French were entering Rome – Garibaldi marched out of Tivoli in a south-easterly direction towards the Neapolitan frontier, in order to confirm the French in their belief that he was heading for the Abruzzi. But after marching south-eastwards for an hour and a half, he wheeled sharp round to the left, and, doubling back on his tracks, marched north-westwards, passing within a few miles of Tivoli on the far side of the hills to the east of the town. Next morning he reached Monte Rotondo, where he was nearer to Rome than he had been at Tivoli, while his rearguard halted at Mentana. It was 4 July, his birthday; he was forty-two.

At Monte Rotondo and Mentana, only thirteen miles from Rome, the Garibaldini rested all day, while they served requisition notices on the inhabitants, requiring them to provide food and wine for 4,700 men. Garibaldi had brought with him from Rome a large stock of the paper money which had been printed under the Republic, and he offered payment in this currency for all the supplies which he requisitioned. But the people of Monte Rotondo were not eager to accept payment in the banknotes of the Republic, which they rightly guessed would not be honoured by the new authorities in the Papal States; and they were unfriendly. In order to prevent any of them from sending word to Oudinot that the Garibaldini were almost within his reach at Monte Rotondo, Garibaldi posted sentries at the gates of the town and refused to allow anyone to leave Monte Rotondo all day. He posted another sentry on the top of the hill to the west of Monte Rotondo. From there Garibaldi could see, in the distance, the reflection of the sun on the dome of St Peter's in Rome, and had a view of the whole countryside between Rome and Monte Rotondo, and of any troops who might be moving in the area.

There was a monastery on the hill outside the town, and the monks were especially reluctant to contribute their share of the rations. Garibaldi sent Anita and one of his officers – a Swiss volunteer named Hoffstetter – to persuade the monks to co-operate. Hoffstetter, who kept a diary throughout the campaign which he published in Switzerland two years later, wrote that the monks seemed to be terrified of Anita, and they produced the food and wine which was required.[8]

In the evening Garibaldi and his men set off again, continuing towards the north-west. When the French, some days later, heard the news from Monte Rotondo of Garibaldi's arrival and departure, they thought that he was heading for the west coast north of Civita Vecchia and was planning to escape from Italy by sea; but Garibaldi had made another feint. After leaving Monte Rotondo he turned right and marched due north to Terni, which he reached on 8 July. Colonel Hugh Forbes, formerly of the British army and the Grenadier Guards, had resigned his commission and married his second wife, an Italian lady, with whom he settled down in Florence. When the revolution of 1848 broke out, Forbes and his son by his first marriage enrolled a battalion to fight for the Roman Republic. He had hoped to take part in the fighting in Rome, but Avezzana had ordered him to stay in the north and harry the Austrian forces which had invaded the territory of the Republic. He now turned up at Terni, wearing his white top hat, and joined Garibaldi with 650 additional soldiers.[9]

Garibaldi continued north from Terni. On the march his line stretched out for about three miles. Garibaldi and Anita rode in front with about thirty of the cavalry, Anita dressed in man's clothes, wearing a green uniform with a broad-brimmed plumed Calabrian hat, riding a white horse, and not carrying any weapons. Behind them marched the infantry, and behind the infantry came the vehicles carrying the equipment and supplies, the ambulance, and the only cannon which Garibaldi had. The rest of the cavalry brought up the rear. Every night the little army moved off at 2 am and marched with hardly a break for eight hours. They then rested for seven hours, during the heat of the day, from 10 am to 5 pm, while food was requisitioned and eaten in the place where they had halted. At 5 pm they set off again for a shorter march for three hours, and then rested, at dusk, for six hours from 8 pm till it was time to set out again at 2 am.[10]

Garibaldi had succeeded, by his feints, in deceiving the enemy as to his position. The semi-official *Giornale di Roma*, which had been started on Oudinot's orders to replace the suppressed Republican newspaper the *Monitore Romano*, gave completely false reports as to where Garibaldi was. On 7 July, when he was at Confine, twenty-five miles north of Monte Rotondo on the road to Terni, the *Giornale di Roma* reported that he was between Tivoli and Palestrina, more than forty miles to the south. But the French had some idea that he had turned north from Tivoli, and Morris's French force and the Spaniards marched north to find him. On 9 July Garibaldi gave his men a day's rest at Terni; and next day, while Garibaldi was between Cesi and San Gemini, Morris reached Viterbo, thirty-five miles south-west of San Gemini, and the Spaniards reached Rieti, which was only fifteen miles south-east of San Gemini. But the Spaniards were still a day's march behind Garibaldi as he set off northwards from San Gemini to Todi.[11]

Garibaldi was having his difficulties and disappointments. His plan of holding out and waging guerrilla warfare in the Papal States depended on his being joined by many of the young men in the territories through which he passed; but in fact no one had joined him. There had never been much support for the Republicans in the country districts, and the little which had previously existed had disappeared in the hour of defeat; and the inhabitants of the towns at which Garibaldi arrived at ten o'clock each morning did not relish being ordered to supply 4,700 rations of bread, salami, cheese and red wine within a few hours, and being paid in the currency of the defunct Roman Republic.

By this time, Garibaldi had more or less decided that he would soon cross the border into Tuscany, where he could not claim that the paper money of the Roman Republic had ever been legal tender. He therefore required the local authorities in the larger towns through which he passed in the Papal States to change the paper money into gold and silver coin which he could spend in Tuscany. On 6 July Oudinot issued a proclamation requiring everyone to hand in to the banks all the Republican paper money that they held, before 10 July, after which date the money would be valueless; and Garibaldi's order to his troops forbidding looting, which he enforced very strictly, did not do much to appease the indignation of the householders and town councils on whom he foisted the banknotes, not only in payment for supplies, but also in exchange for valuable coin.[12]

The peasants in many areas were so hostile to Garibaldi that they were eager to supply the French with information as to his where-abouts. He tried, often successfully, to win them over by his personal friendliness and charm. 'What are you afraid of?' he asked a terrified peasant whom he met on the road. 'Do we speak German? Do we burn and rob? Are we fighting for or against you? And are we not your fellow-countrymen?' But these methods could only influence those whom Garibaldi met personally, and their friends. The *Giornale di Roma* reported that the Pope's loyal subjects were everywhere assisting the forces of law and order to suppress Garibaldi and his bandits, and this was not entirely untrue. Garibaldi was bitterly disappointed at the lack of support which he received from the people, and as usual blamed it on the priests, whom he described, in the 1872 edition of his memoirs, as 'indefatigable traitors to this land which, to her sorrow, tolerates them'. He contrasted the apathy of the Italians with the enthusiasm which the people of Uruguay had shown in the fight against Rosas. 'When I compare, I say, the strong sons of Columbus with my cowardly and effeminate fellow-countrymen, I am ashamed to belong to these degenerate descendants of a very great people, who are incapable of keeping the field for a month without the bourgeois habit of three meals a day.' But the situation in Montevideo, even in the months after Costa Brava and Arroyo Grande, had never been as desperate as the position in July 1849 of the Garibaldini, outnumbered five to one, as their enemies pressed in on them from all sides.[13]

At Viterbo General Morris was as confident as Garibaldi was worried. On 10 July he wrote to Oudinot's ADC, General de Timon, and after telling him that the monks were offering his men hospitality in their monasteries, which made splendid quarters, he asked for three squadrons of cavalry. 'With these and the information which the local people are supplying, I am encircling and squeezing Garibaldi [*j'arc-pince Garibaldi*]. . . . All the women make eyes at us, the country is very healthy.' The action of the women may not have had much political significance, but it showed a different spirit from that which existed in Milan, where the Austrians complained that the women spat at them and raised their handkerchiefs to cover their faces when they passed an Austrian soldier in the street.[14]

On the same day Morris took a step which he hoped would encour-age Garibaldi's men to desert. During the fighting in Rome the French had treated the Republican troops as lawful combatants, and those whom they captured as prisoners of war; but on 10 July Morris at

Viterbo issued a proclamation announcing that any man found carrying arms after the expiry of twenty-four hours would be shot, and anyone who assisted the armed bandits would be tried by court martial and punished. But though the desertions from Garibaldi's band increased, the spirits of the best of his followers were as high as ever. Anita was especially cheerful, and the men who watched her chatting with the soldiers on the march, or making a tent during the hours of rest when the Legion halted, were inspired by her example, and went out of their way to render small services to her. When she encountered any sign of weakness or grumbling among the men, she lashed them with her tongue, as she had done to the cowardly sailors in the sea-fights at Imbituba and Laguna ten years before.[15]

On 11 July Garibaldi reached Todi, where he waited for more than forty-eight hours while he sent out reconnoitring parties to discover the enemy's position. Here he acquired an unexpected and welcome stock of food. He sent out a detachment of his cavalry to forage, and they captured a convoy of provisions for the French army on the road between Rome and Orvieto. The foragers returned to Todi with 5,000 poultry and 50,000 eggs, which made a pleasant change from their usual diet of cheese and salami.[16] But Garibaldi heard bad news at Todi. An Austrian army at Perugia blocked his road to the north, and with the Spaniards advancing from the south-east and the French from the south-west, he was in danger of being caught between the three converging armies. He decided to turn back and make for Orvieto, twenty miles to the west and a little south of Todi, although this meant moving into the path of the advancing French. From there he could march north into Tuscany. Orvieto was only fifteen miles from the frontier, and Garibaldi could be sure that the French would not follow him into Tuscany, which was in the Austrian zone.

On the road to Orvieto, one of his men stole a hen from a peasant woman's house which they passed. Garibaldi arrived while the woman was protesting, and had the man shot on the spot. When the other soldiers came running up after hearing the shot, Garibaldi told them that he had executed a looter, as he had warned them that he would do; and the men shouted 'Long live Garibaldi!'[17]

They reached Orvieto on the evening of 14 July, and found that the French were expected to arrive next day. General Morris had sent word to the authorities to prepare rations for his army. The Conservatives in the moderate party in Orvieto strongly objected to Garibaldi's arrival, and sent a deputation to ask him not to enter the town; but Garibaldi refused to discuss the matter, and rode up the hill into Orvieto, where he was enthusiastically cheered by the supporters of the Democratic Party, who decided to illuminate the town that night in his honour. Next morning Garibaldi was in no hurry to leave. He calculated, from the information which he had received, that Morris could not arrive before the evening; so he coolly decided that he had time to wait at Orvieto while his men rested and ate the food which had been prepared for the French.

With the French coming nearer every hour, Garibaldi gave his men a few hours' leave, and the Swiss Hoffstetter walked round the town, and found a good café where the waiters were most eager to serve one of Garibaldi's men. When it was time to leave, some of the scouting and raiding parties which Garibaldi had sent out into the surrounding countryside had not yet returned; so Garibaldi, believing that he still had a few hours to spare, waited until they came in before he gave the order to depart. His rearguard left Orvieto at 10 pm, and the first French troops arrived there three hours later, at 1 am. Morris, finding the town still illuminated in honour of Garibaldi, gave orders that it was to be illuminated as a mark of respect to the French. By this time the Garibaldini were marching north-west over the mountains towards Ficulle and the borders of Tuscany.[18]

In Tuscany the revolution of 1848 had been carried through peacefully and constitutionally, thanks to the moderation shown by Guerrazzi on the one side and by Grand-Duke Leopold on the other; but when Guerrazzi proclaimed the Republic, Leopold fled to the north, and asked his cousin, the Emperor Franz Josef, to send Austrian troops to restore him to his throne. In May 1849 the Austrians marched into Tuscany, partly, as D'Aspre wrote to the Austrian Chancellor, Schwarzenberg, because they feared that otherwise Leopold would ask the French to do the job. The Austrians had also occupied Bologna and the north-eastern areas of the Papal States; but Oudinot had warned them very firmly that they must not come any nearer to Rome, and must leave the liberation of the Eternal City to the eldest daughter of the Church.[19]

As Garibaldi marched north towards the Tuscan border, the rumours of his approach caused great excitement in Tuscany. The Tuscan Republicans, not having experienced any of the ordeals of revolution and war, were now in a more militant mood than the Liberals in any other part of Italy, and the Austrians became alarmed that the arrival of Garibaldi would spark off revolutionary resistance to their armies of occupation which had so far been avoided. The Austrian forces in Tuscany and in the Papal States, and their fleet in the Adriatic off Ancona, under its Danish commander, Admiral Dahlerup, were put on the alert; but the Austrian generals were no better informed than Oudinot and the Spanish commander as to where Garibaldi was. They thought that he was trying to reach the west

315

coast in the Maremma region of southern Tuscany. They were also mistaken as to the size of his force, believing that he had 6,000 men; but in fact, even with the 650 men that Forbes had brought, Garibaldi's band had diminished, through desertions, to about 2,500.[20]

D'Aspre was anxious to avoid any clash or misunderstanding with the French, and in a friendly correspondence with Oudinot the two commanders-in-chief fixed the precise limits of the zones in which their two armies would operate against Garibaldi. D'Aspre adhered rigidly to this demarcation line, although he was eager to have a crack at Garibaldi, and was exasperated with the incompetence with which the French and Spaniards had allowed him to slip between their fingers. He suspected that they were not trying to catch Garibaldi, but were shepherding him into the Austrian zone so that the Austrians should have the trouble of destroying him. D'Aspre had every intention of doing this. A year before, at Morazzone, he had refrained from shooting his Garibaldini prisoners because Garibaldi held thirty-three of his own Croats who might have been executed in reprisal; but Garibaldi had not captured any Austrian soldiers this time. On 19 July D'Aspre wrote to Schwarzenberg: 'All my troops have been given orders not to accept any capitulations and to make every effort to destroy this band, treating them like brigands.'[21]

The Austrians were preparing for the triumphal return of the Grand-Duke to his capital at Florence under an escort of Austrian troops. With extreme lack of tact, they demanded that Leopold should ride into Florence wearing the uniform of an Austrian Field-Marshal, because, being a Habsburg Prince, he had been granted this honorary rank in the Austrian army. Leopold was shrewd enough to realize the damage which this would do to his reputation with his subjects, and proposed wearing the uniform of the Tuscan National Guard which had been formed with his authority when he granted the constitution in 1848. D'Aspre objected strongly to the idea of a Habsburg Prince wearing the uniform of the Liberal National Guard, and insisted that as the Grand-Duke had been restored to his throne by the Austrian army, he should enter his capital in Austrian uniform. 'I am told that he is an independent prince,' wrote D'Aspre, 'I can only answer that the moment that this prince detaches himself from Austria his ruin is certain, that he had to fly, that it was Austria that gave him back his state, and that if at this moment the Austrian army was not in Tuscany, Garibaldi would be in Florence.' D'Aspre would have liked to go to Lucca to bully the Grand-Duke into wearing the Austrian uniform; but he reported to Vienna that if he left Florence, Garibaldi would at once go there, and would certainly find many supporters, perhaps even among Tuscan officers in the Grand-Duke's native forces.[22]

Schnitzer-Meerau, the Austrian Minister in Florence, was as alarmed as D'Aspre at 'the proximity of this skilful partisan of the revolution', which was encouraging 'the turbulent spirits in several towns of Tuscany, particularly in Leghorn and Florence'; but he pointed out that there was some consolation to be derived from the menace of Garibaldi. 'The closer Garibaldi approached to Tuscany,' he wrote to Schwarzenberg on 25 July, 'the more the fear grew and the more people were thanking Providence for the presence of our troops in these regions'; he had met people, 'even among the party most opposed to Austrian-Tuscan friendship', who admitted that had it not been for the presence of the Austrians, the Reds would have established the guillotine in the three main squares of Florence.[23]

Garibaldi entered Tuscany on the morning of 17 July after a night march from Ficulle across the marshy plain in pitch darkness through heavy wind and rain. It was still raining when they crossed the Tuscan border, but soon afterwards the sun broke through, and their spirits rose as they thought that here in Tuscany they would find more support than they had done in the territory of the Roman Republic. At first it seemed as if their hopes would be fulfilled. At Cetona, the first Tuscan town which they entered, they had a more friendly reception than at any town in the Papal States except Orvieto. For the first time since they left Rome they slept in houses. Anita bought a woman's dress in Cetona and wore it instead of the man's clothes in which she had ridden from Rome, perhaps because she considered that it was incongruous to wear man's clothes now that her pregnancy was more advanced.[24]

Next day, on 18 July, they discovered that not every town in Tuscany was friendly. As Garibaldi marched north-west to Montepulciano to avoid the Austrian troops to the north-east, he sent out a scouting party to Chiusi, a few miles to the right of his line of march. The local authorities at Chiusi had hastily enrolled in the National Guard when they heard of his approach, and were determined to prevent him from entering Chiusi. When the small detachment of Garibaldini came to Chiusi, the National Guard attacked them, killed one of them, and took two of them prisoners. Garibaldi demanded the release of the two men; but this was refused. There was a monastery just outside Chiusi. Garibaldi rounded up all the fourteen monks in the monastery, and forced them to march to Chiusi at the head of his column; and when a priest and another citizen came to Garibaldi and asked him to release the monks, Garibaldi arrested them also. He told the Bishop of Chiusi that he would shoot the monks unless his two men were released. The Bishop refused to agree to the bargain. No doubt he prided himself on this refusal to surrender to blackmail;

but Garibaldi interpreted it as evidence of the Bishop's callous disregard for the lives of the monks.

When Garibaldi saw that his bluff had failed, he did not shoot the monks or his other two prisoners, but took them with him as far as Filo, near Arezzo, where he released them unharmed four days later. He wrote in his memoirs that he did so because he thought that the Bishop was hoping that he would shoot them and so provide the Catholic cause with martyrs; but Garibaldi's humanity, which had seemed impolitic to General Iriarte in Montevideo, was probably the real reason. He found it as repugnant to kill prisoners at Chiusi as at Gualeguaychú.[25]

The Garibaldini reached Montepulciano on 19 July, and here, like at Cetona, they had a very friendly reception from the local population. Anita, in fact, objected because Garibaldi became too friendly with some pretty girls in the crowd which greeted them, and she made a jealous scene which was noticed by some of Garibaldi's officers. Even the monks were friendly, though Hoffstetter thought that they acted out of fear. They entertained many of the Garibaldini to an excellent dinner in the monastery, and insisted on waiting on them at table. Anita hated monks so much that she refused to be served by them, and special arrangements had to be made in her case; the monks brought her food from the kitchen as far as the door of the dining room, where it was handed over to some of the Garibaldini, who took it to Anita.[26]

Garibaldi issued a proclamation in Montepulciano, in which he appealed to the people of Tuscany to rise and fight for freedom under his banner, which had 'struck terror into the Germans at Luino, the Bourbonists at Palestrina and at Velletri, the French in the campaign of Rome'. He ended with the words which ten years later became the national slogan of Italy: 'Out with the foreigners!' to which he now added: 'Out with the traitors!' But his appeal did not produce any effect. The people of Montepulciano cheered him, but did not join him.[27]

The official press in Tuscany, and in most of the other Italian states, published reports every day about Garibaldi's activities and movements. They described the Garibaldini as deserters, escaped convicts, and young boys, and conveyed the impression that the whole population of Tuscany was united in their fear and hatred of them. They admitted that the citizens of Montepulciano, unlike the brave men of Chiusi, had deemed it wiser not to resist, but they gave no indication that Garibaldi had been welcomed there. They gave full coverage to his seizure of the monks at Chiusi, and also reported that he had arrested the Sub-Prefect of Montepulciano as a hostage, though they admitted that the Sub-Prefect, like the monks, had been released, unharmed, at Fojano. They stated that the Garibaldini had arrested the Archdeacon of Montepulciano in the streets of the town, and after inflicting the grossest insults on him, had demanded a ransom of 5,000 scudi, though they eventually agreed to release him on payment of 1,000 scudi. The best story was an account of how eight Garibaldini, one of them being the son of the former Republican Chief Inspector of Police at Rieti, had kidnapped a number of women and held them prisoner in a barn until they were rescued from an awful fate by some heroes of the Tuscan National Guard. The Tuscan press was nearer the truth when they exposed the report in the Radical Turin newspaper, *La Concordia*, that the people of Tuscany had joined Garibaldi in large numbers, and that he had established himself in Tuscany at the head of an army which already numbered 11,000 men.[28]

One source of friction between the Garibaldini and the local population, in Tuscany as in the Papal States, was the necessity which compelled Garibaldi to requisition food in the towns where he halted. He also levied forced loans on the towns through which he passed in Tuscany, as he had done in the Papal States; and as he could not maintain that the paper money of the Roman Republic was currency in Tuscany, he gave the Tuscan town councils, in return for the supplies and forced loans, receipts and promises of repayment in the name of the Roman Republic. Only those town councillors who were enthusiastic revolutionaries could feel happy with this security.[29]

In view of the lack of active support in Tuscany, Garibaldi decided that the only useful thing which he could now do was to go to Venice and join Manin. He therefore planned to march across Tuscany and over the Apennines to the Adriatic coast and take ship there for Venice. D'Aspre had three army corps in Tuscany which blocked his way; but thanks to extremely skilful manoeuvring, to his fair share of luck, and to Austrian incompetence and their lack of a unified command, Garibaldi managed to slip between them all. The Austrians had realized that Garibaldi would try to reach the Adriatic; but instead of marching east to Ancona, he went due north from Montepulciano to Castiglione Fiorentino. There he turned west, making the enemy believe that he was not, after all, aiming for the east coast, but swung round in a semi-circle and on the night of 22 July reached Arezzo. His men had looked forward to a friendly reception in Arezzo; but they found the gates shut in their faces, and the local National Guard in arms to stop them from entering.

Arezzo was ruled by a Conservative town council of the moderate party; and though the Democratic Opposition demanded that Garibaldi be allowed in, the ruling party would not agree. There were ninety Austrian soldiers in Arezzo, recovering from wounds and illnesses in a convalescent home, but they were fit enough to take part in organizing the defence of the town against the Garibaldini. Garibaldi waited all next day in front of Arezzo, asking to be admitted, and hoping that the Democrats in Arezzo would carry the day in the bitter discussions which were going on. The Garibaldini easily outnumbered the defenders, and many of them urged Garibaldi to attack and capture Arezzo by storm. But he was reluctant to fight against the local inhabitants of a Tuscan town and provide his enemies with the opportunity of portraying him, in their propaganda, as a hated invader who was terrorizing the people of Tuscany. He had another reason for avoiding a fight. He pointed out to Hoffstetter that if he stormed the town, some of his men would certainly be wounded, and he would have to leave them behind in Arezzo to be shot when the Austrians arrived. So on the evening of 23 July he marched away to the east.[30]

His hungry soldiers, who had lost their day's rations through not being admitted to Arezzo, were dejected by the set-back, and a mood of defeatism began to spread. The number of desertions increased. Garibaldi caught a few of the deserters, and had them shot; but the total number of his force had now fallen to about 2,000 – less than half the number with which he had marched out of Rome. He suffered a bitter blow when the Polish revolutionary, Müller, who had fought well in Rome and commanded the cavalry in the retreat, deserted with sixty horsemen and surrendered to the Austrians. Garibaldi appointed Bueno, who had come with him from Montevideo, to succeed Müller as commander of the cavalry.[31]

Those who remained with Garibaldi and Anita included his closest companions and officers – the Swiss Hoffstetter, the Englishman Forbes, and Ciceruacchio and his two sons. Ugo Bassi had fallen ill at Cesi and had been left behind, but when he recovered he managed to slip through the French lines and had rejoined the Garibaldini. He had discarded his clerical costume and wore the red shirt like the others. Garibaldi had also been joined by Captain Culiolo, who was nicknamed Leggero, the nimble, by his friends. Leggero had been wounded in the fighting in Rome, and had been unable to leave with Garibaldi; but by the middle of the month he was well enough to set out after him, and he caught up with the Garibaldini. Leggero limped heavily as a result of his wound.[32]

On 24 July Garibaldi crossed the frontier and re-entered the Papal States to the north-east of Tuscany. That evening he reached Citerna, and quartered his men in the monasteries, despite the protests of the monks. He forced the monks and the inhabitants to supply food for his hungry and exhausted men, whom he allowed a day's rest before proceeding on their journey. Relations between the Garibaldini and the monks were unfriendly, and the Garibaldini looted the monasteries and did a good deal of damage. It was the first time since leaving Rome that the men had got out of hand and that Garibaldi was unable to prevent them from looting; there were too many looters at Citerna for him to shoot them all. While he was at Citerna, a delegation from some Republican supporters among the peasants of the district called on him to wish him well. He told them that things were going badly now, but that Italy would be free within ten years.[33]

Garibaldi was now about sixty miles from the Adriatic; but an Austrian army under Archduke Ernst von Habsburg, the cousin of the Emperor Franz Josef, was pursuing him closely. A second force, under Stadion, was coming from Florence in the west to cut him off; and a third Austrian army, under Hahn, was marching south from Bologna to complete the encirclement. On 24 July D'Aspre reported to Vienna: 'Garibaldi is today almost surrounded by my troops . . . One could forecast an immediate solution, but as he is skilful and enterprising he could still escape by a forced march.' Next day Archduke Ernst reached Monterchi, about one mile south of Citerna on the other side of the hill. The Archduke threw a cordon of troops around Citerna to stop Garibaldi from escaping; but one of the byways leading out of Citerna to the north-east was not marked on the Austrian maps, and Garibaldi, seeing that the road was unguarded, slipped out of the ring by following this road on the night of 25 July. He was sure that the monks intended to go straight to Monterchi as soon as he had left, to tell the Austrians where he had gone; so he forced them all to come with him on his silent night march to San Giustino. On the way he had to cross the upper reaches of the River Tiber. He forded the river, forcing the friars, despite their wails and protests, to wade up to their waists in the water.[34]

During the next forty-eight hours the Garibaldini marched on towards the north-east, over the mountains of the Apennines, with the Austrians only a few miles behind them, but pausing nevertheless to rest and eat whenever necessary, and surprisingly avoiding capture by the enemy. 'Garibaldi seems to be going in the direction of Ancona,' wrote D'Aspre on 28 July, 'but, headed off on every side, he will probably switch. His people are beginning to disband. I have given orders not to let him get away again, and to shoot all who are caught with arms in their hands.' A number of stragglers from Garibaldi's band were captured by the Austrians and immediately shot. Some were flogged and then released; others were tortured to get them to divulge information, or ill-treated out of wanton cruelty. The units of Tyrolese light cavalry – the Jäger corps formed from the Tyrolean peasants –

were particularly cruel, especially to the wounded who fell into their hands. A number of boys – the twelve- and fourteen-year-olds – were captured. When they were asked who they were, they proudly replied that they were soldiers of Garibaldi, and were shot.[35]

On 28 July, at San Angelo in Vado, Archduke Ernst's army caught the Garibaldini, and for the first time since leaving Rome Garibaldi, after avoiding the armed forces of four nations for twenty-six days, was forced to fight a battle against greatly superior forces. He succeeded in retreating to the north-east with most of his men, but the Archduke's cavalry sabred his rearguard in the streets of San Angelo. The feelings of the inhabitants of the area were very divided. In San Angelo there were many Republican sympathizers, who risked their lives by hiding some of the Garibaldini in their houses; but many of the peasants in the country districts joined the Austrians in hunting down Garibaldi's stragglers. Some of them did so under duress, because the Austrians acted on the usual principles of a regular army when acting against guerrillas, of making the local population more frightened of them than they were of Garibaldi, and threatening to burn the farms of those who refused to help them. 'I could not obtain a single guide in Italy,' wrote Garibaldi in his memoirs, 'while the Austrians had as many as they wanted. Let this be a lesson to those Italians who go to mass and make their confession to those wonderful black-robed cockroaches.'[36]

On 29 July Garibaldi reached Macerata Feltria, where he discovered that Bueno, like his predecessor Müller, had deserted, though unlike Müller he had not surrendered to the Austrians, but made his way with twenty companions to Rimini, and took ship to the United States. This was the first time that one of Garibaldi's comrades from South America had deserted. Many of his best officers were out of action from wounds or sickness. Jourdan had received a serious head-wound, and had to be left behind to die at Macerata Feltria; Zambianchi was crippled from a wound in his foot; Cenni was suffering from typhus, and Hoffstetter from gastric fever. Anita had suddenly felt the strain during the last few days, and was in a state of exhaustion. But Garibaldi himself was in the best of spirits, despite the fact that he had almost run out of cigars, having shared his few remaining ones with friends on the road to Macerata Feltria.[37]

His force was now reduced to 1,800 men. His chances of reaching Ancona or any other port, and seizing ships and embarking for Venice, seemed very remote. But ten miles to the north was the frontier of the tiny republic of San Marino, which had been an independent state for nine hundred years. This territory, no more than twelve miles long and at its broadest point four miles wide, might be an asylum for the hunted

Garibaldini. They pressed on northwards, and on the morning of 30 July reached the border. Garibaldi sent an envoy to ask the San Marino authorities if they would admit him and his men. Belzoppi, the Captain-Regent of the Republic, refused. Like all San Marinese, he was concerned above all to preserve the independence of the republic, and did not wish to give Austria any cause to invade their state; nor would it be easy for San Marino to feed and support 1,800 extra mouths for a prolonged period.

Garibaldi waited at the frontier all day, and in the evening sent Ugo Bassi to make a second attempt to persuade Belzoppi to let them in. Belzoppi remained adamant. Bassi was offered hospitality by a Radical café proprietor named Simoncini; but while he was eating his supper in the restaurant he could see, in the moonlight, from the hill on which the town of San Marino stands, the encircling camp-fires of another Austrian army under General Hahn approaching from the north. He quickly sent word to Garibaldi to warn him of the danger in which he stood. Garibaldi then ordered his men to enter the territory of San Marino without waiting any longer for permission, and they began to cross the frontier during the night of 30 July.

On the morning of 31 July Garibaldi rode into the main square of San Marino, and, entering the council chamber, formally asked the government for permission for his men to enter the republic as political refugees, surrendering themselves and their weapons to the authorities of the state. Belzoppi, making a virtue of necessity, granted his request. While Garibaldi was talking to Belzoppi, the Austrians caught up with his men as they waited on the border. The Austrians attacked the rearguard, which was still at the bottom of the hill. It is not surprising, in the circumstances, that the Garibaldini were dispirited. They had been waiting for twenty-four hours, without food or shelter, for permission to be interned in neutral territory; and in Garibaldi's absence their morale cracked completely. They fled in isolated groups up the mountain side, trying to escape from the Austrians and to reach the frontier. Hoffstetter and Anita tried to stop the panic and restore order, with Anita calling for Garibaldi – 'Where is Peppino?' – until at last Garibaldi returned from San Marino. Only the gunners who were guarding the little cannon that they had dragged all the way from Rome remained loyally at their post, and fought fiercely in defence of the gun; but after they had been deserted by their comrades, they were forced to abandon it to the enemy.[38]

Garibaldi was disgusted at the cowardice of his men, which even Anita had been unable to check, and again he thought wistfully of the deeds of heroism which his Legionaries had performed in South America.

The imposing presence of the American Amazon [he wrote eighteen months later] did not avail, at San Angelo in Vado and San Marino, to stop the fugitives. The word 'cowards', uttered by her in contempt, was borne away by the wind, and no longer wounded the ears of men who had lost their spirit. Ah, I must recall the glorious fields of San Antonio to forget the disgrace of San Marino.[39]

He somehow managed to herd the remnants of his shattered band into the territory of the republic. Archduke Ernst, who could have occupied the whole of San Marino in a few hours, halted his men on the frontier, and scrupulously observed the requirements of international law.

CHAPTER 21

THE DEATH OF ANITA AND THE
ESCAPE FROM MAGNAVACCA

THE people of San Marino received the Garibaldini with great kindness. The monks in the Capuchin monastery just outside the town of San Marino, who were not affected by the political passions which had been aroused in the Papal States, offered them hospitality in the monastery, and private citizens brought them comforts. At 2 pm on 31 July Garibaldi, sitting on the steps of the monastery, wrote his last order of the day to his soldiers. He discharged them from his army, and told them that they were free to return to private life. 'But remember,' he added, 'that Italy must not remain in infamy, and that it is better to die than to live as slaves of the foreigner.'[1]

The government of San Marino, out of regard for the interests of its citizens as well as out of sympathy for the Garibaldini, sent envoys to the Austrians to negotiate about the future of the defeated partisans. Archduke Ernst and General Hahn, like the other Austrian commanders, had received orders from D'Aspre not to negotiate or accept a surrender from the bandits; but circumstances had changed a little now that the Garibaldini had escaped to neutral territory. Archduke Ernst told the envoys from San Marino that as the Garibaldini were rebels against the Pope, he could only advise them to surrender unconditionally and trust to the mercy of their Pontiff-Sovereign; but he agreed to an armistice while the envoys discussed his answer with Garibaldi. After Garibaldi had rejected the suggestion that he should surrender unconditionally, the San Marinese sent an envoy to Hahn in Rimini, hoping that he would be more amenable than Archduke Ernst. Their hopes were justified, for Hahn sent a lieutenant to San Marino, who met Belzoppi and presented him with Hahn's surrender terms.

The Garibaldini were to surrender their arms and equipment to the authorities of San Marino, who were to hand them over to the Austrians, though San Marino was to retain the horses of the Garibaldini to compensate them for the trouble and expense which the republic had incurred. Garibaldi and Anita were to be granted a safe-conduct through the Austrian lines to a port, from where they were to take ship for the

United States. The rest of the Garibaldini would be permitted to return to their homes, if they were natives of the Papal States, and to leave the country if they were foreigners, and only those who had committed ordinary crimes would be punished. But Hahn was wise enough to safeguard his reputation against any allegations of bad faith in the future by expressly stipulating that these terms were not to be considered binding unless they were ratified by his commander-in-chief. This was General Gorzkowski at Bologna, for the Austrians had pursued Garibaldi out of the area of D'Aspre's command into Gorzkowski's. An armistice would be granted, which would remain in force until they heard Gorzkowski's decision. During the armistice the Austrians would not enter San Marino or attack the Garibaldini, unless the Garibaldini attacked them; and two officials of San Marino, and two of Garibaldi's highest officers, were to go to Hahn's headquarters at Rimini as hostages to ensure the observance of the armistice by Garibaldi.

Garibaldi rejected Hahn's terms. He objected to the article which exempted those guilty of ordinary crimes from the amnesty, as this could certainly have been used as an excuse to take proceedings against Zambianchi, Ciceruacchio's son Luigi Brunetti, and others of his band, who could have been tried for murder for having executed priests or participated in the assassination of Rossi. He also resented being required to hand over hostages to the Austrians before the terms had been confirmed by Gorzkowski, when the Austrians were not giving any hostages to him. But his secretary, Guerzoni, states that the chief reason why he rejected the terms was his objection on principle to entering into any negotiation with the foreign invader.[2] It was a gesture typical of Garibaldi, unwise but superb, like his decision not to retreat after the first day's battle at Costa Brava, and his rejection of the Howden-Walewski proposals in Montevideo. The outcome at San Marino shows that on this occasion at least his heroic defiance was justified.

Garibaldi decided to try to escape through the Austrian lines and reach Venice with his soldiers. On the evening of 31 July he contacted his men as secretly as possible and asked for volunteers to come with him to Venice. Only about 200 of them were still prepared to follow him. These included one whom he tried hard to persuade not to come – Anita. Despite her pregnancy and the exertions of the March from Rome, she had remained in excellent health and spirits until now; but a few days before, she suddenly became very tired, and on 31 July in San Marino she developed a fever. It was probably malaria, or some other disease which could be caught so easily and quickly in many parts of nineteenth-century Italy. She was obviously in no fit state to go with Garibaldi on the dangerous and arduous journey which lay ahead; but she insisted on coming. 'That manly and noble heart,' Garibaldi wrote in his memoirs, 'was indignant at all my warnings about that enterprise, and reduced me to silence with the words "You want to leave me." '3 Nor can he have been happy at the prospect of leaving her behind, to fall perhaps into Austrian hands. So the pregnant woman with a fever went on an expedition on which no prudent commander would have taken any soldier who was not a hundred per cent fit.

Garibaldi spent the evening at Simoncini's café. After having supper there with Anita, Ugo Bassi and Ciceruacchio, he went outside and sat down on a stone in the warm summer night, smoking cigars, studying a map of the area, and questioning some peasants about the best route to take. He set out at midnight with his 200 followers, after he had persuaded the porter to open the gates of the town secretly to let them out. About half of his men were mounted, and the other half were on foot. They slipped unobserved through the Austrian lines and headed west, away from the coast, following a precipitous route over mountain paths which they could never have found without the help of a local guide from San Marino named Zani, who earned his living by conducting tourists through the mountains, but on this occasion gave his services free. They marched in silence, passing the orders in whispers, and going most of the way in single file – Zani at the head, Garibaldi next, then Anita, then Ciceruacchio, then Colonel Forbes – his son had stayed behind in San Marino – then Ugo Bassi. A number of them lost their way in the darkness, including Hoffstetter, who, realizing that he could not re-establish contact with Garibaldi, made his way home to Switzerland. Early in the morning of 1 August they reached San Giovanni in Galilea, where they turned due north and pressed on towards the Adriatic. It was a hot and beautiful day. They stopped for two hours in the little village of Musano, and rested in the heat of the day in front of the village church. The church was afterwards reconsecrated by the bishop of the diocese, as it was thought to have been defiled by Garibaldi's presence.4

At midnight they reached Cesenatico on the coast, about twenty miles south of Ravenna. It was a fishing port, and there were many small ships in the harbour. Garibaldi decided to commandeer thirteen of them to transport his men to Venice; but as he himself was almost the only sailor in his band, he went to the Mayor's house, woke him up, and ordered him to supply the crews of the thirteen boats. There was a small garrison of nine *carabinieri* of the Papal armed forces in the town; but they were quickly disarmed and taken prisoner. The captain of the *carabinieri* was a keen Papal supporter, and some of the local Radicals, and some of the Garibaldini, urged Garibaldi to shoot him, as they were sure that he would try to send word to the Papal authorities and the Austrians that Garibaldi was there. But Ugo Bassi pleaded strongly for the man's life, and Garibaldi, with his usual humanity, did not shoot any of the prisoners, but took them with him in the boats. Though the Radicals in Cesenatico were glad to see the Garibaldini, the population as a whole was not. The fishermen resented being woken up in the middle of the night and forced to work to prepare their own boats for a journey to Venice, nearly a hundred miles to the north. The Mayor sent messengers to Cesena to ask the Austrian garrison for help; but Forbes had set up patrols at the entrance to Cesenatico, and they sent the messengers back.

Garibaldi wished to sail as soon as possible; but a strong gale had arisen, making it not only dangerous to put to sea, but almost impossible to get out of the harbour. The delighted fishermen said that it would now be impossible to go; but Garibaldi could not wait with the Austrians close behind him, and, to the indignation of the fishermen, ordered them to put to sea. He himself took charge of the operation, but the tackle broke repeatedly in the gale, and it took seven hours before the ships were ready to sail. Garibaldi expected the Austrians to arrive at any moment; but Forbes erected barricades at the entrance to the town, and stationed a force of musketeers there to hold them at bay if they arrived while the Garibaldini were embarking. Anita was exhausted, and her fever was worse. She sat on the pier watching, while Garibaldi ordered the protesting fishermen to work, forcing them to stand up to their waists in the water as they pushed the boats into position. The work had to be done, as he says in his memoirs, 'with sleepy and unwilling people who had to be driven by blows with the flat of our swords to make them achieve what was necessary'. At last they were ready, and set sail soon after dawn. Forbes was the last man to go aboard. The Austrians entered Cesenatico an hour later.

Garibaldi had to leave behind at Cesenatico his white horse, on which he had sat in front of the Porta San Pancrazio under the French fire on 3 June, and which had carried him from Rome to Cesenatico. He gave him to a friendly Republican in Cesenatico, and asked him to shoot the horse rather than let him fall into the hands of the Austrians.[5]

In San Marino the remaining Garibaldini waited to hear whether Gorzkowski would confirm the terms which Hahn had proposed. He repudiated them, and demanded the unconditional surrender of the Garibaldini, to the dismay of the San Marinese, who were left with over a thousand refugees in their 32 square miles of territory. Some of the Garibaldini tried to slip through the Austrian lines and return to their homes; others remained in San Marino for many months until the

Austrians had withdrawn from the frontiers of the republic. They came off better than those who tried to leave earlier. Both D'Aspre and Gorz-kowski had given orders that the captured Garibaldini were to be shot; and D'Aspre insisted that the order was to be carried out even if the victims carried passports issued by the San Marino authorities, or by Freeborn or Brown, the British and United States Consuls in Rome.

> I have ordered that all who are taken carrying arms shall be shot [he wrote on 3 August]. The Tuscans do not dare to order the death penalty, but as they have been placed under General Stadion's command they will carry out their orders on this subject; this is also the view of the Minister of the Interior. This measure will be carried out without regard to nationality or to the English or American passports with which this scum have been furnished by Mr Freeborn, who is more scum than they.[6]

The fate of the captured Garibaldini, as usual in such circumstances, depended largely on the whim of the local Austrian commander. Some of the Austrians allowed them to pass unharmed; others, going even further than D'Aspre's order, shot those whom they identified as having been members of Garibaldi's band, even though they had thrown away their arms before they were caught. Many were flogged and then allowed to go. One of these was Demaestri, who had been with Garibaldi in Montevideo and had been wounded and captured at Morazzone in August 1848. He had had his arm amputated, but had nevertheless volunteered to fight for the Roman Republic, and accompanied Garibaldi on the retreat to San Marino. Demaestri was captured by the Austrians at San Marino, and was severely flogged before being released to fight again with Garibaldi in Sicily eleven years later. 'Did I ever treat any of our Austrian prisoners in this way?' Garibaldi wrote in his memoirs.[7]

The Austrian jubilation at the defeat of the Garibaldini was spoilt by the fact that Garibaldi had escaped. 'This morning,' wrote Schnitzer-Meerau in Florence on 3 August, 'official news was received at GHQ of the complete defeat of Garibaldi's corps. The leader nevertheless succeeded in extricating himself once again from human vengeance. It is not known in exactly which direction he has escaped.' D'Aspre blamed Hahn and Archduke Ernst: by granting terms to Garibaldi, even though they had afterwards been repudiated by Gorzkowski, they had allowed Garibaldi twenty-four hours in which to escape from San Marino. D'Aspre believed that the lack of a unified command had been the real cause of the trouble, and that the lesson to be drawn from Garibaldi's escape was that the Austrian armies at Ancona, Bologna and Florence should be brought under a supreme commander;

but he did not like it when, three months later, both he and Gorzkowski were removed from their posts and replaced by a unified command under Prince von Liechtenstein. He complained that he had not even been thanked for his services against Garibaldi, and demanded a military court of inquiry to investigate his conduct of the campaign.[8]

The Garibaldini in their thirteen boats were able to get away from Cesenatico soon after dawn. The gale subsided, and they made good progress towards Venice. For some reason which Garibaldi does not explain, they were very short of drinking water, having evidently been unable to obtain a good supply at Cesenatico, probably because of a local drought. He and his men, though thirsty after the night's work, had to be satisfied with a small ration of water. Anita, whose fever was becoming worse, asked repeatedly for water, and her condition caused Garibaldi great anxiety and distress. They sailed north all day on 2 August and during the following night, passing Ravenna and arriving in the neighbourhood of the marshes around Lake Comacchio. They were about fifty miles from Venice.[9]

Garibaldi afterwards wrote that it was the moon which was their undoing. It was a clear moonlight night, being only two days short of the full moon. When they ran into an Austrian naval patrol under Captain Scopinich, they were clearly seen in the moonlight, and were ordered to halt. They refused, and the Austrians gave chase. The fishermen, realizing perhaps that this was a chance of liberation, worked as slowly as possible, though Garibaldi and his men threatened and beat them; and the Austrians gained on them. Garibaldi, realizing that they would soon be caught, gave orders to put in to shore and to try to escape overland. Under the Austrian fire, they made for land, aiming at a beach near Magnavacca. Three of the thirteen boats reached the shore. The other ten were captured, and their inmates taken prisoner on the Austrian warship, where they were subjected to the insults of the Austrian sailors and of the liberated fishermen of Cesenatico. Their captors spat in their faces, but did not shoot them out of hand.[10]

About thirty of the Garibaldini reached the beach. They included Garibaldi, Anita, Ugo Bassi, Ciceruacchio and his two sons, Livraghi and the lame Leggero. Anita was too ill to climb out of the boat, and Garibaldi had to carry her in his arms as he waded ashore. He gently laid her down on the beach to rest. They were out of sight of the Austrians, but knew that their pursuers would arrive at any moment, apart from the danger that there would be Austrian land patrols in the area. Some of the *carabinieri* whom they had brought as prisoners from Cesenatico were in the three boats which had reached the shore, including the Chief of Police; and as Garibaldi could not take them any further, and would not kill them, they had to be released, though it was obvious that they would immediately inform the Austrians that Garibaldi and his comrades were on the beach.[11]

Garibaldi ordered his men to scatter and make their escape as best they could. He advised them that the wisest course would be to go in groups of two or three, and try to make their way to Venice overland. He knew that their position was very serious, but in fact it was worse than he thought. He did not know that they had landed on an island, which was surrounded on the inland side by the waters of Lake Comacchio and the River Po, and that it was impossible to get away without a boat.

They bade each other goodbye, and the others went off, leaving Garibaldi alone on the beach with Anita and Leggero, who was to stay in his party. Garibaldi carried Anita into a maize field near the shore, and here they lay and rested, concealed by the maize. After a while Leggero went off to spy out the land. Garibaldi and Anita talked as they lay among the maize, and she asked him to take care of the children.[12]* Her spirit was unbroken, but her instinct told her that she would die and that Garibaldi would survive.

Soon afterwards Leggero returned with a man whom Garibaldi recognized at once. By a great stroke of luck the local squire in the area where they had landed was a friend of Garibaldi's, Giacomo Bonnet. He and his younger brother had fought for the republic in Rome under Garibaldi's command. The younger Bonnet had been killed in the attack on the Villa Corsini, but the other brother had survived. He had not followed Garibaldi out of Rome, but like most of the Republican soldiers had handed in his arms and had been allowed to return to his home.

In the early morning of 3 August Bonnet had heard gunfire from the direction of the sea. It had occurred to him that Garibaldi and his companions might be trying to make their way north to Venice, and when he heard the sound of firing he guessed that it was because the Austrian ships had caught up with the Garibaldini. He went down to the sea in case he could be of any help to Garibaldi. He arrived at the beach where Garibaldi landed just in time to see the party disperse, and Garibaldi go off with Anita in his arms, and with Leggero, towards the maize field. He had shouted to them, but they had not heard him. He realized that they were trapped on the island, and knew that he

---

*Garibaldi states that Anita's last words were about the children, and many writers have assumed that she spoke them in the cart on her way to the Guiccioli farm just before her death; but it would appear, from the sequence of Garibaldi's narrative, that it was in the maize field on the previous day. Anita seems to have been delirious and incoherent during the last thirty-six hours of her life.

must find them before the Austrians or the Papal police did. He went in search of them, and had met Leggero.[13]

Bonnet realized that it would only be a matter of hours before the Austrians began a systematic search of the island. The Papal government's troops and police would be eager to assist the Austrians, and so would many of the local people in this period of 'fierce reaction', as Garibaldi afterwards called it. The Papal supporters were spreading stories about the misdeeds of the Garibaldini, and the Public Health Officer of Cesenatico had written a heart-rending account of the horrors which had been inflicted on the peaceful inhabitants of the fishing port during the night when the Garibaldini were there. The priests denounced Garibaldi from the pulpits, and told their congregations that it was their duty to give all possible help to the authorities and the Austrians in catching him and his followers. Everyone knew that the Austrians would offer a large reward for information which led to Garibaldi's capture, and would severely punish anyone who helped him to escape. But there were revolutionaries and Radicals in the area who were prepared to risk their lives to save him.[14]

Bonnet took Garibaldi, Anita and Leggero to a nearby hut, where he left them while he went off to make arrangements for their further progress. When he returned, he found that Garibaldi and Leggero had changed out of their red shirts and put on peasants' clothes. It is not clear where they obtained these peasants' clothes; perhaps they were working clothes which some peasants kept in the hut, which may have been the reason why Bonnet took the three fugitives to the hut. The red shirts were afterwards found, and taken to Admiral Dahlerup.[15] Bonnet led Garibaldi, Anita and Leggero across the island to the Cavallini farm, which was in the charge of one of his Republican friends named Patrignani. Anita was too ill to walk, and Garibaldi, with the help of Bonnet and Leggero, had to carry her for two miles across the fields. The necessity of carrying Anita slowed down their progress very greatly, but they reached the farm safely, and laid Anita on a bed to rest. Patrignani provided her with some food and drink, but she could only swallow a little water and broth.

Bonnet warned Garibaldi that he had no chance of reaching Venice; and as the Austrians would certainly be guarding the roads to the north, he suggested that he and his Republican friends should try to lead Garibaldi and Leggero south to Ravenna, where there were still many Republican supporters and where they could hide until they had an opportunity to escape abroad. As for Anita, Bonnet told Garibaldi that he would have to leave her behind. It was essential for her to see a doctor at once, and if she went with them she would certainly not survive the journey; and her presence, by slowing them down and making them so easily identifiable, would greatly reduce their chances of escape. Bonnet said that they could go to the Zanetto farm, which was on the lake at the northern end of the island, where they could leave Anita in the care of a Republican doctor who could be trusted. Garibaldi agreed to go to Ravenna instead of Venice, and eventually reluctantly accepted Bonnet's arguments about the necessity of leaving Anita at the Zanetto farm.

Bonnet left Garibaldi, Anita and Leggero in Patrignani's care, and arranged to meet them in a few hours' time at the Zanetto farm. He went to the town of Comacchio, where he arranged for two boatmen to take Garibaldi and Leggero off the island. While he was in Comacchio he heard that Ugo Bassi was staying at the inn, the Albergo della Luna, in the town. Bassi had not attempted to hide, because he thought that, as a non-combatant who had never borne arms, he would not be harmed by the Austrians. Bonnet was convinced that Bassi's confidence was misplaced, and went to the inn to warn him. He arrived just too late. He found Bassi in bed, and persuaded him to dress at once and fly; but at that moment Austrian soldiers surrounded the inn and caught Bassi as he tried to escape through the window.

Meanwhile Patrignani had found a cart in which Anita could travel, and after dark led Garibaldi and Leggero, pushing Anita in the cart, from the Cavallini farm to the Zanetto farm. Earlier in the day a troop of Austrian soldiers, who were looking for Garibaldi, had marched past the gate of the Zanetto farm; but Garibaldi and his party did not encounter them on their journey. Garibaldi explained to Anita that he would have to leave her at the Zanetto farm. But Anita was now delirious. She clung to him hysterically, and whispered her usual reproach: 'You want to leave me.'

This made it impossible for Garibaldi to go without her. When Bonnet arrived at the Zanetto farm, Garibaldi told him that Anita had done so much for him that he could not refuse her last request, and would have to take her with him. It was a mad decision, but in such circumstances sentiment is stronger than reason. The idea of leaving Anita to fall perhaps into Austrian hands while he himself escaped, was too painful for Garibaldi to contemplate; for though the Austrians might have let her go unharmed, there had been cases in which they had flogged women revolutionaries. From Garibaldi's point of view, it is well that he did not take a decision which he might have regretted all his life; for he would never have forgiven himself if he had left Anita to die alone or in an Austrian prison.

Before leaving the Zanetto farm, Garibaldi changed into a suit of clothes of Bonnet's, which was evidently thought to be a more suitable disguise then the peasant clothes. There is a conflict of evidence as to whether he shaved off his beard. Then the boatmen arrived, and Garibaldi, Leggero and Anita embarked. As the boatmen were not active Republican supporters, Bonnet did not tell them the identity of their passengers; but he had no reason to distrust the boatmen, and returned to his house at Comacchio thinking that the fugitives were in safe hands. But while the boatmen were rowing across the lake they realized whom they were carrying – perhaps because they identified Anita. They refused to take them any further, saying that they would be shot if the Austrians found out what they had done, and they landed Garibaldi, Leggero and Anita on a small island in the lake, called the Tabarra di Agosta, and rowed away. It was three o'clock in the morning. The fugitives were marooned, and could not escape. They would have to wait there until the Austrians found them, which was likely to be soon if the boatmen went to the nearest police station or Austrian army post and claimed the reward for Garibaldi's capture. There was nothing that Garibaldi and Leggero could do except to try to keep Anita warm as she lay, feverish and delirious, on the ground.

But though the boatmen were too frightened to help Garibaldi, they did not wish to claim the reward, perhaps because the idea had not occurred to them. They went back to Comacchio, and next morning told everybody whom they met that they had left Garibaldi with his wife and a friend on the Tabarra di Agosta. One of the people whom they told was Bonnet's sister-in-law. She went at once and told Bonnet. Bonnet found a boatman named Guidi, who was a convinced Republican, and explained to him that he must rescue Garibaldi, Leggero and Anita; and it was Guidi and his brother, not the Austrians, who found them there at 8 am on the morning of 4 August, and took them off the island after five anxious hours.[16]

That same day Admiral Dahlerup issued a jubilant communiqué which in due course was published in most of the leading newspapers throughout the world. It announced that on the night of 2 August the Imperial and Royal brig of war, the *Oreste*, had sighted more than twenty boats off Comacchio proceeding in the direction of Venice. The commander of the *Oreste*, thinking that it might be a desperate attempt on the part of Garibaldi to reach Venice, gave chase, and after firing a few shots captured most of the boats.

It was learnt from the prisoners that the notorious Garibaldi, with his wife, a doctor, a priest and a small number of the officers of his staff, seeing the danger which threatened them, had run their boats ashore on the beach between Magnavacca and Volacca, and boats were immediately sent to pursue them. According to some of the countrymen who were there, Garibaldi, his wife and his companions took refuge on land, almost naked and without arms, and are followed by a hundred individuals at most, of whom twenty or twenty-five are armed. They say that most of them have retired into a wood five or six miles from the shore.

This information was so inaccurate that it is possible that the countrymen who supplied it may have been Republican sympathizers wishing to mislead the Austrians. The official Austrian newspaper, the *Gazzetta di Milano*, after publishing Dahlerup's communiqué, added: 'The necessary steps have already been taken to secure Garibaldi and the other fugitives.'[17]

Guidi rowed Garibaldi, Anita and Leggero from the Tabarra di Agosta to the mainland. Anita was barely conscious; she was moaning softly and foaming a little at the mouth. Guidi realized that she must get to a doctor at once. He fetched a cart with a mattress for Anita from a neighbouring farm, and then took her, with Garibaldi and Leggero, to a large and isolated farmhouse eleven miles away on the Marquis Guiccioli's dairy farm, which was one of the collection of scattered farms which were known as the village of Mandriole. The Guiccioli farm was managed by the Marquis's agents, two brothers named Ravaglia, who were Republicans. They met several peasants on the way, but no Papal police or Austrian troops. After stopping at various farms on the way to get water for Anita, they reached the Guiccioli farm at about 4 pm. Guidi had arranged for a Republican doctor named Nannini to be brought to the farm, and he arrived at almost the same moment as his patient.

Garibaldi appealed to Nannini to do all he could to save Anita. Nannini said that she must be put to bed at once. Garibaldi, Leggero, Guidi and the doctor each took hold of one corner of the mattress on which Anita was lying and carried her into the farmhouse and up the stairs to a bedroom on the first floor. On the stairs Anita gave a last gasp. As they put her down on the bed, they realized that she was dead.[18]*

Guidi did not find it easy to persuade Garibaldi to leave Anita's body; but at last Garibaldi agreed to go, after he had asked the Ravaglia brothers to give Anita a decent burial. Guidi took Garibaldi and Leggero to the village of Sant' Alberto, where they hid in the house of a Republican supporter. When Garibaldi woke next morning, he peeped through the shutters and saw some Austrian soldiers walking in the village street. He and Leggero were moved for safety to a second house in Sant' Alberto; but his friends thought that it was too dangerous to stay in a village in which Austrian soldiers were quartered, and

*There is a conflict of evidence as to whether Anita died at 4 pm or at 7 pm.

Garibaldi and Leggero were taken to a hiding place in the great pine forests north of Ravenna.[19]

On 5 August General Gorzkowski in Bologna issued a proclamation which was published in the press and printed on placards which were fixed to the walls in the towns and villages throughout the district. It declared that though most of the Garibaldini had been captured off Magnavacca, a number of them had escaped inland,

> among them this same Garibaldi, who has with him his wife in a fairly advanced stage of pregnancy. All right-thinking people, and particularly those in the country districts, are alarmed that this dangerous individual is at large. Everyone is reminded that it is forbidden to aid, shelter or show any favour to the criminals, and that it is the duty of all good citizens to repulse them, and to give all possible help in finding them and in delivering them up to justice; *and warning is given that Summary Military Justice will be inflicted upon anyone who knowingly aids, shelters or shows favour to the fugitive Garibaldi or to any other individuals of the band led and commanded by him.*[20]*

Although the Italian Republicans, and most historians, have stated that Gorzkowski announced that anyone who helped Garibaldi would be shot this is not strictly accurate, because the Austrians always distinguished, in their proclamations under martial law, between offences for which 'summary military justice' would be inflicted and those which were punishable by death. But the wording of the proclamation was ferocious enough to make the inhabitants of the district believe that their lives would be in danger if they helped Garibaldi.

Ugo Bassi was taken to Bologna with Captain Livraghi, one of Garibaldi's officers, who had also been arrested at the Albergo della Luna. In several of the villages through which they passed, Bassi was insulted and mocked by the parish priest. He was remembered and admired in Bologna, where he had lived for most of his life, for his austerity and self-sacrifice, and for his devotion to the poor; but as a 'renegade priest' he had aroused the violent hatred of the ecclesiastical authorities. According to the Republicans, the Austrians handed over Bassi for one night of torture to the priests in the penitentiary prison in Bologna. He was tried by an Austrian court martial on the charge of bearing arms in defiance of the Commander-in-Chief's proclamation. He denied that he had ever borne arms, though he had accompanied the Garibaldini as their chaplain. The court was not interested in fine distinctions, and immediately found him guilty and sentenced him to death. Livraghi, who was a Lombard, was an Austrian subject, and had been called up for military service in the Austrian army

*The passage in italics was printed in italics both in the press and on the placards.

while he was fighting for the Italian cause. He was now charged with desertion to the enemy in wartime, and like Bassi was condemned to death.

General Gorzkowski knew the feelings of the Papal authorities towards Bassi, and was anxious to obtain their endorsement of the death sentence. The matter was referred to the Papal Legate in Bologna, Cardinal Bedini, who had been the Nuncio in Montevideo. Less than two years before, Garibaldi and Anzani had written to Bedini, when they heard the first news of Pius IX's reforms, offering the services of their Italian Legion to the Pope; and Bedini had thanked them for their 'devotion and generosity towards our Supreme Pontiff'.[21] Bedini afterwards stated that he had made great efforts, behind the scenes, to save Bassi's life; but according to the Liberals he summoned a meeting of the Ecclesiastical Council of Bishops in Bologna, and asked them to sign a document consenting to Bassi's execution. The Council consisted of nine Italians and three Hungarians. All the Italians signed; the Hungarians refused. On 8 August, within twenty-four hours of reaching Bologna, Bassi and Livraghi were taken to a place about a mile outside the town, and shot.

Before his execution, Bassi was degraded from the priesthood. The Liberals alleged that the priests, while performing the ceremony of degrading the hands that had consecrated the Host, scraped the palms of his hands with knives until they were covered in blood.[22] D'Aspre tried to dismiss this as the propaganda of the newly appointed British Vice-Consul at Bologna, McCarthy, and complained to Schwarzenberg that McCarthy had written to Palmerston and to the British Minister in Florence 'that a priest who was a member of Garibaldi's band was shot at Bologna after he had first had his fingers cut off. I suppose he refers to the religious ceremony which perhaps precedes the execution. I shall be surprised if this pretty story does not appear in the newspapers.' D'Aspre urged Schwarzenberg to insist that McCarthy be recalled.[23]

Ciceruacchio and his two sons, with several companions, managed to get off the island, and made their way towards Venice. For ten days they travelled northwards, and had covered about twenty-five miles and had entered the province of Venetia before they were betrayed to the Austrians by an informer. Nine of them were sentenced to death. They included Captain Parodi, who had come from Montevideo with Garibaldi; the burly wine-merchant, Ciceruacchio, the hero of the Trastevere; his eldest son, Luigi Brunetti, who had perhaps murdered Rossi; and the younger son, a boy of thirteen. They were marched to the place of execution, and stood waiting, while some peasants, at the orders of the Austrian commanding officer, dug nine graves. Then they were all shot, including the thirteen-year-old child, though for many years afterwards there were rumours that they had escaped and were still alive.[24]

But the man whom the Austrians most wanted to shoot was not caught. Garibaldi owed his life to the members of the underground Republican organization. He and Leggero hid by day in a concealed place in the pine forests of Ravenna. At night a member of the underground came to find them, and guided them along paths through the forest till they saw a fire burning. The men around the fire were not woodcutters, as they pretended to be, but revolutionary supporters. The guide made sure, by code whistles, that it was safe to approach the fire, and then led Garibaldi and Leggero to the group around the fire and handed them over to their care. One of the group led Garibaldi and Leggero on through the wood to another hiding place, where they lay hidden all next day, till nightfall, when the man came for them again, and led them to another guide at another fire. One day, when they were lying in their hiding place, a body of Austrian soldiers came by. They were close enough for Garibaldi and Leggero to hear them talking in German; but the soldiers did not see the fugitives.

Garibaldi and Leggero reached a suburb of Ravenna in safety, and hid there in a worker's house for several days. They then set off again, travelling mostly by night, led on by one supporter to another, south-westwards into Tuscany – the direction in which the authorities would least expect them to go. One of their helpers was the parish priest of Modigliana, Don Giovanni Verità, who hid them in his house and acted as their guide.

It was almost inevitable that one day something should go wrong with the arrangements, and this occurred near Filigare. For some reason, the guide whom they were to meet did not come, and they found themselves left to their own resources. This was a serious set-back, as they did not know the country; but they had to go on. As dawn came, they found themselves on the main road from Bologna to Florence. They knew that it would be dangerous to be on the road during the daytime, because they expected it to be patrolled by Austrian soldiers; but they decided to risk it, and hired a cart with a driver, who drove them along the road towards Florence. On the way they passed a corps of Austrian soldiers marching towards Bologna, who paid no attention to them.

In the evening they came to an inn at Santa Lucia, paid off their driver, and entered the inn. They ordered a cup of coffee, and sat down at a long table in the dining room of the inn. Garibaldi was so tired that he fell asleep at the table, resting his head on his arms. A few minutes later, Leggero woke him with a gentle nudge. Raising his head, Garibaldi saw that some Croat soldiers of the Austrian army had entered the inn. Garibaldi lowered his head and pretended to go to sleep again. After a while, the Croats left. 'As soon as the inn was cleared,' wrote Garibaldi, 'and we had had our coffee, after our masters had been served, we crossed the road, and sought and found shelter in a peasant's house to the right of it.'*[25]

This is the story that Garibaldi wrote in his memoirs eleven years later. A different version of what is certainly the same story was afterwards told by the innkeeper's daughter, Teresa Baldini, who was a beautiful girl of twenty in 1849. Her story was not published until 1892 – twenty years after Garibaldi's memoirs had appeared, and ten years after his death; and though it has since become one of the most famous incidents in Garibaldi's career, its authenticity must be questioned. Teresa says that as soon as Garibaldi entered the inn, she recognized him, because she had seen him in the previous November when he called at the inn with his men on his march from Florence to Ravenna; and she accosted him with the words: 'The Austrian and Tuscan soldiers are looking for you.' Before he could hide, some Croat soldiers had entered the inn, and sat down at the same table with Garibaldi and Leggero. The only light in the inn was from a lamp on the long table. Garibaldi, realizing that it was shining in his face, went up to the lamp, under pretence of needing a light for his cigar, bent down to light the cigar from the flame, taking care as he did so to put his head between the lamp and the soldiers so that they should not see his face, and turned the lamp round so that he and Leggero would now be in the shadow. He sat silently smoking his cigar while the Croats boasted of how they would soon capture 'the infamous Garibaldi'; but they were looking at the girl, not at the two men sitting at their table. After the Croats had left, the innkeeper's daughter took Garibaldi and Leggero to a peasant's hut, where they could hide in safety before proceeding on their way.[26]

Although this story has been generally accepted, it seems almost impossible to reconcile it with Garibaldi's version in the memoirs. Garibaldi might no doubt have forgotten various points of detail; but it is very difficult to believe that he would have failed to mention that the innkeeper's daughter tried to save him, and would instead have impliedly criticized the staff at the inn for serving the Croats first. It seems more likely that Teresa, having identified the inn from Garibaldi's description of it in the memoirs, not only added a few colourful

---

*The account of Garibaldi's escape from Sant' Alberto to Santa Lucia follows his own account in his memoirs. Other authors give additional details, some of which are almost certainly fictitious, having been invented in some cases in order to uphold a bogus claim by the story-teller of having helped Garibaldi to escape.

details, but told a version in which she played an active part in saving
the hero's life. It is also difficult to believe that the Croat soldiers
were actively searching for Garibaldi in Santa Lucia on 24 August,
because it had not occurred to the Austrian authorities that he had
gone that way.

No one outside the secret revolutionary organization had any idea
where Garibaldi was. On 16 August the Piedmontese Radical newspaper, *La Concordia*, published a full report of Garibaldi's arrival in
Venice with Anita. It described how Garibaldi had stood with Manin
on the balcony of Manin's residence, acknowledging the cheers of the
crowd, while Signora Manin was welcoming Anita and supplying her
with all her needs. Next month, when the true facts were known, *La
Concordia* was mercilessly ridiculed for this report by the Conservative
satirical newspaper of Turin, *Smascheratore*; but the journalist of *La
Concordia* may have published it in order to help Garibaldi by misleading the Austrians into believing that he had safely reached Venice,
and therefore into calling off their search for him. But this news of the
Garibaldis' arrival in Venice was received with great scepticism by the
Austrian military authorities in Italy and by many other people.[27]

On 21 August D'Aspre in Florence wrote to Schwarzenberg that
he had just been informed by an Englishman whom he employed as a
spy that Garibaldi and Anita were hiding in San Marino, where the
spy had seen Garibaldi on 16 August, and that Garibaldi was planning
to escape to the coast, with about twenty Americans in his band, and to
take ship to the Ionian Isles – which were then British territory – and
from there to go on to England. D'Aspre considered the possibility of
sending a small party of cavalry to make a raid into San Marino to
seize Garibaldi; but he hesitated to create an incident by violating the
territory of the republic without more reliable evidence of Garibaldi's
presence there. D'Aspre was very ready to believe that Garibaldi was
heading for British territory, because, like many other Austrian officials
and European Conservatives, he was convinced that Palmerston and
the British government were responsible for the revolutionary movements in Italy and Europe. He wrote to Schwarzenberg on 15 August
that he had no doubt that Garibaldi and his followers 'enjoy the secret
protection of England'.[28]

The *Gazzetta di Milano* and the *Gazzetta di Bologna*, after confidently
reporting for two or three days that Garibaldi's capture was imminent,
had lapsed into complete silence about where he was. But on 20 August
they were able to publish a story which was given full prominence in
the world press. Some peasants working on the Guiccioli farm in the
village of Mandriole had seen a dead hand protruding from the ground,
and had found that it belonged to the corpse of a woman. The woman

was in the sixth month of pregnancy, and appeared to have been strangled. None of the local inhabitants could identify the body; but the authorities had no doubt that she was 'the wife or woman who was accompanying Garibaldi'. The managers of the farm, two brothers named Ravaglia, had been arrested and charged with her murder.[29]

In fact what had happened was that the Ravaglias had secretly buried Anita's body during the night of 4 August in a sandy waste on the farm, intending to give it a better burial later; but they had not buried it deep enough, and some dogs, burrowing in the sand, had found the corpse and begun eating it, in the course of which they bit through the larynx, thus making it appear that Anita had been strangled. The Ravaglia brothers, facing a murder charge, were in a very unfortunate position, as they could not expect either Garibaldi, or the other persons who had been present when Anita died, to come forward as witnesses for the defence. But Dr Nannini courageously went to the authorities and told them a story that was partly true. He said that on the afternoon of 4 August he happened to be visiting the farm, and that while he was there a party of people whom he did not know, but whom he now realized must have been Garibaldi and his supporters, arrived carrying a woman who was suffering from a severe fever and was at the point of death; and she died soon after she arrived. This story was eventually believed by the authorities after the medical evidence had confirmed that Anita had died of natural causes and that the neck wounds were caused by dogs; and the Ravaglias were released. But unofficially the Papal supporters circulated the story that Anita had been strangled by the Republicans because she was impeding Garibaldi's escape. The Papal judicial authorities received two anonymous letters accusing the Ravaglias of murdering Anita. She was portrayed by the writers of these letters as an innocent female who had fallen victim to the wickedness of Radical revolutionaries; and as Dr Nannini had disappeared after making his statement to the police, this was seen as a proof of his guilt by the local Papal supporters.

Both the Austrian and the Papal authorities acted with more restraint and impartiality than they have ever been given credit for by the Italian Republicans. The Papal judicial authorities decided to drop all charges of murder against the Ravaglias in view of the medical evidence; and on 5 September they were informed by the Austrian High Command in Bologna 'that considering that the temporary shelter granted to the fugitive spouse of Garibaldi in the Ravaglias' house for reasons of humanity' occurred before the publication of Gorzkowski's proclamation of 5 August, which announced that all who sheltered the Garibaldini would be punished, it was not possible to take any action against them on this account. On 5 October Bedini, who has been so criticized for his brutality in the case of Ugo Bassi, wrote to the Minister of the Interior in Rome pointing out that the offence of the Ravaglias in giving shelter 'to Garibaldi's woman, to Garibaldi himself and to his followers' was committed on 4 August, the day before Gorzkowski's proclamation of the 5th, and that he saw no reason why the Papal authorities should be more zealous than the Austrians themselves in punishing Garibaldi's supporters.[30]

Bonnet was arrested on suspicion of having helped Garibaldi to escape; but he was released. He lied convincingly during his interrogation, and gave nothing away; but he was sure that he was going to be shot. Soon after his arrest he happened to catch a glimpse of a local newspaper in his prison, and saw a report that he, with Ugo Bassi and other Garibaldian bandits, had been taken to Bologna to be shot; and his worst fears were confirmed when he was placed in the cell which Bassi had occupied before his execution. But after he had spent a few weeks in prison he was suddenly told that he could go free. He probably owed his freedom to the fact that General Gorzkowski had been replaced by a more lenient Commander-in-Chief, Prince von Liechtenstein, at Bologna. Many years later, the government of a liberated and united Italy, after much obstruction and after repeated demands from Garibaldi, agreed to pay Bonnet a pension for the rest of his life as a reward for his services to Italy in August 1849.[31]

The 169 Garibaldini who had been captured at sea after leaving Cesenatico were also eventually released. They were fortunate to have been captured at sea and not in the Papal States, and to fall into the hands of Admiral Dahlerup and not of Field-Marshal D'Aspre or General Gorzkowski. Dahlerup ruled that as they had been captured, not as rebels in the Papal States, but at sea on the way to fight for Venice, they must be regarded as prisoners of war, and he sent them to Pola, in Austrian territory in Dalmatia. They had to run the gauntlet of a hostile crowd of civilians when they landed, being spat on by the women of Pola; but in October Forbes was released after the British government had intervened on his behalf, and all his colleagues were freed soon afterwards.[32]

From Santa Lucia, Garibaldi and Leggero travelled on through Tuscany. They were planning to reach the frontier of the Kingdom of Sardinia, which was the only state in which the Liberal régime had not been overthrown, and to cross into the Sardinian province of Liguria. Their chief anxiety was that they had lost contact with the revolutionary organizations, and as they did not know the country they could not go along the footpaths and byways, but had to follow the main roads, where there was much more likelihood of capture.

On the evening of 25 August they reached an inn near Prato. A young man named Sequi was drinking in the inn, and telling everyone that he hoped that Garibaldi would escape. Garibaldi's intuition told him that the young man could be trusted. He drew him aside and told him that he was Garibaldi. Sequi immediately offered to help him escape, and to put him in touch with his friends. Garibaldi was right to trust Sequi, and Sequi was right to trust Garibaldi, who might have been an *agent provocateur* trying to trap revolutionaries. A man's physical appearance is often a good clue to his political affiliations, and if Sequi looked like a Radical, Garibaldi was justified in taking a calculated risk, in view of the importance of getting into touch with the revolutionary organizations.[33]

From now on, Garibaldi and Leggero were again in the hands of reliable local guides, who led them, from one guide to another, across Tuscany and towards safety. But their new contacts told them not to aim for the Sardinian frontier, which was well guarded by the Tuscan and Austrian forces, who expected that Republican supporters would try to escape that way. It would be much safer to make for the coast further south, and find a fisherman who would take them to Liguria by sea. So at Prato they turned south. At Volterra they passed under the walls of the prison where Guerrazzi and many other political prisoners were awaiting trial. D'Aspre and the Austrian government had prevented Grand-Duke Leopold from pursuing a policy of reconciliation with the Liberals, and had insisted that Guerrazzi be tried for treason, though the death sentence was respited, and Guerrazzi was allowed to go into exile after three years in prison. To D'Aspre's indignation, Leopold had insisted on entering Florence in the uniform of the National Guard; but under pressure from D'Aspre he had worn Austrian uniform at a gala performance at the opera a few days later. This association with Austria was to cost him his throne in 1859.[34]

In the last days of August, Garibaldi and Leggero reached the village of San Dalmazio in a remote spot in the hills above the sea near Follonica. It was nearly three weeks since there had been any mention of Garibaldi in the newspapers. In San Dalmazio, twenty miles from the west coast, they waited for several days while their friends made the final arrangements for their departure by sea. By 1 September all was ready, and they set out at 9 pm with half a dozen companions. They carried sporting guns, pretending to be hunters out for a night's shooting, though the guns could be used in combat if they met the enemy.

At 2 am they reached a farmhouse four miles from the sea, where they had arranged to wait and rest. Suddenly a stranger appeared at the door. He was a Hungarian soldier in the Austrian army. He said that he was a revolutionary, a supporter of Kossuth, that he wished to desert from the army, and that he had heard that Garibaldi was embarking that night and hoped to escape with him. Garibaldi wished to take the man with them, but his friends would not take the risk, in case the Hungarian was an Austrian agent; they said that they would arrange for his escape some other time, but not in a boat which was carrying Garibaldi. It was disturbing that a soldier in the Austrian army, however well-intentioned, had heard about Garibaldi's plans for departure.[35]

They set off through the night, walking through a thick and almost impenetrable forest in order to avoid a coastguard station on the road, and at dawn reached the coast at an isolated spot on the Cala Martina. The island of Elba, clearly visible from the coast, was twenty miles away. The fishermen were waiting for them in the boat. Garibaldi and Leggero went aboard, and waving to their friends on shore and calling out 'Long live Italy!' sailed away. They landed at Elba to take on supplies, and then sailed north along the coast, without meeting any enemy ships; and two days after leaving the mainland, on the morning of 4 September, they landed at Porto Venere, near Spezia, in the Kingdom of Sardinia. They travelled overland from Porto Venere northwards along the coast to Chiavari, where they lodged at the house of one of Garibaldi's relatives. On 7 September *La Concordia* revealed that they had reached Chiavari; and the news spread all around the world that Garibaldi was safe.[36]

CHAPTER 22

FROM CHIAVARI TO NEW YORK

THE government of Sardinia was not pleased that Garibaldi had arrived at Chiavari. Their armies had been soundly beaten by the Austrians at Novara in March, and after Charles Albert had abdicated and escaped to Portugal, his son, the new king, Victor Emanuel II, tried to obtain the best possible terms from the victors. At his famous interview with Radetzky at the Austrian headquarters, the young King had won better terms than he could have hoped for, including the right to maintain a Liberal constitution in his kingdom, chiefly because he had persuaded Radetzky that he was determined to stamp out Republicanism and Radicalism in Sardinia and crush the Mazzinian party. Victor Emanuel and his ministers did not wish to antagonize Austria by showing friendship to Garibaldi, or to outrage public opinion in the country by repudiating him. Garibaldi was not expecting a friendly welcome from the Sardinian government, and therefore considered asking for asylum in a British ship in Leghorn instead of landing on Sardinian soil; but he was eager to see his children in Nice, if only for a short time.[1]

When the Intendant of Chiavari heard that Garibaldi had arrived, he asked him not to leave the town for the time being, and not to stir up any popular demonstrations. Garibaldi agreed to both these requests; but next day, on the evening of 6 September, the Intendant arrested Garibaldi after consulting the government in Turin, on a charge of entering the country illegally. The police called at the house where Garibaldi was staying, and, with the greatest courtesy, asked him to accompany them; and during the night he was taken to Genoa. The Intendant had hoped to keep the matter secret; but news of the arrest leaked out at once, and a considerable crowd gathered to see Garibaldi and his escort leave Chiavari at 10 pm. They reached Genoa at 4 am. Garibaldi was imprisoned in a room in the Ducal Palace, which was the headquarters of General La Marmora, the Military Governor of Genoa.[2]

The news of Garibaldi's arrest caused a great outcry in the country. *La Concordia* demanded his release, and the campaign was taken up in the Parliament in Turin. The Left-wing parties had a majority in Parliament, but they were in Opposition, because Victor Emanuel, believing rightly that he had the support of the electorate, had appointed a Conservative government to ratify the peace treaty with Austria, which the Radicals were opposing. The Opposition MPS argued that Garibaldi, as a Sardinian subject, was free to enter the country at all times; but the government was able to quote against the Liberals the constitution of 1848 which they were so anxious to preserve in the face of Austrian pressure. It laid down that a Sardinian subject would forfeit his nationality if he served in the armed forces of a foreign power without the consent of the Sardinian government, and Garibaldi had not obtained the government's consent before entering the service of the Roman Republic. He had therefore forfeited his Sardinian nationality, and as an alien who had entered the country without permission, he could be arrested and deported without trial.

This statement aroused even more indignation in Parliament and in the press, and the rumour spread that the Sardinian government was about to hand over Garibaldi to the Austrians. The government hastened to deny that they had any such intention; but they insisted that Garibaldi must leave the kingdom, though he could go to any other country that was willing to receive him. The MPS demanded that he should be allowed to stay. The government then reminded them that a year ago, during his guerrilla campaign in the Lake Maggiore district, Garibaldi had seized money from the town council at Arona, on the Sardinian shore of Lake Maggiore, without any lawful authority, and that he faced a prosecution for theft, or for obtaining money by menaces, if he remained in the country. The Opposition moved a vote of censure on the government for its treatment of Garibaldi, and after an angry debate the motion was carried without a division with only a handful of MPS opposing it.* The Turin Conservative newspaper, *Armonia*, reported that when Parliament discussed a government bill two days later, the Opposition MPS were much quieter than usual, because they had all lost their voices through shouting so much during the debate on Garibaldi two days before.[3]

One of the few MPS who supported the government in the debate on Garibaldi's arrest was Count Camillo di Cavour. He explained his attitude at length in an article in his newspaper, *Il Risorgimento*, in which he deplored the rudeness and hysteria which the Opposition MPS had shown in the debate, and accused them of using Garibaldi as an excuse to attack and embarrass the government at a time of national

---

*Jessie White Mario states that eleven members, including Cavour, voted against the motion, and that four abstained. The official report states that the motion was agreed without a vote being taken.

emergency. Garibaldi, he wrote, had been ill-served by those who claimed to be his friends.[4]

The Right-wing Catholic press adopted a much more hostile attitude than Cavour did towards Garibaldi. The Genoese newspaper, *Il Cattolico di Genova*, went so far as to imply, by sly phrases and an ironical exclamation mark, that Garibaldi was a party to Anita's death. They reported that when Anita died at Mandriole, 'Garibaldi for the first time, according to what he himself says, shed some tears(!)'[5]

Garibaldi was treated with every consideration by the prison authorities in Genoa. He was allowed to receive as many visitors as he wished, and his friends, his supporters and journalists flocked to see him. The prison authorities moved him into a larger room so that there would be less congestion at his press conferences. General La Marmora visited him, and was most friendly. Garibaldi told La Marmora that he did not wish to embarrass the Sardinian government, and was quite willing to go to the United States, provided that he could be allowed to visit his children in Nice before he left. La Marmora agreed that Garibaldi should spend twenty-four hours in Nice if he gave his word of honour to return after this time to Genoa and to take ship for Tunis, from where he could proceed at his leisure to Gibraltar, Liverpool and New York.[6]

After five days in detention, Garibaldi was released, and he embarked at Genoa for Nice. The people of Genoa had heard that he would be sailing on the steamer *San Giorgio*, and great crowds turned out to see him go aboard. Many of them hired small boats, and clustered around the steamer as she lay at anchor in the harbour, waiting to sail; and they demanded to see Garibaldi. The sailors told them that Garibaldi was not on board; he had in fact been smuggled on board the Sardinian warship, the *San Michele*, on the evening before. When the *San Giorgio* moved off, she sailed across the harbour, and stopped at the harbour entrance near where the *San Michele* was anchored. A boat set out from the *San Michele* with Garibaldi on board, and transferred him to the *San Giorgio*. The crowd at the other side of the harbour realized what was happening. There was a great shout of 'There's Garibaldi!' and the boats in the harbour and the people on the quay hurried to the harbour entrance where the *San Giorgio* lay; but before they reached her she had sailed for Nice with Garibaldi on board. The ship's master was Garibaldi's old friend, Captain Pesante, with whom he had made his first voyage as a young sailor. Pesante showed him every consideration during the voyage, and insisted on vacating his own captain's cabin and handing it over to Garibaldi's use.[7]

On 13 September the *San Giorgio* arrived at Nice, to find that the harbour was full of boats and the quayside crowded with people awaiting Garibaldi. He received another enthusiastic welcome. The Intendant of Nice was less friendly to Garibaldi than the officials in Genoa had been. He referred to him, in a letter to La Marmora, as 'ex-General Garibaldi', and angered Garibaldi by preventing him from landing for several hours, thus shortening the time available for him to spend with his mother and children; but eventually he was allowed to land, and was escorted by the cheering crowds to his mother's house. After seeing his mother, he went to the Deiderys' house, where Anita had left the children when she set out for Rome. Menotti would be nine in a few days' time; Teresita was four, and Ricciotti two and a half. Teresita said to Garibaldi: 'Mother has been to Rome; she will have told you how good I have been.' When they asked where their mother was, Garibaldi was too overcome by emotion to answer them, and left the task of telling them to the Deiderys.[8]

He spent the night in his mother's house, and then, as he had promised, returned to the *San Giorgio*, which had waited for him in the harbour. For the second time his mother saw him go into exile – not, this time, as an unknown young revolutionary hothead, but as a national hero. They were never to meet again. Garibaldi reached Genoa during the night of 14 September, and transferred to the *San Michele*, where General La Marmora visited him next day. Garibaldi and La Marmora had a long talk, and both were very understanding of the other's position. In this hour of defeat Garibaldi, rejected on all sides and suffering from the bitter personal loss of Anita, showed qualities of realism and statesmanship which were in great contrast to the attitude which Mazzini and the Piedmontese Radicals were adopting. He had perhaps realized, as a result of his experiences, that the liberation of Italy was going to be a very difficult task, in which the Republicans would need the help of all possible allies; and his attitude in September 1849 paved the way for his policy of support for the King and government of Sardinia which he adopted ten years later.

La Marmora was impressed by Garibaldi's attitude, and reported to Pinelli, the Minister of the Interior, that Garibaldi had been most co-operative. He had kept his word and returned from Nice at the agreed time, and had done nothing to incite disorders; indeed, all the gatherings of the people who had come out to see and cheer him in Chiavari, Genoa and Nice had been peaceful and orderly.

Garibaldi is not an ordinary man [wrote La Marmora to General Dabormida], his features, though uncouth, are very expressive. He speaks briefly and well; he has great insight; and I am more than ever convinced that if he was driven to fight for the Republican party, it was because the State rejected his services. I do not believe him to be a Republican out of principle. It was a great mistake not to make use of him. If there is another war, he will be a man to employ. How he managed to save himself on this last occasion is really a miracle.[9]

When Pinelli heard that Garibaldi was being so amenable, he asked La Marmora to get Garibaldi to sign a statement declaring that he was going into exile of his own free will. Such a statement would have been useful to Pinelli, who had had to bear the brunt of the Radical attack in Parliament and in the press for the arrest and deportation of Garibaldi; but La Marmora did not receive Pinelli's letter until after Garibaldi had sailed; and in any case, as he told Pinelli, he would have hesitated to strain Garibaldi's goodwill by asking him to sign the statement.[10]

La Marmora, on behalf of the Sardinian government, offered to pay Garibaldi a pension for the maintenance of his mother and family in Nice, and for his own use during his first months of exile. The Mazzinian writers, and the historians who followed them, stated that Garibaldi refused the pension, thus showing both his contempt for money and his refusal to accept a bribe from the hated royal government of Sardinia. The Sardinian Prime Minister, Massimo d'Azeglio, wrote in later years that although Garibaldi had refused the pension for himself, he had accepted it on behalf of his family, which led Jessie White Mario to declare that Garibaldi had not accepted any pension, and that if his family in Nice received anything, it could only have been because the Sardinian government sent them money without Garibaldi's knowledge. In fact Garibaldi, quite legitimately, accepted pensions both for his family and for himself, and signed receipts for both payments. On 11 September, before his departure for Nice, he received 2,000 lire from La Marmora in fifty-lire notes, which he gave to his mother in Nice; and after his return to Genoa, during his talk with La Marmora on board the *San Michele* on 15 September, he agreed to accept a pension of 300 lire a month for himself. La Marmora paid him 1,200 lire as the first quarterly payment.[11]

La Marmora also agreed to Garibaldi's request to allow Leggero and Cucelli to sail for Tunis with Garibaldi at the government's expense.[12] Cucelli, who had been with Garibaldi in Montevideo, was the musician of the Italian Legion, and had composed the revolutionary patriotic songs which they had sung in the ship on the journey back to Europe.

They sailed from Genoa on the afternoon of 16 September in the Sardinian steamship *Tripoli*, under Captain Millelire. They reached Tunis at 4.30 pm on 19 September, only to find that the Bey's government refused to allow Garibaldi to land. Tunis, though in theory a dependency of the Sultan of Turkey, had been very largely infiltrated by French commercial interests. Garibaldi stated in his memoirs that the Bey refused to allow him to enter the country as a result of pressure from the French government; but there is no record of any such pressure in the French diplomatic correspondence, and it seems that the Bey's decision not to annoy France by admitting Garibaldi was a quite spontaneous one.

The Bey suggested that Garibaldi should go to British territory in Malta; but the *Tripoli* was due to sail next day for Cagliari, on the south coast of the island of Sardinia, on her return journey to Genoa. The Sardinian Consul in Tunis, realizing that his government would not be pleased if Garibaldi was on board the *Tripoli* when she arrived at a Sardinian port, asked permission for Garibaldi to land and stay in Tunis for a few days until the steamer *Minos* sailed for Malta. The Bey would only agree to this if he could obtain a definite undertaking from the British authorities that Garibaldi would be allowed to land in Malta; and as this could not be obtained before the *Tripoli* was due to sail, Captain Millelire had no choice but to take Garibaldi with him to Cagliari.

They reached Cagliari on 21 September. The Intendant of Cagliari refused to allow Garibaldi to land, and ordered Millelire to take him on to Genoa; but after Millelire had convinced the Intendant that the government would be most displeased if Garibaldi returned to Genoa, the Intendant gave Millelire an escort of thirty-five naval personnel and twenty dragoons and ordered him to sail to the little island of La Maddalena, off the north-east tip of the island of Sardinia, where he was to land Garibaldi, Leggero, Cucelli and the dragoons. They arrived at La Maddalena on 25 September. Garibaldi was lodged in the house of Lieutenant-Colonel Falchi, the Governor of La Maddalena, who treated him with every consideration. Falchi wrote to Admiral D'Auvare, who had been put in charge of the operation of getting rid of Garibaldi, that he was not holding Garibaldi in detention, though he was keeping him under very strict surveillance.[13]

The island of La Maddalena, which is about two miles off the coast of Sardinia, is some four miles long and three miles wide. On the eastern side of La Maddalena, across a strip of water less than half a mile wide, is the island of Caprera, a little smaller than La Maddalena. Today there is a causeway between the two islands, but this did not exist in Garibaldi's lifetime. La Maddalena and Caprera, surrounded on all sides by the sea and by the hills on the neighbouring islands, may have aroused sentimental memories for Garibaldi, because they resemble in many ways Anita's home town of Laguna. After his first visit to the district in 1849, he wrote that he had found peace in La

Maddalena after the upheavals of a tempestuous life; and five years later he settled down in Caprera, which was uninhabited in 1849, and made it his permanent home. During his stay in La Maddalena he became friendly with his host, Colonel Falchi, and with the Mayor of La Maddalena, Susini, who was the father of Major Susini of the Italian Legion in Uruguay, whom Garibaldi had left in command of the Legion in Montevideo when he went to Salto in 1845, and to whom he had finally handed over the command when he returned to Italy. For Leggero, it was a home-coming, for he was born in La Maddalena.[14]

But some of the Conservatives in Turin were worried about Garibaldi's presence on La Maddalena. They started a rumour that he was planning to carry through a revolution and seize power in the island. The country was affected to some extent by the general mood of reaction in Italy and throughout Europe; in the general election next month, the Left-wing Opposition lost many seats, and the Conservatives gained a majority in Parliament. The government was determined not to let Garibaldi remain anywhere in the kingdom; and Garibaldi was still willing to go to Malta, Marseilles, or preferably to the United States. He was eager to earn his living, and became worried to an almost obsessional extent at the prospect of living on the charity of others. He wished to return to the sea as a merchant seaman, and believed that his friends in the United States could provide him with the necessary capital to acquire his own ship.[15]

The Sardinian government asked the British Minister in Turin, Mr Bingham, if Garibaldi could go to England. Bingham replied that Garibaldi, like all foreign political refugees, was free to come to England, from where he could proceed, if he wished, to the United States; and Bingham promised to write to the Governor of Gibraltar, asking him to assist Garibaldi to do this.[16]

Garibaldi stayed on La Maddalena for a month. On 6 October the Sardinian government ordered a warship, the sailing brig *Colombo*, to sail specially to La Maddalena and take Garibaldi to Gibraltar; but though the *Colombo* left Genoa at once, she was held up by contrary winds, and did not reach La Maddalena till 23 October. Garibaldi embarked next day with Leggero and Cucelli, and after a voyage of sixteen days reached Gibraltar on 9 November; but to Garibaldi's surprise and distress, the British authorities there made difficulties about allowing him to land.[17]

The Governor of Gibraltar, Major-General Sir Robert Gardiner, was aged sixty-eight and had served under Wellington in Spain and at Waterloo. He was much less sympathetic to Garibaldi and Italian revolutionaries than the younger British diplomats in Rome, Florence and Turin. He was a hard man, who, a few weeks earlier, had aroused a controversy by ordering a convict in the hulks at Gibraltar to receive forty-eight lashes for insubordination, although Lord Grey, the Secretary of State for the Colonies, had thought that a period of solitary confinement would have been a sufficient punishment. He also had a brusque manner which sometimes caused offence, and which led Grey to deplore the fact that Gardiner 'was wanting in that courtesy which a Governor might properly combine with a firm refusal of application which he may consider it his duty not to grant'.[18]

The Sardinian Consul at Gibraltar asked Gardiner for permission for Garibaldi to land and remain in Gibraltar till he could proceed to England. The Consul found it very difficult to persuade Gardiner to agree, even though he showed him Bingham's letter on Garibaldi's behalf. The British government had been involved in disputes in the past with Spain about the presence of revolutionaries in Gibraltar; and Gardiner believed, as he wrote both to Lord Grey and to Bingham, that 'Gibraltar is certainly no place for Political Refugees'. Eventually Gardiner agreed that Garibaldi should land in Gibraltar and stay there until 15 or 16 November, when the next ship was due to leave for England, provided that the Sardinian Consul gave the usual security that Garibaldi would leave by that date; and Garibaldi landed on 10 November. Garibaldi was therefore quite right when he wrote in his memoirs that the British authorities only allowed him to stay in Gibraltar for six days; and the statement that he was granted permission to remain there for fifteen days, which has been made by some historians, is based on an inaccurate report from Captain Demoro, the commander of the *Colombo*, to Admiral D'Auvare.[19]

Although Garibaldi knew that he would be allowed to enter England, he was not eager to go there. As he had lived all his life in countries with warm climates, he did not wish to spend the winter in either England or the United States, but would have preferred to stay in Spain or Tangier and proceed to the United States next spring. He applied to the Spanish Consul for permission to go to Algeciras and from there to Cadiz; but, not surprisingly, this was refused. The United States Consul then offered to send Garibaldi to the United States in an American warship which was in the harbour at Gibraltar; but Garibaldi preferred the Mediterranean winter. He then heard that the government of the King of Morocco was prepared to allow him to go to Tangier, and that the Sardinian Consul there, Giovanni Batta Carpeneto, was ready to offer hospitality to him, and to Leggero and Cucelli, in his house.[20]

Meanwhile General Gardiner had heard from Captain Demoro of Garibaldi's change of plan. He immediately wrote to the Sardinian Consul in Gibraltar and warned him that if Garibaldi wished to go to

Tangier, the Consul must see to it that he was put on board a ship which left Gibraltar before the next ship for England sailed on 15 or 16 November, because Garibaldi's permit to stay in Gibraltar could not be extended.[21]

The tone of Gardiner's letter was somewhat abrupt, and it was even more curt and offensive in the Italian translation into which it was rendered by the officials at the Sardinian consulate. If Garibaldi saw the letter, it is not surprising that he resented Gardiner's attitude; but the Governor's decision was approved by Lord Grey, and presumably by Palmerston, who received copies of the correspondence from Grey. Garibaldi still resented his treatment in Gibraltar when he wrote his memoirs eleven years later. 'If this kick to the fallen had been given by the vile or the weak – never mind! But from a representative of England, the land of asylum for all – that knocked me considerably.' It is surprising that there was no outcry in Britain about the attitude of the authorities at Gibraltar; but the incident was not reported in the British press. After having been hot news all over the world for many weeks, Garibaldi had suddenly ceased, for the moment, to interest the foreign press, and only the Italian and Spanish newspapers reported his movements after his departure from La Maddalena.[22]

On 14 November, the day before the next ship sailed for England, Garibaldi left Gibraltar in the Spanish steamer *La Nerea*, and crossed to Tangier.[23] He stayed there for seven months. For the first time in his life, he felt dejected, though he made every effort to maintain his spirits. He was physically exhausted, and liable to rheumatism and arthritis. He was bitterly disappointed at the developments in Italy, not so much by the victory of the Austrians and the French and the triumph of the counter-revolution, as by the apathy, and in many cases the hostility, which so many of the Italians had shown to him and his men and to the revolutionary nationalist cause. There was also the personal tragedy of Anita's death, and the separation from his children, and from his mother, to whom he had always been deeply attached, despite their political differences, and to whom he wrote affectionate letters during his exile. Perhaps he was more conscious of the loss of Anita now, in the calm of Tangier, than he had been in the exciting and dangerous weeks immediately after her death, though it was not until he published his memoirs that he revealed to the world how much her death had affected him. In his letters from Tangier he lamented only the political disasters which had occurred and the sorrows of Italy. In none of them did he refer to his personal tragedy, or make any reference to Anita; but his grief at her death, and his general depression, is shown by the fact that, according to all the available evidence, the years which followed 1849 was the only period of his life, until his old age, in which he had no love affairs and showed no interest in women.

He became friendly in Tangier with his host, the Consul Carpeneto. He admired Carpeneto for his refusal to have social contact with the Austrian Consul in Tangier. In a letter to Valerio, the editor of *La Concordia*, he described Carpeneto as a 'true champion of Italian honour', and added: 'We Italians should be grateful to anyone who refuses to associate with the tyrants who drink our mother's blood.' This policy of non-fraternization with the oppressor was being effectively pursued in Italy, especially in Milan and Venice, where the members of Italian high society were refusing all invitations to the Austrian balls and receptions, and where even the prostitutes, in most cases, were refusing to have anything to do with Austrian soldiers; but it was not the official policy of the Sardinian government. Carpeneto had in fact acted without consulting his government in offering hospitality to Garibaldi; but though the Prime Minister, d'Azeglio, informed him that he would have preferred it if Garibaldi had not been staying in his house, d'Azeglio thought that this did at least have the advantage that Carpeneto could keep Garibaldi under close observation. D'Azeglio told Carpeneto to inform him immediately if Garibaldi left Morocco, and to discover his destination.[24]

Garibaldi became friendly in Tangier with the British Vice-Consul, Murray, who often invited him to his house. At least twice a week Garibaldi went on shooting expeditions in the Atlas Mountains behind Tangier, as he had done in the hills near Nice when he was a child, or went fishing in a boat at sea. Carpeneto and Cucelli sometimes accompanied him on these shooting and fishing expeditions; but he felt lonely, and described his life in Tangier as 'savage and solitary'. In his loneliness he came to value the friendship of a dog, Castore. When he left Tangier he gave Castore to Murray, and afterwards heard that the dog had pined away and died of grief at his absence.[25]

Garibaldi wrote his memoirs in Tangier. He did not intend, at this time, to publish them; but the manuscript which he wrote in Tangier was published nine years later, in an English translation, by Dwight in New York, and in the following year in Italian by Carrano. The manuscript, which ran to about 60,000 words, covered the whole period from Garibaldi's birth to his departure from Montevideo, though he virtually ignored the last two years in South America, after the Battle of the Daimán. He made very few alterations in the text when he published the final version of the memoirs in 1872. The manuscript which he wrote in Tangier did not deal with his recent experiences in Italy, and it was not until eleven years later that he continued the story beyond April 1848.

On 24 November 1849, ten days after he arrived in Tangier, he wrote to his old friend and colleague, Pacheco y Obes, who had once more been removed from power in Montevideo by being given the post of Uruguayan Minister in Paris. In his letter, Garibaldi freely expressed his grief at the political situation in Italy, but made no reference to Anita, though Pacheco had known her well. 'As for Italy, she is today, to put it mildly, in the most shameful slavery, and there is no hope at present of liberating her from her foreign and native tyrants. God, time, and a generation of punishment will avenge her.' He expressed his friendship for Pacheco and his love for Montevideo. 'God protect Montevideo! . . . my glorious and martyred country of adoption . . . that land of freedom and sacrifice.'[26]

At about this time Pacheco, in Paris, became involved in a controversy which led to one of those political libel actions which, then as now, were a feature of French public life. The French government was still supporting the Unitarians in Montevideo in their war against Rosas and Oribe, but those French newspapers which were subsidised by Rosas continued their propaganda on his behalf and their attempts to persuade the French government to abandon Montevideo. They launched a violent campaign against Pacheco, whom they denounced as a murderer and war criminal; and he sued them for libel. Both sides used the courtroom as a forum for their political propaganda. The defendants relied chiefly on Pacheco's order of 12 February 1843 for the shooting of native-born Uruguayans who were captured fighting for Oribe, on the reprisal decree of 7 October 1843, and his action in executing the four prisoners of war at the Cerro and the shooting of Baena for communicating with the enemy;* but they also brought Garibaldi into the libel action. They reminded the court and the public that one of Pacheco's leading collaborators in the defence of Montevideo had been the notorious Garibaldi, who had fought against the French in Rome; and they declared that for France to give support to Garibaldi's friends in Montevideo was an affront to the widows and orphans of the French soldiers who had fallen at the gates of Rome. Pacheco resisted the temptation to dissociate himself from Garibaldi, though he referred to him as little as possible at the trial. He declared that Garibaldi was a gallant, honourable man whom he was proud to call his friend, and that every French soldier who had fought at Rome respected Garibaldi as a brave and chivalrous enemy. The result of the case, as so often in French political libel actions, was inconclusive. The jury acquitted the defendants on the criminal charge, but vindicated Pacheco, and the defendants were ordered to pay his costs.[27]

*See, *supra*, Chapter 11, pp. 152–3, 165.

Alexandre Dumas also championed the cause of the Unitarians in Uruguay in his book *Montevideo, or a new Troy*, which was published, almost simultaneously with three of his long novels, in 1850. In his book he paid tribute to Garibaldi, though he deplored the fact that tragic circumstances had led to Garibaldi fighting against France.[28]

In June 1850 Garibaldi left Tangier, bound for the United States. He left behind in Tangier Leggero, who had been with him throughout, since they slipped out of San Marino, and Cucelli, because he could not afford to pay their fares to the United States; but he took with him Major Bovi, who had lost his right arm in the defence of Rome and had recently arrived in Tangier, because he thought that Bovi would find it difficult to earn his living without his right hand.[29]

On 13 June Garibaldi arrived in Gibraltar from Tangier; but General Gardiner was able to report that he had left the same day for Liverpool in the British steamship *The Queen*. He reached Liverpool on 22 June, and stayed for four days at the Waterloo Hotel. He kept his visit as quiet as possible, and it was almost ignored in the press. The Liverpool newspaper, *The Albion*, reported his arrival in a very short paragraph which was reproduced in the London *Daily News*; but *The Times* did not think it worthy of mention. The *Red Republican*, the Chartist weekly edited by George Julian Harney, reported his visit after he had left, and regretted that a suggestion made in its correspondence columns, that a presentation should be made to Garibaldi, had come too late to be acted on.[30]

The only newspaper which gave any prominence to Garibaldi's visit was the *Liverpool Mail*. Garibaldi went shopping in Liverpool, and talked to the shopkeepers in his halting English; and in the course of the conversation he told some of them that he was Garibaldi. A reporter on the *Liverpool Mail* got to hear of it, and found Garibaldi in the Waterloo Hotel. 'His manners are pleasing and lively,' wrote the reporter, 'but in general his demeanour is staid and grave.' The proprietor of a concert hall in Liverpool, who had also discovered that Garibaldi was in the city, announced, without consulting Garibaldi, that Garibaldi would be attending the performance at the concert hall on the following Saturday; but Garibaldi, who had never had any intention of going to the concert hall, had already sailed on Thursday 27 June for New York in the United States steamship *Waterloo*.[31]

The *Waterloo*, a steamer of 1,200 tons owned by the New York shipping line Spooner Sparks and Co., and flying the United States flag, was one of the many ships which sailed regularly between Liverpool and New York. At this time, when steam navigation was making rapid progress, speed records for the Atlantic crossing were being continually broken; the record was eleven days in June 1850. Earlier in the year the *Waterloo* had made the crossing in eighteen days; but on this voyage she took thirty-three days. This was fortunate for Garibaldi and the other passengers, as it enabled them to avoid the hurricane which struck shipping off the Atlantic coast of the United States on 20 July. One of the victims of the hurricane was Margaret Fuller Ossoli, coming home from Leghorn on the *Elizabeth*, which was wrecked off Fire Island, within sight of land, and went down with no survivors. The Marchioness of Ossoli had with her the almost completed manuscript of a book which she had written on her experiences under the Roman Republic. Her friend Thoreau searched the beaches for the manuscript, but could find no trace of it. The loss was as great for twentieth-century historians as for the nineteenth-century Radicals.[32]

Whatever Garibaldi's personal desires may have been, there was no chance that his arrival in New York would pass unnoticed like his visit to Liverpool. The Italian Committee in the United States had made full preparations for his coming. The President of the Committee was the old revolutionary of the Carbonari, Felice Foresti, who had spent eighteen years in the dreaded dungeons of the Spielberg in Moravia, and in other Austrian prisons, and since 1837 had held the Chair of Italian Literature at Columbia College. After the collapse of the Roman Republic, Avezzana and Filopanti, who had been secretary to the Triumvirs in Rome, had come to the United States and joined Foresti as the leaders of the Italian community. Another prominent member of the community was Antonio Meucci, a prosperous business man who had succeeded in a number of commercial ventures and gave a considerable part of his profits to help the cause and the Italian refugees in the United States. The Italian leaders had friendly contacts with the chief American supporters of Italian freedom, such as Theodore Dwight and Henry Theodore Tuckerman, and with many influential citizens of New York.

Foresti and his committee had arranged a civic welcome for Avezzana, and the former Minister for War of the Roman Republic had been welcomed by the Mayor of New York at a great banquet at the Astor Hotel after a ceremonial parade through the streets of the city. The New York authorities now planned a similar reception for Garibaldi and for General Paez, who arrived in New York a few hours before Garibaldi. This Venezuelan leader, of pure Indian blood, had been one of Bolivar's lieutenants in the struggle for freedom against Spain in South America, and after being dictator of Venezuela had been overthrown, imprisoned and exiled.

The city dignitaries and the public had been ready to welcome Garibaldi on 25 July, because the press had incorrectly reported that his ship was due to arrive on that day; but next day they announced that he would not be arriving for another four or five days. Mayor Woodhull announced that he would meet the ship when she arrived. The management of the Astor Hotel suggested to the Italian Committee that Garibaldi should stay at the hotel as their guest. The French and German Socialists in New York planned a joint project to participate in the welcome to Garibaldi and to try to give it a peculiarly Socialist flavour. On 28 July the United Committees of the Democratic Socialist Republicans of the French and German Nations issued a statement that at 'the reception of this beloved General' only persons wearing red badges would be admitted. The Italian Committee did not wish to see the welcome to Garibaldi turned into a purely Socialist affair, and promptly told the press that the organizing committee 'hope to see Republicans of all nations and shades of opinion together on that occasion, and do not think of prescribing any other distinctive badges than the flags of their respective countries'.[33]

At 10 am on 30 July the *Waterloo* docked at Staten Island, five miles from New York, where all persons arriving from abroad had to wait for a few days in quarantine. Soon after leaving Liverpool, Garibaldi had suddenly experienced a violent attack of rheumatism which prevented him from walking, and he had to be carried off the ship. He had last been crippled with rheumatism eighteen months before, when he was in Rome in February 1849 for the proclamation of the Republic; it was fortunate that he had not had an attack in the neighbourhood of Lake Comacchio. The passengers were met on arrival by Dr Doane, the Health Officer of the port, who made a long speech welcoming Garibaldi, to which Garibaldi made a very brief reply. Dr Doane then ordered that the red, white and green tricolour, the flag of the Roman Republic, should fly, together with the Stars and Stripes, over the Quarantine Buildings in honour of Garibaldi.

Garibaldi was carried to a sofa in the Quarantine Buildings, where he received a stream of visitors who called on him during the afternoon, among them General Paez, who was also waiting in quarantine on Staten Island. The two refugee-generals talked to each other in Spanish for a little while. Dr Doane examined Garibaldi, and told the press that the rheumatism was improving, and that it would be possible for Garibaldi to attend the civic reception in a few days' time.[34] But Garibaldi, who had not authorized the Health Officer's statement, had no intention of taking part in a civic reception. He showed his usual self-effacing modesty, which so endeared him to his friends, and was undoubtedly sincere, though it was sometimes interpreted as a sanctimonious pose by his critics, and occasionally caused inconvenience and disappointment to his supporters, and damaged the Republican cause. Ignoring the propaganda value, in the United States and in

Europe, of a great public demonstration in his honour, he was determined that no civic reception or banquet at the Astor should be held.

As soon as the period of quarantine expired, on Sunday 4 August – it was the first anniversary of Anita's death – Garibaldi left Staten Island without telling anyone, and took the ferry-boat to Manhattan, hoping to arrive in New York without anyone noticing. He might have succeeded had it not been for the fact that some prominent Italians and Germans were on their way to visit him on Staten Island, and ran into him at the very moment when he arrived at South Ferry on the Manhattan shore. 'The Germans were introduced to him as European Republicans,' wrote the *New York Daily Tribune*, 'and welcomed him to the Model Republic. The General replied that he looked upon them as brothers; that all true Republicans were so; that through the brotherhood of the people ultimate freedom would be secured.' Garibaldi then went in a carriage to the house of a friend in Hastings Village, some ten miles north of New York City; and the *New-York Daily Tribune* announced that he had agreed to take part in the civic welcome on 10 August. The civic reception for Paez had been held on 2 August.[35]

On 7 August Garibaldi wrote a letter to the Italian Committee, which was published in the press next day. He refused to have a civic welcome. He announced his intention of applying for United States citizenship, and thanked the people of America for their feelings of sympathy for the Italian cause.

> Though a public manifestation of this feeling might yield much gratification to me, an exile from my native land, severed from my children, and mourning the overthrow of my country's freedom by means of foreign interference, yet believe me that I would rather avoid it, and be permitted, quietly and humbly, to become a citizen of this great Republic of Freemen, to sail under its flag, to engage in business, to earn my livelihood, and await a more favourable opportunity for the redemption of my country from foreign and domestic oppressors.[36]

CHAPTER 23

NEW YORK, LIMA, CANTON

GARIBALDI stayed for a fortnight in Hastings Village, and then lived for six weeks with Foresti in the house of an Italian named Pastacaldi in Irving Place, where Foresti rented a room. New York had grown, within the lifetime of its older inhabitants, from a town with a population of 60,000 to one of 700,000, and the population had doubled in the last ten years, owing chiefly to immigration from Europe. Fifty years before, woods and fields had covered the ground which now contained the imposing red-brick Gothic buildings of Upper Broadway, Fifth Avenue, Fourteenth Street, Union Place and Madison Square.[1]

Garibaldi was visited in Pastacaldi's house by Theodore Dwight, who met him for the first time. Like most other people who met Garibaldi, Dwight was greatly impressed at first sight by his quiet strength.

> He has a broad and round forehead; a straight and almost perpendicular nose, not too small, but of a delicate form; heavy brown moustaches and beard, which conceal the lower part of his face; a full, round chest; free and athletic movements, notwithstanding ill health, and a rheumatism which disables his right arm . . . an easy, natural, frank and unassuming carriage, with a courteous nod and a ready grasp of the hand.

Dwight was one of the few people who realized that Garibaldi's eyes were dark, and not blue. He was impressed by 'the courtesy of his movements . . . the freedom of his utterance and the propriety and beauty of his language'. When he talked about the situation in Italy, he spoke calmly but quickly and with great clarity, never hesitating for a word, and completely without pose or pretention.

Dwight tried to persuade Garibaldi to allow him to publish the memoirs which Garibaldi had written in Tangier. Garibaldi agreed to give his manuscript to Dwight, but would not agree that it be published. From time to time during the next nine years, Dwight pressed Garibaldi to change his mind; and eventually in 1859 Garibaldi authorized Dwight to arrange with A. S. Barnes and Burr for it to be published in an English translation in New York, and by Sampson Low and Co. in London.[2]

Soon after he arrived in New York, Garibaldi, at Dwight's request, wrote a number of short biographical essays about some of his comrades-in-arms. The first essay which he wrote was about Anita. It contained some additional material about Anita's activities in South America which he had not mentioned in his memoirs; and he added a brief account of her courage during the retreat from Rome and of the events leading to her death. For the first time he expressed in writing his grief at the loss which he had suffered through the death of 'the American amazon, the martyr of Italian liberty', and called on God to protect his children. 'And, my Sons! when you are asked, Where are your parents? say, We are orphans for Italy.'[3]

In his short sketch of Ugo Bassi, Garibaldi not only praised Bassi for his Christian virtues, but contrasted them with the vices of the orthodox clergy, whom he never forgave for their treatment of Bassi.

> Bassi fell the victim of the priests, who directed the Austrian bullets. Infamous priests! sellers of Italy! you sold the life of Bassi, as you have sold the life of Italy. Priests! the religion of Bassi shall yet be the religion of Italy. But your religion! ah, yes! it can be nothing else than the religion of hell! . . . The Pope is Lucifer. . . . The watchword, in the day of vengeance, shall be 'Bassi!'

These passages appealed strongly to the violent anti-Catholic feeling which was widespread among American Protestants in 1850.[4]

On 1 October Garibaldi left Irving Place and moved to Meucci's house in a little side street in the village of Clifton on Staten Island, which is now part of Richmond Borough. He wished to return to his old career as a merchant seaman. He had never taken his master's first-class certificate, because his call-up into the Sardinian Royal Navy in 1833, and his subsequent exile and revolutionary preoccupations, had prevented him from qualifying for it; but his second-class certificate was sufficient to allow him to command a ship in the merchant navy. A more serious difficulty was the fact that he was not an American citizen; but he made a formal application for American citizenship, and hoped that in the meantime he would be allowed to command an American ship, for permission to do this could be granted to aliens in special cases. Meanwhile his friends arranged for him to go on a pleasure cruise to the isthmus of Panama in the *Georgia*, a fast steamship. She left New York on 11 November and reached Savannah on the 14th and Havana, in the Spanish colony of Cuba, on the 16th. Garibaldi went on to Chagres, on the Atlantic coast of the isthmus of

Panama. He had returned to Havana by 30 November, and reached New York on 7 December.[5]

Garibaldi was unhappy about living at Meucci's expense, and was determined, whatever his friends might say, to work for his living. He suggested to Meucci that he should open a sausage factory at Clifton in which Garibaldi and other penniless Italian refugees could be employed. Meucci started the sausage factory; but Garibaldi was no better as a business man now than he had been when he was in Rio de Janeiro, and the sausage factory was a financial failure. Meucci, who was a good business man, quickly closed it down and opened a candle factory instead, which prospered and continued for nearly fifty years. It was on the premises immediately adjoining Meucci's house in Clifton, and, like the sausage factory, gave employment to poor Italians. Despite Meucci's efforts to dissuade him, Garibaldi insisted on working in the candle factory. He was almost useless when he tried to make the candles, because he was not skilful at dipping the wick into the tallow; but as he was physically strong he could perform the unskilled labour of carrying barrels of tallow from the Vanderbilt landing wharf to the boiling vat in the factory.[6]

He took some recreation while he was living in Clifton. He sometimes played bowls on an open-air bowling ground frequented by Italians in New York Avenue, by the water's edge. He would go for walks along St Mary's Avenue in Rosebank and Richmond Terrace in Livingstone, and went shopping in the market at Stapleton. He sometimes went to New York and played dominoes, or joined in the conversation, at Ventura's Bar in Fulton Street, near Broadway, which was frequented by journalists and writers, and by actors from the nearby Park Theatre. He went fishing with Meucci in a fishing smack which they named the *Ugo Bassi*, and went shooting by himself in the woods on the Dongan Hills on Staten Island. On one occasion when he was out shooting, he broke some local by-law, and was hauled before the district magistrate. When the magistrate discovered who the defendant was, he dismissed the case immediately. Garibaldi appeared in court on another occasion, when he volunteered to give evidence for the plaintiff in an action of assault arising out of an incident on the ferry-boat between Staten Island and Manhattan. A large crowd assembled in the courtroom to see Garibaldi. He gave his evidence in Italian, and it was translated into English. He spoke very quietly, but was effective as a witness.[7]

He took a keen interest in the welfare of the Italian community in New York, and allowed his name to be used in connexion with charitable appeals. One of these was on the occasion of a charity concert to raise money to help the Italian refugees. The star attraction was a child prodigy of Italian origin, Adelina Patti, who in 1850, at the age of seven, began a career as a singer which continued until 1914.[8]

Garibaldi agreed to sit on a committee which was set up to decide how to spend the remains of the money which had been raised by donations to assist the cause of Italian liberation at the time of the revolutions of 1848. Henry Theodore Tuckerman first met him at a meeting of this committee at Foresti's house in Irving Place. When Tuckerman first arrived at the meeting, he did not know who Garibaldi was, but was immediately struck by the powerful personality of the short, broad-shouldered man who sat in the corner of the room, and who spoke quietly, briefly, and very much to the point when he made his contribution to the discussion.

> Without the superficial vivacity and the exaggerated manner so common to the Italian temperament [wrote Tuckerman], there yet was revealed a latent force and feeling all the more impressive from the contrast it afforded to the voluble and dramatic utterance of his countrymen. His calm manner, comparatively slow movement, and almost Saxon hair and beard, might have seemed characteristic of a northern rather than a southern European; yet his eye, voice and air were essentially Italian.

It was decided to spend the money in assisting the Italian political refugees.[9]

Garibaldi was eager to contribute personally to the relief of the poorer refugees, though he had very little money or property of his own to spare. On one occasion he was visited at Meucci's house by a poor Italian who told him that he was so poor that he could not afford to buy a new shirt to replace his tattered one. Garibaldi said that he would give the man one of his shirts; but he had only two shirts, the one which he was wearing and another that was in the wash. He then remembered that he had with him in a trunk the red shirt that he had worn during the fighting in Rome, and he offered to give it to the man. Meucci protested against Garibaldi giving away so valuable a souvenir, and said that he would give the poor man one of his own shirts if Garibaldi would let him have the red shirt. Garibaldi agreed, and the red shirt is still preserved in the museum of the Masonic lodge in Richmond Borough.[10] This, at least, was the accepted tradition, which had already been published in writing in the lifetime of the people who knew Garibaldi on Staten Island; but it is difficult to explain how Garibaldi could have had with him on Staten Island one of the red shirts which he wore in Rome, all of which would presumably have been left behind in Rome, San Marino or in the hut at Magnavacca.

Garibaldi also concerned himself with the political quarrels which were disrupting the harmony among the Italian refugees in New York. In England and Switzerland, nearly all the Italians were followers of Mazzini; but in the United States Foresti and the Italian Committee, though Republicans, were not Mazzinians. Mazzini's followers were so passionately devoted to him that they could never forgive any Italian who did not look to him, and to him alone, for leadership; and they consequently played a disruptive role in any movement which was not completely under his influence. After the collapse of the Italian revolutions in 1849, a few Mazzinians came to New York, and started a newspaper, *L'Esule Italiano*, which praised Mazzini and attacked *L'Eco d'Italia*, the newspaper of the Italian Committee, for not doing likewise.

The Mazzinians gained very little support in New York, and *L'Esule Italiano* soon ceased publication; but the quarrels between the Mazzinians and the official Committee continued. Garibaldi tried to persuade both sides to be tolerant, and to preserve unity. He made no public statement at this time in favour of either faction. Garibaldi was almost the only non-Mazzinian whom Mazzini and his supporters did not criticize in public. In 1850 Mazzini published an adulatory article about Garibaldi in *L'Italia del Popolo*, in which he declared that 'there is around the name of Garibaldi a halo which nothing can extinguish'. Mazzini felt that he was performing an act of personal self-sacrifice in publishing this article, because he resented the way in which Garibaldi had treated him in Rome under the Republic. 'If Garibaldi has to choose between two proposals,' he said privately, 'he is sure to accept the one that isn't mine.'[11]

After Garibaldi had lived in Clifton for six months, his spirits were at their lowest level. All the people who met him commented on his silence and his sad appearance, and the many women of all nationalities who tried to approach him in New York found that he showed no interest in any of them, though he always had a friendly word for the children whom he met on Staten Island. The chief reason for his depression was his inability to earn his living. He believed that he was living on Meucci's charity, because he felt that he was of no real use in the candle factory, where Meucci and Bovi, who had been appointed foreman, tried to prevent him, as far as possible, from doing any menial work. One day he strolled down to the harbour and offered to sign on as an ordinary seaman on a ship. He was told that no additional hands were needed, and the same occurred when he offered his services to a second ship. He then approached some dockers who were loading a third ship, and offered to help them with their work; but they told him rather brusquely that he was too old to be able to do such heavy physical work. Garibaldi, who was not yet forty-four, was deeply hurt, and returned to Meucci's house in great gloom. He reflected bitterly that he, who only three years before had been Commander-in-Chief of the fleet of Montevideo, was now unable to obtain work even as an ordinary seaman.[12]

The statesmen and diplomats of Europe had a higher opinion than the dockers of New York of Garibaldi's capabilities. In January 1851 the French government received reports from agents in New York that three shiploads of Italian refugees had embarked, under the leadership of Garibaldi, and were intending to land on the Italian coast. The story, which may have been prompted by Garibaldi's departure from New York in November on his pleasure-cruise to Panama, caused great alarm in Paris and Florence. The French government sent naval vessels to patrol the west coast of Italy. A month later, the Austrian Minister in Florence, Hügel, heard other news which seemed to confirm the rumour. A tailor in Leghorn reported that an Italian in Genoa had ordered 116 red shirts to be made; and soon afterwards the same man ordered another 116 red shirts. Hügel was convinced that the red shirts had been ordered for the Italians who were coming from New York with Garibaldi, and that as soon as they had put them on they would have started a revolution in Tuscany, had they not been prevented from landing by the French warships patrolling the coast.[13]

In April 1851 Garibaldi received heartening news. His friend Francesco Carpanetto arrived in New York. Carpanetto and a number of other Italian emigrants in various parts of the world had been making plans to buy a ship for Garibaldi; and they had found a way to get round the difficulties caused by the high price of ships on the eastern sea-board of the United States and the fact that Garibaldi was not an American citizen. They arranged to buy a ship at San Francisco in California, sail her down the Pacific coast to Callao in Peru, and after registering her there under the Peruvian flag, appoint Garibaldi as her master.[14] California had been ceded by Mexico to the United States after the war of 1846-7; and two years later, the discovery of gold at Sutter's mill had sent thousands of 'Forty-niners' hurrying to California from all over the world. Several of the soldiers who had fought under Garibaldi in Rome had gone there to look for gold. Although this influx of population had caused a rapid rise in prices in San Francisco, ships could be bought cheaply, because many ships were lying idle in the harbour, having been abandoned by their crews, who were digging for gold.

Garibaldi set out to join his ship at Callao. There was no particular hurry, because it took several months to travel from New York to

California, and it would therefore be some time before Garibaldi's friends could buy the ship in San Francisco and sail her to Peru. As Carpanetto had to go to Nicaragua in connexion with his business interests, Garibaldi decided to accompany him, and spend the next few months sightseeing in Central America.

On 28 April 1851 he sailed from New York for Chagres as a passenger in the steamship *Prometheus*. He tried to travel incognito, taking the name of Captain Anzani, and stating that he was going on the voyage in order to study astronomy, in which he really had always been interested; but his pseudonym was perhaps too revealing, for his identity was discovered before he left New York. His departure was reported in the press on the day that he sailed, and everyone on board knew who he was. After he reached Chagres he adopted a different pseudonym, and called himself Joseph Pane – the name under which he had lived illegally in Marseilles in 1834, when he had obtained false identity documents from an English sailor.[15]

He spent the voyage from New York to Chagres studying the stars through a telescope, and telling one of the other passengers many details about his escape from Genoa in February 1834 which he had not recorded in his memoirs.[16] He reached Chagres on 8 May, and sailed from there, with Carpanetto, to San Juan del Norte (Greytown), on the Atlantic coast of Nicaragua. They travelled in a canoe up the River San Juan to Castillo, and on into Lake Nicaragua. Crossing the lake diagonally – a journey of a hundred miles – they reached Granada on 12 June, and after crossing the narrow isthmus which separated Lake Nicaragua from Lake Managua, sailed across the smaller lake and visited Leon and Realigo on the Pacific coast.

After spending four months travelling in Nicaragua, they returned to San Juan del Norte, and sailed for Chagres on 2 September. From Chagres they set out on the forty-mile land journey across the isthmus of Panama; but when they reached Gorgona, Garibaldi fell seriously ill of a tropical fever which was often caught by travellers in Panama. He became delirious, and for a few days his life seemed to be in danger; but his excellent physique enabled him to recover, and once the crisis was past, he was soon well enough to set out for Panama, which he and Carpanetto reached on 10 September. They sailed from Panama in a British steamer, bound for Callao. They called at Guayaquil in Ecuador and at Payta in Peru. The ship waited for a day at Payta, and Garibaldi spent it visiting Manuela Saenz de Thorne, who, after marrying an English doctor, had become the mistress of Bolivar and had fought at his side in a manner worthy of Anita Garibaldi. She had recently suffered a stroke which had paralysed her legs, and she was confined to her bed. Garibaldi, who had not yet fully recovered from his illness at Gorgona, lay down on a couch in her bedroom, and the two invalids spent the afternoon talking together. Garibaldi felt a great affinity with Manuela Saenz, and described her as 'the most charming and graceful lady that I have ever met'.[17]

Garibaldi and Carpanetto reached Callao, the port of Lima, on 5 October. Peru, which had experienced a series of revolutions and *coups d'état* since it had gained its independence from Spain, was at that moment governed by the Liberal government of General Echenique. In 1851 the Peruvian economy was in a most flourishing state, owing to the world demand for guano as a fertilizing manure. As the Peruvians had a monopoly of guano, they could demand what price they wished, and their buyers could only complain, while they tried to find other sources of supply.[18] Callao, from where the guano was exported, was one of the busiest ports on the Pacific coast of South America, and for the past few months had been linked with Lima, eight and a half miles inland, by a railway which continued for another ten miles to Chorrillos, and was the only railway in South America. There was a large Italian colony in Lima and Callao, and Sardinian ships often called at Callao. There was also a somewhat smaller French colony.

The Italian community in Lima was largely under the influence of Republican and Radical leaders, and this caused some anxiety to the Sardinian Consul, Canevaro. One of the most active Republicans was a young Mazzinian doctor, Solari, who had escaped to Lima after trying to incite a mutiny in the Sardinian navy. He had brought with him from Europe a large quantity of the banknotes issued by the Roman Republic, which alarmed Canevaro, although the banknotes were no longer accepted as legal tender in any country. Like most Mazzinians, Solari greatly admired Garibaldi, and had notified the Italians in Lima and Callao that Garibaldi was due to arrive.[19]

Garibaldi therefore received a great welcome from the Italians in Peru; and the *Correo de Lima,* the leading Peruvian newspaper, also greeted him warmly. They wrote on 6 October:

> Garibaldi. Illustrious defender of LIBERTY! We salute you. As we view with horror the cowardly tyrants, so we venerate the valiant defenders of the rights of humanity. . . . As we hate the TRAITOR who looks to the monarchy as the means of destroying the Republic, so our love turns to the intrepid defender of the Republic, of liberty, of democracy. . . . Illustrious defender of LIBERTY, we salute you.[20]

If the *Correo de Lima* adopted a different attitude two months later, this was partly Garibaldi's fault.

Canevaro was less happy about Garibaldi's arrival. He reported to d'Azeglio in Turin that Garibaldi had come under the influence of Dr Solari, who had 'always been an Apostle of the Mazzinian party', and of 'other Italians who are unstable and are avowed Communists'. He employed an agent to trail Garibaldi during his stay in Peru. Garibaldi found this out, and was angry. When he met Canevaro on a social occasion, he would hardly speak to him.[21]

Soon after Garibaldi reached Callao, his ship arrived from California. She was a sailing-ship of 400 tons, and was registered as a Peruvian vessel and named the *Carmen*. Denegri, an Italian business man in New York, who had put up most of the money, was the owner of the ship, and Garibaldi was appointed as her master. On 31 October he sailed from Callao in the *Carmen* with a cargo for the Island of Chincha off the Peruvian coast, 150 miles south of Callao. Carpanetto also left Callao, sailing north for Nicaragua. Garibaldi never saw him again. Carpanetto died of cholera a few years later.[22]

After returning from the Island of Chincha before the end of November, Garibaldi stayed at Lima in the house of an Italian resident. This Italian often invited to his house a French factory owner in Lima, Charles Ledo. Garibaldi took an instant dislike to Ledo, who was garrulous and quarrelsome, and he tried as far as possible to avoid talking to Ledo. On 30 November both Garibaldi and Ledo, as well as the Consul Canevaro, were invited to a wedding reception on the occasion of the marriage of a prominent member of the Italian community to the daughter of a wealthy Peruvian. According to Garibaldi, Ledo began taunting him at the reception about the siege of Rome, denouncing the Italians as traitors and cowards. He was obviously trying to pick a quarrel with Garibaldi; but Garibaldi tried to change the subject, not wishing to quarrel with Ledo at a wedding reception in their host's house.

Canevaro gave a rather different account of the incident. He stated that Garibaldi was holding forth to the guests standing around him about the fighting in Rome in 1849, and that when Ledo interrupted him with sarcastic remarks, Garibaldi called Ledo a 'pig' and 'scum' ('*animale*' and '*canaglia*'). Jessie White Mario adds the information, which she claims to have been told by Garibaldi, that when Ledo asked Garibaldi to admit that the French fought like heroes at Rome, Garibaldi replied, 'I don't know about that, sir, I only saw their backsides.' But as Canevaro was in the next room, and did not hear the conversation himself, we are justified in accepting Garibaldi's version; and the ridiculous statement about only seeing the French backsides, which was of course quite untrue, is much more likely to have been invented by Jessie White Mario than spoken by Garibaldi.[23]

Four days later, the *Correo de Lima* published an anonymous letter which was signed 'A Gaul', but was in fact written by Ledo. It was headed 'Heroes of the Mob'. 'In times of revolution and disturbance,' he began, 'the most vulgar type of men are raised above the multitude, men without education or talent.' Garibaldi was one of these; and although certain writers in Europe had tried 'to make this pigmy into a giant', he was 'a caricature of a brave man, and has no intellect'. After condemning Garibaldi's conduct in the defence of Rome and harping on the rapine committed by his men during the retreat to San Marino, the letter referred to Garibaldi as 'an obscure sailor', and called him 'the grotesque Garibaldi'.[24]

Next day the *Correo de Lima* published an indignant letter from a Peruvian, and another from an Argentine Unitarian refugee in Lima, strongly criticizing Ledo's letter, and defending Garibaldi; and this was followed by another letter from a Peruvian supporting Garibaldi on 6 December.[25] But Garibaldi did not wait for these letters to be published. He read Ledo's letter in the *Correo de Lima* in his ship in port at Callao, and guessed that it was Ledo who had written it. He immediately travelled to Lima and went to the large warehouse which Ledo owned. He found Ledo apparently alone on the premises, and proceeded to thrash him with the light cane which he usually carried. But a French dentist, who was a friend of Ledo, was in another room in the warehouse, and he came to Ledo's assistance, armed with an iron crowbar and a swordstick. While Garibaldi was beating Ledo, the dentist hit Garibaldi on the head from behind with the crowbar, cutting open his head and almost knocking him out; but Garibaldi recovered himself, and with the blood streaming down his face he fought both the Frenchmen with his cane, and succeeded in wrenching the iron bar from the dentist. Both the dentist and Ledo, who was also bleeding from a head wound, retreated into another room, leaving Garibaldi wounded but victorious.* Garibaldi left the warehouse and went to recuperate in the house of an Italian who lived on the other side of the street.

Ledo and the dentist called the police, who arrived soon afterwards, intending to arrest Garibaldi on a charge of assault. They discovered that Garibaldi was in the Italian's house; but by now a large crowd of other Italians had gathered in the house to hear Garibaldi's story and to congratulate him on his action, and they refused to allow the police to enter the house and arrest Garibaldi. The police decided that it would be wiser to withdraw. That night the French residents in Lima marched to the Italian quarter and attacked the Italians, and the

*Canevaro, who of course was not present, gave a slightly different account of the fight in the warehouse, stating that it was Ledo who hit Garibaldi from behind with the crowbar, while Garibaldi was dealing with the dentist.

fighting between the two communities became so serious that the Peruvian army sent a squad of cavalry to restore order. President Echenique summoned the Sardinian Consul and the French Minister and asked both of them to restrain their fellow-countrymen; but the communal riots continued for several days.

Ledo brought an action for assault against Garibaldi before the local magistrate, who fined Garibaldi 200 pesos. But next day a crowd of Italians marched to the court-house, where the magistrate was dealing with another case, and became so threatening that the magistrate agreed to reverse his decision of the previous day and remit the fine on Garibaldi. The French Minister then approached Canevaro and suggested that the matter could be settled if Garibaldi would make a voluntary gift of the 200 pesos to a charity; but Canevaro rejected this proposal on the grounds that it would be an admission that Garibaldi had been in the wrong. In his report to the Sardinian government he stated that he did not approve of what Garibaldi had done, but that in view of the clash that had occurred between the French and Italians in Lima, he thought that the national honour was involved, and that this made it necessary for him to champion the Italian cause, though he was obviously a little anxious that his government would not endorse his action. Rather surprisingly, the French accepted the situation, and although Napoleon III was as capable as Palmerston of acting vigorously in defence of his nationals in distant countries, no French gunboats sailed to Callao to uphold Ledo's claims. 'The matter was at last concluded,' wrote Garibaldi, 'without fine and without apology.'[26]

According to Canevaro's report to Turin, both the government and public in Peru sympathized with Garibaldi in the dispute; but the *Correo de Lima* did not, and the editor regarded Garibaldi's action in beating-up Ledo on account of his letter to the newspaper as an affront to the freedom of the press. On 6 December the *Correo de Lima* published an article headed 'Garibaldi the Murderer', in which they declared that though they had acclaimed him as a hero when he arrived in Lima, they now realized that it would have been more correct to have called him a murderer. Aggrieved by a letter to their paper, which he imagined had been written by Ledo, he had not brought an action for libel in the courts, but had gone to Ledo's house, armed with pistols, and had tried to murder him; and they hoped that the Peruvian authorities would not be negligent in performing their duty.[27]

The editor of the *Correo de Lima* had evidently been persuaded by Ledo that Garibaldi's conduct had been considerably worse than it really was; perhaps, like so many other newspaper editors of the period, he had been bribed to put forward a new line by the French embassy. But Garibaldi's action had been headstrong and unjustifiable, however great the provocation. When he wrote and thanked Canevaro for his support, the Consul told him severely that he had only supported him out of regard for the national honour, and not because he approved of his conduct, which had been blameworthy; and Garibaldi himself, in his memoirs, described it as a 'regrettable incident'.[28]

Garibaldi's imbroglio with Ledo was not reported in the press outside Peru; but journalists in other countries knew that he had gone to Lima, and many foreign newspapers published a completely untrue report that he had been appointed Commander-in-Chief of the Peruvian army. This story afterwards found its way into many biographies of Garibaldi. Further south on the American continent, the war between the Rosistas and the Unitarians was at last coming to an end with the sudden and total victory of Garibaldi's comrades. In May 1851 Urquiza deserted Rosas and joined with the Unitarians of Montevideo, who were now commanded by Bartolomé Mitre; and Brazil also intervened against the Rosistas. On 3 February 1852 Urquiza and Mitre defeated Rosas at Monte Caseros, and Rosas fled to England. A Liberal government was established in Argentina, and the Italian Legion under the command of Olivieri, patrolled the streets of Buenos Aires.[29]

On 10 January 1852 Garibaldi sailed from Callao in the *Carmen* with a cargo of guano for Canton. The voyage across the Pacific took ninety-three days. It was on the whole a calm and uneventful journey, but Garibaldi had a strange emotional experience on the seventieth day out. On the night of 19 March the *Carmen* encountered a minor typhoon. Garibaldi, who was suffering from an attack of rheumatism, was lying on his bunk in his cabin, as the ship tossed in the storm, when he had a blurred vision of Nice and of his mother, and of what appeared to be a funeral procession. It was nearly a year later before he heard that on the same night Rosa Garibaldi had died in Nice. The funeral of this devout Catholic woman was attended by the Russian Socialist refugee, Alexander Herzen, who later became a friend of Garibaldi, but had not yet met him in 1852, and by several other Socialists living in Nice, out of respect for Garibaldi.[30]

Garibaldi took the north-west route to China, passing within sight of Hawaii, and after sailing between Luzon in the Philippines and Formosa, arrived at Canton on 12 April. At this time, during the period between Palmerston's first and second war against China in support of the opium merchants, Canton was in a state of great unrest and of almost constant friction between the Imperial government and the British and other foreign communities. There was also continual trouble with pirates. According to local tradition, Garibaldi arrived at the entrance to Canton harbour at the moment when a battle was in progress between a pirate junk and a coastguard vessel. W. C. Hunter, the vigorous young agent of the United States shipping company, Perkis and Co., came on board the *Carmen* to warn her Peruvian captain that he was sailing into the firing zone. Hunter found, to his surprise, that the captain was Garibaldi, who was standing on deck, completely unconcerned as the bullets whizzed past his head.[31]

Garibaldi stayed in Chinese waters for more than six months, but very little is known about his stay there apart from the few lines which he wrote in his memoirs. More information might have been obtained from the records of the port authorities and the foreign shipping companies at Canton if anyone had consulted the documents during the next eighty-six years; but in 1938 all the records were destroyed or lost during the intensive bombing of Canton by the Japanese air force. Garibaldi found that he could not sell his cargo of guano in Canton, probably because he had been instructed to ask too high a price for it, and buyers all over the world were beginning to refuse to buy guano at the price which the Peruvian sellers demanded. Garibaldi therefore sailed to Amoy, some 500 miles to the north on the China coast, and succeeded in selling the guano there. He returned to Canton, and made a voyage to Manila in the Philippines; and after returning again to Canton, finally sailed for Lima about 15 October.[32]

He took the longer, southern route in order to avoid the hurricanes which were usual on the direct route at that time of year, and sailed to the west of Australia. He then turned east and proceeded along the southern coast of Australia through the Bass Strait, between Melbourne and the British penal colony of Tasmania, or Van Diemen's Land. He landed on one of the Hunter Islands in the Bass Strait in order to pick up an additional supply of water. It was uninhabited, but contained an abandoned farmhouse; a notice on the door stated that the farmer and his wife had returned to Van Diemen's Land because they had been unable to bear the solitude. Garibaldi therefore felt justified in picking the potatoes and vegetables which he found in the garden. He was charmed by the beauty and quiet of the island, and in later years often thought of it 'when fed up with this civilized society, so well furnished with priests and police spies'.[33]

He sailed to the south of New Zealand, passing between South Island and the Auckland Islands, and headed north-east for Lima. On the last lap of the journey, the *Carmen* encountered contrary winds and was sometimes becalmed. After a while the supplies began to run low, and though there was no real cause for anxiety, Garibaldi put his crew on short rations. He also organized rat-hunts in the ship, telling his men to catch any vermin which they could find and keep it for food in an emergency; and he told them to collect any rain water which might fall. His men became anxious that they might stay becalmed for so long that they would die of starvation, which was not an unknown occurrence in the days of sailing-ships; but Garibaldi was in excellent spirits, and treated the rat-hunts as an amusing entertainment. This was the first occasion since 1849 on which anyone had described Garibaldi as being gay, so it seems that the danger had a bracing effect on him. The winds, in fact, changed after a short time, and the *Carmen* reached Callao on 24 January 1853, about a hundred days after leaving Canton, and just over a year since they had begun their voyage from Callao.[34]

From Lima Garibaldi sailed to Valparaiso in Chile, where he arrived on 25 March and stayed for two months. It struck him as a place of extraordinary natural beauty. Here he loaded a cargo of copper for Boston, and on 25 May sailed north for a thousand miles to Islay in southern Peru to load an additional cargo, calling at the Chilean ports of Coqumbo, Huasco and Herradera on the way. After loading up with wool at Islay to complete the cargo, he sailed for Boston, rounding Cape Horn, where he encountered a fierce gale, and reaching Boston on 6 September, after a journey from Islay of nearly 10,000 miles.[35]

Garibaldi travelled by train from Boston to New York and on arriving there he found himself in an unpleasant situation. When he presented his accounts to Denegri, his shipowner, on 1 October, they were 1,601 pesos and 77 cents short. Garibaldi had obviously not embezzled the money, but the discrepancy was probably due to his complete lack of capacity for business. Denegri was prepared to give Garibaldi the benefit of every doubt, but his accountant was less tolerant, and made aspersions on Garibaldi's honesty and competence which annoyed Garibaldi so much that he resigned his command of the *Carmen*. His dispute with Denegri's firm about the sums due from him on the China voyage continued for nearly thirteen years, and from time to time, when Garibaldi was not engaged in liberating Sicily or in other campaigns, he resumed the argument with Denegri, until the matter was eventually settled in 1866.[36]

Another source of worry to Garibaldi, when he reached New York, was the quarrel between the Italian Committee and the Mazzinians, which had reached new heights of bitterness. Garibaldi tried to act as a peacemaker between the two factions, but he refused to join in the controversies on either side.[37]

But there was good news as well as bad awaiting Garibaldi in New York. In the autumn of 1852 a new government had come to power in Turin; the Conservative Prime Minister, d'Azeglio, resigned, and was replaced by a coalition government with Cavour as Prime Minister and including the Left-wing Opposition leader, Rattazzi. The Sardinian Consul in New York hinted to Garibaldi that the Sardinian government would have no objection if he returned to the kingdom and took up residence there. Garibaldi decided to set out for his homeland as soon as possible. A few weeks later Captain Figari, who had met Garibaldi in Taganrog in 1832 when Garibaldi was the mate on the *Clorinda* and Figari was a cabin boy, arrived in New York from Europe. He had come to the United States to buy a ship, and offered to appoint Garibaldi as master of the ship for the journey to Genoa.

In November 1853 Garibaldi left New York and went with Figari to Baltimore, where Figari was negotiating for the purchase of a ship. By the beginning of January, the arrangements were completed, and Garibaldi was appointed master of Figari's ship, the *Commonwealth*, flying the American flag. On 16 January he sailed from Baltimore, bound for London and Genoa.[38]

CHAPTER 24

LONDON AND NEWCASTLE

THE *Commonwealth* reached the West India Dock in the Port of London on 11 February 1854. Garibaldi's arrival aroused even less interest than his first visit to England four years before. The *Daily News* reported his arrival in one line;[1] but *The Times* again failed to report it, and the British Radical journals were equally silent. The British press and public were absorbed with the Crimean War. Every day the press reported the departure of troops for the Levant.

Garibaldi stayed in London for five weeks. He met Mazzini for the first time since Rome in 1849, and through Mazzini came into contact with other foreign revolutionary leaders in London. Apart from Mazzini, Saffi, Orsini and the Italians, other prominent European revolutionaries were living in London in 1854 – Ledru-Rollin and Louis Blanc from France, Vogt and Marx from Germany, Kossuth and Pulszky from Hungary, Worcell from Poland, and Alexander Herzen from Russia. Mazzini was friendly with Ledru-Rollin and Kossuth, but he had broken off relations with Louis Blanc and the Socialists after he had published a bitter polemical pamphlet against them in 1852, in which he accused them of splitting the unity of the democratic revolutionary struggle against monarchical despotism, of driving the petty bourgeoisie into the arms of reaction, and of being responsible for the success of Napoleon III's *coup d'état* in France.[2] This was doubtless the reason why Garibaldi did not meet Marx during his stay in London; but he met Herzen, who managed to remain on friendly terms with everyone.

Through Mazzini and his friends, Garibaldi met several of the English supporters of Italian freedom. These included some influential personages. Antonio Panizzi, who later became Sir Anthony Panizzi, had come to England as a political refugee in 1823, and was now Deputy to the Chief Librarian of the British Museum, Sir Henry Ellis, whom he succeeded in 1856, and was engaged in the work which led in 1857 to the opening of the modern Reading Room and the preparation of the British Museum Catalogue of Books. Panizzi was a personal friend of Palmerston, Lord John Russell, Gladstone, and other British statesmen, as was Giacomo Lacaita – afterwards Sir James Lacaita – who had come to London as a refugee from Naples a few months earlier. A more Mazzinian supporter of the Italian cause was William Ashurst, a solicitor living in Muswell Hill, outside London, with his four gifted daughters, who were champions of Italian freedom and women's rights, and smoked cigars. James Stansfeld, who married Caroline Ashurst and was elected a Liberal MP in 1859, also supported the Italians.

Another of Mazzini's ardent women supporters was Jessie White, the daughter of a Gosport shipbuilder, who in 1857 married the Italian Mazzinian revolutionary, Alberto Mario. Jessie White was a beautiful young woman of twenty-two in 1854, with a splendid crop of red hair. She was an excellent platform speaker, and made a great impression at the public meetings which she addressed all over Britain; when she spoke in Newcastle, the *Northern Daily Express* commented that 'her quiet, graceful and thoroughly feminine manners must have agreeably disappointed those who expected in a lady-lecturer something violent, out of keeping, and out of nature'.[3] She became the first woman journalist in Britain, having persuaded the *Daily News* in 1856 to appoint her as their foreign correspondent in Genoa. On her journalistic visits to Italy she sometimes carried pistols and hand grenades hidden in her bodice. Despite her many attributes she had, from the historian's point of view, one defect: her Mazzinian enthusiasm and her vivid imagination made her almost incapable of accurately reporting facts, or even of transcribing documents correctly; and a biographer of Garibaldi is reluctantly compelled to reject all her statements as completely unreliable.

Sympathy for the Italian cause was growing in Britain. It had received a filip from the new wave of anti-Catholicism which had followed the success of the Oxford Movement in the Church of England and the appointment of English Catholic bishops, and the grant of a cardinal's hat to Wiseman, by Pius IX in 1850. The Prime Minister, Lord John Russell, had denounced it as 'Papal aggression', and legislation had been introduced to prohibit the use of Papal ecclesiastical titles in Britain. Mazzini and the Italian refugees had had considerable influence in this campaign. When British Catholics pointed out that there was no reason for alarm, because it was three hundred years since Bloody Mary had burned Protestants, Mazzini and his supporters wrote to the newspapers reminding the British public that Ugo Bassi and other Italian patriots had been martyred much more recently by Catholic persecutors.

During his stay in London, Garibaldi met George Jacob Holyoake, who afterwards became the secretary of the committee which organized the sending of British volunteers to fight with Garibaldi in 1860. Holyoake, one of the most remarkable characters in the British Radical movement in the nineteenth century, had served a sentence of six months' imprisonment in 1842 because he had said, in reply to a question at a public meeting, that he did not believe in God; but by 1854 he was already becoming a respected public figure. He met Garibaldi at a party at the Star Brewery in Fulham, and was asked to escort him to lodgings in Regent Street, presumably because, as on some other evenings, it was too late for Garibaldi to get back to his ship.[4]

Garibaldi met Herzen on several occasions during his stay in London. He talked to Herzen with enthusiasm about his life at sea, and suggested that it was the only acceptable existence for an Italian refugee. The Italians should not remain in Europe, and grow used to slavery; nor should they go begging in England.

> Settling in America is worse still – that's the end, that's the land of 'forgetting one's own country'. . . . Men who stay in America fall out of the ranks. What is better than my idea ['his face beamed', notes Herzen], what could be better than gathering together round a few masts and sailing over the ocean, hardening ourselves in the rough life of sailors, in conflict with the elements and with danger? A floating revolution, ready to put in at any shore, independent and unassailable.

He seemed to Herzen to be 'a hero of antiquity, a figure out of the *Aeneid*'.[5]

While Garibaldi was in London, the United States Consul, Saunders, gave a dinner party to which he invited all the leading foreign Radical revolutionaries in London to meet the Minister of the United States, James Buchanan. No European government in 1854 would have permitted one of its Consuls to hold such a dinner party; but the United States was regarded by European Radicals as the model republic where monarchy and aristocracy had been overthrown and democracy prevailed, although the controversy over negro slavery, which was becoming more bitter every year, constituted a nasty slur on the image of the United States in the eyes of European democrats. The United States government was prepared to permit its consular officials to gain the goodwill of European revolutionaries; and many of these officials, including Saunders in London, had gone far beyond what was permitted by diplomatic usage in actively helping the revolutionaries by smuggling revolutionary correspondence and literature in the United States diplomatic mail, and by offering United States passports and other assistance to Radical refugees.[6]

The guests at the dinner were Garibaldi, Mazzini, Orsini, Kossuth, Ledru-Rollin, Worcell, Pulzsky and Herzen, and one Englishman,

Joshua Wolmsley MP, as well as Buchanan and several officials of the United States legation. Buchanan, who was aged sixty-two, was one of the most eminent of the American elder statesmen, having been a United States Senator for Pennsylvania, Minister in St Petersburg, and Secretary of State under President Polk at the time of the Mexican war. Two years after the dinner party he became President of the United States, and pursued a pro-slavery policy as the nation drifted into civil war. In 1854 he was already trying to secure the Democratic nomination for the presidency, and with this end in view was drawing nearer to the slave-power on the abolitionist issue. Herzen described the dinner party as 'the *red* dinner, given by the defender of *black* slavery'.

Saunders was lavish with the wine and cigars, and Buchanan was charming, saying the right thing to everybody. He told Garibaldi that he had the same reputation in America as he had in Europe, but that in America he had another title to fame, being known as a distinguished sailor. Herzen suspected that Buchanan had been just as charming to the Tsarist ministers when he dined with them in St Petersburg.[7]

Garibaldi and Mazzini maintained friendly relations during Garibaldi's visit to London, but politically they were on the verge of a serious disagreement. As soon as Mazzini had returned to London after the fall of the Roman Republic, he had resumed his old conspiratorial activity, planning revolutionary uprisings and political assassinations in all the Italian states. In Italy, where desultory guerrilla activity was being carried on by small bands of political and non-political bandits in the mountainous districts, and where there was a good deal of sullen and passive opposition in the towns to the reactionary governments, the authorities hit back savagely at the resistance movements, particularly in the Kingdom of Naples and in the Austrian provinces of Venetia and Lombardy. In 1852 the Austrian authorities discovered the names of a number of subscribers to a patriotic loan which Mazzini had secretly organized; nine of the subscribers were hanged in a pit at Belfiore, and many others were sentenced to imprisonment.

Mazzini now took a step which he was to repeat with sad regularity on a number of occasions during the next twenty years. Hearing that a revolutionary plot was brewing in Milan, he travelled from London to Lugano, only four miles from the frontier of Lombardy, and tried to get in touch with the revolutionaries. On 6 February 1853 a number of revolutionary artisans in Milan attacked the Austrian soldiers. The eighty-six-year-old Field-Marshal Radetzky was attending the Countess Wallmoden's ball in Verona, and returning to his headquarters in excellent spirits in the early hours of the morning – he thought that the

378

ladies had looked very handsome at the ball – he was informed that the conspirators had killed ten soldiers and gouged their eyes out, and had wounded 54. 'The officers ran to the barracks,' Radetzky wrote to his daughter, 'and sent out strong patrols, as a result of which 449 young rascals were brought in; on the 8th, six were hanged before the castle with their faces towards the town, and one was shot; on the 10th another five, and so it will go on. Milan is paying a contribution every day to the garrison.'[8] The executions increased the hatred of the Italians for the Austrian oppressor; but many of them blamed Mazzini for irresponsible adventurism in instigating the Milan rising, because, though he was not directly responsible, his political teaching and his presence at Lugano seemed to implicate him in the bloody fiasco. The Sardinian government prevented any assistance being sent from Piedmont to the revolutionaries in Milan.

Cavour had become Prime Minister of Sardinia three months before, at the age of forty-two. A Piedmontese landowner and Count, he had spent a few years as a royal page at court, as a young gentleman in London and Paris, and as an officer in the Sardinian army, before returning to his family estates, where he made a good deal of money by introducing up-to-date methods of farming. During the years before 1848 he had no sympathy with the revolutionary activities of Young Italy. When he spoke of 'my country', he meant the Kingdom of Sardinia, not Italy; but he favoured the idea of Italian unity if it could be achieved in such a way as to increase the power and prosperity of Sardinia. As far as methods were concerned, he believed that the building of railways would do more than political assassinations to achieve Italian unity;[9] but when the revolution of 1848 broke out, he became an enthusiastic champion of war against Austria, and advocated this policy in his newspaper *Il Risorgimento*. After the defeat of Novara, he realized the necessity of making peace and of suppressing the anti-Austrian activities of the Radical party, and for this reason had supported the decision to arrest and banish Garibaldi in September 1849.

His ungainly figure, his round fat face and spectacles, and his slovenly dress, gave the impression of a shrewd and slightly dishonest tradesman rather than an aristocratic landowner. He was an efficient administrator, and a very skilful and unscrupulous diplomat; but he had serious weaknesses as a statesman. He was liable to succumb to emotional outbursts which clouded his judgement, and he was often influenced by personal prejudices and hatreds; and he was not always tactful in handling people.

Cavour won the support of the Liberals by breaking off diplomatic relations with Austria when the Austrian authorities in Lombardy

379

confiscated the property of all the refugees who had fled to the Kingdom of Sardinia, and by forcing a bill through Parliament which suppressed monasteries and ecclesiastical corporations in the realm. Pius IX, by calling in French troops to restore him to power in Rome and by his policy of political repression, had made every Liberal an enemy of the Church hierarchy.

Several leading Republicans, including some of the famous heroes of 1848, began to pin their hopes on Cavour and the government of Sardinia. Manin, who had escaped to Paris after the fall of Venice in 1849, had always been a Republican; but he began a propaganda campaign in favour of achieving Italian unity, not by a Republican revolution, but by bringing all the other Italian states under the government of King Victor Emanuel of Sardinia. He summarized his policy in the simple phrase, 'Victor Emanuel, King of Italy'. 'Gentlemen,' he wrote to the National Action Committee in November 1854, 'you wish, as I wish, national independence, without which it is impossible to have liberty in any form. To win independence, you call for war. For this we need arms, cavalry, and all sorts of munitions for 100,000 soldiers. . . . Do you think you will receive them from Giuseppe Mazzini or from Victor Emanuel?'[10] Manin believed in the advertiser's principle of achieving results by popularizing a simple slogan; he hardly ever wrote a letter without somehow or other introducing the phrase '*Vittorio Emanuele re d'Italia*'.

Mazzini thought that Manin was a traitor who had betrayed the Republican cause to the royal house of Savoy. He did not wish to see Italy united under the King of Sardinia, and believed that Victor Emanuel would betray the national cause like his father, Charles Albert, had done. He rejected Manin's line, attacked him strongly in his pamphlets and newspaper articles, and intensified his revolutionary plots in Italy. He also organized secret revolutionary groups in the Kingdom of Sardinia. But other Italian leaders, like Pallavicino and Foresti, supported Manin's policy, and agreed with the Tuscan poet, Giusti, that Mazzini's watch had stopped in 1848.[11]

One great uncertainty in the situation was the attitude of Garibaldi. Manin and Pallavicino were very eager to win his support for their pro-Sardinian policy. Garibaldi did not commit himself publicly. Privately he was very sympathetic to Manin's line, which appealed to his common-sense realism; but his Republican principles and his past links with Young Italy made him reluctant to repudiate Mazzini publicly. Nor had he any intention of breaking off his personal friendships with his Radical and Republican friends.

The Sardinian Minister in London, Emanuel d'Azeglio, informed Cavour that Garibaldi had arrived in London, and that he was associating there with Mazzini and men like Ledru-Rollin and Herzen. Cavour became suspicious of Garibaldi, and wondered whether it would be wise to allow him to return to Nice. 'If he is coming solely in order to see his family and children again,' he wrote to d'Azeglio on 4 April 1854, 'we will not disturb him in any way; but if his idea is to come here on Mazzini's business, we will not tolerate his presence here for one moment.' But by now d'Azeglio was able to reassure Cavour about the attitude which Garibaldi had adopted in London. He told Cavour that he had kept Garibaldi under surveillance, but that it seemed unlikely that Garibaldi, in his present mood, would engage in revolutionary activity. 'I was preparing to use my most paternal and persuasive style,' he wrote to Cavour, 'but it seems that it would be completely superfluous.'[12]

Mazzini himself had indeed believed, when Garibaldi first arrived in London, that he could send Garibaldi to Italy to further his plans. On 16 February, five days after Garibaldi's arrival, Mazzini wrote to a friend: 'Garibaldi is here: ready to act. Garibaldi's name is all powerful among the Neapolitans, since the Roman affair of Velletri. I want to send him to Sicily, where they are ripe for insurrection and wishing for him as a leader.'[13]

But Garibaldi had no intention of playing the part which Mazzini had assigned to him. Two days later, on Saturday 18 February, he entertained Mazzini, Orsini, Herzen and Haug, the Prussian officer who had served on his staff in Rome, to a lunch on board his ship. He told Mazzini that he strongly condemned the abortive uprising at Milan on 6 February 1853. The same evening, when he again met Mazzini and Herzen at a party at a friend's house, Mazzini showed him an article attacking the Sardinian government which he had published in *L'Italia del Popolo*. 'Yes, it is vigorously written, but it's a very mischievous article,' said Garibaldi, and he added that he considered it a crime to publish the article, and that the writer should be prosecuted.

After the party, Herzen took Garibaldi to his house in Westbourne Terrace, as it was too late for Garibaldi to go back to his ship that night. Garibaldi told Herzen that he condemned Mazzini's policy, as he believed that Mazzini was driving Victor Emanuel into the arms of the reactionary powers.

I have been a Republican all my life, but it is not a question of a republic now. I know the Italian masses better than Mazzini for I have lived with them and lived their life. Mazzini knows the educated classes of Italy and sways their intellects; but there is no making an army from them to drive out the Austrians and the Pope; for the mass, for the Italian people, the only banner is 'Unity and the expulsion of the foreigners!' And how is that to be attained by pulling on to one's head the one powerful kingdom in Italy which, for whatever reasons it may be, wishes to stand by Italy, and is afraid to do so; instead of inviting its co-operation, they push it away and insult it. On the day when the young man [he meant Victor Emanuel] believes that he has more in common with the Archdukes than with us, a brake will be put on the destiny of Italy for a generation or two.

Next day, which was a Sunday, Garibaldi forgot about Mazzini and politics, and took Herzen's young son out for a walk. He also went to Caldesi's and, for the first time, had his photograph taken by the new daguerrotype process.[14]

During these five weeks that he spent in London, Garibaldi developed a very intimate friendship with Mrs Emma Roberts. She was a wealthy English widow, with a London house in Arlington Street and a country house in Yorkshire, and played quite an active part in society when she was in town. She was a charming and cultured middle-aged woman, with a great love of music, and a grown-up son, as well as other children. According to Jessie White Mario, who knew Mrs Roberts well, she and Garibaldi became engaged to be married, though the marriage was postponed, and the engagement finally broken off, because of the opposition of Emma Roberts's son, and Garibaldi's reluctance to live on her money. Jessie White Mario states that Garibaldi told her that another reason why he did not marry Emma Roberts was because he could not bear the idea of sitting for three hours at dinner every day and being waited on at table by servants, as was always the case when he dined in Mrs Roberts's house.[15]

Less is known about Garibaldi's relationship with Emma than with most of the other women with whom he established friendships. He makes no reference to her in his memoirs, and she published no book of reminiscences about him, as did some of his other women friends. It is clear from her correspondence with Garibaldi, on political and other subjects, which continued for many years after the engagement was broken off, that she was a very intelligent and balanced woman. She was therefore discreet about Garibaldi; and he was silent about her. But she obviously meant much more to him than did those ladies to whom he makes some complimentary reference in his memoirs.

On 17 March Garibaldi sailed from the Port of London for Tynemouth to load a cargo of coal for Genoa. He reached Shields Harbour on 20 March, where he received a warm welcome, which was organized by the younger Joseph Cowen, who was aged twenty-four in 1854. Cowen and his father, Joseph Cowen, were leading Radicals on Tyneside. The father, a poor man who had built up a prosperous family business as a fire-brick manufacturer, was one of the MPs for Newcastle. The son, who succeeded his father as MP when the father died, was even more active as a champion of Radical causes, supporting electoral reform, the rights of the working man, the national struggles in Ireland, Poland and Hungary, and above all the Italian fight for freedom. He was a well-known and controversial personality. According to Holyoake, Cowen shocked people as much by his unconventional dress as by his political views, and when he stood as a candidate for Parliament he lost more votes through wearing a soft felt hat, instead of a top hat, than by his Radical opinions.[16]

Cowen was a close friend of Mazzini, but Mazzini apparently did not tell Cowen that Garibaldi was coming to Newcastle. Cowen heard about it from the Polish refugee Worcell, who had met Garibaldi at Saunders's dinner party. Cowen wrote to Garibaldi inviting him to stay, and a week before Garibaldi arrived at Tynemouth his reply to Cowen had been published in the *Gateshead Observer*. The Radicals in Newcastle, if not the general public, were therefore ready to welcome Garibaldi when he arrived. The Radical monthly, the *Northern Tribune*, published, during the next two months, a short serial biography of him, in which fiction was freely mixed with fact. It included the unlikely story that when Garibaldi was fighting for Montevideo, Rosas hated him so much that he made the guards at his palace shout 'Garibaldi is dead' every hour throughout the night.[17]

The *Commonwealth* stayed for three weeks at Tynemouth. Garibaldi spent a good deal of the time with the younger Cowen, who took him to see his father at Blaydon, the mining village four miles west of Newcastle, on the south bank of the Tyne. Garibaldi spent several nights at Cowen's house of Blaydon Burn, talking to the younger Cowen, who spoke fluent Italian. As well as discussing Italian and European politics, Garibaldi told Cowen about his personal experiences and his travels, about the fleas in Tangier, and how he would have enjoyed working in Meucci's candle factory on Staten Island had it not been for the unpleasant smell. Sarah Cowen, the daughter of Joseph Cowen, Junior, who wrote an unpublished biography of her father in 1911, states that Cowen described Garibaldi 'as a typical sailor in appearance, and he had the sailor's faculty of spinning yarns. He used to sit bending slightly forward, his hand resting on his knees, and relate his adventures. He never boasted of his achievements, and what struck everyone who came in contact with him was his kindliness, simplicity and extreme modesty.' Sarah Cowen adds the somewhat cryptic statement that 'his stories were not always of the romantic order'.

Cowen took Garibaldi to visit the Blaydon Mechanics Institution, which he had opened a few years before, where the working men of the district were taught reading and writing, geography and arithmetic, and acted historical dramas. The walls were decorated with portraits of Cobbett, Shakespeare, Milton and Kossuth, and with suitable slogans – 'Let labour be honoured', 'Temperance and beneficence contain all virtues'. Garibaldi was impressed with the Institution, and spoke to several of the members. Cowen also showed Garibaldi the town of Newcastle. In the street they met an elderly gentleman who, to Garibaldi's great amusement, was wearing the stock and high collar of the Regency period, which Garibaldi had never seen before. Cowen introduced the old gentleman to Garibaldi, who was too polite to show his amusement, but, after they had walked on, turned round two or three times to have another look at him.[18]

Cowen would have liked to organize a public demonstration in honour of Garibaldi; but as Garibaldi refused to take part in a public reception in Newcastle as resolutely as he had done in New York, Cowen thought of another way of honouring him. At a public meeting organized by Cowen and his society, the Friends of European Freedom, in the Exhibition Room in Nelson Street in Newcastle, 'it was resolved to Present the glorious defender of the Roman Republic' with a sword, a telescope and a declaration of welcome. The sword cost £4 10s 0d, with an extra 7s 6d for the engravings on it; the telescope and case cost £2 17s 3d; and the address of welcome, inscribed on parchment, the substantial sum of £30 12s 6d. The money for the sword and telescope was raised by the subscriptions of working men, with no one giving more than a penny; and 1,047 of them contributed, raising most of the money needed for the cost of the sword and telescope and the expenses, Cowen paying the deficit of £1 16s 10d and the whole cost of the parchment address, out of his own pocket. The address saluted Garibaldi as 'the glorious defender of the Eternal City' and the 'worthy helpmeet of Mazzini', and assured him that 'when they who drive out the Austrian build up again a Republican Capitol upon the Seven Hills, the heirs of Milton and Cromwell will not be the last to say, God defend your work'.[19]

The ceremony of making the presentation to Garibaldi took place in his ship in Shields Harbour on 11 April, the day before he sailed. The deputation consisted of fourteen men, including the younger Cowen and nine local working men, the Polish refugee Constantine Lekawski, who lived in Newcastle, and Harney, who had come from London for the occasion. Garibaldi thanked them in a short speech in English, apologizing for his inadequacy in the language, and then entertained his guests to drinks on board his ship.

Next day, before leaving Tyneside, Garibaldi wrote a letter of thanks to Cowen. He declared his devotion to the cause of 'universal liberty, national and world-wide', and his admiration for the English, having fought with them against Rosas in Montevideo.

> England is a great and powerful Nation – independent of auxiliary aid – foremost in human progress – enemy to despotism – the only safe refuge of the exile – friend of the oppressed; but if ever England, your native country, should be so circumstanced as to require the help of an ally, cursed be the Italian who would not step forward with me in her defence. . . . Should England at any time in a just cause need my arm, I am ready to unsheathe in her defence the noble and splendid sword received at your hands.

This statement was unearthed in 1914 and used in the propaganda of the parties in Italy who wished to bring Italy into the First World War on the Allied side.[20]

Though Garibaldi's memories of his stay on Tyneside were very happy, it had involved an alarming experience for his crew. Most of his men were Italians who had come with him from New York, and even in the cool climate of London and Newcastle in February and March they continued their usual practice of working barefoot on board ship. When the cargo of coal was being loaded into the ship at Shields Harbour, they were disconcerted by the large hobnailed boots worn by the English dockers. Garibaldi had warned them that if a docker trod on their bare toes with those boots, they would be crippled for life.[21]

The *Commonwealth* called at London on her way to Genoa, and Garibaldi spent a few more days with his friends there. On the evening before he sailed, he gave a farewell party on board ship, to which he invited Herzen and Mazzini. He produced a bottle of special wine, which he proudly told his guests was the best wine of Nice;[22] because though Garibaldi himself normally drank water, he was generous with the wine on special occasions. This was the last occasion for some years that Garibaldi and Mazzini met on terms of friendship.

CHAPTER 25

NICE AND CAPRERA

GARIBALDI reached Genoa on 7 May 1854. There was cholera in the city, and Garibaldi volunteered to serve in the hospitals, as he had done when he was an unknown young man in Marseilles in 1835; but the local authorities did not accept his offer. He would have been of little use, because he had a crippling attack of rheumatism as soon as he arrived in Genoa; but after a fortnight he was well enough to proceed to Nice, and saw his children again after a separation of nearly five years. After Rosa Garibaldi's death, her nephew Gustavini had taken over her house on Quai Lunel, to which the Garibaldis had moved when Garibaldi was a boy of eight. As the house was too large for Garibaldi, he moved into a little cottage near the Lazzaretto. Menotti, who was nearly fourteen, was still at his boarding-school in Genoa. Garibaldi left Teresita, who was nine, in the Deiderys' house, but took the seven-year-old Ricciotti to live with him in the cottage. He taught Ricciotti to write by tracing letters on paper on which he had drawn lines to make it easier for the child; and, according to Jessie White Mario, he washed the squealing Ricciotti under the cold water pump.[1]

Garibaldi allowed himself a holiday that summer, spending it with his old friends in Nice; but the holiday was interrupted by a political and personal controversy which led to a complete rupture with Mazzini. Garibaldi heard reports which forced him to abandon his political silence. Rumours were circulating that Mazzini was planning another revolutionary outbreak somewhere in Italy. It was said that the young men whom he was urging to revolt had told him that they would only rise if Garibaldi was prepared to be their leader, but that they were ready to move directly Garibaldi gave the word; and that consequently some of Mazzini's followers were saying that Garibaldi supported them.

Garibaldi was anxious to prevent another premature rising like 6 February in Milan. On 4 August 1854 he wrote a letter to Mazzini's *L'Italia del Popolo,* which was edited by Savi in Lausanne.

Since my return to Italy, I have on two occasions heard my name connected with an insurrectionary movement of which I do not approve. I think it my duty to speak and warn our young men, who are always ready to risk danger for the redemption of our country, not to allow themselves to be easily deceived in this way by false insinuations of cheats and swindlers who are inciting intemperate attempts which will ruin, or at least discredit, our cause.

Savi published Garibaldi's letter in *L'Italia del Popolo*; but he also published, in the same issue, an article by Roselli about the battle of Velletri in May 1849. Roselli brought up all his old criticisms of Garibaldi's indiscipline during the battle, when he had attacked the Neapolitans with his advance guard before the main body of the Roman army had arrived. Roselli said that Garibaldi had needlessly sacrificed the lives of his men, and had prevented, by his premature attack, the total destruction of the Neapolitan army; and he declared that Garibaldi had been guilty of a more serious dereliction of duty on this occasion than that for which the Sardinian commander, General Ramorino, had been shot after the battle of Novara.

Garibaldi was indignant at the article, and he did not think that it was coincidence that it had been published in the same issue of *L'Italia del Popolo* as his statement repudiating premature insurrections. He wrote to both Roselli and Savi, challenging them to a duel. The Mazzinians, like most Radicals of the period, did not share Garibaldi's enthusiasm for duelling, which they regarded as an antiquated remnant of aristocratic militarism. The challenges were not accepted, and Garibaldi was somehow pacified; but he believed that Mazzini had been responsible for Roselli's article, and he no longer considered Mazzini to be his friend.[2]

In the autumn, Emma Roberts and her daughter came to Nice with Jessie White, who now met Garibaldi for the first time. Emma Roberts rented the Garibaldi house on Quai Lunel from Gustavini, and Garibaldi saw a great deal of them. Garibaldi rose at dawn every morning, and went walking and shooting in the hills behind Nice for four hours. He lunched at twelve, slept for some hours during the afternoon, played bowls with anyone who wanted a game, and visited Teresita at the Deiderys' every day. He spent the evening with Emma Roberts and Jessie White at the Garibaldi house, playing draughts, or listening to Emma playing the piano. He played draughts well, but did not play chess, because he thought it took less time to learn to be a general than to learn to play chess.[3]

After Emma Roberts and Jessie White had spent some weeks in Nice, they went with Garibaldi for a holiday in the island of Sardinia. Here Garibaldi was entertained by several of the leading aristocratic landowners in the island, who had always admired him for his courage and patriotism, and no longer mistrusted him as a Radical revolutionary since his repudiation of Mazzini. They organized boar-hunts for him and his English friends, with the huntsmen and servants wearing their national costume, which Jessie White greatly enjoyed. According to Jessie, many of the young men whom they met in the island criticized Garibaldi for his breach with Mazzini and his over-cautious attitude about instigating insurrections. Jessie White may have exaggerated the extent of this criticism, because she supported Mazzini in the dispute, though it did not interfere with her personal friendship for Garibaldi. Emma Roberts, on the other hand, was not a Mazzinian, and entirely agreed with Garibaldi's political line; and she warned Garibaldi to be careful of Miss White, 'who is completely lacking in discretion'.[4]

From Sardinia, Emma Roberts and Jessie White went on to Rome, Naples and Florence. Garibaldi, of course, could not accompany them, and returned to Nice; but he gave them letters of introduction to several of his revolutionary friends, with whom they made discreet contacts. In Florence they visited Robert and Elizabeth Barrett Browning, who were strong supporters of Italian freedom, and had engaged one of Garibaldi's old soldiers to be their manservant.[5]

A new disagreement had arisen between Mazzini and Garibaldi about Sardinia's participation in the Crimean War. Mazzini, like all the other European revolutionaries, had strongly supported the war against Russian Tsarism, the 'gendarme of Europe' and the mainstay of the international counter-revolution from 1815 to 1849, though he and Kossuth unsuccessfully urged the British and French governments to declare war on Austria as well as on Russia, thus extending the war into a crusade for the liberation of all the oppressed nationalities in Europe. At the start of the war the British government, which had a long tradition of fighting its wars with foreign mercenaries under English aristocratic officers, tried to recruit volunteers in many foreign countries, including Sardinia; but Cavour was determined that if any Sardinian subject fought in the Crimea, it should be as soldiers in the Sardinian army after Sardinia had been accepted as an ally, at a price, by Britain and France. The price which he hoped to receive was Lombardy and Venetia, or a part of them, from Austria, who had been Russia's ally in 1849; but Napoleon III and Palmerston were hoping that Austria, as well as Sardinia, would join them against Russia, and told Cavour that this price would not be paid. Cavour then decided to join the Allies without any reward, in the hope that Italian blood shed in the Crimea would win the goodwill of Britain and France, and a seat at the Peace Conference for Sardinia.

Mazzini was opposed to Sardinia joining the Allies in these circumstances. He believed that Italians should fight for the liberation of their country in Italy, not for Britain and France in the Crimea; and if Austria joined in the war against Russia, this would be a good opportunity for Sardinia to attack Austria and free Lombardy and Venetia. Even Manin agreed with Mazzini on this point; but Garibaldi supported Cavour's policy. He thought that just as his Italian Legion in Montevideo had acquired battle experience, and had won military glory for Italy, as a preparation for the fight for the national freedom of their own country, so the soldiers of Sardinia could gain military experience and glory in the Crimea which would be an asset in the war with Austria which lay ahead.[6]

In the spring of 1855 Emma Roberts and Jessie White returned to Nice after their visit to Rome and Florence. They found Garibaldi greatly excited by the Crimean War. The Sardinian troops had arrived at Sevastopol in February, and the Piedmontese newspapers were proudly reporting their activities, though the war was unpopular in the country. Garibaldi avidly read the newspapers, and was sure that the soldiers would cover themselves with glory.[7] The Sardinian troops did in fact distinguish themselves in several battles, though, to Cavour's disappointment, peace was made before they could win greater renown and greater advantages for Sardinia.

Garibaldi was worried about the health of Ricciotti, who had developed an ailment in his legs. The doctors in Nice had been unable to cure it, and Garibaldi feared that the eight-year-old boy would grow up a cripple. Emma Roberts offered to take Ricciotti to England, and to pay for him to be treated by the best London specialists. Ricciotti travelled to London with Emma and Jessie White, and the London doctors brought about a complete cure. Garibaldi and Emma then arranged for Ricciotti to be educated in England, and he was sent to a boarding-school in Liverpool. His enterprising and independent conduct caused some anxiety to his schoolmaster and guardians; on one occasion, when he was supposed to be staying with Garibaldi's friend, Colonel Chambers, in Manchester, he disappeared without telling anyone, and made his way to Newcastle to see Cowen. He grew up to be a remarkably healthy and virile young man.[8]

In August 1855 Garibaldi went to sea again. On 8 August he obtained his first-class master's certificate from the Sardinian authorities, and five days later sailed from Genoa in command of the *Salvatore*.[9] But he had had enough of long voyages. During the autumn of 1855 he engaged in the coastal trade, going on a number of short voyages between Genoa, Nice and Marseilles, in order to raise some money for a new project on which he had set his heart. He had not forgotten La Maddalena, where he had stayed for a month on his journey into exile in 1849, and the uninhabited island of Caprera; and he now wished to settle on Caprera, build himself a house there, and cultivate a small-holding in peace and solitude. Caprera belonged to an Englishman named Collins, who lived on La Maddalena, but had bought Caprera for the shooting and fishing rights.

In November 1855 Garibaldi's brother Felice died; he was only forty-two, but had enjoyed life to the full. Felice left Garibaldi a legacy in his will, and with this money, and his savings from his pay as a ship's master during the last few years, Garibaldi bought half of Caprera from Collins. Whenever he was not at sea during 1856 he went to Caprera with Menotti and four or five friends, one of whom, Basso, had sailed with him to Canton. They built a house there, doing the work themselves with materials which they brought from Genoa. At first they camped out, living in a tent, while they built the outhouse which now lies on the south side of the buildings; when the outhouse was finished, they lived in it while they built the house itself – a charming four-room stone bungalow, with white walls and green doors and shutters. The rooms were large and high, and reminiscent of the South American style. Around the house they built a number of out-houses, a windmill for grinding corn, and a hut which Garibaldi could use as an observatory for his hobby of astronomy. Over the front door they put a metal grill showing the date of completion, '1856', in metal figures.[10]

It almost seemed as if Garibaldi, after a life of travel and fighting, now wished to retire, at the age of forty-eight, from the turmoil of the world, and take no part in politics except occasionally to issue statements urging the youth of Italy to abstain from revolutionary uprisings. But though he was longing for the quiet happiness of life on Caprera, he was ready to risk death, or a long term of imprisonment, for the cause of Italian freedom whenever he believed that there was a chance of success and that he was not risking his life and the lives of his men on a mad venture. When the occasion came in the summer of 1855, he did not hesitate.

The Italian revolutionaries and their foreign friends had for some years been indignant at the treatment of political prisoners in the Kingdom of Naples. In 1851 Gladstone, after visiting Naples, had shocked the public with his descriptions of the Neapolitan dungeons, where eminent intellectuals were kept permanently chained in pairs to common criminals. The British Minister in Naples, Sir William Temple, who was Lord Palmerston's brother, had tried to use his influence to obtain the release of the prisoners or an improvement in their conditions, but without success. Some of the prisoners were held in the dungeons on the island of San Stefano, seventy miles out at sea to the west of Naples. The most prominent among them was the writer, Luigi

Settembrini, who had been condemned to death for his support of the revolution of 1848, but had had his sentence commuted to life imprisonment.

A group of Italian refugees in England, and their English supporters, planned to liberate the prisoners. They hoped to buy a ship, with money obtained from their wealthy English supporters, to man the ship with a crew of armed Italian volunteers, and make a raid on the island prison of San Stefano, overpower the guards, free the prisoners, and sail away with them to safety in England. The chief organizer of the plan was Panizzi in the British Museum. Lord and Lady Holland and Mrs Gladstone subscribed for the venture, and Sir James Hudson, the British Minister at Turin, and Sir William Temple at Naples, were in the plot. Panizzi invited Garibaldi to command the expedition, and he eagerly accepted.

Garibaldi waited for nearly a year, while he sailed along the coast between Genoa and Marseilles, and began to build his house on Caprera, for the word to come from Panizzi that it was time to sail on the very dangerous expedition to San Stefano. But it took time to prepare the expedition, and there were delays. The money was raised, and a suitable ship, the *Isle of Thanet*, was purchased; but when the preparations were nearly complete, the *Isle of Thanet* sank off Yarmouth. Panizzi and his friends had to start all over again. More money was raised to buy a second ship, and the contributors to the fund were as generous as before. In March 1856 Garibaldi went to England to see Panizzi, to find out what was happening; he was told that he would only have a few more months to wait. Then, in July, he and the other participants in the plot received a coded telegram from Panizzi: 'Our commercial speculations must be suspended.' Sir William Temple had persuaded Panizzi not to go ahead with the scheme for the time being, because he thought that at last there was a real possibility of persuading the Neapolitan government to grant an amnesty to the prisoners on San Stefano, and he feared that an unsuccessful attempt to escape might ruin the chances of an amnesty. But the British government's negotiations on behalf of the prisoners were unsuccessful; and though Britain broke off diplomatic relations with Naples, the plan to rescue the prisoners was not revived. At last, in 1859, the King of Naples granted an amnesty, and the prisoners were deported. By this time, the régime in Naples was on the point of collapse.[11]

There were several reasons for Garibaldi's visit to England in March 1856. Apart from wishing to find out the reason why the rescue attempt was delayed, he went in order to see Emma Roberts and Ricciotti. After staying with Emma Roberts in London and seeing Panizzi there, he went to Portsmouth, and stayed for a few days with Jessie White's father at Gosport. He talked to the workers in White's shipbuilding yard, and met other people in Gosport. Jessie White states that he showed great consideration for the servants in her father's house, and was loved and admired by everyone who met him.[12]

The Allies had won the Crimean War, and during Garibaldi's visit to England the Peace Congress was being held in Paris. Cavour attended as the Sardinian delegate, but gained nothing for his country. As Russia had finally been persuaded to accept the Allied armistice terms by an Austrian ultimatum, there was no question of Britain and France penalizing Austria in the peace treaty; and though Palmerston contemplated giving the Crimea to Sardinia as a colony, or giving her either Parma or Modena in a series of territorial exchanges in Italy and the Balkans, nothing came of the proposal.[13] Cavour was disappointed, but he had achieved his aim of winning Anglo-French goodwill and great-power status for Sardinia.

During Garibaldi's visit to Gosport, Jessie White asked him whether, if Sardinia gained nothing from the Peace Congress in Paris, he would agree that Republican revolutions would be the only way of liberating Italy. Garibaldi said that he did not believe that Italy or Sardinia would gain anything substantial in Paris, but that this would not cause him to change his policy about insurrection. 'If a general rising of the people of Italy could be ensured,' he told her, 'there would be no necessity of waiting for kings or diplomacy; but, at this moment especially, no one will stir hand or foot.'[14]

He adhered to this policy in 1857 when Mazzini planned a simultaneous armed uprising in the kingdoms of Sardinia and Naples and the grand-duchy of Tuscany. A few hundred Mazzinians were to seize the arsenals in Genoa and Leghorn, while a few hundred more, under the leadership of Pisacane, were to land in Sicily and call on King Ferdinand's subjects to revolt. Mazzini had no hopes of winning Garibaldi's support for this enterprise; but Jessie White had, and she wrote to Garibaldi, urging him to lead the party that was to invade Sicily. He refused. On 3 February 1857 he wrote to her, explaining again that he was ready to take all reasonable risks for Italy, and would go on any expedition that had a fair chance of success, but would not participate in, or encourage, any wild-cat ventures that were certain to end disastrously. It is clear from the tone of his letter that Jessie White's appeal had moved him deeply, and that he was unnecessarily afraid that his refusal to join the expedition would be attributed to cowardice or apathy.[15]

The uprisings took place in June 1857 in the usual circumstances of muddle which had marked every insurrection which Mazzini had planned since 1833. At the last moment, Mazzini tried to put off the insurrection, as he had done with the rising in Milan in February 1853; but on this occasion, too, he was unable to prevent it from going off at half-cock, although he had gone to Genoa himself for the purpose. Pisacane and Nicotera led the invasion of Neapolitan territory, which was diverted from Sicily to the mainland. They landed in Calabria and marched inland, calling on the peasants in the villages to rise. Hardly anyone joined them, and many of the peasants helped the Neapolitan army to round them up. Most of them were captured and shot, or sentenced to long terms of imprisonment. Pisacane committed suicide.

In Leghorn and Genoa, the revolts were quickly stamped out, and many Mazzinians and Radicals were arrested. The police in Genoa looked everywhere for Mazzini, but he walked out of a house which they were searching, without being recognized, and escaped to London. He was condemned to death in his absence by the Sardinian court. Among those arrested in Genoa was Jessie White, who had come from England to take part in the plot, though Garibaldi had sent Medici to urge her not to become involved; but she was soon transferred from prison to a mental hospital, and then released and expelled from the country. In 1857 governments had not yet adopted the twentieth-century practice of treating political opposition as a sign of insanity or psychological perversion, and Jessie was indignant that her sanity should be questioned, ascribing it to a pernicious intervention by Sir James Hudson. Immediately after her release from custody in Genoa, Jessie White married Alberto Mario, who had also been involved in the insurrection in Genoa.[16]

Garibaldi's political disagreements with Mazzini and with Jessie Mario did not weaken his personal ties with Jessie. It is typical of Garibaldi that at this time, when the Liberal as well as the Conservative press throughout Europe, and most of Garibaldi's friends in the Italian national movement, were denouncing Mazzini and all the Mazzinians as criminals, he never repudiated the friendship of men and women whom he considered to be sincere Italian patriots and revolutionaries, however misguided they might be.

After the abandonment of the project to free the prisoners of San Stefano in the summer of 1856, Garibaldi spent three uneventful and happy years in his new island home on Caprera. He left his cottage in Nice, handing it over, as well as the Garibaldi house, to his cousin Gustavini. The Garibaldi house was demolished before the end of the century, when its grounds were incorporated into the garden of a neighbouring house belonging to a German Baron; but the cottage where he lived from 1854 to 1856 still remains. He took Menotti and Teresita, who were aged sixteen and twelve, to live with him in Caprera;

Ricciotti remained at school in Liverpool. Garibaldi also took to Caprera a young woman from Nice of peasant stock, Battistina Ravello, to cook and keep house for him. She was betrothed to a sailor, but broke off the engagement when she went to Caprera. The visitors who came to Caprera had no doubt that she was Garibaldi's mistress.

In the summer of 1856 Emma Roberts bought a ship, a 42 ton cutter, for Garibaldi, which he named the *Emma*. According to Jessie White Mario – who, despite her close friendship with both Garibaldi and Emma, cannot be considered a reliable witness – it was about this time that Garibaldi broke off his engagement to Emma, because of 'the disdainful attitude assumed by her eldest son'; and if this is so, the ship was perhaps a parting gift from Emma, though she and Garibaldi remained good friends. He used the ship not only to travel from Caprera to the mainland, but also to trade as a carrier of goods.[17]

In August 1856 Garibaldi went to Turin and met Foresti, who had come to Piedmont from New York. On 13 August Foresti took Garibaldi to see Cavour, whom Garibaldi now met for the first time. Nothing took place except an exchange of courtesies, but it showed that Garibaldi's relations with the Sardinian government were very different from what they had been seven years before. Foresti wrote to Pallavicino, who passed on the good news to Manin, that Cavour had treated Garibaldi with great courtesy and familiarity, and that Garibaldi had parted from Cavour as if he were an old friend. Cavour was encouraging the Manin-Pallavicino movement, though he privately told his friends that he thought that their ideas about a united Italy were nonsense.[18]

During the last six months of 1856, Garibaldi made thirteen short journeys between Caprera, Genoa, Nice, Marseilles and Cagliari; but he no longer yearned for the life of a sailor, and wished to cultivate his holding on Caprera. In January 1857 the *Emma* sank off the island of Sardinia, and Garibaldi took this opportunity finally to retire from his career as a merchant seaman. He did not buy another ship, and henceforth made do with a rowing boat on Caprera, in which he crossed to La Maddalena, from where he travelled to Genoa, when he wished to do so, by the ordinary passenger steamer.[19]

In the autumn of 1857 the Baroness Maria Esperanza von Schwartz visited Garibaldi on Caprera. Tall and handsome, with golden hair, she was the daughter of a Hamburg banker, but claimed to be English because she had been born in England, and had spent much of her life in England and Italy. Her first husband had committed suicide, and her second husband, the Baron von Schwartz, had divorced her.[20] She travelled all over Europe in search of sexual and other adventures, and wrote about them in entertaining travel books which she published under the name of Elpis Melena. She had heard that Garibaldi had written his memoirs, and wished to obtain his permission to translate them into German and arrange for them to be published. She became acquainted with Captain Dodoro, who had met Garibaldi in Constantinople nearly thirty years before, and she persuaded Dodoro to give her an introduction to Garibaldi.

Dodoro took her to Caprera and introduced her to Garibaldi. The Baroness and the General made a very favourable impression on each other. When Garibaldi heard that she had arranged to stay the night in a peasant's cottage on La Maddalena, he said that she would be more comfortable if she slept in his house; and when she declined his invitation and insisted on staying on La Maddalena, he arranged to meet her again next day before her departure for Genoa.

He sent Menotti to row her across to Caprera; she found Menotti a very handsome young man. Garibaldi showed her his house and estate. They discussed the politics of the day and the latest news about the Indian Mutiny. Speranza von Schwartz was interested to note that Garibaldi showed great sympathy for the British in India and much understanding of their difficulties. This surprised her, as in her experience members of oppressed nationalities did not usually appreciate the problems of governing a great empire; though if she had had more political experience, she would not have found it strange that the leader of a national revolutionary movement would hear no criticism of a foreign imperialist power which sympathized with him and his fellow-revolutionaries. Garibaldi was not enthusiastic about having his memoirs published in German, and Speranza von Schwartz found him as difficult on this subject as Dwight had done in New York. Speranza's German edition of the memoirs, under her name of Elpis Melena, was eventually published in Hamburg in 1861, and was based both on Dwight's English edition and on the Dumas French edition. Before Speranza left Caprera, Garibaldi promised to take her on a trip to Sardinia at some future date.[21]

On 28 November 1857 – less than two months after Speranza's visit to Caprera – Garibaldi wrote to her in Rome, taking care not to sign the letter in case it should be opened by the Papal authorities: 'My Speranza, How can I find words to express my gratitude and my other feelings towards you? If I have ever felt ambitious to be of some consequence and worth, it is now, that I may lay all my merits at the feet of a certain lady.' He wrote her fourteen more love-letters in the course of the next fourteen months, all of which she published thirty years later, soon after his death. Jessie White Mario, who liked to portray Garibaldi as an innocent victim of designing women, stated that Garibaldi always wrote in this style to 'his sisters in the faith', and commented that 'it is most amusing to see the perfect good faith with which she [Speranza] considers them "love-letters".'[22]

In August 1858 Speranza visited Caprera again, Garibaldi having urged her to do so – 'You will . . . take the baths here, not in La Maddalena, will you not?'[23] – and spent several days with him. One day, Garibaldi took her for a walk, and suddenly asked her to marry him; she asked for time to consider his proposal. They walked back to the house arm in arm, but when they came in sight of the house, he withdrew his arm, explaining that on such occasions the women in the house were in the habit of observing him through his telescope. This confirmed Speranza's worst suspicions about his relationship with his housekeeper, Battistina. She had thought that Battistina – whom she described, unobjectively, as 'small and rather ugly' – might be Garibaldi's mistress, because Battistina sat with them at table, and whenever Garibaldi showed Speranza any special attention Battistina 'fell into a passion which she had difficulty in dissimulating'.[24]

Garibaldi continued to write love-letters to Speranza. He made plans to go on a visit to South America with her and Teresita.[25] But he suddenly heard that there was work for him to do in Italy.

CHAPTER 26

THE WAR OF 1859

IN July 1858 Cavour, who was on holiday in Switzerland, crossed the French frontier secretly and met Napoleon III at Plombières in the Vosges. The meeting was so secret that not even Napoleon's Foreign Minister, Walewski, knew about it; and Cavour, on his side, told no one except Victor Emanuel and La Marmora. The Emperor and Cavour agreed that in the spring of next year France and Sardinia should make war on Austria, after Sardinia had provoked Austria into attacking her by invading the Duchy of Modena in response to an appeal for help by the Duke of Modena's oppressed subjects. After the defeat of Austria, the Austrian provinces of Lombardy and Venetia should be ceded to Sardinia, while Sardinia should cede the province of Savoy and the town of Nice to France. Cavour made no difficulty about the cession of Savoy; but he only agreed with great reluctance to give up Nice, which was likely to involve him in a good deal of criticism at home, not least because of the unfortunate fact that Nice happened to be Garibaldi's birthplace.

Nothing definite was decided at Plombières about the future of the rest of Italy; but Napoleon and Cavour were in general agreement that the peninsula should be divided into four states – Sardinia, Tuscany, the Papal States and Naples. The small duchies of Parma and Modena, with their Habsburg rulers, might well be absorbed into Sardinia at a later date; and Napoleon seemed prepared to agree that Sardinia could also take the Romagna, the north-eastern province of the Papal States. The rest of the Papal States, and Tuscany, were to remain inviolate; but Grand-Duke Leopold was to be turned out of Tuscany, which was to be given to the Duchess of Parma. There was no immediate design on the Kingdom of Naples, but Napoleon hoped that ultimately it would be possible to overthrow King Ferdinand and replace him by Napoleon's cousin, Prince Lucien Murat, the son of Napoleon I's general who had been King of Naples fifty years before. Cavour was quite willing to agree to this.[1]

Cavour's meeting with Napoleon III at Plombières came six months after Mazzini's friend, Orsini, had adopted a less successful method of dealing with Napoleon. In January 1858 Orsini left London, went to Paris, and threw a bomb at Napoleon and Eugénie as they stepped from their carriage to enter the Opera House. Neither the Emperor nor the Empress was injured, but eight of the bystanders were killed, including an American visitor to Paris and one child, and 148 people were wounded. Orsini, who had no idea that Napoleon was considering intervening in Italy in support of Sardinia, was executed, and Cavour took the opportunity to take new repressive measures against the Mazzinians in Turin and Genoa.

The Mazzinians afterwards claimed that Napoleon had decided to join Sardinia against Austria because he was afraid that otherwise he would be assassinated by revolutionaries. Others have attributed his change of policy to the influence of Cavour's cousin, the beautiful young Countess of Castiglione, whom Cavour had sent to Paris, as he himself put it, 'to flirt with, and if possible to seduce, the Emperor'.[2] But as early as the Congress of Paris in 1856 the British government had suspected that Napoleon was intending to make war on Austria; and there is no need to find complicated reasons to explain why he reverted to the traditional French policy of waging war against Austria in northern Italy.

The Plombières agreement was kept a strict secret for four months. In November 1858 Mazzini somehow discovered or suspected what had happened, and wrote an article in his new newspaper, *Pensiero ed Azione*, outlining the agreement and denouncing it as a betrayal of Italy to 'Mr Bonaparte'. It was perhaps only a lucky guess on Mazzini's part, and the world at large was quite prepared to accept Cavour's denial of its truth. But in December Cavour decided to let Garibaldi into the secret to some extent, though he gave no hint about the agreement to cede Savoy and Nice to France. He invited Garibaldi to visit him in Turin, and told him that a war of liberation would be waged against Austria next year. He asked Garibaldi if he would be willing to train regiments of volunteers and be ready for action by the spring. He also told him of the plan which had been agreed at Plombières of provoking war with Austria by sending a band of guerrillas to invade Modena and Parma. Cavour had worked out the details of the plan in a secret memorandum which he had drawn up in October, and which provided that Garibaldi should lead one of the guerrilla bands. Garibaldi eagerly agreed to the proposals.[3]

After his meeting with Cavour, Garibaldi went off in a state of great excitement to visit his friend, Dr Bertani, in Genoa. Bertani, who was a Radical revolutionary, was close enough to Mazzini to be viewed with great suspicion by Cavour and the Sardinian government, though he had never been involved in any Mazzinian conspiracy. 'One wintry day,' wrote Bertani, 'Garibaldi entered my consulting-room; his face was radiant, his voice was broken with emotion, as, extending his arms, he exclaimed: "This time we shall do it! I have been satisfied in high places. I am authorized to tell my friends to hold themselves ready." '[4]

While he was in Genoa, Garibaldi went to a party one evening. Among the guests was the composer, Luigi Mercantini. Garibaldi asked Mercantini to write a war-hymn for his volunteers. Ten days later, Mercantini handed his *Hymn of Garibaldi* to Bertani. Within six months it was being sung all over Italy, and soon afterwards churned out on barrel-organs in London and New York. 'The graves have opened, and all our martyrs have come out, marching under our banners, with sword and steel, and all with the name of Italy in their hearts. Get out of Italy! Get out, foreigner!'[5]

On New Year's Day Napoleon III said to the Austrian Ambassador, at a reception in the Tuileries: 'I regret that our relations with your government are not as good as they were in the past; but please tell the Emperor that my personal feelings for him have not changed.' These words, which an official at the British embassy in Paris repeated to the other diplomats in an exaggerated form, were taken as a sign that France was about to go to war with Austria; and when Reuter, gaining a march on all other reporters, cabled the news to London and the report appeared in *The Times*, the effect on the international Stock Exchanges was sensational. Ten days later, Victor Emanuel declared in Parliament in Turin that he could not for long remain indifferent to the 'cry of anguish' which reached him from all over Italy. His statement was taken as a sign that war was near, and aroused great enthusiasm among Italians everywhere. Garibaldi was in England at the beginning of January, on a short and secret visit to London and Liverpool, presumably to see Emma Roberts and Ricciotti; but according to Mazzini – who is the only source of information about the visit – he stayed for only a few days before hurrying back to Caprera so as to be nearer the scene of action.[6]

The enthusiasm for war was stirred up by the Italian National Society, which Manin and Pallavicino had founded in the summer of 1857 to work for their policy of Victor Emanuel King of Italy. Manin had died a few days after the society was formed, but Pallavicino became the President, with Garibaldi Vice-President, though Cavour very largely controlled its policy through his friend Giuseppe La Farina, who was the secretary of the society. Membership was open to all Italians in every part of Italy, and members joined it secretly in the territories of the absolutist sovereigns as well as openly in the Kingdom of Sardinia. In the states where it was illegal, the members adopted the slogan *'Viva Verdi'*. They were not saluting the composer, Giuseppe

Verdi, as they pretended to the police, but the initials VERDI – *Vittorio Emanuele Re d'Italia*. Verdi himself was an ardent supporter of the National Society.[7]

At the end of February 1859 Garibaldi arrived in Turin,* having come from Caprera in response to a secret invitation from Cavour. Cavour was told by his servant that a man wearing a big hat and carrying a big stick, who refused to give his name, was at the door, claiming that he had an appointment to see the Prime Minister. Cavour ordered his servant to show the man in at once, and asked Garibaldi to begin immediately enrolling and training the volunteers.[8]

While Garibaldi was in Turin, Cavour presented him to the King. Victor Emanuel was afterwards regarded, along with Garibaldi, Mazzini and Cavour, as one of the four great architects of Italian unity; and although, since the overthrow of his royal house in Italy, it has become fashionable to denigrate him, his role in the *Risorgimento* was of vital importance. In 1859 he was aged thirty-nine – handsome, dashing, and already known throughout Italy as the *Re Galantuomo*, the gentleman king, though some of the staid diplomats thought that he was a little ridiculous. He enjoyed hunting and taking physical exercise, and preferred eating large quantities of peasant garlic dishes to the expensive dainties provided at state banquets. His appetite for women was as strong as his appetite for food. Though he was selfish, indiscreet, and in some ways incompetent, he had one quality which Mazzini, Garibaldi and Cavour all lacked – the art of handling people. When he visited London, he charmed Queen Victoria, who had been strongly prejudiced against him, by his gentlemanly behaviour; but in Paris he delighted the lecherous courtiers of Napoleon III by the coarseness of his jokes and the audacity of his advances to the ladies. In 1849 he had persuaded Radetzky that he would collaborate with Austria in suppressing the revolution throughout Italy; but he convinced Garibaldi that, unlike his ministers, he was a true Italian patriot, who could be trusted to lead the national revolutionary struggle.[9]

Throughout all the frustrations and bitterness of the next twenty years, Garibaldi remained loyal to Victor Emanuel, and, apart from a few occasions when there was minor friction, he always spoke favour-

*Trevelyan and all modern authors follow Guerzoni in giving the date of Garibaldi's arrival in Turin and meeting with Cavour as 2 March; but Guerzoni assumed that this was the date because Garibaldi's arrival was reported in *Diritto* on 3 March. It is clear, however, that Garibaldi had arrived in Turin and seen Cavour some days before, because his Instructions to the volunteers (see p. 402) was dated 1 March 1859, and was sent by Cavour to Nigra already on 6 March (*Scritti*, IV.161; *Carteggio Cavour-Nigra*, II.64). In view of the secrecy of Garibaldi's visit, it is not surprising that the press did not discover about his arrival for some days. Garibaldi himself says that he was summoned to Turin by Cavour in February 1859.

ably of his king. Mazzini and other revolutionaries thought that Garibaldi had been tricked by Victor Emanuel. No doubt Garibaldi, to some extent, blinded himself to Victor Emanuel's faults, like he had done to those of Pacheco y Obes in Montevideo; but in both cases it was because he had correctly judged these two leaders to be men who could be relied upon to be loyal to the cause for which he was fighting, and more likely to achieve results than the politicians who surrounded them.

Although a born revolutionary [he wrote in his memoirs] because who can remain quiet or settled when he is suffering? And who does not suffer, seeing his country enslaved and plundered? – yet nevertheless I have not failed, when necessary, to submit myself to that necessary discipline which is indispensable to the good success of any enterprise; and as I was convinced at that time that Italy should march with Victor Emanuel to free herself from foreign domination, I thought that I should subject myself to his orders at all cost, and silence my Republican conscience.[10]

Victor Emanuel, on his side, liked and respected Garibaldi. The gentleman king had far more sympathy than the Liberal Parliamentarian Cavour for men like Garibaldi and his volunteers. He even extended his broad tolerance to Mazzini. 'Leave Mazzini alone,' he said, 'if we make Italy, he is powerless; if we cannot, let him to it, and I will be Mr Savoy and clap my hands for him.'[11] He had no intention of allowing Mazzini and the Republicans to deprive him of his throne; but he did not hate them, vindictively and instinctively, as Cavour did.

In 1859 Garibaldi believed, as he had done ten years before, that in time of war all power should be vested in a dictator. Already before he met Victor Emanuel, he had thought that the King was the man for this job. On 22 December 1858, on the eve of his return to Caprera after first hearing from Cavour that war was imminent, he wrote from Genoa to La Farina:

I think it is necessary that the King should be at the head of the army, and let us have done with those who say he is incapable. This will quieten the jealousy and the bickering which is unfortunately a quality of us Italians. He knows today what must be done. Everyone is convinced that we need a military dictatorship; so, by God, let it be absolute. I have recommended it for Lombardy and Tuscany; *no trouble-makers at any cost.*[12]

Cavour disagreed. He did not believe in military dictatorship, but in government by Right-wing Liberal politicians, ruling constitutionally through Parliament, if necessary after fraudulently manipulating the elections, and upholding the rule of law, though sometimes surreptitiously violating it when dealing with Radicals. He was working to prevent Victor Emanuel from taking personal command of the army, and hoped that he himself, as Prime Minister, would run the war.[13] From this time onwards, he distrusted Garibaldi, not only as a Radical revolutionary, but also as a potential supporter of royal dictatorship. Apart from political differences, there was the personal factor. There was an instinctive antipathy between Garibaldi and Cavour, just as there was an instinctive sympathy between Garibaldi and the King.

Cavour and General La Marmora did not make the mistake of Charles Albert in 1848 and slight Garibaldi; but they were very suspicious of him, and knew that their ally Napoleon III was equally suspicious. The Sardinian forces were raised by a system of selective conscription, with a provision, which was usual in the middle of the nineteenth century, for the wealthier classes to buy their exemption from military service with a payment of money; but Cavour was anxious to attract volunteers as an addition to the armed forces, and knew that many volunteers would come to serve under Garibaldi but under no one else. The Sardinian generals did not like the idea of having Garibaldi as their colleague in the regular army; but their military convention with France, under which it had been agreed that France should provide 200,000 soldiers and Sardinia 100,000, with Napoleon III as Supreme Allied Commander, had stipulated, at French insistence, that no irregular forces should be employed. Cavour therefore decided to appoint Garibaldi as a Major-General in the Sardinian army; but his commission, instead of being signed in the usual way by the King, was signed by Cavour, who, in addition to being Prime Minister and Foreign Minister, had now become Minister of the Interior and Acting War Minister. Though Garibaldi interpreted this as a deliberate slight, it may equally have been because Cavour was anxious to interfere as much as possible in the running of the army.[14]

Garibaldi immediately began to train his men, and to lay down the principles on which they should act when they invaded Lombardy. 'When hostilities begin between Piedmont and Austria, you will rise to the slogan of "Long live Italy and Victor Emanuel! Out with the Austrians!"' If they encountered any Italian or Hungarian units of the Austrian army, they were not to open fire unless fired upon first; and any Austrian deserters who came over to them were to be sent immediately into Piedmont. In the territories which they occupied, disobedience was to be severely dealt with under martial law, but no one was to be punished for any act which he had committed before the outbreak of war. No political parties or newspapers would be permitted, except one official newspaper to be published by the occupying forces.[15]

Garibaldi was ordered to train his men at Susa, some forty miles west of Turin. He resented this, and thought that he was being kept in the background so as not to offend Napoleon III. 'Garibaldi was to be a peep-show,' he wrote in his memoirs, 'to appear and disappear when wanted. The volunteers ought to know that he was at Turin, so that they would answer the call; but at the same time Garibaldi was asked to hide himself, so as to give no offence to diplomacy.' He was even more resentful when he discovered that while he was 'kept as a flag to attract the volunteers', the men between the ages of eighteen and twenty-six, who flocked to join when they thought that he would be leading them, were sent to serve under other commanders, and that only those who were too young, too old, or unfit were allotted to him.[16]

His allegations are fully confirmed by Cavour's own correspondence. 'I will tell you confidentially,' wrote Cavour to Nigra, the Sardinian Minister in Paris on 9 March 1859, 'that we intend to give the deserters to Garibaldi, who will know how to make use of them.' But Cavour was under pressure from Napoleon III about Garibaldi, and was stoutly defending him from the Emperor's criticisms. In February 1859 the French intelligence agents in London obtained possession of a letter which was said to have been written by Garibaldi to the Mazzinian, Caldesi, who had fought under Garibaldi in Rome. Napoleon, who remembered Garibaldi as his enemy of 1849, was alarmed to find that his Sardinian allies were planning to give a high military command to a man who was still corresponding with Mazzinians.

Cavour assured the Emperor that the letter must be a forgery, because Garibaldi was now strongly anti-Mazzinian. He pointed out that Garibaldi was collaborating in the Italian National Society with La Farina, whom Mazzini detested more than anyone in the world; and he mentioned that on 5 March, in a discussion which had taken place between Garibaldi, Medici and General Cialdini as to what the position would be if Garibaldi were to occupy part of the Papal States on the outbreak of war, 'Medici said to Garibaldi: "If you took part, you might find yourself facing Mazzini; this would embarrass you, perhaps." "Not at all," answered Garibaldi, "it is, on the contrary, what I should most want, because then I could finish once and for all with that man whom I consider to be the greatest enemy of Italy." ' Cavour may, of course, have been lying.[17]

The plan for Garibaldi to start the war by leading a guerrilla raid into Modena did not materialize. The British Conservative government of Lord Derby worked strongly in favour of peace, and succeeded in persuading Napoleon III to abandon the Plombières agreement and agree to submit the Italian problem to an international conference. One element in the British plan was that Sardinia should agree to disarm. All Cavour's hopes seemed to have been shattered when on 23 April 1859 the Austrian government, intending to drive home its diplomatic advantage in the face of the French hesitations, presented an ultimatum to Cavour threatening war unless Sardinia agreed within three days to disarm. Cavour could hardly conceal his joy. He rejected the ultimatum, and on 27 April Austria declared war. France declared war on Austria on 3 May. The British attempts to preserve peace had failed, and the Plombières agreement was again in operation.

On 22 April Speranza von Schwartz came to Turin to see Garibaldi, knowing that he would soon be leaving for the front. She had the greatest difficulty in gaining access to him, being told by the sentries and officials that he was busy with the Minister of War and the officers of the High Command. Eventually she managed to see him, and he found time to express his love and devotion to her. The weather was cold and wet, and Speranza was depressed at the thought of war; but Garibaldi was enthusiastic for the war and for the King. When she mentioned the Republicans, Garibaldi said: 'Give a Republican a million francs today, and you may be sure that tomorrow he will be a Republican no longer.'

On 25 April Garibaldi left Turin for Brusasco, twenty miles to the north-east. On the evening before his departure, he called at Speranza's hotel, and knocked gently at the door of her bedroom. She had to call 'Come in' twice before he ventured to do so; and in her *Recollections* she gives a moving description of the dauntless hero, on his way to war, standing timidly on her threshold, afraid to approach her. But she was kind to him, and next day went with him to the station to see him off. The streets and the station were packed with cheering crowds calling for war. Garibaldi was suffering from an acute attack of rheumatism in his knee, and asked the stationmaster to bring him a couch on which he could lie down in the waiting-room while he waited for his train. He received a great ovation at the station, and Speranza saw his train leave, while the crowds chanted in unison '*Guerra, guerra!*'[18]

Turin was only fifty miles from the frontier of Lombardy, and the Austrian armies rapidly advanced, and within a few days were within twenty miles of the Sardinian capital. The French armies would not arrive for nearly a fortnight, and the Sardinians, who had been defeated by Radetzky in four days in 1849, were afraid that they would be crushed before their allies came to the rescue. Every available man was sent to cover the approaches to Turin, and Garibaldi was ordered to march south from Brusasco and place himself under General Cialdini's orders at Casale. But Radetzky, who had died the year before at the age of ninety-one, had been succeeded by Marshal of Artillery Gyulai, who showed a lack of resolution; and though Garibaldi, at Casale, had his first sight of the Austrian troops, they did not attack, and the danger to Turin passed when 100,000 French troops arrived.

On 8 May Garibaldi saw the King at his headquarters at San Salvatore. Victor Emanuel was sensible enough to realize that there would be trouble if Garibaldi were appointed to serve under any of the officers of the regular army, and he ordered him to go to the district around Lake Maggiore and wage guerrilla warfare against the Austrian right flank. He signed an order authorizing Garibaldi to take whatever men, arms and equipment he needed for this operation. When Garibaldi reached Chivasso, some fifteen miles north of Turin, he found that Cavour had, in effect, countermanded the King's order, and was obstructing the delivery of men and supplies; but after a few days of irritating delays and pinpricks, he assembled the 3,600 men who had been allotted to him. Six hundred of them were unfit to march, but Garibaldi set off for the north-east with the remaining 3,000, crossed the River Sesia after thwarting the attempts of an Austrian raiding party to seize the ferry in order to prevent him from crossing, and marched towards Lake Maggiore.[19] He had with him a number of excellent officers – Medici, who had held the Vascello at the siege of Rome; Nino Bixio, who had ridden his horse up the steps of the Villa Corsini on 3 June, and had been severely wounded; Cosenz, who had fought under Manin in Venice in 1849; and Türr, a Hungarian who had deserted from the Austrian army in Italy. He also had Menotti, who at the age of eighteen was the first of Garibaldi's sons to fight under his command.

Garibaldi was now operating in the district where he had conducted his first campaign in Italy for a fortnight in August 1848; but things were very different from what they had been eleven years before, when the local authorities at Arona had appealed to the King of Sardinia to protect them from the robber who was unlawfully requisitioning their ships and levying forced contributions on the inhabitants. Instead of the apathy and hostility which he had encountered in 1848, he was now received in most places with great enthusiasm.

Realizing that the Austrians would have spies in the area, Garibaldi sent word to the authorities at Arona – this time with the King's authority behind him – to be ready to supply his men with food when they arrived. But this was a trick to deceive the Austrians into thinking that he was going to Arona; in fact he passed to the south, and camped at Castelletto Ticino, where he had issued his manifesto denouncing Charles Albert's armistice in 1848. Here he crossed the Ticino, and marched east towards Como. On the evening of 23 May he entered Varese, and spoke to the people from the same balcony at the town hall where he had addressed them in 1848. Then there had been only a few cheers and no one had joined his band; now, as he entered Varese, he found that the Imperial Austrian flag had already been removed and replaced by the Italian tricolour, and that the inhabitants had formed a National Guard to fight the Austrians. Although it was raining when he reached Varese, nearly the whole population – men, women and children – came out to cheer him.[20]

He was told in Varese that an Austrian army of 40,000 men under Marshal Urban was advancing towards Varese. The inhabitants feared that the Austrians would commit atrocities if they entered the town, and appealed to Garibaldi to save them. This put Garibaldi in a difficulty. Although he had little doubt that the estimate of Urban's numbers had been greatly exaggerated, he would not ordinarily have chosen to fight a defensive battle at Varese against an Austrian force, superior in numbers and training; but he feared the effect on the morale of the people of Varese, and of his own untrained soldiers, if he avoided an engagement. He therefore decided to stay and face the Austrians.

Urban's forces advanced on Varese along the road from Como. Garibaldi had prepared defence posts in various farm buildings along the roadside, building up a good defensive position in depth, and placing the troops who manned them under Medici's command, while he himself waited in the rear with the reserves. Urban had sent only 3,200 Croats from Como. He sent 1,200 of them to outflank Garibaldi, but they lost their way and played no part in the engagement, while the remaining 2,000 Croats advanced along the road from Como against Garibaldi's 3,000 men, suffering casualties at every defence post. Garibaldi, who had a clear view of the whole battle area from his position in the rear, waited until the enemy had reached a disadvantageous position at the foot of rising ground, and then gave the order to Medici to charge them with the bayonet. The Croats broke and fled, terrified, as one of Garibaldi's friends expressed it, of 'the terrible bayonets of the Garibaldi Brigade'. The Austrians lost 19 killed. Eighteen Austrians were wounded and taken prisoner, and another 200, less seriously wounded, were able to follow their retreating comrades, and were sent to hospitals in Milan. Garibaldi lost 18 killed and 63 wounded.[21]

The victory had an excellent effect on the morale of the people of Varese. The wounded were taken to the hospital there, and nursed by the women of Varese. Anaesthetics had been invented since Garibaldi's last campaign, but they were not yet obtainable in a small local hospital like Varese. 'If any cry was uttered by those undergoing operations under the surgeon's knife,' wrote Garibaldi, 'it was the cry of "Long live Italy!" When a people has reached this point, the Papal tiara, the power of the foreigner, and domestic tyranny may pack up and go.' Garibaldi was moved to tears by the death of a young boy who was fighting, along with his elder brother, under his command. He apologized, in his memoirs, for his weakness in this respect, but said that he was no longer as tough as he had been when he was twenty. The boy who died was the youngest of the Cairoli brothers, four of whom were killed while fighting under Garibaldi, while the fifth survived the hazards of war to become Prime Minister of Italy. Their mother's bravery in bearing the loss of four of her five sons made her the prototype of heroic Italian motherhood.

The Austrian prisoners were also taken to the hospital and given the same care as the Italians. Garibaldi believed that though he would have been justified in treating the Austrians as they had treated Ugo Bassi and Ciceruacchio, it was the duty of Italy to show humanity towards her executioners.[22]

Next day, on 27 May, Garibaldi marched from Varese towards Como. At San Fermo he encountered Urban's main force. It was more than twice Garibaldi's in numbers; Urban had 6,400 infantry, a handful of cavalry, and two light cannon, whereas Garibaldi had no cannon or artillery. But Garibaldi knew that in mountainous country, and fighting at close quarters, Urban would not be able to use his cavalry or his cannon; and acting on the principle that it is always possible to attack even a superior force successfully if the attack is made at night, he waited until dark, and then ordered Medici, Cosenz and Bixio to charge the enemy. He directed the attack sitting on his horse, with his cap pushed down over his forehead, which was always recognized by his soldiers as a sign of nervous tension. Again, as at Varese, he relied almost entirely on the bayonet in attack; and again the Croats fled, unable to resist the 'red devil', as they called Garibaldi, though Garibaldi gives them the credit for a brave and prolonged resistance at San Fermo. Garibaldi lost 11 men killed, including Captain De Cristoforis, one of his best officers, and about 45 of his men were wounded. After the victory, in the middle of the night, the Garibaldini entered Como, where the inhabitants, once they had found out that the soldiers were Garibaldi's men and not the Austrians, gave them a great welcome.[23]

After resting for a day in Como, Garibaldi marched west, through Varese, towards Laveno on Lake Maggiore, where a small Austrian force had occupied a fort, and, having seized the Sardinian steamers on the lake, were threatening to disrupt Garibaldi's communications with Piedmont and his supply of munitions. Garibaldi launched a night attack on the fort, sending in two storming parties; but one of them lost its way in the darkness, and though the other, under Major Landi, entered the fort, they were driven out, and Landi was severely wounded. According to Garibaldi's Chief of Staff, Major Carrano, Garibaldi lost his temper and abused Landi as a coward for not renewing the attack, but later apologized to him when he realized that he had been wounded; and he gave unstinted praise to Landi in his memoirs. He had sent a raiding party under Bixio to recapture the steamers, but Bixio was as unsuccessful as Landi. Garibaldi did not renew his attempt to capture the fort, and next day heard the bad news that Urban had received reinforcements and had occupied Varese with 14,000 men.[24]

On entering Varese, and finding the tricolour flying in this Austrian town, Urban asked the Mayor, Carcano, whether the Radical revolutionaries of the Garibaldi band had been there. Carcano replied that the town had been occupied by General Garibaldi of the Sardinian army. This answer was enough to annoy Urban, who fined the town 3,000,000 Austrian schillings. Carcano told him that it would be quite impossible for them to pay the fine, as there was not so much money in the whole of Varese. Urban said that unless the fine was paid within twenty-four hours, Carcano would be shot. The authorities of Varese were only able to raise 618 schillings within the time limit. Urban did not have Carcano shot, but he bombarded the town for a few hours as a punishment for their collaboration with the enemy, while the Austrian military band amused themselves by playing Italian revolutionary songs in derision. But though Urban punished the civilian population of Varese as Austrian subjects who had collaborated with the enemy, he treated the wounded Garibaldini in the hospital with the consideration due to prisoners of war.[25]

The authorities of Varese managed to send word to Garibaldi and appealed to him to save them. He sent them an encouraging message, but knew that he was not strong enough to attack Urban's forces at Varese, so, leaving Laveno, he skirted round Varese to the north. Near Sant' Ambrogio he met a beautiful young girl hurrying towards him in her carriage, escorted only by a priest. Some of Garibaldi's men suspected that she was an Austrian spy; but she was the Marchesina Giuseppina Raimondi, the seventeen-year-old daughter of the Marquis Raimondi, who lived at Fino, near Como, and was an ardent patriot. She brought Garibaldi a message from his supporters in Como, telling him that the authorities there had become alarmed at the news of Urban's occupation of Varese, and that Garibaldi should come at once to Como to prevent the town from going over to the Austrians. Giuseppina had been sent on this errand because it was thought that she had the best chance of getting past the Austrian patrols in the area without being stopped. Garibaldi was deeply impressed by her beauty and her courage, and fell in love with her at once.

He entered Como, and found to his annoyance that the authorities had moved his wounded from the hospital to Menaggio, where there was a less adequate hospital, in order to avoid Austrian reprisals if

Urban entered Como. But once the Garibaldini had re-entered the town, the inhabitants became very friendly. Garibaldi established his headquarters in the Albergo del Angelo on the lakeside. Here he received a visit from Giuseppina Raimondi. He went on his knees to her as he expressed his love and devotion, but found her a little cool when confronted with such ardour.[26]

On 4 June the inhabitants of Varese heard the sound of distant gunfire away to the south. Two days before, Urban had received orders to rejoin the Austrian armies with his troops in the plain of Lombardy; but it was not until the evening of 3 June that he decided to leave 3,000 men in Varese and march south with the rest of his force.[27] He was too late. He arrived on the evening of the 4th in time to meet the Austrians in full retreat after the battle of Magenta, where Napoleon III with 54,000 men had defeated Gyulai's 58,000 Austrians. Urban's 11,000 men would have been useful to Gyulai if they had been there that morning.

Gyulai withdrew his defeated army eighty miles to the River Chiese, where he handed it over to the Emperor Franz Josef, who had arrived to take personal command of the army. On 8 June Napoleon III and Victor Emanuel entered Milan amid the applause of the people. In Modena and Parma, which seemed about to be cut off from contact with the Austrians by Gyulai's retreat in Lombardy, the Habsburg rulers fled to Austria. In Tuscany a revolution had broken out on 27 April, the day of the Austrian declaration of war, and the Grand-Duke had also fled to Austria. When the war began, the Austrian troops in the Papal States withdrew to join the armies in Lombardy, and revolts immediately broke out in Bologna, Ravenna and Perugia. The Pope sent his Swiss troops to suppress the revolt in Perugia, where they murdered a few peaceful civilians,[28] and they also suppressed the risings in Umbria and the Marches; but in the Romagna, the north-eastern province of the Papal States, a revolutionary government was proclaimed. Here, as in Parma, Modena and Tuscany, the revolutionaries demanded union with the Kingdom of Sardinia. Sardinian troops occupied Parma, Modena and the Romagna.

Garibaldi's campaign in the Alps had aroused great interest in Italy and throughout Europe. Cavour's plan to keep him in the background for fear of offending Napoleon III had been a complete failure; and Cavour, not for the first or last time, had based his tortuous policy on a miscalculation. The more Liberal and non-political of the French newspapers, seizing their opportunity now that Garibaldi was fighting for an ally of France, gave him very favourable coverage; and even the Right-wing Catholic newspapers, for the only time during his career after 1848, refrained from attacking him. The semi-official French newspaper, *Les Débats,* as well as the Liberal paper, *Le Siècle,* reported his campaign very sympathetically, stressing his skill as a commander and the very strict discipline which he enforced on his men.[29]

A spate of popular biographies of Garibaldi appeared in many countries. Dwight had at last obtained Garibaldi's permission to publish the memoirs in New York, and they were published later in the year; but meanwhile the biographers relied for their information on Cuneo's biography of Garibaldi, which had been published in Turin in 1850, and even more on their own vivid imaginations. The French novelist, Louise Goëthe, was first off the mark, hurriedly writing a biography which she finished in the first week of June 1859. Her work, which was translated into Italian and Dutch, was shamelessly plagiarized by the German writer, Ludwig von Alvensleben, whose biography, published a few months later at Weimar, was largely an unacknowledged verbatim translation of Louise Goëthe's book, though he added new and wholly fictitious material of his own. Another popular biography, by Claude Pitz, was published in Paris, and several anonymous ones appeared in London.*

Garibaldi had become a hero everywhere except in the government departments in Turin; if Cavour's officials would not praise him, Napoleon III's Second Empire could do so.

> Joseph Garibaldi, the hero of the superb struggles for Italian independence [wrote Louise Goëthe] has never become involved in those infamous conspiracies that a perverted Carbonarism has recently fomented against Napoleon III, this Maccabeus of thrones, this heroic and disinterested

*Louise Goëthe, Pitz and Alvensleben described how Garibaldi was born at sea in a rowing boat in the middle of a thunderstorm, but was somehow miraculously saved when the boat nearly overturned. At the age of nine he was in a ship which was boarded and seized by Moroccan pirates, but 'little Joseph' shot the pirate captain and saved the lives of all his fellow-captives. After being involved in a revolutionary plot with Mazzini, he escaped to the Black Mountains, where he was known as 'the Rob Roy of the Italian Highlands', and was engaged as a tutor to Count Ramsberg's beautiful daughter Margaret. One day the Count returned from hunting to find Garibaldi on his knees before Margaret, making her a declaration of love, and struck Garibaldi across the face with his whip; whereupon Garibaldi set fire to the Count's castle and escaped to the forest with Margaret, where he conveniently found a hermit in holy orders who could perform the marriage ceremony. But Margaret, like a true nineteenth-century heroine, died of consumption, and Garibaldi, after romantic adventures in Tunis with Leila, the Bey's favourite Sultana, arrived in South America. There he met and married a lovely creole girl named Léonta by Pitz and Florita by Alvensleben, and after he and she had survived a series of adventures – some of which, derived from Cuneo, were genuine – he rescued her from Rosas's palace in Buenos Aires, just in time to prevent her from being raped by Rosas. These biographers knew that Anita had died during the retreat from Rome in 1849, even though they could not get her Christian name right.[30]

avenger of the oppressed. We have not seen the firm hand of the modern Jugurtha either in the plots of London or in the regicides of Paris.

But the French writers and journalists made it clear that, great though Garibaldi was, there was one greater than he, and that Garibaldi, outnumbered twenty to one by the Austrians, might eventually be defeated, were it not for the fact that Napoleon III, who was delighted with Garibaldi's achievements, was marching to the rescue.[31]

Enterprising foreigners went to see Garibaldi. Léonce Dupont came from Paris to interview him, and found him in Como. He was most surprised that Garibaldi looked so respectable. All the pictures of Garibaldi that Dupont had seen in Paris showed him looking like a Calabrian brigand.

> A felt hat, a ferocious countenance imbedded in a mass of dishevelled hair, a blouse and large waistbelt adorned with a dozen cavalry pistols, a naked sabre in his hand; such is the personage of the legend. He may have appeared in this condition ten years ago, under the walls of Rome, but times have changed, and Garibaldi with them.

Garibaldi now wore a blue tunic, with silver lace on the collar and cuffs, like all other Sardinian generals. His hair seemed to Dupont to be quite short, and though he had a beard 'it is exactly like hundreds which we may see every day in Paris'. The final proof for Dupont that Garibaldi was a civilized man was the fact that he wore spectacles. From this time onwards he usually carried a pair of pince-nez on a cord around his neck.[32]

A party of English tourists also found Garibaldi in Como, and after they returned home described their visit in a letter to *The Times*. They were on holiday at Lugano, which was invaded by large numbers of wealthy middle-class Italians from the Lake Como and Lake Maggiore districts, who had crossed the frontier into Switzerland, and filled the hotels in Lugano, complaining of the hardships which they were suffering on account of the war. On 5 June the English tourists, who included a group of women, set off for the Lombardy frontier, though both the refugees and the Swiss police told them that it would be unsafe for them to go beyond Lugano. They found the road between Lugano and the frontier deserted, and met no one until they suddenly came on two men in civilian clothes, who looked like tradesmen, one aged about thirty and the other about fifty. The men pointed rifles at them. They were the sentries at Garibaldi's outposts. The sentries allowed them to proceed after taking their British passports, which they said would be returned to them later, and the tourists went on to Como.

We drove through quiet streets, crowded with armed men, to the Albergo del Angelo, and were received and shown rooms just as we should have been a year ago, only there was a guard in the gateway, and we passed a room full of officers writing, for the General had here taken up his head-quarters. We did not consider that it would be a serious breach of the neutrality of the nation if we paid our respects to the Garibaldi who defended Rome, and who, amid all the blunders and disasters of 1848, showed that only time and opportunity were wanting to develop in the Italians a single-minded heroism and constancy worthy of ancient Rome.

Garibaldi was taking an afternoon sleep, but they were told that they could see him if they waited; and in due course he appeared, and talked to them for a little. He briefly discussed the war, and then, turning to the ladies in the party, told them about his experiences in China and the Antipodes. The English were surprised to find that he was not a black-bearded, romantic-looking, Spanish-type guerrilla, but that he had 'a healthy English complexion', and spoke 'without Southern gesticulation', with 'the calm manner and appearance of the English gentleman and officer'.[33]

The victory of Magenta had cleared the Lake Como area of Austrian troops, and Garibaldi, after visiting Varese and congratulating the people on their courage during the Austrian occupation, marched east, through Bergamo and Brescia, dealing with any isolated units of re-treating Austrians whom he encountered on the way. Wherever he passed, he was greeted with wild enthusiasm; people cheered him, knelt to him, tried to kiss his hand or his garments, and in one case asked him to baptize their new-born child. In many cottages the people had hung up his picture and placed candles around it, worshipping it as they had formerly worshipped pictures of the saints. Many observers considered that this worship of Garibaldi was partly due to the fact that, with his long red-brown hair and beard, he looked very like the traditional pictures of Christ. The Church and the Conservatives naturally considered that this adoration of Garibaldi was blasphemous, and cited it as an example of the wickedness of the Liberals.[34]

As soon as Garibaldi linked up with the main body of the army his difficulties began again. On 9 June he was received by Victor Emanuel in Milan, and awarded the gold medal for military valour and created a Grand Officer of the Military Order of Savoy, while his officers and men received corresponding decorations of lower rank; but though his relations with the King were excellent, the high-ranking officers, and Cavour and his representatives, were hostile and jealous of his success. He received an order to attack the Austrians at Lonato; but Lonato, where the Emperor Franz Josef had established his headquarters, was a very strongly defended part of the front. As he marched towards

Lonato his advanceguard, under Türr, attacked the Austrians at Tre Ponti near Castenedolo on 15 June, and was defeated. Both sides lost over 200 men killed and wounded, which were the highest casualties that Garibaldi had suffered during the campaign. He believed that the High Command had ordered him to attack Lonato in the hopes that he and his volunteers would be wiped out; but he was almost as angry when General Cialdini ordered him to take his men to the Valteline, fifty miles to the north of the front line, and mop up any pockets of Austrian troops who might be stationed in the district. He thought that this was an attempt to get him out of the way and out of the public eye.[35]

On 24 June, while Garibaldi was in the Valteline, the French and Austrian advance-guards stumbled on each other in the village of Solferino, to the south of Lake Garda. Before anyone realized what was happening a major battle was being fought, with three monarchs on the battlefield and with a larger number of troops engaged than in any battle in the world since Leipzig in 1813. The French and Sardinians were victorious, but the losses were heavy, the French losing nearly 12,000 men, the Sardinians 5,500, and the Austrians 22,000. The sufferings of the wounded were made much worse because of the gross inadequacy of the ambulance services; many of the wounded lay on the battlefield for three days, in the burning sun, before being taken to hospital, being robbed of their boots, as they lay helpless, by the Lombard peasants. A young Swiss stretcher-bearer, Henri Dunant, was shocked at what he saw, and the disclosures in his book, *Un Souvenir de Solferino*, won public support for his campaign to found the International Red Cross, which was established in Geneva five years later.

Napoleon III was also affected by the carnage of Solferino, and this was one of the reasons which led him to open secret peace negotiations with Franz Josef. After Solferino, the Austrians withdrew into the Quadrilateral, with its chain of defence fortresses, and Napoleon knew that to storm the defences would be at least as costly in human lives as Solferino had been. Also, the heavy field guns, which the Sardinian army had been supposed to supply, had failed to arrive, owing to the inefficiency of the Sardinian military organization; and the French were not satisfied with their allies' contribution to the war effort. At Magenta, owing to a misunderstanding with the Sardinian generals, the Sardinian troops under General Fanti had stood and watched while the French did the fighting, though the Sardinians played a useful secondary role at Solferino, and Victor Emanuel had exposed himself recklessly to the enemy fire in every engagement. But Napoleon's chief reason for wishing to make peace, according to what he told Franz Josef and the Austrian Ambassador in Paris, was that he was 'disgusted at having the revolution at my tail, and Kossuth and Klapka as allies', and at becoming the leader of 'the scum of Europe'.[36]

On 11 July Napoleon and Franz Josef met in a farmhouse near Villafranca, and after talking for an hour agreed on armistice terms. Austria was to cede Lombardy to Sardinia, except for the two fortified towns of Peschiera and Mantua in the Quadrilateral; but, to save Austrian face, the province was to be ceded by Austria to France, which would then give it as a gift to Sardinia. Austria was to retain Venetia, which Napoleon had promised to Cavour at Plombières. The Habsburg rulers were to be restored in Modena, Parma and Tuscany, provided that this could be done without foreign military intervention.

Cavour was furious when he heard about the Villafranca agreement, and believed that Sardinia had been betrayed by Napoleon III. During his audience with Victor Emanuel, he completely lost control of himself, and shouted hysterically at the King, who, unlike Cavour, had been kept informed of Napoleon's meeting with Franz Josef and had reluctantly accepted the armistice. Cavour became so offensive that Victor Emanuel ordered him out of the room, and he resigned as Prime Minister, and was succeeded by General La Marmora.

When the news became known, the people of Italy felt that they had been betrayed by Napoleon III. Anti-French slogans and pictures of Orsini appeared in Turin; the copy of the *Monitore Toscano* containing the armistice terms was burned in Florence; and the Mazzinians claimed that their opposition to the war and to Cavour's policy had been justified.[37] But Garibaldi, surprisingly enough, did not share the general feeling of anger about Villafranca. In view of the muddle and quarrelling in the Sardinian High Command, he thought that it was fortunate that an armistice had been signed; and on 23 July, in the middle of the popular fury against the armistice and the French, he issued a statement in which he referred to 'the gratitude which we owe to Napoleon and to the heroic French nation'.[38]

GIUSEPPINA RAIMONDI

During the eight months which followed the armistice of Villa-franca, a complicated series of political and diplomatic manoeuvres took place to determine the future of Modena, Parma, the Romagna and Tuscany. In all these territories a popular revolutionary movement demanded union with Sardinia under Victor Emanuel. The Sardinian government wished to annex them, but hesitated to offend France by contravening the Villafranca agreement. Austria was demanding that Napoleon should adhere to the Villafranca agreement and restore the Dukes of Modena and Parma and the Grand-Duke of Tuscany. The Pope was indignantly refusing to cede any part of his territory and was insisting that the Sardinians should evacuate the Romagna. Britain, where public opinion was more pro-Italian than ever, and where Garibaldi was becoming a popular hero, had elected a Liberal government with Palmerston as Prime Minister, Lord John Russell as Foreign Secretary, and Gladstone as Chancellor of the Exchequer, which was much more sympathetic to Sardinia and the Italian cause than the Conservative government of Derby and Malmesbury had been, though as always Britain was suspicious of French designs in Italy.

The man who controlled the situation, Napoleon III, was as usual a little uncertain as to what policy to pursue. He did not wish to renew the war with Austria, and still less did he wish to offend the powerful Catholic element in France by turning against the Pope; but he wished to see a settlement of the Italian problem which would end the continual unrest there, and felt that as his troops were still protecting the Pope in Rome, he had a right to ask Pius IX to give up the distant and unruly province of the Romagna. In view of the fact that by making the Villafranca agreement he had failed to carry out the Plombières agreement to obtain Venetia, as well as Lombardy, for Sardinia, he did not feel entitled to insist on Victor Emanuel surrendering Savoy and Nice to France. But he was now considering making a new bargain with Victor Emanuel, by which Sardinia would obtain Parma, Modena, the Romagna and Tuscany in return for Savoy and Nice.

Sardinia had the advantage of being in occupation of Parma, Modena and the Romagna. After the armistice of Villafranca, the Sardinian troops and military governors of the districts were withdrawn; but they handed over power to a provisional revolutionary government which was composed, in most cases, of the former Sardinian governors and officers. In Modena Luigi Carlo Farini, who had been the Sardinian Military Governor of Modena in June, was appointed Dictator. Farini was a Conservative and a friend of Cavour, but Garibaldi paid tribute to his efficiency as an administrator, and of course approved of a dictatorship in an emergency situation.[1] In Tuscany, Baron Bettino Ricasoli, who believed that the welfare of Tuscany and his own political future lay in union with Sardinia, had taken over power and worked closely with the Sardinian government, though Sardinian troops had never entered Tuscany and the revolution there had not been entirely welcome to Cavour.

It was a situation in which the Sardinian government preferred to act indirectly rather than directly, and they thought that Garibaldi would be well suited for employment in the disputed territories. Farini proposed to Garibaldi that he should resign his commission in the Sardinian army and be appointed Commander-in-Chief of the forces of the provisional governments of Parma, Modena, the Romagna and Tuscany, with the task of creating an army there. Garibaldi accepted the proposal; but he was to find his new office a frustrating one. When he arrived in Florence he discovered that he had been appointed, not Commander-in-Chief of the united forces of the provisional governments of Central Italy, but General Officer commanding the Tuscan army; the superior position of Commander-in-Chief of the combined armies had been given to General Fanti at Modena. Farini and Ricasoli were afraid that Garibaldi could not be trusted not to attack the Papal States in defiance of orders, whereas Fanti, after his conduct at Magenta, could almost be trusted not to attack anyone.

Garibaldi visited Farini at Modena, where the intrigues and bickerings continued. Farini suggested that Fanti should become Minister of War in the provisional government, and that Garibaldi should succeed him as Commander-in-Chief; but nothing came of this proposal. Fanti offered to resign his position in favour of Garibaldi, if Garibaldi wished, but then refused to do so when taken at his word. Eventually Garibaldi agreed to accept the position of Deputy Commander-in-Chief, under Fanti, of the combined armies of Central Italy.[2]

Garibaldi, as always, was dissatisfied at having to train troops. He felt at home on the battlefield, but not on the barrack square. 'Organizing troops,' he wrote, 'is a very boring occupation for me, with my innate aversion to the soldier's trade. I have sometimes been a soldier, because I was born in an enslaved country, but always with repugnance, being convinced that it is a crime that men should have to butcher each other in order to reach an agreement.'[3]

He was also angry at the treatment of his volunteers, many of whom had followed him to Central Italy after serving in the Alps with him during the war. He objected to the attempts of Farini and Fanti to prolong their term of service beyond the period of up to six months after the end of the war, for which they had enlisted; and he was incensed to hear of occasions when the volunteers had had to endure hunger and go without shelter for a time owing to the inefficiency of the army administration.[4]

There was also trouble about the Marios. Alberto and Jessie White Mario came to Italy to serve under Garibaldi, Alberto as a guide and Jessie as a nurse; but when they reached Ferrara they were arrested by the Sardinian General Cipriani as Austrian spies; and though Garibaldi sent the Radical politician, Brofferio, to obtain their release, an indignant mob tried to lynch them, and Cipriani insisted on deporting them to Lugano.[5]

The Radical revolutionaries in Tuscany and the Romagna were clamouring to be allowed to attack the Papal States. Mazzini, who had arrived in Florence, urged it vigorously, declaring that a revolution that stands still is lost. Garibaldi had little doubt that he could easily overrun the Marches and Umbria if he marched against the Pope's Swiss troops; but he received orders from Fanti not to attack them unless either they attacked him first, in which case he could pursue them across the border into the Marches, or if there were a rising in Ancona, and the local revolutionary leaders called on him for help. Garibaldi thought that this was a recipe for inaction, because the Papal troops would not dare to attack him, but were nevertheless strong enough to prevent a revolutionary outbreak in Ancona.[6]

Garibaldi's irritation at the obstruction of the miliary and political leaders was partly assuaged by the devotion of his soldiers and of the people. Wherever he went in Central Italy, he was received with enthusiasm. In August he was in Florence and Mirandola; in September, in Ravenna; in October, at Castel Bolognese and Rimini; in November, in Modena. Everywhere it was the same story – a reception on arrival, with cheering crowds, a speech from the balcony of the town hall to a packed audience in the square chanting patriotic slogans in response to his patriotic appeal, and further enthusiastic scenes at his departure.[7]

While he was in Florence he visited the English writer, Thomas Adolphus Trollope, who lived at Ricorboli. Trollope was a friend of

Jessie Mario, who gave him an introduction to Garibaldi. When Garibaldi arrived at Trollope's villa, Trollope's Italian maidservant ran to tell him that 'the General' had come – 'as if he was the only General in the world', wrote Trollope. According to Trollope, Garibaldi said to him that all priests should be put to death because they were murderers. Charles Dickens, who admired Garibaldi as much as most other Englishmen did, was somewhat taken aback when Trollope repeated to him what Garibaldi had said.[8]

In September Garibaldi visited those parts of the Romagna where he had been in August 1849. He met Zani, the guide who had led him and his 200 men out of San Marino; he visited the shoemaker in whose house he had stayed at Sant' Alberto on the night of Anita's death; he met Bonnet and many of the other people who had saved him ten years before. He went to the Guiccioli farm at Mandriole, and attended a banquet in the room in which Anita had died. He made a patriotic speech at the banquet, and denounced the shooting of Ugo Bassi and Ciceruacchio; but he made no reference to Anita, thus showing his usual reluctance to refer to his private grief, and showed great embarrassment, and blushed, when an old man spoke of the great loss which Garibaldi had suffered by her death. After the lunch he visited Anita's grave, over which a small chapel had been erected. Menotti was with him, and he had arranged for Signora Deidery to bring Teresita from Nice, where she had been staying since the outbreak of the war. He had also invited Speranza von Schwartz. He was able to spend a short time alone at the graveside with Menotti, Teresita, Speranza and his intimate friends; but after twenty minutes he was again surrounded by crowds and journalists.

Garibaldi had made arrangements to move Anita's body to Nice, for he still had no knowledge of the secret agreement for the cession of Nice to France. The corpse was carried all the way from Mandriole to Ravenna, a distance of nearly twenty miles, by forty young men dressed in mourning, escorted by the civic band of Sant' Alberto. From Ravenna, Garibaldi and his friends proceeded to Bologna. On the journey to Bologna he was again surrounded by crowds expressing their devotion, asking for his blessing, and producing shirts, handkerchiefs and other objects which they claimed had belonged to him and had been left behind by him somewhere in the district in 1849.[9]

Garibaldi had established his headquarters at Cattolica, to the south of Rimini, on the border of the Romagna and the Marches. Here he was contacted by various revolutionary and Mazzinian enthusiasts, who urged him to liberate the Pope's oppressed subjects in the Marches. His soldiers, too, were eager to march.[10] But though Garibaldi knew that he could overwhelm the Papal troops without the slightest difficulty, he also knew that this might provoke foreign intervention.

It was probably at the suggestion of Victor Emanuel that Garibaldi, in August 1859, wrote to Napoleon III and assured him that he had only accepted the command of the forces in Central Italy because he wished to maintain order and discipline there, and that he had no intention of pursuing an independent policy without the authority of the Sardinian government. But six weeks later he took a step which alarmed Napoleon and many other European statesmen. At the end of September, he went to Cremona and issued a public appeal to the people of Italy. He called for a million rifles and a million men. With a million armed men, Italy would not need to rely on foreign powers and international diplomacy; and those who could not volunteer to serve could contribute to the cost of buying the rifles. Garibaldi seemed to be trying to raise a private army, but his appeal had the approval of the Sardinian government. Farini himself headed the subscription lists with a donation of 500 lire, and the money poured in, as did the offers from young men eager to join the volunteer army. Contributions to the fund came in from abroad, particularly from Britain, where the Friends of Italy collected subscriptions for their Garibaldi Rifle Fund. It was useful for Victor Emanuel and his ministers to have a large force of armed irregulars who would be able to act without involving the Sardinian government and could constitute a useful bargaining factor in their foreign policy – provided that the irregulars could be relied upon not to act independently and provoke war or foreign intervention without consulting Turin.[11]

Garibaldi hoped that the Italian National Society would launch a political campaign to force the government to adopt a forward policy in the Marches. In October Pallavicino resigned as President of the National Society. There could be no doubt who the new President would be, and Garibaldi was elected. He was not able to use the National Society to further his own policy, because La Farina continued, as secretary of the society, to control its day-to-day operations. But Garibaldi's prestige throughout Italy was so great that he did not need to work through any organization; he needed only the press to report his speeches from the balconies of the town halls, and to publish his letters to the editor and his proclamations to the Italian people. On 18 October he issued a proclamation from Rimini in which, after denouncing 'the foreigners, the doctrinaires, the priests', he declared that 'our brothers of the South stretch forth their hand to their brothers of the Centre, to their brothers of the North'.[12]

Farini and Fanti became alarmed that Garibaldi would march into the Marches without waiting for orders. They secretly got in touch with Garibaldi's subordinate officers, and told them that if Garibaldi ordered them to invade the Marches they must disobey. They also took the precaution of transferring some of his most impatient officers from Cattolica to Florence. When Garibaldi discovered what Farini and Fanti were doing, he went to Turin without telling them, and saw the King on 27 October. Victor Emanuel sympathized with Garibaldi's predicament, and promised him that he would remove Fanti and appoint Garibaldi as Commander-in-Chief in Central Italy; but he clearly told Garibaldi that under no circumstances was he to invade the Marches without express orders from the government in Turin.

Garibaldi returned to Cattolica in high spirits; but Fanti remained as Commander-in-Chief. La Marmora and the Right-wing members of the government persuaded Victor Emanuel to change his mind, arguing that Garibaldi could not be trusted not to invade the Marches if he were Commander-in-Chief in Central Italy. They were supported by Cavour, who remained a powerful figure in opposition. At the beginning of November, rumours were circulating that the people of the Marches were on the verge of revolt; and the Radicals in the Romagna, who had been incensed at the stories of the atrocities committed by the Pope's Swiss troops in suppressing the revolt at Perugia in July, demanded that Garibaldi's army should not sit idly by if a revolt broke out in the Marches. As the pressure for intervention from the Radicals grew stronger, Farini, Fanti and Cavour became more alarmed as to what Garibaldi might do. On 12 November Cavour wrote from his farm at Leri to Rattazzi, the Minister of the Interior at Turin: 'The only way of smothering the growing discontent is to invite Garibaldi to resign the command.'[13]

On that same day, Garibaldi attended a top-level conference at the palace of the former Duke in Modena with Farini and Fanti. He demanded that he be given permission to invade the Marches. Farini and Fanti were strongly opposed to this, and asked Garibaldi to give an undertaking not to do so. Their arguments were supported by General Solaroli who had been specially sent from Turin by Victor Emanuel to stop Garibaldi. It was probably only because of Solaroli, the King's special representative, that Garibaldi agreed to their demand and promised not to invade the Marches.

Garibaldi left Modena for Cattolica. When he reached Imola in the middle of the night, he heard the news which had come through a few hours earlier: a revolution had broken out in the Marches. His friends who were with him, and the people at Imola, were in a state of great excitement, demanding that he should march to the support of the revolutionaries. Garibaldi sent a telegram from Imola to Farini in Modena: 'Uprising in the Marches. I am going to the rescue of our brothers.' He continued his journey to Cattolica, where he arrived on 13 November; but Farini had been too quick for him. Garibaldi's headquarters in Cattolica had already received an order from Farini not to invade the Marches, even if ordered to do so by General Garibaldi, and to withdraw the troops at Cattolica a few miles from the frontier. On 14 November Garibaldi received a summons to go to Turin to see the King.[14]

The soldiers at Cattolica were incensed at Farini's order, and at what they considered to be the betrayal of their brothers in the Marches. In fact the people of the Marches had not risen, and the news of the revolt, which was untrue, had been due either to a misunderstanding or to a false report deliberately started by the Mazzinians in the hope of forcing Garibaldi's hand. Garibaldi knew on 13 November that if he ordered the army to invade the Marches, they would disobey Farini and follow him; but he also knew that in that case, as he wrote in his memoirs, 'I should have had to untie every bond of discipline among the soldiers and the people. There, in front and behind me was French intervention; at Rome, at Piacenza, etc. In short, the sacred cause of my country, which I might have compromised, restrained me from acting.' Mazzini thought that Garibaldi had betrayed the revolution. 'The man is weak beyond expression,' he wrote to his friend Taylor, 'and by subscribing himself "Your friend", or patting his shoulder, the King will do anything with him.'[15]

Garibaldi saw Victor Emanuel in Turin on 17 November. In view of what had happened, Victor Emanuel felt that it was necessary to remove Garibaldi from his command in the Romagna. He was as friendly as ever, but he told Garibaldi that, because of the international situation and the attitude of Napoleon III, it would be as well if the command of the army of Central Italy were held by someone less frightening to foreign powers. He offered to reappoint Garibaldi as a general in the Sardinian army. Garibaldi declined; but he gratefully accepted a sporting-gun which Victor Emanuel gave him, and parted from him on very friendly terms. He issued a proclamation, praising Victor Emanuel and denouncing the 'miserable foxy policy' which was preventing Italian soldiers from fighting for national independence, and announced that he would return to Caprera. 'Thus, then, was Victor Emanuel thwarted in his good intentions,' wrote Garibaldi in his memoirs, '(if, that is to say, he was not a trickster), and forced to retreat by Cavourian bullying.'[16]

He did not, however, return to Caprera. At the last moment, when he was about to board the ship at Genoa, he was persuaded by the local authorities in Genoa that it would be politically advisable for hım to stay in Genoa for a short while; and soon afterwards he received a message from Victor Emanuel summoning him to another audience. After seeing Victor Emanuel in Turin, he went to Fino to see Giuseppina Raimondi. It has been suggested by several authors that Garibaldi lied as to his movements, both in his memoirs and in a letter to Speranza von Schwartz, in order to suppress the fact that he left Genoa as early as 29 November to go to Giuseppina in Fino; but this theory rests on a love-letter from Garibaldi to Giuseppina, dated 'Fino, 30 November'. As it seems strange that Garibaldi should have written to Giuseppina from Fino, where he was staying in the same house with her, it is more likely that he wrote the letter of 30 November from Genoa, and wrote 'Fino' in error for 'Genoa' as the place from which he was writing. It is a mistake which could easily have been made by a lover who wished to be in Fino more than anywhere else. If this is so, Garibaldi's account of his delay in Genoa and his meeting with Victor Emanuel was quite correct.[17]

His feelings for Giuseppina were the nearest to an utter infatuation that he ever experienced; but, though it had disastrous consequences for his private life, it did not interfere with his political activities and his national duty. After spending a fortnight in Fino with Giuseppina and her family, he returned to Turin on 27 December to play an important part in a political intrigue which had been instigated by Brofferio and his patron, Rattazzi, almost certainly with the connivance of Victor Emanuel, who probably mentioned the matter to Garibaldi at their meeting at the beginning of December.

The Right-wing elements in Turin were working for a return of Cavour as Prime Minister. General La Marmora had never been considered as more than a stop-gap premier; but Victor Emanuel did not like Cavour, and did not wish to recall him to power. He preferred the Left-wing leader, Rattazzi, the Minister of the Interior in La Marmora's government. Rattazzi was friendly with Victor Emanuel's mistress, Rosina Vercellana. In January 1859 Victor Emanuel, who was a widower, had wished to marry Rosina; but Cavour had objected that it would cause a scandal because of Rosina's reputation and her low birth. This was an additional reason why Victor Emanuel disliked Cavour. In November 1859 he resisted as long as possible the political pressure to accept Cavour as his Prime Minister. He was heard to say that he would prefer to have Garibaldi as Prime Minister rather than Cavour. The courtiers and politicians hoped that he was joking.[18]

On 29 December Garibaldi announced in Turin that he was resigning as President of the National Society; and on New Year's Eve he made the further announcement that he was forming a new political association, which he called the Armed Nation. The idea had been suggested to him by Brofferio at a dinner party. No prominent person, apart from Garibaldi, was openly connected with it, but Garibaldi's name was sufficient to launch a new political party, and his announcement caused anxiety in political and diplomatic circles in Piedmont and abroad. On 2 January the students of Turin University marched to the Albergo di Trombetta, where Garibaldi was staying, with banners and musical bands, and called for the 'hero of Varese' to appear. Garibaldi made a patriotic speech from the balcony of the hotel, which was received with loud applause.[19]

The politicians became increasingly alarmed at the prospect of a royal dictatorship supported by a revolutionary general. They did not know that on 21 December Garibaldi had written, in a private letter from Fino to a friend: 'I believe that for the sake of Italy our good Victor Emanuel should do as Charles XII did and throw one of his boots at the government's head, and place himself alone at the head of the army and of the Italian nation.' But Garibaldi's friend Türr was more indiscreet than Garibaldi. On 25 January 1860 he wrote, in an open letter to the King, which was published in the newspaper *Diritto*: 'Sire, Italy does not need elections or liberty, but battles; assume the dictatorship!'[20]

On 4 January Garibaldi met Alexandre Dumas for the first time. Dumas arrived at the Hotel Trombetta and introduced himself to Garibaldi in a flamboyant manner. Without identifying himself, he walked into Garibaldi's room and said: 'General, what is the time?' Garibaldi told him that it was eleven o'clock. 'What is the day of the month?' asked Dumas. 'Wednesday, 4 January,' said Garibaldi. 'Well, listen carefully, General,' said Dumas, 'I predict that within a year from today you will be the leader of all Italy.' Garibaldi then realized that his mulatto visitor must be Dumas.

While he was talking to Dumas, a messenger arrived from the palace inviting him to come immediately to Victor Emanuel.[21] The King asked him to dissolve the Armed Nation which he had formed four days before. Cavour had persuaded the British Minister in Turin, Sir James Hudson, to intervene. Hudson, who believed that 'that well-meaning goose Garibaldi' had been used as an instrument by 'that astute demagogue and political fox Brofferio', sent Solaroli to tell Victor Emanuel that if Garibaldi's Armed Nation was not broken up, the enemies of Italy 'would have a right to declare that revolutionary doctrine and practice were established permanently in his states and that they consequently must object to its extension by the extension of his states'. Hudson reported that when Solaroli delivered his message, 'the King listened attentively and good-humouredly and rather tried to avoid coming to a decision'; but when Rattazzi threatened to resign, Victor Emanuel gave way, summoned Garibaldi, and persuaded him in five minutes to dissolve the Armed Nation, 'the King to the last insisting that it was not a thing to take seriously'.[22]

At 5 pm on 4 January, Garibaldi issued a statement, announcing that at the request of the King's government he was dissolving the Armed Nation and inviting 'every Italian who loves his country to aid in the purchase of the million rifles', with which they could arm a million soldiers. 'Let Italy arm, and she will be free.'[23]

Two and a half hours later, at 7.30 pm that same evening, Garibaldi wrote to Hudson, asking him to let him know by eight o'clock next morning whether he had raised the matter of the Armed Nation with the King. In his reply, Hudson admitted that he had done so, 'because I did not understand how a government that called itself a government could permit any force or power in the country, or any armed persons, except the King's army'. But Garibaldi did not publish Hudson's letter in the Left-wing press, as Hudson expected.[24]

On 6 January an announcement was published in the press of the forthcoming marriage between General Garibaldi and Giuseppina, the eldest daughter of the Marquis Raimondi.[25]

During the previous year, Garibaldi had been undergoing a disturbing emotional experience. In the first years after Anita's death, he had felt that no other woman had anything to offer him; but now he longed to re-marry. When he proposed to Speranza von Schwartz, he asked her to be a mother to his orphan children; but this was probably the least essential part of the duties that he expected a wife to perform. The children were growing up; Menotti was a soldier, Ricciotti was at a boarding-school in England, and Teresita was about to marry one of Garibaldi's young officers, Major Stefano Canzio. It was Garibaldi, not the children, who needed a woman to love him, to fill a need that neither Emma Roberts nor Battistina Ravello was able to satisfy. Garibaldi was in the unsatisfactory position that, though he was surrounded by adoring women who worshipped him, he had great difficulty in finding a woman whom he loved who was willing to marry him.

In May 1859 Battistina Ravello in Caprera gave birth to Garibaldi's child, a daughter whom they named Anita. Garibaldi thought of marrying Battistina, and just before the outbreak of war he was wondering whether it would be possible to obtain an official certificate of Anita's death from the officials in the Papal States which would enable him to marry again. But if he contemplated marrying Battistina, it was out of a sense of duty, because he was not really in love with her; and his hesitation about marrying her was encouraged by Signora

Deidery, who strongly opposed the idea. She thought that Battistina was a low-minded and common person, and urged Speranza to marry Garibaldi to prevent him from marrying Battistina.[26]

When Garibaldi met Giuseppina Raimondi near Como during the campaign of May 1859, he fell violently in love, and asked her to marry him. She refused. She did not tell Garibaldi, but she was in love with one of his young officers, Luigi Caroli, and was having an affair with him. Garibaldi looked elsewhere for love. When he was in Bologna in October he fell in love with the Marchesa Paulina Zucchini, a beautiful young widow, who was the grand-daughter of King Joachim Murat of Naples. He met her at the Villa Letizia, the house of her sister Carolina Tattini, and walking with her in the garden, he asked her to marry him. Again he met with a gentle refusal; again he had established a friendship which persisted, but he had not found a wife.[27]

Speranza von Schwartz had neither accepted nor refused him when he proposed to her in August 1858, but had asked for time to consider. This was just about the time when Garibaldi and Battistina conceived their daughter Anita; perhaps Garibaldi resumed his affair with Battistina at this time because of Speranza's hesitation. Since that date Garibaldi had not renewed his proposal to Speranza, and she had not made up her mind whether to accept him or not if he did. As he continued to write her affectionate letters, she imagined that he still wished to marry her; but when she visited him in the Romagna in September 1859 she noticed a change in his attitude, and though he gave her a ring as a present, he did not spend as much time with her as she had expected. She then heard from Signora Deidery that Battistina had had a child by Garibaldi. She was upset by the news; but she had lost her chance to marry Garibaldi, if that was what she wanted.[28]

In September Garibaldi wrote a passionate love-letter to Giuseppina Raimondi, and followed this up with further declarations of love. At the end of November he received a much more encouraging reply from Giuseppina than any which she had so far sent him; and as soon as he had finished his business with the King in Turin, he hurried to Fino on Lake Como, where he spent a fortnight with the Marquis Raimondi and Giuseppina.[29]

Garibaldi now became utterly infatuated with Giuseppina; but he had to wrestle with his conscience about Battistina. He had not seen Battistina since the birth of Anita, nor had he yet seen his daughter, having come to Lake Como in pursuit of Giuseppina instead of returning to Caprera to see the mother and child. Garibaldi was not a conventional aristocrat or bourgeois who could without compunction make love to his maidservant and make her pregnant while rejecting as absurd the idea of marrying her; he was a member of the generation of Radicals who considered such conduct to be very reprehensible, and an example of shameful exploitation by the ruling classes. He was also perturbed by the fact that he, a Radical and a disciple of the Saint-Simonian Socialists, had proposed marriage to the Baroness von Schwartz, to the Marchesa Zucchini and the Marchesina Raimondi, but not to the peasant girl, Battistina Ravello. He expressed his dilemma in one of his love-letters to Giuseppina Raimondi. He told her that he longed to marry her, though he felt it was his duty to marry Battistina; and although Giuseppina had not despised him for his poverty, could she, a girl of eighteen, love an old man of fifty-two?[30]

Giuseppina herself, though Garibaldi did not know it, faced the same dilemma; but she was not honest enough to tell him, or too young to venture to do so. Like thousands of other young Italian girls of her age, she admired Garibaldi as a national hero, and she was honoured that he wished to marry her; and her father strongly approved of the match. But though she felt it was her filial and patriotic duty to marry Garibaldi, she wished to marry her young lover, Lieutenant Caroli. So, while Garibaldi's admirers throughout Europe were reading in the popular biographies of how the young Garibaldi had eloped with the Count of Ramsberg's daughter, though the Count despised him for his humble birth, and with Anita, whose father wished to compel her, against her will, to marry an old man,[31] the story was being enacted in real life at Fino in reverse, with Garibaldi as the elderly suitor favoured by the aristocratic father, whom the daughter was being forced to marry, although she was in love with a handsome young man.

The date of the wedding was fixed for early in January 1860, but had to be postponed when Garibaldi broke his kneecap in a riding accident at Fino, and was confined to his bed for some days. Giuseppina showed great affection for him during his convalescence, and he loved her more than ever.[32] On 24 January they were married by the local priest with a Catholic ceremony in the Marquis Raimondi's private chapel at Fino. Teresita was a bridesmaid, and Garibaldi's friend Valerio, the former editor of *La Concordia*, who had been appointed Governor of the Como district, was Garibaldi's best man at the wedding. As the bride and bridegroom left the chapel after the ceremony, young Major Rovelli, who was Giuseppina's cousin, handed Garibaldi a piece of paper. Garibaldi read the contents, showed it to Giuseppina, and asked her if the statement on the paper was true. She said that it was; whereupon Garibaldi, in an outburst of rage, called her a whore and seized a chair which he waved in the air, threatening to bring it down on Giuseppina's head. She faced him without flinching, and told him that though she had thought that he was a hero, she now knew that he was only a brutal soldier. He did not strike her, but led her to her father. He told them that Giuseppina must never use his name, and that though she was the Marquis's daughter, she was not Garibaldi's wife. He never spoke to her again.

Twenty years later, when Garibaldi wished to legitimize his bastard children by marrying their mother, Francesca Armosino, he divorced Giuseppina in January 1880. The evidence in the divorce proceedings, though it was kept secret at the time, was afterwards published, and from this and from several letters of Valerio we know the contents of the note that was handed to Garibaldi as he left the chapel, and the reasons for the immediate breakdown of the marriage. Giuseppina, apparently with the knowledge of her tolerant father, had been the mistress of several men ever since the age of eleven. Soon after she met Garibaldi, she fell seriously in love, for the first time, with Luigi Caroli, who was at Como with Garibaldi in June 1859; and when Caroli was moved to Milan, he often visited Giuseppina surreptitiously at Fino and spent the night with her. After Giuseppina agreed to marry Garibaldi, she probably became Garibaldi's mistress before the wedding, though she was in love only with Caroli. Her cousin Major Rovelli, who wrote the note to Garibaldi, had formerly been one of Giuseppina's lovers; he was madly jealous both of Garibaldi and of Caroli. He revealed to Garibaldi the truth about Caroli in order to wreck the happiness of Garibaldi and Giuseppina, having for this reason deliberately waited until after the wedding before giving Garibaldi the note. It also seems – though this is not so certain – that Rovelli had persuaded Giuseppina, on the night before the wedding, to allow him the final consolation of sleeping with her once more, and that he revealed this also in his note to Garibaldi. Seven months afterwards, Giuseppina gave birth to a still-born child, though whether Caroli, Rovelli or Garibaldi was the father is uncertain.[33]

The events at Fino were reported in the press, but public comment on the breakdown of the marriage was restrained. Cavour, who had just become Prime Minister again, wrote a kind and tactful letter about it to Valerio. 'Garibaldi's case has grieved me,' he wrote on 1 February. 'Although he allowed himself to be dragged into a union with my personal enemies, Brofferio and Company, I none the less recognize that he is one of the greatest forces which Italy is able to use.' Valerio thought that Cavour ought to know that Giuseppina, and not Garibaldi, was to blame, and wrote to tell him the full facts.[34]

The matter was a tragedy for all concerned. Even the contemptible Rovelli can have had little satisfaction from his revenge, because in

June 1879 he wrote to Giuseppina, pleading with her to meet him again after nineteen years and denying that he had written the note to Garibaldi, though it is difficult to believe this in view of the fact that Garibaldi himself wrote to Crispi that it was Rovelli who had informed him about Giuseppina's infidelities. The Marquis Raimondi, who had hoped to have the honour of being Garibaldi's father-in-law, found himself an object of ridicule and contempt. Caroli, who was devoted to Garibaldi, his general, was shocked when he heard that Garibaldi was about to marry Giuseppina, and broke off his association with her. In 1863 he was one of the Garibaldini who volunteered to fight for the revolutionaries in Poland; he was taken prisoner by the Russians and sent to Siberia, where he died soon afterwards.[35]

It was a bitter blow for Garibaldi, as is shown by the fury of his reaction. He did not usually insist that his wives or his mistresses should come to him as virgins; but Giuseppina's deception, even on the eve of the wedding, had wounded him, because he had honestly revealed everything about Battistina to her, and thought that he had at last found someone who loved him. He was perhaps also hurt by the fact that she had preferred one of his young officers to himself, and that, thanks to her, he had been cast, not in his traditional role of the gallant lover, but as the elderly man who was forced on the young beauty against her will. He never forgave Giuseppina. When she sent him a message of sympathy after he was wounded at Aspromonte in 1862, he did not reply; and when on one occasion she came to Caprera to visit him, he refused to see her, and told Signora Deidery to get rid of her.[36]

Giuseppina lost her lover Caroli and her unborn child as well as her position as Garibaldi's wife. She never made any attempt to justify herself during Garibaldi's lifetime, and did not defend the divorce proceedings in 1879, apparently because she did not wish to embarrass Garibaldi and weaken the position of the man whom she always admired as a national hero, even though she was never in love with him. After the divorce she re-married, and lived happily with her second husband, Ludovico Mancini, till his death in 1913. As long as Garibaldi lived, the press did not often refer to Giuseppina Raimondi; and both Guerzoni and Jessie White Mario, in their biographies of Garibaldi which they published very soon after his death, passed over the details of his second marriage with the usual discretion of nineteenth-century biographers. But Speranza von Schwartz revealed a large part of the story, and vilified Giuseppina, in her *Recollections of Garibaldi* in 1884. Thirteen years later Finali published one of Valerio's statements about the case in his book *Le Marche*; but Giuseppina kept silence. She was still living in 1913, when Curàtulo published his book

Garibaldi e le donne, which revealed details of many of Garibaldi's love affairs, and nearly all the facts about Giuseppina.[37]

A few years earlier she had made her only public statement about her relations with Garibaldi.

> It has been suggested that I should have persisted with my refusal of marriage to the very end. But although in those days, as a girl of eighteen, I was allowed sufficient liberty to go between Como and Varese as I pleased in troubled times, and was permitted to choose the men whom I would love, nevertheless the choice of a husband was jealously guarded. How can one expect so much courage from a girl who was abandoned by everyone? Even Caroli, who was sure of my love, left me on my own at the end.

She died in 1918, having four years previously given Garibaldi's love-letters to her, which she had kept since 1859, to the State Archives in Mantua.[38]

CHAPTER 28

THE SICILIAN EXPEDITION:
THE DEPARTURE FROM QUARTO

As soon as Cavour returned to power, he concluded his bargain with Napoleon III. Sardinia was to annex Parma, Modena, the Romagna and Tuscany; the Pope was to retain Umbria and the Marches; Sardinia was to cede Savoy and Nice to France. In each case the cessions were to be approved by a plebiscite in the ceded territory. In March 1860 the plebiscite in Parma, Modena and the Romagna, where nearly all the electorate voted, showed a majority of 426,006 against 1,506 in favour of annexation by Sardinia; in Tuscany 366,571 voted for annexation, 14,925 against, and nearly 153,000 abstained.[1]

The agreement to cede Savoy and Nice to France, subject to the approval of the inhabitants in a plebiscite, was announced on 24 March 1860. If the arrangement with Napoleon was regarded as a bargain, it was a very advantageous exchange for Sardinia; but the cession of the national territory outraged many Sardinians. Garibaldi, who less than six months before had transferred Anita's body from Mandriole to Nice, was indignant at the loss of his home town. On this point, at least, General Fanti agreed with him, and Cavour had great difficulty in preventing Fanti from resigning as Minister of War.

For twenty months since the meeting at Plombières, the agreement about Savoy and Nice had been a well-kept secret. Sir James Hudson had periodically asked Cavour if there was any truth in the rumours which were circulating, and Cavour had always assured him that the cession of Savoy and Nice had never been discussed or contemplated. When the treaty was published on 24 March, the British government were angry, and became very alarmed at the threat of French expansion in Italy. But it did not shake the enthusiasm for the Italian cause in Britain. When the Sardinian Minister in London, Emanuel d'Azeglio, visited the Palmerstons at Lady Palmerston's house at Brocket in Hertfordshire, he found Palmerston very displeased with Cavour, but not anti-Italian. D'Azeglio frankly told Cavour that it would be a long time before Palmerston and Russell believed anything he said; but at the same time he emphasized that Italy was still a favourite country for the British government and people.[2] The chief effect of the cession of Savoy and Nice was to swing the British government against Cavour and in favour of Garibaldi; and as the quarrel between Cavour and Garibaldi developed, British public opinion became increasingly pro-Garibaldi.

In the new, enlarged Kingdom of Sardinia, which had more than doubled its area and population, a general election was held. As the cession of Savoy and Nice was not to take effect until after the plebiscite, these districts were entitled, for the last time, to send MPS to the Sardinian Parliament. Garibaldi was elected as one of the two MPS for Nice. This did not please either Napoleon III or Cavour. On 21 March, three days before the treaty of cession was made public, Cavour wrote to the Governor of Nice that the prospect of Garibaldi standing for Nice was worrying France, and added: 'It may be impossible to prevent him, but if it were possible to achieve this without the open intervention of the authorities, I would be very glad.'[3]

After leaving Giuseppina Raimondi at Fino, Garibaldi returned to Caprera, and saw Battistina and his daughter Anita; but he did not stay there long. At the beginning of April he went to Turin for the meeting of Parliament. In Turin he formed a Nice Committee, composed of several natives of Nice and other strong opponents of cession. A young Englishman, Laurence Oliphant, who was on holiday in Turin, got in touch with some members of the Nice Committee, and, though he was acting quite unofficially, sent reports to the British government of what they were doing. On 10 April he attended a meeting of the Nice Committee. After climbing a long, dark staircase, he entered a large room, somewhere near the top of the house, where he found fourteen or sixteen men seated around a table. Garibaldi sat at the head of the table, wearing his poncho. It was agreed that Garibaldi should speak against the cession of Nice in Parliament.[4] The immediate object of the committee was to get the plebiscite postponed, so that the opponents of cession would have time to counter the propaganda which was being put forward by the officials in Nice in favour of cession to France.

Garibaldi tried several times to persuade the President of the Chamber to allow an emergency debate on Nice, but it was not until 12 April that he was allowed to raise the matter. This was only three days before the plebiscite was due to begin, for voting was to take place on 15 and 16 April. Oliphant spent two hours with Garibaldi helping him to prepare his speech, but he did not expect Garibaldi to make a good impression. 'Certainly politics were not his strong point,' wrote Oliphant. 'He would not make a note or prepare his ideas; he told me several times what he intended to say, but never said twice the same thing, and always seemed to miss the principal points.' When the

431

day of the debate came, Garibaldi's speech received great applause, but did not weigh as much with the MPS as Cavour's cool logic. Apart from pointing out that Nice had been part of the territory of Victor Emanuel's ancestors since 1388, and that it had always been an Italian, not a French, town, Garibaldi gave no reasons against cession, and the government plan for the plebiscite was approved by a large majority. Garibaldi was not surprised, for he had no faith in Parliamentary procedures. 'There, I told you so,' he said to Oliphant, 'that is what your fine interpellations and Parliamentary methods always come to. I knew it would be all a waste of time and breath.'[5]

The Nice Committee worked out a new plan. They knew that there would be no French or Sardinian troops in Nice during the plebiscite, because they were being withdrawn from the town in order to avoid all appearance of intimidation. Garibaldi and his comrades would charter a ship and sail from Genoa to Nice on the last day of the voting, and wait offshore until the hour when the poll closed. After everyone had voted, and before the votes had been counted, they would raid the polling stations, break open the ballot-boxes, and burn the ballot-papers. The authorities would then have to hold a second plebiscite, which would mean a delay of at least a fortnight; and during this fortnight Garibaldi would go to Nice and make speeches against the cession, thus countering the effect of the official propaganda in favour of France.

The committee obtained the ship at Genoa. Oliphant travelled in the train from Turin to Genoa with Garibaldi and his Adjutant. Garibaldi had reserved a private compartment for the three of them, and he spent the journey looking at his large correspondence; after reading each letter, he tore it up and threw the pieces on the floor, so that by the time they reached Genoa the compartment looked like an enormous wastepaper basket. Garibaldi and his friends went to a second-class hotel on the waterfront which Garibaldi used as his head-quarters in Genoa, and prepared to sail to Nice next day. But that evening Garibaldi was persuaded to abandon his plan by a group of friends, and by a Sicilian lawyer, Francesco Crispi, who had come to Genoa to persuade Garibaldi to go to Sicily instead of Nice to help the revolution which had broken out in Sicily eleven days before.

Oliphant went to Nice to observe the plebiscite. The voters were supposed to deposit ballot-papers marked either 'Yes' or 'No' into the ballot-boxes; but Oliphant did not see any 'No' papers available at the polling station. He himself voted 'Yes' as a kind of protest, although his name was not, of course, on the electoral register. 25,943 electors voted for annexation and 260 against, with 4,743 abstentions. In

Savoy, the vote was 130,533 for annexation, 235 against, and 4,610 abstentions.[6]

But Crispi had turned Garibaldi's attention from Nice to Sicily. Crispi, who thirty years later became a Right-wing Prime Minister of Italy, was a Mazzinian in 1860. He had played an active part in the revolution in Sicily in 1848, and had also been involved in the Mazzinian plot of 6 February 1853 in Milan; but he was quite willing to work with Garibaldi to win Sicily for Victor Emanuel if Garibaldi would come to the aid of the Sicilian revolutionaries.

Sicily was the most revolutionary area of Italy; but there were local factors which complicated the situation. In Sicily, as elsewhere, there were Mazzinian intellectuals and idealists, and others who favoured Manin's policy of Victor Emanuel King of Italy; but there was also a strong separatist movement, which demanded independence from Naples, or at least home rule for Sicily, but was equally hostile to all other outside interference. Apart from these revolutionary movements, which were supported by all classes, the extreme poverty of the peasants on the large agricultural estates had produced a state of bitter class war. The rural areas, which were governed on almost feudal lines by the landowning nobility, were always on the verge of a bloody *jacquerie*. There was also great poverty and lawlessness among the urban working classes in Palermo and Messina. In parts of the island, particularly in the area around Palermo, the powerful secret society, the Mafia, exercised a more effective control over the population than did the police officials of the Neapolitan government. It operated as a mutual protection society, and murdered those who opposed it.

King Ferdinand of Naples, the notorious 'Bomba', had died in May 1859, leaving his weak-minded son of twenty-three to succeed him as King Francis II. The new King, influenced by the modern-minded young Bavarian Princess whom he had just married, by a progressive minister, Filangieri, and most of all by the victory of France and Sardinia in the war of 1859, pursued a slightly more Liberal policy than his father on the mainland and in Sicily; but as usual this led to increased revolutionary activity, and to retaliatory outbreaks of savage repression by the police. Mazzini, in London, decided that Sicily would be a good place to try another of his revolutionary adventures. He sent Crispi, with a false British passport and mutton-chop whiskers, to contact revolutionary Radicals in Sicily.

In October 1859 Crispi and La Masa, another Sicilian of somewhat less Radical views, came to Bologna and Turin in an attempt to persuade the Sardinian authorities to allow the impatient revolutionaries in Garibaldi's army in the Romagna, who were clamouring to invade the Marches, to be diverted to an expedition to liberate Sicily. The idea was quite favourably entertained by Victor Emanuel and his Minister of the Interior, Rattazzi, because an invasion of Sicily by irregular forces would certainly arouse less resentment from Napoleon III than an attack on the Papal territory; but it was nevertheless too risky a step to undertake lightly.

In February 1860 Bertani, who was a Mazzinian, wrote to Garibaldi in Caprera and urged him to lead an expedition to liberate Sicily. Garibaldi hesitated, as he had done when Mazzini and Jessie Mario had urged him to support similar expeditions in 1854 and 1857. He thought that the venture would fail as surely as Pisacane's in 1857, and he would not go on a mad adventure; and he insisted that, if he led any expedition, it must be in the name of Victor Emanuel King of Italy.[7]

In March, Mazzini decided to bring matters to a head in Sicily and force Garibaldi's hand. He issued a manifesto calling on the Sicilians to revolt, and sent his friend Rosolino Pilo from London to incite an insurrection and to tell the people that Garibaldi was coming to lead it. His friends in the island acted before Pilo arrived. A Mazzinian plumber named Riso started a revolution in Palermo with seventeen followers on 4 April. The result was a tragic and pathetic failure. When the revolutionaries were attacked by government troops, Riso's home-made bombs failed to explode, and the troops arrested them. Riso was induced to betray the names of other revolutionaries by the threat that otherwise his father would be shot, only to find, after he had given the information, that his father had been executed some days before. But though the revolt was suppressed in Palermo, it continued to smoulder among the peasants in the countryside.[8]

The news of the insurrection of 4 April caused great excitement in the North. A Sicilian Committee was established in Genoa, including Crispi, Bertani, Bixio, Medici and a former priest, Giuseppe Sirtori. This committee invited Garibaldi to lead an expedition to Sicily. Garibaldi went to the King and asked his permission to go. Victor Emanuel listened sympathetically, but postponed giving a decision; and a few days later, apparently after consulting Cavour, he told Garibaldi that he could not go.[9]

Cavour was in two minds about the plan. He was conscious of the pressure of public opinion in favour of action, and hesitated to affront it at a time when he was already unpopular because of the cession of Savoy and Nice, and was in the middle of a general election campaign for a new Parliament which was to be elected on 7 May; but he did not wish to involve Sardinia in difficulties with foreign powers, and he mistrusted the Mazzinians who were surrounding Garibaldi. He therefore contacted the moderate La Masa, and suggested that La Masa should organize an expedition to Sicily without Garibaldi. He authorized his friend La Farina of the National Society to take 1,500 muskets from the arsenal at Milan for the expedition, though, as it happened, the muskets were rusty and antiquated. They were taken to the railway station at Genoa, and kept there under La Farina's control.

Meanwhile Crispi and his colleagues were continuing their pressure on Garibaldi, who could not make up his mind whether to go to Sicily or to raid the ballot-boxes in Nice. On 12 April he decided to go to Sicily with 200 volunteers who had come to Genoa in order to join him. He sent an order to Milan to send 200 of the new Enfield rifles of the most modern type which had been purchased with the money from the Million Rifles Fund. But the Governor of Milan was Massimo d'Azeglio, who had been Prime Minister in 1849 and had ordered Garibaldi's arrest and deportation. He refused to permit the rifles to be handed over to Garibaldi. 'We could declare war on Naples', he wrote, 'but not have a diplomatic representative there and send rifles to the Sicilians.'[10]

But Garibaldi went ahead with his plans for the expedition to Sicily, and abandoned his project to attack the ballot-boxes in Nice. He set up his headquarters in the villa of his friend Agosto Vecchi at Quarto, on the sea about four miles south of Genoa. Vecchi, who had fought with Garibaldi in Rome, was now too old to fight, but played an active part in organizing the Sicilian expedition. The villa was surrounded by crowds of people, including journalists, police agents and spies of foreign governments. Garibaldi was forced to give up his habit of taking a daily walk in the hills above Genoa, in order to avoid the journalists who questioned him whenever he set foot outside the villa grounds. He did not leave the villa for three weeks, and engaged in digging in the garden as an alternative form of exercise. For the first time since 1849, he dressed himself in the red shirt, and adopted it as the uniform of all the volunteers. He no longer wore it hanging loose, as he had done in Uruguay and Rome, but tucked it inside the trousers at the waist. He wore the red shirt for the rest of his life – on campaigns, at home in Caprera, in Parliament, and at banquets in London.

More and more volunteers kept arriving at Quarto. The delay in obtaining arms was fortunate in this respect, because the 200 men with whom Garibaldi might have sailed in mid-April if he had obtained the rifles from Milan had risen to 500 ten days later, and to over 1,000 by the beginning of May. There was a mood of patriotic enthusiasm among the youth which they still remembered with pride forty-five years later, when G. M. Trevelyan went to Italy to do the research for his book *Garibaldi and the Thousand* and met the young men of 1860 in their old age. 'Those who remember the day,' wrote Trevelyan, 'speak of it as something too sacred ever to return. Italy has never seen the like of 1860 again.' Young Giuseppe Abba, coming from Parma to join the expedition, recognized at a glance those of his fellow-passengers in the train who had come, like himself, to volunteer. He also met an old gentleman who was shocked that he was going on an illegal fili-bustering expedition against the Kingdom of Naples.[11]

Garibaldi persuaded La Farina to let him have the muskets at the railway station in Genoa which had been scheduled for La Masa's expedition which had not materialized. He was disgusted at the poor quality of the weapons, but as he was not allowed to have the excellent rifles for which the people had subscribed out of devotion to him, he had to make do with these old muskets. He also had a few modern rifles which were sent direct to him from England, and a hundred revolvers sent by Colonel Colt from the United States. He got in touch with the manager of the Rubattino Steamship Company in Genoa, and persuaded him to connive at the seizure of two steamships for the expedition without Rubattino's authority.[12]

Victor Emanuel and Cavour had two strings to their bow. On 15 April Victor Emanuel wrote a private letter to King Francis of Naples, suggesting that he and Francis should partition the Papal States, leaving only Rome and the Patrimony of St Peter to the Pope, and divide Italy between them, though he added that this could not be achieved unless Francis introduced constitutional reforms in his king-dom. Francis, who was a devoted Catholic, was shocked at the proposal to join the excommunicated Victor Emanuel against the Pope, and rejected the proposal; so Victor Emanuel and Cavour continued to turn the blind eye to Garibaldi's preparations. But the governments of the Great Powers knew what was going on at Quarto, and protested to the Sardinian government. The Neapolitan Minister demanded an explanation. The Russian government intervened, considering it their duty to throw their influence against any encouragement of revolution in any country, and the Tsar sent a personal letter to Victor Emanuel on the subject. *The Times*, though strongly sympathetic to Garibaldi's expedition, wrote that there had rarely been so flagrant a toleration by a government of preparations on its soil for warlike operations against a friendly foreign state.[13]

But Garibaldi hesitated. He would not lead his men on a suicidal expedition which had no chance of success, and he would only go if he were convinced that a serious revolutionary movement was developing in Sicily, because he knew that he could not defeat 25,000 Neapolitan troops with his thousand volunteers, and would have to rely on being joined by substantial numbers of Sicilian revolutionaries after he had landed. He was waiting for news of what was happening in Sicily; but news from Sicily, both then and a few weeks later, after Garibaldi had arrived there, was not easy to obtain, owing to the lack of any railways and an almost complete absence of roads in the interior of the island. On 27 April Crispi, at Quarto, received the famous telegram from his colleague Fabrizi in Malta: 'Offer of 160 casks of America rum 45 pence sold 66 casks English 47 in advance pounds 114 casks 147 brandy without offer. Advise cashing of bill of exchange 99 pounds. Answer at once.' Crispi was the only man at Quarto who knew the cipher, and decoded it: 'Complete failure in the province and city of Palermo. Many refugees received on board English vessels that have arrived at Malta. Do not start.'

Garibaldi called a conference of his chief advisers to decide what to do. Crispi, La Masa and Bixio were eager to go; Sirtori and Medici were against. Garibaldi decided that in view of the telegram from Fabrizi, they could not go, and told the volunteers, with tears in his eyes, that the expedition was off. It was a bitter disappointment to everyone. Bixio made a last attempt to persuade Garibaldi to go, and expostulated angrily with him; but Garibaldi remained adamant.

When the news was known in Genoa, it caused much bitterness. Some of the volunteers angrily packed their bags and went home. Others came to Crispi and Bixio and demanded that they should lead them to Sicily without Garibaldi. Some of them muttered that Garibaldi was afraid, and the Mazzinians said that he had once again betrayed them to the King and Cavour. Bixio and La Masa decided to go without Garibaldi, and Bixio went to tell him so. Garibaldi was deeply hurt, knowing that he would be accused of cowardice; but it did not make him change his mind.

But Crispi, though he had tried to persuade Garibaldi to go, did not want the others to go without Garibaldi. He persuaded Bixio and La Masa to wait for a few days in the hopes that Garibaldi would change his mind. On 29 April he told Garibaldi that he had wrongly decoded Fabrizi's telegram of the 27th. It should have read: 'The insurrection, suppressed in the city of Palermo, maintains itself in the provinces.' He also showed Garibaldi several other telegrams which he had received from Sicily confirming this. In after years both Bixio and Vecchi stated that Crispi had forged these telegrams in order to induce Garibaldi to go to Sicily. If so, his trick was successful. On 30 April at the villa in Quarto, which had been decorated in celebration of the victory at Rome over the French on 30 April 1849, Garibaldi took the decision to go to Sicily, and preparations were made for departure in four or five days.[14]

Meanwhile Cavour was becoming more alarmed at the diplomatic protests. He decided to consult with Victor Emanuel. The King was visiting his newly acquired territories in Tuscany. Cavour ordered a special train to take him on the railway to Bologna, which had only just been completed, and there he met the King, who had come from Florence by road to see him. They discussed the situation for several hours. They were alone, and kept no record of their conversation; but according to a French diplomat who wrote about it two years later, and who may have obtained his information from Nigra, the Sardinian Minister in Paris, Cavour urged Victor Emanuel to authorize the arrest of Garibaldi and the dispersement of his volunteers at Quarto, and said that he would stop the expedition from sailing even if he had to seize Garibaldi by the collar with his own hands. If the King and Cavour did decide to stop Garibaldi, they were too late.[15] On the evening of 5 May Garibaldi sailed from Quarto with 1,150 volunteers in two steamships, the *Piemonte* and the *Lombardo*, which Bixio and a group of volunteers had seized at pistol point from the crew, not all of whom, like the manager of the shipping line, were prepared to collaborate in the seizure of the company's ships. Garibaldi and 350 of the volunteers sailed in the *Piemonte*; the remaining 800 sailed under Bixio in the *Lombardo*. Crispi, La Masa, Sirtori and Türr went with the expedition. Medici, Cosenz and Bertani stayed behind, with orders from Garibaldi to organize another expedition to invade the Papal States as soon as possible.

Garibaldi's party immediately had a serious mishap. They had hired some smugglers to bring the ammunition for their muskets to the ships; but, either from malevolence or incompetence, the smugglers lost their way. Garibaldi nevertheless decided to sail without the ammunition, relying on picking up ammunition on the way. Next day he put in to Talamone on the coast of Tuscany. Although he had sailed from Quarto wearing the red shirt, he had brought a Sardinian general's uniform with him in case it should prove useful, and he sailed into Talamone wearing it, though Abba thought that it did not match his long hair and full beard, and Cavour afterwards complained that he had no right to wear it, as he had resigned his commission in the Sardinian army when he took up his command in Central Italy.

He sent Türr to the Sardinian army barracks at Orbetello, a few miles south of Talamone. Türr bluffed the commandant into believing that he had authority from the King to collect a supply of ammunition and more firearms, and the commandant handed them over – an act for which he was later court martialled by the Sardinian authorities, and acquitted on a technicality. The Garibaldini stayed the night at Talamone, where, to Garibaldi's fury, some of the volunteers got drunk and angered the inhabitants by pestering the girls of the village. But he drove them back to the ships.[16] He relied largely on Bixio to maintain discipline. Abba and Bandi, in their accounts of the expedition, give a vivid picture of Bixio cursing the slackers and breaking a plate in the face of a corporal who muttered some inaudible protest while being reprimanded by Bixio. If his men did not get up at once when reveille sounded in the morning, Bixio would go into their sleeping quarters and flog them with a horsewhip. On one occasion he smashed the head of a troublesome soldier with a rifle-butt.[17]

At Talamone, Garibaldi detached sixty of the volunteers and sent them to invade the Papal States under the command of Zambianchi. He intended this chiefly as a diversion, in order to deceive the enemy as to his intentions, but he also hoped that the local population of Umbria would join Zambianchi, and that Zambianchi would be able to start a revolution there and hold out until Medici, Cosenz and Bertani arrived from Genoa with a new batch of volunteers. In view of Garibaldi's reluctance to go to Sicily until he was convinced that a revolutionary movement was really developing there, it is surprising that he should have sent a band of sixty men to invade the Papal States where there had been no revolutionary uprising for nearly a year. None of the local inhabitants rose, and Zambianchi was forced to retreat into Tuscany, where he and his men were arrested by the Sardinian authorities. The others were released almost immediately, but Zambianchi himself was held in prison, without charge or legal authority, for nearly a year, Cavour having directed that he was to be treated with the greatest rigour.

Garibaldi has been criticized for the diversion in the Papal States, partly because Zambianchi had attained notoriety for having executed the priests in Rome in 1849. Trevelyan and other British Liberals regretted Garibaldi's willingness to collaborate with Zambianchi, both in the retreat from Rome in 1849 and in the 1860 expedition; and as the Mazzinians also disliked Zambianchi, and joined in the condemnation of his excesses in Rome, he has been universally censured, and the failure of the invasion of Umbria has been generally ascribed to his incompetence. Garibaldi certainly committed a great blunder in authorizing it. 'I fear it is a strategic and political error,' wrote La Farina on 12 May, 'let us hope that his good luck, and Italy's, will repair the mistake.' As a diversion it was a complete failure, because everyone had known for the previous three weeks that the expedition which was preparing at Quarto was designated for Sicily; it depleted Garibaldi's small force by sixty men; it alarmed Napoleon III and Catholic opinion in France, and led to an increase in French diplomatic pressure on the Sardinian government; and it increased Cavour's belief that Garibaldi was irresponsible, and that his expedition was too dangerous to Sardinian interests to be given any encouragement.[18]

Victor Emanuel, though he was much more sympathetic to the expedition than Cavour was, found it something of an embarrassment. Soon after Garibaldi sailed, Victor Emanuel said to d'Ideville, the French Minister in Turin, in his usual jovial manner: 'Of course it would be a great misfortune, but if the Neapolitan cruisers were to capture and hang my poor Garibaldi, he would have brought this sad fate upon himself. It would simplify things a good deal. What a fine monument we should erect to him!'[19]

Garibaldi himself and his supporters had boundless confidence that he would succeed against all odds, having a superstitious belief in his invulnerability and success. When he gave the order to go ahead at Quarto on the night of 5 May, despite the fact that the ammunition had gone astray, it was because he had an inner certainty that the expedition was going to succeed. The *Times* correspondent reported that in Turin, where the crowds gossiping under the porticos talked of nothing else except the expedition, the universal feeling was that as Garibaldi had survived worse dangers than this, he would come through in Sicily unharmed and victorious. This attitude was shared in Britain, where the sailing of the Thousand aroused great interest and sympathy. The leader-writer of *The Times*, after writing that even if Garibaldi failed in Sicily 'he will have lighted a candle in the south of Italy which will never be put out', added:

This time twelvemonth, when it was announced that Garibaldi was rushing in on the Austrian territory with a handful of men, the universal feeling was, that . . . the foolhardy leader would be crushed by the masses of the enemy which were concentrated about the lakes. But he was not crushed.[20]

Cavour cannot be blamed if, as a statesman guiding the destinies of his country, he adopted a less optimistic and Messianic attitude. His attitude to the expedition of the Thousand was a subject of dispute at the time, and has been ever since. A week after Garibaldi sailed from Quarto, the *Times* correspondent in Turin reported that, while the Neapolitan and Russian Ministers were repeatedly protesting to Cavour and accusing him of having instigated the expedition, 'the ultra-Liberals who are called Mazzinians, whether they belong to the association of Young Italy or outstrip Mazzini himself, are very loud and savage in their invectives against the supineness and, indeed, downright treachery, as they call it, of Count Cavour's Cabinet, by whom Garibaldi is abandoned to his fate.'[21] After Garibaldi had succeeded in Sicily and Naples, the dispute was carried on, in the Italian Parliament and in the press, with Cavour's supporters claiming

that he had always helped the expedition, and that his many statements to the contrary were only diplomatic subterfuges to appease the
indignation of foreign powers, while the Left-wing MPS and pamph-
leteers accused him of having hampered and sabotaged it. Cavour's
correspondence provides abundant evidence for both points of view,
because he wrote in a very different way in his letters to Emanuel
d'Azeglio, his Minister in pro-Garibaldian England, than he did to
Nigra, his Minister at the court of Napoleon III.[22]

Cavour acted with regard to the Sicilian expedition like Elizabeth I
of England in the sixteenth century and like other more modern
statesmen who make use of revolutionaries to further their national
interests. He would not support the revolution until he thought that it
was likely to succeed; thereafter he supported it in order to control it
and reap the rewards of the revolutionaries' daring. He also realized
that there were political advantages in having Garibaldi in Sicily
instead of stirring up trouble about Nice nearer home. Hudson, who
was a friend and admirer of Cavour, reported eight weeks later to Lord
John Russell: 'At the outset nobody believed in the possibility of
Garibaldi's success; and Cavour and *tutti quanti* thought the country
well rid of him and of the unquiet spirits who went with him. The
argument was, if he fails we are rid of a troublesome fellow, and if he
succeeds Italy will derive some profit from his success.' Two of Cavour's
other friends, De la Rive and Castelli, afterwards published statements which, though expressed less forcibly and frankly than Hudson's,
make it clear that Cavour's policy was one of wait and see.[23]

On 7 May Cavour ordered Admiral Persano, the Commander-in-
Chief of the Sardinian navy, to arrest Garibaldi and his volunteers if
they put in to any port in Sardinian territory on the mainland or in the
island of Sardinia. This order – perhaps intentionally – was sent out
too late to enable the authorities in Tuscany to detain Garibaldi at
Talamone; and next day Cavour ordered Persano not to interfere with
the Garibaldini if he encountered them on the high seas outside
Sardinian territorial waters. This was afterwards explained by Cavour's
apologists, notably by Persano himself, as a clear hint that he was not
in fact to arrest Garibaldi, but was to allow him to proceed unmolested;
but Garibaldi never accepted this theory. It seems more likely that
Cavour was afraid to offend foreign governments by not arresting
Garibaldi if he entered Sardinian waters, and to offend public opinion
at home by arresting him on the high seas, and therefore adopted a
strictly legalistic attitude which was well-suited to his double policy.

On 7 May Cavour wrote to Nigra that as soon as he heard that
Garibaldi had sailed from Quarto, he had cabled his orders to Persano
and to all Sardinian authorities to arrest Garibaldi if he entered

Sardinian waters. He added that the British Consul in Genoa was behind Garibaldi's expedition. Cavour did not tell Nigra that he had delayed for twenty-four hours before sending the order to arrest Garibaldi; nor did he ever explain why no attempt was made to arrest Garibaldi at Talamone, where the Thousand remained until the evening of 8 May – seventy-two hours after they had embarked at Quarto.[24]

CHAPTER 29

FROM MARSALA TO PALERMO

At Talamone, Garibaldi lost the sixty men whom he sent off under Zambianchi to invade Umbria. He also lost another half-a-dozen fanatical Republicans who were indignant that he had raised the flag of Sardinia at the flagmast of his ships instead of the Republican tricolour, and that he had declared that they would be fighting in Sicily for Italy and Victor Emanuel. He was joined at Talamone by another four or five volunteers, and sailed for Sicily with a total of 1,089 men and one woman – Crispi's mistress, who had come with him and cooked for the men.

These 1,089 were to become known, not very inaccurately, as 'the Thousand'. All except seventeen were Italians, and most came from the cities of the North – 160 from Bergamo, 156 from Genoa, 72 from Milan, 59 from Brescia, and 58 from Pavia, though only 7 came from Turin. There were about 50 Sicilians and 46 Neapolitan subjects from the mainland, and several refugees from the Austrian province of Venetia; but only 11 came from Rome and the Papal States. The oldest member of the Thousand was over sixty; he had fought in the army of Napoleon I. But most were young; more than half were under twenty. As in 1849, Garibaldi had a considerable number of boys who were little more than children; the youngest was aged twelve.

About 500, nearly half the total force, were members of the urban working class. Of the others, 150 were lawyers, 100 doctors, 100 business men, 50 engineers, 30 sea-captains, and the rest artists, authors, journalists, civil servants, barbers and cobblers; though, in the case of the professional and business men, many of them were still students, and only embarked on these professions in later years. The only class not represented was the peasantry.

> How splendid were your Thousand, O Italy! [wrote Garibaldi] . . . and variously dressed, as if they had been found in their place of work when they were summoned by the trumpet-call of duty. Splendid! They were splendid in the dress and cap of the student, and in the more humble dress of the bricklayer, the carpenter and the smith. I wish from my heart that I could have added 'and of the peasant'; but I will not distort the

truth. That sturdy and hard-working class belongs to the priests, who keep them in ignorance. There was not one case of them joining the volunteers.[1]

At 1.30 pm on 11 May Garibaldi arrived off Marsala on the west coast of Sicily, and his men saw the white houses and green gardens of the little port above them, as the fifty Sicilians among the Garibaldini ran to the ship's rail to get the first glimpse for many years of the native land from which they had escaped as refugees. There now took place the first of a series of extraordinary occurrences which led to the conquest of Sicily and the defeat of 25,000 Neapolitan troops by 1,089 Garibaldini. In earlier centuries, these events would have been unhesitatingly attributed to the direct intervention of Providence; in the hundred years since 1860 they have been seen as evidence of the power of international Freemasonry, of the influence of the Mafia, of English gold, or simply as remarkable coincidences which were very fortunate for Garibaldi. As the Neapolitan government, like everyone else, had known for some weeks that Garibaldi was planning to invade Sicily, they had guarded the coasts, and had reached the conclusion that he would probably choose the neighbourhood of Marsala as the place for a landing. They had therefore sent General Letizia with a body of troops to occupy Marsala and disarm all the inhabitants, on 6 May. On the same day the authorities in Palermo sent General Landi with another force to Marsala; but on 10 May, before these reinforcements arrived, the troops already in Marsala were withdrawn, and for twenty-four hours the port was undefended.

There were two Neapolitan warships in the harbour of Marsala. On the morning of 11 May, for no reason, they sailed away to the south. When Garibaldi arrived, he saw the ships in the far distance. He also saw two other warships just off-shore at Marsala, but these he recognized at once as British warships. One of them, by a strange coincidence, was commanded by Captain Winnington-Ingram, who had known Garibaldi in Montevideo. He and Captain Marryat had been sent to Marsala at the request of the British business community there. These British subjects, who engaged in the wine trade, had felt a little insecure at the presence of the Neapolitan troops. There were also a number of British merchant ships at Marsala. One of them sailed out as Garibaldi's two ships arrived. Bixio shouted to them as they passed to send news to Genoa that Garibaldi had landed at Marsala. The British crew responded with rousing cheers.

Garibaldi began to disembark his men and supplies. Ten years before, during the retreat from Rome, he had dodged the pursuing French and Austrian armies, which sometimes did not know that he

444

was only a few miles away; but since then, the telegraph had come to Italy, and even to Sicily. Garibaldi therefore sent a unit to seize the telegraph office at Marsala. When the Garibaldini arrived in the office they found that the telegraph clerks had fled, but they had left a note of the last cable that they had sent out. It stated that two Sardinian warships had arrived and were disembarking troops, and that it appeared that an armed invasion had begun. At that moment a message came in over the wire from the neighbouring town of Trapani: it asked for confirmation of the last message about the landing of Sardinian troops. The Garibaldini in the telegraph office cabled back that the last message had been sent in error, and that the ships which they had mistaken for warships were really merchant ships unloading sulphur. Back came a further message from Trapani: 'Idiots!' The Garibaldini then cut the telegraph wires, and left.

The Neapolitan warships had looked back and had seen the arrival of Garibaldi's ships, and turned round. One of them was unable to sail quickly, so the other steamed ahead and soon reached Marsala. Her commander was Captain Acton, a member of the English Catholic family which for several generations had served the King of Naples. He believed, like all other Neapolitan officials, that England was behind all the troubles in Italy; and when he saw the two English warships off Marsala, he deduced that the British navy was supporting Garibaldi's invasion. His opinion was confirmed when he saw the red shirts of the Garibaldini on the *Piemonte* and the *Lombardo*, because he thought, at a distance, that they were the red coats of the British army. He tried to get in touch with the British commanders, but had some difficulty in doing so, as Captain Marryat and Captain Winnington-Ingram had gone on shore to quieten the anxieties of the British inhabitants of the town. When eventually Acton found them, he told them that he would be forced to open fire on the Garibaldini, and hoped that no British ship would be damaged in the process. The British captains offered no objection to Acton's announcement.

By this time, the Garibaldini had nearly finished disembarking, but they were all lined up on the jetty, waiting to go inland, when Acton opened fire. Most of the shells fell short, and though one of the Garibaldini was knocked over by the blast, none of them was killed, and only two men and one dog were wounded. But Winnington-Ingram thought that if Acton had opened fire sooner, and at closer range, Garibaldi would have suffered heavy losses, and the whole future of the expedition would have been different.[2]

Crispi immediately took charge of the political side. He summoned a meeting of the town council of Marsala, and persuaded them to sign a declaration which he had drafted. It announced that the rule of the

445

Bourbon King was abrogated in Sicily, and invited Garibaldi, as the representative of Victor Emanuel King of Italy, to assume the office of Dictator of Sicily. Garibaldi accepted the invitation, and was proclaimed Dictator.[3]

His first act as ruler of Sicily was to give his usual strict orders against looting, which he enforced as strictly as in 1849, for in this campaign, too, he occasionally shot one of his own soldiers whom he caught stealing fruit in an orchard. At Marsala he forbade his men to requisition anything from the population except from the Jesuits, whom he soon afterwards expelled from Sicily. Apart from the Jesuits, who were hated by all the Liberals in Europe on account of their Conservative ideology at this period, he did not allow his men to treat the clergy as enemies. Despite his hatred of priests, he appreciated the fact that in Sicily, unlike in other parts of Italy, most of the clergy were on the side of the revolution. 'True, they are enemies to modern ideas of progress,' he said, 'but above all they are enemies to the Bourbons.'[4]

Next day, he set off with his volunteers for Palermo, the capital, which was about sixty miles to the north-east. The Garibaldini had found the population of Marsala a little cautious and unenthusiastic; but at Salemi, some twenty miles east of Marsala, where they arrived on 13 May, they were enthusiastically welcomed by the people, and from this time onwards they were continually joined by volunteers, and came into contact with partisan bands operating on their own. At Salemi, Garibaldi was joined by a revolutionary Franciscan friar, Father Pantaleo, whom Garibaldi called 'our new Ugo Bassi'. The friar stayed at Garibaldi's side throughout the campaign, despite the fact that he was subjected to a good deal of rudeness from some members of the Thousand when Garibaldi was absent.[5]

On 14 May Garibaldi learned that a Neapolitan army of 3,000 men under General Landi was at Calatafimi, eight miles north of Salemi. At 3 am on the 15th he marched out of Salemi to meet the enemy, and as the Garibaldini climbed to the top of a hill to the south of Calatafimi, they saw the Neapolitans across the valley at the top of the opposite hill. Landi had sent only 2,000 of his men to meet Garibaldi, having held the remaining thousand in the village of Calatafimi to guard against an attack by local partisans. Garibaldi, who had already been joined by over a hundred Sicilians since he left Marsala, had 1,200 men. The rain of the previous days had given way to very hot weather, and at midday, in a heat almost as great as that which he had experienced at San Antonio, the two armies advanced to meet each other in the valley. The Neapolitans quickly retreated to their previous positions on the heights of the Pianto dei Romani.

Garibaldi faced an enemy which outnumbered him by five to three, in a superior position, and equipped with modern rifles which were much better than the muskets which La Farina had provided for the Thousand. But he was, as usual, confident of victory, and believed that it was essential for the morale of the Sicilians that he should fight and win a battle. He ordered his men to advance up the hill with fixed bayonets in the face of the enemy fire. Sitting on his white mare, which he had named Marsala, he led the attack with his sword drawn, though Bixio tried to dissuade him from exposing himself so recklessly to the enemy fire. He told his men that here at Calatafimi they must make Italy or die.

The hillside was broken by terraces covered with vineyards, and as they reached each terrace the Garibaldini found some cover from view, if not from fire, and a place where they could pause for a slight rest. Pressing on up the hill, parched with thirst, and suffering casualties, they eventually reached the highest terrace below the summit. Here, because of the angle of the ground above them, they were virtually out of range of the enemy on the hilltop, though they were well within earshot and could hear the Neapolitans talking. The Neapolitans dared not charge down on to the terrace and sweep the Garibaldini down the hillside to certain destruction; and in this extremely precarious position, Garibaldi rested his men for nearly a quarter of an hour. Bixio advised him that there was no alternative except to retreat; but Garibaldi realized that this would be suicidal.

The Neapolitans, seeing that their bullets were passing over the heads of the Garibaldini, threw stones over the crest of the hill on to the Garibaldini on the terrace. One stone hit Garibaldi in the back. In a moment of inspiration, Garibaldi called out to his men that the Neapolitans were throwing stones because they had run out of ammunition, and ordered a last charge to reach the summit. The Garibaldini stormed up the hill. The Neapolitans had plenty of ammunition left, and put up a stiff resistance – stiffer than any that Garibaldi had encountered from the Austrians in the Alps in the previous year; but although their rifles were superior to the old muskets of the Garibaldini, they feared the bayonet, and eventually broke before the charge of the Thousand.

Garibaldi had won the victory which he needed, though he lost 30 men killed, among them a boy of thirteen, and 200 wounded. One of these was Menotti, who was struck by a bullet in the wrist. The Neapolitans lost 36 men killed and 150 wounded.[6] As they retreated through the villages, where they had terrorized the people a few days earlier, the inhabitants fell on them and slaughtered them.

A miserable sight! [wrote Garibaldi in his memoirs] we found the corpses of the Bourbon soldiers along the road, devoured by dogs! They were the corpses of Italians slaughtered by Italians. If they had grown up as free citizens, they would have rendered effective service to the cause of their oppressed country; and instead, as the fruit of the hatred excited by their perverse masters, they ended their lives lacerated, torn in pieces by their own brothers with a fury which would have horrified the hyenas.[7]

The outside world found it difficult to get reliable news of what was happening in Sicily. There was much anxiety about the fate of the expedition in Piedmont and in England, where the events in Sicily had aroused the greatest interest. *The Times*, instead of the half-column which was the maximum space which they normally allotted to any item of foreign news, devoted several columns nearly every day to the Garibaldi expedition, and on thirteen of the thirty days on which the paper appeared between 12 May and 15 June, had a lengthy editorial discussing his prospects and wishing him well.

On 21 May they published news which brought gloom to thousands of British breakfast tables. 'The following telegrams have been received at Mr Reuter's office. THE EXPEDITION OF GARIBALDI (Official). NAPLES, MAY 18. The bands of Garibaldi have been attacked at the point of the bayonet by the Royal troops near Calata Fimi, and totally routed, leaving on the battle-field their flag and a great number of killed and wounded, among whom was one of their chiefs.' The second telegram was only slightly less depressing; it was from an unofficial source in Naples, and said that there was some doubt as to the result of the battle of Calatafimi. Placards were posted up in the streets of Palermo and other towns announcing the complete defeat of the Garibaldini; but rumours that it was the Neapolitan troops who had been routed at Calatafimi were spreading rapidly through Sicily.[8]

The only real success of the Bourbon troops was on 21 May, when they found Mazzini's envoy, Pilo, who, since the defeat of the rising in Palermo on 4 April, had been holding out with his guerrilla band in the mountains and waiting for Garibaldi to come. The Neapolitan soldiers caught him in a surprise attack. Pilo was shot dead while he was writing a letter to Garibaldi, and his men scattered and fled.[9]

After the Battle of Calatafimi, Garibaldi moved on Palermo, thirty miles to the north-east. In the villages through which he passed, the Sicilians acclaimed him, kneeling to kiss his hand and his garments, like the people in the Alps had done in his campaign in the previous year. But Garibaldi discouraged them from paying him such honours, and, being eager to retain the goodwill of the clergy, he attended mass celebrated by Father Pantaleo, and knelt at the shrines of the local saints.[10]

The capture of Palermo appeared to be an almost impossible task. Nearly all the Neapolitan forces in Sicily were in Palermo, where General Lanza had an army of some 20,000 men well equipped with heavy artillery; but Garibaldi carried out the greatest strategic triumph of his career. He believed that he could capture Palermo and defeat a force nearly twenty times greater than his own if he could infiltrate his men into the city, unobserved by the enemy, and rouse the civilian population to insurrection. He advanced to within fifteen miles of Palermo, approaching from the west, and then swung to the south, disappearing into the mountains and making Lanza believe that he was retreating towards the centre of Sicily, but then turned north; and while a Neapolitan force under the Swiss mercenary, Colonel von Mechel, went searching for him as far south as Corleone, he approached Palermo from the south-east.[11]

Although the Neapolitan commanders had no idea where Garibaldi was, the Hungarian nationalist, Colonel Eber, whom *The Times* sent out as their war correspondent, had no difficulty in finding him in the hills to the south-east of Palermo, with the help of friendly peasants. In his report to *The Times*, Eber described his encounter with the Thousand in their camp at Misilmeri. When Eber arrived, Garibaldi had gone out for his morning walk, but he soon came back and talked to Eber. He was calm and relaxed, and completely confident of victory. Eber described how the Garibaldini were

all collected round a common nucleus – a smoking kettle with the larger part of a calf in it, and a liberal allowance of onions, a basket with heaps of fresh bread, and a barrel containing marsala. Everyone helped himself in the most communistic manner, using fingers and knife, and drinking out of the solitary tin pot. . . . The long marches and countermarches, rains, fights and sleeping on the ground had made almost everyone worthy to figure in a picture by Murillo, with all those grand Sicilian mountains, not unlike those of Greece, forming a background such as no picture can reproduce.[12]

At Gibilrossa, two miles beyond Misilmeri, Garibaldi met two British naval officers who happened to be sight-seeing at the monastery there. Garibaldi was very relaxed, and mentioned that he had been impressed to see, from the hills two days before, the British fleet in the harbour at Palermo when they fired a salute in honour of Queen Victoria's birthday.[13]

While Garibaldi waited at Gibilrossa on 26 May, everyone in Palermo knew that he was there and was going to enter the city that night – except the Neapolitan General Lanza and his staff. The word was passed round in the streets, shops and houses of Palermo; it reached the British fleet in the harbour and the prisoners in the jails. A delegation from the Revolutionary Council of Palermo came to Gibilrossa to discuss the plan for the rising with Garibaldi; but even when a man told Lanza that the red-shirts had been seen at Gibilrossa, he did not believe it.[14]

At 2 am on 27 May the Garibaldini entered Palermo and attacked the sentries and the handful of soldiers whom they encountered in the streets. Garibaldi was in the city where the European revolutions of 1848 had begun, and the people rose again. 'The people of Palermo,' wrote Garibaldi, 'ran to erect those citizens' bulwarks which make the mercenaries of tyranny turn pale – the barricades!'[15]

By midday on 27 May, after eight hours' fighting, most of Palermo was in the hands of the revolutionaries. The prison was captured, and all the prisoners, both the politicals and the common criminals, were released. The Neapolitan army replied by withdrawing to the royal palace and bombarding Palermo. They also held the cathedral nearby, and occasionally sent out raiding parties into the Toledo, the wide street which ran from the palace to the sea, and attacked the barricades there. The Garibaldini crept closer to the palace and the cathedral, erecting their barricades as near as possible and sniping at the royal troops. Sometimes, on their sorties, the Neapolitan troops massacred groups of civilians whom they captured. The revolutionaries committed no atrocities against the soldiers, but about thirty men, accused of being police spies, were lynched.

The street fighting and the bombardment continued for three days. The bombardment inflicted heavy casualties in the streets and the houses, and whole areas of the town were flattened; but the spirit of resistance of the population was roused. Garibaldi set up his headquarters at the city hall, in the Piazza Pretorio. He himself spent most of the time sitting on the fountain in the square, writing orders and smoking cigars under an enemy fire which was close enough that several men fell dead at his side. He had another lucky escape when the pistol in his pocket, which he had evidently been careless enough to keep loaded, was fired accidentally as he was dismounting from his horse, but it did no harm beyond making a hole in his trousers. Bixio was badly wounded, and, bleeding heavily and in a very excited state, cried out that it was now or never, and offered to lead any body of twenty men in an assault on the royal palace. Garibaldi calmly told him to get his wounds dressed and go to bed.

Garibaldi's chief anxiety was the shortage of ammunition; but he opened powder-mills in Palermo, and the population worked day and night to produce the ammunition required. The men came out into the streets with daggers, knives, spits and all kinds of iron instruments when they could not obtain muskets; and the women helped build the barricades, throwing down chairs, mattresses and furniture from the windows to provide the materials for the barricades, and pouring boiling water on the small detachments of Neapolitan troops who ventured out of the palace and the cathedral.[16]

On the morning of 30 May, after three days' bombardment and street fighting, Garibaldi had almost exhausted his stock of ammunition, and was considering whether it would be advisable to withdraw from Palermo and carry on guerrilla warfare in the countryside. Suddenly, at 9.15 am, he received a letter from Lanza, who on the previous day had tried to open negotiations through Admiral Mundy, the commander of the British squadron at Palermo, without dealing directly with Garibaldi. To Garibaldi's surprise, Lanza's letter was addressed to 'His Excellency General Garibaldi', and asked Garibaldi to agree to an immediate ceasefire and to send envoys to meet Lanza's officers on Mundy's flagship, the *Hannibal*, to discuss the possibility of a truce. Lanza, who did not know the desperate straits in which the revolutionaries were placed as regards ammunition, was suffering from a shortage of medical supplies and food for his 18,000 soldiers, who were packed, in very overcrowded conditions, in the palace and the cathedral and a few other strongpoints, and his wounded were suffering greatly. Garibaldi agreed to meet Lanza's representatives in the *Hannibal* at 2.30 that afternoon, and the ceasefire came into operation at 10 am.

At 9.30 am, a quarter of an hour after Lanza had sent his letter to Garibaldi, he was informed that Colonel von Mechel with 3,000 men, who had been searching for Garibaldi near Chiusa thirty miles to the south, had re-entered Palermo in the revolutionaries' rear. Lanza had been told on the previous evening that von Mechel would arrive next day, but had apparently not believed it. The presence of von Mechel's forces completely changed the military situation, and some of Lanza's officers urged him to abandon negotiations for a truce and renew the attack; but Lanza refused. Many years later, Türr told Trevelyan that if von Mechel had arrived on the previous day the revolution would have been defeated and the Garibaldini would have been wiped out.

At 2.30 pm Garibaldi, dressed in his Sardinian general's uniform, went on board HMS *Hannibal* and met Lanza's envoys, General Letizia and General Chretien. Letizia, who had been most embarrassed at finding himself in the same boat with Garibaldi on their journey from the shore to the *Hannibal*, at first refused to talk directly to Garibaldi, and asked Mundy to act as an intermediary between them: but Mundy refused, and said that he would only be the host, not the mediator, and he also insisted, with Garibaldi's consent and to Letizia's annoyance, that the commanders of the French, United States and Sardinian squadrons at Palermo should be present to witness Letizia's humiliation, the Austrian commander having refused Mundy's invitation to attend. Letizia proposed a truce for twenty-four hours, during which time Garibaldi would permit the Neapolitan wounded to be transferred from the palace to the Neapolitan ships in the harbour, and for provisions to be sent into the palace; and he also proposed that the people of Palermo should send a humble petition to the King of Naples professing their loyalty to the throne. Garibaldi refused to consider this last proposal, and said that the time for humble petitions was passed; and Letizia, whose offensive and bullying manner towards Garibaldi was only a mask to conceal what he wrongly believed was the weakness of his position, agreed to waive the demand. Garibaldi then agreed, after a show of reluctance, to a twenty hours' truce until noon on 31 May. In fact he was delighted to have a breathing-space in which to obtain more ammunition.

He spent the twenty hours searching everywhere for the ammunition. The men and women of Palermo worked continuously in the powder-mills to produce it. But Garibaldi got no help at all from the Sardinian warships in the harbour. The officers of the British squadron offered him their pistols, and a Greek warship sold him an old cannon; but when he sent a representative to ask for ammunition from the Sardinian warships, it was refused. 'The ratings of the English squadron here,' wrote Abba in his diary, 'seem much friendlier than our own men from the Piedmontese ships.'[17]

That evening, Lanza held a council of war with his officers, and decided that, in view of von Mechel's arrival, he would attack Garibaldi as soon as the truce expired next day. But in the morning he changed his mind, and to the indignation of some of his officers he sent Letizia to Garibaldi's headquarters at the town hall, where he signed an agreement with Crispi to extend the truce, on the same terms, for seventy-two hours. Lanza's officers had been impressed, on their visits to Garibaldi's headquarters, with the number and strength of the barricades in the streets, for the ramshackle barricades of furniture and mattresses of 27 May had by now been replaced with well-built obstructions of stone and brick. Lanza was doubtless also affected by the open signs of respect and sympathy which Mundy had shown to Garibaldi at the talks on the *Hannibal*. On 3 June Garibaldi and Letizia met again on the *Hannibal*, and the truce was extended for another seventy-two hours to 6 June. By now Lanza was receiving reports of risings at Catania and throughout the interior of Sicily.[18]

On 6 June Letizia, after going twice to Naples to consult with King

Francis and his government, met Garibaldi again, and signed an agreement by which Lanza and his 20,000 troops capitulated to Garibaldi, to the Thousand and to the citizens of Palermo. The Neapolitan troops were to evacuate Palermo and sail to Naples after surrendering their prisoners. The first 15,000 left next day, marching down the Toledo from the palace to the harbour, watched by Menotti, seated on a black horse with his escort of youths in red shirts. The remaining Neapolitans embarked on 19 June, which was the last day allowed for their departure under the terms of the capitulation. Before leaving, Lanza paid a courtesy visit to Mundy in the *Hannibal*; but next day, when the British squadron was dressed over all in honour of the twenty-third anniversary of the accession of Queen Victoria, it was General Garibaldi, Dictator of Sicily, who was the guest of honour in the *Hannibal*.[19]

The capitulation of 6 June was the last of a series of inexplicable moves by Lanza and the Neapolitan commanders in Sicily. There is no evidence for the theory of an intervention by international Freemasonry or the hidden hand of the Mafia; and if there is any truth in Duke Ernest of Saxe-Coburg's statement that the mystery of Garibaldi's success in Sicily is wrapped in English banknotes,[20] the State papers and the private correspondence of the British statesmen show clearly that the banknotes were handed over without the knowledge of Palmerston or Russell. None of these theories is as far-fetched as what is probably the true explanation – that Garibaldi won in Sicily because his daring and genius were helped at every stage by extraordinary and unforeseeable luck.

The only Neapolitan forces which remained in Sicily were 5,000 troops in Messina and a small area surrounding it, some ten miles in depth, in the north-east corner of the island. All the rest of Sicily was under the control of the new Dictator's government; and the leader-writer of *The Times* could tell Garibaldi's English admirers: 'He has done it.'[21]

CHAPTER 30

FROM PALERMO TO THE FARO

O N 2 June Garibaldi, who had moved into the royal palace in
Palermo, appointed the Cabinet that was to govern Sicily for the
time being under himself as Dictator. Crispi was Secretary of State and
Minister of the Interior. Garibaldi appointed Baron Pisani, a Conservative landowner, to be his Minister for Foreign Affairs and Commerce, and there was a Conservative majority in his government.[1] He
did not concern himself much with the government of Sicily, because
he was planning to cross the Straits of Messina as soon as possible and
liberate the mainland, and he devoted all his energies to the military
preparations. The government of Sicily was left chiefly to Crispi,
who drew up a number of decrees in the Dictator's name, though there
is no reason to believe that Garibaldi was a mere figure-head, or that
he did not approve of the orders issued in his name.

Garibaldi's victory had been helped by the fact that all classes of
Sicilians had united behind him, and that neither the landowners nor
the peasants had helped the Neapolitan government out of hatred for
their class enemies, as the peasants had done in 1848 and the landowners on several other occasions. But this united front against King
Francis and his soldiers did not put an end to the class struggle in the
Sicilian countryside; and, once Garibaldi had won in Sicily, it presented him with problems. Both landowners and peasants now expected
him to be on their side.

Garibaldi wished to maintain national unity in Sicily and to appease
and postpone the class struggle until after he had invaded the mainland,
because for him Sicily was primarily a stepping-stone to the achievement of the liberation of all Italy. But his decrees also expressed his
broad ideas of natural justice and fair play for all. He issued a proclamation promising to carry through a land reform and to give the
land to the peasants, not only because he wished to win the support
of the peasantry, but also because he believed that the Sicilian peasants, in their extreme poverty, were entitled to a share of the land.
He appealed to them to avoid violent attacks on the mansions of the
aristocrats and illegal seizures of the land, and imposed the death

penalty for looting, theft and kidnapping, not only because he wished to retain the support of the landowners and to avoid rural anarchy, but also because he believed it right that violence and illegality should be suppressed, except when these methods were used in the fight against a despotic government which he hoped to overthrow. He won the support of the merchants by abolishing the tariffs and restrictions on imports and exports, but he also believed that these measures would help raise the living standards of the Sicilian people.

Two of his measures, however, were unpopular. He introduced military conscription, based on the law of the Kingdom of Sardinia, and he tried to collect the taxes. In general he replaced the laws of the Kingdom of Naples, either by introducing Sardinian law or by re-enacting the decrees of the autonomous revolutionary Sicilian Parliament of 1848.[2] Unfortunately, he was quite unable to stamp out corruption in the civil service. Commander Forbes, a retired British naval officer who visited Sicily as half journalist and half tourist in the summer of 1860, stated that the subordinate officers of Garibaldi's government would do nothing unless they were first offered a bribe.[3]

Cavour believed that the solution to the difficulties in Sicily was immediately to annex the island to the Kingdom of Sardinia. When he heard that Palermo had fallen to Garibaldi, he switched his policy at once, and instead of attempting to stop Garibaldi's expedition and placing obstacles in his path, he tried to gain the benefits of Garibaldi's efforts for Victor Emanuel and the Kingdom of Sardinia. At the same time he tried to prevent Garibaldi from embroiling Sardinia with France. When Garibaldi sailed from Quarto, he had left Bertani, Medici and Cosenz behind, with instructions to organize another expedition to invade the Papal States. Cavour now assisted Bertani to recruit his volunteers, and issued the best modern rifles to them, but persuaded them to go to Sicily instead of invading the Papal States. He was thus able to claim the credit for sending reinforcements to Garibaldi, while preventing an attack on the Pope which would have caused great difficulties with France.

Garibaldi, though he always professed to be acting on behalf of Victor Emanuel, did not wish for immediate annexation to Sardinia. He wished to continue to run things himself for the time being; he believed that until Italy had been liberated, it was better for Sicily to be under his dictatorship than swept into the political controversies of Turin under Cavour; and, above all, as long as he was using Sicily as a base for his campaign to free the mainland, he did not wish to have Cavour sabotaging in his rear, depriving him of rifles again, and preventing him from crossing the straits. Events proved that he was right, because in July and August Cavour tried to stop him from invading the mainland, just as he had tried to stop him from sailing to Sicily in April and May.

Cavour had another source of anxiety. When Mazzini heard of Garibaldi's preparations at Quarto for the expedition to Sicily, he decided to join it, and came secretly from London to Genoa, although he was under sentence of death in the Kingdom of Sardinia. He arrived too late, for despite the fact that Garibaldi's departure was repeatedly delayed, the expedition had sailed three days before Mazzini reached Genoa on 8 May. This saved Garibaldi from the great embarrassment of having to decide what to do if Mazzini had arrived at the villa at Quarto.

Cavour ordered the police to make every effort to arrest Mazzini, and asked Napoleon III to search for Mazzinians in France and to collaborate with the Sardinian government in catching them. But he did not succeed in finding Mazzini in Genoa, and came to the conclusion that Mazzini might be in Sicily with Garibaldi. In June Cavour wrote to Nigra in Paris: 'I have made it known to Garibaldi that if he tolerates the presence of Mazzini in Sicily, I will recall the squadron and will no longer have the slightest contact with him.' Knowing the feelings in Britain about both Mazzini and Garibaldi, Cavour put it a little differently in his letter to Emanuel d'Azeglio, the Sardinian Minister in London.

> I see with pleasure the lively sympathies which Garibaldi's enterprise has aroused in England, and I am in no way jealous of his success. On the contrary, I have given the strictest orders to stop Mazzini from going to Sicily to spoil the work of the famous guerrilla leader. I am ready to do everything rather than tolerate that he should go and organize a republic in Sicily.[4]

The great enthusiasm for Garibaldi in Britain was causing anxiety to Cavour and to the French government, and they were a little alarmed at the possibility that Garibaldi might be in secret communication with the British government and planning to make Sicily a British protectorate. The Catholic press in France was denouncing Garibaldi as an English agent. 'At Marsala,' wrote a Catholic pamphleteer, 'we have seen him land, with a great apparent audacity, but really in the most favourable conditions under English protection, and on soil prepared from afar-off for every sort of cowardice.' The pamphleteer wrote that after staging a number of mock battles on the road from Marsala to Palermo in order to prove to the world that he had seven lives, Garibaldi had accepted the surrender of 25,000 soldiers in Palermo in one of the most cowardly capitulations in history.[5]

Palmerston, on his side, was worried that Cavour might have made a new secret bargain with Napoleon III by which Napoleon permitted Victor Emanuel to annex Sicily and Naples in return for the cession of Genoa and the island of Sardinia to France. When Cavour told Hudson that there was no truth at all in this rumour, Palmerston pointed out that Cavour had denied, with equal conviction, that he had made an agreement to cede Savoy and Nice to Napoleon, and had persisted in his denial until the day before the cession was announced. Palmerston considered that it would constitute a threat to British interests if France obtained a naval base at Genoa or in the island of Sardinia, and on 17 May he suggested to his Foreign Secretary, Lord John Russell, that they should send the British navy to the Straits of Messina to stop Garibaldi from crossing to the mainland, unless Cavour was prepared to sign a treaty with Britain, promising not to cede any more Sardinian territory without Britain's consent. Russell realized that British public opinion would never tolerate such a policy, and eight weeks later Palmerston suggested a completely different one: he proposed to Russell on 10 July that Britain should point out to Garibaldi that it would not further the liberation of Italy if Sicily were acquired by Victor Emanuel and Cavour, and that Garibaldi ought to govern Sicily as Governor for the King of Naples, who would be compelled, if necessary by the British navy, to grant home rule to Sicily and constitutional reforms throughout his dominions. Again Russell dissuaded Palmerston from putting the proposal to Garibaldi.[6]

The Mazzinians decided to make the most of the British government's fears. In June Bertani and his friends in Genoa either obtained or forged a draft of a secret treaty between Cavour and Napoleon III under which Genoa was to be ceded to France in return for Sicily. They sent a copy to Crispi, who showed it to Garibaldi; and Garibaldi, in great indignation, authorized Crispi to send it to the British government. Russell raised the matter with d'Azeglio, but it was not long before he and the British government decided that the document was a Mazzinian forgery.[7]

British public opinion was much more straightforward than Palmerston's thinking, and was so strong that it made it virtually impossible for the British government to do anything else except support Garibaldi in every action which he chose to take. Neither before nor after 1860 has any foreign leader aroused the enthusiasm of the British people as Garibaldi did during the Sicilian expedition. The ordinary Englishman had always disapproved of Mazzini as a Republican and a supporter of political assassination; since the cession of Nice and Savoy, he distrusted Cavour as a diplomatic trickster, and, what was worse, as pro-French. Garibaldi personified all that was pure in the Italian *Risorgimento*, shorn of revolutionary terrorism and of dishonest Francophile diplo-macy. The romantic personality of Garibaldi attracted support in Britain among far wider classes than the aristocrats and intellectuals who knew and loved Italy, and the Radicals who supported all revo-lutionary national struggles for freedom against absolutist governments. Nearly everyone in the country cheered him on. Women wore red Garibaldi blouses, and round, kepi-shaped Garibaldi hats.

As early as 12 May Emanuel d'Azeglio had told Cavour of the contradiction between the attitude of the British government and British public opinion. Whereas Russell had expressed the hope that the government of Sardinia would not be drawn into hostilities with Naples on account of Garibaldi's expedition, 'the other day, when it was believed that we had stopped Garibaldi from leaving, I found myself the object of universal reprobation in high society'. On 24 May d'Azeglio wrote to Cavour: 'Everywhere in England there is the greatest enthusiasm for Garibaldi's expedition. Even in the most Conservative circles they allow themselves to be swept along by the torrent; and the most beautiful ladies of high society are the first to clap their hands, and above all to dig into their pockets.' On 6 June d'Azeglio wrote to Cavour that the British 'are not very Cavourian; they are more Garibaldian than you could possibly imagine. Above all, the women; Lady John [Russell] can no longer sleep because of him, and Mrs Gladstone told me that two days ago, at the Duchess of Sutherland's, they drank Garibaldi's health.' Mrs Sidney Herbert told d'Azeglio that she, too, had drunk Garibaldi's health; and she was standing quite close to Apponyi, the Austrian Ambassador, when she spoke. 'Garibaldi is here a demi-god,' wrote d'Azeglio.[8]

Whatever Cavour's personal feelings might be, he realized that this British enthusiasm might be used to help Sardinia to acquire Sicily. On 18 June he sent a cable in cipher to d'Azeglio: 'Support openly everything that is done in favour of Garibaldi.'[9]

On 22 May a public meeting was held at St Martin's Hall in London to organize support for Garibaldi. A resolution was moved, 'that, in order to afford the friends of the brave Garibaldi an opportunity for showing their high admiration of his pure patriotism and heroic valour', a committee should be elected to organize the collection of subscriptions for a testimonial to be presented to him. The resolution was carried by acclamation, and Holyoake and other Radicals were elected to the committee. Everyone knew that the reference to a testi-monial to Garibaldi was a subterfuge, and that the subscriptions were in fact to be used to finance Garibaldi's expedition against the govern-ment of Naples, a state with which Britain was at peace.

The legality of giving such help to Garibaldi was raised by the small minority of people in Britain who were opposed to Garibaldi and the Italian cause. These consisted chiefly of Irish Catholics, who were particularly incensed because they had been threatened with prosecution under the Foreign Enlistment Acts if they recruited in Ireland for volunteers for the Foreign Legion of the Papal army, which Pius IX was forming to defend the Papal States from an attack by Garibaldi or by the Sardinian army. When Irish Catholic MPs raised the question in the House of Commons, the government law officers were embarrassed; the Attorney-General said that the collection of subscriptions in Britain to help Garibaldi was legal, while the Solicitor-General said that it was illegal. But the government continued to allow money for Garibaldi to be raised in Britain, while preventing the Catholics in Ireland from sending money to help the Pope and the Irishmen in his army.[10]

Contributions poured into the Garibaldi Fund. The second Duke of Wellington – the great Duke's son – sent £50, though he stipulated that the donation was to be anonymous. Florence Nightingale sent £10, and Charles Dickens £5. £300 was raised in one night at the Athenaeum Club. Gladstone, the Chancellor of the Exchequer, even hinted to Panizzi that the British government might make a secret contribution from public funds, but withdrew the offer for fear that Palmerston would object. In the North, where Cowen organized the collection of the money, there was a particularly enthusiastic response; in Berwick alone the initial response was disappointing, but here, too, the money came in later. In Darlington, posters in the streets advertised 'the greatest event of the year in Darlington, the Garibaldi Fund Soirée', tickets one shilling, 'the profits arising therefrom to be devoted to the Garibaldi Fund which is being raised in England for the purpose of assisting him in his heroic endeavours to liberate Italy from the Yoke of Tyranny'. In Newcastle, the shipping company, the Red Star Line, in which the Polish refugee, Lekawski, was a partner, placed their passenger boat, the *Garibaldi*, at the disposal of the Garibaldi Fund Committee for one day, all the takings on that day to go to the Fund. In Glasgow, John McAdam, the secretary of the Glasgow Friends of Italy, organized a special 'Working Men's Fund for Garibaldi', and held a meeting at Bell's Coffee House 'to consider how we can best support the Middle Class Friends of the Cause, who have already remitted to Italy and are preparing for another still larger remittance to which every true patriot should contribute without delay'.[11]

For many of the British people, the personality of Garibaldi had an even greater appeal than the Italian cause. One supporter wrote to Cowen: 'Garibaldi, remember, is THE *man of action* at *the present* moment, and he deserves all the support we can collect. I have nothing to do with the Italian Committee here or Mr Fabricotti or Mr Ashurst and Mr anybody else – I work for and with *Garibaldi & no one else* at PRESENT. The money that I receive shall be sent to HIM direct *if possible.*'[12]

There were men in Britain who were not content to give money, but wished to fight for Garibaldi. One of the first to volunteer was Colonel John Peard, a member of an Irish Protestant family from Tallow in County Waterford, who had fought for Garibaldi in the Alps in 1859. Peard was one of thirty-three Englishmen who reached Genoa in time to sail for Palermo with the relief expedition under Medici and Cosenz. Another was Colonel Forbes, Garibaldi's old comrade of 1849, who since then had fought for John Brown against the slaveowners in Kansas. Colonel Dunne, a veteran of the Crimean War, was in command of the little group.[13]

The Garibaldi Committee were careful not to break the law and antagonize the British government by inciting members of the British armed forces to desert and enlist for Garibaldi. When Gunner Brown of the Royal Artillery in Woolwich wrote to the committee, asking whether it would be legal for him to buy his discharge from the British army, at his own expense, and then join Garibaldi, he received a discouraging answer from the committee stating that they were sure that Garibaldi, with his love of England, would not wish any of the Queen's soldiers to leave her service.[14]

The efforts in Britain to raise a British Legion for Garibaldi did not have altogether happy results. An unscrupulous gentleman, calling himself Captain Styles, went to Sicily and obtained a letter signed by Garibaldi, authorizing him to raise a Legion of volunteers in Britain. Armed with this letter, he went to London and gulled the Garibaldi Committee into accepting him as Garibaldi's official agent in Britain. He established himself in Anderton's Hotel in Fleet Street, and spent day after day interviewing volunteers, having made it clear that neither he nor the committee would pay the volunteers' fares to London. In many cases, without any authority from Garibaldi or the committee, he granted them commissions in Garibaldi's army in return for money which he pocketed himself.[15]

At the end of August, an attempt was made to prevent the recruitment of volunteers by the small group who supported David Urquhart, a former member of the British diplomatic corps, whose hatred of Palmerston and his fear of Russian Tsarism had led him to imagine that everyone was a Russian agent, and to react violently against the selectivity of the sympathies of the British public for the oppressed subjects of the King of Naples. The Mayor of Gateshead, George Crawshay, who had formerly been a member of the Friends of Italy but had resigned and joined Urquhart's group, prosecuted the editor of the Newcastle *Daily Chronicle* for publishing an article in the paper under the heading 'Who will fight for Garibaldi?' The case was heard before the Justices of the Peace at Gateshead, when Garibaldi's letter appointing Styles as his recruiting agent in Britain, as well as the article in the *Daily Chronicle*, were given in evidence by the prosecution to prove a breach of the Foreign Enlistment Acts. The magistrates dismissed the case somewhat summarily, and Crawshay was subjected to violent abuse in the *Daily News*, the *Sunday Times*, and many other British papers, the *Newcastle Guardian* declaring that Crawshay had earned the contempt of everyone who, 'in common with almost every newspaper in the country, supports the chivalrous Garibaldi in his gallant effort to rid the Italians of a foreign yoke, and especially to free the Neapolitans from the detestable tyrant who sits upon their throne'. A similar fate befell a Mr Ironside, another associate of Urquhart's, and the prosecution which he brought against the Garibaldi Committee in Sheffield. When Crawshay appealed to the Court of Queen's Bench to direct the Gateshead magistrates to convict, his application was dismissed on the technical grounds that a prosecution under the Foreign Enlistment Acts could only be brought by the Attorney-General, and not by a private person.[16]

The 'excursionists', as the volunteers of the British Legion called themselves to obviate the difficulties with the Foreign Enlistment Acts, sailed from Harwich to Palermo. By the time that they arrived in Sicily, Garibaldi was fighting on the Volturno, and by the time that they reached the Volturno the campaign was over. By now, many of the volunteers were discontented with the conditions which they had experienced on board ship, and others were angry to find that Garibaldi did not recognize the validity of the commissions which they had purchased from Styles. On the Volturno, five of them robbed a peasant, and in compliance with Garibaldi's orders Peard sentenced them to be shot for looting, though the men complained that they had been short of food. The other British volunteers protested, and threatened to mutiny. Garibaldi then commuted the sentences to two years' imprisonment. He and his officers adopted a tolerant attitude to the misconduct of the British volunteers, because, not being used to Italian wines, the British got drunk more easily than the Italians.[17]

Although the enthusiasm for Garibaldi was greatest in Britain, there were men all over the world who volunteered to fight for him. Men wrote to Garibaldi offering their services from Nice, Germany, Hungary, Spain, Algiers and Bulgaria. Four Turkish officers in Constantinople offered to come. A British officer in the Indian Army wrote from Noukhali in East Bengal, and Captain Litchfield, of the Volunteer Rifles, from Kingstown in Canada. General Wheat, who had retired from the United States army after distinguished service in the war against Mexico, was one of several American officers who approached the Italian Committee in New York. Most of these offers arrived too late for Garibaldi to be able to make use of them; but Avezzana, Garibaldi's Commander-in-Chief in Rome in 1849, could not stay away, and, though he was over sixty, came from New York in time to join Garibaldi in Naples for the last battles of 1860.[18]

Those who could not offer to fight gave assistance in other ways. Mr Joseph Whitworth, the English armaments manufacturer who had invented the Enfield rifle, offered the Garibaldi Committee a cannon for Garibaldi free of charge. The munition workers in Glasgow and the dockers in Liverpool worked without pay on their Saturday afternoon half-holiday to make munitions and load medical supplies for Garibaldi. Money came from all sources – from New York and San Francisco, from the Italians in Montevideo and from Valparaiso in Chile, and from the convicts in the hulks in Genoa, who were allowed to make a collection among themselves for Garibaldi. Manufacturers wrote offering a new kind of gun, a submarine, or a steam engine which they had patented. Many poets, musicians and playwrights sent their verses and compositions as a sign of moral support. The Reverend Lane Fox wrote from his vicarage in Dorset enclosing a hymn which he had specially composed asking for God's protection for Garibaldi. A spiritualist wrote from Brussels to inform Garibaldi that they had got in touch with him at a séance. Father Verità, the priest of Modigliana, who had helped him escape in 1849, sent his best wishes, as did a man who had met him in Liverpool in 1850. Among all these messages of greeting there came an indignant letter from Rubattino, the owner of the steamships in which Garibaldi had sailed from Quarto, complaining of the financial loss which he had incurred through the unauthorized action of his manager in allowing Garibaldi to take the ships. A few months later, Rubattino was claiming the credit for having patriotically given the ships to Garibaldi.[19]

Support for Garibaldi appeared in the most unlikely places. Bismarck, who was then the Prussian Minister in St Petersburg, wrote to his government that Garibaldi's expedition had had an extraordinary effect at the Russian court, and that, apart from a small circle around the Prime Minister, Nesselrode, everyone had become pro-Italian. At Irkutsk, in Siberia, the revolutionary Anarchist, Bakunin, found that the whole population – the artisans, the middle classes, and even the Tsarist officials – waited eagerly for news of Garibaldi's progress, and supported him enthusiastically against the Tsar's ally, the King of Naples. There was considerable support for Garibaldi even in France, though here the enthusiasm of Le Siècle and the Liberals was countered by the Catholic propagandists, who violently attacked Garibaldi. It was not surprising that the old Socialist, De Flotte, who had fought on the barricades in Paris against Cavaignac during the four days in June 1848, should have joined Garibaldi in Sicily; but it was more remarkable that several officers in Napoleon III's army should have offered to fight for him.[20]

This enthusiasm for Garibaldi did not extend to Napoleon's court. When Nigra went to an evening party given by the Empress at Fontainebleau in June, and they played the fashionable game of charades, Eugénie did not react favourably to the suggestion that they should act the word 'Garibaldi'. She rejected it on the implausible grounds that it would be impossible to act some of the syllables, and chose instead the word 'Gargantua'. After they had acted 'gare', 'gant' and 'tua', and it was time to act the whole word, she asked Nigra if he would permit one of the gentlemen present to put on a pair of spectacles and dress up as Monsieur de Cavour, as he was the Gargantua of the modern world. The Empress's views on Garibaldi were shared by Queen Victoria, who had been angered by the report that the British navy had helped Garibaldi at Marsala and Palermo. When Prince Albert saw a photograph of the young Queen of Naples in her hunting costume, and heard that she was an excellent shot, he commented that it was a 'pity she didn't shoot Garibaldi'.[21]

Napoleon III and Cavour were becoming increasingly alarmed at the Mazzinian and Radical elements in Garibaldi's entourage in Sicily. They considered Crispi to be particularly dangerous. As soon as Cavour heard that Garibaldi was master of Palermo and Sicily, he sent La Farina to Palermo to take over the running of the government and to hurry through the annexation of Sicily by Sardinia. Cavour was warned by several of his friends and political colleagues, including Ricasoli, and by Victor Emanuel himself, that it would be a serious error to send La Farina, with whom Garibaldi had been on bad terms since his split with the National Society; but Cavour ignored these warnings, and with that obstinacy and tactlessness which he sometimes showed, he insisted on sending La Farina.[22]

On 10 June La Farina sent his first report to Cavour. 'Most esteemed Signor Count,' he began, 'the impression which Palermo produces at this moment is a mixture of wonder and horror.' There followed a catalogue of complaints against Garibaldi and his government, particularly Crispi, who were accused by La Farina of administrative and financial incompetence. 'Garibaldi is loved, and the gratitude of the Sicilian people to him is immense; but there is no one who thinks him capable of governing the state.' He accused Garibaldi of being too merciful, and of having angered the Sicilians by protecting some hated Neapolitan officials from popular vengeance. He wrote that Garibaldi was unbelievably tired, and that 'the government (or rather Crispi and Raffaele)' were universally hated. In view of Garibaldi's prestige, this was a good line for La Farina and Cavour to take – that Garibaldi, well-meaning but politically inexperienced and physically exhausted, was being used as a tool by the unscrupulous Radical revolutionary, Crispi. La Farina hinted, too, at Mazzinian influences at work in Garibaldi's government.

La Farina got in touch with Baron Pisani, Garibaldi's Conservative Foreign Minister, and with the municipal authorities in Palermo, and organized an agitation for immediate annexation by Sardinia. But Garibaldi would not agree. He told a deputation from the Palermo city council that he favoured a united Italy under Victor Emanuel, but that immediate annexation would place Sicily under the control of diplomats, and would impede his advance; it must wait until all Italy was free, when the diplomats would no longer be able to prevent the unification of the country; if the Sicilians continued to agitate for immediate annexation, he would go away.[23]

Cavour sent La Farina instructions to see Garibaldi and to demand that he arrest Mazzini, whom Cavour believed to be in Sicily, and place him on board one of Admiral Persano's ships, so that he could be taken as a prisoner to Genoa. La Farina was shrewd enough to delegate this duty to Persano; and when Garibaldi, in a strained interview with Persano, objected to the demand that he surrender Mazzini, and said that in any case Mazzini was not in Sicily, La Farina and Persano did not threaten to break off all relations with Garibaldi, as Cavour had instructed them to do, because they knew that this would only exasperate Garibaldi and destroy all hope of his agreeing to immediate annexation.[24]

After trying unsuccessfully for some time to see Garibaldi, La Farina was eventually granted an interview on 25 June. Admiral Persano was present at their talk, but said nothing. La Farina denounced the misdeeds of Garibaldi's ministers, but he only succeeded in angering Garibaldi. 'His reply,' wrote La Farina to Cavour, 'was to make a panegyric of Crispi and his other colleagues . . . He passed to recriminations against me, accusing me of having voted for the treaty of cession of Savoy and Nice, and of having betrayed Central Italy.'

La Farina did not conceal from Cavour that he was responsible for what followed. On 27 June a demonstration against the government, which was certainly organized by La Farina, took place in the streets of Palermo. A crowd marched up the Toledo shouting 'Long live Garibaldi! Down with Crispi! Down with the government!' The demonstrators demanded to see Garibaldi, and Garibaldi received a deputation from them. He refused to remove Crispi, and said that Crispi had played a great part in organizing his expedition to Sicily; and when they demanded that he should appoint some Sicilian Conservatives as members of his government, he objected to all the Conservatives whom they suggested. But next day he reorganized his government, bringing in all the Conservatives whose names had been put forward by the deputation, and dismissing Crispi from his post of Secretary of State and Minister of the Interior.[25] He also ordered that steps should be taken to begin the preparation of an electoral register throughout Sicily, so that a plebiscite could be held on the question of annexation by Sardinia. This, however, proved to be a long job, because it was not easy to compile a register in the remote country districts; and many Sicilians objected to having their names put on the register, thinking that it was a step to facilitate conscription and the gathering of taxes.[26]

La Farina was very satisfied, but not for long. Not for the last time during the year 1860, Garibaldi showed the great indecisiveness in political matters which Oliphant had commented upon two months earlier, before Garibaldi left Genoa. 'He is the most amiable, innocent, honest nature possible,' wrote Oliphant, 'and a first-rate guerilla [sic] chief, but in council a child. The worst of him is that he puts his trust in anybody, and unless you stick to him you lose your influence; but he has a name with the people that may be turned to any account.' La Farina's conduct had aroused great resentment among all the members of the Thousand, and Crispi persuaded Garibaldi that he was a subversive influence who was fomenting unrest in Sicily and was disrupting the unity which was necessary if the preparations for the invasion of the mainland were to continue. On 7 July Garibaldi signed a deportation order against La Farina, who was escorted to a Sardinian warship in the harbour, and returned to Turin to make his complaints to Cavour in person.

At the same time, Garibaldi ordered the arrest and deportation of two men who were spies of the Neapolitan government – one of them was also a double-agent acting for Cavour – and who were suspected, probably wrongly, of having been sent by the Neapolitans to assassinate Garibaldi. To the indignation of La Farina and his supporters, Garibaldi referred to the expulsion of La Farina and the two spies in the same official communiqué in the press, and stated that La Farina had hindered, not helped, the cause for which the Thousand had fought at Calatafimi and Palermo. Ten days later, he reappointed Crispi as Secretary of State.[27]

The expulsion of La Farina confirmed Cavour's fears of Garibaldi, though he was careful to adopt La Farina's line and portray Garibaldi as a well-meaning dupe of the unscrupulous Crispi. He decided that it was essential to prevent Garibaldi from crossing the straits and liberating the mainland, and he now set out to prevent the expedition to Calabria just as he had tried to prevent the expedition from Quarto to Sicily in May. 'We must stop Garibaldi from conquering Naples', he wrote to Nigra on 12 July, 'and try to bring about the annexation of Sicily as soon as possible. . . . It is of the greatest interest for us, and I will say for Europe, that if the Bourbons have to fall, they should not fall through the action of Garibaldi. The annexation of Sicily is a way of annulling Garibaldi.' On the same day he wrote to d'Azeglio and suggested that the British government might use its influence with Garibaldi to dissuade him from crossing the straits, because 'if counsels of moderation reached him from England, for which he has a great respect, it would be very advantageous'.[28]

On 9 July Napoleon III put forward a proposal that the King of Naples and Garibaldi should agree to a six-month truce while the problem of Sicily and Naples was settled by the Great Powers. Cavour said that he approved, but was sure that Garibaldi would not agree. The British government supported the French proposal, and, as Cavour had requested, asked Garibaldi not to cross the straits. But it was the leader-writer in *The Times* who expressed British public opinion on 15 June, when, after stating that 'Garibaldi has made war like a Christian gentleman', denounced the attempts to win a breathing-space for the King of Naples, 'this King of torture-chambers and prisons. . . . Garibaldi has not yet done all his work. . . . The true diplomacy of this crisis is not to diplomatize. There is a knot which none but Garibaldi can untie, and it is better to leave him alone to untie it.'[29]

Before crossing the straits, Garibaldi had to destroy the Neapolitan forces in their bridgehead near Messina. He sent three bodies of troops to converge on Messina and mop up resistance on the way – one, under Medici, moving east from Palermo along the north coast; the second, under Bixio, following the south and east coast up to Messina; and the third, under Türr, going across the interior from Palermo and linking up at Catania with Bixio. On the north coast, Medici encountered a Neapolitan force under Colonel Bosco, and by dint of very skilful manoeuvring, and by fooling Bosco into thinking that his army was nearly four times larger than it was, Medici, with 2,000 men, succeeded in bottling up Bosco's 6,000 troops in the town of Milazzo. But Medici knew that he could not keep Bosco there for long with his inferior numbers, and sent to Garibaldi for reinforcements.[30]

On 18 July Garibaldi left Palermo, and sailed along the north coast to Patti with a force which he had hastily assembled at Palermo, including a body of volunteers who had just arrived from Genoa and were shipped off from Palermo to Patti without setting foot on shore. At Meri, near Milazzo, Garibaldi linked up with Medici.[31] There are considerable discrepancies between the Neapolitan and the Garibaldian figures as to the numbers in the armies which faced each other at Milazzo; but though both sides claim to have been outnumbered by the enemy, it seems certain that there were approximately 5,000 men engaged on each side. The Neapolitans, unlike Garibaldi, had a body of cavalry, and their artillery outnumbered Garibaldi's and was superior in range.[32]

Milazzo is situated on the neck of a promontory about three miles long and half a mile wide, which is surrounded on three sides by the sea and can only be approached by land through the town to the south. Bosco's men took up their positions outside the promontory to the south of Milazzo in a semicircle stretching about two miles wide and two miles deep beyond the isthmus, and protected on both flanks by the sea. Between them and the Garibaldini approaching from the south were fields covered with the cactus of prickly-pear trees and with cane, which was so high that it almost concealed the armies from each other. Here, on 20 July, for eight hours on a very hot day at the peak of the Sicilian summer, Garibaldi and Bosco fought a very bloody battle among the prickly-pear trees and the high cane, on the sands along the seashore, and eventually in the streets of Milazzo.

Garibaldi launched his attack at dawn, sending in his men with the bayonet and firing their rifles against Bosco's line all along the semicircle. On Garibaldi's left wing, his first attack was repulsed with substantial losses, because the Garibaldini found that they had charged right into the mouth of Bosco's artillery, which shot down many of them; but Cosenz rallied them and attacked again, while on the right wing Medici's men edged their way slowly forward near the shore under heavy fire. Garibaldi, who at first directed the battle from the roof of a wine shop in the rear, afterwards joined Medici's wing, where he exposed himself recklessly to the enemy fire throughout the day. Realizing that many of his men were going into action for the first time, and would be suffering heavy casualties, he thought that the most useful thing that he could do would be to set an example of coolness and courage. He stood there, saying words of encouragement to each soldier as the man went into the attack; and on several occasions he led the charge himself like a platoon commander. As he watched his men in action he noticed a boy of twelve, a street urchin from Palermo, who was fighting with great courage. After the battle Garibaldi promoted the boy to be a sergeant.

He sent his battalion of Genoese carbineers into the most important and dangerous sector, and went with them, with his walking-stick in his hand and a cigarette in his mouth. They came to a wall from behind which the enemy were discharging a heavy rifle fire at them. Garibaldi's carbineers, for the first time, halted and hesitated. Garibaldi walked ahead, going straight for the wall without once looking back to see if his men were following; and as the Garibaldini advanced, the enemy abandoned the position. Garibaldi emerged with only a very slight wound.

Bosco sent in a squadron of cavalry in a counter-attack against Medici. They were driven back by the Garibaldini, but in returning to their lines they rode past the point where Garibaldi was standing with the carbineers. The rest of Garibaldi's party dived for cover, but Garibaldi himself and his young ADC, Colonel Missori, were left standing in the road. As the Neapolitan horsemen rode by, one of them struck at Garibaldi with his sabre. Garibaldi, who had drawn his own sabre, killed the horseman with his sabre, while Missori brought down several others with shots from his pistol. Meanwhile the small group of English volunteers, facing very heavy fire, were doubting whether their Sicilian colleagues could stand it for much longer. One of the Englishmen whispered to his friend: 'Garibaldi is here, or all would be lost.'[33]

By 2 pm, after eight hours' fighting, the Garibaldini had stormed their way into the heart of Bosco's defence position, and were fighting in the streets of Milazzo. Garibaldi went to the extreme right wing of his army, on the seashore. The midday heat was at its height, and Garibaldi was bathed in sweat. Judging that it would be a little while before any enemy attack could come that way, he took off his red shirt and washed it himself in the sea. The shirt dried almost immediately in the sun, while Garibaldi ate a hurried lunch of bread, water and fruit, and smoked a cigar. He then put on the shirt, and went on board one of his ships. He sailed round the promontory, right under the guns in the castle of Milazzo, and bombarded Bosco's right wing from the rear, just as it was beginning to crack under Cosenz's attack. This broke the resistance of the Neapolitans, who fled into the castle, leaving Garibaldi victorious and in possession of the town.

In proportion to the numbers engaged, Garibaldi's casualties were heavy. He lost 200 killed and a total of 750 casualties, or about one in six of his men, the same proportion as at the Villa Corsini, as compared with one in two at San Antonio, and two out of three at Costa Brava. Among the Genoese carbineers, with whom Garibaldi had spent most of the day, the casualty rate was as high as in the slaughter on the Paraná, with 50 out of the 82 carbineers being killed or severely wounded. The wounded Garibaldini were taken to field hospitals in the town of Milazzo and at Barcellona, five miles to the south. The conditions in the hospitals were horrible. Jessie White Mario had come from England to nurse the wounded, but her courage and compassion were not enough to overcome the maladministration; and as Garibaldi always acted on the principle that courage was more important than organization, the medical services were almost as inadequate as the catering arrangements in his army. There were no anaesthetics, the surgical instruments were inadequate, and the dirt abounded. Some of the British volunteers who had been in the Crimea found conditions worse than anything they had known at Sevastopol or Scutari, and were filled with admiration for the courage which revolutionary zeal could instil into the Italians and Sicilians. A boy of twelve had an arm amputated. Jessie Mario held him in her lap while the operation was performed. Her husband, who had fought in the battle and watched the scene in the hospital, wrote that Jessie wept more than the boy.[34]

The Neapolitans suffered fewer casualties than the Garibaldini, losing only 200 killed and wounded; but their morale was shattered, and although they could still have held out in the castle of Milazzo, they had lost the will to do so. The garrison in the castle capitulated with the honours of war, and the Neapolitans in Messina followed their example a few days later. They evacuated their forces by sea to the mainland, leaving Sicily clear of Neapolitan troops.[35]

FROM THE FARO TO NAPLES

WHEN Cavour heard of the fall of Messina, he wrote to Emanuel d'Azeglio, criticizing the Neapolitans for their 'cowardly surrender' of Messina, which 'by allowing Garibaldi his freedom of action will make it impossible for us to prevent his landing in Naples'. Cavour's policy now became more tortuous than ever. He opened negotiations with the Neapolitan government and proposed that the King of Naples should cede Sicily to Sardinia in return for Sardinian assistance against Garibaldi; but as it would hardly have been possible for Cavour to persuade the people of Sardinia to agree to such a policy, the Neapolitan government was probably right in thinking that this was just a trick on Cavour's part. He pinned his real hopes on instigating a Right-wing Liberal revolution in Naples before Garibaldi could arrive there.[1]

On 1 August he wrote to d'Azeglio in London, with instructions to destroy the letter rather than run any risk of it getting into other hands.

> I do not flatter myself that England will approve very much of my plan [he wrote to d'Azeglio]. I think that she would prefer to see Garibaldi reach Naples, even if he brought anarchy and revolution in his train. She thinks that he is the enemy of France, which is enough to make him lovable in her eyes. But as we cannot risk death to please England, we will have to put up with any embarrassment that this may cause.

He added, in a postscript: 'I send you, so that you can show off before the beautiful Garibaldian ladies, a lock of the hair of the Hero of Sicily. You can guarantee its authenticity.'[2]

Cavour's plan of inciting a revolution in Naples was a complete failure. The Neapolitans had no wish to make a revolution, and preferred to wait for Garibaldi to come.

Garibaldi had not improved his relations with Cavour by an unfortunate venture in diplomacy in which he engaged at the end of June. Bertani had entered into negotiations with Mr Thomas Parker, a ship's broker of Liverpool, for the purchase for £20,000 of a British

ship, the *Queen of England*, by Garibaldi, who wished to use the ship for the crossing of the straits and for other naval operations against the King of Naples. A slight hitch having arisen in the negotiations, owing to a disagreement as to whether the purchase money should be paid in advance or on the delivery of the *Queen of England* in Sicily, Garibaldi wrote a personal letter to Parker, in which he stated that it was in Britain's national interest to help him to liberate Italy, because 'having once achieved union and liberty, Italy would ally herself with England against the ambitious designs of the Emperor of the French'. Parker gave the letter to the English newspapers, who published it early in July.[3]

The letter was seized on by the French Catholics, who gave it great publicity, and it aroused indignation in France. The French Liberals and pro-Italians were dismayed. Count de la Varenne, a French Liberal who had come to Palermo as a journalist, told Crispi that the publication of the letter had hardened Napoleon III and his ministers against Garibaldi, had alienated public opinion, and had been a serious set-back for the work of Garibaldi's supporters in France. As a result, the government had banned the collection of funds for Garibaldi, and the formation of Garibaldi Committees in France.

> Italy with England against France so soon after 1859! [wrote La Varenne to Crispi] Without the open or secret support of France, without her moral consent, the Italian movement, in spite of the determination of Garibaldi and his volunteers, has no probability of success. It will not be England, the natural ally of the Germans, the furious adversary in the war of 1859, who now flatters Italy only to betray her tomorrow – it will not be England who will ever do anything for you. If France withdraws her hand, Italy must succumb.

Garibaldi's letter to Parker was undoubtedly a blunder. He did not need to win the goodwill of his enthusiastic supporters in Britain by telling them that it was in Britain's interest to support Italian freedom as a move against France; and his statement was certain, not only to weaken the position of the French Liberals, but also to confirm Cavour's worst fears that Garibaldi's gaucheries would endanger the Sardinian-French alliance. Crispi, for all his Mazzinian principles, was already a more skilful politician than Garibaldi, and he tried to repair the damage.

> You know how I detest Napoleon [he wrote to Garibaldi on 2 August] nevertheless it is necessary to outdo him in dissimulation. . . . Frankness is a first requisite when honest men are dealing with honest men, but when one has to do with the butchers of humanity, who are strong in arms and

rich in means, frankness is but a poor policy. Now, in order to neutralize the effects of the Parker letter, do you see your way clear to writing another letter in which – while leaving Bonaparte entirely out of the question – you declare your sympathy for France?

Garibaldi was not prepared to issue any such statement in favour of the nation which had taken Nice; but he allowed Crispi and his new Foreign Minister in Palermo, Count Amari, to issue statements to the press which, without directly denying the authenticity of Garibaldi's letter to Parker, did so by implication. On 6 August Crispi wrote:

> I have not the slightest knowledge of the letter to Mr Parker. I am aware that the General is much gratified by the sympathy which the English people are at last showing for the cause of Italy, but at the same time I feel fully justified in assuring you that this does not blind him to the strong and generous support lent by the Emperor Napoleon in helping us to achieve independence. Our cause is that of nationalism, of civilization and of humanity, and it is precisely Napoleon III, the man of his century, who has laid down the principle that every nation has a right to govern itself. . . . The General will certainly find a means of reassuring public opinion on the subject of his true sentiments towards the Emperor and towards France.

Four days later, Amari stated that he had good reason to doubt the authenticity of Garibaldi's letter, because he could not find a copy of it, and Garibaldi had never mentioned it to him. Other letters of Garibaldi

> give abundant proof that the great Italian chieftain cherishes sentiments differing widely from those attributed to him for the brave and generous nation whose sons shed their blood for our independence on the fields of Magenta and Solferino. In any case I can assure you that the opinions of the Dictator's government coincide in every way with those of His Majesty's government at Turin.[4]

As Garibaldi, having cleared Sicily of the enemy, massed his troops at Cape Faro, on the north-east tip of Sicily and prepared to cross the Straits of Messina, Napoleon III proposed to the British government that an Anglo-French squadron should be sent to the straits to prevent Garibaldi from invading the mainland. According to the well-known incident which was afterwards revealed by Sir James Lacaita, and which became one of the favourite stories of the pro-Cavourians, Russell was only prevented from agreeing by the intervention of Lacaita who, at the instigation of Cavour and d'Azeglio, went round to Russell's house while Russell was discussing the proposal with the

French Ambassador. Luring Russell upstairs on the pretext that Lady John, who was ill in bed, wished to see him urgently, he persuaded Russell to refuse to agree to the French Ambassador's plan. In view of the falsifications to which some of the Cavourian supporters resorted in order to prove that Cavour helped Garibaldi's expedition, one might be tempted to doubt the truth of Lacaita's story, were it not for the fact that Trevelyan states that it was vouched for by Lady Russell in later years. It must therefore be accepted, and shows that Cavour was pursuing three contradictory policies in the last week of July 1860. As well as negotiating with the government of Naples and trying to organize a revolution there to forestall Garibaldi, he was also eager to prevent the French and British governments from making it impossible for Garibaldi to cross the straits. It would therefore seem, as Trevelyan has suggested, that his policy was to win Naples, if possible without Garibaldi, but if necessary through Garibaldi's efforts.[5]

On 22 July Victor Emanuel ordered his orderly officer, Count Litta-Modignani, to deliver a letter to Garibaldi at Cape Faro. In the letter, the King ordered Garibaldi not to cross the straits. But forty-nine years later, a sealed envelope was found among Litta's papers. It contained another letter from Victor Emanuel to Garibaldi, telling him to disregard the order not to cross the straits, and to write a letter to Victor Emanuel explaining that for the welfare of Italy he could not obey him. There is no doubt as to the genuineness of the letter, because it is in Victor Emanuel's handwriting; and although it has been suggested that it was written afterwards in order to give Victor Emanuel the credit for the liberation of the South, and then not used for this purpose, this seems unlikely. As the envelope containing the letter was still sealed in 1909, the letter cannot have been seen by Garibaldi in 1860; and the obvious, and very plausible, explanation is that Victor Emanuel, having been persuaded by Cavour to write the first letter to Garibaldi forbidding him to cross the straits, instructed Litta, probably without the knowledge of Cavour, to tell Garibaldi verbally to disregard the letter, and that Victor Emanuel gave the second letter to Litta with orders not to show it to Garibaldi unless Garibaldi insisted on having written confirmation of Litta's verbal message from the King. As Garibaldi was prepared to accept the verbal message, it was unnecessary for Litta to show him the second letter, and the envelope was never opened until after Litta's death. It is surprising that Litta did not destroy the second letter in these circumstances, but he did not do so, perhaps because he wished to safeguard his own position. If this is what occurred, it is probable that Litta's verbal message from Victor Emanuel, and the unopened second letter, were kept secret from Cavour, because throughout 1860 Victor Emanuel was more sympathetic to Garibaldi, and more prepared to support him, than Cavour was; and there is no doubt that Victor Emanuel corresponded directly with Garibaldi, without Cavour's knowledge, on several occasions while Garibaldi was in Sicily.[6]

Garibaldi wrote to Victor Emanuel in almost identical terms to those which the King had suggested in the letter which Garibaldi never saw;[7] but he did not cross the straits as early as many people expected. He knew that crossing the three-mile stretch of water under enemy fire could be a costly business, and he spent several weeks preparing his ships, men and equipment at the Faro, which had become the focal point for all the statesmen and journalists of Europe. Meanwhile he had to deal with an outbreak of class war in the country districts of Sicily, where the overthrow of the Neapolitan rule had increased the disorders. Garibaldi's appeal to the peasants to observe the law, and his promise of a land reform, may have quietened the trouble to some extent, but this was more than countered by the spirit of revolution and the breakdown of the accepted authority. There were outbursts of violence by peasants against landlords, and seizures of the land by the peasants, in different parts of Sicily during the summer; and several landowners, including some British residents of Marsala, and the Count of Lampedusa's daughter, Princess Niscemi, asked Garibaldi's government for protection.[8]

The worst incident was at Bronte, near Mount Etna in the east. In 1799 Admiral Nelson had been created Duke of Bronte, and given large estates at Bronte by the King of Naples as a reward for his services in suppressing the Jacobin revolutionaries in Naples. Nelson's conduct had aroused great resentment at the time among Radicals and Liberals, who criticized especially his action in hanging the revolutionary leader, Admiral Caracciolo, on his warship, and his alleged breach of faith in repudiating the capitulation terms granted by the Neapolitan commander and in punishing the revolutionaries who had surrendered in reliance on them. But Britain, who in 1799 had supported the Neapolitan Bourbons, was now enthusiastically supporting Garibaldi against them; and although the traditional Italian Republican view was still to regard Nelson as the blackest of villains, Garibaldi, either because he was a sailor or because of his sympathy for England, makes several very favourable references to Nelson in his memoirs.

Nelson's estates at Bronte had been inherited by his niece, Charlotte, Lady Bridport, who had succeeded to the Bronte, though not to the Nelson, title. The Duchess of Bronte, who was seventy-three in 1860, was an absentee landlord living in England. Her Bronte estates were managed by a resident land agent, who had for many years been a supporter of the national revolutionary movement against the King of

Naples, and many secret meetings of revolutionaries had been held in the Duchess's country house at Bronte. In the summer of 1860 the peasants at Bronte seized the Duchess's land and divided it amongst themselves, though they did not enter the house, where the British flag had been hoisted. A local lawyer named Lombardo emerged as the leader of the peasants and of the opposition to the Duchess's land agent; and when the National Guard was formed throughout Sicily after Garibaldi's capture of Palermo, the Bronte unit came under Lombardo's control.

The Duchess's agent appealed for protection to the British Consul at Catania, who asked Garibaldi's government to maintain order at Bronte; but there were no serious disorders there until 2 August, when a small-scale massacre took place. It is not altogether clear what happened, but several supporters of the Duchess's faction were murdered by the peasants and by Lombardo's partisans, some of them in a most horrible manner, though Lombardo claimed that he had tried to prevent the killings. The British Consul visited Garibaldi in Messina, and appealed to him for aid; and Garibaldi sent Bixio with a detachment of troops to suppress the disturbance.

Bixio arrived at Bronte on 6 August. By this time, the local priest and the National Guard of Catania had succeeded in restoring order; but Bixio arrested many of the peasants. He announced that he would impose a fine on the community for every hour that he remained in Bronte, and he seized the leading members of the local council as hostages. Seven of the ringleaders, including Lombardo, were tried by court martial on a charge of waging civil war and committing murder and arson. They were informed of the charges at midday on 9 August; the trial began at 1 pm; by 5 pm Lombardo and four of the accused had been sentenced to death. Lombardo's family asked permission to see him before he was executed, and to send him some eggs for his last meal; but Bixio refused both requests. He told the boy who brought the eggs that Lombardo did not need any eggs, because he would receive two bullets in his head next morning. The five men were shot at 8 am on 10 August, Lombardo declaring that he was innocent, like Jesus. Bixio watched the execution sitting on his horse.

Many of the other prisoners were sent to Catania. They were held in prison for three years, and eventually tried by the courts of Victor Emanuel's kingdom in August 1863, when thirty-seven of them were sentenced to life imprisonment for their part in the events at Bronte.

Bixio acted on his own authority in executing Lombardo and the other revolutionary leaders at Bronte; but Garibaldi endorsed his action when Bixio reported to him in Messina. Garibaldi's firmness in upholding law and order won the approval of the Sicilian landowners and middle classes, and it was especially popular with his British supporters. Commander Forbes, in his book which he published in London next year on his return from Sicily and Naples, congratulated Garibaldi on sending Bixio 'to trample out a small dash of communism that had raised its head in Bronte and one or two other adjacent towns'. Crispi and the Mazzinians, who hated Communism as much as Commander Forbes, approved as much as anyone of Bixio's actions. But three years later, at the time of the trial at Catania, articles vindicating Lombardo and his fellow-victims appeared in the press; and various Socialist writers have hailed Lombardo as a martyr and accused Garibaldi of betraying the revolutionary peasants who had trusted him, and of acting as an executioner for the Sicilian and foreign landlords and exploiters.

There is no doubt that Lombardo's followers committed some atrocious murders of the Duchess of Bronte's supporters, though whether those who were executed so summarily by Bixio were the worst offenders is much less certain. The political significance of their action is also doubtful. Lombardo and his colleagues were officially described as 'Bourbon reactionaries' at their court martial and in the official records of Garibaldi's government; but Lombardo had been a Liberal and a revolutionary supporter for many years. He had played an active part in the revolution of 1848, and after the news of Calatafimi reached Bronte, he had proclaimed Garibaldi as Dictator. At his court martial, he strongly denied being a Bourbon reactionary, and claimed that he was loyal to the revolution. Abba, one of Garibaldi's Thousand, who strongly approved of Bixio's executions at Bronte, commented disgustedly in his diary that the murderers had cried 'Long live Garibaldi!' as they committed their crimes, believing that Garibaldi would support them against the Duchess and the landlords' party. There was also a large element of private vengeance, of local factional quarrels, and of inter-family warfare and vendetta, in the killings.

But whatever the motives of the murderers, Garibaldi could not allow them to proceed. The later Socialist writers compared his action to that of Cromwell in suppressing the Levellers, and of Robespierre in destroying the Communists, Roux and Varlet. They could also have compared it to the suppression of the Anarchist rising at Kronstadt in 1921 by the Communist government of Lenin and Trotsky, who, like Garibaldi, accused the Left-wing extremists whom they were crushing of being counter-revolutionary supporters of the old régime. Like every other revolutionary leader, Garibaldi, once he had come to power, suppressed other revolutionaries by methods which were at least as ruthless as those used by the old régime.[9]

Before crossing the straits, Garibaldi had to make arrangements for the government of Sicily during his absence on the mainland. He made a wise appointment. Instead of appointing Crispi to rule Sicily during his absence, which would have strained relations with Cavour and the government in Turin still further, he wrote to Victor Emanuel in July, before leaving Palermo for the operations at Milazzo, and asked him to send Depretis to Sicily. Depretis, who in his youth had been a member of Young Italy, had become a politician of the Parliamentary Left, politically close to Rattazzi; and though Cavour considered that neither the electorate nor foreign powers would accept Depretis as a member of the government, he was no longer a Mazzinian. Victor Emanuel had been intending to send Valerio to Sicily as his representative, knowing that he was an old friend of Garibaldi; but at Garibaldi's request, he was willing to send Depretis.

Depretis did not arrive in time to take over the government when Garibaldi went to Milazzo, and Garibaldi appointed Sirtori to be his deputy during his absence from Palermo on that occasion. But Depretis arrived while Garibaldi was at Milazzo, and on 21 July, the day after the battle, Garibaldi appointed him as Pro-Dictator, with all his dictatorial powers to govern Sicily during his absence on the mainland. He gave Depretis Crispi as his Secretary of State, though Crispi had hoped to cross the straits with Garibaldi. Before Depretis left Turin, Victor Emanuel had given him instructions to work for the annexation of Sicily as soon as possible, and appointed him as the Royal Commissioner to govern Sicily as soon as the annexation had taken place; but at Depretis's first interview with Garibaldi, Crispi, who was also present, said very firmly that no annexation must take place during Garibaldi's absence, and Garibaldi agreed with this; so Depretis said nothing about annexation or his appointment as Royal Commissioner, and ruled as Garibaldi's Pro-Dictator.[10]

Garibaldi continued his preparations at the Faro. At least once a day, and sometimes twice a day, he would climb to the top of the lighthouse and look across at Calabria through his telescope. Sometimes he stayed up in the tower all day and overnight, in a very small room containing nothing except a low trestle-bed, two stools and a box, with Garibaldi's sword hanging on a nail in the wall, and a spare shirt and a pair of trousers hanging on another nail. But his delay in crossing the straits made the Mazzinians fear the worst. Mazzini had already written to Crispi on 18 July: 'I cannot understand Garibaldi. When an enemy has become demoralized, then is the time to follow up one's advantage. Three thousand volunteers and the name of Garibaldi, descending not upon a remote corner of Calabria but upon the Salerno-Naples road, would take the kingdom in one week.'[11]

Under the pressure of the Mazzinians, Garibaldi's mind turned to another project. He had never abandoned the plan, which he had formulated before leaving Quarto, of launching an attack on the Papal States. Whether he went by way of Calabria or direct by sea from Genoa, he intended to enter Rome as well as Naples; and at the beginning of August, he gave serious consideration to his original idea of sending a body of volunteers, raised by Bertani in Genoa, to invade the Papal States from the sea on the west-coast.

Cavour was determined to prevent such an expedition at all costs. He sent Farini to tell Bertani that the Sardinian navy would use force to prevent the expedition by sea against the Papal States, and that the government insisted that Bertani's new batch of volunteers should join Garibaldi in Sicily. Bertani pretended to agree, and arranged with Farini that the 5,000 volunteers whom he had assembled should sail to the Gulf of Aranci on the east coast of the island of Sardinia, only a few miles south of Caprera, and from there proceed to Palermo. But Bertani, apparently at Mazzini's instigation, decided to trick Cavour. Leaving the volunteers in the Gulf of Aranci, he went to the Faro to fetch Garibaldi, intending to bring him to the Gulf of Aranci and to persuade him to lead the new volunteers in an attack on the Papal States.[12]

Garibaldi had meanwhile made an attempt to cross the straits. At the beginning of August he received a secret communication from some Radicals in Calabria which made him believe that the Neapolitan soldiers in the fort at Scilla, on the mainland just opposite the Faro, would be prepared to join the revolution. On the night of 8 August he sent Missori and Alberto Mario with 200 men to cross the straits, get into contact with the garrison at Scilla, and capture the fort. If the operation were successful, he himself would then cross to the mainland with his troops at the Faro. Missori crossed the straits a little to the south of the Faro, and landed safely in Calabria; but before he and his men could reach Scilla, they met a superior force of Neapolitan soldiers, and retreated into the mountains of Aspromonte, where they kept together and held out as a guerrilla band, and made contact with friendly Calabrian peasants. In view of Missori's failure to capture Scilla, Garibaldi did not attempt to cross the straits with the main body of his men.[13]

It was apparently because of this failure that Garibaldi was prepared to listen favourably to Bertani's proposal when Bertani arrived at the Faro on 12 August. Without telling his men, or even his staff, at the Faro, he slipped away at night and sailed with Bertani for the Gulf of Aranci. They avoided the Neapolitan cruisers off the Faro, and reached Sardinia in safety. Bertani certainly thought that Garibaldi was intending to lead the 5,000 men at Aranci in an expedition against the Papal States; but Garibaldi, in his memoirs, states that he was only pretending to fall in with the plans of the Mazzinians, and had decided to lead the volunteers at Aranci in a landing on the Neapolitan mainland near Naples. This would have had the advantage of surprise, for the enemy was expecting him to invade Calabria. But when he sailed into the Gulf of Aranci at dawn on 14 August he found that only about half of the volunteers were still there; the rest had already sailed for Palermo, having been compelled to do so by the Sardinian navy, which had broken up the concentration of Bertani's ships in the gulf at the orders of Cavour. Cavour had guessed that Bertani might be intending to double-cross him and invade the Papal States, though a spy whom Cavour had put on board one of Bertani's ships had not discovered this, and had told Cavour nothing except the information, which was certainly false, that the volunteers in the ship had cried 'Death to Garibaldi, to Victor Emanuel, to Cavour, Long live the Republic, Communism, etc.' Garibaldi, finding that half the volunteers had left the Gulf of Aranci, reverted to his original plan to invade from the Faro, and sailed for Palermo. As they had to call at La Maddalena for coal, he granted himself a few hours' leave and landed at Caprera, where he saw Battistina and their fifteen-month-old daughter, and inspected his herd of cattle and his vines.[14]

On the morning of 18 August he arrived at the Faro after six days' absence. From there he set off in his carriage to the south, ostensibly to visit the city of Messina, where he drove through the streets in the afternoon of the 18th amid the cheers of the people. Instead of returning to the Faro, he went on to Taormina. Bixio had secretly assembled an army of 3,360 men out of sight in the woods behind Taormina. That night Garibaldi crossed to the mainland with Bixio's force in two unarmed steamers, the *Torino* and the *Franklin*, relying on the fact that the Neapolitan warships would be waiting for him forty miles to the north between Faro and Scilla. Just as they were about to sail from Taormina, Bixio discovered a leak in the *Franklin* which the crew did not know how to repair. He angrily decided to leave the *Franklin* behind, and to pack as many of the men as possible into the *Torino*. But Garibaldi was an old sailor. He ordered a pile of manure to be brought from the shore, and plugged the hole on the *Franklin* himself in a way that he had learned to do in an emergency many years before.[15]

After a thirty-hour journey, the two ships landed safely at Melito on the southern tip of Calabria, soon after dawn on 19 August. There was no sign of any Neapolitan forces in the neighbourhood. Later in the day, some Neapolitan warships appeared off Melito and bombarded the Garibaldini; but though the Garibaldini suffered a number of casualties, they avoided the enemy fire by marching inland. Their greatest ordeal on the first day was lack of provisions, and some of them went without food for thirty-six hours.

The Neapolitan government had 16,000 troops in Calabria, but their generals were even more incompetent than those in Sicily had been. Although the government in Naples ordered them to advance and crush Garibaldi as soon as they heard, on 19 August, that he had landed, the generals did not attack him, and Garibaldi was able to march on the Neapolitan garrison at Reggio di Calabria, which was only 1,000 strong, and had not been reinforced when the Neapolitan command had learned that Garibaldi was in the area. The local Neapolitan commander had stationed his men in a good defensive position on the outskirts of the town; but his superior commander, the aged General Gallotti, ordered him to retire to the centre of the town and await the Garibaldini in the cathedral square.

Garibaldi and his men broke into Reggio before dawn on 21 August, and engaged in some fierce fighting with the Neapolitan troops, who withdrew to the castle. Later on the 21st a Neapolitan force of 2,000 men under General Briganti marched to the relief of Reggio. Garibaldi waited for them outside the town. His chief anxiety was that while he was fighting with the relieving force, he would be attacked in the rear by the garrison of Reggio; but though some of the soldiers of the garrison demanded to be led on a sortie against Garibaldi, General Gallotti refused to move out of the castle. Garibaldi defeated Briganti's relieving army after a sharp fight, and marched back into Reggio. The Garibaldini sharpshooters fired at the sentries on the parapet of the castle, wounding and killing one or two of them. This was enough for General Gallotti, who surrendered the castle to Garibaldi. The Garibaldini suffered 150 casualties in killed and wounded in the fighting in the cathedral square and the action against Briganti.[16]

Meanwhile the Neapolitan warships guarding the Straits of Messina had sailed south towards Melito, having been informed that Garibaldi had landed there. During their absence, Cosenz crossed from the Faro with 1,500 men, without meeting any of the enemy warships, on the night of 20 August, while Garibaldi was fighting in the streets of Reggio. The warships came back to the straits when they heard about Cosenz's movements, and arrived in time to sink many of the fishing craft in which Cosenz's men had crossed, while the boats were returning to the Faro. Soon after Cosenz's men landed, they were attacked by the enemy, but drove them off and marched up the mountain side of Aspromonte to link up with Garibaldi's force at Monte San Giovanni, to which Briganti had retired after his failure to relieve Reggio. In one of the actions on Aspromonte, the French Socialist, De Flotte, was killed.

After uniting with Cosenz's men, Garibaldi had about 4,500 men at Monte San Giovanni, nearly twice Briganti's force, and on 22 August Garibaldi sent an envoy under a flag of truce to demand the surrender of the town. His envoy was shot dead, but soon afterwards Briganti came out in person to assure Garibaldi that this shooting of the envoy was a regrettable error, and offered to surrender if he was allowed to march out with the honours of war. Garibaldi demanded unconditional surrender, and Briganti complied. Briganti himself, who was politically something of a Liberal, slipped away, disguised in civilian dress, but on reaching Mileto was recognized by his own soldiers, who denounced him as a coward, and lynched him, mutilating his body and burning his horse.[17]

In Lower Calabria the poverty was almost as great as in Sicily, and the peasantry, like the townspeople, were revolutionary by tradition. In the course of the next few days, the people rose in revolt against the Neapolitan authorities. In Catanzaro the citizens proclaimed Garibaldi as Dictator while the town was still occupied by government troops; in the countryside, guerrilla bands were formed to fight for Garibaldi; and many of the Neapolitan troops refused to fight, and went off to their homes. Within less than a week, 6,000 Neapolitan soldiers had either surrendered or deserted, and the remaining 10,000 of the Neapolitan troops in Calabria were concentrated under General Ghio in the town of Monteleone, forty miles north of Reggio.

On 26 August Garibaldi walked seven miles across sandy wastes and swamp land, accompanied by only a few officers, to Nicotera, to meet another contingent of his forces under Medici, who landed there after sailing from Messina. At Nicotera he received a message from Ghio, offering to surrender Monteleone if he were allowed to sail to Naples with the honours of war. Garibaldi sent back the messenger with a demand for unconditional surrender, and marched north to Monteleone, where he found that Ghio and his 10,000 men – who outnumbered all Garibaldi's forces on the mainland – had retreated as rapidly as possible to the north. After receiving a tumultuous welcome from the inhabitants of Monteleone, Garibaldi set out in pursuit of the retreating enemy.[18]

The resistance of the royal Neapolitan forces was crumbling before Garibaldi. Commander Forbes crossed the Straits of Messina a few days after the Garibaldini, and set off to find Garibaldi. He happened to meet six of Garibaldi's men who had lost their way. As the seven of them were walking along a road in Calabria, they ran into a battalion of Neapolitan troops, who ordered them, at rifle point, to halt. The six Garibaldini told the Neapolitan commander, quite untruthfully, that they were scouts whom Garibaldi had sent on ahead, and that Garibaldi and his men would arrive in a few minutes. The whole Neapolitan battalion thereupon offered to surrender to the six Garibaldini, and soon afterwards laid down their arms, disbanded, and went home.[19]

Forbes came across Garibaldi near Pizzo, a few miles north of Monteleone, sitting in a grove of oak-trees a few yards from the road, surrounded by his staff and studying a map. Forbes thought that Garibaldi, at the age of fifty-three, was the most active man in the army, and he attributed this to Garibaldi's frugal diet. Garibaldi seemed to live solely on bread, water, fruit and cigars. He went to bed, whenever possible, at 8 pm, rose at 2 am, and took a siesta of two or three hours during the heat of the midday sun. On the night before Briganti surrendered at Monte San Giovanni, Garibaldi told the orderly officer to wake him at 2 am. When the officer mentioned that he did not have a watch, Garibaldi, whose hobby of astronomy now came in useful, told the officer to watch a certain star, and that when that star was hidden from sight by a particular tree, it would be two o'clock.[20]

The only impediment to Garibaldi's advance was his lack of cavalry, for, apart from himself and a few officers, none of his men had horses. Telling his soldiers to follow as quickly as possible, he set off with a small mounted escort and a number of English tourists of both sexes in their carriages, to pursue 10,000 retreating enemy soldiers. The Neapolitans did not stop till they reached the village of Soveria, on the road up to the Agrifoglio pass. Here Ghio heard that several thousand Calabrian partisans, who had risen in support of Garibaldi, were blocking his retreat at the top of the pass, and rather than face them he decided to wait for Garibaldi. On 29 August Garibaldi caught up with them, and next morning, after surviving a minor earthquake in the village of San Pietro on the previous evening, he was joined by 2,000 local partisans and a few of his own men from Cosenz's forces. He sent Alberto Mario and Colonel Peard with a small escort to see Ghio and demand his unconditional surrender. While Ghio hesitated, Garibaldi drew up the partisans in a semicircle around Soveria and moved in on Ghio's men. When the Neapolitans saw the Garibaldini coming, they laid down their rifles and surrendered to a force one-fifth of their number. It was of course impossible for Garibaldi to capture and guard prisoners, but whenever Neapolitan troops surrendered, he gave them the choice of joining his army or surrendering their arms and going home. Nearly all of them chose to go home.[21]

Since landing on the mainland, Garibaldi had travelled 120 miles in twelve days, and he had another 200 miles to cover before reaching Naples. He pressed northwards along the west coast, travelling in an open carriage when the road was good enough, but once crossing mountainous country on a mule, and going for a short part of the journey by boat across the Gulf of Policastro. He was accompanied by his staff on their horses, by a body of cavalry which he had succeeded in mounting on captured horses, and by English journalists and tourists, including Jessie Mario and Lord Shaftesbury's son, Evelyn Ashley, who was Palmerston's secretary, and was spending his summer holiday in Italy. Ashley put on a Garibaldian red shirt, as being the most suitable garment in the circumstances. Colonel Peard went ahead, travelling even faster than Garibaldi. Peard bore a physical resemblance to Garibaldi, and in many places was mistaken for the Dictator. Crowds gathered round Peard, knelt to him, and kissed his hands and clothes, and Neapolitan troops surrendered to him as soon as they saw him. When he realized that he was being mistaken for Garibaldi, he deliberately impersonated him, and ordered the clerks in the telegraph offices to send out the news that Garibaldi had already arrived in the district. This added to the demoralization of the enemy.[22]

In Naples, King Francis and his ministers had watched the situation with increasing gloom. After Garibaldi's victories in Sicily, Francis had granted a constitution to his people in June; but this came much too late to win the goodwill of the Liberals, and its only effect was to demoralize the Right-wing clerical party, who were the only section of his subjects who were still eager to fight for him. It did not alter the realities of power in Naples, which continued to lie largely in the hands of Liborio Romano, the Chief of Police. Apart from having the secret police at his disposal, Romano also controlled the secret society, the Camorra, which was the counterpart in Naples to the Mafia in Sicily. Far from making any effort to weaken Romano's hold over the country, King Francis in June 1860 appointed him Minister of the Interior, thus formally giving him the power which he already held in practice.

On 23 August Alexandre Dumas arrived in Naples from Palermo in his yacht, and called on Romano. He told him that Garibaldi, who had landed in Calabria four days before, was going to win, and he suggested that Romano should betray the King and join Garibaldi. Romano eagerly accepted the proposal. On 30 August, when Garibaldi was in the village of Soveria, where he had just accepted the surrender of Ghio's 10,000 soldiers, he received a letter from Dumas telling him that Romano was ready to join him. Garibaldi accepted Romano's offer to help, but told him to remain in Naples for the moment, and not to show his hand until Garibaldi was on the point of entering the city.[23]

Francis and his other ministers suspected Romano's treachery, but were powerless to do anything about it. The King's hopes rested in his army in the capital and in the peasantry in the north of his kingdom, who were more prosperous than the peasantry in Sicily and Calabria, and much more ready to listen to the exhortations of their parish priests and to defend the King. Garibaldi and the Liberals had no more support among these peasants than they had had in the rural districts of the Papal States in 1849. But Francis did not wish to turn the city of Naples into a battleground like Palermo, and decided to abandon it to Garibaldi, to retreat to Gaeta with his family and personal entourage, and to build up an army in the north with which he could launch a counter-offensive against Garibaldi. On 5 September he left Naples, having placarded the city with posters announcing his temporary absence. On the same day, Garibaldi reached Salerno, thirty-five miles to the south-east of Naples, where 20,000 people came out to cheer him. The town was illuminated, and the people danced in the streets all night.[24]

Next day the Mayor of Naples and the Commander of the National Guard set out for Salerno to invite Garibaldi to enter the capital. Garibaldi waited for them at Salerno, and on the morning of 7 September cabled to Romano that he would come to Naples as soon as the Mayor and his companions arrived. Romano cabled in reply:

> To the invincible General Garibaldi, Dictator of the Two Sicilies, Liborio Romano, Minister of the Interior and Police. Naples awaits your arrival with the greatest impatience to salute you as the redeemer of Italy and to place in your hands the power of the State and her own destinies. . . . I await your further orders and am, with unlimited respect for you, invincible Dictator, Liborio Romano.[25]

Salerno and Naples were connected by one of the only two railways in the kingdom. Garibaldi, despite the apprehensions of his friends for his safety, decided to catch the train to Naples. At 9.30 am on 7 September he drove out of Salerno, through the streets packed with cheering crowds, to the railway terminus outside the town, and boarded a special train. With him on the train were Cosenz, about twenty members of the National Guard of Salerno, and a few English visitors – Evelyn Ashley, Edwin James QC, and W. G. Church, the Public Orator of Cambridge University. It was a very hot and cloudless day. The train moved slowly towards Naples, stopping repeatedly when the line was blocked by excited villagers who had come to cheer Garibaldi. At Nocera they encountered a trainload of Bavarian troops who were on their way to Capua to join King Francis's army; but the stationmaster shunted the troop train on to a siding to let Garibaldi pass. About three miles from Naples Garibaldi's train was stopped by a naval officer who warned him that it would be dangerous for him to proceed, because the railway station at Naples was within the range of the King's cannon in the Carmine fort, and the commander of the fort had trained his guns on the station and was intending to bombard it when Garibaldi arrived. Garibaldi replied: 'What cannon? When the people greet us like this, there are no cannon.'

In Naples, like in Salerno, the railway terminus was an open space just outside the city. Garibaldi's train arrived at 1.30 in the afternoon, and Garibaldi was greeted by Romano and the city council, while a vast crowd surged round him, cheering him and trying to touch him as he entered his carriage. The welcoming authorities had carefully planned his route to the city centre avoiding the Carmine fort; but in the confusion caused by the large crowds, they took the wrong road, and Garibaldi passed right under the cannon of the Carmine fort. As the King had ordered the garrison not to resist Garibaldi's entry into the city, no shot was fired. Most of the 500,000 inhabitants of Naples seemed to be in the streets to welcome Garibaldi. The royal palace was still occupied by Francis's guards, so Garibaldi was taken to the palace annexe nearby, where the King's guests had often been lodged. From there he went to the cathedral, where Father Pantaleo, who had come with him from Sicily, conducted the thanksgiving service, and the blood of St Januarius liquefied in Garibaldi's honour. A few days later, *The Times* expressed the hope of Garibaldi's Protestant supporters in Britain that he would expose and suppress the Papistical fraud of the liquefying blood; but Garibaldi said nothing to offend the religious feelings of the Neapolitans.

He returned to the palace annexe, and made a speech and repeated appearances on the balcony. For the first time, he made the gesture which soon came to be known as the 'Garibaldi sign', raising one finger – the forefinger – on his right hand to signify 'One Italy'. Eventually he retired to bed. One of his red-shirted Garibaldini stepped out on to the balcony and laid his cheek on his hand to show that Garibaldi was asleep; and the crowds quietly dispersed, and continued the all-night celebrations in other parts of the city. They cheered, and drank his health, and shouted '*Viva Garibardo*', as they pronounced his name in their Neapolitan dialect, soon shortening this to '*Viva Bardo*', while the revolutionary sailor from Nice, whose name was pronounced 'Garibaldi' in most of Italy and in Montevideo, 'Garibawldi' in England, 'Gareeboughji' in Rio Grande do Sul, and 'Bardo' in Naples, slept in the palace annexe, Dictator of the southern half of the Italian peninsula.[26]

CHAPTER 32

THE DICTATORSHIP

FOR sixty-two days, from 7 September to 8 November 1860, Garibaldi ruled all except a small area of the Kingdom of Naples, and most of its 9,000,000 inhabitants, as Dictator; but his greatest difficulties began on the day that he entered the capital. At Capua, fifteen miles to the north of Naples, King Francis was assembling an army of 50,000 men; and in Tuscany and the Romagna, 200 miles further north, were the armies of Victor Emanuel and Cavour.

Cavour, who had been temporizing all the summer, realized that the situation now called for decisive action. A week after Garibaldi landed in Calabria, Cavour sent Farini and General Cialdini to Napoleon III, who was on holiday at Chambéry in his newly acquired province of Savoy. According to the information given by the French Foreign Minister, Thouvenel, to Lord Cowley, the British Ambassador, they tried to exculpate Cavour from the responsibility for Garibaldi's expedition by throwing the blame on Victor Emanuel. Farini and Cialdini also pointed out to Napoleon that the only way to stop Garibaldi from consolidating his power in Naples and from attacking Rome was for the Sardinian army to invade the Kingdom of Naples from the north. This could only be done by invading the Papal States too; but they promised that Sardinian troops would not enter Rome. Napoleon said that there would be a great diplomatic outcry, but that he would not intervene, and added that if Cavour decided to act, he should act quickly.[1]

On 11 September 33,000 Sardinian troops under Fanti and Cialdini invaded the Marches and Umbria, and the Sardinian fleet bombarded Ancona. The Papal troops put up a valiant defence, but they were greatly outnumbered by the Sardinian troops, and capitulated on 29 September.

There was a fundamental difference in the aims and methods of the three men – Cavour, Garibaldi and Mazzini – who influenced the Italian *Risorgimento* in 1860. Mazzini wished to unite all Italy, preferably under a republic, and though he was prepared, for the time being, to fight under the slogan of Victor Emanuel King of Italy, he was sure that Victor Emanuel and his ministers would betray the Italian cause and sell out to Napoleon III, while he rejected any kind of compromise or retreat as unnecessary and a betrayal of the cause. Cavour wished to annex all Italy to the kingdom of Victor Emanuel, and believed that this could only be achieved by an alliance with Napoleon III, and that French goodwill must be retained at all costs. He thought that the support of Napoleon III was much more valuable than popular revolutionary zeal or than British public opinion, for although in his youth he had admired British institutions, he knew that Napoleon III had gone to war to obtain Lombardy and Central Italy for Sardinia, and that Palmerston and Russell had not. 'The French alliance is for us an absolute necessity,' he wrote to d'Azeglio in London on 4 June 1860. 'If England had wished to give us effective help, if she still wished to give it, she would guarantee, quite cheaply, the independence of Europe. Unfortunately, her platonic sympathies are not enough.'[2]

Garibaldi's position was in some ways more illogical than Mazzini's or Cavour's. He wished to achieve Cavour's objective by Mazzini's methods, to annex Italy to Victor Emanuel's realm by popular revolution without hesitation or retreat or Napoleon III's goodwill. He succeeded in achieving precisely this in Sicily and Naples; but it placed him in great personal difficulties, and was the cause both of his military effectiveness and of his political ineffectiveness. He acted with great decision and boldness in war because he was acting against the enemy; but he would not consider either Victor Emanuel or the Mazzinians as enemies, and would not crush any Italian who was in favour of national liberation. He therefore appeared to be trying to placate both factions, and succeeded in antagonizing both. A dictator who was politically skilful, like Cromwell or Napoleon I, could have exploited this situation to his own advantage, and consolidated his power at the expense of both factions; Garibaldi could not, and did not wish to do so.

Cavour had correctly diagnosed Garibaldi's attitude in July, when, after receiving La Farina's reports from Palermo, he had decided that, though Garibaldi was personally loyal to Victor Emanuel, he had fallen under the influence of Mazzinians. Mazzini, living illegally in Genoa, was in contact with Bertani, and saw him secretly nearly every day. Bertani wrote regularly to Crispi in Palermo, and Mazzini himself sometimes wrote to Crispi. On most occasions, the political line which Crispi was urging Garibaldi to adopt in Palermo had been laid down by Mazzini in Genoa. There was a germ of truth in the theme of the satirical play, *L'Âne et les Trois Voleurs*, which was published in

Paris in the autumn of 1860, and fictitiously stated to have been acted at the Théatre des Marionnettes Italiennes. In the play Garibaldi, after being reminded by Alexandre Dumas of how he once strangled a tiger with his bare hands in South America, and praised with sickening flattery by the correspondent of the London *Times*, falls out with Cavour as to which of them should ride the donkey, Naples, which they have stolen, only to find that while they are quarrelling, Mazzini rides off on the donkey, declaring 'I am the one you cannot stop, I am the one you cannot kill, I am the Revolution!' The theory that Garibaldi and Cavour were merely dupes of Mazzini was reactionary propaganda; but Mazzini was exercising his influence behind the scenes. The decision to expel La Farina from Sicily was originally Mazzini's, and was suggested to Crispi and Garibaldi by Bertani on Mazzini's direction; and it was Mazzini who encouraged Garibaldi's plans for an invasion of the Papal States by urging Bertani to continue with his preparations for this invasion instead of sending all the new volunteers and equipment as reinforcements for Garibaldi in Sicily.[3]

Bertani had gone to Sicily with Garibaldi after he had been forced to abandon the project of invading the Papal States from the Gulf of Aranci. On 31 August he joined Garibaldi at Cosenza with 1,500 new troops, on the day after Garibaldi had accepted the surrender of Ghio's 10,000 men at Soveria. From then on, he stayed close to Garibaldi, entering Naples with him, acting as his secretary, and, according to the Cavourians, hardly allowing Garibaldi out of his sight. He urged Garibaldi to pursue the policy, which had been suggested to him by Mazzini, of an immediate advance against the King of Naples's troops at Capua, and after defeating them to press on and invade the Papal States. Garibaldi eagerly accepted this suggestion; he established his headquarters in the royal palace at Caserta, and prepared to conduct the campaign before the autumn rains came.

On 10 September Garibaldi issued a proclamation from Naples addressed to the people of Palermo, in which he stated his intention of proclaiming Victor Emanuel King of Italy in the Quirinal Palace in Rome.[4] The publication of this statement alarmed Cavour, who feared that Garibaldi would embroil Sardinia with Napoleon III before the royal Sardinian army could reach Naples; and knowing the influence which the British government had over Garibaldi, he asked them to try to dissuade Garibaldi from attacking the Papal States. Russell, despite his anti-Catholic prejudices, realized that an attack on Rome would cause international complications. Admiral Mundy, who had sailed with his squadron from Palermo to Naples when Garibaldi's advance and the spread of the fighting northwards seemed to make Naples a more dangerous place than Palermo for British subjects, and Elliot, the British Minister in Naples, who remained in the capital when the King withdrew to Gaeta, got in touch with Garibaldi. Mundy invited Garibaldi to meet Elliot in his flagship.

Garibaldi arrived on board escorted by Bertani and his staff. Elliot asked to speak with Garibaldi alone, and after Garibaldi's escort had withdrawn, and Mundy had with some difficulty persuaded Bertani to go too, Mundy, Elliot and Garibaldi were left alone together. Elliot said that though he could not be officially accredited to Garibaldi's government, the British government wished Garibaldi well, and had ordered him to remain in Naples to help Garibaldi; but he urged Garibaldi not to march into the Papal States, and warned him that though British public opinion was strongly sympathetic to him, it would change rapidly if it were thought that he was provoking a European war. Garibaldi became rather heated, and said that Rome was an Italian city and that neither Napoleon III nor anyone else had any right to keep him out of it.[5] Garibaldi's attitude somewhat disconcerted Mundy, and in the course of the next few weeks Cavour saw to his delight that the British government, if not the British people, was becoming less enthusiastic about Garibaldi, though the English ladies in Naples clustered around him, and, to Türr's disgust, asked him to kiss them and give them a lock of his hair.[6]

Matters were made more difficult by the fact that Mazzini himself arrived in Naples on 17 September. He was tactful enough to remain quietly in the background, but he was able to exercise direct influence on Bertani; and Garibaldi, with his usual generosity and lack of political sectarianism, refused to ostracize Mazzini, but met him and greeted him warmly in the King's palace in Naples. This increased the anxieties of Cavour, Victor Emanuel, Napoleon III and the British government.[7]

But Garibaldi, as Cavour knew very well, was not a Mazzinian, and some of his actions as Dictator in Naples disappointed the Mazzinians, although other steps which he took alarmed the Cavourians. When he entered Naples, he found the King of Naples's navy in the harbour. The Neapolitan fleet, which consisted of 90 ships with 786 guns and more than 7,000 sailors, was far more powerful than the Sardinian navy, and Cavour immediately sent Admiral Persano to Naples to take control of it. Garibaldi's first action on reaching Naples was to hand over the Neapolitan fleet to Persano.[8] Bertani and the Mazzinians realized that this was a disaster from their point of view; it not only weakened Garibaldi's bargaining position as against Cavour, but deprived him of a navy which would have been invaluable in any campaign against the Papal States. There is very little doubt that if Garibaldi had retained control of the Neapolitan navy, he would have been treated with more courtesy and consideration by Victor Emanuel's government during the next two months; but the surrender of the fleet was the consequence of the equivocal position which he was adopting towards Victor Emanuel in trying to be, at one and the same time, a loyal subject of the King of Sardinia and a power independent of the King's government. He neither placed himself unreservedly at the orders of the King and his government, like any ordinary general would have done, nor did he take all necessary steps to safeguard his position as an independent dictator.

At the same time as he disappointed the Mazzinians by handing over the fleet to Cavour, he alarmed Cavour and all the Neapolitan and Sardinian Conservatives by appointing Bertani to be Secretary-General of the Dictatorship. The Conservatives considered Bertani to be an even worse Mazzinian than Crispi. But when Garibaldi appointed his government for the Neapolitan territory on the mainland, the majority of his ministers were Neapolitan Conservatives who for some time had been in close contact with Cavour and supported Cavour's policy. Garibaldi kept Liborio Romano as Minister of the Interior and Chief of Police. He thus had a Cavourian majority in his Cabinet, a Mazzinian in the key position of power, and a Bourbonist in the vitally important post of Minister of the Interior. It was a situation which could have been cleverly exploited by a politically cunning and ambitious Dictator, but not by Garibaldi.

Garibaldi also wrote to Victor Emanuel and asked him to send Pallavicino to act as his Pro-Dictator in Naples, like Depretis in Palermo, so that he could entrust the government of the mainland to Pallavicino while he was conducting his campaign against the Papal States. Victor Emanuel, with Cavour's consent, agreed and sent Pallavicino to Naples. Three years earlier, Garibaldi had collaborated successfully with Pallavicino in the Italian National Society, and Pallavicino, who with Manin had been responsible for the concept of Victor Emanuel King of Italy, was certainly not a Mazzinian, though he was too Radical for Cavour's taste. But when Pallavicino arrived in Naples, Garibaldi did not appoint him as Pro-Dictator, but merely brought him in as a new member of the government, while Bertani still remained as the all-powerful Secretary-General.[9]

On Bertani's advice, Garibaldi took a number of steps which angered the Conservatives. Some of his decrees promising land reform, granting unemployment relief, and fixing maximum prices of goods in the shops, along the lines of the decrees which he had promulgated in Sicily, seemed to Cavour and the Conservatives to be the first steps on the road to Socialism. The newspaper *Il Nazionale* described them as 'a challenge to society, a negation of the moral principles on which society rests', and as an 'exaggeration of popular sovereignty, of the

490

absolute right to work, of a contempt for every social distinction'; and Cavour thought that the decree which provided work in the arsenal at Naples for the unemployed was 'worthy of Louis Blanc'. Garibaldi shocked the Conservatives in Naples and Turin, and many of his admirers in Britain, by granting a pension to the mother of Agesilao Milano. Milano had been a soldier in the Neapolitan army who in 1856 had tried to assassinate King Ferdinand by stabbing him with his bayonet when the King was inspecting Milano's regiment on the parade ground. He had only inflicted a slight wound on the King, but had been executed and hailed as a martyr by Mazzini. The pension to Milano's mother was cancelled a few months later when Cavour's government replaced Garibaldi's. Garibaldi also aroused disapproval and ridicule by appointing Dumas to be Director of the National Museum and of Excavations in Naples. Elliot thought, though apparently without any justification, that Dumas was using his position to embezzle the public funds.[10]

Relations between the Garibaldini and the citizens of Naples were unfriendly, for though 'Bardo' the Dictator was still very popular, his red-shirts were not. The Garibaldini despised the citizens who had done nothing to free themselves, and now overcharged and cheated their liberators while pretending to admire them; and the Neapolitans, especially the wealthier classes, resented and feared the boisterousness of the Garibaldini, who swaggered around the streets and interrupted the performances at the opera by demanding that the orchestra should play the Garibaldi Hymn in the middle of the acts, and leaped into the orchestra pit to enforce the demand at the point of the bayonet.[11]

Cavour's solution to these problems was to press for the immediate annexation by Sardinia of both Sicily and the Neapolitan territory on the mainland, as this would immediately end Garibaldi's dictatorship and bring the former Neapolitan kingdom under the government in Turin. This involved the holding of a plebiscite, like those which had been held in Tuscany, Central Italy, Nice and Savoy, because the principle of the referendum had become an accepted part of the cession of territory in 1860, and made it possible for Cavour and Victor Emanuel to state that they were not seizing this territory without the consent of the population.

The Mazzinians opposed annexation by Sardinia, knowing that all their influence would be lost if Garibaldi ceased to be Dictator and Cavour's government took over. Although hitherto Garibaldi had adopted the attitude that annexation must be postponed in Sicily until the Neapolitan mainland had been conquered, the Mazzinians now argued that both in Sicily and on the mainland it must be further postponed until Rome and the Papal States, and perhaps Venetia too, had been liberated. They therefore opposed the idea of a plebiscite, and proposed instead that the question of annexation should be referred to a Constituent Assembly in Sicily and Naples. Cavour and his agents strongly opposed this suggestion. In a plebiscite, with open voting after an intensive propaganda campaign in favour of annexation, and opposition to the proposal being construed as support for the Bourbon King, a large majority for annexation was certain; in a Constituent Assembly, with MPS forming into parties and groups, with some in favour of annexation, some of independence, and others of federal union, there would be endless opportunity for delay, and the result would be doubtful. Cavour's supporters demanded an immediate plebiscite, and denounced the opposition to their demand as an attempt to thwart popular sovereignty.

At Caserta, Garibaldi was making his preparations for his offensive against King Francis's army and his march on Rome. The palace at Caserta was the largest royal palace in Europe, having been built in the middle of the eighteenth century in direct imitation, architecturally, of Versailles, and on purpose made a little larger than the King of France's palace. Garibaldi moved into one of the smaller rooms in the palace, and there, dressed in his red shirt, lived as simply and frugally as he had done in his one room in Montevideo and in the house he had built in Caprera. He appointed a platoon of red-shirts to be his personal bodyguard in order to give him some protection from the hordes of office-seekers, business speculators, political intriguers and admiring English women who tried to force their way into his presence at all hours of the day. He spent as much time as possible away from the palace, riding along the front line, reconnoitring in person the enemy's positions. On the top of Monte Tifata he could not only look down on the enemy lines, but could be alone, away from the politicians and the suitors.[12]

The King of Naples's troops were drawn up to the south of Capua along the line of the River Volturno to a width of some twenty miles. The commander of the royal troops, Marshal Ritucci, had an army of 50,000 men, who were loyal to their King and far more determined fighters than the soldiers who had opposed Garibaldi in Calabria. Garibaldi's forces had now grown to 25,000 men, consisting of the survivors from the original Thousand, the reinforcements which had come with Medici and Bertani, the partisans who had joined him in Calabria, and more volunteers who had now joined him in Naples, though many of these, according to hostile critics, were more eager to show themselves in their red shirts in the streets and cafés of the capital than to fight the enemy. Garibaldi kept 3,000 of these troops in the city of Naples to maintain order and guard the city from enemy raids. He sent 1,500 men under Türr to the Ariano district in the central highlands, fifty miles north-east of Naples, where peasant guerrillas – who Garibaldi thought were stirred up by the priests – had launched a counter-revolutionary uprising, and were massacring any-one whom they suspected of being a Radical or Liberal. Türr curbed the revolt by some summary executions, though on a far smaller scale than those which Cialdini and the royal Sardinian troops were carrying out in the Papal States, where they were shooting all guerrillas who took up arms for the Pope, as they were later to shoot the royalist guerrillas in Neapolitan territory. The rest of Garibaldi's troops, about 20,000 in number, were drafted to the Volturno to face King Francis's army.[13]

But Garibaldi, to his annoyance, had to deal with a political dis-traction. Before he left Sicily in August, he had told his Pro-Dictator in Sicily, Depretis, on Crispi's advice, not to take any steps for holding a plebiscite until he received orders from Garibaldi. But at the beginning of September, after Depretis received news of the surrender of Ghio's army at Soveria and of Garibaldi's rapid advance on Naples, he thought that the time had come to hold the plebiscite, as Garibaldi's original objection to it – that Sicily must remain under his dictator-ship and not be annexed by Sardinia as long as he needed it as a base for operations against the mainland – no longer seemed to apply.

Depretis wrote to Garibaldi, asking for permission to fix a date for the plebiscite, and sent Piola, his Minister for the Navy, to find Gari-baldi on the mainland and give him the letter. Piola found Garibaldi on 4 September, the day before Garibaldi reached Salerno, at the wayside inn of Il Fortino, on the road between Sapri and Casalnuova, some fifty miles south-east of Eboli. After reading Depretis's letter, Garibaldi agreed to his suggestion, and had begun to dictate a reply to Depretis to his secretary, Basso, when Bertani, who had joined Gari-baldi four days before at Cosenza, entered the room. Bertani wrote in his diary for 4 September:

> I come in just as the General is dictating the following words to Basso: 'Dear Depretis, let annexation take place as soon as you like.' I gave a start of amazement and exclaimed: 'General, you are abdicating!' He fixed that penetrating, questioning glance of his upon me. 'Yes, General, you are hamstringing the revolution, and relinquishing all possibility of carrying out your programme.' . . . The argument waxed hot. . . . 'You are right,' the General said, and turning to Basso once more, he dictated as follows: 'Dear Depretis, I think we will let Bonaparte wait a few days longer. Meanwhile get rid of half a dozen agitators.'

This last order meant that Depretis was to deport some Cavourian supporters from Sicily.[14]

Garibaldi's reply was cabled to Palermo, whereupon Depretis summoned a meeting of his Cabinet. Crispi proposed that Garibaldi's reply postponing the plebiscite should be published in the Official Journal, and that two Cavourians should be deported; and when Depretis refused, Crispi resigned, and announced his intention of joining Garibaldi on the mainland. When Crispi sailed for Naples on 11 September, Depretis went with him, and they both saw Garibaldi at Caserta. After a long discussion, Garibaldi told them that he would announce his decision later; and on 16 September he decided in Crispi's favour, almost certainly on Bertani's advice. Depretis immediately resigned as Pro-Dictator, and Garibaldi, thinking that he would have to straighten out the position in Sicily in person, left Caserta on the evening of 16 September and sailed from Naples to Palermo with Depretis. He arrived at Palermo at 3 pm next day, and stayed there for only five hours, during which he appointed Mordini to be the Pro-Dictator there. Mordini was a little more Radical than Depretis, and closer to the Mazzinians, and he was opposed to a plebiscite. During his brief stay in Palermo, Garibaldi addressed the people from the balcony of the royal palace, being received with the wildest enthusiasm. He spoke against an over-precipitate annexation, but attacked 'those wretches' who alleged that he was not in favour of annexation, and urged the 'generous people of the barricades' to 'have faith in me and in Victor Emanuel'.[15]

It was probably Depretis's attempt to hold the plebiscite in Sicily, and the use which Bertani and Crispi made of it in their anti-Cavourian propaganda to Garibaldi, which caused Garibaldi to take a step which incensed Cavour, distressed his supporters in the British government, and for the first time damaged his friendly relations with Victor Emanuel. He published a statement in the Official Journal in Naples that he would never again collaborate with Cavour, the man who had sold an Italian province, and sent Pallavicino to Turin with a letter to Victor Emanuel, in which he asked the King to dismiss Cavour as Prime Minister. Bertani stated later that he had tried to dissuade Garibaldi from writing this letter, which he thought would annoy the King and strengthen Cavour's position; but Garibaldi, convinced that the King was his friend, was now attributing all his difficulties to Cavour's personal malevolence. Victor Emanuel wrote a moderately worded reply, telling Garibaldi that as a constitutional monarch he could not dismiss Cavour 'at the moment', and sent a copy of his letter to Cavour with the words 'at the moment' left out; but Pallavicino noticed that Victor Emanuel was very angry with Garibaldi.

CAMILLO DI CAVOUR

FRANCESCO CRISPI

GARIBALDI AT HIS HOUSE ON CAPRERA, 1861

GARIBALDI'S BEDROOM TODAY

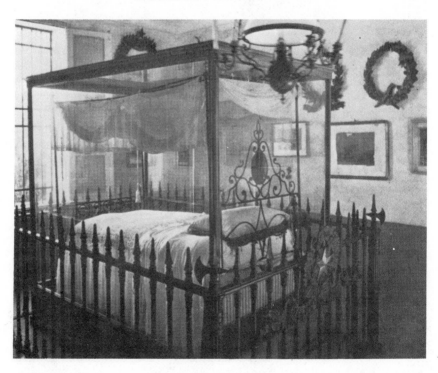

Cavour wrote to the Prince of Carignano, Victor Emanuel's cousin, on 27 September that the King had decided 'to march on Naples at the head of his army to bring Garibaldi to his senses and to throw into the sea this nest of Red Republicans and Socialist demagogues that has formed around him. . . . It is the insolent ultimatum brought by that idiot Giorgio Pallavicino which has decided the King.'[16]

CHAPTER 33

THE VOLTURNO:
THE SURRENDER OF POWER

GARIBALDI had returned from Palermo to Caserta by 19 September, but during his absence his troops had suffered a defeat. Türr, whom he had left in command of the army on the Volturno, had, with his usual impetuosity, attacked the enemy at Caiazzo on the morning of the 19th. After capturing Caiazzo, he advanced to the gates of Capua, and became involved in what appeared to be an attempt to capture Capua by assault. He was repulsed with a loss of 130 men. Some of Cavour's supporters in Naples and Turin hardly concealed their delight at the defeat of the Garibaldini, which took place on the same day as Cialdini's victory over the Papal troops at Castelfidardo. Garibaldi, in his memoirs, blamed Türr, who by the time that Garibaldi wrote the memoirs had become a supporter of Cavour's party, and he accused the Cavourians of being responsible for the defeat by having caused the political difficulties in Sicily which made it necessary for him to go to Palermo and leave Türr in command.

On 21 September Marshal Ritucci launched a counter-attack on Caiazzo, which had been Türr's only gain from the attack of the 19th. The village was defended by 300 Garibaldini, who were attacked by 7,000 royalist troops. Garibaldi sent up 650 men as reinforcements, and the 950 defenders held the position with great heroism for several hours, suffering 250 casualties, many of them young boys, against the enemy casualties of 100. Commander Forbes criticized Garibaldi's tactics in this engagement, and the wasted bravery of the Garibaldini, who should either have been sent adequate reinforcements or ordered to retreat; but ever since Costa Brava in 1842, this refusal to retreat in any circumstances had been a strength and weakness of Garibaldi as a commander. Ritucci did not press home his advantage after the recapture of Caiazzo, and did nothing for more than a week, while Garibaldi brought up more artillery from Naples and strengthened his defences. It was not until 1 October that Ritucci, under insistent orders from King Francis at Gaeta, launched his offensive along the Volturno in front of Capua, his objective being to defeat Garibaldi's army and recapture Naples before the Sardinian army arrived from the north.[1]

The battle of the Volturno was the first time in his life that Garibaldi commanded a large army and fought a pitched defensive battle. Although he was outnumbered by more than two to one by the Bourbonist troops in the area, the enemy only threw in about 28,000 of his total forces of 50,000, while probably about 20,000 Garibaldini were engaged, the numbers being of a size comparable to those in all except the largest battles in the major European wars of the early nineteenth century. Garibaldi's chief task was to induce his men to stand fast and not retreat, and this he succeeded in doing, despite the fact that the army under his command was too large for him to be able to come into personal contact with every soldier, as he had been able to do in most of his other battles.

He benefited from the mistakes of his opponent, which were forced on Ritucci by the High Command at Gaeta. Ritucci drew up his forces in a wide semicircle around Caserta, which gave Garibaldi the advantage of being able to fight on a shorter interior line and to switch his reserves from one sector of the battle to the other. On Garibaldi's left wing, near Capua, he had 7,000 men under Medici and Milbitz, holding the village of Santa Maria and the advance post of San Angelo. His right wing, under Bixio, with 5,000 men, held Maddaloni, while Bronzetti and 280 men held an outpost at Castel Morrone on the extreme right, beyond Bixio. Türr was in Caserta in the centre with the reserves.

On the night of 30 September Garibaldi visited his advance post at San Angelo, and saw a rocket fired into the sky in the enemy lines at Capua. He guessed that this might be the signal for an attack, and sent word to all his commanders to be on the alert. The enemy moved at midnight, and in the early hours of 1 October the Garibaldini could hear them coming, though they could see nothing because of a thick autumn fog which settled over the whole battlefield. By dawn the fighting had started on both wings. Ritucci sent von Mechel, who had fought against Garibaldi in Sicily, to attack Bixio at Maddaloni, but von Mechel made a tactical error and divided his forces, sending 5,000 men to outflank Bixio and 3,000 into the frontal attack. The outflanking forces, instead of marching against Bixio, went off and attacked Bronzetti at Castel Moronne; and Bixio's 5,000 men were attacked by only 3,000 of the enemy. Bixio was therefore able to hold his position, despite the fact that some of his men, who were in action for the first time, lost their nerve and ran, as did some of the Garibaldini officers, for which they were afterwards publicly degraded by Garibaldi. At Castel Morrone, Bronzetti's 280 men held out for four hours against

5,000 of the enemy, and did not surrender until one third of them had been killed, thus preventing these 5,000 Neapolitan troops from being thrown into the attack on Bixio.

On Garibaldi's left wing, Medici held out in the face of even heavier attacks. Garibaldi himself spent most of the day in this part of the battlefield, riding, or travelling in his carriage, between Medici's headquarters in Santa Maria and the advance post at San Angelo. Once, near San Angelo, his carriage ran into an ambush and was surrounded by Bourbon troops; but Garibaldi jumped out of the carriage, drew his sabre, and led the charge against the enemy, who turned and fled. On several other occasions he led various units into the attack, and he was with some battalion of his troops on the left wing all day, pausing only for a few minutes to eat a bunch of grapes handed to him by Jessie Mario, who was in charge of the front-line hospital at Caserta. He was reconnoitring with a unit consisting of about twenty Calabrian riflemen when two squadrons of enemy cavalry made a charge against a battalion of Garibaldi's gunners in an attempt to capture a howitzer. Garibaldi made his carbineers lie down in the furrows and ditches, and as the enemy dragoons charged by above them, they discharged a volley, which, coming from under the horses' bellies, caught the enemy unawares, and scattered them.

At about 4 pm Garibaldi saw that the enemy's right wing was tiring, and he ordered Medici to launch a counter-attack. The Garibaldini charged down the road leading to Capua, between Santa Maria and San Angelo, with Garibaldi going with the vanguard, and the enemy fell back into Capua. On the other wing, the Bourbonists had also retreated, and Ritucci ordered a general retreat; but about 2,000 of his troops in the centre had broken through into Türr's reserves, and were on the point of capturing Caserta and Garibaldi's headquarters at the palace. Excited at this prospect, they did not obey the order to retreat, and Garibaldi and Medici, returning from their pursuit of Ritucci's right wing, and Bixio coming from the other side, were able to surround them and cut off their retreat.

Garibaldi stopped the action at nightfall, but next day, on 2 October, renewed the attack on the encircled enemy at Caserta. On this second day, a number of reinforcements arrived by train from Naples, including some of the battalions of the troops of the Sardinian army who had been stationed during the last three weeks on Admiral Persano's ships in the Bay of Naples. Garibaldi and the Mazzinians afterwards pointed out that Persano had not sent them to Garibaldi in time for them to take part in the vital battle of 1 October; but on the 2nd, Garibaldi led them in person into action against the enemy, who surrendered at 11 am.

Garibaldi lost 306 men killed, 1,328 wounded, and 389 prisoners and missing, of whom 1,400 were killed or wounded on the left wing at Santa Maria and San Angelo, and 200 on the right wing under Bixio, apart from the 280 men of the garrison of Castel Morrone. The Garibaldini suffered less than 50 casualties on the second day. The Bourbonists lost 260 men killed, 731 wounded and 74 prisoners in Santa Maria and San Angelo, and 200 casualties on their left wing, on 1 October, and 2,089 prisoners in their encircled forces on 2 October.[2] Garibaldi's wounded filled the hospitals at Caserta, where Jessie Mario and her helpers earned the gratitude of the men, but were unable to deal with the numbers, or to cope with the dirt and the incompetence of the Neapolitan hospital organization. Many of the wounded were evacuated to Naples, where they complained bitterly of their treatment by the inhabitants. Some of them lay unattended in the streets, as the Neapolitans refused to take them into their houses or even bring them water to drink. The Garibaldini also noted with disgust that, though Garibaldi's forces on the mainland had increased to about 43,000 by the end of October through volunteers who came in from all parts, only 80 of the 500,000 inhabitants of the city of Naples enrolled.[3]

The Battle of the Volturno had saved Naples from the Bourbon troops; but Garibaldi knew that he was not strong enough to destroy the enemy in Capua and Gaeta and advance on Rome. When Mazzini urged him to invade the Papal States, he told Mazzini that it would be quite impossible for him to advance while 60,000 enemy troops were in Capua and Gaeta.[4] Whatever his weaknesses as a politician, Garibaldi was a military realist.

On 9 October Victor Emanuel took personal command of his troops at Ancona, which he had carefully avoided doing as long as they were fighting against the Pope, and led them across the Neapolitan frontier, after issuing a proclamation stating that he was taking possession of his Neapolitan province. Cavour sent Farini, the Minister of the Interior at Turin, to accompany the King at his headquarters; so Victor Emanuel's advisers, as he entered the Kingdom of Naples, were Farini, Fanti and Cialdini, of whom Farini and Fanti had been particularly obnoxious to Garibaldi since their encounter at Modena twelve months before.

The undesirability of angering Garibaldi by sending Farini to Naples had been pointed out to Cavour; but Cavour no longer needed to conciliate Garibaldi, and hardly wished to do so. On 22 September he wrote to Emanuel d'Azeglio that Garibaldi had 'surrounded himself with Mazzinians and Republicans of the worst kind'; and on the same day he wrote to Nigra: 'If Garibaldi perseveres in the ominous course upon which he has embarked, we will go in a fortnight to re-establish order at Naples and at Palermo, even if we have to throw all the Garibaldini into the sea to do it.' Two days later, he wrote to d'Azeglio that he had lost all hope of conciliating Garibaldi, because Garibaldi had 'made his peace with Mazzini'. Fanti and Farini, in their letters, used even more hostile language, repeatedly threatening to use force against the Garibaldini. But Garibaldi wrote to the King and declared that all the troops under his command would submit to the King's authority.[5]

The British government urged Cavour not to antagonize Garibaldi unnecessarily, and pointed out to d'Azeglio the harm that would be done to the Italian cause if civil war were to break out between Victor Emanuel's army and Garibaldi's.[6] Cavour was sufficient of a statesman to see this, and tried to restrain the hatred of Fanti and Farini for Garibaldi.

As Victor Emanuel's troops marched on Naples, it was clear that the days of Garibaldi's dictatorship were drawing to a close. On 4 October the editor of the Left-wing Opposition newspaper *Il Diritto* wrote to Mordini that Garibaldi should now hold the plebiscite in Naples and Sicily, declare annexation, and resign as Dictator, and then take his place as an MP on the Opposition benches in Parliament in Turin, from where he could expose the policy of Cavour.[7] Politically this would have been sound advice if Garibaldi had had any desire or ability to be an influential force in political life in the new Kingdom of Italy; but he had no more desire to do this than to adopt the alternative Mazzinian policy of installing himself as the head of a Republican government in Naples and the South, which he could in any case only have done successfully if he had adopted it some months earlier and with the backing of the British government.

During his last weeks as Dictator, Garibaldi showed an extraordinary lack of decision, being pulled to and fro by the Conservatives and the Radicals in his government like the most feeble-minded of hereditary monarchs at the mercy of scheming favourites. Colonel Ponsonby, whose friend Lord Mark Kerr was in Naples, wrote to Prince Albert's equerry, General Grey, in a vain attempt to persuade him that Garibaldi was 'a most noble, straitforward [*sic*], honest man' who was 'not a man who is perpetually talking of having saved his washerwoman or other more wonderful exploits'; but Ponsonby admitted that Kerr had said that 'the stories told in Naples of his utter incapacity for civil Govt. were extraordinary. He signed almost anything which the Ministers gave him, and next day would sign a decree cancelling the former, because others had got round him and told him to do so.'[8] The explanation is probably that he had acquired a deep distrust of both the Mazzinians and the Cavourians, and had no more wish to be an instrument of the Parliamentary Opposition in Turin than he was willing to co-operate with the man who had given Nice to Napoleon III.

During the last week of September, while Garibaldi was on the Volturno waiting for the battle to begin, he made a number of political decisions which disconcerted both the Cavourians and the Mazzinians in Naples. On 23 September he appointed Crispi to be his Minister of Foreign Affairs. The Conservatives had not recovered from their annoyance at this appointment, and at Garibaldi's continued delay in appointing Pallavicino to the post of Pro-Dictator, when suddenly, on 25 September, Bertani resigned in protest against Garibaldi's refusal to support him in his demand for the dismissal of some Conservative ministers who had attacked him, and at Garibaldi's decision not to resist the entry of the Sardinian army into Neapolitan territory. Bertani thereupon returned to Turin to take his place on the Opposition benches in Parliament, and Mazzini despaired of achieving anything in Naples. On 30 September, Garibaldi damped the hopes of the Conservatives by appointing Crispi to succeed Bertani as Secretary-General to the Dictatorship; but on 3 October, the day after his victory on the Volturno, he at last appointed Pallavicino as Pro-Dictator.[9]

As Victor Emanuel's army advanced through the Papal States and approached the Neapolitan frontier, the Mazzinians played their last card. If Garibaldi could be persuaded to issue a decree for elections to be held for a Constituent Assembly in Sicily and on the mainland, it would seriously embarrass Cavour, and make it difficult for him to proceed to immediate annexation. On 2 October Cavour, in a speech in Parliament in Turin, rejected the idea of a Constituent Assembly and stated that a plebiscite should be held immediately throughout the Kingdom of Naples; but on 5 October Mordini in Sicily, at the instigation of Bertani and the Mazzinians in Turin, drafted a decree ordering elections for a Constituent Assembly to be held in Sicily on 21 October, and sent his draft to Garibaldi for his approval. On Crispi's advice, Garibaldi approved the decree, and it was published by Mordini as Pro-Dictator in the Official Journal at Palermo.[10]

During the next week, Garibaldi showed extraordinary vacillation in reaching a decision between the two political factions in his government. On 2 October Crispi raised the question of elections to a Constituent Assembly on the mainland at a meeting of the Cabinet in Naples, when Pallavicino and a majority of the ministers were against it; but on 6 October Crispi again raised the matter in the Cabinet, using Mordini's decree in Sicily and Garibaldi's approval of it as his chief argument, and after two days of discussion, despite the strong opposition of Pallavicino, the Cabinet by 3 votes to 2 accepted Crispi's proposal that a decree be immediately issued for elections to the Assembly to be held on the mainland on 26 October.

Pallavicino left at once for Caserta, and persuaded Garibaldi not to accept the resolution of the Cabinet in Naples, but to issue a decree ordering that a plebiscite should be held on the mainland on 21 October. A few hours later, Crispi arrived at Caserta and persuaded Garibaldi to change his mind and accept the Cabinet decision that elections for a Constituent Assembly should be held on the mainland on 26 October. Garibaldi told Crispi that he believed that a plebiscite should not be held until Rome and Venice had been liberated.

Next day, on 8 October, Pallavicino came again to Caserta, where he and Crispi saw Garibaldi together. News had reached Naples that morning of Cavour's speech in Parliament on 2 October, and this was used by Pallavicino as a strong argument in favour of a plebiscite. He thought that if Garibaldi summoned a Constituent Assembly, it might lead to civil war between the Garibaldini and Victor Emanuel's troops. Farini was indeed thinking along these lines. On 13 October he wrote to Cavour: 'It is said that they intend to proclaim a Constituent Assembly. Just let them try it! I shall then carry out another "2 December" on 26 October,'[11] – a reference to Napoleon III's *coup d'état* in Paris on 2 December 1851.

After a long discussion, Crispi gave way and agreed that a plebiscite on the mainland should be held on 21 October, whereupon Garibaldi also agreed. The decree ordering the plebiscite was published next day in the Official Journal. But Crispi was not beaten yet. That afternoon, on the 9th, he came to Caserta and persuaded Garibaldi to approve of a decree ordering elections for a Constituent Assembly to be held on 26 October. Crispi thought that it would be possible to elect a Constituent Assembly as well as holding a plebiscite, so that it could be argued that the vote for annexation in the plebiscite was merely a recommendation to the Assembly, or at least that the annexation would not take place until after the Assembly had ratified the popular vote, which would have prolonged the duration of Garibaldi's dictatorship. Garibaldi himself apparently did not realize that he had acted inconsistently in ordering both the plebiscite and elections for the Assembly, because he wrote a note to Pallavicino on the bottom of Crispi's draft of the decree for the elections to the Constituent Assembly: 'This appears to me to represent precisely what we agreed upon together, and is perfectly satisfactory to me. If you consent to all this, send me a copy of the above decree, duly endorsed, and I will sign it also.'

Pallavicino was astounded at Garibaldi's decision. Next day he was again at Caserta, and according to Dumas, who wrote an account of the events in the newspaper *L'Independente*, Pallavicino, Crispi, Mario and other prominent persons spent 10 October trying to get access to Garibaldi and to prevent the others from seeing him. On the 11th Crispi saw Garibaldi at dawn, and Garibaldi summoned a meeting of the whole Cabinet at Caserta at 6 pm that evening. A heated discussion took place. Pallavicino threatened to resign, and warned of the danger of civil war. Pointing at Crispi, he said that 'that man' was to blame for the whole crisis, and that unless Crispi and Mazzini were expelled from Naples immediately, he would leave for Genoa on the next boat. This was bad tactics, because nothing annoyed Garibaldi more than personal attacks on his friends and allegations against the character of an Italian patriot. He became very angry with Pallavicino, and stated that Crispi was his friend who had shared the dangers that he had run since they sailed from Quarto, and that Crispi was chiefly responsible for the success of the Sicilian expedition. Pallavicino broke down, resigned, and became hysterical when Garibaldi refused to accept his resignation; but by the time he reached Naples he had recovered sufficiently to attend a meeting of his supporters at the Café d'Europa and plan the demonstrations which took place next day.

On the morning of 12 October, Pallavicino's resignation was announced in the press. Later in the day thousands of demonstrators marched through the streets of Naples demanding a plebiscite and no Assembly, and shouting 'Death to Mazzini!' In the fashionable streets, placards were erected in nearly every window with the word '*Sì*' written on them, indicating that the occupier would vote Yes in the plebiscite in favour of annexation by Sardinia. There is no doubt that public opinion in Naples, particularly in the middle-class districts, was strongly in favour of immediate annexation, as the inhabitants hoped that Victor Emanuel and his government would rescue them from both Francis II and the Garibaldini; and the demonstrations had been well organized, with the collaboration of the chief of the city police. The Mazzinians feared for their safety, and rushed to Caserta to ask Garibaldi to come to Naples to restore order. Before leaving Caserta, Garibaldi signed a decree fixing 11 November as the date for the meeting of the Constituent Assembly.

Next day, on 13 October, Garibaldi came to Naples, to be greeted with cries of 'Long live Garibaldi! Down with Mazzini! Down with Crispi!' He ordered the arrest of the chief of police who had organized the demonstrations, and addressed the crowd from the balcony of the royal palace.

Do you know who are those who are causing disorder in the country? They are those who last year prevented me from coming to liberate you when I was in the Romagna, who opposed the expedition to Marsala, who sent La Farina to me to end the dictatorship in order to stop me from crossing the straits.

He was interrupted with shouts of 'Death to Mazzini!' and continued: 'I heard someone cry "Death!" The Italians ought to live, to create Italy. We are united. In a few days we shall see our King, Victor Emanuel.'

He then received a deputation from Pallavicino and his supporters. They presented him with a petition signed by thousands of signatories in favour of a plebiscite and against a Constituent Assembly; and Türr, who was the most pro-Cavourian of Garibaldi's generals, gave him a similar petition signed by many of his officers. Garibaldi had never wished to rule as a dictator against the wishes of the people, and he was shaken at this evidence of the extent of popular opposition to his latest decision. He summoned a meeting, not of the Cabinet, but of a group of his personal advisers, at which Crispi, Mario and Pallavicino and a few others were present. All the old arguments were resumed, with the spokesmen on both sides shouting angrily, while Garibaldi sat at the head of the table, silent, depressed, and worn out with fatigue. When the matter was put to the vote, there was a majority of 5 to 2 in favour of an Assembly; but Pallavicino would not accept the decision, and stated that he would not withdraw his resignation unless the decision to hold the Assembly was revoked. Eventually Garibaldi said: 'If you will not have the Assembly, to hell with the Assembly; I am off to Caprera.' No one made any comment. Garibaldi revoked the decree for the elections to the Assembly, and decided to proceed with the plebiscite on 21 October.[12]

The Radicals walked out of the meeting, refusing to shake hands with Pallavicino. Crispi resigned from the government. Mazzini had already despaired of Garibaldi. On 25 September he had written to Catherine Stansfeld in London: 'The weakness of the man is something fabulous.' Garibaldi himself made only a brief public comment on the incident, in a short footnote which he inserted in the 1872 edition of his memoirs.

At other times it would have been possible to convene a Constituent Assembly; at that epoch it was impossible, and would have achieved nothing except a waste of time and a ridiculous solution of the question. Annexations through plebiscites were then the fashion. The people, deceived by the factions, placed all their hopes in the reforming government.[13]

While Garibaldi was making these conflicting decisions about the future of Naples, he would make no decision at all about Sicily.

Mordini, who on 9 October had published his decree for elections to a Constituent Assembly under the impression that Garibaldi had authorized this, was taken aback to hear on 11 October that Garibaldi had issued a decree for a plebiscite to be held on the mainland, because he could not understand why Garibaldi should pursue conflicting policies on the mainland and in Sicily. He immediately cabled to Garibaldi for instructions as to whether to proceed with the elections for the Assembly; but he received no reply. During the next two days he sent more cables to Garibaldi, but still received no answer. Then, on the morning of 14 October, he received news from Naples that Garibaldi had issued a decree for elections for a Constituent Assembly as well as for a plebiscite to be held on the mainland, and a message from Crispi that the decree for a plebiscite applied only to the mainland, and that Garibaldi wished Mordini to go ahead with the preparations for elections to an Assembly to be held in Sicily. This confused Mordini more than ever. On 14 October he sent seven telegrams to Garibaldi, complaining that at such a crisis he had been left without instructions for four days, and threatening to resign as Pro-Dictator. Eventually, on 15 October, Garibaldi replied to Mordini's telegrams. He gave Mordini a free hand to act as he thought fit, and to exercise his own discretion as to whether to hold a plebiscite or elections for a Constituent Assembly in Sicily.

On the same day, Mordini heard that Garibaldi had revoked the decree for elections to a Constituent Assembly on the mainland, and that Crispi had resigned. He thereupon revoked his earlier decree and ordered that a plebiscite, not elections for the Assembly, should be held on 28 October. This decision was welcomed by the local authorities and the middle classes in Sicily, who, like their counterparts in Naples, were now attributing the disorders and social unrest to the weak and incompetent government of the dictatorship. Cavour did not forgive Mordini for having complied with what he thought was Garibaldi's wish in issuing the decree for the elections to the Constituent Assembly, and for his delay in authorizing the plebiscite. Unlike Depretis and Pallavicino, Mordini did not receive any award of honours from the Sardinian government for his services as Pro-Dictator.[14]

The people of Sicily voted in favour of annexation by 432,053 votes to 667, and on the mainland the vote was 1,302,064 in favour and 10,312 against; but a large number of the electorate abstained. The voting was open, and Admiral Mundy, who watched it, thought that it required a brave man to vote No, though in no case did he see anyone punished or insulted for doing so. The vote undoubtedly reflected the general feeling at the time. In the Papal States, Umbria and the Marches were also annexed by Sardinia, the vote being 133,072 to

1,212 in favour of annexation in the Marches, and 99,628 to 380 in favour in Umbria.[15]

Garibaldi was persuaded to stay on as Dictator until Victor Emanuel arrived. On 25 October he rode north with his army to meet the King. The Garibaldini spent the night in the valley between the Caianello and the Vairano hills, where Garibaldi, like all his men, slept on the ground, wrapped in his poncho and with only his aim for a pillow. At dawn on the 26th, the two armies met at the crossroads by the Taverna del Catena near the village of Marganello, about thirty miles north of Naples. As the King and Garibaldi, on their horses, came face to face, Garibaldi took off his hat, and said: 'I salute the first King of Italy.' 'How are you, dear Garibaldi?' said the King. 'Well, your Majesty, and you?' 'Excellent.' Victor Emanuel and Garibaldi rode side by side for eight miles to Teano, followed by their escorts, with the soldiers of the royal army and the red-shirts riding two abreast, side by side. But as the King and Garibaldi rode away together, after the first friendly greeting, the King told Garibaldi that he himself would take over operations against Capua and Gaeta, and that the Garibaldini would be sent to the rear. Garibaldi accepted the order, and placed his men at the King's disposal, while allowing his name to be used in the orders given to them, and taking care not to let them know that he was no longer in command of them; but he deeply resented being deprived of the opportunity of fighting at Capua and capturing it.[16] But if his red-shirts had been sent to the front, he would probably have allowed the Mazzinians to persuade him that Fanti and Farini were trying to get them all killed off.

The next fortnight was painful for Garibaldi. On 2 November the Bourbon troops surrendered at Capua, and the royal Sardinian army proceeded to besiege Gaeta, which eventually capitulated in February; but Garibaldi stayed in Naples, and his men were stationed at Calvi in the rear. Garibaldi and the red-shirts were repeatedly slighted by the army officers and the civilian officials in the King's entourage. Farini refused to hold any discussions with Garibaldi, or to speak to him or shake hands when they met; and he outraged the Garibaldini by banning the Garibaldi Hymn, though this was perhaps not altogether unwelcome to the citizens of Naples, who had heard it played incessantly during the previous two months. Garibaldi blamed Cavour for Farini's attitude; but Cavour was not responsible. Cavour, having gained control in Naples, was ready to be generous to the Garibaldini. He had already, on 11 October, persuaded Parliament in Turin to pass a unanimous resolution of congratulation to Garibaldi; and he wrote to Farini on 8 October that Garibaldi would never oppose the King. 'The King ought to be inexorable about Mazzini and the

Mazzinians whether open or disguised. Crispi, Mordini and all their followers must be swept away.' But the government must show magnanimity to Garibaldi's army.[17]

But Fanti and the generals, as well as Farini, were bitter against Garibaldi. This was interpreted by Garibaldi and the Mazzinians, as well as by Cavour, as a case of prejudice by the brass-hats of the army against revolutionary irregulars; but this is an over-simplification. Both Fanti and Cialdini were old revolutionaries. Fanti had belonged to Mazzini's Young Italy. He had been condemned to death for his part in Ciro Menotti's conspiracy in Modena in 1831, had taken part in Mazzini's invasion of Savoy in 1834, and had fought for the Liberals in the Spanish civil war. Cialdini, too, had been involved in Menotti's plot, and had fought in Spain. Farini was another old revolutionary, though he had never been a Mazzinian or as far to the left as the generals. Their hatred for Garibaldi was as much the hatred of the ex-revolutionary for his past and of one Radical for another as of the regular soldier for the guerrilla. The only one of Garibaldi's opponents in 1860 who had never been associated with the Mazzinians and the revolutionaries was Cavour himself, who in November was certainly more disposed than the others to be conciliatory to Garibaldi.

An unfortunate incident occurred on 6 November. Victor Emanuel had agreed to come and review the Garibaldini at Caserta; but though the red-shirts and Garibaldi were all lined up, ready to receive him, he did not come. The reason for his absence is not known. Commander Forbes did not hesitate to write in his book, which was published in London only a few months later, that it was because Victor Emanuel was flirting with a woman at Capua; but it has been generally assumed that it was because Fanti and Farini had persuaded him to administer a public snub to Garibaldi and his men. It is not easy to reconcile this with Victor Emanuel's attitude to Garibaldi, because, however incensed he may have been in September, after he had received Garibaldi's letter demanding the resignation of Cavour, he had been very friendly at the meeting at the crossroads on 26 October, and was friendly again a few days after the affront of 6 November. The flirtation at Capua is a more likely explanation of his absence. Abba mentions in his diary that while the Garibaldini were waiting for the King to arrive and inspect them, some of the men who were refugees from Venetia said to each other, apparently half-seriously, that when the King came it would be a good idea to kidnap him and take him to the mountains, where they would hold him until he promised to declare war on Austria. If these Garibaldini had been saying such things a few hours earlier, this might be an explanation of why Victor Emanuel did not come.

Whatever the reason may have been for Victor Emanuel's absence, this unfortunate incident, which could have been patched up and forgotten if there had been goodwill on both sides, was greatly resented by Garibaldi. He did not make any protest at the time, but allowed the sore to fester for years, and to be publicized and magnified by the Mazzinians and the Left-wing Parliamentary Opposition in Turin, while at the same time he directed his resentment, not against the King, but against Cavour, Farini and Fanti.[18]

On 7 November Victor Emanuel entered the city of Naples. He invited Garibaldi to ride beside him in his carriage; but though Garibaldi might have interpreted this invitation as a gesture of reconciliation by the King, the Mazzinians convinced him that it was a sly attempt to make use of his popularity for the advantage of Victor Emanuel, Cavour and the government. At first, Garibaldi refused to come, but was persuaded to come by Cialdini, whom at this time he regarded, unlike Fanti and Farini, as being his friend, though within six months they were bitter enemies. When Cialdini urged him to come, he broke into a furious denunciation of Cavour and Fanti, but eventually agreed; and Victor Emanuel and Garibaldi, sitting side by side in an open carriage, drove gloomily into Naples in a thunderstorm, with the rain pouring down, amid the somewhat muted enthusiasm of the King's new subjects. Garibaldi accompanied the King to the cathedral, and stood behind him, next to Farini and Pallavicino, while Victor Emanuel knelt at the high altar; and he was present at a reception at the palace, where he stood, a little apart, with his hat on, like a grandee of Spain. But he refused to attend the gala performance at the opera. His chair was removed from the royal box a few minutes before Victor Emanuel and the royal party arrived.[19]

Next day, at a ceremony in the royal palace, Garibaldi resigned the dictatorship and handed over the power to Victor Emanuel and his government. His parting from Victor Emanuel was friendly. Victor Emanuel appointed him a full general in the Sardinian army, and offered to create the rank of Field-Marshal for him, to grant an estate to Menotti, to make Ricciotti one of his royal ADCs, to provide a dowry for Teresita when she married, and to give Garibaldi a castle and a private steamer, which in 1860 was an accepted symbol of power and affluence. Garibaldi refused all these gifts, but asked to be appointed as the first Governor of the former Kingdom of Naples. Victor Emanuel would not agree to this. The Mazzinians and Radicals later argued that if Garibaldi, with his great popularity in Naples and his kindly tolerance, had been appointed Governor instead of Farini, who obtained the post, a great deal of the hatreds and civil wars in the South would have been avoided; but in view of the way in which

Garibaldi had acted in connexion with the plebiscite and the Constituent Assembly a few weeks earlier, it is understandable that Victor Emanuel and his ministers did not think that he would be a good political administrator.[20]

There was nothing more for him to do in Naples, so he prepared to sail for Caprera in the morning. Before leaving Naples, he spoke to Mazzini, who had been living in hiding since the arrival of the Sardinian army and government, and he discussed with him the possibility of overthrowing Cavour during the winter and launching a campaign against Rome or Venice next spring. Garibaldi also saw Admiral Mundy before he left Naples. He invited Mundy to visit him at Caprera. Mundy said that he would be pleased to do so, but that he was not likely to get leave for the next eighteen months. Garibaldi said that by that time he would no longer be in Caprera, because within five months he would be fighting in other campaigns for the liberation of Italy.[21]

In his farewell message to his red-shirts, he showed that the events of the previous fortnight had not shaken his faith in Victor Emanuel.

> Providence has given Italy Victor Emanuel. All Italians must rally around him and close ranks behind him. At the side of the Gentleman King, all rivalry must disappear, all rancour must be dissipated. I have only one cry, which I repeat: To arms, all of you, all of you! If March 1861 does not see a million Italians in arms, alas for liberty! alas for the Italian way of life!

Then, coupling the victories of the royal Sardinian army with his own, he declared that 'the Italians of Calatafimi, of Palermo, of the Volturno, of Ancona, of Castelfidardo, of Isernia', were not cowards or slaves.[22]

Garibaldi left Naples for Caprera on the steamship *Washington* before dawn on 9 November. He chose this hour as being the time when he was least likely to encounter a demonstration of support, which would have embarrassed both him and the Sardinian government. Only a few friends, including Menotti, Coltelletti, and his secretary, Basso, sailed with him. He took with him a bag of seed-corn for his animals; as his followers often pointed out in after years, this was the only material benefit which he had acquired for himself during the months when he had been Dictator of the Two Sicilies. As he sailed out of the harbour, the ships of the British squadron fired a salvo as a salute. The Sardinian ships did not.[23]

CHAPTER 34

CINCINNATUS ON CAPRERA:
THE CLASH WITH CAVOUR

BY resigning his office of Dictator and returning to Caprera, Garibaldi had bitterly disappointed the Mazzinians without appeasing the suspicions and the jealousy of the Cavourian politicians and the army leaders; but his admirers in Britain were delighted. They had feared, for a few weeks, that he would try to hold on to power, to become a dictator like other successful generals, and to cause international complications; instead, he had proved himself to be a modest and selfless patriot as well as a gallant and successful military leader. The retirement to Caprera increased the Garibaldi cult in Britain, and made him a more romantic character than ever – an Achilles withdrawing, but only temporarily, from the struggle; a Cincinnatus called from his farm to exercise the dictatorship, and returning to his farm when he had done his duty; a giant renewing his strength by his contact with the soil; the hero living in solitude on a lonely isle.

Caprera, however, rapidly became less lonely as a result of Garibaldi's presence there. After November 1860 it was constantly being visited by envoys from the government in Turin and from local government bodies, by English peers and peeresses in their yachts, by politicians, journalists, authors and many ordinary sightseers, and on one occasion by suspected assassins. A hotel was opened on the island of La Maddalena for the sightseers, who walked to the eastern shore of the island to look across the half-mile stretch of water to Caprera in the hopes of catching a glimpse of Garibaldi as he broke stones, planted his vines, or tended his cattle. Several of Garibaldi's visitors wrote books about Caprera, and their readers all over the world became familiar with Garibaldi's life there. Accounts of Garibaldi on Caprera were published between 1861 and 1866 by his old friend Vecchi, by the French author Félix Mornand, by Sir Charles McGrigor, a Scottish baronet, and by John McAdam, the secretary of the Glasgow branch of the Friends of Italy. McAdam, who visited Garibaldi at the end of December 1860 and published an account of his life on Caprera in the

North British Daily Mail, was at one time considered to be Garibaldi's unofficial representative in Britain.[1]

Garibaldi's life at Caprera was as simple as could have been expected. His own room, on the ground floor on the right after entering the front door, was barely furnished. When he first built the house, a few years earlier, he had had very few chairs; but after his 1860 campaign a number of United States army officers sent him chairs with their names engraved on them, and as a result he had more chairs in the house than he had room for. In his bedroom he had a plain metal four-poster bed, a table covered with books and newspapers, and a piano at which he often sat and played, accompanying himself while he sang his favourite Italian operatic arias in his tenor voice. On the walls there were pictures of his daughter Rosita, who had died in infancy in Montevideo, and of two of his officers who had been killed, one at Milazzo and one on the Volturno. There was a box in the room containing a lock of the hair of his first wife, Anita. A clothes-line hung across the room, and it nearly always contained one or two drying red shirts. Garibaldi had acquired the habit, during the hot summers in South America, of changing his shirt several times a day, and he often did this at Caprera, washing the shirts himself, as he had done during the Battle of Milazzo, and hanging them on the clothes-line to dry. They did not dry as quickly here as in the July sun on the Sicilian battlefield, because Garibaldi's room was damp, having been built over a well, and he was obliged to keep a fire always burning in the room. The dampness cannot have been good for his rheumatism, which, as usual, had not troubled him at all when he was busy fighting in the summer of 1860, but which came on again after he returned to Caprera. Garibaldi relieved the rheumatism by spending three-quarters of an hour every day in a steam bath.

He needed only five hours' sleep, going to bed at 10 pm and waking at 3 am. After waking, he dealt with his correspondence, reading the incoming letters in bed, and at about 5 am he would wake his secretary, as he was ready by this time to begin dictating his answers to his correspondents. He had a number of secretaries, including Vecchi and Guerzoni; but his principal secretary was Basso, who had not only been one of the Thousand, like Guerzoni, but had also sailed with him from Lima to Canton.

Garibaldi received a large number of letters. There were invitations to accept the freedom of the borough from countless towns in Italy, including some, like San Marino, Arezzo and Cesenatico, which were more eager to acclaim him as an honorary citizen now than they had been to admit him and his defeated army in 1849. There were appeals for support from charitable foundations and from progressive and

Radical organizations; requests for his opinion about new causes, such as disarmament, international arbitration, and women's rights; applications for permission to use his name to advertise goods which the manufacturers sent him; long letters discussing national and international politics from his Italian and foreign friends; letters containing unasked-for political advice from Mazzini; letters from Herzen, Victor Hugo, the editor of the *Siècle* in Paris, McAdam in Glasgow, and President Mitre in Buenos Aires. But nearly half the total correspondence which he received came from English women, who expressed their devotion to him, and usually asked him to send them a lock of his hair. He could not satisfy them all; but some of them were favoured with a gallant answer. 'My dear Madame Crispi', he wrote in French to Rosalia Montmasson on 5 November 1866, 'I am proud that you wanted to hold my cushion. As for my hair, although white, it will all be at your disposal on the first occasion that I shall have the pleasure of kissing your hand.'[2] He spent most of the morning dealing with his correspondence, often dictating and signing more than forty letters a day.

As soon as he had finished dictating the letters, he went out and worked in his orchards and fields. Like many other members of his generation, Garibaldi firmly believed in the virtues of labour, particularly of physical labour. He broke stones, built walls, herded his sheep, and above all planted and tended his vines and the wonderful display of red carnations which surrounded the house, dressed in his red shirt, and always with a cigar in his mouth. He loved his plants, and tended them, not only with care, but with real affection, and seemed to be hurt if anyone broke them or handled them roughly. Ever since his childhood he had been fond of animals, and had been outraged by the cruelty to animals which he had encountered in so many parts of the world, especially in South America, among the primitive peasants and rough soldiers with whom he had lived. He loved each of his animals on Caprera. When a baby calf died, he grieved over its mother's loss. Once, when a young lamb strayed from the fold, he mounted a search party to find it, and long after all the other searchers had given up, he went on looking by himself, after dark, in the rain, and eventually returned carrying the lamb in his arms at 10 pm.

His favourites among the animals were his dogs and horses. He had brought two of the horses with him from Naples. One was Marsala, the white mare that he had ridden in Sicily, and the other was a stallion named Bourbon, which Menotti had captured from the enemy in Calabria. Garibaldi kept Marsala for many years, and when she died he buried her at the crossroads of the paths at the foot of the hill leading down from his house towards the west side of the island, facing La

Maddalena. He also had four donkeys, whom he named Pius IX, Napoleon III, Oudinot and the Immaculate Conception. The publication of Vecchi's book, with its revelations about Garibaldi's kindness to animals, endeared him even more to the English readers; but the revelation of the names which he had given to his donkeys aroused the greatest indignation among the French Catholics, who denounced him in the press and in their publications as violently for this as for any of his other actions.

The meals at Caprera were a feature of the life there. Speranza von Schwartz had been surprised that Battistina had sat with them at table; but it was one of Garibaldi's maxims that if someone was good enough to work for him, he was good enough to eat with him,[3] and the whole household dined together, even when the Duke of Sutherland or some Italian statesman was a guest, with Garibaldi presiding at the head of the table like an ancient patriarch. He would serve himself and his immediate neighbours in person, always serving the women first, and then push the dishes down the table for the other guests to serve themselves. The food was excellent – macaroni, the local fish, roast meat, and many salads, served with an abundant quantity of oil, with a very pleasant local wine for the guests, though Garibaldi himself always drank water with his midday meal, and cold milk at supper, drinking from an earthenware mug which he kept covered with a sheet of paper. After supper, the guests were offered the choice of tea or white coffee, and lingered around the supper table, talking and smoking, until Garibaldi retired to bed at 10 pm; but sometimes, if some sad or painful subject was referred to, Garibaldi would suddenly rise from the table and retire for the night without saying another word. Vecchi, who mentions this, does not give any example of the painful subjects of conversation which caused Garibaldi to retire prematurely; but one can hazard a guess that Anita's death was one of them.

Although Ricciotti was still at school in England, Menotti and Teresita lived at Caprera, and Teresita enlivened the place. Menotti was twenty in the winter of 1860–1; Teresita was sixteen, and was already married. Her husband was Major Stefano Canzio, one of the more Radical of Garibaldi's young red-shirts. She had become a beautiful girl, with her father's blonde hair, very soft and feminine in manner, but also very determined, and, if necessary, obstinate. She was fond of dancing, and often went to the village dances on La Maddalena; at Caprera, Garibaldi would sometimes dance round the room with her. Once, when Türr came to Caprera on a mission from Victor Emanuel to Garibaldi, he brought some diamonds as a gift to Teresita from the King. Teresita accepted them with some embarrassment, but thanked the King most charmingly for his kindness.

Sometimes there was singing in the evening, with Teresita accompanying on the piano. One evening, when Vecchi was there in January 1861, Teresita, Vecchi and one of the other guests sang arias from *Il Trovatore* and *L'Elisir d'amore*, and Garibaldi followed with a song from *I Puritani*. Then the company sang their old Italian patriotic songs. Finally, someone suggested that they should end by singing the *Marseillaise*. The *Marseillaise*, the French revolutionary song of 1792, had afterwards been banned in France under both the Bonapartist and the Bourbon régimes. It had become recognized all over the world as the song of the Revolution, though ten years later it would become the national anthem of the Third French Republic, and be superseded by the *Internationale* as the international revolutionary hymn. 'The world went on turning peacefully on its axis,' wrote Vecchi, 'although, to end the evening, we sang the *Marseillaise* at the top of our voices.'

When Garibaldi first settled on Caprera, he had purchased only half the island. The other half had been retained by Mr Collins, the former owner. Collins was a quarrelsome Englishman who drank too much, and was said to have been originally employed as a groom by the charming lady whom he had married. Garibaldi and Collins soon fell out over straying animals. Garibaldi's cows wandered on to Collins's land, and Collins complained that they did some damage there. Garibaldi apologized, but soon afterwards Collins's pigs strayed on to Garibaldi's land and damaged his vines. It was now Garibaldi's turn to protest; but Collins's pigs continued to trespass, and eventually Menotti shot at the pigs and captured one of them. Collins was very angry, and sued Garibaldi in the local court. This was the kind of dispute which, in Palmerston's time, sometimes ended with the British navy putting in an appearance; but Collins had no chance of persuading the British government to act against Garibaldi.

Garibaldi approached Captain Roberts, a former British naval officer, who had first visited Caprera when he was serving under Nelson more than sixty years before, and had settled on La Maddalena after retiring from the navy. Garibaldi suggested to Roberts that it would be more fitting if he and Collins settled their dispute by fighting a duel. Roberts succeeded in reconciling Garibaldi and Collins, who became good friends; and when Collins died soon afterwards, his widow continued the friendship with Garibaldi. He often invited her to dinner, and on these occasions always gave her the place of honour. After Collins's death, Mrs Collins could no longer farm on Caprera, and was very willing to sell her half of the island; and when *The Times* got to hear of this, they opened a fund in England to enable Garibaldi's admirers to contribute to the cost of buying Mrs Collins's property and presenting it as a gift to Garibaldi. Although Garibaldi was normally reluctant to accept gifts, he made no objection to accepting this one, which benefited Mrs Collins as well as himself.[4]

During the winter of 1860–1, while Garibaldi cared for his flocks and fruit on Caprera, he had continued to take an active interest in national affairs. His letters to workers' and patriotic women's associations were published in the press, as were his speeches to the delegations from the town councils who visited him on Caprera. These letters and speeches were all on the same theme – a strong pledge of loyalty to Victor Emanuel, some express or implied criticism of politicians, diplomats, and the French alliance, and a call to young Italians to volunteer for a people's army which would liberate Venetia and Rome in the spring. In March he made a speech to a delegation from the town council of Sassari, in the island of Sardinia, in which he attacked Napoleon III. This did not please Cavour.[5]

In February 1861 Victor Emanuel assumed the title of King of Italy. His realm had increased in eighteen months to more than five times its previous area. He had ruled 4,000,000 subjects in April 1859; in November 1860 he ruled 22,000,000, of whom 9,000,000 had been given to him by Garibaldi in the former Kingdom of Naples. But these new subjects in the South were causing trouble. The former King of Naples, who had taken refuge in Rome, sent secret agents to organize revolts and resistance among the peasants, and they succeeded in stirring up a serious guerrilla movement, which Farini and Cialdini tried to suppress by summary executions on a much larger scale than Garibaldi's government had adopted during the dictatorship. The Left-wing Opposition in Parliament in Turin criticized the government for its failure to keep order in the South, just as Cavour and Farini had complained of the anarchy which had prevailed when Garibaldi ruled the area. Garibaldi issued a number of statements to the press in which he condemned the misgovernment of Naples by Farini. Privately, he expressed much sympathy for Francis II, whom he referred to as a 'poor young man', because he had been driven out of his kingdom as a punishment for the crimes of his fathers. One of his guests commented that if Cardinal Antonelli, Francis II and Pius IX were seeking asylum as refugees, Garibaldi would welcome them at Caprera, and give up his room and his bed to them.[6]

His most serious cause of conflict with the government was what he considered to be the shabby treatment meted out to his red-shirts. Garibaldi wanted the government to incorporate them all into the regular Italian army, with the ranks which they had held in his forces. Fanti and the generals strongly objected to this; and though Cavour was eager to conciliate Garibaldi on this point, there were difficulties about doing so. By the time that Garibaldi resigned as Dictator, the number of his red-shirts had increased to 43,000 men, as compared with the total numbers in the peace-time royal Sardinian army of 1860 of 60,000 men. Many of these volunteers, as the veterans of the original Thousand were the first to agree, were worthless as soldiers; they had joined Garibaldi only in order to swagger in the cafés of Naples, and had never been in action. Garibaldi had been as lavish in granting commissions in 1860 as in 1849, and in Naples, as in the campaign in Rome eleven years before, he had one officer to every six or seven men. The officers of the regular army did not want these Garibaldian officers to swamp the officer corps in the army. There was the further difficulty that, in order to win the goodwill of the Neapolitans, many of the officers and men of King Francis's army were taken into the Italian army, so that, in some cases, the Garibaldini were passed over in favour of the soldiers whom they had fought and beaten a few months earlier.

Some of the Garibaldini were put on the reserve, and about 1,500 of them were taken into the regular army. These included most of the members of the original Thousand who wished to continue in a military career; many of Garibaldi's leading officers, Bixio, Medici, Cosenz and Türr, were made generals in the Italian army. All of these – except for the Hungarian Türr, who became Victor Emanuel's ADC – were also elected to Parliament, where they sat on the government benches and became Cavourian supporters. As the Radicals and Mazzinians saw it, Cavour's appointment of Garibaldi's generals to high military positions in the royal army was simply a trick to separate them from Garibaldi and from their former comrades-in-arms, and to buy their support for the government.[7]

The annexation of Naples led to yet another general election being held in the new Kingdom of Italy, and Garibaldi was elected as MP for several constituencies. He chose to sit for Naples, but he did not take his seat when Parliament met. This Olympian detachment from Parliamentary life, which impressed the Radicals, was the subject of sour comment from his critics: instead of playing his part in Parliament and in the royal Italian army, like Bixio and the other generals, he was adopting a superior attitude, and criticizing from Caprera those humbler individuals who were trying to run the country. Then suddenly, in April 1861, Garibaldi came to Turin to take his seat in Parliament. The whole business showed every sign of having been brilliantly stage-managed, though if it was, we may be sure that someone other than Garibaldi was the producer of the show.

On 13 April, two days before Garibaldi arrived in Turin, Rattazzi, who was the President of the Chamber of Deputies, read out in Parliament a letter which Garibaldi had addressed to him in his official

capacity. In the letter, which was widely publicized in the press, Garibaldi asked the Chamber to throw out the government's plans for the organization of the army. In another statement, which his supporters gave to the press, he demanded that the government should maintain a separate corps of volunteers, side by side with the regular army. These statements gave notice to the public that Garibaldi was going to attack Cavour and the government in Parliament. When Cavour read the statements, he was relieved, because he had expected that Garibaldi would concentrate on the government's failure to incorporate the red-shirts into the regular army, on which Cavour himself admitted that Garibaldi had a case; but the proposal to maintain a separate corps of volunteers, as distinct from the regular army, seemed to Cavour, and to many other people, to be a plan to maintain a private army for Garibaldi to use whenever he wished to attack some foreign power without the consent of the Italian government.[8]

After arriving in Turin, Garibaldi stayed in his hotel for five days, being unable to attend Parliament because of an attack of rheumatism. During this time, while political tension and speculation mounted, he refused to meet the press; but he agreed to receive a visit from Ricasoli, the Tuscan leader, who was one of Cavour's most prominent supporters. The rumour spread that, at the eleventh hour, Ricasoli had persuaded Garibaldi not to attack the government; but when Garibaldi announced that he would take his seat in the House on 20 April, no one knew what was going to happen.

The public galleries were packed with former Garibaldini, all wearing their red shirts. Baroness Bunsen, the wife of the Prussian Minister in Turin, had tickets for the diplomatic box, but nearly gave up hope of getting in when she saw the crowd of people, including two Countesses, who were crowding the corridor outside the box in an unsuccessful attempt to enter; but her French friend, Madame Bartholeyns, forced a way through the crowd for herself and Baroness Bunsen. Two gentlemen gave up their standing room in the front row of the box to the two ladies, and Baroness Bunsen stood there for five hours. 'To give you an idea of the crowding in the gallery,' she wrote, 'I had, when I first came in, *one* person between me and a column. Before the end, although I was not aware of having changed my position at all, there were *four* between me and the column.' Her neighbour, leaning on the Baroness's shoulder, told her that she had travelled from the other side of Italy in order to hear the debate.

Rattazzi opened the session at 1.30 pm. The benches were crowded with deputies, but Garibaldi was not there. The debate on the army reorganization began, and as Garibaldi still did not appear, the rumour spread that he was not coming, because of the agreement which he had reached with Ricasoli. Then at ten to two Garibaldi entered by a side door behind the Opposition benches. He was leaning on two friends, and walked with difficulty because of his rheumatism. He made his way to a seat high up on the benches on the extreme Left. He was wearing the red shirt, which made a striking contrast with the black frock-coats of all the other MPS. The French Minister, Count d'Ideville, was not impressed, and wrote in his diary: 'The immortal red shirt, covered by a kind of grey cloak like a chasuble or Mexican poncho, gave him the appearance of a prophet, or, if you prefer, of an old comedian.' As Garibaldi entered, he received a tremendous ovation from the red-shirts in the public galleries, who rose to their feet and applauded for four or five minutes, ignoring Rattazzi's attempts to call them to order. About fifteen deputies of the Left, led by Crispi, joined in the demonstration, rising in their places, and clapping; the other deputies remained seated in icy silence.

Garibaldi took the oath – it was his first appearance in this Parliament – and soon afterwards rose to address the House. He spoke slowly, in a beautiful voice which could be clearly heard in the public galleries, and as always his dignified presence was impressive; but he soon lost the thread of his speech, as he always did when he spoke from notes, and fumbled, putting on his pince-nez and looking through his notes to try to find the figures which he wished to quote about the army units. Then he put away his notes, and, still speaking in his slow and dignified manner, launched an attack on the government, and on Cavour and Fanti, whom he accused of having planned to use the royal army against the Garibaldini in Naples in the previous autumn. Unfortunately for Cavour, the French government had published some of their diplomatic correspondence, which revealed that Farini had obtained Napoleon III's acquiescence in the invasion of the Papal States by the royal Sardinian army by claiming that Fanti's troops were marching south in order to 'fight the Revolution personified in Garibaldi'. As Garibaldi spoke, there were protests and interruptions from the government benches, while Crispi demanded silence for Garibaldi, who calmly proceeded with his speech, and stated that Cavour had been planning to wage 'a fratricidal war'.

This remark caused an uproar. Cavour had one of his fits of temper. He leaped to his feet, from the government front bench, banged the green despatch-box and shouted 'It is not true', demanding that Garibaldi withdraw. The noise subsided, and Garibaldi, still on his feet, paused for a moment, as everyone waited to hear whether he would withdraw the offensive remark. Then he calmly repeated: 'You were planning to wage a fratricidal war.'

Pandemonium broke out. 'The effect was tremendous,' wrote

Baroness Bunsen, 'all the deputies left their seats, crowding down to the centre, all talking, screaming and gesticulating at once.' The red-shirts in the public galleries applauded. The *Times* correspondent wrote that 'in the midst of it all, Crispi was seen bawling, gesticulating like a maniac'. Then a group of Opposition deputies made a concerted rush at Cavour. Cavour's friends blocked their path, and grouped around Cavour, and the deputies struck each other across the face. Rattazzi put on his hat and suspended the session for twenty minutes. Garibaldi remained absolutely calm throughout the uproar, while the Opposition deputies crowded around him to congratulate him, and the government supporters crowded around Cavour to express their sympathies. Other deputies walked over to the diplomatic gallery to discuss the situation with their friends, and Baroness Bunsen was spoken to by an Englishman who said that he had commanded a unit under Garibaldi in Sicily – it must have been Colonel Dunne – and that there was no doubt that Cavour's government had treated the volunteers in a 'beastly manner'.

When the session was resumed, Cavour spoke. He had taken complete control of himself, and speaking quietly, in sorrow not in anger, he deplored the quarrel that had arisen between him and Garibaldi, and proceeded to explain why Garibaldi's proposals for the maintenance of a separate army of volunteers was impracticable. He was followed by Bixio, who appealed for unity in the national interest. He deeply regretted the quarrel which had arisen between the two great Italian patriots, Cavour and Garibaldi, and asked everyone to treat the incidents in the earlier part of the session as if they had never occurred. His speech made a very favourable impression on moderate opinion.

Then Garibaldi asked permission to address the House again. Many deputies expected him to echo the mood of reconciliation, but he calmly repeated his attacks on Cavour, and did not say one word of reconciliation. After he had finished speaking, he left the Chamber without waiting for the vote, and the red-shirts poured out of the public galleries and went into the street to acclaim him as he left the building, and to escort him back to his hotel. But he had offended moderate opinion by his refusal to follow the conciliatory gestures of Cavour and Bixio, and the government had a majority of 194 votes to 79 in favour of their army policy, with 5 abstentions, of which one was of course Garibaldi.[9]

Two days later, Cialdini published an open letter to Garibaldi in the press. 'You are not the man I thought you were,' he wrote, 'you are not the Garibaldi I loved. . . . You dare to put yourself on a level with the King, speaking of him with the affected familiarity of a comrade. You consider yourself too high to be bound by conventions, and you appear in the Chamber in a most outlandish costume.' Victor Emanuel never showed any resentment of the informal language in which Garibaldi expressed his devotion and loyalty; but the former Republican, Cialdini, found it shocking, just as he was shocked to see Garibaldi appear in Parliament in the uniform in which he had won half Italy for the King. In his letter, Cialdini went on to say that when the royal army reached the Volturno, they had found the Garibaldini on the verge of defeat, and had saved them from disaster by winning a brilliant victory at Capua. This was a complete fabrication.[10]

Garibaldi replied in another open letter, in which he repudiated all Cialdini's charges, and ended by challenging him to a duel. But Victor Emanuel intervened. He invited Garibaldi, Cialdini and Cavour to the palace, and asked them all to shake hands and be friends. They all agreed to do so. Garibaldi shook hands with Cialdini, and spoke some words of reconciliation to Cavour, though he did not actually shake hands with him. 'I never saw his hands at all,' Cavour told Ricasoli, 'he held them under his Prophet's mantle all the time.'[11]

But a fortnight later, in one of his sudden changes of attitude, Garibaldi went further than could have been expected in his readiness to be reconciled with Cavour. After he returned to Caprera on 1 May, he received a very friendly letter from Cavour, informing him of the talks which he was intending to hold with Kossuth about the possibility of exploiting the unrest in Hungary. In his reply on 18 May, Garibaldi expressed his admiration for Cavour. He went out of his way to make a derogatory reference to Mazzini, and ended the letter: 'Trusting in your superior capacity and firm will to affect the good of the country. . . . Devotedly yours, G. Garibaldi.'[12]

Nineteen days later, Cavour was dead. He died of a sudden illness on 6 June, at the age of fifty. His supporters, who did not know about Garibaldi's last letter to him, maintained that Garibaldi had hounded him to his death by the viciousness of his attack in Parliament on 20 April. This suggestion was not likely to impress the man who had faced death at Calatafimi and Milazzo.

Garibaldi spent the hot summer of 1861 at Caprera, where he followed with great interest the news of the American Civil War, as did most of the other European Radicals. He had for some years felt strong sympathy with the anti-slavery cause in the United States, and now keenly supported the North in the civil war. Some months earlier, in January 1861, a long article about him had been published in the Boston quarterly, *The North American Review*. It was an anonymous review of a book on the Italian *Risorgimento*, but the author of the review was in fact Henry Theodore Tuckerman; and in the review Tuckerman not only praised Garibaldi's achievements in 1849 and 1860, but also told a number of anecdotes, from his personal knowledge, about Garibaldi's stay in New York in 1850–1. When Vecchi read the article, he wrote from Caprera to thank Tuckerman, and, without consulting Garibaldi, he suggested to Tuckerman that Garibaldi might go to fight for the North in the civil war.[13]

Tuckerman mentioned the matter to his friend Quiggle, the United States Consul in Antwerp, who, with the encouragement of the American government, wrote to Garibaldi on 8 June, and invited him to take a high command in the armies of the North. 'If you do, the name of La Fayette will not surpass yours. There are thousands and tens of thousands of American citizens who will glory to be under the command of the "Washington of Italy".'[14]

On 27 June Garibaldi replied to Quiggle. He said that there were two objections to his going: the first was that Victor Emanuel might need his services in the struggle for the liberation of Italy; the second was President Lincoln's policy with regard to slavery.[15] Lincoln had never been an abolitionist, but had belonged to the moderate group which wished to prevent the extension of slavery into any new state or territory, while taking no steps to abolish it in the states where it was already established. He was vigorously enforcing the Fugitive Slave Law, that measure so hated by the Abolitionists and Radicals, which compelled the authorities in the North to arrest escaping slaves and return them to slavery and punishment in the South. Although his election as President had been the signal for the secession of the South, who feared that he was a secret abolitionist, he continued to assert loudly that the North was fighting to repress rebellion and to preserve the union, and not to abolish slavery, being anxious to retain the support of the three slave states – Kentucky, Maryland and Missouri – which had remained loyal to the Union.

Quiggle handled the abolition question with considerable tact in his correspondence with Garibaldi. He was anxious to persuade Garibaldi to fight for the North, but he had to be careful to say nothing which could be cited by the Southern propagandists to suggest that Lincoln, despite his denials, was really fighting the war in order to abolish slavery. Quiggle wrote to Garibaldi on 4 July saying that he was sure that Garibaldi would realize, on reflection, that grave problems would arise if 4,000,000 slaves were suddenly freed and thrown on to the labour market, but that if the war continued for a long period of time, it might well lead to the abolition of slavery. This was, in fact, what ultimately occurred. On the same day on which Quiggle wrote to Garibaldi, the Garibaldi Guard, consisting of Italian, Hungarian and other European immigrants who had answered the President's call for volunteers, marched past Lincoln, dressed in their red shirts and Garibaldi képis, at the Independence Day parade in Washington.[16]

Lincoln's Secretary of State, Seward, was very eager to get Garibaldi. He wrote to Sanford, the United States Minister in Brussels, and directed him to go to Caprera and secure Garibaldi's services for the American government. Sanford went first to Turin, and wrote to Garibaldi offering him a high command in the US army, and suggesting that he should meet Garibaldi either in Caprera or anywhere else that Garibaldi preferred. Meanwhile great interest had been aroused in the United States by the publication of a report in the *New York Tribune* on 11 August that Garibaldi had agreed to serve in the US army with the rank of Major-General, which was the highest rank in the army, except for the rank of Lieutenant-General which had been specially created for General Scott, the hero of the Mexican War. Interest increased when the government in Washington would neither confirm nor deny the truth of the statement in the *New York Tribune*.[17]

On 31 August Garibaldi replied to Sanford, and told him that if Victor Emanuel did not require his services, and gave him permission to accept the American government's offer, he would go to the United States on certain conditions.[18] On 6 September Sanford, who had kept the government in Turin informed of his correspondence with Garibaldi, was told that Victor Emanuel had written to Garibaldi giving him permission to go, and Sanford travelled to Caprera with the King's ADC, who took the King's letter to Garibaldi. When Sanford arrived at Caprera, he was a little taken aback to find that Garibaldi was completely crippled with rheumatism, and unable to move out of his chair; but he realized that this was only a temporary impediment to Garibaldi's serving in the US army.

A much more serious difficulty arose in the course of his conversation with Garibaldi. Garibaldi said that he was accepting the American government's offer on the clear understanding that he was appointed Commander-in-Chief of the Union army and given the powers to abolish slavery. Sanford explained that this was quite impossible, because under the Constitution of the United States the President was Commander-in-Chief, and no US general had the legal power to abolish slavery in United States territory. Sanford's point about the Commander-in-Chief was a pedantic evasion of the issue, because Lincoln's constitutional position as Commander-in-Chief did not prevent him from appointing a general to be supreme commander of the Union armies under the President – a post which was then held by McClellan and afterwards by a succession of generals and eventually by Grant; but Sanford obviously realized that it would affront the feelings of the

West Point generals if a foreigner, even Garibaldi, were given supreme command above them.

Sanford offered Garibaldi the rank of Major-General and an independent command of sufficient importance to be worthy of his abilities and fame. He urged him to accept, if he felt that the cause of democracy, freedom and constitutional government, for which the North was fighting, was worthy of his support; but Garibaldi insisted that unless Lincoln would declare that he was fighting for the emancipation of the slaves, the civil war would be fought for issues which were of interest only to the citizens of the United States, and not to the rest of the world. Sanford stayed the night at Caprera, but though he tried again next morning, he could not persuade Garibaldi to come to the United States, except on these terms which no American diplomat had authority to accept.[19]

Sanford was very disappointed at his failure to obtain Garibaldi's services; but the US Minister in Turin, Marsh, thought that it was not an unmitigated disaster. Marsh had seen, at closer quarters than Sanford in Brussels, the difficulties which Garibaldi could cause to a government which he served. Marsh wrote to Seward that there were serious objections to employing the services of a general who believed, quite rightly, that his achievements and prestige had placed him in a position in which he could negotiate as an equal with kings and governments. By now, the Italian press had published the report in the *New York Tribune* that Garibaldi was coming to the United States; and patriotic, political and other organizations were writing and cabling to Garibaldi urging him not to go. His Scottish friend, John McAdam, who had lived for fourteen years in the United States, wrote to him that the American Civil War was being fought, not for negro emancipation but for 'dollars & cents – *and trade protection*', and told him that he would have been 'despised' if he had been 'entrapped by the poor spirited wretches, who dare not come out boldly and honestly for the *entire* abolition of Negro Slavery'. 'You may be sure,' replied Garibaldi, 'that had I accepted to draw my sword for the cause of the United States, it would have been for the abolition of Slavery, full, unconditional.'[20]

It is difficult to estimate what Garibaldi would have achieved if he had been appointed to a high military command in the US army during the civil war. The nature of the warfare on the main front in the East was completely different from the kind at which Garibaldi excelled. Until the Battle of the Volturno, Garibaldi had never commanded a force of more than a few thousand men; but in the course of the American Civil War, larger forces became involved than had ever been conceived of in modern warfare, and by April 1865 Grant had 950,000 men in the armies of the North. The civil war was also a landmark in warfare in temporarily establishing the superiority of the defence over the attack. Grant's attacks against Lee in Virginia in the campaign of 1864 were very costly in casualties, and the mind boggles at the thought of what the cost would have been in human life if Garibaldi had been in command, sending in wave after wave of infantry to charge with the bayonet against Lee's positions. But Garibaldi had shown, on the Volturno, that he could learn from experience, and it must not be assumed that he would have repeated the errors of the Villa Corsini if he had been in command in the Wilderness or at Cold Harbor. In the West, along the Mississippi, or in the Shenandoah Valley, he would have been in his element, and probably at least as successful as Grant and Sheridan; and if he had fought in the American Civil War, he would have avoided the failures and disappointments of the next few years in Italy.

CHAPTER 35

ASPROMONTE

B Y 1861, only the Austrian provinces of Venetia and Tyrol, and the remaining part of the Papal States, the Patrimony of St Peter, remained to be liberated and annexed to Victor Emanuel's kingdom; but there were serious difficulties in the way of an immediate solution to the problems of Rome and Venice. Ricasoli, who had succeeded Cavour as Victor Emanuel's Prime Minister, was as conscious as Cavour that Italy would lose a war against Austria if she fought without French help; and Napoleon III made it clear to the Italian government that he would not go to war with Austria again to win Venetia for Italy. The liberation of Rome presented even greater difficulties, despite the fact that the Italian army could defeat the Papal forces, unlike the Austrian; for the French troops were still in Rome, where they had been since 1849, and the powerful force of the Catholic Church in France was determined to prevent Napoleon III from abandoning the Pope.

But Garibaldi, having been disappointed in his hopes of liberating Rome and Venetia in March 1861, was determined not to allow another spring and summer to go by without taking action. As he made no secret of his intentions, the press was full of speculation, and foreign agents sent reports to their governments containing all sorts of rumours as to his plans. Cavour, shortly before his death, had described Garibaldi as a bear looking for prey to devour; and during the winter of 1861–2, every Foreign Office in Europe was alarmed as to where Garibaldi would strike in the spring. Count Vimercati, the Italian Military Attaché and Victor Emanuel's personal agent in Paris, wrote that Garibaldi was the nightmare of the French Foreign Minister, Thouvenel. On 17 January, the Turkish Grand Vizier asked the Italian Minister in Constantinople to take steps to prevent Garibaldi from landing on the coast of Montenegro and placing himself at the head of a national rising against the Sultan's government. The Austrian government had also received reports that Garibaldi was planning to cross the Adriatic, but they believed that his destination was not Montenegro, but Dalmatia, where he would lead a revolution of

Franz Josef's Croat subjects. Ricasoli, like Cavour, had been in touch with Kossuth, who was continually planning revolution in Hungary; and the Austrian government believed that Victor Emanuel's government had planned a simultaneous outbreak under Kossuth in Hungary and under Garibaldi in Dalmatia for the spring or early summer of 1862. The French government had heard, in October 1861, that Garibaldi was intending to land in Catalonia and start a revolution in Spain.[1]

Another rumour was that Garibaldi was intending to lead a revolution in Greece. For thirty years, the Greek Liberals had suffered under the autocratic rule of King Otho, the Bavarian Prince whom the Great Powers had given them as their King after the Greeks had won their independence from Turkey; and although Otho, supported by Russia and buffetted by Palmerston, had so far withstood the storm, the discontent in Greece had reached a point, by the beginning of 1862, where a revolution was expected daily. The Greek throne was expected to be vacant shortly for a prince of some other foreign dynasty, and the rumour spread that Victor Emanuel coveted it for his second son, and would send Garibaldi to Greece to lead the revolution and obtain the crown for the Duke of Aosta. At the same time, the Turkish government believed that Garibaldi was in touch with King Otho of Greece, and was to lead an expedition financed by King Otho to liberate the Ionian Isles from British rule. In fact, King Otho was overthrown a few months later by a revolution without Garibaldi's assistance, and a Danish prince was chosen by the Great Powers to be the new King of Greece; and Garibaldi gave no help to any revolt in the Ionian Isles against his friends the British.[2]

In March 1862 Ricasoli's government fell, owing to a dispute between Ricasoli and Victor Emanuel, who, unlike Ricasoli, believed that the immediate objective should be the acquisition of Venetia rather than Rome. Rattazzi, who had always been Victor Emanuel's favourite politician, became Prime Minister at the head of a Left-wing government. This was everywhere interpreted as a sign that Victor Emanuel and the new government would pursue a more daring policy about Venetia, and would give more support than Cavour and Ricasoli to Garibaldi's projects. Rattazzi had visited Napoleon III shortly before he became Prime Minister, and had gained the impression that although Napoleon would not permit Italy to attack the Pope, he would not mind if they attempted to seize Venetia from Austria; and Rattazzi decided to give up all attempts to liberate Rome for the time being, and to cause trouble for Austria in Venetia and also, with the assistance of Hungarian and Croat revolutionaries, in Hungary and the Balkans.[3]

GARIBALDI
WOUNDED
IN 1862

KING VICTOR EMANUEL

KING VICTOR EMANUEL RECEIVING THE PLEBISCITE OF THE PEOPLE OF ROME, 1870

Meanwhile, Crispi had been making an attempt to unite Garibaldi and Mazzini. The events of the past two years had drawn Garibaldi closer to the Mazzinians. In the fifties, the failure of Mazzini's badly planned and adventurist risings in Milan, Genoa and Calabria had made Garibaldi very sceptical of Mazzini's methods and resolved to stay clear of his reckless enterprises; but in 1860 the mad Mazzinian adventure in Sicily had been unbelievably successful. The rising of the seventeen revolutionaries in Palermo in April 1860 had been completely Mazzinian in method and personnel. The Mazzinians had induced the people to rise by spreading the untrue rumour that Garibaldi was coming to lead them, and had persuaded Garibaldi to go to their aid by forging telegrams and falsely telling him that the people had everywhere risen in revolt. Yet this Mazzinian venture had succeeded, unlike all their previous attempts; and Garibaldi was ready to believe the Mazzinians when they told him that the difference in Sicily was that he had, for the first time, agreed to lead the rising. This encouraged him to think that any call for a rising would succeed if he were there to lead it; and as he had become bitterly disillusioned with Cavour and Victor Emanuel's ministers, he was more favourably disposed to a reconciliation with Mazzini than at any time since the days of the Roman Republic of 1849.

During the winter of 1861–2, Crispi and a number of his friends visited Garibaldi on Caprera, and invited him to preside at a conference at which representatives of various Radical organizations would meet to discuss the possibility of uniting in a common organization to work for the liberation of Rome and Venetia. Garibaldi agreed, and the conference was held in Genoa on 9 March 1862. It was one of the first modern political party conferences, and attracted a good deal of criticism and ridicule. Political commentators and journalists commented on the absurdity of holding a mock Parliament, with a President, delegates, speeches, and voting on resolutions urging action on political matters, when the body had no legal standing and was convened simply at the call of private individuals. Others took the view that to hold such a conference was not farcical, but highly dangerous and seditious, and a contempt of Parliament.[4]

The conference in Genoa lasted two days. It was opened by a short speech by Garibaldi, in which he declared that Liberals and democrats must be like the fasces of the lictors of ancient Rome – the bundle of sticks which, singly, could be broken, but were unbreakable when united together. The delegates decided to unite all their organizations and form the Association of Italian Emancipation, with Garibaldi as its President. They passed resolutions demanding the immediate liberation of Venetia and Rome, and the grant of a pardon and amnesty to Mazzini, which would set aside the sentence of death which had been passed upon him in 1857 for his part in the insurrection in Genoa. The chief difficulty about granting a pardon to Mazzini was Mazzini himself. A few weeks earlier, Ricasoli had offered to grant Mazzini the pardon; but Mazzini refused to accept it, arguing that he could not be pardoned when he had done no wrong.[5]

Though the Mazzinians were pleased to have obtained Garibaldi's support, they still considered him to be unreliable, and likely at any time to capitulate to Victor Emanuel. When he came to the conference, he was besieged by newspaper reporters, who asked him for his opinion on the resignation of Ricasoli and the appointment of Rattazzi as Prime Minister three days before. Garibaldi, who had always thought that Rattazzi stood for a more vigorous and Radical policy than Cavour and Ricasoli, told the press that he welcomed the change of government; but the Mazzinians had recently attacked Rattazzi for his visit to Napoleon III, and were indignant that Garibaldi should speak well of a man who had visited Napoleon.[6]

Garibaldi went from Genoa to Turin, where he had several interviews with Rattazzi, and one with the King. There has been a great deal of speculation ever since as to what was said in these talks. According to Rattazzi, he and Victor Emanuel asked Garibaldi not to lead an expedition against any foreign state without Victor Emanuel's permission, and Garibaldi promised not to do this. The Mazzinian version is very different. The Mazzinians have been as anxious to assign responsibility to Victor Emanuel and the government for the unsuccessful Garibaldian expedition of 1862 as they have been to deny them the credit for having supported the successful Garibaldian expedition of 1860; and the failure of the government to take effective steps to stop Garibaldi, and their vague statements of sympathy for him, which are ignored with regard to 1860, are cited as proof of their complicity in 1862. The Mazzinian theory – which, like so many Mazzinian theories, has come to be accepted as undisputed fact by many twentieth-century scholars – is that Victor Emanuel and Rattazzi led Garibaldi on, encouraging him to attack Austria or the Papal States in 1862, and then shamefully betrayed him at the last moment.[7]

After leaving Turin, Garibaldi went to Milan for the celebration of the anniversary of the revolution of March 1848. In a series of speeches in the great square, at factories, and to revolutionary organizations, he praised the revolutionary heroism of the people of the City of the Five Days, and called for new revolutionary exertions in the future. Without making any specific declaration of his intentions, he often repeated the slogan 'Rome and Venice'. He went on from Milan to other towns in Lombardy and northern Italy. At Monza, Parma, Bozzolo, Cremona and Brescia, he was greeted with the greatest enthusiasm by the population, and addressed great demonstrations from the balcony of the town hall. He adopted his own particular method of oratory, a sort of duologue with the crowds in the city squares, addressing rhetorical questions to them, with the crowds shouting back the expected answer – a method of oratory which was afterwards adopted by Mussolini in conscious imitation of Garibaldi, just as he adopted the black shirt and the Fascist salute in imitation of the red shirt and the Garibaldi salute, as well as the fasces and the title of 'Duce', which the Garibaldini sometimes used in reference to Garibaldi. At Casalmaggiore, Garibaldi proclaimed what Guerzoni called 'the religion of St Rifle', and launched the slogan: 'Young men, to your rifles!' At his meeting in the San Giovanni Theatre in Parma he was greeted with shouts of 'Long live Mazzini!' He answered: 'Long live Victor Emanuel!'[8]

Garibaldi called on the people to form rifle clubs, on the Swiss model, where they could meet on Sundays and practise shooting, thus ensuring that Italy, like Switzerland, would have a popular militia of trained riflemen to supplement the army in case of war. Thousands of young men answered the call, and formed the clubs, with rifles supplied by the Garibaldi Rifle Fund and with the tacit consent of the Italian government. The Great Powers feared that the Italian rifle clubs, under Garibaldi's leadership, would be much more dangerous to the peace of Europe than the Swiss rifle clubs. The Austrian government protested against Garibaldi's speeches and the formation of the clubs in Lombardy, so near the frontier with Austrian Venetia and Tyrol, at a time when the Emperor Franz Josef was on an official visit to Venice. When Palmerston said to Apponyi, the Austrian Ambassador, that the Italian government was wisely allowing Garibaldi and the hotheads to hold their demonstrations and form their rifle clubs as a harmless outlet for their energies, Apponyi replied that he feared, on the contrary, that Garibaldi would succeed in dragging the Italian government along the path of revolution.[9]

At the end of April, Garibaldi had an attack of rheumatism, and went to the health resort of Trescore, near Bergamo, for a cure. He summoned the executive committee of the Association of Italian Emancipation to a meeting at Trescore on 5 May, the second anniversary of his departure from Quarto on the expedition to Sicily. The meeting at Trescore aroused intense speculation in the European Foreign Offices and press. It was widely believed that the story of Garibaldi's attack of rheumatism was an invention, and that he had gone to Trescore to establish a headquarters from which he would invade the Tyrol. In fact, the meeting at Trescore degenerated into a bitter wrangle between Garibaldi and the Mazzinians.

Mazzini wrote to Garibaldi from London, offering to join him in any expedition which he might lead; but he sent Mario to represent him at Trescore. When Garibaldi proposed that they should organize an expedition against Venetia, Mario opposed it strongly, as did Bertani and Crispi and the other Mazzinians. They said that it would fail, as there was no revolutionary movement in Venetia at present, and they urged Garibaldi not to allow himself to be used by Victor Emanuel and Rattazzi to attack Venetia, or in any expedition to the Balkans or to anywhere else outside Italy. They urged him, instead, to launch an attack on the Papal States. Their argument about the difficulties of an attack on Venetia was sound, but was so unlike the usual Mazzinian arguments that it is difficult to avoid the conclusion that Mazzini opposed an expedition against Venetia or Dalmatia only because he believed that the Italian government might support it, and preferred an attack on Rome, which would be purely Mazzinian in inspiration, and would be opposed by everybody else.

Garibaldi became angry when Mario opposed his plans for immediate action against Venetia. He cried out that Mario was a Mazzinian. Mario replied that he was neither a Mazzinian nor a Garibaldian, but thought with his own head. 'That's the worst of it,' said Garibaldi. But the opposition of the Mazzinians persuaded him to call off his plans for an immediate invasion of Austrian territory.[10]

Some of his followers were dissatisfied with his decision, though whether they went so far as to plan to invade the Tyrol is uncertain. The Austrian agents reported to Vienna that an invasion of the Tyrol by Garibaldian bands was imminent, and the Austrian Minister in Turin asked the Italian government to take steps to prevent any violation of the frontier. Rattazzi conveniently was away from Turin, and could not be contacted by cable. His officials at the Foreign Office were therefore compelled to take the decision themselves, and sent orders to the Italian army at Bergamo to take all necessary measures to stop the Garibaldini from crossing the Austrian frontier.[11]

On the evening of 14 May a group of about a hundred Garibaldini under Colonel Nullo assembled at Sarnico on Lake Iseo, and in the early hours of the morning set off to march towards the Austrian frontier. The Italian army caught Nullo and 55 of his followers at Palazzolo, and another 48 who were just leaving Sarnico were also stopped by the army. They were all arrested and taken to the prisons in Bergamo and Brescia. The authorities thought that Bergamo and Brescia were unsuitable places in which to hold the prisoners, because both these towns had a militant Left-wing tradition; so it was decided to transfer the captured Garibaldini to the military prison at Alessandria near Turin.

The news of the arrests caused great indignation among the Radicals. Garibaldi sent a strong protest to the government, and went to the prison at Bergamo, where he demanded that the prisoners should be released on his standing security for them. The prison governor refused to agree, and sent the prisoners to Alessandria. Next day, Nullo and the prisoners at Brescia were also transferred to Alessandria. At both Bergamo and Brescia the Radicals organized demonstrations next day, protesting against the transfer of the prisoners. At Bergamo the demonstration was peaceful; at Brescia, the demonstrators became violent, and the army opened fire, killing four men and wounding others. Garibaldi accused the troops of killing and wounding several citizens, including women and children. The Mazzinian writers incorrectly stated that some of the captured volunteers had been shot while attempting to escape, and, like so many of the Mazzinian propaganda stories, this version has found its way into most of the history books.[12]

The French government were pleased about the incident at Brescia. Thouvenel hoped that it would lead to a Mazzinian rising in Genoa, which Rattazzi would be compelled to suppress; this would cause an irreconcilable split between the Italian government and the Radicals which would put an end to the influence of Garibaldi and the Left wing over Rattazzi. But Rattazzi himself was embarrassed. He let it be known that the decision to arrest the Garibaldini had been taken by the permanent officials while he was away from Turin, but at the same time he clearly stated that he would maintain law and order and would not permit a private army to invade the territory of a neighbouring state. The last thing which he wished to do was to arrest Garibaldi, and he was embarrassed by the fact that Garibaldi insisted on identifying himself with Nullo and the arrested Garibaldini. The Secretary-General of the Foreign Office reported to the Foreign Minister, General Durando, that Garibaldi was determined to take the responsibility for Nullo's attempt to invade the Tyrol. He added that he had sent Plezza, an official of the King's household, to Trescore to ask Garibaldi to leave the district, but that in the official report of the incident, and in the statement to the press, 'we have handled Garibaldi by saying that the agitators had made use of his name, which is the only way of excusing ourselves in the eyes of Europe for not having arrested him'. But on the same day, Garibaldi issued a statement which was published in the Radical newspaper, *Il Diritto*, on 18 May: 'As Colonel Nullo was arrested in Palazzolo yesterday, I think it my duty to say that this gallant officer went there and acted in obedience to my orders.'[13]

Garibaldi followed this up with another statement to the press, protesting against the shooting of the demonstrators at Brescia. 'Italian soldiers! I would not have believed that Italian soldiers could kill and wound unarmed women and children. The killers must have been assassins masquerading as soldiers.' He then suggested that the people of Brescia should erect a monument in honour of a Russian officer named Popoff, who had attracted attention a few months earlier by breaking his sword and refusing to obey orders when ordered to open fire on civilian demonstrators in Warsaw.[14]

Garibaldi's statement caused great resentment in the Italian army, and his old comrades Bixio, Medici, Cosenz and Türr were disturbed. On 23 May *Il Diritto* published another statement by Garibaldi, stating that his previous statement had been misinterpreted. 'Italian soldiers, I did not have, I could not have, the intention of pouring scorn on the Italian army, which is the glory and the hope of the nation. I only wished to convey, by my words, that Italian soldiers should fight the enemies of the country and the King, and not kill and wound unarmed citizens.'[15]

After leaving Trescore, Garibaldi went to Belgirate on Lake Maggiore to the house of Signora Cairoli. One of her sons had fallen at Varese in 1859, and one in Calabria in 1860; two other sons were to die when fighting under Garibaldi in 1867. Garibaldi addressed a number of meetings in the towns on Lake Maggiore, and published statements to the press, calling for Rome and Venice, and urging the formation of rifle clubs.[16]

On 8 June he went to Locarno, on the Swiss shore of the lake, in response to an invitation from the working men of Locarno, who had elected him an honorary member of their trade union. The Italian Minister in Berne reported that the Swiss government were a little anxious about Garibaldi's visit to Locarno, because some months earlier the Italian Foreign Minister had stated that the Italian-speaking population of the Swiss canton of Ticino ought to be united with their brothers in the Kingdom of Italy. Political passions ran high in Ticino, where the population was about equally divided between the Ultramontane Catholics and the Radicals, and the news that Garibaldi was coming caused some protests from the Catholic party.

The visit passed off without any unpleasant incident. The President of the canton, Battaglini, made the speech of welcome to Garibaldi, and stated, in the course of his speech, that the people of Ticino were determined to remain members of the Swiss Confederation. In his short reply, Garibaldi paid tribute to Switzerland as a land of freedom, and thanked the Swiss for having granted him refuge after his retreat from Morazzone in 1848, and for the asylum which they had always granted to political refugees from Italy and from other lands. The Italian Minister in Berne reported that Garibaldi had made a very favourable impression with his speech at Locarno, because the Swiss always liked to hear praise of their institutions; but there was a renewal of suspicion and ill-feeling when the Italian press, in reporting Garibaldi's meeting at Locarno, omitted those passages in Battaglini's speech in which he had declared that the people of Ticino wished to remain Swiss. A Locarno newspaper was so incensed that it published a passionate editorial, declaring that if Ticino were annexed by Italy, it would only be after a bloody struggle.[17]

A few days later, Garibaldi was visited at Belgirate by Plezza, who had presumably been sent there by the government. Plezza was entertained to lunch by Signora Cairoli, and spent some time with Garibaldi in his room, and he then went out alone with Garibaldi in a rowing boat on the lake.[18] No one knows what they discussed, out of earshot, on the lake, and whether Plezza urged Garibaldi, on behalf of Victor Emanuel, not to proceed with any attack on Venetia, or whether, as the Mazzinians afterwards maintained, he encouraged Garibaldi to go ahead with a filibustering expedition into the Balkans, or even against Rome. One can only say that, despite all the allegations of the Mazzinians and their successors, there is not a shred of evidence that, either on this occasion or on any other, Victor Emanuel or Rattazzi urged Garibaldi to go ahead. It is, however, quite probable that Plezza tried to placate Garibaldi's wrath over the arrest of Nullo and the Brescia shootings by vague assurances of sympathy from the King and Rattazzi, and that this, as well as the experience of 1860, encouraged Garibaldi in his belief that they would connive at some new venture and support him if it turned out to be successful.

Immediately after this meeting with Plezza, Garibaldi returned to Caprera after a three months' absence; but he stayed there less than ten days. On 27 June, to everyone's surprise, he issued a statement that he was leaving immediately for Sicily,[19] which he had not visited since 1860. There had been considerable discontent in Sicily in the last few months, and there were rumours that a new separatist movement was developing there in favour of independence from the Kingdom of Italy. Garibaldi hoped to use his influence to appease the discontent.

He arrived at Palermo next day. The Governor of Sicily was his old colleague Pallavicino, his Pro-Dictator at Naples, and Pallavicino immediately invited him to stay as an honoured guest in the palace at Palermo. Next day Garibaldi spoke to a delegation of students from the university. The leader of the delegation, in his speech of welcome, said that Italy was a nation of 22,000,000 people, all united in loyalty to Victor Emanuel. Garibaldi, in his reply, stated that there were not

22,000,000 Italians, but 25,000,000, and that all of them would soon
be united in one country. He then said: 'Let us go to Rome and Venice.'
On 1 July he addressed a great rally at the Garibaldi Theatre in Palermo, and declared: 'We will liberate Rome and Venice!'[20]

All this was a little embarrassing for Pallavicino; but worse was to
come. In the course of the next three weeks, Garibaldi travelled all over
Sicily, addressing great rallies at Misilmeri, Corleone and elsewhere,
and being greeted everywhere with shouts of 'Long live Garibaldi! To
Rome and Venice!' On 19 July he addressed a meeting at Marsala.
After hailing Marsala as the cradle of freedom from whence his
liberating march of 1860 had begun, he spoke the words 'Either Rome
or death' which were to become the slogan of his supporters during the
next five years. The crowd took up the slogan, and amid the shouts of
'Roma o morte!' he closed his speech, and turned as if to leave the
platform. But he was called back to the rostrum by the applause of the
audience, and then, in this postscript to his speech, and obviously on
the spur of the moment, made a violent personal attack on Napoleon III.
Dealing with the usual French claim that the Italians owed a debt of
gratitude to France for the war of 1859, he declared: 'We do not owe
gratitude to the tyrant of France, we owe it rather to the French people.
Yes, the French people are with us, and are our brothers, because they
groan as slaves under a despot, and pant for liberty. Napoleon is a
thief, a robber, a usurper.' Garibaldi said that Napoleon had made
war in 1859 for his own interests, whereas Italy had fought for him in
the Crimea and had given him Nice; and he ended his speech: 'Get
out, Napoleon, get out! Rome is ours!'[21]

Garibaldi's statements in Sicily alarmed Napoleon III and every
government in Europe, especially as it was known that volunteers were
assembling in a camp in the Ficuzza forest near Palermo, and that arms
were being distributed to them. Some governments and journalists
thought that Garibaldi's talk about Rome was a blind, and that he was
really preparing to lead an expedition from Sicily across the Adriatic
to the Balkans; but the Pope and Napoleon III believed that he meant
what he said, and was planning an attack on the Papal States. The Pope,
indeed, believed that Napoleon III was behind Garibaldi, and had
planned the whole thing. When the commander of the French troops
in Rome strengthened the defences of Civita Vecchia, Pius IX became
even more convinced of this, because he thought it obvious that
Garibaldi would not attack Civita Vecchia, but would march up from
Sicily through Calabria and Naples and attack the Papal States from
the south, and that the French preparations at Civita Vecchia were
all part of the trick. He thought that Napoleon III had again arranged
for Victor Emanuel to send in the Italian army to rescue Rome and

the Patrimony of St Peter from Garibaldi, as they had done in the Marches and Umbria in 1860, and that Napoleon and Victor Emanuel had arranged with Garibaldi for him to threaten the Papal States in order to give them this excuse to intervene. On 26 July Pius confided his fears to Lord Odo Russell, the British Minister in Rome, and asked whether he would be granted political asylum in England after the Italian troops had marched in. Odo Russell assured him that he would be granted asylum if the need arose, but said that he was sure that the Pope's fears were unfounded.[22]

Napoleon III and Thouvenel had in fact been hoping for a *détente* in the situation which would enable them to reach some agreement with Victor Emanuel and Rattazzi and withdraw their troops at last from Rome; but they considered that Garibaldi's campaign made it impossible for them to do this for the moment without a complete loss of prestige and an outburst of fury from the French Catholics which they dared not face. Napoleon III stated that 'a nation like France does not give way to the threats of a Garibaldi'.[23]

At the end of July, the French government definitely decided that Garibaldi must be stopped from attacking Rome. When the Empress Eugénie, who was a powerful representative of the Catholic party at Napoleon's court, heard of the Garibaldini slogan 'Rome or death', she is alleged to have said: 'Death if they like, but Rome never.' Napoleon instructed the French Consul at Palermo to warn all his consular colleagues that they would lend ships and equipment to Garibaldi at their peril, as the French navy would act against the Garibaldini if they tried to attack the Papal States. The French Minister in Rome, the Duke of Gramont, believed that if the Italian government proved to be incapable of preventing Garibaldi from disturbing the peace of Europe with a private army with which he was constantly threatening to attack Rome, Venice or the Balkans, it might be necessary for the Great Powers to send a joint expeditionary force to deal with him.[24]

On 3 August Victor Emanuel issued a proclamation in which he stated that he, and he alone, would decide when the next step should be taken to secure the liberation of the remaining Italian territory, and that his government would not permit any individual, however eminent, to defy the law and conduct warlike operations against a foreign state with a private army. He said that anyone who formed an armed body without his royal authority was guilty of high treason and was waging civil war. But Garibaldi went ahead with his military preparations in the Ficuzza forest, and in his speeches in Sicily he continued to threaten to march on Rome. He apparently believed that, like in 1860, Victor Emanuel did not mean what he said; and it was widely believed among his men that the King was secretly encouraging Garibaldi. The failure of the military authorities to arrest Garibaldi or break up the camp in the Ficuzza forest seemed to prove it. A story was spread around that Garibaldi had a tin box with him in which he had a document sealed with a red seal, which he showed to everyone who attempted to stop him; and this was said to be an order from the King to let Garibaldi pass unhindered.[25]*

Garibaldi's lack of political understanding now had disastrous results. He did not have Crispi or any shrewd political adviser with him, and the Opposition MPS who hastened from Turin to Sicily were the most irresponsible of the Radical politicians. They egged him on without considering the consequences. Garibaldi repeatedly asserted that he wished to liberate Rome from the French troops, and would never under any circumstances fight against the Italian army; and he proclaimed his loyalty to Victor Emanuel in his speeches.[26] He therefore could not understand how Victor Emanuel could think that he was guilty of high treason or order the army to act against him. He believed that when it came to the point, the Italian army would melt away before his advance, as the Neapolitan army had done two years before. He did not realize that no king or government could draw back after issuing a declaration in the terms of Victor Emanuel's proclamation of 3 August.

On 1 August Garibaldi broke up his camp in the Ficuzza forest, and moved south to Mezzojuso; and on 6 August he began his march towards the east coast with the 3,000 men who had joined him. His old friend Pallavicino, who realized that the government must now use force to stop Garibaldi, resigned as Governor of Sicily rather than implement such a policy, and was succeeded by General Cugia. As Garibaldi approached the port of Catania, Cugia, who was receiving constant exhortations from the government in Turin to disperse the Garibaldini by force, sent troops to prevent Garibaldi from entering Catania. But Cugia was very reluctant to fight Garibaldi, and knew that all the officers and men in the army would be equally reluctant. Several of them deserted, and joined Garibaldi. Cugia sent a succession of telegrams to Turin, promising that the Garibaldini would be rounded up in a day or two; but the army did not attack Garibaldi's main force, and merely arrested any stragglers or small bands of Garibaldini whom they happened to encounter. On 18 August Garibaldi and his volunteers entered Catania without any opposition from the small body of troops in the town, and were enthusiastically welcomed by the population, who illuminated the town, and cheered Garibaldi till 3.30 am. The people erected barricades in the streets to prevent any attempt

*Although Guerzoni refers to the document with the red seal, it is clear from his statement that he did not see it himself.

by the royal army to capture the town from the Garibaldini. Cugia and his officers shrank from the idea of capturing Catania after bloody street fighting on the barricades.[27]

The only alternative was for the royal warships to bombard Catania from the sea; but there were two British merchant ships at Catania. The British government, although they had authorized the bombardment of Canton a few years earlier, always protested strongly against any bombardment of a civilian population in Europe, particularly when damage to British property was likely to result; and fear of the British reaction deterred Cugia from bombarding Catania, apart from the fact that he was sure that Victor Emanuel would not wish to became a second King Bomba.[28]

Cugia therefore did nothing against the Garibaldini in Catania, and Garibaldi became more confident than ever that the government would not use force against him. The rumour spread that the British government had prevented the bombardment of Catania, and that Britain was backing Garibaldi; and the Italian government ordered the seizure of a British ship at Catania which they suspected of helping Garibaldi. On 8 August Cugia informed Rattazzi that Garibaldi had stated, in a speech at Roccapalumba, that he would go to Rome whatever the French and Victor Emanuel might say, because he had the support of the British government. This was a complete distortion of Garibaldi's speech at Roccapalumba, in which Garibaldi had merely stated that Britain had supported him in 1860 when France and the government in Turin had wished to stop him; but it is very likely that Cugia's agents had heard some of the Garibaldini claiming that Britain was supporting them against the French and Italian governments. In fact, neither the British government nor British public opinion supported Garibaldi this time. When d'Azeglio informed Palmerston of Victor Emanuel's proclamation of 3 August, Palmerston expressed his strong approval of it; and the British government ordered the navy to be ready to stop Garibaldi from crossing the straits. *The Times* reprimanded Garibaldi, though more in sorrow than in anger.[29]

On 24 August, two years and six days after he had sailed from Taormina in 1860, Garibaldi again crossed to the mainland. He sent some of his men to seize a French and an Italian packet ship in the harbour at Catania. When the Garibaldini took over from the French captain at pistol point, the captain demanded to see Garibaldi, and told him that he would demand the protection of the French Consul. Garibaldi calmly replied that the captain must do his duty, and he would do his. He crossed to the mainland in the two ships and landed, as in 1860, at Melito. The failure of the royal navy to intercept him was afterwards cited as proof of Victor Emanuel's connivance in his expedition. It may well be proof of the sympathy and connivance, as well as the incompetence, of the local naval officers, who were later court martialled for negligence, and acquitted. There was certainly a reluctance among the Italian military authorities to fight Garibaldi.[30]

But the government in Turin had decided that Garibaldi must be stopped, and they sent one of the few men whom they knew would have no hesitation in fighting Garibaldi. On 24 August General Cialdini sailed from Genoa with sixty battalions, with orders to fight and capture Garibaldi and his men in Sicily. On the way, Cialdini put in at Naples, where he learned to his astonishment and anger that Garibaldi had crossed to Calabria, although Cialdini had been confident that the authorities would prevent him from leaving Catania. In Naples Cialdini met La Marmora, who was Commander-in-Chief of the royal armies in Naples and Calabria, and obtained his permission to operate against Garibaldi on the mainland as well as in Sicily. He then sailed with his army to Reggio di Calabria. Hearing that Garibaldi was in the mountains of Aspromonte, he sent Colonel Pallavicino with six or seven battalions to find Garibaldi, and ordered Pallavicino 'to pursue him constantly without giving him a moment's rest; to attack him if he sought to escape, and destroy him if he accepted battle'. He sent other units to surround Garibaldi and cut off his escape, so that the royal army 'would have a bigger chance of meeting him and destroying him'.[31]

Before leaving Catania, Menotti wrote to a friend in Liverpool that Garibaldi would be in Rome in three weeks without firing a shot. The Garibaldini believed that the Pope would abandon Rome, as Francis II had abandoned Naples. But once Garibaldi had reached the mainland, things worked out differently from 1860. Once again he had landed at Melito, and once again his men went without food for the first thirty-six hours; but this time, the local peasants did not bring him provisions, and neither joined him nor formed their own guerrilla bands. The greatest difference was that in 1860 the Neapolitan army had no will to fight; in 1862 it was Garibaldi who had no will to fight, being resolved not to fire on the Italian army. On 24 August, before leaving Catania, he had issued a proclamation, in which he declared: 'I bow to the Majesty of Victor Emanuel', and ended with the words: 'Long live Italy! Long live Victor Emanuel in the Capitol!' When the small garrison of Reggio di Calabria marched against him, Garibaldi retreated into the mountains of Aspromonte, being determined to avoid a battle with the Italian army.[32]

On 29 August, Garibaldi encountered the royal army under Colonel Pallavicino on Aspromonte. From his position on the plateau, he could see Pallavicino's men through his telescope as they advanced up the hill, and he watched them approach for three-quarters of an hour. There are three conflicting stories of what happened next – the first official report published by the Italian government; the reports of Colonel Pallavicino and Cialdini, which were published twelve days after the battle; and the statement made a few days afterwards by a group of Garibaldi's officers, which is substantially but not exactly the same as the account published subsequently by Garibaldi in his memoirs. The first official report was certainly untrue; but the Garibaldian version ought not perhaps to be accepted as uncritically as it has been.

The royal troops came up the hill, firing as they advanced. Garibaldi called on his men not to return the fire, as he had always said that he would not fire on the Italian army; but Colonel Pallavicino's men continued to fire as they came closer. Garibaldi noted in his memoirs that it was only to be expected that the absence of resistance would encourage the attacking force to press home their attack and increase their fire. It is typical of Garibaldi that his military experience and the offensive spirit which he showed as a commander caused him to reach this conclusion, but that his political incapacity had led him into a position where he had to adopt an attitude which he knew would be militarily disastrous. No doubt he hoped that if he could make contact with the royal troops, he would be able to fraternize with them and win them over; but Cialdini and Pallavicino did not give him this opportunity.

As Garibaldi stood in front of his men, urging them not to fire, a bullet fired by the advancing soldiers struck a tree, ricochetted, and entered Garibaldi's right ankle. Almost simultaneously, another bullet hit him in the left thigh; but he stood erect in front of the line, and, drawing himself up to his full height, continued to call on his men not to fire. Most of the Garibaldini obeyed Garibaldi's orders; according to the statement by Garibaldi's officers, the Garibaldini just stood still: 'he who is standing continues to stand, he who is sitting continues to sit'. But on the right wing, the Garibaldini under Menotti, finding that they were being shot at, returned the fire. According to the Garibaldini officers, those who fired were chiefly young boys, who were unable to control their excitement on going into action for the first time. A group of royalist officers, pressing ahead of the rest of their troops, came to Garibaldi, who ordered them to be taken prisoner. Their leader told Garibaldi that he had come to parley. Garibaldi said that he had far more experience of war than this young officer, and that in all his experience he had never known an envoy present himself in this way when he came to parley.

The wound in Garibaldi's thigh was not serious; but the foot wound was painful and severe, and after a short time Garibaldi could no longer stand. His men laid him down under a tree, and his old surgeon, Dr Ripari, who had served under him in Rome in 1849, attended to the wound. Garibaldi lit a cigar, and told Ripari that if it was necessary to amputate the foot, he should go ahead with the operation at once; but Ripari and the other surgeons agreed that amputation would not be necessary. Menotti had also been wounded, and he was brought and laid down beside Garibaldi.

After a while, Garibaldi ordered his men to release the royalist officer whom he had captured, to restore his sword to him, and send him to Colonel Pallavicino with an offer of parley. Soon afterwards Pallavicino came himself to Garibaldi. He treated Garibaldi with the greatest respect, and Garibaldi agreed to surrender. He asked to be taken to Scilla, and put on board an English ship. Pallavicino said that he had no authority to negotiate, but that he would try to persuade Cialdini to agree to this. Garibaldi asked Pallavicino to show mercy to all his men, including those who had deserted from the royal army in order to join him. Pallavicino again promised to exert himself to obtain this from Cialdini, but said that he could offer no hope of mercy for the deserters, because he knew that it was intended to deal severely with them.

Garibaldi was carried down the mountainside on a stretcher, and taken to Scilla. Cialdini refused to allow him to go in a British ship, and ordered that he was to be sent as a prisoner in the Italian ship, the *Duca di Genova*, to the fortress of Varignano at Spezia. As Garibaldi went aboard, he pulled himself up by a rope next to the gangplank, and those who watched him were astounded at his agility in the circumstances. Cialdini stood and watched the embarkation in silence from the bridge of another ship. Garibaldi saluted him when he saw him, but Cialdini did not return the salute. The other Garibaldini officers did not salute the officers of the royal army, and were not saluted by them.

Next day, the official government journal in Turin published an account of the battle of Aspromonte.

> Garibaldi was summoned to surrender; when he refused, the fight began. It was long and desperate. The volunteers made a resistance which could not have been expected from such young and inexperienced troops. The position was carried at the point of the bayonet. . . . When the regulars came up, the volunteers fired; the Bersaglieri fired a few shots, then charged the position with the bayonet, and a terrible mêlée ensued. Garibaldi evidently sought for death. His son fought with extreme courage and determination.

This report was certainly a travesty of the truth, either from a deliberate desire by the government to justify the attack on the Garibaldini, or from journalistic inaccuracy. The falsity of the report is clearly shown by Colonel Pallavicino's report to Cialdini, and Cialdini's report to the War Office, which were at first suppressed by the government, but were afterwards published on 10 September.

But the account of the battle by Garibaldi's officers cannot be wholly accurate. There seems no doubt that the Garibaldini were not as passive as they made out. The Garibaldini officers themselves admitted that the royalist casualties and their own were about equal. The royalists lost 5 killed and 24 wounded, and the Garibaldini 7 killed and 20 wounded.[33] They explain this by the fact that although the royal troops fired far more rounds than the Garibaldini, the Garibaldini were much more accurate marksmen, which seems difficult to reconcile with their other assertion that the only Garibaldini who returned the royalist fire were inexperienced young boys. Again, Garibaldi's action in taking prisoner the royalist officer who came to parley, on the grounds that his method of approach was technically incorrect, hardly seems compatible with a desire to avoid bloodshed at all costs. On the other hand, it is clear that Garibaldi did not have the will to fight and win; if he had, and if the Garibaldini, in their superior position on the plateau, had fought at Aspromonte as they fought at Calatafimi and Milazzo, the result would have been very different.[34]

When the news of Aspromonte was received in Vienna, the value of commercial shares on the stock exchange rose by ten per cent in less than an hour.[35]

CHAPTER 36

THE VISIT TO ENGLAND

THE journey from Scilla to Varignano was a painful one for
Garibaldi. He was in no way ill-treated by his captors, and ten of
his officers were allowed to accompany him; but the medical services
were inadequate, and he suffered much from his wound. In his memoirs, he bitterly reproaches the authorities for sending him straight
to Varignano instead of taking him to the nearest hospital in Reggio di
Calabria or Messina; and his supporters at the time complained that
when he arrived at Varignano, he was kept waiting on board the
Duca di Genova for another twenty-four hours until his quarters in the
prison were made ready for him.[1]

While he was on board the *Duca di Genova*, he wrote an account of
Aspromonte to the newspaper *Il Diritto*.

> They thirsted for blood, and I wished to spare it. Not the poor soldiers
> who obeyed, but the men of the clique who cannot forgive the Revolution
> for being the Revolution – it is that which disturbs their Conservative
> digestion – and for having contributed to the re-establishment of our
> Italian family.

His declaration was published in *Il Diritto*, as a result of which the
editor was prosecuted for sedition, and sentenced to eighteen months'
imprisonment and a fine of 2,000 lire.[2]

There were demonstrations of support for Garibaldi all over Italy.
As Rattazzi had feared, his government could not survive an armed
clash with Garibaldi, and he was forced to resign after a bitter debate
in Parliament. At first it seemed as if Garibaldi and the other prisoners
would be prosecuted for high treason; but as early as 11 September the
government tried to appease the popular anxiety and indignation by
announcing that the captured Garibaldini would be treated as prisoners
of war. Only the men from the army and navy who had deserted to join
Garibaldi were put on trial. They were tried for desertion by court
martial, and sentenced to death. Eventually, after great public protests,
the sentences were commuted to imprisonment for life; but a few
deserters were summarily shot in Sicily, in the days immediately after

Aspromonte, by a major who, to the indignation of the Radicals, was not punished for his action.[3]

The question of the treatment of Garibaldi and the other prisoners became a matter of great controversy. The government and their supporters insisted that Garibaldi was being treated with every consideration compatible with his safe detention. The Radicals alleged that he was being ill-treated, and complained about the smallness and bareness of his cell and the hardness and simplicity of his bed. He and Menotti and the other eight officers who were imprisoned with him had six rooms between the ten of them, and many of them had to sleep on mattresses on the floor; but the discomfort of his quarters at Varignano was not much worse than that to which he had voluntarily submitted in his houses in Montevideo and Caprera. His greatest consolation in prison was the view of the sea from the window of his room.[4]

The news of his arrest and his sufferings from his wound aroused great sympathy in Britain, where all the criticism of him for his actions in the weeks before Aspromonte was forgotten. A British ship's broker in Genoa, John Nimmo, wrote to McAdam that he was organizing a collection among British and American sea-captains to provide Garibaldi with bare necessities in prison, 'without which his own physician (poor man) cannot guarantee the issue of the cure'. Nimmo added that Garibaldi's followers 'are being treated by the Ratazzi [sic] government as so many galley slaves'.[5]

Stansfeld, Ashurst and Jessie Mario went to Spezia to visit Garibaldi and to inquire about his health. Mazzini wrote a letter to the British newspapers in which he declared that 'the royal bullet that wounded Garibaldi has torn the last line of the contract entered into by us Republicans with monarchy'. On Sunday, 5 October, a protest demonstration was held in Hyde Park in which, according to the organizers, 100,000 people took part. A small group of Irish Catholics took possession of the mound from which the speakers had intended to address the demonstration, and they enraged the demonstrators by shouting 'Long live the Pope!' to which the demonstrators responded with 'Long live Garibaldi!' A battle ensued between the Garibaldian supporters and the Irish, which ended when a group of Guards officers arrived and charged the Irish, with shouts of 'Long live Garibaldi!' The conduct of the demonstrators, and especially the Guards officers, in attacking the Irish was severely condemned by the *Morning Star*, the organ of the pacifist Cobdenite wing of the British Radicals.[6]

In other countries, too, the Liberals and Radicals showed great sympathy for Garibaldi. The Swiss poet, Wulliémoz, commemorated the tragedy of the defeated hero of Aspromonte with an epic poem.

In Italy, opinion was divided on political lines. There were certainly many Italians who believed that the government had been right in making it clear that not even a national hero would be allowed to defy the law; and Massimo d'Azeglio pointed out to Panizzi that whereas in the last general election Garibaldi had been nominated as a candidate by acclamation in thirty constituencies, only two constituencies selected him, and after a secret ballot, in the next general election after Aspromonte. But the decisions of political constituency associations are an even less reliable guide than the vociferous Radical demonstrators to the feelings of the silent majority of Italians about Garibaldi's action in 1862.[7]

Almost everyone showed sympathy, real or feigned, for Garibaldi on account of his wounds. Visitors flocked to see him, some of whom succeeded in gaining admission, although others did not. But the wound in his foot showed no sign of healing, and it was this which caused the greatest anxiety among his admirers. His supporters paid for the most eminent surgeons in Italy, Britain and Germany to visit him in Varignano. There were almost too many eminent surgeons, for the twelve doctors in attendance could not agree about the best treatment. The chief cause of disagreement was whether the bullet was still in his foot, and the fact that his foot had swollen with rheumatism made both the diagnosis and the treatment more difficult.[8]

On 5 October Victor Emanuel announced that he had granted an amnesty to Garibaldi and to all the prisoners of Aspromonte except the army deserters. The prisoners all objected to being amnestied, as this implied that they were guilty, and argued, as Garibaldi did, that they were no more guilty of high treason in 1862 than in 1860. One of them challenged the government to prosecute them for treason for fighting, not only at Aspromonte, but also at Calatafimi and the Volturno, and added that many of the volunteers regretted now that they had committed these acts of treason in 1860 for Victor Emanuel's benefit. The Radicals and Mazzinians asserted that the reason why they were not prosecuted for treason was because Garibaldi had documents which implicated the King in the Aspromonte expedition to liberate Rome, and which showed the duplicity of the King and Rattazzi, so that Victor Emanuel dared not risk exposure at Garibaldi's trial.[9]

Contrary to the belief of the Radicals, and of most other observers, Napoleon III and the French government used their influence to persuade Victor Emanuel and Rattazzi to pardon Garibaldi. They feared that the Italian government would make a martyr of Garibaldi, and that France would be blamed for his martyrdom. The Radicals would also have been surprised if they had known of the anger with which their most reactionary enemies had received the news of Aspromonte. While Napoleon III's pro-Italian Foreign Minister, Thouvenel, was as pleased as Palmerston and Russell that Victor Emanuel's government had asserted its authority and proved itself to be a responsible government, the Empress Eugénie and the Duke of Gramont, who both represented the extreme Right-wing Catholic faction in French official circles, and also the Pope's ministers in Rome, regretted that the Italian army's victory over Garibaldi had removed the excuse for the Great Powers to intervene in Italy by force and crush the *Risorgimento*.[10]

On 22 October Garibaldi was released from Varignano, being carried out of the prison on a special bed which Lady Palmerston had sent him. He was taken to the house of a friend in Spezia, where all the doctors could attend on him more easily than in the prison. Some of them believed that it would be necessary to amputate the foot, and as this became known it caused great sadness among Garibaldi's supporters; but the majority of the surgeons decided that this was not necessary. Eventually the Italian specialist, Dr Zanetti, extracted the bullet from the wound. Garibaldi clenched Jessie Mario's hand and bit on his cigar while the operation was performed, but it was only later that the doctors realized how great the pain had been. The story of his sufferings spread throughout Italy and the world, and Garibaldi became a martyr as well as a hero. Thousands of bloodstained handkerchiefs, said to have been used to staunch Garibaldi's wound, were sold and treasured as relics.[11]

From Spezia, Garibaldi sailed to the mouth of the Arno, and was towed up the river to Pisa, where he stayed for a few weeks' convalescence. On 19 December he left for Caprera. He did not leave his island for more than a year. After his release from Varignano, he was again approached by the United States government and offered a high command, with the rank of Major-General, in their army. Lincoln had just issued his proclamation liberating the slaves, and the war was now openly stated to be a war to end slavery as well as for the preservation of the Union; but though the difficulty about slavery was removed, Garibaldi was forced to decline the invitation on account of his wound. For more than a year he could walk only with the aid of crutches. Sympathy was therefore the only aid which he could give to the Polish revolutionaries whose struggle against Russia aroused the enthusiasm of all European Radicals in 1863. Several of his former redshirts went to fight for the Poles.[12]

The Russian Socialist, Alexander Herzen, wrote to Garibaldi and expressed another point of view. While agreeing with all the strictures passed by international Liberal opinion on Russian Tsarism and its actions in Poland, Herzen pointed out to Garibaldi that there were

545

Socialists and Radicals in Russia, while on the other hand many of the foremost Polish revolutionaries were Catholic nationalists and landowners who oppressed their peasants. In his reply on 23 December 1863, Garibaldi told Herzen that he knew that the Russian people were not responsible for the tortures of Vilna and the gallows of Warsaw, and that many Russian officers had preferred Siberia and death to acting as the executioners of Poland; but he thought that Poland, where women were flogged and young men were hanged, should arouse a more solemn protest than mere words from the Russian people.

> The powers-that-be have always profited from nationalist and religious prejudices to make their system triumph and to poison the fraternal links which unite the people. But at a time when blood is flowing, the strong must nevertheless have compassion for the weak. Preach this to the Russians, and I will say to the Polish nobility: Give up the land to the peasants. I will say to all Poles: Stop giving your heroic struggle a religious and antique character which alienates sympathy from you and provokes bloody reactions against you.[13]

By the spring of 1864 Garibaldi had sufficiently recovered from his wound to accept the long-standing invitations which he had received to visit Britain, though he still limped and walked with the aid of a stick. According to Jessie Mario, his reason for coming to Britain was to enlist British sympathy for Denmark in her war against Prussia and Austria, though this sympathy was already strong; but Garibaldi denied that he went for any other reason than to express his gratitude to the British people for the aid which they had given him in 1860, and he made no public statement while he was in England about the Danish war.[14]

On 19 March he sailed from Caprera for Malta, and proceeded from there on the Peninsula and Oriental steamship *Ripon* to Southampton. He was accompanied by Menotti and Ricciotti, by his doctor Basile, and his secretaries, Basso and Guerzoni.[15] From the beginning his visit caused controversy between two groups of his supporters. His aristocratic admirers, especially the Duke and Duchess of Sutherland and Lord Shaftesbury, wished to introduce him into London society and honour him at banquets in the City; the Radicals and the Mazzinians wished to organize mass demonstrations in the provinces, particularly in the north, at which he could make Radical speeches. Garibaldi, with his usual amiability, was willing to associate with both the aristocrats and the Radicals, but ended by being rather disillusioned with both of them.

When his ship docked at Southampton on 3 April 1864, she was immediately overrun by crowds of journalists, sightseers and representatives of Italian business and other organizations in England, who swarmed on to the ship and pushed their way into Garibaldi's cabin before he had time to leave it. Holyoake, who was among the crowd, wrote that the only people who behaved with dignity were the Duke of Sutherland and Cowen. Several of the observers thought that Garibaldi seemed a little bewildered by the reception, though this may have been their imagination, because Garibaldi was well used to this kind of welcome in Italy. He barely had time to say a few words of greeting to Cowen and his other old friends before he was taken away to a civic reception given by the Mayor of Southampton, from where he was taken to Brook House, near the west coast of the Isle of Wight, where he was to be the guest of Charles Seely, the Liberal MP for Lincoln.[16]

Mazzini intended to run the Garibaldi visit. On 22 March he had written to Cowen about Garibaldi: 'I have urged him to come here two months past. He came late, but we must try to make the best of it. He must not linger in England beyond 20 April. We want him in Italy at that time, and he must if possible carry away from England some two or three thousand pounds.' In view of the indignation which Mazzini expressed a month later when Garibaldi was compelled to leave England on 28 April by what was, according to Mazzini, a plot of Napoleon III's, it is interesting to observe that on 22 March Mazzini thought it imperative that Garibaldi should be back in Italy by 20 April. Mazzini was determined that Garibaldi should tour the provinces and not go to London until after he had spoken at rallies in Birmingham and the north. Ashurst thought that it was essential that Garibaldi should be made to realize 'the importance of *coming out* as much as possible as a *pro-Mazzite* – and this is less likely if he begins with the Londoners and the aristocrats'.[17]

Mazzini was convinced that Seely would try to stop him from gaining access to Garibaldi, so he sent Cowen, Holyoake and his friends the Nathans to visit Garibaldi at Brook House to urge him not to go to London, but to go to the North. No one at Brook House made any attempt to prevent the Mazzinians from seeing Garibaldi, and they seem to have had the run of the house while Garibaldi was there, with Holyoake walking with Garibaldi in the garden nearly every day. Mazzini himself went twice to Brook House at Garibaldi's invitation, and saw Garibaldi for the first time since they had met in the royal palace in Naples when Garibaldi was Dictator. But the Mazzinians could not persuade Garibaldi to cut out his visit to London; he said that everything had been arranged for him to stay with the Duke of Sutherland in London. The Mazzinians were worried that Garibaldi was succumbing to aristocratic influence. Mazzini, writing to Cowen in his slightly quaint English, wrote three times in the course of five days that Garibaldi 'is badly surrounded'.[18]

Seely and the aristocrats, on their side, were becoming worried that Garibaldi was going to be used by Mazzini and the Mazzinians for seditious purposes. But Lord Shaftesbury put the best possible interpretation on Garibaldi's meeting with Mazzini at Brook House. He told Palmerston that Garibaldi had said that ' "had he found Mazzini in prosperity he would have avoided all misunderstanding by not seeing him; but finding him in adversity, he could not throw him aside". This is truly generous if not politic.'[19]

Garibaldi stayed at Brook House for eight days. During his stay there, he drove over for the day to Freshwater, a few miles west of Brook House, to visit Alfred Tennyson, the Poet Laureate. Tennyson, who was always a mouthpiece of British public opinion, had written poems in praise of the 'warrior of Caprera'; and he now welcomed Garibaldi warmly. Garibaldi planted a wellingtonia tree in the garden of Tennyson's house, as he did at other houses where he stayed in England. At Freshwater, he met Tennyson's friend, Julia Margaret Cameron, the well-known photographer. According to Mrs Tennyson, when Mrs Cameron went down on her knees to Garibaldi to ask him to allow her to take his photograph, Garibaldi, with his weak knowledge of English, thought that she was asking for alms; but from Garibaldi's experiences of kneeling women in Italy, it is more likely that he thought that she was asking for his blessing.[20]

During his stay at Brook House, Garibaldi visited Portsmouth, where he was entertained at a civic reception at the Guildhall, and inspected the naval dockyards. He also visited Jessie Mario's stepmother, the widow of his old friend Thomas White, at Gosport.[21]

On 11 April Garibaldi left Brook House, escorted by Seely and his entourage, and travelled from Southampton to London in a train draped with the Italian flag. After being greeted on the platform at Winchester by the Mayor and the city council, and by cheering crowds at Basingstoke station, he continued towards London. From Clapham onwards, the crowds were standing shoulder to shoulder all along the railway line. An enormous crowd was waiting at Nine Elms. The Metropolitan Police had been warned that 100,000 people were likely to be on the streets to welcome Garibaldi, and they had made preparations to deal with them; in fact, it was estimated that the crowds numbered about half a million, and were even larger than the crowds which had welcomed Princess Alexandra of Denmark when she came to London the year before to marry the Prince of Wales.[22]

The members of the military band at the station greeted Garibaldi with the Garibaldi Hymn, which was well known in Britain, and amid tumultuous cheering he was escorted to his carriage. A number of business men of the Italian community in London pushed their way to the front, and entered Garibaldi's carriage, although they had never met Garibaldi, and took their seats in the carriage beside him. As a result, there was no seat for Menotti or Basso, and they found themselves stranded at Nine Elms in the middle of half a million Englishmen, not knowing their way about London, and unable to speak any English. They were found by Holyoake, who had travelled in Garibaldi's train from Southampton with other journalists, despite an attempt by Seely and other Liberal MPs to eject him from the train at Micheldever. The MPs were afraid that Holyoake would attach himself to Garibaldi at Nine Elms and convert Garibaldi's reception into a Radical demonstration. Holyoake took Menotti and Basso to Stafford House, the Duke of Sutherland's residence at St James's, which today is known as Lancaster House. But Menotti and Basso were not invited to stay there with Garibaldi, and were given rather uncomfortable accommodation at the Bath Hotel.[23]

Garibaldi in his carriage, accompanied by the Duke of Sutherland and his self-invited companions, made his way to Stafford House by way of Wandsworth Road, Westminster Bridge, Parliament Street and Trafalgar Square. The crowds were so thick that the horses were often prevented from proceeding, and the three-mile journey took six hours. The crowds pressed against the carriage doors on both sides, and when finally the carriage reached Stafford House, and Garibaldi and his fellow-travellers alighted, the carriage fell in pieces; the sides had been lifted from their hinges by the pressure of the crowds, but held in position by the people pressing against the carriage.[24]

Next day Garibaldi began a busy week in London society. The Duchess of Sutherland and the Dowager Duchess were enraptured by him, and after he returned to Caprera they wrote love letters to him. The Duchess gave a dinner party for him at Stafford House at which Palmerston and other members of the government were present. After dinner the Duchess showed the guests round the house, even taking them into that inaccessible place, her boudoir, where Garibaldi, to the consternation of Lord Malmesbury, lit a cigar without incurring any sign of displeasure from the Duchess.[25]

Garibaldi dined at Panizzi's, where he met Gladstone. He was taken to the opera at Covent Garden to see Bellini's *Norma*, and was applauded by the audience. He travelled by train to Bedford, and was shown the new steam-roller factory. At his special request, he was taken to see Barclay and Perkins's brewery in Southwark, where the Austrian General Haynau, the butcher of Brescia and Hungary in 1849, had been assaulted by the workers when he visited the brewery in 1850.

He went to St Pancras, and told the reception committee that there was also a San Pancrazio in Rome, where he had established his head-quarters during the fighting in 1849. He was introduced to many distinguished persons, including Florence Nightingale and the Archbishop of Canterbury. He dined with the Palmerstons at Cambridge House in Piccadilly; and he also had a private talk with Palmerston, which lasted for over an hour. Some observers thought that Garibaldi looked angry as he left Cambridge House after his talk with the great British statesman, whose background, political opinions and character were utterly unlike his own, and who had used his power to thwart Garibaldi in Montevideo and, on the whole, to help him in Italy. The Prime Minister had been urging him not to attack Rome or Venetia.[26]

Garibaldi also had a private talk with the Foreign Secretary, Lord Russell, who, like Palmerston, asked him not to start a European war. Garibaldi assured Russell that he had no intention of doing so, but told him that he believed that Napoleon III would attack Britain in the near future, and that when this occurred he would lead his red-shirts to fight at Britain's side. He added that any revolutionary intrigues in the Balkans were not instigated by him, but by Napoleon III and the Emperor's cousin, Prince Napoleon.[27]

On 16 April he attended a rally at the Crystal Palace at Sydenham, four miles to the south of London. The great hall in the building, which was 536 yards long and 128 yards wide, was packed to capacity with enthusiastic supporters of Garibaldi, some of whom had come to London on cheap excursion trains from places as far afield as Hull. Garibaldi spoke from a rostrum in the centre of the hall, making a short speech in his halting English. One feature of the demonstration was when a group of Polish refugees entered, and presented an address of welcome to Garibaldi, who called on the British people to do all in their power to rescue the oppressed people of Poland. A delegation of Italian residents in London, who were in fact Mazzinians, handed him a banner inscribed with the words 'Rome and Venice'. Two days later, Garibaldi attended another demonstration and concert at the Crystal Palace, at which 30,000 people were present.[28]

There was a small minority in Britain who did not approve of Garibaldi's visit. Henry Manning, the future Cardinal, was indignant at the reception which Garibaldi received. Manning was the representative of the extreme Ultramontane element among the British Catholics, and next year was appointed to be the Catholic Archbishop in England, the opposition of the more moderate British Catholic hierarchy to his appointment having been overcome by the personal intervention of Pius IX. But Lord Shaftesbury led a deputation from the Low Church Evangelical Society to interview Garibaldi, though he was distressed that Garibaldi's anti-Catholicism had not made him a good Protestant. He gave Garibaldi an Italian edition of the New Testament, and made him promise to read it.[29]

Disraeli refused to meet Garibaldi. With his superior intelligence and his understanding of long-term political principles, he realized the absurdity of the supporters of an aristocratic and Conservative social order who cheered a revolutionary leader. But Disraeli's party leader, Lord Derby, and the former Conservative Foreign Secretary, Lord Malmesbury, met Garibaldi. When Malmesbury discussed politics with Garibaldi and a few of the other guests over cigars after dinner at Lady Clanricarde's, someone said that Napoleon III had been more successful than the great Napoleon. 'We must wait for the end,' said Garibaldi.[30]

Queen Victoria strongly disapproved of Garibaldi, being encouraged in her attitude by Sir Charles Phipps, the Keeper of the Privy Purse, though in this matter she was in opposition not only to the feelings of the great majority of her subjects, but also to several members of her own family. She was distressed at the attitude of her intimate friend, the Dowager Duchess of Sutherland. Whereas *The Times* hailed the great reception that Garibaldi had received on his arrival, when a vast but orderly working-class crowd had escorted a revolutionary leader to the mansion of a Duke, as something which could only happen in England, the Queen wrote in her diary:

> The people of England have gone really quite mad about Garribaldi,* who made a sort of triumphal entry into London yesterday! driving in the Duke of Sutherland's state carriage & being received by the good (I must say, foolish) Duchess, at the foot of the stairs! A tremendous crowd, but of the lowest riff raff! Honest, disinterested & brave, Garribaldi certainly is, but a revolutionist leader![31]

The Duchess of Sutherland suggested that she should bring Garibaldi to Windsor Castle. This led Phipps to report to the Queen that 'It appears to him an extraordinary thing that anybody should think of bringing Garibaldi to Windsor Castle', because apart from the fact that he was planning to attack a sovereign with whom the Queen was in alliance, 'nothing could be more unseemly than the noise and excitement at Your Majesty's Palace Gates which such a Visit would create'. But the Queen's daughter, Victoria, the Princess Royal, who had married the Crown Prince of Prussia, and who carried on a frequent and intimate correspondence with her mother, wrote to her from

---

*Queen Victoria, like the Rosista newspapers in Buenos Aires, usually wrote 'Garribaldi' with a double r.

Berlin on 30 March: 'Garibaldi's visit in England is very strange – as you know I have a secret weakness for that individual. I feel much interest in what he is about.'[32]

At the other political extreme, Karl Marx ridiculed the welcome to Garibaldi. Marx had a higher opinion of Garibaldi than he had of Mazzini, whom he hated and despised both for his anti-Socialist doctrines and for the rash adventurism of his revolutionary tactics; and Marx's great friend and colleague, Friedrich Engels, who was a shrewd commentator on military affairs for various British and American newspapers, admired Garibaldi as a revolutionary guerrilla leader. But Engels had foretold as early as 1859 that Garibaldi would be used, and then discarded, by Victor Emanuel; and Marx, being by instinct a *Realpolitiker manqué*, had little sympathy with a romantic revolutionary of the Garibaldi type. During Garibaldi's visit to London in 1864, he thought that Garibaldi was allowing himself to be made use of by Palmerston and the aristocracy. Writing to Engels on 19 April, in his usual mixture of German and English, he commented that, this year, April Fool's Day had been extended to cover the whole month, with 'Garibaldi and Palmerston for ever' being the slogan on the walls in London, and Garibaldi visiting Palmerston and being acclaimed by English policemen at the Crystal Palace. Garibaldi, he wrote, 'halb killed ist von John Bull's embrace'. The organization of German Socialists in London asked him to present a message of greeting to Garibaldi; but he refused.[33]

Foreign governments, as Queen Victoria had realized, were not pleased at the reception accorded to Garibaldi in England; and none was so annoyed as the Italian government. Elliot, the British Minister in Turin, reminded Russell that no one in Italy now thought of Garibaldi as the man who had given Sicily and Naples to Victor Emanuel, but remembered only his attack on Cavour in Parliament and his rebellion of 1862. 'The effect of a red rag on a bull or a turkey cock has long been known,' wrote Elliot, 'but that the whole British Nation should have gone mad at the sight of a red shirt has astonished the Italians not a little.' He added that the Italians felt that Garibaldi's reception in London had weakened the Italian government's position as against Garibaldi and the revolutionaries in Italy. Elliot thought that the worst result would be that when Garibaldi went on his next filibustering expedition, it would be impossible to persuade anyone in Italy or in Europe that he was not incited and financed by the British government. Victor Emanuel and his ministers were so angry that they cancelled the plans for the forthcoming visit of Prince Umberto to England.[34]

The Mazzinians, too, were becoming anxious about the visit,

fearing that Garibaldi had fallen completely into the hands of London society. They were eager to get him out into the provinces. Cowen and McAdam arranged for him to speak at large public meetings in Newcastle, Glasgow and Birmingham. In Manchester, the Temperance Society of Manchester and Salford planned to hold a rally at the Free Trade Hall to be addressed by Garibaldi, because they had heard that Garibaldi drank water or milk, but not wine.

> We have admired your ardent patriotism [they wrote in their address to Garibaldi], your unselfish devotion and generous enthusiasm in the holy cause of human liberty. . . . And we have also reason to believe, not only that your own habits and tastes are of an extremely pure and simple character, true to nature's primary laws of life and health; but that you most sincerely sympathize with the efforts of Social and Temperance Reformers, to abrogate the absurd and pernicious Drinking usages of Society, to prohibit that most foul and iniquitous system of temptation and corruption – the Traffic in Intoxicating Liquors, and thus roll away the curse of our modern civilization, and the greatest obstruction to all efforts to elevate, ameliorate, and bless mankind.

But a few days later, the secretary of the Manchester branch of the United Kingdom Alliance for the Total Suppression of the Liquor Traffic Offices wrote in some alarm to Cowen about Garibaldi: 'I see the papers say now that he takes a glass of wine at breakfast. Hope it is the pure juice and unfermented. Our English victims may seduce him.'[35]

But neither the temperance reformers of Manchester nor the Radical artisans of Glasgow or Newcastle were destined to see Garibaldi. On 18 April it was announced that Garibaldi had cancelled his plans to visit the provinces, and was returning to Caprera almost immediately. The government stated that this was because of the state of his health. The Mazzinians stated that it was because Gladstone, at Palmerston's instigation, had persuaded Garibaldi to leave, as the government feared that Garibaldi's speeches in the provinces would stir up revolution and anger Napoleon III.

Within a few days of Garibaldi's arrival in London, his more moderate supporters became anxious about his health, as well as about the political consequences of his tour of the provinces under Mazzinian auspices. As early as 13 April Robert Dalgleish, the Liberal MP for Glasgow, urged McAdam to ensure that when Garibaldi came to Glasgow not only were no extremist speeches made which might embarrass the Italian cause, but also that Garibaldi was not kept at the meeting for much more than an hour, as his health would not stand any more.[36] On Friday 15 April Seely mentioned to Colonel Chambers, Garibaldi's English Mazzinian friend who had come with him from

Caprera, that it might be advisable if the provincial tour were cancelled. He may have been worried about Garibaldi's health, but he certainly also wished to prevent Garibaldi from speaking at the Mazzinian propaganda meetings in the provinces. Next day, on Saturday 16 April, Mrs Chambers visited Garibaldi at Stafford House. She found him very tired after his exhausting round of social engagements and the ordeal of the public acclamation in London. Colonel Chambers had called in William Fergusson, the famous surgeon, to see Garibaldi. Although Fergusson was surgeon to Queen Victoria, he was politically sufficiently Radical and sympathetic to the Italian revolutionaries for Mrs Chambers, herself a zealous Mazzinian, to write that Fergusson's 'politics were always understood Mazzinian'.

Fergusson told Chambers that he was anxious about Garibaldi's health. Mrs Chambers suggested that as next day was Sunday, when Garibaldi would have no engagements, they might all go to Windsor for a quiet day in the country. Garibaldi said that he would have liked to go, but felt too tired, though he added that he was only tired, and not ill. Mrs Chambers told Cowen that she then said to Garibaldi: ' "*Generale*, there is one thing that you ought to know and that is that Mr Seely came to John [Colonel Chambers] yesterday, and tried to induce him to endeavour to prevent you from visiting the provinces." "How very singular," observed the General, "however, we go to Bristol on Tuesday next, therefore that question is settled." '* She then told Garibaldi that if he went to the provinces, he would obtain plenty of money to finance his campaign to liberate Venetia, and that the organizers of the rally in Manchester were expecting to raise at least £5,000.

Next morning, on the Sunday, while Chambers and his wife were at Windsor, Lord Shaftesbury visited Fergusson and told him that he was very anxious about Garibaldi's health. The Duke of Sutherland sent a note to Fergusson to the same effect. Fergusson came at once to Stafford House and examined Garibaldi. He wrote a statement which was published next day in the *Daily Telegraph*, stating that because of Garibaldi's health it would not be possible for him to go to the provinces, as he had planned, and that he must return to Caprera immediately.[37]

Mazzini had already heard about it on the Sunday. He immediately deduced that it was due to the pressure which Napoleon III had placed on Lord Clarendon, the Chancellor of the Duchy of Lancaster, who had just returned from a visit to Paris, and wrote to Cowen on

---

*In order to assist the reader, punctuation has been inserted in this and in subsequent quotations from Mrs Chambers's letters. There is no punctuation at all in the original holograph letters.

17 April that it was 'A cowardly concession to Napoleon. Garibaldi weak as good has yielded.' He urged Cowen to come to London at once, bringing a deputation from Newcastle with him if possible, to persuade Garibaldi to change his mind.[38]

On the previous day, Mazzini had visited Garibaldi and had invited him to a lunch at Herzen's house in Teddington on this Sunday, 17 April, where Garibaldi would meet all`the old Radical revolutionaries whom he had met during his less publicized visit to London in 1854. Garibaldi accepted the invitation, and asked Mazzini to arrange that Ledru-Rollin should be present. Ledru-Rollin declined the invitation, telling Herzen that as the official representative in Britain of the French Republic of 1849, it was necessary, for reasons of protocol, that Garibaldi should call on him at his own house, and not meet him elsewhere.

On the morning of 17 April, Herzen came to Stafford House to fetch Garibaldi. A member of the Duke of Sutherland's household objected to Garibaldi going to the revolutionary luncheon party in Teddington, and said that he could not permit the Duke's horses and carriage to be used for the journey. Herzen said that he had brought his own horses and carriage, and that Garibaldi could travel with him. The Duke's gentleman did not like this proposal any better, and he engaged in a somewhat heated argument with Guerzoni; but Garibaldi announced that he had quite decided to go, and the Duke's coachman, who had driven him around on all his excursions while he had been staying at Stafford House, drove him and Herzen to Teddington.

On the way, Herzen explained to Garibaldi why Ledru-Rollin would not accept the invitation to the dinner. Garibaldi said that he quite understood Ledru-Rollin's attitude, and suggested that he should tell the Duke's coachman to drive to Ledru-Rollin's home on the way to Teddington. Herzen said that this would be impossible, because it would involve going in the opposite direction, as they were now passing through Wandsworth, and Ledru-Rollin lived near Regent's Park.

Garibaldi was greeted at Teddington by a crowd of local inhabitants who had been waiting for him in front of Herzen's house. Many of them were Italian residents, and some of the women knelt and kissed his hand, like the people did in Italy. The lunch was a happy affair. Afterwards there were speeches, with Mazzini saluting the international revolution, and especially the struggle of the people of Poland. Garibaldi, in his speech, referred to Mazzini as his first teacher who had brought him into the struggle for Italian freedom more than thirty years before; he, too, spoke about the heroic struggle of the Polish revolutionaries, and saluted Herzen as the representative of all that was progressive and noble in the Russian people. Then the guests left, and Garibaldi was driven back to Stafford House in the Duke's carriage. Next day the Duke's coachman drove him to the homes of Ledru-Rollin and Louis Blanc.[39]

Garibaldi's visit to Teddington, which was reported in the press, disturbed his aristocratic friends; but the Radicals were delighted, and were prepared to forgive Garibaldi for his previous association with the aristocracy. The Polish revolutionary, Shawk, had written from Malaga on 23 April, having read in the papers about Garibaldi's visit to England, which 'seems to interest the Spanish editors more than anything else', to complain that 'Garibaldi has not done that which was required of him as the representative of the people. He has fallen into the hands of the Reigning class.' But next day, having read about the Herzen lunch in the *Glasgow Sentinel,* he was greatly relieved to hear 'that Garibaldi has paid his visit to the humble lodgings of his pariah friend and master'.[40]

On the Monday morning, 18 April, Colonel and Mrs Chambers came to Stafford House, with an invitation which Chambers had received for Garibaldi to visit yet another provincial town. When Chambers told Garibaldi about this invitation, Garibaldi said: 'The programme is changed, I do not visit the provinces.' Chambers asked what answer he should give to the provincial Mayor who had invited him. 'Say I cannot go', said Garibaldi. At that moment Fergusson came in, and, taking Mrs Chambers aside, told her that Garibaldi's health was much worse than he had stated in the letter published in the *Daily Telegraph,* and that he feared that Garibaldi would have a paralytic stroke if he did not rest and return at once to Caprera. After discussing the matter with his wife, Chambers very reluctantly wrote out a statement for Garibaldi to sign: 'Colonel Chambers is directed by General Garibaldi to state that in consequence of fatigue and by the advice of Mr Fergusson his medical adviser, he is reluctantly compelled' to cancel his visit to the provinces. Garibaldi took his pen and scratched through the words 'in consequence of fatigue and by the advice of Mr Fergusson his medical adviser', and inserted instead 'for various reasons'.

Chambers went to see Fergusson, and asked if he had made his statement about Garibaldi's health because he had been asked to do so for political reasons. Fergusson solemnly declared that there had been no political pressure of any kind, and that he had made his own medical diagnosis without discussing the matter with anyone. 'I went to the General,' wrote Mrs Chambers, 'Dearest *Generale,* if you are really so weak and tired, don't you think John's note to the Mayors was the best?' 'It read the best, but mine was the truth, his was not,' replied Garibaldi. 'Are you not leaving England on account of your health?' she asked. He replied with another question: 'What do you and John suppose?' 'We fear that you must have been ill on Sunday, dear General.' 'No, I was not, and you are both very stupid to think so and believe these people.' 'I don't, now. But do tell me, why then do you go?' 'Because I am not wanted,' said Garibaldi.[41]

On the same day, Palmerston wrote to the Queen that though Garibaldi had accepted invitations to visit a large number of provincial towns, 'those who have taken an interest about him, and especially Lord Shaftesbury, thought that politically, and with regard to his health, it was very desirable that these visits should not be made.' Mr Fergusson had given a written opinion that these visits to the provinces would be harmful to Garibaldi's health, and Garibaldi's friends had therefore decided that Garibaldi should return at once to Caprera with the Duke of Sutherland in the Duke's yacht, and that they would leave next Friday. 'This,' Palmerston told the Queen, 'is on every account a good arrangement.' Lord Granville, the Lord President of the Council, agreed, and wrote to the Queen that Garibaldi's departure 'will be a comfort to most people, always excepting Lord Granville's Ducal female relations.'[42]

The Queen thought that it was high time that Garibaldi left, especially after she had read the report in *The Globe* of the speeches of Garibaldi and Mazzini at the lunch at Teddington.

It appears to the Queen [she wrote to Granville on 21 April] that the object for which it was declared that the Government should receive and honour Garibaldi, namely that of keeping him out of dangerous hands, has hardly been attained when he boasts himself to have been the pupil of Mazzini, after calling upon Ledru-Rollin and Louis Blanc.[43]

Granville wrote to the Queen immediately to explain the government's attitude.

Garibaldi has all the qualifications for making him a popular idol in this country. He is of low extraction, he is physically and morally brave, he is a good guerilla soldier, he has achieved great things by 'dash', he has a simple manner with a sort of nautical dignity, and a pleasing smile. He has no religion, but he hates the Pope. He is a goose, but that is considered to be an absence of diplomatic guile. His mountebank dress, which betrays a desire for effect, has a certain dramatic effect. His reception at Southampton and in London shows that no amount of cold water would have damped the enthusiasm of the middle and lower classes. His political principles, which are nearly as dangerous to the progress and maintenance of real liberty as the most despotic systems, are thought admirably applicable to foreign countries. The joining of the aristocracy, including some

Conservative leaders, in demonstrations in his favour, although making the affair more offensive and more ridiculous to foreign nations, has been of great use in this country. It has taken the democratic sting (as to this country) out of the affair.

He denied that the red cloth had been put down for Garibaldi at Stafford House; it was only the red carpet which was always there.

The Duke of Sutherland . . . likes Garibaldi, but he says he cannot comprehend how he can be a good general or an able organizer. He described his belongings, the doctor, the secretary and the eldest son, as ruffians. He has the real merit of getting him away. The ladies of the family and Lord Shaftesbury are temporarily a little out of their minds.[44]

On 19 April, Cowen arrived from Newcastle, in response to Mazzini's summons, and visited Garibaldi at Stafford House. He tried to persuade Garibaldi to stay and go ahead with his provincial tour; but Garibaldi told him that Gladstone had made it clear that the British government were embarrassed by his presence, and Garibaldi stated that he would not stay in England as an unwelcome guest. According to Cowen, Garibaldi told him that he had never felt in better health at any time in his life; but whatever Garibaldi may have said, it is clear from the statements of both Mrs Chambers and Herzen that he was suffering from exhaustion, if not from ill-health, at this time.[45]

Meanwhile the Mazzinians had told the press that Garibaldi was being forced to leave England by the British government because of pressure from Napoleon III, and that Fergusson's statement about Garibaldi's health was an excuse. The allegation about Napoleon III is certainly not borne out by Clarendon's confidential report to Queen Victoria on his talk on the subject with the Emperor, and it was immediately denied by the government. Palmerston stated in the House of Commons that Garibaldi's health had been affected by his heavy round of social engagements in London, and by the late hours which he was obliged to keep, which were upsetting to Garibaldi, who normally went to bed at 8 pm and rose at 2 am. Palmerston added that Garibaldi had still not fully recovered from the wound which he had received 'two years ago' – he tactfully did not specifically refer to Aspromonte. The Glasgow Herald and other newspapers made a strong attack on Cowen's Newcastle Daily Chronicle for suggesting that so eminent a surgeon as Fergusson could have been persuaded to issue an untrue medical report at the request of the government. But Garibaldi's regular medical attendant, Dr Basile, informed the press that in his opinion Garibaldi was well enough to go to the provinces. A protest

GARIBALDI AT THE CRYSTAL PALACE, 1864

THE MEETING OF GARIBALDI AND TENNYSON
AT FARINGFORD HOUSE, ISLE OF WIGHT, 1864

GARIBALDI IN TRAFALGAR SQUARE, 1864

demonstration against Garibaldi's expulsion was held at Primrose Hill in London, but it was broken up by the police.[46]

To the distress of the Mazzinians, Garibaldi spent his remaining time in England with the aristocrats and the Establishment. He left Stafford House and stayed for a few days with Seely at his town house at 26 Prince's Gate. Mrs Seely fell even more in love with him than the two Duchesses of Sutherland. A reception was held for him at Seely's house on the evening of 19 April. Herzen, who had visited Garibaldi there during the afternoon, but was unable to spend more than a few minutes alone with him, stayed for the reception, at Garibaldi's insistence, and watched the guests arrive. He later wrote mockingly about the Right Honourables and the Lordships who were so solemnly announced as they stepped down from their carriages, and of the many MPs, each of whom seemed to be bringing with him three ladies belonging to three different generations. An endless number of guests seemed to be arriving, and their carriages blocked Kensington Gore. They all queued up to be presented to Garibaldi, who stood near a little sofa and shook hands with each guest as he arrived. After a while he became very tired, and sat down on the sofa for brief moments to rest before rising again to greet another guest; but eventually he became so tired that he could no longer rise, and greeted his guests sitting down.[47]

Next day Garibaldi drove through great crowds from Prince's Gate to the Guildhall, where he was given the Freedom of the City of London. He thanked the Lord Mayor in a speech in English, in which he referred to his collaboration with the British forces in Montevideo and to the kindness which he had received from the British residents in China, as well as to the help which the British people had given to him during his campaigns for the liberation of Italy. The crowds outside the Guildhall were so great that Menotti was unable to gain admission, though Ricciotti was at Garibaldi's side throughout the ceremony. On 21 April Garibaldi went with Panizzi to visit Ugo Foscolo's tomb at Chiswick. Panizzi, who hated the Mazzinians so much that he would not even speak to Mazzini when he met him in the street, spent the journey from the British Museum to Chiswick urging Garibaldi to go home as soon as possible; and he persuaded Garibaldi not to make a speech to the crowds who had gathered to see him at Ugo Foscolo's tomb, on the grounds that it would be an impropriety for him to do so. After a lunch at the Reform Club, where one of the trustees, Lord Ebury, referred to him, in his speech, as an instrument of God, Garibaldi visited the House of Lords. The peers received him with every mark of respect. Samuel Wilberforce, the Bishop of Oxford, who had recently distinguished himself by his vigorous opposition to Darwin's theory of evolution, and was one of the most reactionary churchmen in Britain, was particularly demonstrative in his warm welcome of Garibaldi. 'Soapy Sam' and Garibaldi could at least agree in detesting the Pope.[48]

In the evening, Garibaldi attended a banquet at the Fishmongers Hall. Menotti and Ricciotti were not allowed in, because they were not wearing evening dress; they had thought that they would be dining with some fishmongers at a dockside restaurant, and had dressed accordingly. As they were the subject of the ninth toast of the evening, the Prime Warden hastened to find them and assure them that they would be welcome in any dress; but they had already left. Garibaldi appeared among all the guests in their full evening dress, wearing his red shirt, and escorting the Dowager Duchess of Sutherland. After the dinner he shook hands, sitting down, with another 350 guests who had not been invited to the dinner. Among them was Lady Ouseley, his old admirer in Montevideo. Garibaldi had not been able to accept Ouseley's invitation to visit him at his house in Berkeley Square; but Lady Ouseley had come without her husband to see him for a moment.[49]

Next day, on 22 April, Garibaldi left London at 3 pm and went to stay with the Duke and Duchess of Sutherland at their country house at Cliveden in Buckinghamshire. His last morning in London was a busy one; after having breakfast at the United States Consulate, he visited, in succession, Mazzini at his home in Onslow Terrace in what is now South Kensington and the Prince of Wales at Stafford House.[50] The Prince – the future King Edward VII – who was aged twenty-two, had insisted on meeting Garibaldi, though the Queen his mother was intensely displeased, and afterwards made her feelings very plain to him. The Prince explained to her that though he realized that she could not meet Garibaldi, he saw no harm in his doing so. 'I called at Stafford House & went in by the garden gate, so that not a soul saw me either go out or in', he told the Queen, and he had thought that as Garibaldi had left Stafford House it would not be known that he had met him there; but the visit was in fact reported in the press, and warmly welcomed by nearly every newspaper.

> I was much pleased with him [wrote the Prince to his indignant mother]. He is not tall, but has such a dignified & noble appearance, & such a quiet & gentle way of speaking, especially never of himself, that nobody who sees him cannot fail to be attracted by him. . . . He speaks French very well – better than any Italian I have yet heard.

Queen Victoria was particularly annoyed that the Prince had discussed the Danish war with Garibaldi, because the Queen, unlike her son and her Danish-born daughter-in-law, supported Prussia and Austria against Denmark. The Prince told the Queen that Garibaldi referred to Denmark, & said how much he felt for all the brave soldiers who had perished in the war – He also said he felt for the Austrian & Prussian soldiers who had also fallen – as *they* were not to blame for the war. He ended by begging me to present 'ses hommages' to you – & he asked also a great deal after dear Alix [Alexandra, Princess of Wales] & wrote his name for her on a piece of paper, as Alix begged me to ask him for it.[51]

Garibaldi not only expressed his respect for Queen Victoria in his talk with the Prince of Wales, but also made a favourable reference to her in his speech at the Crystal Palace. His admiration for England led him to exempt Queen Victoria, like Victor Emanuel, from the criticisms which he levelled at monarchies, and to take the surprising attitude, with which the Queen certainly did not agree, that Britain under Victoria could be classed as a republic, because the Queen was loved by the majority of her subjects.[52]

McAdam, who like Garibaldi was a Freemason, came to London to present him with a message of greeting from the Masonic Lodge St Clair in Glasgow, and to give him a walking stick as a gift from the working men of Glasgow. When McAdam arrived at Stafford House, Garibaldi was talking to the Prince of Wales; and as Garibaldi left London immediately afterwards, McAdam followed him to Cliveden, where he met Garibaldi just as Garibaldi and the Duchess of Sutherland, and her daughter the Duchess of Argyll, were leaving in the Duchess of Sutherland's carriage to visit Prince Albert's model farm at Windsor. Garibaldi recognised McAdam and spoke to him, and the Duchess of Sutherland asked him to wait and make himself at home until they returned. McAdam walked around the garden, though the police and the detectives guarding the house told him that they had orders not to admit 'men of your stamp'. When Garibaldi returned, McAdam gave him the message from the Lodge St Clair and the walking stick, and Garibaldi told McAdam how much he regretted being unable to visit Scotland.[53]

Garibaldi spent a quiet weekend at Cliveden, and on Monday 25 April visited Eton with the Sutherlands for a brief visit to the school. He travelled in a coach-and-four with the Duke, the Duchess and the Dowager Duchess, and was greeted by the Provost and the Headmaster and a group of distinguished people, among them Mrs Gladstone. He stayed for only ten minutes, driving round the school yard with the boys clustering around him, trying to shake his hand, and clinging to his carriage in very dangerous positions. Some of them still held on as the carriage, gathering speed, drove off down the road, until the last remaining boy tumbled off into the road. Surprisingly, none of the boys was hurt.[54]

Next day Garibaldi left Cliveden for Cornwall with the Duke and Duchess of Sutherland, and after visiting the naval base at Weymouth, and attending civic receptions at Exeter and Plymouth, he went on to Penquite near Fowey, the home of his old friend Colonel Peard, who had fought under him in 1860 and had impersonated him so successfully in the final stages of the advance on Naples. On 28 April he sailed from Fowey in the Duke of Sutherland's yacht, the *Ondine*, accompanied by the Duke, Ricciotti and Basile, and returned to Caprera. 'Garibaldi, thank God! is gone,' wrote Queen Victoria to the Crown Princess. Menotti and Guerzoni, who had not accompanied Garibaldi to Cliveden and Cornwall, travelled separately to Caprera. According to the Mazzinians, the Duke had planned to take Garibaldi on a cruise to the Middle East, hoping to get him out of the way; but Garibaldi insisted on being taken to Caprera.[55]

Before Garibaldi left England, his aristocratic admirers organized a fund to provide him with money, as a tribute to his achievements and to relieve his poverty. The Duke of Sutherland presided at a meeting at Stafford House to launch the fund, and the money poured in, the Duke and Seely giving £200 each, and Palmerston giving £100. The Mazzinians thought that it was a bribe to get Garibaldi to go home, or perhaps a kind of conscience money. Garibaldi had told the Prince of Wales as early as 22 April that he would refuse to accept the gift, and on 6 May it was announced that all the money would be paid back to the donors after deducting the organizers' expenses.[56]

The Mazzinians felt bitter about the cancellation of the provincial tour and Garibaldi's acquiescence in it. In Warwick, Blyth and Manchester the cancellation of the meetings, after everything had been arranged, did some harm to the Italian cause. 'It is very provoking,' wrote Mrs Chambers to Cowen, 'Manchester had promised £6,000. I know we could get £5,000 out of Liverpool, and so on.' She thought that Garibaldi had lost the opportunity of raising £140,000 which could have been used to buy arms for his next campaign. But J. M. McFarlane, of the *Glasgow Herald*, wrote to Cowen that if Garibaldi had visited the city, 'there would have been trouble in Glasgow', as the demonstration planned by the working men's council on his arrival would have been 'a general shouting exhibition of the advanced Radical type.'[57]

Manning stated that if Garibaldi had gone on his provincial tour, there might have been riots. It was one thing to have him in London, where the Catholics were a small minority of the population; 'but London is not Manchester, and Manchester is not Liverpool, and Liverpool is not Glasgow. The follies of the last month may pass off quietly in London, where the minority to be goaded and insulted is as one in twenty; not so where they are one in four, or one in three.' He declared that Garibaldi was a Socialist, who had hoped to see the English people 'stimulating and assisting the seditious and Socialist revolutions which at this present moment threaten every government, absolute or constitutional, throughout Europe'. Manning wondered whether the Duke of Sutherland had realized that he was inviting the principles of 1789 to Stafford House; and he reminded his readers of the blasphemous Radical in Naples who, when Garibaldi was there in 1860, had stuck up above Garibaldi's photograph the letters 'INRI' – Joseph of Nice, Redeemer of Italy.[58]

Mazzini and his British friends tried to organize a campaign of protest, and wrote a pamphlet accusing Gladstone of having forced Garibaldi to go home in order to please Napoleon III. But on 24 May Garibaldi wrote a letter to the editor of the newspaper *Il Movimento* of Genoa, which had published an article from the *Morning Post* about the controversy in Britain over his departure. Garibaldi's letter, which was published, stated that he had gone to England only in order to repay a debt of gratitude which he owed to the English people, and that there had been no pressure of any kind to induce him to leave. This threw the Mazzinians in England into consternation. They decided that in view of Garibaldi's statement, it would be impossible to publish their pamphlet about his departure. 'So with the help of Garibaldi himself,' wrote Mazzini's friend, C. A. Taylor, on 11 June, 'Gladstone, Seely, Shaftesbury will triumph. The saddest part of the affair is Garibaldi's part in it.'[59]

The bitterest comment came from Mazzini's friend, Emilie Venturi.

Garibaldi has done much to pervert the moral sense of the Italians [she wrote to Cowen on 29 June]. His admirers are so dazzled and blinded by his glory on the only place where he is great – the battlefield – that they lose all perception of the painful fact that wherever moral courage is required, he is utterly deficient. He has no respect for truth or friendship; at the slightest difficulty or irritation, he abandons his word, or his friends, and all men cry bravo! because he is a great soldier. I know no subject more painful and depressing to me than the contemplation of the careers of Mazzini and Garibaldi, and the effect produced by each on our toadying, cowardly generation.[60]

It seems clear that neither the British government nor the Mazzinians told the whole truth about the reasons for Garibaldi's departure. Palmerston's statement in the House of Commons, that the only reason was Garibaldi's state of health, was not true; and although John Morley in his biography of Gladstone in 1903, made strenuous efforts to maintain that Gladstone did not use his influence to get Garibaldi to go, he ignored the evidence. But the Mazzinian version, that Garibaldi was in perfect health and was compelled to go by Gladstone and the government, is not reconcilable with the evidence of Mrs Chambers and of Herzen, to say nothing of Fergusson's statement, nor with Garibaldi's letter to *Il Movimento* of 24 May. Garibaldi was sufficiently tired for a reputable specialist like Fergusson – whom Colonel and Mrs Chambers considered was a pro-Mazzinian and was first called in by them – to be able to state, in perfect good faith, that Garibaldi's health would be seriously endangered if he went ahead with his tour of the provinces, even though Dr Basile took a different view. The Mazzinians, on the strength of Cowen's statement, seem also to have exaggerated the personal role of Gladstone, as opposed to that of the Duke of Sutherland and Seely. Garibaldi's statement to *Il Movimento* shows that another factor in the situation was that Garibaldi was not prepared to be used as a pawn by Mazzini and his English friends, any more than he was prepared to let anyone stop him from visiting Herzen, Ledru-Rollin and Louis Blanc.

Garibaldi's statement to *Il Movimento* was his last word on the subject. He made no reference whatever, in his memoirs, to his visit to England.

CHAPTER 37

THE WAR OF 1866: THE VISIT TO GENEVA

GARIBALDI stayed at Caprera for only six weeks. On 19 June he sailed for the island of Ischia, just outside the entrance to the Bay of Naples, where he stayed for a short holiday and rest cure. Very few people were prepared to believe that this was the real reason for his visit to Ischia; the press and the agents of foreign governments reported that he had gone there to plan an expedition to the Balkans. Victor Emanuel had sent an emissary to London in April, when Garibaldi was there, to get into contact not only with Garibaldi but also with Mazzini and the Hungarian refugees, in order to instigate a simultaneous uprising in Poland, Hungary and Dalmatia; but though Garibaldi met the Hungarian leader, Klapka, at Cliveden, nothing came of these negotiations. On 14 July Garibaldi returned from Ischia to Caprera. From now on, whenever Garibaldi left Caprera, every government in Europe became anxious, and feared that he would attack somewhere.[1]

On 15 September 1864 the Italian government signed a treaty with Napoleon III, under which Napoleon III agreed to withdraw all French troops from Rome within two years, and the Italian government guaranteed the inviolability of the frontiers of the Papal States. At the same time, the Italian government agreed to remove the capital from Turin to Florence, in order to make it clear that they were not planning to establish the capital in Rome. The treaty was violently attacked, both by the Pope and the French Catholics on the one side, and by Garibaldi and the Mazzinians on the other, who continued to call for the immediate liberation of Rome and Venice.

Napoleon III's spies sent constant reports about Garibaldi's plans to invade Venetia, Tyrol or Dalmatia. In May 1865 both the Austrian and the French governments received reports of preparations by a joint committee of Mazzinians and Garibaldini to invade Venetia. The Mazzinians were alleged to be preparing an insurrection in the Friuli in Venetia, with the full support of Garibaldi, who was intending to lead the expedition. The spies who sent the report afterwards claimed to have discovered that the invasion had been abandoned because of quarrels between Garibaldi and Mazzini.[2]

Italy now received aid from an unexpected quarter. Prussia, under Bismarck, was preparing to go to war with her Austrian ally in order to settle, not merely their quarrel over the spoils of Schleswig-Holstein, but also the question as to who was to control the German Confederation and be the master of Central Europe. Bismarck offered Italy an alliance against Austria, promising Venetia to Italy as a reward for her assistance in the war which he was preparing. By this enterprising stroke of policy, Bismarck, who had always been an inveterate enemy of European Liberalism and revolution, became the instrument by which the final stages of the *Risorgimento* were achieved, and not only compelled Austria to fight on two fronts in the war, but weakened the influence in Italy of Napoleon III and France, Bismarck's next intended victim.

Bismarck and Victor Emanuel were ready to begin the war by the beginning of June 1866. Victor Emanuel and his Prime Minister, General La Marmora, thought that they could again make use of Garibaldi, now that the moment had come to liberate Venice. 'I soon forget injuries,' wrote Garibaldi in his memoirs, 'and the opportunists realized this.' On 10 June General Fabrizi, who had always been a friend of Garibaldi, came to Caprera to invite him, on behalf of Victor Emanuel, to serve in the war against Austria, and also urged, on behalf of the Left-wing Opposition to which Fabrizi belonged, that Garibaldi should forget Aspromonte and fight once again for Italian liberation. Garibaldi agreed, and sailed from Caprera on the same day.[3]

Victor Emanuel's original plan had been for Garibaldi to command an expedition of 30,000 men whom Admiral Persano was to transport to Dalmatia, and who would open up a third front against Austria in the Balkans; but La Marmora objected, and to Garibaldi's disappointment the plan was abandoned, though Garibaldi believed, somewhat optimistically, that 30,000 men in Dalmatia, who would be joined by the local population, could have finished off the Austrian Empire in 1866. Instead, as in 1859, Garibaldi was sent to wage a guerrilla war in the Alps. The area of his operations was the mountainous country on the frontier of Italy and Austria to the west of Lake Garda, in the district, fifteen miles wide, between the lake and the Giudicarie valleys. He was placed in command of about 10,000 men and a flotilla on Lake Garda, consisting of one warship. The Austrians had 16,000 men in the area and eight warships on the lake. These were larger forces than had been involved in Garibaldi's campaign in the Alps in 1859; but the new Kingdom of Italy was able to place larger forces in the field than the old Kingdom of Sardinia. Victor Emanuel and La Marmora had 350,000 men under their command, of whom 210,000 were in the battle area, 120,000 being stationed along the Mincio, and 90,000 on the Po. The Austrians, with their main armies facing Moltke's Prussians in Bohemia, could spare only 80,000 men to fight the Italians.[4]

Garibaldi established his headquarters at Salò, on Lake Garda, and after issuing a proclamation in which he called on his soldiers to show themselves worthy of Victor Emanuel, 'the hope of all Italy', he advanced north-westwards into the Tyrol; but within a week the regular army on the Mincio had clashed with the Austrians at the Battle of Custozza, the site of Radetzky's victory in 1848. The incompetent Austrian army, which had been defeated by the French in 1859 and was about to be defeated even more decisively by the Prussians, was nevertheless good enough to beat a superior number of Italians, when the Italians were fighting under Victor Emanuel's regular generals and not under Garibaldi. On 24 June the Italians were routed at Custozza, and fell back twenty miles, retreating across the Mincio. Garibaldi received orders from La Marmora to retreat from the Tyrol, and to evacuate the southern shore of Lake Garda; but he disregarded these orders, and having occupied Lonato and Desenzano, on the south side of Lake Garda, on 26 June, two days after Custozza, he decided to try to hold both villages, and wait there for any Austrian attack. The attack did not come, and after a week Garibaldi felt able to renew the offensive, and advanced into the Tyrol.[5]

On 3 July he marched north from Salò, intending to capture the Caffaro and the Austrian position on the heights of Monte Suello. He launched the attack on Monte Suello at 3 pm; he afterwards stated that it might have been wiser to wait until next morning, after his troops had rested after their march from Salò. The Austrian troops in the area consisted of Tyrolese riflemen, who proved to be tougher adversaries than any Austrian troops whom he had faced in his earlier campaigns; and they were led by an able commander, General Kuhn. They were also better armed than his own men, who as usual had been provided with antiquated muskets by the Italian High Command. Garibaldi's attack on Monte Suello was repulsed, and he suffered heavier losses than the defenders, losing 14 killed and 66 wounded. He himself was struck in the thigh by a bullet as he was directing operations, and because of his wound he was forced to retire from the battlefield and leave Colonel Corte in command. At the end of the day, the Austrians still held Monte Suello, though Garibaldi's other units had succeeded in capturing Bagolino and the Caffaro.[6]

On this same day, 3 July, the war was decided by the Prussian victory at Königgrätz in Bohemia, after which Moltke's armies advanced rapidly on Vienna. The main body of the Italian army did nothing more in the Seven Weeks War, and the fleet under Admiral Persano was annihilated by the Austrian navy at Lissa off the Dalmatian coast on 20 July; but Garibaldi advanced into the Tyrol, winning and losing a number of skirmishes against an enemy who was far more able than Urban, and who, unlike Urban in 1859, himself used guerrilla tactics against Garibaldi. Garibaldi acted on the principle, which he considered always applied in warfare in mountainous country, of occupying the heights and making no attempt to advance in the valleys; and the only thing which disconcerted the brave Austrian Tyrolese was to see the Garibaldini above them, higher up the mountain.

Garibaldi himself was too incapacitated by his wound to be able to walk, or to mount a horse, and had to direct operations sitting with his foot up in a carriage.[7] He was able to entrust the execution of his orders to a number of reliable subordinate commanders – the Prussian Radical, General Haug, who had been with him in Rome in 1849; Avezzana; Colonel Chiassi; and Menotti Garibaldi. Ricciotti, now aged nineteen, fought in his first campaign.

On 21 July the Garibaldini fought their fiercest battle of the campaign at Bezzecca, some ten miles north-east of Garibaldi's head-quarters at Storo. The Austrians attacked Garibaldi's vanguard under Haug, and after some hard fighting the Garibaldini, who were in danger of being surrounded, retreated in some disorder. The retreat was not a rout, but the Garibaldini suffered unnecessarily heavy casualties because of the manner of the retreat. As usual, the arrangements for treating the wounded were grossly inadequate, and McAdam in Britain published horrifying reports of their sufferings, and appealed for volunteers to help Jessie Mario and the nurses;[8] but Garibaldi at least had the benefit of the assistance of a Swiss doctor, Appia, and a team of helpers sent by the Swiss Red Cross. Appia brought a number of horse-drawn ambulances, each capable of holding eight men, five lying down and three sitting in the coupé. Two of the beds in the ambulances were above the other three, and could be lowered by levers to the level necessary to enable the patient to be lifted in and out of the ambulance.

Appia and his team joined the Garibaldini in time to render good service at the battle of Bezzecca. Appia met Garibaldi on the day before the battle, on the road near Storo, where Garibaldi spent the day from 6 am onwards reviewing his whole army, who were lined up along the road while Garibaldi drove past in his carriage. Next day, on 21 July, the Swiss doctors moved forward as they heard the sound of the battle. As they approached, they met Ricciotti galloping towards them; he had come to find them, and told them that they were urgently needed up in front, as there were many wounded men at Tiarno. Appia found them in the village church, lying on straw, some of them in great pain. Every minute, two or three wounded men were brought in on two-wheel hand-carts from the direction of Bezzecca, three miles to the north-east. The litters went endlessly from the church to the carts and from the carts to the church. Soon the church was so full of wounded men that it was difficult for the medical orderlies to avoid stepping on them. Appia was able to prevent the army surgeons from carrying out a number of amputations, because he believed that only in the most exceptional cases was it necessary to carry out amputations on the battlefield. He authorized only two amputations at Tiarno.

During the afternoon, the Garibaldini launched a series of counter-attacks. Haug, Ricciotti and Chiassi led their men against the Austrian positions at Bezzecca, but were repeatedly repulsed. Garibaldi himself arrived at Tiarno in his carriage, and drove on from there towards Bezzecca, although the road was under bombardment from the Austrian artillery. As he advanced, he became involved in the thick of the fighting, with units of Garibaldini and Austrians fighting all around his carriage. He remained completely cool and unruffled. He said, as he had said at Salto and Calatafimi: 'Here we will conquer or die.' In the last hour of the battle, Chiassi, leading the Garibaldini in one last attack, was killed.

According to Garibaldi and Guerzoni, the Garibaldini succeeded in regaining all the ground which they had lost in the fighting earlier in the day, and won a victory at Bezzecca; but Appia states that despite the valour of Haug, Ricciotti, Chiassi and their men, all the counter-attacks failed, and that Bezzecca cannot be considered to be a victory for Garibaldi. It is universally agreed that neither side was in a position to renew the fighting next day, so it is clear that the results of the action of 21 July were indecisive. The losses were heavy. Garibaldi lost 500 killed and wounded – as many as at the Villa Corsini in 1849 – and 400 of his men were taken prisoner. The Austrian losses in killed and wounded were about the same as Garibaldi's, but only 100 Austrians were taken prisoner.

Next day, Garibaldi discovered that one of his regiments had spent the whole of 21 July immobile a few miles away, within earshot of the gunfire at Bezzecca, because their commanding officer had not received any orders as to what to do. Garibaldi placed him under arrest and ordered him to be court martialled for neglect of duty. He states in his memoirs that if a commander hears gunfire, or knows that a battle is in progress, it is in all cases his duty to march towards the battlefield and go to the assistance of his comrades, unless he has received express orders not to do so, even if he has no ammunition, as he will always be able to pick up the ammunition of the dead men on the battlefield. Garibaldi also court martialled, on Appia's advice, a surgeon who had carried out an amputation in a hut near the battlefield at Bezzecca, which in Appia's opinion was unnecessary, or at least could have been postponed until the wounded soldier had been taken to a base hospital.[9]

Kuhn had suffered so heavily in the fighting at Bezzecca, and in his action against Fabrizi at Condino, that he felt unable to continue resistance in the area; and as Garibaldi moved his headquarters forward to Pieve di Ledro, Kuhn prepared to withdraw from the district, evacuating Riva and falling back on Trent.[10] But on 25 August Garibaldi received orders to withdraw, as the war was over. Bismarck had decided to grant the Austrians a soft peace, wishing to preserve Austria as a chastened ally and junior partner in Central Europe; and he insisted that though Austria must cede Venetia to Italy, she should retain South Tyrol. The loss of Venetia was a bitter blow to Austria, although it was agreed, to assuage Austrian pride, that Austria should cede Venetia to France, who would then give it as a gift to Italy.

There was great indignation throughout Italy at the peace terms. The Italians wished to liberate the Tyrol as well as Venetia, and were affronted at having to receive Venetia as a gift from Napoleon III. But when Bismarck declared that he intended to sign a separate peace with Austria if Italy did not accept the terms, Victor Emanuel and La Marmora gave way, because after Custozza and Lissa it was obvious that they could not continue the war alone; and Italy reluctantly adhered to the peace terms. When Garibaldi received the orders to withdraw from the Tyrol, he sent his famous one-word telegram to La Marmora: '*Obbedisco*' (I obey). Mazzini and the Mazzinians accused him of having once again betrayed the Italian cause to Victor Emanuel, and argued that he should have marched on either Vienna or Florence and proclaimed the Republic. Garibaldi, in his memoirs, dismissed this as 'the usual complaints of the Mazzinians'.[11]

Venetia was liberated at last. On 18 October 1866 it was ceded by Austria to France, and after being part of the French Empire for twenty-four hours, it was ceded next day by France to Italy. The usual plebiscite gave a majority for union with Italy of 647,246 votes against 69. South Tyrol remained Austrian territory for another fifty-three years, and was not acquired by Italy until 1918.

After the conclusion of peace, Garibaldi returned to Caprera, where he stayed for four months, during which time he again enraged the French Catholics by sending a contribution to the cost of erecting a monument to Voltaire in France under the auspices of the French Liberal newspaper, *Le Siècle*.[12] In February 1867, to the alarm of every Foreign Office in Europe, he left the island again. On 13 February the Italian Parliament, which now sat in Florence, was dissolved, and new elections were fixed for 10 March; and on 22 February Garibaldi sailed from Caprera and arrived in Florence. On the evening of his arrival in the new capital, he issued a statement to the press, calling on all Italians not to vote for candidates who were enemies of freedom or satellites of the fallen dynasty of Naples, and declared that 'the priests are subjects and soldiers of a foreign power'.[13] He himself was as usual nominated in several constituencies, although he had not attended a session of Parliament since his attack on Cavour in April 1861. Instead of taking his place in Parliament, he wrote letters from time to time to the President of the Chamber, and arranged for one of the other Left-wing MPs to read out the letter in the course of a debate. In these letters, Garibaldi demanded, in somewhat peremptory language, that Parliament should insist on the government changing its policy on some matter or other. This method of procedure did not make a good impression on the majority of MPs, who thought that Garibaldi was acting like a king sending messages from the throne.

On 24 February Garibaldi left Florence by train for Venice, a city which he had never visited in his life, though he had tried so hard to reach it in 1849. He was accompanied by Teresita and her husband, Canzio, and by three Left-wing politicians. He stopped at Bologna, where he received a great welcome from the population, and made a speech from the balcony of the San Marco Hotel, which was owned by Ugo Bassi's sister. Next day he and his party went on to Ferrara, where he received another great ovation from the crowds which filled the vast square in front of the Strozzi Palace. In his speech, he called on the population to vote for his doctor, Riboli, in the general election.

He proceeded towards Venice, being greeted by great crowds at Rovigo, the first stop in Venetian territory, where he declared, in his speech, that the slogan in the elections must be 'War on clericalism'. At 5 pm on 26 February he reached Venice, and received a welcome which exceeded even the reception which he had received in Palermo, Naples and London. The people filled the streets and the gondolas on the canals. They pressed so closely around him that it was feared at one moment that he might be crushed to death, but, alone of all his party, he did not show any alarm. An American woman presented him with the Stars and Stripes. Two beautiful women in a gondola blew kisses at him. According to the Italian press, they were two ladies from the highest ranks of society, one of them being a Venetian and the other representing the people of unliberated Trent; but the French Catholic writers stated that they were two well-known local prostitutes.

Garibaldi made a speech from the balcony of the Mayor's house, where he was staying. 'You belong to a great country,' he told the Venetians, 'but our country still lacks one tit-bit, Rome.' Rome must become the capital of Italy; 'Rome is ours, and ours legally, so we can go to Rome as we can go into a room in our own house.' He said that although they could easily go to Rome with arms in their hands, he hoped that it would not be necessary to do this; they should go there legally, and at the general election the Venetians must elect MPs who would voice this demand in Parliament. After his speech, a section of the crowd attacked and damaged the palace of the Cardinal Patriarch, who, according to the Catholic propagandists, was rescued from the rioters by his 'devoted ones'.

Garibaldi repeated this demand for Rome in a speech next day at Chioggia, where he met one of the fishermen who had sailed with him in the boat which was driven ashore at Magnavacca in 1849. The seamen of Chioggia elected Garibaldi as their MP in the general election. But these demands for Rome caused anxiety to foreign governments, especially since the last French troops had left Rome in December 1866 under the provisions of the treaty of 15 September 1864.[14]

After leaving Venice, Garibaldi went to Verona, in Venetia, where he received another great welcome from the people of the liberated city. In Verona there occurred an incident which was widely reported, particularly in the Catholic press in France; a woman in the crowd brought her three-week-old baby to him, and asked him to baptize it. The Catholic newspapers reported that Garibaldi put his hand on the baby, and said: 'I baptize you in the name of God. May Christ, the Legislator of Humanity, bless you. Grow up to be free and virtuous, and an enemy of hypocrites, whether they call themselves priests or Jesuits. Be free of prejudices, and prodigal with your blood if your country requires it. Kiss me. I salute you.' The mother then asked him what name they should give to the child, and Garibaldi said 'Chiassi', after his officer, Colonel Chiassi, who had been killed at Bezzecca.

Next month, at Alessandria, Garibaldi baptized three children, though this time by remote control. As he was leaving Alessandria after another great reception, a friend reminded him that he had promised to baptize three babies. Garibaldi wrote in pencil on a sheet of paper: 'In the name of God and of the Legislator, Jesus, name your children by the glorious names of three martyrs for the Italian cause – Rottini, Lombordi, Cappellini. 14 March 1867.' The Catholic propagandists denounced these Garibaldi baptisms as hideous blasphemy. Garibaldi's supporters did not deny that they had taken place, but claimed that they had been misinterpreted.[15]

In the summer of 1867, the hostility between Garibaldi and the Catholic Church rose to new heights. Garibaldi made no secret of the fact that his target was Rome and the one province of the Papal States which still remained to Pius IX. As the French troops had been withdrawn from Rome, he could no longer claim that he was fighting against the foreigner, so he directed his attack against the Papacy and the priests, who, he claimed, had always been the agents of the foreign and domestic oppressors of Italy. The Catholic hierarchy throughout the world, but particularly in France, sounded the alarm, and called on all Catholics to rally to defend the Pope against Garibaldi. The French Catholic writer, Mirecourt, published a biography of Garibaldi in which he attacked him viciously, sneering at him as the 'limping general' who had hobbled along 'cloppety-clop' throughout his Tyrolean campaign of 1866. Mirecourt thanked God for sending Garibaldi his frequent attacks of rheumatism, as a punishment for his sins and in order to hinder, for a time at least, his campaign against the Holy Father.[16]

Garibaldi did not return to Caprera during the spring and summer of 1867, but remained on the mainland, to the alarm of the Catholics and of the governments of Europe. He spent the time quietly resting at San Fiorano, near Parma; but though he himself might be resting, it was clear that the Papal States were being threatened. A secret Centre of Insurrection was set up in Rome, being largely under the control of the Mazzinians, in association with the Committee of Romans in Emigration at Bologna. The refugees in Bologna published the proclamations of the Centre of Insurrection in Rome, which announced that they would shortly issue a call for an armed uprising in Rome, and expected to receive assistance, when that time came, from their brothers in free Italy. In March, the Centre of Insurrection offered Garibaldi the post of 'Roman General', and invited him to lead the insurrection. Garibaldi accepted. The proclamation of the Centre of Insurrection of 1 April 1867, which announced his acceptance of the post, stated that Garibaldi had been appointed Commander-in-Chief of the armies of the Roman Republic on 2 July 1849, and that he was now about to make Rome the capital of Italy.[17]

The Left-wing parties had done well in the general election, and Rattazzi had become Prime Minister. Once again, as in the year of Aspromonte, a Left-wing government under Rattazzi half-encouraged and half-restrained Garibaldi as he planned to march on Rome. Pius IX and his Secretary of State, Cardinal Antonelli, protested to Napoleon III against the action of the Italian government in tolerating Garibaldi's preparations on Italian soil for an attack on the Papal States. On 15 April Rattazzi made a long-awaited statement in Parliament about the situation; but his only comment about Rome was that 'time will solve the question', which was capable of being interpreted in more ways than one.[18]

In June, forty young revolutionaries crossed the frontier of the Papal States and attacked a police station at Terni. They were taken prisoner, and a letter of encouragement from Garibaldi was found in their possession. There were fresh protests to Rattazzi from the French government. The Pope formed a legion of volunteers, which was known as the Antibes Legion, to protect the Papal States now that the French troops had been withdrawn. The commander of the Legion, General Dumont, and several members of the Legion, were serving officers and soldiers of the French army. When some of the rank-and-file of the Legion deserted, General Dumont warned them, in a speech on the parade ground, which was reported in the press, that as they were still members of the French army, they could be court martialled for desertion after they returned to France. Dumont's speech created an international incident, with both the Italian and the British government protesting to France that by creating the Antibes Legion, Napoleon III had broken the Franco-Italian treaty of 15 September 1864 under which he had promised to withdraw the French troops from Rome.[19]

In July, Garibaldi went into action again. On 15 July he visited Pistoia, and on 11 August Siena, being received in both towns with the usual enthusiasm. He was getting nearer to the frontiers of the Papal States. On 27 August he arrived at Orvieto, where he had been received with so much enthusiasm in 1849 during his retreat from Rome. At that time, Orvieto was in the Papal States; now it was in Italy five miles from the Papal frontier. Garibaldi made a speech at Orvieto, in which, after denouncing the Jesuits and Napoleon III, he declared: 'Without Rome, Italy cannot be.' He received a great ovation from the crowd, in which some soldiers of the Italian army, who were standing in the square listening to him, joined enthusiastically. The soldiers shouted: 'We want Rome! Long live Italian Rome!' Turning to the soldiers, Garibaldi said: 'With me or without me, you must go to Rome.'[20]

Suddenly, to everybody's surprise, Garibaldi announced that he was going to Geneva for the Congress of Peace. The Congress of Peace had its roots in an attempt, which had been made by a few advanced thinkers in the years after the Napoleonic wars, to persuade the Great Powers to renounce war as an instrument of policy and settle disputes by arbitration and peaceful negotiation. The first Congress of Peace had been held in Geneva in 1820, and had been followed by similar Congresses in London and elsewhere between 1843 and 1850; but by 1867 such ideas attracted much more support than in earlier times, though they were still rejected as utopian by European statesmen. A committee for convening the Congress of Peace was established in Paris, and it was decided to hold the Congress at Geneva from 9 to 13 September.

A number of prominent persons accepted the invitation to attend.

Apart from Garibaldi, they included the Genevan elder statesman, James Fazy, who had first participated in politics as a Radical student in Paris during the Hundred Days in 1815, but by 1867 had become a Right-wing Liberal; the French Radical historian, Edgar Quinet, who had resigned his professorship at the Collège de France in Paris and had emigrated to Switzerland when Napoleon III came to power; the Hungarian revolutionary, Colonel Frigyesi, who had fought under Garibaldi in 1866; the moderate Liberal, Prince Dolgorukov, and the famous novelist, Dostoievsky, as well as Herzen and the Anarchist leader, Bakunin, from Russia; the German Radical, Goegg, who had been Minister of Finance in the revolutionary government of Baden in 1848; and the Swiss Anarchist Guillaume, who represented Marx's International Association of Working Men. The country least adequately represented was Britain, for only Cremer and Odger, two trade unionist members of the executive committee of Marx's International, attended the Congress. The call to hold the Congress had been supported by John Stuart Mill and by the Quaker and Cobdenite Peace Committee, which exercised some influence in British politics; but Mill and the Peace Committee refused to attend at the last moment, chiefly because in the preliminary programme the convening committee had listed, among its objects, the achievement of a 'free democracy', and had refused to change 'free democracy' to 'liberty' at the request of Mill, who knew that 'democracy' was an objectionable word in British politics. Jessie Mario was present as a press correspondent for several British newspapers. Not surprisingly, Mazzini refused to come. He wrote to the Congress to say that what was needed was a people's war of liberation against tyrants, and not talk of peace.[21]

It was clear to some observers, even before the Congress opened, that there were likely to be disagreements, because two different trends of thought were represented. The one consisted of Liberals like Fazy, who wished to persuade the governments of Europe that it would be in their interests to avoid war and settle international disputes by peaceful means; and the other, of Radical Republican revolutionaries, who believed that wars were caused because kings forced their unwilling subjects to fight for their dynastic interests, and that the only way to avoid war was to overthrow the European monarchies by revolution, and establish a federal union of European democratic republics.

As far as the population of Geneva was concerned, by far the most interesting thing about the Congress was that Garibaldi was attending it; but although his acceptance of the invitation had been published in the press, there was a good deal of speculation as to whether he would in fact be coming. He was known to have accepted invitations before, and then not come, and the organizers appeared to be very vague about when he would be arriving. Many Catholics thought that his acceptance of the invitation was a trick, and that at the time when he was expected to be in Geneva, he would in fact be leading an invasion of the Papal States. But on 5 September it was announced that he would be arriving on the evening of Saturday the 7th.[22]

Garibaldi travelled by train from Orvieto. At Florence, Milan and Domodossola his train was delayed by the great crowds which gathered to greet him, and his arrival at Geneva was postponed until the Sunday morning. At Lausanne, 1,500 people crowded the station platform and the railway line in order to see him. The train stopped at every wayside station between Lausanne and Geneva, and Garibaldi got out of the train, drank a glass of the local wine with the peasants, and allowed the children, at their mothers' request, to touch him. When he reached Geneva, the square outside the central station had been packed to capacity already two hours before 9.30 am, when his train was due to arrive.

As he entered his carriage amid the cheers of the crowd, an unfortunate incident occurred, reminiscent of what had happened at Nine Elms in London. Fazy, who headed the reception committee and made the welcoming speech at the station, was supposed to sit beside Garibaldi in the carriage; but Barni, the chairman of the organizing committee of the Congress of Peace, pushed Fazy aside and sat down beside Garibaldi in the carriage, so that there was no room for Fazy, who had to travel in another carriage. The Radicals afterwards attributed Fazy's subsequent attitude at the Congress to his resentment at having been excluded from Garibaldi's carriage.

The carriage moved down the Avenue Mont Blanc from the station to the lake, with the snow-capped summit of Mont Blanc visible in the far distance ahead. Every window in the wide street was full of people waving and cheering. Garibaldi arrived at the Hotel Dumont on the lakeside, and appeared on the balcony with Fazy and other notables of Geneva. He made a speech to the large crowd. He thanked Switzerland, the land of 'the nephews of Rousseau, the descendants of Tell', for the asylum which she had granted to him in 1848 and to so many other political refugees, and continued: 'The magnificent reception which you have given me in your city perhaps makes me a little too bold. Someone will perhaps say that I have committed an impertinence.' Then, amid cries of 'No, no!' he said that he would tell the truth 'in the country from which freedom of thought spread out across all the European plains like the streams which pour out of your glaciers'. The people of Geneva had been the first to attack 'that pestilential

institution which is called the Papacy'; and he asked them to join him now, 'when we give the final blow to the monster.'[23]

Garibaldi may have thought that Geneva, the city of Calvin, was solidly Protestant; but in the city, and in the countryside of the small canton which surrounded it, half the population were Catholics in 1867, and their leaders were outraged by Garibaldi's words. Already that same evening there were shouts of 'Down with Garibaldi!' from the crowds who assembled beneath his window at his hotel. Next day, another large crowd assembled to see him arrive at the Electoral Palace – today the Salle du Conseil Général – in the Place Neuve for the opening session of the Congress. The speeches on the first day showed the clear split between the moderate Liberals and the revolutionary delegates; while Fazy and Schmidlin, the Director of the Central-Suisse Railway Company, spoke in favour of peaceful co-operation between states, Guillaume, representing Marx's First International, called for the revolutionary overthrow of capitalism as being the only way of avoiding war, and the French refugee lawyer, Acolles, denounced Pius IX and Napoleon III as enemies of humanity.[24]

When Garibaldi rose to address the Congress, he accepted the President's suggestion that he should speak from his place, as 'the consequences of his glorious wounds' made it impossible for him to go to the rostrum. In his speech, he put forward an eleven-point programme to prevent future wars.

1 All nations are sisters. 2 War between them is impossible. 3 All quarrels which may arise between nations shall be judged by the Congress. 4 The members of the Congress will be nominated by the democratic societies of all the peoples. 5 Each nation will have one vote in the Congress, whatever its population may be. 6 The Papacy, being the most harmful of sects, is declared to be overthrown as a human institution. 7 The religion of God is adopted by the Congress, and everyone of its members undertakes to propagate it across the world's surface.

When a delegate interrupted Garibaldi to ask what he meant by the religion of God, Garibaldi replied: 'Religion of God, religion of truth, religion of reason, are synonymous.'

He then declared his four remaining points.

8 The Congress ordains to the priesthood the men of the élite of science and intelligence. 9 Propaganda for democracy, by instruction, education and virtue. 10 Only democracy can remedy the scourge of war by overthrowing lies and despotism. 11 Only the slave has the right to make war, against tyrants.

Garibaldi ended his speech by saying that some of his remarks about religion might be a little controversial, but they should remember that the Crimean War, which involved four nations and cost 200,000 lives, was started by two priests, one a Greek Orthodox and one a Roman Catholic, who had quarrelled about the right to hold their religious services in the Temple of Jerusalem. This was a somewhat over-simplified explanation of the dispute between France and Russia as to which of them should be the protector of the Christian holy places in the Turkish Empire, which was one of the causes of the dispute which led to the Crimean War. [25]

While the discussions at the Congress became increasingly un-friendly, and soon degenerated into wrangles between the Left and the Right about points of procedure, the Catholics in Geneva mounted a campaign against Garibaldi. Under the leadership of Monsignor Mermillod, Bishop of Hebron, whose diocese included Geneva, they organized protest deputations to the city and cantonal authorities and to the Federal government in Berne, and called for a great demonstration against Garibaldi in front of his hotel. They claimed that Garibaldi, coming to Geneva on the pretext of taking part in a Congress of Peace, had abused Swiss hospitality by attacking the Pope, who was both the head of a foreign sovereign state and the religious father of all Swiss Catholics. There were also many non-Catholic Swiss who, being as always very sensitive to any infringement of Swiss neutrality, were alarmed both at Garibaldi's attack on the Pope and at many of the revolutionary speeches and attacks on Napoleon III at the sessions of the Congress, though on the other hand many of them condemned the attempt of the Catholics to suppress Garibaldi's right of free speech. Meanwhile Garibaldi drove to the suburb of Carouge, two miles to the south of Geneva, to visit the Polish revolutionary leader, Count Bossack-Hauké, the hero of the revolution of 1863. A large crowd was waiting to see Garibaldi as he alighted at Hauké's house in the Rue de Lancy. Garibaldi shook hands with Hauké, and, turning to the crowd, said to Hauké: 'I want it to be known that if Jesuit and diplomatic Europe has abandoned you, the democracy will never forget you.' [26]

Next day, Garibaldi left Geneva early in the morning. An hour after his departure, the Catholic placards appeared in the streets, calling on the people to join the demonstration in front of Garibaldi's hotel; the police had prevented the placards from being posted up until after Garibaldi had left. As the Congress was still in session, and Garibaldi was seen off by his reception committee with much less ceremony and publicity than had marked his arrival, the Catholics claimed that he had hastily departed in order to avoid the hostile demonstrations, and claimed the credit for having driven him out of Geneva. Pius IX sent a

578

message of congratulation to the Bishop of Hebron. But Garibaldi and his Radical and Liberal supporters denied the truth of the Catholic boast. They pointed out that Garibaldi had said, in his speech to the Congress on the opening day, that he would not be able to stay until the end of their proceedings; and his departure was certainly not secret, because, though the hour of his departure was not announced in advance, and consequently no large crowd gathered to see him off, he drove to the station accompanied by all the members of the committee, and there were farewell speeches at the station.[27]

Garibaldi's speeches at Geneva shocked Catholic and Conservative Europe. Felix Dupanloup, Bishop of Orleans, the greatest of the French Catholic leaders of the period, appealed to Rattazzi to stop this general bearing the honoured military rank of General Bonaparte, General Menabrea and General MacMahon, this MP, this Italian, from going ahead with his plans, on Italian soil, to make war on the Pope. At Geneva, Garibaldi and his fellow-delegates to the Congress of Peace had demanded 'a religion without cults and without priests', and had opposed to the despotism of sovereigns the universal fraternity of peoples. The conclusion was clear: 'Impiety, demagogy, Socialism, all of these are united today. Garibaldi declares war on the Pope, but also on all sovereigns. . . . Garibaldi is only one of the mouths of the infernal machine with twenty cannon, each of which is aimed against a throne.'[28]

CHAPTER 38

MENTANA

GARIBALDI took the train to Belgirate, where he stayed with Signora Cairoli, and then to Pallavicino's house at Ginestrelle. He reached Florence on 17 September, and made his final plans to attack the Papal States. But his speech in Geneva had convinced Rattazzi that he was about to march on Rome, and on 21 September the government published a proclamation in the Official Gazette, calling on all Italians to respect the authority of Parliament, and not to violate the frontiers of a foreign state. The members of the Committee of Romans in Emigration hurriedly met to discuss what to do. Some said that they should abandon their plans to attack the Papal States; others thought that Rattazzi's statement, by exculpating the government from all responsibility in the eyes of foreign powers, made it easier for the Garibaldini to go ahead with the invasion. Garibaldi decided to go ahead.[1]

On the same day, he issued his order of the day to his volunteers, telling them to invade the Papal States. One body, under the command of himself and Menotti, were to invade from Orvieto in the north; the other, under Nicotera, from the former Neapolitan territory near Tivoli in the south. After crossing the frontier the volunteers were to converge on Viterbo; if they met superior bodies of Papal troops, they were to avoid battle if possible. They were to treat the inhabitants of the Papal States as brothers, and were to avoid fighting the Italian army at all costs.[2] It was twelve days since Garibaldi had made his speech against war at the Congress of Peace in Geneva. He had no doubt in his mind that this campaign against Rome came within Clause 11 of the programme that he had put forward in Geneva; it was a war of the slave against the tyrant.

Next morning, on 22 September, he left Florence by train for the south, his destination being Arezzo and Orvieto. His train was as usual delayed by large crowds at every wayside station. At Compiobbi, the first station where he stopped, he told the crowds, in his speech, that he was on his way to Rome, and he repeated this at the other stations. He stayed the night at Arezzo, where he received a great reception;

in his speech, he thanked the population for having given him a better welcome than in 1849, when they had refused to allow him and his men to enter the town. From Arezzo he wrote a hurried note to McAdam in Glasgow, who was trying, with much less success than in 1860, to organize volunteers and other support for Garibaldi in Britain: 'I count on your activity, and beg you to do much and do it quickly.' Next day he went on to Orvieto, but as his train was delayed by crowds he decided to stay the night of 23 September in the village of Sinalunga, about forty miles north of Orvieto.[3]

The Governor of Perugia had received orders from the government to arrest Garibaldi if he went to Orvieto. When the Governor heard that Garibaldi had left Arezzo for Orvieto, and was staying the night at Sinalunga, he ordered a company of troops in Orvieto to proceed to Sinalunga and arrest Garibaldi. The unit arrived at Sinalunga very early in the morning of 24 September and surrounded the house where Garibaldi was staying. As the lieutenant began to mount the stairs outside the house which led to the room on the first floor where Garibaldi was sleeping, a group of Garibaldini, hurriedly putting on their red shirts, blocked his path in an attempt to protect Garibaldi. The lieutenant arrested them, and went up to Garibaldi's room, where he told Garibaldi, very courteously, that he had orders to arrest him and take him to the prison at Alessandria, near Turin. Garibaldi said that he was about to have a bath, and the lieutenant agreed to wait for half an hour while he had his bath. The lieutenant nearly regretted his consideration, because by the time that Garibaldi had finished his bath and had dressed, the square in front of the house was full of local inhabitants protesting against the arrest, and shouting 'To Rome!'; but fifty of the soldiers held them back from the house, and the lieutenant was able to take Garibaldi to the station of Lucignano at the foot of the hill on which Sinalunga stands. Three of Garibaldi's friends, including Basso, travelled on the train with him. It was still only 6 am when the train left Lucignano for the north.

At Pistoia, Garibaldi's friends were ordered to leave the train, while Garibaldi was taken on to Alessandria; but before the rest of his party left the train at Pistoia, Garibaldi was able to give them a hurriedly written note for publication in the press. '24 September. The Romans have the right of slaves to revolt against their tyrants, the priests. The Italians have the duty to help them, and I hope they will do so, even if the government imprisons fifty Garibaldis.'[4]

Many volunteers were arrested in Orvieto, Siena and elsewhere. Frigyesi was escorted to the Swiss frontier, and deported. A crate belonging to the Garibaldini, containing 298 rifles, with ammunition and bayonets, was seized at the station in Florence. But protests broke out immediately all over Italy. Twenty-five Opposition MPs, including Crispi, Guerrazzi, Fabrizi, Guerzoni and Benedetto Cairoli, signed a protest against the arrest of Garibaldi, which they claimed was a breach of Parliamentary privilege, as Garibaldi was an MP. Radical supporters demonstrated in the streets in Florence, Turin, Genoa, Pavia, Modena, Bologna, Verona, Venice and Naples, shouting 'Long live Garibaldi! Death to Rattazzi! Give us arms!' In Florence, an angry crowd tried to storm Rattazzi's residence. The demonstrations were particularly violent in Genoa, where the troops were called out, and used their bayonets to disperse the demonstrators.[5]

At Alessandria, Garibaldi was treated with great courtesy by the prison governor and by the soldiers who guarded him. His prison consisted of three large and very well-furnished rooms; and though at first the governor had strict orders not to allow any visitors to have access to him, this order was soon countermanded by Rattazzi under pressure from Parliament, and he received many visitors. The soldiers of the Modena Brigade who guarded him at Alessandria demonstrated in front of his prison window, shouting 'Long live Garibaldi, free! Long live Rome, the capital!' Garibaldi, who was deeply touched, went out on to the balcony and addressed the soldiers. 'Yes, my sons, we are going to Rome, but not with your bayonets, because they are not worthy of them; we will sweep them away with the butts of our rifles.' The soldiers cheered loudly. The governor sent a telegram to the government describing what had happened, and the government thought that there had been a mutiny.

Although the French government congratulated Rattazzi on his firmness in dealing with Garibaldi, the Prime Minister was very embarrassed at being obliged to hold Garibaldi in prison, and by the feeling which the arrest had aroused in the country. Two days after the arrest, on 26 September, he sent General Pescetto, the Minister of Marine, to see Garibaldi at Alessandria, and offered to release him if Garibaldi would give his word of honour to return to Caprera and make no attempt to leave the island. Garibaldi rejected the offer. Pescetto then cabled to Rattazzi in Florence that in view of the feelings of the garrison at Alessandria, he did not think that they could hold Garibaldi in custody for very much longer, and that unless he received other instructions from Florence by midnight, he proposed to release Garibaldi unconditionally. Rattazzi cabled back that Garibaldi was not to be released unless he gave his word to return to Caprera and not to try to leave it; but the clerks at the telegraph office at Alessandria had decided to go to bed earlier than usual, and when Rattazzi's cable reached Alessandria just before midnight, there was no one there to deliver it to Pescetto. As Pescetto had not received any instructions by midnight, he released Garibaldi, but took him immediately under escort to Genoa, and at 4 am placed him in a ship bound for Caprera.[6]

The government sent the navy to blockade Caprera. Though Garibaldi was not under arrest or any legal detention on Caprera, the navy prevented him from leaving and any visitor from landing there. On the east of Caprera, where the island faces the open sea, a constant patrol was kept up; on the western side, in the narrow strip of water between Caprera and La Maddalena, and to the west of La Maddalena, between La Maddalena and the island of Sardinia, there was a slightly less intensive watch. All ships leaving and approaching the area were liable to be stopped and searched, and letters to and from Garibaldi were censored. Garibaldi nevertheless succeeded in sending a letter on 2 October to his volunteers on the borders of the Papal States. He asked them to accept his son Menotti as their leader in his absence. But the Garibaldini had not waited for Garibaldi's orders. On the afternoon of 30 September they crossed the frontier of the Papal States, Menotti invading from the north-east, Acerbi from the north-west, and Nicotera from the south. They tried to avoid clashes with the Papal troops and the French Antibes Legion, and established themselves as guerrillas in the mountains; but on 7 October Acerbi occupied the village of Torre Alfina, and, in compliance with Garibaldi's instructions, proclaimed Garibaldi as Dictator in the Papal States and himself as Pro-Dictator.[7]

Meanwhile, off Caprera, on the late afternoon of 2 October, the men of the naval patrol noticed a small rowing boat pushing off from Caprera in the direction of La Maddalena. They called on her to halt, and when she failed to do so, they fired first a salvo of cannon and then a rifle shot across her bows. The boat then stopped, and the commander of the patrol boat discovered that Garibaldi and a few companions were in the boat. He ordered Garibaldi to return to Caprera. Garibaldi asked whether he was being arrested. The officer answered no, but that he had orders to prevent Garibaldi from leaving Caprera. He allowed Garibaldi's friends to proceed to La Maddalena without Garibaldi, but he would not allow them to take a box of Garibaldi's documents with them. The officer believed that there had been a plot to enable Garibaldi to escape, because soon afterwards the steamer from La Maddalena to Genoa passed Caprera, and the officer saw Jessie Mario standing on the bridge waving to Garibaldi, who returned her salute. The officer thought that this was very significant, and promptly sent a full report to his superiors of how, when the steamer passed Caprera, Signora Mario had waved to Garibaldi, and he had waved back.[8]

Garibaldi's friends on the mainland, realizing how important it was to have him in personal command of the volunteers in the Papal States, made their plans to help him escape from Caprera. His son-in-law, Canzio, got in touch with Adriano Lemmi, a wealthy banker in Florence who was a supporter and friend of Garibaldi. Lemmi put up the 4,000 lire needed to buy a little fishing trawler, and with this, Canzio and a few friends set out for the neighbourhood of Caprera to reconnoitre. They had to be very cautious, for they knew that if they were caught by the naval patrol, they would be arrested and their trawler would be confiscated. They sailed round by Elba, Montecristo and Corsica, and on 10 October approached La Maddalena and Caprera from the north; but they could not get through, either to Caprera or to the house of Garibaldi's friend, Mrs Collins, on La Maddalena. At 2.30 am that night they were stopped and boarded by a warship north of La Maddalena, but were allowed to proceed when they told the marines that they were fishermen; and next day they managed to reach La Maddalena, and met a friend of Mrs Collins, who in his turn succeeded in meeting Basso and Teresita in Mrs Collins's house. But the only result of their discussions was that they decided that there was no possibility of arranging Garibaldi's escape, and Canzio and his friends sadly went to Brandinghi on the north-west coast of Sardinia, where they tried to think of a new plan. There, on the morning of 17 October, to their joy and astonishment, Garibaldi arrived, and they heard about his escape from Caprera.[9]

On the night of 13 October, a thick mist covered the area of Caprera and La Maddalena. At 10 pm, Garibaldi entered his rowing boat, alone, wrapped rags around the oars to deaden the sound, and rowed across the narrow strip of water between Caprera and La Maddalena. As usual, a gunboat of the naval patrol was stationed in the narrow channel, and Garibaldi passed so close to her that he could hear the marines talking and could distinguish what they said; but they did not see him in the fog. It reminded him of the night in 1843 when he had sailed as close as this to Admiral Brown's flagship in the Bay of Montevideo on his way from Rats Island to Montevideo. He reached the Punta della Moneta on the east side of La Maddalena, and landed on Mrs Collins's beach, where he hid his rowing boat. He slept at Mrs Collins's house, and remained there all next day; the naval authorities did not know that he had left Caprera. After dark, at 7 pm on 14 October, he rode three miles on horseback across La Maddalena to the little port at Cala Francese on the south-west side of the island; he was accompanied by his friend Susini, who had returned from Montevideo to his birthplace on La Maddalena. They met Basso and a sailor friend, Captain Cuneo, and stayed the night in a house at Cala Francese; and early next morning, they set out for Sardinia in

Cuneo's fishing boat. They were stopped on the way by a naval patrol boat but the marines, who had not been told that Garibaldi had left Caprera, did not recognize him, and Cuneo persuaded them that all the passengers were members of his crew, and that they were on a fishing expedition. To avoid suspicion, they did not cross directly to Sardinia, but went by the island of San Stefano and the Punta Rossa, as if they were fishing, and after six hours landed in Sardinia between Liscia and Araschena.

They spent the night of 15 October and all next day in a grotto near the east coast of Sardinia, and on the evening of the 16th, having obtained horses, they rode across the island, through the wild highlands of Gallura and the wasteland of Terra Nuova – an area which was almost completely uninhabited in 1867. After riding for seventeen hours, they reached the little fishing port of San Paolo near Brandinghi; and Cuneo, leaving Garibaldi to rest in a house at San Paolo, went to Brandinghi, where he contacted Canzio and his friends and told them about Garibaldi's escape. They were all astonished that Garibaldi could have had the strength to ride from Araschena for seventeen hours through the rough and mountainous country. They thought that only a man who had spent his youth among the gauchos of South America could have accomplished such a feat at the age of sixty.

At 3.30 that same afternoon, well refreshed with a good meal of local fish and Tuscan wine, and after Garibaldi had had a good rest, they sailed in Canzio's trawler for Italy. They were outside the area of the naval patrol, who still did not know that Garibaldi had left Caprera, and after sailing by Montecristo and Elba, they reached Vado at 7 pm on 19 October, after a journey of fifty-one and a half hours. They hired two carriages, and travelled to Leghorn, and from there to Florence. Once they were stopped for a routine road check, and Garibaldi gave his name as Joseph Pane. They reached Florence at 11.30 am. The news of Garibaldi's escape from Caprera had been published in the press that morning.*[10]

Later in the day, Rattazzi resigned. Two days before, the French government had informed him that they considered that his failure to prevent Menotti Garibaldi from invading the Papal States constituted a breach of the treaty of 15 September 1864. The French government

---

*This account of Garibaldi's escape from Caprera is based on the story told by Canzio to Cavallotti, and published by Cavallotti in his *Storia del Insurrezione di Roma nel 1867* in 1869. Speranza von Schwartz, in her *Recollections of Garibaldi* in 1884, published an account of the escape by Garibaldi, which she claimed to have taken down verbatim from Garibaldi himself; and Garibaldi wrote a third version in his memoirs. The three versions conflict on a few points of detail.

therefore considered that they were no longer bound by the treaty, and were sending an expeditionary force to Rome to protect the Pope. Rattazzi offered to fulfil his obligation under the treaty of protecting the Papal States from invasion by sending the Italian army into the Papal States to protect them from Garibaldi; but this was too crude an approach, and did not achieve the same result as Cavour's subtleties in 1860. Rattazzi's proposal was indignantly rejected by Napoleon III.[11]

Victor Emanuel asked Cialdini to form a government, while demonstrations were held in Florence and other Italian cities in protest against the French decision to send troops to Rome. Garibaldi spent 21 October in Lemmi's house, and on the 22nd moved to Crispi's house. Crispi and his other friends among the Opposition MPS had discovered that Cialdini had no intention of arresting Garibaldi, but on the contrary wished to meet him; and Garibaldi, Crispi and other MPS issued manifestoes to the press in which they called for volunteers to join Garibaldi and liberate Rome. On the morning of the 22nd, a crowd gathered in front of Crispi's house and called for Garibaldi to appear. Garibaldi made a speech to them, and declared: 'We have the right to have Rome; Rome is ours.'[12]

Garibaldi then visited Cialdini. It is not known what Cialdini said to him. Perhaps he tried to dissuade him from attacking the Papal States, though one theory is that Cialdini encouraged him to go ahead, and discussed plans by which the Italian army could march to his assistance. It seems clear that Victor Emanuel and the government, angered at the French intervention in Rome and alarmed by the patriotic and pro-Garibaldian demonstrations all over Italy, did not contemplate arresting Garibaldi and preventing the volunteers from joining their comrades in the Papal States; and it is certainly possible that Cialdini thought that the best solution now would be to let his old enemy Garibaldi fight it out with the French and get the worst of it.[13]

On the afternoon of 22 October, Garibaldi left Florence for the Papal frontier. On his journey he heard that the right wing of his volunteers, under Acerbi, and the centre under Menotti had joined together, and had defeated the Papal forces at Monte Rotondo, twelve miles from Rome; and on the 24th Garibaldi joined his men at Monte Rotondo. He had last been there eighteen years before, on 4 July 1849, when he had spent his forty-second birthday resting all day, without the French troops in Rome knowing that he and his volunteers were there, and he and Anita had seen the reflection of the sun on the dome of St Peter's. This time he made no attempt to conceal his presence from the enemy, and next day, on 25 October, he attacked the Papal garrison at Monte Rotondo. After three hours' hard fighting, he took the place by storm at 4 am, capturing 300 prisoners. He ordered them all to be given bread and water – the only rations immediately available – and they cried 'Long live Garibaldi!'[14]

But he found, to his disappointment, that he was not joined by the local population in the Papal States, though he could count on their passive support; in a plebiscite organized by the Garibaldini in Velletri on 31 October, the vote in favour of union with Italy was 4,057 against 0. In the city of Rome, the Mazzinian leadership of the Centre of Insurrection started a revolution on 22 October, and Garibaldi sent some of his best men to Rome to join the revolutionaries. The revolutionaries attacked the Capitol and occupied the Piazza Colonna; but the Papal troops of the Antibes Legion drove them back to the Trastevere, and after a last desperate fight in the Piazza di Santa Maria, the revolutionary district was occupied and the revolt suppressed. Thirteen of the revolutionaries were killed, including one of the Cairoli brothers and a boy of twelve. Another of the Cairolis was severely wounded, and taken prisoner, but was eventually released and sent home to die in his mother's arms – the fourth of her sons to die fighting for Garibaldi.[15]

Garibaldi's total forces in the Papal States amounted to about 8,000 men, of whom 6,529 were under Garibaldi and Menotti at Monte Rotondo. Garibaldi occupied a strong defensive position at Monte Rotondo, and waited there for the enemy to attack. On 26 October – the day after Garibaldi had captured Monte Rotondo – the French expeditionary force of 2,000 men left Toulon for Civita Vecchia, while the Papal troops and the Antibes Legion marched towards Monte Rotondo.[16]

The morale of Garibaldi's volunteers was not as good as usual, perhaps because Garibaldi himself had been absent during the first three weeks of the campaign, and Menotti and Acerbi and his other officers did not have his experience at handling men, or at least not the magic of his name. Some of the Garibaldini were as trustworthy as the best of the red-shirts of the earlier campaigns; but others began to grumble after their three weeks' inaction, and there were many desertions. The victories at Monte Rotondo on 22 and 25 October had revived morale, but the dissatisfaction and the desertions continued during the eight days that Garibaldi waited for the enemy at Monte Rotondo. Garibaldi afterwards blamed Mazzini for having incited his men to desert; but this was strongly denied by Jessie White Mario and other Mazzinians, who claimed that, as in Garibaldi's other revolutionary expeditions, his most valiant fighters were mostly Mazzinians.[17]

On 28 October, Rattazzi sent the Italian army into the Papal States on the pretext of maintaining order. When Garibaldi heard the news, he reacted by issuing a proclamation on 1 November which marked a return to a more Republican position than any which he had adopted for thirteen years. His presence once again on Roman soil, and his resentment at Rattazzi's proclamation, reawakened in him the spirit of 1849.

> The government of Florence has invaded the Roman territory which we have acquired with precious blood from the enemies of Italy. We must greet our brothers of the army with nothing but love, and help them to chase from Rome the mercenaries who uphold tyranny. But if they infamously intend to continue the vile convention of September [1864] with Jesuitism, and by an obscene agreement will place their arms in obedience to the orders of the men of 2 December, then I must remind the world that I alone am the Roman General, with plenary powers from the only legal government of the Roman Republic elected by universal suffrage, and I have a right to maintain an army in this territory under my jurisdiction.

Victor Emanuel, who afterwards told the French Minister in Florence, Malaret, that he had intended to attack the Garibaldini and 'massacre them so that not one would be left', was forced to withdraw his troops from the Papal States when he received an ultimatum requiring this from Napoleon III.[18]

On 2 November, Garibaldi set out to march towards Tivoli, intending to link up with Nicotera's forces. In the morning, he reviewed his troops, and told them that they would advance that afternoon. This immediately revived morale, and the desertions stopped; and Garibaldi felt encouraged as he galloped along the whole line of his army drawn up along the Mentana road. He had no idea that the enemy were in the vicinity, and did not even know that the French expeditionary force had arrived in Rome. On the same day, he sent Jessie Mario to Rome to propose an exchange of the wounded prisoners whom he had captured at Monte Rotondo for the wounded Cairoli and the corpse of his brother. The Papal commander agreed to the exchange, but he detained Jessie Mario in Rome. She was therefore unable to let Garibaldi know that the French troops had arrived.[19]

On 3 November, as Garibaldi marched from Monte Rotondo to Tivoli, he met the Papal forces at Mentana, three miles south-east of Monte Rotondo. The Papal troops, who numbered 9,000 men against the 4,652 Garibaldini, attacked Garibaldi's right flank, and Garibaldi ordered his men to take up defensive positions in and around the village of Mentana. As the Papal soldiers advanced through the corn fields, the Garibaldini, sheltering behind haystacks and other cover, put up a stout defence; but though some of the Garibaldini had all the courage of their predecessors in Garibaldi's earlier campaigns, others were less experienced and resolute, and fell back into the village in panic. Garibaldi became anxious about the result of the battle. He decided to bring his artillery into play. This consisted of two cannon at Monte Rotondo, and Garibaldi, hurrying back from Mentana to Monte Rotondo, loaded and fired the cannon himself. The shells did some damage to the Papal troops, and had an even greater effect on their morale; and the Garibaldini, encouraged by the cannonade, took the offensive, and pouring out of Mentana, drove back the Papal troops. By 3 pm the Garibaldini seemed to be at the point of victory; but then the 2,000 French troops of the expeditionary force arrived.

Once again, as in the campaign of 1849, Garibaldi found that fighting against French troops was a different matter from fighting Austrians or Neapolitans. As usual, the weapons of the Garibaldini were inferior to those of their enemy, and the discrepancy was never more marked than at Mentana, where the French riflemen were armed with the new *chassepot* rifle, which had a much longer range than the muskets of the Garibaldini. The French did not advance, but merely fired at the Garibaldini, and their aim was deadly. At about 4 pm, when the November day was beginning to close in, the Garibaldini broke and retreated in disorder. The French continued to fire at the Garibaldini without advancing. Guerzoni wrote that it was a battle between men who fled and men who would not advance.

Old General Fabrizi, who was present, described how several of Garibaldi's officers, including Mario, Frigyesi, Menotti, Missori and Guerzoni, tried to rally the fleeing soldiers, and succeeded in stopping many of them from running away; but Garibaldi himself was less decisive. 'Garibaldi appeared to be transformed,' wrote Fabrizi, 'gloomy, hoarse, pale; only his eye was still firm and clear. . . . I have never seen anyone age so quickly as he did at that moment.' The nightfall saved the Garibaldini from utter destruction. They had lost 150 killed, some of whom had been bayoneted by the French as they lay wounded on the battlefield, and 240 wounded and 900 prisoners. The Papal troops lost 230 killed and the French 26, with 200 wounded.[20]

Garibaldi abandoned all hope of continuing the campaign, and decided to retreat into Italian territory. He succeeded in restoring discipline among his men; but the Garibaldi of 1867 who gave up the struggle after Mentana was not the Garibaldi of the retreat of 1849. Next day, on 4 November, the 3,500 defeated Garibaldini crossed the frontier at Passo Corese, where they surrendered to the Italian army. The remaining Garibaldini in the Papal States surrendered to the enemy, being careful to stipulate that they were surrendering to the French and not to the Papal forces; and they were granted the privileges of prisoners of war. Garibaldi told the Italian commander at Passo Corese that he had given up all hopes of invading the Papal States, and intended to return to Caprera; and he took the train to Leghorn, accompanied by Crispi, who had come to greet him at Ponte di Corese. But the new government of General Menabrea, who had become Prime Minister when Cialdini failed to form a government, decided to imprison Garibaldi. When his train reached Perugia, Garibaldi was arrested, despite violent protests from Crispi, and was taken to the fortress where he had been imprisoned after Aspromonte. On 5 November a government statement in the Official Gazette stated that Garibaldi had invaded the Papal States, in breach of the law, and that although he had asked to be allowed to return to Caprera, 'the King's government, determined to maintain the rule of law and to remove any cause for the disturbance of public order, have thought it necessary to hold General Garibaldi safe in custody at Varignano in the Gulf of Spezia.'[21]

Garibaldi's arrest did not succeed in achieving this object of removing 'any cause for the disturbance of public order'. There were protests from MPs and demonstrations in favour of Garibaldi's release, as there had been after his arrest at Sinalunga six weeks before. This time the government did not give in so quickly to the public clamour; but the United States Minister in Florence intervened on Garibaldi's behalf, and on 26 November Garibaldi was released from prison on condition that he gave his word of honour to return to Caprera and not to leave the island for six months. Garibaldi was now quite willing to give this undertaking, and reached Caprera at 8 pm on 27 November. 'The Revolution personified in Garibaldi' had been finally defeated.[22]

GARIBALDI AFTER HIS SPEECH TO THE WORKERS IN ROME, 1875

GARIBALDI WITH HIS THIRD WIFE, FRANCESCA ARMOSINO

CHAPTER 39

FRANCESCA ARMOSINO

GARIBALDI had given his word of honour not to leave Caprera for six months; in fact, apart from occasional visits to La Maddalena and the island of Sardinia, he did not leave his island for nearly three years. Mentana had caused him, for the first time in his life, to give way to something close to despair. The moral effect of his defeat was greater, on both friends and foes, than any of his previous set-backs. General de Failly, the French commander at Mentana, coolly reported to his government that the new *chassepot* rifle had worked 'marvels'; and the French Prime Minister, Rouher, gave a pledge in the French Parliament that 'Italy will not get possession of Rome; France will never tolerate this violent affront to her honour and to Catholicism'. Two days after Mentana, Queen Victoria wrote in her diary: 'I heard that Garribaldi had been completely routed. . . . This is a great thing.' The French Catholic writer, Mirecourt, gloated that God had preserved Garibaldi's life at Mentana so that he should limp for ever through the world, another Wandering Jew, hobbling on his crutches in a vain attempt to get to Rome.[1]

As a result of the events of 1867, Garibaldi for the first time lost faith in Victor Emanuel, although he had suffered less in 1867 than in 1862 from the actions of the King and the Italian government. This disillusionment with the King was probably largely due to the influence of Garibaldi's son-in-law, Canzio, who was a Left-wing Radical and Republican. In the summer of 1869 Canzio was arrested on a charge of planning a Republican revolt in Italy, and imprisoned at Alessandria. Garibaldi energetically took up Canzio's cause. He briefed Crispi and other prominent Left-wing lawyers to appear for the defence at Canzio's trial, and wrote letters to the press in support of Canzio, as well as writing frequently to Canzio in prison to comfort and encourage him. In one of his letters to Canzio he declared that 'when a government breaks all their promises, and acts arbitrarily, the people have the right to revolt'. The government released Canzio under an amnesty after he had spent some months in prison.[2]

Although Garibaldi lived a very simple life on Caprera, subsisting largely on the milk and fruit which he produced on his farm, he was nevertheless in need of money, having spent all the profits of his voyages as a sea-captain in the years between 1851 and 1855, and having at last, in 1866, settled his debt to Denegri in New York for the takings of his voyage to China. He decided to earn money by writing a novel, which he began in the winter of 1866–7 after his return from his campaign in the Tyrol. His name alone was of course sufficient to ensure that the book was accepted by publishers in Italy, Germany, Britain and the United States; and though he did not receive the large advances which any author in his position would receive today, he made a considerable amount of money from the book. It was called *Clelia, or The Rule of the Monk (Rome in the Nineteenth Century)* – a title which appealed to British Protestant readers as much as to Italian Radicals and Freemasons.

The heroine of the story, Clelia, is the daughter of a Left-wing sculptor of the Trastevere in Rome, and is known throughout the district as the 'Pearl of the Trastevere'. But it is a dreadful fate for any girl in Rome to be born beautiful, for she is then likely to fall a victim to the agents of Cardinal Procopio – a thinly veiled portrait of Cardinal Antonelli – who kidnap the beautiful girls of Rome and take them off to the Cardinal's brothel. In Clelia's case, she falls into the Cardinal's hands because her father Manlio, the honest sculptor, is arrested on a charge of being a revolutionary, and Clelia goes to the Cardinal to beg for mercy for her father. The Cardinal proceeds to make love to her; but she scornfully repulses him, and threatens to stab herself if he ventures to approach her. She is rescued in the nick of time by the arrival of her lover and another young revolutionary, who kill the Cardinal and his two henchmen.

Apart from Clelia, there are other heroines. One of them is Camilla, a peasant girl from the countryside near Rome, who was 'too beautiful and too innocent to live in safety near this metropolis of corruption', and had been noticed by the Cardinal's agents. She, too, barely escapes being raped. Another is Julia, a girl from an aristocratic English family, who is in Rome studying art, and falls in love with a young Italian revolutionary artist. On many occasions in the book Garibaldi praises Julia's English virtues, and on one of these occasions he digresses into a panegyric of the British as a nation and an apologia for British imperialism. 'The British race has its vices and defects – for who is perfect among the human family? But if there is a people whom I am pleased to compare with our ancient fathers of Rome, it is certainly the English. Being egotists and conquerors, like our ancient fathers, their history overflows with crimes – crimes committed on their own shores and on the shores of other nations. Many are the peoples whom they have enclosed in their iron coils in order to satisfy their insatiable thirst for gold and domination; but I cannot deny that they have contributed enormously to human progress and to laying the foundations of individual dignity, and that they present a picture of man standing upright, inflexible and majestic in the face of all the compelling exigencies that govern the human race.' Above all, he praised the English for their part in freeing the negro slaves.

Clelia, Julia and their lovers take refuge in the woods and mountains, where they encounter a notorious bandit chief; but he befriends them, and tells them his life-story, from which it transpires that he only became a bandit because he was being hunted by the police, who wished to arrest him for assaulting a priest who was trying to rape a girl. Afterwards they take refuge on a small island which is undoubtedly Caprera. Here 'the small number of inhabitants make police and government superfluous, and the absence of priests is the greatest blessing of the island. God sees himself worshipped as he should be, with the cult of the spirit, without pomp, in the magnificent temple of nature that has the sky for a dome and the stars for lights'.

The head of the family who inhabit the island is called 'the Recluse'. 'He is a man like other men, with his fortunes and misfortunes. He has had the luck to have been able sometimes to serve the cause of the people. Like all human beings, he has his share of defects. He is a cosmopolitan, but passionately loves his own country, Italy, and Rome he loves to adoration. He hates the priests as a lying and mischievous institution', but will eagerly forgive all priests who renounce the priesthood and turn to a life of honest toil. He is a Republican, but does not wish to see the republic governed by five hundred governors; he believes that the people should choose some leader to rule them as Dictator. 'But woe to those who, instead of a Cincinnatus, choose a Caesar!' The Recluse 'wishes the Dictatorship to be limited to a fixed period, and only in an exceptional case, like that of Lincoln in the recent war of the United States, will he consent to its prolongation. In no case will he agree to it becoming hereditary. But this is not the only system. He thinks that the system which he really desires for the majority of nations is the English system of government, which is the equivalent of a republic.'

On the island, the fugitives find safety and complete happiness for a time; but the young men, knowing that beautiful women will forgive sin, but never cowardice, in a man, return to the mainland to fight for freedom under the Recluse. The last part of the book is an account of Mentana and the Roman insurrection of 1867, in which the heroes are killed, because not even for the love of Clelia and Julia will they escape and relinquish the opportunity to die a martyr's death for

Italy. Julia takes Clelia to live with her in England, where they vow that they will not return to Italy until Rome is freed from the priestly plague.[3]

Garibaldi finished the novel in 1868, and sent a copy of the manuscript to Speranza von Schwartz, so that she could arrange for a German translation to be published. She thought that the novel was so bad that she travelled to Caprera in order to try to persuade Garibaldi not to publish it in any language. She seems to have succeeded in causing him to have second thoughts about whether to publish it, because it was not in fact published until two years afterwards, in 1870; but Garibaldi told her frankly that he knew that he was not a great novelist, and had written it only to make money. When the book appeared, it received some very bad reviews in the better-class literary papers. The London *Saturday Review*, which had been one of the few journals to ridicule the popular acclamation which Garibaldi had received during his visit to London in 1864, published a particularly devastating criticism of the crudity of the propaganda and the characterization, and stated that this 'strange mixture of absolute childishness with genuine heroism would make Garibaldi a far better hero, than author, of a romance'.[4]

In fact, *Clelia* is not as bad as it is generally thought to be. It is better than many popular novels of the period. Even more than Garibaldi's other writings, it suffered severely in the English edition; for the translator not only translated Garibaldi's Italian very freely into grandiloquent and stilted English, but also added whole passages of his own, so that the English version is nearly twice as long as the Italian. Nearly all the most ridiculous phrases and passages are found only in the English edition. Garibaldi's text was written in a comparatively simple, straightforward style which was considered in the nineteenth century to be a sign of lack of writing ability, but is today thought to be in better taste than the rodomontade of many nineteenth-century authors. There is an exciting narrative, and some of Garibaldi's digressions into politics and moral philosophy throw an interesting light on his outlook and character; and it brought in some much-needed money.

In the same year, Garibaldi published another novel, which he had written after he had finished *Clelia*. The title was *Cantoni il volontario*, and is the story of Cantoni, the volunteer, who joins Garibaldi's forces in 1848. Real people, such as Garibaldi himself and Anita, come into the novel, as well as the fictional characters. This mixing of real and fictitious characters and events was of course very common in the nineteenth-century historical novel; but the unusual feature of *Cantoni il volontario* is that the fictional episodes occupy a very small part of the book, which consists chiefly of a description of real events during the period covered by the story, from Garibaldi's arrival at Leghorn in October 1848 to the disaster at Magnavacca and Anita's death in August 1849. For this reason, it is definitely a better book than *Clelia;* but, unlike *Clelia*, it was not translated into English, or into any foreign language except French and German.

Garibaldi needed the money which he obtained from his books because he had once again become entangled in personal difficulties with women. After his unhappy experience with Guiseppina Raimondi in 1860, he turned his back on the elegant aristocratic ladies who had attracted him in the first years after his return from the United States, which was probably the reason why he failed to respond to the encouragement which he received from his society hostesses during his visit to London. He settled down with his housekeeper Battistina Ravello in Caprera, and though he could not marry her, because he was married to Giuseppina Raimondi, he executed a document in which he accepted Anita, his daughter by Battistina, as his legitimate child. This had the effect, under Italian law, of legitimizing Anita, and making her father Garibaldi, and not her mother Battistina, her legal guardian. But soon after the birth of Anita, Garibaldi was informed that Battistina was having an affair with a young man on La Maddalena. Garibaldi was very angry, and Battistina left Caprera, taking Anita with her, and returned to her native town of Nice, where she and the child lived on an allowance provided by Garibaldi.[5]

Garibaldi's daughter Teresita had married Canzio when she was only sixteen, after Canzio returned to Caprera with Garibaldi from the war of 1859, and before he sailed with the Thousand to Sicily.[6] In the autumn of 1862, when Garibaldi and Canzio were prisoners after Aspromonte, Teresita was pregnant with her third child, who was born when Teresita was just nineteen; and by the time that she had reached the age of twenty-seven, she had given birth to nine children. She brought a nursemaid to Caprera to help her to look after the children. The nursemaid was a young peasant woman, Francesca Armosino, who, to judge from her photograph, had no trace of refinement or beauty, but was a shrewd and domineering character. She soon became Garibaldi's mistress. On 16 February 1867 she gave birth to Garibaldi's daughter, who was conceived shortly before Garibaldi left Caprera for the campaign in the Tyrol, and was born six days before he left again for his visit to Venice and his political and military campaigns of 1867. The daughter was named Clelia, after the heroine of the novel which Garibaldi had begun to write shortly before her birth.

Francesca Armosino had so forceful a personality that nearly every-

one who knew her either liked or disliked her very much. Her friends
and her enemies tell a very different story about her background and
her relations with Garibaldi. According to Speranza von Schwartz,
who disapproved of her as much as she did of Battistina, she had had
an illegitimate child as a result of a casual affair with a soldier; but
Mrs Chambers told McAdam that exhaustive inquiries in Francesca's
native village in Piedmont had established that this allegation was
false. Speranza states that Teresita was so disgusted that her nursemaid
had become her father's mistress that she left Caprera and went to
live in Genoa with Canzio; and certainly Francesca's relations with
Anita Garibaldi's children became so bad that Teresita, Menotti
and Ricciotti all left Caprera soon after Francesca came to live
there.

On 5 December 1875 Mrs Chambers wrote a long letter to McAdam
giving details about Garibaldi's three marriages. Her accounts of
Garibaldi's marriages to Anita and Giuseppina Raimondi are such a
travesty of the truth that one is tempted to reject her story about
Francesca as equally unreliable; but it must be remembered that
though Mrs Chambers was not at Laguna in 1839 or at Fino in
1860, she spent much time in Caprera when Francesca first came
there.

According to Mrs Chambers, Garibaldi's relationship with Teresita
became strained at the time when Francesca arrived. Teresita had
given birth to a boy, who was named Lincoln after Abraham Lincoln,
and, like several of Teresita's children, died in infancy. Teresita wished
to engage a wet-nurse to feed the baby. Garibaldi, like many other
nineteenth-century Radicals, strongly objected to wet-nursing as a
particularly flagrant example of the oppression of the poor by the rich,
and he was encouraged in this attitude by Mrs Chambers, who had
had a guilty conscience about wet-nursing ever since she herself had
employed a wet-nurse whose child had died, perhaps as a result.
Teresita was so upset by Garibaldi's refusal to allow her to have a
wet-nurse that she became a little unbalanced. She complained that
she was disturbed by the noise made by Garibaldi's four guinea-fowls,
to whom Garibaldi was greatly attached. Without telling Garibaldi,
she gave orders that the fowls were to be killed and served up for
dinner; but Garibaldi was so distressed by the death of the fowls
that no one in the household would eat them.

Garibaldi eventually gave way to Teresita's pleas and allowed her
to have a wet-nurse; but he could not forgive her either for the wet-
nurse or the guinea-fowls. Mrs Chambers states that it was soon after
this that Teresita, who had at first thought very highly of Francesca,
began to resent Francesca's friendship with Garibaldi. She accused

Francesca of stealing the produce at Caprera; and after the real thief had been discovered, and Francesca vindicated, Teresita accused Francesca of being Garibaldi's mistress. When Ricciotti returned to Caprera from England, he made fresh accusations against Francesca; but Garibaldi reacted to the unjust attitude of Teresita and Ricciotti by falling in love with Francesca. Soon Francesca was the mistress of Caprera, and Teresita and Ricciotti had departed.[7]

Both Mrs Chambers and Speranza von Schwartz are so unreliable that it is impossible to believe either version of the rights and wrongs of the family disputes which arose from Garibaldi's relationship with Francesca. It is equally unsafe to accept Speranza's story about his daughter Anita, though most readers of Speranza's *Recollections* have been so antagonized by Speranza's affectation of callousness that they have interpreted her actions, not in a favourable, but in the worst possible light.

There had been a second flowering of Speranza's friendship with Garibaldi. After her disappointment in 1859 and 1860 about his marriage to Giuseppina Raimondi and his affair with Battistina, their relations had become sufficiently strained that when he wrote to her about the German edition of his memoirs, he began his letters, no longer '*Speranza mia*', but '*Gentilissima Signora*'. During 1863 their correspondence became warmer; and Garibaldi, having begun his letter of 4 March 1863 '*Gentilissima Signora*', was writing '*Speranza carissima*' by 17 July.[8] Next year, Speranza visited Caprera again. Her chief reason for going was to take steps for the welfare of Garibaldi's daughter Anita, who was then aged five. Speranza, who had always objected so strongly to Garibaldi's association with Battistina, was distressed that Anita was in the charge of an uneducated and immoral peasant girl like Battistina, and urged Garibaldi to entrust Anita to Speranza's care, so that Anita could be brought up as an educated lady of quality.

In the sorry story of his daughter Anita, Garibaldi showed as much hesitation, and was as liable to be influenced by the latest person to see him, as in the days when he was taking political decisions as dictator in Naples. After much hesitation he allowed Speranza to persuade him to use his parental authority to order Battistina to hand over Anita to Speranza, and appointed Speranza as Anita's guardian, though both Battistina and Anita strongly objected when Anita was removed from her mother, at the age of nine, and placed by Speranza in a school for young ladies at Winterthur in Switzerland. When Battistina reluctantly came to Caprera to hand over Anita, the child sobbed and rolled hysterically in the sand; and when Speranza took her to the mainland, she struck Speranza in public. Speranza, who had nineteenth-century

German ideas about the upbringing of children, thought that Garibaldi was much too lenient with Anita, and that the girl needed the strict discipline of the school in Winterthur.

But the school caused more problems than it solved. Garibaldi found, to his disgust, that Anita was acquiring expensive tastes and a snobbish attitude in the establishment for young ladies in Winterthur. He wrote to Anita and to the headmistress to say that he could neither afford, nor would he tolerate, that Anita should be trained to lead an idle life of luxury. He turned strongly against Anita. He endorsed all Speranza's complaints about his daughter, wrote that Speranza had done much more for her than she deserved, refused to read Anita's letters, and stated that if he could use Anita as a crutch with which to walk, with his rheumatism, she might be of some use in the world. He eventually agreed to Speranza's suggestion that she should take Anita to her house in Crete; and Anita, having been almost forcibly removed from her protesting mother on the grounds that she would thereby receive a good education, seems to have ended up as Speranza's unpaid servant in Crete.[9]

There were other illegitimate children. As long as his wife Anita lived, Garibaldi does not seem to have been conspicuously unfaithful to her. Although he made her jealous by flirting with other women, there is no evidence of his having had mistresses and bastards, apart from the story of Lucía Esteche at Santa Lucía in Corrientes, which rests only on the unreliable source of local tradition. In the first years after Anita died, he showed no interest in women; but after his return to Italy from his second exile in 1854, when he was aged forty-seven and had been a widower for five years, his old interest revived. Most of his famous love affairs took place during this period, and rumour made out that the affairs were far more numerous than they really were. By the 1870s, many young men and women in Nice and Genoa were writing to Garibaldi, claiming that he was their father. Garibaldi asked his old friend and officer of the Thousand, Luigi Coltelletti, to handle the matter. The correspondence with these real or pretended bastards was kept in the Coltelletti family for fifty years; but soon after the First World War, Coltelletti's son, Giuseppe Garibaldi Coltelletti, burned all the letters with the help of his little boy, the present Comandante Coltelletti.[10]

On 10 July 1869 Francesca Armosino gave Garibaldi a second daughter, whom they called Rosa after Garibaldi's mother and his daughter Rosita who had died as a child in Montevideo. Some of Garibaldi's friends and neighbours spread malicious gossip about Rosa's parentage. Garibaldi was only sixty-two when she was born, but he had aged greatly in the past few years, and the combined effect of his

Aspromonte wound and of his rheumatism had made him virtually an invalid. The gossipmongers said that he could not have procreated a child, and that Garibaldi the philanderer had now become Garibaldi the cuckold.[11] But Garibaldi was about to show that his active life was not quite over.

THE FRANCO-PRUSSIAN WAR

I<small>N</small> July 1870 Bismarck skilfully manoeuvred Napoleon III into launching an unprovoked attack on Prussia. Political observers throughout the world, who did not know that Bismarck had opened a bottle of champagne to celebrate when he heard that the French had declared war, rightly considered that France was the aggressor. Most Liberals and Radicals strongly sympathized with the Germans, even under the reactionary Bismarck, in their fight against the hated enemy, Napoleon III. But Victor Emanuel and his government, who had Napoleon III to thank for giving them Lombardy and Bismarck to thank for Venetia, were motivated by other considerations. They offered to enter the war on France's side if Napoleon would withdraw his troops from Rome and allow them to annex it. Napoleon refused. He repeated his pledge to protect the Papal States, where at this very time, in July 1870, the doctrine of Papal Infallibility was being proclaimed by an Oecumenical Council; and despite the pressure on French manpower caused by the war against Germany, he maintained the French garrison in Rome.

The Italian government therefore maintained a policy of strict neutrality, while continuing to hint to Napoleon III that Italy might join France for a suitable reward. But among the Left-wing Opposition and the Garibaldini, sympathy was strongly pro-German. Many of Garibaldi's former officers and volunteers went to the Prussian legation in Florence and offered to fight against France. Bismarck neither needed nor wanted Garibaldini volunteers to supplement Moltke's large and well-equipped armies, and preferred to win the goodwill of the Italian government by informing them of the offers of the Garibaldini, and that they had been declined; but as he told the Italian government, quite truthfully, that Garibaldi himself was not among the officers who had volunteered to fight, the Italian government believed that Bismarck was hiding the fact that Garibaldi had volunteered because he was planning to make use of his services. In August the Italian government was alarmed by a report in *The Times* that the Prussian Chargé d'Affaires in Florence had paid a secret visit to Caprera; and the

Italian government, knowing of Garibaldi's hatred for Napoleon III and his resentment over his defeat at Mentana, was sure that he was intending to lead an expedition to capture Nice or to raid the south of France, or otherwise to help the Germans in some way. They therefore sent a naval patrol to prevent Garibaldi from leaving Caprera; and on 2 August Garibaldi wrote to his friend Biassioli that he was once again a prisoner on Caprera.[1]

On 1 September the German armies annihilated the French at Sedan, taking prisoner Napoleon III and 82,000 soldiers. Three days later, revolution broke out in Paris, and the Third Republic was proclaimed under the leadership of Gambetta and Left-wing Radicals. The new Republican government immediately withdrew the French garrison from Rome. Within a fortnight, Victor Emanuel had informed the Pope that he was sending his armies to occupy the Papal States in order to prevent the outbreak of revolution there. When Pius IX indignantly rejected Victor Emanuel's offer of protection, the Italian army, one division of which was commanded by Bixio, marched on Rome, and, showing less consideration for the Roman historical monuments than the French had shown in 1849, blew a breach in the Aurelian Wall and bombarded the city defences. As usual, the action of the Italian government was criticized from both sides; while the Catholic propagandists accused Bixio of deliberately turning the blind eye and continuing the bombardment when the Papal government raised the white flag of capitulation on St Peter's, Jessie White Mario, with equal indignation, accused the Italian government of ordering Bixio not to bombard the Vatican, but to direct his fire at other objectives.[2]

It was a sweet revenge for Bixio, the old Garibaldino of 1849; but for reasons of international policy, as well as from their normal motives of personal envy, it was essential for the Italian government to prevent Garibaldi from having any share in the final liberation of Rome. The naval blockade of Caprera was intensified. As for Mazzini, he travelled from London to Sicily in the summer of 1870; but in this hour, when the dream of a united Italy and a free Rome, which he had first put forward forty years before, was at last being realized, he was arrested by the Italian police and held in prison at Gaeta for several months, though in due course he was released, and spent the last months of his life in Italy.[3]

Meanwhile the French Republican government had opened peace negotiations with Bismarck; but they found, to their dismay, that Bismarck was not disposed to be any more lenient to a Republican government than he would have been if Napoleon III had still been in power. He demanded the cession of Alsace and Lorraine to Prussia, the surrender of Belfort and the border fortresses, and the payment of a large indemnity. When Jules Favre, the French Foreign Minister, protested that it was unjust to punish the new French Republic for the aggression of Napoleon III, Bismarck replied that he liked Napoleon III personally, and that if Favre made difficulties about agreeing to his terms, he would reinstate Napoleon III as Emperor and sign a peace treaty with him. The French rejected the terms, and prepared to carry on the war as a people's war in defence of the Republic against German imperialism.

The sympathies of the international Republicans and Radicals swung round to France's side. Already on 23 August, before Sedan, Garibaldi had written to a friend that Napoleon III, and not the French people, was the enemy, and he now shared the universal sympathy of international revolutionaries for Republican France. As usual, he decided, unlike the others, to show his sympathy in practical form; he offered to fight for France. On 7 September, within three days of the revolution of 4 September in Paris, he wrote to the *Movimento* of Genoa: 'Yesterday I said to you: war to the death to Bonaparte. Today I say to you: rescue the French Republic by every means.' A few days later, he sent a cable to the French government: 'What remains of me is at your service; dispose of me.'[4]

But the French government hesitated to accept Garibaldi's offer. They hoped that the French Catholics and Conservatives, however incensed they might be at the fall of the Second Empire, would still rally to the new government as long as it was fighting a patriotic war against Germany; and they did not wish to antagonize them, and alarm foreign governments, by having Garibaldi as an ally. They did not reply to Garibaldi's cable; and in any case the Italian navy prevented Garibaldi from leaving Caprera, though the Italian government could not believe that Garibaldi, who had for so long regarded the French government as his enemy, really wished to fight for the French. They thought that his offer to do so was a ruse, and that he was really intending to lead an expedition to seize Nice.[5]

But the French Radicals were determined to bring Garibaldi to France. The matter was taken in hand by Bordone, an adventurous French Radical doctor who had come with De Flotte to fight for Garibaldi in Sicily and Naples in 1860. The French Conservatives and Catholics accused Bordone of being an ex-convict, a thief, a pimp, and an abortionist. He had, in fact, been convicted by a criminal court in France on three occasions between 1857 and 1860 – once for assaulting a man who had insulted his wife at a coach station, for which he had been fined 10 francs; once for receiving stolen goods of very small value, which he claimed had occurred without his knowledge, for which he was fined 50 francs; and once for defrauding his partner in a clock-manufacturing business, of which he was convicted in his absence when serving under Garibaldi in Sicily. For this offence, of which he claimed he was innocent, he was sentenced to two months in prison; but he did not return to France until the sentence had lapsed by passage of time.[6]

In September 1870 Bordone cabled to Garibaldi, urging him to come to France; and after receiving a reply from Garibaldi – 'My dear Bordone, if I can get out of my prison I will be with you. Yours, G. Garibaldi' – he set out to fetch Garibaldi. He took a steamer to Corsica, and before dawn on 4 October he sailed in a small skiff from Bonifacio and landed on Caprera without anyone seeing him. When Basso and Garibaldi came out of the house to see why the dogs were barking, they met Bordone, who said to Garibaldi: 'Well, General, here I am, I have come to fetch you.' As the naval patrol seemed to be off duty for the moment, they decided to leave at once; and within a few minutes Garibaldi was in Bordone's skiff, bound for Corsica, which they reached without mishap the same evening. Next day, after spending the morning looking at the magnificent grottos at Bonifacio, they sailed for France at 5 pm in the French yacht *La Ville de Paris*.[7]

To the surprise of the Italian government, Garibaldi proceeded to Marseilles, not to Nice; and instead of embroiling Italy with France, he forced the Italian Foreign Minister to explain to Bismarck that the Italian authorities had not connived at his escape from Caprera. On 7 October he landed in the port of Marseilles, where he received a great welcome; the Radical Mayor greeted him on landing, ordered the cannon at the fort to fire a salvo in salute, and placed a special train at his disposal to take him to Tours. The Germans had advanced to Paris, and were besieging the city, and the French government had established the temporary capital at Tours.[8]

Garibaldi was welcomed at Tours by a cheering crowd of Radicals; but his arrival was greeted with a storm of protest from the Catholic Right wing, and even the more Liberal politicians were embarrassed. The aged Jewish Liberal, Crémieux, who was a member of the Republican government, declared, when he heard of Garibaldi's arrival at Marseilles: 'Oh my God! he has arrived; this was all that was lacking!' But Crémieux himself had to bear the brunt of the criticism from the Archbishop of Tours for having accepted Garibaldi's services. The Archbishop said to him: 'I thought that Divine Providence had filled to the full the cup of the humiliations which it was imposing on our country. I was wrong. A further supreme humiliation was reserved for us – that of seeing Garibaldi arrive here, giving himself the mission in the world of saving France.' The well-known Catholic writer, Count Armand de Pontmartin, asked:

What will go on in patriotic and Christian hearts when they face this essentially demoralizing spectacle: France at war saluting a foreigner as her saviour; the France of St Louis, of Joan of Arc, of Fénelon, prostrating herself before the man who called the Catholic religion and the Church of Rome a cancer and an ulcer? . . . In the eyes of all Europe, Garibaldi personifies, if not Communist demagogy and pillage, at least the revolution to the last extremity, the international revolution which takes as its password: 'No more kings! no more Popes! no more priests!'[9]

Bismarck, on his side, used the bogey of Garibaldi for propaganda purposes. He instructed his press secretary, Busch, to insert articles in the newspapers stating that the Germans were no longer fighting against the French nation, but against 'the Red Republicans Garibaldi and Mazzini, who are with Gambetta and act as his counsellors'. This association of Mazzini with the French Republican government was pure invention.[10]

The day after Garibaldi reached Tours, Gambetta arrived there, after escaping from Paris in a balloon, and he became the leading spirit in the Government of National Defence. He was quite ready to welcome Garibaldi; and Freycinet, the Minister of War, was equally sympathetic. But difficulties arose as to how Garibaldi should be employed. He was at first offered the command of a unit of 300 volunteers, and rejected this as being too unimportant a duty; and as the government were not prepared to offer him any higher position, he announced a few days later that he would return to Caprera, as the French Republic obviously had no use for his services. The French Radicals demanded that he should be appointed Commander-in-Chief of the forces in the Vosges area. Freycinet then stepped in with a compromise proposal. He thought that it would cause too much resentment among the Conservatives and Catholics if Garibaldi were appointed Commander-in-Chief in the East; but he appointed him to be the commander of the Army of the Vosges, consisting of about 10,000 *francs-tireurs*, and directed him to co-operate with General Cambriels's regular forces in the East. Neither Garibaldi nor Cambriels was placed in command over the other; Gambetta merely expressed the optimistic hope that they would work very well together.[11]

The *francs-tireurs* had originated three years before, during the Luxemburg crisis of 1867, when the men in eastern France formed rifle clubs, on the model of the Swiss rifle clubs and Garibaldi's in Italy, to act as auxiliary defence forces in their districts in wartime. During the German advance on Paris in 1870, they operated as guerrillas along the lines of communications, blowing up railway lines and bridges, sniping at German columns, and sometimes launching attacks in strength on small bodies of German troops. As they had not been incorporated into the French regular army, and did not wear uniform, Bismarck refused to treat them as lawful combatants, though they acted under the orders of the French High Command; and all who were captured were hanged as murderers. Bismarck spoke with great bitterness about Garibaldi, who was fighting for his old enemies the French against the Prussians who had given Venetia to Italy, and on one occasion expressed the hope that if Garibaldi and his men were taken prisoner, they would all be shot.[12]

In practice, however, despite Bismarck, the German High Command drew a distinction between the *franc-tireur* sniper and guerrilla, and those who fought openly in large armies under Garibaldi. The captured Garibaldini were treated as prisoners of war. Jessie White Mario, who came to France to organize Garibaldi's front-line hospitals, and was sometimes sent by him to negotiate with the German commanders, paid special tribute to the excellent medical treatment which the Germans gave to their wounded Garibaldini prisoners. This is in marked contrast to Jessie Mario's usual complaints about the cruelties of the Neapolitans, Austrians and French to the captured Garibaldini in earlier campaigns.[13]

On 14 October Garibaldi established his headquarters at Dôle, near Dijon, and soon afterwards moved to Autun, some sixty-five miles to the west. Here he gathered around him a corps of volunteers composed of Italian, Polish, Hungarian and other revolutionaries, including the Polish revolutionary, General Bossack-Hauké, whom he had visited at Carouge during the Geneva Congress of Peace. There were also many French Radicals and revolutionaries among the volunteers, some of whom had been political prisoners under the Second Empire, and were to be so again under the Third Republic; and his corps in France in 1870, like his units in Uruguay and in Italy in earlier years, included some common, non-political criminals. The Catholics and Conservatives repeatedly referred to the criminal record of Bordone, whom Garibaldi appointed as his Chief of Staff, and pointed out that Garibaldi's volunteers were not fighting out of patriotic love of France, but for the French Republic as a branch of their concept of an international democratic republic.[14]

Throughout his life, it had been Garibaldi's fate to fight, in particularly disadvantageous and dangerous circumstances, for the benefit of allies who not only appropriated the gains which Garibaldi had won at so high a price in blood and effort, but also failed to show any trace of gratitude, and gave him nothing but abuse and hatred in return for his services. But neither Iriarte and the generals in Montevideo, nor Fanti and Cialdini in Italy, had shown such malice and ingratitude to their benefactor as the French Catholics and Conserva-

tives showed to Garibaldi for his assistance in 1870. While Garibaldi
and his men were risking, not only their lives in battle, but the hang-
man's rope or the firing squad if captured, in defence of the country
which had done them so much harm in the past, the Right wing on
the one hand vilified them for coming, and on the other complained that
they had not fought well enough.

Gambetta had authorized Garibaldi to requisition any property
and supplies which he needed, and ordered the local authorities in
the Côte-d'Or region to comply with all his requisitions. The local
councils at Lyons and Autun protested against Garibaldi's requisitions,
though Ordinaire, the Prefect of the Doubs district, at Besançon, was
a staunch supporter of Garibaldi. The railway officials complained
that Garibaldi insisted on requisitioning a special train for himself and
his headquarters' staff when he travelled, and the Conservative critics
sneered that 'the invalid of Caprera' was unable or unwilling to travel
anywhere except in a special train. There were the usual complaints
about the boisterous and lawless behaviour of the Garibaldini, as
there had been about their conduct in Montevideo, Colonia, Macerata
and Naples.[15]

The strongest complaints came from the Church authorities, who
claimed that Garibaldi, though pretending to make war on the Germans, was in fact making war on the Church. He and his officers
tended to adopt the attitude that priests, especially Jesuits, were
certain to be enemies of the new Republic, and should therefore be
treated as actual or potential German spies. Garibaldi sent a unit to
arrest three aged Jesuit priests who guarded a small chapel on the
summit of Mont Roland, near Dôle, on the grounds that they might be
signalling to the Germans from the chapel. He closed down the Jesuit
College at Dôle on the same grounds, in order to prevent the Jesuits
from signalling to the Germans from the bell-tower of the College, and
served an order on them, requiring them to leave the district and not
come within sixty miles of his headquarters.[16]

The Bishop of Autun protested against these measures; but on the
night of 8 November the Garibaldini forced their way into the Bishop's
palace and searched every room, including the Bishop's bedroom
where the Bishop was in bed, claiming first that they were looking for
German soldiers who were hiding in the palace grounds, and afterwards that they were searching for correspondence between the
Bishop's servants and the Germans. The Bishop and the Archbishop
of Besançon sent a strong protest to the Government of National
Defence, and were not appeased when Bordone sent a fulsome apology and
explained that the entry into the palace had been due to an excess of zeal
by young and untrained soldiers, who had only recently enlisted.[17]

Garibaldi also angered the French Conservatives by a letter which he wrote on 16 November to a friend in Belgium, which was published in an Italian newspaper, in which he stated that he had supported the Prussians until Sedan, that Prussia deserved the credit for having rid humanity of the Papal protector, Bonaparte, and that although he was now fighting for the French Republic against the reactionary German government, he regarded the German people as his brothers.[18]

Garibaldi's enemies accused him of military incompetence, and even, by implication, of cowardice in the face of the enemy. In the summer of 1871, after the end of the war and the defeat of the Paris Commune, when Gambetta's Government of National Defence had been replaced by the much more Conservative government of Thiers, an official Parliamentary inquiry was opened into the causes of the defeat and the conduct of the war by the Government of National Defence. The main object of the witnesses and of the members of the Committee who conducted the inquiry was to vindicate the honour of the French army and the reputation of the French generals, and to throw the blame for the defeat on the Left wing. The Conservatives and the military hierarchy, stung by the praise which the Radicals had lavished on Garibaldi, and above all by Victor Hugo's statement that Garibaldi was the only French general who had not been defeated by the Germans, made serious allegations against Garibaldi before the Committee, accusing him of unwillingness to fight the Germans. Although it is impossible to believe this malicious and evilly motivated evidence, there seems no doubt that Garibaldi, who was old and crippled, did not show the energy which he would have done in his younger days. His account of the campaign in his memoirs contains several references to occasions when he was forced to retreat without engaging the enemy, because it would have been too risky to fight a superior force. This may well have been true, but it reads very differently from Garibaldi's accounts of his campaigns in South America and in Italy.

In the last week of October, the Germans advanced on Dijon. The French forces in the town prepared for a ferocious defence, and other French armies marched to their support. General Cambriels asked Garibaldi to march at once to Dijon. Garibaldi set out from Dôle, but on the way, as he marched through the Forest of La Serre, he heard that a skirmish was in progress nearby, and marched to the assistance of the French unit which was engaged in it. By the time he arrived, the French had beaten off the German attacks; and Garibaldi spent the next few days skirmishing with the Germans in the Forest of La Serre, and then returned to Dôle. On 30 October Dijon fell to the Germans. The French Conservatives claimed that Garibaldi's failure to march at once to the relief of Dijon was responsible for the loss of the town.[19]

On the night of 18 November, shortly before dawn, a band of Garibaldini under the command of Ricciotti attacked 800 German soldiers who were stationed in the town of Châtillon-sur-Seine. They routed the Germans, killing 120, and capturing 167 prisoners of war, 82 horses and a regimental flag. Garibaldi was delighted at Ricciotti's achievement, and wrote proudly to tell Teresita about it. The French Conservative witnesses before the Parliamentary Committee, and the Catholic writers, paid full tribute to Ricciotti, either from a genuine respect for him or from a desire to belittle the father by praising the son; the Conservative writer, Vuilletet, wrote that Ricciotti's attack on Châtillon was the only success which the Garibaldini achieved during the whole campaign. The Germans recaptured Châtillon a few days later, and revenged themselves by imposing a heavy fine on the inhabitants.[20]

Garibaldi then decided to attack the Germans at Dijon, and to recapture the town. On 24 November he sent part of his forces to launch a night attack on Dijon, but the attack was repulsed. He established his headquarters on the plateau of Lantenay, and there, on the night of 25 November, he was visited by General Cremer's Chief of Staff, who discussed with him the plans for the recapture of Dijon. According to Cremer, his Chief of Staff told Garibaldi that Cremer would not be ready to take part in the attack until 29 November, but Garibaldi refused to wait, and next morning marched on Dijon without waiting for Cremer. Garibaldi, in his memoirs, makes no reference to Cremer, but admits that it was rash to attack the Germans in Dijon with only 5,000 men.[21]

Setting out for Dijon on 26 November, Garibaldi met the Germans on the plateau of Lantenay, and after an artillery duel, in which the Garibaldini gunners emerged victorious, the Germans retreated to Dijon. On the night of the 26th, which was a dark and rainy night, Garibaldi launched the attack on Dijon at about 7 pm. He relied on the effect of a surprise attack, and on the darkness of the night to cover his retreat in the event of failure; but a German officer in Dijon noted scornfully that the surprise attack failed because the Garibaldini went into the attack singing the Garibaldi Hymn, as if they wished to frighten children. The song was not, in fact, the Garibaldi Hymn, but a song which had been adopted as a battle-song by the Army of the Vosges – 'Aux armes, aux armes, aux armes, l'étranger veut nous envahir'; and Garibaldi, who according to Bordone sang louder than anyone, knew the effect which singing had on the morale of his volunteers.

Garibaldi, who had told his men not to fire, but to go in with the bayonet, cheered them on as he sat in his carriage, and renewed the attack repeatedly, being confident of success; but the Germans resisted with a courage and discipline to which Garibaldi pays tribute in his memoirs, and at 10 pm Garibaldi reluctantly ordered the retreat in the face of heavy enemy rifle fire. The losses on both sides were heavy.[22]

The Germans were unable to pursue the retreating Garibaldini through the night, but next day, on the 27th, they caught up with them on the plateau of Lantenay. This time, unlike the battle on the same site on the previous day, the Germans had the best of the engagement, and Garibaldi retreated to Autun. According to the French Conservatives, he did not expect the Germans to follow up their victory with an attack on Autun; and when, on the morning of 1 December, some officials of the French railway company and of the National Guard went to Garibaldi's headquarters to report that a German attack was imminent, they found that Garibaldi had gone out to reconnoitre in the neighbourhood, and that the staff at his headquarters refused to believe the report of a German attack, and threatened to arrest the officer of the National Guard for spreading false rumours. Garibaldi, on his ride, saw that the Germans were about to attack, and hurried back to his headquarters; but by the time that he arrived there, the Garibaldini had driven off the attackers. The French Conservatives sneered over the fact that Garibaldi had been absent during the battle. They denied that it was a victory for the Garibaldini, and claimed that the Germans withdrew from Autun only because they feared that General Cremer's troops would arrive and cut off their retreat.[23]

Some of the units under Garibaldi's command which had taken part in the attack on Dijon did not retreat with him to Autun, but retreated further away, and did not come when Garibaldi ordered them to join him at Autun. Garibaldi decided to make an example of one of them. He arrested Colonel Chenet, the French commander of a regiment of engineers from Eastern France, and had him court martialled for cowardice. The court martial, at which Bossack-Hauké presided, convicted Chenet and sentenced him to be shot.

There were great protests in the district. Chenet, who had a distinguished war record in the Crimea and in Mexico, claimed that he was not under Garibaldi's orders, but was exercising his judgement as the head of an independent guerrilla band as to where he should operate against the enemy; and he complained that his conviction was illegal, because he had been tried by a court martial composed of foreigners, and had been denied the right to call essential witnesses in his defence. The local Conservatives became very indignant that a patriotic French *franc-tireur* was going to be shot by the foreigner

Garibaldi; but Garibaldi refused all demands for a reprieve. At the last moment, after Chenet had been told to prepare for execution at midday on 14 December, Garibaldi granted him a pardon at 11 am, and commuted the sentence to a public degradation.

> This Colonel Chenet [wrote Garibaldi in his memoirs] whom I was so stupid as to extricate from the death to which the court martial had sentenced him, this poltroon, I say, became the top hero of the priests and the chauvinists, who only just failed to canonize him [like] St Domenic Arbuès and similar riff-raff.

In April 1871, after the end of the war, Chenet's conviction was quashed by the Court of Appeal in Lyons, and he was cleared of the charge of cowardice. Next year he brought a libel action against Bordone for repeating the charge in his book *Garibaldi and the Army of the Vosges*. Bordone counter-claimed against Chenet, who had accused him of being a criminal. The jury gave a verdict for the defendants in both actions.[24]

On 12 December Garibaldi attended a conference at Chalon-sur-Saône with General Bressoles, General Cremer and General Pélissier. The other generals presented a plan for an attack on Dijon; but according to Cremer's evidence to the Parliamentary Committee, Garibaldi said that he could not take part in the attack because he was short of the necessary equipment. Cremer believed that Garibaldi refused to join in the attack out of resentment that Cremer had not taken part in Garibaldi's attack on Dijon on 26 November. On 18 December Cremer attacked the Germans at Nuits-sous-Ravière, near Dijon, and was repulsed after fierce fighting. That same evening, Cremer cabled to Garibaldi, asking for reinforcements to enable him to resume the attack next day; but as Garibaldi sent only a token force, and remained at Autun, Cremer did not attack again.

On 21 December Freycinet cabled to Garibaldi from Bordeaux, where the French government had retreated as the Germans advanced on Tours. Freycinet's cable was mildly critical in tone, and urged Garibaldi to leave Autun and establish his headquarters further north, at Bligny, and he reminded him that his target was the recapture of Dijon. But Garibaldi did not leave Autun.[25]

The French armies were now in a desperate situation. Paris was being starved into surrender and was being subjected to heavy bombardment from the big Prussians guns. A second Prussian army was advancing on Le Mans and against the French armies in south-west France; and a third, under General Manteuffel, was sent against General Bourbaki's troops in the East. As Manteuffel advanced, Garibaldi received orders from General Cambriels and from the government to harass Manteuffel and prevent his progress. Garibaldi sent Ricciotti to hold the passes in the mountains between Grancey and Dijon; but, according to his French Conservative critics, he did nothing more, and during the first three weeks of January 1871 showed a lack of energy and an unwillingness to fight which was the cause of the disaster which befell Bourbaki's army.

On 27 December the Germans, who were outnumbered by the French armies which were converging on Dijon, evacuated Dijon, and withdrew to the north to link up with Manteuffel. Freycinet ordered Garibaldi to advance with his 13,000 troops from Autun to Dijon; but the weather had turned very cold, with 18 degrees Fahrenheit of frost, and Garibaldi informed Freycinet that he could not move his men to Dijon unless railway transport was made available. On 3 January Freycinet cabled to Garibaldi: 'I am very surprised that as you are so near Dijon, your army has not gone there, and that it insists on being transported there by railway.' But Garibaldi, though he went himself to Dijon with his staff on 7 January, would not move his army unless trains were made available, as his men were inadequately clothed for the cold weather. The weather was almost certainly the reason for Garibaldi's ineffectiveness in January 1871, because, although Garibaldi had often fought battles in a temperature bordering on 100 degrees Fahrenheit, he had never had to fight in a colder climate than that of the Paraná in August, the Volturno in early October, and the Roman Campagna on 3 November. At the beginning of January he was almost put out of action by a severe attack of rheumatism; and a few days later he experienced another great personal tragedy in his life, when he heard that his seventeen-month-old daughter Rosa had died at Caprera on New Year's Day. She was the second Rosita Garibaldi to die in infancy while her father was away at the war.[26]

With some difficulty, the Paris–Lyons–Marseilles Railway Company provided the necessary railway transport, sending eighteen special trains between 7 and 11 January to take Garibaldi's 13,000 men from Autun to Dijon. There Garibaldi linked up with the 17,000 soldiers under Pélissier. On 13 January Manteuffel began his march from Grancey; but Ricciotti, finding himself hopelessly outnumbered by Manteuffel's 70,000 men, made no attempt to hold the passes, and retreated to Dijon. On 15 January Monsieur de Laborie, the Chief Engineer for Roads and Bridges in eastern France, visited Garibaldi's headquarters at Dijon in some alarm after hearing the news of Manteuffel's advance. According to Laborie's evidence to the Parliamentary Committee, Garibaldi was in a wretched state, suffering acutely from rheumatism, complaining about his health, deeply worried over

Ricciotti's safety, and insisting on referring every decision to Bordone, his Chief of Staff; but even allowing for Garibaldi's age and state of health, and his paternal anxiety about Ricciotti, it is impossible to believe that he could ever have been the pitiable wreck of a man which Laborie made him out to be. Laborie stated that Garibaldi said to him: 'Oh, you can be sure that Dijon will not be attacked', to which Laborie replied: 'But I am not thinking about Dijon, I am thinking about the Army of the East.' But this is very unlikely, because Garibaldi and Bordone, far from being complacent about the danger to Dijon, were pressing Freycinet to send them additional cannon for the defence of the town. [27]

The government in Bordeaux was disturbed at Garibaldi's failure to help Bourbaki. At 2.15 pm on 19 January, Freycinet cabled to Bordone:

> You are the only one who is constantly creating difficulties and conflicts, no doubt to justify your inaction. I will not hide from you that the government is far from satisfied with what has just occurred. You have given no support to Bourbaki's army, and your presence at Dijon has had no effect at all on the enemy's march from the west to the east. In short, fewer explanations and more acts, this is what is asked of you.

Two days later, Freycinet sent another cable to Bordone, threatening to take disciplinary action against him. [28]

Bordone received this cable in the middle of a battle. That same day, 21 January, the Germans attacked Dijon. Garibaldi's men drove them back, after fierce fighting with the bayonet. The enemy renewed the attack next day, and again on the 23rd, when their attack was finally repulsed, and they retreated from Dijon. Garibaldi's Polish comrade, Bossack-Hauké, was killed in the second day's fighting. Garibaldi claimed that he had won a great victory, and Freycinet and the government congratulated him. But the Conservative witnesses before the Parliamentary Committee, though they admitted that the Garibaldini had gained a success at Dijon, interpreted the fight of 21–23 January in a very different light. They stated that the Germans attacked Dijon with only 6,000 men, and that Garibaldi had 30,000 troops to defend it; and they claimed that the German objective was not the capture of Dijon, but to detain Garibaldi there for three days so as to prevent him from impeding Manteuffel's march against Bourbaki. If the German commander, General von Kettler, and 6,000 men succeeded in keeping 30,000 Garibaldini and *francs-tireurs* in Dijon, while Bourbaki's army was being destroyed, he was even more successful than Garibaldi had been in 1859 when he prevented Urban from taking 11,000 soldiers to Magenta. [29]

On 28 January Freycinet sent a final appeal to Garibaldi to advance on Dôle, recapture the town, and occupy Forêt-de-Chaux in an attempt to relieve the pressure on Bourbaki. He told Garibaldi that he appreciated that this was a difficult task, but added: 'It is worthy of your genius; do you think you can try it?' Garibaldi set out for Dôle next day, but after he had passed Auxonne he heard reports from his scouts that led him to believe that the Prussians were at Dôle in much too great strength for it to be possible for him to attack them, and he retreated to Dijon. The witnesses before the Parliamentary Committee claimed that he retreated at the first sight of a handful of German snipers.[30]

On 29 January an armistice was signed between the German and French High Commands, the French having surrendered Paris and agreed to all the German demands; but a clause in the armistice agreement provided that it was not to apply in the eastern region near Dijon. According to Bismarck's press secretary, Busch, this was because Bismarck refused to include Garibaldi's forces in the terms of the armistice, and wished to give the German army the opportunity to destroy them. Jules Favre, who had established almost friendly personal relations with Bismarck, was alarmed at Bismarck's refusal to include Garibaldi in the armistice, and feared that the Garibaldini would be exterminated; but though Bismarck ordered Moltke to exclude the Garibaldini from any armistice which he concluded in the East, he assured Favre that if Garibaldi were captured, he would not be hanged, but would be exhibited in Germany beneath a placard containing the words 'Italian ingratitude', and then sent home to Caprera.[31]

The armistice terms gave rise to the most bitter of all the disputes about the campaign of 1870–1 between the Garibaldini and the French Conservatives, who alleged that as soon as he heard about the armistice, Garibaldi hurriedly transferred himself and his army to a region where the armistice was in force, out of a cowardly desire to find an excuse for not fighting. On 1 February Bourbaki's army, hemmed in by Manteuffel's, crossed the frontier into Switzerland and was interned by the Swiss authorities. On 31 January Garibaldi evacuated Dijon, and the Germans entered it next day; and in the course of the first week in February, Garibaldi retreated to Chagny, Chalon-sur-Saône and Courcelles. In his memoirs, he claims that he had no alternative but to retreat before the overwhelming superiority of the Prussians; but the report of the Parliamentary Committee stated that if Garibaldi had been a French general, they would have recommended that he be brought before a court of inquiry 'to answer for his conduct in having abandoned to the enemy, deliberately and without fighting, the positions that he had been given the mission to defend, and thus having caused the loss of a French army, and brought about a military disaster with which the only comparison in history were the disasters of Sedan and Metz'. This malicious judgement ignores the fact that Garibaldi did not begin his retreat from Dijon until 31 January, the same day on which the commanders of Bourbaki's army had agreed with the Swiss authorities to surrender to internment in Switzerland.[32]

While Garibaldi was still in Dijon, the Government of National Defence ordered that elections should be held for the new National Assembly. Garibaldi was elected as MP for Dijon, Paris, Nice and Algiers. The Conservatives asserted that, as an alien, he was ineligible for election; but the Radicals claimed that he was eligible because he was born in the French town of Nice. As soon as he reached Courcelles, he left his army under the command of Menotti and went to Bordeaux for the meeting of the Assembly; but he believed that, with the signing of the armistice, his mission in France was over, and he decided to return to Caprera. On 13 February he wrote to the Minister of War, resigning his command in the French army.[33]

The electors had returned a majority of Conservatives and monarchists to the Assembly, because of their dissatisfaction with the Government of National Defence, which was held responsible for carrying on the war and leading France to defeat. Many observers expected that the Assembly would vote to restore the monarchy; but the Conservatives could not agree amongst themselves as to whether to choose a Legitimist Bourbon, or an Orleanist, king, and they also thought that it would be better to allow the Republic to bear the onus of signing the humiliating peace treaty with Germany.

Garibaldi and his companions arrived at the station in Bordeaux on the morning of Sunday 12 February. Bordone states that the reaction was already beginning in Bordeaux, and it was becoming dangerous to be known as a Garibaldino; but Garibaldi was cheered by his Radical supporters at the station, and at the Hôtel de Nantes, where he lodged. When the crowds in front of the hotel cried 'Long live the Republic! Long live Garibaldi!' Garibaldi called out to them: 'Friends, cry "Long live France! Long live Republican France!"' He was cheered again in the afternoon, when he went sailing in a small boat in the harbour; but these Radical demonstrations increased the resentment of the Conservatives.[34]

Next day, on the afternoon of 13 February, Garibaldi attended the opening session of the National Assembly. He was cheered as he entered the building by the Radicals in the streets; but his entry into the Chamber provoked a hostile reception from the Conservative deputies. They demanded that Garibaldi, who as usual was dressed in his red shirt, poncho and képi, should remove his hat; but he refused, saying that it was as proper for him to wear it as it was for the priests among the deputies to wear their black or green velvet skull-caps. Garibaldi delivered a letter to the President of the Assembly in which he stated that he was rendering his last service to France by casting his vote in the Assembly for a republic, and was herewith resigning his seat as a deputy.

When the President read out the letter to the Assembly, there was a hostile reception from the Conservative majority. They protested that Garibaldi could not resign, because, being a foreigner, he had not been validly elected. Garibaldi then rose to address the Assembly. The President told him that he could not speak, because he had just resigned his seat in the Assembly. This led to strong protests from the Left-wing deputies, and Garibaldi began to address the House. The President ordered him to sit down, and the Right-wing deputies shouted at Garibaldi, thus provoking counter-protests from the Left. The President declared the session closed, and left the Chamber, while Garibaldi continued to try to speak, though his words were quite inaudible amid the hubbub. Eventually Garibaldi walked slowly out of the Chamber in silent dignity. There was another uproar in the Assembly three weeks later, when Victor Hugo protested against the refusal to permit Garibaldi to speak. When he denounced the Conservative deputies for denying free speech to a man who had come to fight for France, he was interrupted by mocking cries from the Right: 'To pretend to fight for France.' He then said that Garibaldi was the only general in the French army who had not been defeated in the war – a statement which was received with howls of protest from the Conservatives. Victor Hugo, like Garibaldi, was shouted down, and was unable to finish his speech.[35]

Louis Blanc, who had been elected to the Assembly, was as disgusted as Victor Hugo at the treatment of Garibaldi, and four years later referred to it in a speech. He said that he had been in London on 11 April 1864, when 'a whole town – and what a town! – went to meet a man in a sort of delirium, with their hearts full of emotion'. The man was not a potentate, but a Republican named Garibaldi.

This happened in London on 11 April 1864; and at Bordeaux, on 13 February 1871, what happened there? On 13 February 1871, at Bordeaux, the day after a war in which Garibaldi had come to offer to France in her distress his blood and the blood of his two sons, the voice of the hero was smothered, in a French Assembly, by protests.[36]

Garibaldi left Bordeaux for Marseilles the same evening. On 15 February he embarked at Marseilles, and reached Caprera next day.

In France, the controversy about his visit continued for some time. The Bishop of Autun declared that honest French soldiers were 'groaning under the humiliation, which necessity had imposed upon their faith and their patriotism, of serving under the orders of a chief whom some of them had formerly fought victoriously in Italy in defence of the Church, and whose presence among us served only to draw down upon France the maledictions of Heaven'. Bordone commented that soon the priests would be teaching the young that it was the Archbishops of Autun and Dijon who had driven back the Prussians with their bayonets on 1 December and 21, 22 and 23 January.[37]

Garibaldi's army, which he had disbanded, disintegrated. The Poles and the Hungarians went to Switzerland or England or other places of exile; the Italians returned to Italy; and the French scattered all over France, some going to Paris to fight for the Commune, which seized power there in March, and sharing the fate of the massacred Communards, while others experienced the hard life of Radicals and Left-wing sympathizers in the first years of the Third Republic.

Two years later, one of them made a pathetic appearance in a local court at Lons-le-Saunier, near Dôle. A young girl, Lucie B—, was charged under the harsh vagrancy laws with wandering around the country as a vagabond with no fixed address. Her only defence was to hand in a certificate of discharge from the army, signed by Bordone as Garibaldi's Chief of Staff; it was authenticated by the printed notepaper and the seal of the headquarters of the Army of the Vosges. The document stated that Madame B—, canteen-worker, had performed her duty as a private soldier in the Army of the Vosges to the satisfaction of all her officers, and had been wounded at Dijon on 21 January 1871. It did not help her with the magistrates, but was a reminder of the days when the outcasts of French society had been given the opportunity to perform useful service, and inspired to acts of valour, by Garibaldi.[38]

CHAPTER 41

THE LAST YEARS

GARIBALDI was less disappointed about his campaign in France than were most of his friends. They were indignant at the treatment which he had received from the French whom he had gone to help, and some of them were also disappointed that he had conducted a campaign when he was in poor health and past his prime and therefore unable to do himself justice; but he himself was satisfied that he had made a gesture of friendship with France and of loyalty to the cause of international Republicanism. In July John McAdam wrote to Cowen: 'Our old friend Garibaldi is sick, body and mind – his going to France at all was a great blunder, but he and his sons came out of it better than could have been expected.' McAdam had written to Garibaldi, warning him not to go to France 'and risk assassination in a country that had done nothing for Italy unless to serve its own purposes'. Garibaldi had answered from Dôle on 19 October 1870, writing on the official notepaper of the Army of the Vosges: 'I think that the Democracies of all the nations must help the French Republic.'[1]

But Garibaldi realized that he was too old to fight again. A month after he returned to Caprera from France, the Paris Communards rose in revolt against Thiers's government at Versailles, and Thiers prepared for civil war. The Communards wrote to Caprera to invite Garibaldi to become Commander-in-Chief of their army. If Garibaldi had been the Garibaldi of 1849 and 1860, his services would have been invaluable to the Commune; he would not have allowed the Communards to wait behind the barricades in their districts of Paris until the Versailles troops arrived and slaughtered them, but would have marched on Versailles, as Marx and Engels were urging the Communards to do. Garibaldi, with his belief in the importance of attack at all costs, was just the leader that the Communards needed. But the old, rheumatic Garibaldi of 1871 would have been of little use to the Commune; and he declined the invitation on the grounds of his age and health.[2]

At the end of May, Paris fell to the Versaillese after savage street fighting, during which the Communards set fire to part of Paris and shot several hostages, including the Archbishop of Paris, and the Versaillese executed at least 20,000 Communard prisoners without trial. The Commune had been led by old Republican revolutionaries of 1848, steeped in the French Jacobin tradition, and Marx and the International had very little influence over them. But two days after the fall of the Commune, when the overwhelming body of Liberal, and even Radical, opinion was joining the Conservatives in denouncing the crimes of the Communards, Marx delivered a speech to the Council of the International in London, in which he warmly defended the Commune, criticizing it only for not having been sufficiently revolutionary, and violently denouncing the atrocities of the Versaillese troops. Marx's speech, which was later published under the title of *The Civil War in France*, and became one of the leading classics of Marxist literature, attracted a good deal of attention. The French government denounced the International for having instigated the Communard revolt, and the enemies of the Commune associated it firmly with the International.

In July 1871 Mazzini published an article in the Mazzinian newspaper, *La Roma del Popolo*, which enraged the Socialists in every country. Mazzini had always been a strong opponent of Socialism, and he attacked the Commune and the International with great vehemence, denouncing them for having committed three unpardonable offences; they were against God, which meant being against morality; they were against nationality, which meant betraying the people; and they were against property, which meant being against liberty. Mazzini's attack, which he continued in other articles and pamphlets, was particularly resented by the Socialists, coming at a time when the Communards had so recently been massacred and the International was under attack from so many enemies.[3]

Garibaldi's broad sympathy with revolutionaries, and his vaguely Socialist leanings, made him sympathetic to the Commune; and the fact that Mazzini had attacked it was perhaps all that was needed to bring Garibaldi firmly down on its side. He vigorously supported the Commune and the International, and denounced Mazzini with more than usual bitterness.[4] Mazzini had come home to Italy only to die; he was in the last year of his life as he entered into the fifth stage of his relationship with Garibaldi. In the first stage, after 1833, Garibaldi had been Mazzini's devoted pupil; in the second stage, in Rome in 1849, they fought together against the French, but personal differences divided them; in the third stage, after 1854, they became opponents, because Garibaldi supported Victor Emanuel and Mazzini remained a Republican; in the fourth stage, after Aspromonte, they once again drew closer together as Garibaldi became disillusioned with the Italian monarchy; in the fifth stage, they disagreed about the Commune and the International, with Victor Emanuel's champion supporting Marx and the Communards.

Garibaldi stated his opinion in a letter to Arthur Arnold, the editor of the London *Echo*, in September 1871. He supported the International for four reasons – because it believed in the principles of internationalism and of brotherhood between European, American and African; because it was against priests; because it favoured the abolition of large national standing armies, and their replacement by a national militia; and because it supported the Paris Commune. But he condemned what he called the doctrine of the International that 'property is theft, the right of inheritance is theft'.[5]

A month later, Garibaldi wrote to Petroni, the editor of *La Roma del Popolo*. In this letter which, like his letter to Arnold, was published, he attacked the critics of the Commune, who had denounced it for demolishing the Vendôme Column and Thiers's house; and he asked whether these critics had ever seen a whole village destroyed merely because it had harboured a *franc-tireur*, which had occurred not only in France, but in Lombardy, Venetia and everywhere. He hoped that when a cooler judgement could be made, there would be less criticism of the Commune and more of the 'assassins of Versailles'; his own criticism of the Commune was for having had too many leaders who quarrelled amongst themselves, though he did not expressly state, what he clearly implied, that they would have done better under one dictator. He attacked Mazzini, and stated that he would never again be reconciled with him; the only way of being reconciled with Mazzini was to obey him in everything. He declared that he had fought for the welfare of humanity in South America; he had been prepared to fight for it under Pius IX; he had fought for it under Victor Emanuel; he had fought for it under Gambetta and Trochu. He was now ready to fight for it under the International, because he had read the statutes and the programme of the International, and was prepared to adhere to them; but he stated that he believed that private property should be protected, and that the International should proclaim that it came to ensure that the worker obtained his rights, but not to expropriate the wealthy classes. He also declared that he would not accept the discipline of the International, and that though he believed in the principles of internationalism, he would never belong to a party which required him to accept orders from the leadership of an international organization.[6]

Garibaldi's friends among the British aristocracy preferred to ignore the letter, and treated it as one of his typical idiosyncrasies which must not be held against him. The Mazzinians reacted much more strongly. Cowen censured Garibaldi's action in an article in the *Newcastle Daily*

Chronicle, and Jessie White Mario denounced Garibaldi more severely for his support of the Commune and the International than for anything else that he did. Mazzini himself commented: 'Garib. would not support the International if I had written in favour of it.'[7]

Pallavicino, who feared that Garibaldi would lose all his popularity if he became identified with the International, wrote to warn him that he was becoming the tool of a movement whose objects he did not understand or support. Garibaldi clarified his position in a letter to Pallavicino of 14 November 1871, which was published in the newspaper *Il Gazzettino Rosa*. He stated that he had belonged to the International long before this society was created in Europe. He would imprison the supporters of the International if they persisted in their policy of 'War on Capital – property is theft – inheritance another theft. . . . But if the International, as I understand it, proves to be a continuation of the moral and material betterment of the working class . . . I shall be with the International'; and he told Pallavicino: 'If you once saw me as the gentle and humane dictator, I am still in favour of honest dictatorship, which I consider the only antidote for eradicating the cancers of this corrupt society'. Pallavicino deleted this reference to dictatorship in the copy which he gave to the press for publication.[8]

The reaction of the supporters of the International was more complex. Although Engels, as a military theorist, had always admired Garibaldi, Marx was less enthusiastic, and took no steps to contact Garibaldi and draw him into the active leadership of the International. Apart from the fact that by temperament Marx was more egocentric than Engels, and more likely to fear being overshadowed in the International by the overwhelming figure of Garibaldi, there was another reason for his hesitation: if Garibaldi joined the International, he would have to become a member of the Italian section, which was under the control of Marx's great rival, Bakunin, with whom Marx was engaged in a bitter faction fight which was to lead to the destruction of the International within three years.

Bakunin's role in the revolution in Saxony in 1849, and his long years of imprisonment in Russia and Siberia, had made him a hero in the eyes of revolutionaries all over Europe. Bakunin, on his side, had admired Garibaldi as a revolutionary ever since the day in 1860 when he and his fellow-exiles in Irkutsk in Siberia had heard with joy of Garibaldi's achievement in Sicily and Naples. After Bakunin had been pardoned by the Tsar and allowed to emigrate to London, he had visited Garibaldi at Caprera in January 1864, and had met him again at the Congress of Peace in Geneva in 1867.[9]

By 1871, Bakunin was engaged in a faction fight with Marx beside which the quarrels among the Mazzinians and Garibaldians were mild. This faction fight reflected the different attitudes of the various sections of the International. The British section, which Marx dominated, consisted chiefly of pacific trade union leaders who disapproved of violence and revolution. The German and French sections, which were also under the control of Marxist leaders, in theory believed in a proletarian revolution, but rejected assassination and terrorism as a useless method of struggle, and, like Marx and Engels themselves, were in practice becoming a good deal less revolutionary than they had been in their younger days in 1848. In southern Europe, especially in Spain and Italy, the sections of the International were imbued with the traditional Italian and Spanish belief in revolutionary terrorism and assassination which the Carbonari and Mazzini had advocated and practised for the last sixty years. They were very responsive to Bakunin's Anarchist doctrine of the abolition of the State and its overthrow by individual acts of terrorism.

Despite Bakunin's admiration for Garibaldi, he did not wish to have him in the International, because he did not believe that Garibaldi really understood and accepted the principles of the International. He was even more disturbed by Garibaldi's views on dictatorship, which he believed were diametrically opposed to his own on the question of the power of the State. His belief was confirmed in 1873, when Bismarck began his struggle against the Catholic Church in Germany for the control of education and other cultural activities – the famous *Kultur-kampf* which was carried on for several years before Bismarck quietly abandoned his efforts to subordinate the Catholic Church in Germany to the State. Garibaldi supported Bismarck enthusiastically in the *Kulturkampf*. Bakunin believed that Garibaldi's hatred of priests had blinded him to the fact that the absolutist state was a greater danger than the Catholic Church. He was afraid that the members of the Italian section of the International, dazzled by Garibaldi's fame and his past revolutionary achievements, would allow themselves to be dominated by Garibaldi; and he warned them that Garibaldi was not a Socialist, and that his internationalism was no different from that of many bourgeois Liberals.[10]

In the autumn of 1871 the struggle between the Marxists and the Bakuninists in the International was in full swing, and Engels launched a bitter campaign against Bakunin in Italy, even attacking him in the columns of the Mazzinian *Roma del Popolo*. While Mazzini attacked the International and Engels attacked Bakunin and Bakunin warned the Socialists against Garibaldi, everyone waited to see whether Garibaldi would support Marx or Bakunin in the fight within the International. He refused to support either faction, but in a letter to Valzania on

3 April 1872 appealed for an end to this conflict, which was splitting the revolutionary youth of the Romagna. Nor would Garibaldi take an active part in any revolutionary political organization. At the foundation of the Workers Federation of Turin in October 1871, the meeting closed amid shouts of 'Long live Garibaldi! Long live the International!' but Garibaldi did not give the organization active support. He also refused an invitation to preside at the Democratic Congress at Bologna in March 1872, which the Mazzinians had convened in order to offer the revolutionary youth an alternative to the International, and partly because of his refusal the Congress was not held.[11]

By the beginning of May 1872, the bitterness between the Mazzinians and the Socialists had reached such a pitch that Francesco Piccinini, a prominent Socialist of the Romagna, was stabbed to death by two Mazzinians in Bologna. Garibaldi could only repeat his call for the union of all Italian progressives, whatever party they might adhere to, in a letter to Celso Ceretti on 1 August 1872. Ceretti had been one of Garibaldi's boy-soldiers, having fought under him in the campaign of 1859 when he was aged fifteen. He was now one of the leaders of the Bakuninist section of the International.[12]

In September 1872 the International split irrevocably at its Congress at The Hague, where Marx succeeded with great difficulty in defeating Bakunin; and in 1876 it was quietly dissolved. Thirteen years later, it was succeeded by the Second International, and in due course by the Third and the Fourth. The Swiss, Italian and Spanish sections, over which Bakunin gained control, continued to exist for a while, and in 1873 the Spanish section led an unsuccessful revolution at Cartagena; but Garibaldi never played any active part in the work of the Italian or any other section of the International, and despite his personal friendship with Bakunin, and their mutual respect for each other, he was politically even further removed from Bakunin than he was from Marx.

Garibaldi referred to the International in the preface to his third novel, *I Mille*, which was published in Milan in 1873. Like *Cantoni il volontario*, it is a historical novel in which the fictional part occupies only a small section of the book. It is a factual account of the expedition of the Thousand from Quarto to the Volturno; but the narrative of the Sicilian and Neapolitan campaign is periodically interrupted by chapters which deal with the imaginary adventures of a fictional heroine in Rome, the beautiful Marzia, who, though she believes that she is the daughter of a kindly Jew who has brought her up, is in fact the illegitimate child of an influential Jesuit priest and a Roman Countess. She is raped by her father the Jesuit, and, after being forcibly converted from Judaism to Catholicism, is ill-treated by the nuns in the convent where the Jesuit has incarcerated her; but, like the other heroines in the book, she is repeatedly rescued from danger by brave young Garibaldini, and eventually dies fighting for Garibaldi near Naples. Crude and banal though these fictional chapters are, they show the sincerity and intensity of Garibaldi's desire to liberate Rome.

In the introduction, addressed to the 'Youth of Italy', and dated 21–22 January 1873, Garibaldi called on all young Italians to support the International, though the International had nothing whatever to do with the novel. The introduction was a clear statement of Garibaldi's attitude to the International. He said nothing about Socialism or the discipline of the International over its sections, but mentioned the two points which had attracted him to the International. He stated that if the workers who engage in the honourable profession of labour are denied the just rewards of their toil, and are exploited by their employer, they are as much enslaved as the inhabitants of a nation which is occupied by a foreign conqueror; and he expressed his belief in internationalism and the brotherhood of the peoples of different lands, repeating the slogan which had been used in the chorus of the anthem *L'Internationale* which Eugène Pothier had written in 1872: 'The International unites the human race.'[13]

After 1873, Garibaldi separated increasingly from the Italian Bakuninists. By 1874 Ceretti, the Garibaldino of Varese and the Thousand, was describing Garibaldi and Saffi as 'two coryphées of bourgeois Republicanism'; and when Garibaldi died in 1882, the Bakuninist-Anarchist Malatesta wrote that Garibaldi had been a more dangerous enemy of the working class than Mazzini. But Garibaldi was always ready to defend the Bakuninists from persecution. In 1875 the Italian government arrested the Bakuninists throughout Italy and prosecuted them in a series of much-publicized trials, all of which ultimately resulted in the triumphant acquittal of the defendants by a sympathetic jury. In the trial of the Bakuninists at Florence, Garibaldi submitted a written statement in favour of the defendants. 'Unlike Mazzini,' he stated, 'I am an internationalist. . . . What difference is there between an American and an Italian? They are the same men, and morally they must be brothers. I had the good fortune to fight for the American people, as for my people; therefore I am for the fraternity of the human race.' He added that if a man who has earned 100 scudi by the fruit of his own labour is required to share this money 'with another who demands to live slothfully on his shoulders, the latter is a thief; such is my internationalism.'[14]

Garibaldi's argument with Mazzini about the International was the last which he was to have with his great teacher, colleague and adversary. In March 1872 Mazzini died at Pisa in the arms of his most ardent women admirers. When Garibaldi heard the news, he forgot, for a moment, all his quarrels with Mazzini, and cabled from Caprera to the devoted Mazzinians at Genoa: 'Let the flag of the Thousand wave over the bier of the great Italian!'[15] But this did not prevent him from renewing his attacks on Mazzini in the new edition of his memoirs, which he published in the summer of 1872. After stating that he regretted that the necessity of speaking the truth required him to write ill of the dead, he criticized Mazzini with considerable bitterness throughout the book – in the account of his campaign in the Alps in 1848, of the Roman Republic, of the events of 1860, and of Mentana.

He had set to work on this last edition of the memoirs as soon as he returned from France in 1871. Since 1859, forty-six editions of the memoirs had been published in eleven languages, all of them being editions and translations of either the Dwight, Dumas or Speranza von Schwartz editions. In the 1872 edition, which Garibaldi edited himself, he made only a few minor corrections in the Dwight edition, and included none of the additional material in the Dumas or Speranza editions, which is a strong indication that the Dwight and 1872 editions are more reliable than Dumas's or Speranza's. In the 1872 edition he published the story of his life up to the Mentana campaign, which he had written at various periods since 1860, and wrote an additional section on his campaign in France of 1870–1. There are a number of striking omissions in the story. Apart from the fact, which has often been commented on, that there is no mention of his visit to England in 1864, he also avoids all reference to the political controversies in Sicily and Naples in 1860 and to his clash with Cavour in Parliament in 1861, and makes only a passing reference to his visit to Geneva for the Congress of Peace. In fact, from 1860 onwards he refers to nothing except his military campaigns, all of which are described in considerable detail. He had always been at his best on the battlefield, and it was the battles that he remembered and chose to write about. In the preface to the book, dated 3 July 1872, he quoted, a little ashamedly, the words of his old ally and adversary, General Rivera of Montevideo: 'War is the true life of man.'

But in principle he was a pacifist, and he repeatedly expressed anti-militarist opinions at the most unexpected places in the memoirs. Describing his last desperate defence at Costa Brava, he wrote: 'We still had powder and ammunition on board, and were bound to fight on, not for victory, not to save ourselves, but for honour.' But then immediately he added:

Honour! I feel inclined to laugh with contempt when I think of a soldier's honour! the honour of the Bourbons, the Spaniards, the Austrians, the

French, who attack like the murderers attack poor travellers on the road. The honour of slaughtering our fellow-countrymen, our political co-religionists, while a monster, a prostitute, or a young scoundrel on the throne enjoys the sight and laughs up his sleeve amid the lurid orgies of Naples, Vienna, Madrid and Paris.[16]

Apart from the memoirs and his novels, Garibaldi wrote other works which he never published during his lifetime. These include thoughts on various political and social subjects – dictatorship, monarchy, capital punishment, the position of women – about which he expressed the Liberal and humanitarian views which he had always held. His opposition to capital punishment had led him in 1867 to join in the unsuccessful attempts to persuade the revolutionary Liberal President of Mexico, Benito Juarez, to reprieve the Emperor Maximilian, Franz Josef's brother, from the sentence of death for treason which had been passed on him at Querétaro. Although Garibaldi had written, only a few months earlier, that he hoped that Franz Josef would share his brother's fate, he did not wish that fate to be death.[17] Like other opponents of capital punishment among revolutionary Radicals and Socialists, Garibaldi distinguished between capital punishment as a judicial method of punishment, and the summary executions in wartime which he himself had often ordered and had sometimes carried out. He also wrote memoranda on military organization, on the irrigation of the Tiber valley, and on agricultural plans for Caprera. He made many notes about logarithms and astronomy, which had always been a favourite hobby.[18]

He wrote poetry. Ever since he was a young man he had recorded in verse the recent experiences which he had undergone. He had written a poem when he was a prisoner at Gualeguay in 1837, and this had been followed by other poems, which taken together form an autobiography in verse – poems on life as a privateer, Rio Grande do Sul, Montevideo, San Antonio, the Return of the Seventy-three (from Montevideo to Italy in 1848), Luino and Morazzone, the defence of Rome, the retreat to San Marino, and a special poem on the death of Anita, whom he does not mention in any of the other poems which have survived. These were followed by poems on his second exile and journey to China, on Caprera, on Calatafimi and on Aspromonte. The style is agreeably romantic; it is not great poetry, but is quite inoffensive, and suggests that Garibaldi was a better poet than a novelist.[19]

He was still a Freemason, having maintained his connexion with the society ever since he had first joined it in Rio de Janeiro in 1836. After 1860 he was elected as an honorary member of many Italian lodges, and Grand Master of the Freemasons of Italy. In 1865 he was made a member of a lodge in New York; and in 1876 the Freemasons of Alexandria in Egypt appointed him as their Honorary Grand Master. His children also became Freemasons. In 1871 Menotti was elected as a member of the joint Philadelphia and Concorde lodge, which had been formed by Polish, Hungarian and other immigrants in the United States; and Teresita became an honorary member of the Naples lodge in 1867.[20]

It is sad to think that his last years were unhappy, but many of his friends believed this. For many years he had got the better of his rheumatism by taking a great deal of exercise; but now, as a result of his wound at Aspromonte, he could no longer ride, or leap from rock to rock on the beach at Caprera; and the rheumatism became much worse. It confined him to a bath-chair, and, what was almost more inconvenient, it spread to his right hand, which made it very difficult for him to write. But a treatment which he received from a Swiss doctor, who wrote to him in 1876 offering to help him, had considerable effect, at least for a short time. His greatest grief was for the two children who had died. On 1 January 1872, the first anniversary of Rosa's death, he wrote to Speranza von Schwartz:

Rosa, like my other little daughter whom I lost in America, was too beautiful, too good for this wicked world. It seems to me that such beings are exotic plants, who willingly leave this vale of tears for happier regions. . . . Clelia has a good heart, but otherwise she is like Anita; these two children are very far from rivalling the two Rosas.[21]

His sorrow for his dead children had to some extent soured his affection for the surviving ones; but when, in October 1872, the five-year-old Clelia fell seriously ill of a fever, he realized how greatly he loved her. 'I hope I am not to lose our little fish, else I shall be in despair,' he wrote to Speranza.[22] But Clelia had another eighty-seven years to live.

On 23 April 1873 Francesca Armosino gave birth to a third child by Garibaldi, a son named Manlio, after the father of the heroine of Garibaldi's novel *Clelia*. Garibaldi became very fond of the boy, though he sometimes complained querulously of the noise which Clelia and Manlio made in their play. His grief for the loss of Rosa went deep; he frequently referred to it in his letters, and often walked down to her grave under the juniper tree off the track which led across Caprera.[23]

In November 1874 a general election took place, and as usual Garibaldi was elected as an MP for several constituencies. Italian politics had now settled down to comparative quiet after the heroic age of the *Risorgimento*, with only occasional disputes over the Pope's pension and the privileges of the Church, and over labour unrest and the rising Socialist movement, disturbing the consensus politics of the Liberal centre parties. Nearly all the moderate statesmen who took it in turn to govern Italy had been Garibaldini volunteers in their youth; Benedetto Cairoli, Crispi, Depretis and Mordini all became Prime Minister in the seventies and eighties. These old Garibaldini, in their government departments, completely abandoned the revolutionary doctrines to which their General still adhered on his island. When Depretis, Cairoli, Crispi and the Left came to power, they were as active as the Right in suppressing the Socialists and Bakuninists; and the old Garibaldino, Nicotera, was forced to resign as Minister of the Interior in 1877 when it was discovered that he had ordered the police to interfere illegally with the telegraph in their pursuit of revolutionaries.

In March 1875 Garibaldi, to everyone's surprise, came to Rome to take his seat in Parliament. It was the first time that he had been in Rome since he marched out of the beleaguered city on 2 July 1849; and it was the first time during the seventeen years that he had been a member of the Parliaments of Uruguay, the Kingdom of Sardinia, the Roman Republic, the Kingdom of Italy, and of France, that he had taken part in Parliamentary life as an uncontroversial MP. After speaking at a number of public meetings in Civita Vecchia, Velletri, and his constituency of the Trastevere, he took his seat in Parliament and spoke in a debate on the naval estimates in favour of a certain type of vessel as opposed to other kinds of ships. He introduced a bill for the utilization of the waters of the Tiber for irrigation purposes, which was adopted in principle by the government. In Parliament he was warmly received with prolonged applause by all the deputies; and Medici, who with all the other leading generals had met him at the station on his arrival in Rome, took him to the Quirinal to see Victor Emanuel, who greeted him warmly. The Quirinal was a suitable place for a reconciliation between the King and the guerrilla general, who had been wounded and imprisoned by the officers of the King on account of his efforts to place Victor Emanuel in the Quirinal, where Victor Emanuel would never have arrived if Garibaldi's methods alone had been used.[24]

Victor Emanuel, as usual, offered Garibaldi gifts and privileges, all of which Garibaldi refused. He asked only one favour of the King, that he would legitimize his children, Clelia and Manlio. Victor Emanuel said that this was impossible, and told Garibaldi that he was unable to legitimize his own bastards.[25]

Garibaldi's visit to Rome was widely reported in the world press, and his daughter Anita read about it in Crete. She asked Speranza to take her to Rome to see her father. Garibaldi had written to Speranza, asking her and Anita to come to see him in Rome; but Speranza did not respond. Anita then wrote a letter to Garibaldi, telling him how unhappy she was with Speranza, and threw it out of the window of her room in an envelope addressed merely to 'General Garibaldi'. It was picked up in the street of the Cretan village, and delivered at Caprera within a week. Garibaldi sent Menotti to Crete to bring Anita to Caprera. When she arrived, they found that her hair was crawling with lice. She spent six happy weeks with Garibaldi and his family on the island. Then, one day in August 1875, when she was playing with her half-brother Manlio by the seashore, she was seized by an attack of the malarial fever which not uncommonly affected newcomers to an area where malaria was rife until well into the twentieth century. She died that night, at the age of sixteen.[26]

This was yet another personal tragedy for Garibaldi. He not only lost another of his children, but also lost faith in Speranza, on whom he had depended so much for solace and friendship during recent years. Speranza made no reference in her book to the manner of Anita's departure from Crete, or of Garibaldi's letter to her about the lice in Anita's hair. She ended her book, after publishing an affectionate letter from Garibaldi written in Rome on 7 May 1875, with the comment:

> This was not the last letter I received from Garibaldi, but I stop here. In accordance with her father's wish, Anita left Crete. I prefer to throw a veil over the treatment with which father and daughter requited me for all I had done for them, as well as over Anita's mysterious death. . . . I owe it to the memory of the dead. . . . In history, Garibaldi will always shine resplendent as a sun; but even the sun has its spots.[27]

The whole tone of Speranza's book, in which lavish praise of Garibaldi is intermingled with discreditable revelations about him which are confirmed by no other writer, suggests that she intended not only to make money by publishing revelations about Garibaldi's private life, but also to blacken the memory of the man who had not repeated his proposal of marriage after she had refused him, and who, in the end, opened his eyes to the spiteful side of her nature and the unkind way in which she had treated his daughter and his former mistress.

Garibaldi was still troubled from time to time by financial difficulties. He sold his yacht to the government in order to pay his debts; but his ever-trusting nature, and the misfortune which always attended his business enterprises, caused a further disaster on this occasion, for his agent ran off to America with the purchase money. In 1874 the government and the public found out that he was in debt, and a National Gift was organized to help him. The money poured in, with thousands of people giving sums varying from 100 to 3,000 lire. At first he refused to accept the money, but after the victory of the Left-wing parties in the general election, and his happy visit to Rome in 1875, he was persuaded with difficulty to accept the gift from Depretis's government.[28]

He continued to interest himself in national and international politics. He strongly supported the revolt of the Bosnians, Herzegovi-nians and Bulgarians against Turkey. He had never accepted the argument of those revolutionaries, like Marx, who supported the Sultan because he was against the Tsar. 'It is time to have done with this carcass which is called Turkey,' he wrote to McAdam on 9 January 1867, 'not in favour of Russia, which we will fight when there will be need of it, but in favour of the oppressed Christians.' He remembered how, as a young sailor forty years before, he had seen the olives rotting on the ground at Olivieri in the island of Mytelene because the peasants were forced to sell the olives to the local Pasha at so low a price that it was not worth their while to pick them. During the revolt of 1876 some of his Garibaldini, under Canzio's leadership, went to fight for the Balkan revolutionaries; and Garibaldi denounced Disraeli and the decisions of the Congress of Berlin of 1878. He had also criticized Gladstone's government in 1873 for their failure to recognize and sup-port the Republican government of Spain; but he always expressed his regret whenever he felt bound to criticize the policy of Britain.[29]

He had not forgotten that the Trentino was still under the Austrians. In October 1876 he sent a message to the people of the Trentino to be ready for action next spring; but nothing more happened. He gave no support to the other Italian aspiration, which began to be in evidence after 1870, of overseas colonial expansion. In 1879 a report appeared in the Italian press that Menotti was preparing to lead an expedition to seize and colonize New Guinea. Garibaldi wrote to the editor of *Il Capitale* denying the rumour, ridiculing the plan, and stating that if the British had not colonized New Guinea, it could only be because it would not be advantageous to do so. He was more sympathetic to the idea put forward by the French Socialist, Henri Rochefort, that Menotti should lead an expedition to liberate the Communard priso-ners who had been deported to the penal settlements in New Caledonia; but the project did not materialize.[30]

In the spring of 1879, Queen Victoria visited Italy for the first time, spending a month's holiday in a villa at Baveno on Lake Maggiore. Neither the Prince of Wales nor the Dowager Duchess of Sutherland had ever told Garibaldi that Queen Victoria did not approve of him;

and Garibaldi saw her as the representative of the nation that he so greatly admired. He therefore wrote to her on 1 April:

> To the official welcome offered to the august sovereign of England the Italian people hold it to be their duty to add their own, offering her their good wishes and an expression of deeply felt gratitude for all that the noble English nation, so worthily governed by her, did for the unification of our country. G. Garibaldi.[31]

This letter caused some alarm at the British embassy in Rome, where it was feared that Garibaldi might call on Queen Victoria at her villa. On 5 April the Queen's secretary, General Ponsonby, who personally admired Garibaldi, informed the Queen that he had received a telegram from the British Ambassador, Sir Augustus Paget, 'who asks if he may answer that Your Majesty will certainly not receive General Garibaldi: and that should he ask to see Your Majesty that Sir A. Paget should reply that he cannot be received'. Paget was haunted by visions of enthusiastic demonstrations at the Queen's gate in honour of Garibaldi by his local admirers; but Ponsonby realized that any refusal to receive Garibaldi would have to be tactfully worded if Anglo-Italian relations were not to be endangered, and suggested referring the matter to the Foreign Secretary, Lord Salisbury. Paget's fears were groundless, as Garibaldi did not ask for an audience.[32]

A few days later, Garibaldi surprised everyone by launching a new political campaign. After travelling to Rome and announcing that he intended to reside permanently in the city, he proclaimed that 'the fasces of democracy have been formed', and founded the League of Democracy in April 1879. Most of the Left-wing organizations adhered to the League, and a number of prominent Radical leaders, including Bertani, Saffi, Avezzana, Alberto Mario and Cavellotti, served with Garibaldi on the executive committee. The objects of the League were the introduction of universal suffrage, the abolition of the constitutional guarantees which protected the position of the Pope, the confiscation of ecclesiastical property, and the abolition of the standing army and its replacement by a people's militia. Depretis's government was hostile to this programme; and while the new King, Umberto, who had succeeded to the throne on Victor Emanuel's death in 1878, visited Garibaldi's bedside when he heard of his illness, the police tore down the manifestoes of the League of Democracy which had been posted on the walls in the streets throughout Italy.[33]

On 1 September Garibaldi unexpectedly returned to Caprera, and here, at the age of seventy-two, he married Francesca Armosino. After a great deal of effort by Garibaldi's lawyers, his proceedings for divorce against Giuseppina Raimondi were successful; for although his petition was rejected by the High Court in July 1879, the Court of Appeal reversed the finding, and dissolved the marriage, on the grounds of non-consummation, on 14 January 1880. The marriage with Francesca took place twelve days later, in a civil ceremony at Caprera. Garibaldi described himself as a farmer (*agricoltore*) on the marriage register. King Umberto sent his congratulations. Menotti and Teresita came back to Caprera for the wedding; Ricciotti, who had married an English girl, Constance Hopcraft, in London in 1874, was in Melbourne with his family. On the morning of his wedding to Francesca, Garibaldi told his daughter Clelia of his first love affair with Francesca Roux in Nice fifty years before, and said that his first and his last love had both been called Francesca. Clelia, who was nearly thirteen, had emulated her father by saving a man from drowning at Civita Vecchia in the previous summer.[34]

In the autumn of 1880 Garibaldi bestirred himself again when he heard that Canzio had been arrested and charged with sedition. He immediately travelled from Caprera to Genoa and visited Canzio, being loudly cheered by the people as he passed through the streets on his way to the prison. At the same time, he resigned his seat in Parliament. 'Today', he wrote to his constituents in Rome, 'I can no longer act as a legislator in a country where liberty is suppressed, and the law serves only to guarantee freedom to the Jesuits and to the enemies of the Italian unity for which the bones of her best sons have been strewn on the battlefields during sixty years of struggle.' The MPs refused to accept his resignation, and the government released Canzio under an amnesty.[35]

Garibaldi was worn out physically, and conscious that his work was done. On 3 November he was in Milan for the unveiling of the monument to the men who had fallen at Mentana; but he was so ill that his speech had to be read for him by Canzio, and after the ceremony, to the government's relief, he returned to Caprera. In 1881 he joined in the protests of the international Radical movement against the French conquest of Tunisia, which led to great friction between France and Italy, and to riots in Marseilles in which members of the Italian minority were killed. The pro-French policy of Benedetto Cairoli, the Prime Minister, was discredited, and Cairoli fell, and was replaced by Depretis. Garibaldi shared the national indignation, and took the occasion to warn the Italian government and people, in letters to the press, about the danger of French imperialism and the need for a strong army and navy. He still resented the loss of Nice; and on the clear days, when he could see Corsica from his bed, he reflected that it ought to be an Italian, not a French, possession.[36]

In March 1882 there were official celebrations in Sicily to mark the six hundredth anniversary of the Sicilian Vespers, when the people of Sicily rose and massacred the Norman French garrison and freed the island from the rule of Charles, Duke of Anjou. Garibaldi decided to attend the celebrations in the 'land of the Vespers', as he had so often called Sicily in his speeches in 1860 and 1862. On his way he visited Naples, for the first time since 1860, and was received with tremendous enthusiasm; but when, after travelling through Calabria, he arrived at Palermo, and was carried on his litter from the steamer to his hotel along the Toledo, where the barricades had stood during the three days in May twenty-two years before, the people were asked not to cheer, lest the excitement prove too much for him. He was too ill to attend the official commemoration of the Vespers on 31 March. During his stay in Palermo, he received over 1,500 telegrams of greetings and support.[37]

He sailed for Caprera on 17 April. Six weeks later, on the morning of 1 June, he suddenly fell ill with a bronchial complaint, and during the night his condition became much worse. The next day, a hot and glorious summer day, he realized that he was dying. Menotti, who happened to be staying at Caprera, and Francesca were with him; but though cables were sent at once to Ricciotti and Teresita in Rome, they arrived too late. Garibaldi saw a ship sail past his window, and asked whether she was the ship bringing Ricciotti and Teresita. They told him that it was not; but he smiled when they said that the ship was bound for Sicily. Two finches flew in through the open window, and he told his friends not to drive them away, as they were perhaps the souls of his two baby daughters, the two Rosas, who had come to fetch him. At twenty past six, he asked them to fetch his nine-year-old son, Manlio; but he died before Manlio came, at 6.22 pm on Friday, 2 June 1882. In another month he would have been seventy-five.[38]

The news of his death, and the obituary notices, were the principal features in nearly every newspaper in the world. The praise was almost universal, even in journals which had been hostile to him during his lifetime. The Italian Parliament adjourned for a fortnight in tribute. The United States Congress and the Hungarian Parliament passed unanimous resolutions of sympathy; in Berne, thanks to the opposition of the Catholics, a similar resolution in the Swiss Parliament was contested, but passed by 63 votes against 20. The Common Council of the City of London voted unanimously for a resolution of condolence on the death of the revolutionary to whom they had given the freedom of the City. Queen Victoria, who often commented in her diary on the death of famous men, made no reference to Garibaldi's death; but her daughter Victoria, the German Crown Princess, disagreed with her about Garibaldi. 'So poor old Garibaldi has died at last,' wrote the Crown Princess to Queen Victoria on 4 June, 'in spite of all the ridiculous humbug and mischief that was mixed up with his name, he *was* a hero and a Patriot and his Country owes him Much. I was never able to withhold a certain degree of admiration & sympathy for him.'[39]

On several occasions since 1870, Garibaldi had told his friends that he wished to be cremated when he died; and in a document which he signed on 17 September 1881, he directed that his corpse was to be burned, and his ashes placed in the graves of his daughters Rosa and Anita. He did not wish to be cremated in a crematorium, because he had wished to be burned on an open fire ever since Jessie Mario had told him that Shelley's corpse had been burned in such a manner; and he told Francesca to keep the news of his death secret for a few days, until his body had been burned on the pyre, in case anyone tried to prevent it. But the news was known immediately, and his fears were realized. Apart from the fact that cremation had only recently been introduced, and aroused strong religious objections, the idea of burning Garibaldi's corpse outraged his admirers, and the Radicals and Left-wing politicians were the first to demand that he be buried at an official funeral. The matter was discussed at a meeting at Caprera of Francesca, Menotti, Teresita and Canzio, Crispi, Alberto Mario, Garibaldi's doctor Albanese, and his friend Fazzari. Francesca and Fazzari, who had both been asked by Garibaldi to ensure that his wish to be cremated was carried out, argued strongly that his corpse should be burned; but the others took the view that his body belonged to Italy and to his Garibaldini, and that the demand for an official funeral should prevail.[40]

Garibaldi was therefore buried at Caprera on 8 June, in the presence of Prince Tommaso, representing King Umberto, of the Presidents of both Houses of Parliament, of high-ranking officers of the army and navy, of members of the government, and of many of the survivors of the Thousand.* In the middle of the ceremony the fine weather ended in a great thunderstorm, which some people believed was a protest by the elements against the defiance of Garibaldi's wish to be cremated. A more serious disaster marked the memorial service in Montevideo, where a fire broke out and caused a panic in which twenty-seven persons lost their lives.[41]

Garibaldi's death left Francesca in possession of Caprera, and

*Garibaldi's body lies buried on the little terrace among the vine-trees, just outside the house at Caprera. For more than eighty years, through two world wars, a sentry stood permanently on guard at the grave. On Garibaldi's left lie the graves of his daughters Rosa, Anita and Teresita; on his right, those of his wife Francesca, and Manlio and Clelia. The body of his first wife Anita has never been brought to Caprera. In 1932 it was transferred from Nice to Rome, and buried under the statue of Anita on the Janiculum.

severed the last links of Anita's children with the island. Menotti lived in Rome with his family. He entered the royal Italian army, and was given the rank of General. In 1895 he gave vent to those sympathies with Italian imperialism which Garibaldi had checked in 1879. The Governor of Eritrea, General Baratieri, who had been one of the Thousand, seized Tigre from Ethiopia. Crispi, as Prime Minister, gave full support to Baratieri, and Baratieri claimed that both he and Crispi had Garibaldian blood in their veins. Menotti joined in, and toasted Baratieri at a banquet as the man who had 'renewed in Africa the splendour of Garibaldi's victories'. Baratieri's defeat at Adowa in 1896 led to his being censured by a court martial, and to the fall of Crispi's government.[42]

Teresita, on the other hand, associated herself with the campaign to free the Left-wing revolutionary leaders who were sentenced to long terms of imprisonment by military tribunals after the street-fighting in Milan in 1898. When King Umberto paid an official visit to Caprera a few months later, Teresita caused a sensation by calling out 'Sire, pardon the political prisoners!'[43] They were all pardoned within three years.

Teresita died in January 1903, at the age of fifty-eight. Menotti died seven months later, in August, a month before his sixty-third birthday. Canzio, who had become a General and the Governor of the Port of Genoa, died in 1904.

Ricciotti, after returning from Australia, lived in Rome, and carried on his father's tradition of irregular warfare in defence of the freedom of other countries. In 1897 he led a corps of volunteers, in their red shirts, to fight for Greece against Turkey; and in 1912 he fought at Yannina in the war of Greece, Serbia and Bulgaria against Turkey. In 1914 his sons led the Garibaldini to fight for France in the First World War, before Italy joined the Allies. Ricciotti died in July 1924, aged seventy-seven.

Manlio entered the Italian navy, but died in January 1900, when he was only twenty-six. His mother, Francesca, died in 1923. Clelia, who never married, lived on at Caprera, occasionally granting interviews to journalists and to biographers of her father, and publishing articles and a book of reminiscences about him as she remembered him during the first fifteen years of her life. After her mother's death she had a reconciliation with the children of Ricciotti and Teresita. When she died in February 1959, a fortnight before reaching the age of ninety-two, Caprera passed into the possession of Ricciotti's son, General Ezio Garibaldi, whose widow lives there today.*

*Menotti left four daughters, but no sons. Ricciotti had eight children, but only one of his sons left a surviving son. There are numerous Canzio descendants of Teresita's

Garibaldi is still today an inspiration to the Italian people, and the Fascists, the Communists and the Liberals have all tried to claim him as their own. All have some justification for doing so. The Fascists can claim him as an Italian patriot and a believer in dictatorship; but his profound internationalism was utterly repugnant to Fascist doctrine. The Communists can claim him as a revolutionary leader who combined revolutionary nationalism with internationalism, who sympathized with Socialism and supported the International, and who was always ready to fight under any King or Republican leader in a united front against the main enemy of the moment; but the Communist concept of the disciplined political party and the totalitarian state would have disgusted Garibaldi. The Liberals have a better claim to Garibaldi, because of his belief in the nineteenth-century Liberal values of freedom and humanitarianism, even though he adopted revolutionary methods and had no respect for Parliament or the rule of law. Garibaldi believed in a temporary dictatorship, and distrusted professional politicians; but his idea of a dictatorship was not the twentieth-century totalitarian kind. If Garibaldi had been told that, to preserve himself in power as a dictator, he would have to build concentration camps or create a secret police, he would immediately have quitted and gone home to Caprera.

It is quite impossible to place Garibaldi in any of the political categories of the twentieth century. He was a product of nineteenth-century Radicalism, with its hatred of priests, which today is out-of-date even among revolutionaries, its passionate belief in a high, though anti-clerical, morality, and in the perfectability of the human race. His political doctrines, like his military tactics, belonged to the age before the invention of the machine-gun, to say nothing of the hydrogen bomb. As a military leader, he was a great commander on the battlefield, irrespective of whether or not he can be considered as a great general in the technical sense. In an age when, perhaps more than in any other before or since, victory was won less by technical efficiency than by the dogged courage of the infantryman, Garibaldi was unequalled in inspiring small and large bodies of men under his command to fight to the end, to snatch victory wherever possible, and if necessary to die rather than to retreat.

In recent times, his reputation has suffered to some extent from the exaggerated claims of his over-zealous admirers. Garibaldi did not win every battle in which he fought, and did not always fight against overwhelming odds. Of the fifty-three more important engagements in

nine children, most of whom still live in Genoa; but Signor Giuseppe Garibaldi, the twenty-five-year-old son of General Ezio Garibaldi, is the only descendant from Garibaldi's twenty-two grandchildren who still bears the family name of Garibaldi.

which he took part – not always as supreme commander of operations – he may be said to have won thirty-four, lost fifteen, and drawn four.* It is very doubtful whether Velletri and Bezzecca, which are considered as great victories, were really victories at all. In some of his victories – for example, Colonia, Luino, Varese and second Dijon – he had decisive superiority in numbers; and in others, like Morazzone, he was outmanoeuvred and defeated by a force no larger than his own. But it should be sufficient for his reputation as a David who could overcome a Goliath that he won at San Antonio and in Palermo, where he was outnumbered on the first occasion by about six to one and on the second occasion by nearly twenty to one; and it does not detract from his achievement that in both these battles, the enemy, as is self-evident, contributed to his victories by their incompetence and cowardice.

But it is not for his political doctrines, or for his great military achievements, that Garibaldi is still loved, in Britain nearly as greatly as in his native Italy, but for the warm personality and the absolute integrity and sincerity by which he, in his red shirt and with his long hair, could win the respect of the most strait-laced English aristocrat or naval officer, who denounced foreign revolutionaries in the same breath in which he praised Garibaldi. It was this warm-heartedness and love of human beings which made him as completely at home with the Prince of Wales and the Duke of Sutherland at Stafford House as with a group of Continental revolutionaries in Herzen's house at Teddington, though these qualities were also responsible for his only real fault – his excessive trust in his fellow-creatures, which made it impossible for him to believe that there was any guile or malice in Pacheco y Obes, Victor Emanuel or Speranza von Schwartz.

He did not deny that he enjoyed the excitement of war, but he never fought except for what he believed was the cause of human freedom. He declared at the Congress of Peace in Geneva that just as he would leap into their lake to save someone from drowning, so he would go to the aid of any nation which cried out to be rescued from

---

*The victories: the fight with the pirates in the Aegean, with the gunboats off Montevideo, Camaqua, first Laguna, Imbituba, Imarui, Santa Vitória, Serra do Espinasso, Taquari, Paraná, the Cerro, Tres Cruces, Colonia, Itapebí, Salto, San Antonio, first and second Daimán, Luino, Rome (30 April), Palestrina, Varese, San Fermo, Calatafimi, Palermo, Milazzo, first and second Reggio di Calabria, the Volturno, Bagolino, Monte Rotondo, first Lantenay, Autun, second Dijon.
The defeats: second Laguna, Curitibanos, San José do Norte, Costa Brava, Morazzone, Villa Corsini, Porta San Pancrazio (21 June), the Aurelian Wall (30 June), Laveno, Tre Ponti, Aspromonte, Monte Suello, Mentana, first Dijon, second Lantenay.
Indecisive: La Boyada, Machado, Velletri, Bezzecca.

oppression; and both in his life-saving activities and in waging war he put his principles into practice. He was not surprised that his actions were rewarded with ingratitude in Uruguay, Italy and France. He told Vecchi that human beings are divided into two types, 'the selfish ones, who never sacrifice anything for the common good, and the true patriots, who freely sacrifice what is most dear to them for the benefit of others. The latter are always misunderstood, insulted and dragged through the dirt, while the former rule the world.'[44]

There have been wiser politicians and greater generals than Garibaldi; but none has been more lovable or more loved.

BIBLIOGRAPHY

MANUSCRIPT SOURCES

Aberdeen MSS (British Museum)
Colección Pablo Blanco Acevido (Museo Histórico Nacional, Montevideo)
Autografos Colección Casavalle (Museo Histórico Nacional, Montevideo)
Cowen MSS (Central Library, Newcastle-upon-Tyne)
Cowen, Sarah – 'Life of Joseph Cowen'. See Cowen MSS
F. Frias MSS (Archivo General de la Nación, Buenos Aires)
Garibaldi MSS (Museo del Risorgimento, Milan)
Fondo Archivo General Administrativo (Archivo General de la Nación, Montevideo)
Ministerio de Guerra y Marina MSS (Archivo General de la Nación, Montevideo)
Liber Mortuarium, 1846–1880 (Mandriole Parish Church)
Libra de Casamentas, Laguna, 1832–1844 (Church of Santo Antonio de los Anjos, Laguna)
Lodge St Clair MSS (Glasgow)
McAdam MSS (Bedlay Castle, Chryston, Scotland)
Ministerio de la Marina MSS (Ministerio de la Marina, Buenos Aires)
Instituto Magnasco MSS (Gualeguaychú)
Ministério da Marinha: Capitania dos Portos do Estado de Santa Catarina: Directoria de Portos e Costas 1516–1944 (Florianópolis)
Mitre MSS (Museo Mitre, Buenos Aires)
Señora Pirretti de Novikov's MSS (Buenos Aires)
Correspondencia de Oribe con Rosas y Arana 1841–9 (Archivo General de la Nación, Buenos Aires)
Palmerston MSS (British Museum)
Alberto Palomque MSS (Museo Histórico Nacional, Montevideo)
Public Record Office MSS (London)
Senhor Desembargador Dr Belisário Nagueira Ramos's MSS (Florianópolis)
'Register of Marriages for the Church of St James's, Piccadilly', 1873–75 (Westminster City Library)
Correspondencia particular de Rosas (Archivo General de la Nación, Buenos Aires)
Royal Archives (Windsor Castle)
Church of San Francisco de Asis MSS (Montevideo)
Shaftesbury MSS (Broadlands Papers, Historical Manuscripts Commission, London)

639

NEWSPAPERS

The Albion (Liverpool, 1850)
L'Apostolato Popolare (London, 1842–3)
Archivo Americano y Espíritu de la Prensa del Mundo (Buenos Aires, 1843–8)
El Avisador Federal Extraordinario (Corrientes, 1843)
The Britannia and Montevideo Reporter (Montevideo, 1842–4)
British Packet and Argentine News (Buenos Aires, 1837–52)
Comercio del Plata (Montevideo, 1847–8)
El Conservador (Montevideo, 1847–8)
El Constitucional (Montevideo, 1843–7)
Correo de Lima (Lima, 1851)
Il Costituzionale Romano (Rome, 1848–9)
The Daily Chronicle and Northern Counties Advertiser (*Newcastle Daily Chronicle*
  (Newcastle-upon-Tyne, 1860–4)
Daily News (London, 1850–64)
The Daily Telegraph (London, 1864)
Defensor de la Independencia Americana (Miguelete, 1844–8)
La Démocratie Suisse (Geneva, 1867)
The Evening Standard (London, 1864)
The Falkirk Herald (Falkirk, 1860)
Il Felsineo (Bologna, 1846–8)
La Gaceta Mercantil (Buenos Aires, 1837–52)
The Gateshead Observer (Gateshead, 1854–60)
Gazzetta di Milano (Milan, 1848–9)
Gazzetta di Roma (Rome, 1848)
Gazzetta Piemontese (Turin, 1849)
Giornale Costituzionale del Regno delle Due Sicilie (Naples, 1860)
Giornale del Regno delle Due Sicilie (Naples, 1860)
Giornale di Roma (Rome, 1849)
Giornale Officiale di Napoli (Naples, 1860)
Glasgow Herald (Glasgow, 1864)
The Globe (London, 1845)
El Guerrillero de la Linea (Montevideo, 1843)
L'Italia del Popolo (Lausanne, 1850)
Jornal do Commercio (Rio de Janeiro, 1837–43)
Journal de Genève (Geneva, 1867–1912)
Il Legionario Italiano (Montevideo, 1844–6)
The Liverpool Mail (Liverpool, 1850)
The Liverpool Times (Liverpool, 1850)
Le Messager Français (Montevideo, 1842)
Il Mondo Illustrato (Turin, 1848)
Le Moniteur Universel (Paris, 1849–67)
Monitore Romano (Rome, 1849)
Morning Chronicle (London, 1846)
The Morning Star (London, 1862–4)

Muera Rosas! (Montevideo, 1842)
El Nacional (Montevideo, 1840–6)
The Newcastle Daily Chronicle. See *Daily Chronicle*
Newcastle Guardian (Newcastle-upon-Tyne, 1860)
Newcastle Journal (Newcastle-upon-Tyne, 1860)
New York Daily Tribune (New York, 1850–1)
North British Daily Mail (Glasgow, 1860–4)
The Northern Daily Express (Newcastle-upon-Tyne, 1857)
The Northern Tribune (Newcastle-upon-Tyne, 1854)
The Observer (London, 1862)
O Povo (Piratini and Caçapava, 1838–40)
Le Patriote Français (Montevideo, 1843–9)
The People's Paper (London, 1854)
Le Peuple (Paris, 1851)
Le Proscrit (Paris, London and Brussels, 1850)
The Red Republican (London, 1850)
The Saturday Review (London, 1864–70)
The Sheffield Daily Telegraph (Sheffield, 1861)
The Sun (London, 1864)
The Sunday Times (London, 1860)
El Tambor de la Linea (Montevideo, [1843?])
The Times (London, 1848–83)
The Western Daily Press (Bristol, 1860)
The Windsor and Eton Express (Windsor, 1864)

BOOKS AND ARTICLES

ABBA, G. C. *The Diary of one of Garibaldi's Thousand* (Oxford, 1962)
— *Ricordi Garibaldini* (Turin, 1913)
— *Ritratti e Profili* (Turin, 1912)
Affaire Bordone. *Cour d'Assises de la Seine. Affaire Bordone. Procès en diffamation* (Paris, 1872)
A.G.P. 'Santa Lucía de los Astos: La ciudad que conoció a Garibaldi' (in *Historium* (Buenos Aires, Dec. 1968–Jan. 1969))
ALVENSLEBEN, L. VON. *Garibaldi, seine Jugend, sein Leben, seine Abenteuer und seine Kriegsthaten* (Weimar, 1859)
L'Ane et les Trois Voleurs (Paris, 1860)
Annales du Congrès de Genève 9–12 septembre 1867 (Geneva, 1868)
The Annual Register: a preview of public events at home and abroad for the year 1864 (London, 1865)
APPIA, L. *Souvenirs de la Campagne de Garibaldi dans le Tyrol en 1866* (Paris, no date)
Atti del Parlamento Subalpino 2ᴬ Sessione del 1849 – Discussioni della Camera dei Deputati (Turin, 1862)
Atti Ufficiali del Parlamento Italiano – Camera dei Deputati (Turin, no date)
BAKUNIN, M. *Archives Bakounine: Bakunin-Archiv* (Leyden, 1967)

BALLEYDIER, A. *Histoire de la révolution de Rome* (Paris, 1851)

BANDI, G. *Anita Garibaldi* (1st ed., 1889; 1932 (Florence) ed., with Preface by G. Doria, cited as 'Doria-Bandi')

— *I Mille* (Florence, 1903)

BARRAZA, C. F. 'Brown y Garibaldi' (in *Anuario de História Argentina* (Buenos Aires, 1943))

BATLLE, L. 'Biografia del general Pacheco y Obes' (in *Revista Historica*, vol. I, Montevideo, 1907)

BELLUZZI, R. *La ritirata di Garibaldi da Roma nel 1849* (Rome, 1899)

BELZOPPI, EMILIA. Diary. See Franciosi

BENT, J. T. *The Life of Giuseppe Garibaldi* (2nd ed., London, 1882)

BERTANI, A. *L'Epistolario di Giuseppe La Farina: Ire politiche d'oltre tomba* (Florence, 1869)

BESEGHI, U. *Il Maggiore 'Leggero' e il 'Trafugamento' di Garibaldi* (2nd ed., Ravenna, 1932)

BIANCHI, C. *Il barone Ricasoli, Mazzini, Garibaldi* (Turin, 1862)

BIASE, C. DE. *L'Arresto di Garibaldi nel settembre 1849* (Florence, 1941)

BIDISCHINI, F. *Garibaldi nelle vita intima* (Rome, 1907)

Biografias Navales (Buenos Aires, 1963)

BISMARCK, O. VON. *Werke in Auswahl* (vol. VIII) (Stuttgart, 1963)

BLAKISTON, N. *Garibaldi's visit to England in 1864* (Milan, 1964)

— *The Roman Question* (London, 1962)

BLANC, LOUIS *Garibaldi, discours prononcé le 4 juillet 1875* (Paris, 1875)

BOGGIO, P. A. *Da Montevideo a Palermo: Vita di Giuseppe Garibaldi* (Turin, 1860)

BOITEUX, H. *Anita Garibaldi* (Rio de Janeiro, 1933)

BONNET, G. *Lo sbarco di Garibaldi a Magnavacca* (Bologna, 1887)

BORDONE, J. P. T. *L'Armée des Vosges et la Commission d'Enquête sur les actes du Gouvernement de la Défense Nationale* (Paris, 1875)

— *Garibaldi* (1807–1882) (Paris, no date)

— *Garibaldi et l'armée des Vosges* (Paris, 1871) (cited as 'Bordone')

— *Garibaldi, sa vie, ses aventures, ses combats* (Paris, 1878)

See Affaire Bordone

BOSCH, BEATRIZ. 'Entre Ríos a mediados del Siglo XIX' (in *Cronicas de Entre Ríos* (Buenos Aires, 1967))

BOURGIN, G. 'Le dossier du Saint-Simonisme' (in *Revue d'histoire économique et sociale*, vol. XIX (Paris, 1931))

BRENTARI, O. *Garibaldi a Milano* (Turin and Milan, 1907)

BROOKE, W. B. *Out with Garibaldi, or From Milazzo to Capua* (London, [1861])

BROSSARD, A. DE. *Considérations historiques et politiques sur les Républiques de la Plata dans leurs rapports avec la France et l'Angleterre* (Paris, 1850)

BROWN, W. *Documentos del Almirante Brown* (Buenos Aires, 1958–9)

BUNSEN, MADAME C. DE. *In Three Legations* (London, 1909)

BUSCH, M. *Bismarck – some secret pages of his history* (London, 1898)

CAILLET-BOIS, T. *Ensayo de Historia naval argentina* (Buenos Aires, 1929)

— *Los marinos durante la Dictadura* (Buenos Aires, 1935)

CALMON, P. *História do Brasil* (Rio de Janeiro, 1959–61)

CALONNE, A. DE. *M. Rattazzi et la Crise Italienne* (Paris, 1862)

CAMPANELLA, A. P. 'Ammiratori di Garibaldi in Inghilterra' (in *Nuova Antalogia,* vol. 486, (Rome, 1962)

— *Garibaldi and the first Peace Congress in Geneva in 1867* (Amsterdam, 1960)

— *Giuseppe Garibaldi e la tradizione Garibaldina: Una Bibliografia dal 1807 al 1970* (Geneva, 1971)

— *Joseph Cowen, Garibaldi e Mazzini* (Milan, 1966)

— *La legione Britannica nell' Italia Meridionale con Garibaldi nel 1860* (Palermo, 1964)

CARMAGNOLE, A. J. 'Garibaldi à Genève pour le Congrès de la Paix de 1867' (in *Journal de Genève,* 23 Sept. ,1912)

CARR, E. H. *Michael Bakunin* (London, 1937)

CARRANO, F. *I Cacciatori delle Alpi comandati dal generale Garibaldi nella guerra del 1859 in Italia* (including Garibaldi's Memoirs) (Turin, 1860)

CARRANZA, A. J. 'Campanias Navales de la República Argentina: Costa Brava 15 y 16 de agosto de 1842' (in *Revista Nacional,* vols. XXIX-XXXIII, Buenos Aires, 1900–2)

— 'Garibaldi' (in *Revista Nacional,* vol. XLIV (Buenos Aires, 1907))

Carteggio del governo Provvisorio di Lombardia con i suoi rappresentanti al Quartier Generale di Carlo Alberto (ed. A. Monti) (Milan, 1923)

CASARETTO, P. F. 'Il ritorno di Garibaldi del secondo esilio' (in *Nuova Antalogia,* vol. 235, Rome, 1911))

CASTELLANI, G. A. 'Come Garibaldi fu liberato dal Varignano nel 1867' (in *Nuova Antalogia,* vol. 254 (Rome, 1914))

CASTELLI. See Chiala

CAVALLOTTI, F. *Storia del Insurrezione di Roma nel 1867* (completed by B. E. Maineri) (Milan, 1869)

CAVOUR, C. DI. 'Des Chemins de Fer en Italie'. See Chiala

Cavour e l'Inghilterra: Carteggio con V. E. d'Azeglio (Bologna, 1933)

Cavour-Nigra. *Il Carteggio Cavour-Nigra dal 1858 al 1861* (Bologna, 1929) See also Chiala; *Liberazzione del Mezzogiorno*

CESARESCO, EVELYN MARTINENGO. *The Liberation of Italy 1815–1870* (London, 1895)

CHAMBERS, O. W. S. *Garibaldi and Italian Unity* (London, 1864)

CHIALA, L. *Lettere edite ed inedite di Camillo Cavour* (Turin, 1883–7) (cited as 'Chiala')

— *Ricordi di Michelangelo Castelli* (Turin and Naples, 1888)

CHIAMA, LETIZIA. 'La Fuga di G. Garibaldi da Genova nel 1834' (*Nuova Antalogia,* vol. 266 (Rome, 1916))

CIAMPOLI, D. *Giuseppe Garibaldi: scritti politici e militari ricordi e pensieri inediti* (Rome, 1907)

CILIBRIZZI, S. *Storia Parlamentare Politica e Diplomatica d'Italia* (Naples, 1923–40)

CLOUGH, A. H. *Prose Remains of Arthur Hugh Clough* (London, 1888)

COLLOR, L. *Garibaldi et a Guerra dos Farrapos* (Rio de Janeiro, 1938)

CORNELI, A. *Giuseppe Garibaldi nell' Uruguay* (Buenos Aires, 1951)

COSTA, C. *O Visconde de Sinimbú* (São Paulo, 1937)

CRIOLLO VIEJO. 'José Garibaldi en Entre Ríos.' See Villanueva

CRISPI, F. *The Memoirs of Francesco Crispi* (ed. T. Palamenghi-Crispi) (London, 1912)

Cronicas de Entre Ríos. See Bosch

CUNEO, G. B. *Biografia di Giuseppe Garibaldi* (Genoa, 1876 ed.) (first published Turin, 1850)

CUNNINGHAME-GRAHAM, R. *Three Fugitive Pieces* (ed. H. F. West) (Hanover, New Hampshire, 1960)

CURÀTULO, G. E. 'Ancora dell' autografo segreto di Vittorio Emanuele II a Garibaldi del passaggio in Calabria' (in *Risorgimento Italiano*, vol. II Turin, 1909)

— *Autografi, Documenti storici e Cimeli riguardanti Garibaldi e il Risorgimento Italiano* (Garibaldi MSS) (Rome, 1917)

— *Garibaldi e le donne* (Rome, 1913)

— *Garibaldi, Vittorio Emanuele, Cavour nei fasti della patria* (Bologna, 1911)

CUYÁS Y SAMPERE, A. 'Apuntes Históricos sobre la Provincia de Entre Ríos' – see Villanueva

DABADIE, F. 'Episode inédit de la vie de Garibaldi' (in *Revue Française*, vol. XVII (Paris, 1859))

DAHLERUP, H. B. *Mit Livs Beginenheder* (Copenhagen, 1908–12)

DANDOLO, E. *The Italian Volunteers and Lombard Rifle Brigade* (London, 1851)

Dearest Child. See VICTORIA, QUEEN

DELLA ROCCA, E. *The Autobiography of a Veteran* (London, 1899)

DELLA VALLE, G. *Varese, Garibaldi ed Urban nel 1859* (Varese, 1863)

DE-MARIA, I. *Anales de la Defensa de Montevideo 1842–1851* (Montevideo, 1883)

Der deutsch-französische Krieg 1870–71 (War Office, Berlin, 1874-81)

DES PORTES, R. BITTARD *1849: L'expédition française de Rome sous la Deuxième République* (2nd ed., Paris, 1905)

DIAZ, A. *Historia politica y militar de las Repúblicas del Plata* (Montevideo, 1877–8)

DIAZ, C. *Memorias inéditas del General Oriental Don César Diaz* (Buenos Aires, 1878)

DIERAUER, J. 'Eine Erinnerung an Garibaldi (nach Briefen eines Schweizers in Catania 1862)' (lecture in 1912, published in *Festgabe für G. Meyer von Knonau* (no place or date))

DUMAS, ALEXANDRE THE ELDER. *Causeries* (Paris, 1860)

— *Les Garibaldiens – révolution de Sicile et de Naples* (Paris, 1861)

— *Montevideo, ou une nouvelle Troie* (Paris, 1850)

See also Garibaldi; Garnett

DUPANLOUP, F. A. P. *Lettre à M. Ratazzi* [sic] *Président du Conseil des Ministres du Roi d'Italie sur les Entreprises de Garibaldi* (Paris, 1867)

DURAFORD, J. *Avant Pendant et Après, ou Garibaldi à Genève* (Geneva, 1867. 1st ed.)

DWIGHT, T. See Garibaldi

ELLESMERE, LORD. See Meyer

ELLIOT, SIR H. *Some revolutions and other diplomatic experiences* (London, 1922)

Enciclopedia Italiana (Rome, 1936)

Enciclopedia Universal Illustrada Europeo-Americana (Barcelona, 1930)
Encyclopaedia Britannica (13th ed., London and New York, 1926)
ENGELS, F. and MARX, K. *Der Briefwechsel zwischen Friedrich Engels und Karl Marx, 1844 bis 1883* (ed. A. Bebel and E. Bernstein) (Stuttgart, 1913)
Enquête Parlementaire sur les actes du Gouvernement de la Défense Nationale (Assemblée Nationale) (Paris, 1875)
'Extracts from the Journal of an Englishwoman at Naples' (in *Macmillan's Magazine*, vol. III (Cambridge, 1860))
FAGAN, L. *The Life of Sir Anthony Panizzi* (London, 1880)
— *The Reform Club* (London, 1887)
FARRAGUT, L. *The Life of David Glasgow Farragut* (New York, 1879)
FAZY, J. *Les Mémoires de James Fazy* (Geneva, 1947)
FERRÉ, P. *Memoria del Brigadier General Pedro Ferré* (Buenos Aires, 1921)
FILIPUZZI, A. *La pace di Milano (6 agosto 1849)* (Rome, 1955)
FINALI, G. *Le Marche* (Ancona, 1896)
FLETCHER, J. C. and KIDDER, D. P. *Brazil and the Brazilians* (9th ed., London, 1879). See also Kidder
FOGLIETTI, R. *Garibaldi in Macerata negli anni 1848 e 1849* (Macerata, 1888)
FORBES, C. S. *The Campaign of Garibaldi in the Two Sicilies* (Edinburgh, 1861)
FORTINI, P. *Giuseppe Garibaldi Marinaio Mercantile* (Rome, 1950)
FRANCIOSI, P. *Garibaldi e la Repubblica di San Marino* (Florence, 1949)
FRANCIS, J. W. *Old New York, or Reminiscences of the Past Sixty Years* (lecture of 1857) (New York, 1865)
FRAY, MOCHO, (J. S. Alvarez) *Obres Completas* (Buenos Aires, 1954)
FREITAS, N. *Garibaldi en América* (Buenos Aires, 1946)
GALTON, F. *Vatican Tourists and Notes of Travel in 1860* (London, 1861)
GARIBALDI, ANITA I. *Garibaldi en América* (Buenos Aires, 1930)
GARIBALDI, CLELIA. *Mio Padre* (Florence, 1948)
GARIBALDI, G. *Cantoni il Volontario* (Milan, 1870)
— *Clelia, ovvero Il governo del monaco (Roma nel secolo XIX)* (Milan, 1870)
— *Edizione Nazionale degli scritti di Giuseppe Garibaldi* (Bologna, 1932–7) (cited as 'Scritti')
— 'From General Garibaldi to his English Friends' (*Cassell's Magazine*, New Series, vol. I (London, 1870))
— I Mille. See *Scritti*
The Memoirs:
— *The Life of General Garibaldi written by himself. With sketches of his Companions in Arms. Translated by his friend and admirer Theodore Dwight* (London and New York, 1859) (cited as 'Dwight')
— *Mémoires de Garibaldi, par Alexandre Dumas* (Brussels, 1860–2) (cited as 'Dumas')
— *Garibaldi's Denkwürdigkeiten* (ed. Elpis Melena) (Hamburg, 1861) (cited as 'Melena')
— *Le memorie di Garibaldi nella redazione definitiva del 1872.* See *Scritti* (cited as 'Scritti, II')
— *Autobiography of Giuseppe Garibaldi. Authorized translation by A. Werner. With a supplement by Jessie White Mario* (London, 1889) (cited as 'Werner.')

645

Vols. I and II are Werner's translation of the Italian 1872 edition; vol. III is an original work by Jessie White Mario
— *The Memoirs of Garibaldi, edited by Alexandre Dumas. Translated and with an introduction by R. S. Garnett* (London, 1931)
See also Carrano; Ciampoli; Ximenes
— *Poema Autobiografico* (ed. Curàtulo) (Bologna, 1911)
— *The Rule of the Monk, or Rome in the Nineteenth Century* (London and New York, no date) (English translation of *Clelia*)
Garibaldi condottiero (Rome, 1932)
Garibaldi en América (Buenos Aires, 1888)
GARNETT, R. S. *On Board the Emma* (London, 1929) (English translation of Dumas's *Les Garibaldiens*, with additional material)
See also Garibaldi, Memoirs
GAY, H. NELSON. 'Lincoln's offer of a command to Garibaldi' (in *Century Magazine*, vol. LXXV (New York, 1907)
— 'Il Secondo Esilio di Garibaldi' (*Nuova Antalogia*, vol. 231 (Rome, 1910)
General Garibaldi at Fishmonger's Hall. See Weston
GERNSHEIM, H. *Julia Margaret Cameron* (London, 1948)
GERSON, B. *Garibaldi e Anita* (Rio de Janeiro, 1953)
GIAMPAOLO, L. and BERTOLONE, M. *La prima campagna di Garibaldi in Italia* (Varese, 1950)
GIANELLO, S. 'El asunto de Garibaldi en Gualeguay'. See Villanueva. See also Biografias Navales
GILLEY, S. 'The Garibaldi riots of 1862' (in *Historical Journal*, vol. XVI) (Cambridge, 1973)
GIORGIONI, M. 'Garibaldi vince sempre!' (in *La Nuova Sardegna*, 21 Dec. 1972)
GOËTHE, LOUISE. *Garibaldi: sa Vie, son Enfance, ses Moeurs. ses Exploits Militaires* (Paris, 1859)
GORCE, P. DE LA. *Histoire du Second Empire*, vol. IV (Paris, 1901)
GRADENIGO, G. *Garibaldi in America con il diario della legione Italiana di Montevideo* (Montevideo, 1967)
La Grande Encyclopédie (Paris, 1887–1902)
Grandes Personagens da nossa història (ed. V. Civita) (São Paulo, 1969)
GRUBER, E. *Giuseppe Mazzini, Massoneria e Rivoluzione* (Rome, 1901)
GUERRAZZI, F. D. *Lo Assedio di Roma* (Leghorn, 1864)
GUERRINI, D. 'La missione del conte Giulio Litta Modignani in Sicilia (1860)' (in *Il Risorgimento Italiano*, vol. II (Turin 1909))
— 'Riposta del colonello D. Guerrini' (in *Il Risorgimento Italiano,* vol. II (Turin, 1909))
GUERZONI, G. *Garibaldi* (Florence, 1882)
HALES, E. Y. Y. *The Catholic Church in the Modern World* (London, 1958)
— *Mazzini and the Secret Societies* (London, 1956)
— *Pio Nono* (London, 1954)
Halte-là, Garibaldi! (Paris, 1860)
Hansard (London, 1844–64)
HARRISON, F. *Autobiographic Memoirs* (London, 1911)
HAUSSONVILLE, G.D', 'M. de Cavour et la crise italienne' (in *Revue des Deux*

Mondes, vol. XLI (Paris, 1862)

HERZEN, A. *Camicia Rossa: Garibaldi à Londres* (Brussels, 1865)

— *My Past and Thoughts: the Memoirs of Alexander Herzen* (London, 1968)

HIBBERT, C. *Garibaldi and his Enemies* (London, 1965)

HODDER, E. *The Life and Work of the Seventh Earl of Shaftesbury* (London, 1886)

HOFFSTETTER, G. VON. *Tagebuch aus Italien 1849* (Zürich and Stuttgart, 1851)

HOLT, E. *Risorgimento: the Making of Italy 1815–1870* (London, 1970)

HOLYOAKE, G. J. *Bygones worth remembering* (London, 1905)

— *Sixty Years of an Agitator's Life* (London, 1893)

HOSTETTER, R. *The Italian Socialist Movement* (Princeton, N. J., 1958)

HOWARD, M. *The Franco-Prussian War* (London, 1960)

HÜBNER, A. VON. *Neuf Ans de Souvenirs d'un Ambassadeur d'Autriche à Paris* (Paris, 1904)

IDEVILLE, H. D'. *Journal d'un diplomate en Italie* (Paris, 1872)

I documenti diplomatici Italiani (Rome, 1952–68)

The Illustrated Life and Career of Garibaldi (London, 1860)

INDARTE, R. *Efemerides de los deguellos asesinatos y matonzas del degollador Juan Manuel Rosas* (Montevideo, [1842?])

— *Rosas y sus opositores* (Montevideo, 1843) (incorporating his *Tables de Sangre*)

Instructions to Mr Ouseley, Her Majesty's Minister at Buenos Ayres (Parliamentary Papers) (London, 1846)

IRAZUSTA, J. *Vida Politica de Juan Manuel de Rosas a través du su correspondencia* (Buenos Aires, 1941–7)

IRIARTE, T. DE. *Memorias* (ed. E. de Gandía) (Buenos Aires), 1944–72)

JOLIVAUD, L. *Victor-Emanuel et Garibaldi* (Paris. 1862)

KIDDER, D. P. *Sketches of Residence and Travels in Brazil* (Philadelphia and London, 1845)

See Fletcher

KING, BOLTON. *Mazzini* (London, 1902)

KLEIN, P. S. *President James Buchanan* (Pennsylvania, 1962)

KOELMAN, J. P. *In Rome 1846–1851* (Arnhem, 1869)

KOLOWRAT-KRAKOWSKY, L. *Meine Erinnerungen aus dem Jahre 1848 und 1849* (Vienna, 1905)

Kossuth, Mazzini, Garibaldi (Vienna, 1861)

KRASINSKY, H. *Italy, Venetia and Hungary* (London, 1861)

LA FARINA, G. *Epistolario di Giuseppe La Farina* (Milan, 1869)

LAMAS, A. *Escritos Politicos y Literarios de D. Andres Lamas* (ed. A. J. Carranza) (Buenos Aires, 1877)

LA MESSINE, JULIETTE. *Garibaldi, sa vie d'après des documents inédits* (Paris, 1859)

LA RIVE, W. DE. *Le Comte de Cavour* (Paris, 1862)

LAZZARI, A. *Il Capitano Angelo Pesante di San Remo e Giuseppe Garibaldi* (San Remo, 1907)

LEECH, MARGARET. *Reveille in Washington* (London, 1942)

LESSEPS, F. DE. *Mémoire présenté au Conseil d'Etat* (Paris, 1849)

Lettere ad Antonio Panizzi di uomini illustri e di amici Italiani 1823–1870 (ed. L.

Fagan) (Florence, 1880)

LEYNADIER, C. *Mémoires authentiques de Garibaldi* (Paris, 1864)

La liberazione del Mezzogiorno e la formazione del regno d'Italia: Carteggio di Camillo Cavour (Bologna, 1949–54)

The Life of Garibaldi: including his career in South America, Rome, Piedmont and Lombardy (London, 1864)

LINTON, W. J. *European Republicans* (London, 1893)

LOEVINSON, E. *Giuseppe Garibaldi e la sua legione nello stato romano 1848–49* (Rome and Milan, 1902–7)

LOWE, C. *Bismarck's Table Talk* (London, 1895)

LUBBOCK, B. *The China Clippers* (Glasgow, 1919)

— *The Opium Clippers* (Glasgow, 1933)

LUTYENS, MARY. *Effie in Venice* (London, 1965)

LUZIO, A. *Garibaldi, Cavour, Verdi* (Turin, 1924) (cited as 'Luzio')

— *Giuseppe Mazzini Carbonaro* (Turin, 1920)

— *La Massoneria e il Risorgimento Italiano* (Bologna, 1925)

— 'Per un' edizione critica delle Memorie di Garibaldi' (in *Corriere della Sera*, Rome, 15 Sept. 1907)

MCGRIGOR, SIR C. *Garibaldi at Home: notes of a visit to Caprera* (London, 1866)

MACK SMITH, D. *Cavour and Garibaldi 1860* (Cambridge, 1954)

— *Garibaldi* (London, 1957)

— *Garibaldi: Great Lives Observed* (Englewood Cliffs, N. J., 1969)

— *The Making of Italy* (London, 1968)

— *Victor Emanuel, Cavour, and the Risorgimento* (London, 1971)

MAGARINOS DE MELLO, M. J. *La Misión de Florencio Varela a Londres, 1843–1844* (Montevideo, 1944)

— 'La política exterior del Imperio del Brasil y les intervenciones extranjeros en el Rio de la Plata' (in *Miscelanea Americanista* (Madrid, 1949))

MAINERI, B. E. See Cavallotti; Manin

MALLALIEU, A. *Buenos Ayres – Monte Video and affairs in the River Plate* (London, 1844)

— *Rosas and his Calumniators* (London, 1845)

MALMESBURY, THIRD EARL OF. *Memoirs of an ex-Minister* (London, 1885)

MANIN, D. *Documents et Pièces Authentiques laissés par Daniel Manin* (Paris, 1860)

— *Daniele Manin e Giorgio Pallavicino: Epistolario Politico 1855–1857* (ed. B. E. Maineri) (Milan, 1878)

MANNING, H. *Miscellanies* (London, 1896)

MARCHESE, P. S. *Giuseppe Garibaldi* (Turin, 1861)

MARIO, A. *The Red Shirt* (London, 1885)

MARIO, JESSIE WHITE *Agostino Bertani e i suoi tempi* (Florence, 1888)

— *The Birth of Modern Italy* (ed. Duke Litta-Visconti-Arese) (London 1909)

— *Garibaldi e i suoi tempi* (Milan, 1884)

— Supplement to Werner's edition of Garibaldi's Memoirs. See Garibaldi

MARX, K. *The Civil War in France* (London, 1933). See Engels

MAZZINI, G. *Edizione Nazionale degli Scritti di Giuseppe Mazzini* (Imola, 1906–43)

— *The Life and Writings of Joseph Mazzini* (London, 1864–70)

— *Mazzini e l'Internazionale* (Rome, 1871)

MELENA, ELPIS. *Garibaldi: Recollections of his Public and Private Life* (London, 1887)

See also Garibaldi, Memoirs

MERCANTINI, L. *Inno di Garibaldi* (London, 1861)

MEYER, W. *Die kriegenschen Ereignisse in Italien im Jahre 1848* (Zürich, 1848)

— *Die kriegenschen Ereigbisse in Italien im Jahre 1849* (Zürich, 1850) (English translation of both vols. by Lord Ellesmere)

MIRECOURT, E. DE. *Garibaldi* (Paris, 1867)

MITRE, B. *Paginas de Historia* (La Plata, 1944)

— 'Un Episodio Troyano'. See *Garibaldi en América*

MÖGLING, T. *Ein Besuch bei Garibaldi im Sommer 1859* (Zürich, 1860)

MONTI, A. 'L'"Agricoltore" Giuseppe Garibaldi (con inediti del "Diario Agricolo" di Caprera)' (in *Nuova Antologia,* vol. 375 (Rome, 1934)

— *La Vita di Garibaldi giorno per giorno narrata e illustrata* (Milan, 1932))

MONYPENNY, W. F. and BUCKLE, G. E. *The Life of Benjamin Disraeli, Earl of Beaconsfield* (London, 1929 ed.)

MORLEY, J. *The Life of William Ewart Gladstone* (London. 1903)

MORNAND, F. *Garibaldi* (Paris, 1866)

MULHALL, M. G. *The English in South America* (Buenos Aires, 1878)

MUNDY, SIR R. *H.M.S. 'Hannibal' at Palermo and Naples during the Italian Revolution 1859–1861* (London, 1863)

ODINICI, B. Diary. See Gradenigo

OLIPHANT, L. *Episodes in a Life of Adventure* (Edinburgh, 1887)

OLIPHANT, MARGARET. *Memoir of the Life of Laurence Oliphant and of Alice Oliphant, his Wife* (Edinburgh, 1892)

'Le onoranze garibaldine a Cesenatico' (in *Rassegna Storica del Risorgimento,* vol. XXV (3) (Rome, 1938))

ORIBE, A. B. *Brigadier General Don Manuel Oribe* (Montevideo 1913)

OSSOLI. *Memoirs of Margaret Fuller Ossoli* (London, 1852)

PACHECO Y OBES, M. *Rectification de Faits Calomnieux attribués à la défense de Montevideo* (Paris, 1849)

— *Réponse aux Détracteurs de Montevideo* (Paris, 1849)

— *Rosas et Montevideo devant la Cour d'Assises* (Paris, 1851)

PALASCIANO, F. *La Palla nella Ferita del Generale Garibaldi* (Naples, 1862)

PALÉOLOGUE, M. *Un grand réaliste: Cavour* (Paris, 1926)

PALLAVICINO, G. *Memorie di Giorgio Pallavicino* (Turin, 1882–95). See also Manin

PARRIS, E. *The Lion of Caprera* (London, 1962)

PAZ, J. M. *Memorias Postumas* (Buenos Aires, 1892)

PECORINI-MANZONI, C. *Storia della 15A Divisione Türr* (Florence, 1876)

PEMBERTON, W. B. 'Garibaldi's Englishman: the story of Colonel John Peard' (*History Today*, vol. IX (London, 1959))

PEREDA, S. E. *Garibaldi en el Uruguay* (Montevideo, 1914–16)

PERRENS, F. T. *Deux Ans de la Révolution en Italie (1848–1849)* (Paris, 1857)

PERSANO, C. DI. *Diario privato-politico-militare*, (2nd ed., Florence, 1869)

PIERI, P. *Storia militare del Risorgimento* (Turin, 1962)

PISACANE, C. *Guerra combattuto in Italia negli anni 1848–49* (Genoa, 1851)

PITZ, C. *Biographie du Général Garibaldi* (Paris, 1859)

PRADERIO, A. *Indice Cronologico de la Prensa Periodica del Uruguay 1807–1852* (Montevideo, 1962)

Il Problema veneto e l'Europa 1859–1866 (ed. R. Blaas, N. Blakiston and G. Dethan) (Venice, 1966–7)

PROUDHON, P. J. *Garibaldi et l'unité italienne* (Brussels, 1862)

RADETZKY, J. VON. *Briefe des Feldmarschalls Radetzky an seine Tochter Friederike 1847–1857* (ed. B. Duhr, S. J.) (Vienna, 1892)

RADICE, B. *Nino Bixio a Bronte* (Caltanisetta and Rome, 1963)

RAMA, C. M. *Garibaldi y el Uruguay* (Montevideo, 1968)

RATTAZZI, LETIZIA. *Rattazzi et son temps* (Paris, 1881)

RATTO, H. R. *Almirante Guillermo Brown* (Buenos Aires, 1961)

— *Historia de Brown* (Buenos Aires, 1939)

RAVA, L. *Vittorio Emanuele e Garibaldi nella spedizione dei Mille* (Rome, 1911)

REICHARDT, H. C. *Bento Gonçalves* (Porto Alegre, 1932)

— *Ideas de liberdade no Rio Grande do Sul a guerra dos Farrapos* (Rio de Janeiro, 1928)

Le Relazioni Diplomatiche fra l'Austria e il Granducato di Toscana (ed. A. Filipuzzi) (Rome, 1966–9)

Le Relazioni Diplomatiche fra l'Austria e il Regno di Sardegna e la Guerra del 1848–49 (ed. A. Filipuzzi) (Rome, 1961)

Le Relazioni diplomatiche fra la Francia e il Granducato di Toscana (ed. A. Saitta) (Rome, 1959–60)

RETA, E. Diary. See Chiama

RIBO, J. J. *Retrato Histórico del Rey de las Dos Sicilias Francisco II* (Barcelona, 1864)

RICCIARDI, G. *Da Quarto a Caprera* (Naples, 1875)

RODRIGUEZ, V. *Memorias Militares del General Don Ventura Rodríguez* (Montevideo, 1919)

Rome and Venice: Memoirs of Albert and Jessie White Mario (London, 1861)

SACCHI, C. 'Batalla de San Antonio, relato del Gral. Cayetano Sacchi' (in 'Homenaje a Garibaldi en campos de San Antonio', in *Revista Military Naval* (Montevideo, Nov.–Dec. 1934))

SACERDOTE, G. *La Vita di Giuseppe Garibaldi* (Milan, 1933)

SAINT-HILAIRE, A. DE. *Voyage dans les provinces de Saint-Paul et de Sainte Catherine* (Paris, 1851)

SALDANA, J. M. F. 'Retrato de Rugendas Garibaldi' (in *La Prensa*, Buenos Aires, 16 Nov. 1941)

SALDÍAS, A. *Historia de la Confederación Argentina* (Buenos Aires, 1930–1 ed.)

SALVEMINI, G. *Scritti sul Risorgimento* (Milan, 1961)

SARDAGNA, F. *Garibaldini in Lombardia 1848* (Milan, 1927)

SARMIENTO, D. F. *Life in the Argentine Republic in the Days of the Tyrants: or, Civilization and Barbarism* (New York, 1868)

SCHNEIDAWIND, K. *Aus dem Hauptquartiere und Feldleben des Vater Radetzky* (Stuttgart, 1856)
— *Radetzky-Lieder* (Leipzig, 1858)
SCHWARTZ, ESPERANZA VON. See Melena.
SETON WATSON, C. *Italy from Liberalism to Fascism 1870–1925* (London, 1967)
SFORZA, G. *Garibaldi in Toscana nel 1848* (Rome, 1897)
STOCHI, G. 'Un paragrafo inedito della vita di Giuseppe Garibaldi' (in *La Rassegna Nazionale*, vol. LXV (Florence, 1892))
TENNYSON, ALFRED LORD. *Poetical Works of Alfred Lord Tennyson* (London, 1926)
TENNYSON, HALLAM. *Alfred Lord Tennyson: a memoir by his son* (London, 1897)
THAYER, W. R. *The Life and Times of Cavour* (London and New York, 1911)
THOUVENEL, L. *Le Secret de l'Empereur* (Paris, 1889)
TONELLI, J. B. *Garibaldi y la Masoneria Argentina* (Buenos Aires, 1951)
TOWNSEND, G. A. *The Life and Battles of Garibaldi and his March on Rome in 1867* (New York, no date)
TREVELYAN, G. M. *Garibaldi's Defence of the Roman Republic* (London, 1907) (cited as 'Trevelyan, vol. I')
— *Garibaldi and the Thousand* (London, 1948 reprint of 4th ed. of 1910) (cited as 'Trevelyan, vol. II')
— *Garibaldi and the Making of Italy* (London, 2nd ed., 1911) (cited as 'Trevelyan, vol. III.')
— 'Garibaldi in South America; a new document' (in *The Cornhill Magazine*, New Series, vol. XXX (London, 1911))
— 'War Journals of "Garibaldi's Englishman"' (in *The Cornhill Magazine*, New Series, vol. XXIV (London, 1908))
TROLLOPE, THOMAS ADOLPHUS. *What I Remember* (London, 1887)
TUCKERMAN, H. T. 'Giuseppe Garibaldi' (anonymous book review of Arthur's *Italy in Transition* in *The North American Review*, vol. XCII (Boston, Mass., 1861)
TYRRELL, H. 'Garibaldi in New York' (in *The Century Magazine*, vol. LXXIV (New York, 1907))
VAILLANT, J. A. *Grammaire dialogues et vocabulaire de la langue des Bohémiens ou Cigrains* (Paris, 1868) (containing his 'Lettre au Général Garibaldi')
VAILLANT, J. B. P. *Siège de Rome en 1849 par l'armée française* (Paris, 1851)
VARZEA, V. *Garibaldi in America* (Italian translation by C. Petti) (Rio de Janeiro, 1902)
VASQUEZ, A. S. 'Andanzas de D. José Garibaldi por Entre Ríos'.
— See Villanueva
VECCHI, C. A. *Garibaldi et Caprera* (Utrecht, 1862)
— *La Italia – Storia di due anni 1848–49* (2nd ed., Turin, 1856)
VICTORIA, QUEEN. *Dearest Child – Letters between Queen Victoria and the Princess Royal 1858–1861* (ed. R. Fulford) (London, 1964)
— *The Letters of Queen Victoria* (London, 1907–32)
VILLANUEVA, A. *Garibaldi en Entre Ríos* (Buenos Aires, 1957)
VISCONTI-VENOSTA, G. *Ricordi di Gioventù* (Milan, 1904)
Vita di Giuseppe Garibaldi (Florence, 1864)

651

VUILLETET, A. *Garibaldi en France* (Paris, 1876)

WALSH, R. *Notices of Brazil in 1828 and 1829* (London, 1830)

Was ist der St. Simonismus? (Quedlingburg and Leipzig, 1832)

WERNER, A. See Garibaldi, Memoirs

WESTON, J. *General Garibaldi at Fishmongers' Hall* (1864, no place)

WINNINGTON-INGRAM, H. F. *Hearts of Oak* (London, 1889)

WRIGHT, A. *Montevideo: Apuntos históricos de la defensa de la República* (Montevideo, 1845)

WULLIEMOZ, C. *Garibaldi* (Lausanne, 1862)

XIMENES, E. E. *Epistolario di Giuseppe Garibaldi* (Milan, 1885)

YABEN, J. R. *Biografías Argentinas y Sudamericanas* (Buenos Aires, 1938–40)

REFERENCES

Chapter 1

1. Garibaldi, *Memoirs* (1872 edition, in *Scritti di Giuseppe Garibaldi*, II. 19; Melena's German edition, I.6; Dumas's French edition, I. 51); Sacerdote, *La Vita di Giuseppe Garibaldi*, pp. 25–26, 31; Werner's English translation of Garibaldi's Memoirs, Supp., III. 4–5n. Angelo Garibaldi gave his age as 65, not 73, when he signed Giuseppe Garibaldi's birth certificate as a witness. Dumas's French edition of the memoirs (I. 51) wrongly gives the date of Garibaldi's birth as 22 July 1807.
2. J. W. Mario, *Garibaldi e i suoi tempi*, p. 7.
3. Guerzoni, *Garibaldi*, I. 5–8; *Scritti*, II. 17; Melena, I. 3; Dumas I. 52; Werner, III. 1–5, 5n.; Parris, *The Lion of Caprera*, p. 14.
4. *Memoirs* (Dwight's edition, p. 13).
5. Guerzoni, I. 6; Parris, p. 326.
6. Parris, pp. 13–14; *Scritti*, II. 19.
7. *Memoirs* (Dumas, I. 51; cf. the Dwight and 1872 editions); Parris, p. 326; Guerzoni, I. 5.
8. Werner, III. 16.
9. Parris, pp. 14, 326; Guerzoni, I. 5.
10. *Garibaldi en América*, App., pp. vii–ix; Werner, III. 9; *The Times,* 4 June 1883; Morley, *Gladstone,* II. 110; *Scritti*, II. 14, 19; Dwight, pp. 14–15; Melena, I. 6; Dumas, I. 55; J. W. Mario, *Garibaldi*, pp. 8, 11.
11. *Scritti*, II. 19–20; Dwight, p. 15; Melena, I. 6–7; Dumas, I. 55–56; Werner, III. 10.
12. Bent, *Life of Giuseppe Garibaldi*, pp. 43–44; Guerzoni, I. 10; J. W. Mario, *Garibaldi*, p. 7; Werner, III. 7, 65; Parris, p. 326
13. *Scritti*, II. 18–19; Dwight, p. 14; Melena, I. 4–5; Dumas, I. 53–54; Werner, III. 9.
14. Parris, p. 14; *Scritti*, II. 17, 20; Dwight, pp. 13, 15–16; Melena, I. 4; Dumas, I. 53; Bent, p. 100.
15. Werner, III. 10; *Scritti*, II. 17; Dumas, I. 52–53.
16. *Scritti*, II. 21; Dwight, p. 16; Melena, I. 8; Dumas, I. 57; *The Times,* 4 June 1883; Morley, II. 110. In Werner, I. 13, *'perseguire'* is translated by 'to persecute', which is too strong.
17. *Scritti*, II. 22–23; Dwight, pp. 17–18; Melena, I. 10; Dumas, I. 58–59; Fortini, *Giuseppe Garibaldi marinaio mercantile*, p. 16.

18. Fortini, pp. 16, 20–21; *Scritti*, II. 22–24; Dwight, pp. 17–19; Melena, I. 11–12; Dumas, I. 59–60; J. W. Mario, *Garibaldi*, pp. 28–29; Parris, p. 16. In all the editions of his memoirs, Garibaldi states that his second voyage was to Rome; but see Fortini, p. 21, and Parris, p. 16.

19. Cf. Garibaldi's account in *Scritti*, II. 23–27; Dwight, pp. 18–21; Melena, I. 10–15; Dumas, I. 59–63 with the official records, given in Fortini, pp. 16–18, 20–27, which conflict as to the sequence in which the journeys were made and the names of the ships and ship's masters, but basically agree as to the places to which Garibaldi travelled.

20. Werner, III. 11.

21. Fortini, pp. 17, 24, 26, 35; *Scritti*, II. 26.

22. Fortini, pp. 17, 24, 47; *Scritti*, II. 26; Melena, I. 13.

23. For Garibaldi's encounters with the pirates, see Melena, I. 13; Dumas, I. 62; *Cassell's Magazine* (New Series), I. 264–5; Fortini, pp. 30–37.

24. Fortini, p. 24.

25. Fortini, p. 24; *Scritti*, II. 28; Dwight, p. 22; Melena, I. 24.

26. Fortini, pp. 17, 24.

27. For Garibaldi's stay in Constantinople, see *Scritti*, II. 26–27; Dwight, pp. 20–21; Melena, I. 14; Dumas, I. 63; J. W. Mario, *Garibaldi*, pp. 29–30; Cuneo, *Giuseppe Garibaldi*, pp. 15–16; information from Signor Sperco.

28. See 'Registre des Mousses de Nice', 1821–25, 1826–30, and 1831–35 (in Fortini, pp. 16–18), and the particulars of his service in the Sardinian Royal Navy (given by Guerzoni, I. 40n. and Jessie White Mario in Werner, III. 12). These descriptions all agree, except that the colour of his hair is given sometimes as chestnut and sometimes as fair; and in the records of the Royal Navy, in 1834, there is no mention of his beard.

29. If Garibaldi stayed in Constantinople from August 1828 to February or March 1831, this would be consistent with all the entries in the maritime records at Nice that refer to his voyages and to his appointment as a ship's master, and also with Clelia Garibaldi's story of his broken engagement to Francesca Roux (see *infra*).

30. Clelia Garibaldi, *Mio padre*, pp. 109–10; Parris, pp. 19, 328.

31. J. W. Mario, *Garibaldi*, p. 31; Werner, III. 449. In the English text of her Supplement to Werner, Jessie White Mario gives Garibaldi's words in French: '*Est ce que tu m'aime? Je t'aime! Tu ne m'aime pas? Tant pis pour toi*' (Jessie White Mario's spelling). In *Garibaldi e i suoi tempi*, she gives Garibaldi's words in Italian.

Chapter 2

1. *Scritti*, II. 27; Dwight, p. 21; Melena, I. 15; Dumas, I. 63; Fortini, pp. 18, 25.

2. Fortini, pp. 18, 26; *Cassell's Magazine* (New Series), I. 265; M.R.M., Garibaldi MSS., C. 110; Sacerdote, pp. 68–69; Fortini, pp. 30–37.

In his article in *Cassell's Magazine*, Garibaldi wrote that the fight with the pirates occurred when he was sailing eastwards in the *Clorinda* in 1830. In his list of battles, he dated it '1831'. But if it was in the *Clorinda*, it must have been in 1832. Garibaldi spent 1830 in Constantinople. As far as we know, his only voyage through the Aegean in 1831 was westwards.

3. Fortini, pp. 26–27.
4. *Nuova Antalogia,* 5th Ser., CCXXXV. 632–3.
5. Fortini, pp. 18, 27.
6. Salvemini, *Scritti sul Risorgimento*, p. 531.
7. Werner, III. 16–17; Dwight, p. 113.
8. Bolton King, *Mazzini*, p. 46.
9. Mazzini, *Works*, VI. 276–7.
10. J. W. Mario, *The Making of Modern Italy*, p. 22.
11. Dumas, I. 64–65; see also Melena, I. 16.
12. Mazzini, *Works*, VI. 98–186. See also his criticism of the Saint-Simonians in his 'On the duties of Man' (*Works*, IV. 344–5).
13. Mornand, *Garibaldi*, pp. 231–5; Bordone, *Garibaldi*, pp. 3–4.
14. *Revue d'histoire économique et sociale*, XIX. 369–74.

Chapter 3

1. Cuneo, p. 16 and n.; *Scritti*, II. 27; Dwight, p. 21; Melena, I. 15–16; Dumas, I. 64; Guerzoni, I. 33–35; Werner, III. 31. In some versions, the meeting at Taganrog was a discussion around a table; but Cuneo's account seems the most reliable. The evidence that Cuneo himself was the speaker who impressed Garibaldi seems overwhelming.
2. Melena, I. 17; Dumas, I. 66.
3. Melena, I. 17; Dumas, I. 66; Mazzini, *Works*, I. 340n.; Werner, III. 31, 35–36; Guerzoni, I. 35–36; Parris, pp. 38–40, 329.
4. Mazzini, *Works*, I. 340n.; Werner, III. 14; J. W. Mario, *Birth of Modern Italy*, p. 23.
5. Werner, III. 32–35.
6. Fortini, pp. 18, 67; Guerzoni, I. 40n.; Sacerdote, pp. 89–90; Werner, III. 12.
7. Melena, I. 17–18; Dumas, I. 72; Werner, III. 36; J. W. Mario, *Birth of Modern Italy*, p. 23; Guerzoni, I. 1–3; Sacerdote, pp. 90–91.
8. For the Savoy expedition, see Mazzini, *Works*, I. 355–68; J. W. Mario, *Birth of Modern Italy*, pp. 21–22; Hales, *Mazzini and the Secret Societies*, pp. 111–35. Mazzini states that there were 223 men in the invading force on 1 February. Other accounts give the figures as 160 and 270.
9. For Garibaldi's experiences in Genoa on 4–5 February, see *Scritti*, II. 27; Melena, I. 18–19; Dumas, I. 72–73; Dwight, p. 21; *Nuova Antalogia*, CCLXVI. 199–200; Sacerdote, pp. 100–3.
10. Melena, I. 19; Dumas, I. 73; Sacerdote, p. 38; Cuneo, p. 17.
11. Guerzoni, I. 31 and n.

12. For Garibaldi's journey from Nice to Marseilles, see Melena, I. 19–22; Dumas, I. 73–77.
13. *Scritti,* II. 27; Dwight, p. 22; Melena, I. 22–23; Dumas, I. 77–78.
14. Guerzoni, I. 1–3.
15. Fortini, pp. 18, 38–39, and unpaginated pages following p. 72; *Scritti,* II. 28; Dwight, p. 23; Melena, I. 23–24; Dumas, I. 78–79.
16. *Scritti,* II. 28; Dwight, p. 22; Melena, I. 23–24; Dumas, I. 78–79.
17. Fortini, pp. 38–40, 68–70; *Scritti,* II. 28; Dwight, p. 23; Melena, I. 24; Dumas, I. 79; *The Illustrated Life and Career of Garibaldi,* p. 4; Alvensleben, *Garibaldi,* pp. 45–57.
18. *Scritti;* Melena; Dumas, ibid.; Bent, p. 27.
19. Guerzoni, I. 48.
20. Fortini, p. 43.
21. Fortini, pp. 44–45, 74; Kidder, *Sketches of Residence and Travel in Brazil,* I. 21.

Chapter 4

1. Kidder, I. 24, 41, 66–67, 98, 106, 133.
2. Kidder, I. 66; *Scritti,* II. 29; Dwight, p. 23; Melena, I. 24–25; Dumas, I. 81; Luzio, *Garibaldi, Cavour, Verdi,* pp. 28–30.
3. Luzio, p. 17.
4. Luzio, pp. 24–27.
5. *Scritti,* II. 30; Dwight, p. 23; Kidder, I. 95; II. 11–12, 389–90; Fletcher and Kidder, *Brazil and the Brazilians,* p. 175.
6. Luzio, p. 18.
7. Varzea, *Garibaldi in America,* pp. 16–18, 18n.; Doria's preface to Bandi, *Anita Garibaldi,* pp. 15–16, 18.
8. For freemasonry and the Radical movement, see Luzio, *La Massoneria e il Risorgimento Italiano,* pp. 111–23, 213–16, 258–66. For Garibaldi's membership of the Rio lodge, see Pereda, *Garibaldi en el Uruguay,* III. 19
9. Cuneo, p. 19; Kidder, I. 66, 161, 174–5; Walsh, *Notices of Brazil in 1828 and 1829,* II. 354.
10. Ximenes, *Epistolario di Giuseppe Garibaldi,* I. 2–3; Werner, III. 41; *Scritti,* II. 30; Dwight, p. 23; Melena, I. 25; Dumas, I. 82.
11. Ximenes, I. 2–3; Werner, III. 40–41.
12. Werner, III. 42.
13. *British Packet* (Buenos Aires), 14 Dec. 1839.
14. Kidder, II. 9.
15. For Gonçalves and the struggle in Rio Grande do Sul, see Reichardt, *Bento Gonçalves,* pp. 65–127; Salmon, *História do Brasil,* V. 1605–12; *Grandes Personagens da nossa História,* pp. 397–405.
16. Varzea, pp. 31–33; *Scritti,* II. 30, 54; Dwight, p. 24; Melena, I. 25; Dumas, I. 82; Doria-Bandi, p. 17; Cuneo, p. 19; Guerzoni, I. 61; Parris, p. 331.
17. Doria-Bandi, p. 18; *Gaceta Mercantil* (Buenos Aires), 15 July 1844. For the conflicting statements as to the number of Garibaldi's crew, see

Scritti, II. 30; Dwight, p. 24; Melena, I. 26; Dumas, I. 82; Doria-Bandi, p. 18; Pereda, I. 40, 42.

18. Reichardt, p. 129; *Grandes Personagens da nossa História,* p. 406; *British Packet,* 6, 27 May 1837.

19. *Scritti,* II. 30–31; Dwight, pp. 24–25; Melena, I. 26–27; Dumas, I. 83–84; *Jornal do Commercio* (Rio de Janeiro), 14 June 1837; Doria-Bandi, p. 19. The *Jornal do Commercio* gave the date of the capture of the Luisa as 17 May and the place as off Point Itapacaroi; but Garibaldi's own account is more reliable. For the tonnage of the *Luisa,* see *British Packet,* 28 Oct. 1837.

20. *Scritti,* II. 30, 43; Dwight, p. 24; Melena, I. 26; Dumas, I. 84–85; *Jornal do Commercio,* 30 June 1837. In Garibaldi's petition to Rosas, 27 June 1837 (Arch. Gen., B.A., Sala X/C.16/A.1/No. 4), he calls the *Luisa* the *Mazzini.*

21. See infra, pp. 161, 214, 227.

22. *Jornal do Commercio,* 30 June 1837.

Chapter 5

1. Sarmiento, *Civilization and Barbarism,* pp. 6, 20, 22–23, 55, 153–5.

2. Sarmiento, pp. 137–42.

3. See, e.g., in Irazusta, *Vida politica de Juan Manuel de Rosas* IV. 141–2, 325–8.

4. Sarmiento, pp. 73–90, 171–2, 206–10.

5. *Scritti,* II. 31–32; Dwight, p. 26; Melena, I. 27–29; Dumas, I. 85–89; *Jornal do Commercio,* 30 June 1837; *British Packet,* 24 June 1837.

6. *Scritti,* II. 38–41; Dwight, pp. 26–28; Melena, I. 33–37; Dumas, I. 93–96.

7. *Scritti,* II. 41–43; Dwight, pp. 28–30; Melena, I. 37–39; Dumas, I. 96–98; Pereda, I. 36–38.

8. *Scritti,* II. 43–46; Dwight, pp. 30–32, 238–9; Melena, I. 39–43; Dumas, I. 99–102.

9. Pereda, I. 40, 42.

10. *Scritti,* II. 47; Dwight, p. 33; Melena, I. 44; Dumas, I. 102–3; Arch. Gen., B.A., Sala X/C.16/A.1/No. 4, Garibaldi to Rosas, 27 June 1837.

11. *Crónicas de Entre-Rios,* pp. 153–5.

12. Arch. Gen., B.A., Sala X/C.16/A.1/No. 4, Rosas to Echague, 5 Aug. 1837; Garibaldi to Rosas, 27 June 1837; *British Packet,* 28 Oct. 1837. The date on Garibaldi's petition, '26 of Independence', is a slip of the pen. Year 22 was intended.

13. Pereda, I. 43–44; *Scritti,* II. 47–48; Dwight, pp. 33–34; Melena, I. 44–45; Dumas, I. 103–4; Villanueva, *Garibaldi en Entre-Rios,* pp. 131, 144. Garibaldi says that he was allowed to ride up to twelve miles from Gualeguay; but see infra, p. 67n.

14. *Scritti,* II. 48, 51; Dwight, pp. 33–34, 37; Melena, I. 45, 49; Dumas, I. 104, 109; Arch. Gen., B.A., Sala X/C.16/A.1/No. 4, Rosas to Echague, 5 Aug. 1837; Echague to Rosas, 21 Aug. 1837.

15. *British Packet,* 28 Oct. 1837.
16. Local tradition at Gualeguay.
17. Cuneo, p. 21; Werner, III. 42–43; J. W. Mario, *Garibaldi,* pp. 82–83; Guerzoni, I. 73–74.
18. Garibaldi states that he stayed six months at Gualeguay (*Scritti* II. 47, Dwight p. 33, Melena, I. 44, Dumas, I. 103), and he arrived there on or about 27 June 1837.
19. Cf. Cuneo, p. 21; *Scritti,* II. 48; Dwight, p. 34; Melena, I. 45; Dumas, I. 104.
20. For the account of Garibaldi's escape and torture, see *Scritti,* II. 48–51; Dwight, pp. 34–36; Melena, I. 46–49; Dumas, I. 105–8. This is one of the very few episodes in which the various versions of the memoirs agree in every respect. For the local traditions at Gualeguay, see the various accounts by persons who were either living there as children in 1837, or were born soon afterwards, which were reprinted by Villanueva in *Garibaldi en Entre-Ríos,* pp. 129–45, 151–6. They undoubtedly contain errors, but, as embodying local traditions, have at least some weight.
21. Anita I. Garibaldi, *Garibaldi en América,* p. 20.
22. Cuneo, p. 22; J. W. Mario, *Garibaldi,* p. 84; Pereda, I. 46.
23. *Scritti,* II. 51; Dwight, p. 37; Melena, I. 49; Dumas, I. 108–9.

Chapter 6

1. *Scritti,* II. 37, 51–53, 55–56; Dwight, pp. 38–39; Melena, I. 50–51, 54 Dumas, I. 109–14, 117. In the statement in Werner's translation (I. 53) that Rossetti remained in Montevideo to edit *O Povo,* 'Montevideo' is a misprint for 'Piratinim' in the Italian edition.
2. Mallalieu, *Rosas and his Calumniators,* p. 90.
3. Kidder, I. 346, 358; *O Povo,* 23 Oct. 1839.
4. *Scritti,* II. 54–55; Dwight, p. 39; Melena, I. 52–54; Dumas, I. 114–15.
5. Dumas, I. 121. These anti-Austrian sentiments are deleted from Melena's German edition of the memoirs.
6. Kidder, I. 358.
7. *Scritti,* II. 62; Melena, I. 63; Dumas, I. 140–1.
8. *Scritti,* II. 56; Melena, I. 53; Dumas, I. 117. In the Melena (I. 55) and Dumas (I. 117) editions of the memoirs, Garibaldi says that the tonnage of the *Rio Pardo* was 18 tons, and the *Republicano* (the *Seival*) 15 tons. But from the remains of the *Seival,* which was at Laguna until she was broken up in 1918, we know that she was 25 metric tons.
9. *Scritti,* II. 57.
10. Varzea, p. 201; *O Povo,* 20 Oct., 28 Nov., 22 Dec. 1838; *Scritti,* II. 56; IV. 3; Dwight, p. 40; Melena, I. 55–56; Dumas, I. 117–18.
11. See, e.g., the oath of loyalty to the Catholic religion taken by the Minister of War, Marine and Foreign Affairs, and the regulations for the Parliamentary elections (*O Povo,* 21 Nov. 1838, 12 Feb. 1840).

12. *Scritti*, II. 58–60; Dwight, pp. 40–42; Melena, I. 57–60; Dumas, I. 119–21; Doria-Bandi, pp. 22–23; Garibaldi to Doña Anna, 3 Feb. 1839 (dated '3 Fevereiro 4', i.e. Year 4 of the Republic of Rio Grande do Sul), holograph in possession of Dr Belisario Nequeira Ramos, of Florianópolis, Brazil.

13. For the fight with Moringue, see *O Povo*, 22 May 1839; Varzea, pp. 209–10; *Scritti*, II. 61–66; IV. 4–5; Dwight, pp. 44–49; Melena, I. 61–69; Dumas, I. 121–7. The various versions of the memoirs conflict with regard to the number of casualties.

14. Kidder, I. 346.

15. *Scritti*, II. 67–68; Dwight, pp. 50–51; Melena, I. 71–73; Dumas, I. 129–30; *O Povo*, 10 Aug. 1839. Garibaldi states that the distance overland across which the ships were carried was 54 'miglia', which Dwight and Warner translate as 54 'miles', Melena as 54 'Miglien', and Dumas as 'cinquante-quatre milles, c'est-à-dire dixhuit lieues' (see supra, p.67n.) The distance in fact is a little less than 50 English miles.

16. *Scritti*, II. 69–74; Dwight, pp. 52–56; Melena, I. 73–79; Dumas, I. 131–40; Santa Catarina Register of Wrecks, entry for 15 July 1839.

17. *O Povo*, 10 Aug. 1839.

18. *O Povo*, 20 Aug. 1839.

19. *Scritti*, II. 74–75; Dwight, pp. 57–58; Melena, I. 79–80; Dumas, I. 141–2; *O Povo*, 20 Aug. 1839; information from Senhor W. L. Rau.

20. *Scritti*, II. 76. For a shortened version of this passage see Melena, I. 82 and Dumas I. 143, where it is stated that the lagoon referred to is the lagoon of Santa Catarina, i.e. Laguna. In the 1872 edition, the use of the word '*laguna*' leaves the matter open. The passage is omitted in the Dwight edition.

Chapter 7

1. Winnington–Ingram, *Hearts of Oak*, p. 93; Dwight, p. 225; Varzea, pp. 242–3n.; Boiteux, *Annita Garibaldi*, p. 52; Alvensleben, *Garibaldi*, pp. 77, 86.

2. Information from W. L. Rau.

3. Saint-Hilaire, *Voyage dans les provinces de Saint-Paul et de Sainte-Catherine*, II. 255, 371, 387.

4. Varzea, p. 243n.

5. Dwight, p. 215.

6. Boiteux, pp. 53–54.

7. The marriage certificate, in 'Libra de Casamentas, Laguna, 1832–1844', f. 83; information from Father Claudino of Laguna; Saint-Hilaire, II. 386.

8. Corneli, *Giuseppe Garibaldi nell' Uruguay*, p. 45, states that Anita had a daughter named Cristina; but this book contains many errors.

9. *Scritti*, II. 78–79.

10. See, e.g., *O Povo*, 22 May 1839; Garibaldi to Anna do Silva Santos, 3 Feb. (1839) (holograph letter in possession of Dr Ramos of Florianó-polis).
11. Dumas, I. 145, 146n.
12. Melena, I. 85.
13. Guerzoni, I. 94; cf. Melena, I. 84–85.
14. Werner, III. 44–46; See also J. W. Mario, *Garibaldi*, pp. 91, 91–92n.
15. Alvensleben, *Garibaldi*, p. 77.
16. In the public libraries at Brescia, Milan, Nice and São Paulo.
17. Varzea, pp. 242–3n.
18. Boiteux, pp. 54–55; Trevelyan, I. 28, 30–31; Anita I. Garibaldi, pp. 37–39; personal information from Senhor Rau and from Señora Pirretti de Novikov of Buenos Aires.
19. Senhor Rau.
20. See, e.g., *O Povo*, 2 Oct. 1839.

Chapter 8

1. *Scritti*, II. 79; Melena, I. 86; Dumas, I. 146–7; Dwight, p. 215.
2. Museo Annita Garibaldi, Laguna; Senhor Rau.
3. *Scritti*, II. 79–83; Dwight, pp. 61–64, 216–17; Melena, I. 86–90; Dumas, I. 146–50.
4. *Scritti*, II. 84.
5. For the events at Imarui, see *Scritti*, II. 84–86; Dwight, pp. 65–66; Melena, I. 91–92; Dumas, I. 151–3; *O Povo*, 23 Nov. 1839.
6. *Scritti*, II. 86–89; Dwight, pp. 67–69, 216–17; Melena, I. 93–97; Dumas, I. 153–7; *British Packet*, 21 Dec. 1839. In his 'Biographical Sketch of Anna Garibaldi' (in Dwight), Garibaldi confuses the sea-battle at Imbituba and the second battle of Laguna, which he does not do in the Dwight edition of the memoirs.
7. *Scritti*, II. 90; Dwight, p. 69; Melena, I. 98; Dumas, I. 158.
8. *Scritti*, II. 90–91; Melena, I. 99, 104; Dumas, I. 158–9, 162, 183–4; Dwight, p. 218; *O Povo*, 18 Jan. 1840; *El Nacional* (Montevideo), 15 Jan. 1840.
9. *Nacional*, ibid.
10. For the fight in the wood, Senhor Rau. This is the engagement to which Garibaldi refers in *Scritti*, II. 96–98, Melena, I. 106–9, Dumas I. 164–6. For other skirmishes, see *Scritti*, II. 91–95, 98–102; Dwight, pp. 70–84; Melena, I. 99–106, 110–13; Dumas, I. 159–64, 168–71. The fullest account is in Melena's edition.
11. Dumas, I. 184–8; Dwight, pp. 219–22; Hoffstetter, *Tagebuch aus Italien*, pp. 339–40; Cuneo, pp. 24–25. The site of the battle is identified by Senhor Rau.
12. *Scritti*, II. 101–2; Dwight, pp. 83–84; Melena, I. 112–14; Dumas, I. 169–71.
13. *Scritti*, II. 104–5; Dwight, pp. 85, 222; Melena, I. 116; Dumas, I. 172–

3; *Nacional*, 4 June 1840. In Werner, I. 110, the figure of 8,000 for the Imperial cavalry is a misprint.

14. *Scritti*, II. 106–7. An almost identical passage is in Dwight, p. 87.

15. *Scritti*, II. 107, 109–10; Dwight, pp. 84–90; Melena, I. 119–20; Dumas, I. 175, 177–8. For the battle of Taquari, see also Cuneo's article in *Nacional*, 5 Sept. 1840.

16. *O Povo*, 6 May 1840.

17. *Scritti*, II. 111–14; Dwight, pp. 92–93; Melena, I. 123–7; Dumas, I. 179–81.

18. *O Povo*, 9, 19 Oct. 1839, 8 Jan. 1840.

19. Anita I. Garibaldi, pp. 53–54.

20. *Scritti*, II. 114–17; Dwight, pp. 93–96; Melena, I. 127–31; Dumas, I. 182–3, 188–90. In Melena's edition, the date of Menotti's birth is given, through a misprint, as 6 Sept. Dwight gives it as 10 Sept.

21. *Scritti*, II. 118; Dwight, p. 98; Melena, I. 132; Dumas, I. 192.

22. *Scritti*, II. 119–25; Dwight, pp. 98–105, 223–4; Melena, I. 132–41; Dumas, I. 191–200, 202–9.

23. *Scritti*, II. 125; Dwight, p. 105; Melena, I. 141; Dumas, I. 201. In the Dwight, Dumas and Melena editions, Garibaldi wrote that he had decided to go to Montevideo 'at least for a time'. In the 1872 edition, he wrote that he had decided to go there 'for a time'.

24. *Scritti*, II. 125–7; Dwight, p. 106; Melena, I. 141–3; Dumas, I. 200–2, II. 5–6.

25. *Nacional*, 19 June 1841.

26. *Nacional*, 25 May 1843.

27. De-María, *Anales de la Defensa de Montevideo*, I. 60.

28. *Scritti*, II. 127; Dwight, pp. 106–7; Melena, I. 143; Dumas, II. 6; Ferré, *Memoria*, p. 917.

29. Marriage register of the church of San Francisco de Asis of Montevideo, 1842, f. 20. The entry has been printed in Werner, III. 46–47; Pereda, III. 6; and elsewhere.

30. Guerzoni, I. 152.

31. Bent, p. 48; McAdam MSS., Mrs Chambers to McAdam, 5 Dec. 1875; Parris, pp. 346–7.

32. *Nacional*, 19 June 1841. Pereda, I. 25, says that Garibaldi arrived in Montevideo at the beginning of 1842, and has been followed by most biographers of Garibaldi, who were not aware of the report of his arrival in the *Nacional*; but Cuneo, p. 25, had stated that Garibaldi arrived in Montevideo about the middle of the year 1841.

33. Corneli, pp. 54–55.

34. See e.g., Saint-Hilaire, II. 388; Iriarte, *Memorias*, IX. 16, 250.

Chapter 9

1. Werner, III. 48; *Scritti*, II. 129; Dwight, p. 112; Melena, I. 145–6.

2. For French designs in Uruguay, see the secret anonymous memorandum

(undated, 1843), 'Notes relatives aux Affaires de la Plata' (Mus. Hist., Mont., MSS. 433/147).

3. For Admiral Brown, see Ratto, *Almirante Guillermo Brown;* Gianello, in *Biografías Navales,* pp. 13–21; Mulhall, *The English in South America,* pp. 144–54.

4. *Scritti,* II. 128, 139; Dwight, pp. 115, 125; Melena, I. 157; Dumas, II. 61.

5. *Scritti,* II. 132; Barraza, 'Brown y Garibaldi' (*Anuario de Historia Argentina,* V. 166–8, 173); Carranza, 'Costa Brava' (*Revista Nacional* (Buenos Aires), XXIX. 277–80).

6. *Scritti,* II. 128; Dwight, p. 107; Melena, I. 145; Pereda, II. 69. Seguí reported to Oribe on 19 July 1842 that the *Constitución* carried 20 guns, the *Pereyra* 10, and the *Prócida* 5 (*Gaceta Mercantil,* 20 Sept. 1842); but see infra, p. 117. The Montevidean French-language newspaper, *Le Messager Français,* of 5/6 Sept. 1842 stated that Garibaldi's three ships had a total of 32 guns at the battle of Costa Brava; but as its figures for Brown's ships, guns and losses were quite inaccurate, its report cannot be relied on. Melena, I. 145, states that the *Pereyra,* like the *Constitución,* had 18 guns and 2 decks; but this is obviously a misprint for two 18-calibre guns.

7. *Scritti,* II. 144.

8. Ferré, pp. 917–18.

9. M.H., Mont., Acevido MSS. 139, ff. 60–62; Pereda, I. 249–50, 261–3; *Scritti,* IV. 7–13; Ferré, pp. 925–6; Barraza, op. cit., V. 169.

10. Carranza, op. cit., XXIX. 185–91; Ratto, *Historia de Brown,* p. 238.

11. The story is accepted by Carranza, op. cit., XXIX. 279, and Pereda, I. 224, and in part at least by Saldías, *Historia de la Confederación Argentina,* VI. 14, and Caillet-Bois, *Ensayo de Historia naval argentina,* p. 374; but see Barraza, op. cit., V. 174, who rejects it, chiefly on the strength of Crespo's report to Brown, 27 June 1842 (in Carranza, op. cit., XXX. 94). For the origin of the story, and the untrue report that Garibaldi had succeeded in taking Seguí prisoner by this ruse, see *Nacional,* 8 Aug. 1842; *British Packet,* 20 Aug. 1842.

12. For the action at Martín García, and the grounding of the ships, see *Scritti,* II. 130–2; IV. 5–6; Dwight, pp. 116–17; Melena, I. 147–9; M. H. Mont., Acevido MSS. 139, f. 63; *Nacional,* 5, 9 July 1842; Carranza, op. cit., XXX. 94; Barraza, op. cit., V. 173–9, 193, 197–8; Ratto, p. 238; Pereda, I. 231–7; *British Packet,* 2 July 1842; *The Britannia* (Montevideo), 9 July 1842.

13. *Scritti,* II. 132; Dwight, p. 118; Melena, I. 149–50; Barraza, op. cit., V. 171–2.

14. *Nacional,* 9 July 1842; *Scritti,* IV. 5–6.

15. For the engagement at Paraná, see *Scritti,* II. 133; IV. 7–8; Dwight, pp. 118–20; Melena, I. 150–1; Pereda, I. 249–50; *Gaceta Mercantil,* 22 Aug., 20 Sept. 1842; Barraza, op. cit., V. 184–5, 210–11; *Nacional,* 24 Aug., 5 Sept. 1842; *Britannia,* 13 Aug. 1842; *British Packet,* 20 Aug. 1842.

16. For the action at El Cerrito and the link-up with Villegas, see *Scritti,*

II. 134-5; IV. 9-13; Dwight, pp. 120-1; Melena, I. 151-3; *Nacional*, 9 Sept. 1842; *Gaceta Mercantil*, 20, 26 Sept. 1842; Barraza, op. cit., V. 185-6.

17. Scritti, II. 136, 141; Dwight, pp. 121-2; Melena, I. 154.

18. Barraza, op. cit., V. 179-82, 189.

19. Barraza, op. cit., V. 172, 189-90, 192.

20. *Gaceta Mercantil*, 20 Sept. 1842; Pereda, II. 132; *Scritti*, IV. 16. For Pereda's controversy with Carranza about the dates, see Pereda, II. 289-308; but Pereda overlooks Ferré's letter of 22 Aug. to the Military Commandant of Esquina, which he himself had quoted in another context.

21. *Scritti*, II. 138; *Nacional*, 10 Sept. 1842; Barraza, op. cit., V. 192.

22. *Scritti*, II. 137, 140-2; Melena, I. 158-60; Pereda, II. 33-38.

23. For the battle of Costa Brava, see *Scritti*, II. 137-45; IV. 16-17; *Gaceta Mercantil*, 20 Sept. 1842; Dwight, pp. 122-9; Melena, I. 155-62; Dumas, II. 64 (where the battle is thought by Dumas to have been fought near Martín García); Barraza, op. cit., V. 186-96; Carranza, op. cit., XXX. 171-9, 251-8, 349-56, 403-14; XXXI. 5-12, 107-21, 333-40; XXXII. 5-15, 101-10, 199-210; Caillet-Bois, *Los marinos durante la Dictadura*, pp. 118-22; Pereda, II. 17-56. The best account is by Caillet-Bois, who had seen Admiral Bartolomé Cordero's unpublished diary, which I have been unable to trace.

24. *Gaceta Mercantil*, 20 Sept. 1842; *Scritti*, II. 143-4.

25. *Scritti*, II. 141; Pereda, II. 69.

26. *Gaceta Mercantil*, 3 Oct. 1842.

27. Pereda, II. 36.

28. *Scritti*, II. 145; Dwight, p. 129; Melena, I. 161-2; Dumas, II. 65; Caillet-Bois, *Ensayo de Historia naval argentina*, p. 375; and his *Los marinos durante la Dictadura*, p. 177; Pereda, II. 67-68, 142-3; Carranza, op. cit., XXIX. 108-10; XXXI. 108-19; Iriarte, X. 198-208.

29. *Gaceta Mercantil*, 20, 26 Sept. 1842; Caillet-Bois, *Los marinos durante la Dictadura*, p. 122.

30. *Gaceta Mercantil*, 20 Sept. 1842; *British Packet*, 3 Sept. 1842; Gianello, in *Biografías Navales*, p. 88.

31. *British Packet*, 3 Sept. 1842.

32. *Britannia*, 3 Sept. 1842; *Nacional*, 5, 9, 10, 14 Sept. 1842; *Le Messager Français*, 5/6, 9/10 Sept. 1842; Iriarte, VII. 389.

33. *British Packet*, 10, 24 Sept. 1842; Carranza, op. cit., XXXI. 11; Pereda, II. 176; L. Farragut, *Life of David Glasgow Farragut*, pp. 147-9; B.M. Add.43153, Mandeville to Aberdeen, 16 Sept. 1842.

34. *Scritti*, II. 145-6, 16-17. Dwight, p. 129; Melena, I. 162-3; Pereda, II. 70.

35. Pereda, II. 75-77, 107; A. Diaz, *Historia política y militar de las Repúblicas del Plata*, V. 321n.; *Messager Français*, 21 Sept. 1842.

36. *Histonium*, Dec. 1968-Jan. 1969, pp. 24-25.

37. *Scritti*, II. 146; IV. 19, 22; Dwight, pp. 129-30; Melena, I. 163; Pereda, II. 107-13.

Chapter 10

1. *British Packet*, 17 Dec. 1842; C. Diaz, *Memorias inéditas*, pp. 103–5; *Britannia*, 25 Feb. 1843.
2. *Britannia*, 4 Mar., 12 Aug. 1843; Dumas, *Montevideo, ou une nouvelle Troie*, pp. 109–10.
3. *Scritti*, II. 147–8.
4. *British Packet*, 3 Dec. 1842.
5. *Scritti*, II. 151; Dwight, pp. 131–3; Melena, I. 169; Pereda, III. 207.
6. *Nacional*, 3 Feb. 1843; *Britannia*, 4 Feb. 1843; *Scritti*, II. 154–9; Dwight, p. 138; Melena, I. 172–3; C. Diaz, p. 107; De-María, I. 123.
7. *Nacional*, 17 Feb. 1843; *Britannia*, 18 Feb. 1843; C. Diaz, pp. 71, 105; Wright, *Apuntos históricos de la defensa de la República*, p. 114.
8. C. Diaz, p. 111. The figures in the Dumas edition of the memoirs of 9,000 men in the defence forces, of whom 5,000 were freed negro slaves, is completely wrong.
9. C. Diaz, pp. 98, 139; *Scritti*, II. 156–7; Dwight, p. 140; Melena, I. 174–5; De-María, I. 57. See also *British Packet*, 19 Apr. 1845.
10. *Scritti*, II. 153; Melena, I. 171.
11. De-María, I. 60–61; II. 27; Wright, App. (unpaginated).
12. *Patriote Français*, 8/9 May, 2 June 1843; *Nacional*, 8 May 1843.
13. *Nacional*, 7, 8 Apr. 1843; De-María, I. 96.
14. *Britannia*, 8 Apr. 1843; Gradenigo, *Garibaldi in America*, p. 119; *Nacional*, 13 May 1843; Pereda, III. 320.
15. Werner, III. 49–50; Cuneo, p. 31.
16. *Patriote Français*, 7 Jan. 1844.
17. *Le Patriote Français*, which was first published on 1 Feb. 1843, succeeding a previous French-language paper, *Le Messager Français*, appeared every day except Mondays till 1849, when for a time it appeared only three times a week. The four issues of *Il Legionario Italiano* are undated, but internal and other evidence shows that they were published on 27 Oct., 11 Nov. and 26 Dec. 1844, and on 15 Mar. 1846; see Prederio, *Indice Cronologico de la prensa periódica del Uruguay*, p. 99. See also *Nacional*, 31 Oct. 1844.
18. *Apostolato Popolare*, 25 Nov. 1842, 31 Sept. [*sic.*] 1843.
19. Delacour was frequently named as editor in *Le Patriote Français* until 1848, when Arsène Isabelle succeeded him. Prederio (p. 87) seems prepared to accept the opinion expressed by Zinni in *Historia de la prensa periódica de la República Oriental del Uruguay* (Buenos Aires, 1883), that Arsène Isabelle was always in fact the editor; but De-María (I. 70), who as editor of another Montevidean newspaper, *El Constitucional*, should have known, states that Delacour was the editor.
20. *Britannia*, 23, 30 Dec. 1843, 6, 13, 20 Jan., 16, 30 Mar., 13, 20 Apr. 1844; De-María, I. 294–301.
21. *Garibaldi en América*, App. iii; *Scritti*, II. 179, 181, 187–8; Dwight, pp. 159, 167–8; Melena, I. 208, 216–17; Dumas, II. 75; *British Packet*,

16 Sept. 1843, 26 Oct., 14 Dec. 1844, 19 July 1845; *Patriote Français,* 18/19 Nov., 30 Nov. 1844, 27/28 Jan. 1845; *Defensor de la Independencia Americana* (Miguelete), 26 Nov. 1844.

22. *Britannia,* 17 Dec. 1842, 25 Feb. 1843; *Nacional,* 28 May 1842.
23. Gradenigo, pp. 119–20; Pereda, III. 315–26; *Constitucional,* 4, 7 Apr. 1843.
24. *Scritti,* II. 127, 146, 160; Dwight, p. 143; Melena, I. 179–88; Dumas, I. 202–10; Rodríguez, *Memorias militares,* pp. 191–2; Werner, III. 54.
25. *Scritti,* II. 157.
26. *Scritti,* II. 154; Melena, I. 172.
27. De-María, I. 122; M.H. Mont., M.H.MSS. 953/90/155, Garibaldi's memorandum, 15 Feb. 1844.
28. *Scritti,* II. 144.
29. Brossard, *Considérations historiques et politiques sur les Républiques de la Plata,* p. 280; Werner, III. 50–51; Rodríguez, p. 191.
30 Pereda, I. 92–93; M.H. Mont., Acevido MSS. 139, ff. 60–62.
31. *Nacional,* 29 Feb., 6 Sept. 1844, 5 Nov. 1845; Indarte, *Rosas y sus opositores,* pp. 317–63; Mallalieu, *Rosas and his Calumniators,* pp. 43, 56, 61–62.
32. *Morning Chronicle,* 4 Feb. 1846.
33. *Britannia,* 25 Feb. 1843.
34. *Scritti,* II. 161–3; Dwight, pp. 144–5; Melena, I. 188–90; *Nacional,* 8 Apr. 1843; *Constitucional,* 2 May 1843.
35. *British Packet,* 15 Apr. 1843; *Documentos del Almirante Brown,* II. 194–5.
36. *Documentos del Almirante Brown,* II. 197–8, 200–2, 210; *British Packet,* 15 Apr., 20 May 1843; *Scritti,* II. 164–5; VI. 304; Dwight, pp. 146–7; Melena, I. 190–2 (where Purvis is wrongly named Pierce).
37. *Britannia,* 22 Apr. 1843; *British Packet,* 6, 13, 20 May 1843; *Nacional,* 15 Apr. 1843; *Documentos del Almirante Brown,* II. 193–4, 196–7, 199, 203–7.
38. Gradenigo, p. 119; *Nacional,* 8 June 1843; *Patriote Français,* 8 June 1843; *British Packet,* 10 June 1843; *Scritti,* II. 158; Dwight, p. 141; Melena, I. 177; Werner, III. 51.
39. *Nacional,* 12, 14, 16, 17 June 1843; Gradenigo, p. 120; *Scritti,* II. 158–9; Dwight, pp. 141–2; Melena, I. 177–9; Cuneo, pp. 29–31; Werner, III. 52.
40. Gradenigo, p. 120; *Nacional,* 1, 11 July 1843; *Patriote Français,* 9 July 1843; *Scritti,* II. 159; Dwight, p. 143; Melena, I. 179; Dumas, II. 70; Werner, III. 52.
41. Gradenigo, p. 120; *Gaceta Mercantil,* 5 July 1843. For the Unitarian allegations of atrocities committed by Oribe's men in the village near the Cerro, see *Patriote Français,* 11 June 1843.
42. *British Packet,* 31 May 1845; De-María, I. 108–17; *Miscelanea Americanista* (Madrid), III. 475–7.
43. For the Regis–Garibaldi incident, see *Britannia,* 24 June, 1 July 1843; *Patriote Français,* 26/27 June 1843; *British Packet,* 1 July 1843; *Jornal do Commercio,* 8 July 1843; *Gaceta Mercantil,* 5, 13 July, 6 Sept., 1 Dec. 1843;

Wright, pp. 273–6; *Miscelanea Americanista,* III. 481; Magariños de Mello, *La misión de Florencio Varela a Londres,* pp. 272–5; De-María, I. 172–3.

44. M.H. Mont., Acevido MSS. 139, ff. 114–15.
45. *Gaceta Mercantil,* 5 July 1843.
46. M.H. Mont., M.H. MSS. 434, f. 51; Costa, *O Visconde de Sinimbú,* pp. 44, 46–47, 82–83.
47. *Patriote Français,* 30 Aug. 1843; Wright, pp. 273–6; Costa, pp. 92–94.
48. *Miscelanea Americanista,* III. 487, 490, 492–4; Costa, pp. 94–95.
49. Varzea, p. 313.

Chapter 11

1. *Hansard,* 8 Mar. 1844.
2. *Revista Historica* (Montevideo), I. 186.
3. *Britannia,* 18 Feb., 3 June 1843; De-María, I. 158–61; *British Packet,* 10 June 1843.
4. *Britannia,* 7, 14, Oct., 4, 11 Nov. 1843; *Patriote Français,* 8, 11, 12 Oct., 9 Nov. 1843; *Nacional,* 14 Oct. 1843; De-María, I. 234–40; Mallalieu, *Rosas and his Calumniators,* pp. 66–67; *Defensor,* 8 Apr. 1847.
5. Mallalieu, *Buenos Ayres, Monte Video and affairs in the River Plate,* pp. 34–35, 38n., 45; Pacheco y Obes, *Rectification de Faits Calomnieux attribués à la défense de Montevideo,* pp. 6–10.
6. *Nacional,* 3 July 1844.
7. *Britannia,* 2 Dec. 1843; *Patriote Français,* 6, 12, 21 Dec. 1843; B.M. Add. 43130, f. 358; *Nacional,* 18 Apr. 1845.
8. C. Diaz, p. 107; De-María, I. 56.
9. *British Packet,* 28 Dec. 1844.
10. Dumas, *Montevideo, ou une nouvelle Troie,* pp. 85–86, 109, 156–9, 166; private information from Señor J. L. Borges. For the official casualty figures of the French Legion, see *Patriote Français,* 31 Oct., 1 Nov. 1844, 8 June 1845.
11. Dumas, ibid., pp. 87–89; Pacheco, *Réponse aux détracteurs de Montevideo,* p. 30.
12. Pereda, III. 73–74.
13. Dumas, ibid.; Pacheco, ibid.; Pereda, ibid.; Werner, III. 56n., *Cornhill Magazine* (New Series), XXX. 394.
14. *Nacional,* 17 July 1843; *Patriote Français,* 8/9, 19 May, 2 June, 23 July 1843.
15. *Scritti,* IV. 28–29; Melena, I. 196–201; Dumas, II. 76–78; De-María, II. 253–4.
16. Parris, p. 330. Clelia Garibaldi's statement that her father's eyes were brown is confirmed by the official note of his physical characteristics in the 'Registre des Mousses de Nice 1831–35' (in Fortini, p. 18, see supra, p. 13).
17. For Mitre's account of Garibaldi and the fight at Tres Cruces, see Mitre,

'Un episodio Troyano', in *Garibaldi en América,* App. vi-xv, published in Buenos Aires in 1888. The article has often been reprinted, most recently (with a few omissions) in the selection of Mitre's writings published under the title *Paginas de Historia* in Buenos Aires in 1944. For Tres Cruces, see also *Scritti,* II. 166; Dwight, p. 149; Melena, I. 193–4; Dumas, II. 71–72; *Nacional,* 20 Nov. 1843; *Patriote Français,* 19 Nov. 1843; *British Packet,* 25 Nov. 1843; Rodríguez, pp. 92–94; Cuneo, p. 32.

18. *Nacional,* 29 Mar., 1 Apr. 1844; *Britannia,* 30 Mar. 1844; *Patriote Français,* 6/7 Apr. 1844; *British Packet,* 6 Apr. 1844; *Scritti,* II. 168–70; Dwight, pp. 150–2; Melena, I. 196–8; Dumas, II. 73–75, where the battles of 28 March and 24 Apr. are confused; Cuneo, pp. 31–32.

19. *Nacional,* 26 Apr. 1844; *Scritti,* II. 166–8; Dwight, pp. 149–50; Melena, I. 194–5; Dumas, II. 73; *Britannia,* 27 Apr. 1844; *British Packet,* 4 May 1844.

20. *Nacional,* 23, 26 Aug., 17 Sept. 1844; Iriarte, VIII. 206; Rodríguez, p. 181; De-María, II. 98–101; Pacheco, *Réponse aux détracteurs de Montevideo,* p. 31.

21. De-María, II. 106–7, 126; *Nacional,* 20 Sept. 1844; Dumas, II. 83; *Patriote Français,* 17/18 May 1844; *Britannia,* 11 May 1844; Dumas, *Montevideo, ou une nouvelle Troie,* p. 89; Pacheco, *Réponse aux détracteurs de Montevideo,* p. 29; Cuneo, pp. 36–37.

22. *British Packet,* 22 July, 24 Aug. 1844.

23. *Nacional,* 24 Apr. 1843; *Patriote Français,* 22 June, 28 Dec. 1843, 8, 20/21 May, 27 Sept., 26 Oct., 4/5 Nov. 1844, 16 Jan., 8 June, 19/20 July 1845; De-María, II. 30–32; Wright, pp. 227, 254.

24. *Patriote Français,* 22/23 Apr. 1844.

25. Guerzoni, I. 379.

26. Dwight, p. 224.

27. For the Baena case, see *Patriote Français,* 16/17, 19 Oct. 1843; De-María, I. 233, 240–2.

28. *British Packet,* 28 Oct. 1843.

29. M.H. Mont., Acevido MSS. 140, ff. 15–16.

30. For the desertions from the Italian Legion, see *Nacional,* 1, 2, 6, 20 July 1844; *Patriote Français,* 30 June 1844, 6 Jan. 1845; Gradenigo, pp. 124–5; *British Packet,* 6, 13, 20 July 1844; *Gaceta Mercantil,* 2 July 1844; Iriarte, VIII. 198–9; *Scritti,* II. 171; IV. 26–27; Dumas, II. 69; Werner, III. 53–54; J. W. Mario, *Garibaldi,* p. 123.

31. *Patriote Français,* 30 June 1844.

32. *Defensor,* 15 July 1844; *Gaceta Mercantil,* 15 July 1844, where the statements are slightly abbreviated.

33. Iriarte, IX. 19–34; De-María, II. 152–69.

34. For the incident with Grenfell and the resignation and exile of Pacheco, see De-María, II. 171–93; *Nacional,* 7, 9, 11, 12, 13, 14, 15, 16 Nov., 9 Dec. 1844; *Patriote Français,* 10, 14 Nov. 1844; *Gaceta Mercantil,* 23 Nov., 21 Dec. 1844; *Defensor,* 26 Nov. 1844, 11 Jan. 1845; *British Packet,* 16, 23 Nov. 1844; Iriarte, VIII. 242–50; 272–7; Rodríguez, pp. 179–89.

35. Gradenigo, p. 125.

36. *British Packet,* 16, 23 Nov. 1844; *Defensor,* 26 Nov. 1844; *Patriote Français,* 1, 4 Dec. 1844.

Chapter 12

1. Iriarte, VIII. 278–84, 376, 379–80, 386–7, 390; IX. 326.
2. Iriarte, VII. 389; VIII. 377; IX. 51, 74–75.
3. *Gaceta Mercantil,* 28 Nov. 1845. For a more recent attack on the Argentine Liberals, Garibaldi and the Freemasons, see Tonelli, *Garibaldi y la Masoneria Argentina* (Buenos Aires, 1951). See also De-María, II. 320–1; III. 179.
4. Pereda, III. 18–20.
5. B.M. Add. 43152, Aberdeen to Ouseley, 20 Feb. 1845; B.M. Add. 43153, Ouseley to Aberdeen, 12, 21 May, 28 June 1845; De-María, II. 302–9, 312; *British Packet,* 27 Sept. 1845.
6. *British Packet,* 9, 23 Aug. 1845; De-María, II. 310–11; III. 29–38.
7. De-María, III. 45–46; *Cornhill Mag.,* N.S., XXX. 392.
8. Iriarte, II. 271; *British Packet,* 14 June 1845.
9. See Garibaldi's memorandum of the numbers of his forces on 1 Oct. 1845, to which must be added the garrison left in Colonia (A. Diaz, VII. 138–40).
10. Rodríguez, pp. 208, 211–12.
11. Winnington-Ingram, *Hearts of Oak,* p. 93; Werner, III. 52; *Garibaldi en América,* App., p.x.; Gradenigo, pp. 79–81.
12. For the capture of Colonia, see *Scritti,* II. 172–4; IV. 31–32; Dwight, pp. 154–6; Melena, I. 203–5; Dumas, II. 84–85; Gradenigo, p. 126; *Nacional,* 6, 9 Sept. 1845; *Patriote Français,* 13 Sept. 1845; *Gaceta Mercantil,* 4, 9 Sept. 1845; *Defensor,* 14 Sept. 1845; B.M. Add. 45153, Ouseley to Aberdeen, 2 Sept. 1845; A. Diaz, VII. 144.
13. *Archivo Americano,* No. 23, pp. 27–33; Iriarte, X. 83–84, 142.
14. *Gaceta Mercantil,* 16 Sept., 21 Oct. 1845; *British Packet,* 1 Nov. 1845; *Archivo Americano,* No. 1, pp. 59–60; No. 23, p. 33; *Globe,* 18 Nov. 1845; *Defensor,* 9 Oct. 1845.
15. *British Packet,* 6 Sept. 1845; *Defensor,* 27 Mar. 1847; *Archivo Americano,* No. 32, p. 78.
16. *Patriote Français,* 15, 19 Oct. 1845.
17. *Scritti,* IV. 33; De-María, III. 46–53; *Nacional,* 9, 10 Sept. 1845; *Patriote Français,* 10, 11, 12 Sept. 1845; Gradenigo, p. 126; *Gaceta Mercantil,* 18 Sept., 14 Nov. 1845; A. Diaz, VII. 137–8.
18. *Nacional,* 23 Sept. 1845; *Patriote Français,* 25 Sept. 1845; *Scritti,* II. 182; IV. 34–46 (where, following De-María, III. 70–72, Garibaldi's letter of 15 Sept. is wrongly dated 19 Sept. and published with several omissions); Dwight, p. 161; Melena, I. 211. For the treatment of British and French civilian internees, see A. Diaz, VII. 145–9, 193, 225–7; *Patriote Français,* 24/25 Nov. 1845; B.M. Add. 43153, Ouseley to Aberdeen, 25, 28 Jan. 1846; Iriarte, X. 141–2.

19. *Nacional*, 23 Sept. 1845; *Patriote Français*, 25 Sept. 1845; *Scritti*, IV, 38–9.
20 Iriarte, X. 142.
21. *Nacional*, 3 Oct. 1845; *British Packet*, 11, 18 Oct. 1845. This letter of Garibaldi to Bauzá of 25 Sept. 1845, unlike another letter of the same date, is not published in *Scritti*.
22. For the occupation of Gualeguaychú, see *Nacional*, 3 Oct. 1845; *Patriote Français*, 3 Oct. 1845; *Gaceta Mercantil*, 14, 23 Oct., 14 Nov. 1845; *Defensor*, 9 Oct., 2, 5 Nov. 1845; Villanueva, *Garibaldi en Entre-Rios*, pp. 120–1; A. Diaz, VII. 144–5n.; 157, 165; Tonelli, *Garibaldi y la Masoneria Argentina*, pp. 28–31; Gradenigo, p. 127; *British Packet*, 11 Oct. 1845; *Scritti*, II. 183–4; Dwight, pp. 163–5; Melena, I. 213–14; Dumas, II. 86–87; private information from Señorita Garciarena and Señora Chaparro, and local tradition at Gualeguaychú. In *Scritti*, IV. 46–49, where (following De-María, III. 73–76) Garibaldi's reply to the business men of Gualeguaychú is published in part, it is wrongly stated to be written to the business men of Salto.
23. *British Packet*, 1 Oct. 1842.
24. Iriarte, X. 184–5, 195.
25. Fray Mocho, *Obres Completas*, pp. 133–6.
26. Dumas, I. 109; II. 86; Cunninghame-Graham, *Three Fugitive Pieces*, pp. 14–15. For Sergeant Millan, see *Defensor*, 14 Sept. 1845.
27. B.M. Add. 48574, Ouseley to Aberdeen, 6 June 1846; Machiavelli, *The Prince*, chap. xvii; *Archivo Americano*, No. 23, pp. 35–36.
28. *Gaceta Mercantil*, 23 Oct. 1845; *Defensor*, 5 Nov. 1845; *Patriote Français*, 24/25 Nov. 1845; A. Diaz, VII. 147–9; B.M. Add. 48574, Ouseley to Aberdeen, 17 May 1846; De-María, III. 130–1.
29. Arch. Nav., B.A. MSS., Caya 1321–1845, No. 73; A. Diaz, VII. 157–8, 165–8, 168–9n.; *Nacional*, 13 Nov. 1845; *Defensor*, 15 Oct. 1845; *Gaceta Mercantil*, 23 Oct., 5 Nov. 1845; *British Packet*, 18, 25 Oct. 1845; *Archivo Americano*, No. 23, pp. 35–36.
30. See Garibaldi's three memoranda on the number of his forces and ships, 1 Oct. 1845 (A. Diaz, VII. 138–40). In the lists of his total forces, where Garibaldi gives the total of his naval forces as 279, Garibaldi's total (including the garrison of Martín García) in fact adds up to 630, though Garibaldi gives the total as 675. But if the total of the naval forces of 323, given in the list of ships, is taken, instead of the total of 279 given for the naval personnel in the lists of all the forces, then the grand total comes to 674, which, if Garibaldi himself is included, gives the correct total of 675. In the other list, Garibaldi included himself among the naval forces, not among the Italian Legion.
31. *Defensor*, 2 Nov. 1845; *Scritti*, IV. 49–50. In the letter, Garibaldi, like all the Spanish-speaking inhabitants at the time, translated the name of the French ship, *L'Eclair*, as *El Relámpago*.
32. M.H. Mont., M.H. MSS. 953/90/No. 38; *Gaceta Mercantil*, 14 Nov., 6 Dec. 1845; *Nacional*, 13, 17 Nov. 1845; *Patriote Français*, 17/18 Nov. 1845; De-María, III. 82–83; *Scritti*, II. 185–90; IV. 52–53; Dwight, pp. 165–70; Melena, I. 215–20; Gradenigo, p. 128; A. Diaz, VII. 159–

60n., 161–3n., 171, 173–5; *British Packet*, 22 Nov. 1845. The text of Garibaldi's letter to Bauzá, published by De-María and followed in *Scritti*, omits certain passages which are included in the shorter version in the *Nacional*; but both these Spanish texts are less complete than the French translation in the *Patriote Français*.

33. *Scritti*, II. 191–5; IV. 55–58; Dwight, pp. 171–6; Melena, I. 220–4; Dumas, II. 87; *Nacional*, 24 Dec. 1845; *Patriote Français*, 24 Dec. 1845; A. Diaz, VII. 177; *Gaceta Mercantil*, 24 Dec. 1845; *British Packet*, 3 Jan. 1846; *Archivo Americano*, No. 25, p. 41.

34. *Gaceta Mercantil*, 24 Dec. 1845; *British Packet*, 3 Jan. 1846; *Archivo Americano*, No. 25, p. 41; B.M. Add. 43130, f. 362.

35. For the siege of Salto by Urquiza, see *Scritti*, II. 195–9; Dwight, pp. 178–80; Melena, I. 225–8; Dumas, II. 88–90; Gradenigo, pp. 129–30; *British Packet*, 20 Dec. 1845; A. Diaz, VII. 178–81.

36. *Nacional*, 24 Dec. 1845; A. Diaz, VII. 188.

37. A. Diaz, VII. 179n.

38. M.H. Mont., M.H. MSS. 953/90/No. 39; *Nacional*, 3 Feb. 1846; A. Diaz, VII. 228; *Patriote Français*, 31 Jan. 1846; *Scritti*, II. 199–202; IV. 63–70; Dwight, pp. 181–5; Melena, I. 228–32.

39. Guerzoni, I. 376n.; Werner, III. 66–67; Pereda, III. 29–35.

Chapter 13

1. Gradenigo, p. 131.

2. Garibaldi gives the number of his Italian Legionaries as 186 in the Dwight, Melena and 1872 editions of the memoirs, and as 190 in the Dumas version. Cuneo says that there were 184 Legionaries; Sacchi, 190; and the anonymous Legionary in the *Legionario Italiano*, 170 (see n.3, infra). Garibaldi, in his report to Muñoz and in all the editions of the memoirs except Dumas's, gives the number of the cavalry as 100, as does Baez himself; only Sacchi says 200, which is the figure given by the Blanco commander, Gomez. The anonymous Legionary in the *Legionario Italiano* gives the figure of 80 cavalrymen. No figure is given in the Dumas edition of the memoirs, or by Odinici.

3. For the battle of San Antonio, see *Nacional*, 25, 28 Feb., 4 Mar. 1846; *Patriote Français*, 23/24/25/26, 27 Feb. 1846; *Scritti*, II. 202–9; IV. 72; Dwight, pp. 185–93; Melena, I. 231–8; Dumas, II. 90–97; Gradenigo, pp. 131–3; *Legionario Italiano*, No. 4; *Revista Militar y Naval* (Montevideo), Ano XVI, Nos. 171 and 172, Supp., pp. 19–28; *Gaceta Mercantil*, 7 Mar. 1846; A. Diaz, VII, 244–56; *British Packet*, 14 Mar. 1846; Cuneo, pp. 33–35, 38.

4. Garibaldi states this in a footnote to his novel *Clelia*, p. 458n.

5. *Scritti*, II. 209–11, 223–4; IV. 75–76; Dwight, pp. 193–5; Melena, I. 238–40; Dumas, II. 97–98; *Nacional*, 25 Feb. 1846; Gradenigo, p. 133.

6. *Nacional*, 25 Feb. 1846; *Scritti*, IV. 70–74; Dumas, II. 98–99.

7. *Legionario Italiano*, No. 4; *Nacional*, 25, 28 Feb., 4 Mar. 1846; *Patriote Français*, 23/24/25/26, 27 Feb. 1846.
8. *Gaceta Mercantil*, 7 Mar. 1846; A. Diaz, VII. 249–52.
9. *Nacional*, 2 Mar. 1846; *Patriote Français*, 5 Mar. 1846; Werner, III. 56n.
10. *Cornhill Mag.*, N.S., XXX. 396; *Il Felsineo*, 21 Aug. 1846; *Il Mondo Illustrato*, 5 Feb. 1848; Mazzini, *Scritti*, XXX. 235, 271, 278–80, 298, 308, 312, 319, 329; *Nacional*, 28 Feb., 9 Mar., 17 Apr. 1846; *Comercio del Plata*, 3 Feb., 18 May, 8 July 1847; Dumas, II. 112; Cuneo, p. 35; Werner, III. 55–56n. Cuneo, who had Lainé's autograph letter in his possession, published an Italian translation, from which Dumas retranslated it into French.
11. *British Packet*, 28 Feb., 7 Mar. 1846; *Gaceta Mercantil*, 7, 13, 30 Mar. 1846; *Defensor*, 24 Feb., 8, 14 Mar. 1846; *Patriote Français*, 28 Feb. 1846; *Nacional*, 28 Feb. 1846.
12. *Patriote Français*, 23/24/25/26 Feb. 1846; *Nacional*, 25 Feb. 1846.
13. Iriarte, XI. 180–1, 183–5, 192–5, 197, 202, 205, 214–15, 238–9.
14. De-María, III. 217–18; *Scritti*, IV. 79–80; *Patriote Français*, 8 May 1846; Ximenes, 1.9.
15. Werner, III. 57–8.
16. *Patriote Français*, 4/5, 8 May 1846.
17. Garibaldi was called 'Colonel Garibaldi' in the *Patriote Français* of 6 Sept. 1846, the *Constitucional* of 8 Feb. 1847, and the *Courrier de la Plata* of 16 Apr. 1848. All other references to him in the press after February 1846 are to 'General Garibaldi'.
18. Werner, III. 56n.; *Rev. Mil. y Nav.*, Ano XVI, Nos. 171 and 172, Supp., p. 28; A. Diaz, VII. 255; J. W. Mario, *Garibaldi*, pp. 132–3, where she gives completely different casualty figures from those which she gives in Werner.
19. Iriarte, XI. 193–4; *Gaceta Mercantil*, 7 Mar. 1846; A. Diaz, VII. 249–52.
20. A. Diaz, VII. 243–4, 255.

Chapter 14

1. *Nacional*, 16, 17 Feb. 1846; De-María, III. 219–35.
2. De-María, III. 246–310; Iriarte, XI. 267; *Nacional*, 11, 15 Apr. 1846; *Patriote Français*, 4/5, 9, 16 Apr. 1846; Dumas, *Montevideo, ou une nouvelle Troie*, pp. 145–51.
3. *Scritti*, II. 211, 213; Dwight, p. 194; Melena, I. 239; A. Diaz, VII. 313, 315; Werner, III. 61–62.
4. *Gaceta Mercantil*, 23 Jan. 1847; A. Diaz, VII. 314; Werner, III. 60.
5. For the battle of the Daiman, see *Scritti*, II. 214–21; Dwight, pp. 199–207; Melena, I. 243–51; *Patriote Français*, 5 June 1846; *Nacional*, 4, 10 June 1846. Garibaldi's report to Costa is not included in *Scritti*, and was published in full only in the French translation in the *Patriote Français*. A shortened version was published in the *Nacional* of 10 June.

6. *Gaceta Mercantil,* 23 Jan. 1847; A. Diaz, VII. 315; Werner, III. 60–61; Gradenigo, pp. 134–5. Jessie White Mario's account conflicts with all the other versions.

7. A. Diaz, VII. 315.

8. *Scritti,* II. 213–14; Dwight, p. 199. For Ouseley's support of the Pachecists, see A. Diaz, VII. 236–7; Iriarte, XI. 488.

9. Gradenigo, p. 135; *Patriote Français,* 6 Sept. 1846.

10. Pereda, III. 74; Werner, III. 56n.

11. Iriarte, IX. 393.

12. *Cornhill Mag.,* N.S., XXX. 392–5.

13. Winnington-Ingram, *Hearts of Oak,* p. 94.

14. Brossard, *Considérations historiques et politiques sur les Républiques de la Plata,* pp. 279–80.

15. *Gaceta Mercantil,* 10 Oct., 9 Nov. 1846; *Defensor,* 11 Nov. 1846; *British Packet,* 14, 21 Nov. 1846; Iriarte, XI. 488, 511–12; *Scritti,* II. 228.

16. *Gaceta Mercantil,* 6, 10, 16, 22 Oct. 1846; *Defensor,* 27 Sept. 1846.

17. For the Howden–Walewski proposals and negotiations, see B.M. Add. 48554, Normanby to Palmerston, 5 Feb. 1847; B.M. Add. 48555, Palmerston to Normanby, 11 Jan. 1848; *British Packet,* 8, 15, 22, 29 Mar. 1847; De-María, IV, 49, 55, 59; A. Diaz, VIII. 29, 31–32, 38.

18. B.M. Add. 43127, ff. 167–8.

19. A. Diaz, VIII. 174–6; *Constitucional,* 15 June 1847.

20. *Constitucional,* 26 June 1847; *Comercio del Plata,* 26 June 1847; *Gaceta Mercantil,* 30 June 1847; *British Packet,* 3 July 1847.

21. *Defensor,* 1, 5 July 1847.

22 Gradenigo, p. 137; Werner, III. 54–55; *Hansard* (House of Lords) 10 July 1849; *British Packet,* 20 Oct. 1849.

23. A. Diaz, VIII. 177; *Comercio del Plata,* 8 July 1847; *Scritti,* II. 228.

24. *Comercio del Plata,* 18 July 1847.

25. *Comercio del Plata,* 26 July 1847; De-María, IV. 76; Dumas, II. 65; Werner, III. 49.

26. De-María, IV. 66–75; A. Diaz, VIII. 40–44; *British Packet,* 24, 31 July 1847; Winnington-Ingram, p. 107; *Comercio del Plata,* 21 July 1847; *Scritti,* II. 227, 229.

27. *Comercio del Plata,* 3 Aug. 1847.

28. For the peace agitation, the Larraya mutiny, and the banishment of Flores, see *Comercio del Plata,* 4, 7, 20 Aug. 1847; *Constitucional,* 20 Aug. 1847; *Defensor,* 9 Sept. 1847; A. Diaz, VIII. 177–8; De-María, IV. 83–105 (where the official documents published in the *Comercio del Plata* are included in a shortened form); Werner, III. 63.

29. De-María, IV. 117–42; *Scritti,* II. 213, 226.

30. *Defensor,* 22 Aug. 1847; *Gaceta Mercantil,* 28 Aug. 1847; *British Packet,* 4 Sept. 1847, 22 Jan. 1848.

Chapter 15

1. For the Bandiera plot and the opening of Mazzini's letters, see J. W. Mario, *Birth of Modern Italy,* pp. 67–81; *Hansard,* 24 June, 2 July 1844.
2. Pereda, III. 29, 35; Werner, III. 69.
3. Dumas, II. 118–19. Though the story of Teresita's toy appears only in the Dumas edition of the memoirs, Dumas expressly states that he was told the story by Garibaldi himself.
4. Werner, III. 67.
5. *Scritti,* IV. 82–85; Cuneo, p. 43; Werner, III. 69.
6. Instructions to Garibaldi, 6 Nov. 1847 (Arch. Gen., Mont., Caja 1398); *Comercio del Plata,* 9 Nov. 1847; *Defensor,* 11, 15, 18, 22 Nov., 16 Dec. 1847; *Gaceta Mercantil,* 25, 26 Nov. 1847; *British Packet,* 13 Nov. 1847; *Conservador,* 18 Nov. 1847; A. Diaz, VIII. 185.
7. *Comercio del Plata,* 7 Dec. 1847; *Conservador,* 7 Dec. 1847.
8. Garibaldi's application for a passport for Anita, 27 Dec. 1847 (Arch. Gen., Mont., Caja 1399); *Scritti,* II. 233; IV. 85–87; Werner, III. 70–71.
9. *Conservador,* 8, 10 Feb. 1848; *Comercio del Plata,* 8 Feb. 1848; *Gaceta Mercantil,* 10 Feb., 8 Mar. 1848; *Defensor,* 22 Feb. 1848.
10 *Scritti,* IV. 85–87.
11. *Conservador,* 1 Mar., 10 Apr. 1848.
12. *Conservador,* 22 Mar. 1848; A. Diaz, VIII. 197–202; Indarte, *Rosas y sus opositores,* App., i-lxxii.
13. *Scritti,* II. 233; Melena, II. 9–10; Dumas, II. 105; Werner, III. 72; Cuneo, p. 44.
14. Gradenigo, p. 107.
15. *Scritti,* II. 234; Werner, III. 72–73; Cuneo, p. 45.
16. *Patriote Français,* 15, 16 Apr. 1848; *Conservador,* 15, 18, 19, 26 Apr. 1848; *Defensor,* 2, 22 Apr. 1848; *British Packet,* 29 Apr. 1848; *Gaceta Mercantil,* 2 May 1848; *Scritti,* II. 235.
17. *Conservador,* 13 Apr. 1848; *Patriote Français,* 30 Apr. 1848.
18. *Scritti,* II. 234.

Chapter 16

1. *Scritti,* II. 235; Dumas, II. 105–6.
2. *Memoirs of Margaret Fuller Ossoli,* III. 162; *Gazzetta di Roma,* 29 Apr. 1848.
3. Ossoli, III. 155, 173.
4. Sardagna, *Garibaldi in Lombardia 1848,* pp. 30–31; Werner, III. 71–72.
5. *Scritti,* II. 236–8.
6. Parris, p. 347.
7. *Scritti,* II. 238; IV. 87.
8. *Scritti,* II. 238–9; Giampaolo and Bertolone, *La prima campagna di Garibaldi in Italia,* p. 408.
9. *Scritti,* IV. 88; Sardagna, pp. 36–39; *Gazzetta di Milano,* 1 July 1848.
10. Werner, III. 75; *Letters of Queen Victoria,* I(ii). 207.

11. Werner, III. 77–78.
12. *Scritti,* II. 239.
13. *Scritti,* II. 240–1; Pieri, *Storia militare del Risorgimento,* p. 328n.
14. Brentari, *Garibaldi a Milano,* pp. 6–7; J. W. Mario, *Garibaldi,* p. 204; Werner, III. 76.
15. Pieri, p. 328n.
16. Werner, III. 76.
17. *Scritti,* II. 241; *Gazzetta di Milano,* 15 July 1848; Brentari, pp. 6–8; J. W. Mario, *Garibaldi,* p. 204; Werner, III. 76; *Carteggio del governo provvisorio de Lombardia,* pp. 236, 244.
18. *Scritti,* II. 244–5; Werner, III. 76–78.
19. *Scritti,* II. 242.
20. Pieri, p. 321.
21. *Scritti,* II. 244.
22. *Scritti,* II. 244; Werner, III. 79–80.
23. *Scritti,* II. 247; Giampaolo and Bertolone, p. 410.
24. *Scritti,* IV. 92–94.
25. Giampaolo and Bertolone, pp. 316, 318–19.
26. Giampaolo and Bertolone, pp. 309–10, 318.
27. *Scritti,* II. 251.
28. *Scritti,* II. 248; Giampaolo and Bertolone, p. 414.
29. Sardagna, pp. 144–5; *Scritti,* IV. 94.
30. *Scritti,* II. 248–9; Giampaolo and Bertolone, p. 375.
31. *Scritti,* II. 249–50; Giampaolo and Bertolone, pp. 94, 151; 313–15, 335, 370. For Garibaldi's movements, day by day, after the fight at Luino, see Giampaolo and Bertolone, pp. 96–115.
32. *Scritti,* II. 251–2; Giampaolo and Bertolone, pp. 416–20; *Gazzetta di Roma,* 22 Aug. 1848.
33. Giampaolo and Bertolone, pp. 322–3.
34. *Scritti,* II. 252; Giampaolo and Bertolone, pp. 318–99, 321, 345, 405.
35. For the battle of Morazzone, see *Scritti,* II. 253–6; Giampaolo and Bertolone, pp. 328–33; Werner, III. 81n.
36. *Scritti,* II. 257.
37. *Gazzetta di Milano,* 29 Aug. 1848; Vecchi, *La Italia, storia di due anni 1848–49,* I. 265.
38. Giampaolo and Bertolone, p. 330.
39. Giampaolo and Bertolone, pp. 334–7; *Scritti,* II. 256.
40. *Scritti,* II. 257–8.
41. Dumas, II. 129–42; *Scritti,* II. 244, 248, 251, 253; Werner, III. 80–82n.
42. Pisacane, *Guerra combattuto in Italia negli anni 1848–49,* pp. 158–62.
43. Giampaolo and Bertolone, pp. 336–7; Schneidawind, *Radetzky-Lieder,* pp. 30, 33–37, 57–59.

Chapter 17

1. Sardagna, p. 217.
2. Parris, p. 78.

3. *Scritti*, II. 258; IV. 95.
4. Sardagna, pp. 217–18.
5. *Scritti*, IV. 95–96.
6. *Scritti*, II. 260.
7. Luzio, pp. 34–35.
8. *Le relazione diplomatiche fra la Francia e il Granducato di Toscana*, III. 113.
9. For the events during Garibaldi's stay in Leghorn, see Sforza, *Garibaldi in Toscana nel 1848*, pp. 5–14. See also *Scritti*, II. 260.
10. Sforza, pp. 14–16; *Scritti*, IV. 98–99.
11. Sforza, pp. 22–25, 51–60; *Scritti*, IV. 99–101.
12. *Rel. dip. Francia-Toscana*, III(i). 111; *Scritti*, II. 261.
13. For the incidents at Filigari and Bologna, see *Scritti*, II. 261–4; IV. 102–3; Sforza, pp. 36–39.
14. For the events at Ravenna, see *Scritti*, II. 264–5, 267–9.
15. Schneidawind, *Aus dem Hauptquartiere und Feldleben des Vater Radetzky*, p. 124.
16. Balleydier, *Histoire de la Révolution de Rome*, I. 196–206.
17. Balleydier, I. 237; see also Ossoli, III. 185–6.
18. *Scritti*, II. 266–7.
19. Balleydier, pp. 265–77.
20. *Scritti*, II. 269–73; Loevinson, *Garibaldi e la sue legione nello stato Romano*, I. 43–77.
21. *Scritti*, II. 272–3; Dandolo, *The Italian Volunteers and Lombard Rifle Brigade*, p. 206.
22. Balleydier, I. 324–43.
23. *Gazzetta di Roma*, 26 Jan. 1849; Foglietti, *Garibaldi in Macerata negli anni 1848 e 1849*, pp. 4–5; *Scritti*, II. 274.
24. *Scritti*, II. 275–6; Loevinson, I. 139; *Gazzetta di Milano*, 13 Mar. 1849.
25. Loevinson, I. 130–1.
26. Pisacane, pp. 299–302.
27. Balleydier, I. 324–7, 344–5.
28. *Scritti*, II. 277–8; IV. 106–10; *Monitore Romano*, 10 Feb. 1849; *Costituzionale Romano*, 7 Feb. 1849.
29. Dwight, p. 229; Melena, II. 144; Loevinson, III. 128, 331. As Anita was five months pregnant when she died in August 1849, her fifth child must have been conceived as soon as she arrived at Rieti at the end of February.
30. *Scritti*, II. 276; Pieri, p. 420.

Chapter 18

1. Werner, III. 103–4; Loevinson, I. 131.
2. Werner, III. 92–93n.; Koelman, *In Rome 1846–1851*, I. 324–5.
3. *Monitore Romano*, 19 Feb. 1849.

4. *Monitore Romano*, 25, 27 Apr. 1849; Vaillant, *Siège de Rome en 1849*, pp. 8, 173; Des Portes, *L'expédition française de Rome*, pp. 46–47.

5. *Monitore Romano*, 27, 28, 30 Apr. 1849; Balleydier, II. 89–91; Des Portes, pp. 69–70.

6. Balleydier, II. 99; Des Portes, pp. 48–49; Werner, III. 95.

7. Balleydier, II. 70.

8. Pieri, pp. 416, 420; Werner, III. 113.

9. Ossoli, III. 215, 243–4.

10. Koelman, II. 310–16; Trevelyan, I. 169n.

11. Koelman, II. 314.

12. Pieri, p. 417; Trevelyan, I. 149–50; Des Portes, p. 63; Loevinson, II. 185–6n.

13. Dandolo, pp. 191–5.

14. Vaillant, p. 8; Des Portes, pp. 63–71.

15. *Scritti*, II. 280; Pieri, p. 421.

16. Balleydier, II. 103.

17. For the battle of 30 April, see *Monitore Romano*, 1, 5 May 1849; *Scritti*, II. 280–4; Hoffstetter, *Tagebuch aus Italien 1849*, pp. 11–13; Vaillant, pp. 9–11; Vecchi, *Storia di due anni*, II. 195–8; Cuneo, pp. 56–57; Guerzoni, I. 269–70; Loevinson, I. 160–7; Balleydier, II. 104–7; Des Portes, pp. 73–95; Werner, III. 96–98; Trevelyan, I. 128–34; Hibbert, *Garibaldi and his enemies*, pp. 55–57.

18. Guerrazzi, *Lo Asedio di Roma*, p. 698.

19. *Scritti*, II. 284; Werner, III. 98–99; *The Times*, 9 May 1849.

20. Balleydier, II. 110–14.

21. *Monitore Romano*, 7 May 1849; Des Portes, pp. 114–15; Balleydier, II. 155; *The Times*, 21 May 1849.

22. *Le Moniteur Universel*, 8 May, 7 June 1849; Vaillant, p. 174; Des Portes, pp. 117–20.

23. Balleydier, II. 122–4.

24. Hoffstetter, pp. 20, 32; Vaillant, p. 14; Loevinson, I. 171–3; Des Portes, p. 139.

25. Dandolo, pp. 204–8.

26. Dandolo, pp. 208–9; Hoffstetter, pp. 29–30; Guerrazzi, p. 722.

27. For the battle of Palestrina, see *Monitore Romano*, 11 May 1849; Hoffstetter, pp. 30–33; Dandolo, pp. 210–14; *Scritti*, II. 284; Loevinson, I. 175–8.

28. Lesseps, *Mémoire présenté au Conseil d'Etat*, pp. 17–20; Des Portes, p. 133; Balleydier, II. 134, 136–7; *Scritti*, II. 283–4. For the Polish Legion, see *Monitore Romano*, 30 May 1849.

29. *Scritti*, II. 287–8n.; Werner, III. 94–95.

30. Balleydier, II. 143.

31. For the battle of Velletri, see *Monitore Romano*, 21, 22, 24, 25 May 1849; Hoffstetter, pp. 69–80; Dandolo, pp. 218–19; Vecchi, II. 235–40; Cuneo, pp. 61–62; Guerzoni, I. 282–91; Loevinson, I. 180–6; Trevelyan, I. 153–7.

32. Mirecourt, *Garibaldi*, pp. 36–38, 71–72.

33. *Scritti*, II. 287–8; Werner, III. 100; Hoffstetter, pp. 75–76; Pisacane, p. 270; Loevinson, I. 182–4, 190–2.
34. Scritti, II. 289–91.

Chapter 19

1. Lesseps, pp. 23–24; Des Portes, p. 171n.
2. *Monitore Romano*, 1, 2 June 1849; Lesseps, pp. 26–73; Balleydier II. 166–82, 187–90; Des Portes, pp. 149–74, 178–201.
3. Des Portes, p. 200, 207–9; Balleydier, II. 199–200, 205; *Scritti*, II. 291–2
4. Ximenes, I. 37; Werner, III. 101n.; *Scritti*, II. 291; Pisacane, p. 301.
5. For the battle of 3 June, see *Scritti*, II. 293–4; IV. 132–6; *Monitore Romano*, 3, 4, 8 June 1849; Dandolo, pp. 229–55; Hoffstetter, pp. 105–35; Vaillant, pp. 32–33; Pisacane, pp. 285–6; Vecchi, II. 260–3; Balleydier, II. 200–3; Cuneo, pp. 62–64; Guerzoni, I. 302–13; Loevinson, I. 213–36; Des Portes, pp. 211–37; Trevelyan, I. 167–93, 336–41, 344–6; Hibbert, pp. 71–77; Pieri, pp. 428–30.
6. Hoffstetter, p. 162.
7. Balleydier, II. 250–6; *Monitore Romano*, 14, 26, 28 June 1849; *The Times*, 7 July 1849; Dwight, pp. 271–2; *Prose Remains of Arthur Hugh Clough*, pp. 152–3, 156.
8. *The Times*, 20 Feb., 11 May, 19 June, 5 July 1849. See also 18, 22, 24 May, 1, 23, 30 June, 3 July 1849.
9. *Le Moniteur Universel*, 13, 14 June 1849; *Monitore Romano*, 22 June 1849; Balleydier, pp. 240–1; Des Portes, pp. 295–6, 315–16.
10. *Scritti*, II. 295; Hoffstetter, pp. 135–224; Dandolo, pp. 249–53; Vaillant, pp. 18, 36–98; Balleydier, II. 225–6, 229–39; Des Portes, pp. 245, 251–2, 272–3, 278–83, 297–300, 311–14, 317–18; Loevinson, I. 242–51.
11. *Monitore Romano*, 22, 24, 25 June 1849; Hoffstetter, pp. 224–34; Dandolo, p. 255; Balleydier, II. 243–6; Des Portes, pp. 322–36; Vaillant, pp. 98–99, 102–7; Loevinson, I. 252–3; II. 197.
12. Vecchi, II. 285; Guerzoni, I. 322–3; Loevinson, I. 254–5; III. 318; Dandolo, pp. 167–8; Guerrazzi, pp. 827–8.
13. Werner, III. 105–7; J. W. Mario, *Birth of Modern Italy*, p. 200; Guerzoni I. 320–2; Loevinson, I. 253–6; Dandolo, pp. 257–9; Pisacane, p. 292; Vecchi, II. 283–5; Mazzini, *Scritti*, XL. 157.
14. *Scritti*, IV. 141–3; Werner, III. 106–7; *The Times*, 14 July 1849.
15. *The Times*, 9 July 1849; Vaillant, pp. 9, 25, 27, 109–33, 143, 196; Balleydier, II. 218; Des Portes, pp. 311, 339–42, 349–54; Clough, pp. 156–7.
16. Dwight, p. 225; Melena, II. 144; Werner, III. 113; J. W. Mario, *Birth of Modern Italy*, p. 204; Guerzoni, I. 381–2; Loevinson, II. 214–15. Guerzoni is wrong in giving 14 June as the date of Anita's arrival in Rome, because Garibaldi had written to her on 21 June, believing that she was still in Nice; see Loevinson, II. 214–15n.; III. 106.

17. Ximenes, I. 40; Hoffstetter, p. 270; Loevinson, II. 126–7.
18. Des Portes, pp. 359–65.
19. *Monitore Romano,* 2 July 1849; *Scritti,* IV. 146–7; Dandolo, pp. 267–78; Hoffstetter, pp. 288–305; Vaillant, pp. 133–45; Balleydier, II. 262–71; Loevinson, I. 261–3; Des Portes, pp. 364–83; Werner, III. 108; Trevelyan, I. 217–26.
20. Vaillant, p. 142; Balleydier, II. 266.
21. *Monitore Romano,* 1, 2 July 1849; *Scritti,* II. 296; Werner, III. 108–9; Balleydier, II. 271–7; Loevinson, I. 262–6; Des Portes, pp. 384–91; Mazzini, *Scritti,* XL. 189–90.
22. Des Portes, p. 352; *The Times,* 17 July 1849; P.R.O., F.O. 43/45, Palmerston's memoranda, 20 July, 2, 13 Aug. 1849; Freeborn to Palmerston, 4 Aug. 1849.
23. Dwight, p. 296; *Scritti,* II. 297.
24. The text of Garibaldi's speech given here was the first version to be published; see Loevinson, III. 114; Cuneo, p. 69; *Scritti,* IV. 148. For other versions, see Hoffstetter, p. 307; *Scritti,* IV. 147.
25. Dandolo, p. 285; Pisacane, p. 302; *Scritti,* II. 297–8; Hoffstetter, pp. 314–15; *The Times,* 17 July 1849; Des Portes, pp. 392–4.

Chapter 20

1. *Monitore Romano,* 1, 2, 3, July 1849; Dwight, pp. 310–11.
2. Des Portes, pp. 406–7, 423–4; Balleydier, II. 281–3, 286–7, 308–10, 325, 376–8, 387–8; *Giornale di Roma,* 6 July 1849; Werner, III. 110; J. W. Mario, *Birth of Modern Italy,* p. 201; Trevelyan, I. 235.
3. Balleydier, II. 381–3; *Giornale di Roma,* 6 Nov. 1849.
4. Vaillant, pp. 130–1; *The Times,* 14, 17 July 1849.
5. Pieri, pp. 436–7; *The Times,* 20 July 1849; Clough, p. 166.
6. Hoffstetter, p. 318.
7. Balleydier, II. 257–8.
8. Hoffstetter, pp. 325, 328–9; Trevelyan, I. 243–5.
9. Hoffstetter, pp. 329, 334, 340, 342; *Scritti,* II. 299; *Gazzetta di Milano,* 17 July 1849; Pieri, p. 439; Trevelyan, I. 252, 349–50; Hibbert, p. 104. Other sources say that Forbes joined Garibaldi with 800 or 900 men; Hoffstetter, who was present and almost certainly noted the fact on that very day, says that he came with 600 infantrymen and about a dozen horsemen, though elsewhere he states that Forbes brought 600 or 700 men.
10. Hoffstetter, pp. 317, 325–7. Hoffstetter, writing in German, says that Garibaldi's line stretched for three or four 'Miglien', not 'Meilen', and must therefore be referring to the Italian mile. The scale given on Map 2 at the end of his book makes it clear that this is the ordinary Italian mile of 1,850 metres, not the shorter Roman, or the longer Piedmontese, mile.
11. *Giornale di Roma,* 7, 13 July 1849; *Gazzetta di Milano,* 13 July 1849; *The*

Times, 21 July 1849; *Rel. dip. Austria-Sardegna*, II. 409–10; Hoffstetter, pp. 343, 345, 347–8, 352; Trevelyan, I. 245–7, 253.

12. *Giornale di Roma*, 7 July 1849; *Gazzetta di Milano*, 22 July 1849; Hoffstetter, p. 324.

13. Hoffstetter, p. 365; *Giornale di Roma*, 13 July 1849; *Gazzetta di Milano*, 18 July 1849; *Scritti*, II. 299–300.

14. Des Portes, p. 413n.

15. *Giornale di Roma*, 13 July 1849; Hoffstetter, pp. 325, 331, 339–40, 359, 363; *Scritti*, II. 303; Dwight, pp. 225–6.

16. Hoffstetter, pp. 352–3, 359.

17. Hoffstetter, p. 365.

18. Hoffstetter, pp. 366–72; *Giornale di Roma*, 18, 21 July 1849; *Gazzetta di Milano*, 22 July 1849.

19. Des Portes, p. 159; Balleydier, II. 306.

20. *Rel. dip. Austria-Tosc.*, III(i), 177–9, 240; Dahlerup, *Mit Livs Beginenheder*, III. 88; Hoffstetter, p. 375.

21. *Rel. dip. Austria-Tosc.*, III(i). 178, 201.

22. *Rel. dip. Austria-Tosc.*, III(i). 182–3, 185, 187, 192; *Rel. dip. Francia-Tosc.*, III(i). 276–7; Kolowrat, *Meine Erinnerungen aus den Jahren 1848 und 1849*, II. 194–5.

23. *Rel. dip. Austria-Tosc.*, III(i). 181, 184.

24. Hoffstetter, pp. 377–81; *Giornale di Roma*, 23, 24 July 1849; *Gazzetta di Milano*, 23 July 1849.

25. *Scritti*, II. 302; Hoffstetter, pp. 384–6; Vecchi, II. 317; *Giornale di Roma*, 21, 24, 26, 27 July 1849; *Gazzetta di Milano* 22, 27 July 1849; Iriarte, X. 184.

26. Hoffstetter, pp. 386–8; Guerzoni, I. 380.

27. *Scritti*, IV. 148–9.

28. *Giornale di Roma*, 21, 23, 24, 25, 26, 27, 31 July, 4 Aug. 1849; *Gazzetta di Milano*, 23, 24, 25, 26 July, 5 Aug. 1849.

29. *Giornale di Roma*, 23, 25, 26, 27, 28 July 1849; *Gazzetta di Milano*, 23, 26, 27, 29 July 1849.

30. Hoffstetter, pp. 393–403; Vecchi, II. 318; *Giornale di Roma*, 25, 26, 27, 30 July 1849; *Gazzetta di Milano*, 26, 27 July 1849; Trevelyan, I. 261–2.

31. *Scritti*, II. 302; Hoffstetter, p. 414; *Rel. dip. Francia-Tosc.*, III (i). 277. There does not appear to be any justification for the statement by Trevelyan and other authors that Müller and afterwards Bueno, 'sold himself' to the Austrians, which implies that they joined the Austrian forces and fought against Garibaldi.

32. Hoffstetter, p. 350; Loevinson, II. 239.

33. Hoffstetter, p. 408; *Giornale di Roma*, 27, 28, 30 July 1849; *Gazzetta di Milano*, 28, 29, 30, 31 July 1849; Trevelyan, I. 264.

34. *Rel. dip. Austria-Tosc.*, III(i). 183; *Giornale di Roma*, 28, 30 July, 1 Aug. 1849; *Gazzetta di Milano*, 29 July, 3 Aug. 1849; Trevelyan, I. 265–6.

35. *Rel. dip. Austria-Tosc.*, III(i). 188; Trevelyan, I. 266.

36. Hoffstetter, pp. 415–18; *Scritti*, II. 301; *Giornale di Roma*, 3 Aug. 1849; *Gazzetta di Milano*, 3 Aug. 1849; Trevelyan, I. 269.

37. Hoffstetter, pp. 391–2, 405–9, 414, 418–19, 422, 424, 426, 429–30.
38. Hoffstetter, pp. 431–6; Guerzoni, I. 349–50; Franciosi, *Garibaldi e la Repubblica di San Marino*, pp. 47–48, 59–61; *Scritti*, II. 302–3.
39. Dwight, p. 226.

Chapter 21

1. *Scritti*, II. 304; IV. 150; Trevelyan, I. 277. In the memoirs, Garibaldi slightly misquotes the words of his order of the day.
2. For the negotiations with the Austrians, see Franciosi, pp. 48–49, 61; *Scritti*, II. 304; IV. 152; Guerzoni, I. 351–6; Hoffstetter, pp. 436–9; *Gazzetta di Milano*, 6 Aug. 1849; *Giornale di Roma*, 7 Aug. 1849.
3. *Scritti*, II. 304.
4. Hoffstetter, pp. 440–2, 444–55; *Scritti*, II. 304–5; Trevelyan, I. 279–85; *Gazzetta di Milano*, 6 Aug. 1849; *Giornale di Roma*, 6 Aug. 1849.
5. *Scritti*, II. 305–7; Guerzoni, I. 357–8n.; Trevelyan, I. 283–6.
6. Franciosi, pp. 50–52, 57, 61–62; *Rel. dip. Austria-Tosc.*, III(i). 200–2.
7. *Scritti*, II. 256; Trevelyan, I. 280–1; Loevinson, II. 243.
8. *Rel. dip. Austria-Tosc.*, III(i). 183, 199, 207, 254, 370–3.
9. *Scritti*, II. 307–8.
10. *Scritti*, II. 308–9; *Giornale di Roma*, 13 Aug. 1849; *Gazzetta di Milano*, 7, 8, 11 Aug. 1849; *The Times*, 14, 18 Aug. 1849; Dahlerup, III. 166–7; Trevelyan, I. 291–2, 351–3.
11. *Scritti*, II. 309; Bonnet, *Lo sbarco di Garibaldi a Magnavacca*, pp. 24–25; Trevelyan, I. 295–6.
12. *Scritti*, II. 311.
13. Bonnet, pp. 13-16; *Scritti*, II. 311.
14. *Scritti*, II. 309, 311; Guerzoni, I. 357–8n.
15. Dahlerup, III. 167.
16. Bonnet, pp. 16–33; Trevelyan, I. 294–8.
17. *Gazzetta di Milano*, 7 Aug. 1849. The communiqué was published in a slightly inaccurate translation in *The Times* of 14 August.
18. *Scritti*, II. 312; Guerzoni, I. 369n.; Beseghi, *Il Maggiore 'Leggero' e il 'Trafugamento' di Garibaldi*, pp. 189–216, 224–5; Trevelyan, I. 298–9.
19. *Scritti*, II. 312–13; Bonnet, pp. 45–46.
20. *Giornale di Roma*, 10 Aug. 1849; Beseghi, p. 76.
21. See supra, p. 226.
22. *Scritti*, II. 310; *Giornale di Roma*, 8, 13 Aug. 1849; *Gazzetta di Milano*, 8 Aug. 1849; *The Times*, 18, 20 Aug. 1849; Trevelyan, I. 307–9; Melena, *Recollections of Garibaldi*, pp. 76–77.
23. *Rel. dip. Austria-Tosc.*, III(i). 208.
24. *Scritti*, I. 310; Trevelyan, I. 306–7; Curàtulo, Garibaldi MSS., Nos. 665, 688.
25. For Garibaldi's escape from Sant' Alberto to Santa Lucia, see *Scritti*, II. 313–18.
26. *La Rassegna Nazionale*, LXV. 678–86.

27. *Gazzetta di Milano*, 28 Sept. 1849; *Giornale di Roma*, 13, 16 Aug. 1849; *The Times*, 17, 18, 22 Aug. 1849.
28. *Rel. dip. Austria-Tosc.*, III(i). 210, 222.
29. *Gazzetta di Milano*, 20, 23 Aug. 1849; *Giornale di Roma*, 21 Aug. 1849; *The Times*, 23 Aug., 17 Sept. 1849.
30. For the proceedings and accusations against the Ravaglia brothers, see Beseghi, pp. 219–53; Guerzoni, I. 367–9n.
31. Bonnet, pp. 54–65.
32. Trevelyan, I. 292, 350–1.
33. *Scritti*, II. 318; Trevelyan, I. 314.
34. *Scritti*, II. 318–20; Trevelyan, I. 314–17; *Rel. dip. Austria-Tosc.*, III(i). 186–7, 190, 192, 200; *Rel. dip. Francia-Tosc.*, III(i). 277, 279.
35. *Scritti*, II. 321; Trevelyan, I. 317–21.
36. *Scritti*, II. 322; Trevelyan, I. 321–3; *Gazzetta di Milano*, 10 Sept. 1849; *Giornale di Roma*, 11 Sept. 1849; *The Times*, 14, 17 Sept. 1849; Gay, *Il Secondo Esilio di Garibaldi*, p. 8 and n.

Chapter 22

1. *Scritti*, II. 322.
2. Biase, *L'Arresto di Garibaldi nel settembre 1849*, pp. 2–7, 77–79, 86; *Scritti*, II. 322–3; *Gazzetta di Milano*, 10 Sept. 1849; *Giornale di Roma*, 11, 13 Sept. 1849; *The Times*, 14, 17 Sept. 1849; Gay, p. 8.
3. *Atti Parl.*, 10 Sept. 1849; *Gazzetta Piemontese*, 11 Sept. 1849; *The Times*, 17 Sept. 1849; *Gazzetta di Milano*, 16 Sept. 1849; Werner, III. 116–18; Guerzoni, I. 387–8; Biase, pp. 13–31.
4. *Gazzetta di Milano*, 13 Sept. 1849.
5. *Giornale di Roma*, 18 Sept. 1849.
6. Biase, p. 86; *Scritti*, II. 322; *Patriote Français*, 5 Dec. 1849.
7. Biase, pp. 108–9, 111, 114–15; *The Times*, 19 Sept. 1849; Gay, p. 8.
8. *Scritti*, II. 323; Biase, p. 116; *Giornale di Roma*, 21 Sept. 1849; *TheTimes*, 24 Sept. 1849; Werner, III. 119.
9. Biase, pp. 86, 116–18.
10. Biase, pp. 123–4.
11. Biase, pp. 108–9, 112, 117–19, 124, 141; Werner, III. 118 and n.
12. Biase, p. 122.
13. Biase, pp. 125–32; *Scritti*, II. 324; *Gazzetta di Milano*, 19, 28 Sept. 1849; *Giornale di Roma*, 2 Oct. 1849; *The Times*, 24 Sept., 4, 5 Oct. 1849; Gay, pp. 11–13.
14. Biase, pp. 149, 151–2; Gay, pp. 13–14; Beseghi, p. 12.
15. *Scritti*, II. 324; Biase, pp. 132–3.
16. Biase, p. 138.
17. Biase, pp. 139; 141, 147–8, 154; Gay, pp. 13–14.
18. P.R.O., C.O. 92/18, ff. 415–16; C.O. 92/20, f. 58.
19. Biase, pp. 150–1; P.R.O., C.O. 91/194, No. 104; *Scritti*, II. 324.
20. Biase, pp. 151–3, 155; *Gazzetta di Milano*, 2 Dec. 1849; Gay, p. 14.

21. P.R.O., C.O. 91/194, No. 104; Biase, pp. 152–3.
22. P.R.O., C.O. 91/194, No. 104; C.O. 91/197, No. 69; *Scritti*, II. 324.
23. Biase, pp. 153, 155.
24. Gay, p. 16; Biase, pp. 156–7.
25. *Scritti*, II. 325–6, 329.
26. Garibaldi to Pacheco y Obes, 24 Nov. 1849, holograph letter in possession of Señora Pirretti de Novikov of Buenos Aires.
27. Pacheco y Obes, *Réponse aux Détracteurs de Montevideo*, pp. 28–32; and his *Rosas et Montevideo devant la Cour d'Assises*, p. 107. See also Pacheco, *Rectification de Faits Calomnieux attribués à la défense de Montevideo*.
28. Dumas, *Montevideo, ou une nouvelle Troie*, pp. 84–92, 101.
29. *Scritti*, II. 328–9.
30. P.R.O., C.O. 91/197, No. 69; *The Albion* (Liverpool), 24 June 1850; *Daily News* (London), 25 June 1850; *The Red Republican*, 6, 13 July 1850.
31. *Liverpool Mail*, 29 June 1850.
32. *The Albion*, 24 June 1850; *Daily News*, 27 June 1850; *Liverpool Mail*, 27 July 1850; *New-York Daily Tribune*, 23, 30 July, 11 Aug. 1850; Fortini, p. 98.
33. *New-York Daily Tribune*, 25, 26, 27, 29, 30 July 1850.
34. *New-York Daily Tribune*, 31 July 1850; *Scritti*, II. 326.
35. *New-York Daily Tribune*, 2, 5 Aug. 1850.
36. *New-York Daily Tribune*, 7 Aug. 1850; Gay, pp. 17–18.

Chapter 23

1. Gay, p. 19; Francis, *Old New York*, p. 13.
2. Dwight, pp. 5, 317–19.
3. Dwight, pp. 5–6, 215–27; for the passages cited, see p. 227.
4. Dwight, pp. 232–7; for the passages cited, see pp. 233–5. An Italian translation of part of this essay, but excluding the passages cited, is published in *Scritti*, I. 395–8.
5. Gay, pp. 19–21; *Scritti*, II. 327–8; *Century Magazine*, LXXIV. 174; Fortini, p. 105.
6. *Century Mag.*, LXXIV. 177; Gay, pp. 21–22.
7. *Century Mag.*, LXXIV. 179–80, 182.
8. Gay, p. 24.
9. *The North American Review*, XCII. 34–36; Gay, p. 22.
10. *Century Mag.*, LXXIV. 180.
11. Gay, p. 25;
12. *Scritti*, II. 327–8; Gay, p. 22; Vecchi, *Garibaldi et Caprera*, p. 67.
13. *Rel. dip. Francia-Tosc.*, III(ii). 39–40; *Rel. dip. Austria-Tosc.*, III (ii). 394–5, 411–12, 420.
14. *Scritti*, II. 326–7, 329; Fortini, pp. 104, 129–30.
15. *New York Daily Tribune*, 29 Apr. 1851; *Scritti*, II. 329–30; Fortini, p. 106; Gay, p. 25.

16. *Nuova Antalogia*, CCLXVI. 193–202.
17. *Scritti*, II. 330–2; Fortini, p. 106.
18. James Caird's letter in *The Times*, 16 Feb. 1854.
19. Fortini, pp. 129–30.
20. *Correo de Lima*, 6 Oct. 1851.
21. Fortini, pp. 129–30.
22. *Scritti*, II. 332–3; *Correo de Lima*, 31 Oct. 1851; Fortini, p. 133.
23. *Scritti*, II. 333; Fortini, pp. 161–2; Werner, III. 157.
24. *Correo de Lima*, 4 Dec. 1851.
25. *Correo de Lima*, 5, 6 Dec. 1851.
26. *Scritti*, II. 333–5; Fortini, pp. 162–3.
27. *Correo de Lima*, 6 Dec. 1851.
28. Fortini, p. 163; *Scritti*, II. 333.
29. *Comercio del Plata*, 26 Jan. 1853.
30. *Scritti*, II. 336; Guerzoni, I. 398–9; Werner, III. 119–20n.; Herzen, *Memoirs*, p. 919.
31. *Scritti*, II. 336; Lubbock, *The Opium Clippers*, p. 326. Lubbock, who wrote in 1933, gives no reference for his statement about Garibaldi's encounter with Hunter, but states that most of the information in his book was obtained from persons in China who had personal knowledge of the events.
32. *Scritti*, II. 336; Fortini, pp. 144, 166–9; Lubbock, *The China Clippers*, pp. 121–2.
33. *Scritti*, II. 336–8.
34. *Revue Française*, XVII. 509–12; Fortini, pp. 147–50; *Scritti*, II. 338.
35. *Scritti*, II. 338; *Boston Daily Journal*, 9 Sept. 1853; Fortini, pp. 154, 156; Gay, p.27.
36. *Scritti*, II. 338–9; Fortini, pp. 177–85.
37. Gay, p. 27.
38. *Scritti*, II. 339; *Nuova Antalogia*, CCXXXV. 630–2, 634–7, 639; Fortini, p. 194.

Chapter 24

1. *Daily News*, 13 Feb. 1854.
2. J. W. Mario, *Birth of Modern Italy*, pp. 234–7.
3. *Northern Daily Express*, 25 Apr. 1857. For Jessie White Mario, see Duke Litta-Visconti-Arese's preface to her *Birth of Modern Italy*.
4. Holyoake, *Bygones worth remembering*, I. 231–3; II. 218–19.
5. Herzen, p. 701.
6. Klein, *President James Buchanan*, p. 235.
7. Herzen, pp. 1165–9.
8. *Briefe des Feldmarschalls Radetzky an seine Tochter Friederike*, p. 110.
9. Chiala, *Lettere di Cavour*, I. lxxiv–xciii.
10. *Daniele Manin e Giorgio Pallavicino: Epistolario politico*, p. 329.
11. Bolton King, *Mazzini*, p. 162.

12. *Cavour e l'Inghilterra*, I. 22–23 and n.
13. Mazzini, *Scritti*, L. 273–4.
14. Herzen, pp. 1032–4.
15. Werner, III. 125, 132; J. W. Mario, *Birth of Modern Italy*, p. 246.
16. Holyoake, *Bygones worth remembering*, II. 52–77, 285.
17. *Gateshead Observer*, 11 Mar. 1854; Cowen MSS., E. 436, Chap. VII, f. 1; *Northern Tribune*, Apr., May 1854.
18. Cowen MSS., E. 436, Chap. IV, ff. 12–13, 15, 22–24, 26; Chap. VII, ff. 9–11; *Newcastle Daily Chronicle*, 14 Sept. 1859.
19. Cowen MSS., A. 210–11, A. 213–17, A. 219–21; Werner, III. 123.
20. Cowen MSS., E. 436, Chap. VII, ff. 6–8; A. 986; Werner, III. 123–5.
21. *Century Mag.*, LXXIV. 182.
22. Herzen, p. 700.

Chapter 25

1. Mazzini, *Scritti*, LIII. 46; Werner, III. 132.
2. *Scritti*, IV. 160; J. W. Mario, *Birth of Modern Italy*, pp. 248–9.
3. Werner, III. 132; J. W. Mario, op. cit., p. 249; *Rome and Venice: Memoirs of Alberto and Jessie White Mario*, p. 9; Mack Smith, *Garibaldi*, p. 59.
4. J. W. Mario, op. cit., p. 250; *Rome and Venice*, p. 10; Curàtulo, Garibaldi MSS. No. 673.
5. J. W. Mario, op. cit., pp. 250–1.
6. Ibid., p. 247.
7. Ibid., p. 252.
8. Ibid., pp. 253, 260; Werner, III. 135; Cowen MSS., A. 889.
9. Fortini, p. 199; Guerzoni, I. 400.
10. Guerzoni, I. 401–4; J. W. Mario, op. cit., p. 255; Guràtulo, *Garibaldi, Vittorio Emanuele, Cavour*, p. 15; information from Mrs Anita Hibbert, Signor Antonio Putzu, and from personal observation at Caprera.
11. J. W. Mario, op. cit., pp. 255–6; Werner, III. 134–7; Guerzoni, I. 404–5.
12. J. W. Mario, op. cit., pp. 254, 256.
13. B.M. Add. 48579, Palmerston to Lewis, 7 Oct. 1855; B.M. Add. 48580, Palmerston to Clarendon, 7, 9 Mar. 1856.
14. J. W. Mario, op. cit., p. 254.
15. Ibid., pp. 264–5; Werner, III. 139–41.
16. J. W. Mario, op. cit., pp. 263, 266–73; Werner, III. 141–3; *Rome and Venice*, pp. 4, 11.
17. Werner, III. 135; J. W. Mario, op. cit., p. 255.
18. *Manin e Pallavicino, Epistolario*, pp. 163–4, 172; Guerzoni, I. 405–7, 411–12.
19. Fortini, pp. 207–8.
20. Hibbert, p. 128.
21. Melena, *Recollections*, pp. 2–9, 15.

22. Ibid., p. 15.
23. Ibid., p. 21.
24. Ibid., pp. 22–26.
25. Ibid., pp. 18, 29–30.

Chapter 26

1. For the negotiations at Plombières, see *Carteggio Cavour–Nigra*, I. 103–10; Mack Smith, *The Making of Italy*, pp. 238–47; Thayer, *Life and Times of Cavour*, pp. 528–33.
2. *Cavour e l'Inghilterra*, II. 108.
3. Guerzoni, I. 417–19; Werner, III. 151–2.
4. Werner, III. 148.
5. Werner, III. 155–6; J. W. Mario, *Agostino Bertani e i suoi tempi*. I. 285–7; Trevelyan, II. 82.
6. Hübner, *Neuf ans de souvenirs d'un Ambassadeur d'Autriche à Paris*, II. 244–5; Mack Smith, *The Making of Italy*, p. 256; Mazzini, *Scritti*, LXIII. 108, 114.
7. Trevelyan, II. 65.
8. *Scritti*, II. 340; Guerzoni, I. 420; De la Rive, *Le Comte de Cavour*, p. 390; Trevelyan, II. 83.
9. Guerzoni, I. 420. For Victor Emanuel and his visits to London and Paris, see Mack Smith, *Victor Emanuel, Cavour, and the Risorgimento*, pp. 38–55; Paléologue, *Cavour*, pp. 64–65; Hibbert, pp. 134–5.
10. *Scritti*, II. 392.
11. Bolton King, p. 188.
12. *Epistolario de La Farina*, II. 98–99; Guerzoni, I. 418n.
13. See Mack Smith, *Victor Emanuel, Cavour, and the Risorgimento*, pp. 56–76, for Cavour's relations with Parliament.
14. *Scritti*, II. 344; Mack Smith, op. cit., p. 95.
15. *Scritti*, IV. 161–3; Mack Smith, *The Making of Italy*, pp. 261–2; see supra, p. 400n.
16. *Scritti*, II. 342, 390.
17. *Cavour–Nigra*, II. 53, 60–61, 64, 74.
18. Melena, *Recollections*, pp. 35–45.
19. *Scritti*, II. 345–9; Guerzoni, II. 430–3; Carrano, *I Cacciatori delle Alpi*, pp. 180–234.
20. *Scritti*, II. 349–52; IV. 170; Carrano, pp. 234–55; Della Valle, *Varese, Garibaldi ed Urban nel 1859*, pp. 38–39.
21. *Scritti*, II. 352–7; IV. 172–3 (where, following Ciampoli, *Scritti politici e militari*, p. 93, Garibaldi's report is dated 29 May; but the report refers to 'ieri, 2 giugno' on p. 175); Carrano, pp. 261–82; Della Valle, pp. 65, 67, 70; Trevelyan, II. 94–95, 331.
22. *Scritti*, II. 358–60; Carrano, pp. 282–6; Della Valle, pp. 74, 79–81; Trevelyan, II. 95.
23. *Scritti*, II. 360–3; IV. 173–5; Carrano, pp. 295–324; Trevelyan, II.

96–101, 331–2; *Cornhill Mag.*, N.S., XXIV. 106–9; *Illustrated Life and Career of Garibaldi*, p. 94.

24. *Scritti*, II. 367–9; IV. 175; Carrano, pp. 325–43; Della Valle, pp. 91–96, 100.
25. Della Valle, pp. 104–24.
26. *Scritti*, II. 369–71; Della Valle, pp. 99–100; Guerzoni, I. 508; Werner, III. 450n.; Curàtulo, pp. 298–9, 303.
27. Della Valle, pp. 138–9.
28. For the 'massacre' at Perugia, see Blakiston, *The Roman Question*, p. 28; Holt, *Risorgimento*, pp. 214–15; Mack Smith, *Victor Emanuel, Cavour, and the Risorgimento*, p. 102; Hales, *Pio Nono*, p. 194n.
29. *Illustrated Life of Garibaldi*, pp. 82–86, 88–90, 94–96.
30. Louise Goëthe, *Garibaldi*, pp. 8, 12–51; Alvensleben, *Garibaldi*, pp. 9–13, 23–57, 77, 81–82, 85–86, 104; Pitz, *Biographie du Général Garibaldi*, p. 40.
31. Louise Goëthe, pp. 73–74; *Illustrated Life of Garibaldi*, p. 89.
32. *Illustrated Life of Garibaldi*, p. 84. Garibaldi's pincenez are preserved at Caprera.
33. *The Times*, 26 July 1859; *Illustrated Life of Garibaldi*, pp. 96–102.
34. *Scritti*, II. 373–7; Carrano, pp. 376–91, 398–411; Venosta, *Ricordi di Gioventù*, pp. 544–6; Trevelyan, II. 103–5, 107; Mirecourt, *Garibaldi*, pp. 61–63.
35. *Scritti*, II. 377–80; Carrano, pp. 392–3, 412–31, 499–503; Trevelyan, II. 105–6, 109n. For Garibaldi's operations in the Valteline, see *Scritti*, II. 384–6; Carrano, pp. 445–84. The full itinerary of Garibaldi's volunteers during the whole campaign from 26 April to 19 July is given by Carrano, pp. 497–8.
36. *Il problema veneto e l'Europa*, I. 30.
37. For the agreement of Villafranca and the Italian reaction, see Mack Smith, *Victor Emanuel, Cavour, and the Risorgimento*, pp. 104–12; Paléologue *Cavour*, p. 246; Holt, pp. 217–19.
38. *Scritti*, IV. 184.

Chapter 27

1. *Scritti*, II. 400.
2. Ibid., II. 389–94.
3. Ibid., II. 393.
4. Ibid., II. 394–6.
5. J. W. Mario, *Birth of Modern Italy*, pp. 289–90.
6. *Scritti*, II. 395–7; Holt, p. 220.
7. *Scritti*, II. 395; IV. 187–8, 191–3, 197–8, 201–2, 210–11.
8. Thomas Adolphus Trollope, *What I remember*, II. 229, 231.
9. Melena, II. 165–81; and her *Recollections*, pp. 63–75, 78; Trevelyan, I. 283; *Scritti*, IV. 194–6; Bandi, *Anita Garibaldi*, pp. 71–73, 109; *Illustrated Life of Garibaldi*, pp. 108–12.
10. *Scritti*, II. 397.

11. *Il problemo veneto e l'Europa*, I. 23; *Illustrated Life of Garibaldi*, p. 112; Luzio, *Garibaldi, Cavour, Verdi*, pp. 75–77, 89.

12. La Farina, II. 222; Trevelyan, II. 165; Luzio, p. 76; see also *Scritti*, IV. 188, 190–1, 193–4, 196–200, 203–4, 207–8.

13. *Scritti*, II. 398; Guerzoni, I. 492–6, 503.

14. Guerzoni, I. 499–501, 503; Werner, III. 202–3.

15. *Scritti*, II. 401; Trevelyan, II. 121.

16. *Scritti*, II. 399, 401; IV. 211–12; Guerzoni, I. 503; Werner, III. 203.

17. *Scritti*, II. 401–2; Melena, *Recollections*, p. 129; Luzio, p. 50; Parris, pp. 190–2.

18. Massari, *Diario*, p. 463; Mack Smith, *Victor Emanuel, Cavour, and the Risorgimento*, pp. 93–94, 225–7.

19. *Scritti*, II. 402–3; IV. 222–3; Guerzoni, I. 506; Werner, III. 245; Trevelyan, II. 165.

20. Luzio, pp. 81–82.

21. Dumas, *Causeries*, pp. 259–62; Garnett, *Garibaldi's Memoirs (Dumas edition)*, p. 5.

22. RA: J25/40.

23. *Scritti*, II. 403–4; IV. 223–4; *Illustrated Life of Garibaldi*, p. 116; Luzio, pp. 80–84; Guerzoni, I. 507; Werner, III. 220, 245; Mack Smith, *Victor Emanuel, Cavour, and the Risorgimento*, p. 227.

24. RA: J25/41-42. See also Luzio, pp. 82–83; Werner, III. 245–6; J. W. Mario, *Birth of Modern Italy*, pp. 294–5; *Hansard*, 3 Feb. 1860.

25. Luzio, p. 54. See also RA: J25/40.

26. Melena, *Recollections*, pp. 79–80, 134; Werner, III. 449.

27. Sacerdote, p. 600. The story of Garibaldi's proposal to Paulina Zucchini appears to rest on oral tradition only. Sacerdote gives no reference for his statements, but shows a picture of the tree under which the proposal is supposed to have been made.

28. Melena, *Recollections*, pp. 51, 55–56, 78–80, 87–88, 92, 95, 121, 129.

29. Luzio, p. 47; Curàtulo, p. 303.

30. Luzio, p. 50.

31. See supra, pp. 91, 410n.

32. Curàtulo, pp. 305–7; Luzio, p. 55.

33. The best account of the incidents at Fino on 24 Jan. 1860 and the breakdown of the marriage is in Luzio, pp. 41–45, 55–60, 63–73; see especially Volpi's letter, pp. 65–71. See also Finali, *Le Marche*, pp. 108–12; Curàtulo, pp. 297–302, 307–9; Sacerdote, pp. 601–12; Melena, *Recollections*, pp. 131–2, 147–9; Werner, III. 246, 450; Guerzoni, I. 509.

34. Chiala, III. 208; Luzio, pp. 72–73.

35. Luzio, pp. 57, 66–67; Melena, *Recollections*, p. 148; Abba, *Ritratti e profili*, pp. 175–87; Curàtulo, pp. 299, 310–14.

36. Curàtulo. p. 308; Melena, *Recollections*, p. 147; Luzio, p. 63.

37. Luzio, pp. 65–71; Melena, *Recollections*, pp. 131–2, 147–9; Werner, III. 246, 450; Guerzoni, I. 509; Finali, pp. 109–12; Curàtulo, pp. 293–314.

38. Curàtulo, pp. 298–9; Luzio, pp. 46n., 71.

Chapter 28

1. Holt, p. 224.
2. *Cavour e l'Inghilterra*, II (ii). 64–67.
3. *Cavour-Nigra*, III. 208.
4. Luzio, p. 95; Trevelyan, II. 333; Oliphant, *Episodes in a Life of Adventure*, p. 168.
5. Oliphant, p.171; *Scritti*, IV. 227–31.
6. Oliphant, pp. 172–3, 176, 179; Holt, p. 224.
7. *Scritti*, II. 412–13; *Memoirs of Francesco Crispi*, I. 132–6; Trevelyan, II. 163–4, 167–8.
8. Trevelyan, II. 152–61, 332.
9. Trevelyan, II. 171–2.
10. *Scritti*, II. 414–15; Luzio, pp. 101–6; Guerzoni, II. 30–33; Trevelyan, II. 176, 181–5; Mack Smith, *Victor Emanuel, Cavour, and the Risorgimento*, pp. 185–6; Chiala, IV. cxxix.
11. Trevelyan, II. 195; Abba, *The Diary of one of Garibaldi's Thousand*, pp. 4–6.
12. Trevelyan, II. 171, 185, 200–1, 340; Luzio, pp. 113–14, 119; *Scritti*, II. 415; Curàtulo, *Garibaldi, Vittorio Emanuele, Cavour, nei Fasti della Patria*, p. 177.
13. Chiala, IV. cxx–cxxi; Trevelyan, II. 185–6.
14. Crispi, I. 148–55; Guerzoni, II. 34–36; Trevelyan, II. 189–93, 337–8.
15. *Revue des Deux Mondes*, XLI. 420 (1862); Trevelyan, II. 196–7, 338.
16. *Scritti*, II. 416–19; IV. 239; Crispi, I. 156–9; Abba, pp. 9–16; Curàtulo, Garibaldi MSS., No. 1010; Guerzoni, II. 45–47; Trevelyan, II. 200–16.
17. Abba, p. 19; Trevelyan, II. 222; III. 125, 188.
18. *Scritti*, IV. 244–5; Guerzoni, II. 50–57, 56n.; Crispi, I. 159–60; Abba, p. 16; La Farina, II. 320; Trevelyan, II. 216–18; Mack Smith, *Cavour and Garibaldi 1860*, p. 27.
19. D'Ideville, *Journal d'un diplomate en Italie*, I. 53–61.
20. *Scritti*, II. 417–18; *The Times*, 14, 18 May 1860.
21. *The Times*, 15 May 1860.
22. For the controversy as to Cavour's attitude to the Sicilian expedition, see especially *Atti Parlamentari*, 19 June 1863; Bertani, *Ire politiche d'oltre tomba*, pp. 51–55; Trevelyan, II. 195–8, 225–7, 335–7; Mack Smith, *Victor Emanuel, Cavour, and the Risorgimento*, pp. 176–89; Guerzoni, II. 30n.
23. *Il problema veneto e l'Europa*, II. 273–4; De la Rive, *Le Comte de Cavour*, pp. 411–13; Trevelyan, II. 338–9.
24. Chiala, III. 245–6; *Cavour-Nigra*, III. 287, 294–5; Curàtulo, *Garibaldi, Vittorio Emanuele, Cavour*, pp. 139–50; Trevelyan, II. 225–6; Mack Smith, *Victor Emanuel, Cavour, and the Risorgimento*, pp. 186–8.

Chapter 29

1. Trevelyan, II. 212, 218–19; Hibbert, p. 199; *Scritti*, II. 412.
2. For the landing at Marsala, see *Scritti*, II. 422–4; Ximenes, I. 104; Crispi, I. 172–4; Abba, pp. 22–25, 31; Guerzoni, II. 58–64; Trevelyan, II. 229–39; Winnington-Ingram, *Hearts of Oak*, pp. 197–8.
3. Crispi, I. 174–5; Scritti, II. 424–5.
4. Trevelyan, II. 241–2; Forbes, *The Campaign of Garibaldi in the Two Sicilies*, p. 179. See also Ximenes, I. 103–4.
5. Trevelyan, II. 249–50.
6. For the battle of Calatafimi, see *Scritti*, II. 425–32; IV. 252–3; Ximenes, I. 105; Abba, pp. 33–40; Trevelyan, II. 247–62, 342–3; Bandi, *I Mille*, pp. 164–70.
7. *Scritti*, II. 433.
8. *The Times*, 21 May 1860; Abba, p. 63; Trevelyan, II. 292–3.
9. Trevelyan, II. 274; *Scritti*, II. 435; Abba, p. 50. For Pilo's letter to Garibaldi, see Curàtulo, Garibaldi MSS., No. 1225.
10. Dumas, *Les Garibaldiens*, pp. 89–92; Trevelyan, II. 268.
11. For the advance from Calatafimi to Gilibrossa, see *Scritti*, II. 433–4, 436–9; Abba, pp. 41–63; Guerzoni, II. 82–91; Trevelyan, II. 270–82, 344–6.
12. *The Times*, 8 June 1860; Trevelyan, II. 286–7.
13. Mundy, *H.M.S. Hannibal at Palermo and Naples*, pp. 107–8; Abba, p. 63; Trevelyan, II. 285–6.
14. Mundy, pp. 106–7; Trevelyan, II. 286, 292–4.
15. *Scritti*, II. 441.
16. For the fighting in Palermo, see *Scritti*, II. 440–3; Abba, pp. 64–75; Guerzoni, II. 96–105; Mundy, pp. 110–16. Trevelyan, III. 296–313, is the best account, derived from conversations with survivors of the fighting, as well as from written reminiscences.
17. Abba, p. 80.
18. For the events of 31 May–3 June and the negotiations between Garibaldi and the Neapolitans, see *Scritti*, II. 443–9; Guerzoni, II, 106; Mundy, pp. 117–69; Abba, pp. 74–79; Trevelyan, II. 313–24. See also *Scritti*, IV. 254–9; Crispi, I. 216–17.
19. *Scritti*, IV. 261–2; Mundy, pp. 171–3, 175, 178–83; Trevelyan, II. 324–6.
20. Countess Martinengo Cesaresco, *The Liberation of Italy*, p. 266.
21. *The Times*, 5 June 1860.

Chapter 30

1. Mundy, p. 185; Dumas, *Les Garibaldiens*, p. 36; Crispi, I. 479; Mack Smith, *Cavour and Garibaldi*, pp. 21, 41.
2. For the social policy of Garibaldi and Crispi, see Crispi, I. 221–9;

Mack Smith, *Victor Emanuel, Cavour, and the Risorgimento*, pp. 203, 206–10, 219–21.
3. Forbes, pp. 80–81.
4. *Cavour-Nigra*, IV. 26–27; *Cavour e l'Inghilterra*, II (ii). 81.
5. *Halte-là, Garibaldi!*, p.4.
6. Palmerston to Russell, B.M. Add. 48581, 17 May, 10 July 1860.
7. Crispi, I. 332–4; *Il problema veneto e l'Europa*, II. 290, 292.
8. *Cavour e l'Inghilterra*, II (ii). 68, 77 and n., 84.
9. Ibid., II (ii). 82.
10. Cowen MSS., C.1403; *Hansard*, 11, 17 May 1860; *The Times*, 19 May 1860.
11. Mack Smith, *Victor Emanuel, Cavour, and the Risorgimento*, p. 165; *Cavour e l'Inghilterra*, II (ii). 77n.; Cowen MSS., C.1378, C.1403, C.1521, C.1524, C.1532, C.1543.
12. Cowen MSS. C.1403.
13. For Peard, see *Cornhill Magazine*, N.S., XXIV. 812–30; see also Cowen MSS., C. 1504. For Colonel Hugh Forbes 'not to be confused with Commander Charles Stuart Forbes) see Trevelyan, I. 349–51; III. 98.
14. Cowen MSS., C.1508.
15. *Newcastle Journal*, 25 Aug. 1860 (report of Crawshay v. Baxter); Cowen MSS., C.1488; Holyoake, *Bygones worth remembering*, I. 245; Campanella, *Le Legione Britannica nell' Italia Meridionale*, pp. 5–8.
16. *Daily Chronicle and Northern Counties Advertiser* (Newcastle-upon-Tyne), 13, 21, 27 Aug. 1860; *Newcastle Journal*, 25 Aug. (editorial and report of Crawshay v. Baxter), 24 Nov. 1860; *Newcastle Guardian*, 25 Aug. 1860; *Sunday Times*, 26 Aug. 1860; *Gateshead Observer*, 25 Aug. 1860; *Falkirk Herald*, 30 Aug. 1860; *North British Daily Mail*, 25, 27 Aug. 1860; *Western Daily Press*, 23 Aug. 1860; *Daily News*, 22 Aug. 1860.
17. Holyoake, *Bygones worth remembering*, I. 243–58; Brooke, *Out with Garibaldi*, pp. 265–74, 286–9, 291, 293–4, 323–4, 342n.; Campanella, pp. 28–32.
18. Curàtulo, Garibaldi MSS., Nos. 724, 752, 755, 760, 771, 847, 859, 860, 861, 997, 1042, 1076, 1163, 1180, 1181, 1183, 1222, 1357.
19. *Cavour e l'Inghilterra*, II(ii). 79, 115–16; Curàtulo, Garibaldi MSS., Nos. 778, 831–3, 877, 894, 957, 1014–15, 1025, 1041, 1049, 1091, 1127–8, 1143, 1149, 1154, 1184, 1238, 1252–3, 1262–3, 1284, 1322, 1329, 1347, 1350; Luzio, p. 108.
20. Bismarck, *Werke in Auswahl*, VIII. 344–5; Curàtulo, Garibaldi MSS., Nos. 1236, 1292. For De Flotte, see Abba, pp. 121–2; Forbes, p. 168.
21. *Cavour-Nigra*, IV. 29; RA: C 12/46; *Dearest Child*, p. 286.
22. Mack Smith, *Cavour and Garibaldi*, pp. 37–39; see also his *Victor Emanuel, Cavour, and the Risorgimento*, p. 243.
23. La Farina, II. 324–6, 330, 333, 336–7, 339.
24. Chiala, III. 263; Persano, pp. 31–34; Trevelyan, III. 49–52.
25. La Farina, II. 341–4; *Scritti*, IV. 272–3; Crispi, I. 296–8, 302–7; Mack Smith, *Cavour and Garibaldi*, pp. 57, 76–86.

26. Abba, p. 94; Mack Smith, *Cavour and Garibaldi*, p. 59.
27. Mundy, pp. 189–90; Margaret Oliphant, *Life of Laurence Oliphant*, p. 148; La Farina, II. 345–6, 355–7, 359–60; Persano, pp. 60–64; Crispi, I. 311; Guerzoni, II. 128–32; Trevelyan, III. 57–58; Mack Smith, *Cavour and Garibaldi*, pp. 87–89.
28. *Cavour-Nigra*, IV. 70–71; *Cavour e l'Inghilterra*, II (ii). 93.
29. *Il problema veneto e l'Europa*, II. 278–9, 284, 293–6; *Cavour e l'Inghilterra*, II(ii). 90, 92; *The Times*, 15 June 1860.
30. *Scritti*, II. 452; IV. 276–7; Forbes, pp. 83–88; Trevelyan, III. 74–77.
31. *Scritti*, II. 453; Trevelyan, III. 77–78.
32. For the battle of Milazzo, see *Scritti*, II. 453–8; Forbes, pp. 89–101; Brooke, pp. 30–34; *The Times*, 4 Aug. 1860; Trevelyan, III. 82–90, 331–5. For Garibaldi's speech to his soldiers before the battle, see *Scritti*, IV. 277–9.
33. Brooke, pp. 30–31.
34. A. Mario, *The Red Shirt*, pp. 38–40; Trevelyan, III. 96, and caption to picture opposite.
35. *Scritti*, II. 458–9; Ximenes, I. 118–19; Forbes, pp. 102–22; Trevelyan, III. 91–96, 99–100.

Chapter 31

1. *Cavour e l'Inghilterra*, II(ii). 109; *Cavour-Nigra*, IV. 122–3.
2. *Cavour e l'Inghilterra*, II(ii). 118–19.
3. Crispi, I. 326–8.
4. Crispi, I. 379–81, 387–9.
5. Trevelyan, III. 104–8, 105n., 315.
6. *Cavour-Nigra*, IV. 98; Trevelyan, III. 101–3; Mack Smith, *Cavour and Garibaldi*, pp. 125–7; *Il Risorgimento Italiano*, II. 1–48, 652–62 (1909); Curàtulo, *Garibaldi, Vittorio Emanuele, Cavour*, pp. 150–4; Crispi, I. 373–5. Trevelyan, writing soon after the discovery of Victor Emanuel's second letter to Garibaldi, believed that it was shown to Garibaldi by Litta.
7. Trevelyan, III. 102. The original of the letter is lost, and there are five versions of it; see Mack Smith, *Cavour and Garibaldi*, p. 125.
8. For the agrarian disorders, see Mack Smith, *Victor Emanuel, Cavour, and the Risorgimento*, pp. 190–224; Crispi, I. 399–401.
9. For the events at Bronte, see Radice, *Nino Bixio a Bronte*, pp. 31, 34–35, 37, 39–43, 45, 49, 52, 68–70, 101, 104–7, 110–23, 125, 133–6, 140–2, 144–7, 150–1, 153, 155–64; Abba, pp. 124–5; Forbes, pp. 126–7.
10. Crispi, I. 316–19, 321–4, 335.
11. Mario, *The Red Shirt*, p. 43; Abba, p. 118; Forbes, pp. 124, 131–3; Trevelyan, III. 109–11; Crispi, I. 362.
12. Guerzoni, II. 154–6; Trevelyan, III. 117–20.
13. *Scritti*, II. 459; Forbes, pp. 130–1; Abba, pp. 119–20; Trevelyan, III. 111–14.
14. *Scritti*, II. 460; Forbes, pp. 123–4, 135–6; Abba, pp. 123, 126; Bertani,

Ire Politiche, pp. 66–67; J. W. Mario, *Agostino Bertani e i suoi tempi*, II. 165–70; Luzio, p. 189; Guerzoni, II. 157–9; Trevelyan, III. 120–2.

15. *Scritti*, II. 461–2; Forbes, pp. 146–50; Trevelyan, III. 125–7.
16. *Scritti*, II. 462–6; Forbes, pp. 151–8; Trevelyan, III. 127–31.
17. *Scritti*, II. 466–7; Forbes, pp. 159–70; Abba, pp. 129–31; Ximenes, I. 123; Trevelyan, III. 131–7, 142–3.
18. A. Mario, *The Red Shirt*, pp. 148–51; Trevelyan, III. 141–4.
19. Forbes, pp. 161–3.
20. Forbes, pp. 193–5; Abba, pp. 129–30.
21. *Scritti*, II. 467; Forbes, pp. 192, 207, 213, 215; A. Mario, *The Red Shirt*, pp. 156–69; Trevelyan, III. 144–9.
22. Forbes, pp. 217–26; Trevelyan, III. 151–7, 160–4; *History Today*, IX. 783–90 (Dec. 1959).
23. Trevelyan, III. 17–19, 149–50.
24. Trevelyan, III. 163, 166–77; Mundy, pp. 231–2.
25. Trevelyan, III. 177.
26. *Scritti*, II. 467–8; Forbes, pp. 231–4, 238; Guerzoni, II. 168–70; *The Times*, 13, 15, 18 Sept. 1860; Galton, *Vatican Tourists in 1860*, pp. 16–28; Elliot, *Some Revolutions and other Diplomatic Experiences*, pp. 68–72; Trevelyan, III. 178–85. See also Garibaldi's proclamation from Salerno and his speeches at Naples on 7 Sept. 1860 (*Scritti*, IV. 295–7).

Chapter 32

1. *Il problema veneto e l'Europa*, II. 336–7; Chiala, III. 353–4; IV. 3; VI. 582–3; Thouvenel, *Le secret de l'Empereur*, I. 237–8, 252; Trevelyan, III. 209–14.
2. *Cavour e l'Inghilterra*, II(ii). 75.
3. *Cavour-Nigra*, IV. 55, 70; Crispi, I. 252–6, 258–66, 268–79, 362–7; *L'Ane et les Trois Voleurs*, pp. 1–3, 8–9, 15.
4. *Scritti*, IV. 299.
5. Mundy, pp. 239–45.
6. *Macmillan's Magazine*, III. 154 (1861); *Cavour e l'Inghilterra*, II(ii). 122–4, 130; *The Times*, 21 Aug. 1860; Trevelyan, III. 190.
7. Trevelyan, III. 192; *Cavour e l'Inghilterra*, II(ii). 128–9.
8. Guerzoni, II. 170n.; Mack Smith, *Cavour and Garibaldi*, pp. 210–11.
9. Crispi, I. 439–40.
10. Mack Smith, *Cavour and Garibaldi*, p. 250n.; Trevelyan, III. 195; Elliot, pp. 78–79.
11. Brooke, pp. 178–82;
12. Forbes, p. 278; Trevelyan, III. 199–202.
13. Pecorini-Manzoni, *Storia della 15a. Divisione Türr*, pp. 161–71; Abba, p. 137; Trevelyan, III. 187–8.
14. Crispi, I. 403–8, 404n.; Guerzoni, II. 177; Bertani, pp. 72–77; Trevelyan, III. 157–8; Mack Smith, *Cavour and Garibaldi*, pp. 181–9.
15. Crispi, I. 410–13, 481; *Scritti*, IV. 300–5; Mack Smith, *Cavour and Garibaldi*, pp. 199–202.

16 Ximenes, I. 127; J. W. Mario, *Bertani e i suoi tempi*, II. 219; *Cavour e l'Inghilterra*, II(ii). 127; *Cavour-Nigra*, IV. 223, 235; Curàtulo, *Garibaldi, Vittorio Emanuele, Cavour*, p. 353; Crispi, I. 418; Palavicino, *Memoirs*, III. 605–9; Trevelyan, III. 191; Mack Smith, *Cavour and Garibaldi*, pp. 232–3, 236–7, 253–4, and his *Victor Emanuel, Cavour, and the Risorgimento*, p. 237. Trevelyan, III. 191n., states that Garibaldi's demand for Cavour's dismissal was delivered to Victor Emanuel on 23 Sept., not on the 13th; but the demand is referred to in several letters written before 23 Sept. The explanation seems to be that Garibaldi repeated the earlier demand in the letter delivered to the King by Pallavicino on 23 Sept.

Chapter 33

1. *Scritti*, II. 472–3; Forbes, pp. 269–78; Abba, pp. 138–9; Guerzoni, II. 179–82; Pecorini–Manzoni, pp. 187–211, 438–49; *The Times*, 27 Sept., 2 Oct. 1860; Trevelyan, III. 229–32.

2. For the battle of the Volturno, see *Scritti*, II. 474–87; IV. 320–6; Forbes, pp. 278–308; Abba, pp. 138–48; Guerzoni, II. 187–99; Trevelyan, III. 238–54, 341–5, 348–50.

3. Abba, p. 142; Brooke, pp. 180–1; Trevelyan, III. 198, 255–6, 313.

4. Guerzoni, II. 205; Trevelyan, III. 261.

5. *Cavour e l'Inghilterra*, II(ii). 127–8; *Cavour-Nigra*, IV. 221; *Liberazione del Mezzogiorno*, III. 53, 63–64, 103; Ximenes, I. 135–6; Mack Smith, *Cavour and Garibaldi*, pp. 258–9.

6. *Il problema veneto e l'Europa*, II. 340; *Cavour e l'Inghilterra*, II(ii). 128.

7. Mack Smith, *Cavour and Garibaldi*, pp. 341–2.

8. RA: J30/137.

9. Crispi, I. 420, 424, 482; Mack Smith, *Cavour and Garibaldi*, pp. 254–5.

10. Curàtulo, *Garibaldi, Vittorio Emanuele, Cavour*, p. 386; Crispi, I. 435–7; Mack Smith, *Cavour and Garibaldi*, pp. 296–8, 300–1.

11. *Lib. del Mezz.*, III. 103; Mack Smith, *Cavour and Garibaldi*, p. 339.

12. For the events of 2–13 Oct., the struggle over the decrees for the plebiscite and the elections, and the passages quoted, see Crispi, I. 441–59, 482–5; Pallavicino, *Memorie*, III. 611–33; Pecorini–Manzoni, pp. 267–80; Trevelyan, III. 265–6; Mack Smith, *Cavour and Garibaldi*, pp. 314–18, 356–72.

13. Crispi, I. 459, 485; Mazzini, *Scritti*, LXX. 107; *Scritti*, II. 488n.

14. Crispi, I. 458–9; Mack Smith, *Cavour and Garibaldi*, pp. 347–55, 376–80, 420.

15. Mack Smith, *Cavour and Garibaldi*, p. 389; Holt, p. 255.

16. A. Mario, *The Red Shirt*, pp. 283–6; *The Times*, 6 Nov. 1860; Guerzoni, II. 229–30; Brooke, pp. 316–23; Abba, pp. 160–2; Forbes, pp. 330–2; Trevelyan, III. 269–72.

17. *Lib. del Mezz.*, III. 63–65, 323–7; Mack Smith, *The Making of Italy*, p. 328; and his *Cavour and Garibaldi*, p. 409; and his *Victor Emanuel, Cavour, and the Risorgimento*, p. 239.

18. Abba, pp. 164–5; Forbes, pp. 341–2; Trevelyan, III. 278–9; Mack Smith, *Cavour and Garibaldi*, p. 409; and his *Victor Emanuel, Cavour, and the Risorgimento*, p. 239.

19. Chiala, *Ricordi di Castelli*, p. 340–6; Crispi, I. 487–8; Mundy, pp. 271–5, 284; Forbes, pp. 342–3; Trevelyan, III. 279–80; Mack Smith, *Victor Emanuel, Cavour, and the Risorgimento*, p. 239.

20. Della Rocco, *Autobiography of a veteran*, p. 202; Pecorini–Manzoni, pp. 316–17; Guerzoni, II. 232; Trevelyan, III. 284, 286; Mack Smith, *Cavour and Garibaldi*, p. 407, and his *Victor Emanuel, Cavour, and the Risorgimento*, p. 239.

21. Mazzini, *Scritti*, LXX. 183–7; Mundy, pp. 280–2.

22. *Scritti*, IV. 330.

23. Guerzoni, II. 232–4; Trevelyan, III. 286–7; Mack Smith, *Cavour and Garibaldi*, pp. 408–9, and his *Victor Emanuel, Cavour, and the Risorgimento*, p. 240.

Chapter 34

1. See Vecchi, *Garibaldi e Caprera* (Naples, 1861; French translation, Utrecht 1862; English translation, London 1862; German translation, Leipzig 1862); McGrigor, *Garibaldi at home: Notes of a visit to Caprera* (London, 1866); Mornand, *Garibaldi* (Paris, 1866, pp. 45–154); *North British Daily Mail*, 9 Jan. 1861.

2. Curàtulo, *Garibaldi, Vittorio Emanuele, Cavour*, p. 69.

3. Melena, *Recollections*, p. 43.

4. For Garibaldi's life at Caprera, see Vecchi, *Garibaldi e Caprera*, pp. 3–6, 8–11, 14–16, 23, 28–31, 36, 48–50, 55–56, 58, 63, 72, 94, 100, 121, 123, 149–50, 153, 159, 161, 169–70.

5. Ximenes, I. 143–4, 148–9; *Scritti*, IV. 337, 344–54.

6. Vecchi, *Garibaldi et Caprera*, pp. 61–62.

7. Cavour-Nigra, IV. 290–1; Werner, III. 346–7n.; Trevelyan, III. 281. For Türr's change of attitude, see *Cavour e l'Inghilterra*, II(ii). 190.

8. *Scritti*, IV. 357–60; *I Documenti Diplomatici Italiani*, I(i). 81.

9. For the debate in Parliament, see *Scritti*, IV. 360–82; Mack Smith, *The Making of Italy*, pp. 348–52; Baroness Bunsen, *In Three Legations*, pp. 136–9; *The Times*, 23 Apr. 1861; d'Ideville, *Journal d'un Diplomate en Italie*, pp. 178–88; Guerzoni, II. 257–66.

10. Thayer, *Life and Times of Cavour*, II. 475–6.

11. Guerzoni, II. 268–9; Thayer, II. 478n.

12. Chiala, *Lettere di Cavour*, VI. 710–12; Werner, III. 354–6; Thayer, II. 481–3.

13. *The North American Review*, XCII. 15–56; Vecchi, *Garibaldi et Caprera*, pp. 76–80; Gay, *Lincoln's Offer of a Command to Garibaldi*, p. 66.

14. Gay, p. 66.

15. Gay, pp. 66–67.

16. Gay, p. 67; Leech, *Reveille in Washington*, pp. 85, 88.
17. Gay, pp. 67–68; *New-York Tribune*, 11 Aug. 1861.
18. Gay, p. 68.
19. Gay, p. 69.
20. Gay, p. 70; Curàtulo, Garibaldi MSS., Nos. 1732, 1872; McAdam MSS., McAdam to Garibaldi, 28 Sept. 1861; Garibaldi to McAdam, 3 Dec. (1861).

Chapter 35

1. *Cavour-Nigra*, IV. 373; *Doc. Dip. Ital.*, I(i). 81–82, 86, 291, 316, 409, 443, 452, 534; I(ii). 36–37, 57, 71–72, 119, 125, 142, 175–6, 186, 201, 210; *Il problema veneto e l'Europa*, II. 503, 513, 560; III. 340; Mack Smith, *Victor Emanuel, Cavour, and the Risorgimento*, pp. 287–8.
2. *Doc. Dip. Ital.*, I(ii). 253, 289, 300; *Il problema veneto e l'Europa*, I. 442.
3. *Il problema veneto e l'Europa*, I. 431–3, 439–40; Mack Smith, *Victor Emanuel, Cavour, and the Risorgimento*, pp. 283–6.
4. J. W. Mario, *Birth of Modern Italy*, p. 314; Guerzoni, II. 281–2; Letizia Rattazzi, *Rattazzi et son temps*, I. 617–18.
5. *Scritti*, V. 24–25; J. W. Mario, *Birth of Modern Italy*, pp. 315–16; Guerzoni, II. 281–2.
6. J. W. Mario, op. cit., p. 317; Chambers, *Garibaldi and Italian Unity*, pp. 178–9.
7. *Il problema veneto e l'Europa*, I. 442; J. W. Mario, op. cit., p. 317; Mack Smith, *Victor Emanuel, Cavour, and the Risorgimento*, pp. 287–92.
8. *Scritti*, V. 40–44, 46–51, 53–58, 62–65; Guerzoni, II. 284–6.
9. *Il problema veneto e l'Europa*, I. 443, 445; II. 572–4; III. 347–8.
10. *Scritti*, V. 73–74; J. W. Mario, *Birth of Modern Italy*, pp. 319–20; Letizia Rattazzi, I. 620.
11. Letizia Rattazzi, I. 620–1; *Il problema veneto e l'Europa*, I. 455–6; III. 358–64.
12. *Doc. Dip. Ital.*, I(ii). 353–4, 357–8; Letizia Rattazzi, I. 621; Guerzoni, II. 288–9; J. W. Mario, *Birth of Modern Italy*, pp. 320–1.
13. Thouvenel, II. 304; Letizia Rattazzi, I. 622–5; *Doc. Dip. Ital.*, I(ii). 357–8; *Scritti*, V. 78.
14. *Scritti*, V. 80–81.
15. *Scritti*, V. 81–82.
16. Chambers, pp. 246–7; Guerzoni, II. 297–8.
17. *Doc. Dip. Ital.*, I(ii). 454; *Scritti*, V. 91–92.
18. Chambers, p. 189.
19. *Scritti*, V. 96.
20. Guerzoni, II. 298–302; *Scritti*, V. 97–102.
21. *Scritti*, V. 102–23.
22. Blakiston, *The Roman Question*, pp. 235, 245.
23. *Doc. Dip. Ital.*, I(ii). 593, 607; I(iii). 28–29.

24. J. W. Mario, *Birth of Modern Italy*, p. 322; Thouvenel, II. 341, 374; Letizia Rattazzi, I. 633.
25. *Doc. Dip. Ital.*, I(iii). 5; Guerzoni, II. 310–11.
26. *Scritti*, V. 132–4.
27. Guerzoni, II. 305–11; Chambers, pp. 209–17; *Scritti*, II. 492–3; *Doc. Dip. Ital.*, I(iii). 8, 15–17, 22–23, 25, 46; Dierauer, 'Eine Erinnerung an Garibaldi', in *Festgabe für G. Mayer von Knonau*, pp. 477–8.
28. Chambers, pp. 215–16.
29. *Doc. Dip. Ital.*, I(iii). 5, 14–15, 41–42; *Scritti*, V. 136; *The Times*, 5, 21. 25 Aug. 1862.
30. *Scritti*, II. 493–5; Guerzoni, II. 314–16; Chambers, pp. 219–21, 221n.
31. Chambers, pp. 235–6; Letizia Rattazzi, I. 634–6.
32. Chambers, p. 220; *Scritti*, II. 495–6; V. 143; Letizia Rattazzi, I. 636–7; Guerzoni, II. 316–20.
33. Letizia Rattazzi, I. 637.
34. For the conflicting accounts of Aspromonte, see Chambers, pp. 223–43; *Scritti*, II. 496–8; V. 146–9; Guerzoni, II. 320–4.
35. *Il problema veneto e l'Europa*, II. 617.

Chapter 36

1. *Scritti*, II. 498–9; Guerzoni, II. 324–5; Chambers, pp. 244–5.
2. *Scritti*, V. 146–9; Chambers, pp. 232–4.
3. Guerzoni, II. 325–9; Chambers, pp. 247, 255; Letizia Rattazzi, I. 638–9, 644–5; Werner, III. 367; Mack Smith, *Victor Emanuel, Cavour, and the Risorgimento*, pp. 291–2.
4. Chambers, pp. 245–54.
5. McAdam MSS., Nimmo to McAdam, 15 Sept. 1862.
6. *Morning Star*, 6 Oct. 1862; Guerzoni, II. 326, 328.
7. Wulliémoz, *Garibaldi; Lettere ad Antonio Panizzi*, p. 480.
8. Chambers, pp. 245–6; J. W. Mario, *Birth of Modern Italy*, pp. 324–8.
9. Chambers, pp. 254–5; Guerzoni, II. 329; J. W. Mario, op. cit., p. 329; Werner, III. 367–70; Mack Smith, *Victor Emanuel, Cavour, and the Risorgimento*, pp. 291–2.
10. *Doc. Dip. Ital.*, I(iii). 55, 57–58, 89; *Il problema veneto e l'Europa*, I. 514–16. 618; Thouvenel, II. 374, 384.
11. *La Palla nella Ferita del Generale Garibaldi*, pp. 3–10; Chambers, pp. 256–62; Guerzoni, II. 330; J. W. Mario, *Birth of Modern Italy*, pp. 329–30.
12. Chambers, p. 262; Gay, *Lincoln's Offer of a Command to Garibaldi*, pp. 73–74; Guerzoni, II. 334–8.
13. Herzen, *Camicia Rossa*, pp. 101–22.
14. Werner, III. 371; Herzen, op. cit., pp. 47–48.
15. Cowen MSS., A. 728.
16. *The Times*, 4, 5 Apr. 1864; Cowen MSS., E. 436, Chap. VII, ff. 24–26; Holyoake, *Sixty Years of an Agitator's Life*, II. 119; Guerzoni, II. 349–51;

Herzen, *Camicia Rossa,* pp. 11, 13; *Annual Register for 1864,* II. 45–46; Blakiston, *Garibaldi's Visit to England in 1864,* p. 133.

17. Cowen MSS., E. 436, Chap. VII, ff. 17–20; A. 734.
18. Cowen MSS., E. 436, Chap. VII, ff. 29–34; Herzen, *Camicia Rossa,* pp. 14–29; Holyoake, *Sixty Years of an Agitator's Life,* II. 119, and his *Bygones worth remembering,* I. 238–40.
19. H.M.C., Broadlands Papers, GC/SH/63.
20. Hallam Tennyson, *Alfred Lord Tennyson: a memoir by his son,* II. 1–4; Guerzoni, II. 352 and n.; Tennyson, 'To Ulysses' (*Poetical Works of Alfred Lord Tennyson,* p. 600).
21. *The Times,* 11 Apr. 1864; Guerzoni, II. 352.
22. Guerzoni, II. 353; *Annual Register for 1864,* II. 47; Blakiston, op. cit., pp. 133–4.
23. Holyoake, *Sixty Years of an Agitator's Life,* II. 120–5, and his *Bygones worth remembering,* I. 234; Herzen, *Camicia Rossa,* p. 38.
24. *The Times,* 12 Apr. 1864; Guerzoni, II. 353–7; Holyoake, *Sixty Years of an Agitator's Life,* II. 121; Herzen, *Camicia Rossa,* pp. 35–37; *Annual Register for 1864,* II. 47–51; Blakiston, op. cit., p. 134.
25. Curàtulo, *Garibaldi e le donne,* pp. 276, 289; Malmesbury, *Memoirs of an Ex-Minister,* pp. 593–4.
26. Morley, *Gladstone,* II. 110–11; Guerzoni, II. 358–9, 386; *Daily Telegraph,* 16 Apr. 1864; Manning, *Miscellanies,* I. 131–2; RA: J36/118; Hibbert, p. 342.
27. RA: J36/118, 123.
28. *The Times,* 18 Apr. 1864; Guerzoni, II. 359; Blakiston, op. cit., p. 134; Midland and North-Eastern Railway handbill (Apr. 1864); Manning, I. 133; Cowen MSS., E. 436, Chap. VII. f. 38.
29. Manning, I. 125; Morley, II. 111; Hodder, *Life of Shaftesbury,* III. 174.
30. Monypenny and Buckle, *Life of Disraeli,* II. 61–62; Malmesbury, p. 594.
31. *The Times,* 12 Apr. 1864; RA, Queen Victoria's Journal, 12 Apr. 1864. See also *Letters of Queen Victoria,* II(i). 169.
32. RA: J36/114; RA: Z16/33.
33. *Der Briefwechsel zwischen Friedrich Engels und Karl Marx,* II. 331–2, 358–60, 399–400; III. 37, 156–8.
34. Blakiston, op. cit., pp. 139–41.
35. Cowen MSS., A. 740, A. 812, A. 819, B. 50.
36. McAdam MSS., Dalgleish to McAdam, 13 Apr. 1864.
37. Cowen MSS., A. 823, ff. 2–8; *Daily Telegraph,* 18 Apr. (2nd edition), 19 Apr. 1864.
38. Cowen MSS., E. 436, Chap. VII. ff. 45–46.
39. Herzen, *Camicia Rossa,* pp. 40–57; Guerzoni, II. 359–61.
40. Cowen MSS., A. 806–7.
41. Cowen MSS., A. 823, ff. 9–20.
42. *Letters of Queen Victoria,* II(i). 172; RA: B20/79.
43. *Letters of Queen Victoria,* II(i). 174; see also RA: Y86/25.
44. *Letters of Queen Victoria,* II(i). 175.
45. Cowen MSS., A. 832; E. 436, Chap. VII, ff. 47–50; Herzen, *Camicia*

Rossa, pp. 66–67; Frederic Harrison, *Autobiographic Memoirs*, II. 356–7; Holyoake, *Bygones worth remembering*, I. 241–2 and n.; J. W. Mario, *Birth of Modern Italy*, pp. 335–6.

46. RA: J36/126; *Hansard*, 19 Apr. 1864 (House of Commons and House of Lords); *North British Daily Mail*, 23, 26, 29 Apr. 1864; *Newcastle Daily Chronicle*, 20, 21, 22, 23, 25, 26, 27, 29 Apr. 1864; *Glasgow Herald*, 20 Apr. 1864; *The Sun*, 19 Apr. 1864; *Morning Star*, 22, 25, 28 Apr. 1864; *Evening Standard*, 20, 22 Apr. 1864; *The Times*, 20 Apr. 1864; Herzen, *Camicia Rossa*, pp. 66–67; J. W. Mario, *Birth of Modern Italy*, pp. 335–6; Guerzoni, II. 378–85, 378–80n., 382n.

47. Herzen, *Camicia Rossa*, pp. 70–75; *The Times*, 20 Apr. 1864; Curàtulo, *Garibaldi e le donne*, pp. 260, 289.

48. *The Times*, 21, 22 Apr. 1864; Guerzoni, II. 362–5, 385–6; Fagan, *Life of Panizzi*, II. 250–1 (where the date of the visit to Ugo Foscolo's tomb is wrongly given as 20 Apr.); Fagan, *The Reform Club*, pp. 108–9; *Scritti*, V. 225–6; Manning, I. 132.

49. Weston, *General Garibaldi at Fishmongers' Hall*, pp. 1, 7, 10; *Nuova Antalogia* Vol. 486, pp. 88–89.

50. *The Times*, 17, 23 Apr. 1864; Guerzoni, II. 386–7.

51. RA: J36/137–41.

52. *Scritti*, V. 222–4.

53. McAdam MSS., McAdam's Memoirs, ff. 37–38, published in part in the *North British Daily Mail*, 25 Apr. 1864; Lodge St Clair MSS., No. 362.

54. *Windsor and Eton Express*, 30 Apr. 1864.

55. Guerzoni, II. 388–91 and n.; RA: Add. U32 April 28 1864; J. W. Mario, *Birth of Modern Italy*, p. 337; Werner, III. 373.

56. Cowen MSS., A. 822, A. 824; RA: J36/137.

57. Cowen MSS., A. 803, A. 805, A. 812, A. 814, A. 826–7.

58. Manning, I. 131, 134, 141.

59. Ximenes, I. 253–4; Cowen MSS., A. 810, A. 816, A. 829–30, A. 839.

60. Cowen MSS., A. 844.

Chapter 37

1. Guerzoni, II. 393–408; *Il problema veneto e l'Europa*, III. 444–5, 450–64.

2. *Il problema veneto e l'Europa*, I. 648, 677; III. 465, 471, 474, 477–8, 482–5, 489–91, 493–4, 501–6, 512–16, 519–20, 560–3, 567–8.

3. *Scritti*, II. 499; Guerzoni, II. 423–4.

4. *Scritti*, II. 502–4, 508; Mack Smith, *Victor Emanuel, Cavour, and the Risorgimento*, p. 315.

5. *Scritti*, II. 505–9; V. 278–9; Guerzoni, II. 425–8.

6. *Scritti*, II. 509–12; Guerzoni, II. 430–4.

7. *Scritti*, II. 512–17; Guerzoni, II. 434–52.

8. McAdam MSS., McAdam's Memoirs, f. 40.

9. For the battle of Bezzecca, see Appia, *Souvenirs de la campagne de Garibaldi*

dans le Tyrol en 1866, pp. 10–18; *Scritti*, II. 517–20; V. 306–8; Guerzoni, II. 452–7; Curàtulo, Garibaldi MSS., No. 376.

10. Appia, p. 22; *Scritti*, II. 519–22; Guerzoni, II. 458–62.
11. *Scritti*, II. 521–2; Guerzoni, II. 462.
12. Mirecourt, pp. 70–71; *Scritti*, V. 367.
13. *Scritti*, V. 367–8.
14. For Garibaldi's visit to Venice, see Cavallotti, *Storia del Insurrezione di Roma nel 1867*, pp. 18–23; Mirecourt, pp. 59–61; and see *Scritti*, V. 369–70.
15. Mirecourt, pp. 61–63; Guerzoni, II. 470; Cavallotti, p. 23.
16. Mirecourt, pp. 51, 57–58.
17. Cavallotti, pp. 44–61; *Scritti*, V. 374.
18. Cavallotti, p. 87n.
19. Cavallotti, pp. 98–99n., 103n., 119–28, 131, 132–3n.
20. Cavallotti, pp. 172–3, 213–15, 213–14n., 217–19n., 224, 226; *Scritti*, V. 407–8.
21. *Annales du Congrès de Genève*, pp. 1–6, 10–11, 23–24, 35–37, 40, 336–42; *Journal de Genève*, 19 Sept. 1867; Campanella, *Garibaldi and the first Peace Congress in Geneva in 1867*, pp. 456–9, 471, 478.
22. *Journal de Genève*, 3, 5, 24 Sept. 1867; Duraford, *Avant, Pendant et Après, ou Garibaldi à Genève*, pp. 5–6.
23. *Journal de Genève*, 9 Sept. 1867, 23 Sept. 1912; Duraford, pp. 25–30; *Annales du Congrès de Genève*, pp. 107–14; Campanella, op. cit., pp. 460–5; Cavallotti, pp. 242–4; Melena, *Recollections*, pp. 196–205; *Scritti*, V. 408–10. The fullest version of Garibaldi's speech is in Duraford.
24. *Journal de Genève*, 10 Sept. 1867; *Annales du Congrès de Genève*, pp. 115–35; Duraford, p. 31; Campanella, op. cit., pp. 466–7.
25. *Annales du Congrès de Genève*, pp. 136–41, 139n.; Campanella, op. cit., pp. 467–9; *Journal de Genève*, 10 Sept. 1867; *La Démocratie Suisse*, 11 Sept. 1867; Cavallotti, pp. 246–7; *Scritti*, V. 410–12.
26. *Annales du Congrès de Genève*, pp. 144–202, 205–305; Duraford, pp. 36–46; *Journal de Genève*, 11, 12, 13, 24, 27 Sept. 1867; *La Démocratie Suisse*, 14, 18, 21 Sept. 1867; *Les Mémoires de James Fazy*, pp. 213–14; Campanella, op. cit., pp. 473–81.
27. *Journal de Genève*, 11, 12 Sept. 1867; Duraford, pp. 48–52; *Annales du Congrès de Genève*, pp. 378–9; Campanella, op. cit. p. 472; Cavallotti, pp. 249–50; *Scritti*, V. 412–13.
28. Dupanloup, *Lettre à M. Ratazzi* [sic.] . . . *sur les Entreprises de Garibaldi*, pp. 8, 27.

Chapter 38

1. Cavallotti, pp. 250, 256, 260–1, 263–4.
2. Cavallotti, pp. 268–9; *Scritti*, V, 414–15.
3. Cavallotti, pp. 270, 273–4; McAdam MSS., Garibaldi to McAdam, 23 Sept. 1867. See also McAdam MSS., McAdam's circular, 17 Oct. 1867; Pallavicino to McAdam, 30 Oct. 1867.

4. Cavallotti, pp. 275–6; *Scritti,* II. 524; V. 416.
5. Cavallotti, pp. 278–88.
6. Cavallotti, pp. 292–6, 296–8n., 299.
7. Cavallotti, pp. 300–1, 301n., 312–13, 315, 333, 456–7; *Scritti,* II. 524–5; V. 417–19.
8. Cavallotti, pp. 347, 455–6n.
9. Cavallotti, pp. 459–67.
10. Melena, *Recollections,* pp. 215–18; *Scritti,* II. 526–31; Cavallotti, pp. 468–76; Curàtulo, Garibaldi MSS., No. 311.
11. Cavallotti, pp. 349, 357, 359, 361, 363, 365, 370–1, 371–2n., 373, 375n., 377.
12. Cavallotti, pp. 476–7.
13. Werner, III. 379–80; Mack Smith, *Victor Emanuel, Cavour, and the Risorgimento,* pp. 344–7.
14. *Scritti,* II. 536–9; V. 425–31; Guerzoni, II. 519–23; Cavallotti, pp. 492–5, 500–3.
15. Cavallotti, pp. 506–33, 654.
16. Cavallotti, pp. 595, 602–3.
17. Cavallotti, pp. 613–14; *Scritti,* II. 540, 543; Werner, III. 382, 384–93.
18. Scritti, V. 440–1; Mack Smith, *Victor Emanuel, Cavour, and the Risorgimento,* pp. 345, 348–9.
19. Werner, III. 381n.; Cavallotti, p. 624.
20. For the battle of Mentana, see *Scritti,* II. 541–50; Guerzoni, II. 536–48; Cavallotti, pp. 627–35.
21. Cavallotti, pp. 643, 645.
22. *Scritti,* II. 551–2; Cavallotti, pp. 644, 647–52, 651n.; Guerzoni, II. 548–52.

Chapter 39

1. *Le Moniteur Universel,* 10 Nov., 6 Dec. 1867; RA: Queen Victoria's Journal, 5 Nov. 1867; Mirecourt, pp. 56, 66.
2. Curàtulo, Garibaldi MSS., Nos. 327–36, 338–41.
3. For the passages cited and referred to from *Clelia,* see the Italian edition, pp. 1, 22–23, 80–82, 91, 239, 241, 254, 287–92, 456–63.
4. Melena, *Recollections,* pp. vi–vii, 260, 333–5; *Saturday Review,* XVII. 428, 458–9, 489–90, 518–19 (1864); XXIX. 321–2 (1870); Mack Smith, *Great Lives Observed: Garibaldi,* pp. 141–4.
5. Melena, *Recollections,* pp. 134, 257; Werner, III. 449n.
6. Abba, *Ritratti e Profili,* pp. 64–65.
7. McAdam MSS., Mrs Chambers to McAdam, 5 Dec. 1875; Melena, *Recollections,* p. 256n.; personal information from Mrs Anita Hibbert and from Comandante Coltelletti.
8. Melena, *Recollections,* pp. 168–71.
9. Melena, *Recollections,* pp. 178–80, 184, 254–61, 273–4, 276, 283, 300, 302, 307, 312–14, 316–20, 322–7; Curàtulo, *Garibaldi e le donne,* pp.

162, 173, 184–8; Curàtulo, Garibaldi MSS., Nos. 2281–3, 2398, 2735, 2743, 2801.

10. Personal information from Comandante Coltelletti.
11. Personal information from reliable sources.

Chapter 40

1. *Doc. Dip. Ital.*, I(xiii). 198, 216, 379; *The Times*, 22 Aug. 1870; Ximenes, I. 355.
2. Werner, III. 396; Hales, *Pio Nono*, p. 315.
3. *Doc. Dip. Ital.*, I(xiii). 147, 266, 311; II(i). 32.
4. Ximenes, I. 355; *Scritti*, VI. 46–47.
5. Vuilletet, *Garibaldi en France*, p. 5; *Doc. Dip. Ital.*, I(xiii). 488, 500, 525; II(i). 37.
6. *Affaire Bordone*, pp. 137–9.
7. Bordone, *Garibaldi et l'armée des Vosges*, pp. 13, 16–19.
8. *Scritti*, II. 557; *Doc. Dip. Ital.*, II(i). 179, 186, 188, 202, 235–6, 359.
9. Vuilletet, pp. 6–7, 9–10; Howard, *The Franco–Prussian War*, pp. 253–4.
10. Busch, *Bismarck, some secret pages of his history*, I. 380.
11. *Scritti*, II. 557, 559–61; Vuilletet, pp. 10–11, 13; Bordone, pp. 23–26; Howard, pp. 254–5.
12. Howard, pp. 249–53; Busch, I. 311.
13. Werner, III. 423–4.
14. *Scritti*, II. 559; Vuilletet, pp. 14, 119–20; Bordone, pp. 30–31.
15. Vuilletet, pp. 10, 14–15, 102–3, 105, 109–10.
16. Vuilletet, pp. 87–92, 94–96; Bordone, pp. 50–52.
17. Vuilletet, pp. 88, 96–97; Bordone, pp. 161–6.
18. Ximenes, I. 363–4; Vuilletet, pp. 117–18; Werner, III. 404–5.
19. *Scritti*, II. 562–3; VI. 54–55; Bordone, pp. 53–101; Vuilletet, pp. 19–23.
20. Curàtulo, Garibaldi MSS., No. 399; *Scritti*, II. 561–2; Bordone, p. 173; Vuilletet, pp. 25, 53; Howard, pp. 252, 409.
21. Vuilletet, p. 26; *Scritti*, II. 567; Guerzoni, II. 564.
22. Bordone, pp. 185–6, 197; *Scritti*, II. 563–70; Guerzoni, II. 564–7; Vuilletet, pp. 26–31.
23. *Scritti*, II. 570–7; Bordone, pp. 196–211; Guerzoni, II. 567–9; Vuilletet, pp. 32–40.
24. *Scritti*, II. 571–2, 576; VI. 64–66; Bordone, pp. 225–34, 295–6; *Affaire Bordone*, p. 228.
25. Vuilletet, pp. 41–45; Bordone, pp. 235–6.
26. *Enquête Parlementaire*, VII. 130–2; Vuilletet, pp. 48–50, 106–7; *Scritti*, II. 578; Bordone, pp. 267–70; Werner, III. 451–2; Clelia Garibaldi, *Mio Padre*, pp. 29–31.
27. *Enquête Parlementaire*, VII. 174–9; Vuilletet, pp. 50–71; *Scritti*, II. 578–9; Guerzoni, II. 570–2; Bordone, pp. 271–80, 305–13, 315–23, 325–7.
28. *Enquête Parlementaire*, VII. 162–4.
29. *Enquête Parlementaire*, VII. 146–53; *Scritti*, II. 580–8; VI. 70–72; Bordone,

pp. 328–52; Guerzoni, II. 572–7; Vuilletet, pp. 72–78; Howard, p. 427.
30. Vuilletet, pp. 79–82; Bordone, pp. 353–67; Guerzoni, II. 577–9; *Scritti*, II. 579; Werner, III. 421–2.
31. Busch, I. 531–3.
32. *Enquête Parlementaire*, VII. 187; Vuilletet, pp. 80–83; *Scritti*, II. 589–91; Bordone, pp. 368–74.
33. *Scritti*, VI. 82; Werner, III. 416, 420, 426–7.
34. Bordone, pp. 389–90.
35. *Scritti*, VI. 81–86; Werner, III. 420–1n.; Vuilletet, pp. 84–85; Bordone, pp. 391–3.
36. Louis Blanc, *Garibaldi, discours prononcé le 4 juillet 1875*, pp. 10–11.
37. Vuilletet, p. 85; Bordone, pp. 165, 392, 396–407.
38. Vuilletet, pp. 112–13.

Chapter 41

1. Cowen MSS., A. 917; McAdam MSS., Garibaldi to McAdam, 19 Oct. 1870.
2. *Scritti*, VI. 87–88; see also *La Commune*, 28 Mar. 1871.
3. Marx, *The Civil War in France;* Mazzini, *Mazzini e l'Internazionale*; Werner, III. 429–31; *Archives Bakunin*, I.xl.
4. *Scritti*, VI. 89–93; *Archives Bakunin*, I. 209, 253–4; II(ii). 110; Hostetter, *The Italian Socialist Movement*, I. 175.
5. Curàtulo, Garibaldi MSS., No. 430; *Archives Bakunin*, I. 264–5, 342.
6. Ximenes, I. 384–91; *Newcastle Daily Chronicle*, 7 Nov. 1871.
7. *Newcastle Daily Chronicle*, 7 Nov. 1871; Werner, III. 429–35; Mazzini, *Scritti*, XCI. 220; Hostetter, I. 160n.
8. Hostetter, I. 216–17.
9. *Archives Bakunin*, I.xv; II(ii). 128, 190.
10. *Archives Bakunin*, I. 49, 87, 264–6; II(i), 14; II(ii). lix, lxi, 31–32, 36–39, 46, 64, 202–3, 242, 293–5, 297–300, 306, 308; III. 207, 225, 245, 313, 360–1.
11. Hostetter, I. 201, 216, 242, 255, 273; *Archives Bakunin*, II(ii). lxi, 469.
12. Hostetter, I. 273 and n., 288; *Archives Bakunin*, II(ii). lx.
13. *Scritti*, III. 3–8, 161.
14. Hostetter, I. 346n., 347–51; *Archives Bakunin*, II(ii). lxi.
15. Werner, III. 437.
16. *Scritti*, II. 14, 139.
17. Werner, III. 436; McAdam MSS., Garibaldi to 'a friend near London', 18 Dec. 1866 (copy).
18. For Garibaldi's unpublished writings, see *Scritti*, VI. 329–592; Curàtulo, Garibaldi MSS., Nos. 7–169. See also Werner, III. 442–6.
19. Garibaldi, *Poema Autobiografico*.
20. Curàtulo, Garibaldi MSS., Nos. 590–4, 615–16, 2195, 2235, 2715, 2792–3; Tonelli, *Garibaldi y la Masoneria argentina*, pp. 36–38.

21. Werner, III. 451; Ciampoli, *Giuseppe Garibaldi, Scitti politici e militari*, p. 767; Melena, *Recollections*, p. 302.
22. Melena, *Recollections*, p. 308.
23. Melena, *Recollections*, pp. 302, 312, 316; personal information from Comandante Coltelletti.
24. *Scritti*, VI. 122–38, 142–52, 159–203, 205–21, 224–5, 234–6, 242–4; Guerzoni, II. 589–95; Werner, III. 444.
25. Paris, pp. 319, 345. Parris was told this story by Clelia Garibaldi.
26. Melena, *Recollections*, pp. 328–9; Curàtulo, p. 190; Werner, III. 449n.; Hibbert, p. 365.
27. Melena, *Recollections*, p. 329.
28. Curàtulo, Garibaldi MSS., Nos. 2788–91, 2794–5, 2798–9, 2803–4, 2809–12, 2815–17, 2858, 2864–6; *Scritti*, VI. 233; Werner, III. 452–4.
29. McAdam MSS., Garibaldi to 'a friend near London', 18 Dec. 1866 (copy), Garibaldi to McAdam, 9 Jan. 1867, 24 July 1873, 7 July 1877; *Scritti*, VI. 158–60, 162, 228–30, 241, 261–2, 266–7, 275, 284.
30. C. Seton Watson, *Italy from Liberalism to Fascism*, p. 102; *Scritti*, VI. 282–4; Curàtulo, Garibaldi MSS., No. 2886.
31. RA: W85/10. Garibaldi's letter is printed in *Scritti*, VI. 260, from a copy in the Museo del Risorgimento in Rome, where it is wrongly dated 30 Sept. 1877.
32. RA: Add. 1 12/458.
33. *Scritti*, VI. 288, 299; *The Times*, 9 Apr., 3 May 1879; Cilibrizzi, *Storia Parlamentare Politica e Diplomatica d'Italia*, II. 180–1.
34. Guerzoni, II. 597–8; Melena, *Recollections*, p. 325n.; *The Times*, 7 Aug., 3 Sept. 1879; Hibbert, p. 367; Werner, III. 450–1; Register of Marriages of the Church of St. James, Piccadilly, 1873–75, p. 74; Clelia Garibaldi, *Mio padre*, p. 109; Parris, p. 328.
35. *The Times*, 1, 4, 5, 6 Oct. 1880; *Scritti*, VI. 306; Clelia Garibaldi, pp. 111–12; Cilibrizzi, II. 201.
36. Guerzoni, II. 599–605; Ximenes, II. 318–22, 324–6 (where Garibaldi's letter to Dobelli of 22 June 1881 is wrongly dated 11 Sept.); *Scritti*, VI. 318–19; Werner, III. 443–6, 456–7; Cilibrizzi, II. 201; private information from Mrs Anita Hibbert.
37. Guerzoni, II. 603–6; Werner, III. 455–8; Thomas Adolphus Trollope, *What I remember*, II. 232; Curàtulo, Garibaldi MSS., No. 2905.
38. Guerzoni, II. 607–10; Werner, III. 458–9; Hibbert, p. 367.
39. Guerzoni, II. 611–12; RA: Z36/27.
40. Guerzoni, II. 613–16; Werner, III. 459–61.
41. Guerzoni, II. 617; Werner, III. 461; Tonelli, pp. 52–53.
42. Hostetter, I. 179.
43. Pereda, III. 26.
44. Vecchi, *Garibaldi et Caprera*, p. 144.

INDEX

705